A TRIP THROUGH TIME

A TRIP THROUGH TIME

Principles of Historical Geology

SECOND EDITION

JOHN D. COOPER
California State University, Fullerton
RICHARD H. MILLER
San Diego State University
JACQUELINE PATTERSON
California State University, Fullerton

MERRILL PUBLISHING COMPANY
A Bell & Howell Information Company
Columbus Toronto London Melbourne

Cover Photo: Jack W. Dykinga

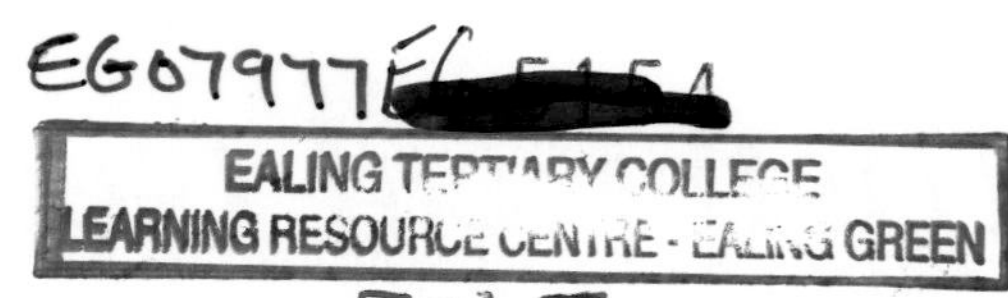

Published by Merrill Publishing Company
A Bell & Howell Information Company
Columbus, Ohio 43216

This book was set in Trump Mediaeval

Executive Editor: Stephen Helba
Production Coordinator: Julie A. Higgins
Art Coordinator: James H. Hubbard
Cover Designer: Brian Deep
Photo Editor: Terry L. Tietz

Photo credits for color inserts: Theme I. I.2A Kirkendall/Spring; I.2B Geoscience; I.2C Geoscience; I.3D J. D. Cooper; I.3E Geoscience; I.3F Geoscience; I.3G B. N. Cooper; I.3H Geoscience; I.3I Geoscience; I.4B John S. Shelton; I.4C J. D. Cooper; I.5A John S. Shelton; I.5B B. N. Cooper; I.5C John S. Shelton; I.6A–C J. D. Cooper; I.7A Breck P. Kent; I.7B J. D. Cooper; I.7C Breck P. Kent; I.8A Craig Watterson; I.8B J. D. Cooper. Theme II. II.1A painting by W. K. Hartmann; II.1B U.S.G.S. Volcano Observatory; II.2A J. D. Cooper; II.2B Harold L. James; II.3A J. D. Cooper; II.3B Breck P. Kent; II.3C J. D. Cooper; II.4A J. D. Cooper; II.4B John S. Shelton; II.4C Thomasson Grant/Stockfile; II.5A–C Breck P. Kent; II.6 National Museum of Natural History, Washington D.C.; II.7A J. D. Cooper; II.7B–D Society of Economic Paleontologists and Mineralogists. Slide Set No. 3, Peter A. Scholle; II.8A J. D. Cooper; II.8B,C Society of Economic Paleontologists and Mineralogists. Slide Set No. 3, Peter A. Scholle; II.8D J. D. Cooper. Theme III. III.1A Craig Watterson; III.1B Kirkendall/Spring; III.2A J. D. Cooper; III.2B Craig Watterson; III.2C J. D. Cooper; III.3A J. D. Cooper; III.3B J. D. Cooper; III.3C Kirkendall/Spring; III.4A,B Kirkendall/Spring; III.4C Geoscience; III.5A B. N. Cooper; III.5B J. D. Cooper; III.6A Breck P. Kent; III.6B J. D. Cooper; III.6C Wards Natural Science Establishment; III.7 Kirkendall/Spring; III.8A Alessandro Montanari; III.8B–D paintings by William K. Hartmann. Theme IV. IV.1A Kirkendall/Spring; IV.1B John S. Shelton; IV.2 photo courtesy of J. B. Minster and T. H. Jordon; IV.3 photo courtesy of Mike Abrams, Jet Propulsion Lab, Pasadena, California; IV.4A–C J. D. Cooper; IV.5A,B J. D. Cooper; IV.5C U. S. Geological Survey; IV.6A NASA; IV.6B,C J. D. Cooper; IV.7A Kirkendall/Spring; IV.7B J. D. Cooper; IV.7C Breck P. Kent; IV.8A,B Breck P. Kent; IV.8C George C. Page Museum of La Brea Discoveries, Los Angeles, California.

Chapter 6 opener photo: View looking upstream at Lower Moses Coulee, a late glacial meltwater flood channel, eastern Washington. This channel was carved by a series of catastrophic floods during the late Pleistocene from waters spilling out from ancient glacial meltwater Lake Missoula. Prominent geomorphologist J. Harlan Bretz argued steadfastly for a natural catastrophic origin for this and many other landscape features in the channeled scablands of eastern Washington. Late in his career he was accorded long overdue respect and acknowledgement for his interpretation that natural catastrophes had carved most of this landscape (photo courtesy of John S. Shelton).

Library of Congress Catalog Card Number: 89–62134
International Standard Book Number: 0–675–21134–4
Printed in the United States of America
1 2 3 4 5 6 7 8 9–93 92 91 90

Preface

Historical geology—the study of the Earth's evolution, including changes in its crust, surface, atmosphere, and life—has experienced its own evolutionary burst during the past two decades as new models for interpreting Earth history have been developed. The *plate tectonics* doctrine has become the new central theme of historical geology and has caused a monumental shift in how Earth scientists view the Earth's evolution.

Traditionally Historical Geology, as a formal course, has been taught at the first- or second-year college level, either in tandem with Physical Geology or as a separate course appealing to a general education audience. Teachers of historical geology always have faced the twofold problem of how to boil down an enormous body of factual information about *what* happened during the Earth's past history and at the same time present a meaningful dose of guiding principles and concepts to facilitate appreciation and understanding of *how* we know about geologic events and their chronology. With the advent of plate tectonic theory and its many ramifications for Earth history, this dilemma of information level and balance has been compounded. Historical geology has become a more complex subject because of greater synthesis of data and integration of ideas from many diverse disciplines. Consequently, in recent years, both teaching and development of text material for historical geology have faced new challenges as well as frustrations—the key elements of plate tectonic concepts and interpretations must be woven into the fabric of geologic time, evolution, ancient seas, mountain building, changing climates, dinosaurs, and extinctions, without losing the student.

Such a course for the geology major, early in the program, provides an opportunity to interpret, to relate cause and effect, and to learn some important principles and methods as a prelude to more advanced courses. It also provides an opportunity to begin to *think geologically,* to develop the resourcefulness and detective approach required to read and decode the rock record, and to develop appreciation of past geologic events set in their chronologic sequence. Such a course for the nonscience, general education student (with or without the benefit of background in physical geology) provides an overview of prehistory and of mankind's evolutionary heritage, promotes an appreciation for the Earth's natural resources (how they form and how long they take to form), and helps in development of a perspective on the Earth's cosmic connection and how the planet was born. A well-designed course also has the potential for acquainting students with the unique aspects of the geological sciences as well as for showing how historical geology relates to the breadth of human knowledge and problems.

Our mission in writing and revising this text has been in part to meet the challenges that historical geology presents for a beginning course, but, more importantly, to share the excitement, beauty, intrigue, fascination, and achievement of historical geology. In our attempt to accomplish this mission we have set the following principal goals:

1. To develop the thought processes and methodologies of historical geology—what the guiding principles are and how they are applied to the interpretation of Earth history. The text is structured so that working principles and concepts are developed in the first part. Plate tectonics, as a unifying theme, is introduced in the first chapter within the context of the grand *geologic cycle* (how the Earth works).

2. To make clear the very important concepts of geologic time. Principles and concepts of relative and absolute time, presented in Chapter 5, are initially set apart from discussions of the birth and development of the geologic time scale and fundamental stratigraphic principles, which are presented in Chapter 6. This separation is intended to focus on the working principles and concepts first in order to facilitate clear understanding of how interpretations of Earth history are made.

3. To strike a healthy balance between *what happened when* (geologic events and their chronology) and *how we know* (the guiding principles employed in the interpretation of Earth history). Historical events are outlined in the second part of the text, with emphasis on the geological evolution of North America. In order to avoid isolating principles and events phases in their own separate vacuums, we have endeavored to tie them together through extensive cross-referencing and by providing case histories from the geologic record.

4. To stimulate the reader by punctuating the text with scientific controversies, personal feuds, amusing anecdotes, and other human interest items. Historical geology has had its own fascinating evolution and many colorful, imaginative, and inventive people have made important contributions to its development. Human interest aspects and the evolution of ideas provide extra dimension to the science and furnish themes for the various chapter openings.

5. To develop as a unifying theme the interaction between physical and organic changes in the history of the Earth and the cyclic nature of many geologic phenomena. The geologic events part of the text has been developed in such a fashion as to illustrate and exemplify important principles and concepts, to downplay detailed facts and figures, and to concentrate on cause and effect. We have tried to emphasize major highlights and how they have been described and interpreted within the limits of state-of-the-art scientific research.

6. Finally, to present information in a logical sequence and to make it appealing and interesting, but also to challenge the mind with a blend of depth and rigor that is in keeping with a college-level learning experience.

In this second, significantly revised, edition of *A Trip Through Time,* we not only have added new material, but also have restructured and streamlined the text. Updated information on the Precambrian-Cambrian transition and boundary, dinosaurs, the terminal Cretaceous mass extinction event, and tectonic history reflect exciting areas of ongoing vigorous research. Regarding the first of the above-mentioned areas, we have returned to a more conventional time scale, wherein the contentious Ediacarian Period is included in the Proterozoic, emphasizing instead the transitional nature of the Precambrian-Cambrian boundary interval (Chapter 9). One addition that we are particularly excited about is the inclusion of four new 8-page, full-color inserts that are designed to illustrate and enhance the main segments of the text with images that exemplify many of the diverse scales and perspectives that geologists use to interpret Earth history. The chapters on the sedimentary record, including facies and environments and paleontology, have been moved forward in the text to provide a more logical sequence of preliminary concepts. Previous chapters on Paleozoic and Mesozoic history have been updated and subdivided for better organization. These changes have been made with the intent of providing you with a more readable, well-illustrated, and informative text.

We feel our text is appropriate for a general education course at the junior college and four-year university level as well as for the geology major early in the program. We hope our text will provide a thread of continuity in learning about the fascinating history of the Earth and about the guiding principles and methods that allow interpretation of that history. But we also realize no text can provide the last word on the subject. It is up to the individual instructor to fill the gaps and catalyze the learning experience, and it is up to the individual student to accept responsibility for the learning.

ACKNOWLEDGMENTS

We are very thankful to the following colleagues for their thoughtful comments and suggestions: Richard L. Bowen, University of Southern Mississippi; Barbara Christian, University of North Carolina at Charlotte; Kraig L. Derstler, University of New Orleans; Douglas H. Erwin, Michigan State University; C. B. Gregor, Wright State University; William S. McLoda, Mountain View College; William Mode, University of Wisconsin—Oshkosh; Joaquin Rodriquez, Hunter College; and Johnny A. Waters, West Georgia College. We also extend our warm appreciation to those individuals who reviewed the first edition of this text: Karl J. Koenig, Texas A&M University; Raymond Sullivan, San Francisco State University; C. John Mann, University of Illinois; Charles Rockwell, Nassau Community College;

Charles J. Mott, St. Petersburg Junior College, Clearwater; William J. Ausich, Ohio State University; William N. Orr, University of Oregon; Thomas H. Dunham, Old Dominion University; Lawrence H. Balthasar, California Polytechnic State University; and San Louis Obispo and E. Joan Baldwin of El Camino College.

Contents

12 Early Mesozoic History 345

13 Late Mesozoic History 377

14 Cenozoic History 413

15 The Big Freeze: Glaciers and Glaciation

A TRIP THROUGH TIME

How the Earth Works

1

Contents

Key Terms

Plate tectonics
Lithosphere
Mesosphere
Asthenosphere
Geologic cycle
Hydrologic cycle
Rock cycle
Tectonic cycle
Uniformitarianism
Actualism
Isostasy
Divergent plate boundary
Magnetic anomaly
Convergent boundary
Subduction zone
Benioff zone
Andesite
Volcanic island arc
Magmatic arc
Wilson Cycle
Transform fault
Triple junction
Orogenic belt
Orogen
Terrane
Craton
Continental margin basin
Miogeocline
Eugeocline
Microplate
Exotic terrane
Sedimentary basin
Wave base
Moho

Continents Adrift, Continents Aground

During the 1960s, Earth scientists reached a new plateau in their understanding of the Earth. An exciting revolution, called **plate tectonics,** gave substance to the once-outrageous hypothesis that the continents have been mobile during much of the Earth's history—at times separating (continents adrift), at other times colliding (continents aground). Plate tectonics is a new and exciting variation on the old theme of moving continents. During the latter part of the nineteenth century, it was observed that many rock sequences of southern-hemisphere continents matched one another, but, in turn, were quite different from the rock sequences of northern-hemisphere continents. Coupled with recognition of this similarity in geologic sequences was the recognition of evidence for late Paleozoic (Table 1–1) glaciation on the southern-hemisphere continents. During the last two decades of the nineteenth century these geologic similarities inspired a brilliant Austrian geologist and synthesist, Edward Suess, to postulate the former existence of a vast southern supercontinent which he called *Gondwanaland,* with the implication that the southern-hemisphere continents had moved.

The recognized father of the moving-continent idea was Alfred Wegener, a German geographer and meteorologist. In a remarkable book, *The Origin of Continents and Oceans,** first published in 1912, Wegener made a cogent case for the nonpermanency of the positions of continents, and "continental drift" was proposed as an actual theory. Wegener based his theory on similarities recognized from a comprehensive comparison of rocks, structures, stratigraphy, paleontology, paleoclimatology, and the geometrical fit of continental margins (particularly the fit between the outer edges of the continental shelves of eastern South America and western Africa).

He maintained that the goodness-of-fit hypothesis could be supported by matching up geologic features across the ocean abyss—much like reading the newsprint across two pieces of torn newspaper (Fig. 1–1). He proposed the name *Pangaea* for a supercontinent composed of today's separated continental masses—a supercontinent that was assumed to have existed prior to the beginning of fragmentation about 180 million years ago. This was a truly brilliant synthesis.

In spite of all the evidence marshaled by Wegener in support of continental drift, the theory suffered from not being explained by a viable mechanism. The geophysicists of the day vehemently attacked the notion as absurd and contrary to the physical properties and laws of the solid Earth. They considered it a theory that represented more fiction than truth, and one that appealed to extremists in geology. How, the geophysicists and most geologists asked, could the lighter continental masses move headlong across the heavier ocean basin crust? Preposterous!

---

*1966 translation by John Biran from 4th German ed. (1929). New York: Dover Publications.

Table 1–1
Major subdivisions of the geologic time scale

Eon		Era	Period		Age in Ma*
PHANEROZOIC		CENOZOIC	Quaternary	Quaternary	2
			Tertiary	Neogene	24
				Paleogene	65
		MESOZOIC	Cretaceous		144
			Jurassic		208
			Triassic		245
		PALEOZOIC	Permian		286
			Carboniferous	Pennsylvanian	320
				Mississippian	360
			Devonian		408
			Silurian		438
			Ordovician		505
			Cambrian		570
CRYPTOZOIC (PRECAMBRIAN)	PROTEROZOIC	Late Proterozoic			900
		Middle Proterozoic			1600
		Early Proterozoic			2500
	ARCHEAN	Late Archean			3000
		Middle Archean			3400
		Early Archean			~3800
HADEAN (Pregeologic history of the Earth)				Origin of Earth	4600

*Ma means numerical ages in millions of years before present or millions of years old.
Source: Data from A. R. Palmer, comp., 1983, The Decade of North American Geology 1983 Time Scale, p. 504: *Geology*, vol. 11, no. 9; G. V. Cohee, M. F. Glaessner, and H. D. Hedberg, 1978, Contributions to the Geologic Time Scale: *American Association of Petroleum Geologists, Studies in Geology*, no. 6; W. B. Harland and others, 1982, *A Geologic Time Scale*, Charts 1.1, 1.2, p. 4, 5: Cambridge University Press, Cambridge, England.

It seems that each line of evidence proposed was squelched by a more definitive counterargument. Wegener and his followers were convinced they were right; they felt the onus of finding a mechanism for drift was to be borne by the geophysicists. Their counter-counterargument was that the geophysicist doubters simply were not smart enough to discover the mechanism for drifting, and thus raged the debate—from the early 1900s on through the teens and twenties. A contingent of southern-hemisphere geolo-

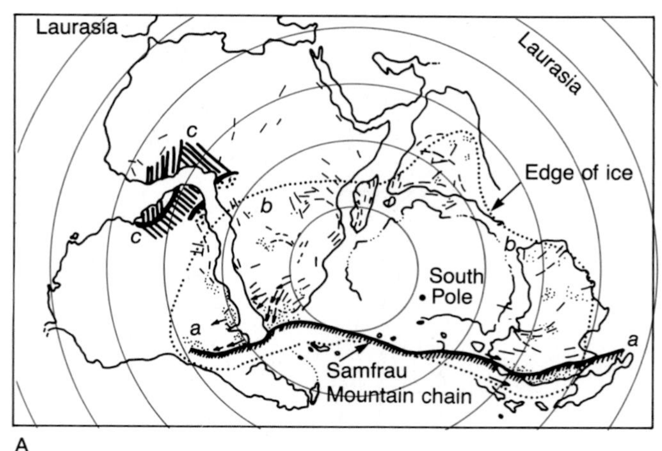

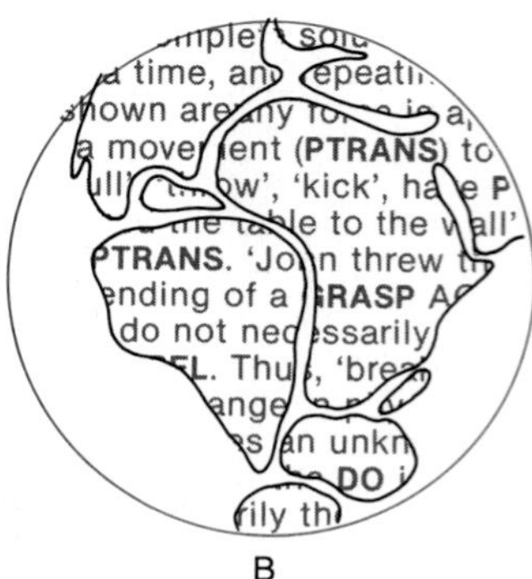

Figure 1–1
A. Reconstruction of Gondwanaland on the basis of alignment of mountain belts (a), distribution of glacial deposits (b), and matching geologic terranes (c).
B. Printed lines across the continents, depicted as pieces of a torn page.
(A from A. L. du Toit, 1937, *Our Wandering Continents,* Fig. 11, p. 93. Oliver and Boyd, Edinburgh. Reproduced by permission of Longman Group Ltd., London; B from H. Takeuchi, S. Uyeda, and H. Kanamori, 1970, *Debate about the Earth,* rev. ed., Fig. 1–16, p. 46. Reproduced by permission of Freeman, Cooper & Company, San Francisco)

gists, proponents of continental drift, continued to assemble evidence in support of their "radical" views. The most vociferous skeptics continued to be the geophysicists, who summarily dismissed what the drifters considered to be geologic facts, as inferences based on inconclusive data.

In 1929, Alfred Wegener died on the Greenland ice cap while engaged in historic research on echo sounding to determine the thickness of polar ice. Ironically, this type of research paved the way to later ocean-floor mapping techniques that ultimately led to recognition that it is the ocean crust that moves, carrying with it the continental masses. The doctrine of *plate tectonics,* with its "continents adrift, continents aground" theme became accepted as gospel in the mid-1960s, nearly 40 years after Wegener's death, rendering just vindication for one of the great pioneers of the Earth sciences.

The New Revolution

The nub of plate-tectonics theory is that the Earth's outer rind, the **lithosphere,** is fragmented, consisting of a mosaic of rigid pieces, called plates (Fig. 1–2), that move and interact. The implications of this theory for evolution of the Earth's lithosphere and surface are great. Plate tectonics provides at last a viable unifying concept that can explain such diverse phenomena as the origin of the Rocky mountains, formation of the Atlantic Ocean, why and where earthquakes and volcanoes occur, and some of the major patterns in the evolution of life. It is perhaps the most important breakthrough in the geological sciences since development of the time scale (Table 1–1).

The knowledge that has come with the plate-tectonics theory is continually interwoven with the

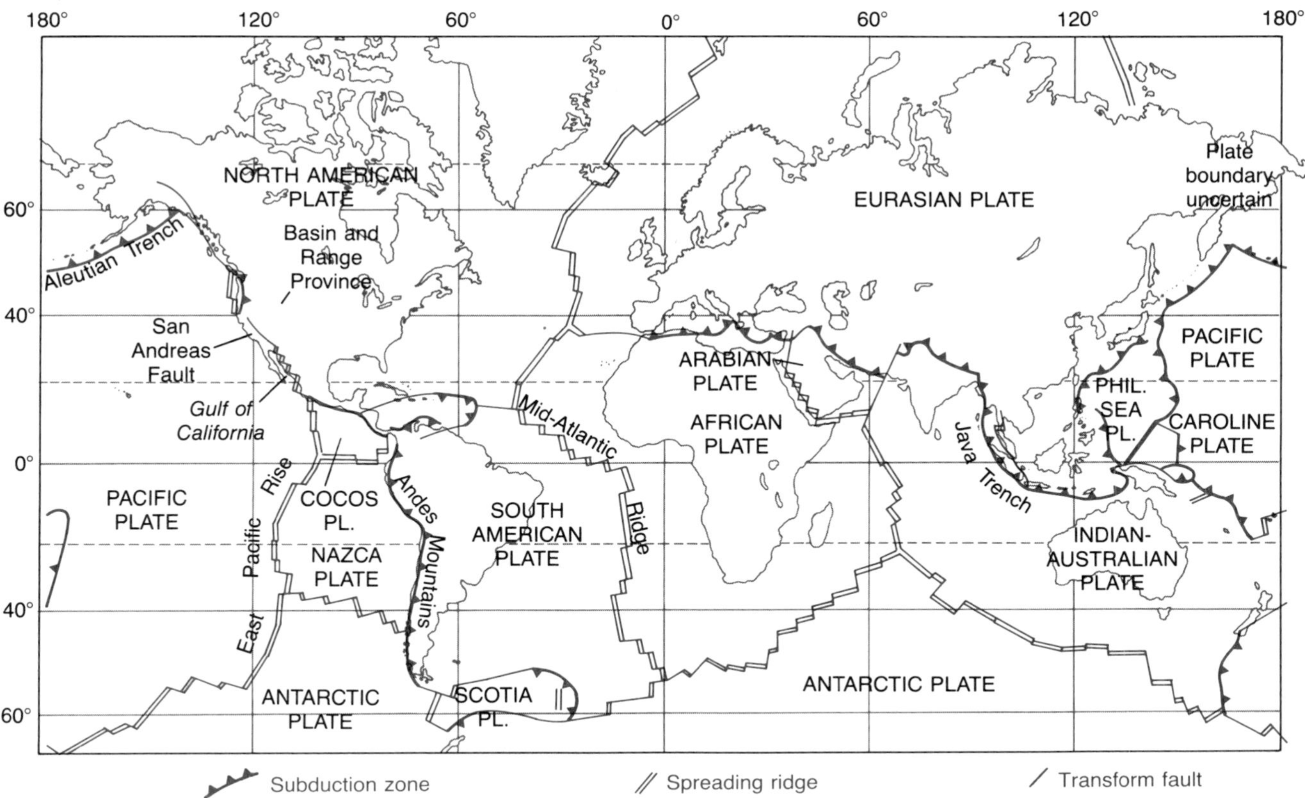

Figure 1–2
Major lithospheric plates of the world.
(From Warren B. Hamilton, 1979, Tectonics of the Indonesian Region, Fig. 2, p. 8: *U.S. Geological Survey Professional Paper* 1978)

fabric of this text. The purpose of this introductory chapter is to explain what plate tectonics is, and its relationship to how the Earth works. Before examining the main tenets of the theory, it is appropriate to become acquainted with the Earth's composition and architecture, and the *cycles* that mold its character.

Architecture of the Earth

The Earth's Interior

The Earth has an average density of about 5.5 grams per cubic centimeter (g/cm^3) and is believed to have a solid inner core and a liquid outer core (both of which are composed predominantly of iron and nickel). Outside the core, the Earth has a solid **mesosphere,** a mushy, almost plastic **asthenosphere** where partial melting occurs, and a rigid lithosphere (Fig. 1–3).

Most of this knowledge has come from the study of *seismic* (earthquake) waves. Two principal wave types—shear (S waves) and compressional (P waves)—have characteristic velocities in solid media. P waves travel faster than S waves (Figs. 1–3B, 1–4), and the velocities of both increase with increasing density of the Earth's interior. S waves, however, are not transmitted in a medium that lacks resistance to shearing deformation (such as a liquid). Thus, the outer core is believed to be in a molten state, due to its failure to transmit S waves, together with the dramatic decrease in P-wave velocity (Fig. 1–4).

Study of seismic waves and of volcanoes in the oceanic regions (e.g., the Hawaiian chain in the Pacific) and direct sampling by means of deep-sea drilling show that the lithosphere that forms the floor of the ocean basins is composed of *basalt.* Basalt is an igneous rock rich in magnesium-bearing *silicate minerals* such as olivine and pyroxene (Table 1–2); it has a density of about 3.0 g/cm^3.

Through seismic-wave studies and other geological investigations, continents have been found to

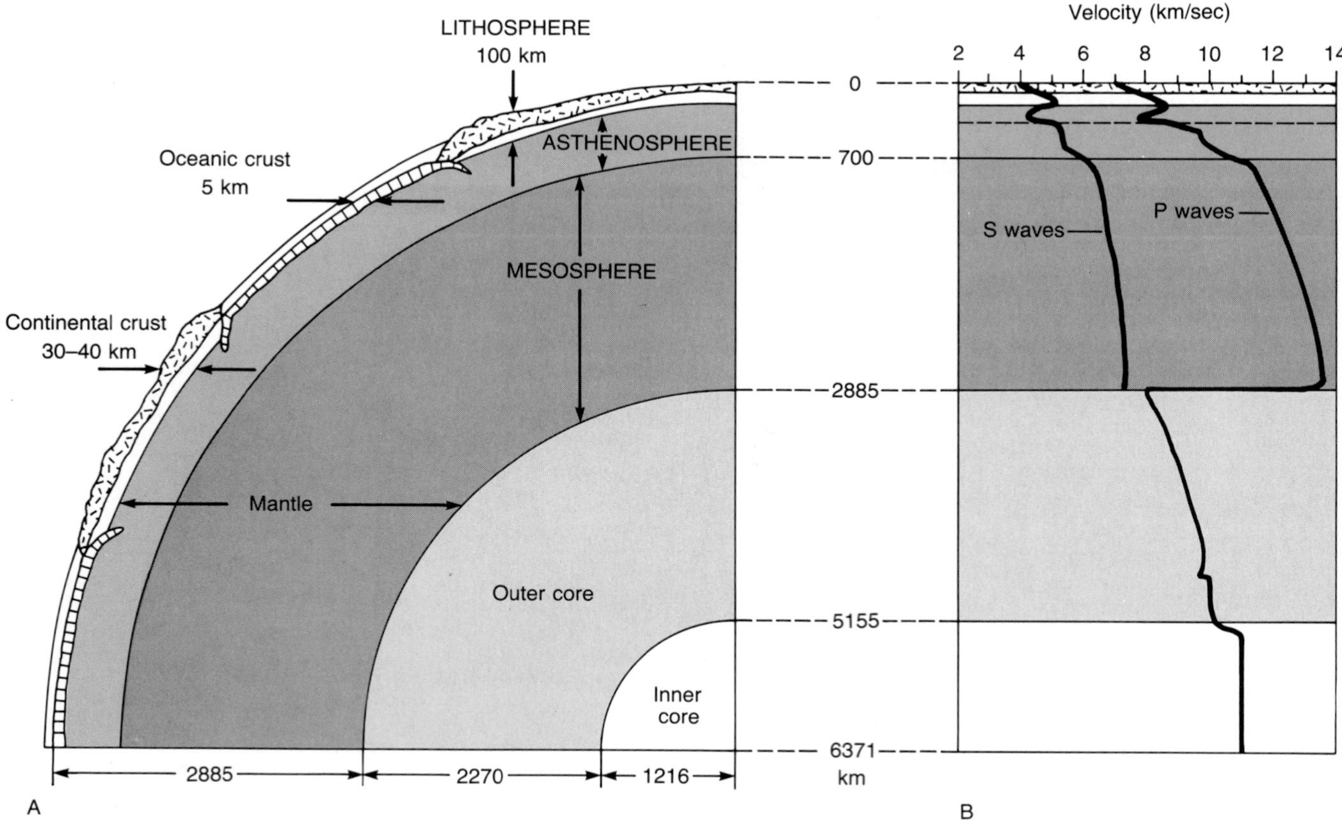

Figure 1–3
A. Schematic cross section of the Earth's interior structure. Note that the traditional mantle includes the mesosphere and lower part of the lithosphere.
B. Same interior structure showing pattern of seismic-wave velocities. Note the disappearance of the S wave at the mesosphere–outer core boundary, the abrupt slowing of P-wave velocity at this same boundary, and the slowing of both P- and S-wave velocities in the upper part of the asthenosphere.
(From E. J. Tarbuck and F. K. Lutgens, 1987, *The Earth,* 2d ed., Figs. 15–6, 15–11: Merrill Publishing Co.)

have an average composition of *granite,* an igneous rock that crystallizes from magma below the surface. However, in their composition and structure, continents are complex, generally more so than oceanic lithosphere. Granites and their close relatives are composed predominantly of silicate minerals that consist mainly of oxides of silicon and aluminum, such as quartz and potassium feldspar (Table 1–2).

Continental lithosphere has a density that averages about 2.7 g/cm^3, significantly less than that of basalt. The density of the bottom part of the continental masses appears to approach the density of basalt (Fig. 1–5). Below the lithosphere lies a zone 100 to 200 km thick in which the velocities of earthquake waves are lower than in the more rigid lithosphere. This low-velocity zone constitutes the upper part of the asthenosphere (Fig. 1–5).

It is the lithosphere, essentially "floating" on the more plastic asthenosphere below, that figures most prominently in our later discussion of how the Earth works. Before examining some of the key elements of the plate-tectonics theory, let us consider the lithosphere in a broader geologic context.

The Geologic Cycle

The lithosphere is composed of a complex assortment of rock types having a wide range of compositions. These different rocks are the products of physical, chemical, and biological processes occur-

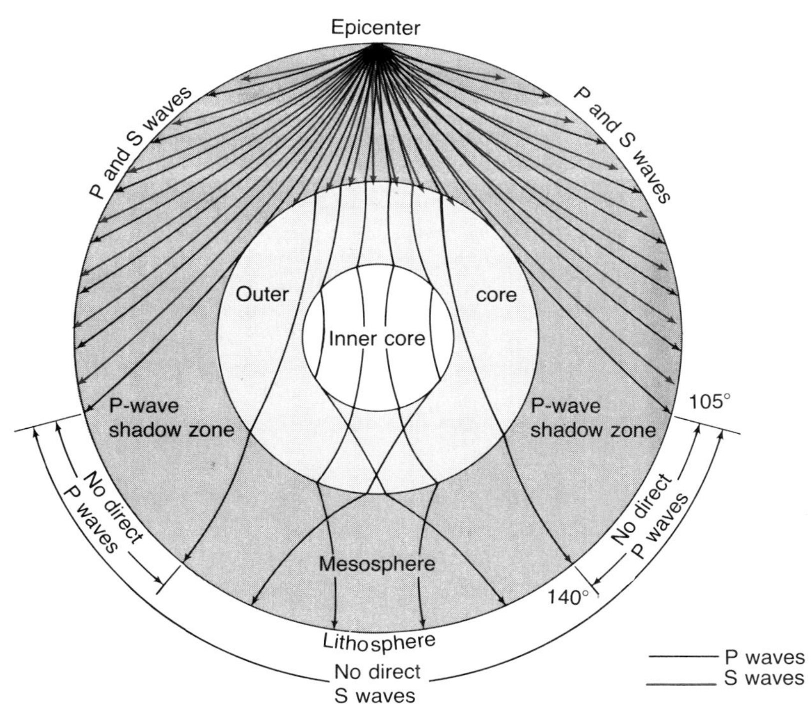

Figure 1–4
View of the Earth showing the paths of P and S waves. Any location more than 105° from the epicenter will not receive direct S waves, because the outer core will not transmit them. A small shadow zone exists (from 105° to 140°) for P waves. The P-wave shadow zone is caused by the bending of these waves as they pass from more rigid mantle material to less rigid core material. The seismic waves that pass through the center of the Earth increase in velocity, revealing the existence of the solid inner core.
(From E. J. Tarbuck and F. K. Lutgens, 1987, *The Earth,* 2d ed., Fig. 15–9, p. 382: Merrill Publishing Co.)

Table 1–2
Simplified classification of igneous rocks showing relationship between mineral composition and texture

← Decreasing temperature of silicate melt

(common rock-forming silicate minerals) Composition / Texture (crystal size)	Mica, Quartz, K-feldspar	Amphibole, Na-Plagioclase feldspar-Ca	Pyroxene, Ca-Plagioclase feldspar, Olivine	Pyroxene
	FELSIC	INTERMEDIATE	MAFIC	ULTRA MAFIC
EXTRUSIVE APHANITIC (finely crystalline; rapid cooling)	Rhyolite	ANDESITE	**BASALT**	
INTRUSIVE PHANERITIC (coarsely crystalline; slow cooling)	**GRANITE**	Diorite	Gabbro	Peridotite
PORPHYRITIC (2-stage cooling; presence of phenocysts, which are relatively (to ground mass) large crystals)	Rhyolite porphyry (>50% phenocysts) porphyritic rhyolite (<50% phenocrysts) Granite porphyry (>50% phenocrysts) porphyritic granite (< 50% phenocrysts)	Andesite porphyry, porphyritic andesite Diorite porphyry porphyritic diorite)	Basalt porphyry porphyritic basalt Gabbro porphyry, porphyritic gabbro	
GLASSY (rapid cooling)	← Pumice (porous) → ← OBSIDIAN (solid) →			
PYROCLASTIC (Explosive; fragmental texture)	Tuff and breccia			

Figure 1–5
Structure of the lithosphere and asthenosphere showing relationship to traditional crust and mantle, relative densities, and low seismic velocity zone in the more "plastic" upper asthenosphere.

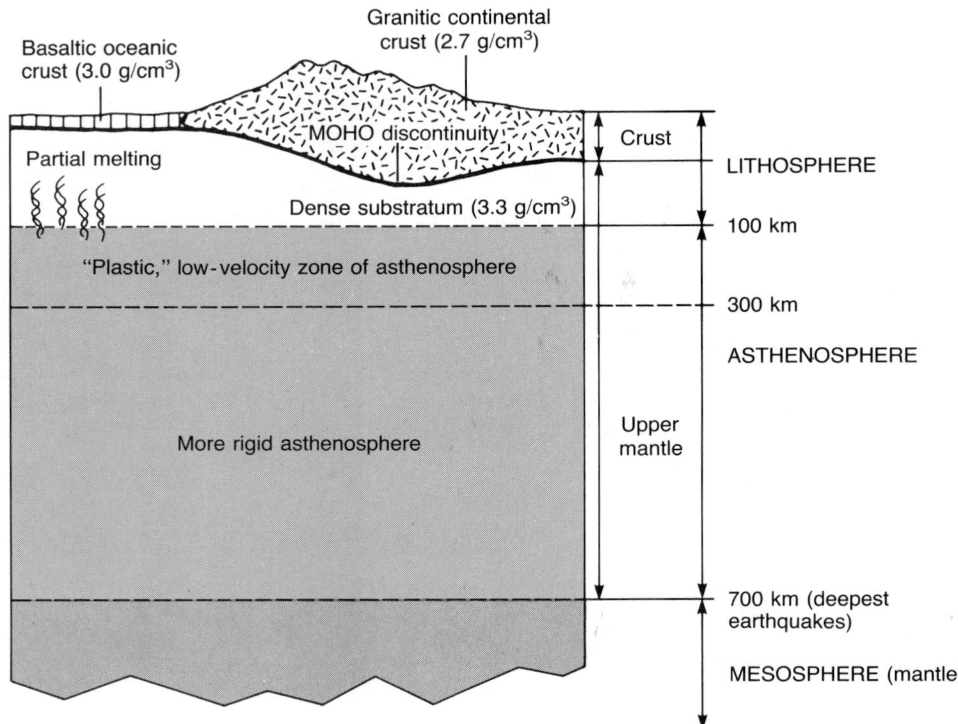

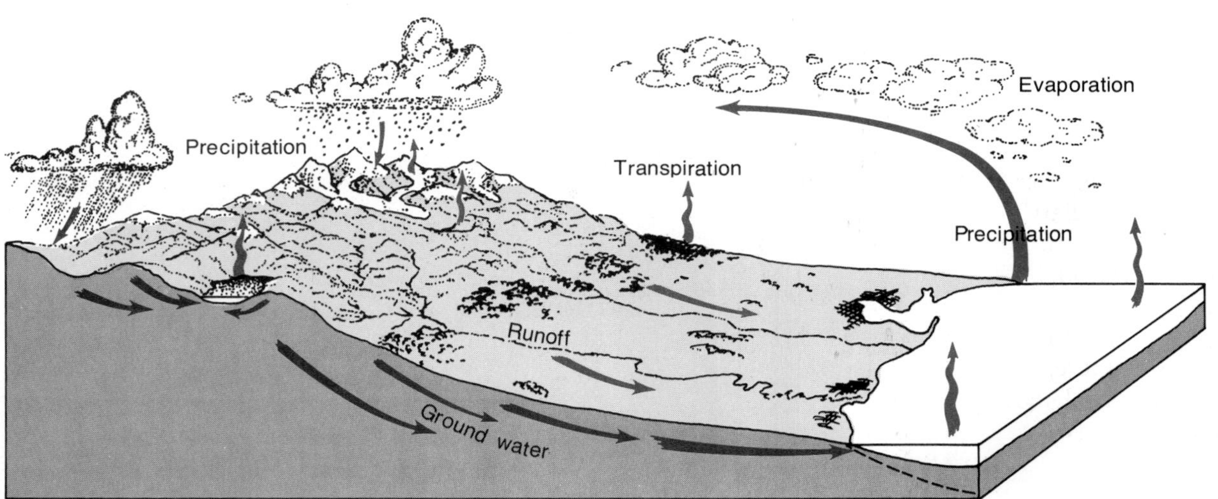

Figure 1–6
The circulation of water in the hydrologic system operates by solar energy. Water evaporates from the oceans, circulates around the globe with the atmosphere, and is eventually precipitated on the surface as rain or snow. The water that falls on the land returns to the ocean by surface runoff and groundwater seepage. Variations in the major flow patterns of the system include the temporary storage of water in lakes and glaciers. Within this major system are many smaller cycles, shortcuts, and two-way paths. Some occur in just minutes, as when rain evaporates before it falls to the surface of the Earth. Others endure for millions of years, as in the case of water locked up in minerals or deposits of sediments.
(From W. K. Hamblin, 1989, *The Earth's Dynamic Systems,* 5th ed., Fig. 2.2, p. 22: Macmillan Publishing Co., New York)

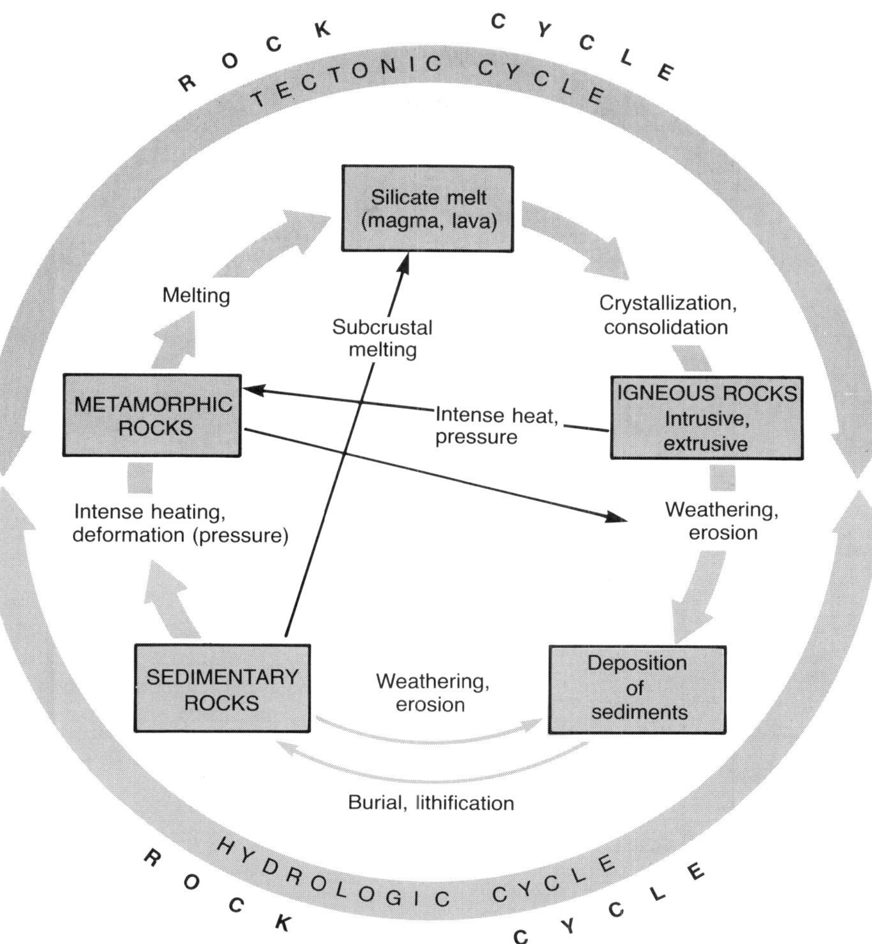

Figure 1–7
The Rock Cycle. The rock (or lithologic) cycle portrays the complex interrelationships among the three main families of rock: igneous, sedimentary, and metamorphic. The rock cycle is intricately related to (1) the tectonic cycle, which involves the generation of magmas, formation of igneous rocks, and dynamic metamorphism; and (2) the hydrologic cycle, whose main influence is in the weathering and eroding of rock and in providing the aqueous medium for sedimentation.

ring within the **geologic cycle,** which simplistically explains the way the Earth works. The components of the geologic cycle are: the **hydrologic cycle** (Fig. 1–6), the **rock cycle** (Fig. 1–7), and the **tectonic cycle.** All three of these cycles interact and, in turn, involve interactions of the lithosphere with the atmosphere, hydrosphere, and biosphere within the framework of internal (igneous and tectonic) processes and external (weathering and erosion) processes.

The interrelationship of these cycles and spheres is a very important concept in Earth history. Fundamental to how we view the history of the Earth is our understanding of observable geologic processes operating at the present. One of the principal credos of historical geology is *"the present is the key to the past,"* which means we believe that the geologic processes operating today also operated in the past. This concept is called **uniformitarianism** (also called **actualism;** see Chapter 6).

The hydrologic, or water, cycle involves the myriad pathways of water from the atmosphere to (and within) the lithosphere, and back again. Water is the most important geologic agent; in that it serves as a solvent for a host of chemical ions and compounds, it accomplishes much weathering and erosion, and it serves as a medium for deposition of sediments.

The rock cycle is the hub of the geologic cycle. Figure 1–7 graphically portrays the interrelationships among the three families of rock that make up the lithosphere: igneous rocks (Fig. 1–8; Table 1–2), sedimentary rocks (Fig. 1–9; Table 1–3), and metamorphic rocks (Fig. 1–10; Table 1–4).

Igneous rocks are those that have solidified (crystallized) from a hot silicate melt (Fig. 1–7). This molten material, generated within the asthenosphere and lithosphere, is called *magma* below the Earth's surface and *lava* on the surface (Fig. 1–8). As the melt cools through a succession of critical temperatures, various silicate minerals crystallize and aggregate to form rocks. Common types of igneous rocks are granite, basalt, rhyolite, and andesite (Table 1–2).

Table 1–3

Simplified classification of sediments and sedimentary rocks*

Composition \ Texture	Gravel	2 mm Sand	1/16 mm Mud (or silt, clay)
TERRIGENOUS CLASTIC (extrabasinal)	CONGLOMERATE (if rounded particles); BRECCIA (if angular particles)	SANDSTONE	MUDSTONE, SILTSTONE, CLAYSTONE; SHALE if fissile
Quartz	Quartz-pebble conglomerate/breccia	If >95% quartz: QUARTZARENITE	Quartz siltstone
Feldspar	Granite rock fragments + coarse feldspar Arkosic conglomerate	If 25% feldspar: ARKOSE	Arkosic siltstone
Rock fragments	Polymictic conglomerate if mixed composition; single source + conglomerate if one clast type; e.g., limestone-pebble conglomerate, volcanic-pebble conglomerate	If 25% rock fragments: LITHIC SANDSTONE	Lithic siltstone
Mica and clay minerals		Micaceous arkose or micaceous lithic sandstone	Micaceous siltstone Mudstone Claystone; and shale
NONTERRIGENOUS (intrabasinal)	Express in terms of grain size if rock is composed largely of transported particles; crystal size if texture is crystalline		
	LIMESTONE		
Calcium carbonate: LIMESTONE	CALCIRUDITE; modify with dominant grain type (e.g., skeletal calcirudite)	CALCARENITE; modify with dominant grain type (e.g., oolitic calcarenite)	CALCILUTITE or MICRITE
	DOLOSTONE		
Calcium-magnesium carbonate: DOLOMITE	Coarsely crystalline DOLOSTONE	Medium crystalline DOLOSTONE	Finely crystalline DOLOSTONE
Silica-cryptocrystalline quartz: CHERT	Includes green and red jasper; white novaculite, and gray/black flint varieties; can form as primary precipitate or secondary replacement		
Calcium sulfate: GYPSUM and ANHYDRITE Sodium chloride: HALITE	Coarsely crystalline gypsum, anhydrite, halite	Medium crystalline gypsum, anhydrite, halite	Finely crystalline gypsum, anhydrite, halite
Carbon: COAL	Includes anthracite, bituminous, subbituminous, and lignite varieties		

*Simplified classification of sedimentary rocks showing relationship between texture and composition for terrigenous clastic and nonterrigenous (chemical) sediments. Terrigenous clastic sediments are composed of particles derived from preexisting rocks. The particles are mainly the more stable silicate minerals such as quartz and K-feldspar, but include rock fragments (grains that maintain the full identity of their parent rocks), particularly in the conglomerates (and breccias). Nonterrigenous sediments are composed of transported particles and minerals precipitated from solution within the basin of deposition. Composition of individual nonterrigenous rocks is generally less complex than that of terrigenous clastic rocks. Limestones commonly have textures analogous to those in terrigenous clastic rock. Most of the other chemical sediments (with the exception of coal) have a crystalline texture.

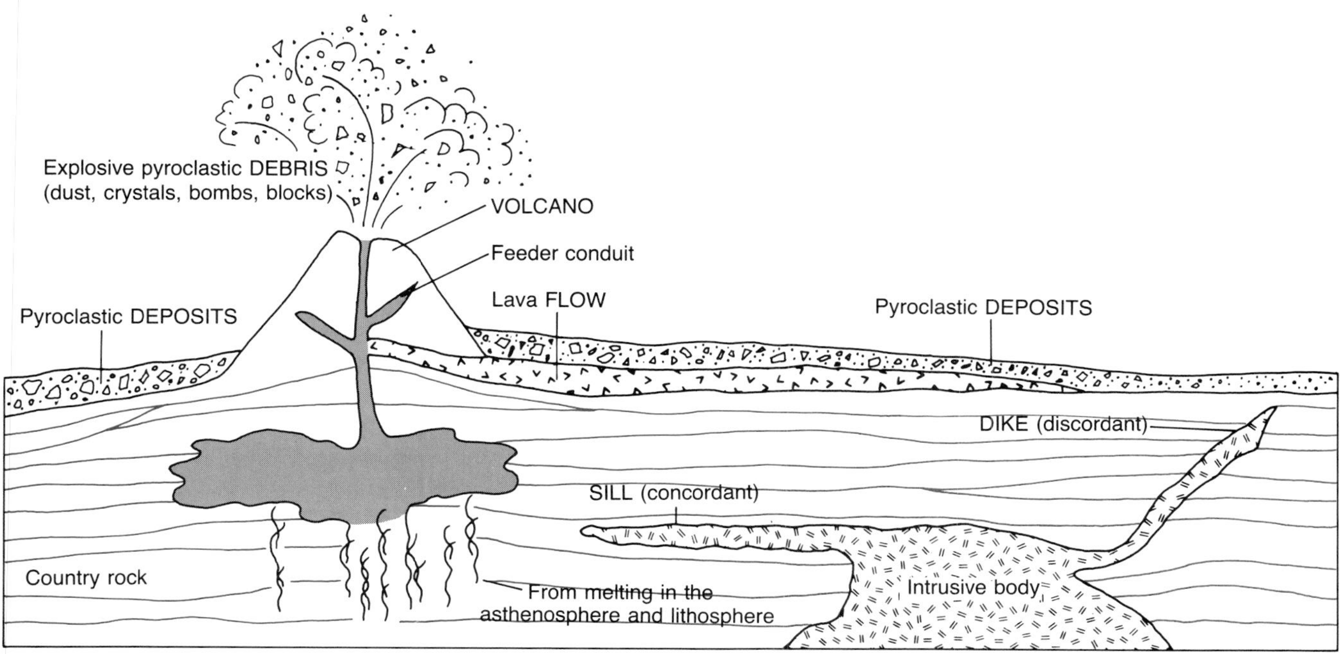

Figure 1–8
Intrusive and extrusive igneous activity and resulting bodies of rock.

Sedimentary rocks result from the accumulation of particles on the Earth's surface through the combined action of the hydrosphere, atmosphere, and biosphere (Fig. 1–7). Most sedimentary particles are *deposited* by the action of water, but some are deposited directly by the wind or by ice (Fig. 1–9). Some common sedimentary rock types are sandstone, shale, conglomerate, and limestone (Table 1–3).

Observing processes of sedimentation in modern-day sedimentary environments provides many examples of the application of uniformitarianism (actualism). Sedimentary rocks are developed characteristically in stratified (layered) sequences, the result of spreading and working by the depositional agent (usually water). It is this layered arrangement, together with the occurrence of fossils (remains of ancient life) in many sedimentary sequences, that

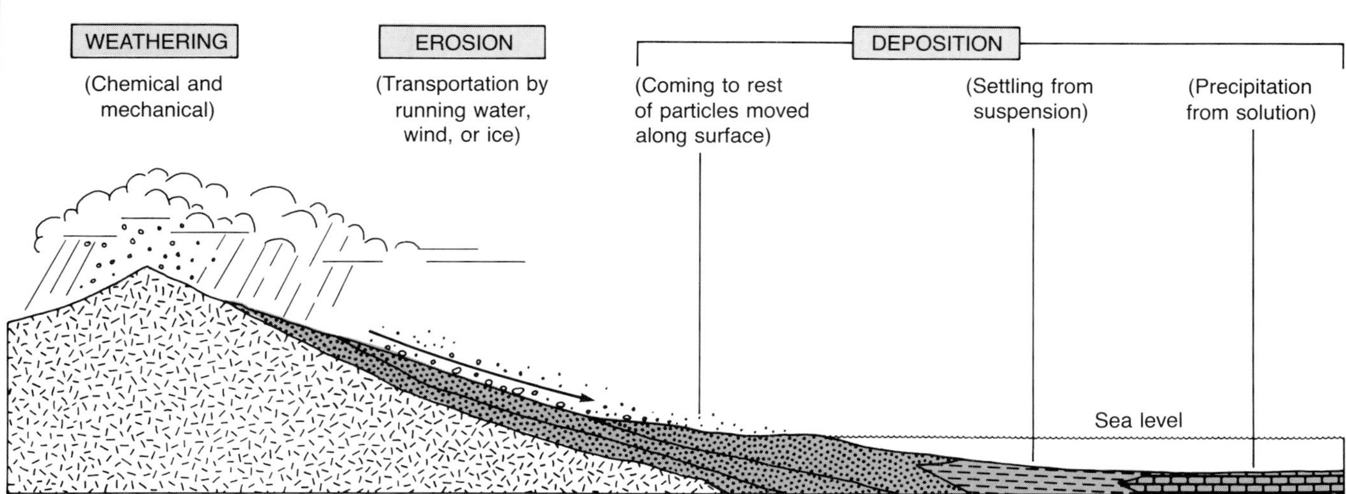

Figure 1–9
Processes active in the formation of sedimentary deposits. Composition of sedimentary particles is related to extrabasinal origin (transported solids derived from preexisting rocks) and intrabasinal origin (formed as biochemical or chemical precipitates within basin of deposition).

make this family of rocks most critical for interpreting Earth history. More detailed discussions of sedimentary rocks are presented in Chapters 2 and 5.

Metamorphic rocks are those that have been changed from their original state by the individual or combined action of high pressure, high temperature, and chemically active fluids, resulting from deformation, deep burial, and igneous activity within the lithosphere (Fig. 1–10). The metamorphic part of the rock cycle occurs only when and where the tectonic cycle is operating. Some of the more common metamorphic rocks are slate, schist, gneiss, and marble (Table 1–4).

The great bulk of the lithosphere is composed of *intrusive* igneous rocks (Fig. 1–8; Table 1–2) and secondarily, metamorphic rocks. Sedimentary rocks are confined to the surface and to the moderately shallow subsurface in the uppermost part of the lithosphere. Through geologic time, all three rock types have been continually recycled: melting of rock produces magma for the formation of new igneous rocks; weathering and erosion of igneous, metamorphic, and sedimentary rocks produce new sedimentary rocks; and intense heating and deformation of igneous and sedimentary rocks result in new metamorphic rocks (Fig. 1–7).

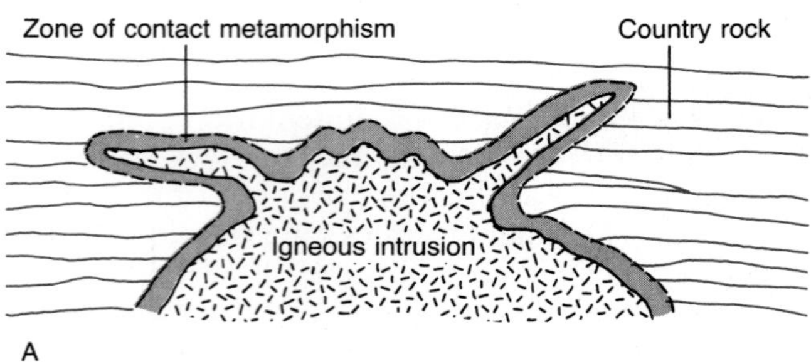

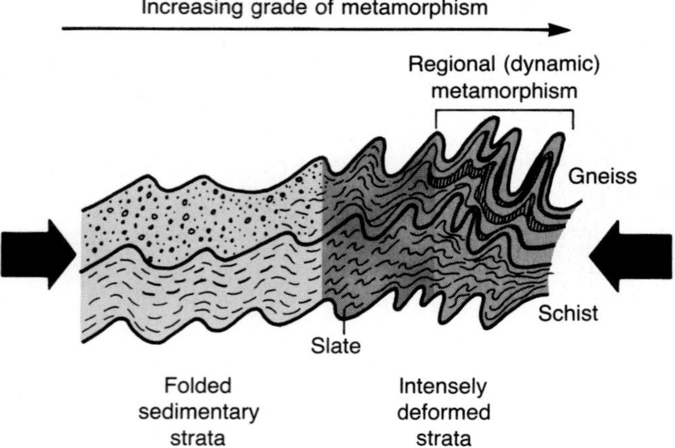

Figure 1–10
A. Contact metamorphism (thermal) of preexisting country rock around margins of igneous intrusion.
B. Regional, dynamic metamorphism (regional high pressure and temperature) resulting from deep burial and intense deformation produced by compression.

The tectonic cycle involves deformation of the lithosphere. Stresses propagated within and through the lithosphere serve to compact, stretch, bend, and break rock. The ultimate source of the stress is the movement of large lithospheric plates, and heat generated in the Earth's interior. Three principal types of stress deform rock: *compression, tension,* and *shear.* The response (strain) to these forms of stress is generally manifested in local-to-regional deformation, in any one or more of three principal styles, respectively: crustal shortening, extension, and lateral slip.

Compression results in shortening of the crust and is commonly expressed by folding, producing *anticlines* and *synclines* (Fig. 1–11A) and *reverse faulting* (Fig. 1–11B). *Thrust faults* (Fig. 1–11C) are reverse faults with a low angle of inclination of the fault plane. Tension results in crustal lengthening or extension, and is commonly expressed by *normal faulting* (Fig. 1–11D). Shear deformation involves "sideswiping" of crustal blocks, and is most commonly expressed by *strike-slip* faulting (Fig. 1–11E, F).

The Earth's Surface

The surface of our planet can be directly observed and sampled. Two of the most apparent features of the Earth's surface are the continents and ocean basins. As mentioned, the continental and oceanic parts of the lithosphere are made of rock of very different composition. The continents represent blocks of lighter rocks that essentially "float" on denser subjacent materials, much as an iceberg floats in water. This so-called "flotational equilibrium" is in accordance with the principle of **isostasy,** which, like Archimedes' principle of buoyancy, says that rock masses sink in denser substrata until the weight of substrata displaced becomes equal to the weight of the rock mass. This creates a state of balance, or equilibrium, illustrated in Figure 1–12A by the blocks of copper floating in mercury.

Approximately 70% of the Earth's surface is covered by the oceans. Figure 1–12B shows the relative percentages of the surface areas that lie at various

Table 1–4

Classification of metamorphic rocks showing relationship between texture and composition for *foliated* rocks (parallel to subparallel layering produced by mineral segregation and orientation of platy minerals such as mica) and *nonfoliated* rocks (generally involving recrystallization of monomineralic rocks such as quartz sandstone, limestone, or dolomite). Metaconglomerates have elongate pebbles (produced by stretching).

	Composition / Texture				
FOLIATED	Composition	Mica (including muscovite, biotite, chlorite)			
		Amphibole			
		Pyroxene			
	Texture	Feldspar			
		Quartz			
	Finely crystalline		SCHIST	PHYLLITE	SLATE
	Coarsely crystalline	GNEISS	SCHIST		
		← Increasing grade of metamorphism			
NONFOLIATED	Composition			Mica	
				Rock fragments	
			Quartz		
	Texture	Calcite/dolomite			
	Finely to coarsely crystalline	MARBLE	QUARTZITE		
	Fine to coarse grained			METACONGLOMERATE	

elevation intervals above or below sea level. Of particular note among the submerged regions of the Earth are submarine mountains (the ocean ridges), the abyssal plains of the ocean floor, and the continental shelves, slopes, and rises, which are major areas of sedimentation in the world's oceans. Sediments and sedimentary rocks that veneer the ocean bottoms, together with the sedimentary rocks on the continents, account for about 75% of the rocks exposed at the Earth's surface. This wide surface distribution and accessibility is yet another feature that makes the sedimentary rock record so important for understanding Earth history.

Within the context of continent and ocean-basin structure, there are various kinds and scales of relief features. The tectonic cycle causes large areas of the Earth's surface to subside (sink) slowly during geologic time, and subsequently to rise slowly through uplift and mountain building. Without these intervals of continental uplift, all exposed rocks would have been worn down by weathering and erosion and redeposited in the oceans long ago. Therefore, the surface morphology of the Earth, at any given time in Earth history, is the net result of internal and external processes operating within the *geologic cycle.*

The hydrologic cycle and the sedimentary part of the rock cycle are driven by external (surface) processes. The igneous and metamorphic parts of the rock cycle and the tectonic cycle are driven by internal (subsurface) processes. The explanation of the tectonic cycle, as well as parts of the rock cycle, lies in the theory of plate tectonics.

The Earth is a dynamic planet with an atmosphere that weathers and erodes, a hydrosphere that transports and collects solid particles and chemical compounds, a biosphere that includes all life processes, including secretion of hard skeletal parts that become incorporated in the rock cycle, and an internal heat engine that is responsible for driving the lithospheric plates. Because of the geologic cycle, and particularly because of plate tectonics, ocean basins and continents have changed dramatically during geologic history. We will examine the outline of the unifying plate-tectonics concept by taking a more detailed look at composition, structure, and surface features of the ocean basins and continents as they relate to the geologic cycle.

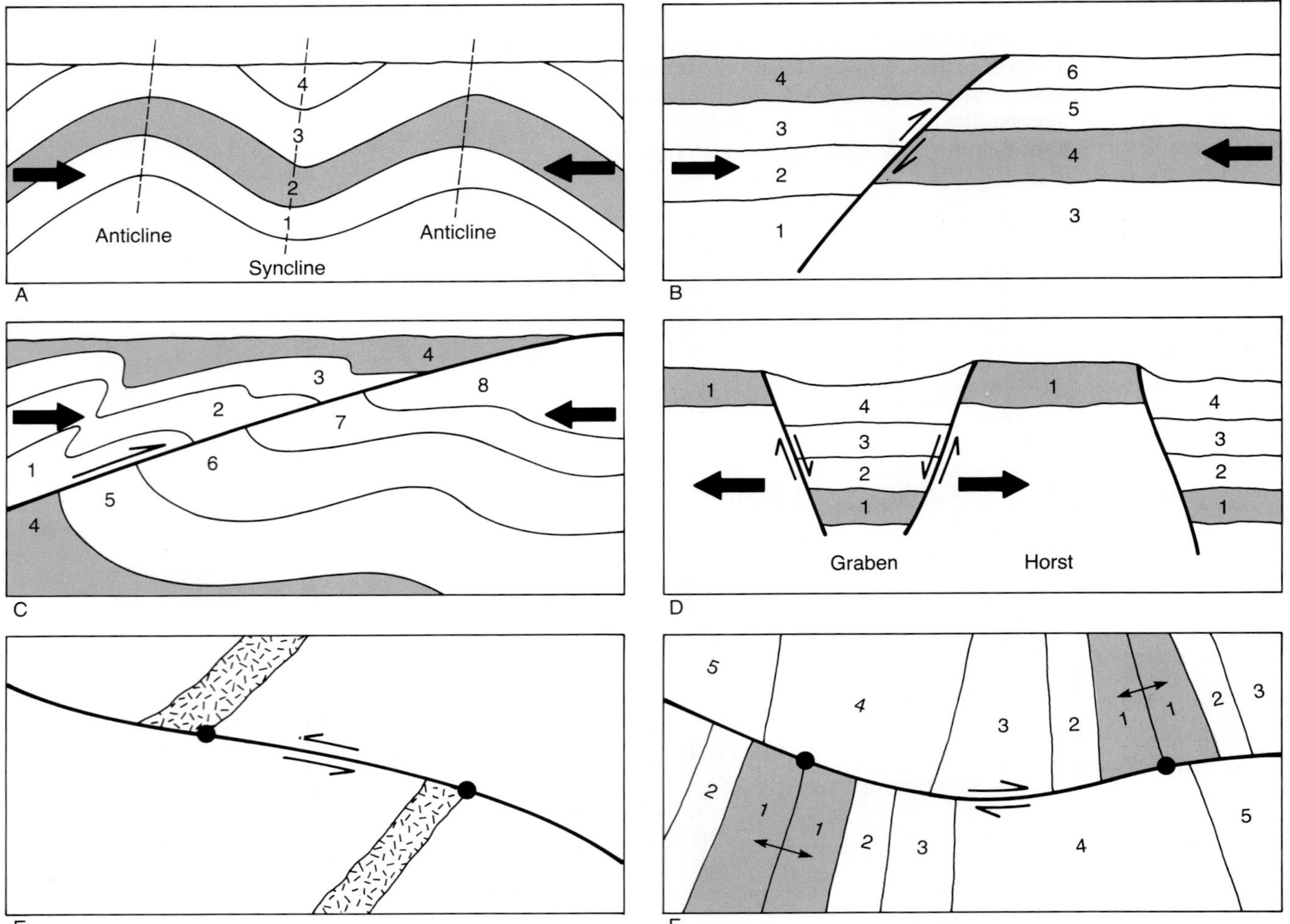

Figure 1–11

Tectonic structures. A. Folding. Folds are expressed in cross section as anticline and syncline. An anticline is an arch-shaped fold with oldest strata in core. Syncline is a trough-shaped fold with youngest strata in core. B–F. Faulting. B, C, D are cross sections of dip-slip faults, in which the main component of movement has been up or down the fault plane (vertical separation). Fault planes are inclined (dip) toward the hanging wall and away from the foot wall. B. Reverse fault. The hanging wall has moved up in relation to the foot wall. C. Thrust fault. The hanging wall has moved up and over the foot wall along a gently inclined (shallow-dipping) fault plane. D. Normal fault. The hanging wall has moved down in relation to the footwall. E and F are plan or map views of strike-slip faults, whereby the main component of movement has been essentially parallel to the surface (horizontal separation). E. Left-lateral strike-slip fault. Horizontal motion has offset the vertical dike in a left-hand sense. F. Right-lateral strike-slip fault. Horizontal motion has offset the axis of the anticline in a right-hand sense.

Plate Tectonics

Ocean Basins

The most prominent feature of the ocean basins is a 70,000 km-long ridge system that constitutes the most extensive mountain range on Earth. This ridge system is fundamentally and significantly different in composition, origin, and structure from the mountain ranges that exist on continents. In the Mid-Atlantic Ridge, there are on both sides of the ridge abyssal plains (Fig. 1–13), which are immense flat regions blanketed by fine-grained sediments at depths of 5000 to 6000 m or more. The sides of the ridge rise gradually from the abyssal

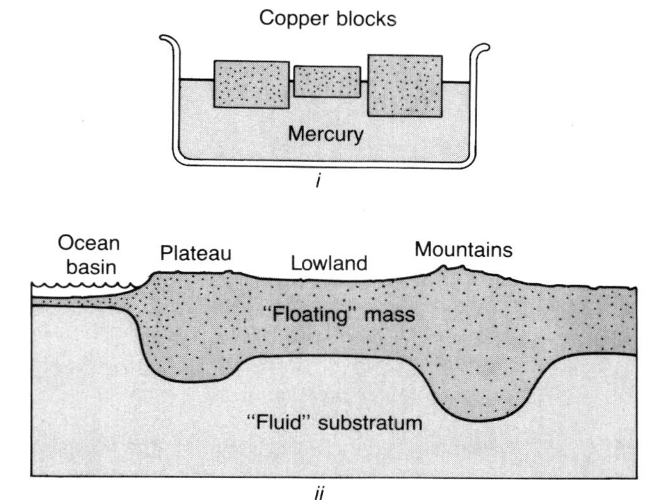

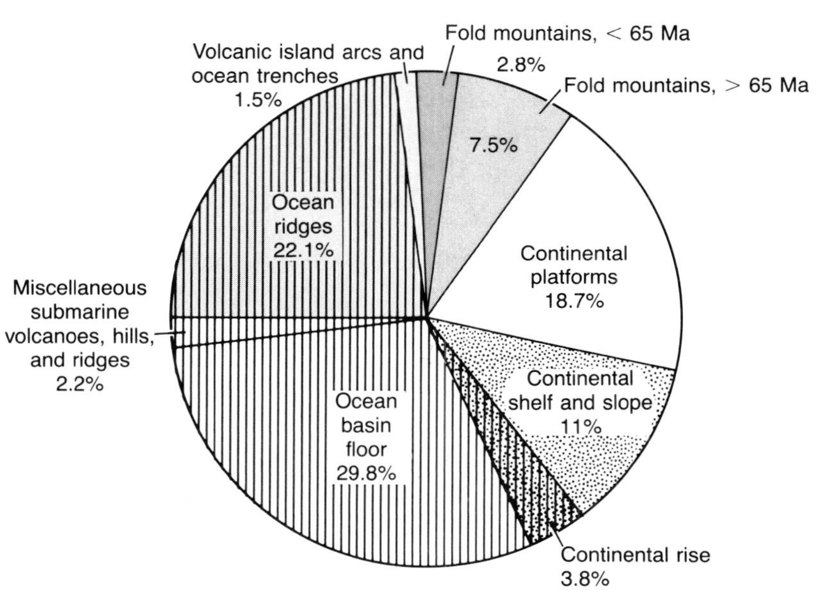

Figure 1–12
A. The principle of isostasy. *i.* Flotation of copper blocks in more dense mercury. *ii.* Flotation of lighter continental crustal blocks in "more fluid" denser substratum. B. Major features of the Earth's solid surface, shown as percentages of the total world surface.
(A from H. Takeuchi, S. Uyeda, and H. Kanamori, 1970, *Debate about the Earth,* rev. ed., Fig. 1–8, p. 33. Reproduced by permission of Freeman, Cooper & Company, San Francisco; B from Peter J. Wyllie, *The Way the Earth Works,* Fig. 3–11, p. 38: Copyright © 1976 by John Wiley & Sons, Inc., New York. Reprinted by permission of John Wiley & Sons, Inc.)

plains to the crest of the ridge, which is generally 1500 m or less below the surface of the ocean, but in places projects to the surface as islands such as Iceland and the Azores. Along the crest is a rift, or structural valley (Fig. 1–13), which has abnormally high heat flow, abundant earthquakes, and submarine volcanism.

The volcanism results from upwelling basaltic material that solidifies and becomes welded onto the inner sides of the rift. This activity creates new lithosphere along the rift. The rift itself continues to exist because newly formed lithosphere separates and moves away on both sides of the rift.

In the language of plate tectonics, the Mid-Atlantic Ridge and the rest of the oceanic ridge system are *ocean floor spreading centers.* They represent **divergent plate boundaries,** where two major lithospheric plates move apart at a rate of a few centimeters per year. This spreading of oceanic lithosphere along the Mid-Atlantic Ridge, for instance, has been responsible for separation of the opposite shores of the Atlantic Ocean. As a divergent plate boundary, the ridge system has played an instrumental role in global tectonics history and patterns.

The signature of this seafloor spreading is the pattern of paired **magnetic anomalies** (irregularities) arranged like stripes on both sides of the oceanic ridge system (Fig. 1–15B). These anomalies are detected by sensitive *magnetometers,* instruments that record the *remanent magnetization* of rocks on the ocean floor.

This "fossilized" magnetism is preserved in many rocks of the Earth's lithosphere, particularly in oceanic basalts, and is an expression of the

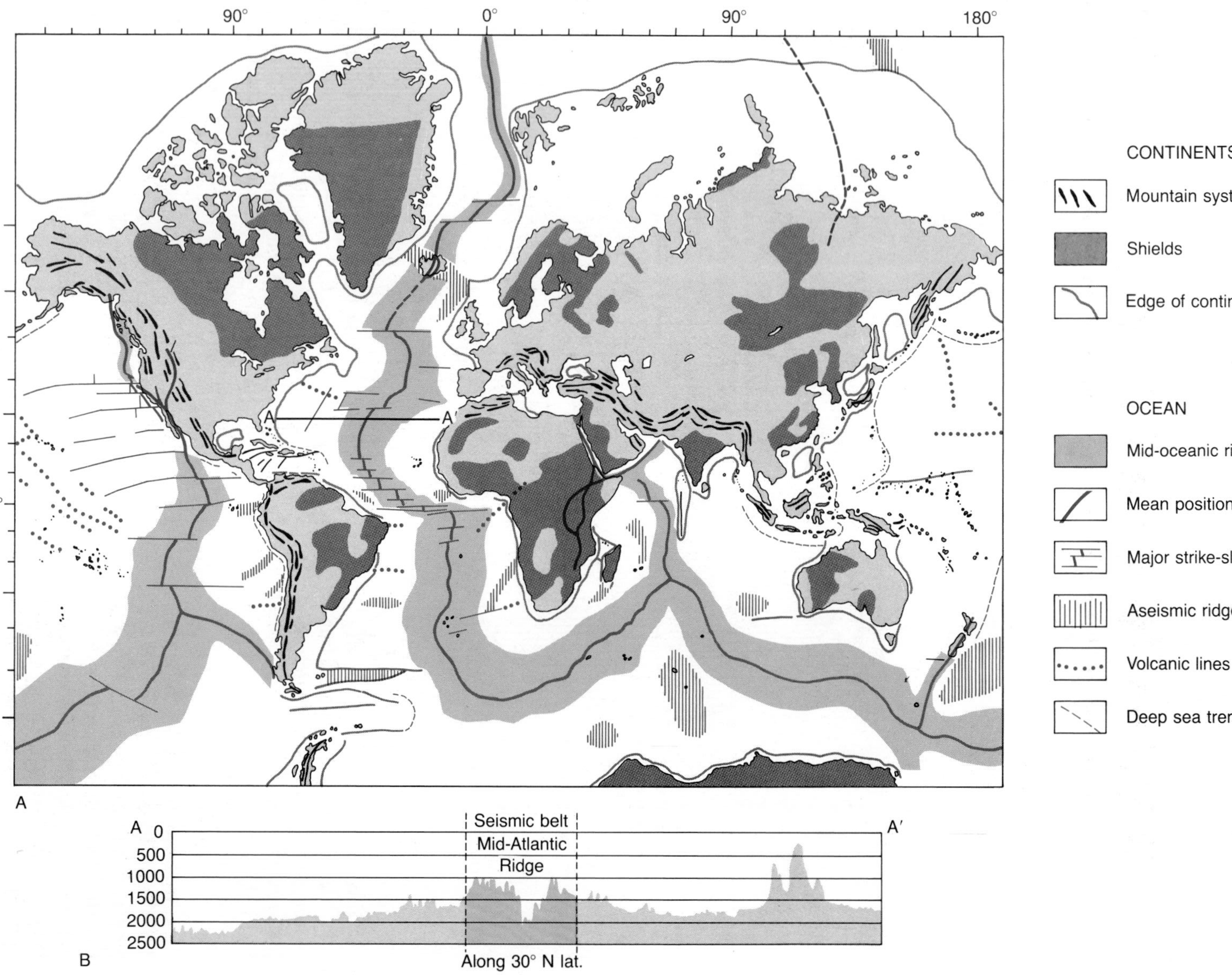

Figure 1–13

A. Mid-oceanic ridge systems of the world. B. Vertically exaggerated cross section across the Atlantic Ocean basin showing Mid-Atlantic Ridge and rift as well as topography of adjacent seafloor. See reference line A–A′ in A for location and orientation.

(From B. C. Heezen, 1962, The Deep Sea Floor, Figs. 19, 20, p. 260, 262, *in Continental Drift*, International Geophysics Series, vol. 3, S. K. Runcorn, ed.: Academic Press, New York. Reproduced by permission of Academic Press, Inc.)

The Geologic Cycle

One of the principal underlying themes in the geological sciences is the geologic cycle, which succinctly explains how the Earth works. The geologic cycle consists of the complex interactions between the lithologic cycle (formation of rocks), the hydrologic cycle (pathways of water), and the tectonic cycle (deformation of rocks). These interactions involve the Earth's lithosphere, atmosphere, hydrosphere, and biosphere. Historical geology treats the history of the geologic cycle—how and when rocks of the Earth's lithosphere formed; how and when mountain ranges formed and changed; how and when the positions of continents changed; how and when changes occurred in the Earth's atmosphere; and how and when major changes in the Earth's biosphere took place.

The Rock Cycle

The rock cycle depicts the complex interrelationships among the three families of rocks that make up the Earth's lithosphere. Special focus is on one representative of each of these three rock families and how they interrelate. These three rock types: granite (igneous), arkose (sedimentary), and gneiss (metamorphic) are illustrated in large, medium-, and small-scale perspectives in the following two plates. These outcrop, hand specimen, and microscopic scale perspectives each provide a different data base, which is necessary for the interpretation of Earth history.

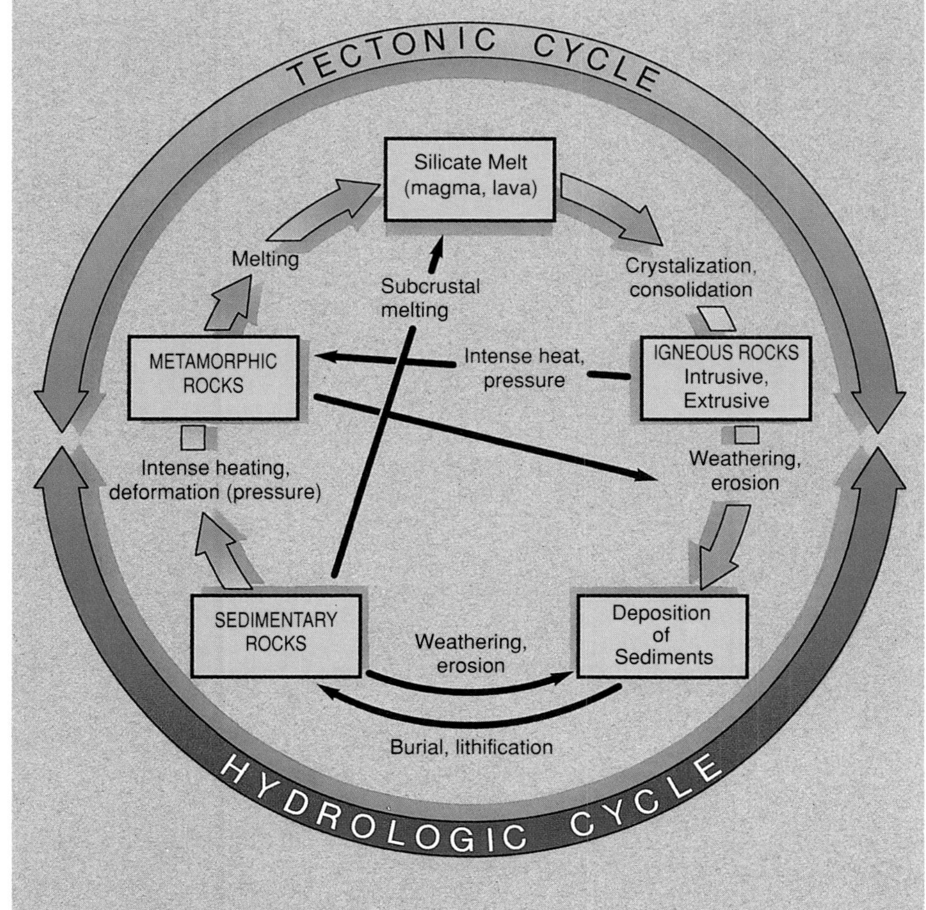

Igneous and Sedimentary Rocks

A.

Scale: width is 10 cm B.

Scale: width is 5 mm C.

A. Outcropping of intrusive granite body, Yosemite National Park, California. Granite similar to this comprises most of the Sierra Nevada Range in California. Granite exposed at the surface indicates uplift (tectonic cycle) and exposure by weathering and erosion (hydrologic cycle) after initial emplacement by intrusion of silicate magma deep below the surface.

B. Hand specimen photograph of typical granite showing the characteristic coarse crystalline texture indicative of slow cooling of silicate magma at depth, as well as mineral composition of quartz (gray), potassium feldspar (pink), and biotite mica (black).

C. Thin-section photomicrograph of granite. A thin section is a thin slice (fraction of a millimeter, so that light can pass through) of the rock mounted on a glass slide so that optical properties of the various minerals can be studied under the light-polarizing petrographic microscope. This microscopic scale allows for more detailed study of the composition and texture of the rock.

D. Sedimentary rocks: arkose. Erosional (hydrologic cycle) spires of steeply tilted (tectonic cycle) arkose sandstone strata, Garden of the Gods, Colorado. Weathering and erosion (hydrologic cycle) of a granite outcrop could produce feldspar-rich detritus deposited as an arkose in a sedimentary environment such as an alluvial fan or stream.

E. Hand specimen photograph of arkose sandstone. In contrast to the granite hand specimen, which has an interlocking crystalline texture, note the grainy, particle texture of this rock. Such detrital sedimentary rocks involve interaction of the hydrologic cycle with the rock cycle.

F. Thin-section photomicrograph of arkose sandstone. Analysis of sedimentary rocks using the petrographic microscope permits more detailed description of detrital composition and texture as well as the occurrence of certain minerals that formed after deposition of the detrital grains.

D.

Sedimentary and Metamorphic Rocks

G.

Scale: width is 16 cm H.

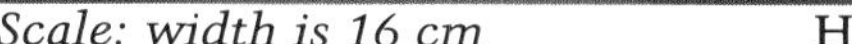

Scale: width is 5 mm I.

G. Outcrop exposure of gneiss from the Blue Ridge Mountains, Virginia. This gneiss could have formed from regional metamorphism (tectonic cycle) of granite or arkose. Metamorphic rocks involve interactions of the tectonic cycle with the rock cycle.

H. Hand specimen photograph of gneiss showing distinct banded foliation pattern.

I. Thin-section photomicrograph showing texture, structure, and mineral composition of gneiss.

Scale: width is 8.5 cm E.

Scale: width is 5 mm F.

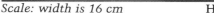

The Tectonic Cycle

The tectonic cycle involves deformation of the Earth's lithosphere by stresses generated primarily by the interaction of large pieces of the lithosphere called plates. These plates are in motion and they interact by separating, colliding head-on, or sideswiping one another. Collision plate boundaries have been the principal zones of mountain-building throughout Earth history. Folding and faulting are two important responses of layered sedimentary rocks to the stresses propagated through the lithosphere by plate interactions.

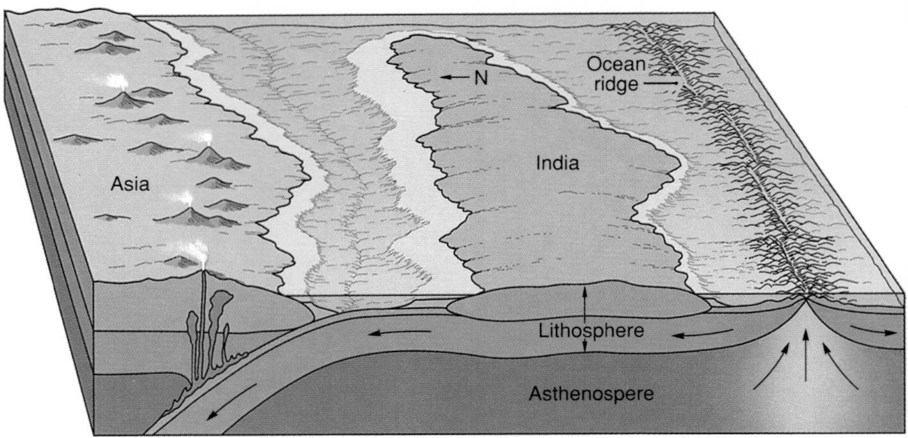

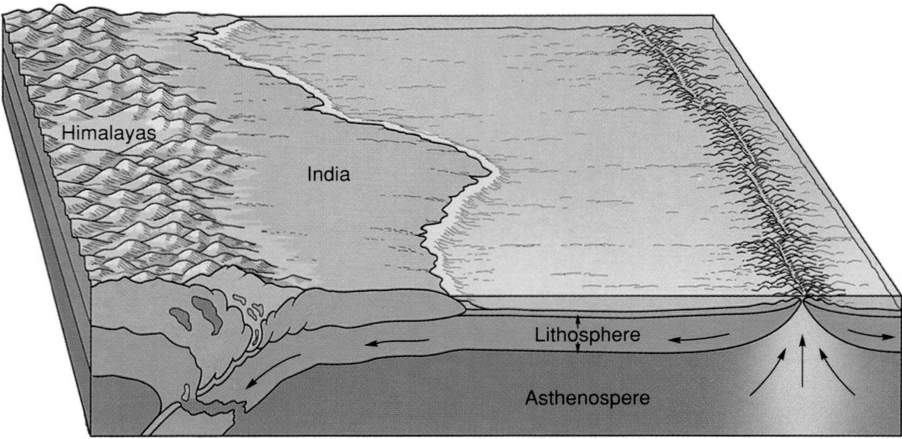

A.

Schematic block diagrams illustrating the collision between two continental masses (India and southern Asia) and the resulting deformation of rock and formation of the Himalayan mountain chain.

Aerial view of Sheep Mountain, Wyoming, which is a breached (eroded) anticline, an arch-shaped fold in which the oldest rocks are in the center. Note the topographic expression, which is related to the relative resistance to erosion of the various strata involved in the fold. Note also the systematic repetition of strata on both sides of the central axis.

B.

C.

Ground-level view of small-scale syncline, a trough-shaped fold in which the youngest strata are in the center, in roadcut near St. George, Utah.

Cross-section view of thrust fault that has moved Precambrian gneiss over Quaternary alluvial sediments, San Bernardino Mountains, California. Thrust faults result from strong regional compressive (shortening) stresses.

A.

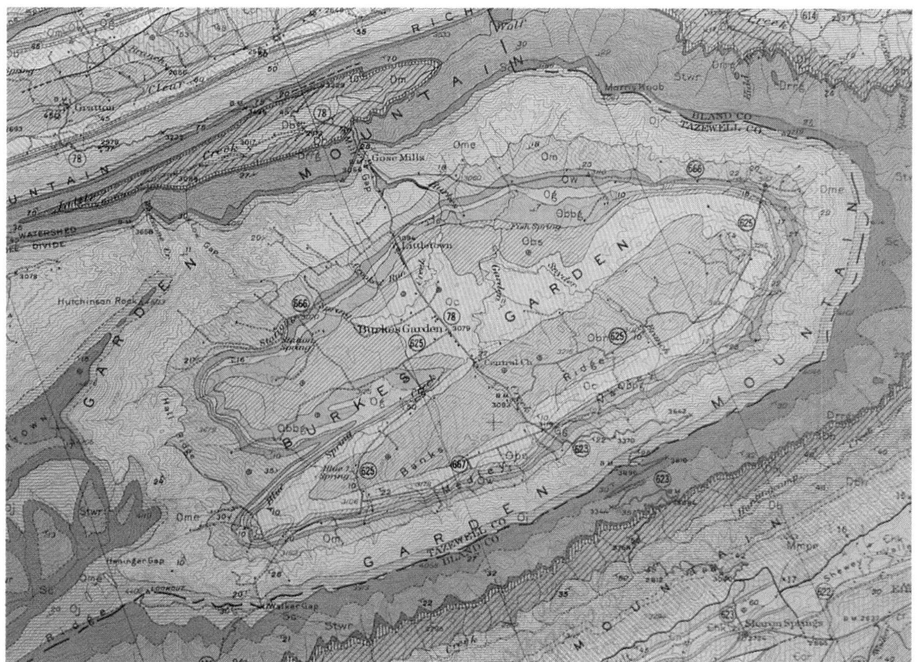

B.

Geologic map showing the plan view geometry of an anticline, Burkes Garden Quadrangle, Virginia. Different colors represent sedimentary units (formations) that express the fold configuration. Note the systematic repetition of formations on both sides of the fold axis. Geologic maps are invaluable for working out the geologic history of a region.

Aerial view showing topographic expression of California's San Andreas fault. This fault, which forms the boundary between the North American and Pacific plates, has resulted from large-scale shearing movements parallel to the Earth's surface.

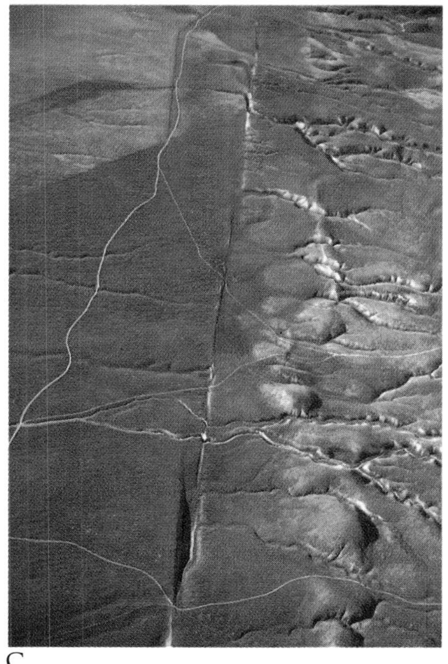

C.

Sedimentary Structures

Sedimentary rocks are of particular importance to the students of Earth history because: 1. they cover 75% of the Earth's surface or immediately accessible shallow subsurface; 2. they represent the depositional products of surface environments; 3. they are layered and developed in sequences, which makes them amenable to organizing and working out history; 4. and they contain fossils, the documents of life on Earth.

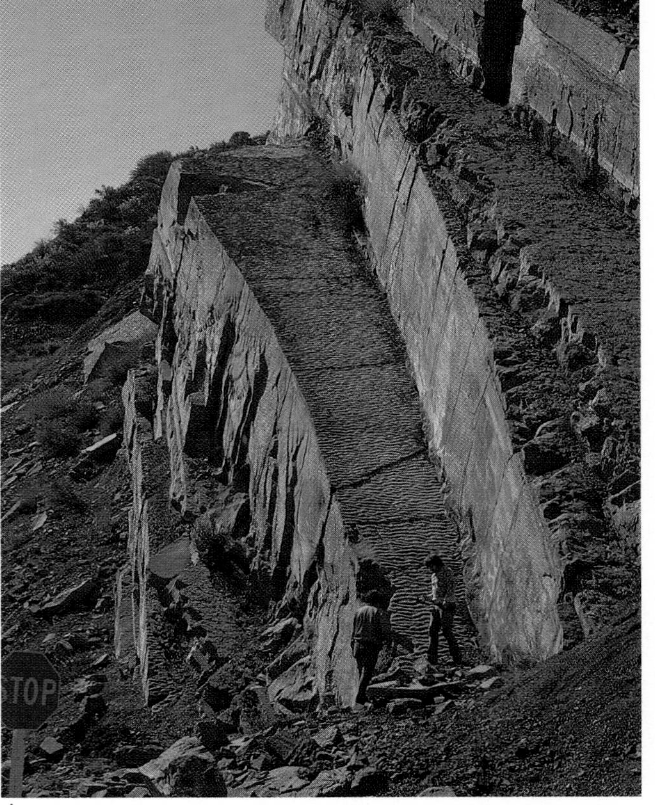

A.

Ripple marks on top surface of thick sandstone layer, Ridge Basin, southern California. Ripple marks are primary sedimentary structures, megascopic features formed in the environment of deposition by moving air or water, and they provide clues about the physical conditions that were operating.

B.

Rippled surface on modern beach, Baja California Norte, Mexico. Sedimentary structures in modern environments aid the interpretation of similar structures in the ancient rock record—an application of the geologic principle of actualism.

Cross-stratified sandstone, Mogollon Rim, Colorado Plateau, Arizona. Cross-stratification in sandstone can give clues about current strength, water depth, and flow direction.

C.

Fossil cephalopod mollusc, from Cretaceous of South Dakota. Certain fossils such as this ammonoid cephalopod mollusc represent groups of organisms that were widespread in their distribution and were rapidly evolving. Such fossils enable geologists to divide strata into time-significant intervals and to make long-distance correlations between sedimentary sequences. (Scale: fossil measures 8 cm across.)

Fossils

One of the most important aspects of sedimentary rocks is the fossil record. Fossils are much more than objects of curiosity—they furnish important information about the evolution of life, the relative age of sedimentary rocks, the kinds of environments that existed in the past, and they aid in reconstructing the positions of continents during various stages of Earth history.

A.

B.

Trace fossil in sandstone, from Cretaceous of northern Mexico. Trace fossils, like this dwelling and feeding burrow of an ancient crustacean, are evidence of organism activity, and they provide information about ancient environmental conditions.

C.

Assemblages of fossils, such as these brachiopods from New York, when viewed in the context of the containing sediment, provide valuable data for the interpretation of age and environment of deposition of sedimentary deposits. (Scale: brachiopod in upper center measures 5.5 cm in length.)

A.

One of the most instructive places on Earth to read a long succession of Earth history is in the marvelous exposures in the walls of the Grand Canyon, Arizona. The Grand Canyon provides a record of an ancient mountain system worn down by erosion; the invasion of shallow seas; withdrawal of seas and extensive erosion; followed by a landscape coursed by rivers and later covered by desert sand dunes.

Stratigraphic Sequences

Sedimentary strata are parts of successions or sequences that reflect the time dimension of Earth history: the oldest layers at the bottom, the youngest at the top. Vertically arranged strata at various localities reveal a record of the changes through time at that place.

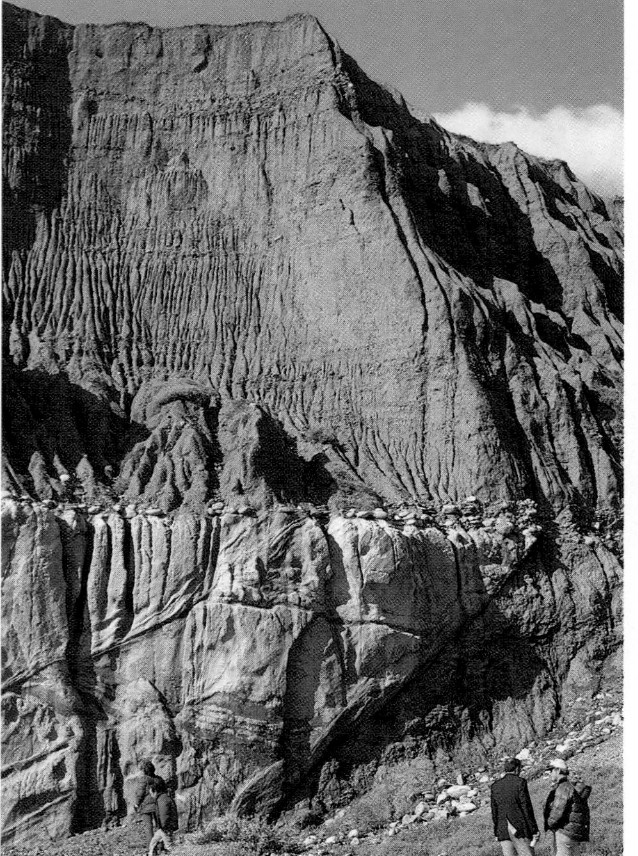

B.

Cliff exposure near San Onofre, southern California. The exposure here reveals the following relative sequence of events: deposition of deep marine sediments; uplift and faulting; erosion; deposition of shallow marine and nonmarine sands and gravels; and later uplift of the deposits into a terrace.

The erosion surface is indicated by the truncation of the fault. This buried erosion surface is called an unconformity and, along with the fault, is a cross-cutting feature that helps in the interpretation of Earth history.

Earth's magnetic field at the time of formation of the rocks (Fig. 1–14). Iron-bearing minerals in the rocks were oriented parallel to the *magnetic field dipole* at the time of final consolidation (Fig. 1–14C). The orientation of the iron-bearing particles is an index to the *paleolatitude* at which the rocks formed.

Magnetized particles in volcanic rocks and sediments (Fig. 1–15) forming at the present time show a progressive range of inclinations from horizontal at the equator to vertical at the poles. The magnetic anomaly stripes record not only differences in magnetic intensity (the initial indication of their existence), but perhaps even more importantly, they show *reversals* in polarity of the Earth's magnetic field.

These positive (present magnetic pole orientation) and negative (reversed magnetic pole orientation) anomalies (Fig.1–15B) are clearly the records of successive polarity reversals—magnetic north became magnetic south, and vice versa—at intervals of several hundred thousand or several million years. The anomalies provide a kind of "tape recording" of the succession of polarity reversals: oceanic lithosphere continually formed along the spreading centers and moved away from the ridge as new material took its place.

The actual dating of seafloor rocks by various methods (Chapter 5) has demonstrated conclusively that the rocks (and their paleomagnetic anomaly patterns) increase in age away from the ridge crests, and that the oldest rocks in the Atlantic Ocean basin are less than 200 million years old (Fig. 1–16). This age is only about one-twentieth that of the oldest known rocks on the continents.

All of the oceanic ridge spreading centers are flanked by magnetic anomalies that can be matched from one side to the other. The most symmetrical pattern is in the Atlantic Ocean, where it appears that the ocean basin has been steadily widening (and the bordering continents separating) since Jurassic time (Fig. 1–16). The continental blocks on both sides of the Atlantic are linked to the spreading Atlantic Ocean lithosphere, and thus are separating as a consequence of spreading.

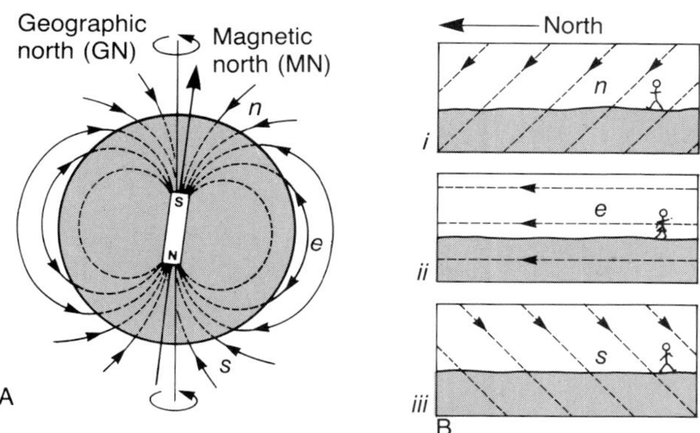

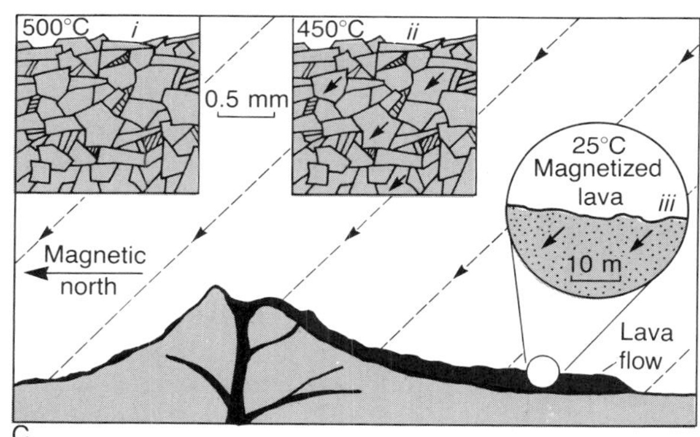

Figure 1–14

The Earth's magnetic field. A. Directions of the lines of magnetic force at the Earth's surface and in space around the Earth (as measured from satellites) are consistent with the presence of a "magnet" within the Earth. The Earth's magnetic field is probably produced by electromagnetic forces generated in the Earth's outer, liquid core. The lines of magnetic force, as they would be measured by a person standing on the Earth's surface at points *n*, *e*, and *s*, respectively, are illustrated in larger scale in B, *i*, *ii*, and *iii*. C. Schematic vertical cross section through a volcano showing directions of the Earth's lines of magnetic force. In this sequence, lava erupts, flows, cools, and crystallizes. Inset (*i*) represents the interlocking crystals in the lava after it has solidified but while it is still hot; the minerals are not magnetized. Inset (*ii*) shows the same rock when it has cooled to 450°C., below the melting point for some minerals. These minerals have become magnetized in the direction of the Earth's magnetic field. Inset (*iii*) represents a larger part of the lava flow after it has cooled further; it contains many minerals, all cooled below their melting points and magnetized as shown in (*ii*). Consequently, the entire rock is magnetized in the direction shown in (*iii*).

(From Peter J. Wyllie, *The Way the Earth Works*, Fig. 8–5, p. 105: Copyright © 1976 by John Wiley & Sons, Inc. Reproduced by permission of John Wiley & Sons, Inc.)

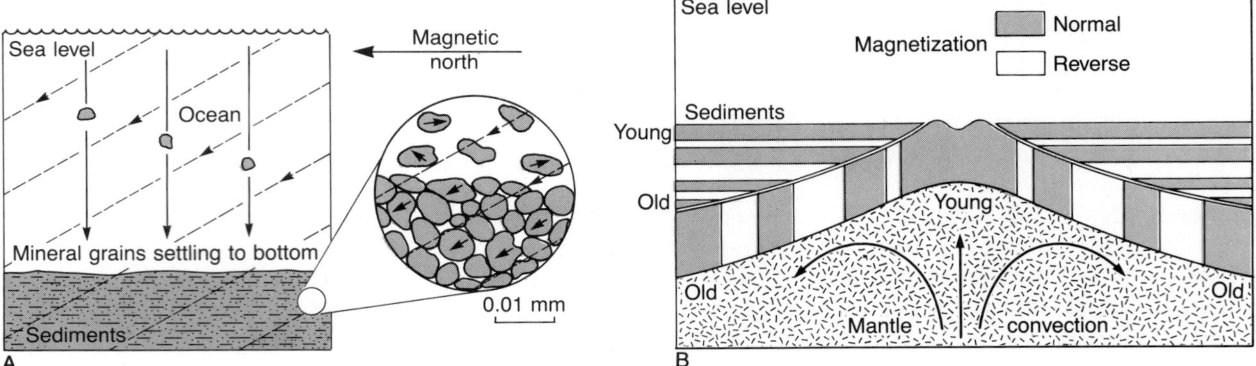

Figure 1–15
A. Schematic vertical cross section through ocean and submarine sediments, showing mineral grains settling slowly to the ocean floor and the direction of the Earth's lines of magnetic force. The inset shows that some of these falling particles have been magnetized at some earlier stage in their history (as in 14–C); as these particles settle on the sediment surface, they become oriented in the direction of the Earth's magnetic field. This magnetic direction is recorded by the sediment layer as a whole when it becomes compacted and consolidated into sedimentary rock. The best results in reading the magnetic signature of sediments are obtained from very fine-grained deposits that accumulated under quiet (free from disturbance by currents) water conditions of settling from suspension. B. Schematic cross section depicting the effect of polarity reversals on magnetization of deep-sea sediments with seafloor spreading. Each magnetized sedimentary layer overlies the older sediments and rests on a portion of the lava crust that was generated at the ridge crest during the same time interval and subsequently migrated away from the ridge.
(From Peter J. Wyllie, *The Way the Earth Works,* Figs. 8–11, 10–7, p. 113, 144: Copyright © 1976 by John Wiley & Sons, Inc. Reproduced by permission of John Wiley & Sons, Inc.)

In the Pacific region, the situation is more complex. There the continents are colliding with oceanic lithosphere, instead of drifting apart, as they are in the Atlantic. In this region, we see the results of actual interaction between plates of different density: those composed of the relatively light, granitic continental lithosphere ($d \approx 2.7$ g/cm^3) and those of the heavier, basaltic oceanic lithosphere ($d \approx 3.0$ g/cm^3). There are also interactions between segments of oceanic crust that have more subtle differences in density. In terms of oceanic-continental lithosphere interactions, the spreading oceanic lithosphere, because of its greater density, gradually moves beneath the edge of the bordering, continental block in the fashion depicted in Figure 1–17A.

Such collision margins constitute a second type of plate boundary called a **convergent boundary.** In the situation described (Fig. 1–17A), the older, leading edge of the oceanic lithospheric plate plunges to destruction at depth as it impinges against the leading edge of the continent. This interface of underthrusting of oceanic lithosphere beneath continental lithosphere is called a **subduction zone.** The underthrusting itself is most commonly referred to as "subduction," and occurs along a zone of high-pressure metamorphism, deep subcrustal melting, and deep-focus seismic activity. *Subduction can occur only beneath an advancing side of a plate, not beneath a retreating one.*

In the context of seismicity, the subduction zone is commonly referred to as a **Benioff zone,** which is a plane beneath a deep-sea trench, inclined toward the continent at an angle of about 45°, along which earthquake foci cluster. Deep-sea trenches (Figs. 1–12B, 1–13, 1–17), such as the Peru-Chile trench in the east Pacific, represent the deepest ocean-bottom environments, and are the seafloor topographic expressions of subduction zones.

The process of subduction, causing subcrustal melting and mixing of continental and oceanic lithosphere, is responsible for considerable volcanism as well as deep-seated igneous activity, and is the most prevalent mechanism for generating a hybrid type of igneous rock called **andesite** (Table 1–2). Andesite forms in (1) **volcanic island arc** chains (Fig. 1–17B), such as the Japanese and Aleutian archipelagos, where two oceanic plates collide, and (2) **magmatic arcs,** which are volcanic and intrusive igneous mountain chains developed along conti-

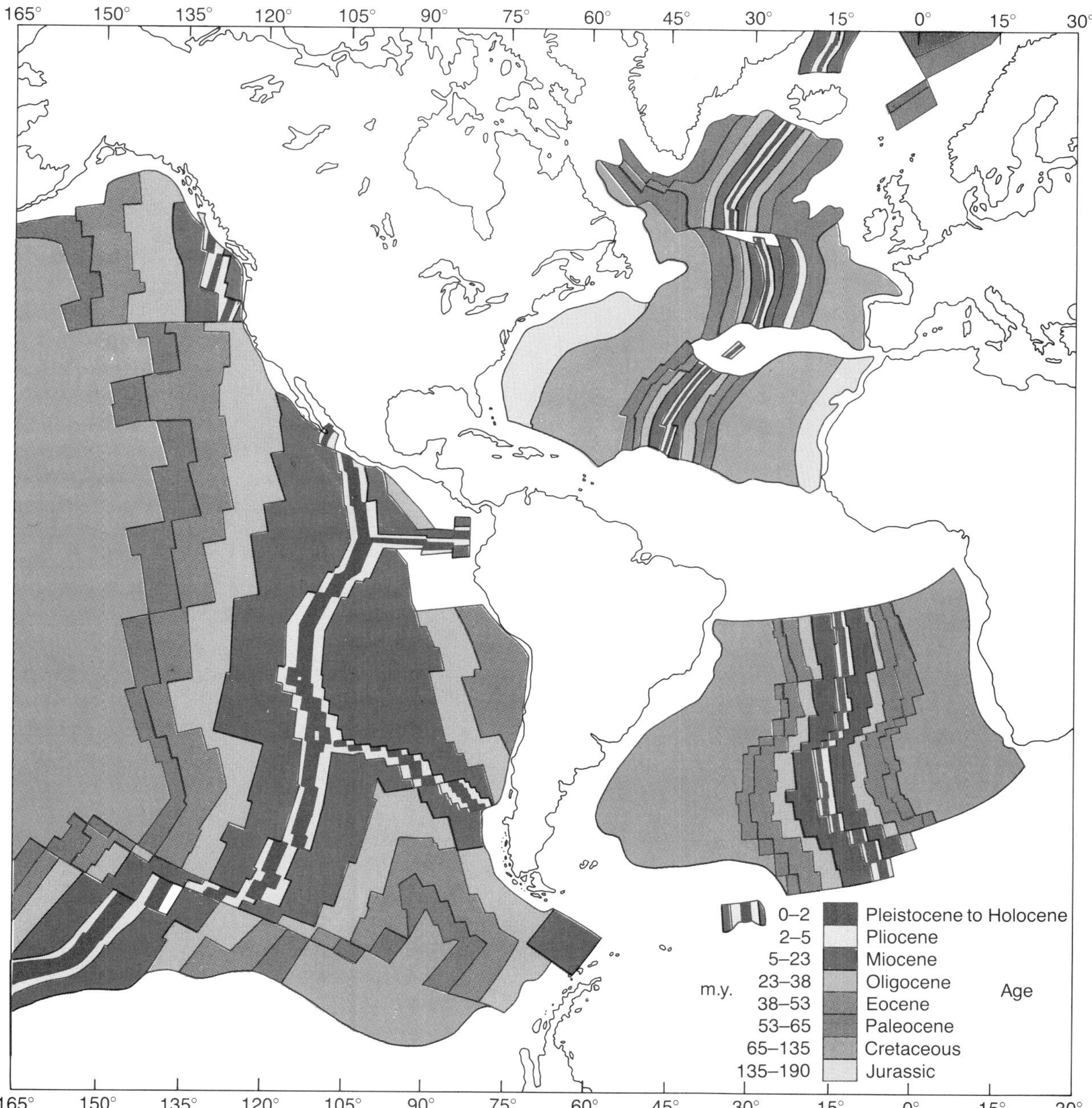

Figure 1–16

Age of the ocean floors in the East Pacific and Atlantic Ocean basins. This pattern is an expression of seafloor spreading since the Mesozoic.

(From W. C. Pitman III, R. L. Larson, and Ellen M. Herron, compilers, 1974, *Age of the Ocean Floors:* Geological Society of America Map. Reproduced by permission of authors and Geological Society of America)

nental margins. The Cascades of the northwestern United States and the Andes of western South America are examples of such mountain chains.

Both volcanic island arcs and magmatic arcs bear testimony to the igneous activity resulting from subduction. The arc configuration results from the intersection of the planar subduction zone with the curvature of the Earth's surface. Old oceanic lithosphere is consumed essentially as fast as new lithosphere is created at spreading centers (rates for both are generally less than 10 cm/year).

The mechanisms of seafloor spreading and subduction demonstrate that the continents are not independent blocks moving across a denser lithosphere, but rather are parts of much larger plates. In a sense, the continents are "passengers" that are

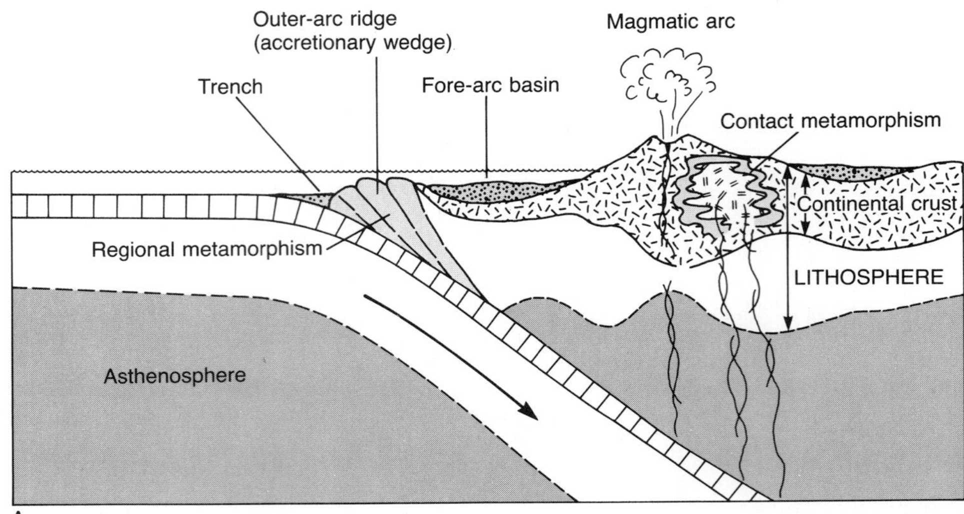

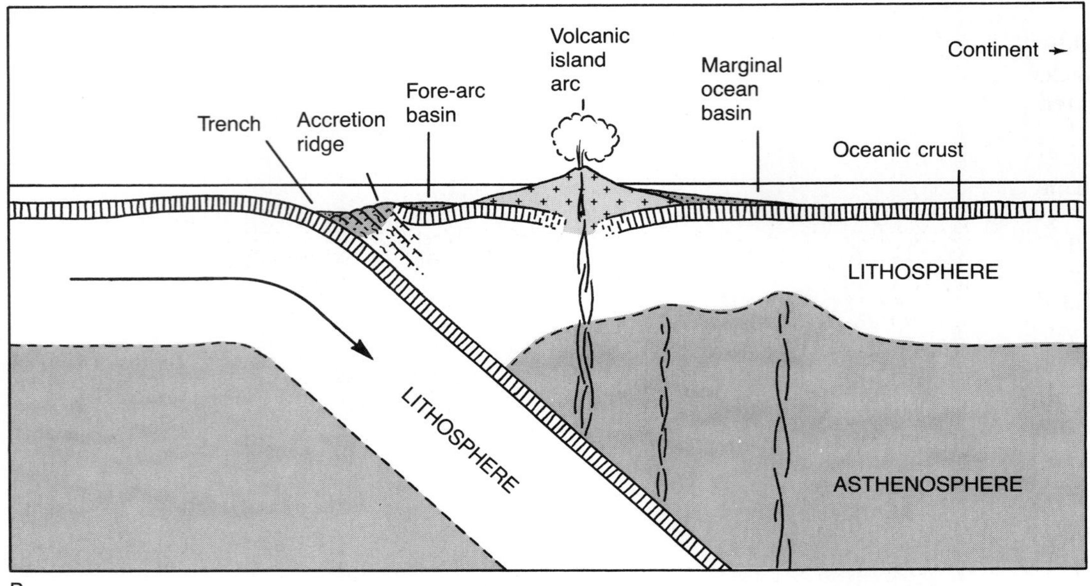

Figure 1–17

Plate collision in the Pacific Ocean. A. Continental margin magmatic arc-trench system. B. Intraoceanic volcanic island arc-trench system. Note the igneous activity generated by subduction into the asthenosphere.

(From Ben M. Page, 1977, Subduction Tectonics, *in Late Mesozoic and Cenozoic Sedimentation and Tectonics in California*, Fig. 1–1B, p. 21: Short Course Syllabus published by San Joaquin Geological Society. Reproduced by permission of San Joaquin Geological Society)

carried along on giant slabs of spreading oceanic lithosphere. North America, in such a context, is one part of a colossal lithospheric plate that extends to the Mid-Atlantic Ridge. As new lithosphere is continually added along the inside of the spreading ridge, the North American plate slowly migrates relatively westward. Along its leading western edge, it impinges upon, and in places overrides, the several plates that comprise the Pacific oceanic lithosphere (Fig. 1–2).

Another manifestation of plate convergence involves the collision of continental masses. Continent-to-continent collisions have occurred when continental lithospheric blocks have interacted with other continental slabs along a subduction margin. Once the continent-to-continent collision

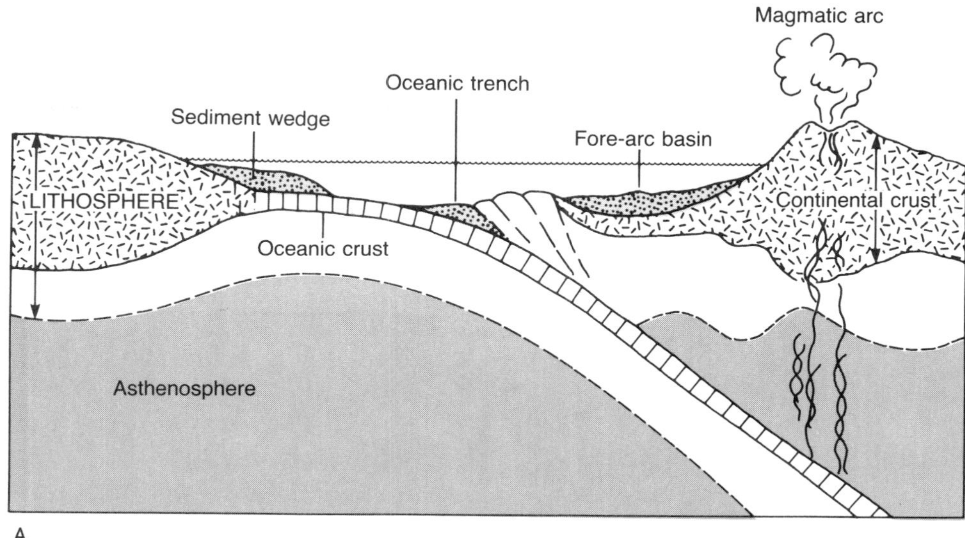

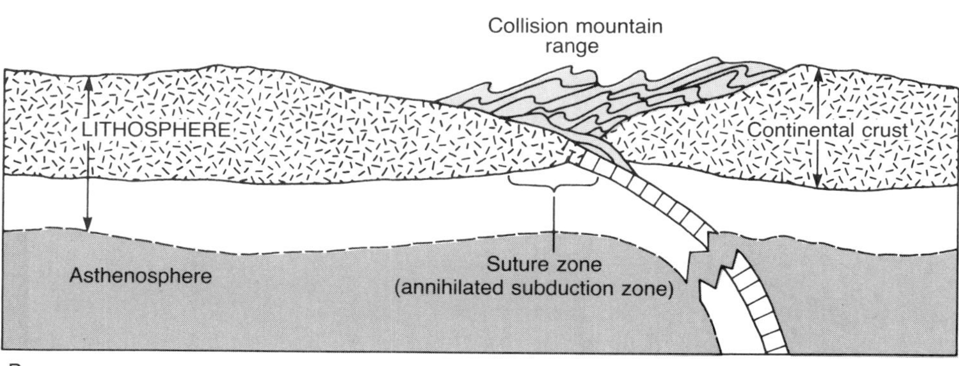

Figure 1–18
Continent-to-continent collision. A. Subduction, at the leading edge of a continent, of an oceanic plate carrying another continent. B. Continued subduction leads to eventual collision. Because of isostasy, the continental block attached to the subducting oceanic plate is not subducted because the continent is too bouyant (owing to its being less dense) to be carried down into the asthenosphere. Such a collision produces a mountain range along the suture (collision) zone. The mountains will be composed mainly of highly deformed sedimentary rocks that originally accumulated along the margins of both continents. The lofty Himalayan mountain chain formed in just such a setting during the last 40 million years: an oceanic plate carrying India collided with the Asian continental plate.

occurs, the oceanic lithosphere as well as the subduction zone are annihilated. One continent is not subducted beneath the margin of the other because of the density similarities between the two masses, although some partial subduction and thickening of continental lithosphere along the suture zone (zone of contact) does occur.

Continental plate collisions (Fig. 1–18), such as that between India and Asia during Cenozoic time, have resulted in the uplift of mountain belts along the sutured margins, and the growth of supercontinents. When two continental masses collide, the ocean basin that once separated them is completely destroyed. Conversely, ocean basins can form where intracontinental rifts occur, followed by separation of the continental masses on either side of a newly developing oceanic spreading center. This cycle of opening and closing of ocean basins through time is known as the **Wilson Cycle.**

A third type of plate boundary involves a lateral or sideswiping motion between rigid plates. Such a boundary, caused primarily by *shearing stress* (Fig. 1–19A), is developed most characteristically in oceanic areas where gigantic fractures cut across and offset oceanic ridges. The formation of new lithosphere does not occur at a constant rate: different segments of an oceanic ridge are volcanically active at varying rates at different times. The variations in spreading motion and differential movement have produced numerous fracture systems (Fig. 1–19B) that are generally quite different from those that appear on geologic maps of continental regions.

These fractures were first recognized and named **transform faults** in 1965 by J. Tuzo Wilson, one of the pioneers of plate-tectonic theory (and for whom the Wilson Cycle was named). The term "transform" refers to the transforming of one type of plate boundary into another. The famous San Andreas fault in California represents a most unusual and

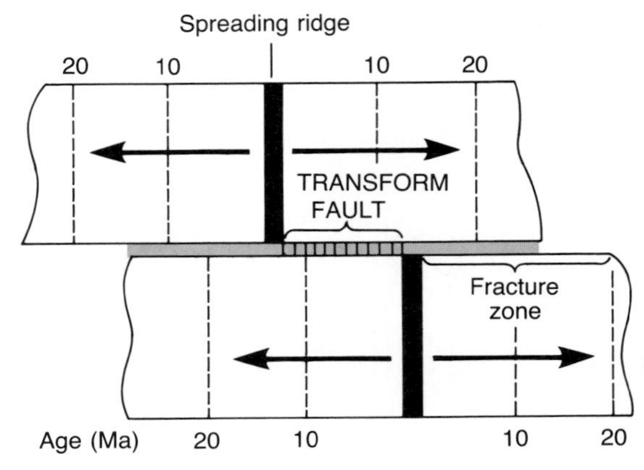

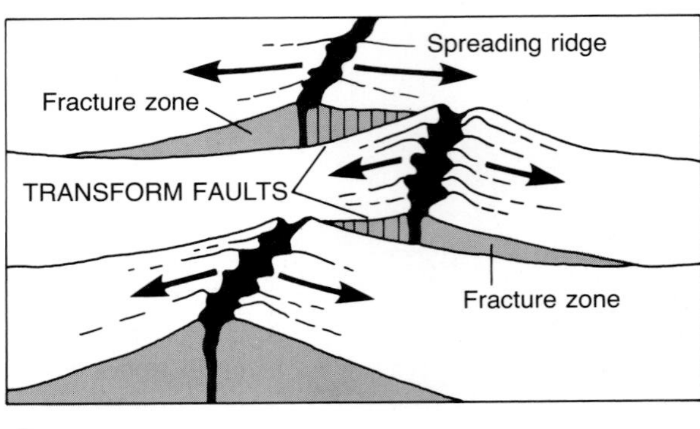

Figure 1–19
Transform plate boundary. A. Note difference between direction of displacement of oceanic ridge segment (transform fault) and direction of seafloor spreading. B. Perspective view of situation illustrated in A.
(From Leigh W. Mintz, 1981, *Historical Geology: The Science of a Dynamic Earth,* 3d ed., Fig. 8–27, p. 113: Merrill Publishing Co.)

significant type of transform fault that will be discussed in some detail in Chapter 14. The San Andreas fault zone separates, or transforms, two segments of the East Pacific spreading center (Fig. 1–20), and therefore forms the boundary between the North American and Pacific plates.

Plate boundaries, in addition to being described as divergent, convergent, or transform, show more complex interactions in some places. Those points that mark the intersection of three lithospheric plates are called **triple junctions.** Examples include those off the coast of Mexico and northern Califor-

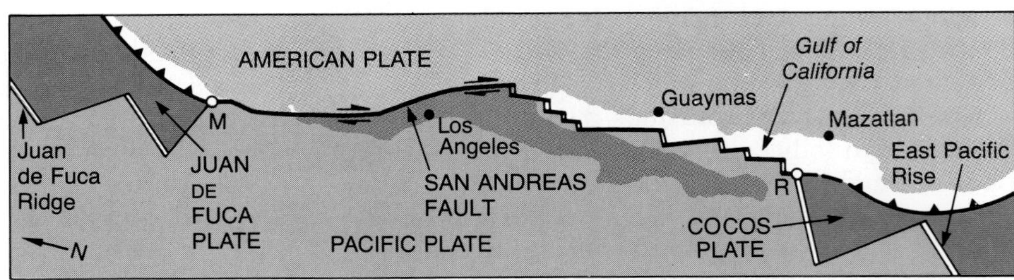

Figure 1–20
The San Andreas fault zone is an oblique transform plate boundary between the North American and Pacific Plates. M is the Mendocino triple junction among the North American, Juan de Fuca, and Pacific Plates, and R is the Rivera triple junction among the North American, Cocos, and Pacific Plates.
(From Tanya Atwater, 1970, Implications of Plate Tectonics for the Cenozoic Tectonic Evolution of Western North America, Fig. 1, p. 3514: *Geological Society of America Bulletin,* vol. 81, no. 12. Reproduced by permission of the author and the Geological Society of America)

nia (Fig. 1–20), where seafloor-spreading ridges intersect both a subduction zone and a transform fault. It is important to realize that the three types of plate boundaries can occur in three principal styles of physiographic and lithospheric settings: ocean basin-to-ocean basin; continent-to-ocean basin; and continent-to-continent. Plate margins are named for the geographic settings where the different kinds of plate interactions occur (e.g., California margin, Andean margin, Japanese margin, Atlantic margin; see Fig. 1–23).

Continents: The North American Example

Although the dynamics of lithospheric plate motion are centered in the ocean basins, it is the continents that contain most of the evidence of past plate interactions. In contrast to the oceanic lithosphere, which is geologically young (rocks less than 200 million years old), the continental lithosphere includes rocks ranging in age from roughly 3800 Ma to yesterday's sand and gravel. Each continent, therefore, is a mosaic of many different kinds of rocks of different ages and different origins.

Figure 1–21 shows the major geologic subdivisions of the North American continent: *shield, interior lowlands, mountains,* and *coastal plains,* each with its own set of rock types, rock ages, structural styles, and physiographic expression. The regions from which structural mountains are born are called **orogenic belts.** These are regions of lithospheric mobility and deformation during intervals of geologic time. Ancient orogenic belts, expressed as deformed mountain systems, are called **orogens,** and are significant parts of the continent. We shall have a good deal more to say about them when we investigate the geological evolution of North America in Chapters 8 through 15.

What is the cause of structural mountains? What produces the forces within the Earth that bend and break rocks? How do mountains form and grow? Why are they located where they are? How important have they been in the evolution of the lithosphere? How do they tie into the tectonic cycle and the geologic cycle? The theory of plate tectonics is bringing us closer to some of the answers.

It has been known for some time that the geologically young, active mountain chains of the world are narrow, elongate belts. Reconstruction of the geologic history leading to the formation of these and older mountain chains indicates that the operation of the tectonic cycle has been mainly confined spatially to similar elongate belts. Nowadays, armed with the concept of plate tectonics, geologists are relating these orogens to convergent plate boundaries. The explanation of the tectonic cycle is seen to lie in the theory of plate tectonics: the volcanism and tectonic deformation that make mountains are generated through lithospheric plate interactions.

The main structural framework of the North American continent is somewhat symmetrical (Fig. 1–21). In the north-central part, mainly in Canada, the areally extensive *Canadian Shield,* composed of a patchwork of ancient lavas, igneous plutons (large bodies of intrusive rock), metamorphic complexes, and sedimentary successions of Cryptozoic (Precambrian) age (Table 1–1), contains the roots of several ancient orogenic belts (orogens).

During the past 1000 million (billion) years of Earth history, the shield has been worn down to a low, rolling surface that plunges southward beneath a cover of younger sedimentary rocks of the interior lowlands (Fig. 1–21). Nearly encircling the shield and interior lowlands are various mountain systems formed at different times during the Phanerozoic (Table 1–1). These include the Appalachian-Ouachita systems to the east and south, the wide Cordilleran system extending the entire western length of the continent, and a prominent chain along the oceanward side of the Arctic islands and Greenland.

Along the continental margin, especially along the east and southeast, coastal plains have been constructed from sediment derived from the mountain belts as these systems have been progressively worn down by erosion. The coastal plains are composed of geologically young sediments deposited across the eroded surfaces of deformed mountain structures (Fig. 1–22). The continental shelves, submerged parts of the same prism of sediments that make up the coastal plains (Fig. 1–22), are inclined seaward at less than 50 m/km (less than 1°), and include the area generally between sea level and about 200 m below sea level. Although now submerged beneath marine waters, the continental shelves are parts of the continental structure.

Seaward of the shelves (Fig. 1–22), and composed of major volumes of sediment, are the continental slopes (inclined at an angle of 1° to 3°) and continental rises (aprons of sediment at the toe of the continental slope and inclined at an angle generally of less than 1°). The transitional boundary between true continental granitic lithosphere and oceanic basaltic lithosphere is beneath the continental slope–rise wedge (Fig. 1–22).

Hence, the generalized plan of continental structure is: shield–interior lowlands–mountains–coastal plains–continental shelf–continental slope

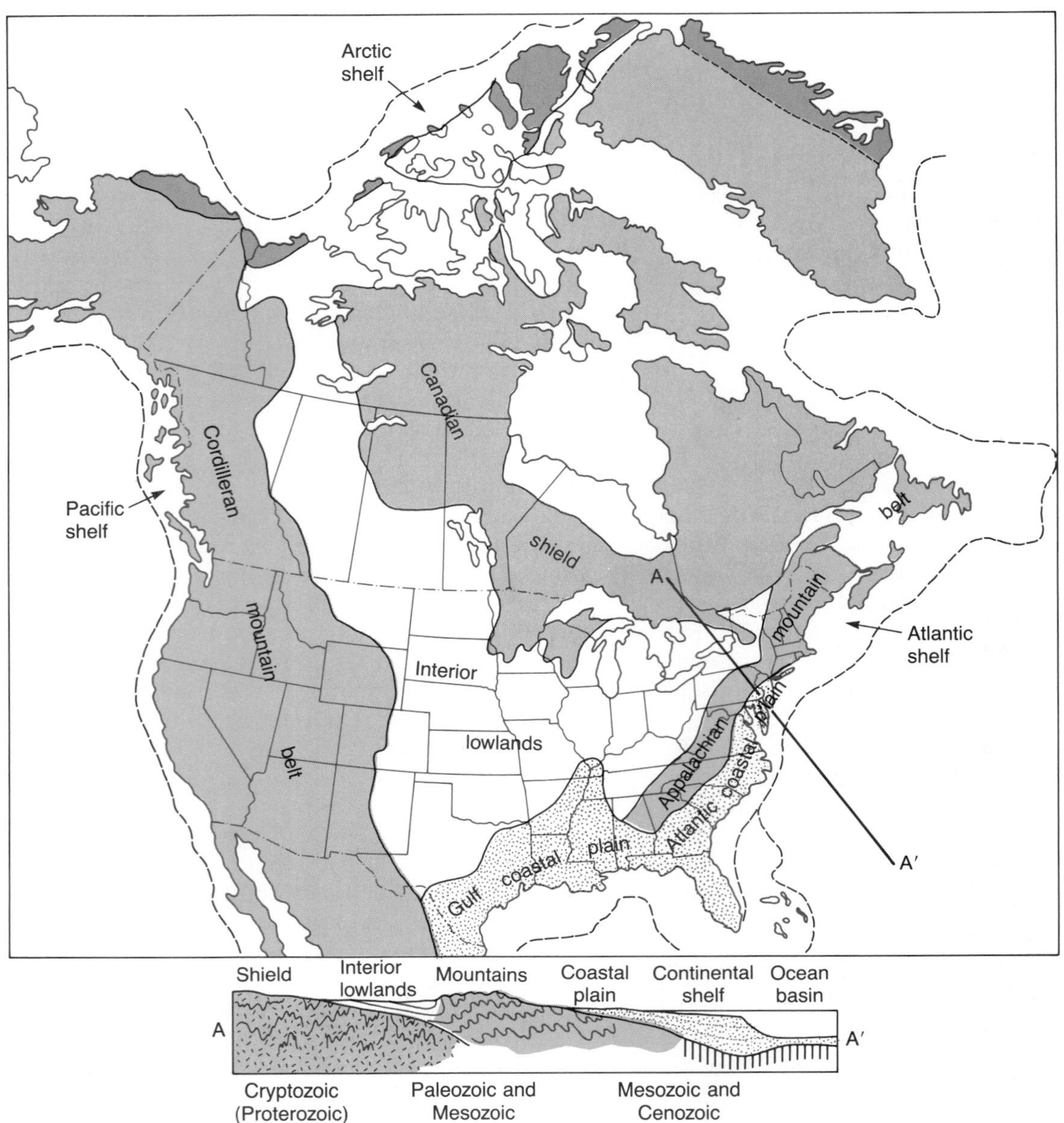

Figure 1–21
Large-scale structure and accretionary elements of North Amerca: Precambrian shield, Paleozoic-Mesozoic interior lowlands, Paleozoic-Mesozoic mountain chains, Mesozoic and Cenozoic coastal plain–continental shelf–continental rise and slope sedimentary wedge. Mountains represent a deformed earlier trailing (Atlantic-type) margin sedimentary wedge.
(Data from *Tectonic Map of North America,* 1969, U.S. Geological Survey)

(Fig. 1–21). From the perspective of the tectonic cycle viewed within the model of plate tectonics, the shield represents the forged-together **terranes** of ancient orogenic belts (orogens), interior lowlands, and coastal plains and shelves, together with pieces of ancient oceanic crust and intrusive complexes. As such, the shield is a patchwork of pieces of ancient lithospheric plates. It is the exposed part of the very foundation or "basement" of the continent, and contains the oldest rocks. The interior lowlands include generally undeformed or only slightly deformed sedimentary rocks that accumulated in shallow seas which periodically invaded the tectonically more stable and topographically subdued continental interior, called the **craton.**

The mountain systems record the geologically more recent—and, consequently, more apparent—collisions between lithospheric plates. The shelf-

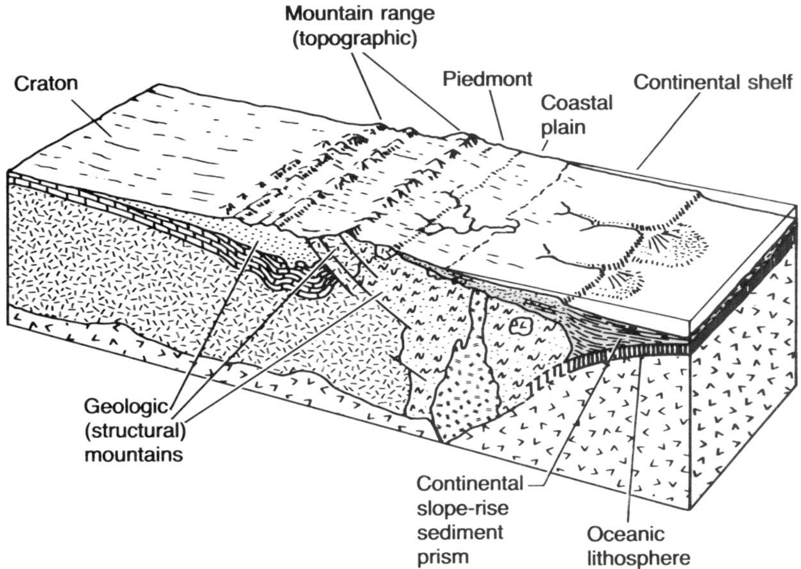

Figure 1–22

Relationship between oceanic and continental lithosphere and the coastal plain–continental shelf–continental slope-and-rise prism of sediments. The continental-shelf sediments have accumulated along the passive, trailing margin of the continental block and on older rocks that were deformed during earlier plate collisions.

(From R. S. Dietz and J. C. Holden, 1974, Collapsing Continental Rises: Actualistic Concept of Geosynclines—a Review, Fig. 6a, p. 22, *in Ancient and Modern Geosynclines,* Society of Economic Paleontologists and Mineralogists Special Publication 19. Reproduced by permission of Society of Economic Paleontologists and Mineralogists)

slope-rise sedimentary prisms making up the continental margin represent the most recent additions to the continent, and have developed mainly upon the tectonically passive, trailing edge of the moving continental block during the past 200 million years (Fig. 1–22). These long, linear **continental margin basins,** including the present-day Atlantic and Gulf margins, are subdivided into (1) a comparatively shallow marine (shelf)-to-nonmarine (coastal plain) depositional setting called the **miogeocline,** and (2) a deeper water, offshore marine (slope-and-rise) depositional setting called the **eugeocline.**

In the geologic future, the trailing eastern margin of North America may become an active collision margin similar to the present-day Pacific borderland. If this happens, the continental shelf (miogeocline)–slope–rise (eugeocline) prism of sediments will be deformed into a mountain belt and *accreted* to the continental structure. In this fashion, subduction of oceanic lithosphere beneath continental lithosphere would compress the thick prism of sediments. This process might be heightened by the closing of the Atlantic Ocean basin and the collision of the Eurasian and North American continents, in accordance with the Wilson Cycle. Hence, the major mountain belts of all the continents represent original passive margin miogeoclinal and eugeoclinal sedimentary prisms that were deformed through subduction, and in some cases, through continent-to-continent collisions.

An interesting sidelight involves the collision of **microplates,** which are smaller than continent-size geologic terranes that are rafted along on moving oceanic lithosphere, but resist subduction along continental margins and thus become accreted to the continents. Microplates that have a foreign origin with respect to the continent of which they become a part are called **exotic terranes.** In such a plate-tectonics context, the continent of North America has grown through the lateral accretion of orogenic belts (orogens), formed by subduction of oceanic lithosphere, the collision of continents, and the addition of microplates.

In terms of the sedimentary record, which is so critical for interpreting Earth history, plate tectonics has been the determining influence on the volumetric importance, size, and location of **sedimentary basins.** Figure 1–23 provides an actualistic model that depicts the various plate-tectonic settings within which the principal kinds of sedimentary basins have formed. The largest-scale basins are the ocean basins and trailing continental margin basins (miogeoclines and eugeoclines). Along collision margins are various kinds of basins asso-

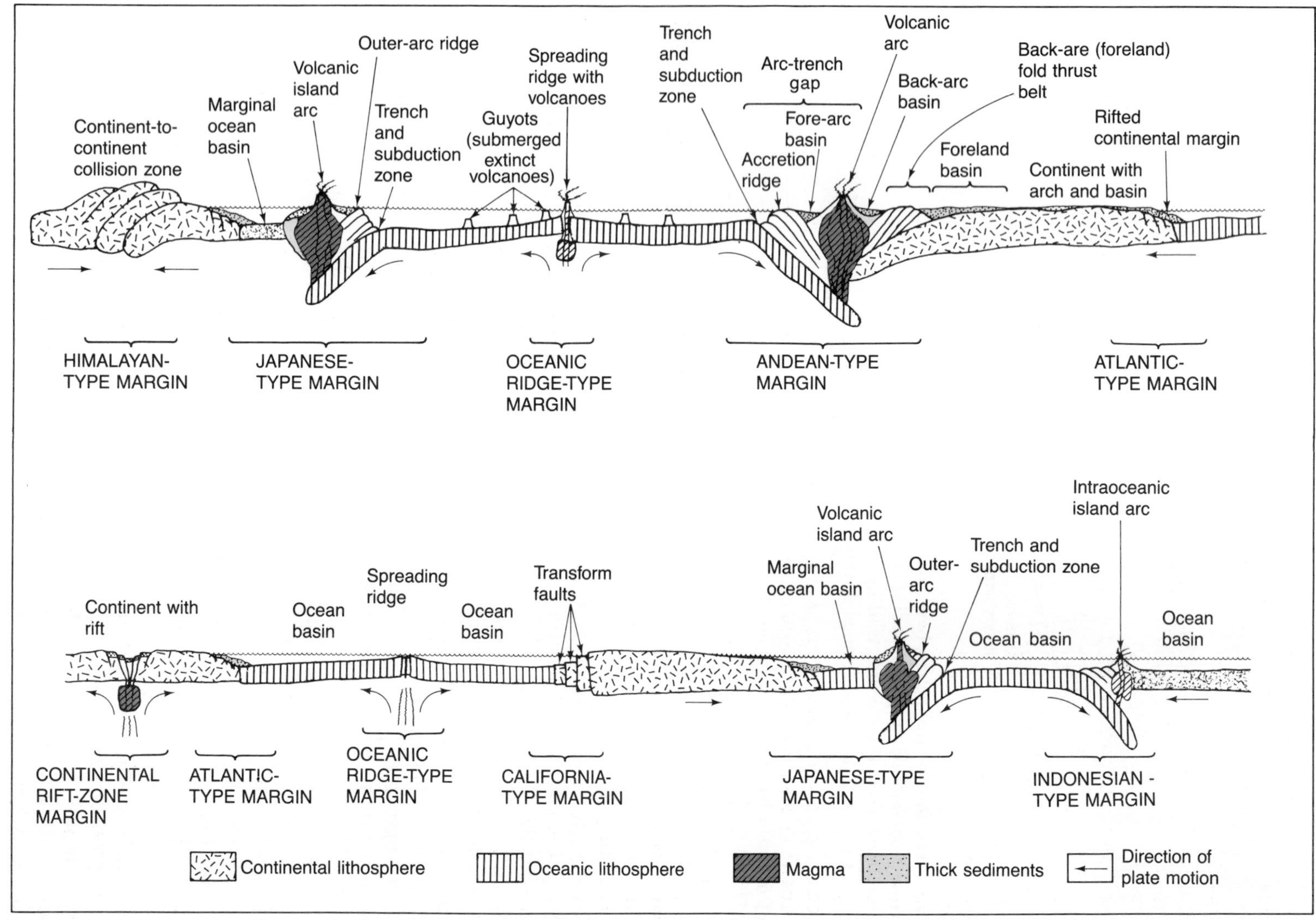

Figure 1–23

Kinds of plates and plate margins, geologic settings for plate interactions, and principal kinds of sedimentary basins.

(From Leigh W. Mintz, 1981, *Historical Geology: The Science of a Dynamic Earth,* 3d ed., Fig. 8–26, p. 211: Merrill Publishing Co.)

ciated with igneous arc systems, including *forearc* and *backarc* basins (Fig. 1–23). These basins occur in the so-called arc–trench gap area between the volcanic arc and the subduction trench, which serves as a basin in its own right. Extinct submerged volcanic mountains (guyots) are logical candidates for future accreted microplates. Basins within continents include downsags, rifts, and *foreland* basins, the latter forming inboard (cratonward) of deformed mountain belts.

These basin types are characterized by particular suites of sedimentary rocks, as controlled by the plate-tectonics setting. For instance, basins in more tectonically quiescent settings tend to accumulate quartz-rich sandstones, mudstones, and carbonate sediments. Such sediments tend to show a high degree of compositional *maturity*, whereby the long transport history, recycling, and working of the sediment enriches the mineral composition of the particles toward the end-products of weathering. In more tectonically active settings, such as forearc basins and deep-sea trenches, the sedimentary suites are characterized by more feldspar and lithic fragment-rich sandstones, volcaniclastic sediments, conglomerates and breccias, mudrocks, and a general lack of carbonate rocks. These sediments are generally compositionally *immature*, because they have a detrital mineral composition which is rich in particles that represent the earliest products of weathering, and are generally rapidly deposited in environments below **wave base.**

Basin subsidence, which accommodates the depositional sedimentary sequences, is an important tectonic activity in its own right. Subsidence of the lithosphere is believed to be related mainly to either one or both of two primary factors (Fig. 1–24): (1) lithospheric cooling and sedimentary loading following a lithospheric thermal, stretching event, and (2) by lithospheric flexure in response to loading by multiple stacked sheets of rock, emplaced by *overthrusting* in an orogenic belt (for example, the classic foreland basin in Fig. 1–24).

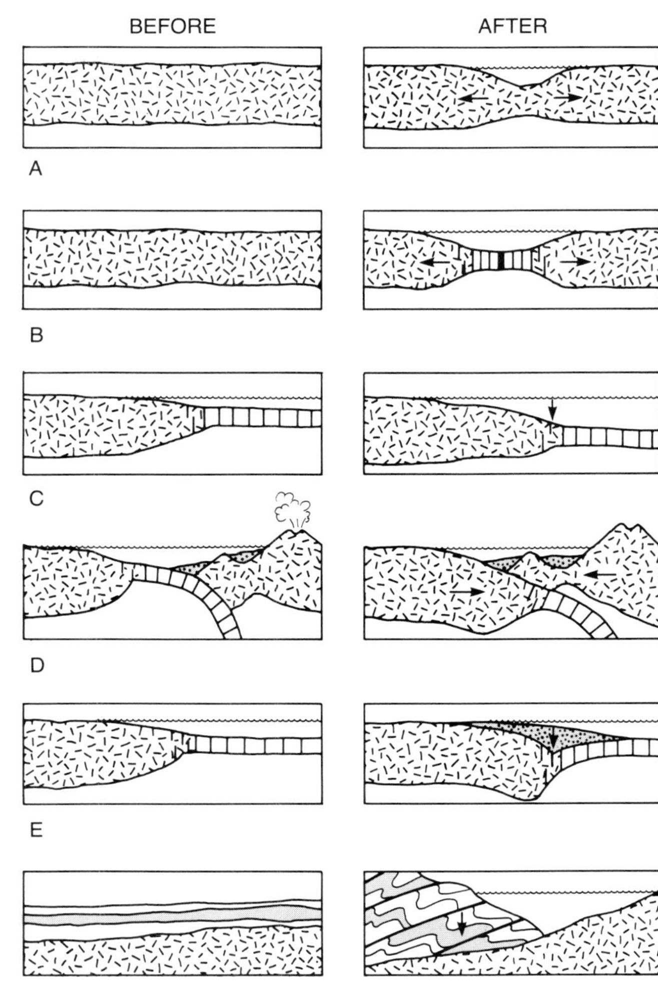

Figure 1–24
Subsidence of continental lithosphere. A. Crustal thinning by extension. B. Crustal thinning during continental separation to form rifted continental margins alongside new ocean basin. C. Thermal subsidence of freshly rifted continental margin adjacent to cooling oceanic lithosphere. D. Flexure of lithosphere accompanying plate consumption (subduction) at converegent plate boundary. E. Flexure of lithosphere along rifted continental margin owing to sediment load in continental margin basin. F. Flexure of lithosphere owing to tectonic loading in fold-thrust belt.
(After W. R. Dickinson, 1975, *Current Concepts of Depositional Systems with Applications for Petroleum Geology,* Fig. 12.3, p. 12–2: Short Course Syllabus published by San Joaquin Geological Society. Produced by permission of San Joaquin Geological Society)

Evolution of a Concept

Historical Perspective

Plate tectonics is a theory that has emerged from a controversy about moving continents. Once the theory became a working principle, the phenomenon of "continental drift" was regarded as merely a byproduct of seafloor spreading. In this light, the continents are viewed as parts of much larger, rigid lithospheric plates that move across the "plastic" asthenosphere. For nearly 100 years after its first serious proposal, the notion of moving continents was a subject of heated controversy. To appreciate how far this theory has come to take its place alongside the great breakthroughs in science, let us look at a brief historical summary of developments in the post-Wegener years. The evolution of great ideas is a necessary and important part of the great ideas themselves.

In 1928, the year before Alfred Wegener's death, the American Association of Petroleum Geologists organized a historic international meeting in New York City, where prominent Earth scientists from around the world gathered to review the theory of continental drift. Both sides assembled their entire arsenal of ammunition and fired volley after volley. But when the smoke had cleared, the opponents of drift held the upper hand and carried the victory banner. It seems that their serious objections were presented more strongly and argued more convincingly than the evidence in favor of drift.

During the 1930s and 1940s, for lack of new or otherwise stimulating evidence, the "continental drift" controversy began to wind down. It would not be until the decade of the 1950s that the controversy would be renewed. During the 25-year period of relative dormancy following the historic 1928 symposium, serious debate was continued in only a few enclaves as some of the more revolutionary geologists continued to support the idea of footloose continents. One of the most brilliant adherents of the outrageous hypothesis was Arthur Holmes, a British geologist who first proposed the existence of convection currents in the solid material of the Earth. Could the large-scale convective motion of heat move continents?

After World War II, a great surge of oceanographic research commenced, and a flood of new data became available. This, combined with information derived from proprietary mapping of the ocean floor during the war, produced a revolution in our understanding of the topographic surface of the ocean basins. One of the most significant revelations came from the charting of great mountain ranges beneath the surface of the oceans. Investigators identified a 70,000 km-long mountain system girdling the world—the oceanic ridge system. (Its significance in terms of the geologic cycle would await further research.) Mapping of the ocean basins demonstrated that the floors of the oceans are not flat, monotonous plains covered by water, but in fact contain more extensive mountains and deeper valleys than can be found on the familiar continents. (The real significance of deep-sea trenches likewise would await further research.) It was the early work on mapping the ocean floor that really paved the way for a new revolution in the Earth sciences.

As new research—very different from that involved in the earlier debate—progressed during the 1950s, there was a revival of interest in the continental-drift theory. One of the principal areas of new research involved *paleomagnetism.* Studies on the paleomagnetism of rocks on the continents revealed some rather astonishing results. For example, in 1954 it was suggested that England was at a lower latitude during the Triassic Period (Table 1–1; Fig. 1–25), and, since the Triassic, not only had moved northward, but had rotated 30° clockwise!

Sets of curves were generated that showed the relation of the continents to the Earth's magnetic poles during successive intervals of time in geologic history. These *polar wandering curves* (Fig. 1–26) suggested either that the poles had changed positions significantly during geologic history, or that

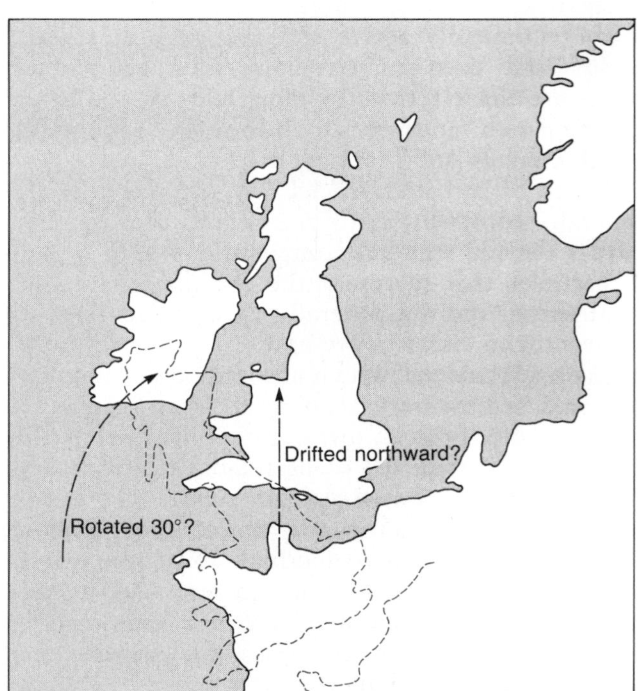

Figure 1–25

Presumed northward migration and clockwise rotation of England since the Triassic, determined on the basis of considerable deviation in Triassic geomagnetic field directions from present field direction. In 1954, this phenomenon was interpreted by a group of University of London geophysicists to represent not a change in geomagnetic field direction, but rather a change in England's position with respect to essentially fixed poles. This study reopened the question of the possibility of continental drift.

(From H. Takeuchi, S. Uyeda, and H. Kanamori, 1970, *Debate about the Earth,* rev. ed., Fig. 5–8, p. 167. Reproduced by permission of Freeman, Cooper & Company, San Francisco)

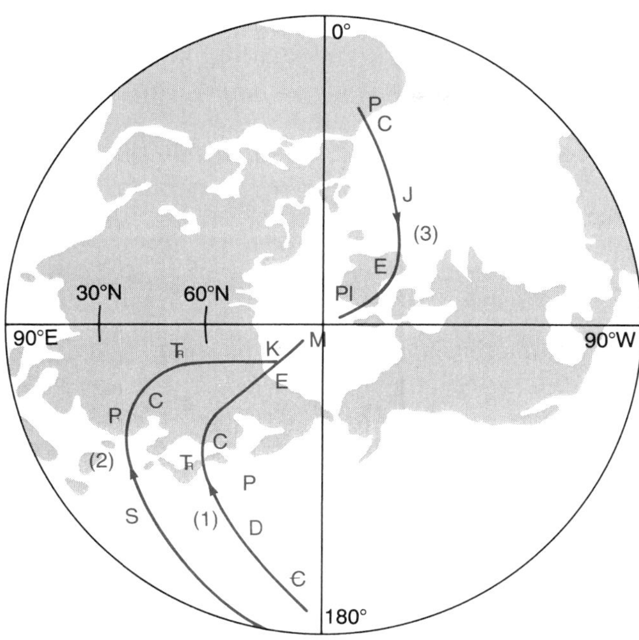

Figure 1–26
Postulated paleomagnetic "polar-wandering" curves for Europe (1), North America (2), and Australia (3). Є = Cambrian, S = Silurian, D = Devonian, C = Carboniferous, P = Permian, Ŧ = Triassic, J = Jurassic, K = Cretaceous, E = Eocene, M = Miocene, Pl = Pliocene. These curves represent the paths of movement of the three continental areas during the Phanerozoic with respect to essentially fixed poles.
(From Allan Cox and Richard Doehl, 1960, Review of Paleomagnetism. *Geological Society of America Bulletin,* vol. 71, no. 6, Fig. 34, p. 759. Reproduced by permission of Geological Society of America)

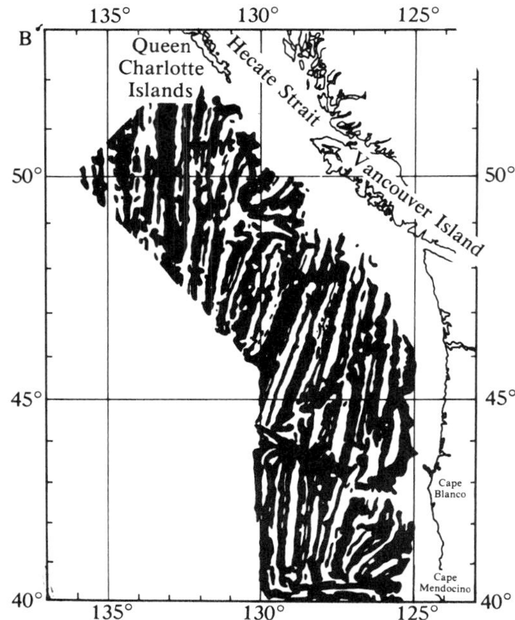

Figure 1–27
Index anomaly map of the total magnetic field for the Northeast Pacific. Positive magnetic anomalies are shown in black. Data from this study led the Canadian geologist L. W. Morley to his "radical" idea that mid-oceanic ridges are loci for creation of new ocean bottom crust. Morley surmised, quite rightly and brilliantly, that the mid-ocean ridge, which should be off California, was, in fact, under California at the location of the San Andreas fault, having been overriden in California by continental drift.
(From Arthur D. Raff annd Ronald G. Mason, 1961, Magnetic Survey Off the West Coast of North America, 32°N latitude to 42°N latitude. *Geological Society of America Bulletin,* vol. 72, no. 8)

the continents had assumed various positions with respect to essentially fixed poles. Slowly, more and more geologists and geophysicists began to look upon the theory of continents in motion with favor.

In 1960 a great American geologist, the late Harry Hess of Princeton University, postulated the hypothesis of seafloor spreading as a mechanism to move continents. This put the emphasis on the oceanic crust, and viewed the continental masses as playing only a very subordinate role. Actual documentation of the phenomenon of seafloor spreading was presented in 1963; it involved interpretation of magnetic anomalies discovered in the eastern Pacific Ocean basin floor some five years previously. It was determined that ocean-floor magnetic stripes (Fig. 1–27) were the expressions of periodic changes in magnetic intensity, that they were successively generated by seafloor spreading, and that they carried the indelible imprint of periodic reversals of the Earth's magnetic field. It was the confirmation of periodic magnetic-field polarity reversals and the association of these with the system of submarine ridges (the spreading centers) that transformed what Harry Hess had called "geopoetry" into geofact.

By 1966, nearly 40 years after the memorable New York City meeting that almost laid to rest the "continental drift" theory, a group of experts reviewed all available evidence on magnetic anomalies, magnetized rocks, earthquakes, and matching continental age/geologic provinces across the oceans. The evidence was persuasive, and the new revolution was proclaimed. The scientific community quickly appreciated that the Earth's outer layer was a dynamic mosaic of separate pieces called plates, and it was the plates moving through the mechanism of seafloor spreading that provided the essence of the new theory. It was apparent that the geophysically defined boundary between the lithosphere and the asthenosphere figured most importantly in the process. The geophysically defined base of the crust, called the **Moho** discontinuity (short for Mohorovičić), took on only secondary importance in the process. *Plate tectonics* became the geological buzzword of the late 1960s and early 1970s.

Let us recapture for the moment the revival of the "continental drift" theory during the 1950s. It is ironic how the dissenting opinions of one period may become the majority opinions of another. But therein lies the beauty and intrigue of the highly interpretive science of geology. It is ironic also that leading the way in the revival were the geophysicists, originally the most vocal opponents. They opposed the idea because no mechanism could be found to move continents, but now we know that the continents did not move independently across more dense basaltic lithosphere: they moved *with it*. In this perspective, continental drift becomes the stepchild of plate tectonics.

Yet another final irony relates to Alfred Wegener, the "father of continental drift" and the central figure in the early debate. When he died in 1929, he was engaged in pioneering echo-sounding techniques that later would be used in ocean-floor mapping that would give the concept of continents in motion strong support.

A Unifying Principle

In 1967 a comprehensive program of deep-sea drilling was inaugurated, using the research vessel *Glomar Challenger.* This proved to be one of the most successful long-term scientific ventures of all time. Hundreds of drill cores of deep-sea sediments and oceanic crust, together with magnetic and other geophysical surveys, have provided important data on spreading rates and directions, and have continuously substantiated the theory that the present ocean basins are indeed comparatively young geologic features.

During the past several decades the theory of plate tectonics has catapulted into the role of a master scheme for the whole Earth—a unifying principle that gives meaning to and helps explain many diverse phenomena. It is a model that seems to accommodate and link together many aspects of Earth science that previously had been treated as subjects for independent study. Plate tectonics has become a unifying concept that is providing a powerful model for interpreting and reinterpreting the vast storehouse of descriptive geology that has accumulated during the past two centuries.

Interaction of lithospheric plates has produced orogenic belts, which, in turn, have been sites of active mountain building. In addition, the distribution over the Earth of major earthquake epicenters and active volcanoes is directly associated with the locations of lithospheric spreading centers, and especially with deep-sea trenches (ocean-floor manifestations of subduction/Benioff zones). Plate boundaries have been loci for the formation of economic mineral deposits, particularly where igneous activity is involved. The occurrences of certain rock types, such as andesite, are related directly to plate-tectonic activity and setting. Plate tectonics has been the determining influence in the origin and evolution of *sedimentary basins* and those depositional and postdepositional environments where fossil fuels (oil, gas, and coal) have formed.

Still another exciting revelation, and an area of active multidisciplinary research, concerns the biological consequences of plate tectonics. The lithosphere and the hydrosphere have been the stage of life, and changes in that stage—separation and coming together of continents, opening and closing of ocean basins, drift of continents into different climatic belts, and changes in environments—have had far-reaching effects on the diversification and extinction patterns of species through time.

Finally, plate tectonics has had a profound influence on world climatic patterns, determined as they are largely by the cycle and periodicity of mountain building, the amount of volcanism, the position of the continents with respect to the poles, the degree of clustering or fragmentation of continental blocks, and oceanic circulation and wind patterns. One of the exciting outgrowths of this new theory is the need for information from a number of disciplines in geology. We are seeing a most significant synthesis of data from traditional areas such as paleontology, stratigraphy, petrography, structural geology, geophysics, geochemistry, and oceanography. Application of the theory to many geological problems has fostered healthy communication among the subdisciplines of geology.

As you progress through this text, particularly the section on the geologic evolution of North America (Chapters 8 through 15), the central theme of plate tectonics will become apparent. It is our hope that you often will think about this central theme as you become acquainted with how our continent came to be as it is. We do not begin to have all the answers; many of the major implications and applications of the plate-tectonics theory still await study. But it is the ability to begin asking the right questions and to search for the elusive answers that provides the real excitement in probing the mysteries of historical geology—the science of a dynamic Earth.

Summary

The planet Earth has a density of 5.5 g/cm^3 and an internal structure that consists of: (1) a central iron-nickel core, the inner part of which is solid, and the outer zone molten; (2) a thick, dense silicate mesosphere; (3) a mushy, almost plastic asthenosphere; and (4) a thin, rigid lithosphere. Historical geology is concerned primarily with the evolution of the lithosphere and the interaction among the lithosphere, atmosphere, hydrosphere, and biosphere during the 4600 million-year history of the Earth.

The lithosphere has evolved within the context of the geologic cycle, which consists of three subcycles and their interactions:

1. The rock cycle involves the interrelationships among igneous, sedimentary, and metamorphic rocks, which give the lithosphere its composition.
2. The hydrologic cycle traces the myriad pathways of water and how it is instrumental in weathering and eroding the lithosphere.
3. The tectonic cycle relates to the mobility of the lithosphere, and involves the deformation of rock.

A new revolution in the Earth sciences has brought the tectonic cycle into clearer focus and has given Earth scientists a better understanding of how the Earth works. Only during the past 25 years has it been appreciated that the Earth's lithosphere is fragmented into a mosaic of plates, which interact by spreading apart at divergent boundaries, colliding at convergent boundaries, and sideswiping at transform boundaries. This dynamic aspect of the Earth's lithosphere is called plate tectonics.

New oceanic lithosphere is formed along mid-oceanic ridges at seafloor spreading centers where fresh basalt, derived from the asthenosphere, wells up into the central rift zone. This new lithosphere is continuously accommodated as older seafloor material glides away on both sides of the rift at rates of several cm/year. The continents, which "bob" higher than the ocean basins because they are lighter, move apart or approach one another as passive passengers attached to spreading oceanic lithosphere. The mid-ocean ridges rise up from the abyssal plains and form an interconnected system some 70,000 km in length—the "mountain chains" of the ocean basins.

Old oceanic lithosphere is destroyed in subduction zones, where it dives (subducts) beneath the edges of continental lithosphere at rates of several cm/year. Oceanic–continental lithospheric collisions result in magmatic arcs, like the Cascades and Andes mountain chains, which form along the edges of continents. Oceanic–oceanic lithosphere collisions result in volcanic island arc chains, like the East Indies and Japanese archipelagos, which form seaward of continental margins. Subduction can occur only along the advancing edge of a plate. Both island arcs and magmatic arcs produce hybrids of basalt and granite called andesite. Deep-sea trenches are the seafloor topographic expressions of subduction zones.

New seafloor crust is created at spreading centers and old crust is destroyed in subduction zones. Through geologic history, oceanic crust probably has been totally replaced by new material every 300 to 400 million years. The oldest rocks yet recovered from any of the present-day ocean basins are less than 200 million years old. The locations of most geological observations, however, are on the continents, where the oldest rocks yet discovered are about 3800 million years old—almost 20 times the age of the oldest ocean basin rocks.

The continents consist of complex patchworks of igneous, sedimentary, and metamorphic rocks. The nuclei of continents are shield areas that consist of Precambrian basement forged from earlier plate collisions. Mountain ranges like the Appalachians and Rockies represent younger plate-collision boundaries where thick accumulations of sedimentary rock were folded and faulted, intruded by igneous plutons, and, in places, regionally metamorphosed as part of the tectonic cycle. Emergent coastal plains and submergent continental shelves (miogeoclines), and slopes and rises (eugeoclines) are the surfaces of giant prisms of sediment deposited in long, linear subsiding continental margin basins along the passive, trailing edge of the continent. In the context of the tectonic cycle, these trailing margins, with their thick sediment wedges, are likely to become the collision margins and resulting mountain belts of the future. Continents have grown by accretion of orogens around continental nuclei; ocean basins have opened and closed through seafloor spreading, subduction, and collision of continents (together with microplates). All are part of the Wilson Cycle.

The theory of plate tectonics provides a unifying concept and model that explains such diverse phenomena as origin and evolution of sedimentary basins and mountain belts, distribution and cause of earthquakes and volcanoes, occurrence of economic mineral deposits, and major patterns in the history of life. Plate tectonics came as a scientific revolution in the decade of the 1960s and represented an about-face in geologic thinking—from belief in a static crust with fixed continents, to advocacy of a dynamic lithosphere with footloose continents.

The turning point came with the discovery of seafloor magnetic anomalies: paired patterns of magnetic "stripes" parallel to mid-ocean ridges. These anomalies represent differences in magnetic intensity, reflecting a history of changes in the Earth's magnetic field. The symmetrically paired magnetic anomaly patterns documented a calendar of seafloor spreading, thus providing a viable mechanism to explain continental drift—an old theory clearly enunciated near the turn of the century by Alfred Wegener.

Suggestions For Further Reading

Condie, K. C. 1976. *Plate tectonics and crustal evolution.* London: Pergamon Press.

Frankel, Henry. 1988. From continental drift to plate tectonics. *Nature* 355:127–30.

Glen, William. 1982. *The road to Jaramillo.* Stanford, CA: Stanford Univ. Press.

Hallam, A. 1973. *A revolution in the Earth sciences.* Oxford, England: Clarendon.

Hamilton, W. B. 1988. Plate tectonics and island arcs. *Geological Society of America Bulletin* 100(10):1503–27.

Marsh, B. D. 1979. Island-arc volcanism. *American Scientist* 67:161–72.

Menard, H. W. 1986. *The ocean of truth—A personal history of global tectonics.* Princeton, NJ: Princeton Univ. Press.

Molnar, Peter. 1988. Continental tectonics in the aftermath of plate tectonics. *Nature* 335:131–37.

Molnar, Peter, and Paul Tapponier. 1977. The collision between India and Eurasia. *Scientific American* Offprint 923. San Francisco: W. H. Freeman.

Redfern, Ron. 1983. *The making of a continent.* New York: Times Books.

Uyeda, Seiya. 1978. *The new view of the Earth: Moving continents and moving oceans.* San Francisco: W. H. Freeman.

Weiner, Jonathan. 1986, *Planet Earth.* New York: Bantam Books.

Wilson, J. T., ed. 1976. Continents adrift and continents aground. *Readings from Scientific American.* San Francisco: W. H. Freeman.

Windley, B. 1984. *The evolving continents.* 2d ed. New York: John Wiley & Sons.

Wyllie, Peter J. 1976. *The way the Earth works: An introduction to the new global geology and its revolutionary development.* New York: John Wiley & Sons.

Shifting Sands and Murky Muds: Ancient Sedimentary Environments and Facies

2

Contents

Key Terms

Sedimentary facies
Diagenesis
Red beds
CCD
Aragonite
Graded bedding
Turbidity current
Turbidite
Biofacies
Lithofacies
Facies tract
Walther's Law
Transgression
Regression
Retrogradation
Onlap
Progradation
Offlap
Sedimentary cycle
Paleogeographic map

From Permian Sea to National Park.

History has been described as a continuous stream of time—the origin and early beginning of the solar system flowing into and merging with the early geologic history of the Earth, and this, in turn, flowing into and incorporating the origin and development of life, including the history of human existence. Guadalupe Mountains National Park in West Texas and southeastern New Mexico provides an excellent example of this stream of history. The park was created because of the natural beauty of the area, its geologic history (outstanding development of ancient sedimentary environments), its long period of associated human history, and more recent events involving the dedication of one person in particular who felt the area should be preserved for future generations to observe, understand, and appreciate.

The rocks of the Guadalupe Mountains are the exposed part of what has been called the largest fossil reef in the world. This feature, Capitan Reef, is a large barrier reef (carbonate buildup) that developed during Permian time. Geologically, the Capitan Limestone and associated rocks provide an outstanding example of the development of a spectrum of depositional environments: reef, back-reef lagoon, and deep basin seaward of the reef (Fig. 2–1). Each of these settings produced distinctive sediments and life forms. One of the principal attractions of this area, the world-famous Carlsbad Caverns, is developed in the deposits of this ancient reef complex. The rocks of this complex will serve as an illustrative example of **sedimentary facies** later in this chapter. Here, let us look briefly at the human history leading to the development of this area as a national park.

Indians were living in the Guadalupe Mountains as long as 12,000 years ago, as indicated by carbon-14 dating of charcoal from their fires. Evidence of their presence is found also in caves and in rock shelters where pictographs were painted on the walls. The first known written references to this area are in accounts from the 1700s of explorations by Spanish conquistadores. It is not known, however, if any of these explorers were within the present park boundaries. The name Guadalupe was first used for these mountains on a map dated 1828. The remoteness of the area, the aridity of the land, and the presence of the Mescalero Apache discouraged settlement.

Recognition of this area as an outstanding section of Permian rocks is reflected in the established names for subdivisions of the Permian System in the United States. The lower part of the Permian is divided into the Wolfcampian and Leonardian Series, both names derived from geographic sites (type areas) in the Glass Mountains of West Texas. The upper part of the Permian is divided into the Guadalupian and Ochoan Series, names also derived from this region. The stratigraphic sections from which these names are derived are examples of *stratotypes* (see Chapter 6): type sections of regional time-stratigraphic units whose boundaries are clearly defined on the basis of paleontologic criteria. The Guadalupe Mountains region is the site of the standard American Permian stratigraphic section, and is one of sev-

A

B

Figure 2–1
A. El Capitan limestone cliff, southern end of Guadalupe Mountains.
B. Rock units in the El Capitan section: (1) Capitan Limestone, consisting of massive reef and fore-reef deposits overlying (2) deeper-water slope and (3) basinal deposits.
(Photo by J. D. Cooper)

eral regional reference sections for correlation and comparison of Permian rocks on a worldwide basis. The original type-Permian section was established by Roderick Murchison in 1821 in the province of Perm, Russia (USSR). It is necessary to have a number of intermediate reference sections to enable worldwide correlation.

Wallace Pratt, a petroleum geologist, was intimately familiar with the Guadalupe Mountains and the impressive historical sequence they display. His enthusiasm for the area was not limited to wishful thinking that something should be done to preserve this rock record. Fortunately, Pratt had considerable landholdings in the region, and in 1961 he donated over 5000 acres to the federal government for the establishment of Guadalupe Mountains National Park. The donated area included McKittrick Canyon, whose north wall is 600 meters high and displays a graphic cross section of the various *carbonate rock* facies that are the lithified products of contemporaneous depositional environments of the ancient reef complex. Over 70,000 acres eventually were purchased by the government and included in the park. The park was opened officially to the public in 1970.

In 1976 Wallace Pratt, then in his ninety-first year, was interviewed and was asked why he had felt moved to donate this land. Pratt's reply expresses the depth of his feelings for this land, and his concern for its preservation:

> The canyon exposes a precise cross section of the Capitan Barrier Reef, which is unique in the Western Hemisphere. There are more than five hundred different fossils to be found here. But of greatest importance, the canyon clearly exposes

> the anatomy of the organic reef. By giving the land to the park service [I have the assurance] of preservation of a record of natural events over a period of two hundred million years.*

To be a "giant" of geology does not require being a nineteenth-century founder of the science!

*From interview printed in *Exxon USA*, fourth quarter, 1976.

Rocks and Environments

The Grand Canyon Succession

The mighty cleft of the Grand Canyon (Fig. 2–2) arouses wonder in the minds of many of those who stand on its rim and look out over the imposing view. Questions arise as to how this "gash" in the Earth's crust was formed: When did all of this begin? What is the significance of the different-colored rock layers? One generally is overcome, too, with a feeling of spaciousness and grandeur, even awe. The eighteenth-century catastrophists would have invoked a great Earth-splitting event to create the canyon, but *actualistically* the Grand Canyon, which exposes more than a billion years of Earth history, is testimony to the long-term erosive downcutting of the Colorado River. It is a marvelous place to take a trip through time.

Joseph Wood Krutch, a well-known English professor and drama critic, reflected on the canyon view:

> As the river sawed slowly through the rising strata, its deepening walls exposed again to sight older and older formations going back more and more millions of years until, finally, they add up to more than a billion. . . . Seated at my point on the rim, I look up and down as well as east and west, and the vista is one of the most extensive ever vouchsafed to man. But I am also at a point in time as well as in space. The one vista is as grandiose as the other. I am small and alone in the middle of these great distances, vertical as well as horizontal. *But the gulf of time over which I am poised is inconceivably more vast and much more dizzying to peer into.* (Italics added)*

The present-day uplifted Colorado Plateau and deeply incised Grand Canyon are geologically young features. During the last billion years, the topography of this region and its *paleoenvironmental* conditions have changed many times. In the Grand Canyon's colorful Paleozoic sedimentary rocks alone, there is exposed a record of about 350 million years of change, of advancing Cambrian seas, of Carboniferous rivers and deltas, of Permian tidal flats and sand dunes. These changing paleoenviron-

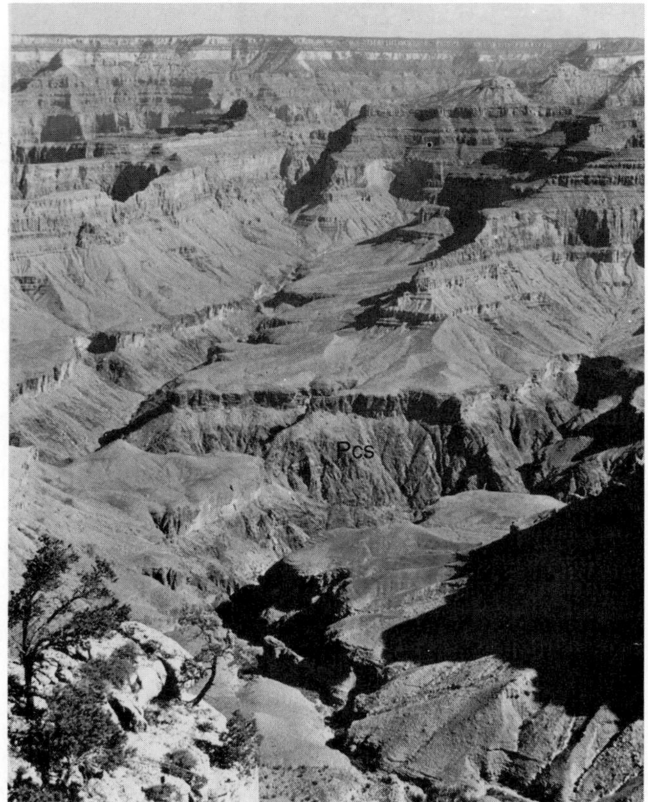

Figure 2–2
View looking north in Grand Canyon. Precambrian schist (Pcs at bottom of gorge) is overlain by a layered sequence of Paleozoic sedimentary rocks.
(Photo by J. D. Cooper)

*J. W. Krutch. 1957. *Grand Canyon: Today and all its yesterdays.* New York: William Morrow.

ments are recognized by reading the rock pages of this historical volume. Each rock layer in the vertical succession of Paleozoic formations in the walls of the Grand Canyon is a product of the paleoenvironment that existed in the district at the time the sediment was deposited.

The Meaning of Facies

Changes in paleoenvironments are documented not only in *vertical* sections, but also may be expressed by *lateral* variation, as exemplified by the Old Red Sandstone in Britain. This formation was recognized by early workers in southern Wales as a product of continental (nonmarine) deposition. The Old Red consists of thick sequences of red conglomerates, sandstones, and shales containing fossils of early land plants and amphibians and of freshwater fish.

By tracing outcrops of the Old Red Sandstone southward through the British Isles, Sedgwick and Murchison determined that the nonmarine beds interfinger with and grade laterally into marine carbonate rocks of the *type Devonian* in northern Devon, England. The regional intertonguing of these units indicates that during Devonian time both marine and nonmarine paleoenvironments existed in different parts of what is now the British Isles and that each paleoenvironmental area was the site of accumulation of distinctively different sediments (Fig. 2–3). This lateral change from nonmarine to marine rocks of equivalent age is an example of a facies change. A **sedimentary facies** refers to the *lateral* variation in lithology of sedimentary rock units that are partly or wholly equivalent in age. The lateral variation is produced by deposition in different, but laterally adjacent, environments. Most commonly, changes between sedimentary facies are gradational transitions, rather than the sharply defined tongues of marine and nonmarine rocks graphically depicted in Figure 2–3.

The original work leading directly to the recognition of sedimentary facies relationships was done in the 1830s by a Swiss geologist, Amanz Gressly. Gressly traced Jurassic sedimentary rock units in the Jura Mountains and found that the lithology of the rocks varied laterally; contemporaneous limestone and shale lithologies were the result of differences in the paleoenvironments in which the original sediments accumulated. Gressly was the scientist who first used the name *facies* for the distinctive units in this sort of lateral relationship.

The Relationship Between Facies and Environments

Introduction

Sedimentary facies represent products of different environments of deposition. Facies analysis involves study of the internal characteristics of facies as well as of distribution patterns and relationships, and is critical for correct interpretation of ancient environments (paleoenvironments). One of the keys

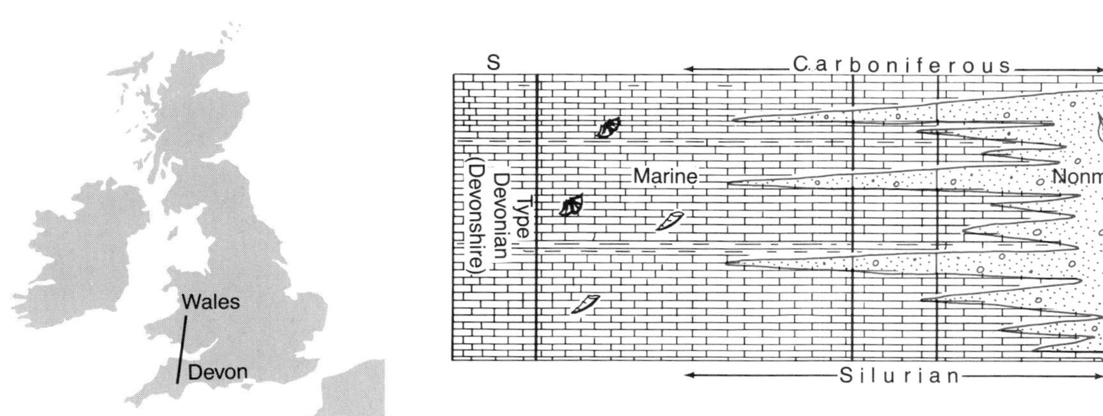

Figure 2–3
Sedimentary facies change in Devonian rocks of Great Britain. To the north in Wales, deposition consisted of nonmarine sandstones and conglomerates of the Old Red Sandstone; southward, in England, marine limestones were deposited. The lateral equivalency of the units is diagrammatically illustrated by the interfingering relationship between the two facies.

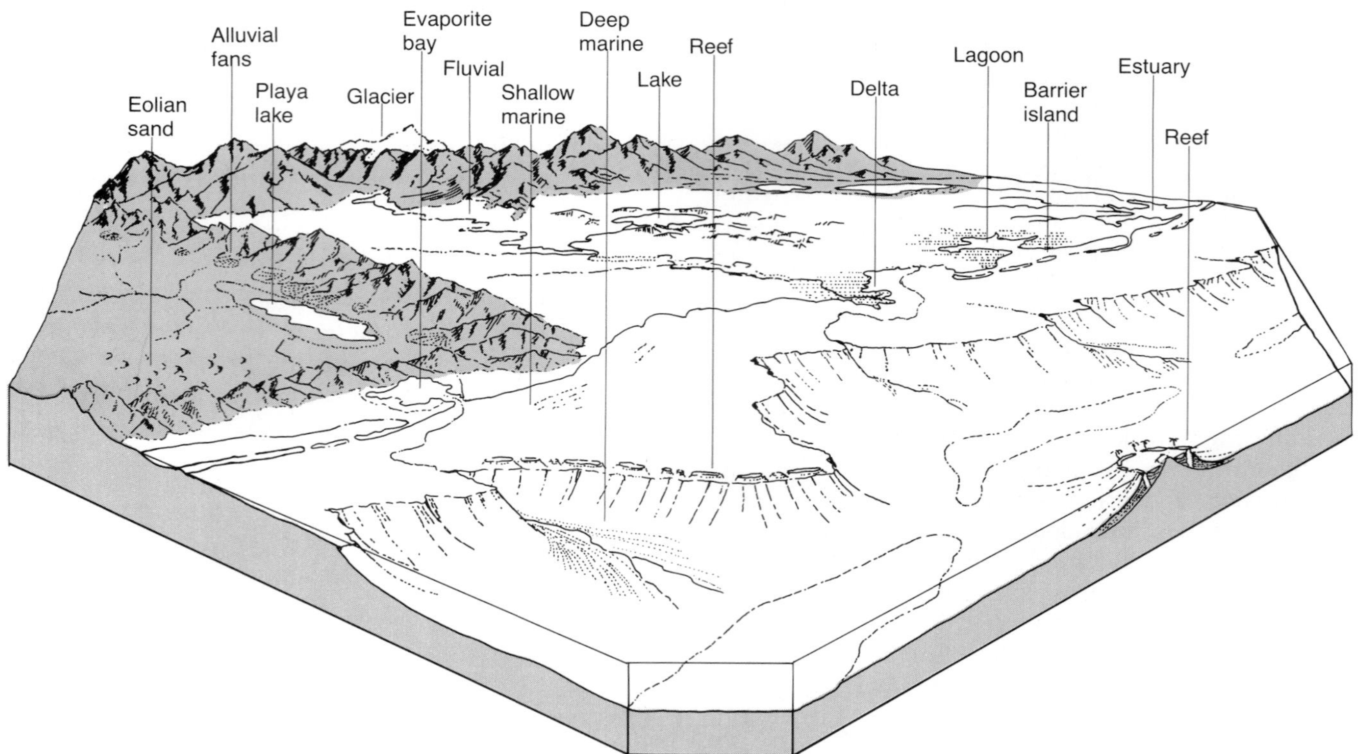

Figure 2–4
Overview of modern sedimentary environments.
(Based on W. K. Hamblin and J. E. Howard, 1980, *Exercises in Physical Geology,* 5th ed., Fig. 98, p. 49: Burgess Publishing Co., Minneapolis)

to recognition of ancient sedimentary environments is understanding present environments; this is an example of the use of modern analogues. On the Earth's surface today there are many different sedimentary environments (Fig. 2–4): river channels and floodplains, deltas, coastal lagoons and beaches, continental-shelf and offshore areas, and various other settings. Each of these environmental settings is an area where sediment accumulates and where organisms live and die. Each of these environmental areas produces a representative sedimentary rock type or assemblage, dependent upon the physical, chemical, and biological processes operating. It is necessary to understand present-day processes and environments in order to identify and interpret their ancient counterparts.

Thus, facies analysis involves numerous applications of the principle of *actualism* ("the present is the key to understanding the past"). Many criteria useful in the recognition of ancient sedimentary environments are determined from study of present-day processes and their depositional products, the most important being lithology, geometric shape of the rock unit, sedimentary structures, and fossils.

Lithology

Lithology refers to the type of sedimentary rock, determined by *composition* and *texture.* These physical characteristics result from several factors related to the rock cycle (see Chapter 1). Some of the factors are the type of source rocks that are weathered to provide terrigenous clastic debris; the method of transport of particles; the conditions prevalent in the depositional environment (where the particles come to rest); and the processes of lithification that convert loose sediment particles into indurated sedimentary rock.

Terrigenous clastic rocks (rocks derived from the accumulation of erosional debris of preexisting rocks) reflect the ancient environment of deposition mainly in their textures. However, because the clastic debris is *extrabasinal* in origin, the composition of the framework particles is controlled mainly by the geology of the source area. *Chemical* sedimentary rocks, such as limestone and evaporites (see Table 1–3, Chapter 1), are *intrabasinal* (within the depositional basin). Their lithologies commonly reflect paleoenvironmental conditions in that these rocks are deposited within their source area and are not composed of solids derived from preexisting rocks. In these sediments, the solid particles are manufactured (precipitated physicochemically or biochemically) and transported within the basin of deposition.

The extrabasinal nature of the terrigenous clastic sedimentary rocks means that the composition of the rocks is largely determined by conditions outside the depositional environment. The composition of the source rock, be it plutonic igneous, volcanic, sedimentary, metamorphic, or a combination of rock types, initially controls the composition of the clastic grains weathered from the outcrops and unleashed into the transport system.

The type and degree of weathering may modify the grains and thus further influence the composition of the *detritus.* If the weathering occurs in a humid climate, the feldspars and other unstable silicate minerals may be chemically altered to clays and soluble components. In humid tropical regions, the weathering of feldspars to clays is especially common. The imprint of mechanical weathering is more prevalent in semiarid-to-arid climates, however, and detrital feldspar may comprise a significant volume of the detritus. *Arkose* (feldspar-rich sandstone; see Table 1–3, Chapter 1) is indicative of "granitic" source rocks, dry climatic conditions and/or high relief, rapid erosion, and rapid burial of the feldspar-rich detritus. *Lithic fragments* (actual pieces of rock that still retain the full identity of their parentage) also tend to accumulate in higher concentrations under conditions of dry climates and/or rapid deposition and burial.

The mineral quartz is chemically relatively stable under surface conditions and typically remains as discrete grains; thus it is the major component of most sandstones. Quartz grains are sufficiently tough and durable to be recycled through rock-forming processes numerous times. For example, suppose that an ancient quartz-rich conglomerate with a sand and mud *matrix* is exposed along the course of a modern stream. Present weathering processes loosen the detrital grains. The competence of the modern stream is such that most of the coarser, gravel fraction is left upstream as channel deposits, and the sand and clay/silt (mud fraction) particles are transported downstream to the ocean. During this transport, many of the more unstable particles, such as silicate minerals and lithic fragments, are destroyed, thus enriching the detrital population in the most stable end products of weathering and erosion, viz. quartz and clay minerals. The winnowing effect of the waves and currents carries the mud fraction out to sea to be deposited in quiet water below wave base, and leaves the relatively pure quartz sand behind as a beach deposit, where it is entrained under high-energy conditions and enriched in quartz even more. In time, this beach sand could be buried and lithified to form a quartz sandstone that is composed of recycled quartz grains.

This reworking of grains to produce a "pure" product introduces the concept of *compositional maturity* in sediments (Table 2–1A). Terrigenous clastic sediments and sedimentary rocks are compositionally mature when they are composed only of the most stable detrital minerals. What began perhaps as an immature mixture of particles of varying stability becomes progressively more mature as the result of changes in detrital composition during erosion and deposition, involving time, energy, climate, and distance.

Postdepositional changes (in the burial environment), such as dissolution and recrystallization, can also further alter the detrital mineral composition. Postdepositional changes, not including metamorphism, occur in the realm of **diagenesis.** One of the most important aspects of diagenesis is the filling of pore space in the fabric of deposits by precipitated mineral *cements* such as quartz and calcite. Diagenetic compaction and cementation are the chief processes that lithify sediments into rock. Early-to-late diagenetic change involving iron in sediments commonly produces colors that reveal information about the geochemical conditions in the depositional and diagenetic (burial) environment. **Red beds** result from the *oxidation* of ferrous iron in sediments exposed to the atmosphere. Black, dark gray, and dark green colors commonly result from *reducing* conditions in stagnant, restricted, low-oxygen environments.

In addition to mineralogic maturity, the quartz sandstone example is also an expression of *textural maturity,* which relates to the amount of mud fraction (silt and clay), the degree of *sorting* (how narrow the size range), and the degree of *rounding* (smoothing of sharp edges and corners) of sand-size and coarser particles in a deposit (Table 2–1B). This involves the relationship between *matrix* (smaller than sand-size particles) and *framework* (sand and coarser fraction), and the condition of the framework. Textural maturity is a rough index to the level of physical, mechanical energy operating at the site of deposition (Table 2–1B).

Deposits containing appreciable amounts of detrital mud (silt and/or clay) are texturally immature and reflect relatively low energy level, characterized by currents of weak strength, such as quiet-water lakes, river floodplains, marine shelves, slopes, and deeper water basins. Deposits that are

Table 2–1
Maturity of Sedimentary Rocks

A. COMPOSITIONAL MATURITY

Maturity	Composition	Possible Implications
Immature	<50% quartz or clay minerals	First cycle; close to source; dry climate
Submature	<90% quartz or clay minerals	long transport and/or humid climate if first cycle; prolonged weathering; multicyclic
Mature	>90% quartz or clay minerals	long transport and/or multicyclic; prolonged weathering
Supermature	>98% quartz or clay minerals	Multicyclic; prolonged weathering

B. TEXTURAL MATURITY

Maturity	Texture	Possible Implications
Immature	Mud matrix or support	Low depositional energy (weak currents of removal)
Submature	No mud matrix; framework poorly sorted	Moderate depositional energy
Mature	No mud matrix; framework well sorted	High, constant depositional energy
Supermature	No mud; framework well sorted, well rounded	Very high, constant depositional energy; recycled if compositionally supermature

generally mud free and whose framework is well sorted are considered to be texturally mature, and reflect higher, more constant energy levels, such as in beaches. Submature sediments were deposited under conditions of moderate energy—strong enough to winnow out the mud fraction, but not strong or constant enough to effectively sort the sand and gravel fraction, such as in stream channels. Sediments that are mud free, well sorted, and well rounded are *supermature,* reflecting the highest, most constant energy levels, such as those occurring in dune fields. Rounding is an index to the amount of abrasion of particles, and is generally enhanced through successive cycles.

Thus, in a simplified spectrum from immature to supermature, there is a connotation of increasing depositional energy conditions. However, the products of various energy levels can be mixed in the depositional environment, producing *textural inversions.* Examples of such textural contradictions or anomalies include well-sorted sand grains in a muddy matrix, or well-rounded but poorly sorted sand and gravel. Most textural inversions are created by energy pulses such as storms, which stir sediment surfaces and sweep particles from one environment to another. Although sorting and winnowing are mainly products of energy at the final depositional site, rounding, to a much larger extent, can be inherited from the source area and may reflect multicyclic derivation. In terms of interpretation, the textural maturity of any deposit is based on the lowest maturity level expressed, because this indicates the latest energy level operating to produce the deposit that we see.

In the idealized model depicted in Figure 2–5A, terrigenous clastic debris from the highland source area becomes generally finer in texture and more mature in composition as it moves downstream. It becomes generally finer because the fines outrun the coarse fraction. It becomes more compositionally mature because attrition enriches the detrital population in the more stable end products of weathering and erosion, such as quartz. Even in this idealized model, however, exceptions do occur, such as the coarser deep-basin sediments transported and deposited by turbidity currents, which short-circuit the "normal" progression from coarser-to-finer in an offshore direction.

Note also that in this idealized model (Fig. 2–5A), depositional energy is generally low to moderate in most environments, producing texturally immature-to-submature deposits. The exceptions are dunes, beaches, and barrier islands, where higher, more constant energy is focused, and mature-to-supermature sediments are the result. Keep in mind that energy in this context refers to the strength of currents of *removal*—not delivery. For instance, a landslide deposit has a high kinetic energy of delivery, but a low energy of removal. The particles come to rest and remain there with little or no subsequent winnowing and working; consequently most landslides are texturally immature.

Carbonate sedimentary rocks, the most abundant of the chemical (nonterrigenous clastic) deposits, are not as abundant as the terrigenous clastic rocks, but are, nonetheless, economically important. Many limestones and dolostones (see Table 1–3, Chapter 1) are *porous* and *permeable*, and form reservoirs for groundwater and petroleum. It is, in fact, due to intensive studies of carbonate rocks by

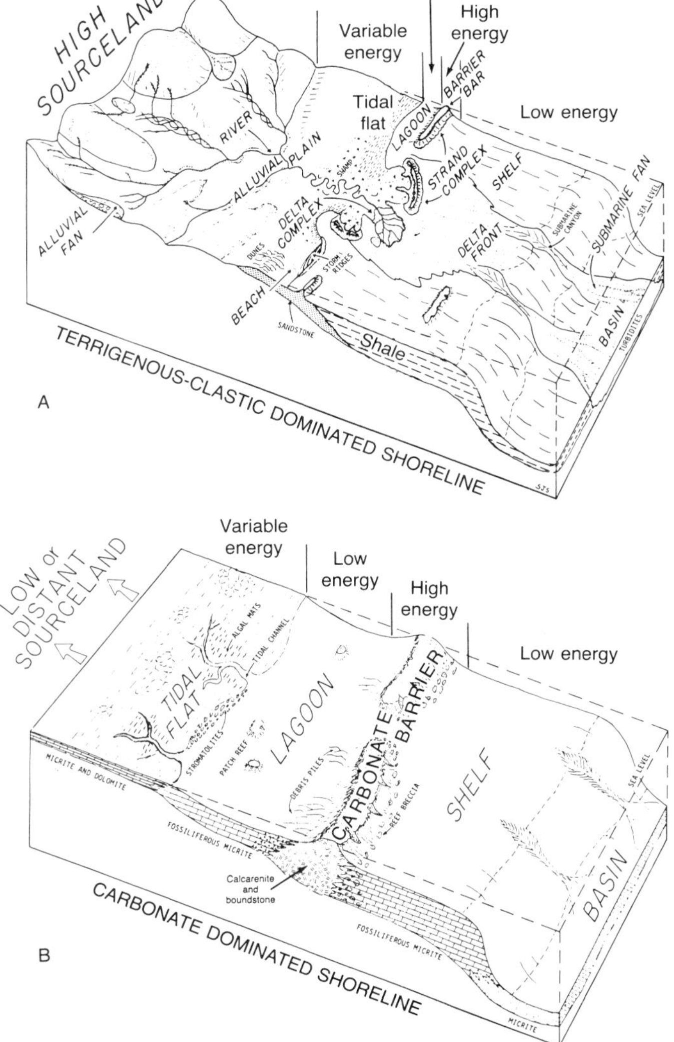

Figure 2–5
Schematic block diagrams depicting idealized spatial arrangement of depositional environments, energy conditions, and sediment types for: A. Terrigenous clastic-dominated shoreline; B. Carbonate-dominated shoreline.
(From Lynn S. Fichter and David J. Poché, 1979, *Ancient Environments and the Interpretation of Geologic History:* Macmillan, New York. Reproduced with permission of publisher)

petroleum geologists in recent years that our understanding of the origin of this important suite of rocks has increased greatly. Carbonates also are the host rocks for some ore deposits and great quantities of them are mined and quarried for agricultural lime, building stone, cement, and other industrial purposes.

The most fundamental concept in understanding the origin of the carbonate rocks is appreciating that the ingredients are intrabasinal—that the carbonate muds, sands, and gravels, for the most part, are formed in place. Modern carbonate sediments are being deposited in several environmental settings: tidal zones, shallow marine shelves, beaches, marine basins (where depositional surfaces are above the calcium carbonate compensation depth—**CCD**), in freshwater lakes, and in association with hot springs activity. The marine deposits are volumetrically the most significant. Two basic types of shelf or platform environments are presently important as depositional sites of carbonate sediments. These are exemplified by the attached shelf south and west of Florida and by the isolated, unattached, shallow-water platform of the Bahama Banks (Fig. 2–6). Both locations are areas in relatively low latitudes (within 30° N or S of the Equator) where waters are warm, carbonate-producing organisms are prolific, and where there is a general lack of influx of terrigenous clastic debris, especially terrigenous mud. These parameters are essential, because most carbonate sediments are biochemically derived and influx of fine terrigenous detritus tends to overwhelm and smother and retard the delicate calcium carbonate depositional mechanism. There are examples of mixed terrigenous clastic-carbonate sedimentary associations in both the ancient and modern record, but the great bulk of carbonate sediments has accumulated under conditions generally free of terrigenous clastics, and most limestones contain less than 5% terrigenous-derived material.

Lime mud (*micrite*), initially formed as minute, needlelike crystals of the unstable mineral **aragonite,** is the most abundant component of limestones. The carbonate mud (remember that "mud" is a textural term) is derived largely from biologic and physical abrasion of larger carbonate particles (such as shells), from inorganic precipitation, and from organic precipitation, mainly by calcareous algae. Recent sedimentologic studies on the Bahama Banks indicate that the formation of lime mud from the disaggregation of calcareous algae is sufficient in quantity to account for the existing sediment on the bank, plus enough to supply about twice the amount of carbonate sediment that is found in the surrounding deeper-water environments.

Most carbonate sediments and rocks, however, are bimodal mixtures of micrite and carbonate sand-size grains (calcarenite), and, to a lesser extent, gravel-size grains (calcirudite). The coarser components are derived from several intrabasinal sources: whole and broken skeletal material of invertebrates and algae (sand and gravel); pieces of semilithified micritic sediment called *intraclasts* (gravel); *ooids* (sand-size carbonate grains that have accretionary inorganic concentric rings or envelopes of micrite around a nucleus of another particle such as a shell fragment); lumps of concentrically laminated blue-green algae accretions called *oncoids* (gravel size); and *peloids* (silt and sand size). The last is a nongeneric term applied to small, structureless, spherical-to-oval micritic particles, many of which probably originated as fecal pellets produced by carbonate mud–ingesting organisms (some worms and crustaceans, for example). It has been suggested that many carbonate sediments have been passed through the digestive tracts of organisms.

Limestones have textures that are analogous to the terrigenous clastic rocks, viz. various combinations of matrix (lime mud) and framework (sand-size and gravel-size particles), generally reflecting the same relationship to energy conditions. Thus, carbonate sediments and rocks generally follow the textural-maturity spectrum (Table 2–1), but the compositional maturity concept does not apply because of the intrabasinal, single-cycle nature of the material. Nearly all dolostones in the geologic record are the products of secondary, diagenetic replacement (the mineral dolomite replaces calcite) of limestone precursors. Some show good retention of original limestone depositional fabrics and textures, but in most, the dolomitization has largely or completely obliterated the original character. In order to determine the depositional conditions of most ancient dolostones, one must "wade through" the diagenetic overprint to try to determine what the original limestone was like. One particular type of limestone called a *boundstone* is unique among the sedimentary rocks, and has a fabric that owes its existence to the organic sediment-trapping and/or binding of material in place by the growth structure of organisms, such as in a coral reef.

In the idealized carbonate model of Figure 2–5B, the variation in sediment character is primarily controlled by differences in organic abundance and wave and current energy levels in the environment. Note that the terrigenous sourceland is subdued or distant, which accounts for a lack of extrabasinal

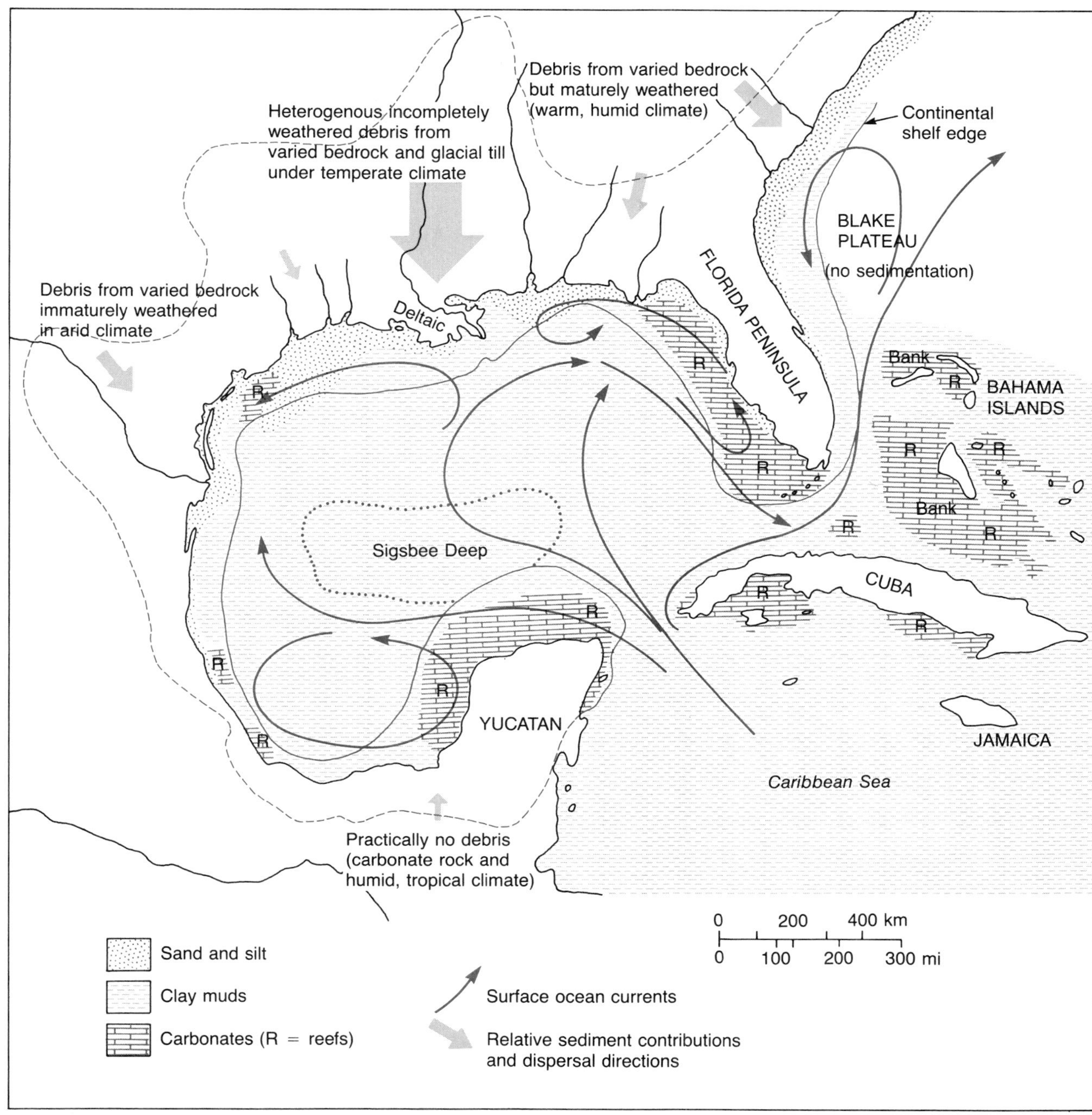

Figure 2–6

Map of present-day southeastern United States and Gulf of Mexico–Caribbean region showing major sediment-dispersal patterns. Most of the sediment being deposited in the marine environments consists of terrigenous clastics, derived from erosion of continental land masses and delivered by major trunk streams. Carbonate sediments are restricted to places such as the Bahama platform and the west Florida shelf, which are relatively free of terrigenous influx. A strict uniformitarian view would hold that such a situation has existed throughout Earth history.

(From R. H. Dott, Jr., and R. B. Batten, *Evolution of the Earth*, 3d ed., Fig. 11.22, p. 247: Copyright 1981 by McGraw-Hill Book Company. Reproduced by permission of publisher)

Table 2–2
Physical characteristics of some sedimentary environments

Environment	Common sediments (texture)	Sedimentary features
NONMARINE (terrestrial)		
Fluvial (stream)	Gravel, sand, mud	Poorly sorted material Rounded pebbles Lenses of sandstone Cross-bedding
Lacustrine (lake)	Silt, clay, lime*, mud	Laminated beds Freshwater fauna
Swamp	Silt, clay, organic debris	Decayed vegetation, peat
Desert		
Dune	Sand	Well-sorted material Frosted, rounded grains Large-scale cross-beds
Playa lake	Mud, evaporite salts	Laminated beds Desiccation cracks
Alluvial fan and debris flow	Boulders, gravel, sand	Poorly sorted material Beds of limited extent Lenticular or wedge-shaped units Cross-beds
Glacial		
Ice deposits	Morainal debris of all sizes	Unsorted debris Striated boulders
Glacial lake	Silt, mud	Varved (annual) layers
Fluvial (meltwater streams)		
TRANSITIONAL		
Delta	Complex intermingling of many subenvironments such as channels, swamps, freshwater lakes (see text discussion)	
Coastal lagoons, bays, estuaries	Silt, mud	Thin beds Brackish-water fauna

debris, allowing the "carbonate factory" to function. The sediment in the tidal flat in this model is predominantly carbonate mud (micrite), because the energy level is low (no strong current activity to produce ooids, for example), and the life forms adapted to this environment are characterized mainly by types that trap and bind fine sediments (see stromatolites, Chapter 3), producing boundstones.

The generally low, but changeable, energy level of the lagoon also typically produces micrite, but organisms are likely to produce skeletal material contributing to calcarenites, skeletal micrites, and limestones with whole fossils. The carbonate muds of this environment are likely to have been pelletized by mud-ingesting organisms, and on a larger scale, disturbed by storms, which provide energy pulses below fair-weather wave base and produce intraclasts and textural inversions.

The carbonate barrier is subject to the highest wave and current energy in this model, and produces skeletal sands of beachlike character as well as a variety of submature-to-mature calcarenites and calcirudites. If the carbonate barrier is an organic reef consisting of boundstone reef framework, associated erosional calcarenite and calcirudite debris piles characteristically develop as flanking facies (forereef and backreef). (Reef framework and related backreef, forereef, and basinal facies are discussed more fully as part of the Permian reef model later in this chapter.) Like the lagoon, the shelf environment, normally below fair-weather wave base, produces micrite and fossiliferous micrite. Depositional products of these two environ-

Physical characteristics of some sedimentary environments

Environment	Common sediments (texture)	Sedimentary features
MARINE Supratidal (typically broad flats occasionally inundated by wind tide)	Evaporites, dolomite, silt, mud	Laminated beds Desiccation cracks Stromatolites
Littoral (intertidal)	Cobbles, sand, mud	Laminated beds Mud cracks Trace fossils Stromatolites (carbonate) Well-sorted sands
Sublittoral Shelf	Sand, silt, clay	Wide geographic extent Thin-to-massive bedding Cross-bedding Diverse fauna
Carbonate platform	Calcareous sediments (lack of land-derived clastic debris)	Ooids Skeletal sands Lime mud Intraformational conglomerates
Also includes the reef environment (see text discussion)		
Bathyal depths (slope, rise) (100+ to 4000 m)	Mud Sand and gravel in submarine fans	Graded bedding (turbidites) Thick, coarse beds Sole marks Deep-water fossils
Abyssal depths (abyssal plains) (more than 4000 m)	Mud, ooze (biogenic)	Relatively thin and even bedding Deep-water fossils

*Carbonate deposition (lime) may occur in a wide spectrum of environments; wherever carbonate material is in solution and there is relatively little influx of clastic debris.

ments may be difficult to distinguish in the ancient rock record unless fossils are present. Lagoonal faunas, because of abnormal salinities, tend to be restricted in diversity, whereas shelf faunas are typically more diverse because of the more normal marine salinities. The deeper basin is a quiet environment where micrite is likely to be interbedded with occasional dark shales. Dark colors of these deeper basin sediments reflect lower oxygen levels and preservation of raw organic matter. Turbidity currents may bring periodic influxes of carbonate debris from the carbonate barrier, producing calcareous turbidites that punctuate the quiet-water mudrocks.

Diagenesis exerts many important controls on carbonate rocks, owing mainly to the metastable-to-unstable nature of the calcium carbonate system, particularly the mineral aragonite. Limestones are very susceptible to diagenetic changes, such as inversion of aragonite to calcite, *dissolution* of aragonite and calcite, *recrystallization* of calcite, *cementation* under marine or freshwater influence to plug pore space, and *replacement* (mainly by *dolomitization*). The important properties of porosity and permeability are more complex in carbonate rocks than in terrigenous clastics, because porosity can be either *inter*particle or *intra*particle, and the unstable nature of the calcium carbonate system is more susceptible to multiple cycles of inversion-recrystallization-dissolution-cementation-replacement.

Table 2–2 shows that identification of ancient environments on the basis of lithology alone may be inconclusive. For example, conglomerates and sandstones (gravel and sand) can form in fluvial, alluvial fan, glacial, littoral, and offshore submarine fan environments, among others. Lithology commonly is a good index to the *kinds of conditions* that operated in the depositional environment. Grain size, sorting, degree of rounding of particles, and color furnish clues about turbulence, current strengths, water depth, and geochemical aspects, but seldom do these features serve as fingerprints of specific environments. The lithology of a sedimentary unit is one of the easiest characteristics to observe directly, but to be useful in paleoenvironmental interpretation, it must be studied *in combination with other parameters.*

Geometric Shape of Rock Bodies

The overall three-dimensional shape of a rock unit is the result of the architecture and topography of the depositional area, of compaction during lithification, and, possibly, of postdepositional erosion processes. A long, narrow, *linear unit* of sandstone may represent an ancient stream channel (Fig. 2–7) or an offshore bar, among other possibilities. A pattern of *radiating* sandstone units might represent deposits in a series of distributary channels on an ancient delta. An extensive *sheetlike* unit of sandstone may represent deposition along the migrating shoreline of an ancient sea, or perhaps may be the product of a laterally meandering stream complex. A thick wedge of sediment may result from accumulation in a slowly subsiding basin.

Figure 2–7
Stream-channel sands and conglomerates of Pleistocene age. Note the linear nature of the sands.
(Photo by J. Patterson)

Unfortunately, postdepositional erosion may destroy the original geometry of a rock unit. Sedimentary sequences deposited in terrestrial environments are particularly vulnerable to erosion, whereas the marine setting is more favorable for preservation.

Where abundant rock outcrops (exposures) are available for direct study, the geometry of a rock unit commonly can be determined. In the subsurface, the geometry must be determined by indirect methods, such as mapping the unit from borehole data or from modern geophysical seismic surveys (see Chapter 6). The latter method can trace the outlines of a reef or of a submarine fan unit, for example, even though the unit may be buried beneath thousands of feet of overlying sediments. This technique is exceedingly useful in the determination of the geometry of units that are potential petroleum traps.

Sedimentary Structures

Primary sedimentary structures, which formed at the time the sediment was accumulating, provide significant clues to the original conditions of deposition, and therefore are valuable for interpretation of paleoenvironments. Reference to Table 2–2 indicates that one such primary structure, stratification, is a helpful feature that has many forms. For example, the laminated strata characteristic of a lacustrine (lake) environment are distinctly different from the large-scale cross-stratification (cross-bedding) typically found in sand dunes (Fig. 2–8). Note, however, that cross-bedding on a smaller scale can be displayed in sediments deposited in a lacustrine environment, as well as in deposits of streams, beaches, deltas, tidal flats, and other environments. Like sediment textures, sedimentary structures overlap environmental categories and generally cannot be used as a single, diagnostic criterion in paleoenvironmental interpretation. Also, like textures, sedimentary structures are signatures of paleoenvironmental conditions, such as current flow. Variations in certain kinds of sedimentary structures, such as cross-bedding, indicate changes in the depositional medium; for example, changes in the energy level of running water or wind in transporting sedimentary particles. Remember throughout that *analysis requires the utilization of multiple lines of evidence,* rather than simply homing in on one feature.

Graded bedding is an *internal* sedimentary structure that typically is formed in sediment deposited by a **turbidity current,** a dense sediment-laden cur-

A

B

Figure 2–8
Sand dune cross-bedding on a massive scale (section 100 m thick) in the Permian Coconino Sandstone, Grand Canyon National Park.
(Photo by J. Patterson)

A

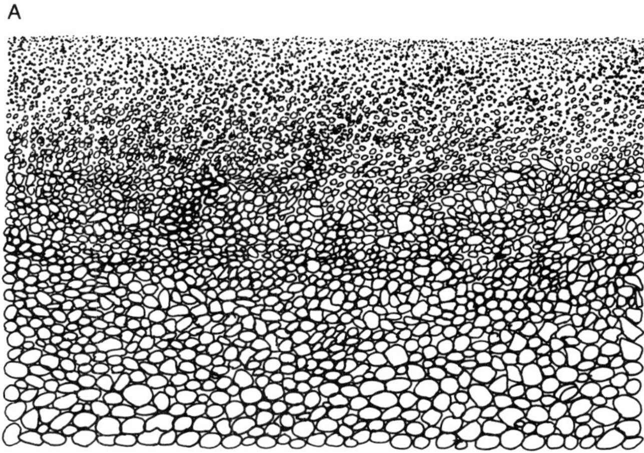

B

Figure 2–9
Turbidite graded bedding illustrating the upward decrease in size of particles formed as clastic debris settled out of suspension from water.
(Photo courtesy of Critter Creations, Gary Peterson collection, no. 4)

rent that moves rapidly down a submarine canyon or basin slope. At the mouth of the canyon or base of the slope, the velocity of the turbidity current is checked; the coarsest particles of the sediment load settle out of the water first, followed by finer and finer debris, resulting in the bottom-to-top, coarse-to-fine grading shown in Figure 2–9. Graded bedding occurs in other kinds of deposits, but it is a characteristic feature of **turbidites** deposited in deep-sea fan settings.

Ripple marks are *external* sedimentary structures that indicate sense or direction of movement of the transporting medium and are helpful features in paleoenvironmental interpretation. *Oscillation ripple marks* are symmetrical in cross section (Fig. 2–10A, B) and indicate a back-and-forth (swash) movement of water, such as the uprush and backwash motions of waves on a beach face.

Current ripple marks are asymmetrical in cross section (Fig. 2–10C, D) and indicate a prevailing direction of current flow either of water (such as in a stream channel or on a submarine surface) or of wind (such as over a dune surface). Detailed studies of ripple marks forming in modern sedimentary environments have resulted in the establishment of criteria that facilitate distinction between water and wind currents, and these criteria can be applied to ancient ripple marks. Ripple marks are *external* sedimentary structures that form at the sediment-air or sediment-water interface. In rocks they are seen on the bedding surfaces, and in cross section they are expressed as various kinds of cross-stratification; thus external ripple marks and internal cross-strata of all scales are genetically related.

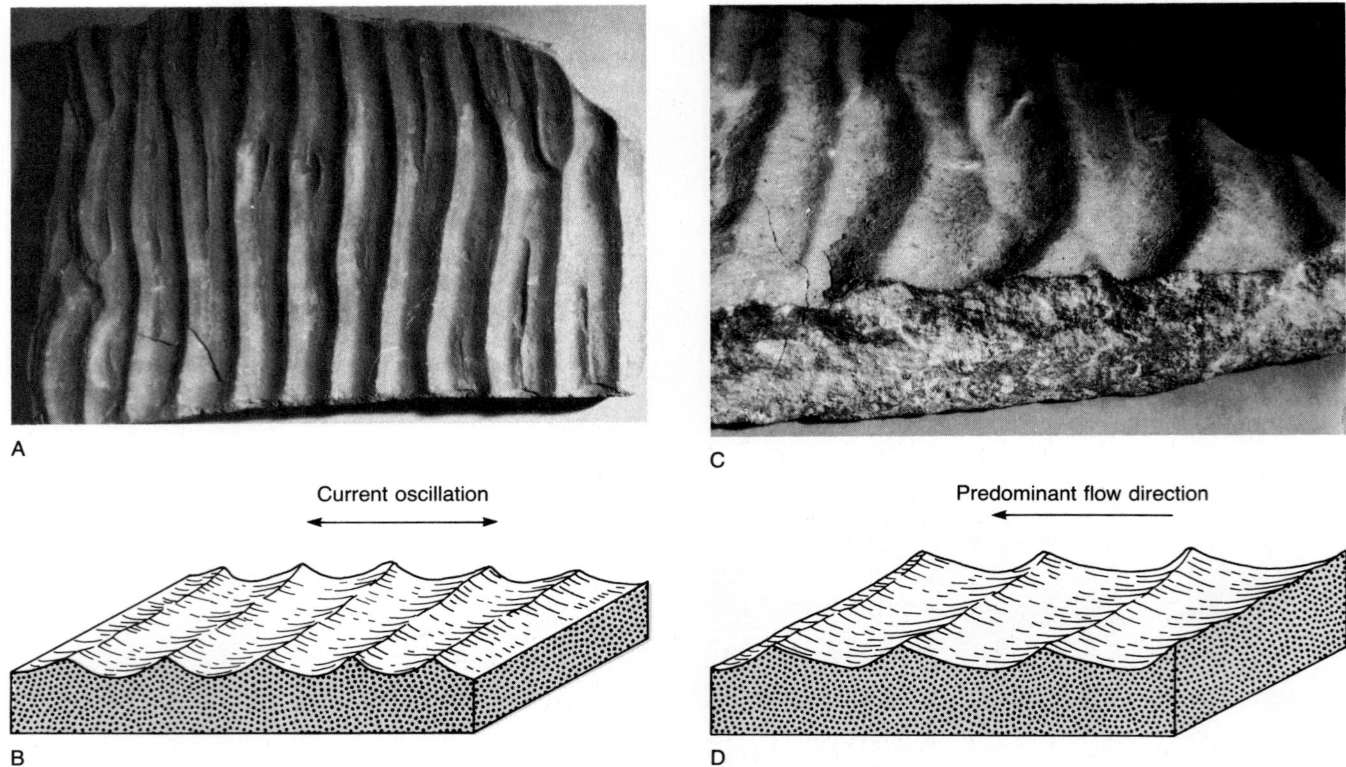

Figure 2–10
A. Oscillation ripple marks. B. In this cross section, note the symmetrical form of this type of ripple mark, indicative of water moving back and forth as on a beach face (specimen 33 cm in length). C. Current ripple marks. D. In this cross section, note the asymmetrical form of this type of ripple mark, indicative of current flow from right to left (specimen 23 cm in length).
(Photos by J. Streng)

Desiccation cracks are shrinkage cracks formed by drying of cohesive sediment. They are good environmental indicators because they generally indicate some subaerial exposure (Fig. 2–11). They imply a sedimentary setting of alternating intervals of wetting and drying of surfaces, such as river floodplains, desert playas, and shorelines.

These are only a few of the more common examples of many different kinds of primary sedimentary structures that can be used to interpret physical conditions operating in the depositional environment, and are a major component of sedimentary facies. Some of the sedimentary structures used as examples in this section, plus others such as various kinds of *sole markings* (e.g., flute casts), are discussed later (Chapter 5) in the context of determining the stratigraphic top of a bed. Sedimentary structures are significant, therefore, in determining *superposition,* as well as in the interpretation of ancient depositional environments.

Fossils

Just as modern-day living organisms reflect the environments in which they dwell, fossils are one of the best indicators of ancient sedimentary environments (see the discussion of the use of fossils in paleoecologic studies, Chapter 3). The concept of facies applies to fossils as well as to physical, or lithologic, aspects of sedimentary rocks. Lateral changes in fossil content within contemporaneous strata are called **biofacies,** as distinguished from the facies defined on lithology, the **lithofacies.** Commonly, these two kinds of facies coincide, because *benthic* (bottom-dwelling) organisms tend to be controlled in their distribution by bottom sediment type; thus, benthic fossils commonly are facies-controlled in their occurrences.

The distinction between marine fossils, such as oysters and corals, and nonmarine fossils, such as dinosaur bones, is an obvious clue to the deposi-

A

B

Figure 2–11
A. Desiccation cracks (mudcracks) on the edge of a modern lake bed. B. Desiccation cracks expressed on a rock surface by ridges of sediment that filled in the cracks (specimen 38 cm in length).
(A, Photo by J. Patterson. B, photo by J. Streng)

tional setting of rocks containing the fossils. The use of fossils as paleoenvironmental indicators, however, does necessitate caution. Fossils are useful in paleoenvironmental interpretation if the paleoecologic organism-sediment relationship can be worked out, either through comparisons with modern counterparts (an application of actualism) or by deducing the adaptive characteristics of the fossilized organisms. Fossils commonly occur in sedimentary rocks that represent *not* where the organisms lived, but where they were transported after death and eventually buried and preserved. A good example of this situation is the wood of Petrified Forest National Park, discussed in Chapter 15. The trees (conifers) lived in an upland area, died, were broken up in transport (probably during flood stage), and eventually accumulated (displaying current orientation) mostly as fragments on floodplains and in stream channels in a lowland area. The site of burial and preservation does not represent the original upland environment where these conifer trees were growing during Triassic time. Marine forms likewise can be subject to postmortem transport.

In some instances, biofacies can be interpreted to represent parts of ancient benthic *communities,* whose members have undergone comparatively little postmortem transportation from their original life habitats. As an example, three benthic paleocommunities are recognized in Upper Ordovician rocks of the Appalachian region:

1. The nearshore paleocommunity, including both *infaunal* (living below the sediment-water interface) and *epifaunal* (living at the sediment-water interface) forms, lived on a sandy bottom and was characterized by inarticulate brachiopods, gastropods, and bivalves (Fig. 2–12A; see Chapter 3 for discussion of these organisms). This type of assemblage appears to reflect coastal, brackish paleoecological conditions.
2. An intermediate paleocommunity, living on a silty substrate, consisted of a more diverse association of thin, smooth-shelled and round-shaped brachiopods, some gastropods, trilobites, infaunal bivalve molluscs, and bryozoans (Fig. 2–12B). This community existed in shallow, nearshore shelf environments of normal salinity.
3. The offshore paleocommunity (Fig. 2–12C) lived on a muddy bottom and was characterized by a lack of infauna, but included a diverse assemblage of epifauna composed of abundant branching bryozoans and several types of brachiopods. Some crinoids, gastropods, and bivalves also were present. This paleocommunity reflects deeper and quieter water, probably below wave base, on the outer part of the shelf.

Preserved evidence of benthic organism behavioral activity on or in sediment has proved to be excellent in paleoenvironmental analysis. These *biogenic sedimentary structures,* called *trace fossils,* are discussed in Chapter 3, but it is appropriate to mention here that they represent in situ (not reworked or transported) organic activity that is sensitive to paleoenvironmental conditions.

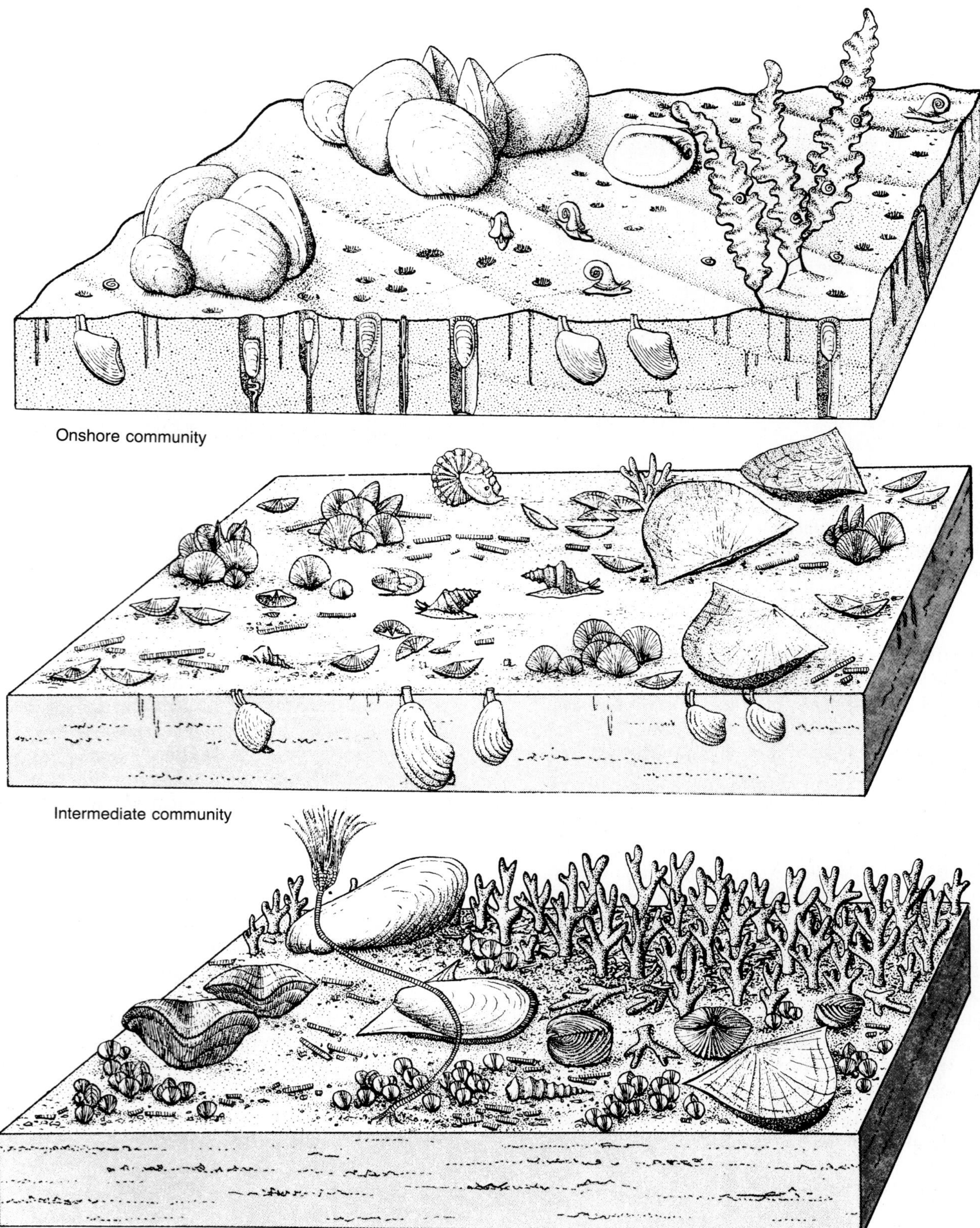

Figure 2–12

Three benthic paleocommunities recognized in Upper Ordovician rocks of the Appalachian area. Analysis of fossil data defines an onshore community of infauna plus epifauna with sturdy hard parts to withstand water turbulence; an intermediate community with forms of greater diversity reflecting a less rigorous environment; and an offshore community including some delicate life forms that require quiet water. (Based on graphics by T. L. Chase, in R. L. Anstey and T. L. Chase, 1979, *Environments Through Time,* 2d ed., Fig. 6.1, p. 54. Burgess Publishing Co., Minneapolis. Original source is P. W. Bretsky, 1969, Central Appalachian Late Ordovician Communities: *Geological Society of America Bulletin,* vol. 80)

Table 2–3
Basic approach to determine how sediment was deposited

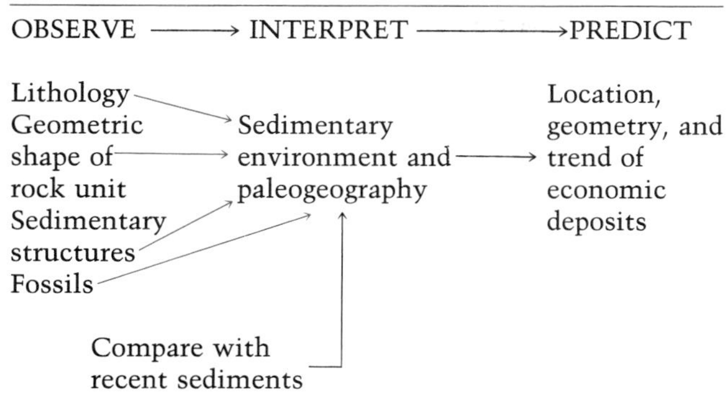

Source: Richard C. Selley, ed., *Ancient sedimentary environments*, 3rd ed., p. 35. © 1970, 1978, 1986 by Richard C. Selley. Used by permission of the publisher, Cornell University Press.

It has been emphasized that the use of only a *single* parameter—lithology, geometry of the rock units, sedimentary structures, or fossils—to interpret ancient sedimentary environments would be shortsighted, and the results inconclusive. A synthesis of information integrating several or all parameters is much more meaningful and definitive (Table 2–3).

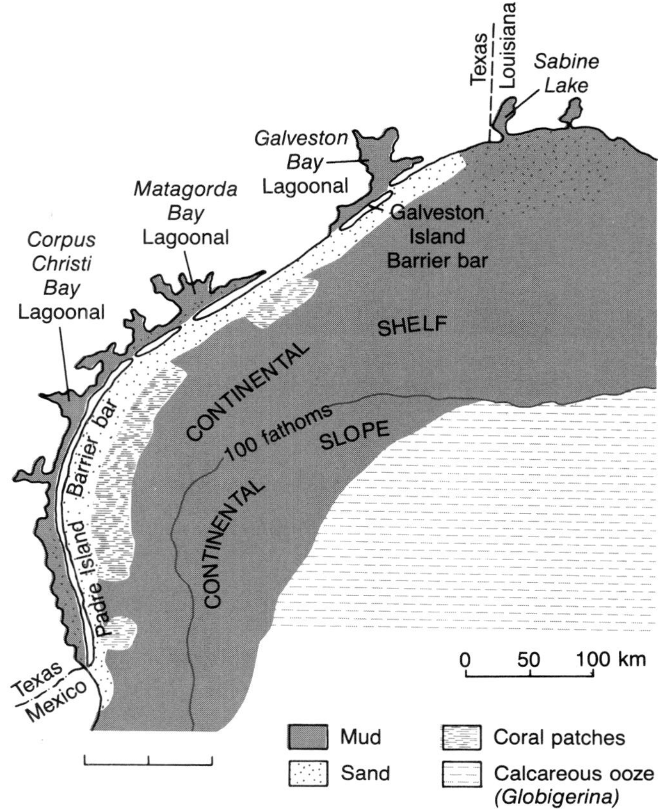

Figure 2–13
Examples of some modern sedimentary environments in the western Gulf of Mexico.

A Present-Day Model

The Delta

Depositional environments along the coast of the western Gulf of Mexico include delta, beach, bay, lagoon, barrier bar, and shallow-marine shelf (Fig. 2–13). Each of these environments has a set of physical and chemical factors, such as water energy (turbulence), circulation patterns, temperature, depth, and salinity, which influence the type of sediment that accumulates and the kinds of organisms that are adapted. Stratigraphers and sedimentologists from all over the world have used the Gulf Coast region as an instructive actualistic model for observing sedimentary processes and the characteristics of depositional environments.

An examination of one particular environment along the Gulf Coast, the delta (Fig. 2–14), reveals a complex association of a number of small subenvironments, such as swamps, sand bars, and stream channels. Deltas are important environments of deposition because they represent the building out of land areas into bodies of water. Because they form at the termini of many major rivers, such as the Mississippi, they also are instrumental in introducing terrigenous clastic sediment into the marine setting. The principle of actualism tells us that ancient deltas likewise were significant as local areas for the feeding of sediments onto marine shelves. Their recognition in the ancient rock record is important for reconstruction of geologic history, as well as for exploration for fossil fuels.

Deltas consist of a mosaic of subenvironments that interact with one another and undergo continuous shifting and changing of position. Rivers flow more slowly as they enter the sea; because they no longer have the capacity to transport their load, they become choked with sediment and their channels are divided. The *subaerial* parts of deltas include *deltaic plains,* which are characterized by a system of bifurcating *distributary channels* that become filled with silts and sands; *natural levees,* which form as ridges of interlaminated sand and mud deposited adjacent to the channels during overbank spreading of flood waters; and *back-swamp* areas where muds transported away from the chan-

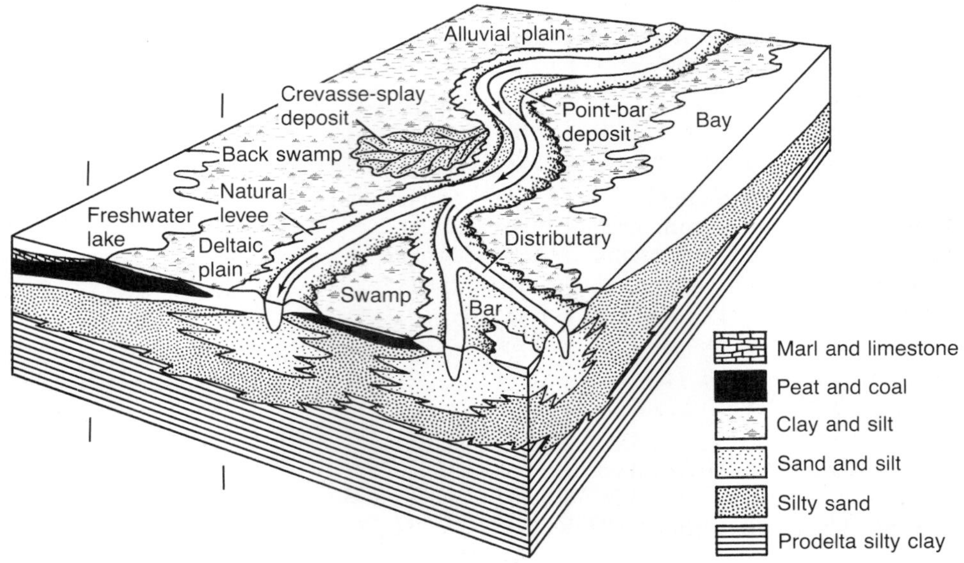

Figure 2–14
Subenvironments associated with a delta. Note the various sediment types associated with the different depositional subenvironments. Changes in position of these subenvironments produce a sedimentary record that illustrates Walther's Law. In the locality represented by stratigraphic section lines, prodelta silty clays are overlain by channel silts and sands, and these, in turn, are overlain by natural levee and then deltaic plain deposits. In the vertical succession of sediments in this section, we observe the record of subenvironments that once were lateral to one another but now are superimposed due to shifting of the delta subenvironments. (Based on graphic by T. L. Chase, in R. L. Anstey and T. L. Chase, 1979, *Environments Through Time,* 2d ed., Fig. 14.2, p. 104: Burgess Publishing Co., Minneapolis)

nels by high water are deposited (they may become sites of luxuriant vegetation, the possible precursor to coal deposits).

The *subaqueous* delta subenvironments include the distributary mouth bars, which are sand bodies deposited as distributaries enter the sea, and the *prodelta,* which is the foreslope of the delta and the site of clay and silt deposition (Fig. 2–14). Prodelta deposits (facies) merge gradually with the muds of the marine shelf. Modern and ancient deltas show a complex association of facies that represent the sediment-response products of the shifting subenvironments of deposition.

Lateral and Vertical Facies Relationships

The Gulf Coast delta model, with its mosaic of coexisting subenvironments, provides a two-dimensional map view of lateral facies changes; this is a **facies tract,** a series of laterally adjacent facies, different but genetically related. As environments shift through time, the migration of facies over the tops of one another produces a superposition of different facies vertically, and results in a complex three-dimensional intertonguing of these facies. If a continuous core could be examined from a well borehole drilled at one particular location on the delta, a vertical succession of facies might include the products of back-swamp, natural-levee, freshwater-lake, distributary-mouth-bar, and prodelta environments. All of these facies at any one time were laterally adjacent to one another and formed a facies tract.

This relationship between lateral and vertical sedimentary facies was expressed at the beginning of this century by the German geologist Johannes Walther (1860–1937), who traveled extensively and studied modern sedimentary environments. Present-day depositional processes, he believed, were the keys to interpretation of paleoenvironments. Walther observed that in a continuous sequence (not punctuated by unconformities), facies that precede or succeed one another in a vertical section were laterally adjacent to one another at any single moment in time (comprising a facies tract). This concept is known as **Walther's Law** of the correlation of facies.

At a single locality, therefore, one is able to determine what the lateral paleoenvironmental relationships were by observing the nature of the overlying and underlying facies (Fig. 2–14). The interpretation of the geologic history of an area commonly involves the recognition both of lateral facies that were contemporaneous and of vertical succession of facies produced through time. *The vertical and lateral facies relationships together provide a three-dimensional stratigraphic view within which to interpret the paleoenvironmental implications of individual facies.* The total depositional context in which the facies occurs is probably the single most important criterion for paleoenvironmental interpretation.

Facies relationships are illustrated by numerous examples in the stratigraphic record of ancient sedimentary rocks. The delta model, for example, has been recognized in rocks of several Paleozoic systems in the Appalachian and midcontinent regions and in rocks of Cretaceous age in the Rocky Mountain region (see discussion of the Devonian and Pennsylvanian, Chapter 11, and the Cretaceous, Chapter 13).

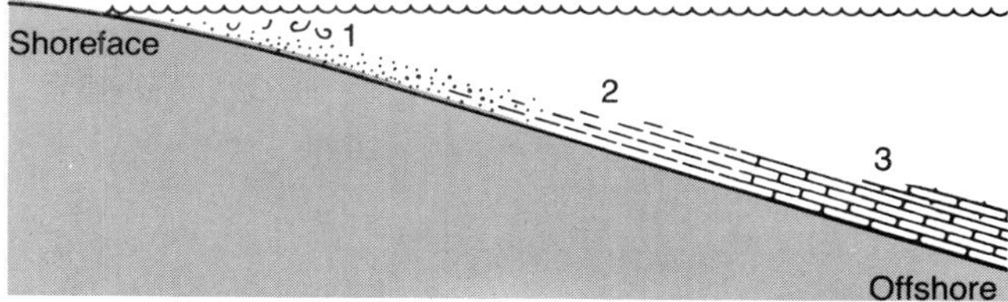

Figure 2–15
Idealized model of marine deposition. Sand is deposited (1) where an influx of clastic debris is available and there is some water turbulence. Farther seaward (2) water is less turbulent and muds settle to the sea bottom. Calcareous sediment (3) is deposited offshore where terrigenous clastic debris is not available. In a shoreward-to-seaward direction, the sediment texture and composition may change.

The Fluctuating Shoreline

Onlap and Offlap

Sedimentary facies patterns have been influenced by changes in position of the shoreline; seas have advanced upon and receded from the continents many times during the geologic past. Migration of shallow-marine environments, evidenced by sedimentary facies changes, accompanied these **transgressions** and **regressions,** respectively.

In a simplified, *idealized model* (Fig. 2–15), sand accumulates in a shoreline or beach environment, with finer muds deposited offshore in less turbulent water. These terrigenous muds, in turn, grade laterally farther seaward into calcareous mud, as the influx of terrigenous clastic material decreases. This example illustrates a facies tract—a lateral change of facies from coarse-to-fine terrigenous sediment, to calcareous sediment—deposited in a shoreface-to-offshore direction.

If the sea transgresses the land, each of these sedimentary environments will shift landward by **retrogradation,** and, in time, a vertical succession of sand, mud, and calcareous mud will be produced (Fig. 2–16). A stratigraphic pattern of this type, which shows progressively more seaward facies *overlying* more landward facies, is called an **onlap** succession. *Stratigraphic onlap is the result of marine transgression and retrogradation of facies.* Note that this vertical succession is an illustration of Walther's Law; the facies in the stratigraphic column (Fig. 2–16) were positioned adjacent to one another at a single moment in time.

In our same hypothetical facies tract model, if the sea regresses, an opposite pattern will be produced (Fig. 2–17), with each of the sedimentary environments shifting seaward by **progradation,** and, in time, a vertical succession of calcareous mud, terrigenous mud, and sand will be produced. A stratigraphic pattern of this type, which shows progressively more landward facies *overlying* more seaward facies, is called an **offlap** succession. *Stratigraphic offlap is the result of marine regression and facies progradation.* In both situations, onlap and offlap, the vertical succession of rock units (lithofacies) at a specific location reflects the shifting or migration (retrogradation/progradation) of depositional environments through time. Both onlap and offlap stratigraphic sequences are expressions of Walther's Law.

A **sedimentary cycle** is a repetition of facies or a sequence of facies (Fig. 2–17) in vertical section, and represents both onlap and offlap cycles, expressing the consequent repetition of depositional environments through time in the area. Recognition of onlap-offlap patterns on a regional scale is enhanced by the *correlation* of a number of stra-

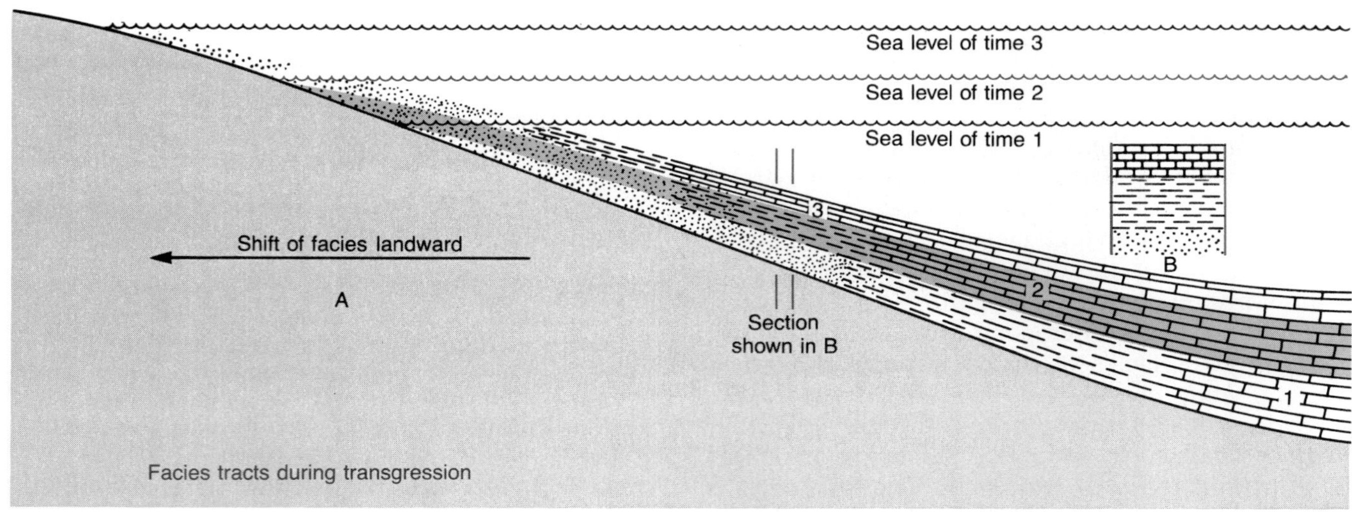

Figure 2–16
Marine transgression sequence. A. As sea level rises, the sedimentary facies shift in a landward direction. B. A sedimentary rock sequence of marine sandstone overlain by marine shale and limestone reflects this transgression and is called an *onlap* succession (section B is not to scale of A).

tigraphic sections (Fig. 2–18). This provides a three-dimensional time-and-spatial framework for understanding facies relationships. The lithofacies patterns make possible interpretation of shoreline fluctuations in a geographic region through time.

It should be emphasized that the foregoing discussion has presented an idealized situation for purposes of explanation, and that actual examples typically are more complex. Also, the lithofacies changes that result from the transgressive-regressive cycle are likely to correspond to *biofacies* changes, because each of the shifting environments carries its own particular assemblage of benthic organisms.

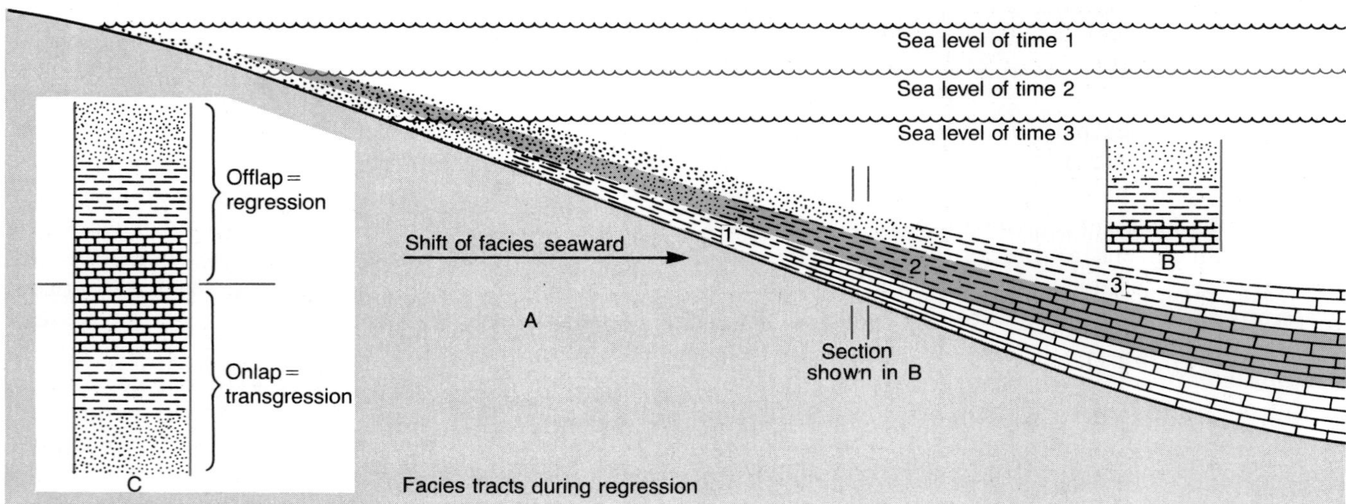

Figure 2–17
Marine regression sequence. A. As sea level falls, the sedimentary facies shift in a seaward direction. B. A sedimentary rock sequence of marine limestone overlain by marine shale and sandstone reflects this regression and is called an *offlap* succession (section B is not to scale of A). C. An onlap sequence followed by an offlap sequence is called a complete *sedimentary cycle.*

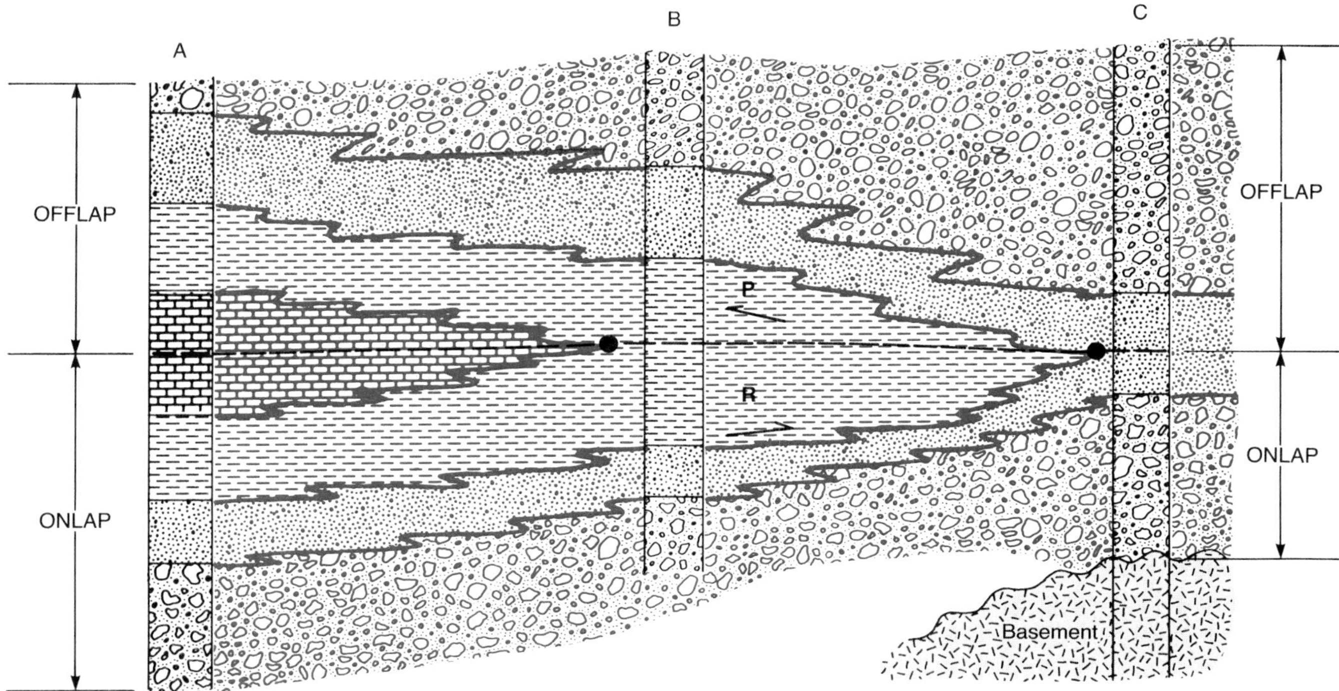

Figure 2–18
Stratigraphic panel depicting dynamic facies patterns in three separate correlated sections (from A—most seaward—to C—most landward). The conglomerate facies represents a continental environment; the sandstone facies represents a shallow marine shoreface environment; the shale facies represents a marine shelf environment; and the limestone facies represents a more offshore, carbonate environment. R is retrogradation and P is progradation. The dashed line is a time line connecting the change from retrogradation to progradation in the three sections. Walther's Law illustrates the lateral arrangement of facies at this time. As the environments and their facies products migrated over one another through time, the vertical arrangement of facies in each section was produced.

In the midwestern United States, the St. Peter Sandstone is a distinctive, widespread rock unit of Ordovician age that crops out in several states. The St. Peter is a well-sorted, mature, cross-bedded quartz sandstone that was deposited as a blanket-like lithofacies in a shallow-marine environment. It represents the deposits of the leading edge of the transgressing Ordovician sea. As such, the lithofacies transgresses time; its outcrops in Illinois, for example, are older than those in Iowa and Wisconsin (Fig. 2–19). In interpreting the depositional history of an area, it is important to remember that sedimentary facies are lithologic units that may have been deposited, as was the St. Peter Sandstone, over an interval of geologic time. Their boundaries generally do *not* coincide with time-stratigraphic boundaries (see discussion of Cambrian transgression in the Grand Canyon region, Chapter 10).

Causes of Transgression and Regression

Geologists have long recognized that changing sea-land relationships caused by transgression and regression have produced onlap and offlap stratigraphic patterns. Actual sea-level changes include *eustatic* (worldwide) fluctuations, as well as smaller local variations. The largest eustatic changes generally have been attributed to cycles of continental glaciation, whereby buildup and advance of ice sheets have resulted in lowered sea-level stands, and melting and retreat of major glaciers have resulted in raised sea-level stands (see Chapter 15). Smaller-scale fluctuations in position of the shoreline may result from tectonic activity or isostatic adjustments involving uplift or subsidence of the lithosphere. The smallest fluctuations generally result from changing sedimentation patterns. Rapid influx of sediment, such as in delta-

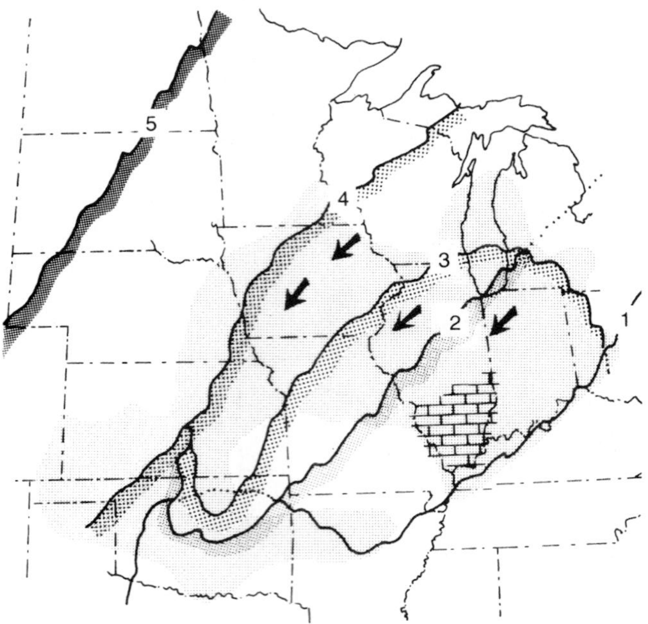

Figure 2–19
Shorelines of the St. Peter Sandstone. The wavy lines (1–4) indicate shorelines during transgression of the sea in which the sediment was deposited. Line 5 represents the possible westernmost extent of the sea. The stippled area indicates areas of outcrop of the sandstone. The St. Peter Sandstone was deposited over a span of time and is *not* everywhere the same age.
(After E. W. Spencer, 1962, *Basic Concepts of Historical Geology*, Fig. 13–6, p. 228: Thomas Y. Crowell, New York. Reproduced by permission of author)

building, can cause local regression of the sea as the land builds seaward. If, however, sedimentation stops, the delta is no longer nourished, and subsidence allows marine waters to transgress its surface.

The present model of plate tectonics accounts for major eustatic sea-level changes in the past, for example, encroachment of shallow seas into continental interiors during Paleozoic and Mesozoic times. As continents have welded together by collision or fragmented by rifting, changes in the cubic holding capacity of the ocean basins have occurred. For example, it has been suggested that fragmentation of continents, accompanied by decreased volume of ocean basins, has caused extensive marine transgression; major regressions have resulted from increases in holding capacity of ocean basins, with corresponding withdrawal of marine waters from continental platforms (see discussion of cratonic sequences, Chapter 10). Transgression and regression have been important influences in forming the stratigraphic record from which we read geologic history.

A Permian Facies Model

Guadalupe Mountains National Park

The beginning of this chapter featured some human history of Guadalupe Mountains National Park, with a reference to the geologic features for which this area was set aside as a unit of the national park system. The park exposes rocks of a Permian reef complex that provides an excellent model for illustrating facies relationships, relationships between facies and paleoenvironments, onlap-offlap sedimentary cycles, distinctions between rock-stratigraphic and time-stratigraphic units, and transition from shallow platform to deep basin. These rocks are developed as four major facies that represent deposition in adjacent reef, back-reef, fore-reef, and basin paleoenvironments (Fig. 2–20).

Reef Facies

The Capitan Limestone, named for its exposure in the massive limestone face of El Capitan Peak at the south end of the Guadalupe Mountains, is a gigantic "fossilized" reef. The Capitan reef was a major carbonate buildup that formed a 600-kilometer loop around the margin of the Delaware Basin during much of Permian time (Fig. 2–21). The east flank of the Guadalupe Mountains exposes just the northwestern edge of this reef structure. The impressive mountain front consists predominantly of massive limestone composed of the exoskeletons of reef-building organisms (boundstones), as well as other kinds of carbonate debris. Much of the reef complex is buried in the subsurface beneath younger sedimentary rock, and can be located only by drilling or seismic profiling.

Geologists working in this area several decades ago interpreted the facies within the Capitan as various parts of a huge barrier reef, similar to the present-day barrier reef of Australia. More recent paleontologic and lithologic studies suggest that the Capitan reef was not so much a structure composed of frame-building organisms as it was a carbonate buildup composed predominantly of fragmented exoskeletons and other carbonate particles. But whether it was an ecologic reef in the strict sense, or a buildup of fragmental material, the important consideration is that it was a wave-resistant, moundlike feature that grew near the edge of a shallow-marine platform and profoundly influenced the development of facies both seaward and landward of it.

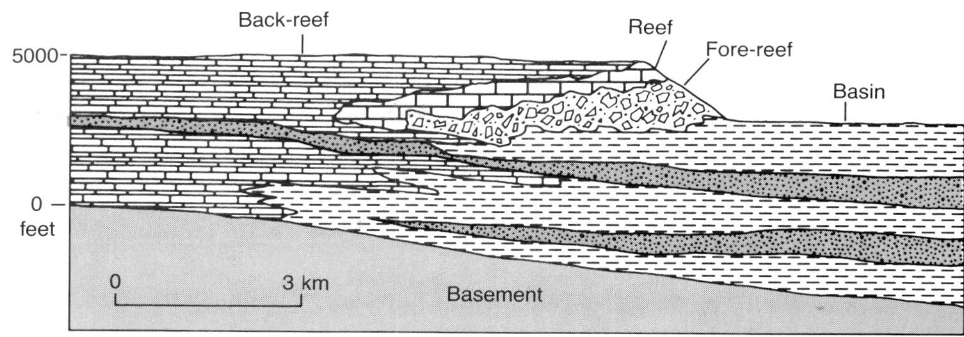

Figure 2–20
Schematic north-south cross section of Permian Reef Complex in Guadalupe Mountains, New Mexico and West Texas. The back-reef, reef, fore-reef, and basin environments are well expressed in the Carbonate facies.
(From N. D. Newell and others, 1953, *The Permian Reef Complex of the Guadalupe Mountains Region, Texas and New Mexico,* Fig. 50, p. 13: W. H. Freeman, San Francisco. Reproduced by permission of author)

Back-Reef Facies

Back-reef facies sediments were deposited in the relatively quiet waters of a platform shelf behind (landward of) the reef. In this back-reef lagoon (Fig. 2–20) the water was shallower and less turbulent than on the seaward side of the reef; the sediments that accumulated were predominantly lime muds and skeletal limestones near the reef, and more saline deposits landward. Within this setting there existed a lateral gradation of subenvironments that produced several subfacies. In a north-to-south direction across the northwestern shelf (seaward direction, see Fig. 2–21) the spectrum of paleoenvi-

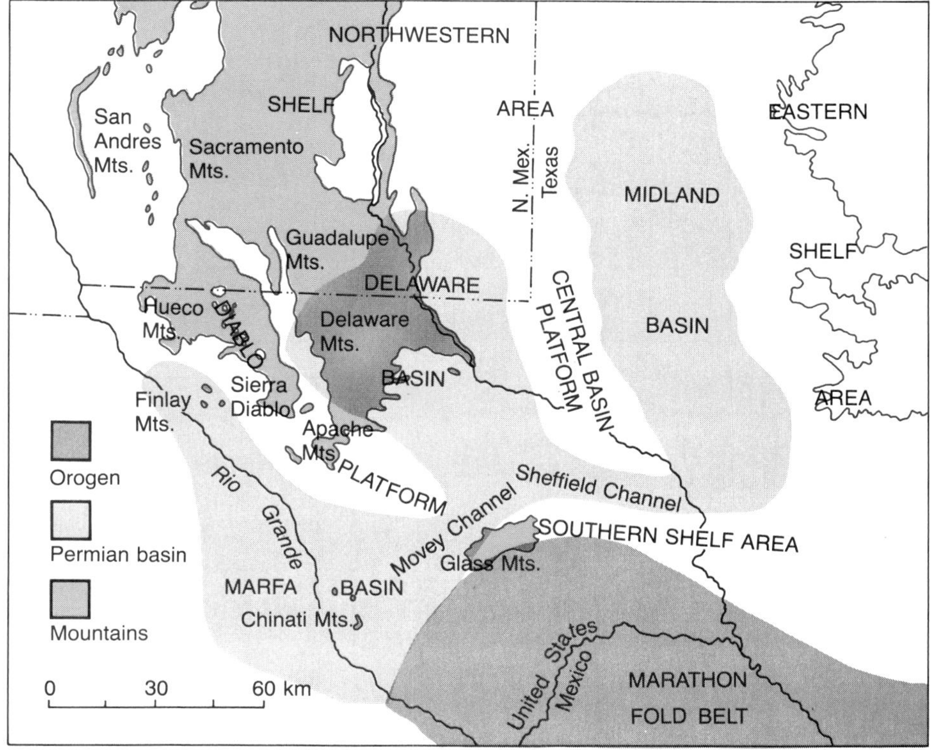

Figure 2–21
Permian-age paleotectonic setting in West Texas and southeastern New Mexico.
(After P. B. King, 1948, Geology of the Southern Guadalupe Mountains, Texas, Fig. 3, p. 25: *U.S. Geological Survey Professional Paper,* no. 215)

ronments included supratidal (sabkha), intertidal flats, and shelf lagoon. The supratidal area, covered by a film of shallow water only during the highest tides, was the site of deposition of reddish terrigenous silt and sand and of evaporites such as dolostone and nodular gypsum. Abundant desiccation features attest to dry, exposed depositional conditions. The intertidal flats were sites of accumulation of algal stromatolites and dolostone, and in the shelf lagoon shelly limestones and lime mudstone accumulated.

Fore-Reef Facies

The fore-reef facies includes the apron of debris eroded from the seaward face of the reef. These limestone beds had original depositional dips of as much as 30° seaward into the deep basin. The fore-reef limestones are composed of bits and pieces of broken skeletal debris from the reef and variously sized clasts and blocks of limestone (Fig. 2–20). Sliding and slumping apparently occurred on this fore-reef slope between the shelf margin (reef) and the basin floor, and dense mixtures of mud and rock fragments accumulated with the broken shells to form a reef *talus.*

Basin Facies

The basin facies was developed seaward from the reef in moderately deep waters of the restricted Delaware Basin (Fig. 2–21). This facies is divided into two interbedded subfacies. One is composed of black, well-laminated claystones and siltstones. This subfacies was deposited in water well below wave base under *anaerobic* conditions. The second subfacies consists of fine-grained sandstones with some graded bedding. These sandstones have been carefully mapped because they are hydrocarbon reservoirs in the subsurface. The sandstones are developed as elongate pods which are oriented perpendicular to the margin of the basin, and have been interpreted as turbidite channel and fan deposits.

Biofacies

The depositional environments that produced the distinctive lithofacies also produced characteristic biofacies. The reef limestones are the most fossiliferous of the facies (Fig. 2–22), containing both the greatest abundance and the greatest diversity of organisms. The reef environment was a well-oxygenated, sunlit, resource-rich setting that was able to

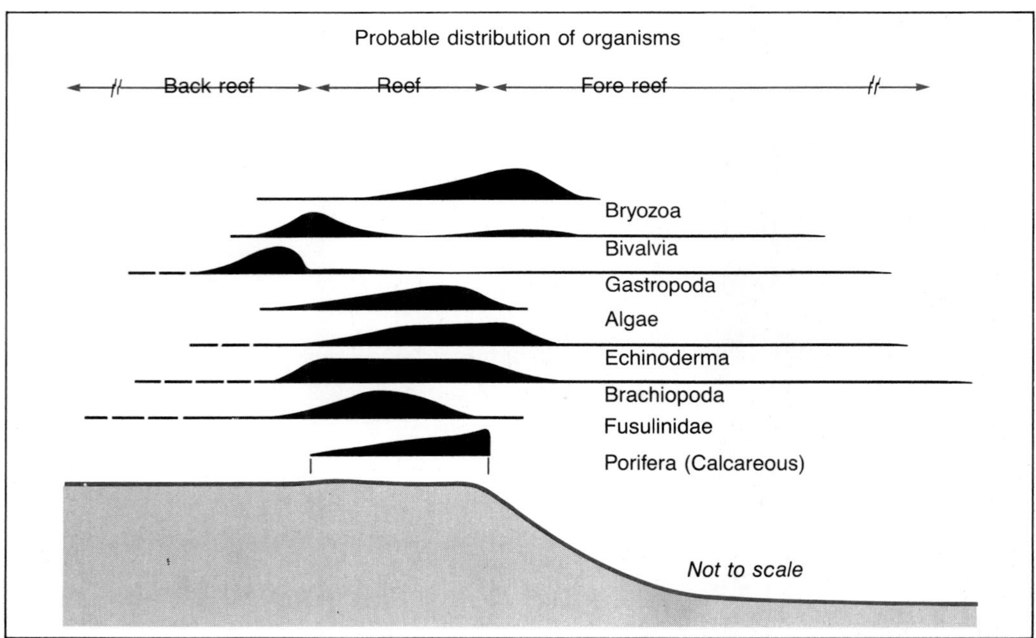

Figure 2–22
Components of the biofacies associated with the Permian reef complex.
(From N. D. Newell and others, 1953, *The Permian Reef Complex of the Guadalupe Mountains Region, Texas and New Mexico,* Fig. 79, p. 203: W. H. Freeman, San Francisco. Reproduced by permission of author)

support a rich community of sponges, bryozoans, crinoids, gastropods, calcareous algae, and rare corals. Because of poor circulation and low oxygen levels on the sea floor of the basinal environment, the rocks of the basin facies contain an impoverished fauna of sponge spicules, radiolarians, and ammonoids. The back-reef deposits carry a moderately diverse assemblage of fusulinids, gastropods, brachiopods, and algae. Particularly significant elements of the biofacies are the fusulinid foraminifers (Chapter 3), which are amenable to biostratigraphic zonation. The sequence of fusulinid biozones has provided time lines that enable time-stratigraphic subdivision and correlation. The lithofacies boundaries cut across the biozonal boundaries, illustrating the fundamental difference among lithostratigraphic, biostratigraphic, and chronostratigraphic units, which will be discussed in more detail in Chapter 6.

The Permian Reef Complex and Walther's Law

The analysis of the described lithofacies and biofacies has defined a paleoenvironmental picture for Late Permian time in West Texas and southeastern New Mexico. The spatial relationships of the various facies show that their environments of deposition shifted through time as fluctuations of sea level occurred. Near the end of the Permian Period the sea gradually retreated from the region. This regression is expressed by the progradational shifting of the marine paleoenvironments to the south, and the gradual replacement of the marine setting by transitional and nonmarine environments (Fig. 2–23).

The depositional pattern resulting from this regression and progradation is an offlap cycle expressed by the vertical facies sequence, from bottom to top:

bottom: dark micrite and shale with interbedded turbidite sandstones (basin);

breccia beds (fore-reef);

sponge-algal boundstones and calcarenites (reef);

thin-bedded micrite, fossiliferous micrite, and dolomite (back-reef);

stromatolitic boundstones and intraclasts (algal flat);

red beds and nodular gypsum (supratidal flat, also called *sabkha,* which is Persian for supratidal flat); and

top: supermature quartz sandstone (eolian dune field).

At the lowest sea-level stand, the deposition of hundreds of meters of delicately laminated evaporites occurred as the original deep-water basin became more restricted. Deposits consisting of very thin alternating laminations of anhydrite and calcite, arranged in varvelike seasonal couplets, accumulated in this setting (Fig. 2–24). As waters became even more saline (about ten times normal salinity), thick deposits of halite (rock salt) formed; these presently are mined as a natural resource. As the seas continued to retreat from the region, the evaporites, in turn, were *offlapped* by continental deposits. In accordance with Walther's Law, facies that formed beside one another in a lateral relationship also lie on top of one another (Fig. 2–23).

On the north wall of McKittrick Canyon in Guadalupe Mountains National Park, the verticolateral facies relationships among the reef, back-reef, fore-reef, and basin facies are clearly displayed (Fig. 2–25). This important location was included in the land donated by Wallace Pratt to the National Park Service (see beginning of this chapter).

Another significant area where part of the Permian reef complex can be observed is Carlsbad Caverns. The caverns were formed by dissolution of the carbonate rocks long after the rocks were initially deposited. The entrance to the caverns and the upper level of the caves have developed in the reef core (Capitan Limestone), but parts of the cavern complex, such as the Big Room, have formed in the fore-reef talus. Thus a walk through Carlsbad Caverns provides a walk through three distinctive sedimentary facies—the back-reef, the reef, and into the fore-reef.

End Products

Paleogeography

Both lithofacies and biofacies are the products of their ancient sedimentary environments. As mentioned previously, these paleoenvironments were areas that had distinctive sets of physical, chemical, and biological characteristics that left their impress on the sediments that accumulated. Reconstruction of these paleoenvironments through facies analysis of the rock record has enabled geologists to fashion an end product, a **paleogeographic map.** Such a map is based on outcrops and/or subsurface sections of rocks of the same age, whose pa-

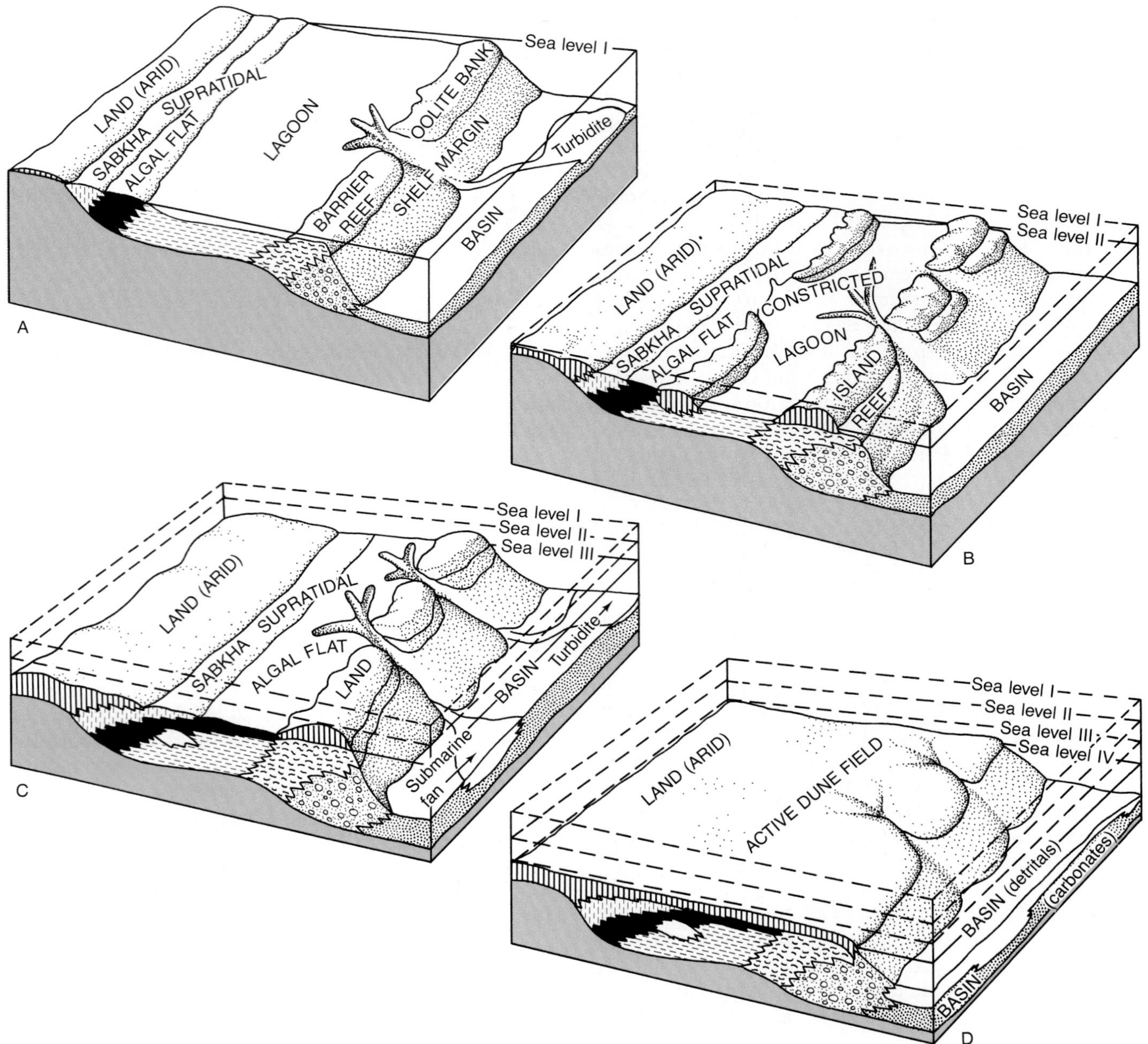

Figure 2–23

Regression of the Permian sea southward (A–D) resulted in replacement of conditions that formed the Permian reef complex by nonmarine conditions. The reef environment and the nonmarine coastal plain environment existed simultaneously in a lateral relationship and these two environments also existed at the same location at different times. The illustrated facies relationships are an example of Walther's Law.

(After B. A. Silver and R. G. Todd, 1969, Permian Cyclic Strata, Northern Midland and Delaware Basins, West Texas and Southeastern New Mexico, Figs. 4–7, p. 2227–2230: *American Association of Petroleum Geologists Bulletin,* vol. 53)

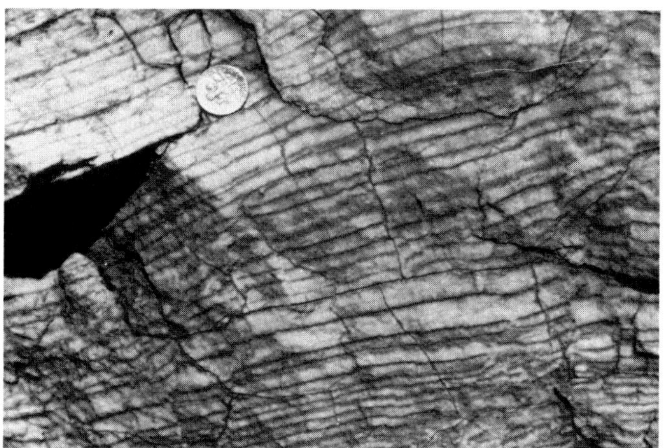

Figure 2–24
Varvelike interlaminated calcite (dark) and anhydrite (light), Castile Formation, West Texas. This delicately interlaminated sequence represents evaporite deposition in the Permian basin during low sea-level stand and conditions of restricted circulation. The anhydrite ($CaSO_4$) was originally deposited as gypsum ($CaSO_4\ 2H_2O$), which was subsequently dehydrated during burial and compaction.
(Photo by J. D. Cooper)

A

B

Figure 2–25
A portion of the north wall of McKittrick Canyon, Guadalupe Mountains National Park, West Texas. Exposed rocks are the Permian Capitan Limestone (Pc). The massive limestone along the skyline (Pc/m) is part of the reef facies and the slopes below (Pc/f) are part of the dipping reef rubble of the fore-reef facies.
(Photo by J. D. Cooper)

leoenvironments have been interpreted. The ideal paleogeographic map is constructed for a single time-stratigraphic level; thus the map surface is a time plane. This ideal time plane is intersected by various facies boundaries, which are translated into paleoenvironmental boundaries. More commonly, however, the degree of refinement possible constrains these maps to various narrow time-stratigraphic *intervals.*

Paleogeographic maps depict the location and distribution of ancient seas, shorelines, basins, rivers, and other paleogeographic features such as mountain belts. Creation of these maps is not purely an academic exercise; this understanding of the geologic past is important in the exploration for mineral resources (Table 2–3). In the Permian model of West Texas, the subsurface mapping of the basinal turbidite sandstones and the reef carbonates is important for hydrocarbon exploration, because these are possible reservoir facies. The surfaces of the block diagrams in Figure 2–23 are pictorial or cartoon paleogeographic maps, and Figure 2–21 is a regional paleogeographic map superimposed on a present-day map which includes cultural features.

With the advent of plate tectonics, *world* paleogeography during successive time intervals of the Phanerozoic Eon has become an exciting and fruitful area of research. The compiling of global paleogeographic maps involves synthesis of many diverse kinds of data from various fields of geology and geophysics: paleontology, sedimentology, paleomagnetism, paleoclimatology, and structural geology (see discussion, Chapter 10).

As pointed out in Chapter 1, we know that continental movement, the result of plate tectonic activity, has caused the geography of the Earth to change slowly and intermittently during the last several billion years. The initial phase of reconstructing scenes of this ever-changing world of the past involves identification of regions that functioned as separate paleocontinents. This is accomplished by integrating a wealth of geologic data. At the heart of world paleogeographic reconstructions is the positioning of these paleocontinents in their correct orientation. The basis for this positioning is paleomagnetic information, which enables determination of paleolatitude (see Chapter 1).

Paleogeographic reconstructions for the ancient North American continent as well as larger-scale world paleogeography will be illustrated and discussed for various parts of the Paleozoic, Mesozoic, and Cenozoic in the chapters on the evolution of North America. The continent of North America will provide the primary model for our trip through time, but appreciating ancient North America in its more global context provides an exciting perspective for historical geology.

An Economic Incentive

As noted previously, some economic mineral deposits such as coal, oil, and natural gas are associated with certain kinds of sedimentary rocks which are products of specific depositional environments. Most of the world's petroleum reserves have been found in sandstones that represent ancient delta and barrier beach complexes, or in carbonates closely associated with ancient reefs. One of the reasons the Capitan reef tract has been studied so intensively is that around the edge of the Midland Basin (Fig. 2–21) the subsurface reef complex contains important oil reservoirs. Because of the economic value of the reef structures, the surface outcrops have been studied to aid interpretation of facies in the subsurface units. In the Texas Permian reef complex, oil is produced mainly from lagoonal calcareous sands. Oil produced from a reef complex of Devonian age in the subsurface beneath the plains of Canada, however, comes directly from a reef-core facies. Much petroleum has been located through paleoenvironmental analysis of facies and prediction of favorable reservoir rocks in the subsurface.

Paleoenvironmental facies analysis is important, too, in locating metalliferous deposits. In the Mississippi Valley region, various limestone facies are laced with ore deposits of lead and zinc that are commercially valuable and are mined. Many of the identified uranium occurrences in the United States are in Mesozoic freshwater sediments of the Colorado Plateau region. The uranium minerals were derived from weathering of uranium-bearing igneous rocks, were transported as detrital grains, and were delivered to fluvial and deltaic depositional environments, where they became incorporated in the sediments. Low-grade uranium resources are contained in marine organic shales in the same geographic region, but these are not mined at present because strip mining of these shales would produce great quantities of rock waste and consequent deterioration of environmental quality.

The recognition of ancient sedimentary environments and sedimentary facies gives us a better appreciation and understanding of the dynamics behind sedimentation, of the relationships of bodies of rock and stratigraphic patterns, and of Earth history—most commonly in answer to an economic incentive. The Guadalupe Mountains are a part of this story, and the national park was created specifically to preserve a portion of the record of the ancient sedimentary environments of the Permian reef complex there.

Summary

The physical, chemical, and biologic characteristics of various depositional environments produce different types of sediments and, after lithification, sedimentary rocks. At a single point in time, distinctive environments exist side by side—for example, a beach environment adjacent to a shallow-marine environment—and so different rock types may form in contemporaneous and adjacent sites. These lateral variations are called *sedimentary facies.* An important part of the study of sedimentary rocks is determination of ancient depositional environments and of interrelationships of facies.

Sedimentary facies analysis involves study of a number of characteristics of rock units: lithology, including compositional and textural maturity of terrigenous clastics and carbonates; geometric shape of rock bodies, such as the narrow and linear shape of a stream-channel sandstone; sedimentary structures, including variations in bedding, ripple marks, and desiccation cracks; and fossils. Facies defined primarily on physical features (lithology) are called *lithofacies;* those defined primarily on fossils are called *biofacies.*

A river delta is an excellent example of a complex interrelationship of subenvironments (channel, swamp, lake, levee) and, therefore, of sedimentary facies. Study of the modern Mississippi River delta has provided a basis for recognition of ancient deltas preserved in the rock record.

Facies change position through time—sea level may rise and produce a *transgression* upon the land, or fall and produce a *regression* of the sea from the land. A transgressive event may be recorded in the rock record by a shifting of a sandy beach facies landward, such as the St. Peter Sandstone in the midcontinent area. A shallow-marine environment then comes into existence where the beach had originally been located, typically depositing finer sedimentary material upon the beach sand. The change of sedimentation from coarse-grained (beach) to fine-grained (shallow-marine) is an *onlap* succession.

A regressive event is exemplified by the rock record of the Permian reef complex of West Texas and southeastern New Mexico. In Permian time a series of adjoining environments formed back-reef, reef, fore-reef, and basin facies. As time progressed, the sea regressed southward and these environments shifted in their locations. In the rock record, consequently, the reef facies is overlain by back-reef facies and, eventually, nonmarine coastal facies rocks, an *offlap* succession. A stratigraphic section at one location exposes vertically a succession of sedimentary facies that were at one time laterally adjacent to one another, an expression of *Walther's Law.*

The cause of specific transgression and regression events is often difficult to determine, but it has been suggested that, in general, fragmentation of continents may be accompanied by decreased volume of the ocean basins and subsequent transgression. Conversely, suturing of continents may be accompanied by increased volume of ocean basins and subsequent regression.

An end product of facies/paleoenvironmental study is the construction of a paleogeographic map of an area. These maps reconstruct ancient shorelines, deltas, and rivers, for example, and are important tools in the quest for Earth-related resources.

Suggestions for Further Reading

King, P. B. 1948. *Geology of the Southern Guadalupe Mountains, Texas.* U.S. Geological Survey Professional Paper 215.

Laporte, Léo. 1979. *Ancient environments.* 2d ed. Englewood Cliffs, NJ: Prentice-Hall.

Newell, N. D. 1972. The evolution of reefs. *Scientific American* 227(6):54–65.

Newell, N. D., and others. [1953] 1972. *The Permian reef complex of the Guadalupe Mountains Region, West Texas and New Mexico.* New York: Hafner. Reprint of original by W. H. Freeman.

Rigby, J. K., and W. K. Hamblin, eds. 1972. *Recognition of ancient sedimentary environments.* Society of Economic Paleontologists and Mineralogists Special Publication No. 16.

Scholle, P. A. 1988. *The Permian reef complex, West Texas and New Mexico.* Society of Economic Paleontologists and Mineralogists slide set no. 3 (80 slides with explanatory text).

Selley, R. C. 1986. *Ancient sedimentary environments.* 3rd ed. Ithaca, NY: Cornell Univ. Press.

Documents of Life: Preservation of Fossils and the Spectrum of Life

3

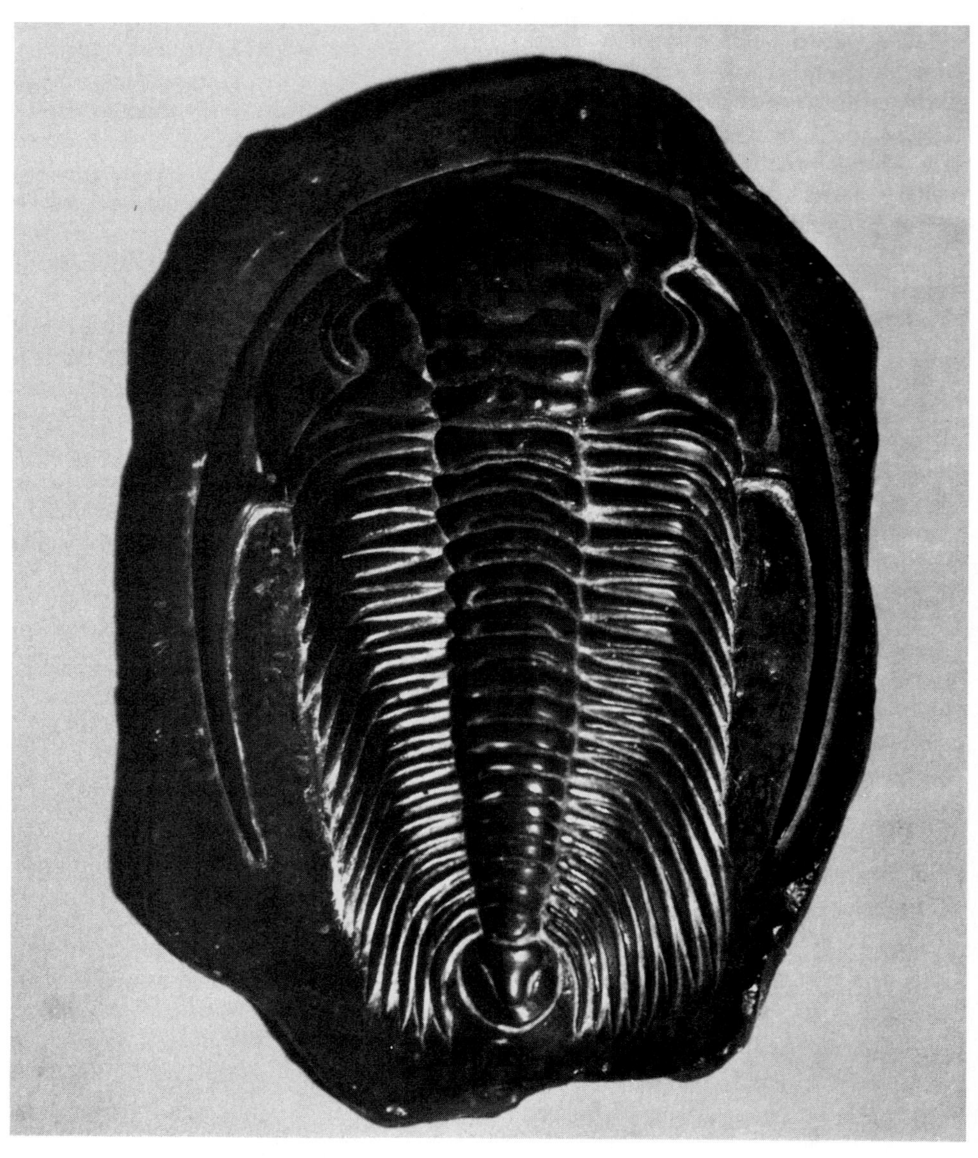

Contents

Key Terms

Stratigraphy
Carbonization
Permineralization
Recrystallization
Replacement
Mold
Cast
Trace fossil
Paleontology
Taxonomy
Kingdom
Phyla (phylum)
Class
Order
Species
Genera (genus)
Family
Taxa (taxon)
Moneran
Protistan
Stromatolite
Invertebrate
Vertebrate
Septa (septum)
Suture
Paleoecology
Habitat
Niche
Community
Ecosystem
Benthos
Epifauna
Infauna
Plankton
Nekton
Food Chain
Producer
Consumer
Autotroph
Heterotroph
Biofacies
Biogeographic province
Endemic
Cosmopolitan
Fossil fuel

The Way It Was

It began, probably, as a practical joke. Colleagues of Professor Johann Beringer were humorously impressed by the professor's dedication in combing the hills for fossils around the University of Würzburg, Germany. Beringer lived during the early eighteenth century. At this time the argument about an organic origin versus an inorganic origin for fossils still was debated, a relic of the so-called "fossil controversy." Beringer opposed the concept of an organic explanation for fossils, favoring an elusive origin as "unique manifestations of nature." Colleagues fabricated a number of artificial fossils by molding masses of clay into forms with various images (Fig. 3–1), and proceeded to salt the hillsides where Beringer was likely to look for his specimens.*

Professor Beringer was enthused with his discoveries; he studied his fossilized finds and described them in detail. Unusual findings spurred him to look further, and his fossils became more and more remarkable. Unusual markings were followed by discoveries of fish, insects, bees actually sucking nectar from fossil plants, birds in flight, figures of astronomical bodies, and finally, unusual letters, some apparently Hebrew and some ancient Babylonian forms. Professor Beringer wrote a treatise in which he described his fossil discoveries, including one that actually had the name of the divine upon it. He illustrated his treatise with 21 folio plates.**

Prior to Beringer's publication of this work, some had expressed the opinion that his specimens were fakes—that they had been made artificially. In his treatise, Beringer devoted a specific chapter to denial of such a possibility. Then came the day when Beringer found on the hillside a fossil form with his name inscribed on it! His dismay was great. He attempted to buy back all the copies of his treatise, and impoverished himself in the effort. Unfortunately, he did not destroy the copies that he so diligently had retrieved, and they were found after his death. An opportunistic publisher purchased them, printed a new title page, and sold them in 1767 as a second edition of Beringer's work. Professor Johann Beringer's name remains as part of the colorful background of the development of our concepts on the nature of fossils. He is remembered as the victim of a classic fossil hoax!

The word *fossil* originally referred to any discrete object dug from the Earth. It did not, at first, have the organic restriction that is associated with it today. Fossils have fascinated humans since ancient times. Prehistoric people buried fossils with their dead; writings of the ancients include references to and drawings of fossil objects. Along with actual fossils of plants

---

*Written accounts of Beringer's "fossils" differ in whether one or more students or another professor made and scattered the clay images. Students are most commonly credited with responsibility for the deed.

**1726. *Lithographiae Wirceburgensis, Specimen Primum.* Würzburg.

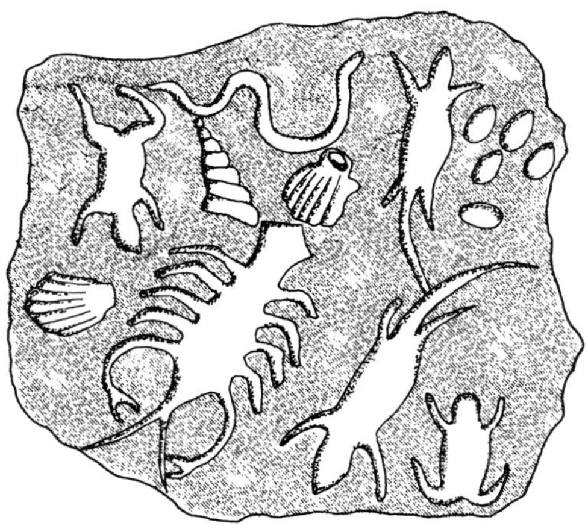

Figure 3–1
Examples of Beringer's "fossils."
(From Johann Beringer, 1726, *Lithographiae Wirceburgensis Specimen Primum*)

and animals, these objects include curious geometric forms and stones with markings that one's imagination is able to convert to clouds, landscapes, and castles. Some ancient writers, especially Greek, did recognize plant and animal fossils as being of organic derivation. Herodotus, journeying in Egypt between 460 and 443 B.C., observed fossil shells on the hillsides and straightforwardly called them shells. Writing much later, in the eleventh century A.D., the Chinese scholar Shen Kua observed that in the cliffs of the Thai-Hang Shan mountain range there were layers of rock containing whelklike animals, oyster shells, and stones (fossil sea urchins) that he described as being like bird eggs. Shen Kua states that this locality, about 500 kilometers from the sea, must once have been marine. Unusual in Shen Kua's statements is his recognition not only of the former marine nature of the area, but also that these fossils were shallow-water forms and that the area had probably been a shoreline.

More influential in the thinking of western cultures, however, were the ideas of Aristotle. As the founder of a highly influential center of learning, Aristotle championed the view that the Earth had been shaped by observable processes which obeyed certain natural laws. However, Aristotle generally believed that fossils formed ("grew") directly in the rock, most often under the influence of celestial bodies. During the Dark Ages and Middle Ages, the early Christian church dogmatically accepted a great deal of Aristotelian thinking, thus strongly hindering acceptance of the organic derivation of fossils.

We chuckle readily today in reading some of the explanations of fossils that come to us from writings in the Middle Ages. To keep our perspective, however, remember that these explanations were made during a historical period when it generally was accepted that "anything" could happen. Some wrote of fossils being formed as a result of the work of a spirit influence in nature, a "Virtu Divina." Pictures perceived in rocks (such as forms of a virgin and child) were considered to be prophetic designs formed in the rocks at the time the Earth itself was created, and thus a direct prophecy from the creator. Other writers suggested that fossils were the result of earlier ill-fated attempts by the creator—discarded abortive models, so to speak. Another opinion that was quite widespread during this time was that fossils were "jokes" of nature, humorous "sport" of a whimsical creator. More ominous was the idea that fossils resulted from the forces of evil; they were created to confound humankind and to terrify people.

One view was that fossils grew in the rocks because of the presence of vapors that were generated by a fermentationlike process. This particular

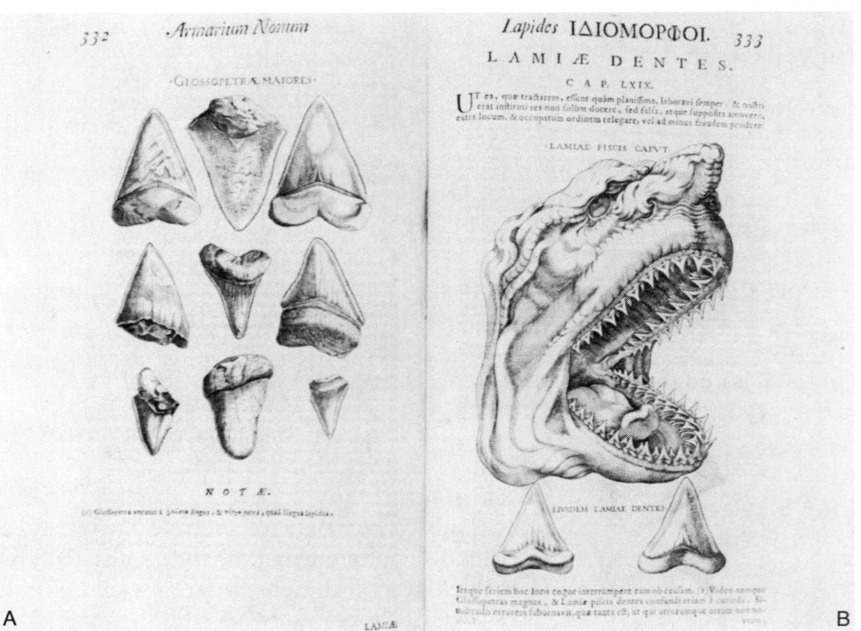

Figure 3–2
A. Head of the lamia fish (shark). B. Glossopetrae ("tongue-stones"). Nicolaus Steno used these plates to demonstrate that the "tongue-stones," which were found in great abundance on the island of Malta, were in fact the teeth of ancient sharks that lived prior to Malta's being uplifted as an island (a former sea bottom, now land). The plates first appeared in Steno's work, but had been prepared in bronze in the previous century by Michele Mercati (1541–1593), who saw no scientific relationship between the "tongue-stones" and the teeth of modern sharks.
(From Nicolaus Steno, 1667, *The Dissection of the Head of a Carcharias Shark;* photo courtesy of F. Stanton Hill)

concept went so far as to ascribe beautiful Etruscan vases and other pottery dug up in Rome to formation from these elusive vapors. These vases had grown in the rocks and did not involve human workmanship at all!

During the Renaissance (fifteenth to seventeenth centuries), scientific thinking changed. A number of individuals, such as Leonardo da Vinci, wrote of the more plausible organic derivation of fossils. Nicolaus Steno, who laid the foundation for the science of **stratigraphy** (see Chapter 6), in the 1660s illustrated the organic nature of what were then called "tongue-stones" (Fig. 3–2). The concept of fossils as organic features was still contrary to church dogma, however, and some who expressed the idea were persecuted. One unfortunate victim, Giordano Bruno, was burned at the stake in 1600 by the Italian Inquisition because of his statements and writings on some aspects of science.

Thus, even into the eighteenth century, the time of Johann Beringer, the "fossil controversy" was still evident. Early in that century it was stated that fossils had been created to fulfill the role of "ornaments" for the inner portion of the Earth, just as flowers had been formed to ornament the surface of the Earth! As the eighteenth century progressed, the concept of the organic nature of fossils prevailed and became widely accepted. The term *fossil* came to mean what it means today: the remains or traces of ancient organisms preserved in rocks or sediments of the Earth's lithosphere.

Bias of the Fossil Record

The Miracle of Preservation

The spectrum of life—from single-celled amoebas to the complex cellular structures of humans—is truly immense and impressive. Biologists have described and classified about 1.5 million living species of plants and animals. New species are being described each year and added to this figure, and the actual number of living species probably will be much higher; estimates have been made that 4.5 million species of living plants and animals eventually will be known. This figure is for only the *present* moment of time. It is not known how many species actually have existed throughout the history of life; the fossil record, as presently recognized, includes about 250,000 described and classified species of organisms. This seemingly is a large sample of past life, but in view of the total number of organisms that must have lived and died during the past several *billion* years, the number is undoubtedly small. Thus the fossil record is a biased record, and does not give a complete picture of life of the past.

When a plant or an animal dies, it is subject to bacterial decay or destruction by scavengers. If the dead organism has hard parts, such as shell or bone material, these parts may remain after this first round of destruction. These hard parts, in turn, may be subject to breakage by abrasion, or may be completely pulverized. However, strong shells and bones, or portions of them, may be buried under and within sediments before destruction; and thus may be preserved as fossils. Common prerequisites for the formation of fossils, therefore, are the existence of hard parts and their relatively rapid burial (Fig. 3–3). However, even at this stage preservation of an organism is not assured.

The buried shells or skeletal parts later may be chemically destroyed by groundwater that percolates downward through the enclosing sediments and leaches the hard organic parts from the sedimentary material. Other destructive processes that may occur include metamorphism of the sedimentary material under conditions of deep burial and/or tectonic events, and destruction by uplift and subsequent erosion of the sedimentary rocks containing the fossils. Thus, fossils can be preserved and can be destroyed by various aspects of the *geologic cycle* (Chapter 1).

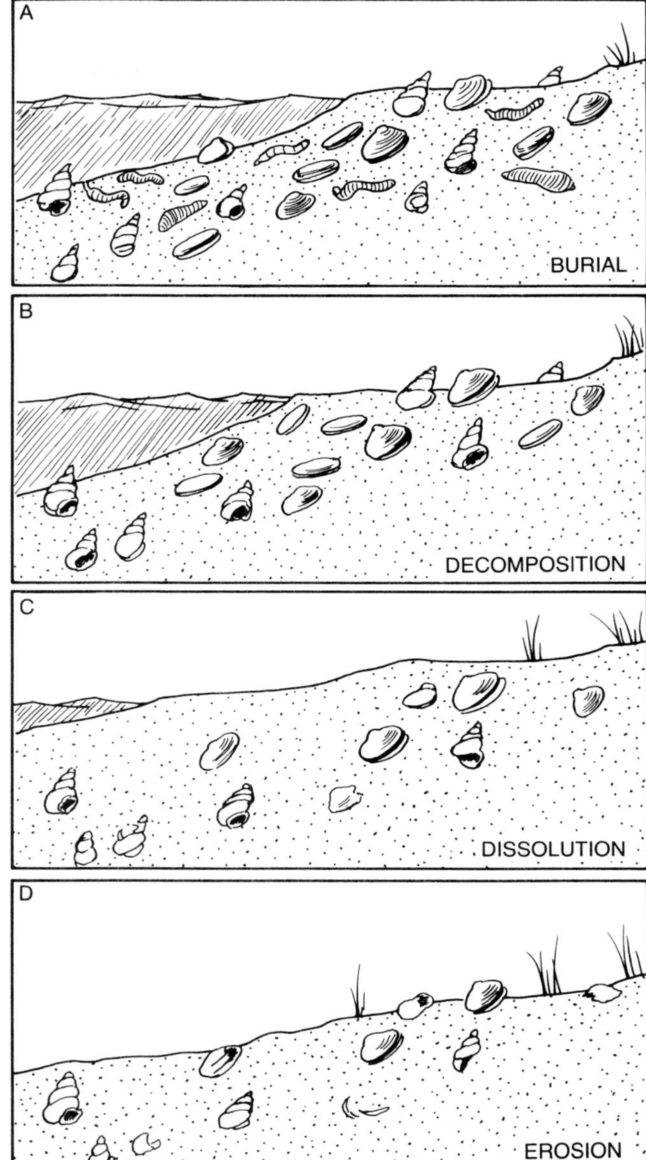

Figure 3–3
Forms of destruction that obscure the fossil record. A. Death assemblage. B. Bacteria decompose soft forms. C. Hard parts are buried and dissolution removes delicate shells. D. Erosion removes part of record, dissolution continues, and only a small part of the death assemblage remains.

An assemblage of dead organisms provides us with an exceedingly distorted glimpse of the variety and abundance in the original assemblage. For example, about three-quarters of a million living species of insects are recognized, but only about 8000 fossil insect species have been classified. The fact that most insects live in terrestrial environments not conducive to rapid burial, and that insects possess fragile exoskeletons, explains why this group of animals is rarely fossilized. Even in more readily preservable groups of animals with shells (such as clams and snails), this bias and distortion of the picture of past life prevails.

Estimates have been made that the known number of fossil species of preservable forms of life represents only 2.5 to 13.5 percent of the total number of preservable species that lived since the beginning of the Cambrian (Table 1–1, Chapter 1). Whichever estimate is accepted, it is clear that the fossil record includes a *small fraction* of the total number of species that have lived in the past. In a sense, preservation is rather miraculous, in light of all the events that may obliterate the record.

In spite of the bias of the fossil record, the significant interrelationships of rocks, fossils, and time have provided the basis for formulation of the concept of fossil succession, and subsequently, development of the geologic time scale (see Chapter 6). Fossils have become a major tool in our ability to look back over the abyss of geologic time. This chapter and the next present an overview of these "miracles" of preservation.

Preservation and Occurrence of Fossils

Most fossils are found in sedimentary rocks; it is the deposition of soft sediments (muds, silts, sands) enclosing the dead organisms that increases the possibility of preservation. Also, the accumulations of sediments throughout geologic history have been in those places (environments) where organisms have lived and died. Because the ocean is the "sink" to which most clastic debris is carried and deposited, there is a selective preservation of marine sedimentary rocks, which, in turn, exerts a direct influence on the fossil record. Because they represent areas of erosion more than of accumulation, continental environments such as mountain and desert areas are less conducive to accumulation of sediments, a condition that has a profound negative effect on the fossil record. Nonetheless, unusual and outstanding occurrences of fossils have been found in some rocks formed in lake and stream environments.

Within the marine realm, the continental-shelf setting (the submerged margins of the continents) has contributed importantly to the sedimentary rock record, which, in turn, has had important implications for the fossil record. Continental shelves, such as those off the coast of the eastern United States and the Gulf of Mexico, are generally wide, shallow, submerged regions within the *photic zone* (the depth of sunlight penetration). The shelf environment supports abundant life and receives sediments from rivers emptying into the sea. Most of the fossil record consists of the hard-part remains of organisms that lived and died on the shallow marine bottoms of continental-shelf environments or other shallow seas during the *Phanerozoic.* Thus, the bias of the fossil record is influenced by preservation of organisms that secreted hard parts and lived in shallow marine environments. The particular type of preservation is dependent upon the physical and chemical characteristics of the sedimentary environment, and upon postdepositional events.

Metamorphism tends to destroy fossil remains through the high pressures and temperatures associated with metamorphic events. Occasionally fossils are found in low-grade metamorphic rocks; here the fossils commonly are deformed and partially altered, but not destroyed. An important occurrence of fossils in metamorphic rocks was located by Clarence King (later to become first director of the U.S. Geological Survey) in 1863 in the western metamorphic belt of the Sierra Nevada, California. The problem of the age of the slates associated with the gold deposits of the region had puzzled western geologists. For many days King had been searching for fossils in the slate beds, as others had previously; then, at the end of a wearying day's search, he picked up his hammer to return to camp, and, in his words:

> . . . noticed in the rock an object about the size and shape of a small cigar. It was the fossil, the object for which science had searched and yearned and despaired! There he reclined comfortably upon his side . . . a plump pampered cephalopoda (if it is cephalopoda), whom the terrible ordeal of metamorphism had spared. . . . The age of the gold-belt was discovered!*

The thrill of discovery is reflected in these expressive words from the 1860s.

Even rarer than fossils in metamorphic rocks are the occasional occurrences of fossils in igneous rocks. A striking example of the latter can be seen in Yellowstone National Park, where stream erosion has exposed a succession of 27 forest levels encased in lava flows. The forests grew between periods of volcanism and then were buried in the fluid lavas (Fig. 3–4). Fossil plant-bearing sedimentary rocks are interstratified with the volcanic materials, and so in this unusual geologic situation a fossil record is found in both sedimentary and igneous rocks. Because of the relative rarity of such occur-

*Clarence King. 1872. *Mountaineering in the Sierra Nevada.* Boston: James R. Osgood.

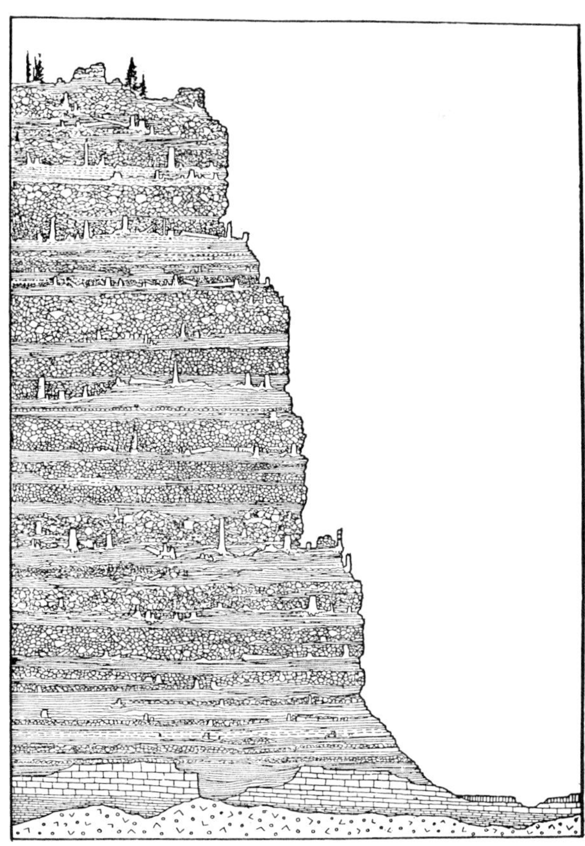

Figure 3–4
Amethyst Cliff, Yellowstone National Park, illustrates a succession of eighteen forests, each one killed when buried by volcanic flows of Paleogene age (section about 700 m thick).
(Courtesy of U. S. Geological Survey)

rences, the discussion of the fossil record in this and succeeding chapters will concentrate on occurrences in sedimentary rocks.

The "miracle" of preservation is considered to be just that because of the vulnerability of organisms to decay and destruction after death, and the resultant loss of record of most individuals or even entire species. When fossilization does occur, it may, in rare cases, involve soft organic parts, but hard-part preservation is much more common. Both soft-part and hard-part preservation can be accomplished by several processes (Table 3–1).

Unaltered soft remains of organisms are relatively rare, and generally are confined to geologically young strata. The frozen mammoths and the other examples of unaltered preservation of soft parts listed in Table 3–1 are restricted essentially to deposits of Pleistocene age (see geologic time scale, Table 1–1). As time passes, of course, it is more likely that alteration will affect the organisms. Although exceedingly rare, these unaltered fossils are significant in that they present a picture of the complete animal. Unaltered hard parts, and hard parts altered just by leaching, also are restricted essentially to comparatively young strata that have *not* been mineralized or severely deformed.

Important and outstanding are the carbonaceous films of organisms found in dark shales deposited in oxygen-deficient environments. Plant material (Fig. 3–5) commonly is fossilized by this **carbonization** mode of preservation. For example, as plant leaves were buried by accumulating muds, volatile materials (such as nitrogen and oxygen) were squeezed out, and chemical action changed the tissues to a thin film of carbon. What remains is a residue forming an outline of a portion of the previously living leaves.

If thick accumulations of plants derived from swampy coastal lagoons and deltas are carbonized more completely, coal deposits may develop. This important economic resource is a sedimentary rock derived from the chemical alteration of plant material that has progressed through a sequence of grades:

peat, a fibrous mat of partially decayed plant material;

lignite, a soft, brownish, lithified form of the original plant material;

bituminous coal, a black, so-called "soft coal" which typically leaves a tarry residue when burned; and

anthracite coal, a black and glossy "hard coal" that provides more heat than bituminous coal when burned, and produces little smoke.

Anthracite coal typically is found in areas where intense folding and low-grade metamorphism have occurred: the original plant material has been compacted and carbonized, then further altered by the heat and pressure of deformation (see Chapter 16).

Alteration by **permineralization** involves the deposition by underground solutions of mineral matter in the pore spaces of organic hard parts (Fig. 3–6). Calcium carbonate (lime), silica, or occasionally the mineral pyrite (an iron compound) may fill the pore spaces of shells or bones. This process has the effect of making the original organic material more indurated or rocklike. Hardening of the original shell or bone increases the possibility of preservation.

The **recrystallization** of unstable forms of mineral material in shells destroys the microstructure

Table 3–1
Modes of fossil preservation

Preservation without alteration	
Soft parts (rare)	Freezing of organisms, such as the mammoths of Siberia Mummification of remains in dry climates Entrapment of organisms in resin (amber) or in oil seeps
Hard parts	Unaltered shells, bones, teeth, most commonly of calcium carbonate, calcium phosphate, silica, and chitin; cellulose
Preservation with alteration	
Leaching	Chemical dissolution of the most soluble portions of the remains, commonly resulting in bleached and pitted shell and bone
Carbonization	Changing by chemical action of original plant or animal material to a thin film of carbon which outlines the shape of part or all of the organism
Permineralization	Deposition by underground solutions of mineral material, unlike original shell or bone compositon, in the pore spaces of buried remains; most commonly calcium carbonate, silica, pyrite, dolomite
Recrystallization	Conversion into a more stable form (such as the calcite form of calcium carbonate) of less stable compounds (such as the aragonite form of calcium carbonate of some clams and snails)
Replacement	Complete (or nearly so) dissolution and replacement by new mineral matter of original organic material (such as shells or bones); common replacement minerals are calcite, dolomite, silica compounds, and iron compounds
Molds and casts	
Molds	Removal by dissolution of organic material buried in sediment; void left in the rock is a mold (e.g., an imprint); molds can be internal (expressing the shape of the inside of a shell or other feature) or external (expressing the shape of the outside of the object)
Casts	Filling of a mold (void) with sediment or mineral material, thus preserving the shape (internal or external) of the organic feature
Trace fossils	
Tracks and trails	Footprints of animals and birds Indications of movements by invertebrates
Burrows	Excavations made by worms and other animals such as clams, crabs, shrimp, fish as they tunnel into sediments
Borings	Drill holes bored through shells by predator snails or other organisms; holes bored into rock by rock-boring organisms such as clams, worms, certain crustaceans
Coprolites	Fossilized animal excrement; may give evidence of diet, animal size, and habit

of the original shell—e.g., calcium carbonate in the form of *aragonite* to a more stable form, such as calcium carbonate in the form of *calcite*. This form of alteration, which typically changes a shell to a mosaic of interlocking crystals, does not involve a change in chemical composition.

Alteration by **replacement** takes place by removal of the original hard part through dissolution, and deposition of new compounds in its place. A familiar result of this process is petrified wood (Fig. 3–7); the woody cellulose material was removed and replaced by silica. This replacement may occur so precisely that even such fine detail as tree-ring structure is preserved.

A common mode of preservation is the formation of **molds** and **casts.** After burial of an organism,

Figure 3–5
Plant fossilization by formation of a carbonaceous film (specimen 14 cm in width; Eocene, Green River Formation, Wyoming.)
(Specimen in Raymond Alf Museum, Webb School, Claremont, CA. Photo by J. Streng)

Figure 3–6
Fossilization by permineralization. Fragile bird eggs are not commonly fossilized, but the eggs in this cluster have had mineral material deposited in the pore space of the organic matter, thus indurating them (Paleogene age).
(Specimens in Raymond Alf Museum, Webb School, Claremont, CA. Photo by J. Streng)

dissolution by groundwater may remove the original material and leave a void that expresses the external shape of the organic feature; this void is an external mold. If this mold is later filled with some type of sediment or mineral matter, a cast is formed (Fig. 3–8A). Molds and casts preserve the shape of an organic feature; either the inside (internal mold or cast) or the outside (external mold or cast) shape of the buried object remains. In addition to being relatively common types of naturally formed fossils, molds and casts can be made artificially in the laboratory to provide specimens for student use, research, and for displays at museums and other institutions.

The modes of preservation that have been discussed and illustrated preserve the actual organisms or the shape of the original organic material; these fossils are referred to as *body fossils.* In addition, there is a group of fossils called **trace fossils,** in which the body parts of the organism are not preserved, but evidence of the former behavior and activity of an individual is. Trace fossils show evi-

A

B

C

Figure 3–7
Preservation by replacement. A. Abundant slabs of petrified wood being exposed by erosion in the Petrified Forest National Park, Arizona. B. Preservation has been so detailed that some slabs have an outer barklike appearance, although no woody bark remains. C. Tree-ring structure is still visible in some petrified logs.
(Photo by J. Patterson)

A

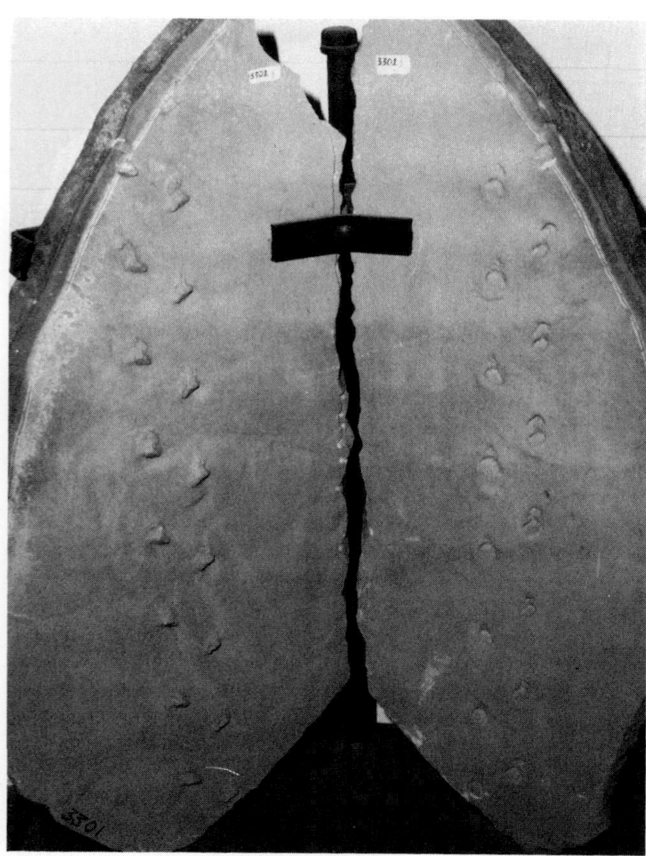

B

Figure 3–8
A. Internal casts of gastropods in mudstone, Cretaceous age. B. A "book" of reptile tracks with external casts (fillings) on the left side and molds (foot impressions) on the right side, Permian age, Arizona.
(A, photo by J. D. Cooper; B, specimen from Raymond Alf Museum, Webb School, Claremont, CA, photo by J. Streng)

dence of activities (Fig. 3–9) such as dwelling, walking, running, digging, resting, feeding, and escape (from sudden sedimentation pulses). Animal tracks (Fig. 3–8B) in sedimentary rocks are examples of fossilized locomotion behavior. Various forms of trace fossils, such as burrows and borings, indicate a disturbance of the original sediments. Burrowing is accomplished in unconsolidated sediments; boring affects "hard" surfaces, such as shell and lithified sedimentary rock. The study of trace fossils is an important and significant subscience (called *ichnology*) within the broad field of **paleontology,** the study of ancient life.

Each fossil, be it a delicate carbonaceous film, a permineralized oyster, the cast of a snail, or merely tracks indicating movement of an individual, is a special occurrence. Fossils contain a potential wealth of data that may provide *paleontologists* with information about where the organisms lived, how they lived, how they grew, and what they ate. Fossils are important tools for the study of the geologic past; they are the link between present life forms and the vast spectrum of life that has lived and died.

Classification of Organisms

Taxonomy

The spectrum of life preserved in the fossil record may at first present a confusing picture. However, this picture becomes clearer when the spectrum of living and fossil organisms is viewed within a framework of organization. Prerequisite to an ability to fully understand relationships among organisms, and to communicate with others about these

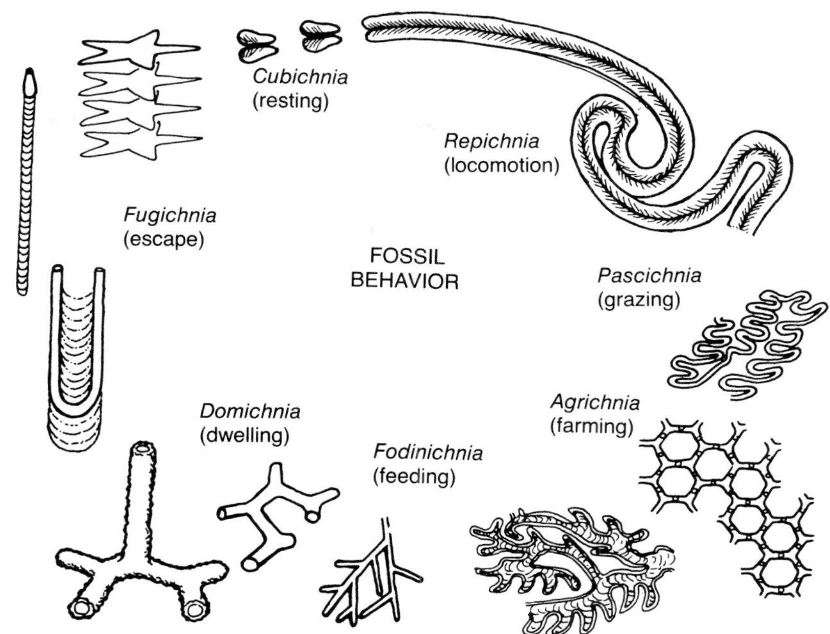

Figure 3–9
Schematic diagram illustrating some of the diverse behavior traces made on or in sediment by various invertebrates. (From A. A. Ekdale, R. G. Bromley, and S. G. Pemberton, 1984, *Ichnology: Trace Fossils in Sedimentology and Stratigraphy:* Society of Economic Paleontologists and Mineralogists Short Course No. 15, Fig. 2–8, p. 24. Reproduced with permission of SEPM)

relationships, is the development of a classification scheme. The science of naming and classifying organisms is **taxonomy.**

Living organisms as well as fossils are classified by a scheme that was developed by the Swedish naturalist, Carl von Linné (better known by the Latin form of his name, Carolus Linnaeus), who lived during the eighteenth century. Linnaeus established a hierarchical classification, published in the tenth edition of his book *Systemae Naturae* in 1758.*

This was a system in which each individual organism was grouped with "like" individuals into various categories (Table 3–2). Progression upward through the hierarchical system shows a succession of categories that are more inclusive and more diverse. These categories within the classification scheme represent groupings based on the degree of similarity or difference among organisms. Especially important for assigning organisms to their proper categories in the hierarchical system are observable features, such as the morphology of the external form (important in both paleontologic and biologic study) and the internal anatomy (biologic study).

The most inclusive category in the Linnaean system is the **kingdom.** Five kingdoms are currently recognized, although only four are well represented in the fossil record: Monera, Protista (also called Protoctista), Plantae, and Animalia. Linnaeus in the mid-eighteenth century differentiated only between plants and animals. The kingdom category is very broad, and each kingdom contains a large spectrum of different-appearing but related organisms. Each category below the level of kingdom becomes less inclusive and thereby more restrictive in the degree of similarity and biological relationship among the included organisms.

Thus, each of the kingdoms is subdivided into various **phyla** (singular **phylum**), and these phyla, in turn, are subdivided into **classes,** which, in turn, are subdivided into **orders.** Further subdivision of each category forms the kingdom-to-species classification scheme shown in Table 3–2. Viewed in the op-

Table 3–2
Linnaean and modern systems of classification of organisms

Linnaean	Modern
KINGDOM* (two: plants and animals)	**KINGDOM**
	PHYLUM
CLASS (six: worms, insects, fish, amphibians, birds, and mammals)	**CLASS**
	ORDER
ORDER	**FAMILY**
	GENUS
GENUS	**SPECIES**
SPECIES (about 4000)	
(variety)†	

*Linnaean system names in boldface.
†Variety indicates a distinctive group of individuals within a species population; not a formal subspecies.

*Stockholm, Sweden.

posite direction (bottom to top), closely related **species** are grouped into **genera** (singular **genus**); closely related genera are grouped into **families**; and so forth. In each situation, as dictated by the hierarchical system, organisms are grouped into broader, more inclusive categories.

The basic, fundamental unit of this classification scheme is the *species.* Biologically a species is composed of related organisms that share a common *gene pool* (all the genes of a particular population). This means that a typical species is a group of organisms whose members are capable of interbreeding (exchanging genetic material) and producing fertile offspring (see discussion of species concept, Chapter 4).

Linnaeus used the categories of kingdom, class, order, genus, species, and variety, and listed about 4000 species in his treatise. Since the time of Linnaeus, however, the number of *known* species has increased greatly, and with this increase the main categories of phylum and family have been added to the original classification. Further refinement of the Linnaean system has introduced subcategories, some of the more common of which are *subphylum, subclass,* and *superfamily.* This further splitting of categories has increased the number of classification "cubbyholes" available for differentiating organisms.

These refinements in the original Linnaean classification reflect increased knowledge about the biological relationships among organisms. A classification of the elements of any subject area can be viewed as an index to the level of understanding of a particular subject. However, the classification of organisms is unique, in that there is a thread of evolutionary continuity that runs through the members of the biosphere. In addition to refinements in the classification of organisms, the assignment of organisms to appropriate categories called **taxa** (singular **taxon**) is neither static nor inflexible, and instead may change with time as knowledge and understanding of evolutionary relationships increase (see Chapter 4). In paleontology, this is particularly true for assignments below the rank of class, but for some enigmatic extinct taxa, correct placement in the proper phylum remains a problem.

Nomenclature

Using all seven major classification categories to name each organism would be cumbersome. One of the main aspects of the Linnaean classification is the *nomenclature,* whereby each species is identified by a two-part or *binomial* name that is latinized. Modern humans belong to a species designated by the binomial *Homo sapiens* (Table 3–3). The first term, *Homo,* is the genus, and by convention is capitalized. The second term, *sapiens,* is the *specific* name, and is not capitalized.

Table 3–3
Classification of humans in the modern hierarchical system

KINGDOM	Animalae
PHYLUM	Chordata (Vertebrata)
CLASS	Mammalia
ORDER	Primate
FAMILY	Hominidae
GENUS	*Homo*
SPECIES	*Homo sapiens*

Two species of early humans, both extinct, also are assigned to the genus *Homo: Homo habilis* and *Homo erectus.* The generic name, *Homo* in this example, can be used only once in naming organisms; once assigned, it cannot be used again in any of the other kingdoms. The specific name, however, is a modifier, and can be used any number of times in association with different genus names.

Rules of *binomial nomenclature* (established by the International Commission on Zoological and Botanical Nomenclature, and set forth in respective codes) require the names (taxa) at every level of the classification to be latinized, thus avoiding the obvious problem of language barriers. It has been decreed that both generic and specific names be *italicized* when printed, and underlined when written. Remember: a name, whether at the species, genus, family, order, or higher level, is referred to as a *taxon.* In paleontology, this classification and nomenclatorial scheme applies to body fossils.

For trace fossils, however, individual forms have been classified into *ichnogenera* and, in some cases, *ichnospecies.* One of the problems in using Linnaean classification nomenclature for trace fossils is that different organisms which are engaged in similar behavior can leave similar traces; conversely, the same organisms engaged in different behavior are capable of making very different traces, each of which would be assigned a different ichnogenus name! The trace-maker will generally have a different name than the trace itself; therefore it is important to keep body fossil names separate from trace fossil names.

A Parade of Characters: Unicells to Plants

Introduction

Recognition of the biases in the fossil record indicates that our knowledge of past life is incomplete. In the continuous parade of life forms that have lived and died during geologic history, we are generally limited in our observation and study to those organisms that secreted hard parts capable of being preserved. Even so, the available fossil record shows tremendous diversity. This chapter presents an overview of the life forms preserved as fossils; a more detailed classification is provided in Appendix B.

The major subdivisions, the kingdoms (Table 3–4), include the **monerans,** the **protistans,** and the more familiar plants and animals. Many biologists recognize a fifth kingdom, the fungi, but this group will not be included in the following discussion because it has left very little fossil record.

Monerans

Monerans are single-celled organisms, different from organisms of all other kingdoms in that the cells lack a distinct nucleus. Common examples of monerans are bacteria and cyanobacteria (blue-green algae), which occur as isolated cells or form colonies. Microscopic monerans are the oldest known forms of life (see Chapter 8). They are found in rocks of early Cryptozoic (Precambrian) age, thus supporting the hypothesis that the origin of life goes back nearly 4000 million years.

Table 3–4

Basic characteristics of the four kingdoms well represented in the fossil record*

Kingdom	Characteristics
Monera (monerans)	One-celled; nonnucleated cells
Protista (protistans)	One-celled, nucleated cells
Plantae (plants)	Multicellular; manufacture food from inorganic materials
Animalia (animals)	Multicellular; obtain nutrients from other organisms

*Synoptic classification, Appendix B.

Organosedimentary structures called **stromatolites** are especially noteworthy in rocks of Cryptozoic age because they are essentially the only *megafossils* (visible without magnification) found in rocks of this ancient time. Stromatolites are layered, mound-shaped structures (Fig. 3–10) formed by the calcium carbonate–binding activities of colonial cyanobacteria. These earliest stromatolites are associated with some of the first limestones, and are important indicators of changing Cryptozoic environmental conditions (see Chapter 8).

Protistans

Protistans are one-celled organisms also, but unlike the monerans, their individual cells have a nucleus. The evolutionary development of the nucleated cell indicates an order of complexity considerably advanced beyond the simplest monerans. The development of the cell nucleus is possibly one of the most important evolutionary steps in the history of life (Chapters 8 and 10). The nucleus contains the heredity-controlling chromosomes, and functions in cell reproduction as well as in regulating other activities of the cell.

An important protistan group in the fossil record is the Foraminifera (Fig. 3–11). The variety of form in this abundant and diverse group is illustrated by the shape of the *test* (internal shell), which can be rod-shaped, globular, coiled, or spiral. Simpler varieties of Foraminifera have a single-chambered test, but a thin-section of a particular form, the *fusulinid* (Fig. 3–12), illustrates the multichambered construction of some more intricate tests. The fusulinids were marine bottom dwellers that became extinct at the end of the Paleozoic Era. They evolved rapidly during the late Paleozoic, and their fossil remains are used for the biozonation of rocks of this age (see Chapter 11). In Mesozoic time floating varieties of foraminifers contributed their tests to the sediments that accumulated on the sea floor. This process occurs also in modern oceans, and millions of square kilometers of present seafloor are carpeted with foraminiferal *ooze.* Because most individuals of this fossil group are so small, they can be retrieved intact from well cuttings and have been used by petroleum geologists in important subsurface stratigraphic studies.

Radiolaria are another group of protistans that have left an important fossil record. These microscopic organisms secrete siliceous tests that form a variety of complex shapes. Photographs of radiolarians taken through a *scanning electron microscope*

Figure 3–10
Domal stromatolite in dolostone of Cambrian age. Note the well-developed curved laminations which represent successive layered increments of fine carbonate sediment trapped and bound in place by colonial mats of cyanobacteria ("blue-green algae").
(Photo courtesy of Critter Creations, Inc., San Diego. Used with permission)

(Fig. 3–13) show the intricacies of the finely detailed tests. Radiolarians are floating marine organisms that typically live in the photic zone of modern oceans and are distributed widely from polar to tropical regions. After death, the tests, like those of some foraminifers, settle to the seafloor and contribute to the sedimentary ooze. Radiolarians are found in marine rocks that range in age from Cambrian to Holocene, and are major components of *radiolarian cherts* that represent deep-seafloor deposition (see Chapter 11).

Diatoms, a group of microscopic protists that have left an important fossil record, secrete siliceous bivalved structures called *frustules* that are commonly ornate (Fig. 3–14). Diatoms appeared during the Mesozoic and thrived throughout the Cenozoic Era, producing an abundant fossil record. A sedimentary rock, *diatomite,* is composed primarily of these tiny frustules that accumulated as "ooze" on the floors of some ancient seas. Diatoms are abundant in modern oceans, but several types have adapted to freshwater environments. These tiny protistans are significant to marine life because they are among the most important *photosynthesizers.* They form the so-called "pasture of the sea," the base of many oceanic food chains.

Various kinds of algae constitute a significant protistan group that has left an important fossil record. This is particularly true of the calcareous green and red algae, which have contributed to many ancient limestones. One group of calcareous marine algae called the *coccolithophorids* (Fig. 3–15) contributed to great volumes of calcareous *oozes* during the Mesozoic and Cenozoic.

Protistans form a diverse kingdom, and have left an abundant fossil record. Most of the forms referred to in the paleontological literature as *microfossils* belong to this group of organisms, but many fossil groups from the other kingdoms have microscopic-sized individuals or microscopic-sized larval specimens, or are represented as bits and pieces of individuals. The term "microfossil" refers specifically to size—those organic remains requiring use of a high-magnification microscope for study—and not to a kingdom or a portion thereof.

Plants

The plant kingdom is composed of life forms that are multicellular, contain nucleated cells, and manufacture their food (autotrophism) from inorganic materials through the process of photosynthesis. In comparison to animals, plants have left a less abundant fossil record, but it is nonetheless an interesting and important one (see Chapter 16). Plant fossils include such familiar forms as a leaf imprint (Fig. 3–16), preserved tree trunks and petrified wood (Fig. 3–7), and various other structures of multicellular and megascopic land dwellers. Some classifications include the unicellular chlorophyll-bearing

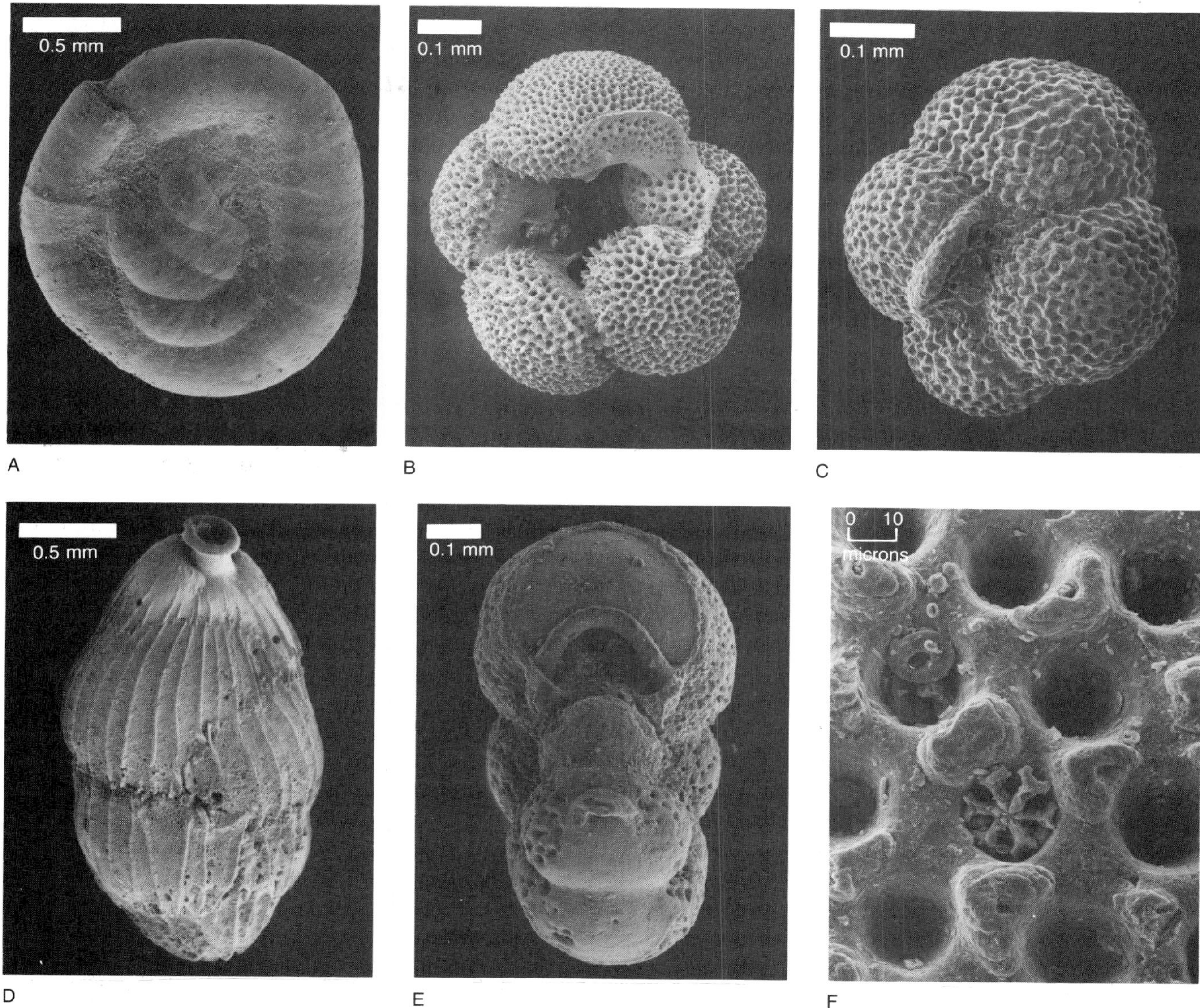

Figure 3–11
Various forms of Foraminifera. A. Agglutinated (sand grains cemented together) benthic foraminifer. B. Calcareous planktonic foraminifer. C. Calcareous planktonic foraminifer. D. Calcareous benthic foraminifer. E. Calcareous planktonic foraminifer. F. Calcareous nannoplankton (extremely small microfossils) in the pore spaces of a foraminifer.
(Scanning electron microscope photos courtesy of Union Oil Science and Technology Division, Brea, CA)

algae and diatoms as plants, but we prefer to make the distinction at the unicellular-versus-multicellular level. (See Chapter 16.)

Less familiar plant fossils include microscopic *spores* and *pollen* of multicellular land plants (Fig. 3–17). The study of plant spores and pollen is a subdiscipline of paleontology called *palynology.* Like the foraminifers, spores and pollen have application in the exploration for petroleum.

The Parade Continues: The Animal Kingdom

The fourth kingdom represented in the fossil record is Animalia, the animals. These life forms possess nucleated cells and are multicellular organisms. They are unable to manufacture their own food from inorganic materials, and thus must obtain their nutrients from other organisms. Both **inverte-**

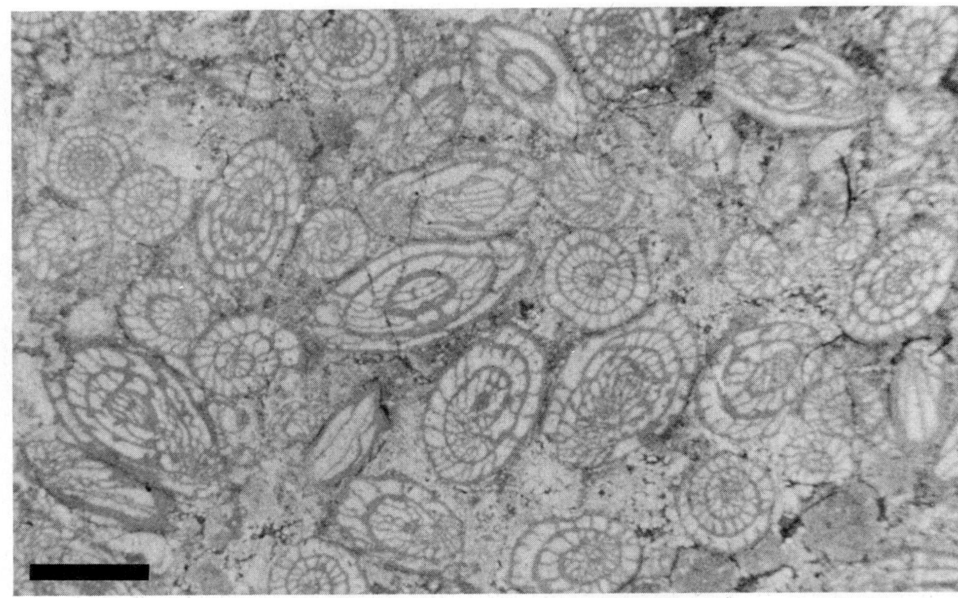

Figure 3–12
Thin section of a fusulinid (a type of Paleozoic Foraminifera) limestone; note the many chambers in the coiled form of one individual. Bar length is 1 mm.
(Photo by J. D. Cooper)

brates, animal forms without backbones, and **vertebrates,** animals with backbones, have left an abundant and diverse fossil record. The invertebrates, however, make up the most important part of this record and are emphasized in this discussion. It is the shallow-marine shelf-dwelling invertebrates that are most commonly preserved because they satisfy the prerequisites of fossilization: the possession of hard parts that were rapidly buried.

Marine invertebrates make up the most accessible part of the fossil record, and are the kinds of fossils most likely to be found in the field. In the following discussion, the major phyla of invertebrates that have left an important fossil record will be surveyed. A more formal and complete classification of organisms is presented in Appendix B.

Invertebrates first appear in rocks of late Proterozoic time, approximately 700 million years old. These early forms were relatively simple and lacked hard parts; the fossils occur as soft-bodied impressions in sandstone (see discussion of Ediacarian Period, Chapter 9). The fact that these soft-bodied creatures were preserved at all is amazing, in light of their vulnerability to decay and destruction

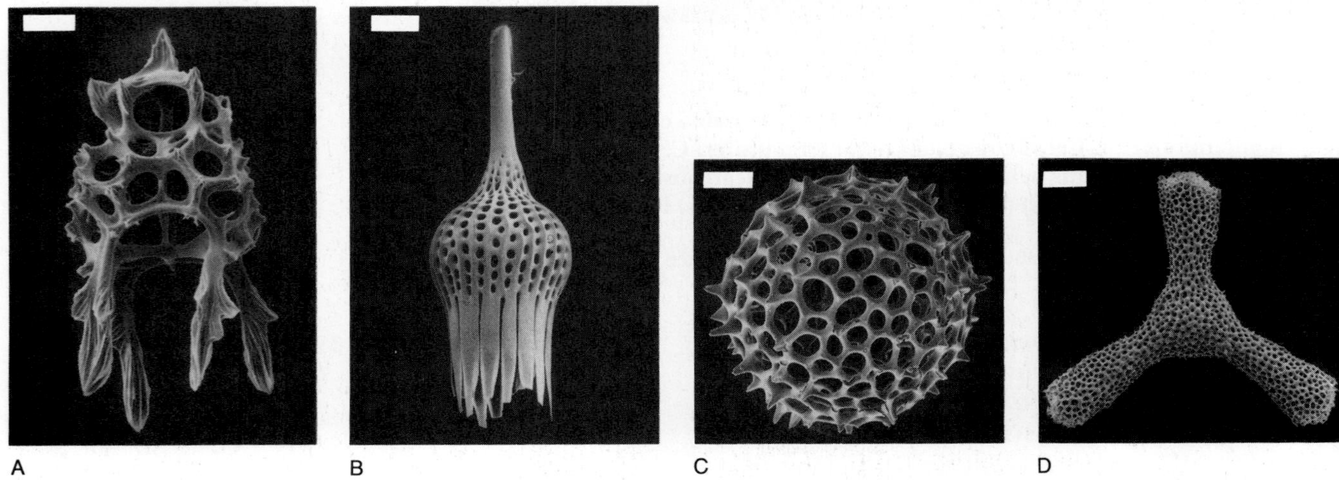

Figure 3–13
Finely detailed tests of Radiolaria. Bar length is 50 microns.
(Scanning electron microscope photos courtesy of Union Oil Science and Technology Division, Brea, CA)

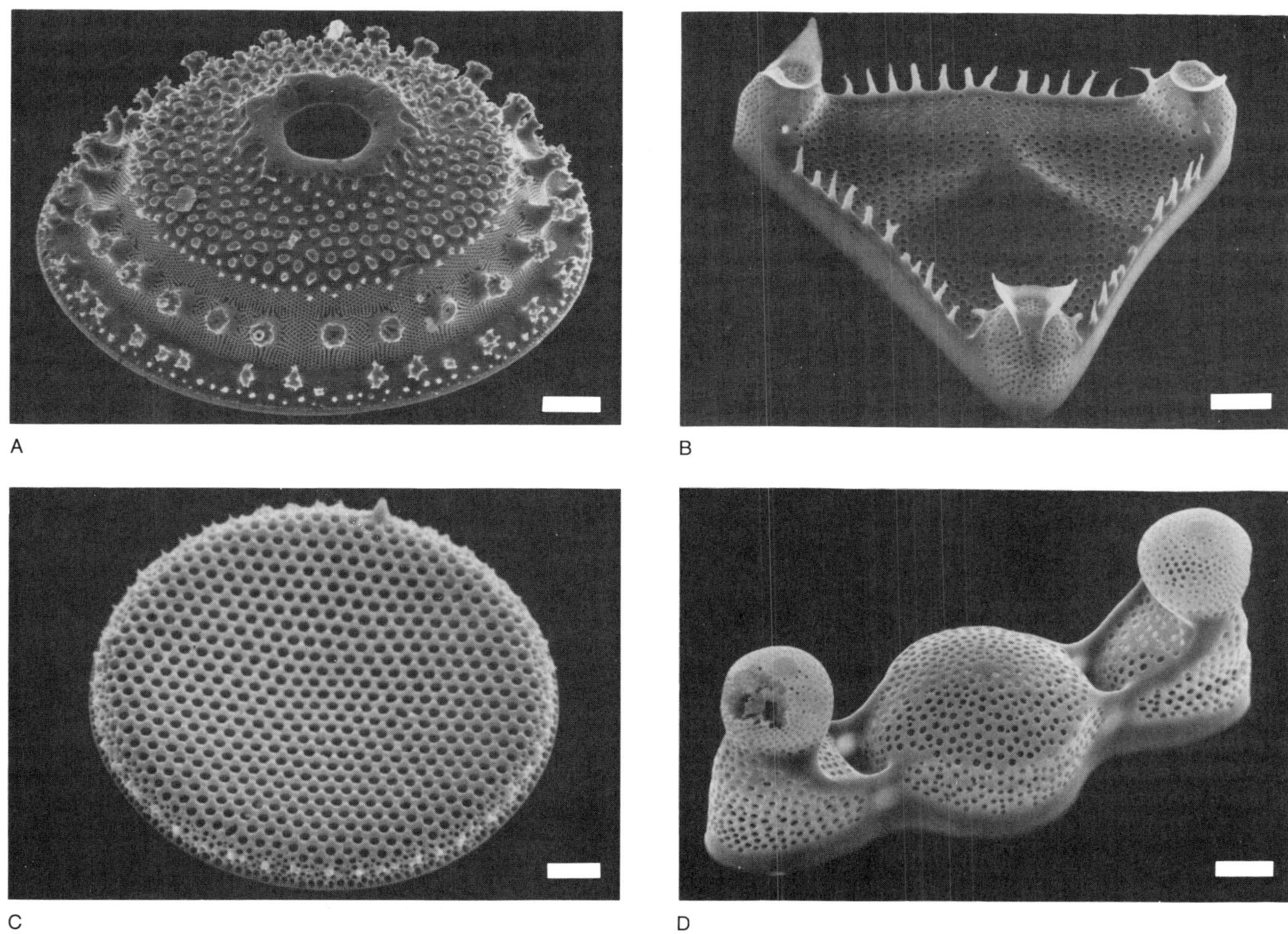

Figure 3–14
Ornate frustules of diatoms. Bar length is 50 microns.
(Scanning electron microscope photos courtesy of Union Oil Science and Technology Division, Brea, CA)

following death. The first appearance in the geologic column of an abundant and diversified shelly invertebrate record reflects the appearance (beginning of the Cambrian Period) of organisms with more easily fossilized hard parts composed of calcium carbonate, silica, or calcium phosphate. The development of such parts is responsible for the abundant and diverse fossil record of the invertebrates.

Sponges (Phylum Porifera)

Biologically, the sponges are the simplest invertebrates. Modern forms possess a saclike-to-globular body, covered with pores. Water intake through the pores provides nutrients; water outflow passes through a larger opening, the osculum (Fig. 3–18A). Although barely multicellular, the sponge cells nonetheless are specialized for various functions such as food digestion, construction of skeletal elements, and reproduction. Yet, each cell has remained so generalized that it is capable of respiration and excretion functions similar to those of the single-celled protistans. The biological relationship of sponges to other animals is not well understood, and apparently no other animal group evolved from this phylum. Modern sponges live attached to the sea floor and are found at all depths.

The skeletal elements of the sponges are either hard *spicules* (Fig. 3–18B) or a mass of organic fibers called *spongin.* The fossil record of the sponges is

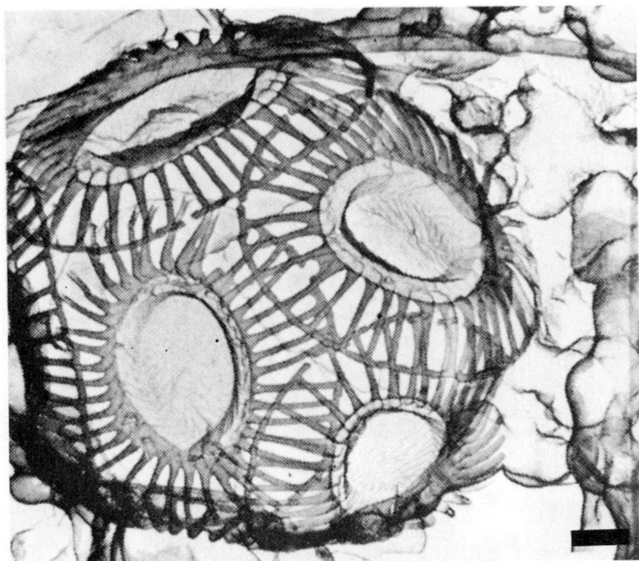

Figure 3–15
Scanning electron photomicrograph of coccolithoporid. Bar length is 25 microns.
(Photo courtesy of Union Oil Science and Technology Division, Brea, CA)

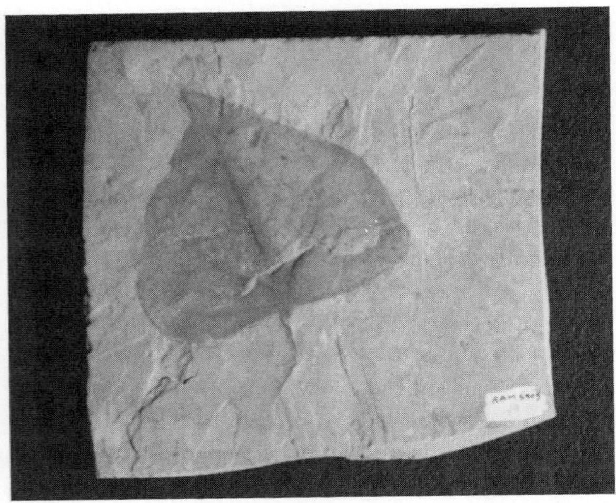

Figure 3–16
Plant leaf (specimen 12 cm in width, Eocene age, from Green River Formation, Wyoming).
(Specimen in Raymond Alf Museum, Webb School, Claremont, CA. Photo by J. Streng)

predominantly spicules, either isolated or in an interlocking mass. Spicules differ widely in form, from rod shaped to star shaped; some are composed of calcite and others are of silica. Siliceous sponge spicules have contributed to the formation of chert during various times in the geologic past. Several subdivisions of sponges are designated on the basis of the types of spicules present. The fossil record of the sponges is found in rocks of late Proterozoic to Holocene age.

Corals (Phylum Coelenterata)

The phylum Coelenterata includes a diverse array of organisms (e.g., corals, sea anemones, jellyfish) of which the corals have left the most important fossil record. The corals (Fig. 3–19A) possess relatively simple saclike bodies with a body wall that surrounds a digestive cavity, to which the mouth acts as both entrance and exit; there is no separate anus. Commonly the body is subdivided by radial, wall-like infoldings (mesenteries) that extend partway into the central digestive cavity. The small individual coral *polyp* secretes a calcareous external skeleton at its base and around the sides of its body. This skeleton reflects the internal body structure

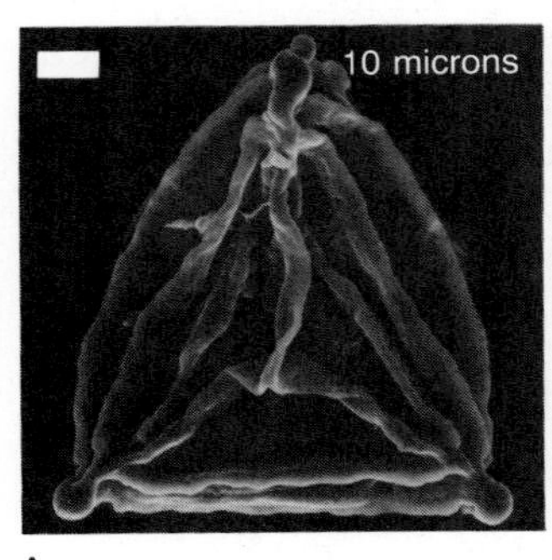

A

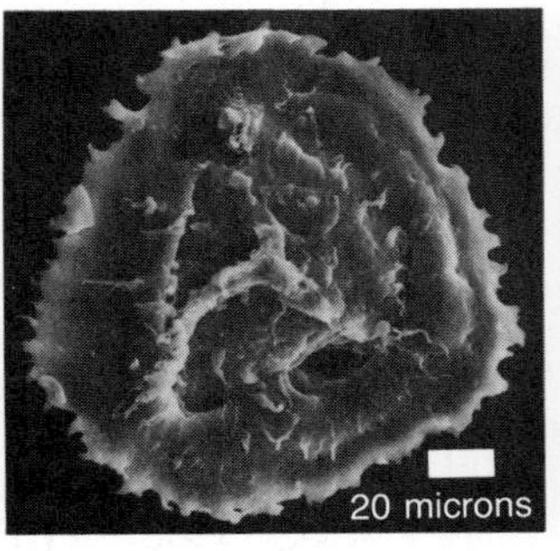

B

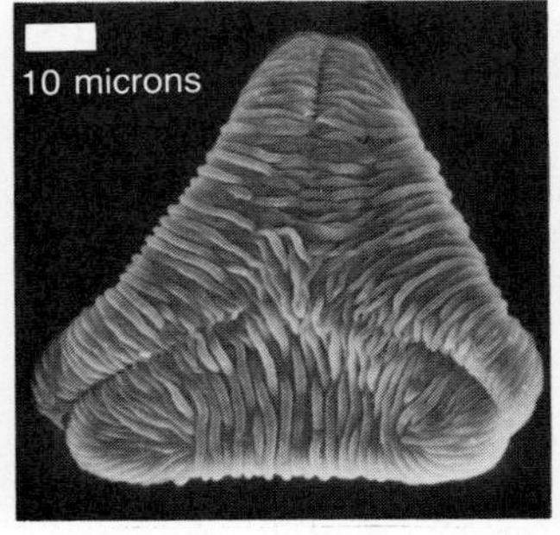

C

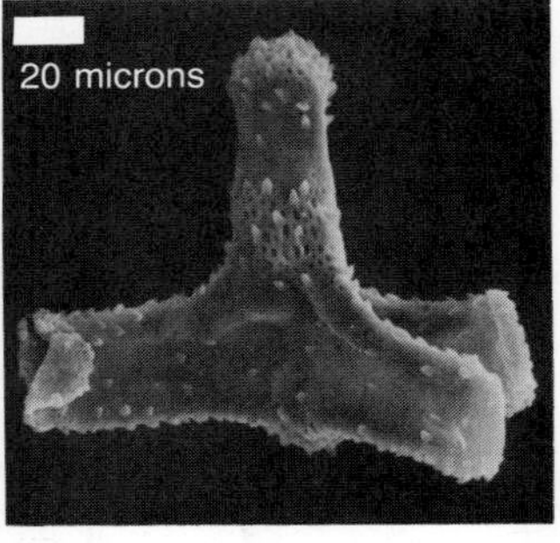

D

Figure 3–17
A, B. Plant spores. C, D. Angiosperm pollen grains.
(Scanning electron microscope photos courtesy of Union Oil Science and Technology Division, Brea, CA)

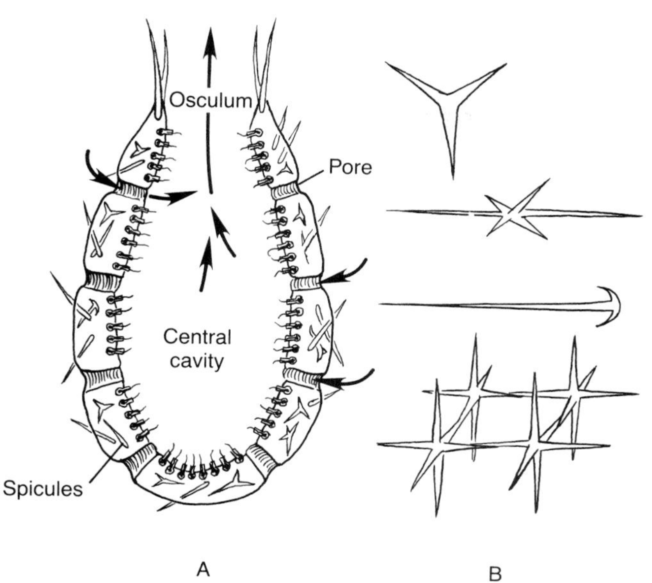

Figure 3–18

A. Basic anatomical features of the sponge include a perforated saclike body, water intake (nutrients) through the pores, and water outflow through the osculum. B. A variety of shapes of siliceous sponge spicules, the predominant sponge structure found in the fossil record. (After R. C. Moore, C. G. Lalicker, and A. G. Fischer, 1952, *Invertebrate Fossils,* Figs. 3–2(1), 3–3, p. 82, 84: McGraw-Hill Book Co., New York. Reproduced by permission of publisher)

with the presence of radiating plates called **septa** (singular, septum) that alternate in position with the internal mesenteries. The septa of the coral skeleton are distinctive features of this animal group.

Some individual coral polyps (such as the horn coral, Fig. 3–19B) secrete a relatively large single shell; others aggregate with many individuals to form a colony and secrete a larger colonial skeletal structure (Fig. 3–19C). Both the single-horn corals and the compound colonial corals are important elements of the fossil record: corals are known from Ordovician time to Holocene.

During several geologic periods corals were very abundant, and in association with other invertebrates and calcareous *algae,* formed massive *reef* structures similar to the present Great Barrier Reef of Australia. The discovery of one of these fossil reefs in sedimentary rocks provides a great deal of information about community life of the past.

An interesting type of fossil called a stromatoporoid was formerly included in the same phylum as the corals, but its biological affinity is uncertain. More recent classifications include stromatoporoids as a type of sponge in the phylum Porifera. The stromatoporoids are an extinct group with a fossil

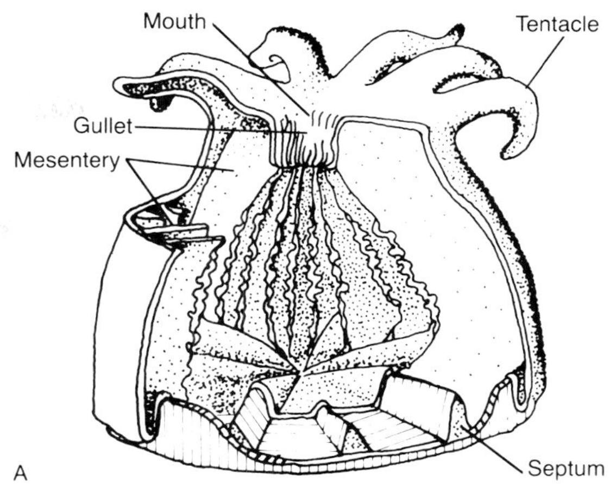

Figure 3–19

A. Basic anatomic structure of a coral polyp includes a saclike body with a mouth that is both entrance and exit for fluids, and infoldings of the body (mesenteries) separated by radiating skeletal plates (septa) B. Solitary "horn" coral. Note the radial septa at the top of each specimen. C. Thin section through a colonial coral showing the radiating septa plus the thin dark walls separating individual corals from one another. (A after R. C. Moore, C. G. Lalicker, and A. G. Fischer, 1952, *Invertebrate Paleontology,* Fig. 4–12(1), p. 117: McGraw-Hill Book Co., New York. Reproduced by permission of publisher; B and C, photos courtesy of National Museum of Natural History)

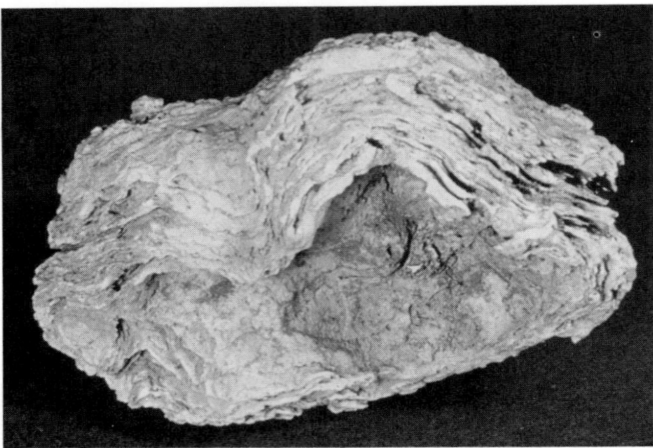

Figure 3–20
Fossil stromatoporoid sponge. Note the well-defined layered (stroma) structure. Although this specimen looks superficially like a stromatolite, the calcium carbonate laminations in the stromatoporoid specimen are part of the secreted skeletal structure; the layers in a stromatolite represent bound sediment. Length of specimen is approximately 15 cm.
(Photo courtesy of Wards Natural Science Establishment, Rochester, NY).

record extending from Cambrian to Cretaceous. The fossils are typically laminated masses composed of calcium carbonate, with vertical structures penetrating the horizontal layers (Fig. 3–20). On the upper surface of the mass are star-shaped features that may have housed polyps. Stromatoporoids, in association with corals, were major contributors to reefs during the Silurian and Devonian Periods, and they are found most commonly as large and irregular masses within the reef structure.

Archaeocyathids (Phylum Archaeocyatha)

Archaeocyathids are yet another fossil group of extinct organisms of uncertain biological affinity. Nothing is known of the soft-part anatomy of these enigmatic creatures, but the hard parts form two conelike structures, one inside the other (Fig. 3–21), connected by septa; both cones and septa are perforated.

Most archaeocyathid fossils are individual calcareous cones, but a few forms are colonial. Archaeocyathids are confined to marine rocks of Early and Middle Cambrian age. Because they possess some structural features similar to those of sponges, corals, and even calcareous green algae, archaeocyathids have been classified with each of these groups at various times. Some experts have

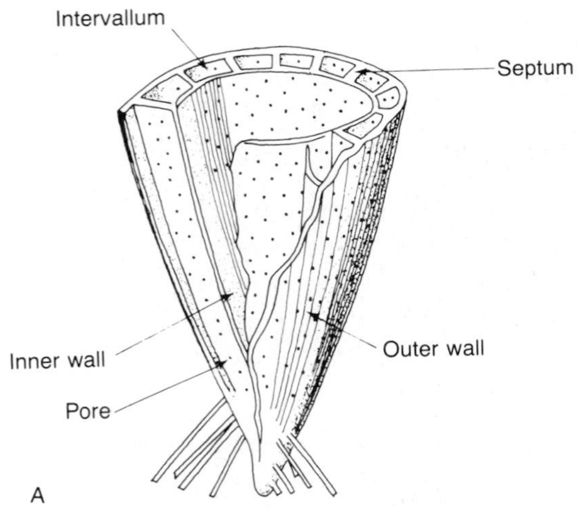

Figure 3–21
Archaeocyathids, extinct organisms of unknown biological affinity. A. Double-wall structure of the cone-shaped shell. B. Cross section of this structure, with visible septa (partitions) is illustrated by the fossil specimen (specimen 2 cm in width; Lower Cambrian, Australia).
(A after R. C. Moore, C. G. Lalicker, and A. G. Fischer, 1952, *Invertebrate Paleontology,* Fig. 3–10, p. 94: McGraw-Hill Book Co., New York. Reproduced by permission of publisher. B, photo by J. Streng)

recently suggested that they should be placed in the phylum Porifera. Archaeocyathids, like the stromatoporoids mentioned previously, are examples of extinct organisms that lack recognized living relatives. A "search for relatives" of these extinct groups is severely hampered by the lack of knowledge of soft-body anatomy, a factor that makes accurate biological classification difficult. Some other groups of extinct organisms also exemplify this problem, which focuses upon yet another element of incompleteness of our knowledge of the fossil record.

Bryozoans (Phylum Bryozoa)

Bryozoans are colonial organisms whose calcareous encrusting masses contributed to limestones during the Paleozoic Era. Their plantlike appearance (Fig. 3–22) has been responsible for their common designation as "moss animals." The individual bryozoan is microscopic in size, but this animal always aggregates into colonies, commonly many centimeters in diameter. The bryozoan soft-part anatomy is more complex than that of the previously discussed life forms. Bryozoa possess a U-shaped digestive tract (rather than the simple saclike cavity of the corals), with esophagus, stomach, and intestinal structures. Both a mouth and an anus are present.

Bryozoa are common in modern marine environments and commonly attach to rocks and seaweed along the shoreline. The significant bryozoan fossil record extends from Ordovician to Holocene.

Brachiopods (Phylum Brachiopoda)

Brachiopods also contributed to the formation of great volumes of limestone during the Paleozoic Era. Brachiopods were abundant animals in the warm, shallow Paleozoic seas, but in the modern marine realm they are rare in comparison to their earlier Phanerozoic abundance. Brachiopods have a stratigraphic range that .xtends from Cambrian to Holocene.

The anatomy of the brachiopod is more complex than that of the bryozoan. In addition to a digestive system, the brachiopod has a nervous system, reproductive organs, and well-developed sets of muscles (Fig. 3–23A). The possession of a *lophophore,* a ciliated armlike structure used in food-gathering, suggests that brachiopods and bryozoa evolved from a common ancestor. These soft parts are enclosed by two separate shells *(valves)* that protect the internal organs. Most shells are hinged at one end and open at the opposite end to allow water to circulate and to bring food to the animal. Protruding from the hinged end is a fleshy stalk, the *pedicle,* by which the animal is attached to the seafloor.

A

B

Figure 3–22
Diversity of form of bryozoans. A. Twig-shaped bryozoans in limestone slab (about natural size; Silurian). B. Distinctive spiral axes of *Archimedes* (Mississippian). Some of the lacy bryozoan fronds scattered on the limestone surface were attached to the spiral axes (slab about 15 cm across).
(Photos courtesy of National Museum of Natural History)

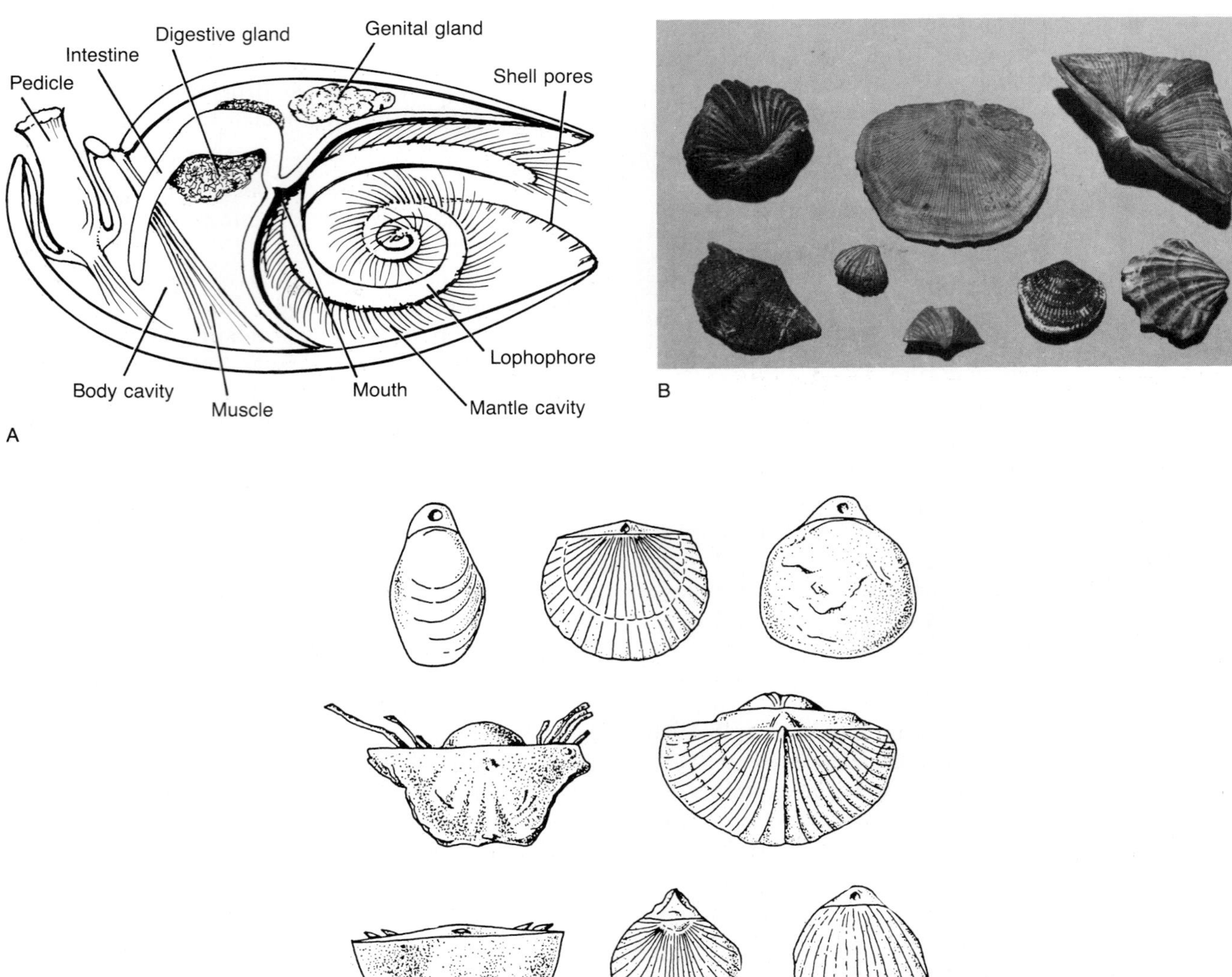

Figure 3–23
A. The complex body of the brachiopod is enclosed between two valves which protect the soft parts. Much of the mantle cavity inside the shell is occupied by the lophophore, the food-gathering structure. The lophophore consists of a pair of extendable "arms," the brachia. Note the position of the pedicle, the fleshy stalk by which the animal is attached to the sea floor. B. Brachiopods were diverse in size and shape (upper right specimen 5.5 cm in length). C. Brachiopods typically display bilateral symmetry, but the valves are unequal in form (unequivalved).
(A after R. C. Moore, C. G. Lalicker, and A. G. Fischer, 1952, *Invertebrate Paleontology*, Fig. 6–3, p. 199: McGraw-Hill Book Co., New York. Reproduced by permission of publisher. B, photo by J. Streng. C, from N. Gary Lane, 1986, *Life of the Past*, 2d ed., Fig. 11–5, p. 174, Merrill Publishing Co., Columbus, OH. Reproduced with permission of publisher)

Brachiopods include two major groups, one of which secretes a calcium *phosphate* shell (class Inarticulata), and the other a calcium *carbonate* shell (class Articulata). The shell has been very diverse through the Phanerozoic and has included smooth, ribbed, and spiny forms as well as those with short or long hinge lines, and convex and concave shapes (Fig. 3–23B). Despite this shell diversity, brachiopods are readily recognized by the facts that the two enclosing valves are different in shape and size from one another (unequivalved) and each individual valve is *bilaterally symmetrical* (the two halves of a single valve are mirror images—Fig. 3–23C).

Molluscs (Phylum Mollusca)

Molluscs make up an animal group that contains many familiar modern examples such as clams, snails, octopi, and squids (Fig. 3–24). Other important members of the phylum, such as ammonoids (Fig. 3–28), are extinct. The molluscs are one of the most significant groups of fossils, and constitute a *major* part of the marine shell-bearing shelf fauna that is favored by the bias of the fossil record. It is a record that extends from Cambrian to Holocene.

Molluscs are so numerous and diverse that it is difficult to pick out a single representative, or even a few, to illustrate this important group. The soft anatomy of molluscs is more complex than that of the brachiopods, and includes internal organs for the functions of digestion, circulation, and excretion, as well as better-developed nervous, reproductive, and muscle systems. A characteristic molluscan feature is the *mantle,* which consists of two fleshy flaps that fold together to form a cavity (mantle cavity) within which the soft body mass is suspended. Body organization includes a fleshy mass that serves as a crawling foot for snails and clams; a well-defined head, with eyes, characterizes the cephalopod molluscs (e.g., octopi, squids). Most molluscs share the characteristic of an external, calcareous shell that is secreted by the mantle, but some types of cephalopods, such as the octopus, have an internal shell. Modern shell-bearing molluscs are commonly referred to as "shellfish."

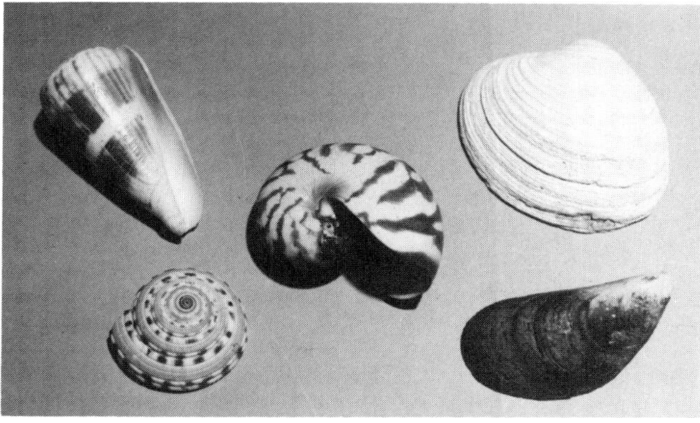

Figure 3–24
The molluscs are an abundant and diverse group. Examples of molluscs include (left) two forms of coiled gastropods or snails; (center) the coiled *Nautilus* cephalopod (specimen 6 cm in width); and (right) two forms of bivalves or clams (the lower specimen is a mussel).
(Photo by J. Streng)

Molluscs show a great range of environmental adaptations to a variety of marine, terrestrial, and freshwater habitats. Some molluscs live attached (e.g., oysters), some are active swimmers (e.g., squids, octopi), many are crawlers (e.g., snails), and many are burrowers (e.g., clams). Because of their tremendous abundance and diversity and their importance as fossils, three separate molluscan classes require closer examination: pelecypods (bivalves), gastropods (univalves), and cephalopods (swimmers).

Bivalve molluscs (also called *pelecypods*) are characterized by a body enclosed within a bivalved shell; common examples are clams, mussels, oysters, and scallops. Typically, the two valves are the same shape and size (equivalved), but individual valves are *not* bilaterally symmetrical (Fig. 3–25). Recall that the two valves of the brachiopod shell have an opposite relationship: the individual valves are bilaterally symmetrical, but the two valves have different shapes and sizes (see Fig. 3–23C). However, not *all* bivalve molluscs are symmetrical. Those that have adopted a sedentary life style, such as an attachment to the sea floor (e.g., oysters), most commonly have unequal, nonsymmetrical valves. This condition results from the mollusc resting or reclining on one valve, or from one valve being cemented to rock or to another shell.

An extreme example of this asymmetry is exhibited by the extinct *rudist* bivalves of the Jurassic and Cretaceous. These forms had a lower elongate coral-like valve, and an upper flattened lidlike valve (see Fig. 3–26). Bivalve mollusc shells are positioned on the left and right sides of the body and are hinged along the *dorsal* (back) margin. The ventral (bottom) unhinged margin of the valves opens to allow for protrusion of the large muscular foot with which many mobile types of bivalves crawl, as well as to allow nutrient waters to enter the shell.

There is great diversity in the mode of life within the class: some forms actively burrow into the bottom sediment; some bore into wood or rock; some forms are cemented to the bottom, while others recline; many are tethered to the bottom by organic threads called a *byssus;* and a few even propel themselves through the water by rapidly opening and closing the valves. Perhaps more than for any other group of invertebrates, this range of life habits among the bivalve molluscs is faithfully reflected

A

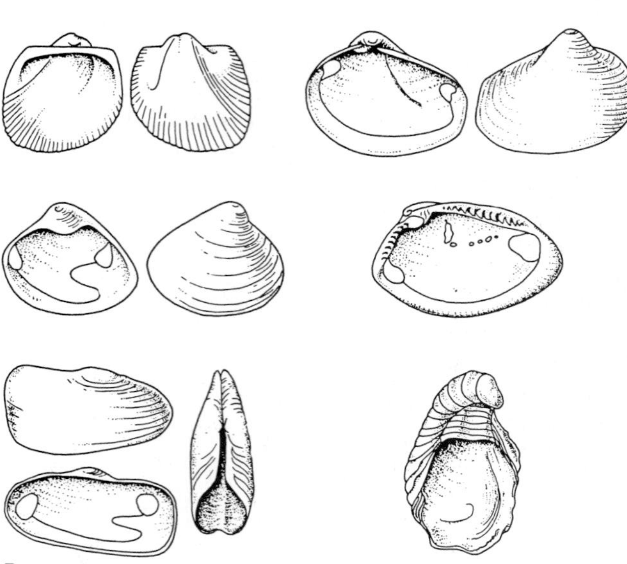
B

Figure 3–25
Bivalve molluscs. A. Specimens illustrate the asymmetrical shape of each valve and the equivalve nature of the shell, whereby both valves are mirror images of each other. Specimens are 7 cm in length. B. Specimens illustrate some of the diversity of shell form in the bivalve molluscs. The more elongate shells are well adapted for a burrowing mode of life.
(A, photo courtesy of Wards Natural Science Establishment, Rochester, NY; B, from N. Gary Lane, 1986, *Life of the Past,* 2d ed., Merrill Publishing Company, Fig. 11–14, p. 182. Reproduced with permission of the publisher)

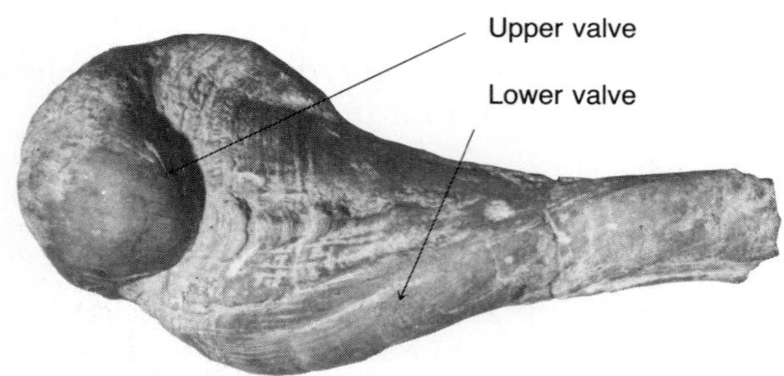

Figure 3–26
Upper Cretaceous rudist bivalve illustrating nonsymmetry of some aberrant forms. Note the elongate lower valve and the lidlike upper valve (specimen 20 cm in length; Baja California, del Norte, Mexico).
(Photo by J. Streng)

A

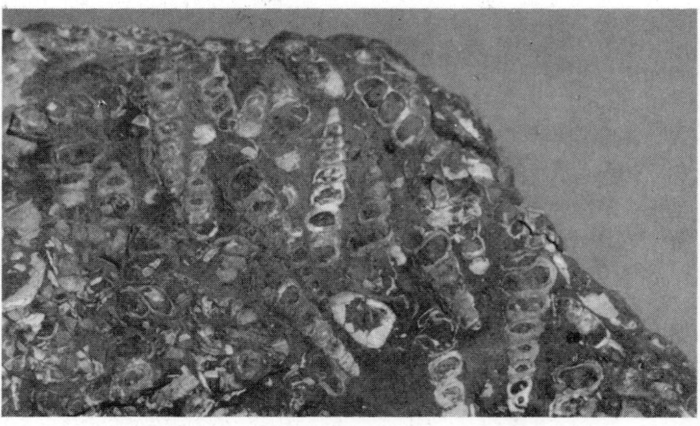
B

in shell shape, thickness, and ornamentation. Bivalve mollusc fossils are found in rocks ranging in age from Cambrian to Holocene, but are most prevalent in strata of the Mesozoic and Cenozoic.

Gastropod molluscs (snails) are *univalved* forms whose bodies are enclosed by a single, spirally coiled shell. Gastropod shells exhibit a vast number of shapes and sizes (Fig. 3–27), including low-spired

Figure 3–27
A. Variety of size and form of the modern gastropod shell; note high-spired form (left, specimen 9 cm in length) and low-spired cone shell (right, specimen 7 cm in length). The muscular foot of the gastropod protrudes from the aperture visible on several of the specimens. B. Upper Cretaceous fossil gastropods from southern California (specimens 2–3 cm in length).
(Photos by J. Streng)

to high-spired forms, those with many whorls or only a few whorls, those ornamented with ribs, knobs, or spines, or those that are unornamented.

The gastropod shell contains only a single chamber into which the animal withdraws its body completely. The body may be protruded (in a manner similar to that of the bivalve) as a muscular foot on which the animal crawls. Anatomically, gastropods have a distinct head with a pair of eyes and a pair of feelers. They also possess a mouth with a strip of material holding filelike teeth (the *radula*). Carnivorous snails are able to drill with their radula directly through the shells of other organisms to gain access to the soft body parts within. Many Cenozoic fossil clams have been found with a smooth circular hole penetrating the shell, a sure sign of the cause of death! Gastropods have a Cambrian-to-Holocene fossil record, and like the bivalve molluscs, were most abundant and diverse during the Mesozoic and Cenozoic.

Cephalopod molluscs, unlike bivalves and gastropods, are swimming forms. These exclusively marine molluscs have the ability to jet-propel themselves through the sea by the expulsion of water from a nozzlelike tube. Because of this ability to swim, cephalopods are agile and are active predators, rather than being confined to slow crawling on the sea floor or passively drifting with currents. The cephalopods possess several other distinctive features: highly developed eyes, tentacles commonly covered with sucker discs, and the ability to eject inky fluid as a defense or escape mechanism. Some modern squids have attained a length of 16 meters and are the largest known invertebrate animals.

Living cephalopods are relatively few in number (octopus, squid, chambered nautilus), but ancient cephalopods were abundant, diverse, and rapidly evolving, and thus serve as important fossils for biozonation and correlation. Most of the important fossil forms had external shells similar to those of their modern-day distant cousin, the chambered nautilus (see Figs. 3–24 and 3–28A).

Most extinct *ammonoids* (Fig. 3–28B), for example, lived in a symmetrical flatly coiled shell that was divided into a series of chambers by *septa.* The animal secreted larger and larger septa as it grew, and the adult body occupied only the large end (living chamber) of the shell. A fleshy tube, the *siphuncle,* extended back through the septal walls, allowing the living animal to maintain communication with the older unoccupied chambers. This communication involved the partial-to-complete filling of some or all of the unoccupied chambers with various gas-fluid mixtures that aided importantly in movement through the water.

In the cephalopod shell, distinct lines, called **sutures,** represent the contact between the septa and

A

B

Figure 3–28
A. Interior of the modern chambered *Nautilus*. Living chamber is at top; note the septa that partition the shell's interior into the earlier-used chambers; a fleshy tube, the siphuncle, extended from the living chamber back through the projection on each septum into the older chambers (maximum width of specimen 13 cm). B. Fossil ammonoid cephalopods illustrating ornamental "ribs" (right) and a complex suture (left; specimen 12 cm in diameter).
(Photos by J. Streng)

the inner wall of the shell. Cephalopod sutures range in form from a simple, slightly curved line in the *nautiloids*, to various types of more complex crenulated designs in the *ammonoids*. This feature is significant in classification of the cephalopods below the rank of class. One group of extinct cephalopods, the squidlike *belemnites*, secreted internal, calcareous, cigar-shaped shells similar to the cuttlebone of the modern cuttlefish.

The geologic range of the cephalopod molluscs extends from Late Cambrian to Holocene, but the extinct ammonoids are confined to rocks of Devonian to Cretaceous age. The ability of the ammonoids to disperse over wide geographic areas, coupled with the evolutionary development of many distinctively sutured forms during the Mesozoic Era, makes them unsurpassed in their usefulness as guides to narrow time subdivisions (chronozones) within rocks of this age (see Chapters 6, 12, and 13).

Arthropods (Phylum Arthropoda)

Arthropods are another group that contains many familiar living forms: crabs, lobsters, shrimp, insects, and spiders. These familiar members, however, have not left as abundant or as significant a fossil record as an extinct class of arthropods, the *trilobites*. As biologically advanced invertebrates, the trilobites are especially important because they developed the ability to secrete a chitinous exoskeleton very early in the Phanerozoic. In fact, the first appearance in the rock record of trilobites previously had been used to define and recognize the boundary between rocks of Precambrian and Cambrian age in some areas. Trilobites are used to subdivide the Cambrian System into series and stages.

Arthropods, in a sense, are the most successful of all animals, because they are the most abundant organisms on Earth—remember that this phylum includes insects!—and because they live in a greater variety of habitats than do the members of any other phylum. As the term arthropod ("jointed" + "leg") implies, the various subgroups in this diversified phylum are characterized by segmented bodies and jointed limbs. Arthropods also have a *chitinous* dorsal exoskeleton that covers the body and is molted as the individual organism grows. Many trilobite fossils probably represent discarded molted exoskeletons. Variation in the arthropod phylum is expressed by the nature of the segmentation; by specialization of appendages; by differences in nervous systems, respiratory systems (marine to air-breathing forms), and other systems; and by differences in locomotion (swimming to flying forms).

The trilobite body is divisible into three sections: *cephalon* (head), *thorax*, and *pygidium* (tail) (Fig. 3–29). In addition, the entire body is further divisible into three longitudinal lobes formed by grooves separating a central portion (axial lobe) from two lateral areas (pleural lobes); hence the derivation of the name *trilob*ite.

Because trilobites are extinct and have no direct living descendants, our knowledge about the soft parts of the animal is incomplete. Sufficient information has been determined from fossilized remains to indicate the presence of well-developed eyes in some trilobites, to determine the placement of soft parts, and to detect the areas of muscle attachment to the exoskeleton. It is noteworthy that trilobites are complex and highly developed invertebrates, and yet they are the major component of some of the oldest Paleozoic faunas. Many paleontologists believe the early appearance of biologically complex trilobites in the abundant Cambrian

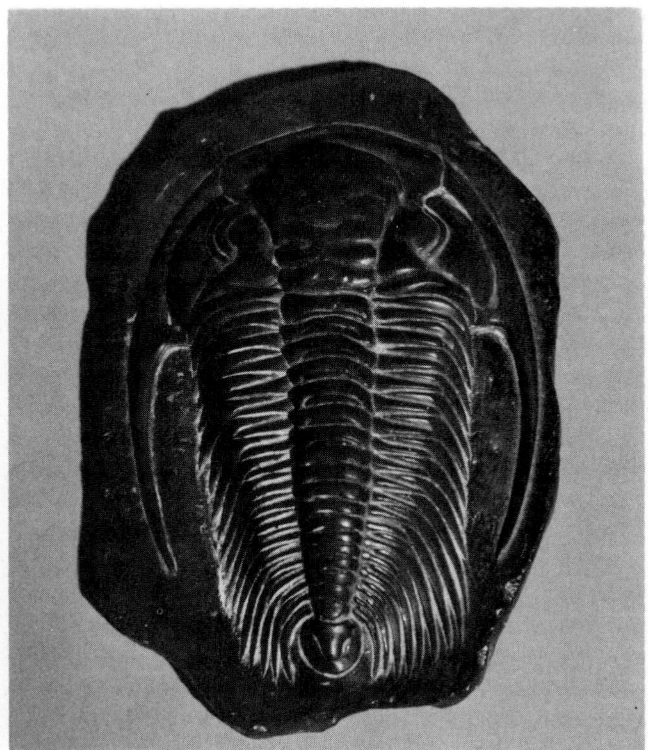

Figure 3–29
Model of a Middle Cambrian trilobite *(Paradoxides harlani)*, an important Paleozoic arthropod fossil. The distinct trilobed structure of the animal gives it its name. In addition, it has a three-part division into cephalon (head), thorax, and pygidium (tail). Note the crescent-shaped eyes located on either side of the central, globular part of the cephalon (specimen about 16 cm in length).
(Photo by J. Streng)

fossil record provides evidence of an "explosive" (dramatically rapid) evolutionary development of multicellular life forms at the beginning of Paleozoic time (see Chapters 9 and 10). Fossil arthropods occur in rocks of Cambrian-to-Holocene age, but the important trilobites are found only in rocks of Paleozoic age, and are especially significant in strata of the Cambrian and Ordovician Systems.

Echinoderms (Phylum Echinodermata)

Echinoderms are a diversified, exclusively marine group that includes starfish, sand dollars, sea urchins (echinoids), and sea "lilies" (crinoids). The echinoderms are distinctive in several aspects: The body is commonly globular; most forms exhibit *pentameral* (five-rayed) symmetry; and the "shell" is actually an internally secreted series of calcareous plates that fit together like a tile mosaic. After the death of the organisms, the plates commonly separate and become dispersed in sediments, although many shells have been preserved intact.

Because the echinoderm phylum contains so many classes of organisms, it is divided into a number of *subphyla;* two are discussed here because of their importance in the fossil record. The subphylum Crinozoa includes forms that are most commonly attached to the sea floor *(sessile).* They have a structure typified by the crinoids (Fig. 3–30), which have a stem, a cup-shaped body, and a series of branching arms extending upward from the body. The long, flexible stems allow the crinoids to bend and wave in an almost plantlike manner (thus the designation sea "lily") in the ocean currents.

Although locally abundant, crinoids are not prominent members of the fauna of modern oceans; they are best known from an extensive fossil record. Some living crinoids are brightly colored in hues of purple, red, yellow, and brown, and have changed their mode of life from predominantly sessile during the Paleozoic and Mesozoic to *vagrant* in the Cenozoic. Although their fossil record extends from Ordovician to Holocene, crinoids were most abundant during Paleozoic time, when they formed abundant gardenlike masses on the warm, shallow seafloor (Fig. 3–30). Some Paleozoic carbonate rocks are so full of crinoid fragments that they are referred to as crinoidal limestones.

Subphylum Echinozoa includes forms that generally are globular and without arms or a stem, as typified by echinoids (sea urchins and sand dollars, see Fig. 3–31). Within the subphylum there are some sessile forms, but most are mobile and move sluggishly along the sea floor; some burrow into the sediments. The pentameral symmetry characteristic of the echinoderms in general is well illustrated by the arrangement of plates on the sea urchins. Fossil echinoids are found in rocks of Ordovician to Holocene age, but are most diverse and abundant in strata of the Mesozoic and Cenozoic.

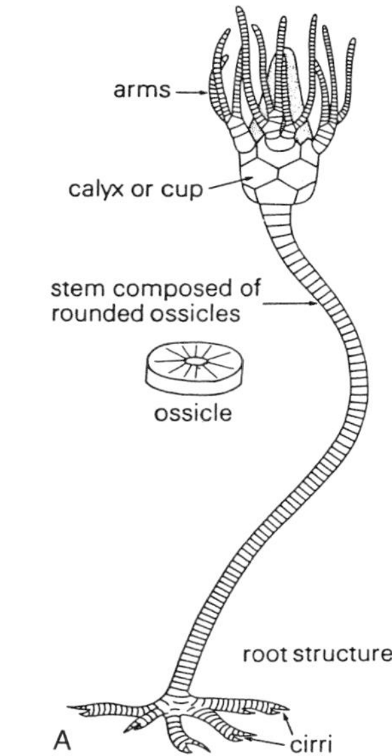

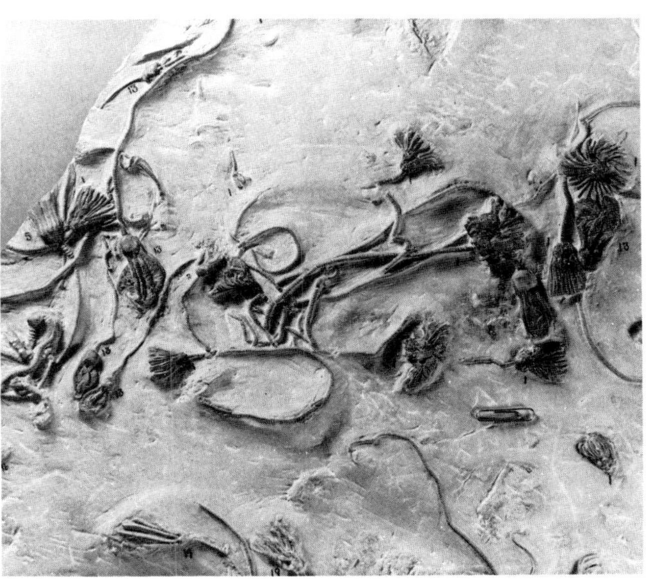

Figure 3–30
A. Crinoids illustrate the sessile (meaning attached to the seafloor) form of echinoderm (subphylum Crinozoa). The crinoid body is enclosed in the cup-shaped calyx. B. Complete fossil crinoids on a slab of Mississippian limestone from LeGrand, Iowa (scale indicated by paper clip).
(A, from Richard Moody, 1977, *The Fossil World*, p. 57, Chartwell Books, Inc.; B, photo courtesy of National Museum of Natural History)

Figure 3–31
Modern sea urchins illustrate the vagrant (mobile) form of echnoid echinoderm, and the radial symmetry (often five-rayed) characteristically displayed by members of this phylum (note petal appearance on specimen on left; specimen is about 11 cm in width).
(Photo by J. Streng)

A

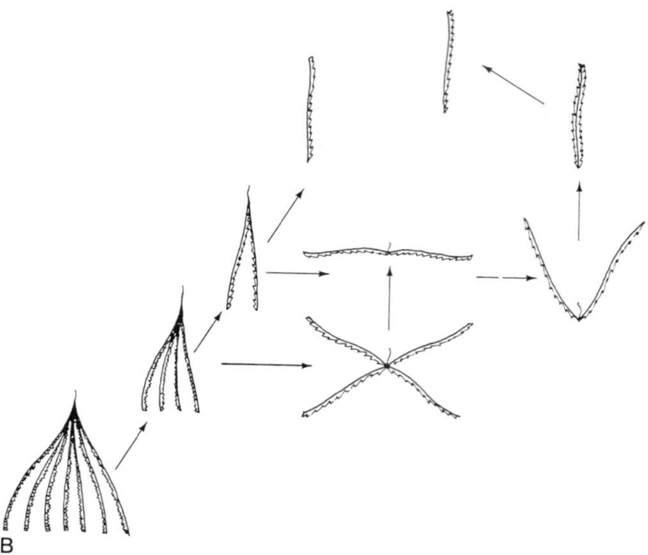

B

Figure 3–32
A. Graptolites are often preserved as carbonaceous films on the bedding surfaces of dark shales, as illustrated by these Middle Ordovician specimens from Canada. On the portion of branching colonies shown, each barblike projection housed an individual; graptolites occur in colonies. B. Changes in form of colonies in planktonic graptolites during the Ordovician and Silurian, showing the two major evolutionary trends: reduction in number of branches, and rotation of the branches.
(A, photo courtesy of National Museum of National History; B, from N. Gary Lane, 1986, *Life of the Past,* 2d ed., Fig. 10–11, p. 161: Merrill Publishing Co. Reproduced with permission of the publisher)

Graptolites (Phylum Hemichordata)

Graptolites are extinct, colonial, floating *(planktonic)* organisms that lived during part of the Paleozoic Era (Cambrian-Mississippian). During that time they were geographically widespread and left a broadly dispersed, but rapidly changing, fossil record which is useful in correlating rock units in various parts of the world. The graptolites (Fig. 3–32) are an excellent example of organisms preserved as carbonaceous films; they occur predominantly as carbonaceous impressions on the bedding surfaces of dark shales. Apparently the colonies floated into an area, died, and settled into the dark muds in an *anaerobic* (oxygen-poor) bottom environment; decay and scavenging were restricted under these conditions.

Graptolites also provide another good example of the problems encountered in attempting to assign some extinct organisms to their proper place in the scheme of biological classification: their biological affinities are not known with certainty. The structure of each graptolite colony was composed of many small cuplike features arranged along branches, each cup housing an individual animal. Living organisms most similar in structure to the extinct graptolites belong to a group known as *hemichordates* ("half chordate"), exemplified by the living *pterobranchs.* Because the hemichordates are characterized by the presence of a dorsal stiffened-rod structure called a notochord, they have been classified as intermediate between the invertebrate and vertebrate condition. It is possible, therefore, that the graptolites represent an extinct group of these intermediate forms.

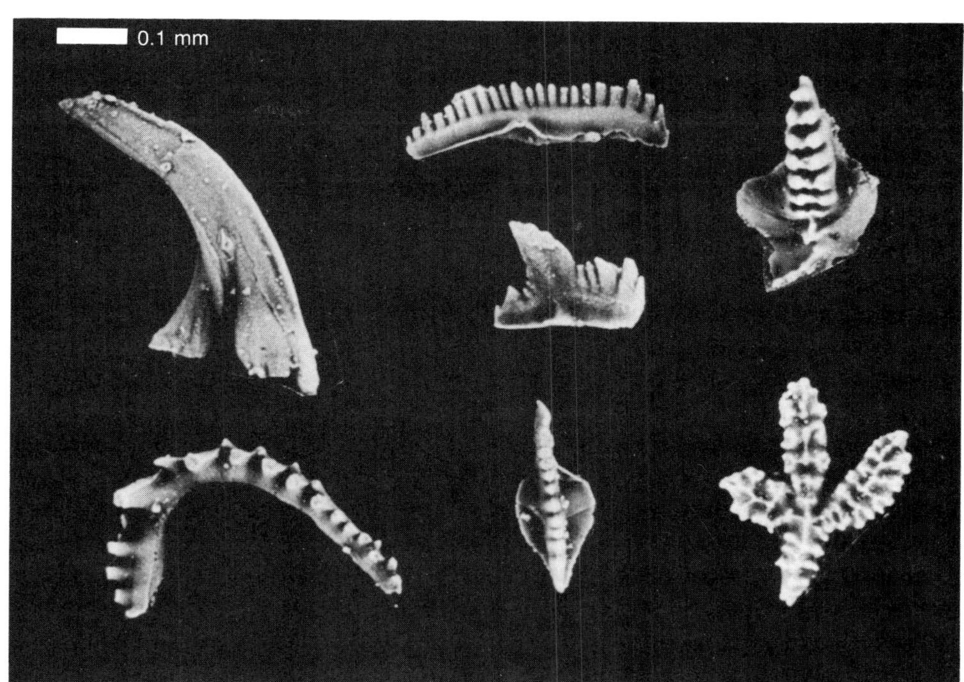

Figure 3–33
Conodont diversity illustrated by Devonian forms: conical form (upper left), bars with denticles, (lower left and upper center), simple platform (lower center), complex platform (right). Conodonts, like graptolites, are of uncertain biological affinity, but are important fossils in dating and correlating Paleozoic rocks. In spite of great diversity of form, each conodont has a toothlike appearance.
(Photo courtesy of Michael A. Murphy, University of California–Riverside)

Conodonts (Phylum unknown)

Conodonts (Fig. 3–33) are another excellent example of an extinct group of organisms having uncertain biological affinities. These tiny toothlike structures have a phosphatic composition that is similar to that of vertebrate bone; however, no similar structure is known to exist in any living or fossil vertebrate. At various times, conodonts have been linked to fishes, gastropods, worms, crustaceans, cephalopods, and most recently, to an eel-like vertebrate. In spite of the problem of the origin of the conodonts, they are important fossils for dating rocks of middle-to-late Paleozoic age. The stratigraphic range of conodonts extends from Cambrian through Triassic.

Vertebrates (Phylum Chordata)

True vertebrates, or animals with backbones, include fish, amphibians, reptiles, birds, and mammals (Fig. 3–34). In addition to the backbone (vertebral column), which is a supporting structure composed of calcium phosphate, the internal vertebrate skeleton typically possesses paired limbs (fins, wings, legs) and a rib cage. Yet another important skeletal feature of the vertebrates is the skull, housing sense organs and a well-developed brain.

Vertebrates make their first known appearance in the fossil record as primitive jawless fish in

Figure 3–34
Examples of vertebrates. Fish, amphibian (frog), reptile (alligator), mammal (man, dog), and bird all share the common structural feature of a vertebral column, the backbone. There is, as illustrated, *great* diversity of form, habitat, and life style within the phylum.

rocks of Late Cambrian age, and they occur in the fossil record throughout the rest of the Phanerozoic. Vertebrates are probably the most dramatic of fossils, and arguably hold the most fascination for humans, perhaps because we are vertebrates ourselves. Who has not been enthralled by a reconstructed dinosaur skeleton in a museum? Certainly such displays have kindled the imagination of writers and moviemakers. Although dramatic and sometimes spectacular, the vertebrate fossils are, nonetheless, comparatively rare and not generally as complete as invertebrate fossils. Many vertebrates live in terrestrial and aerial environments that are not conducive to preservation, and the vertebrate skeleton easily disarticulates and becomes scattered following the death of an individual. The bias of the fossil record tells us that vertebrates have not been selectively preserved as readily as invertebrates.

Mammals, the biological group to which humans belong, are represented by many fossil forms in rocks of Cenozoic age. *Homo sapiens* is a very recent mammal member of the animal kingdom, although there is a fossil record extending back several million years. Human fossils are found most commonly in deposits of Pleistocene age in Africa. Some of the most exciting discoveries in paleontology since the 1950s have been geological and archaeological finds in the Olduvai Gorge of East Africa.

The foregoing has been a brief overview of life forms that have left an important fossil record. The preservation of the spectrum of life forms, from the lowly monerans to the highly developed vertebrates, has been accomplished in many different ways, dependent upon the physical, chemical, and biological conditions that prevailed in the death and burial environments. As we have viewed the parade, however, we also have seen that some fossil forms are of unknown affinity and present problems in classification.

Taxonomic Problems

Paleontologists commonly differ in opinion on the classification of some fossils. Should a fossil in question be "lumped" with a particular previously described taxon, or should this fossil be assigned to another taxon, or perhaps even to a new one? The assignment of fossils to particular taxa on the basis of their morphology has involved the judgment of paleontologists for more than two hundred years—since the time of Linnaeus. However, Linnaeus was a creationist, and assumed that each species was an immutable, nonevolving entity. We still use the Linnaean classification scheme, but the interpretation of the evolutionary thread of continuity that binds the various taxonomic levels is vastly different from the more simplistic Linnaean concept of static taxa which are differentiated solely on the basis of morphologic similarity, much as one would classify coins or barbed wire.

A good, meaningful classification of fossil organisms should attempt, to the full limits of knowledge available, to reflect the evolutionary biologic relationships among the organisms being classified. These evolutionary relationships (phylogeny) are not indicated by morphology alone, but are also dependent upon stratigraphic position and geographic location of the specimens. When a fossil is classified, in effect a statement is made about its evolutionary relationships; i.e., classification is a statement of how we think the evolution of that particular taxon proceeded. There still remains, however, the problem of proper assignment of some extinct taxonomic groups such as graptolites, conodonts, archaeocyathids, and stromatoporoids. Regardless of differences of opinion in paleontologic judgments, the classification scheme used for fossils has been found to be a workable one.

Some Uses of Fossils

Paleoecology

Perhaps the most important aspect of the fossil record concerns the *stratigraphic* distribution of fossils and how they can be used to subdivide sequences of strata, correlate geographically separated sequences of strata, and provide the basis for the Phanerozoic time scale. Concepts and principles of *biostratigraphy* will be discussed in Chapters 5 and 6. For now, let us focus attention upon the environmental and geographic controls on fossil organisms—the kinds of controls that have strongly influenced our biostratigraphic record.

Organisms are influenced in their stratigraphic distribution not only by evolutionary changes through time (Chapter 4), but also by environmental factors. Marine bottom-dwelling organisms are limited in their geographic distribution by environmental parameters (Table 3–5). Swimming organisms, such as fish and cephalopods, or floating forms, such as graptolites, are less affected by bottom environmental conditions. These animals generally are more widely dispersed than bottom dwellers; consequently their fossils are more useful for time-stratigraphic correlation. Recall that the

Table 3–5
Environmental parameters in a marine ecosystem

Physical Parameters	Biologic Parameters
Water temperature	Birth and death rates of organisms
Water composition	Size and number of organisms (biomass)
Salinity	Food supply and nutrients
Dissolved gases (oxygen, nitrogen)	Mode of life (planktonic, nektonic, benthic, sessile, or vagrant)
Trace elements present	
Water depth	
Light conditions	
Pressure	
Turbulence (energy level)	
Turbidity	
Upwelling currents	
Type of substrate (material forming the sea floor)	
Topography of the sea floor	

great bulk of the fossil record is composed of shell-bearing, shallow-marine, *bottom-dwelling* invertebrates; thus most fossils have the potential for providing information about ancient environments.

Paleoecology is that branch of paleontology that is specifically concerned with the study of relationships of fossil organisms to each other and to their ancient environments. It involves applications of principles of modern ecology, thus invoking the concept of *actualism,* whereby studies of living populations of organisms and their interactions with environments provide insight into ancient rocks and their contained fossils. Fundamental concepts in ecologic-paleoecologic study are the **habitat,** which is the specific environment ("address") occupied by a species; the **niche,** which is the specific role ("profession") or lifestyle of the species; and the **community,** which is an association of organisms living in close proximity and having a tendency to be found together. Habitats commonly are occupied by a number of species, with each species having a distinct niche, and each making a contribution to the interrelated activities of the community. Both the living species and the nonliving components of the environment interact with one another to form an **ecosystem.**

In a marine ecosystem such as that illustrated in Figure 3–35, three basic types of organisms typically are recognized. The **benthos** is composed of organisms *(benthic)* that live on or within the seafloor. Benthic forms living *on* the bottom *(substrate)* are the **epifauna,** some of which *(vagrant)* are able to move about and some of which *(sessile)* are attached to or recline on the substrate. Benthic forms that burrow into the substrate make up the **infauna.**

The **plankton** are organisms *(planktonic)* that float freely in the water; planktonic plants and photosynthetic protists are *phytoplankton* and planktonic protists and animals are *zooplankton.* The swimming organisms are referred to as the **nekton;** these organisms (nektonic) are able to control their own movements in the water. The relationships among the phytoplankton, the zooplankton, the nekton, and the benthos, and the relationships between these groups and the physical environment, form complex patterns.

Species existing in communities are fundamental links in **food chains,** which represent the feeding sequence from primary **producers** through various levels of **consumers.** An example of one simplified food chain existing in oceanic environments today is indicated in Figure 3–36A. This example shows a food chain beginning with phytoplankton, which utilize materials in the environment, plus sunlight, to photosynthesize their own food and energy (i.e., use the process of *photosynthesis*). These producer organisms are called **autotrophs;** they have played a significant role in the history of the atmosphere and the biosphere. Microscopic-sized autotrophs that float in the photic zone of the oceans are consumed by organisms on the next higher step of the chain, and these in turn are consumed by other organisms.

The consumer organisms at each step are **heterotrophs** and must ingest their food. Among the marine invertebrates, for example, *filter* (suspension) *feeders* obtain food by filtering quantities of water across membranes to trap small organisms or organic particles; *deposit* (detritus) *feeders* obtain food by ingesting sediment and selectively removing the organic material; *grazers* ingest plants or

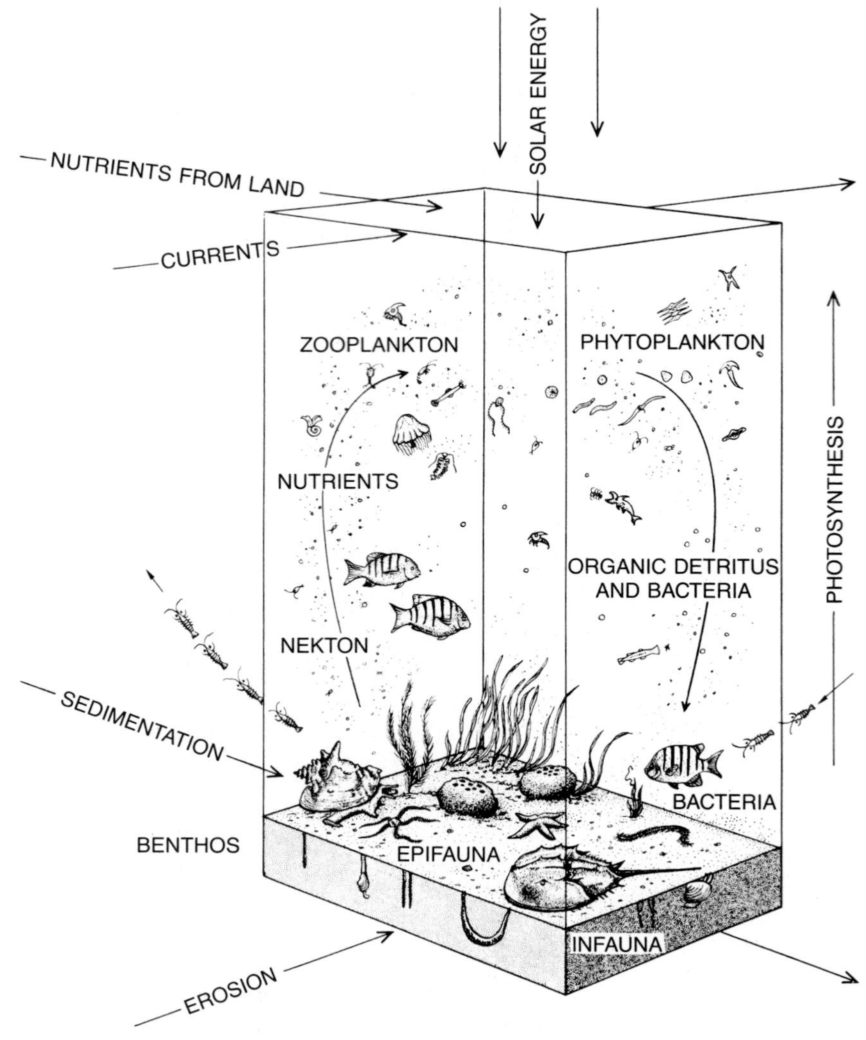

Figure 3–35
Elements of a marine ecosystem (see text for definition of terms).
(Based on graphic by T. L. Chase in R. L. Anstey and T. L. Chase, 1979, *Environments Through Time,* 2d ed., Fig. 3.9, p. 27: Burgess Publishing Co., Minneapolis. Original source is J. W. Hedgpeth, Marine Ecology, *in* R. W. Fairbridge, ed., 1966, *The Encyclopedia of Oceanography,* Van Nostrand Reinhold Co. Inc., New York. Reproduced by permission of publisher)

scrape algae from hard surfaces; and *decomposers* break down organic material. The particular mode of food gathering is a most important aspect of the adaptability of any particular species. Usually there is considerable interaction among the myriad species within food chains; this produces a much more complex association called a food web. A food web can be visualized as a complex energy-flow system progressing through successive levels.

A similar situation exists on land. Although the terrestrial food chain (Fig. 3–36B) is more complex than that depicted for the ocean, both have been highly simplified for this discussion. Note that the base of this food chain is still composed of autotrophic species; there are many separate steps consisting of consumer heterotrophs representing higher and higher levels, eventually reaching the highest level. Where would humans fit into a food chain?

Another way of looking at communities of organisms is by determining the particular function (niche) of the various species. As indicated in Figure 3–37, most communities consist of basic nutrients and producer, consumer, and decomposer species. The nutrients include sunlight as well as organic and inorganic molecules; these are converted into food energy by the producers. This energy is used in the food chain as already described. After death, producers and consumers eventually are broken down by bacterial decomposition, and thus may provide a source of nutrient molecules to help begin the cycle again. (Remember the geologic cycle discussed in Chapter 1?)

By making a large jump in our scale, it is possible to consider the vast number of communities of organisms, that, when considered collectively, represent the Earth's *biosphere.* Each community has been described in terms of food chains or by the

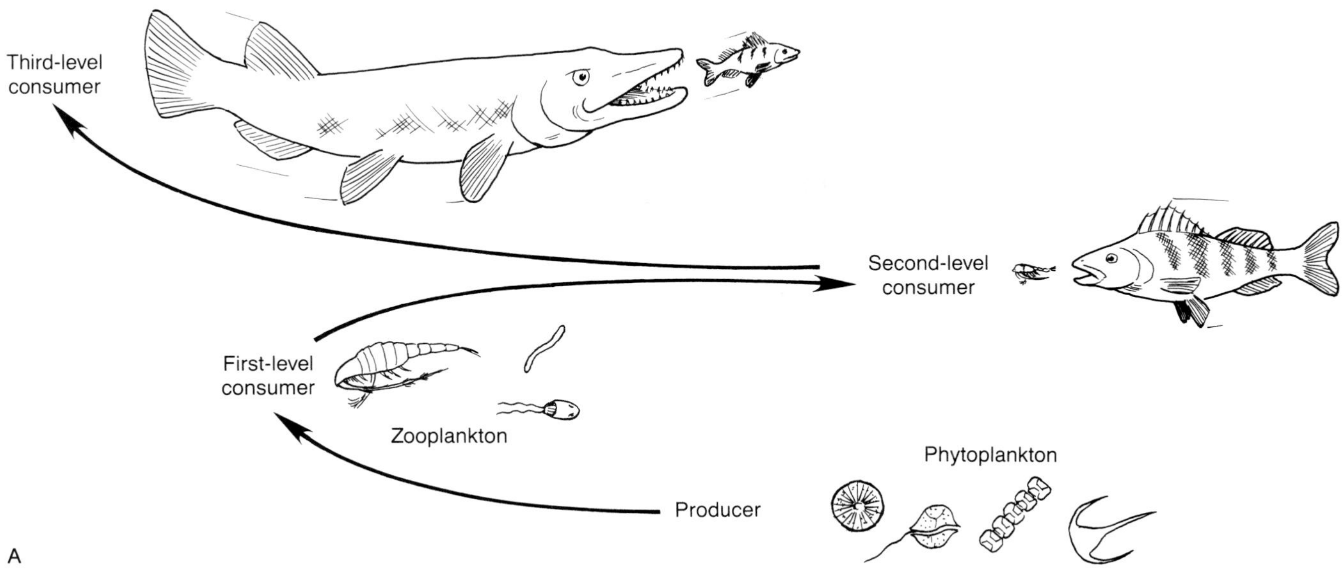

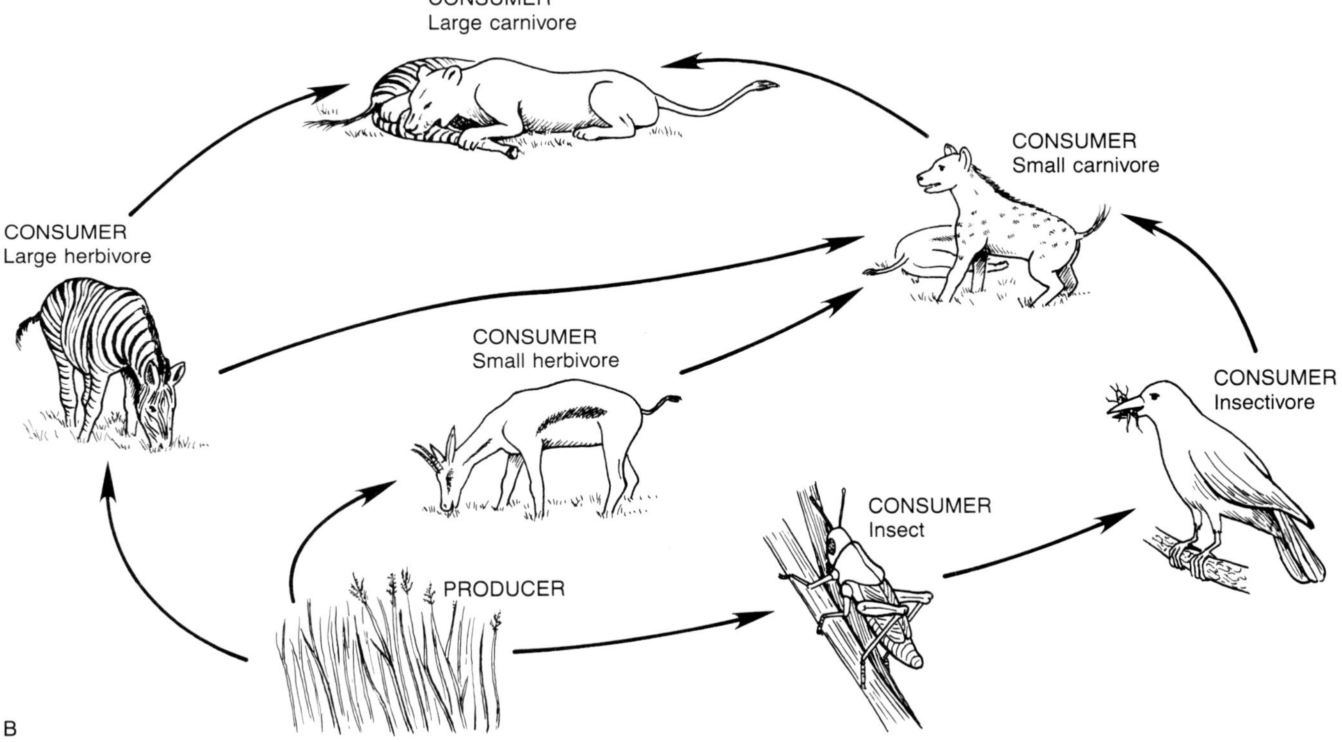

Figure 3–36
A. Basic elements of a simplifed marine food chain representing the feeding sequence from primary producers (phytoplankton) through various levels of consumers (zooplankton, fish). Consumption of the larger fish by humans or another fisheater would add a fourth level of consumer. B. Basic elements of simplified terrestrial food *chain* are illustrated in the sequence: producer = grasses, and consumers = antelope and hyena. A food *web* is also represented by the interrelationships of several food chains; i.e., there are several places where food chains connect with one another. As in the marine food chain, the base of a terrestrial chain is a producer (grasses) with various levels of consumers building upon this base. Humans play many roles in food chains and webs, but the most common role is that of herbivore, because grains and other plant materials compose a major proportion of the diet of most people.

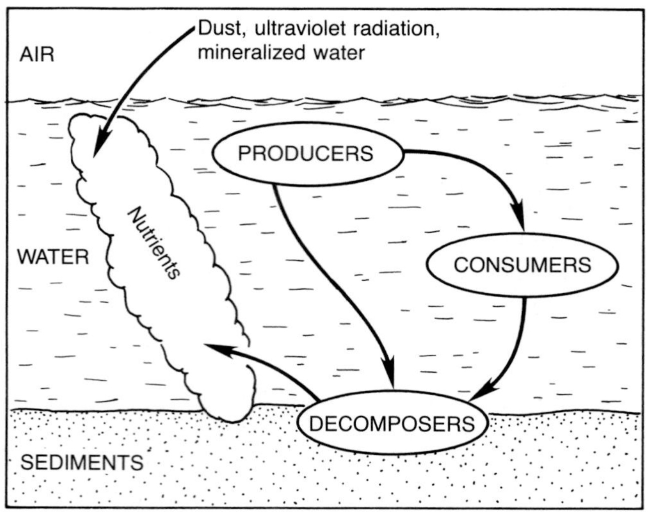

Figure 3–37
Interrelationships within a community based on the function (niche) of various organisms. Note the cyclic nature of the model, with the consumers and producers being decomposed into nutrient materials to be utilized by new organisms.

niche of each member species, but individual communities are not isolated. They are somewhat interdependent, and there is much interaction, one example being the food web. Different regions have communities composed of different species basically performing the same function (occupying the same niche), but acted upon by different environmental factors. Each organism in an ecosystem is controlled in its distribution by these environmental limiting factors (Table 3–5).

Paleontologists, working with fossil assemblages that usually represent only a part of the original community structure, attempt to reconstruct the ancient ecosystem in which the organisms lived. Reconstruction of ancient community structures involves consideration of the kinds and numbers of fossils present, the condition of the fossil material (for example, fragmented or whole fossils, fossils oriented in possible growth position, and so forth), mode(s) of preservation of fossils, and characteristics of the surrounding rock. All of these aspects of paleoecologic study are important in unraveling the life relationships and postdeath history of fossil organisms. Paleoecologic reconstructions, therefore,

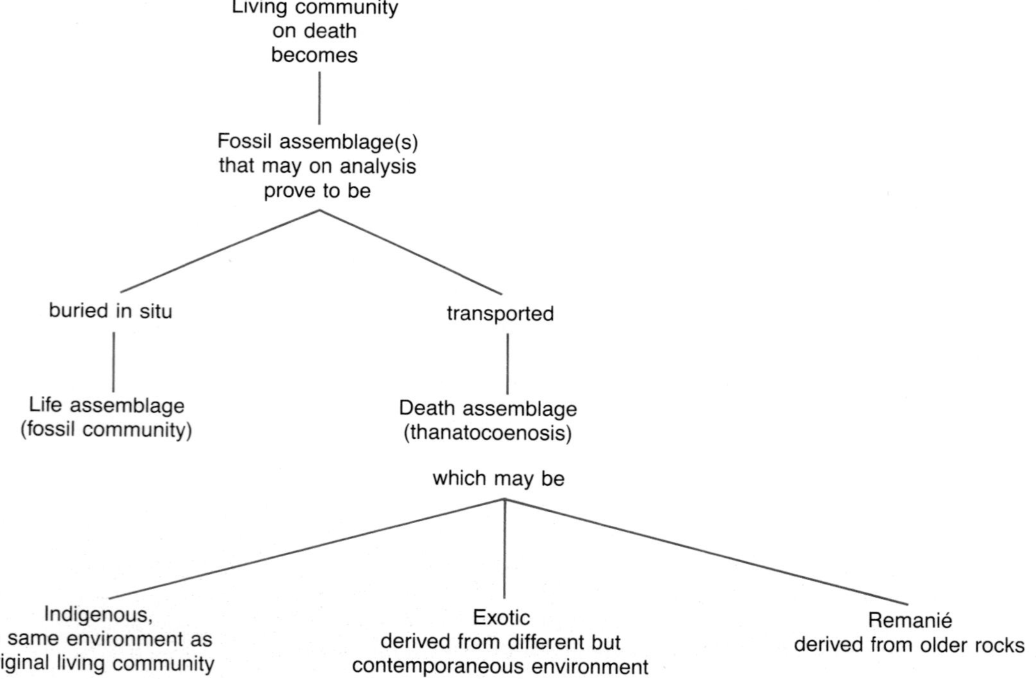

Figure 3–38
Status of a fossil assemblage. From a synthesis of paleoecologic and sedimentologic data it may be determined whether a fossil assemblage represents an original living community, or whether post-mortem events have modified the record.
(From G. Y. Craig and A. Hallam, 1963, Size-Frequency and Growth-Ring Analyses of *Mytilus edulis* and *Cardium edule,* and Their Paleoecological Significance: *Paleontology,* vol. 6. Reproduced by permission of authors)

involve a synthesis of paleontologic and sedimentologic data (Fig. 3–38) and an analysis of **biofacies.**

Trace fossils have taken on a special importance in this regard. Because various biogenic structures are preserved *in situ* (where the animal made them) and are not subject to post-mortem transportation and reworking as are body fossils, they have great potential as paleoecologic tools. Trace fossils of benthic marine organisms have been used, particularly in the absence of body fossils, to aid importantly in analysis of paleobathymetry (water depth) and paleoenvironments. In fact, various associations of trace-fossil form types (behavioral patterns) have been demonstrated to show a close relationship with paleobathymetric setting, and have given rise to the concept of *ichnofacies* (Fig. 3–39).

Synthesis of the data from this complexity of paleoecologic relationships, we emphasize again, is based largely on the important concept of *actualism.* The use of studies of recent examples to provide interpretive comparisons is fundamental. This emphasis on modern-day analogues is a basic tool for geologic interpretation; it is an important part of the ticket that allows us to make this trip through time.

Paleobiogeography

Biologists recognize a basic relationship between the distribution of modern plants and animals and the geographic areas where they are dispersed. Areas characterized by a particular composition of organisms and distinctive climatic factors represent **biogeographic provinces.** Recognition of modern biogeographic provinces had its roots in the Renaissance voyages of exploration. As Europeans discovered new lands, they also found new floras and faunas that were unlike those in their homelands. In the nineteenth century, naturalists journeyed widely specifically to study these different plants and animals and to map their distribution. It was from observations made on one such worldwide voyage that Charles Darwin amassed the documen-

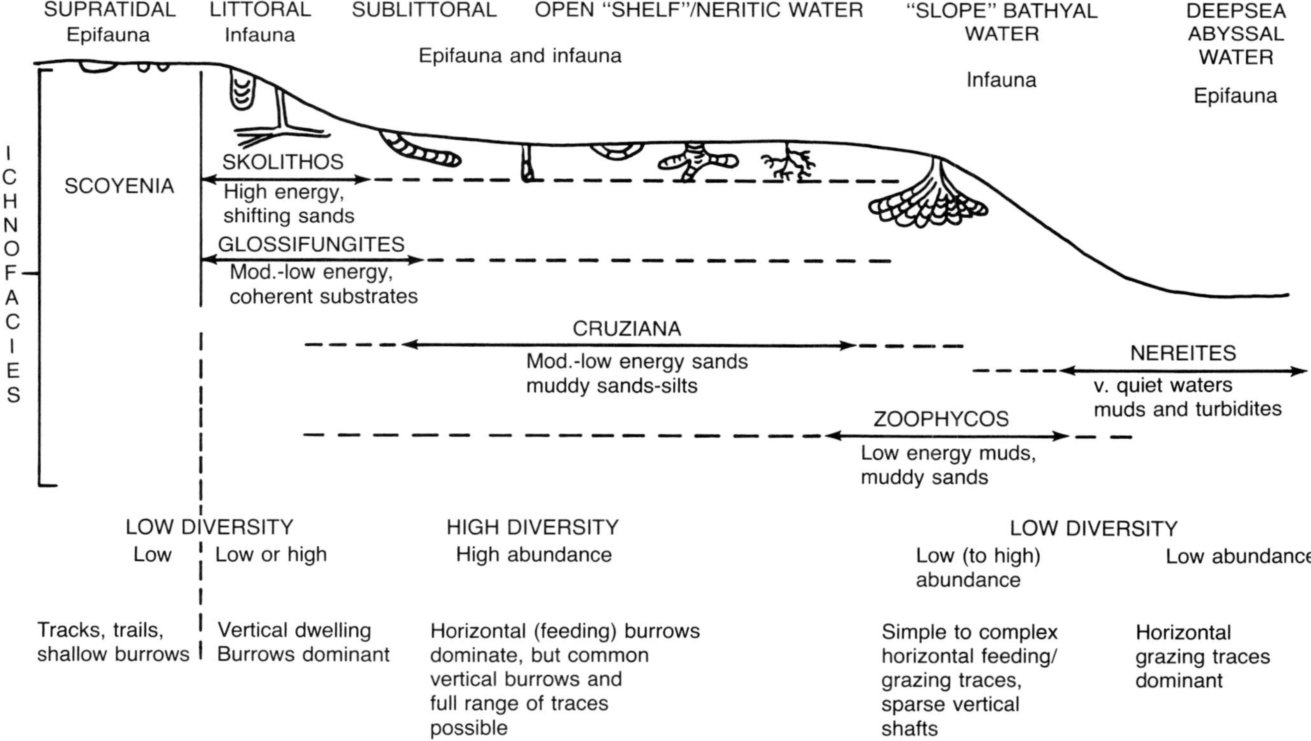

Figure 3–39
Bathymetric profile of marine realm showing ichnofacies, including their predominant trace-form types and diversity, and their relation to water depth and substrate (bottom sediment) type.
(From A. A. Ekdale, R. G. Bromley, and S. G. Pemberton, 1984, *Ichnology: Trace Fossils in Sedimentology and Stratigraphy,* Society of Economic Paleontologists and Mineralogists Short Course No. 15, Fig. 15–2, p. 187. Reproduced with permission of SEPM)

tation to support his concept of organic evolution (see Chapter 4). On the basis of these voyages, a classification hierarchy of areas was defined; on the continents various *realms, regions,* and *provinces* were recognized. Later, this type of biogeographic division was applied to the oceans of the world.

Studies indicate that the latitudinal boundaries or limits of these biogeographic areas are determined primarily by climate, but also by other environmental factors such as topography, availability of food, salinity, and depth of water. An influential factor in the longitudinal separation of biogeographic provinces is the presence of geographic barriers, such as mountains or even entire continents, as well as of bodies of water, such as oceans.

The existence of barriers is directly related to the geologic history of an area. Prior to late Pliocene time, for example, the Isthmus of Panama did not exist, and there was intermingling of the marine life of the Atlantic Ocean and Pacific Ocean. The late Pliocene tectonic uplift of the isthmus created an emergent land barrier between these two oceanic realms, resulting in divergence of the marine faunas on either side.

It is significant that the formation of this land *barrier* between the two oceans simultaneously formed a land *connection* between South America and North America, thus providing a bridge for terrestrial faunas to mix and converge between these two continents. The biostratigraphic record of the areas adjacent to and including the isthmus helps to date the time of this tectonic event as Pliocene.

Several biogeographic provinces are recognized along the present marine shelf of the East Coast (Fig. 3–40). Because of climatic constraints, species characteristic of the present-day Nova Scotian Province are not likely to be found in the Carolinian Province or South Florida Province. Typically, each province has **endemic** species that are confined to it and characterize the province, and some **cosmopolitan** species that have a wider geographic distribution.

Very few, if any, taxa in the fossil record had actual worldwide distribution, but many of them were sufficiently widespread geographically that they provide good indexes for *continentwide* and *intercontinental* correlation. It is unmistakable that most fossil-bearing stratigraphic sequences are

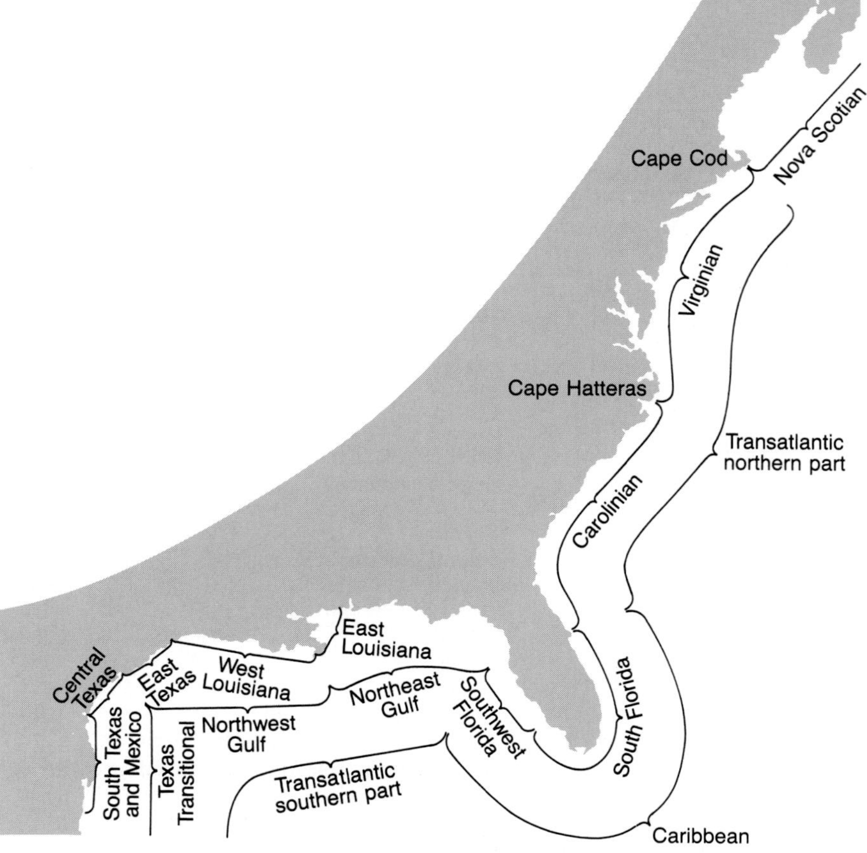

Figure 3–40
Present biogeographic provinces along the east coast of the United States. Climatic factors control the occurrence of species that are typical of each province. Species characteristic of the Nova Scotian Province, for example, would not be expected in the South Florida Province.
(From J. W. Valentine, 1963, Biogeographic Units as Biostratigraphic Units, Fig. 1, p. 459: *American Association of Petroleum Geologists Bulletin,* vol. 47)

preserved as part of continental structure (even though perhaps originally marine). The modern-day ocean basins, remember, do not contain rocks recognized as being older than Jurassic.

It is recognized that widespread cosmopolitan species are not *exactly* the same age everywhere. Dispersal to regions beyond the area of origin must have taken some time. Studies of migrations of modern species, however, have shown that dispersal can occur rapidly once plants or animals have gained access to a new environmentally suitable territory.

Migration histories differ considerably, and are dependent upon the type of organism studied. Migration of planktonic or nektonic forms, for example, occurs more rapidly than dispersal of benthic organisms. But even benthic organisms can achieve widespread dispersal because many groups have larval stages that are planktonic. Research indicates that at least several thousand years are required for a species to reach all areas suitable for its propagation *once* migration routes are open. In terms of geologic time, several thousand or tens of thousands of years is a short interval, and does not negate the apparent contemporaneous nature of cosmopolitan fossils.

The distribution of modern plants and animals defines present biogeographic provinces, and the distribution of fossils defines *paleobiogeographic* provinces. A classic study by British paleontologist J. W. Arkell of the biostratigraphic record of Jurassic ammonite cephalopods indicated a marked change in the provinciality (number of provinces) during the Early Jurassic, compared to the remainder of the period. Early Jurassic ammonites were cosmopolitan: species composition is similar in western North America and Europe, and stratigraphic correlation is precise. However, Middle and Late Jurassic ammonites are less widespread, indicating greater provinciality. This led Arkell to define three faunal provinces (Fig. 3–41) for the Late Jurassic.

There is a direct relationship between provinciality and taxonomic diversity. During times of fewer distinct paleobiogeographic provinces (Early Jurassic, for example) organisms that migrated readily

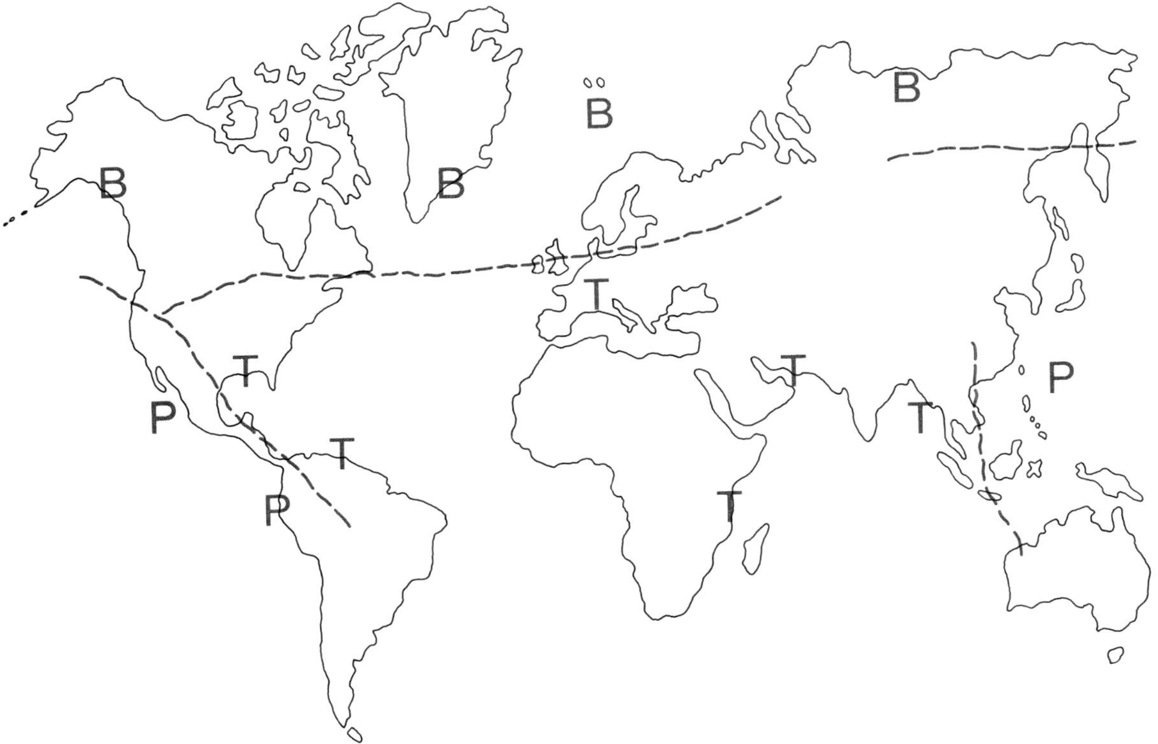

Figure 3–41
Late Jurassic marine realms defined on occurrence of ammonite cephalopods. B = boreal; P = Pacific; T = Tethyan.
(From W. J. Arkell, 1956, *Jurassic Geology of the World:* McGraw-Hill Book Co., New York. Reproduced by permission of Oliver & Boyd, Edinburgh, Scotland)

became cosmopolitan in distribution. Conversely, during times of greater provinciality (e.g., the Late Jurassic) organisms were less cosmopolitan, a greater number of endemic species existed, and there was comparatively greater total taxonomic diversity.

The important paleontologic concept of paleobiogeography relates three aspects of the distribution of fossils: (1) number of paleobiogeographic provinces, (2) provincial-versus-cosmopolitan nature of the taxa, and (3) taxonomic diversity. It also meshes as a fourth component into the interrelationship involving evolution, paleoecology, and biostratigraphy (see discussion in Chapter 6). Furthermore, paleobiogeography provides important insight for understanding the timing of continental drift, as well as the biologic consequences of moving continents. As continents have broken apart or moved together, greater or lesser numbers of paleobiogeographic provinces have formed, and thus the distribution of fossils in the biostratigraphic record, such as in the Jurassic example cited, is related to plate tectonics!

The Fossil Record and Plate Tectonics

The concept of moving continents has tenuous roots going back over two hundred years, long before Alfred Wegener's work early in the present century (see Chapter 1). In the mid-eighteenth century, the French naturalist Comte de Buffon, on the basis of similarity of *modern* flora and fauna, speculated that North America and Europe had once been joined. Distribution of similar *ancient* taxa in the biostratigraphic record of now-separated continents was one of Wegener's major lines of evidence for continental drift. Biostratigraphic correlations and paleobiogeographic distribution of fossils are important in both the former continental-drift model and the present plate-tectonic model, and in this light represent a dynamic aspect of paleontologic interpretation.

A relationship between distribution of fossils and plate tectonics is illustrated by closure of a proto-Atlantic Ocean during the Devonian and Carboniferous Periods, with an accompanying decrease in floral provincialism on the colliding continents leading to the cosmopolitan *Glossopteris* floral *realm* of the Permian (see Chapter 11). During the Mesozoic Era, the biostratigraphic record of terrestrial reptiles appears to indicate land connections during the Triassic, but provides less evidence of this during the later Mesozoic periods as Pangaea was breaking apart (see discussion, Chapter 12).

The northward migration of Australia during the Cenozoic has been accompanied by the progressive adaptation of the flora. The vegetation has adapted to arid and semiarid climates in central Australia as that part of the continent has moved into the dry climatic belt between 20° and 30° south latitude. If Australia's northward movement continues, the flora of central Australia will change to savannah vegetation, and then to rain forest as the continent enters the equatorial belt.

Analyses have attempted to relate major evolutionary events, such as rapid diversification or extinction of taxa to lithospheric plate motions. There is an interesting twofold relationship between fossils and plate tectonics. First, fossils in the biostratigraphic record provide evidence of moving continents and of the timing of opening and closing of ocean basins. Second, plate motions through geologic history have been responsible for large-scale environmental changes that have influenced rates and patterns of organic evolution. Plate tectonics has produced not only a new model for interpretation of Earth's tectonic structure, but also a new framework for paleontologic study.

Economic Geology

Exploration for petroleum and natural gas provides a good example of the use of fossils in industry. Ancient organisms are the raw material from which the **fossil fuels** (petroleum, natural gas, coal) are derived. Burial and transformation of plant material into coal is relatively well understood, but the burial and transformation of predominantly marine phytoplankton and zooplankton into petroleum and natural gas is a more complex chemical process that is not understood as well. The buried organic debris disseminated in bottom sediments has been compacted and chemically changed to *hydrocarbons.* Following development of the hydrocarbon substances in the *source* rock, the processes of burial and compaction, expulsion of fluids into adjacent rock, migration through *permeable* beds, and final entrapment in *porous reservoir* rock result in accumulations of oil and/or gas.

It is the task of teams of petroleum geologists to locate subsurface hydrocarbon traps: anticlines, faults, and stratigraphic facies changes. Microfossils play an important role in the sedimentary-basin analysis that is required for systematically successful exploration ventures. One of the key tools in the exploration for hydrocarbons is the biostratigraphic correlation of rock units in the subsurface, as discussed in Chapter 6.

Exploration for oil and gas must be conducted in deposits buried beneath the Earth's surface, commonly in areas that provide little or no surficial indication of the presence of hydrocarbons. Microfossils such as foraminifers, diatoms, and pollen grains are small enough to remain intact in the well cuttings derived from boreholes. These microfossils serve as valuable aids in correlating subsurface stratigraphic sequences which, in turn, enable geologists to conduct subsurface mapping and to locate geologic structures that are potential petroleum and natural gas traps. It is important to remember that the soft parts of ancient organisms have formed the hydrocarbons, and their fossilized hard parts have made possible the biostratigraphic record aiding us in locating the resources!

Other mineral resources associated with sedimentary rocks—rock salt, gypsum, limestone (for manufacturing cement), phosphates (for making fertilizer), and uranium—are found in geologic settings whose characteristics are understood. Paleontologic studies may provide leads to these geologic settings, and thus to the discovery of potentially valuable resources.

Summary

The fossil record is not a complete picture of the life of the past, because only those organisms with hard parts (shells, bone) that become relatively rapidly buried tend to be preserved on any kind of major scale. These prerequisites for fossilization have most often been fulfilled by animals in a shallow marine (continental shelf) paleoenvironmental setting. Hence, sedimentary rocks formed in this depositional setting tend to be fossiliferous, and the great bulk of the fossil record is comprised of calcium carbonate shell-secreting, benthic, shallow-marine, invertebrate organisms. The fossil record is highly biased toward the organisms with hard parts that lived in shallow marine environments.

Fossils are formed by a variety of methods: preservation without alteration; preservation with alteration, including leaching, carbonization, permineralization, recrystallization, and replacement; formation of molds and casts; and recording of organism activity as trace fossils.

To facilitate study, fossils are classified into categories that correspond to the present biological classification of organisms, based on the hierarchical system of Linnaeus. As one progresses through the categories kingdom, phylum, class, order, family, genus, and species, each subdivision becomes less inclusive (more restrictive). The fundamental unit in this system is the species: a group of related organisms that share a common gene pool and typically are capable of interbreeding and producing fertile offspring. Each species is known by a binomial name; for example, modern humans are *Homo sapiens.* Problems of classification that arise—overlapping of terms or use of synonyms—and recognition of new species are controlled to some degree by an international commission. The science of classifying and naming organisms is taxonomy.

In this chapter an overview of fossil forms belonging to four kingdoms was presented:

1. Kingdom Monera
   Characteristics: one-celled; nonnucleated cells
   Example: cyanobacteria in stromatolites
2. Kingdom Protista
   Characteristics: one-celled; nucleated cells
   Examples: foraminifers, radiolarians, diatoms, algae
3. Kingdom Plantae:
   Characteristics: multicellular; autotrophic
   Examples: trees, ferns, spores and pollen

4. Kingdom Animalia
   Characteristics: multicellular; heterotrophic
   Examples: sponges, corals, stromatoporoids, archaeocyathids, bryozoans, brachiopods, molluscs (bivalves, gastropods, cephalopods), arthropods (trilobites), echinoderms (crinoids, echinoids), graptolites, conodonts, vertebrates (fish, amphibians, reptiles, birds, mammals)

Fossils are more than museum curiosities; they are useful in providing:

1. the basis of biostratigraphic study that led to the development of the relative geologic time scale;
2. an important tool in stratigraphic correlation;
3. the record of evolutionary development of life forms;
4. the basis for paleoecologic studies (recognition of habitats, niches, and food chains within ancient ecosystems);
5. the basis for paleobiogeographic studies (endemic versus cosmopolitan species, and their association with biogeographic provinces);
6. a line of evidence in Wegener's original concept of continental drift and in the modern plate tectonics model; and
7. a tool for exploration for Earth resources, especially hydrocarbons.

Fossils have long fascinated humans. These relics of former life have been articles of religious value and have been items of mere curiosity, but more significantly they are important tools in solving geologic problems.

Suggestions for Further Reading

Case, G. R. 1982. *A pictorial guide to fossils.* Florence, KY: Van Nostrand Reinhold Co.

Fortey, Richard. 1982. *Fossils: The key to the past.* Florence, KY: Van Nostrand Reinhold Co.

Hallam, A. 1972. Continental drift and the fossil record. *Scientific American* 227(5):56–66.

Halstead, L. B. 1982. *The search for the past.* Garden City, NY: Doubleday & Co.

Lane, N. G. 1986. *Life of the past.* 2d ed. Columbus, OH: Merrill Publishing Co.

Laporte, Leo F. 1978. Introductions, *in* Evolution and the fossil record. *Readings from Scientific American.* San Francisco: W. H. Freeman.

MacDonald, J. R. 1978. *The fossil collector's handbook, a paleontology field guide.* Englewood Cliffs, NJ: Prentice-Hall.

MacFall, R. P., and J. C. Wollin. 1983. *Fossils for amateurs.* 2d ed. Florence, KY: Van Nostrand Reinhold Co.

Margulis, Lynn, and K. V. Schwartz. 1987. *Five kingdoms: An illustrated guide to the phyla of life on Earth.* 2d ed. San Francisco: W. H. Freeman.

Marshall, L. G. 1988. Land mammals and the great American interchange. *American Scientist* 76:380–88.

McKerrow, W. S., ed. 1978. *The ecology of fossils: An illustrated guide:* Cambridge, MA: MIT Press.

Simpson, G. G. 1983. *Fossils and the history of life.* New York: Scientific American Books.

Skinner, Brian J., ed. 1981. Paleontology and paleoenvironments. In *Readings from American Scientist.* Los Altos, CA: Wm. Kaufman.

Thompson, Ida. 1982. *The Audubon Society field guide to North American fossils.* New York: Alfred A. Knopf.

Valentine, James W., and E. M. Moores. 1974. Plate tectonics and the history of life in the oceans. *Scientific American* 230(4):80–89.

The Pervasiveness of Change: Evolution and Extinction

4

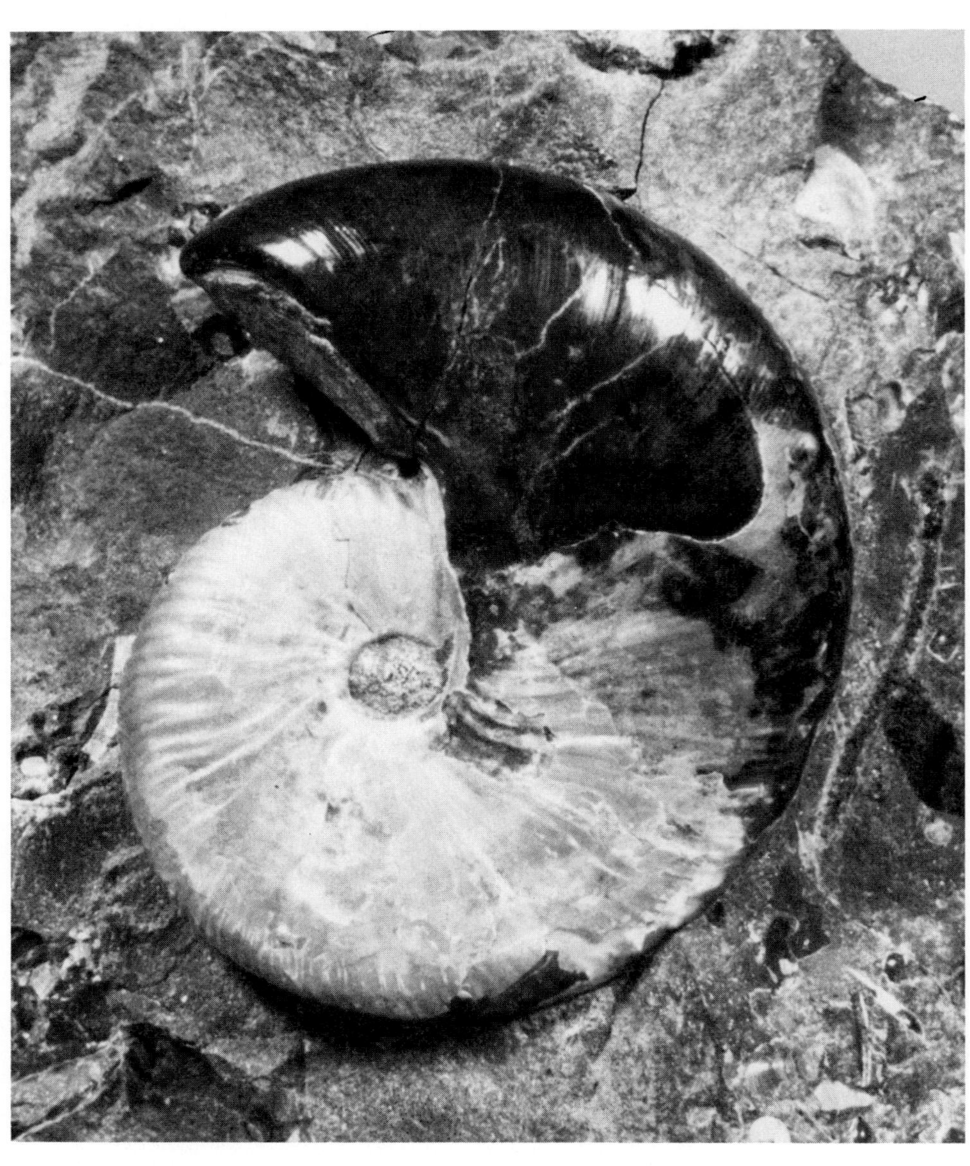

Contents

Key Terms

Evolutionary theory
Natural selection
Heredity
Chromosome
Gene
DNA molecule
Genotype
Phenotype
Mutation
Gene pool
Mitosis
Meiosis
Reproductive isolation
Divergence
Ontogeny
Phylogeny
Lineage
Speciation
Allopatric speciation
Punctuated equilibrium
Phyletic gradualism
Adaptive radiation
Extinction
Stenotopic
Eurytopic
Food web

Too Much Monkey Business

Tennessee, 1925, Chapter 17, House Bill 185. An act prohibiting the teaching of the Evolutionary Theory in all Universities, Normals and all other public schools of Tennessee, which are supported in whole or in part by the public school funds of the State, and to provide penalties for the violations thereof.

The preceding paragraph is the introduction to the Butler Act, which was passed by the General Assembly of the State of Tennessee in 1925. It, and the many other acts subsequently introduced into state legislatures and occasionally passed into law, represented political attempts to control or prohibit the teaching of the theory of evolution in public schools or universities. Evidently, by the early 1900s the concept of evolution had transcended the realms of education and science and entered the world of politics.

As we will see in this chapter, modern **evolutionary theory** provides an explanation for the variety and changes in biological taxa through geological time. The presently understood theory has its own evolutionary history as it developed from bits and pieces and occasional large chunks of knowledge contributed by many scientists. One of the first scientific explanations of evolution was proposed by Jean Baptiste Lamarck in the early 1800s. However, Lamarckian concepts were completely overshadowed following the publication in 1859 of *On the Origin of Species,* by Charles Darwin. Darwin's concepts of evolution represent one of the major milestones in biology, and had a profound impact on science and society in general; thus the following sketch of his background provides an interesting backdrop to the history of evolutionary theory.

Charles Darwin grew up in England in a relatively well-to-do family during the early 1800s. Somewhat typically of his social class, he studied medicine at the University of Edinburgh, and then prepared for the ministry at Cambridge University. However, his main interest leaned toward natural history, and it was this interest that led him to embark as shipboard naturalist on an inauspicious voyage that began in December 1831. Darwin's voyage on the *H.M.S. Beagle* provided a vast amount of data that were later synthesized into his concepts of evolution. One of the most significant areas he visited was the Galapagos Islands, approximately 1000 km west of the coast of South America and lying astride the Equator. On these isolated islands, formed by volcanic activity, Darwin marveled at large marine iguanas, giant tortoises, the great variability of finches, and an array of unusual vegetation.

Upon his return to England in 1835, Darwin moved to the county of Kent and spent more than 20 years carefully analyzing data collected on his voyage and making further studies. Although he planned to write a major treatise on his interpretations and confided many of his ideas to geologist Charles Lyell and botanist Joseph Hooker, it is possible that Darwin never would have published his ideas but for the manuscript sent to him for review by another naturalist, Alfred Russel Wallace, in 1858. To Darwin's surprise, Wallace had independently come up with similar concepts. With this stimulus, a joint paper by Darwin and Wallace was presented to the Linnaean Society of London. Darwin then rapidly completed his major manuscript, and it was published in the fall of 1859. The first edition was sold out on the first day. Reaction to the book in scientific circles and by the public ranged from very favorable to violently negative. The well-known biologist Thomas Huxley commented upon reading the *Origin:* "How extremely stupid not to have thought of that."

Darwin's book was the outgrowth of decades of research and certainly had a profound influence on human thought; it described an elaborately researched and carefully reasoned concept, and was based on a large volume of data. For the biological sciences, the concept was the beginning of a revolution that led to many new ideas and developments. Scientists and the public in general were presented with a new interpretation that provided a coherent and comprehensive explanation for the richness of life on Earth. The major emphasis of the book was its elaboration of **natural selection,** whereby the environment controls the probability of survival for each individual in a population of organisms. Those organisms best adapted to environmental conditions were viewed as having the best chance of survival, and by reproducing offspring they would influence the characteristics of succeeding generations. The appearance of new species occurred by survival and reproduction of successful variants in original populations.

Darwin explained to the satisfaction of many, but by no means all, that life evolves continually through time and is always being modified through various processes of natural selection. To Darwin, and to biologists today, changes by natural selection provide the explanation as to why diverse organisms can have strikingly similar kinds of shells or arrangements of bones and organs, and how plants and animals can be well adapted to particular environments. To geologists, these concepts help explain underlying causes responsible for the recognized succession of different faunas and floras observed in the fossil record.

Because of the far-reaching significance of the theory of evolution, modern scientists such as evolutionary biologists Ernst Mayr and Stephen Jay Gould have attempted to recognize how various scientific, social, and religious trends of the early and middle 1800s may have influenced Darwin's thinking, and what mental steps were involved in the gradual formulation of his concepts. These studies provide an intriguing glimpse into the thought process that operates within the human mind. Evident from these studies is that ideas as momentous as Darwin's hypothesis often involve the assimilation of considerable data from widely diverse sources; thus the ideas are greatly dependent upon previous contributions to total human knowledge.

Since Darwin's time much new information has been added to our understanding of evolutionary processes. For example, Darwin knew nothing of genes or of the science of genetics; the modern concepts of this branch of biology have been formulated only in the twentieth century. Today we have extensive knowledge of biochemistry, population biology, and microbiology, again areas of science not known to Darwin. Our concepts of evolution have, therefore, undergone considerable refinement since Darwin's time, but still can be traced to his original ideas.

Modern concepts of organic evolution have surpassed the hypothesis stage. Evolutionary theory consists of a very considerable body of supporting information, including much experimental data, from many scientific disciplines. Surprisingly, however, we find that a very vocal minority still is convinced that the theory is totally false. Consider the opening paragraph of this chapter, which represents a law passed 60 years after most scientists were no longer concerned as to whether evolution occurs, but rather how it operates.

A result of the Tennessee antievolution law was the 1925 trial of high school biology teacher John Scopes in Dayton, Tennessee. This trial, now known as the "Great Monkey Trial," pitted two well-known historical figures against one another—William Jennings Bryan argued for the prosecution, and Clarence Darrow provided the defense for Scopes. Bryan, a staunch antievolutionist, thundered and preached the state's case, fighting the cutting wit of Darrow. The result of the trial, which became one of the most famous of this century, was a victory for the state, as Scopes was found guilty of teaching evolution. However, in the process, antievolutionists—especially Bryan—were ridiculed. A number of state legislatures introduced antievolution bills during the middle 1920s, but almost all were defeated, and by 1930 most of the outward controversy had died away.

However, even today there are still significant protests against evolutionary theory. These have taken the form of censuring biology textbooks and lobbying in the legislatures to prohibit use of the books by some school districts. A recent tactic used by many fundamentalist groups is to bring legal suit demanding "equal time." These suits ask that religious creation, or "creationism," be given coverage equal to evolution in biology textbooks and in the classroom, conveniently ignoring the facts that creation is not a scientific concept, and that it is not open to modeling or experimentation. Numerous leaflets, pamphlets, and even an antievolution journal are published to discredit the theory.

Let us consider this theory of evolution and determine its effects on the history of life on Earth.

Mechanism of Organic Evolution

Organic Change Through Time

A wide variety of fossils preserved in the lithosphere has provided us with a nearly continuous, but often fragmentary, record of the diversity of life that has existed for over 3500 million years of the Earth's history. One of the most interesting discoveries made by studying this history of life is the evidence of continuous change in the kinds of organisms that have existed throughout this immense interval of time. Studies of the fossil record, especially that part representing what we now term the Phanerozoic Eon, had provided documented evidence of these changes to paleontologists by the late 1700s.

One example of these changes is provided by the history of giant reptiles so familiar to us from museum displays, but not recognized by eighteenth-century paleontologists. These reptiles first appeared during Triassic time, were abundant and diverse in the Jurassic, and disappeared at the end of Cretaceous time. Progressing one step further, we find that all fossil taxa exhibit similar patterns; that is, they appear and then disappear, although some may last considerably longer than others. This paleontological pattern provides strong evidence that evolution occurs, but by itself does not explain the mechanisms controlling the process.

Accumulation and analyses of data from the fossil record raised perplexing questions related to the fossils themselves. A major question of this type, recognized as early as the late 1700s, was how to explain appearances and disappearances of taxa recorded throughout the stratigraphic record—a phenomenon termed fossil succession. The French naturalist Cuvier championed the idea of catastrophism, whereby the Earth's history was interpreted as having been punctuated by episodes of worldwide revolution—in particular, global floods. Catastrophism, as applied to the fossil record, conceptualized a succession of annihilations and subsequent repopulations by new kinds of organisms;

this concept provided the crux of Cuvier's interpretation of the principle of fossil succession (see discussion, Chapter 6).

As discussed in Chapter 6, an alternative to catastrophism was the concept of uniformitarianism, proposed by Charles Lyell in the early 1800s. His concept recognized no worldwide catastrophic events, but emphasized that small, more local changes, taking place over the great length of geologic time and of variable levels of magnitude, were sufficient to produce immense change.

Building on the impetus supplied in the last half of the 1800s by Darwin's evolutionary hypothesis, the concept of evolution was tied to uniformitarianism, and applied to the fossil record to provide a logical, if not completely understood, explanation for the history of various taxonomic groups (Fig. 4–1). These two concepts—evolutionary theory and uniformitarianism—have held sway in biological and geological thought since the late 1800s. We can conclude this section by pointing out that evolution basically describes changes in taxa through time, and is irrefutably documented by the fossil record. The mechanisms by which evolution works, however, are more difficult to decipher, and have been hotly debated since the time of Darwin.

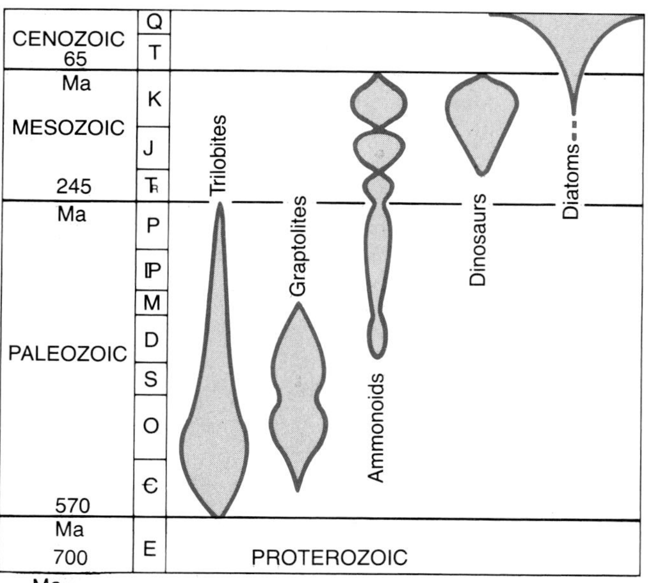

Figure 4–1
Origin and extinction of taxa, including trilobites, graptolites, ammonoids, dinosaurs, and diatoms. The pattern width of each group represents approximate diversity; wide spacing indicates large numbers of species (high diversity). Diversity among various groups is not to scale. Note that each taxon has a distinctly different evolutionary history. (E is Ediacarian.)

The subsequent discussion outlines the development of tenets important to evolutionary theory.

Historical Development: Natural Selection, Genetics, and the DNA Molecule

Three historically important discoveries provide a basis for our discussion of evolution.

The first was Darwin's concept of the process of evolution, which provided an explanation for changes in species, and which Darwin described as "transformation." As he interpreted the process, changes in organisms are brought about by selective survival of individuals whose characteristics are transmitted to successive generations through the process of reproduction.

The second discovery was the mechanism of **heredity,** first described by Gregor Mendel, who published his results in 1866. His conclusions were used in the early 1900s to provide a fundamental basis for the developing science of genetics. The concept of heredity, when coupled with subsequent discoveries of **chromosomes** and **genes** later in the 1900s, provides a powerful tool for explaining the mechanisms by which characteristics are transmitted from one generation of organisms to another.

The third discovery involved unraveling the extremely complex chemical nature of genetic material, namely, the chemistry and structure of the **DNA molecule,** described in 1953 by biologists James Watson and Francis Crick of Cambridge University.

The life of an individual organism and the evolutionary history of a species are controlled by many events and conditions. These can be divided into two categories: the first represents environmental conditions, and the second represents genetic characteristics. Darwin recognized that environmental conditions influenced populations of organisms by effectively determining which, if any, individuals of a species survive, and even more importantly, which members reproduce successive generations, thereby perpetuating their genetic characteristics. This process of selective survival and reproduction he termed natural selection—popularly known by the somewhat misleading slogan, "survival of the fittest."

Natural selection operates so that successive generations of the species will include offspring possessing characteristics similar to those individuals of the previous generation that were best adapted to the environment, and thereby were able not only to survive but also—of the utmost importance—to reproduce. Thus, each generation represents a segment of an evolutionary continuum. Significantly, over many generations the general character of the species can and may change. Darwin recognized these changes on the basis of morphological variations, especially in the populations of distinctive birds and reptiles he saw on the Galapagos Islands during his voyage on the *Beagle.* However, his concept suffered from a lack of information, because he could not explain which mechanisms within the organisms themselves could produce such changes; indeed this difficulty was a source of frustration for him.

This example illustrates a parallel development between the concepts of evolution and continental drift. Both for many years were hypotheses in search of a viable mechanism. Just as seafloor-spreading vindicated early explanations of continental drift, so did the recognition of genetics and the mechanism of inheritance put evolution on a solid footing.

The mechanisms that Darwin sought in vain were being discovered by Gregor Mendel, ironically, at about the same time that the *Origin* was being published. Mendel was an Augustinian monk and taught natural science at a monastery in what is now Brno, Czechoslovakia. After developing an interest in the process of heredity, he experimented over many years with the breeding of sweet pea plants. From these experiments he developed a hypothesis that today represents one of the fundamental principles of genetics (Fig. 4–2).

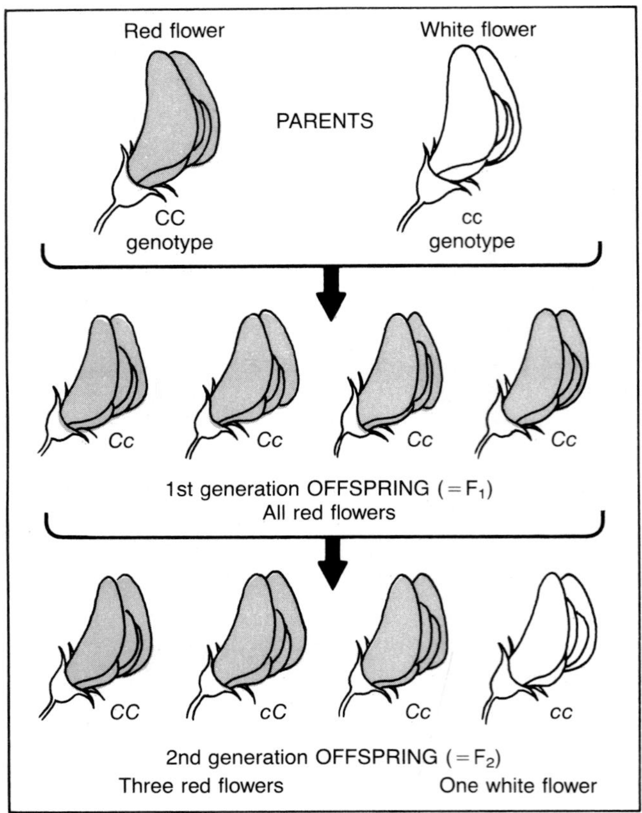

Figure 4–2
Results of Gregor Mendel's genetic experiments, illustrating the mechanisms of heredity and ratios of morphologic features (color of flowers) in offspring from successive generations of sweet pea plants. The genes responsible for the color are represented by C (red) and c (white). This experiment was performed with hundreds of offspring to produce the statistical ratio of 3:1.
(Adapted from *Life, An Introduction to Biology,* Second Edition, by G. G. Simpson and W. S. Beck, copyright © 1965 by Harcourt Brace Jovanovich, Inc. Reproduced by permission of publisher)

Mendel made the following assumptions, based on his experimental results: (1) Each plant contained a pair of hereditary factors that controlled flower color. (2) Both of these factors were derived from the parents, and in each parent the factors separate during formation of germ cells. (3) In pea plants, the red or white color of the flowers represents an alternate form of the same factor, although red was found to be dominant over white. Thus Mendel recognized that variability of traits was transmitted to successive generations of his pea plants, and that the ratios of color (red and white) in each generation could be mathematically predicted.

Mendel published his results in an obscure journal and did no further research on the subject. His results were overlooked by biologists for about 35 years, and then were rediscovered in the early 1900s when the modern science of genetics was in its infancy. This brings to mind that often in the history of science, individual scientists have been ignored and their ideas buried in scientific literature because they were "ahead of their time," or because they failed to publish in appropriate journals. At a later date the ideas may be rediscovered and recognized as historical milestones.

From the published work of Watson and Crick in the 1950s and more recently, as well as from a vast number of contributions by many other scientists, we recognize that genetic information in organisms is contained within comparatively large, complex deoxyribonucleic acid (DNA) molecules. These DNA molecules comprise genes that are located along strands called chromosomes. These complex molecules control critical chemical reactions within cells that play a major role in determining the physical characteristics and responses to environmental changes of individual organisms.

The genetic makeup of an individual organism is described as its **genotype.** Physical characteristics of the organism are due to a combination of genotype and environmental conditions, and are collectively described as **phenotype** (Fig. 4–3). Variation in genes is produced by alterations of the internal chemistry of the DNA molecule, a process called **mutation.** Genetic variation can occur also by structural rearrangement or reordering of the sequence of genes along chromosomes; these processes are known as *recombination* and *crossing over.*

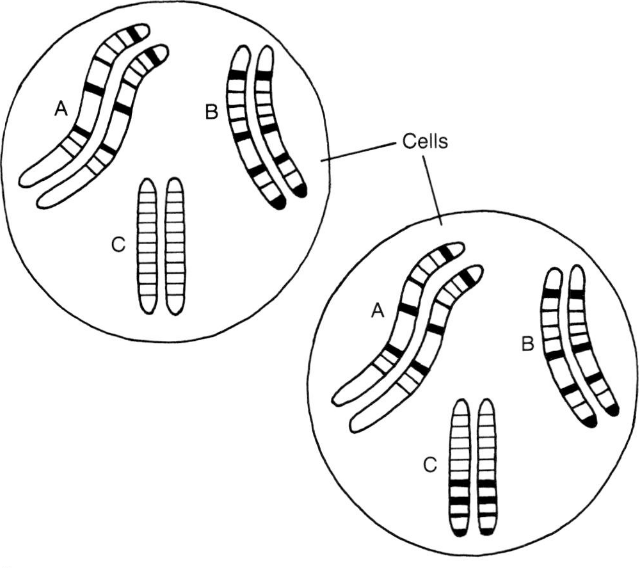

Figure 4–3
Difference between genotype and phenotype within organisms of the same taxon. A. Sketches of two cells, each having three chromosomes containing a variety of genes. Note the variation in genes present in chromosome C between the two cells. This illustrates variation in *genotype.* B. Photograph of a population of individual fossil gastropods, illustrating differences in external morphology. This illustrates variation in *phenotype.*

Modern Synthesis: Population and Reproduction

The collective genetic material of any population of one type of organism (a species) constitutes the **gene pool** of that population. Evolutionary changes in the composition of a gene pool can occur only through successive generations of populations, and do not occur by changes in individual organisms (Fig. 4–4). The key link in this change is reproduction, and sexual reproduction provides the most effective method for recombining genetic information.

Reproduction involves replication (duplication) of a multitude of organic chemical molecules such as DNA; it can be accomplished through **mitosis** or **meiosis.** Mitosis is characteristic of prokaryotic organisms of the kingdom Monera (see Chapter 3). Monerans replicate their DNA and then divide into two smaller cells that contain genetic information

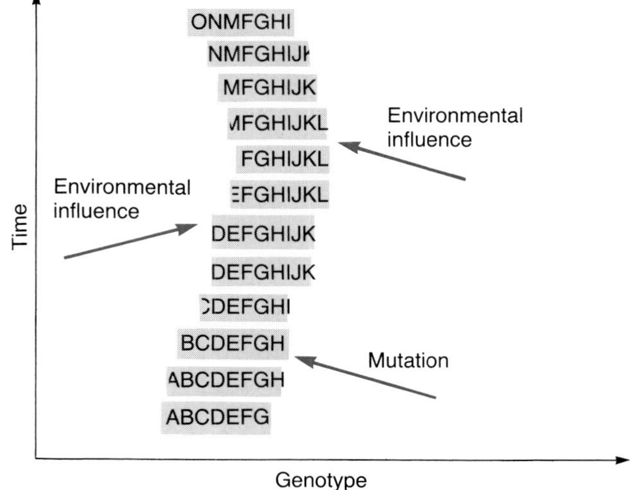

Figure 4–4
Hypothetical example of changing gene pools in successive populations over time, as represented by the changes in letters (= genes). Environmental conditions and other mechanisms such as mutation produce irreversible changes. One difficulty is to determine the point in this continuum of populations where biological speciation has occurred.

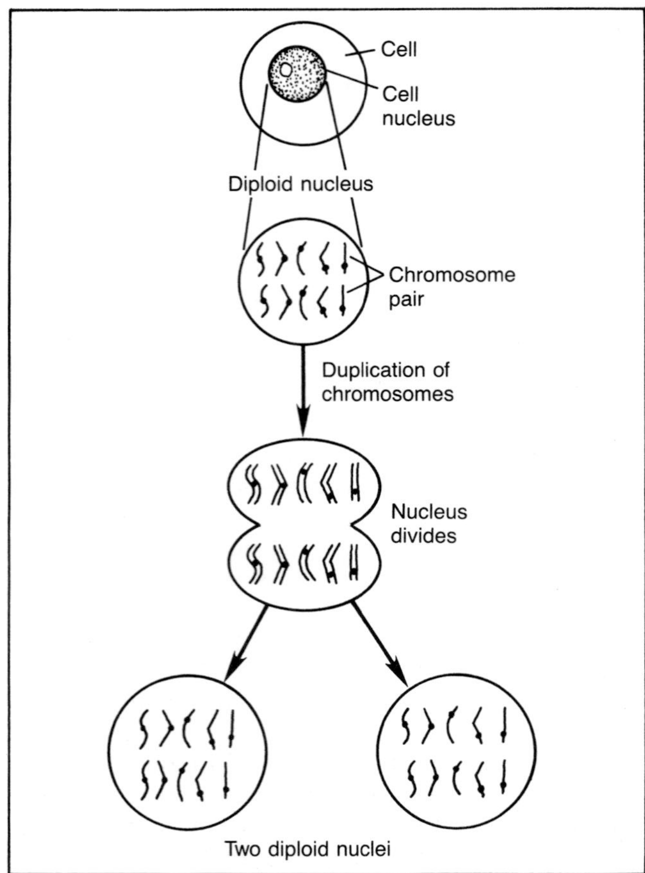

Figure 4–5
Diagram illustrating reproduction by mitosis (essentially cell division), a process which occurs in all kingdoms of organisms. This process tends to produce identical or nearly identical cells.

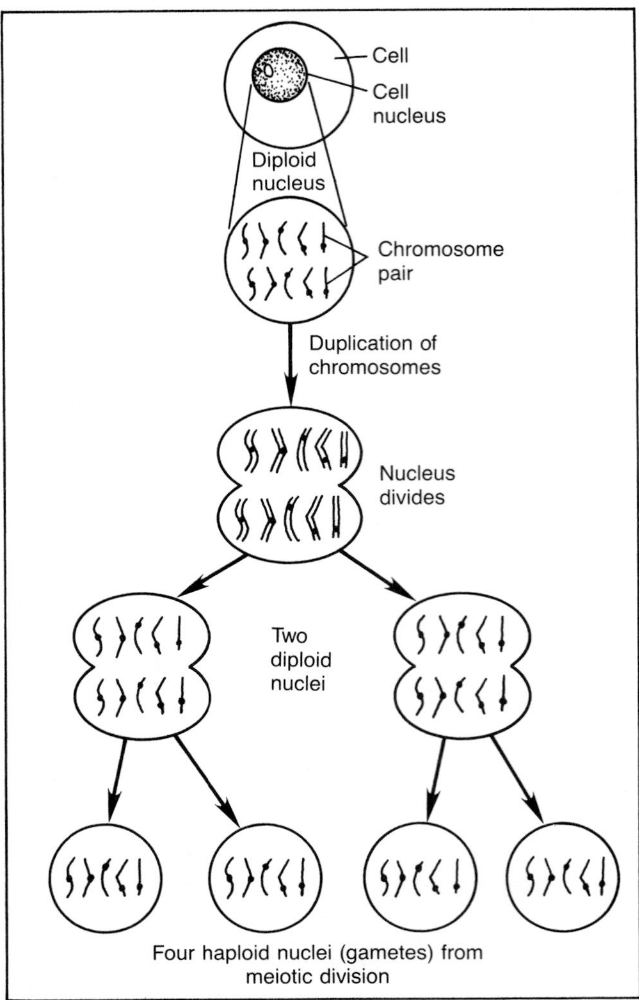

Figure 4–6
Diagram illustrating reproduction by meiosis, or reduction division. This is the process characteristic of sexually reproducing organisms. In this process gametes from different parents unite to produce cells that are genetically distinct from either parent.

which is identical to that of the parent cell (Fig. 4–5); the various groups of prokaryotic bacteria and cyanobacteria illustrate a number of variations of this mitotic process.

Much more complicated is the process of meiosis, or reduction division, which is characteristic of eukaryotic organisms that represent the other four kingdoms of organisms. In meiosis there are two successive divisions of the replicated DNA strands (chromosomes); the products are known as gametes (Fig. 4–6). Each gamete contains only half the genetic information of the parent; offspring are produced by combining gametes from two different parents; thus each offspring is genetically somewhat different from either parent.

Sexual reproduction by meiosis has played an enormous role in the evolutionary diversity of life. This can be illustrated by the following example, provided by the work of paleobiologist J. William Schopf at the University of California, Los Angeles. In a hypothetical asexually reproducing population consisting originally of one genotype, ten mutations will result in eleven different genetic combinations: the original plus the ten mutations. In contrast, ten mutations within a single genotype in the simplest sexually reproducing population could result in over 59,000 different genetic combinations! This large number dramatically expresses the potential for recombining genetic material through sexual reproduction. Evidence of this immense potential variation is provided by the multitude of living species and fossil taxa.

Evolutionary changes from one species to another take a considerable length of time—perhaps a minimum of about 10,000 years—much greater than that of a single human life span. It would therefore be impossible to observe such an event. Nonetheless, it is possible, within existing populations, to document the smaller genetic changes that may lead to the emergence of new species.

A very well-known example that illustrates changes in gene frequency is provided by the color changes in a species of British moth over the last 120 years. The extensive burning of coal for energy in the late 1800s and early 1900s produced considerable pollution that coated the trees, and gradually killed the lichens growing on the outer bark, darkening the trunks. As the trees became darker, light-colored moths became more visible and were easily preyed upon by birds. A strain of darker-colored moths (melanistic variants) gradually became more abundant because they were better camouflaged on the darker trees, were not as intensively preyed upon by birds, and thus were able to produce more offspring than the lighter-colored moths. The melanistic moths were selected for in this environment, and over successive generations became the most abundant strain in the populations.

This classic example, known as industrial melanism, provides a good illustration of the effect of environment and reproductive patterns on population gene pools and is an example of natural selection. Interestingly, the installation of antipollution devices has allowed the lichens to grow again, and lighter moths are becoming more abundant, apparently reversing the earlier trend. This would suggest that the environmental change had influenced the selection of darker variants in the moth populations, but was not of sufficient duration to produce a permanent genetic shift in the moth gene pool. Thus, this example illustrates processes that may lead to speciation.

Evolutionary changes from one species to another can be recognized in the fossil record; in fact, this is one of the most important contributions provided by the fossil record. These changes include appearance and disappearance of species and higher taxonomic groups. Although many taxa such as foraminifera, molluscs, trilobites, and others illustrate evolutionary changes, an excellent example is provided by the history of horses. As discussed in Chapter 17, a very large collection of fossil horses has been painstakingly assembled in Europe, Asia, and North America by many paleontologists. These remains illustrate the many species that have existed through the 50-million-year history of the group. The pattern illustrated by horses provides strong support for evolutionary processes operating over geologic time, and it is noteworthy that the fossil record of many other taxa discussed in this text also provide similar support.

Major Features of Evolution

The Species Problem

In living organisms, species often can be distinguished from one another on the basis of differences in phenotype, and these differences provide the basis of our classification of them. However, the underlying basis of our biological definition of a species is the genotype: more specifically, individuals of a single species must have the potential ability to interbreed and produce fertile offspring. Conversely, members of different species cannot interbreed. As defined by Harvard University biologist Ernst Mayr, species are "groups of actually or potentially interbreeding natural populations, which are reproductively isolated from other such groups."*

The key test for distinguishing among living species, therefore, especially if they closely resemble each other in morphology, is the determination of their potential for interbreeding. That is, different species should not be capable of interbreeding and producing fertile offspring. This isolation among species is known as **reproductive isolation,** but may not be complete in all species. For example, horses and donkeys can interbreed and produce mules, but mules are sterile and cannot reproduce. This reproductive test indicates that horses and donkeys are biologically different species, but are genetically somewhat similar because the evolutionary process of **divergence** of species has not yet become complete in this case. From these examples and many others it becomes evident that naming and recognizing most modern species on the basis of morphologic differences and reproductive capabilities are relatively easy. However, the recognition of species is somewhat more difficult for paleontologists working with fossils, because only morphologic features are available.

The scientist who collects, studies, and identifies fossils obviously cannot determine the ability of the specimens to interbreed! Paleontologists, therefore, rely heavily on the phenotype of the individuals, but also consider geographic proximity and stratigraphic position of the specimens and the range of variation within the entire population undergoing study. We previously made the observation that morphology is influenced to a great extent by genetic control; thus morphological differences or similarities among fossils provide a guide, although occasionally imperfect, to their evolutionary relationships. For example, comparison of the

*1965. *Animal Species & Evolution.* Cambridge, MA: Belknap Press of Harvard University Press, p. 19.

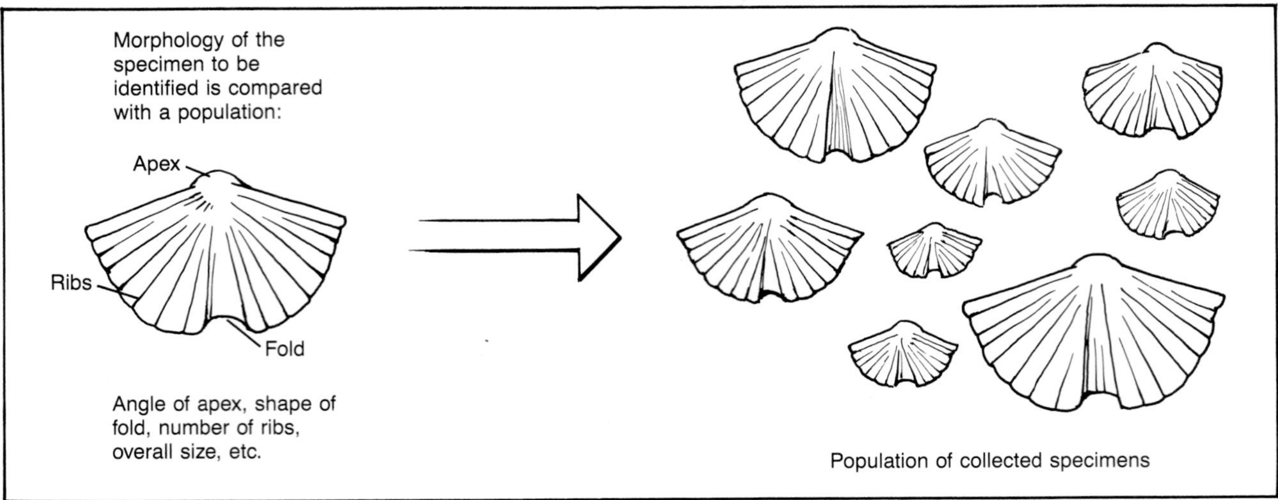

Figure 4–7
Comparison of a single brachiopod specimen with a large population of individuals judged to represent a single species. If the morphology (phenotype) of the individuals falls within the range of the large population, most paleontologists would consider that the individual belongs to the same species.

morphology of an individual specimen with the total variation in morphology observed in a collection of fossils judged to represent a single species can provide a strong clue for proper identification of the specimen (Fig. 4–7). The stratigraphic position of specimens in the geologic column also may provide a clue to species identification of the individual specimens (Fig. 4–8), but by itself is a poor tool for identification.

A further feature related to identification is **ontogeny,** which is growth of an individual organism through its lifetime. In many organisms, considerable changes in phenotype are expressed during ontogeny. For example, amphibians such as the frog have a young stage represented by a larval fishlike tadpole. After metamorphosis and growth of legs and lungs, loss of tail, and other changes, an adult frog has a totally different phenotype. Importantly, however, the organism has not undergone any genetic changes. Many other organisms, including most benthic marine invertebrates, also have a larval stage. Even in the absence of obvious metamorphosis the young and old of the same species may be considerably different in size, ornamentation, and other morphologic features. These morphologic variations present major problems for the paleontologist who attempts to recognize and identify species. Still another difficulty hampering correct identification is presented by the differences in morphology between males and females of the same species, a characteristic known as sexual dimorphism.

Evident from this discussion is that recognition and correct identification of species of fossils is a considerably more subjective process than recognition of living species. Paleontologists attempt to distinguish species on the basis of significant morphologic differences. Traditionally, these kinds of judgments have been made from visual, qualitative comparisons; more recently, mathematical approaches have been used in attempts to provide more objective, if less personal, discrimination of species. Nonetheless, the overall experience and judgment of the paleontologist who has studied a particular group of fossils, and who may be considered a "competent expert," still plays an important role in the recognition of species.

Models and Patterns of Evolution

We have emphasized the genetic and morphologic variability within living species, and the various problems encountered in identification of fossil species. The next step is to consider changes in species and higher taxa through time. Just as an individual organism undergoes ontogenetic changes during its life history, species, genera, families, or higher taxa to which the individual belongs likewise undergo changes during their geologic history. The reconstructed record of these changes is called **phylogeny,** which refers to the evolutionary relationships of species and supraspecific taxa. Phylogenetic relationships are illustrated most com-

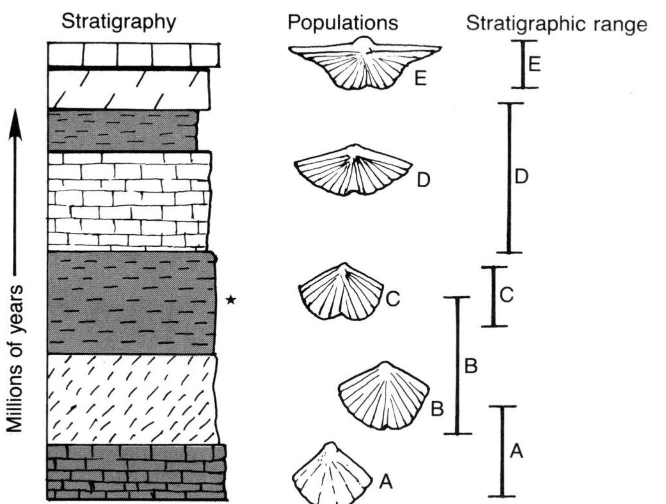

Figure 4–8
The stratigraphic position of a specimen (indicated by asterisk) may provide an important clue to its identification if the stratigraphy and associated fossilized taxa for the region have been worked out in detail. Note that the total amount of geologic time represented by the rocks is too long for these taxa (A–E) to represent variations of interbreeding populations.

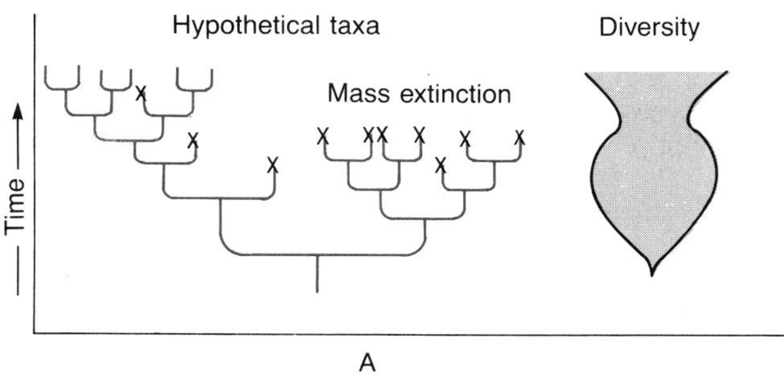

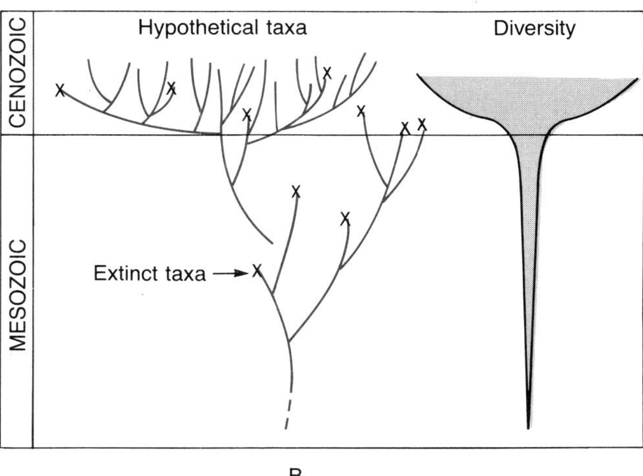

Figure 4–9
Hypothetical relationships of various related taxa (species, genera, and so forth). Each branch represents a separate taxon and the various groupings represent supraspecific taxa. This "family tree" can be expressed by the diversity diagram to the right, and represents the *allopatric model* (punctuated equilibria), where evolutionary change occurs between species. B. Another way of expressing phylogenetic relationships, evolutionary history, and diversity is by *phyletic gradualism,* where evolutionary change occurs within lineages.

monly by the branching "tree of life" (Fig. 4–9), which is a graphic expression of what is known about the phylogenetic relationships of the taxa involved.

The reconstructed geologic history of one or more genetically related species constitutes a **lineage.** If new species result from changes within a lineage, the process is termed **speciation.** A major problem in recognizing the various species within lineages is the difficulty of determining the rates and processes by which speciation occurs. Two models have been proposed to explain speciation.

In one model, proposed in the early 1970s and called **allopatric speciation** (Figs. 4–9A, 4–10), species are envisioned as forming from small parts of large populations that become geographically isolated. Because of mutations, genetic drift and natural selection, over many successive generations these isolated populations eventually become reproductively isolated and genetically distinct from the main population, and thus represent biologically new species. Because this process probably occurs rapidly in small isolated populations, the intermediate steps are rarely, if ever, preserved. This may explain the abrupt appearance of species in the rock record with no apparent intermediate forms. In this allopatric model all evolutionary changes occur rapidly between species. Within each individual lineage, represented by the entire gene pool, few or no evolutionary changes occur because of a dilution factor that tends to dampen any genetic changes. This process, representing rapid, local speciation events and longer-lived unchanging lineages, has been termed **punctuated equilibrium,** or sometimes the punctuational model.

Another, historically more traditional model of speciation is called **phyletic gradualism,** whereby one species of a lineage gradually changes into another through time (Figs. 4–9B, 4–11). In effect the processes are the same as in punctuated equilibria, but in contrast, operate on the entire population. In this model, gradual evolutionary transition from one end-member species to another renders it difficult to recognize exactly where the two lineages

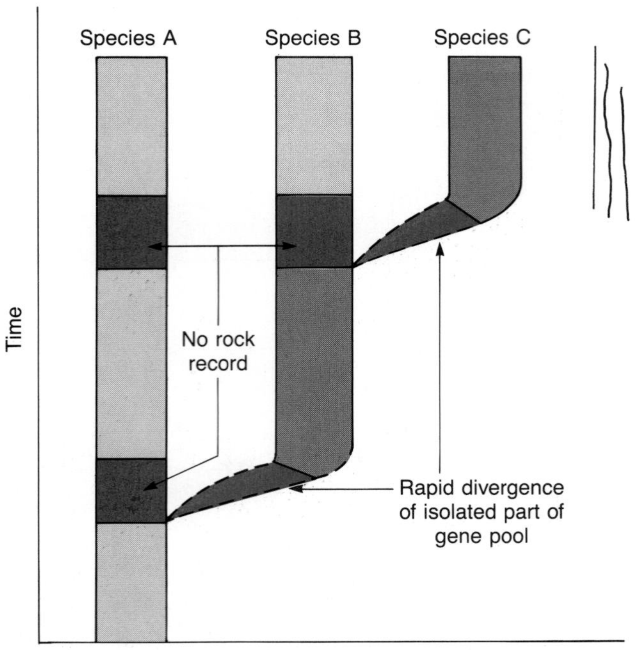

Figure 4–10
Simple model of allopatric speciation, illustrating three species having basically unchanging genotype and phenotype (equilibrium) over a significant length of time (represented by a stratigraphic range in the rock record). Small, reproductively isolated populations tend to undergo episodes of rapid genetic change, resulting in divergence (punctuated equilibrium). These populations become genetically and morphologically distinct from the bulk of the population and represent new species. These new species appear abruptly in the rock rercord.

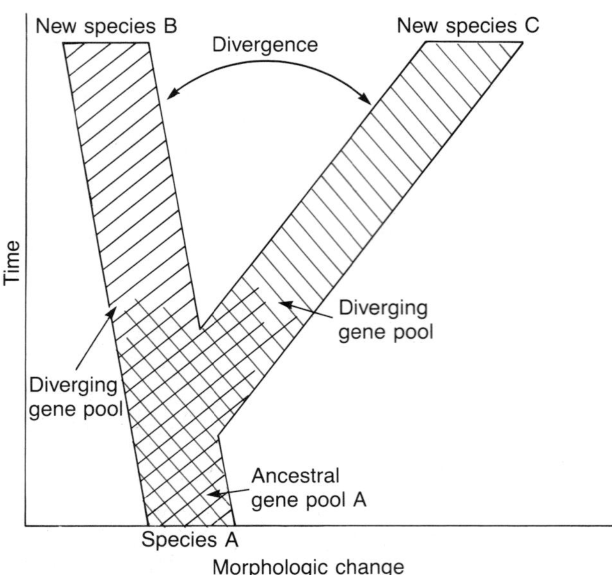

Figure 4–11
Example of phyletic speciation, or gradualism, where gradual divergence in the genetic composition of two populations leads to reproductive isolation and evolution of new species. Note that each species undergoes genetic and morphologic change through time.

separate. This decision, however, commonly is simplified for the paleontologist because of gaps in the fossil and rock record (Fig. 4–12).

Evolutionary biologists and paleontologists currently are engaged in a controversy over which of the two evolutionary models best explains the history of life. As we have seen, the rock and fossil records are incomplete and interpretations of evolutionary events suffer from many biases. However, the fossil record is sufficiently complete to provide enough data for evaluation of evolutionary patterns; the models developed from these patterns are based on how the record is interpreted and how the evolutionary process is viewed. Published work on various groups of fossils seems to indicate that both models have merit. As discussed earlier, what is important to remember is the fact that speciation by evolutionary changes has occurred throughout geologic time and can be documented by the fossil record; the method or methods by which speciation occurs are more difficult to interpret and provide the gist of much research and discussion.

On a larger scale, the geologically rapid proliferation of many new species and higher taxa from one or a few ancestral stocks is called **adaptive ra-**

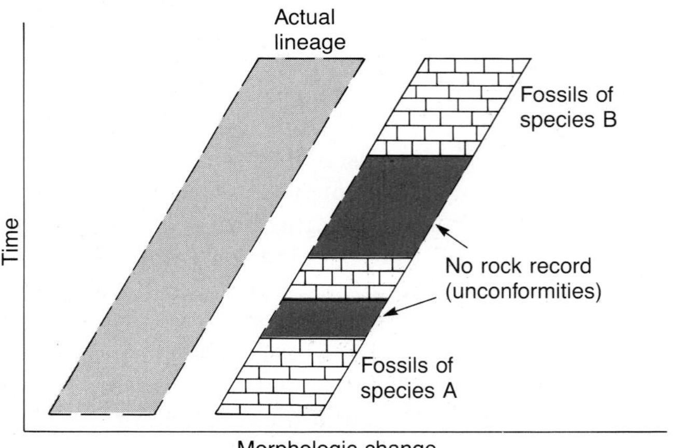

Figure 4–12
Gaps in the sedimentary rock record create apparent "breaks" in the preserved record of a taxonomic lineage. These gaps are used by paleontologists to help recognize new species. In this example fossils of B are morphologically distinct from those of A, and may be genetically distinct as well, thereby representing a distinct species.

diation. Some spectacular examples are the abrupt appearances of shelled invertebrates in the early Paleozoic (Chapter 9), the evolution of ruling reptiles in the Mesozoic (Chapter 13), and the evolution of mammals in the Cenozoic (Chapter 14).

So far our discussion has focused upon the species, but how do we explain the origin of higher taxa? In our discussion of the classification scheme for organisms we recognized that taxonomic categories above species are artificially created by taxonomists; however, these ranks still represent evolutionary relationships among organisms.

At various times in the geologic past, significant environmental changes, coupled with adaptive innovations or breakthroughs, have produced broad new adaptive patterns. As a consequence of these far-reaching evolutionary opportunities, major adaptive radiations have occurred, highlighted by the appearance of new higher taxa—phyla, classes, and orders—in response to the accessibility of new ways of life. Lower taxa within these groups—families, genera, and particularly species—diversified most rapidly at later times within these adaptive radiations, and in the process essentially partitioned the broad adaptive zones invaded earlier. A few examples include the evolution of hard skeletal parts in the early Paleozoic, paving the way for the radiation of invertebrate phyla; the evolution of limbs and lungs in a group of fish that later invaded the land as the class Amphibia; and the evolution of temperature regulation and feathers, which allowed the development of flight, characteristic of birds.

Such patterns of diversification have been clearly recognized within marine invertebrates through the Phanerozoic. At least three episodes of diversification can be recognized; one occurred early in the Phanerozoic and provided a variety of invertebrates, which are collectively known as the "Cambrian fauna." These organisms were replaced later in the Paleozoic with new types of invertebrates, which are known as the "Paleozoic fauna." Yet another replacement occurred, beginning in Triassic time and continuing to the present; these taxa are known as the "Modern fauna" (Fig. 4–13).

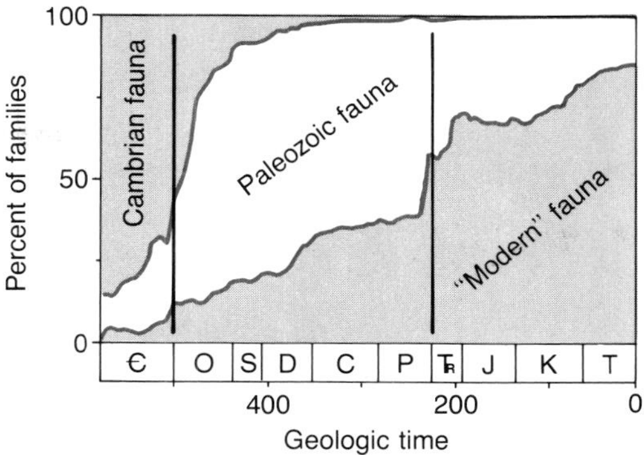

Figure 4–13
Changes in the taxonomic composition of marine invertebrates through the Phanerozoic. Cambrian fauna is represented by trilobites, inarticulate brachiopods, archaeocyathids, hyolithids, and what are termed primitive echinoderms. Paleozoic fauna is represented by articulate brachiopods, corals, stalked echinoderms, cephalopod molluscs, and graptolites. Modern fauna is represented by gastropod and bivalve molluscs, echinoid and asteroid echinoderms, and bryozoans.
(From J. J. Sepkoski, Jr. 1981. The Uniqueness of the Cambrian Fauna, Fig. 2, p. 205, *in Short Papers for the Second International Symposium on the Cambrian System:* U.S. Geological Survey Open File Report 81–743. Reprinted by permission of author)

Crises in the History of Life

Introduction

We have briefly considered some of the processes of evolution that control the appearance, diversity, and distribution of organisms. There is yet another major feature to consider, and that is the phenomenon of **extinction,** which represents the disappearance of a taxonomic group on a global scale. Evidence from our previous discussion of models of speciation suggests that extinction is a major feature of evolution, and furthermore is the ultimate fate of all species (Figure 4–14). Extinction of species appears to be a continuous phenomenon re-

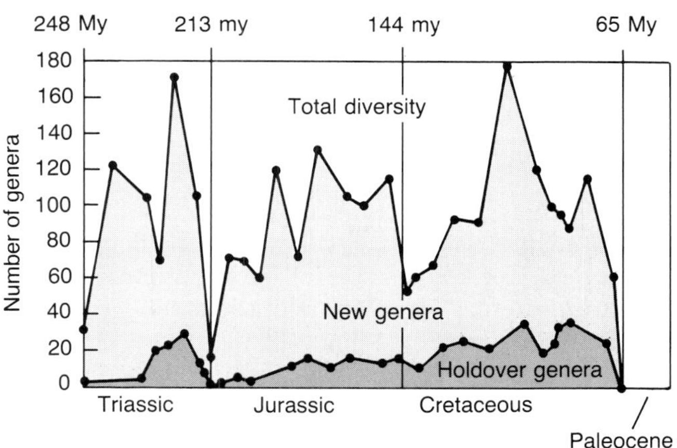

Figure 4–14
Model of the distribution of ammonoid molluscs through Mesozoic time, illustrating major changes in diversity of genera, culminating with final extinction at the end of Cretaceous time. This rapid turnover of taxa is one reason ammonoids are good index taxa.
(Modified from W. J. Kennedy, *in* A. Hallam, ed., 1977, *Patterns of Evolution:* Elsevier, Amsterdam)

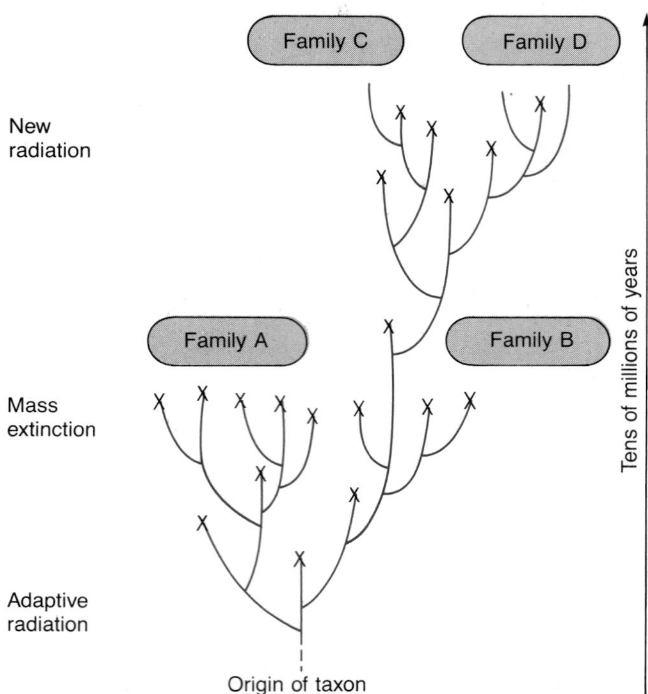

Figure 4–15

Origin and subsequent radiation of taxa classified into distinct families. Families A and B are affected by an episode of mass extinction. Only one lineage survives, and it serves as the ancestor for a new adaptive radiation. Although this is a hypothetical example, the geologic record of ammonoids in the Mesozoic followed a similar pattern (see Chapter 13).

corded in the rock record. However, study of the distribution of extinctions of taxa through time indicates that at certain intervals of time relatively severe waves of extinction affected large numbers of species and higher taxa on a worldwide scale. As paleontologist Norman Newell has aptly pointed out, these times of mass extinctions were "crises in the history of life."*

These mass extinctions are essentially the opposite of adaptive radiations; we can consider extinction to be an expression of environmental foreclosure, whereas adaptive radiation reflects environmental opportunity (Fig. 4–15).

Although extinctions have occurred throughout geologic time, our focus will be upon those that have affected a large number of taxa within a relatively short span of time. The most interesting major episodes of extinction were those that occurred near the ends of the Cambrian, Ordovician, Devonian, Permian, Triassic, and Cretaceous Periods. As we mention in Chapter 6, such events in the fossil record have been used to define and recognize these and other chronostratigraphic boundaries. We will consider as examples mass extinctions at the ends of Permian and Cretaceous time. The events will be discussed more fully in the chapters on Permian and Cretaceous history (11 and 13), but we introduce them here in the fuller context of evolution.

The Permian and Cretaceous Extinctions

A tabulation of the fossil record made by Newell indicates that approximately 55% of the families of invertebrates became extinct within a 5 million-year span at the end of Permian time. A similar tabulation indicates that about 30% of the families of invertebrates became extinct at the end of the Cretaceous. Although this is a lower percentage than for the Permian, the total number of families was greater in the Cretaceous because the total diversity apparently was greater. At both times many land and marine-dwelling vertebrate taxa also became extinct (Fig. 4–16).

During the Permian crisis some groups, such as trilobites and fusulinid Foraminifera, completely

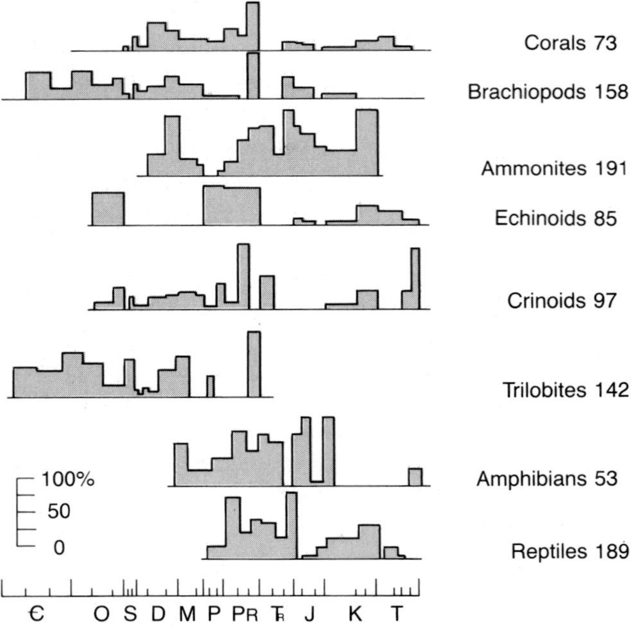

Figure 4–16

Selected representatives of major taxonomic groups that became extinct at the end of the Permian and Cretaceous Periods. Note percentages of families.
(Adapted from N. D. Newell, 1962, Paleontological Gaps and Geochronology, Fig. 6, p. 599: *Journal of Paleontology*, vol. 36, no. 3. Reproduced by permission of Society of Economic Paleontologists and Mineralogists)

*February 1963. Crises in the history of life. *Scientific American.*

disappeared. Many other taxa were severely affected; some of these were brachiopods, crinoids, corals, and terrestrial amphibians and mammal-like reptiles. Surprisingly, this episode of extinction did not greatly affect terrestrial plants. In general, similar kinds of organisms became extinct at the end of the Cretaceous. These included marine invertebrates, such as ammonites and many kinds of bivalves, and planktonic Foraminifera. Many vertebrates also became extinct, especially the large reptiles that lived on land and in the oceans. Again, plant groups were not, for the most part, severely affected.

By comparing these two episodes of extinction, we find that a wide variety of land-dwelling and water-dwelling vertebrates and invertebrates became extinct. The fact that plant groups do not seem to show a similar decline in numbers presents an interesting problem. The fossil record indicates that major extinctions and replacement of plant groups occurred slightly before the Permian and Cretaceous animal extinctions. What, if any, are the relationships between these plant extinctions and the subsequent animal extinctions? This is discussed later in this chapter.

Perhaps one of the most nagging questions in paleontology is what caused extinctions of a wide variety of taxonomic groups during these relatively short intervals of time. Major physical and biological phenomena known from study of the Earth's history and from study of the Earth today might have caused or contributed to major episodes of extinction. Over the years, many geologists have become interested in the phenomenon, and have proposed a number of hypotheses to account for these events. Why are some taxa affected and others not at all? What are the ideas and hypotheses that have been proposed to explain extinctions? Figure 4–17 and the following list indicate some of these proposals:

1. Volcanic eruptions on a very large scale
2. Major episodes of mountain building (orogeny)
3. Heating or cooling of global climate
4. Trace-element changes in oceans
5. Magnetic reversals and solar radiation
6. Meteorite or other large bolide impacts
7. Plate tectonics and associated environmental disruptions
8. Changes in atmospheric composition
9. Food-chain disruptions on a large scale
10. Species competition affecting communities

These explanations for extinction can be divided into two main categories: those proposing a physical cause (1–8), and those proposing a biological cause (9–10). Perhaps a combination of these explanations is involved, or perhaps an event or events not yet recognized may have contributed. One frustrating feature common to all of these hypotheses is that, for the most part, they cannot be tested experimentally; very likely it will never be possible to determine which, if any, is correct.

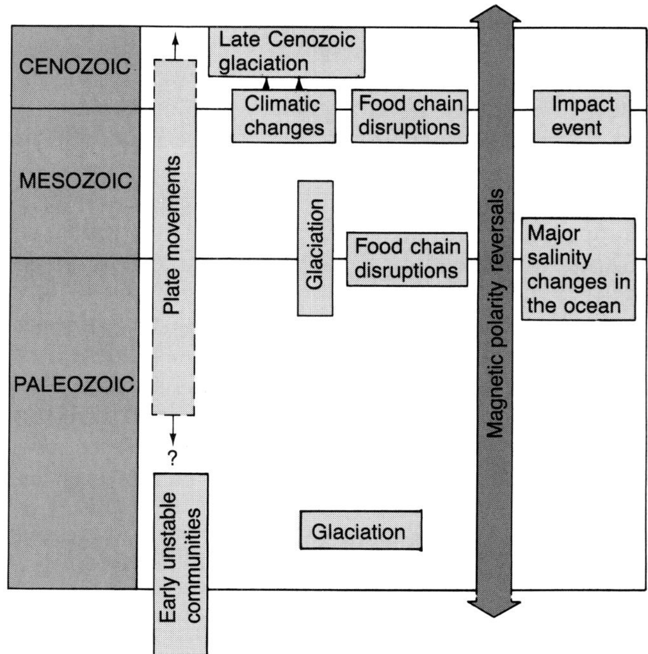

Figure 4–17
Some physical and biological events which have occurred in the last 700 million years and which might have triggered episodes of mass extinction.

Extinctions: Physical Hypotheses

Only two physical causes for extinction will be considered here. Movements of lithospheric plates and catastrophic impact events represent the most recently proposed hypotheses, and they have received much attention in the scientific community as well as much public interest. Both represent physical conditions that could have affected the entire planet, and thus had the potential for producing complete extinction of one or more groups of organisms.

Movement of continents and opening and closing of ocean basins could have played a major role in extinctions. This idea, related to the concept of plate tectonics, has been developed only since the late 1960s. Let us look at some factors involved, and determine their possible consequences for organisms.

Shifting of the lithospheric plates will produce a number of physical changes in the environment. First, we know that movements of the lithospheric plates have influenced mountain-building and volcanic activity, especially at convergent plate boundaries. This has resulted in tectonic uplift of mountain belts and thereby changed the relative position of sea level. Second, any northward or southward movements would result in a change in position of the continents relative to east–west distribution of climatic zones. Finally, the opening and closing of ocean basins, along with changing climate, would create environmental stresses by changing the number as well as the characteristics of habitats to which organisms had become adapted. For example, a clustering of continents would produce more severe climatic conditions on land by eliminating any buffer effect of large intervening bodies of water. Such clustering would also decrease the number of shallow-marine environments by eliminating many thousands of square kilometers of shelf, and additionally would allow greater intermixing of terrestrial communities.

All of these changes tend to decrease diversity of organisms—in effect, producing extinctions. Could such environmental changes, caused by plate tectonic activity, have affected habitats and lowered rates of speciation enough to produce worldwide extinctions of many diverse taxa? Let us consider this possibility further.

Paleontologic, stratigraphic, and paleomagnetic evidence all suggest that the continents were joined together to form Pangaea in late Paleozoic time (Chapter 11). The effects of this movement and joining were:

1. Uplift of land areas and regression of the shallow Paleozoic seas,
2. Reduction in areas of shallow-shelf seas that bordered the continents, and
3. Accentuation of climatic extremes because of the clustering of the continents.

It is quite reasonable to assume that a combination of these events would have placed great stress on existing organisms in the Permian, primarily because of climatic changes on land and reduction in habitats and changes in circulation patterns in the oceans. However, the basic question still remains: were these factors sufficient to produce the extinctions noted in the record?

Moving ahead in time about 150 million years, we find that by mid-Cretaceous time there were considerable changes in the positions of continents and ocean basins, compared with their positions in the Paleozoic (Chapters 11 and 13). In particular, opening of the south Atlantic and partial opening of the north Atlantic had occurred, and Australia and India had moved northward. Corresponding with these changes was the establishment of warm climate, possibly related to formation of widespread, shallow, continental seas reminiscent of those existing during the middle Paleozoic before the formation of Pangaea.

Thus, environmental conditions were considerably different from those that had existed on Pangaea in late Paleozoic-to-early-Mesozoic time. Study of the fossil record indicates that Mesozoic marine and terrestrial environments were filled with a great diversity of organisms. However, in rocks representing the last 30 million years of the Cretaceous Period, the fossil record changes dramatically and provides evidence of another mass extinction.

Major environmental changes that occurred from Middle to Late Cretaceous time resulted from plate motions and fragmentation of Pangaea. Increased tectonic activity associated with subduction of oceanic lithosphere and withdrawal of the extensive interior seas from the continents may have influenced development of drier and cooler climatic zones. These changes reduced the number of terrestrial habitats and very conceivably could have played a major role in the Cretaceous extinctions.

The present positions of the continents and ocean basins indicate that considerable movement has occurred during the 65 million years since the end of the Cretaceous Period. Today continents are still moving; average elevation of land areas is relatively high compared with elevations in the past, and climate is relatively cool. Furthermore, we recognize that there have been considerable changes in kinds of organisms and their geographic distributions in the last few million years of the Cenozoic Era. These changes may reflect continent positions.

Overall, the movements and positions of lithospheric plates through time appear to play an important role in the evolutionary history of taxa, and may indeed have been a major cause of mass extinction. Could there be other mechanisms significant enough to cause mass extinction?

The other extinction hypothesis we will discuss for the terminal Cretaceous event was first proposed in early 1980 by Walter Alvarez and colleagues of the University of California, Berkeley (see discussion in Chapter 13). Study of the sedimentary rocks at the stratigraphic position of the

Cretaceous-Tertiary boundary provided evidence of an unusually high concentration of iridium and other rare elements. Subsequent research has confirmed that in some areas this element occurs in significantly higher concentrations in strata at or very near the boundary than in other strata. This anomaly suggests an extraterrestrial event: an asteroid or comet (bolide) burning through the atmosphere and crashing on Earth, either on land or in the oceans. Disintegration of this iridium-containing bolide, which is calculated to have been 6 to 10 kilometers in diameter, and the force of the impact event would have produced a dust cloud and spread a layer of iridium-bearing dust around the globe. Recent modeling of the proposed dust clouds produced by a nuclear war—the "nuclear winter" hypothesis—provides a scary analogy for the results of a bolide impact.

More controversial than the impact itself is the hypothesis that the Cretaceous extinctions were directly related to this event. Current ideas are tentative and are being revised almost monthly. An impact on land would have produced many cubic kilometers of dust, whereas an impact in water would have produced ice crystals. These materials literally would have been blown into the upper atmosphere, and the resulting clouds would have caused a severe reduction in solar radiation reaching the Earth's surface. As presently calculated, the resulting decrease in sunlight would have lasted a few months—long enough to produce massive extinctions in marine phytoplankton and thus disruption of the entire oceanic food chain structure. Significantly, this length of time would have been insufficient to drastically affect terrestrial plants; this is in accord with the record of plants in the latest Cretaceous.

Current studies have focused upon determining the iridium concentrations in strata bracketing the Cretaceous-Tertiary boundary. Cores from deep-sea bore holes and from outcrops in areas such as the Rocky Mountain region are currently being studied. Along with determination of the iridium content, comparisons of distribution and changes in taxa associated with iridium-rich layers are being made. Relationship of these layers to the established position of the boundary will, perhaps, indicate the validity of this hypothesis (Fig. 4–18).

It is evident that both these physical hypotheses for extinction operate by producing major alterations of the environment, thereby affecting communities of organisms on a regional or global scale. Possibly the changes triggered within and among communities themselves would be important contributions to extinction. This possibility is considered below, as we examine biological hypotheses for extinction.

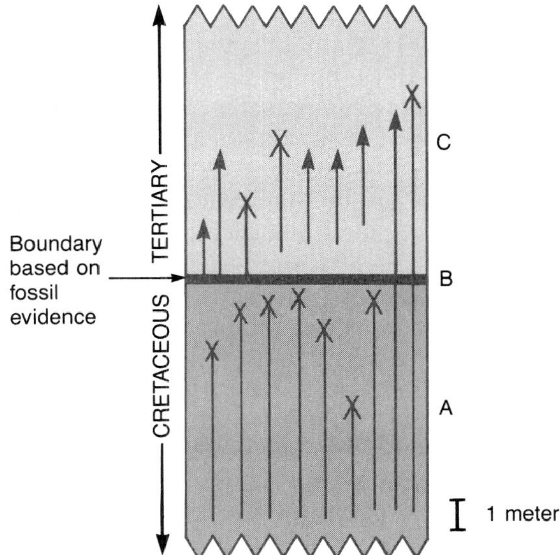

Figure 4–18
Stratigraphic distribution of taxa used to recognize the Cretaceous-Tertiary boundary. X represents an extinction; arrow indicates continued range of taxon. A, B, and C represent potential locations of iridium-rich layers with respect to the boundary. Current research may provide an indication of the stratigraphic position of this layer with respect to the boundary in many geographic locations.

Extinctions: Biological Hypotheses

Biological hypotheses used to explain extinctions invoke mechanisms operating within or among communities of organisms, rather than those involving changes in the physical environment. Some hypotheses within this category are species competition, alteration of community relationships, and changes of food chains among interdependent species. As you will see, these hypotheses are not isolated from one another, but tend to overlap and often must be considered together. In the following discussion we will combine these ideas.

Although each species occupies a *niche* that is generally distinct from that of other species, requirements for various resources create considerable competition among individuals of a single species and among the species themselves. Physical changes in the environment can alleviate or intensify this competition. Just as individuals have different abilities to cope with competition and environmental stress, so do species differ in their ability to survive environmental changes. In general, each species is physiologically adapted to the conditions under which it lives, but some species can survive and reproduce in a much greater range of conditions than others. For example, in oceanic environments those with narrow tolerances are considered **stenotopic,** and those having wide tolerances are considered **eurytopic.** Stenotopic species are specialized taxa that are more vulnerable to changes; eurytopic species are generalists and are able to survive by adapting to changes. Stenotopic species would be more likely to become extinct and have shorter phylogenetic histories than eurytopic species.

Modern organisms exist in complex communities that may consist of tens or hundreds of species and a vast number of individuals. During times of environmental stability, well-established communities consisting of a large number of interdependent stenotopic and eurytopic species develop. Each species exists within a niche, but the boundaries of niches commonly overlap; this creates competition for living space, sunlight, food, oxygen, and other resources. This competition occurs in all communities and promotes strong selective pressure on organisms. Competing species exist in complex systems of interacting communities within major *biogeographic provinces* (Chapter 3). The species, together with the general characteristics of communities in each province, can and do change through time. Perhaps extinctions are explained more easily at the community level of organization than at the individual species level. Let us examine some ancient communities.

Paleontologist Helen Tappan Loeblich at the University of California, Los Angeles, has suggested that mass extinctions at the end of the Paleozoic were caused in part by a breakdown in the stable community structures that had developed earlier in the Paleozoic. This breakdown may have been precipitated by lithospheric plate movements that produced major changes in distribution of land and ocean-basin positions, thereby triggering catastrophic changes in primary producer organisms and in feeding patterns in oceanic **food webs.**

Careful analysis of organisms preserved in the fossil record shows that there has been a trend toward greater efficiency in food gathering through time. The ability of individual organisms and species to obtain food in competition with others determines in large measure which survive, and most importantly, which reproduce. Thus natural selection will favor the most efficient food gatherers. For example, the bivalve molluscs, many of which are efficient filter feeders, rapidly increased in diversity in the Mesozoic and replaced brachiopods (Chapter 12), which had been abundant during most of Paleozoic time but had been affected greatly by extinction in the Permian Period.

The significance of food chains and food webs in development and maintenance of communities is well documented for living organisms. In modern communities, disruptions of food chains or food webs have disastrous consequences for the structure of the community and the survival of its species. For example, changes in climate on land will affect the type of vegetation. Because land plants are the base of terrestrial food webs, changes in these taxa greatly alter the types of consumer species living in a region. In the oceans, phytoplankton blooms such as red tides greatly affect the other organisms, although these changes may be only temporary. We have noted a possible connection between changes in producers and mass extinctions at the end of the Permian. Does this hypothesis of food-chain disruption as a triggering mechanism for extinctions hold for the Cretaceous also?

Reconstruction of a simplified terrestrial food chain for Mesozoic time indicates that it consisted of seed plants such as gymnosperms as the basic producers, and herbivorous and then carnivorous dinosaurs as the consumer groups (Fig. 4–19A). Study of the fossil record provides evidence that during the latter part of Mesozoic time many taxa of gymnosperms became extinct and were replaced by flowering plants (angiosperms). This is particularly evident in rocks of the Cretaceous Period. The dinosaurs also became extinct at the end of the Cretaceous. It is tempting to assume a direct cause-and-effect relationship between changes in gymnosperms and the subsequent extinction of dinosaurs. However, plant replacement took place primarily during the early part of the Cretaceous, and major extinction of dinosaurs occurred only near the end of this time, many millions of years later. Were the dinosaurs decreasing in abundance throughout this interval, and if so, were the changes in plants a significant contributing factor? As yet, we do not know the answers to these questions. Also, this mechanism does not explain the simultaneous extinctions of many marine-dwelling species at the end of the Cretaceous.

A food chain can be reconstructed for Mesozoic marine communities (Fig. 4–19B). This food chain has two more steps than the terrestrial example, and involves more species. The producers consisted of phytoplankton, such as diatoms. These were consumed by various plankton, such as Foraminifera and Radiolaria, and eventually the sequence ended at large marine reptiles, such as plesiosaurs and ichthyosaurs. The fossil record indicates that

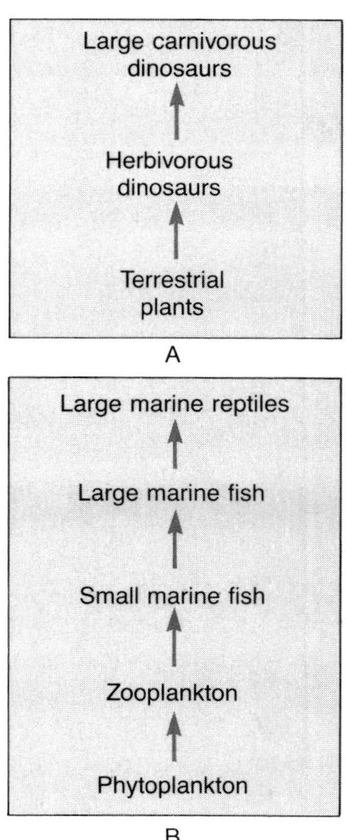

Figure 4–19
A. Simplified terrestrial food chain for Mesozoic time, which had primary producers (land plants) and a variety of consumers up to the level of carnivorous dinosaurs. B. Simplified oceanic food chain for Mesozoic time to illustrate the interdependence of species from the producers (phytoplankton) to the top-level consumers (marine reptiles).

significant changes in phytoplankton occurred near the end of the Mesozoic. We find that the first major diversification of diatoms and other microscopic algal groups occurred during the Cretaceous Period. Drastic changes affected planktonic Foraminifera, algal groups, ammonite cephalopods, and marine reptiles at the end of Cretaceous time; perhaps there is a connection among all of these taxa that explains their similar phylogenetic histories.

After considering these biological explanations as the cause of mass extinction, and recognizing that geologists currently lack sufficient evidence to provide proof for any of these mechanisms, we can suggest an area of research. This would involve detailed study to determine feeding characteristics of the various taxa affected by mass extinction, and then an attempt to reconstruct their community relationships. Perhaps analyses of feeding types would indicate that certain kinds of organisms such as filter feeders were more affected during mass extinctions than organisms having different feeding habits. Evidence that extinction selectively affected taxa on the basis of their feeding type and community organization would provide strong support for the hypothesis that biological events play an important role in mass extinctions.

Armed with these ideas on extinction, we can look at a representation of the relative extinction rates of families of eleven major taxa of vertebrates and invertebrates (Fig. 4–20). Based on a scale of 1 to 100%, it is evident that mass extinction occurred at a number of fairly regularly spaced time intervals within the last 600 million years. Especially evident are the extinctions that occurred at the end of the Cambrian and Permian; slightly less dramatic are those that occurred at the end of Devonian, Triassic, and Cretaceous times.

We have considered those events that occurred in the Permian and Cretaceous, but it is evident that our explanations must account for these other episodes of mass extinction as well. At the present state of paleontological knowledge, we are not yet able to detect a common feature relating all of these episodes to a single event or a combination of events. This is obviously an area of geological re-

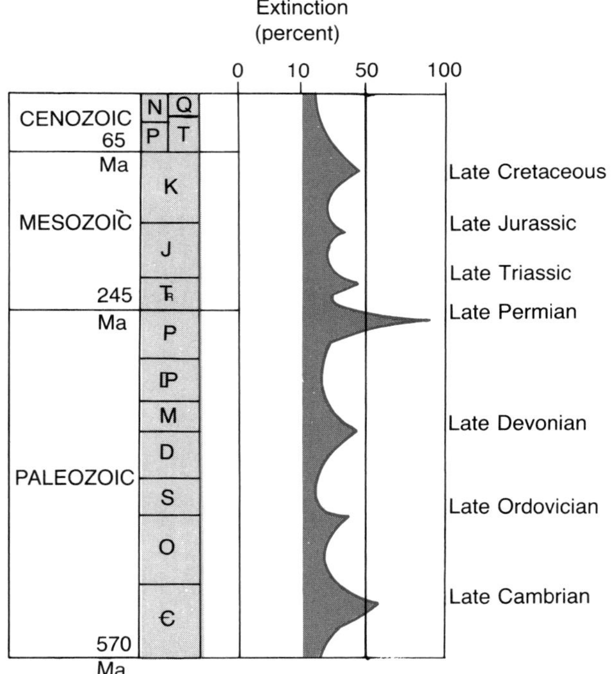

Figure 4–20
Simplified chart illustrating rates of extinction of major taxa during Phanerozoic time. Significant extinction peaks occurred in Late Cambrian, Late Ordovician, Late Devonian, Late Permian, Late Triassic, and Late Cretaceous.

search that will continue to present a challenge for years to come.

Other Ideas on Diversity and Extinction

Perhaps what are seen to be significant episodic mass extinctions are in part a bias of the fossil record. Discussion of the diversity of taxa through the Phanerozoic Eon provides an illustration of this idea. Many tabulations of the number of species in the fossil record of the Phanerozoic indicate that a very rapid, spectacular increase in diversity occurred in the late Mesozoic and in the Cenozoic (Fig. 4–21). However, other interpretations of the same evidence suggest this geologically recent, apparent increase may instead represent a bias in the older rock and fossil record (Fig. 4–22). For example, younger sedimentary rocks are more abundant on the Earth's surface, commonly contain more abundant fossils, and are less altered than older rocks; they also are more intensively studied by paleontologists. Furthermore, the fossil record consists primarily of the remains of organisms having hard parts, and tends to reflect only a small portion of the true diversity existing during any particular interval of time. Consider the large number of modern soft-bodied taxa, few of which would be preserved.

The alternative explanation suggests that the major increase in diversity occurred in the early Phanerozoic, triggered by the appearance of sexual reproduction and aided by the evolution of hard parts and the conquest of land. Support for this idea comes from very recent studies which note much higher diversities of soft-bodied fossils in rocks of Ediacarian and Cambrian age than had previously been recognized.

These models, as well as other explanations of evolution and extinction considered in this chapter, serve to illustrate the many problems of unraveling the complex nature of the history of life. The models also touch on a fascinating aspect of geology: the existence of alternative answers, none of which

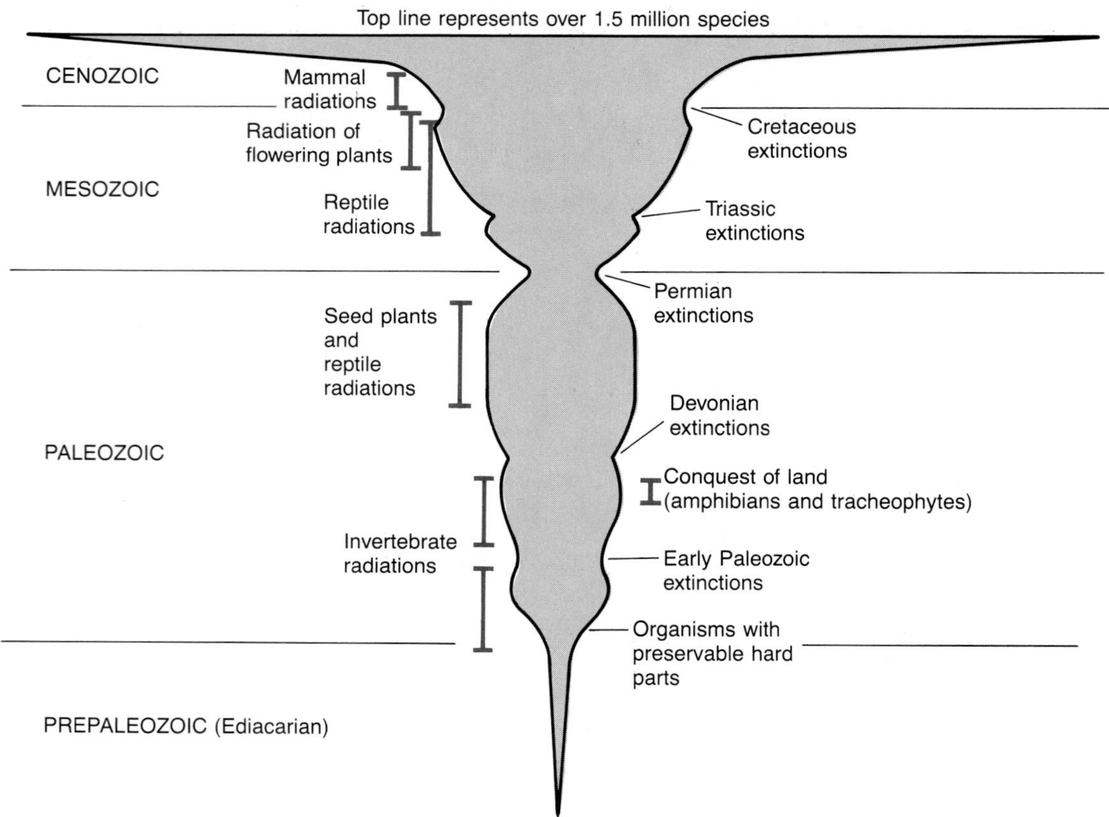

Figure 4–21
Model of diversity changes through the Phanerozoic; based on the known fossil and modern record. Note important events and the extremely rapid increase that has occurred in the last million years.

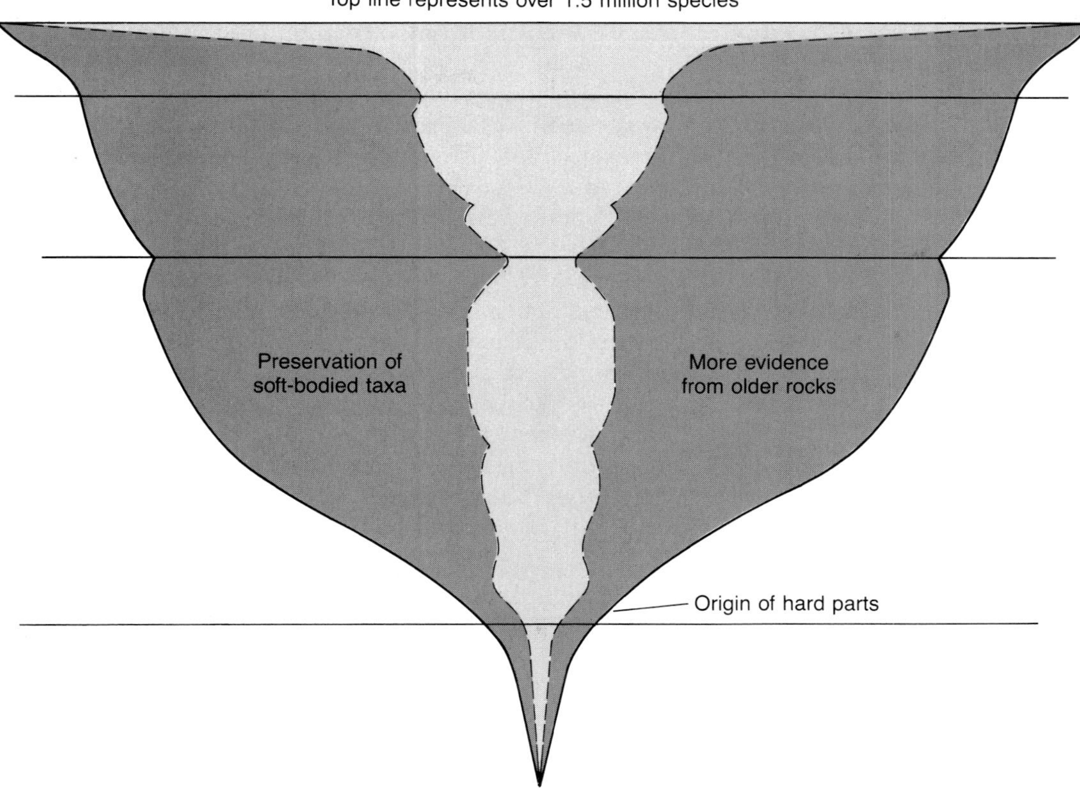

Figure 4–22
Alternative model of diversity changes through the Phanerozoic; based on extrapolation of organisms not preserved. This model and the one in Figure 4–21 represent "end members" in concepts of diversity increase. Perhaps the correct explanation lies between the two.

may be proved correct, and any of which may be evaluated or reinterpreted upon acquisition of new data. Indeed, these examples illustrate the scientific method, and underscore the fundamental differences between scientific and religious explanations for evolution.

Summary

Evolutionary theory has had a stormy history since publication of Charles Darwin's *On the Origin of Species* in 1859. Evidence of natural selection operating on populations, the experiments of Gregor Mendel and later development of the science of genetics, and the unraveling of DNA structure by Watson and Crick provided three important support pillars for the theory. We recognize that environmental influences, coupled to mutation, provide mechanisms for changes which occur through sexual reproduction, or meiosis, over successive generations. These changes in gene pools of populations eventually lead to reproductive isolation, and such reproductively isolated populations represent biologically distinct species.

Speciation events through geologic time, if preserved in the rock record, represent what we call evolutionary lineages. Study of such lineages has provided evidence of immense changes in the biosphere over the last 3500 million years. Two models have been proposed to explain speciation; one is known as phyletic gradualism, and the other is allopatric speciation. Evidence has been put forth to support both models, and possibly both have served as pathways for speciation.

A phenomenon recognized in the study of higher taxonomic ranks is adaptive radiation, characterized by the appearance of many new taxa within a relatively short interval of geologic time. An opposing phenomenon is extinction: the disappearance of taxa from the rock record. Episodes of mass extinction have occurred at a few intervals during geologic time, in particular at the end of the Permian Period (= end of the Paleozoic Era) and at the end of the Cretaceous Period (= end of the Mesozoic Era). Of course, it was the recognition of these extinctions by the early architects of our geologic time scale that inspired the placement of these era boundaries.

Explanations to account for these apparently catastrophic events have called upon a wide variety of physical and biological events. Plate movements, with corresponding changes in the position of ocean basins and land areas and in climate, or possible impacts of large extraterrestrial bodies, are currently the most favored physical hypotheses. Changes in food chains and disruptions of major community structures have been suggested as biologically related hypotheses.

Suggestions for Further Reading

Darwin, C. R. 1859. *On the origin of species.* London: John Murray.

DeCamp, L. S. 1968. *The great monkey trial.* New York: Doubleday.

Laporte, L. F. 1978. Evolution and the fossil record. In *Readings from Scientific American.* San Francisco: W. H. Freeman. (Note especially the articles by Dobzhansky 1950, L. C. Eiseley 1956, and N. D. Newell 1963.)

Mayr, E. 1978. Evolution. *Scientific American* 239(3):46–55.

Newell, N. D. 1962. Paleontological gaps and geochronology. *Journal of Paleontology* 36(3):592–610.

Raup, D. M. 1977. Probabilistic models in evolutionary paleobiology. *American Scientist* 65(1):50–57.

Raup, D. M., and S. M. Stanley. 1978. *Principles of paleontology.* 2d ed. San Francisco: W. H. Freeman.

Watson, J. D. 1968. *The double helix.* New York: Signet.

The Abyss of Time: Concepts and Principles of Geologic Time

5

Contents

Key Terms

Stratigraphy
Superposition
Original horizontality
Lateral continuity
Correlation
Cross-cutting relationships
Unconformity
Hiatus
Nonconformity
Angular unconformity
Diastem
Disconformity
Law of inclusions
Fossil succession
Geochronology
Radiometric
Radioactive decay
Radioactive emission
Nuclide
Atomic number
Isotope
Radiogenic
Half life
Blocking temperature

The Book of Time

> High up in the North in the land called Svithjod, there stands a rock. It is a hundred miles high and a hundred miles wide. Once every thousand years a little bird comes to this rock to sharpen its beak. When the rock has thus been worn away, then a single day of eternity will have gone by.*

This quote from Hendrick Van Loon may be overstating the case, but the point is that geologic time is enormous. Time is on the side of all geologic processes and has accommodated many changes and cycles in the Earth's lithosphere, hydrosphere, atmosphere, and biosphere. We are but some of the latest inhabitants of the third planet from our sun, which occupies the center of a solar system that was born some 5 billion years ago. The Earth and its companion planets belong to a great galactic spiral that formed from a big-bang explosion some 15 to 20 billion years ago and now moves silently through the universe.

Arthur Holmes once said, "Perhaps it is indelicate of us to ask Mother Earth her age." Nonetheless, our latest scientific findings tell us she is some 4600 million years old, and we have learned much about her secretive past. We have learned that a giant supercontinent began to split apart on the Earth's lithosphere about 200 million years ago, and that upright beasts who might reasonably lay claim to the name *Homo* lived along the shores of a lake in what is now Ethiopia about 3 million years ago. In 1492, Christopher Columbus planted his footprint on the shores of Hispaniola in the New World, and in 1969 Neil Armstrong left his footprint on the surface of the Moon (Fig. 5–1A).

The last two dates we can comprehend, but the others we have mentioned are incomprehensible. It stretches the imagination to ponder intervals of time measured in millions, tens of millions, and even hundreds of millions or billions of years. But this vast abyss of time, which popular geoscience writer John McPhee has dubbed "deep time," is reality, not fantasy. What makes intervals of geologic time so staggering is that our personal, everyday calendars deal with increments of time measured in hours, days, weeks, months, and years. Our history books relate events set in a time frame of centuries, but even a century is difficult to appreciate fully.

An individual's lifetime, or for that matter the longevity of our species on this planet, is indeed short by comparison with a time interval such as the Cambrian Period, which lasted for 65 million years (Table 5–1). It is an exciting, yet humbling experience to split open a piece of shale and expose to the light for the first time in 550 million years the fossilized remains of a trilobite (Fig. 5–1B), a crustaceanlike arthropod that once scuttled across a Cambrian mudflat in a world we can never truly fathom. But therein lies

---

*Hendrick Van Loon. [1951] 1962. *The story of Mankind.* Black and Gold ed. New York: Liveright Publishers, p. 2.

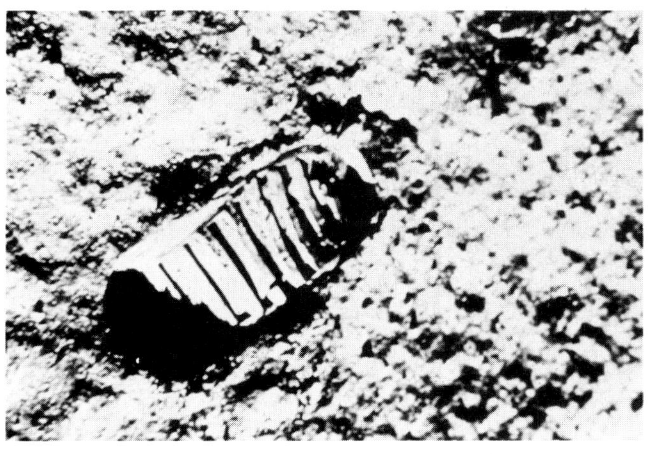
A

B

Figure 5–1
A. Footprint of U.S. astronaut Neil Armstrong on surface of moon. B. Cluster of Cambrian trilobite casts and molds. Trilobite in lower center is 8.5 cm long.
(A, photo courtesy of NASA; B, photo courtesy of Ward's Natural Science Establishment, Rochester, NY)

the intrigue, the challenge, and the beauty of historical geology—to probe the record of the rocks in search of clues for what the world was like long ago.

Deep time is so alien, so difficult to comprehend, that we can only begin to comprehend it when it is portrayed by metaphor or analogy. The following is a feeble attempt to convey the concept of deep time . . .

> If all of tangible Earth history, from 4600 million years ago to the present, were condensed and portrayed in the form of a 460-page book, we would see something like the following: Each page would correspond to 10 million years, but far fewer than half of the pages would even be present, much less easy to read. Certainly the first 80 pages of the book would be missing. On a tattered and smudged page 81 there would be a sketchy description of the formation of the oldest rocks yet discovered on Earth, and on page 110 we would see the first mention of evidence of primitive life on our planet.
>
> The origin of life itself, unless possibly decoded from a few badly smudged lines of type several pages back, probably has been lost forever on one of the missing pages. The attainment of a significant level of free oxygen in our atmosphere, perhaps 1% of the present-day level, would be mentioned on page 260. The first true animals would be discussed on page 390, and the first animals with hard external coverings capable of being preserved would make their appearance on page 400.
>
> Up to this point, seven-eighths of the way through, the book would be dilapidated. Many pages, even whole chapters, would be missing. Remaining would be crinkled fragments of pages with smudged type; the decipherable words would be in cryptic code. But the last 60 pages, although difficult and at times impossible to read, would be easier. A primitive fish, the earliest animal with a backbone, would be described on page 410. The oldest land plants would be mentioned on page 415, and extensive coal-forming swamps inhabited by the earliest reptiles would be described on page 430. The breakup of a giant supercontinent would be discussed on pages 442 to 450; dinosaurs would roam the continents on pages 440 to 455; and the formation of the Rocky Mountains would be mentioned on pages 450 to 456.
>
> Man would not appear until three-fourths of the way down page 460, and Columbus's voyage to the New World and the first walk on the Moon by the *Apollo 11* crew would be mentioned on the last line of page 460.

Table 5–1
Geologic time scale and bar scale showing relative proportions of Cryptozoic and Phanerozoic time

Age (Ma*)		
65	PHANEROZOIC	CENOZOIC
245		MESOZOIC
570		PALEOZOIC
2500	CRYPTOZOIC (PRECAMBRIAN)	PROTEROZOIC
3800		ARCHEAN
		(Pregeologic history of the Earth)
4600		Origin of the Earth

(to scale)

Oldest ←known rocks

Eon	Era	Period		Age (Ma*)	Geologic events
PHANEROZOIC (Age of manifest animal life)	CENOZOIC (modern life)	Quaternary		2	Glaciation in northern hemisphere Dawn of man
		Neogene		24	
		Paleogene		65	Evolutionary expansion of mammals; uplift of Rocky Mountains
	MESOZOIC (middle life)	Cretaceous		144	Extinction of dinosaurs; faunal crisis; first angiosperm plants
		Jurassic		208	Origin of birds
		Triassic		245	Origin of mammals, origin of dinosaurs
	PALEOZOIC (ancient life)	Permian		286	Complete formation of Pangaea, great crisis in history of life; uplift of Appalachians
		Carboniferous	Pennsylvanian	320	Major coal-forming swamps, oldest reptiles; glaciation in Gondwana
			Mississippian	380	
		Devonian		408	Age of fish; oldest amphibians
		Silurian		438	Oldest land plants
		Ordovician		505	Glaciation in Gondwana
		Cambrian		570	Origin of vertebrate animals Origin of exoskeletons
CRYPTOZOIC (PRECAMBRIAN) (age of microscopic life) — PROTEROZOIC	Late Proterozoic			900	Origin of multicellular life Sexual reproduction; oldest known nucleated cells
	Middle Proterozoic			1600	Attainment of 1% present atmospheric level of O_2
	Early Proterozoic			2500	Change from reducing to oxidizing ocean, atmosphere;
ARCHAEN	Late Archean			3000	formation of extensive continental lithosphere
	Middle Archean			3400	
	Early Archean			~3800	Oldest definitive fossils of single nonnucleated cells. – – – – – – – – – oldest known rocks
HADEAN	Pregeologic history of Earth Origin of Earth			4600	Meteoric bombardment; volcanic outgasing; formation of early lithosphere; atmosphere, biosphere; Origin of the Earth

*Ma = millions of years before present.

And the book of Earth history continues to be written: 10 million years hence another page will be added. What will the Earth be like 10 million or 100 million years from now? Will members of our species be here to chronicle the events?

For centuries, scholars have been intrigued by the mysteries of deep time, and many metaphors and analogies have been used in attempts to express it. As described by Stephen Jay Gould, some have viewed time as an arrow, whereby history is regarded as an irreversible sequence of unrepeated events—a story of linked events moving in a direction. Others have viewed time as a cycle, wherein time has no direction and events have no meaning as distinct episodes, but rather apparent motions are parts of repeating cycles. Geologic time has been analogized with various familiar scales such as a 24-hour clock, a calendar year, or the Eiffel Tower (with the thickness of the coat of paint at the top representing recorded human history).

But enough of analogies; let us investigate the fundamental principles that provide the basis for our appreciation of geologic time.

Relative Time

History and Prehistory

One of the most unique and fascinating aspects of any of the sciences is how geologists measure time. The methods of reckoning geologic time are very different indeed from time determinations made during the history of human experience. Human events are chronicled through written testimony, recorded and passed down from generation to generation. We are all familiar with various kinds of historical time scales. At one time or another we have had to learn important dates in human history: the Battle of Hastings, the Boston Tea Party, the treaty signing at Appomattox, and many others. Such events could be arranged on a time scale that shows chronological succession, as well as absolute dates.

Geologic time is illustrated by a *prehistoric* time scale that attempts to accomplish the same thing. Events from the distant past—the origin of the Earth, the first appearance of multicellular life, the formation of the Rocky Mountains, the dawn of humans (Table 5–1)—are arranged in their relative order of occurrence. Dates in "millions of years before present" are assigned to the events (the symbol for millions of years before the present, or millions of years ago, is *Ma*). This record of prehistoric time is written in the rocks of the Earth's lithosphere. The rock record, like the pages and chapters in the book-of-time analogy, contains the secrets of the Earth-shaping events of the past.

How do Earth scientists read and decode the history recorded in the rocks, and how do they place geologic events in a meaningful time frame? In this chapter we shall examine the principal methods by which Earth scientists tell time. In the following chapter, we shall become acquainted with the historical development of geologic time concepts and the birth and subsequent development of the geologic time scale.

The geologic time scale actually incorporates two scales (Table 5–1): The first is a *relative scale* that expresses the order of geologic events as determined from their positions in the rock record. Intervals of geologic time—major chapters in Earth history—have been given names such as Cambrian, Permian, and Cretaceous. The second is an *absolute scale* that designates ages in years, expressed in terms of millions of years before the present (Ma). These ages are based on the natural radioactive decay of various chemical elements which are present in trace amounts in certain minerals in some rocks. Knowledge of the principles of relative and absolute geologic time is essential for understanding and appreciating Earth history. First we shall consider aspects of relative time in geology.

A Science Called Stratigraphy

Of the three main kinds of rocks (igneous, sedimentary, metamorphic) that make up the Earth's lithosphere, sedimentary rocks provide the most complete record of Earth history. Although igneous and metamorphic rocks make up more than 90% of the total volume of the Earth's lithosphere, sedimentary rocks make up more than 75% of the rock record exposed at the surface or present in the upper-

Figure 5–2
Stratification in sedimentary rocks displayed in the walls of the majestic Grand Canyon, Arizona.
(Photo by J. D. Cooper)

most few kilometers. Of singular importance for reconstructing geologic history is the layering or *stratification* of sedimentary rocks. Stratification allows for the ordering, arrangement, and determination of sequence (Fig. 5–2).

The science of layered rocks or strata is **stratigraphy.** It is the study of spatial and time relationships of bodies of rock to one another and the dynamic depositional patterns that can be observed and interpreted. Stratification of sedimentary rocks results from deposition and net accumulation of solid particles that settle through water or air in response to gravity. Particles of individual minerals or fragments of rocks settle according to size, shape, density, and the velocity of the transporting medium (water or air). The resulting layers, also referred to as beds or strata, range in thickness from a few millimeters to several meters or more, and generally are separated by well-defined surfaces called *bedding planes.*

Sedimentation tends to occur in pulses, with depositional events being separated by quiescent intervals. Such episodic activity is largely responsible for the textural differences observed between successive strata and for the bedding planes that separate them. Deposition occurs in *sedimentary basins* of various sizes. Compaction and lithification of the sediments result from postdepositional burial beneath subsequent layers, and this process tends to enhance the bedding and the *contacts* between beds.

Superposition

The most fundamental principle of stratigraphy is **superposition.** In a sequence of layered rocks, the oldest layer is at the bottom and the youngest layer is at the top (Fig. 5–2). Consideration of superposition is the first step in developing relative time sequences in layered rocks.

Superposition is rather straightforward if the rock sequence has not been inverted. In this regard it is appropriate to mention another fundamental law or principle of stratigraphy, that of **original horizontality.** This principle states that not only does sedimentation proceed from the bottom upward (and therefore, so does the net accumulation of sediment in superposed layers), but also that the depositional surfaces, throughout their extent, are essentially flat, generally not departing more than a few degrees from horizontal. Thus, sedimentary strata are originally horizontal because the surfaces (interfaces between sediments and water or air) on which they are deposited are essentially flat, and the sedimentary particles come to rest in response to gravity.

When we see sedimentary successions that depart appreciably from the horizontal, such as those shown in Figure 5–3, it is reasonable to assume that postdepositional events have repositioned the strata. Sedimentary strata tilted from the horizontal at some measurable angle are said to have *dip,* which is expressed as both a direction and an angle. The direction of dip is the compass direction toward which the bedding plane faces (direction of inclination); the angle of dip is the acute angle of inclination measured downward from the horizontal. Dip is perpendicular to the *strike* of the bed, which is the compass direction of a horizontal line on the bedding plane.

The angle of dip can range from 0° to 90°. If a succession of strata is bent or tilted beyond vertical, the direction of dip is reversed (as before, the angle is measured downward from the horizontal), and the succession's superposition is inverted. Such sequences are *overturned.* Tectonic forces (tectonic cycle) within the Earth's lithosphere bend and break rock strata and have been responsible for the tilting and folding of sedimentary rock sequences, particularly in the mountain belts of the world.

How can the superposition of a sequence of strata dipping at a steep or even vertical angle be determined? How can an overturned sequence be recognized? Why is it important to make this determination? The working out of superposition in layered rocks is the essential first step in unraveling the geologic history of sedimentary sequences. However, recognizing correct superposition of layered rocks is not always automatic. For example, how might one determine superposition in a stratigraphic succession such as that shown in Figure 5–4? What are the clues that tell sequence and how are they expressed?

The determination of sequence in layered rocks involves the recognition and correct interpretation of bottom indicators versus top indicators. Such indicators are *primary sedimentary structures:* megascopic features incorporated in the sediment in the

A

B

Figure 5–3

Dipping successions of sedimentary strata. A. Lower Paleozoic succession in Appalachians of southwestern Virginia. B. Pliocene section in southern California. In both photos the superposition is from left to right; the succession is oldest-to-youngest in the direction of dip.
(A, photo by B. N. Cooper; B, photo by J. D. Cooper)

Figure 5–4

View looking north at road cut along U.S. 90 near Marathon, Texas. A vertical sequence of upper Paleozoic sedimentary rocks is exposed.
(Photo courtesy of Critter Creations, Inc., San Diego, CA)

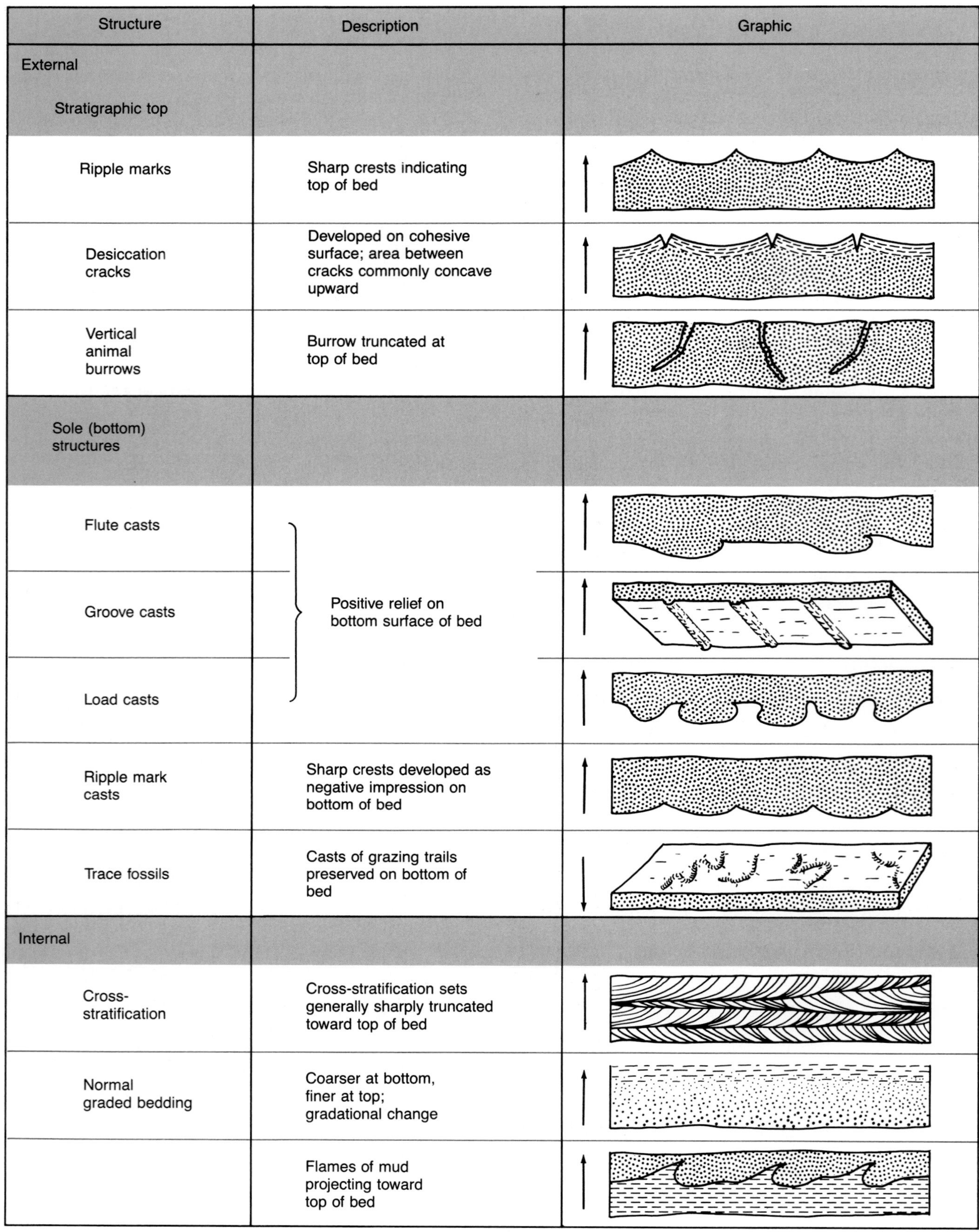

Structure	Description	Graphic
External		
Stratigraphic top		
Ripple marks	Sharp crests indicating top of bed	
Desiccation cracks	Developed on cohesive surface; area between cracks commonly concave upward	
Vertical animal burrows	Burrow truncated at top of bed	
Sole (bottom) structures		
Flute casts	Positive relief on bottom surface of bed	
Groove casts	Positive relief on bottom surface of bed	
Load casts	Positive relief on bottom surface of bed	
Ripple mark casts	Sharp crests developed as negative impression on bottom of bed	
Trace fossils	Casts of grazing trails preserved on bottom of bed	
Internal		
Cross-stratification	Cross-stratification sets generally sharply truncated toward top of bed	
Normal graded bedding	Coarser at bottom, finer at top; gradational change	
	Flames of mud projecting toward top of bed	

Figure 5–5
Primary sedimentary structures useful for determination of stratigraphic bottom versus top.

original environment of deposition (Chapter 2). Primary sedimentary structures are *external* if they are present on the bedding surfaces, and *internal* if they are present within the bed (Fig. 5–5).

An example of an external sedimentary structure is shown in Figure 5–6A. These peculiar structures, called *flute casts,* represent the sand fillings or castings of scours (flutes) formed on the original depositional surface (Fig. 5–6B). Such structures are indicative of the soles or bottoms of beds. Their shape and orientation provide information on the direction of movement of the original scouring current. Flute casts and other related sole marks are most common in successions of interbedded sandstone and mudstone. Depressions formed by currents that scoured the surface of a muddy bottom served as molds for the filling by sand during deposition of the immediately overlying layer. These structures, present on the soles of many of the beds in the sequence of Figure 5–4, indicate the top of the sequence is to the right. A number of additional sedimentary structures can be used to determine stratigraphic top versus stratigraphic bottom (Fig. 5–5).

Lateral Continuity

Another stratigraphic principle is that of **lateral continuity.** Sedimentary strata, when originally formed, are three-dimensional and extend laterally in all directions until they thin to a zero-thickness edge, terminate against the edge of the *depositional basin* in which they accumulate, or change charac-

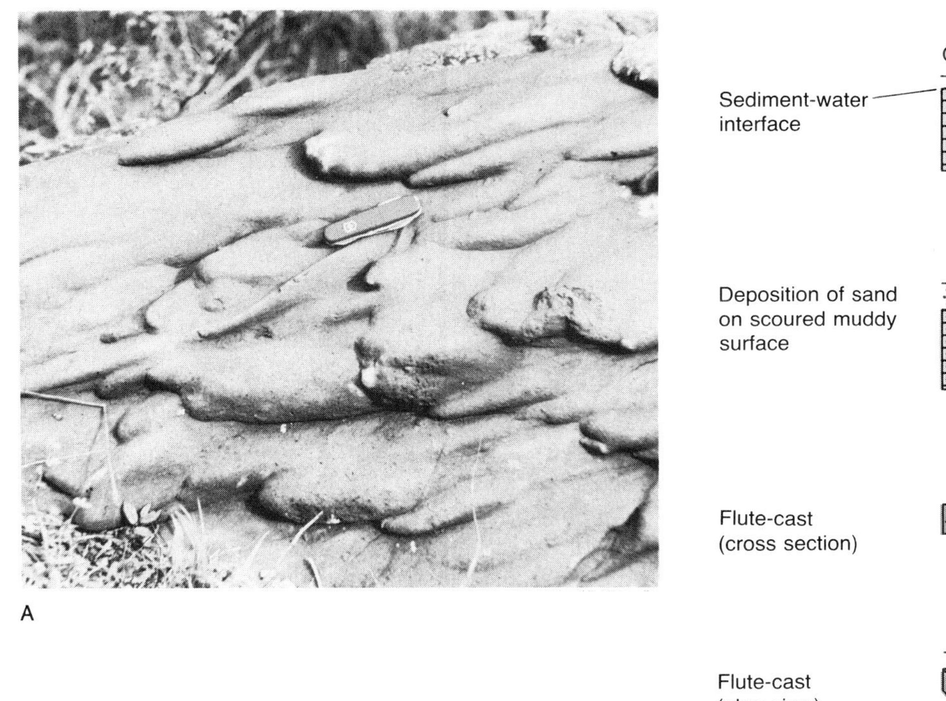

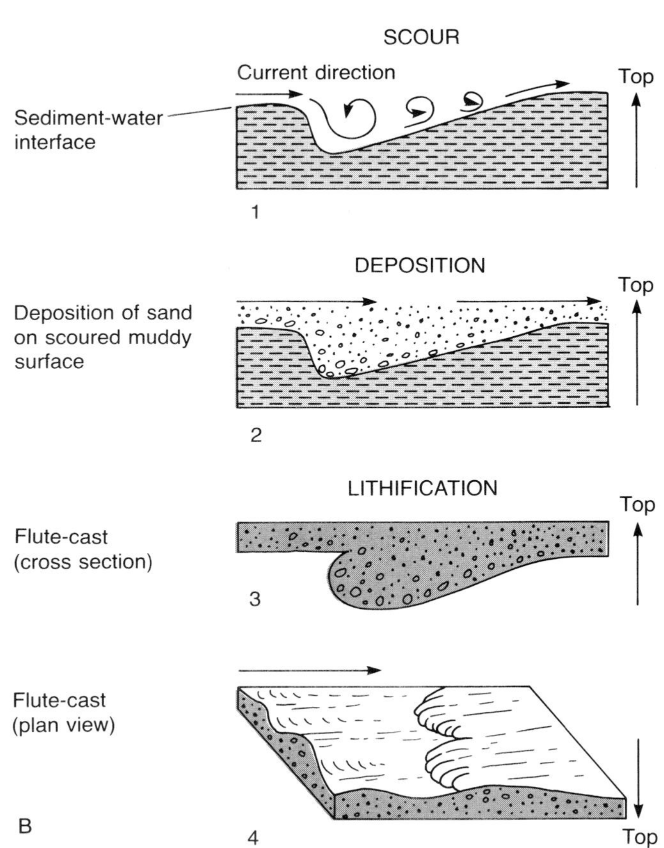

Figure 5–6
A. Flute casts on bottom (sole) of sandstone bed, upper Paleozoic, Ouachita Mountains, southern Oklahoma. B. Sequence (1–4) showing formation of flute cast on sole of sandstone bed. 1. A flute or scour mark is eroded into the surface of a muddy bottom at the sediment-water interface, producing an asymmetrical depression. 2. The scour is filled by deposition of sand from the overlying bed. 3. The sandstone layer is separated from the underlying mudstone, displaying an asymmetrical flute cast on the sole of the sandstone bed. 4. A plan view of the flute cast on the sole of the sandstone bed.
(Photo by J. D. Cooper)

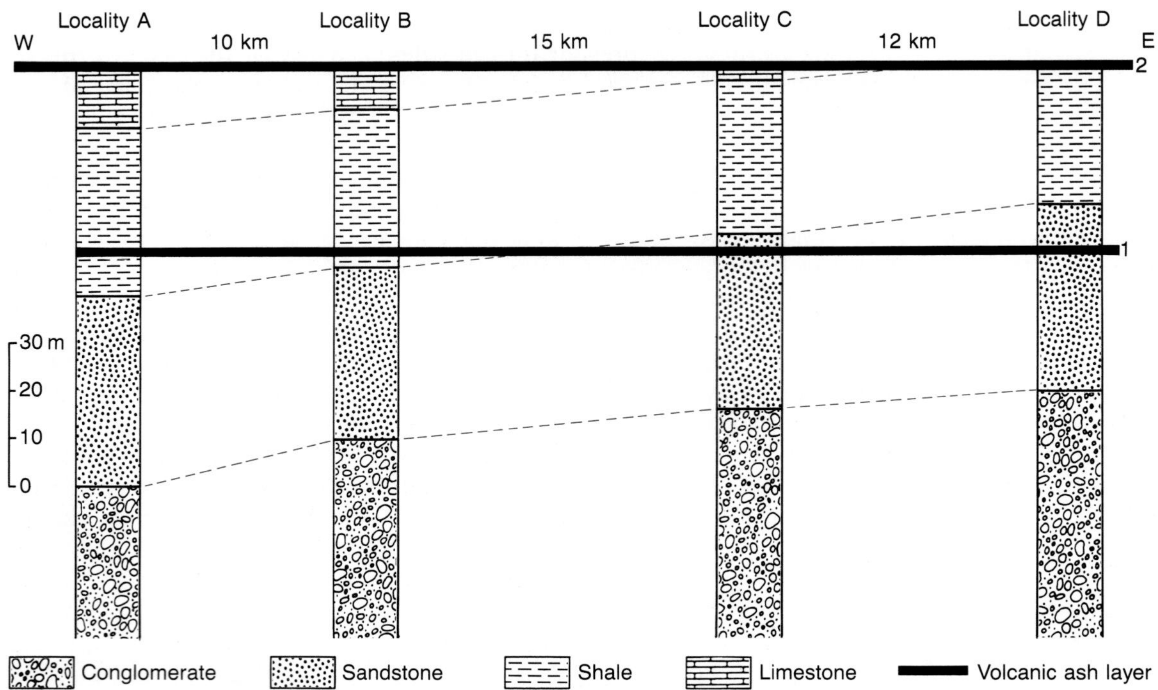

Figure 5–7
Distinctive thin volcanic ash beds (1 and 2) within sequence of conglomerate-sandstone-shale-limestone. The volcanic ash key or marker beds were deposited as fallout of volcanic ejecta that blanketed the area in a geologic "instant" of time. The volcanic ash beds cross the correlated boundaries (dashed lines) separating the sandstone and shale, and shale and limestone units, suggesting that these contacts are *not* time-equivalent from section to section.

ter by merging into laterally adjacent deposits. Strata can be identified laterally by tracing and **correlation** (matching). At the surface, isolated exposures of the same stratigraphic unit, when correctly recognized and correlated, indicate that the exposures are parts of what was once a laterally continuous unit (Fig. 5–7). Position in a superpositional sequence that can be recognized at each outcrop section in Figure 5–7 helps substantiate the physical correlation of the units.

Individual, distinctive, thin stratigraphic intervals or beds can commonly be demonstrated to have time-significant value and can be used to define *time lines.* Such physical units are considered to have formed "instantaneously" (geologically) over the area of lateral continuity. Thin volcanic ash beds, for example, are fallout blankets deposited by volcanic eruptions (Fig. 5–7). Such *key beds (marker beds)* not only provide local to subregional time lines, but their distinctive character allows them to be recognized in separate sections, thus facilitating correlation.

Cross-Cutting Relationships

A most important principle used in the determination of relative geologic time involves **cross-cutting relationships.** Intrusive igneous rock bodies (such as dikes) and faults (fractures in the Earth's crust allowing movement of adjoining blocks of rock) cut across preexisting rocks and structures, and thus are younger than the geologic features they cut. Figure 5–8 illustrates cross cutting and superposition. Using these two fundamental principles, can you arrange the rocks and other geologic features shown in the figure in their relative chronological order?

A very important stratigraphic feature known as an **unconformity** is critical to our discussion of principles of relative time and geologic history. Unconformities are a type of cross-cutting feature (Fig. 5–9), but unlike igneous intrusions and faults, which are structural (tectonic) features, unconformities are stratigraphic surfaces. Simply stated, an unconformity is *a buried surface of erosion or nonaccumulation.* As such, the buried surface repre-

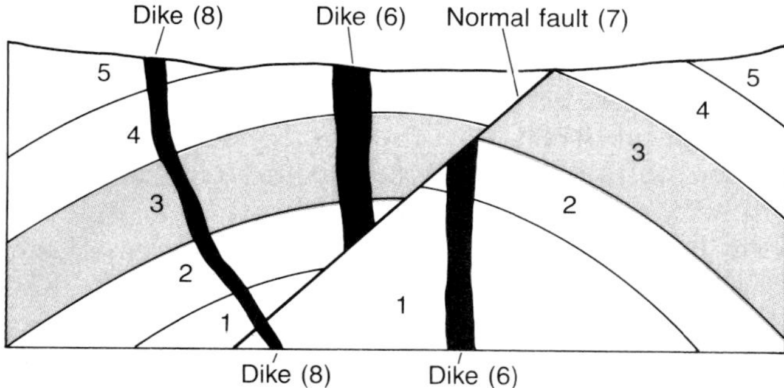

Figure 5–8
Cross-cutting relationships of two dikes, a *normal* fault, and sedimentary strata. The sedimentary sequence formed first (1 = oldest, 5 = youngest in order of superposition), followed by the intrusion of a dike (6), then the occurrence of the normal fault (7) which displaced the strata and dike, and finally the intrusion of dike (8) that crosses the fault. Folding of the strata into an anticline probably occurred after deposition of 5 and before intrusion of 6.

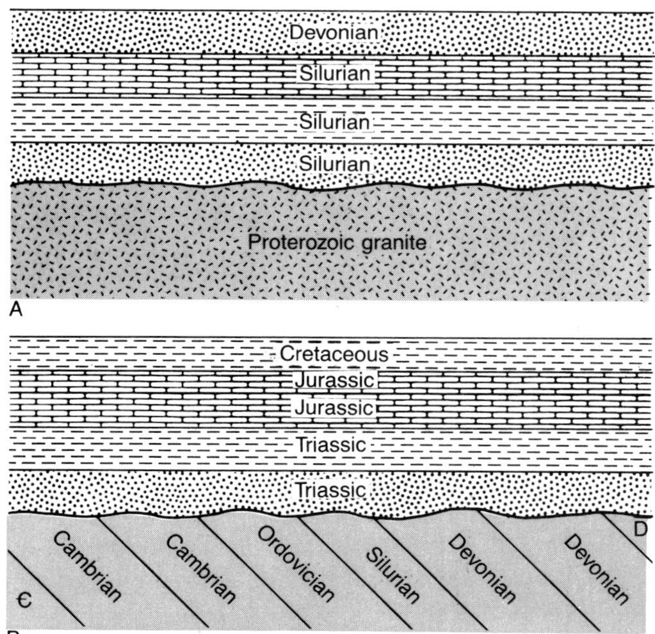

Figure 5–9
A. Nonconformity (wavy line). Note the age difference between the crystalline basement rocks and the overlying sedimentary sequence. If this were an intrusive igneous contact, the igneous rock would have to be younger than the sedimentary sequence. B. Angular unconformity. Note that the unconformity separates two superpositional packages of rock, each with its own internal superpositional arrangement.

sents a significant gap in the geologic record. The time value of an unconformity is called a **hiatus,** which is the difference in age between the rocks directly above and directly below the unconformity surface.

Three main kinds of unconformities occur in the stratigraphic record and can be recognized on the basis of physical relationships. One kind, called **nonconformity** (Fig. 5–9A), is a stratigraphic surface that separates older crystalline rock (igneous or metamorphic rocks) from younger (overlying) sedimentary strata.

A second type of unconformity, the **angular unconformity** (Fig. 5–9B), has an angular relationship between older, deformed sedimentary strata and younger, less deformed strata. In the example shown in Figure 5–9B, the underlying succession appears to be internally conformable, but it is tilted at a sharp angle and abruptly truncated by the unconformity surface. The younger, overlying sequence also appears to be internally conformable, and the stratification is essentially parallel to the unconformity. The strata immediately above an unconformity are always parallel (or subparallel) to the unconformity. (Why? because of original horizontality. The unconformity represents the essentially flat erosion surface upon which the younger strata were deposited.)

The term "unconformity" should be reserved for buried stratigraphic surfaces representing major hiatuses. A large amount of geologic time is required for deposition of a sequence, lithification into coherent rock, uplift and tilting, erosion to develop a surface across the upturned strata, subsidence, and resumption of sedimentation. The surfaces separating successive individual units within conformable sequences represent comparatively very short geologic time durations, and are called **diastems.** Diastems are part of the normal, continuous sedimentation process whereby deposition alternates with nondeposition and erosional removal to result in a net accumulation of sediments. Unconformities generally represent missing records amounting to millions or hundreds of millions of years; diastems represent time periods of weeks, months, years, perhaps even centuries—comparatively short intervals of geologic time that cannot be measured with conventional geologic techniques.

The third kind of unconformity, called a **disconformity,** is more subtle than the other two because it occurs between essentially parallel strata (Fig. 5–10). Disconformities, being not so obvious as angular unconformities or nonconformities, generally require more careful examination for recognition.

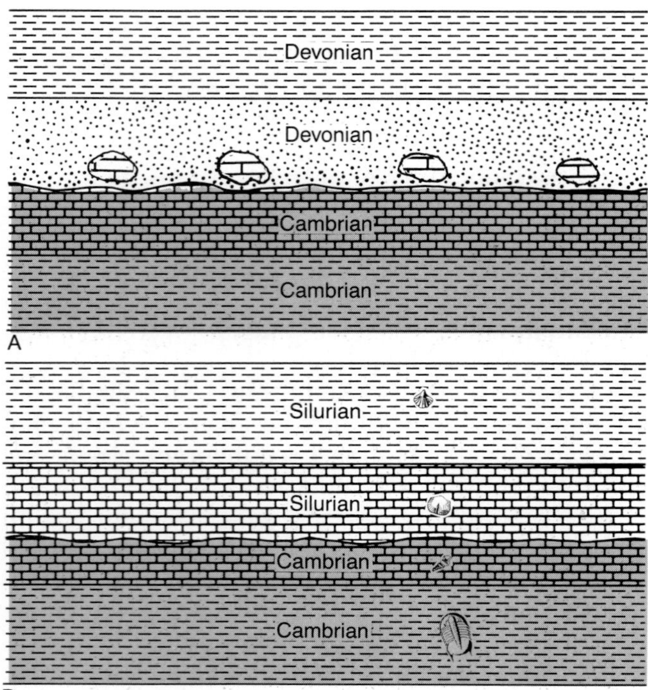

Figure 5–10
Erosional disconformities (wavy lines). The hiatus (time value of the unconformity) is the difference in age between the oldest rock above the erosional surface and the youngest rock below that surface. A. In this cross section, note the absence of at least Ordovician and Silurian rocks, and the inclusions of Cambrian limestone as pebbles in the basal part of the Devonian section. B. The most subtle type of disconformity, showing no change in basic lithology and no inclusions of older rock. The absence of Ordovician strata is determined by comparison of fossils above and below the erosional surface.

Evidence is generally in the form of physical criteria that suggest erosion, such as fragments of underlying rock in the directly overlying strata. This situation involves yet another stratigraphic principle, the **law of inclusions,** which states that the fragments or particles in a terrigenous clastic sedimentary deposit are older than the deposit itself. This is especially significant for the detection of disconformities in the stratigraphic record, because inclusions of underlying strata incorporated in overlying strata represent erosional products. Cross-cutting relationships also can aid in the recognition of disconformities, for example, the erosional truncation of a dike or fault.

A good illustration of the three kinds of unconformities can be seen in the Grand Canyon of the Colorado River (Fig. 5–11). This spectacular canyon exposes a stratigraphic succession spanning more than 1000 million years. An impressive *nonconformity* occurs between the Tapeats Sandstone and the Vishnu Schist; an *angular unconformity* is present between the Tapeats Sandstone and the tilted units of Upper Proterozoic strata. A *disconformity* occurs between the Redwall Limestone and the Bright Angel Shale; the Redwall is Mississippian in age and the Bright Angel is Cambrian. Reference to Table 2–1 indicates that strata of Ordovician, Silurian, and Devonian ages are missing at this boundary. However, note that in a few places, strata of the Temple Butte Formation of Devonian age are preserved in eroded channels between the Redwall and Muav formations. The Temple Butte is bounded by two disconformities that merge into one where Redwall directly overlies Muav.

Unconformities have their advantageous and disadvantageous aspects. The fact that they represent missing geologic record and loss of information for certain localities and regions would seem to be a negative factor. This is tantamount to the absence of some pages, sections, or entire chapters from our book-of-time analogy. In reality, unconformities, as evidence of erosional events, are an important part of geologic history. In addition, they commonly can be used to bracket parts of the stratigraphic record and thus provide convenient, recognizable stratigraphic boundaries for large-scale superpositional packages of rock. The use of unconformities in organizing the stratigraphic record will become more apparent in our discussion of the evolution of North America.

Fossil Succession

A stratigraphic principle that has had a most profound effect on the science of historical geology is **fossil succession.** Simply stated, fossil succession refers to the changes in fossil content (kinds of organic remains or evidence) upward through superpositional sequences of rock. As documents of life (Chapter 3) and the products of organic evolution (Chapter 4), fossils provide the key to recognizing the relative ages of sedimentary strata. As mentioned previously, sedimentary rocks provide the most complete record of Earth history, especially because of the layered, superpositional arrangement of strata. The presence of fossils in sedimentary rocks contributes greatly to recognition of relative time sequence.

The principle of fossil succession transcends the principle of superposition. Fossils, unlike inorganic particles such as rock fragments or quartz grains, are objects that do not occur in random or haphazard fashion, but rather in a regular, irreversible or-

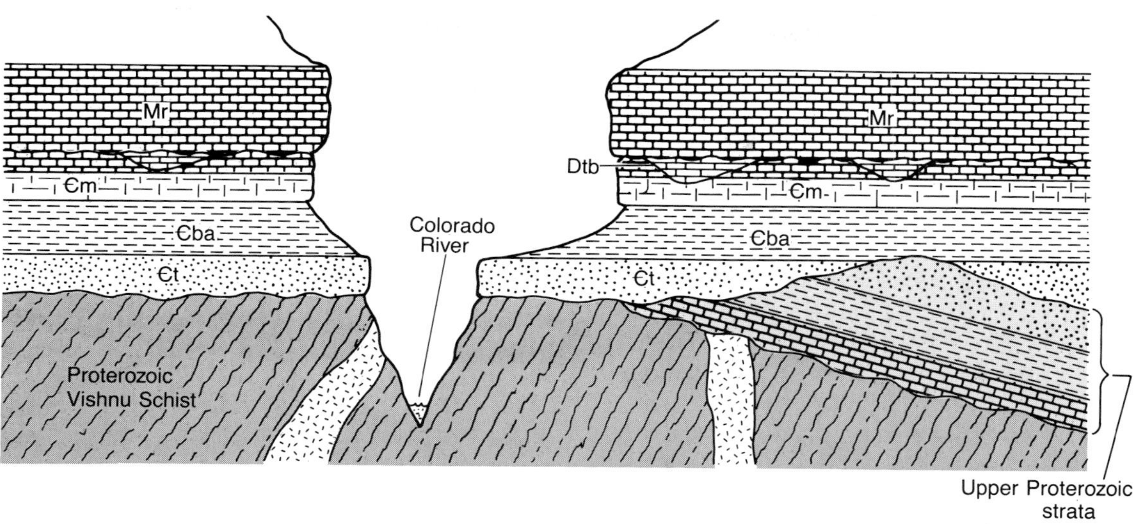

Figure 5–11

Rock succession in Grand Canyon illustrating three main kinds of unconformities. Locate and identify them. Ꞓt = Cambrian Tapeats Formation; Ꞓba = Cambrian Bright Angel Formation; Ꞓm = Cambrian Muav Formation; Dtb = Devonian Temple Butte Formation; Mr = Mississippian Redwall Formation.

der. Rock types can be repeated many times in vertical succession (Fig. 5–12A) because of recurrence of the sedimentary environments that produced the rocks; but fossil assemblages change progressively in vertical succession, and assemblage compositions are nonrepetitive because of evolution (see Chapter 4).

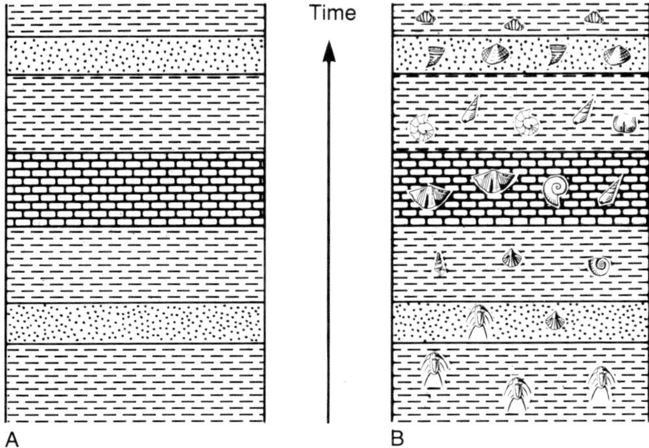

Figure 5–12

Lithologic and fossil succession. A. The vertical change in rock type and repetition of rock type is an expression of the patterns of changing yet repeating environments through time. A bed of a particular lithology might be thought to correlate with a later bed of the same lithology in another location. B. Note the change in fossil assemblages through the vertically repeating succession of lithogies shown in A. Even though some forms persist through more than one lithology, the combination of forms in any particular lithology is definitive.

With few exceptions, fossils represent the preserved remains of organisms that lived and died and became preserved in the same or nearby contemporaneous environments in which the containing sediments accumulated. Some exceptions involve fossils that represent inclusions derived from the erosion of older fossil-bearing rock (Fig. 5–13).

Paleomagnetic Signatures

An important twentieth-century addition to stratigraphy has been the discovery of *magnetic signatures* in rocks. We have previously discussed (Chapter 1) the importance of seafloor magnetic anomalies in the recognition and understanding of the seafloor-spreading process. Sequences of layered rocks also show a succession of magnetic-polarity events (normal and reversed polarities), or anomalies, if you will. This provides yet another means of subdividing stratigraphic sequences (Fig. 5–14) and, as we shall see in the next chapter, serves as a powerful tool for correlating layered sequences, both in the present-day ocean basins and between ocean basins and certain sequences on the continents.

In Chapter 6, we will trace the development of these fundamental principles and their historic influence on the birth, development, and later refinements of the *geologic time scale*.

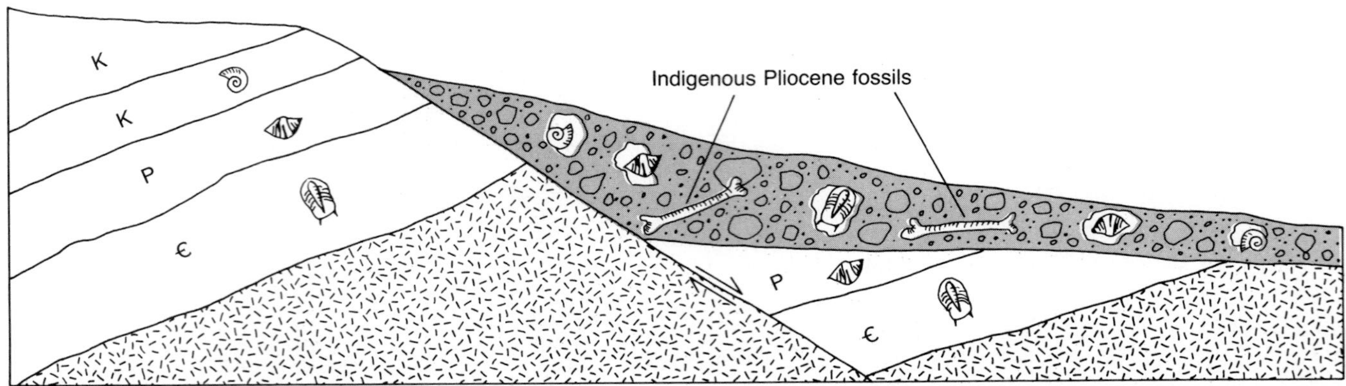

Figure 5–13
The law of inclusions, as exemplified by reworked fossils. A Pliocene nonmarine alluvial deposit contains marine Cambrian, Permian, and Cretaceous fossils, and nonmarine Pliocene fossils. A deposit can be no older than its youngest fossil; thus the deposit in question is Pliocene, as determined from the indigenous Pliocene fossils. The Cambrian (Є), Permian (P), and Cretaceous (K) fossils have been reworked into the Pliocene alluvial deposit as erosional debris from older source rocks.

Absolute Time

How Long Ago?

Up to this point, the emphasis has been on concepts of relative time: the determination of sequence in layered rocks and the relative order of geologic events as they can be read from a rock record that involves superposition, cross-cutting relationships, and fossil succession. As shown in Table 5–1, the geologic time scale includes not only a relative scale, but also an absolute scale, expressed by dates in years before present and superimposed on the relative scale. Although expressed in years (gen-

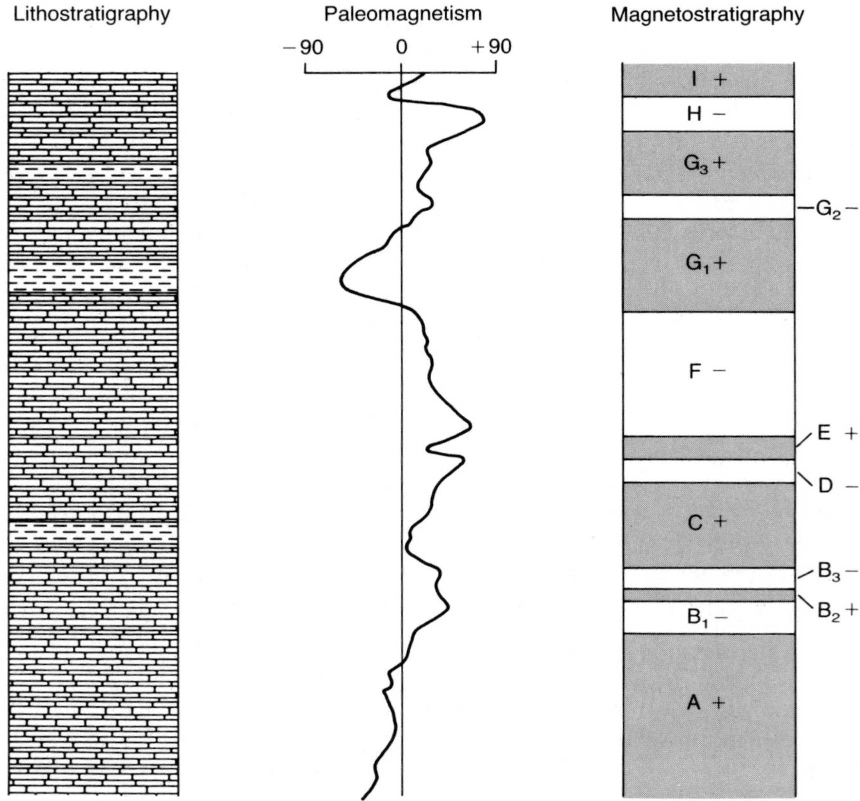

Figure 5–14
Stratigraphic section showing vertical sequence of lithologies and succession of magnetic polarity events recorded from the sequence. The paleomagnetism, recorded by a sensitive magnetometer, provides another means of stratigraphic subdivision and correlation.

erally millions) before present (Ma), the dates are not absolute in the strict sense, because there is a small percentage of error in their calculation. Absolute dates such as 4600 Ma for the age of the Earth and 245 Ma for the boundary between Paleozoic and Mesozoic Eras give us an appreciation of the antiquity and duration of the relative time-scale subdivisions.

As we shall explore further in Chapter 6, the relative time scale was gradually pieced together and was completed, in essentially its modern form, by the end of the nineteenth century; the absolute time scale, developed through the science of **geochronology,** became a reality in the early decades of the twentieth century, spurred by the discovery of radioactivity and its application to mineralogy. Refinements of both scales have continued to the present day. Relative and absolute geologic time-scales represent two of the great achievements in the history of science.

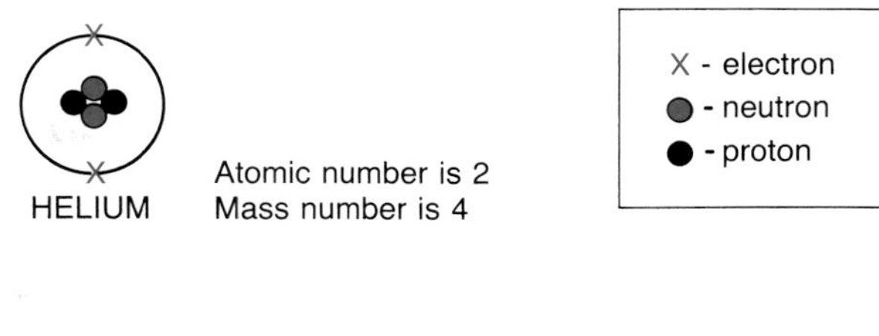

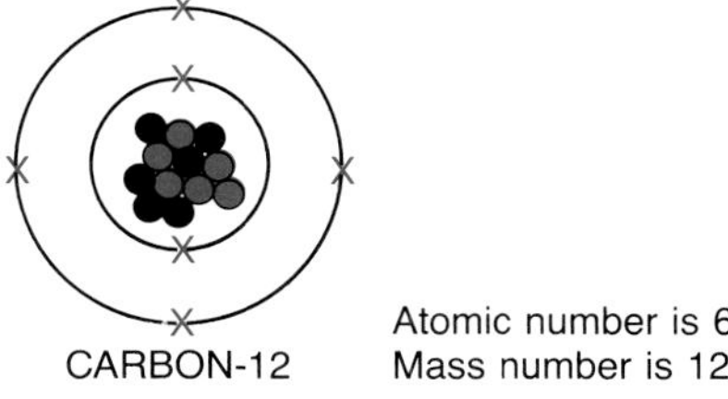

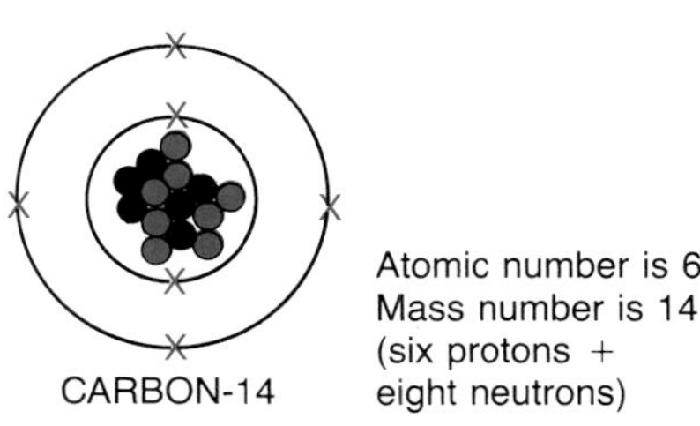

Figure 5–15
Atomic structure, atomic number, mass number, and isotope.

Principles of Radiometric Dating

Radiometric age determination is based on the phenomenon that many kinds of atoms are unstable, and consequently change spontaneously to a more stable, lower-energy state. The process of change involves **radioactive decay,** which results in **radioactive emissions.** Particular atoms called **nuclides** are different from others according to the number of *protons* (positively charged particles) and *neutrons* (neutral particles) in the atomic *nucleus* (Fig. 5–15).

Each chemical element of the standard periodic table (see Appendix A) is defined by the number of protons in its nucleus, which gives the **atomic number.** For example, helium (He), the number-2 element in the period chart (Appendix A), has two protons in its nucleus; uranium, element number 92, has 92 protons. The *mass number* of an atom is the number of protons plus the number of neutrons (Fig. 5–15). Orbitals around the nucleus are filled with electrons (negatively charged particles), whose number equals the number of protons. Thus, each individual nuclide has a unique atomic number.

A chemical element, which is a nuclide with fixed atomic number, can have alternate forms, called **isotopes,** which are distinguished on the basis of the number of neutrons; thus, different isotopes of the same element have different mass numbers (Fig. 5–15).

Uranium-235 and uranium-238 are examples of nuclides that contain the same number of protons but different numbers of neutrons (and therefore have different masses). These two isotopes of the element uranium figure importantly in the concept of radioactive decay and the radiometric dating of some kinds of igneous rocks.

Radioactive isotopes decay to more stable nuclides: a nuclide, called the *parent,* changes through a series of steps to a more stable end product, the *daughter nuclide.* Radioactive decay involves *alpha decay* (the emission of two protons and two neutrons from the nucleus); *beta decay* (the emission of a high-speed electron from the nucleus); and, in some cases, *electron capture* (Fig. 5–16).

In alpha decay, the nucleus of the parent atom, by losing two protons and two neutrons, assumes a new mass number that is decreased by four and a new atomic number that is decreased by two, making it a different element. In beta decay, the nucleus, by emitting a high-speed electron, has one of its neutrons turned into a proton. Thus the mass remains unchanged, but the atomic number increases by one, and a new element results. In electron capture, a proton in the nucleus picks up an orbital electron and changes into a neutron, thereby decreasing the atomic number by one (forming a new element), while the mass number remains unchanged.

Individual radioactive isotopes, such as uranium-238, have particular decay products (e.g., uranium-

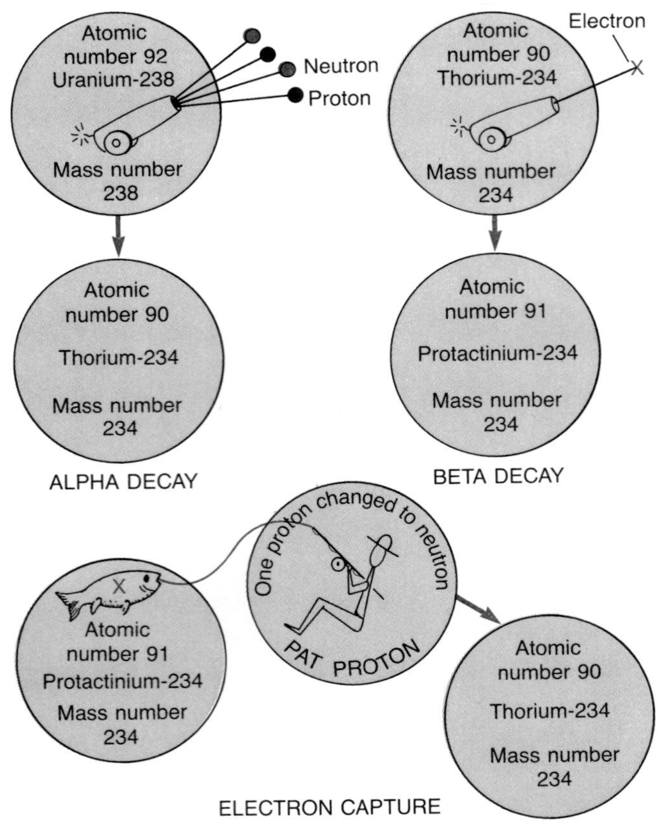

Figure 5–16
Three kinds of radioactive decay: alpha decay, beta decay, and electron capture.

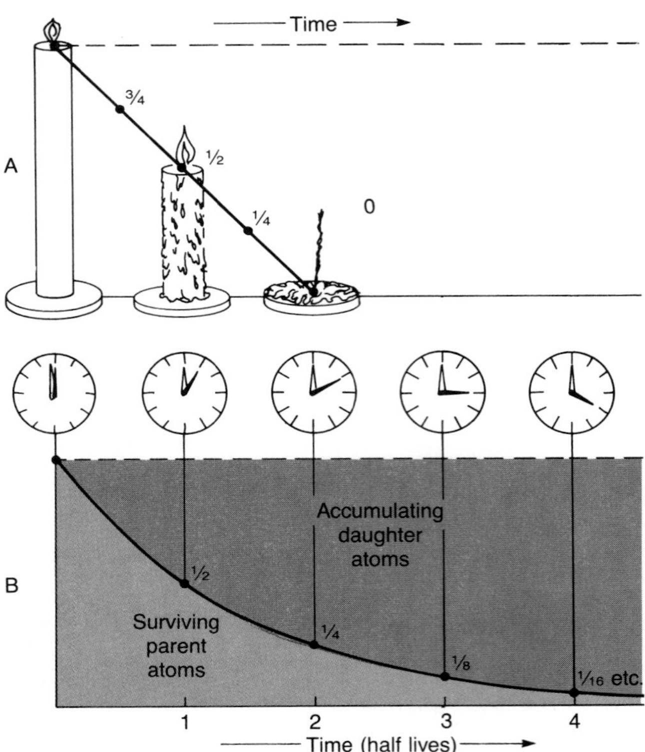

Figure 5–17
A. Uniform, straight-line depletion characteristic of most everyday processes. B. The radioactive decay curve, which approaches the zero line asymptotically: the end of one half-life is the beginning of another.
(From Don L. Eicher, *Geologic Time,* 2d ed., © 1976, Fig. 6–1, p. 120. Reprinted by permission of Prentice-Hall, Inc., Englewood Cliffs, NJ)

238 decays to lead-206 through 10 alpha-decay steps and 7 beta-decay steps). Important to radiometric age determination is the fact that the rates of decay from element to element are unique and unchanging (decay constant). Ideally, then, as applied to mineralogy, if a radioactive nuclide becomes incorporated into a mineral upon crystallization, the amount of radioactive parent that decays to **radiogenic** daughter (e.g., uranium-238 to lead-206) is a function only of the *passage of time.* However, for accurate data, it is absolutely essential that both parent and daughter nuclides be fully retained within the lattice structure of the mineral; if accurate parent:daughter ratios are to be observed, the mineral must be a closed system.

What is so significant about parent:daughter ratios, and how do we determine the amount of time that has elapsed since the radiometric clock started ticking?

A time interval called **half-life** is unique to each radioactive nuclide. Half-life is the time required for one-half of the atoms of a particular radioactive nuclide to decay (Fig. 5–17). Radioactive decay occurs at a geometric rate: for a given quantity of radioactive nuclide (N_0), half the original number of atoms ($N_0/2$) remain after one half-life; half of those, or one-fourth of the original ($N_0/4$), are present after the next half-life; half of those, or one-eighth of the original ($N_0/8$), are present after still another half-life; and so on, theoretically to infinity (Fig. 5–17).

Simply stated, the radiometric age of a geologic sample is the amount of elapsed time since crystallization of the mineral lattice that contains the radioactive atoms. The starting point is age zero, and the ratio—radioactive parent:radiogenic daughter nuclide—is zero at the setting of the radiometric clock. The amount of elapsed time since crystallization is determined by measuring the ratio of radiogenic daughter to radioactive parent nuclides in the mineral. (Of course, the half-life of the radioactive parent must be known; this is multiplied by the ratio.)

For example, in a particular sample in which the uranium-238–lead-206 decay series is used, the uranium-238:lead-206 ratio is found to be 1:1. This means that half the original parent has decayed to

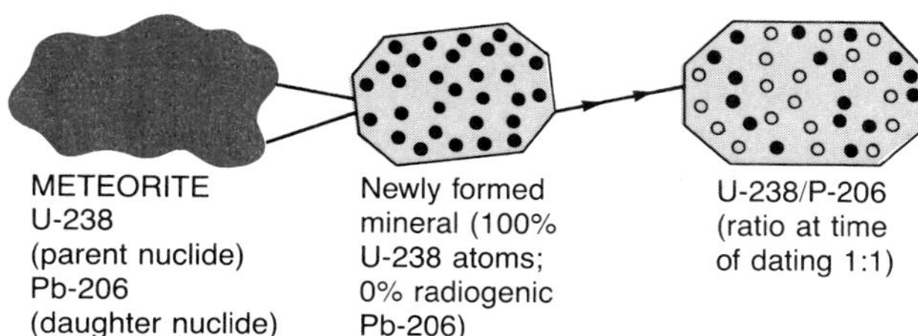

Figure 5–18
Radiometric dating of meteorite. U-238 has a half-life of 4510 million years. Because one half-life has elapsed, the age of the meteorite is 4510 million years.

daughter product (i.e., one half-life has elapsed); and because uranium-238 has a half-life of 4510 million years, this is the age of the sample (Fig. 5–18).

The Main Isotopic Decay Series

The half-lives of radioactive nuclides have been determined with sensitive analytical instruments in the laboratory; some half-lives are only fractions of a second long, and others are measured in minutes, days, or years—in some cases, tens, hundreds, and even thousands of millions of years. For example, in the uranium-238 decay chain, half-lives range from 0.00016 second to 4500 million years. The dating of most geologic events by radiometric methods necessarily involves those radioactive isotopes that have long half-lives; the choice of specific dating method must be tailored to the particular problem that must be solved.

Table 5–2 lists the radioactive isotopes uranium-238, uranium-235, potassium-40, and rubidium-87, their decay processes, their half-lives, and their daughter nuclides. These isotopes constitute the chief decay series used in determining radiometric ages of ancient rocks. Also included are the minerals and rocks that most commonly provide the raw materials for dating, and some of the most important applications. Just four radioactive nuclides of a great multitude that have existed since the origin of the Earth have provided *most* of the radiometric ages for ancient rocks.

Radiometric dates for igneous and metamorphic rocks are ages of cooling to a critical threshold called the **blocking temperature,** where a particular mineral becomes a closed chemical system for a particular decay series. Igneous rocks generally yield the best results because rocks of this family are the products of crystallization of a silicate melt. As such they are primary rocks. Metamorphic rocks can yield radiometric dates, but the ages obtained are ages from the time of metamorphism; such dates generally do not give the ages of the original, unmetamorphosed rock. Metamorphic changes generally include recrystallization of existing minerals as well as formation of new minerals, and result in a resetting of the radiometric clocks.

Sedimentary rocks, in general, are not amenable to radiometric dating because the detrital grains

Table 5–2
Four of the most important radiometric decay series used in age-dating ancient rocks

Parent nuclide	Daughter nuclide	Half-life of parent nuclide (million years)	Chief minerals	Applications
Uranium-238	Lead-206	4510	Zircon Uraninite Pitchblende	Dating of lunar samples, meteorites, old Precambrian rocks
Uranium-235	Lead-207	713	Same as U-238	Same as U-238
Potassium-40	Argon-40	1300	Muscovite Biotite Hornblende Glauconite Whole metamorphic rock	Dating of ocean-floor basalts, lava flows, some sedimentary deposits
Rubidium-87	Strontium-87	47,000	Muscovite Biotite Lepidolite Microcline Whole metamorphic rock	Dating of oldest rocks on Earth, meteorites, Precambrian rocks

have been derived ultimately from older igneous or metamorphic rocks. Dating of detrital zircon or microcline, for example, would give the age of the original rock rather than the age of the sedimentary deposit itself. However, glauconite, a green potassium-iron silicate mineral that forms as a primary mineral in certain marine sedimentary environments, can yield reliable potassium-argon dates for some sedimentary rocks.

Sources of Error

The most reliable radiometric dates are provided by the *concordant* results of two decay series. For example, if a uranium-bearing crystal has remained a closed system, the uranium-238:lead-206 and uranium-235:lead-207 ages should agree. Perhaps the greatest source of inaccuracy in *geochronology* is the failure of rocks and minerals to remain closed systems. In particular, loss of radiogenic daughter product such as argon-40 (because argon is a gas, it is more easily lost) can be detected only by checking results from more than one dating method. In addition, original nonradiogenic daughter nuclide is commonly present as a contaminant in the mineral to be dated. This daughter nuclide was incorporated when the mineral first crystallized; its presence must be detected and its exact amount precisely determined.

Yet another source of error is in the laboratory analyses. The determination of ratio of parent nuclide to daughter product is generally accomplished by a *mass spectrometer*, a highly sensitive analytical instrument that has the capacity to separate and measure the proportions of minute particles according to their mass differences. Intermediate steps that attempt to calculate the presence of original daughter product can, for example, introduce small errors that may become compounded during successive steps. The amount of error depends on the amounts of radioactive parent, radiogenic daughter product, nonradiogenic original daughter, half-life of the parent, and true age of the sample.

Thus, radiometric ages commonly are expressed as a number with amended plus-and-minus values. The date of 475 ± 15 million years incorporates the stipulated total error (insofar as it can be determined); the error range of 30 million years is a statistically determined expression of the precision of the measurement. In addition to the systematic and analytical errors, the spread also reflects the scatter of dates obtained in conducting several analyses. For our example, the range 460 to 490 Ma expresses the statistical precision of the age determination. Should another sample of the same rock be analyzed, there is a very high statistical probability that it will give a date that falls within this 30-million-year time range. This statistical repeatability, however, may not be an accurate measure of the true age of the rock. Accuracy is a measure of the departure of the determined age from the true age.

Radiocarbon Dating

Carbon is an important element, both in nature and for absolute dating of geologically very young organic material. The most common carbon atom has six protons and six neutrons in its nucleus, thus an atomic number of 6 and a mass number of 12. Carbon has two isotopes, carbon-13 and carbon-14, both of which behave chemically like carbon-12. The significance of this is that plants and animals do not distinguish among the various forms of carbon and consequently use them all in the manufacture of such diverse organic substances as cellulose, the calcium phosphate of bones and teeth, and the calcium carbonate of shells (Fig. 5–19). Carbon-14, however, is unstable and decays by losing a beta particle from its nucleus. The result is the formation of a daughter nuclide, nitrogen-14.

The basic justification for all radiometric techniques is that decay proceeds at a uniform rate, unique to each radioactive nuclide, and is not changed by variations of heat, pressure, or chemical reactions. Therefore, knowing the half-life of carbon-14 (5730 years) and the decay constant, it should be a relatively simple matter to calculate when an animal or plant died by measuring the

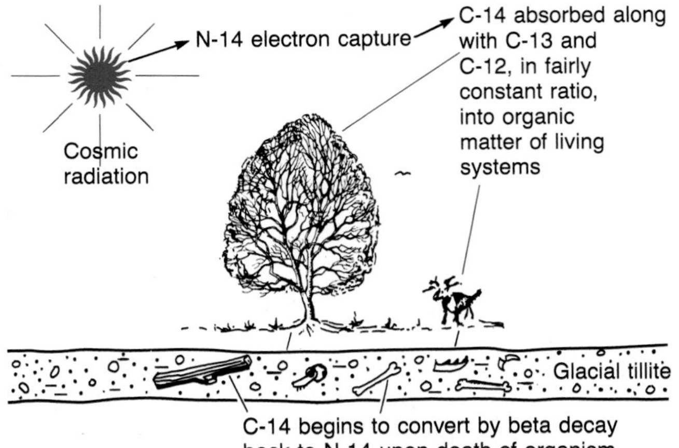

Figure 5–19
Part of the carbon cycle and the formation, incorporation into living systems, and decay of carbon-14.

amount of carbon-14 in the fossil remains. Carbon-14 decays to nitrogen-14, but the age of the carbon-bearing material is not determined from the parent:daughter ratio as in uranium-lead age determinations. Instead, age is computed from the ratio of carbon-14 to other carbon in the sample. Therefore, if the original proportion of carbon-14 to carbon-12 and carbon-13 is known, the fossil can be dated according to the amount of carbon-14 that remains. The critical measurements are not accomplished with a mass spectrometer, but rather with a highly sensitive geiger counter.

With carbon-14's half-life of 5730 years, radiocarbon dating is limited to a maximum age of about 50,000 years. Remember that a decay curve is an exponential curve; accordingly, the amount of carbon-14 diminishes rapidly with time. After about 17,000 years only one-eighth of the original carbon-14 remains; after about 50,000 years, the amount becomes too small to measure accurately. Despite this age constraint, radiocarbon dating has become indispensable for archeology and a valuable technique for late Pleistocene geology. One of the earliest applications, after the technique was devised in 1947, was to date accurately the time of the last advance of continental glacial ice in North America. The results showed that the ice advanced 11,400 years ago, a figure less than half that estimated previously by use of stratigraphic criteria.

Two other short-lived radioactive isotopes that have been used with some success in furnishing dates in the recent geologic past are thorium-230 and protactinium-231. Thorium-230 is a decay product in the Uranium-238 series and has a half-life of 75,000 years. Protactinium-231 is a product of the Uranium-235 decay series and has a half-life of 34,000 years. Both accumulate in marine bottom sediments, and their respective concentrations or comparative ratios in different layers of a drill core (such as those extracted by *Glomar Challenger*) can be measured and compared to the isotopic content in a surface layer, thus providing the age of the sediment layers.

Fission Track Dating

A dating technique that has proved successful involves *nuclear fission tracks,* minute tunnel-like features in some mineral crystals that can be detected only under high magnification. The fission tracks are produced when high-energy particles from the nuclei of uranium-238 atoms are discharged during spontaneous fission of the atom into two or more lighter atoms and nuclear particles. The particles speed through the lattice structure of the mineral crystal, leaving a pathway signature that is only a few atoms wide. The natural rate of fission-track production by uranium atoms is extremely slow, and occurs at a constant rate; thus, in theory, the tracks can be used to determine the number of years that have elapsed since the uranium-bearing mineral crystallized, provided that the original number of uranium atoms and the number of uranium atoms that have already disintegrated can be determined.

The minerals apatite, sphene, and zircon seem to work best, and the method has been used to date specimens as young as a few centuries as well as rocks several billion years old. However, like other dating methods, fission tracks have their limitations. High temperatures may cause the tracks to disappear and cosmic ray bombardment could accelerate fission rates, both of which could result in erroneous ages.

Amino Acid Dating

A rather recently developed technique that involves analyzing the proportion of D-amino to L-amino acids in fossil bone and shell material of Quaternary age has proved to be a viable age determiner. Pioneering research during the 1970s has shown that a process called *amino acid racemization* reaction can be used, with certain limitations, to give the age of the skeletal material. Only the so-called L-amino acids are generally found in the proteins of living organisms, but with the passage of time, after death of the organism, these L-amino acids convert to the nonprotein D-amino acids through a process known as racemization. The proportion of D-amino to L-amino acids in skeletal material steadily increases with time until the L/D ratio reaches 1.0. Beyond this, the ratio is spurious, because, unlike radiometric decay series, the reaction is reversible. By determining the extent of racemization in a sample of skeletal material, its age can be determined, provided that the sample can be calibrated with a dated sample whose exposure temperature has been determined.

Proponents of the technique claim that, relative to radiocarbon dating, much smaller quantities of raw material are required in the racemization-dating method, and the range of applicability exceeds that of radiocarbon dating. Also, elaborate scientific instruments are not required to run the analyses. Applications have included the dating of early human fossils, and the dating of marine terraces that formed during the last several hundred thousand years.

Summary

Relative geologic time relates to the order of occurrence and sequence of geologic events and stratigraphic units. The fundamental principles used to place rocks and structures in a relative time frame are:

1. Superposition, which means the oldest strata are at the bottom and the youngest at the top of a layered sequence.
2. Original horizontality and lateral continuity, which provide for a better understanding and visualization of the superpositional arrangement of strata.
3. Cross-cutting relationships, which give the relative age of faults, intrusive igneous rock bodies, unconformities, and the sedimentary sequences that are cut by them.
4. Unconformities, which are cross-cutting features, but, as buried surfaces of erosion or nonaccumulation, not only are the products of missing record, but also provide convenient stratigraphic boundaries that aid in organization of the record.
5. Law of inclusions, which gives the relative age relationships between inclusions in sedimentary rocks and the "parent" rocks that represent the source of the inclusions.
6. Fossil succession, which is the change in fossil assemblages from bottom to top (the time dimension) in superpositional sedimentary sequences. Superposition and cross-cutting relationships allow determination of relative sequence of geologic events on a local scale, but fossil succession permits the recognition of relative age and the correlation of isolated sections of rock on a larger scale. Fossil succession also provides the basis for the relative geologic time scale.
7. Paleomagnetic signatures in rock result from the sequence of polarity reversals in the Earth's magnetic field through time. These polarity events can be used to subdivide sequences and to correlate from place to place.

Absolute time involves the age in years before present of rocks and geologic events. In radiometric determinations, the age of a datable mineral or rock is determined by analyzing the original number of parent atoms of a particular radioactive nuclide, the number of such atoms remaining at present, and the half-life of the parent radioactive isotope. The age is the elapsed time since the decay process began which was at the time of crystallization.

Four principal methods of radiometric dating are used to determine the age of ancient igneous and metamorphic rocks:

uranium-238 : lead-206
uranium-235 : lead-207
potassium-40 : argon-40
rubidium-87 : strontium-87.

The most reliable dates come from concordant results using several different methods. Applications of radiometric dating have included determining the age of the Earth, dating the Earth's oldest rocks, dating lunar rocks, and measuring seafloor spreading rates and lithospheric plate movements.

Radioactive isotopes with short half-lives include carbon-14, thorium-230, and protactinium-231. Ages are determined from the amounts of these nuclides that remain in the sample relative to the amounts present originally. Techniques involving these isotopes have been successful in dating rocks less than several million years old, seafloor sediments, glacial deposits, and archaeologic sites. Nuclear fission tracks and amino acid racemization are other absolute dating techniques.

Techniques of relative and radiometric dating and the geologic time scale that has evolved represent major scientific achievements. Knowledge of these techniques and of the time scale that is based on them are fundamental to interpretation of Earth history.

Suggestions for Further Reading

Cloud, Preston, ed. 1970. *Adventures in Earth history.* San Francisco: W. H. Freeman.

Dunbar, C. O., and John Rodger. 1957. *Principles of stratigraphy.* New York: John Wiley & Sons.

Eicher, D. L. 1976. *Geologic time.* 2d ed. Foundations of Earth Science Series. Englewood Cliffs, NJ: Prentice-Hall.

Fleisher, R. L. 1979. Where do nuclear tracks lead? *American Scientist* 67:194–203.

Gould, Stephen Jay. 1987. *Times's arrow, time's cycle: Myth and metaphor in the discovery of geologic time.* Cambridge, MA: Harvard Univ. Press.

Harbaugh, J. W. 1968. *Stratigraphy and geologic time.* Foundations of Earth Science Series. Dubuque, IA: William C. Brown Co.

Harper, C. T., ed. 1973. *Geochronology: Radiometric dating of rocks and minerals.* Stroudsburg, PA: Dowden, Hutchinson and Ross.

Krumbein, W. C., and L. L. Sloss. 1963. *Stratigraphy and sedimentation.* 2d ed. San Francisco: W. H. Freeman.

Laporte, Leo. 1979. *Ancient environments.* 2d ed. Foundations of Earth Science Series. Englewood Cliffs, NJ: Prentice-Hall.

Pettijohn, F. J., and P. E. Potter. 1964. *Atlas and glossary of primary sedimentary structures.* New York: Springer-Verlag.

Ralph, E. K., and Henry N. Michael. 1974. Twenty-five years of radiocarbon dating. *American Scientist* 62:553–60.

Schaeffer, O. A., and J. Zahringer, eds. 1966. *Potassium-argon dating.* New York: Springer-Verlag.

Schrock, R. R. 1948. *Sequence in layered rocks.* New York: McGraw-Hill Book Co.

Birth and Development of the Geologic Time Scale

6

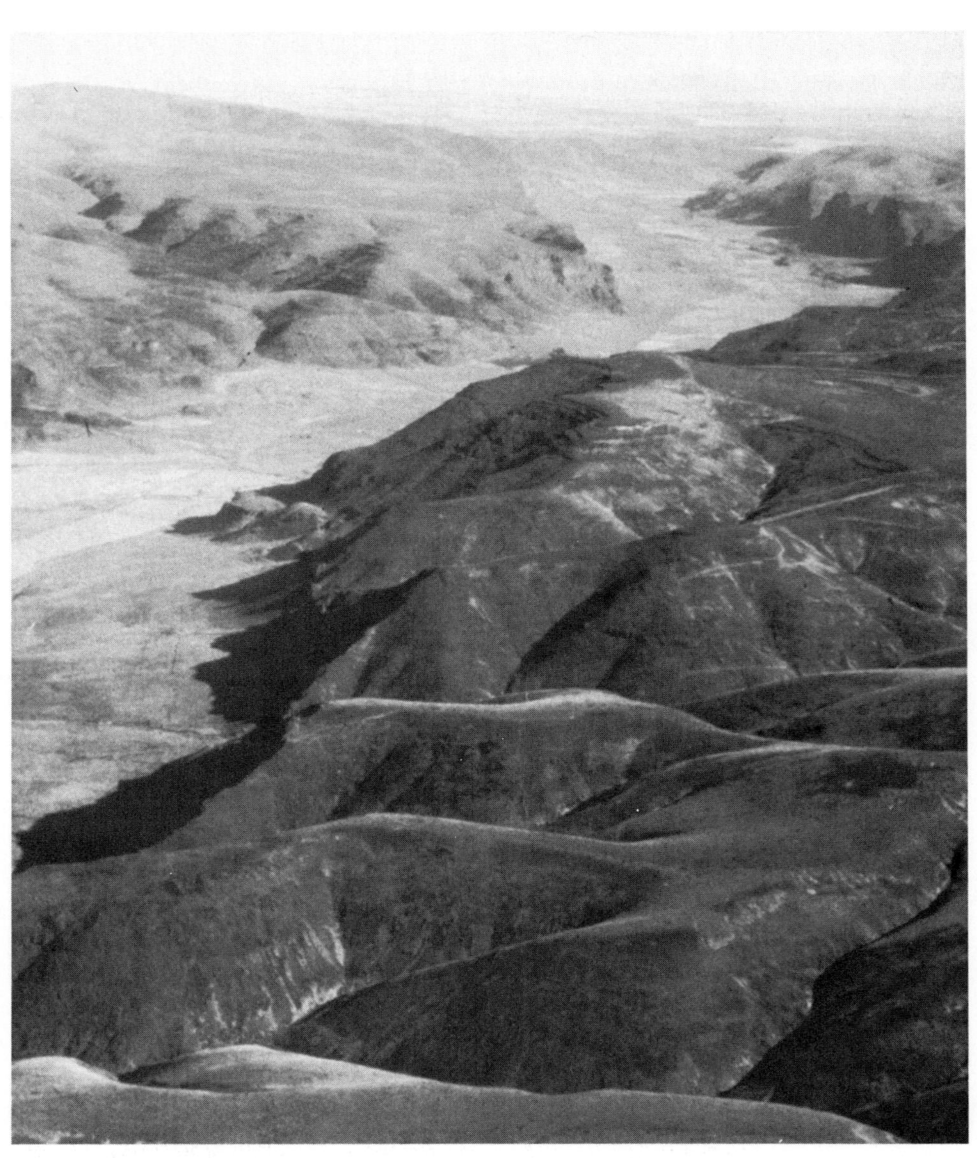

Contents

Key Terms

Neptunism
Catastrophism
Uniformitarianism
Geotectonic cycle
System
Stratotype
Erathem
Era
Series
Stage
Zone
Chronostratigraphic unit
Geochronologic unit
Period
Lithostratigraphic unit
Formation
Member
Group
Supergroup
Biostratigraphic unit
Biozone
Chronozone
Magnetostratigraphic unit
Actualism

Two Giants

Georges Cuvier in France and William Smith in England made major contributions to our understanding of how fossils can be used in stratigraphy—both in subdivision of stratigraphic sequences and correlation of geographically separated sequences. The lives of these two contemporaries were very different and their paths did not cross, but in their individual ways each utilized fossils in a manner that was to have a profound effect on how we view geologic history.

Georges Cuvier (1769–1832), scientist, anatomist, writer, politician, and historian, was arguably the finest intellect in nineteenth-century science. Among his many scientific contributions was a major impact on historical geology made by his work on the stratigraphic succession of Cenozoic units in the Paris Basin (Fig. 6–1). He recognized that distinctive fossils and assemblages of fossils were confined to specific strata, and realized further that many of these fossils were of extinct animals. The concept of extinction was not widely accepted during Cuvier's lifetime, but he believed that the causes of extinction were sudden, catastrophic events, and that successive levels of extinct fossils could be explained by a series of catastrophic happenings. Interestingly, he argued that many faunal changes following catastrophes represented migrations of preexisting biotas from distant areas.

Keep in mind that the prevailing Church dogma of the time embraced the notion of a very young Earth. In 1654, Archbishop Ussher of Ireland had proclaimed, "in the year of our Lord 4004 B.C., he created the earth." This pronouncement was based on biblical scriptures and literal acceptance of ancient Hebrew writings, and was the accepted age of the Earth. Cuvier was a product of the French Enlightenment and viewed dogmatic theology as an impediment to scientific advancement. However, he was also a pragmatist and a diplomat, so in order to accommodate early eighteenth-century church dogma, he proposed a three-part history of the Earth: (1) a Diluvian period, which represented the time of the Noachian flood; (2) a post-Diluvian period that included all time since the flood; and (3) an ante-Diluvian period that included all the time *before* the flood.

Cuvier accepted that the time of the flood and the time since the flood were interpreted accurately by biblical scholars. He placed his extinct fossilized animals in the period of time prior to the flood—a time characterized by prevailing darkness, and strange, now-extinct creatures. Although believing in a much more ancient Earth, and believing in the literal interpretation of geologic phenomena rather than the literal interpretation of the Bible, his view of Earth history explained many catastrophic events and complete new assemblages of life forms without offending the position of the Church.

Cuvier's compromising ideas were widely accepted because he was influential in both scientific and political circles. His academic background included studies in entomology and comparative anatomy. He was appointed professor at the Collège de France in 1800, and in 1803 he became perpetual

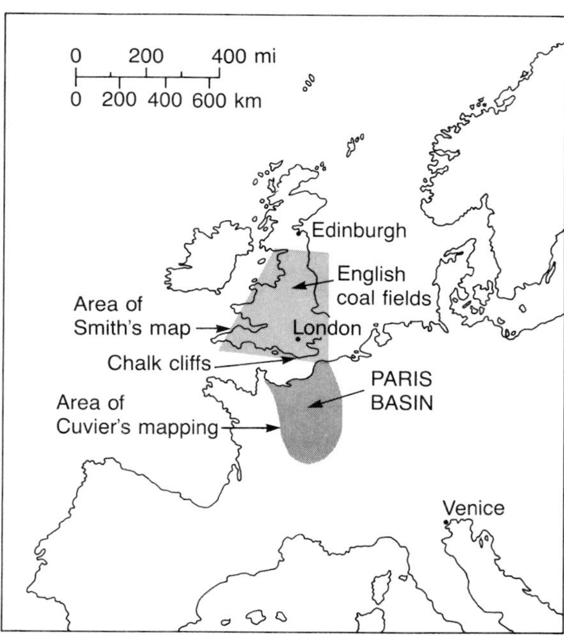

Figure 6–1
Index map of a portion of Europe, illustrating the geographic areas where Cuvier (Paris Basin) and Smith (England) did their late eighteenth century–early nineteenth century studies on fossils.
(After R. H. Dott, Jr. and R. L. Batten, 1981, *Evolution of the Earth,* 3d ed., Fig. 2.8, p. 25: McGraw-Hill Book Co., New York. Reproduced by permission of publisher)

Secretary to the Division of Physical and Mathematical Science of the National Institute. In 1818 he was elected a member of the prestigious French Academy.

William Smith (1769–1839) contributed to historical geology principally through his work as a civil engineer, as he surveyed and built canals (Fig. 6–1). Like Cuvier, he recognized an association of certain fossils and fossil assemblages with particular stratigraphic intervals. As canals were dug and layers of sedimentary rock were exposed, Smith recognized the interrelationship of fossils and stratigraphic units. What a contrast, however, in the directions from which Smith and Cuvier came in their recognition of *fossil succession!* Cuvier was academically educated, was a member of the French court, and worked within its pomp and grandeur. Smith was born in a small village in England, was raised by an uncle in a more casual farm setting, and received no formal education beyond the local village school. His understanding of geology and the nature of fossils was self-acquired through his own countryside wanderings as a boy and later through his work on the canals.

As a young man of eighteen, Smith became an assistant to a surveyor; later he pursued this work on his own. At this time in England, prior to the invention of the steam locomotive, there was active interest in the construction of canals to be used for transportation of coal. Smith traveled widely in England, making survey lines for these canals, and later was employed during construction of the waterways. Recognizing the importance of the strata-fossil associations he observed in the canal walls, Smith compared these associations in many locations in England. These observations led him to formulate independently the principle of fossil succession, and the correlation of strata using fossils.

Perhaps Smith's greatest single contribution to the science of stratigraphy was his geological map of England, one of the first geological maps ever published (1815).* The map included cross-sections and stratigraphic col-

**Map of Strata of England and Wales with a Part of Scotland.* Birmingham, England: Studio Press.

umns, and consisted of 15 sheets compiled at a scale of about three km/cm (roughly 1:300,000); the completed map measured about 2 × 2.5 m. Twenty colors were used in printing it, plus various degrees of shading. It was a map without precedent, a monumental and original work, and the result of more than 20 years of geological observations in the field. (A simplified portion of his map is shown in Fig. 6–8.)

Smith's map units were based on fossil content, and thus are essentially biostratigraphic units. Smith's map demonstrated conclusively that stratigraphic sequences could be subdivided and correlated on the basis of fossil content. This particular application of the principle of fossil succession provided a foundation for the development of the relative geologic time scale during the nineteenth century.

William Smith was not a member of the academically oriented Geological Society of London, but fortunately during his lifetime the significance of his work was recognized and he was honored by this prestigious society. Smith's imaginative vision saw beyond the local use of fossils to identify stratigraphic position. He was able to grasp a greater significance for this inference: an application of fossil succession on a regional scale. During his later years when he was being honored for his original work, he was given the designation "Father of English Geology and Stratigraphy."

Beginnings of the Relative Time Scale

Early Ideas

In the preceding chapter we reviewed the fundamental principles and methods used in telling geologic time: superposition, original horizontality and lateral continuity, inclusions, cross-cutting relationships, fossil succession, correlation, paleomagnetism, and radiometric dating. In this chapter we shall consider these principles in historical perspective with reference to the discovery of *deep time,* the birth and development of the geologic time scale, and the evolution of historical geology as a science.

The beginning of scientific thought and recording of scientific observations in the Western world probably dates back to the sixth century B.C. when Greek scholars began to record and analyze data within the context of assumed principles that governed nature. Some of these early classical Greek thinkers optimistically assumed that natural phenomena within their world could be understood. This attitude kindled the search for guiding principles and natural laws and led to some interesting conclusions regarding causes and effects.

Some of the earliest recorded observations were geological and even stratigraphical. It was observed that shells, not unlike those of clams and snails then living along coasts, were found on mountain tops and other places far inland. This inspired the conclusion that the ocean had once extended to the places where the fossils were found. Herodotus, a Greek historian who lived just prior to 400 B.C., concluded from scientific observation that the Mediterranean Sea was at one time more widespread, and that the Nile delta was constructed from great volumes of sediment that had been transported and deposited by the Nile River. Such students of natural history were impressed by the repeatability of certain processes that shape the face of the Earth, as well as by the impermanence of details of the Earth's surface. This style of thinking about natural phenomena presaged Hutton's philosophy of uniformitarianism.

Grecian theories of scientific inquiry transcended time and cultures and were inherited by Roman scholars. Some of the more notable Greek-influenced Roman scholars, such as Pliny the Elder (A.D. 23–79), came to conclusions similar to those of the Greeks about past positions of land and sea, comparisons of modern sea shells with fossils, volcanic eruptions, earthquakes, and floods. But after the decline of the Roman Empire, the principle of uniformity of nature's processes, along with scientific inquiry in general, suffered a critical blow. The Dark and Middle Ages witnessed a major recession in scholarly activity, and interpretation of natural history took a giant step backward. A few Byzantine and Arab scholars borrowed some ideas from the Greeks and Romans, but did not advance them. Other scientific writings during this nearly thousand-year span of Western history were limited to monasteries and various cloisters. Religious dogma held sway, and any departure from the strictures of the time was considered a serious offense.

The Renaissance witnessed advances in many different fields of science, spawned mainly by development of scientific principles. The stimulus provided by such scientific thinkers as Copernicus, Kepler, and Galileo put the Earth in a new cosmic context. Unfortunately, the religious climate of the times created a barrier to rapid advances in geology, the science of the Earth itself. The Book of Genesis portrayed an Earth that was only a few thousand years old and that was formed during the creation. The creationist viewpoint considered the Earth to have been in a stable state ever since a single great catastrophe, the Noachian flood.

Steno's Principles: The Foundation

Like other sciences, geology and its subdiscipline, stratigraphy, are based upon principles that have been derived by *induction* from the masses of data that have accumulated from observations of natural phenomena. For example, the modern concept of plate tectonics represents a major principle developed from observations of many aspects of the oceanic lithosphere. Principles are the very essence of science, and they provide the basis for interpretation.

The first stratigraphic principles were formulated and clearly enunciated in the last half of the seventeenth century by Niels Stensen, better known as Nicolaus Steno, a Danish physician who settled in Florence, Italy. Steno observed layered strata in Tuscany in northern Italy, and witnessed the process of deposition of layers in an aqueous medium. He noted that when any layer was forming, only the fluid from which its particles came was above it, and therefore no overlying layers could have been present when the lower layers were formed. From this observation he concluded that the lower layers must be older than the upper layers in any sequence of strata. Steno arrived at the principle of *superposition* (see Chapter 5) through inductive reasoning. In time, a set of criteria involving recognition and interpretation of sedimentary structures (Chapter 5) was gradually established, allowing stratigraphers to recognize the tops and bottoms of beds in deformed sequences.

Many naturalists before Steno had observed that certain rocks were layered, and perhaps some of these naturalists tacitly assumed the correct superposition. But Steno is credited with being the first to put the idea of sequence in perspective. He also stated the principles of *lateral continuity* and *original horizontality* of strata (Chapter 5) and recognized that tilted and deformed strata were the result of postdepositional Earth movements such as might be caused by volcanic eruption and cave-ins. Steno's principles laid the foundation for placing rocks in relative order, a first step toward unraveling the history of the Earth.

First Attempts at Subdivision: An Economic Incentive

Geology, as a science based on inductive principles, received its earliest stimulus during the Renaissance because of interest in mining and mineralogy. Mining had been practiced for centuries throughout much of the Western world, and many techniques for extracting metals had been devised. As the economic aspects and uses of metals and gems broadened during the beginning of the industrial revolution in the eighteenth century, more and more emphasis was placed on natural occurrences of minable rocks and minerals. The science of mineralogy itself had its greatest early stimulus from the writings of George Bauer, better known as Agricola, a sixteenth century student of the Earth. He is commonly referred to as the "Father of Mineralogy" because of his classification scheme and vivid descriptions of minerals and mining activity.

During the seventeenth and eighteenth centuries, as more attention was focused upon the study of minerals and rocks, mining academies were established with teaching positions in mineralogy. Knowledge expanded regarding the origin, occurrence, and relationships of ore minerals. In time, there developed a critical need for a scheme by which the time of formation of economically important rocks in one mining area might be related to the time of formation in other areas. And so it was that early attempts to subdivide and organize the rock record had an economic incentive.

The earliest attempts to unravel Earth history used only superposition as a guide. The targets for study were mainly sedimentary rock successions in areas of mining activity. Then early eighteenth-century geologists began to use the local sequences in attempting to develop a history of the entire Earth. This was a noble ambition; it led not only to some good descriptive generalizations, but also to some faulty hypotheses. Superposition was a valid and necessary principle, but it alone would not be the tool for deciphering Earth history.

One of the generalizations that resulted from this attempt to order the rocks of the entire Earth was this: stratified, younger-looking sedimentary rocks that form low mountains and foothills must overlie the older-looking, more complex igneous and metamorphic rocks that form the cores of topographically higher mountain ranges. This led to a stratigraphic subdivision that carried the use of superposition beyond the local scale to a larger scope. Use of large-scale superposition was valid for individual areas, but it led to the fallacious assumption that *all* the crystalline rocks formed at one time, and that *all* the layered, sedimentary rocks formed later. What started out as a good descriptive generalization, applicable to individual mountain belts, was stretched to a faulty, unfounded principle and perpetuated.

In the mid-1750s, Johann Lehmann, who taught mining and mineralogy at a mining academy in Berlin, proposed a broad threefold subdivision of the rocks of the Earth's crust (Fig. 6–2). He referred to each subdivision as a "mountain," a designation that included the topographic expression, kinds of rocks, and sequence of events that had acted collectively to form it. According to Lehmann's scheme, the cores of the highest mountains were made up of the oldest rocks—crystalline rocks that he called "ore mountains" because they were the source of so many valuable mineral deposits. These rocks he judged to have formed at the time of the Earth's origin.

Outward from the ore mountains and superpositionally above them were a second class of mountains which he termed "stratified mountains." The rocks of the stratified mountains consisted of layered sedimentary rocks such as limestone, sandstone, and shale (many with fossils), some beds of coal and marble, and mineral veins. The stratified rocks were assumed to have formed at the time of the Noachian flood. Lehmann interpreted the fossils as the remains of animals and plants that had inhabited the slopes of the older ore mountains and subsequently were swept up by the floodwaters and deposited along with the sediment as the water receded from the mountain flanks. His third class of mountains, called the "alluvial mountains," consisted of loosely consolidated rocks that Lehmann presumed to represent accidents of nature—volcanic eruptions, earthquakes, storms, landslides, cave-ins, and so forth—that occurred after the flood.

Lehmann's scheme, although simple, was based on arduous field work and research, and was truly a monumental work for its time. The mountains, with their individualistic topographic expression and rock makeup, were interpreted as representing a set of geologic events unique in time. To apply the scheme, one could determine the relative age of a rock simply by identifying it and relating it to one of the three mountain types. However, as a means of subdividing the history of the Earth, there are inherent problems with such a scheme because similar rock types can form at vastly different times.

It is a point of interest, though, that Lehmann correctly observed the general large-scale stratigraphic relationships that exist in many of the world's mountain ranges and adjacent foothills and plains:

- a central core of metamorphic and intrusive igneous rocks, commonly referred to as *basement complex;*
- overlain nonconformably by folded and faulted, well-indurated sedimentary strata; and
- the sedimentary strata separated by an angular unconformity from overlying, more loosely consolidated sediments that flank the mountains and commonly represent the erosional debris of the mountains themselves.

Lehmann's scheme, however, perpetuated the erroneous principle that geologic time could be told by what rocks look like.

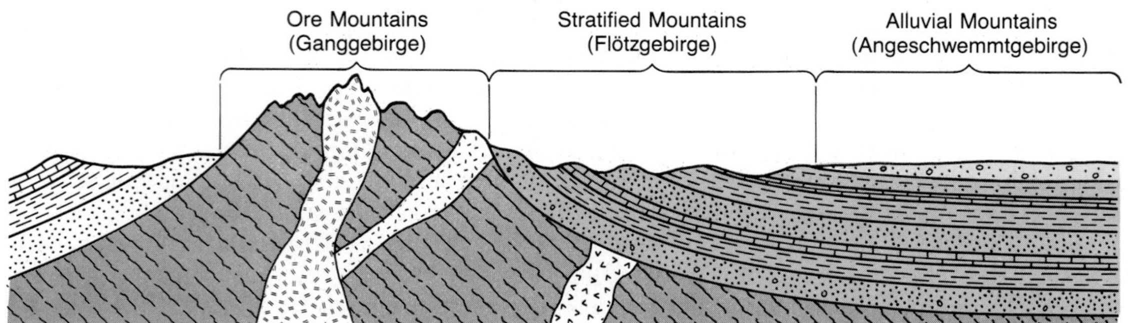

Figure 6–2
Johann Lehmann's subdivisions of rocks of the Earth's crust.

Giovanni Arduino, a contemporary of Lehmann, was professor of mineralogy at the University of Padua, Italy. He was an ardent student of the rocks in Tuscany, where Steno, a century before, had formulated the principle of superposition of strata. Arduino was an active researcher and was influential among other geologists. During the 1760s and 1770s, as had Lehmann before him, Arduino described three kinds of mountains formed from different suites of rock that he called *Primary, Secondary,* and *Tertiary.*

His primary rocks, analogous to the ore mountains of Lehmann, included igneous and metamorphic rocks making up the cores of high mountains (Fig. 6–3). His secondary rocks were described as fossiliferous limestone, claystone, and other kinds of sedimentary rocks exposed on the flanks of the high mountains. Tertiary rocks consisted of a younger, generally less consolidated succession of fossiliferous limestone, sandstone, clay, and marl (clayey limestone) forming lower mountains and hills. Arduino included a fourth class of rocks, *Volcanic,* as a subdivision of the Tertiary mountains; these rocks included lavas and volcaniclastic sediments.

Arduino did not consider this scheme to be applicable universally, but only to the area he studied. He maintained that rock type alone was not a sufficient criterion to make a relative age assignment, and that rocks had to be studied and sequences analyzed on a local basis. His open-mindedness is to be admired, considering the prevailing tendency to organize the rocks of the world solely on the basis of their appearance.

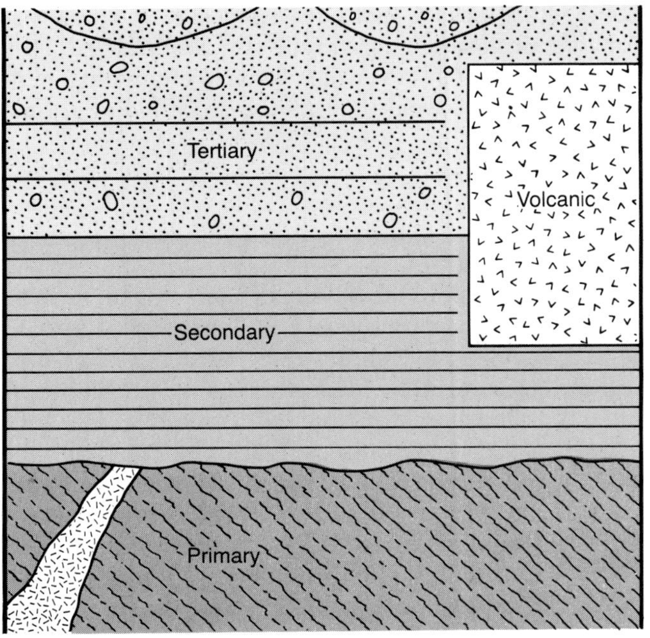

Figure 6–3
Arduino's subdivision of rocks of the Earth's crust.

Werner and Neptunism

The viewpoint—that all crystalline rocks formed at one time, and that all sedimentary rocks formed at successive later times—was carried to an extreme during the last quarter of the eighteenth century. The foremost individual associated with attempts to determine the Earth's history from superposition alone, and to tell the age of rocks by their composition, was Abraham Gottlob Werner, professor of mineralogy at the Freiberg School of Mining in Germany. He zealously nurtured the idea that all rocks of the Earth's crust, regardless of composition, were precipitates of a world-encompassing primeval ocean. As this original ocean gradually shrank, it left behind precipitated layers arranged in superpositional order (Fig. 6–4). Each major layer was considered to have its own unique composition, and to be the same age everywhere. Because water was invoked to explain the formation of all rocks, this school of thought became known as **neptunism.**

As the most influential of all eighteenth-century geologists, Werner recognized a succession of four main groupings of rocks (Fig. 6–5) that he believed revealed the four primary stages in formation of the Earth's crust. He visualized the Earth's crust as being granite at the bottom of the stack, followed in superpositional order by a thick sequence of gneisses, schists, and other crystalline rocks, together constituting the *Primitive* Series. Above these primary precipitates of the Earth-encompassing ocean, Werner recognized a sequence of slates, graywackes, quartzites, and limestones that he called the *Transition* Series. Fossils in these rocks were considered the earliest forms of life. As we shall see later, this recognition of the Transition series was an important contribution.

In terms of original lateral continuity, Werner considered the Primitive and Transition rocks to have covered the entire global surface at one time. Next in order were the stratified rocks of Lehmann. Werner believed that this fossiliferous succession of sandstone, limestone, slate, and coal, called the *Secondary* Series, had formed by chemical precipitation and settling as the sea began to shrink in size, with some of the rock being reworked by surface running water.

Werner's universal sequence was topped by the *Alluvial* rocks, consisting of sand, gravel, clay, peat, and ash and cinder beds, interpreted as the deposits that formed as the primeval ocean waters retreated well below the mountain tops, leaving major areas

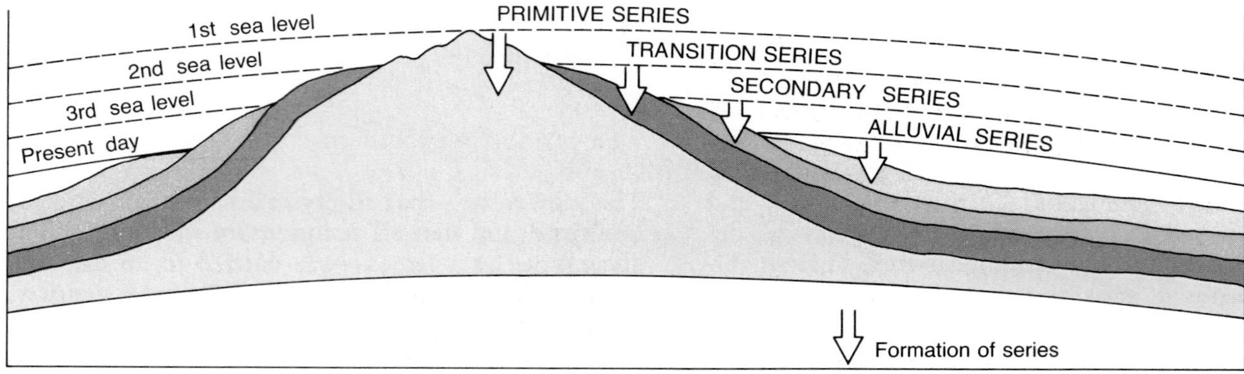

Figure 6–4
Illustration of Werner's neptunist view concerning history of formation of the Earth's crust. As precipitates and deposits from a gradually shrinking but once all-encompassing primeval ocean, the subdivisions of the Earth's crust were envisioned as having formed in the superposition sequence: Primitive Series, Transition Series, Secondary Series, and Alluvial Series.

of bare land. The deposits themselves were formed in the remaining parts of the original ocean, in large part from materials delivered to the sea by running water that coursed over the land. Werner's concept of the sequence of formation is shown in Figure 6–5.

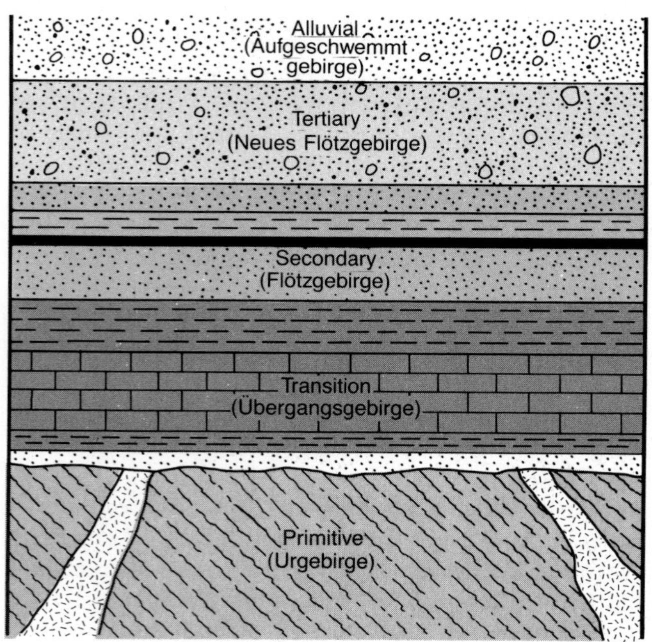

Figure 6–5
Werner's subdivision of rocks of the Earth's crust (his subdivision names are shown in parentheses). Although Werner was misguided in many of his geological interpretations, he was, nonetheless, a great pioneer in the geological sciences and made an important contribution in his definition of the Transition Series.

The appeal of the neptunist philosophy was that, even without mentioning Noah or the Bible, a picture of the history of the Earth was presented that anyone could reconcile with prevailing religious opinion that the Earth was only about 6000 years old. The religious climate of the times dictated that natural processes were controlled by providence, and that the history of the Earth and processes of nature were regarded as having neither great antiquity nor variability. All things—animal, vegetable, and mineral—had been placed by the creator upon the Earth following the last great catastrophe, the Noachian flood (the Great Deluge). The belief that the Earth's surface had been shaped by various major supernatural catastrophes conditioned the thinking of most seventeenth- and eighteenth-century naturalists, making this the so-called age of **catastrophism.**

Hutton and the Roots of Uniformitarianism

Werner's fourfold division of the rocks of the Earth's crust became widely known, but with time its application to separate rock sequences ran into difficulty. Neptunist ideas were extremely vulnerable to field scrutiny and commonly came into sharp conflict with the observations of less provincial, more far-sighted workers. Foremost among these was James Hutton, a Scottish physician-farmer-turned geologist who was not bound by the arithmetic of biblical chronology.

Hutton and a handful of others were able to demonstrate from field relationships that rock units were not worldwide and that each region had its own sequence. To exemplify the conflict, basalt, considered by the neptunists to have formed during a particular time in the Primitive Series as a precipitate from the primeval ocean, was proved to have an igneous origin. Arduino had appreciated the igneous origin of basalts (Fig. 6–6A) when he named the Volcanic subdivision of the Tertiary Series, and Hutton himself demonstrated that basalt could form as an intrusive body. He correctly interpreted the picturesque Salisbury Craig in his native Scotland as a basalt sill. In addition, Hutton's observations of granite dikes cutting through stratified rocks led him to the conclusion that they had an igneous origin and were molten when they forced their way into fissures and cracks in other rocks "like a thicket of fingers." Most certainly, plutonism represented a contradiction to the tenets of neptunism.

From his studies of rocks along the Scottish coast, Hutton observed that every rock formation, no matter how old, appeared to have been derived from other rocks, still older. Hutton's departure from biblical chronology was prompted by his approach to the history of the Earth: he was convinced that geologic processes in ages past were no different from the processes now active. This is the principle of **uniformitarianism.** (Although he is generally credited with formulating the principle, Hutton never actually used the term *uniformitarianism.*) Based on phenomena open to observation, geology could be interpreted without recourse to postulated catastrophes such as the Noachian flood. Hutton openly challenged neptunist ideas (Fig. 6–6B) with his view that the Earth was constantly changing (although its basic nature remained the same). Observable processes such as weathering, erosion, deposition, and volcanic activity were recognized by Hutton as being recorded in the rocks of his native Scotland. He believed that the present provided the key to understanding the past.

James Hutton was a remarkably perceptive observer who clearly recognized the stratigraphic significance of *unconformities* (Fig. 6–7) and other cross-cutting features. He also appreciated the relationship between the grains in sedimentary rocks and the parent rocks from which they were derived. Hutton died in 1797, two years after the publication of a two-volume expansion of his philosophy

A

B

Figure 6–6
A. Geologically recent volcanic activity in the Auvergne region of south-central France: an early graphic testimonial to the igneous origin of basalt. B. James Hutton, trusty rock hammer in hand, contemplating a rock outcrop whose weathered profile simulates the faces of some of his antagonists.
(A, from Faujas de Saint-Fond, 1778; B, from John Kay, Edinburgh Portraits, 1842; photos courtesy of F. Stanton Hill)

A

B

Figure 6–7
A. John Clerk of Eldin's celebrated engraving of James Hutton's unconformity at Jedburgh, Scotland. B. Siccar Point, along the North Sea coast, where Hutton correctly identified and interpreted the unconformity relationship between underlying highly deformed Silurian slates and graywackes and overlying, less deformed Old Red Sandstone. Upon visiting this site in 1805, John Playfair stated, "The mind seemed to grow giddy by looking so far into the abyss of time."
(Photo by J. Patterson)

entitled *Theory of the Earth, With Proofs and Illustrations.** Unfortunately, his writing was cumbersome, and much of the thrust of his arguments was lost in excess verbiage, detail, and convoluted sentence construction. However, John Playfair, a devoted friend and colleague of the Royal Society, assumed the task of clarifying and defending Hutton's ideas. In a clear, concise style, he set forth the observations and conclusions in a brilliant summary, published in 1802: *Illustrations of the Huttonian Theory of the Earth.*** It was through this effort that Hutton's views became widely known, although acceptance of his ideas was slow.

One of the key ingredients in the Huttonian theory of the Earth was the concept of long geologic time. His pronouncement in 1788—"The result, therefore, of our present inquiry is that we find no vestige of a beginning and no prospect of an end"*—was unsettling for those who subscribed to the notion of a 6000-year-old Earth. This statement, more than any other, has been responsible for Hutton's being credited with the discovery of *deep time.* However, most scientists know Hutton through Playfair, and it was Playfair who, in his lucid style, attached a description of the historical significance of unconformities that was lacking in Hutton's original, convoluted treatise. In fact, as Stephen Jay Gould has pointed out in his revealing book, *Time's Arrow, Time's Cycle,**** Hutton did not grasp the power, worth, and distinction of history, and seemed to disdain the recording of sequential events. It was Playfair who added this flavor to what unconformities represented (Fig. 6–7).

Hutton tried desperately to give fixed principles to geology, attempting to emulate what Newton had done for astronomy. But in reality, Hutton's theory of the Earth was based too much on theory and too little on hard field data. Even so, Hutton's philosophy represents the real beginning of progress in geologic thinking, and he will forever stand tall as one of the giants in the history of geology—the "Father of Modern Geology."

As geologic evidence accumulated, the biblical concept of time faded, and the Wernerian viewpoint lost ground because assumed principles had not been verified by experience. The Lehmann-Werner time scales were no more valid than the assumptions on which they were based. There still remained the problem of relating the rocks and structures of one region to those of another, on any kind of meaningful time basis. How could geologic events be correlated from place to place and put into a viable, universal scheme of chronology? Development of a time scale beyond one based on layer-cake appearance would have to wait the development of a new principle—the recognition in rocks of ingredients that had time significance.

*W. Creech, Edinburgh.

**Theory of the Earth: *Royal Society of Edinburgh Transactions.*

***Cambridge, MA: Harvard Univ. Press.

Smith, Cuvier, and Fossil Succession

The answer lay in the fossil record. Fossils had been observed with curiosity for centuries. They were also the center of controversy between the believers in uniformity in nature and the creationists (see Chapter 3). Fossils were mentioned in the rock subdivision schemes of Lehmann and Werner, but only as adjuncts to the compositions of the series. Even Hutton, as enlightened as he was, never suggested that fossils might record a vector of historical change. Interestingly, it was Robert Hooke, the brilliant seventeenth-century British physicist, inventor, and keen student of nature, whose studies of fossils led him to reason that they might be used to determine a record of past ages. He believed that extinctions of old life forms and appearance of new life forms had taken place. At the time such an idea received little serious attention, but in retrospect it amounts to an initial step toward fossil succession as a valid principle.

The discovery by William Smith that fossil assemblages change upward through sequences of strata and that isolated sequences of strata, no matter how different they might appear, are of the same age when they contain the same fossils, provided an efficient means of establishing sequence. Smith not only independently formulated the hypothesis of fossil succession; he also demonstrated its broad applicability through his 1815 geologic map of Britain (Fig. 6–8), and thus established it as a working principle.

The time-significant aspects of fossil succession were put into even clearer perspective for early nineteenth-century geologists by Georges Cuvier in France. Cuvier, from his stratigraphic work in the Paris Basin, also appreciated the reality of fossil succession, but he related the individual faunas to a succession of catastrophic annihilations (extinctions) and subsequent new creations. This view, no doubt, was greatly influenced by the presence of numerous unconformities in the stratigraphic succession.

Fossil succession demonstrated that vertical changes in fossil content in a stratigraphic sequence could be recognized from place to place and that rocks could be correlated on the basis of the fossils they contained. During the early decades of the nineteenth century in Western Europe, fossil succession stood the test of repeated observation

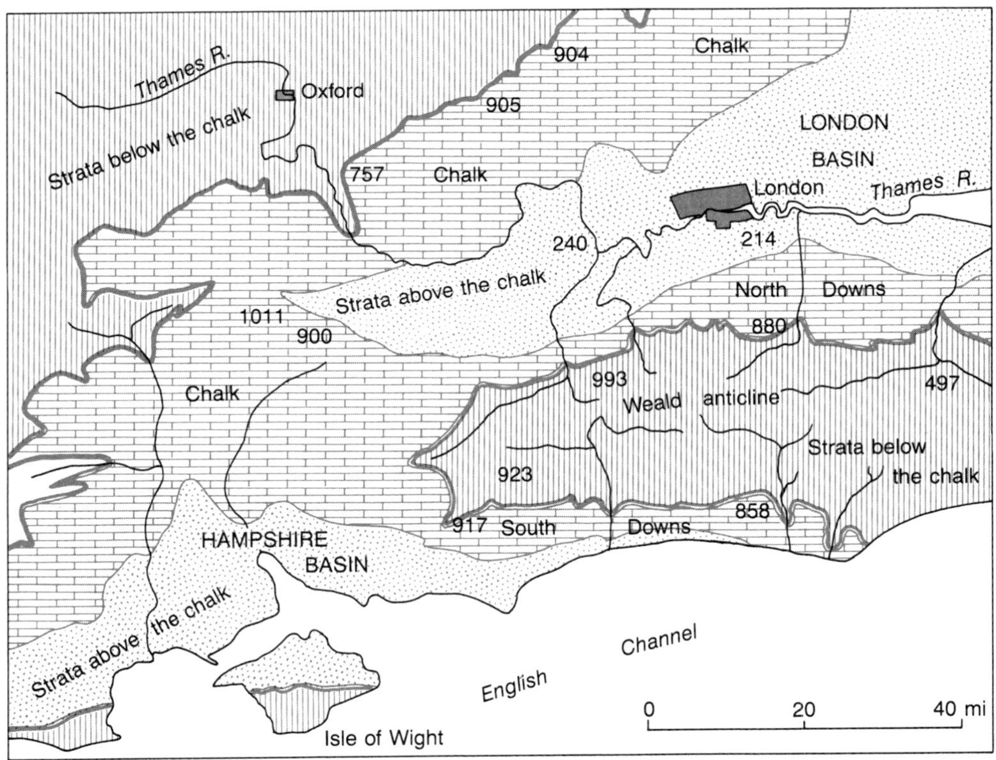

Figure 6–8
Simplified version of William Smith's 1815 geologic map of part of southwestern England. Numbers are spot elevations in feet.
(From A. D. Woodford, 1965, *Historical Geology*, Fig. 3–4, p. 48: W. H. Freeman, San Francisco. Reproduced by permission of author)

and experience. Fossil succession, and correlation using fossils, became the keys that unlocked the door to developing a chronology of Earth history.

The widespread application of the principle of fossil succession was immediate. It provided a real point of departure from the confusion that had resulted from the diversity of geologic opinion existing at the end of the eighteenth century and into the early part of the nineteenth century. Geologists all over Europe were engaged in tracing strata, collecting and describing fossils from them, and establishing fossil succession and lithologic detail of local stratigraphic sequences. These studies generated new interest, geology became popular, and geologic knowledge expanded rapidly. It was through such endeavors that the relative geologic time scale was gradually pieced together.

Lyell: The Champion of Uniformitarianism

In the year 1830, while the modern geologic time scale was beginning to take shape, a milestone and seminal volume in geology was published: *Principles of Geology.** Its author, Charles Lyell, clearly and forcefully presented all the documentation he could marshal in support of the doctrine of uniformitarianism. James Hutton's view of the Earth and Playfair's brilliant clarification of it were slow in being fully accepted. Lyell launched a crusade to lay to rest once and for all the idea that the Earth and all things on it were the product of divine creation. His attack advanced on two fronts: (1) establishment of uniformitarianism at the expense of catastrophism as the acceptable philosophy for interpreting the history of the Earth, and (2) establishment of geology among the sciences as a discipline based on inductive principles.

Lyell gave the uniformitarianism theory its biggest boost, and by effectively reintroducing the concept of unlimited time, he founded modern historical geology. Uniformitarianism then successfully nourished progress in historical geology, because unlike Hutton, Lyell was a historian. He realized the primary task of geology was the unraveling of the sequence of actual events in time, using the key that Cuvier and Smith had provided. Lyell also was a devotee of Darwin's gradualistic evolutionary theory and was one of Darwin's most vocal supporters. Lyell embraced a concept of time that saw a succession of cycles within a framework of sequential development—in essence, a unification of time's cycle and time's arrow. The true codification of deep time was deeply rooted in his complete *Principles of Geology* (Vol. I–III, 1830–1833), which enjoyed eleven editions between 1830 and 1872 and stands as one of the truly monumental tomes in the history of science.

*J. Murray, London.

Growth of the Relative Time Scale

Stratigraphic Systems

As William Smith had shown, fossils could be used to establish the time equivalency of rocks even where lithologies differed. The principle of fossil succession led gradually to the recognition of large-scale aggregates of fossils upon which the major stratigraphic divisions of the time scale were based. With this recognition we see the transition from purely descriptive stratigraphic units to interpretive units.

Today we refer to these main divisions as **systems,** but as the geologic column was being assembled, various other designations such as group, formation, order, and series were used to denote these major packages of rock. These stratigraphic systems were established one by one by different people working in Western Europe (Fig. 6–9, Table 6–1). The systems were based on particular stratigraphic sections, called *type sections,* which today are referred to as **stratotypes.** The geographic areas or districts that contain the stratotypes are called *type areas.*

Some of the systems originally were established on lithologic grounds, reflecting the influence of Wernerian philosophy; some were based on unconformities in the stratigraphic record, an artifact of catastrophist thinking; and some were based on distinctive fossil content. Regardless of how they were defined originally, they were subsequently refined and recognized on every continent through application of fossil succession. They became interpretive units based on unique fossil content.

The modern relative geologic time scale (Table 6–1) was firmly established by the beginning of the twentieth century as a scale based on a succession of fossiliferous units, each with its own type section and type area and unique aggregate of fossils. The system names in common use today are essentially the same as those employed at the turn of the century, and with few exceptions, have received worldwide usage. The large-scale stratigraphic names have remained stable, testimony to universal confidence in the validity of the units and their

Figure 6–9
Map of western Europe showing type localities of the stratigraphic systems. (From Leigh W. Mintz, 1981, *Historical Geology: The Science of a Dynamic Earth,* Fig. 2–18, p. 27: Merrill Publishing Company)

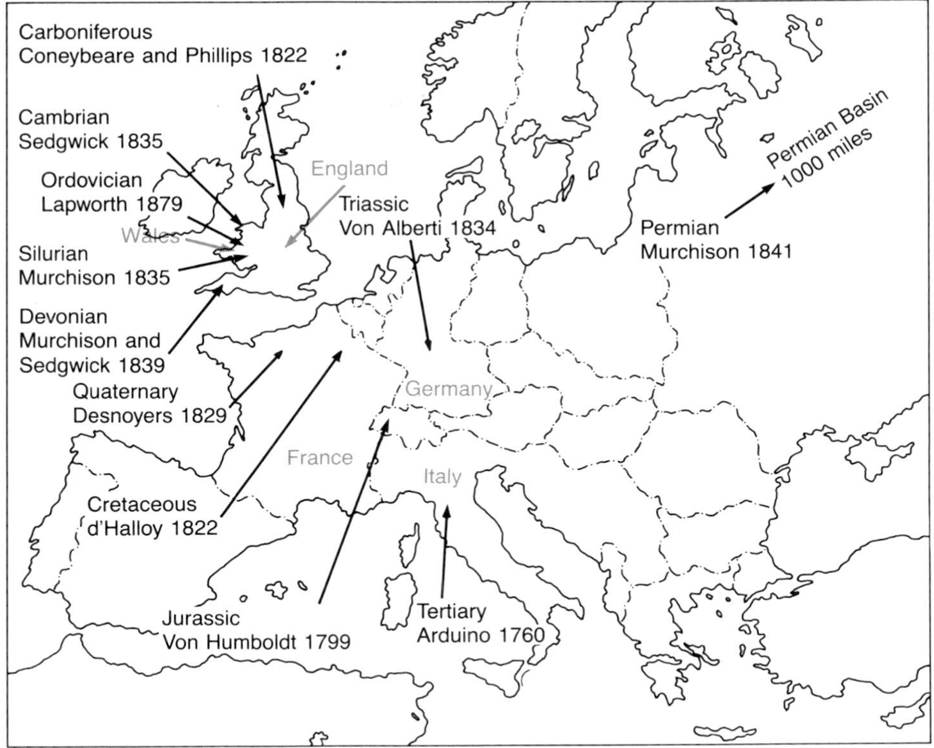

worldwide applicability. Over the years, however, many workers have abandoned the term Tertiary in favor of a more equal time subdivision of the Cenozoic, and have employed the terms *Paleogene* and *Neogene* (Table 6–2).

In the early 1840s it was proposed that the systems be lumped together into three larger-scale units that represented the major subdivisions of the fossil record (and thus fundamental chapters in the history of life). Today these subdivisions are called **erathems,** which correspond to the time term **era.** The names of the eras—Paleozoic, Mesozoic, and Cenozoic—are derived from the Greek word meaning "to live" combined with the Greek words for ancient, middle, and new, respectively. The eras are convenient large-scale generalized units useful for distinguishing large segments of prehistoric time.

It is interesting to note how the major subdivisions of the Arduino–Lehmann–Werner time scale correspond, in a broad sense, with the eras of the modern time scale (Table 6–1). Note also the correspondence of the Transition Series with the lower Paleozoic, and the Primitive Series (= Primary of Arduino) with the Precambrian. However, it is important to bear in mind that application of the principle of fossil succession has demonstrated that many rock units have turned out to be either older or younger than would have been assumed solely on the basis of their appearance.

Other Subdivisions of the Time Scale: Series, Stage, Zone

Once the large-scale systems were established, they were, in turn, subdivided into smaller units. As the systems became more easily recognized from place to place and correlation of fossil-bearing sections established a reliable web of continuity, relative age assignments were made away from type sections, and smaller scale subdivisions were recognized.

In 1833 Charles Lyell defined four subdivisions of the Tertiary System and called them the Eocene, Miocene, older Pliocene, and new Pliocene Periods, in ascending order (Table 6–2). This represents one of the earliest attempts at recognizing time-significant stratigraphic units defined on fossil content. The definition was based on the relative proportion of living and extinct species of fossils that each unit contained. This ingenious technique served to separate the units more conveniently. Lyell, although having confidence in the technique, stated that more detailed work on the type-Tertiary beds of France very likely would refine the subdivisions and additional ones would be defined.

In 1854 the Oligocene and in 1874 the Paleocene were added to the succession (Table 6–2). Subsequent workers demoted the Tertiary subdivisions to the rank of **series** because they felt the magnitudes were too small compared to magnitudes of

Table 6–1
Different vintages of geologic time scales

<table>
<tr><th colspan="4">Early Subdivisions</th><th colspan="4">Modern Usage</th></tr>
<tr><th>Arduino
1760</th><th>Lehmann 1756
Füchsel
1760–1773</th><th>Werner
ca. 1800</th><th>English
Equivalents</th><th>Eras</th><th>Periods</th><th>Epochs</th><th>Alternate
Periods</th></tr>
<tr><td rowspan="3">Volcanic
Alluvium
Tertiary</td><td rowspan="3">Angeschwemmtgebirge</td><td rowspan="3">Aufgeschwemmtgebirge
Neues Flötzgebirge</td><td rowspan="3">Alluvium
Tertiary</td><td rowspan="3">CENOZOIC
Phillips 1841</td><td>QUATERNARY
Desnoyers 1829</td><td>Holocene
Pleistocene</td><td>QUATERNARY</td></tr>
<tr><td>NEOGENE
Hoernes 1853</td><td>Pliocene
Miocene</td><td rowspan="2">TERTIARY
Arduino 1760</td></tr>
<tr><td>PALEOGENE
Naumann 1866</td><td>Oligocene
Eocene
Paleocene</td></tr>
<tr><td rowspan="6">Secondary</td><td rowspan="6">Flötzbirge</td><td rowspan="6">Flötzgebirge</td><td rowspan="6">Secondary</td><td rowspan="3">MESOZOIC
Phillips 1841</td><td colspan="3">CRETACEOUS
d'Halloy 1822</td></tr>
<tr><td colspan="3">JURASSIC
von Humboldt 1799</td></tr>
<tr><td colspan="3">TRIASSIC
von Alberti 1834</td></tr>
<tr><td rowspan="7">PALEOZOIC
Sedgwick
1838</td><td colspan="3">PERMIAN
Murchison 1841</td></tr>
<tr><td>PENNSYLVANIAN
Williams 1891</td><td colspan="2" rowspan="2">CARBONIFEROUS
Coneybeare and Philips 1822</td></tr>
<tr><td>MISSISSIPPIAN
Winchell 1870</td></tr>
<tr><td rowspan="5">Primary</td><td rowspan="5">Ganggebirge</td><td rowspan="4">Übergangsgebirge</td><td rowspan="4">Transition</td><td colspan="3">DEVONIAN
Murchison, Sedgwick 1839</td></tr>
<tr><td colspan="3">SILURIAN
Murchison 1835</td></tr>
<tr><td colspan="3">ORDOVICIAN
Lapworth 1879</td></tr>
<tr><td colspan="3">CAMBRIAN
Sedgwick 1835</td></tr>
<tr><td>Urgebirge</td><td>Primitive</td><td colspan="4">PRECAMBRIAN</td></tr>
</table>

Table 6–2
Cenozoic subdivisions—Lyell and modern*

<table>
<tr><th>Era</th><th>Period</th><th>Lyell's Scheme</th><th colspan="2">Modern Usage</th><th>(Age in Ma)</th></tr>
<tr><td rowspan="7">CENOZOIC (1841)</td><td rowspan="2">QUATERNARY (1829)</td><td>Recent (time since first appearance of humans)</td><td rowspan="2">QUATERNARY (1829)</td><td>Holocene (1885)</td><td>0.01</td></tr>
<tr><td>New Pliocene (1833) 90% living species</td><td>Pleistocene (1839)</td><td>1.8</td></tr>
<tr><td rowspan="5">TERTIARY (1760)</td><td>Older Pliocene (1833) 33–50% living species</td><td rowspan="2">NEOGENE (1853)</td><td>Pliocene</td><td>5.3</td></tr>
<tr><td>Miocene (1833) 18% living species</td><td>Miocene</td><td>24.0</td></tr>
<tr><td rowspan="3">Eocene (1833) 3.5% living species</td><td rowspan="3">PALEOGENE (1866)</td><td>Oligocene (1854)</td><td>37.0</td></tr>
<tr><td>Eocene</td><td>58.0</td></tr>
<tr><td>Paleocene (1874)</td><td>65.0</td></tr>
</table>

*Lyell's units defined on percentage of living species found as fossils. Paleogene and Neogene are preferred to Tertiary, although in certain contexts Tertiary is acceptable. Dates show when names were established. Charles Lyell, 1830, 1832, 1833, *Principles of Geology*, vols. 1–3, J. Murray, London.

other systems of the geologic time scale. These series subdivisions of the Tertiary System have had essentially worldwide application. Other stratigraphic systems have been subdivided into formal series, most commonly designated by stratigraphic position terms such as Lower, Middle, and Upper (e.g., Lower Cambrian Series; Upper Cretaceous Series). Some series have names based on *type* sections and type areas (e.g., Guadalupian Series of the Permian System, with type locality being the Guadalupe Mountains of southeastern New Mexico). Although there is generally universal agreement in concept, the individual series names themselves have only regional-to-continentwide application (with the exception of those of the Cenozoic).

As work continued on a wider scale, it was realized that understanding the history of the Earth demanded even smaller-scale time-stratigraphic units. Many local stratigraphic sections that had been worked out represented only isolated pieces of the composite puzzle. How could more refined time correlations be effected, and how could the vast number of local formations and fossiliferous sequences that had been studied be related to one another?

Careful work in France, Germany, Switzerland, and England demonstrated the reliability of plotting the vertical ranges of fossil species for the recognition of smaller-scale, paleontologically defined units which could be correlated. From such painstaking work emerged the concepts of faunal **stage** and **zone** (Fig. 6–10). The recognition that rock types change laterally within the same time-stratigraphic interval spawned the concept of sedimentary facies (discussed in Chapter 2), which are deposits produced by different (but laterally adjacent) environments of deposition.

By the beginning of the twentieth century the relative geologic time scale had been laboriously pieced together, and the stratigraphic principles for working out Earth history had been formulated. Notions about a 6000-year-old Earth appealed only to those who had (and who still have) a fundamentalist interpretation of biblical scriptures. However, it would not be until after the discovery of radioactivity and its application to age-dating that realistic determinations of the age of the Earth would be made, and that the antiquity and duration of the relative subdivisions of the geologic time scale would be appreciated.

America's First Major Geologic Concept

One very important outgrowth of this ability to subdivide and correlate strata using fossil content led to a theory of mountain building, and represents

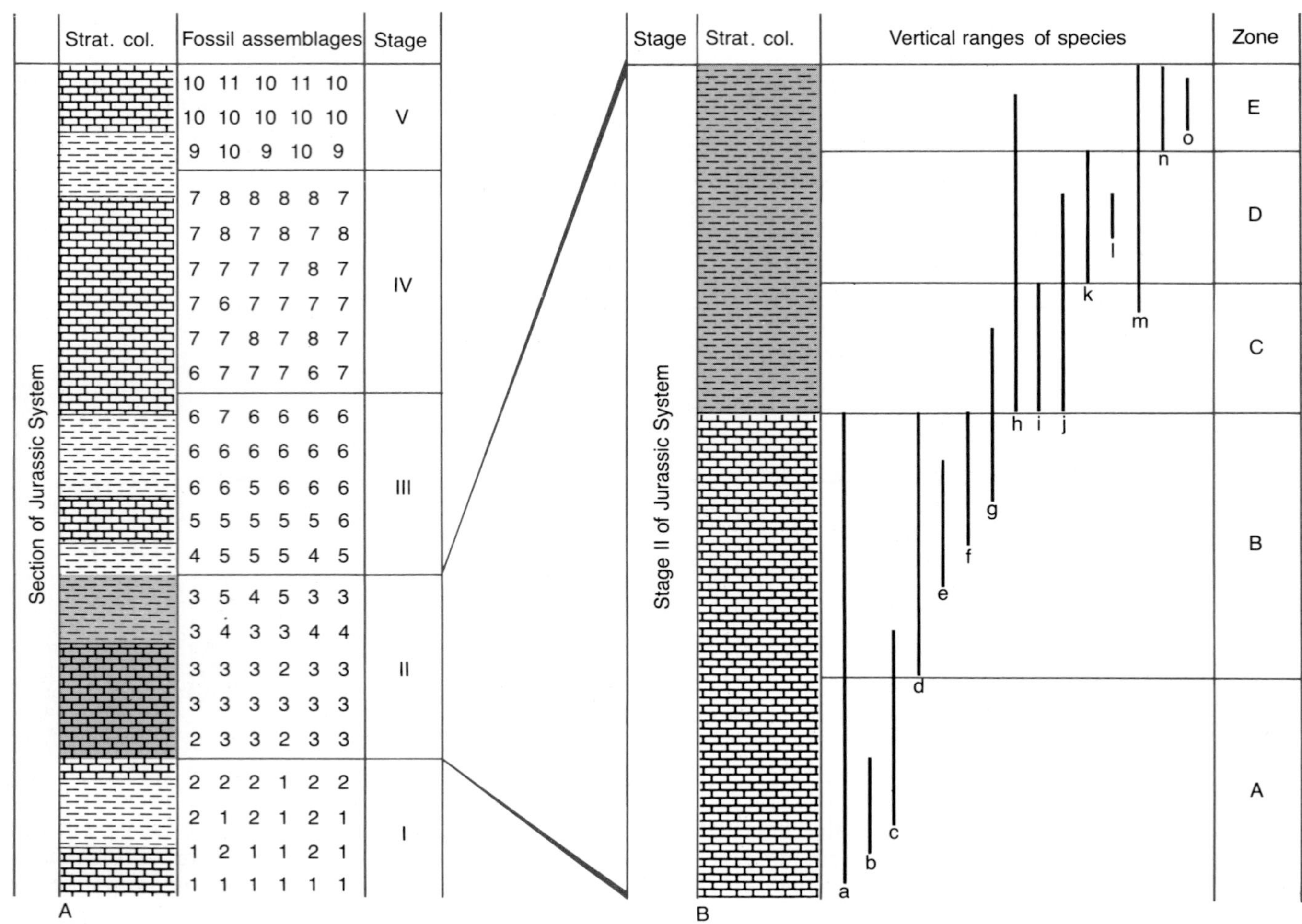

Figure 6–10

A. Subdivision of Jurassic System into stages based on smaller aggregates (assemblages) of fossils; concept developed by A. d'Orbigny in 1842. Numbers 1–11 represent assemblages of fossils composed of species (a, b, c, etc.) shown in B. B. Subdivision of stage into zones, based on still smaller aggregates of fossils defined by overlapping ranges of individual fossil species; concept developed by A. Oppel in 1856–1858. Species a, d, f, g, h, and m make up assemblage 3; species b, c, and e make up assemblage 2; species i, j, k, and l make up assemblage 4; species n and o make up assemblage 5.

the first American contribution to the rapidly burgeoning science of geology. In his presidential address to the American Association for the Advancement of Science in 1859, James Hall, a great pioneer American geologist and state geologist of New York, submitted the observation that Paleozoic strata in the Appalachian Mountain belt are comparatively much thicker than their time-equivalent counterparts in the Mississippi Valley region of the mid-continent, and they are much more deformed. Hall reasoned that there must be a causative relationship between the greater thickness of sediments in the Appalachians and their deformed character. From this he drew the conclusion that all large mountain chains must represent areas of inordinately thick accumulations of sediments. He also observed that the character of the sediments in both the Appalachians and midcontinent was unmistakably similar—they both bore the earmarks of shallow-water deposition.

Hall maintained that the greater thickness of shallow-water sediments in the Appalachians had to be an expression of greater crustal subsidence there than in the continental interior (craton). He believed the crust gradually yielded under the weight of the sediments themselves; subsidence then kept pace with sedimentation so that the depositional surface was constantly in the shallow-water realm. Mountain building was envisioned as a cyclic process whereby sedimentation resulted in further subsidence, which in turn accommodated more sediment. Eventually along the axis of the subsiding belt, sediments were folded and faulted, occasionally intruded by plutons, and, in places, metamorphosed.

In 1873, James Dwight Dana, professor of geology at Yale University, gave Hall's theory a name—"geosynclinal" (later changed to *geosyncline*)—but not without some additional ideas of his own. Dana took exception to the role that sediments were assumed to play in the deformation of geosynclinal sequences into mountain belts. Dana was one of the first geologists to recognize the fundamental differences between oceanic and continental crust, and he subscribed to the notion that the Earth's crust was subjected to constant compression due to the general contraction (through cooling) of the interior. He believed that the greatest yielding to this compressive stress should be along the interfaces between continents and ocean basins. Such yielding would manifest itself by downwarping to form geosynclines. In Dana's hypothesis, thick masses of sediment were able to accumulate because the crust, downwarped by forces *within* the Earth, subsided to create a place for them.

In a sense both Hall and Dana were correct, and their ideas formed the basis for the concept of the **geotectonic cycle** and an understanding of the relationship between tectonic framework, sedimentation, and stratigraphy. Plate tectonics has given us new insights and new models within which to view ancient geosynclines, and new terminology such as *continental margin basin* to replace the antiquated term geosyncline. Plate tectonics has also provided modern (actualistic) analogues to allow for advancing the "geosynclinal" concept from a descriptive one to a genetic one.

As an example, genetically distinct sedimentary prisms form on tectonically passive edges (Fig. 6–11) of diverging continents, in contrast to those deposits that accumulate on tectonically active leading edges of lithospheric plates. Plate tectonics demonstrates how these two different depositional settings, with their contrasting stratigraphic successions, ultimately may become deformed into *orogens*. Characteristics of these continental margin basins are understood better now in terms of the Wilson Cycle.

Historical Geology Matures

Stratigraphic Classification

Through the late nineteenth century and into the twentieth, establishment of a worldwide stratigraphic correlation network and refinements in the geologic time scale continued, but various stratigraphic concepts and terms such as series, stage, group, formation, and zone were used interchangeably and became confusing. Through the years, a number of symposia have been held and various national and international stratigraphic commissions have been organized in an attempt to achieve consistency in formal stratigraphic nomenclature and stratigraphic practice.

In the spirit of such concern, the North American Commission on Stratigraphic Nomenclature, in collaboration with the American Association of Petroleum Geologists, has published several editions of a Code of Stratigraphic Nomenclature. This code

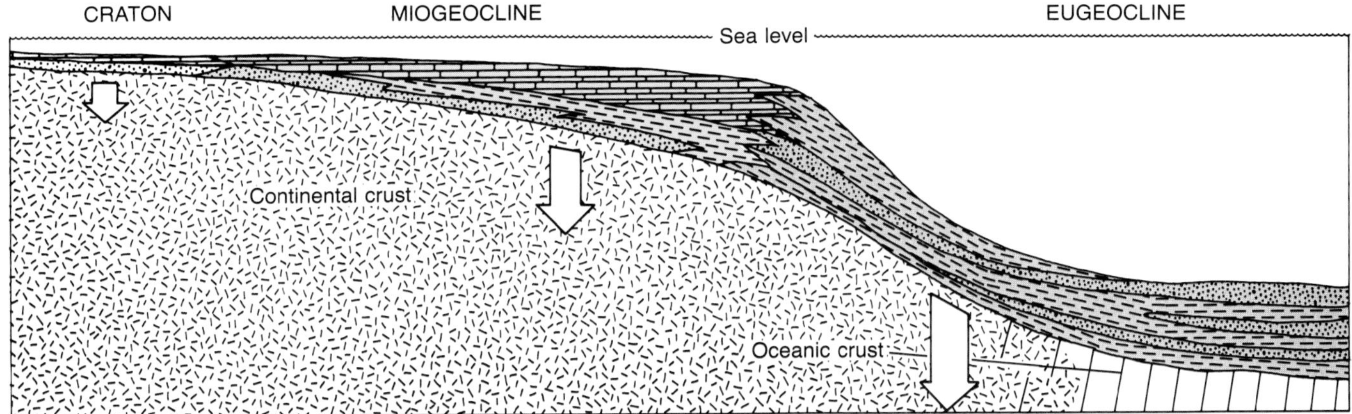

Figure 6–11
Miogeocline (shelf) and eugeocline (slope and rise) divisions of continental-margin basin (also commonly referred to as a geosyncline).

Table 6–3
Principal categories of formal stratigraphic units

A. Material Units (Descriptive)*

LITHOSTRATIGRAPHIC	BIOSTRATIGRAPHIC	MAGNETOPOLARITY
Supergroup	B	Polarity Superzone
Group	I	
FORMATION	O	POLARITY ZONE
Member	Z	Polarity Subzone
Bed	O	
	N	
	E	

B. Temporal (Time) or Related Chronostratigraphic Units (Interpretive)*

Biostratigraphic (or *radiometric) Data			Magnetostratigraphic Data		
CHRONOSTRATIGRAPHIC		GEOCHRONOLOGIC GEOCHRONOMETRIC**	POLARITY CHRONOSTRATIGRAPHIC		POLARITY CHRONOLOGIC
Eonothem	=	Eon			
Erathem	=	Era	Polarity superchronozone	=	Polarity superchron
SYSTEM	=	PERIOD	Polarity chronozone	=	Polarity chron
Series	=	Epoch			
Stage	=	Age	Polarity subchronozone	=	Polarity subchron
Chronozone	=	Chron			

*In the above scheme, the brown background highlights lithologic criteria, the gray highlights paleontologic criteria, and the white highlights paleomagnetic criteria. **Geochronometric units are geochronologic units, based on radiometric dates, for which there are no tangible reference sections.

has evolved primarily to clarify the unequivocal distinctions among the principal categories of formally named stratigraphic units, and has resulted in a classification (Table 6–3) whose utility involves the organization of the stratigraphic record so that geologists can communicate and nomenclature is consistent. For our purposes, the Code classification is simplified to emphasize five principal categories of formal stratigraphic units. These are based upon chronostratigraphic, geochronologic, lithostratigraphic, biostratigraphic, and magnetostratigraphic data, and are described below.

Chronostratigraphic units (or time-stratigraphic units) are intervals of strata formed during specific intervals of time and are demarcated by *isochronous* (synchronous) boundaries as defined by synchronous events in the fossil record. These are the fundamental units of the standard chronostratigraphic scale, such as eonothem, erathem, system, series, and stage. **Geochronologic units** (or time units) are abstract units that correspond to chronostratigraphic units (Table 6–3). The time concept of the Cretaceous **Period,** for example, is based on the tangible chronostratigraphic record of the Cretaceous System. Geochronologic (time) terms are necessary to refer accurately to historical events and circumstances.

Lithostratigraphic units are based on the physical (nonbiological) aspects of rocks. The fundamental unit in this category is the **formation,** defined as a body of strata that has characteristic properties by which it can be identified. This definable character is based on mappable physical criteria such as color, mineral composition, texture, thickness and geometry of contained beds, sedimentary structures, and topographic expression. Fossils are included in the set of identifying criteria only if they are used as lithologic adjuncts (e.g., a fossiliferous limestone formation) without regard to the ranges of individual species.

Formations are formally named for geographic locales where the stratotypes are defined. In terms of lithologic homogeneity, formations are descriptive units, recognized for their individuality because they are different from adjacent bodies of rock. They represent parts of or complete sedimentary *facies,* and their boundaries, also defined on physical criteria, may be sharp or gradational (Fig. 6–12). Formations are the fundamental stratigraphic units on geologic maps of conventional (7½-minute and 15-minute) quadrangle scale. They are units of convenience, designated to aid in organization and communication of the stratigraphic record in a physical sense. Formations commonly are subdivided into **members** (Table 6–3) or, conversely, may be lumped together into **groups.** Some closely related groups are combined into very thick **supergroups.** Such procedures and practices enhance recognition and correlation of lithostratigraphic units.

A lithostratigraphic unit of any rank can be recognized away from the type section. More precisely stated, isolated outcrop or subsurface sections can be assigned to the same lithostratigraphic unit, if it

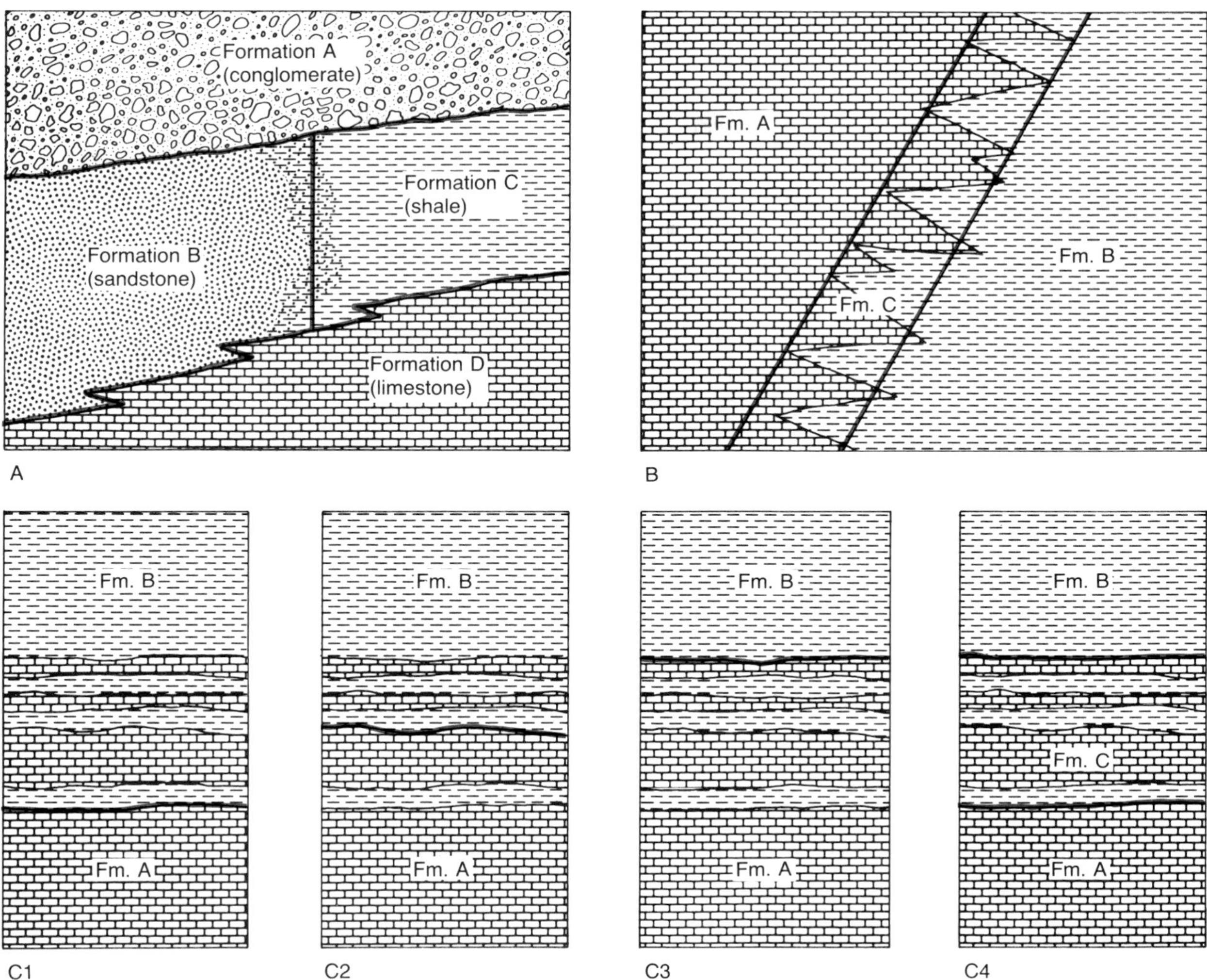

Figure 6–12
Lithostratigraphic formations and some of the different ways that formation boundaries can be drawn. Remember, the boundaries should be mappable and formation names cannot be repeated in vertical sequence. A. Vertical separation by abrupt lithologic change; arbitrary lateral separation within gradational facies change. B. Two laterally interfingering facies divided into three formations, including limestone, shale, and interbedded limestone-shale. C1–C4. Different ways of selecting boundaries within a transitional (interbedded) change from one lithology (limestone) to another (shale) in a vertical sequence. Individual choice reflects stratigraphic judgment. C1. Boundary selected at lowest occurrence of shale. C2. Boundary selected at top of uppermost *prominent* limestone unit. C3. Boundary selected at top of uppermost limestone unit. C4. Transitional (interbedded) interval designated as separate formation. The interbedded transition is a local expression of regional interfingering of limestone and shale facies.
(Modified from North American Commission on Stratigraphic Nomenclature, 1983, North American Stratigraphic Code, Fig. 2, p. 857; *American Assoc. Petroleum Geologists Bulletin*, vol. 67, no. 5. Used with permission of American Association of Petroleum Geologists.)

can be demonstrated that they were once part of the same contiguous body of rock and bear sufficient similarity to the stratotype (Fig. 6–12).

The boundaries of lithostratigraphic units, selected on lithologic criteria, are not intended to be isochronous. Such units are fundamentally different from the interpretive chronostratigraphic units and are defined by different criteria. This fundamental distinction may seem obvious, but the tendency of many stratigraphers to recognize formations on the basis of fossil content or to consider formations and groups as chronostratigraphic units has resulted in much poor stratigraphic practice, creating the necessity for clarifying the distinction.

A fourth category of formal stratigraphic classification is the **biostratigraphic unit** (Table 6–3). The fundamental unit is the **biozone** (originally called zone), which is simply a body of rock whose boundaries are defined by fossil content. Most biozones are formally named after a particular characterizing species. Biozones are descriptive units; however, a biozone that has chronostratigraphic utility is an interpretive unit and the designation **chronozone** is commonly used (Table 6–3). As originally defined, such biozones are the smallest formal chronostratigraphic units that can be recognized.

Again, biozones are descriptive units first. However, certain biozones can be interpreted to have chronostratigraphic value; that is why the distinction is necessary between chronostratigraphic and biostratigraphic units. It is important to remember, however, that it is biostratigraphic data that provide the underpinnings for our relative chronostratigraphic scale.

As shown in Figure 4–1 (Chapter 4), patterns of first and last appearance and diversity of taxa give us the information for drawing the erathem, system, series, and stage boundaries for the chronostratigraphic scale. These biostratigraphic patterns are evolutionary patterns, and the biostratigraphic record—deeply rooted in the principle of fossil succession—is a record of organic evolution through time. Here we see the interrelationship among biostratigraphy, evolution, and paleoecology. The biostratigraphic record of fossil succession is a reflection of evolution; the paleoecology relates to the living environments of populations of organisms, where the selective pressures for evolutionary change and the sites of accumulation of the biostratigraphic record itself occurred.

Yet a fifth, but relatively new, category of formal stratigraphic nomenclature concerns **magnetostratigraphic units** (Table 6–3). In a sense, magnetostratigraphic units, based on magnetic signatures in rock, are analogous to biostratigraphic, chronostratigraphic, and geochronologic units. In this perspective, the descriptive "fossil" magnetism data, expressed as a *polarity zone,* are analogous to fossils. The polarity signature takes on chronostratigraphic significance in terms of the *polarity chronozone,* which, in turn, has its geochronologic or abstract time counterpart when expressed as a *polarity chron* (Table 6–3). This chronostratigraphic significance of paleomagnetic events and polarity intervals has enabled the construction of a geomagnetic time scale (see later discussion).

The Meaning of Correlation

The classification of stratigraphic units has evolved as a result of the progressive awareness by stratigraphers that there are fundamentally different kinds of units: different rock types (facies) can be found within a time-stratigraphic unit; formations can be of different ages in different places; and only those biostratigraphic units that have become interpretive in a time sense can be designated chronostratigraphic units. Additionally, magnetopolarity events are judged to be geologically synchronous, and thus provide another expression of chronostratigraphy. This philosophy of unequivocal distinction among the kinds of stratigraphic units has important overtones for correlation. Correlations can be based on material units and on temporal and related chronostratigraphic units (Table 6–3).

Lithostratigraphic correlation refers to the matching of physical lithologic units which may be, but generally are not, time equivalent (Fig. 6–13). (An example of where they *are* time-equivalent is the case of matched volcanic ash layers, or "tephra chronology.") Most practical chronostratigraphic correlations are biostratigraphic in nature, but they are interpretive biostratigraphic, whereby fossils are used in an interpretive sense to establish time equivalency (Fig. 6–13). Recognition of magnetopolarity units from place to place has provided another means of chronostratigraphic correlation because of the geologically synchronous nature of changes in the Earth's polarity through time.

Yet another aspect of chronostratigraphic correlation involves certain geochemical signatures in sediments and sedimentary rocks. These include stable isotope ratios such as O^{18}/O^{16}; C^{13}/C^{12}; and Sr^{87}/Sr^{86}, and trace elements such as *iridium.* The idea here is to match departures (called excursions) from standard curves that have been developed for particular abundances or abundance ratios. This involves the matching of geochemical *events.*

Another example of correlation using recorded events is the matching of relative sea-level changes from place to place, such as in comparison of the kick-off points between transgressive and regressive events.

The fundamental principles of stratigraphy (Chapter 5) and stratigraphic classification apply to subsurface sequences as well as to surface outcrop exposures. Subsurface geology presents some spe-

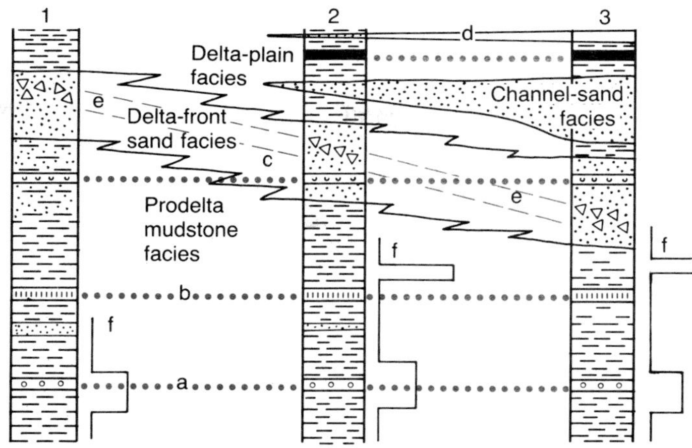

Figure 6–13

Chronostratigraphic correlation with interpreted time-significant fossil horizons (a, b) and with blanketlike geologically "instantaneous" volcanic ash beds (c, d). Note that the correlated lithofacies boundaries cross the time lines defined by the time-stratigraphic markers. Note also that the biostratigraphic correlation (e) is not chronostratigraphic—probably a result of the lithofacies control on the distribution of the fossils. Magnetostratigraphic correlations are shown by f, where excursion to right represents reverse polarity.

cial problems because the rocks are seldom observed directly. However, countless thousands of wells have probed the subsurface realm, mainly to depths of less than 10,000 meters below the surface, in the search for and in the production of oil and gas. Well cuttings, cores, and various kinds of electrical and radioactivity logs (Fig. 6–14) have provided a twentieth-century dimension of stratigraphic information not available to the pioneer architects of the geologic time scale. Logs can be matched from locality to locality, just as surface sections are matched (Fig. 6–14).

Subsurface basin analysis and correlation also have been greatly enhanced by the application of seismology. Seismic profiles have greatly facilitated the interpretation of stratigraphy and structure of subsurface sedimentary basins within and marginal to the present-day continents, and *seismic stratigraphy* has become a major force in sedimentary basin analysis. Seismic stratigraphy is based on the premise that a single seismic reflection horizon approximates a single bedding surface and therefore a synchronous horizon—yet anther means of subsurface chronostratigraphic subdivision and correlation.

Formal classification has facilitated the necessary and improved organization of the stratigraphic record and consistency in terminology. However, the most important advances in sedimentary geology, from the standpoint of understanding sedimentary processes and natural stratigraphic patterns, have been in the area of informal stratigraphy. This has involved the development of sophisticated models for analysis of sedimentary facies and for interpretation of ancient environments (Chapter 2). Here the emphasis is on genetic units rather than on formal ones, although formal stratigraphic classification provides the framework for correlation and analysis. Much of this work has centered around developing models for exploration for oil and gas and other mineral deposits—the rationale being that formation of many economic mineral deposits is critically influenced by depositional and postdepositional environments.

Geomagnetic Time Scale

Figure 6–15 is a *geomagnetic time scale* for the last 160 million years. This scale shows magnetopolarity events indelibly imprinted in diverse assemblages of rocks: terrestrial lava flows, oceanic basalts, deep-sea sediments, and even certain nonmarine sediments. Radiometric dating has pro-

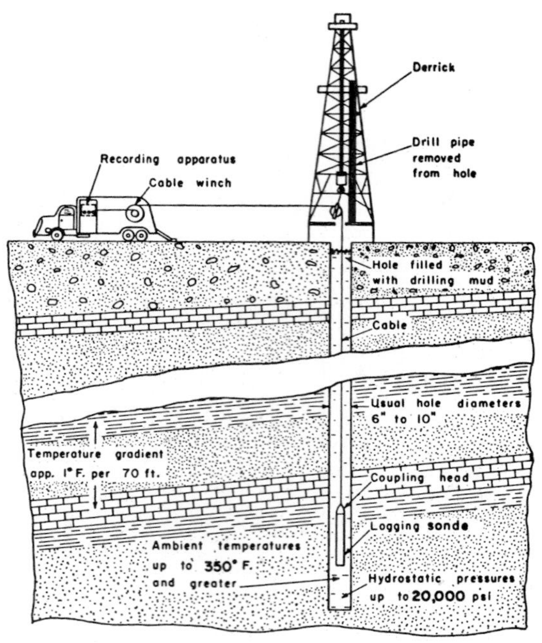

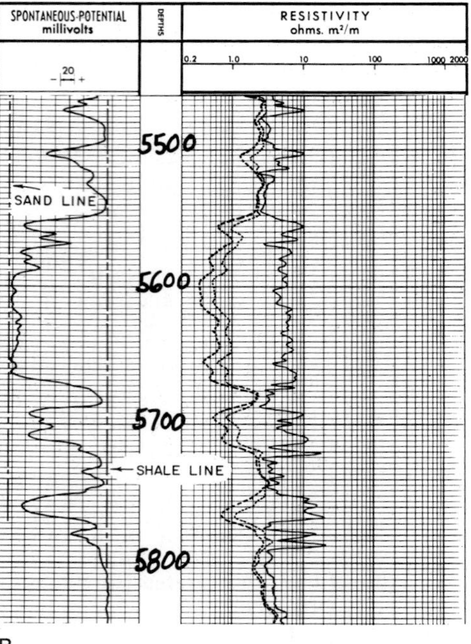

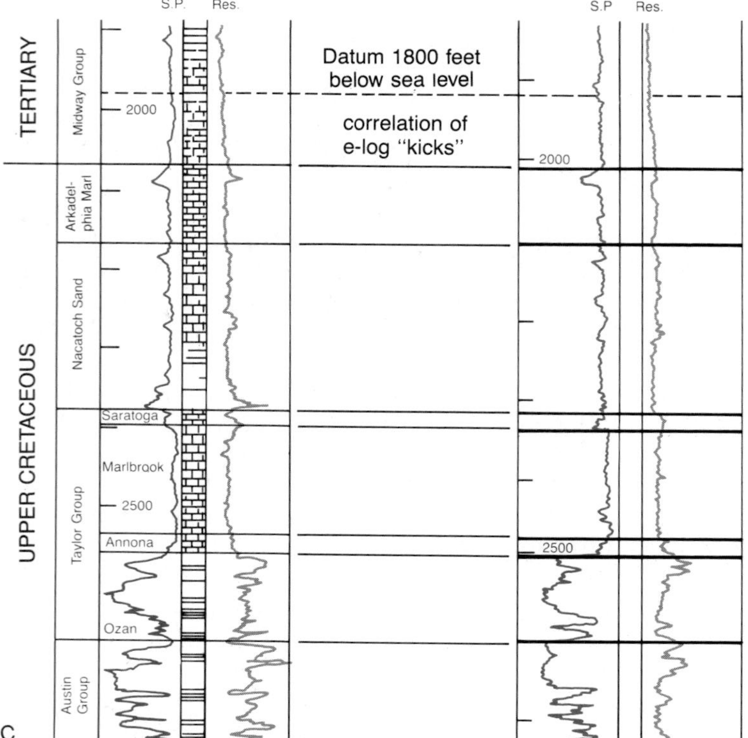

Figure 6–14

A. Instrument truck logging a well. Specially equipped truck lowers electrical recording device (sondes) by cable down the borehole. As sondes are slowly raised back to the surface, electrical impulses are recorded on a sensitive drum and fed to a computer, which gives a printout as in B. B. Portion of an electric well log showing lithology in a sandstone-shale sequence. The spontaneous potential curve is a recording versus depth of the difference between the potential of a movable electrode in the borehole and the fixed potential of a surface electrode. The resistivity curve is a measure of the resistivity of contained fluids in strata in the borehold. C. Subsurface correlation of Upper Cretaceous and Paleogene rocks in southern Arkansas using electric logs from wells.

(A, from F. Segesman, S. Soloway, and M. Watson, 1962, Well logging–the Exploration of Subsurface Geology, p. 2228: *Proc. IRE*, vol. 50, no. 11; B, modified from Schlumberger, Ltd. 1972, *Log Interpretation*, vol. 1, *Principles*, 7; C, from Morris S. Peterson and J. Keith Rigby, *Interpreting Earth's History*, 3d ed.)

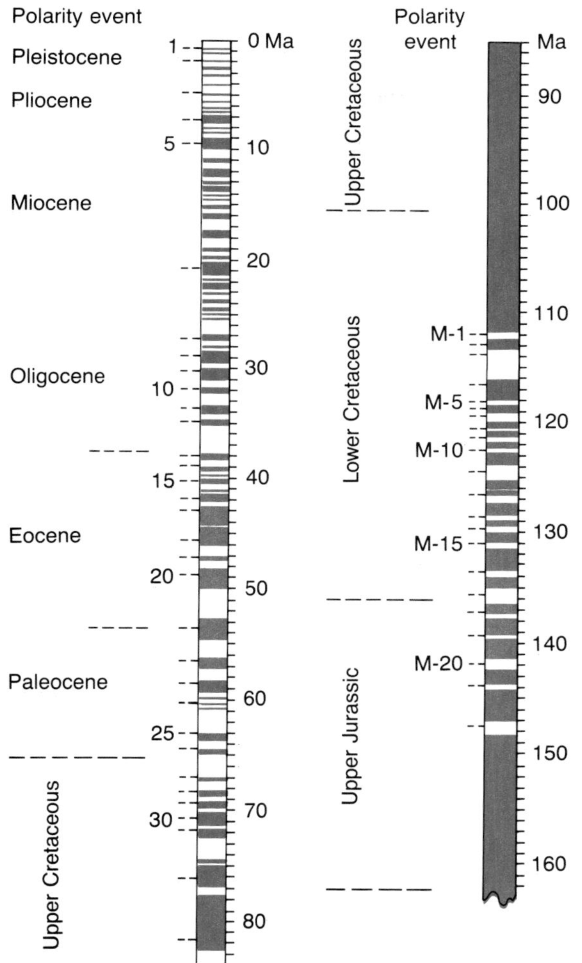

Figure 6–15

Geomagnetic reversal time scale from the present to the beginning of the Late Jurassic, 162 Ma. Brown is reversed polarity.

(From Robert L. Larsen and Walter C. Pitman III, 1972, World-Wide Correlation of Mesozoic Magnetic Anomalies and Its Implications, Fig. 5, p. 3651: *Geological Society of America Bulletin*, vol. 83. Reprinted by permission of authors and Geological Society of America)

vided an absolute time frame for the magnetopolarity events, whose time intervals are called *polarity chronologic units* (Table 6–3). In deep sea sediment, the time value of the polarity chronologic units has also been verified in many places by their constant relationship to chronostratigraphic units based on fossils (chronozones).

Thus, paleomagnetism, as mentioned previously, is yet another property of rocks that shows time sequence and permits time-significant correlation. If particular paleomagnetic events can be identified and related to other means of correlation, we have a powerful tool for correlating deep-sea sediments on a worldwide scale (Fig. 6–16). In fact, paleomagnetism has proved to be an excellent chronostratigraphic technique for the Cenozoic and last half of the Mesozoic, but its routine application to older rocks suffers from the lack of a well-documented global standard. In other words, the geomagnetic time scale is reliable only as far back as the age of the oldest rocks in our modern ocean basins. But with a geomagnetic time scale (Figs. 6–15, 6–16) calibrated with the later part of the conventional radiometric time scale, we have a global standard with which we can determine the *age* of sedimentary rocks in the mid-Mesozoic and Cenozoic time range that do not contain age-diagnostic fossils.

With today's sophisticated and highly sensitive magnetometers, geomagnetic events are being determined for many oceanic stratigraphic sequences. For example, a geomagnetic *stratotype* for the Cretaceous-Paleogene boundary has been designated near Gubbio, Italy (Fig. 6–16). Here an exposed section of deep marine limestone, representing continuous deposition and with excellent microfossil control and well-defined microfossil biozones, has yielded exceptionally good paleomagnetic data, facilitating correlation with sections in several ocean basins and other continent-based sections. (The Cretaceous-Paleogene boundary in the Gubbio section is also marked by an *iridium* anomaly that has been widely correlated with other sections, and is the subject of the introduction to Chapter 13.) Additional stratotypes utilizing polarity chronostratigraphy no doubt will be recognized for other parts of the Mesozoic and Cenozoic record.

A New Look at Uniformitarianism

As so often happens when one philosophy displaces another, the pendulum swung a bit too far from catastrophism to uniformitarianism. Lyell, in refuting the catastrophist view of Earth history, argued quite rightly for the invariability of natural laws. Unfortunately, he also argued for uniformity in rate of change. He held steadfast to the notion that rates of change or relative importance of geologic events had never been different from what they were perceived to be within the context of human experience. This strict interpretation of uniformitarianism stressed uniformity in rate and magnitude, and somewhat overstated the theme of "the present is the key to the past."

Today the basic tenets of uniformitarianism are viable: the present does give us insight into past history, and the physical, chemical, and biological

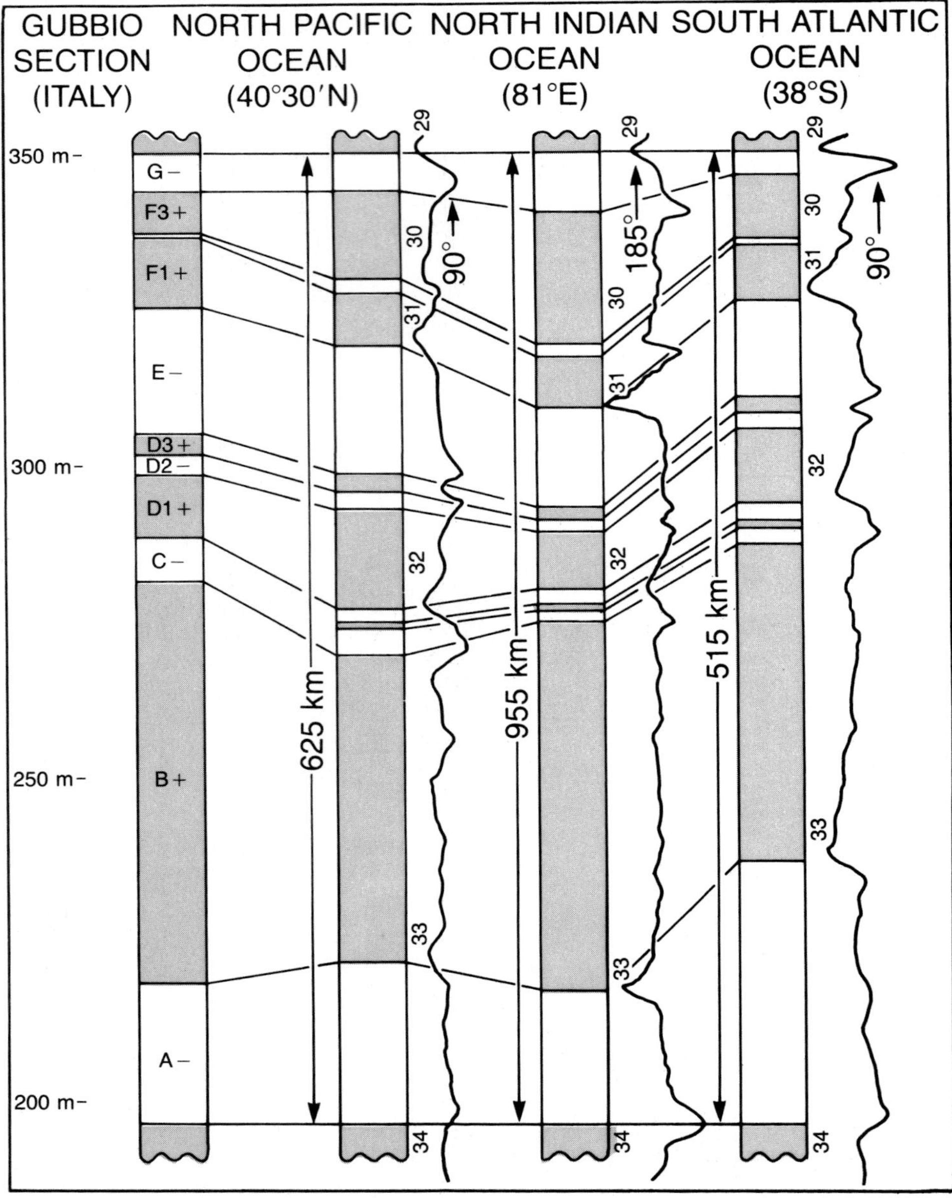

Figure 6–16
Comparison of the Late Cretaceous geomagnetic polarity sequence of Gubbio, Italy, with marine magnetic profiles and interpreted geomagnetic polarity sequences from three oceanic areas. Here brown represents normal polarity epochs. Numbers and letters represent polarity events.
(From William Lowrie and Walter Alvarez, 1977, Upper Cretaceous-Paleocene Magnetic Stratigraphy at Gubbio, Italy, III. Upper Cretaceous Magnetic Stratigraphy, Fig. 2, p. 376: *Geological Society of America Bulletin*, vol. 88. Reprinted by permission of the authors and Geological Society of America)

laws that govern activity and change are viewed as permanent. However, we no longer demand an Earth model where rates, intensities, and relative importance of processes have prevailed unwaveringly through geologic history. Many Earth scientists have dropped the word uniformitarianism and have adopted in its place the term **actualism,** in accordance with viewing the Earth in terms of actuality (Fig. 6–17). Actualism removes the "uniformity" from uniformitarianism and views the Earth in the more realistic perspective of the *geologic cycle* (see Chapter 1).

Lyellian uniformitarianism lulled geologists into accepting an Earth undergoing gradual, almost imperceptible change. It was assumed that major changes resulted only from accumulation of small changes. Until recently, any mention of catastrophic change was anathema to most geologists because of this vise-like grip that Lyellian Uniformitarianism held on geologic thinking. Today, however, most Earth scientists believe in punctuational change and appreciate that uniformity of natural law does not preclude *natural* catastrophes or *episodes* such as floods, storms, volcanic eruptions, asteroid impacts, and others. Actualism accommodates such natural punctuations in geologic history (Fig. 6–17).

As Derek Ager, a British geologist, writes: "The history of any one part of the Earth, like the life of a soldier, consists of long periods of boredom and

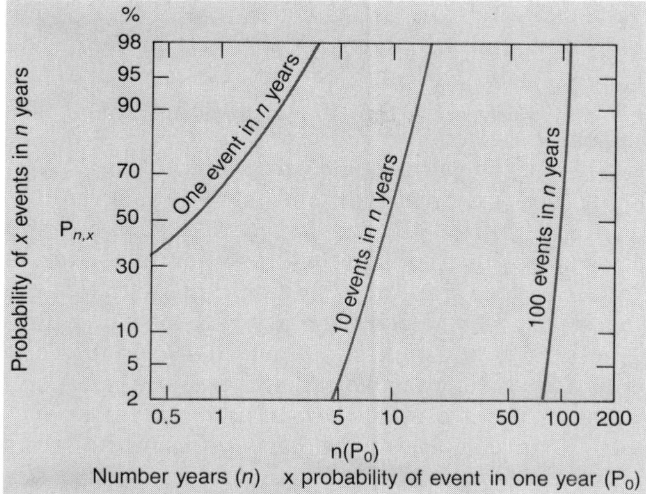

Figure 6–17
Plot showing probability ($P_{n,x}$) of a rare event to occur at least x times in n years. P_0 is the probability that the event will take place in a single year. Such a plot lends credence to the certainty of occurrence of natural catastrophes (volcanic eruptions, earthquakes, intense storms, and floods) during certain intervals of geologic time. Such episodic events have been instrumental in the evolution of the Earth's lithosphere.
(From P. E. Gretener, 1967, Significance of the Rare Event in Geology, Fig. 1, p. 2198: *American Association of Petroleum Geologists Bulletin,* vol. 51, no. 11. Reproduced by permission of American Association of Petroleum Geologists)

short periods of terror."* And in the words of Stephen Jay Gould, "Lyell, by the power of his intellect and the strength of his vision, deserves his status as the greatest of all geologists. But our modern understanding is not his, either unvarnished or even predominantly, but rather an inextricable and even mixture of uniformitarianism and catastrophism."**

Age of the Earth: A Uniformitarian Approach

The eminent Lord Kelvin, perhaps the most esteemed physicist of the nineteenth century, proposed estimates of geologic time expressed with elaborate and impressive mathematical detail. His estimates, based on calculations of heat loss from the Earth, were always less than 100 million years. Kelvin's calculations, employing physical measurements, used known temperature gradients from the Earth's surface into the progressively warmer subsurface (as observed in deep mines in many areas) to arrive at the rate of heat loss from the Earth's interior to the surface. This rate of heat flow and subsequent loss was then extrapolated back in time to when Kelvin believed the Earth to have been in a completely molten condition—less than 100 million years ago.

Lord Kelvin and a number of other scientists believed that the sun's energy was burning out at a uniform rate. Lord Kelvin himself reasoned that the amount of solar energy reaching the Earth had been much greater only a few tens of millions of years ago and that several million years hence it would be much less than now. Accordingly, the amount of time available for the Earth to have been sufficiently cooled to support life was judged to be between 20 and 40 million years, much less than Darwin needed to defend his theory of evolution. Darwin's biological reasoning about geologic time was mostly intuitive and not amenable to quantitative verification. Paleontologists and evolutionary biologists could offer only qualitative estimates in reply to Kelvin's calculations on heat dissipation from the Earth and on the sun's history. By the turn of the century, most geologists reluctantly adjusted their ideas on the age of the Earth to conform more with Kelvin's estimates.

Age of the Earth: Radioactivity and Radiometric Dating

No principle or theory is any more valid than the basic assumptions on which it is founded. As it turned out, the seemingly vague intuitive hunches of the evolutionists would be vindicated; the tide would turn against the quantitative proofs of Lord Kelvin. One of the first serious challenges to Lord Kelvin's elegantly quantified experiments on the age of the Earth was presented in 1899 by T. C. Chamberlin, professor of geology at the University of Chicago. Chamberlin had been working on the hypothesis that the Earth and other planets of our solar system had never been completely molten, but rather had accumulated from small cold pieces that he called *planetesimals.* In addition, he threw open the question about whether the internal constitution and energy aspects of atoms were completely known. The thrust of his argument concerned the thermal possibilities for keeping the sun alive for much longer than Lord Kelvin had calculated. This turned out to be a rather prophetic good guess about the nuclear energy source for the sun.

*1981. *Nature of the Stratigraphical Record.* 2d ed. MacMillan Press Ltd., p. 106–107.
**1987. *Time's Arrow, Time's Cycle.* Cambridge, MA: Harvard University Press, p. 178.

Prior to Chamberlin's postulation, Henri Becquerel discovered the radioactive property of uranium. In 1903, Pierre and Marie Curie discovered that radioactive radium was a source of heat. Three years later, R. J. Strutt, in England, showed that the amount of helium in uranium minerals was larger than what would have accumulated from alpha decay within the time frame of Lord Kelvin's calculations. Strutt estimated the quantity of heat that is continuously generated by radioactive minerals in the Earth's crust and showed that this could easily account for the flow of heat from the surface.

This was indeed a monumental scientific breakthrough. With it came the realization that the heat escaping from the Earth's surface no longer needed to be considered residual; instead, it is always being produced within the Earth by radioactive decay. The fact that heat loss from the Earth's surface probably had been about the same for a very long time destroyed the accuracy of Kelvin's measurements. In 1906, Lord Rutherford, in England, made the first attempt to measure the age of minerals from their helium-uranium ratio. This was the real beginning of the science of *geochronology.*

Quantitative measurements suggested that the Earth was considerably older, and that the length of geologic time during which the Earth was capable of supporting life was considerably greater than Lord Kelvin's estimates. In spite of the overwhelming evidence, Lord Kelvin remained unimpressed; he died in 1907 convinced it was all wrong.

That same year, Bertram Boltwood, an American chemist at Yale University, discovered that lead was also a stable end product of uranium decay. He demonstrated that the ratio of daughter lead to parent uranium increased with increased age of the mineral. He collected a large amount of data on published analyses of pure uranium minerals, and calculated their age from the lead content. Although his uranium half-life value of 10^{10} years was more than twice that known at present, and the uranium decay series was still incompletely known, and chemical techniques were severely limited, Boltwood's age determinations clearly established that the geologic time scale was very long.

In 1911, Arthur Holmes, a brilliant young English geologist and student of Strutt, summarized all available data on radiometric age determinations, presented evidence that radioactive decay rates are constant for particular nuclides, and pointed out the tremendous potential of radiometric dating for unraveling Precambrian history. He also clearly predicted that periods of the relative geologic time scale might one day be defined by accurate radiometric dates. Years later, he published such a scale, with subsequent revisions, and was one of the scientists most instrumental in combining the relative and radiometric time scales.

A major breakthrough came in the late 1930s with the invention of the *mass spectrometer,* which permitted the mass spectra of uranium and lead to be clearly resolved. This allowed for calculation of the uranium-238:uranium-235 ratio, the decay rate of the rarer uranium isotope uranium-235, and the ratio of lead-206:lead-207. One of the main byproducts of this discovery was measurement of the age of the Earth. Our present knowledge about the age of the Earth is derived directly from interpretations made during the 1940s of the primordial ratios of lead-207:lead-206:lead-204.

All common lead contains a blend of four lead isotopes: lead-204, lead-206, lead-207, and lead-208. Fortunately, in most minerals used for radiometric dating, the proportions of these lead isotopes are nearly constant. Although the quantities of radiogenic lead-206 and lead-207 have increased during geologic time (through decay of uranium-238 and uranium-235) in relation to unchanging nonradiogenic lead-204, these two lead isotopes have changed progressively in ratio with respect to one another because of the different decay rates of their parent isotopes.

Regarding the age of the Earth, we must know what the lead-206:lead-207 isotopic ratio was at the time the Earth formed. Extrapolation of ratios back in time to the point where, theoretically, there was no lead-206 or lead-207 shows a date of 5600 million years ago for zero lead-207, and 6700 million years ago for zero lead-206 (Fig. 6–18). The discordance of these dates indicates that some portion of the Earth's accumulated lead-206 and lead-207 was furnished along with other nonradiogenic nuclides when the Earth formed. Thus, the Earth must be younger than 5600 million years (the theoretical time of accumulation of lead-207), yet older than the oldest lithospheric rocks (gneisses from Greenland), which have yielded radiometric dates slightly younger than 4000 million years.

Data from iron and stony *meteorites,* which are believed to represent the primordial materials from which our solar system is made (and thus are the same age as the Earth), have filled the gap. Meteorite samples containing trace quantities of lead but no uranium have been compared to those containing both lead and uranium (mixtures of primordial lead and radiogenic lead). Thus, primordial lead is shown to have isotopic ratios of 1.0 for lead-204,

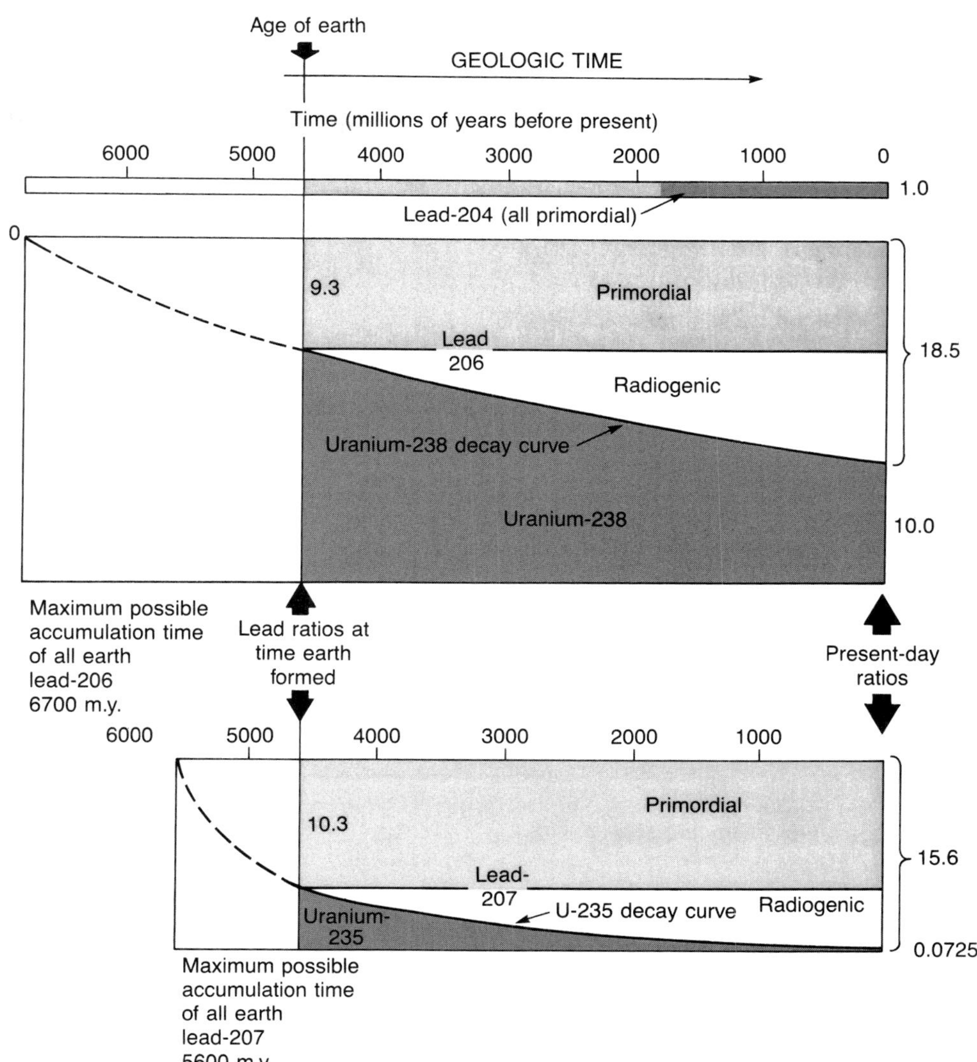

Figure 6–18
Radioactive decay of the Earth's uranium has added significant lead-206 and lead-207 and has changed their proportions throughout geologic time. Left margin of lead-207 curve shows that it cannot have been accumulating for more than 5600 million years, and similarly, lead-206 cannot have been accumulating for more than 6700 million years. Indicated ratios are based on lead-204 = 1.0. Extrapolating back to the appropriate lead ratios at the time the Earth formed gives an age of approximately 4600 million years.
(From Don L. Eicher, *Geologic Time*, 2d ed. © 1976, Fig. 6–11, p. 137. Reprinted by permission of Prentice-Hall, Inc., Englewood Cliffs, NJ)

9.3 for lead-206, and 10.3 for lead-207, indicating an age of 4600 million years on lead-evolution curves (Fig. 6–19).

Supercharged research on radioactivity during World War II boosted nuclear analytical technology to a point where the very minute quantities of radiogenic daughter products in radioactive minerals could be measured. Accurate mass spectrometers and other sophisticated tools were developed and refined. After the war, when information pertaining to radioactivity was not so restricted, it became possible to measure the accumulation of argon from the decay of potassium and the accumulation of strontium from the decay of rubidium for determination of the age of ancient rocks. By the early 1950s, laboratories for isotopic age determination were established in research centers in the United States and abroad. By the late 1950s, isotopic age determinations on rocks securely tied to the fossil record (Fig. 6–20) were becoming more and more available, and refinements have continued to the present, highlighted by radiometric dating of lunar samples and of the oldest known rocks on Earth (Fig. 6–21A).

In 1947, Nobel laureate W. R. Libby and associates devised radiocarbon dating, which provided the first technique for obtaining absolute dates from the uppermost part of the geologic column. Subsequently, techniques involving thorium-230 and protactinium-231, as well as amino-acid racemization (not a radiometric method) and fission-track dating, have allowed the filling of significant age-determination gaps between 50,000 years before present (the lower limit for radiocarbon dating) and

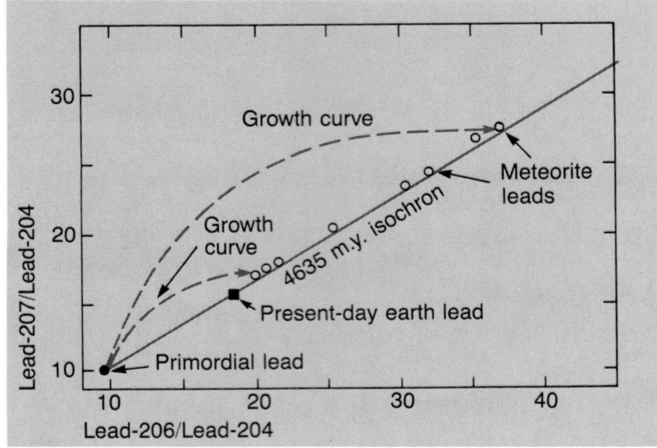

Figure 6–19
Lead isochron diagram for meteorites gives an age of 4635 million years. Present-day Earth lead falls on the isochron, indicating it came from the same primordial meteorite source and at the same time.
(From G. R. Tilton, 1973, Isotopic Lead Ages of Chondritic Meteorites, p. 325: *Earth and Planetary Science Letters*, vol. 19. Reprinted by permission of Elsevier Science Publishers)

about 3 million years (the upper limit of potassium-argon dating). Thus, quantitative dating techniques have spanned the entire geologic column.

Not only has the network of radiometric dates improved the radiometric time scale for the Phanerozoic part of the geologic column; it has facilitated age correlations within the very complex Precambrian rocks (Fig. 6–21B), which are widely distributed in many parts of the world and comprise more than 15% of all surface exposures. As radiometric dating became a reality, we soon learned that the Precambrian was a much longer geologic time interval than previously had been estimated.

James Hutton would probably be delighted to know that we have found some "vestige of a beginning": we have reliable dates on the age of the Earth (4600 million years), on the oldest exposed rocks of the Earth's lithosphere (3800 million years), and on lunar samples (dates ranging between 3800 and 4300 million years). We also have 4200-million-year dates on detrital zircon grains from

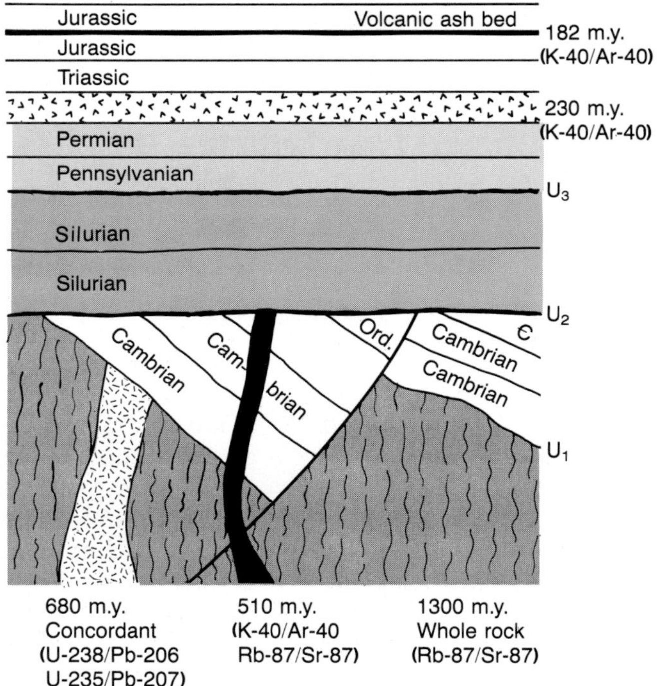

Figure 6–20
Relative and absolute dating applications. The sedimentary sequences are assigned relative ages such as Cambrian, Silurian, Permian, or Jurassic on the basis of their fossil content. Radiometric dates on the bracketing igneous rocks provide information on the antiquity and duration of various parts of the sedimentary sequences. For example, the Paleozoic sections can be no younger than 230 million years and no older than 680 million years. $U_{1,2}$ represent unconformities. This is how absolute ages are determined for boundaries of the relative time scale: the radiometric dating of igneous rocks that bracket the boundaries.

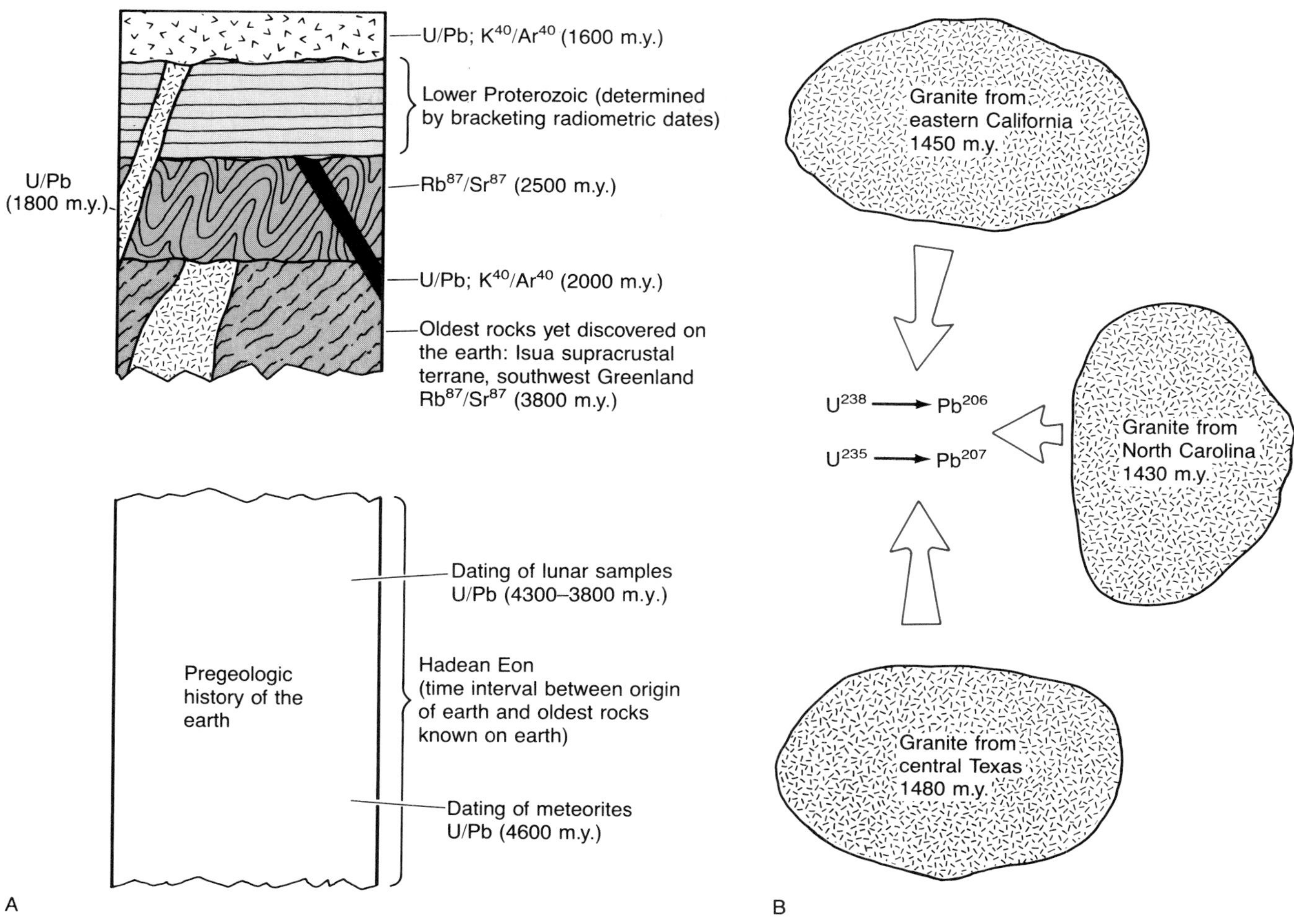

Figure 6–21
A. Applications of radiometric dating of Precambrian rocks and the pregeologic (Hadean Eon) history of the Earth. B. Radiometric correlations between separated Precambrian terranes.

Precambrian rocks in Australia, which suggests the erosion of granite-like crust older than the oldest known preserved crust.

Radiometric dating paved the way for the principle of plate tectonics, perhaps the greatest conceptual breakthrough in the history of geology. Radiometric age determination of volcanic rocks on land and in the ocean basins, combined with measurements of the magnetic signatures in those same rocks, has shown that the Earth's magnetic polarity has reversed itself frequently in the geologic past, that oceanic lithosphere has moved away from seafloor-spreading centers, and that land masses have rotated and moved with respect to the poles. This discovery inaugurated a new era in human understanding of the Earth and its history.

Summary

Although the science of historical geology has its roots in ancient Greece, the first stratigraphic principles were formulated in the last half of the seventeenth century by Nicolaus Steno in Italy. The principles of original horizontality, lateral continuity, and particularly superposition paved the way for development of the geologic time scale. Earliest attempts at subdivision of the rocks of the Earth's crust were motivated by the economic incentive of mining activity in western Europe. These subdivisions were based on the superposition of stratified, younger-looking sedimentary rocks above the supposedly underlying, older-looking, more complex igneous and metamorphic assemblages.

Although such simplified subdivisions represented monumental achievements for the time and worked for local stratigraphic sequences, they were destined for ultimate failure as universal schemes for telling geologic time. The fallacy that all crystalline rocks formed at one time and that all stratified rocks were formed at a later time continued to be perpetuated through the eighteenth century, mainly by Werner and his followers. The religious climate of the time was one of strict adherence to the notion of a 6000-year-old Earth—one that had been shaped by various catastrophes, such as the Noachian flood, wrought by a provident creator.

The legitimate father of modern geology was James Hutton, a Scotsman, who took a more realistic, albeit heretical, view of the Earth by placing no time constraints on the age of the Earth and by invoking natural laws rather than supernatural catastrophes to explain geologic history. "The present is the key to the past" became the slogan for the principle of uniformitarianism, which slowly displaced catastrophism as the guiding philosophy of the geological sciences.

Early in the nineteenth century, William Smith in England and Georges Cuvier in France independently articulated the principle of fossil succession. During the early decades of the nineteenth century in western Europe, application of fossil succession withstood the test of repeated observations and became the key that unlocked the door to development of a chronology of Earth history.

The principle of fossil succession led gradually to the recognition of large-scale stratigraphic units that contain unique aggregates of fossils upon which the stratigraphic systems—the major subdivisions of the modern chronostratigraphic scale—are based. By the beginning of the twentieth century, the modern relative geologic time scale was firmly established as a scale based on a succession of fossiliferous units, each with its own stratotype and unique aggregate of fossils. The stratigraphic systems were subsequently lumped into three larger-scale aggregates corresponding to three major chapters in the history of multicellular life: the Paleozoic, Mesozoic, and Cenozoic Eras. More precise, refined stratigraphic correlations necessitated subdivision of the systems into smaller increments, including series, stages, and zones—all based on aggregates of fossils. Sir Charles Lyell, the father of modern historical geology, subdivided the stratigraphic succession of the Cenozoic into units based on the relative percentages of fossil species still living today. He is also responsible for putting uniformitarianism on solid footing as a guiding principle of geology.

Twentieth-century refinements of the geologic time scale and stratigraphic principles and practice include, among others: stratigraphic classification, delineation of subsurface stratigraphy, paleomagnetism, and radiometric dating. Classification of formal stratigraphic units was necessary to avoid confusion and to clearly distinguish between material units—lithostratigraphic, biostratigraphic, chronostratigraphic, and magnetostratigraphic—in order to facilitate organization of the stratigraphic record and to establish consistency in terminology and communication.

Principles of stratigraphy have been applied to the subsurface as well as to outcrop sections. Exploration of subsurface sedimentary basins has been in response to a twentieth century economic incentive: the search for oil and gas. Deep drilling and seismic studies have delineated facies and formal stratigraphic units. Abandonment of strict Lyellian uniformitarianism has freed geologists to take a more realistic posture in the interpretation of geologic history. Actualism allows a more liberal application of "The present is the key to the past" by accepting changes in rate, magnitude, and intensity of geologic processes. It also accommodates the episodic event, which gives Earth history a punctuated tempo.

The greatest twentieth-century contribution to the geologic time scale is the radiometric scale, which has provided an understanding and appreciation of the antiquity and duration of the relative subdivisions and the age of the Earth. The discovery of radioactive decay and its application to mineralogy launched the science of geochronology, and soon demonstrated the age of the Earth to be at least an order of magnitude greater than turn-of-the-century estimates of about 100 million years. Continued advances in age dating highlighted by the development of the mass spectrometer promulgated a vast network of uranium-lead, rubidium-strontium, and potassium-argon dates from throughout the world, resulting in tighter bracketing of the relative time-scale subdivision boundaries and assignment of absolute dates. Radiocarbon dating, together with other techniques applicable to the late Neogene and Quaternary (last 3 million years), have completed the spanning of the geologic column with absolute dates that show greater reliability than once believed possible.

Paleomagnetism has proved to be another property of rocks that shows time sequence and is amenable to global correlation. With the advent of plate-tectonics theory, paleomagnetic studies on land and across the ocean basins have resulted in a reliable late Mesozoic and Cenozoic geomagnetic time scale whose magnetopolarity units can be plugged into the radiometric and relative times scales. Stratotypes for various parts of the upper Mesozoic and Cenozoic stratigraphic column combine magnetopolarity units with traditional chronostratigraphic units (utilizing fossils) to provide powerful correlation tools and refined land-land, ocean-ocean, and ocean-land global correlation for the last 180 million years of Earth history.

Suggestions for Further Reading

Ager, Derek. 1981. *The nature of the stratigraphical record.* 2d ed. New York: John Wiley & Sons.

Berry, W. B. N. 1968. *Growth of a prehistoric time scale.* San Francisco: W. H. Freeman.

Eicher, D. L. 1976. *Geologic time.* Foundations of Earth Science Series. Englewood Cliffs, NJ: Prentice-Hall.

Eiseley, Loren. 1969. *Charles Lyell.* Scientific American Offprint No. 846. San Francisco: W. H. Freeman.

Faul, Henry. 1978. A history of geologic time. *American Scientist* 66:159–65.

Geikie, Archibald. [1905] 1962. *The founders of geology.* New York: Dover. Unabridged and unaltered republication of 1905 2d. ed. of work first published by Macmillan Co., New York, in 1897.

Gillispie, Charles C. [1951] 1959. *Genesis and geology.* Harper Torchbook ed. New York: Harper. Originally published as vol. LVIII of Harvard Historical Studies, 1951.

Gould, Stephen Jay. 1965. Is uniformitarianism necessary? *American Journal of Science* 263:223–28.

Gould, Stephen Jay. 1987. *Time's arrow, time's cycle: Myth and metaphor in the discovery of geological time.* Cambridge, MA: Harvard Univ. Press.

Origins of Earth and Its Spheres

7

Eon	Era	Period		Age in Ma*
PHANEROZOIC	CENOZOIC	Quaternary	Quaternary	2
		Tertiary	Neogene	24
			Paleogene	65
	MESOZOIC	Cretaceous		144
		Jurassic		208
		Triassic		245
	PALEOZOIC	Permian		286
		Carboniferous	Pennsylvanian	320
			Mississippian	360
		Devonian		408
		Silurian		438
		Ordovician		505
		Cambrian		570
CRYPTOZOIC (PRECAMBRIAN): PROTEROZOIC	Late Proterozoic			900
	Middle Proterozoic			1600
	Early Proterozoic			2500
CRYPTOZOIC (PRECAMBRIAN): ARCHEAN	Late Archean			3000
	Middle Archean			3400
	Early Archean			~3800
HADEAN (Pregeologic history of the Earth)			Origin of Earth	4600

Contents

Key Terms

Coacervate droplet
Lithosphere
Hydrosphere
Atmosphere
Biosphere
Protoplanet
Jovian planet
Terrestrial planet
Nova
Supernova
Planetesimal
Astrobleme
Outgassing
Anaerobic
Ozone
Red bed
Banded iron formation
pH
Cell
Fermentation
Photosynthesis
Respiration
Organic macromolecule

Origin of Life

Perhaps the most fascinating phenomenon of planet Earth is the almost bewildering array of organisms that exist in virtually every nook and cranny. As far as we presently know, neither these kinds of organisms nor any others are known to exist on any other planet within our solar system. Investigation of other solar systems has not even begun; in fact, direct evidence for existence of other solar systems is exceedingly sparse. The possibility that life is not unique to Earth is the subject of a number of proposed studies (Fig. 7–1), but little information is presently available. Our understanding of life on Earth, however, has progressed tremendously since the mid-1800s. New techniques have given us much information about the way life works, when and how it originated, and its geological history.

Because of its significance to us, many people have contemplated the meaning of life and how it may have originated. These speculators have diverse backgrounds: philosophy, psychology, biology, geology, chemistry, and religion. Each ponders the questions and apparent mysteries of life and develops explanations and interpretations that are colored by his or her training and temperament. Such diversity of ideas, coupled with the great antiquity of life and its history, makes for a provocative and often perplexing field of study.

The fossil record provides an important account of the history of life. With the tremendous increase in our knowledge of fossils in the last 200 years has come recognition of amazing changes in types of organisms that have populated the Earth. Many scientists have observed evidence of the sudden appearance and proliferation of hard-part–bearing fossils in the rock record, and have recognized extinctions of such creatures as trilobites and dinosaurs. How are these events explained on a scientific basis?

Since publication of Darwin's momentous *On the Origin of Species,* various scientific hypotheses used to explain the observed changes and to account for the origin of life have focused upon evolutionary theory. In recent years, teams of scientists have attempted to determine the history of the earliest life on our planet, to search for evidence of life on other planets, and to reconstruct models of the ancient Earth on which life originated. The complexities of these models require synthesis of evidence from many disciplines, such as astronomy, biology, chemistry, and geology, and such cross-fertilization has provided added insights.

Most scientists agree that life originated by a sequence of chemical reactions that produced aggregates of organic molecules under environmental conditions significantly different from those existing on the planet today—conditions, in fact, that would be lethal for most presently living organisms. These models provide a logical complement to the theory of organic evolution, in that they suggest that many of the same mechanisms that control populations today—competition, replication of molecules, natural selec-

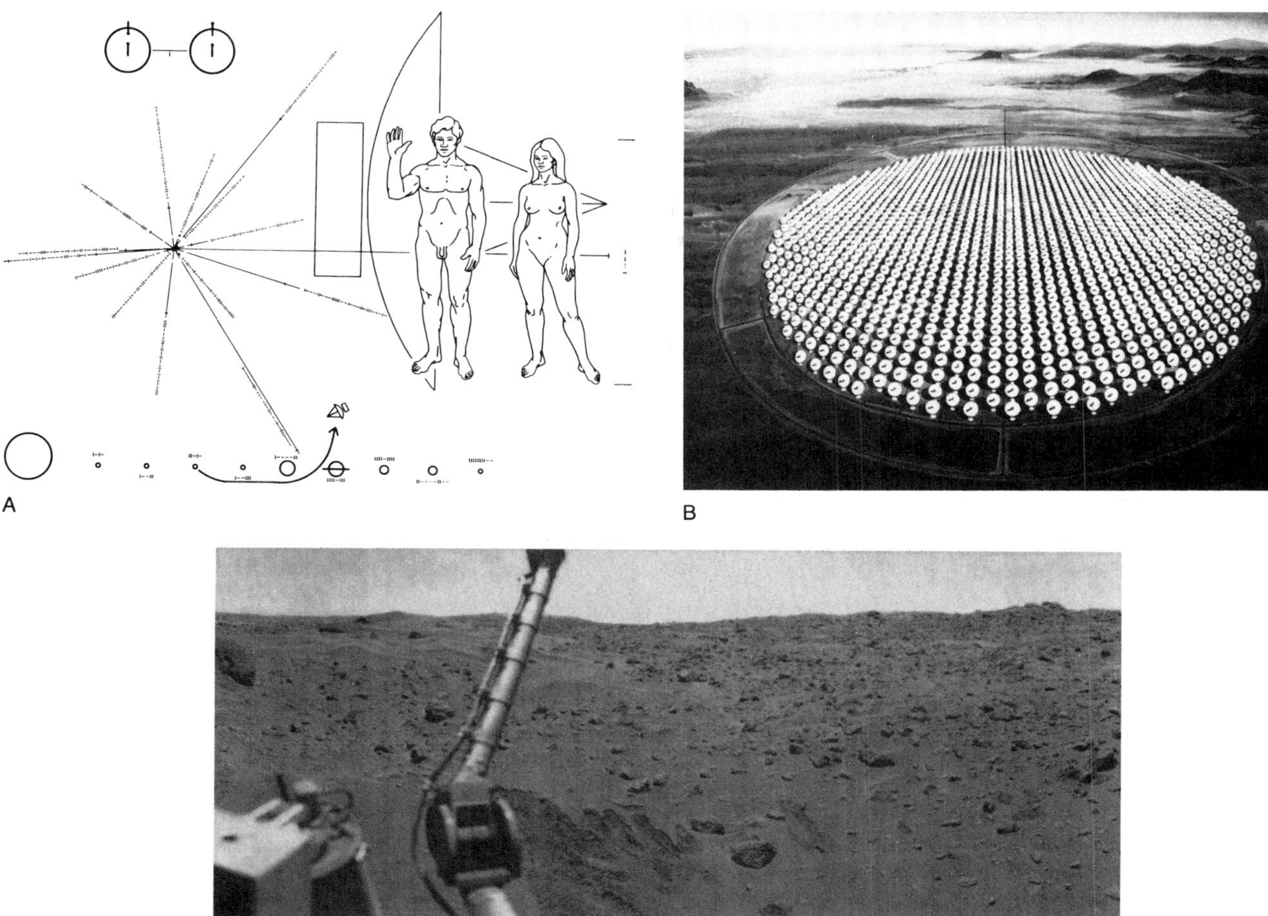

Figure 7–1
Attempts to search for and communicate with extraterrestrial life. A. Aluminum plaque (15 × 23 cm) placed on the *Pioneer* spacecraft, which was launched in 1972 and is heading to the fringes of our solar system and beyond. The plaque, designed by Carl and Linda Sagan, is much like the proverbial message in a bottle. B. Large array of radio telescopes, such as that of the proposed *Project Cyclops,* will be used to search for broadcast signals from space, presumably from other civilizations. C. Experiments to test for evidence of organic activity on Mars were part of the *Viking* landings of 1976; no evidence of Earth-type organic molecules or cells was found.
(A, reproduced by permission of Carl Sagan; B and C, courtesy of National Aeronautics and Space Administration)

tion—influenced the development of nonliving, or abiologic, organic molecules that preceded the first living cells.

In 1870, English biologist T. H. Huxley presented a stimulating presidential address to the British Association for the Advancement of Science. He discussed the perplexing and controversial idea that biological systems evolved from abiological molecules in primitive oceans resembling dilute organic soup. At the time of his speech most scientists had become convinced from many previously reported experiments that life could come only from previous life—the hypothesis of spontaneous generation. As Huxley carefully pointed out, this ancient concept, whereby life supposedly developed from decaying organic matter, had been disproved, but only through a variety of experiments performed at various times over hundreds of years.

Huxley lauded the invention of the microscope and its gradual improvements through the eighteenth century. Better resolution and magnification aided in the performance of many of these experiments, in that they allowed studies of tiny single-celled organisms. The tests by Spallanzani in the 1700s and Pasteur in the 1800s, among many others, were noted as simple but significant experiments which demonstrated clearly that any organisms appearing on decaying organic matter were either brought in by other organisms, or were carried in by air currents. Similar experiments with nonliving organic material sealed off from the atmosphere illustrated that no new organisms developed.

Having made his point, Huxley then strongly hinted that he believed life had in fact originated from nonliving chemicals. He was at a loss to explain the method by which this may have happened, but felt that, were he present on primitive Earth, he "should expect to be a witness of the evolution of living protoplasm from not living matter."*

Perhaps because of a lack of models for primitive Earth, studies on the origin of life languished in the late 1800s and early 1900s. However, beginning in the late 1920s and continuing in the 1930s the work of two biologists provided stimulus for more detailed investigations into the origin of life. A. I. Oparin, a Russian, and J. B. S. Haldane, an Englishman, published thought-provoking ideas which supported hypotheses that life began on Earth as a result of chemical reactions in oxygen-deficient environments.

As Oparin envisioned the process, a transitional step between nonliving chemicals and living cells may have resembled what are today known as **coacervate droplets.** These microscopic-sized droplets consist of large, organic-but-nonliving molecules which remain suspended in water. Under appropriate conditions these droplets behave like living cells. They can be used to simulate the reactions that may have occurred in prebiologic molecules, and therefore they provide clues for understanding how the first cells may have developed.

Haldane was a pivotal figure in promoting subsequent research into the origin of life. In a paper published in 1954, he considered four possible explanations to account for the appearance of life, and judged as most reasonable a process in which life arose by chemical evolution in oxygen-poor paleoenvironments. His ideas stimulated a number of laboratory experiments in which attempts were made to duplicate conditions thought to exist on primitive Earth.

A key experiment was performed in the 1950s in the laboratory of Harold C. Urey at the University of Chicago. Earlier work had suggested that in the early stages of Earth's history, its atmosphere lacked oxygen gas, instead consisting of ammonia and methane, and therefore was a reducing atmosphere. One of his graduate students, Stanley L. Miller, constructed an apparatus containing these gases and water and energized the mixture with electrical discharges (Fig. 7–2). Within a short time, a variety of organic molecules had formed, including many types that occur in living organisms. This experiment provided strong evidence for a method by which complex organic molecules and possibly living cells could develop from simple chemicals in appropriate environments.

Since these pivotal experiments in the 1950s, studies have suggested that the early atmosphere on Earth was probably not composed of ammonia and methane—compounds that had been vaporized early in the evolution of the planet—but rather was a mixture of nitrogen, carbon dioxide, and water va-

*1896. *Discourses biological and geological.* New York: D. Appleton.

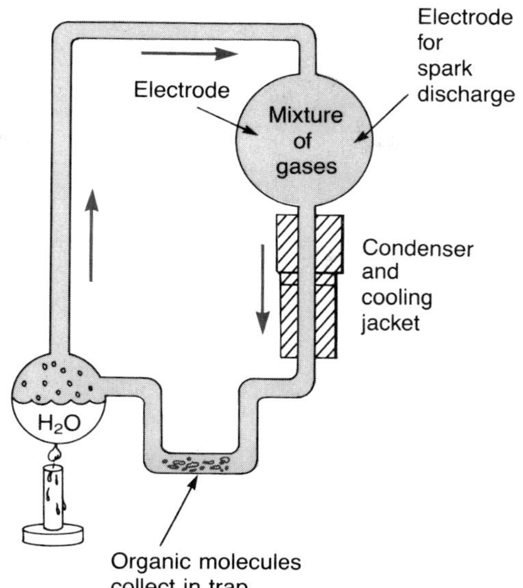

Figure 7–2
Type of apparatus used by S. L. Miller at the University of Chicago. Methane, ammonia, water vapor, and hydrogen gas were circulated in a system sealed off from the atmosphere and subjected to electric discharge. Amino acids formed in a relatively short time and collected in the trap.
(Adapted from S. L. Miller, 1953, A Production of Amino Acids under Possible Primitive Earth Conditions, Fig. 1, p. 528: *Science*, vol. 117. Copyright 1953 by the American Association for the Advancement of Science)

por. Subsequent workers have agreed that there was a virtual absence of free oxygen gas. Further laboratory experiments using these newer ideas have also been successful in producing a variety of complex organic molecules such as amino acids. These molecules represent the major building blocks for cells. Although a complete living system has yet to be produced, these experiments have clearly demonstrated a process by which life could have evolved. Thus, over a hundred years later, we find strong support for Huxley's concepts at the time of his presidential address in the 1870s.

During the 1980s a variety of new hypotheses have been added to these older ideas. Geologists such as A. S. Carins-Smith and E. S. Nisbit have offered stimulating ideas suggesting that life may have evolved in close association with clay minerals or zeolites, and perhaps first formed in hot springs. These ideas require further investigation.

Beginnings

Earth's Spheres

This chapter is concerned with origins. We will consider ideas and models for the origins of Earth and some of its spheres, including the lithosphere, atmosphere, hydrosphere, and biosphere. Accumulated evidence indicates these spheres developed early in Earth's history: it appears that all were present at least 3800 million years ago, near the beginning of Archean time, and we have geologic evidence for their existence. Very probably, some if not all of these spheres have a much older origin, but evidence for this is much more tentative. During and since their formation, each sphere has been affected by the others, and a change in one will eventually be reflected by changes in one or all of the others.

This interconnection of spheres provides the context for the geologic cycle and has implications for us. Developing awareness of what has come to be thought of as spaceship *Earth* has suggested to many people that our rapid development, exploitation, and alteration of these spheres may initiate long-term changes unfavorable to us, but which we only dimly perceive at the present time. Some modern problems involve the greenhouse effect, depletion of the ozone layer, and buildup of various chemicals in soil and the oceans.

In Chapter 1 we discussed Earth's spheres, and it will be helpful to briefly review them here. The **lithosphere** represents the outermost layer of the Earth's internal structure (Fig. 7–3). It consists of a

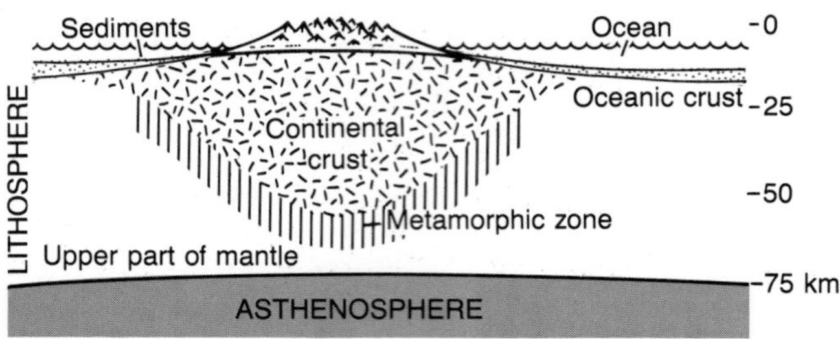

Figure 7–3

Earth's lithosphere (maximum thickness about 75 km) includes mantle rock, oceanic crust, and in some areas continental crust. The lithosphere is thickest where the continental crust has been deformed into mountains; examples are the Rocky Mountains and the Himalayas.

variety of rocks that make up the continents and floors of the ocean basins, and is divided into about a dozen large plates which have a maximum thickness of about 75 km but are generally much thinner. Generally overlying the lithosphere are the **hydrosphere** and the **atmosphere.** We recognize the hydrosphere as including water in oceans, freshwater lakes, streams, and rivers, along with groundwater and water vapor in the atmosphere. Part of this sphere is locked up in solid form as glacial ice. The atmosphere is the gaseous envelope surrounding Earth and consists mainly of nitrogen and oxygen gases. The final sphere, known as the **biosphere,** represents life on Earth. Living organisms are generally restricted to areas containing water.

Origin of the Solar System

Earth is but one planet in the solar system. To consider its origin, we must look to the initial formation of the sun and all the planets. Our solar system is believed to have formed from a cold, swirling, contracting cloud of cosmic gas and dust. As gravitational contraction of this cloud began, it started to heat up, and its speed of rotation increased so that the mass gathered into a disclike form with a dense central zone. This central globular core ultimately became the sun, which represents over 99% of the mass of our solar system and acts as a nuclear-fusion furnace.

Remaining dust particles and gas of the primeval solar disc separated into belts. Within these belts, accretion of adjacent dust and gas particles through gravitational attraction produced swarms of larger masses which rotated about their own centers and revolved around the globular core of the cloud (Fig. 7–4). These orbiting masses, called **protoplanets,** gradually condensed into solid bodies that were precursors of the present-day planets. A time framework places this formational stage around 4600 million years ago.

This hypothesis actually represents a synthesis of various earlier ideas. It represents an attempt to account for various physical characteristics of our solar system: mass and patterns of angular momentum of the sun compared to the planets, distinct differences in size and composition of the inner planets and outer planets, and distances and similar rotational directions of the planets relative to each other and to the sun. Earlier hypotheses, some of which date back to the mid-1600s, suggested possible collisions between a sun and a passing comet; a condensing gas cloud; a near-miss between two suns; and an exploding sun in a double-star system.

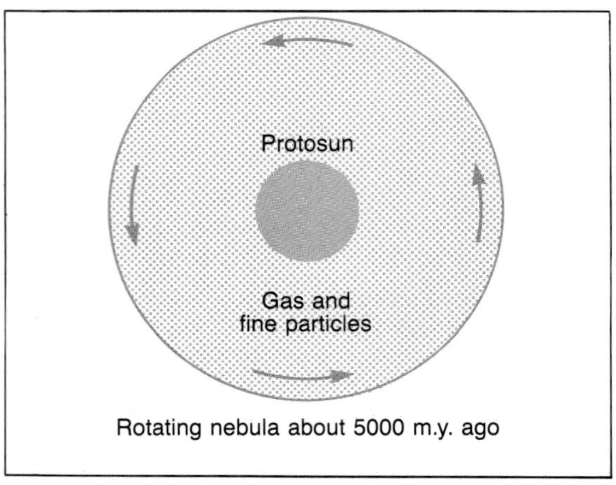

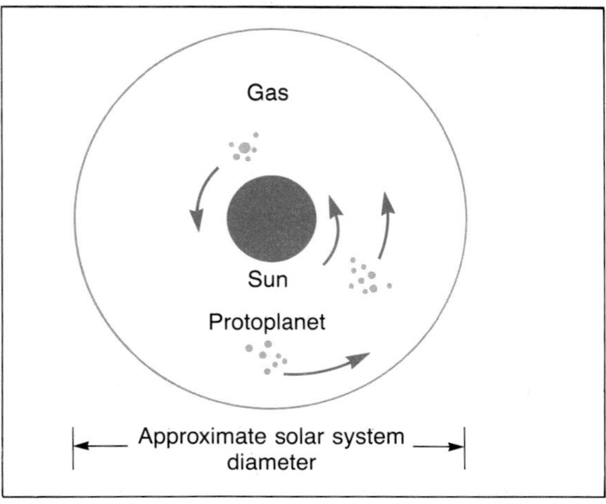

Figure 7–4

Hypothetical succession of events in the formation of our solar system. A. Condensation of primordial sun and beginning of formation of the disc. B. Central portion has collapsed and heated to the point of thermonuclear reactions; remaining particles collide and form protoplanets which have fixed orbits around the sun.

The next step is to interpret what events may have led from protoplanets to planets. Since the late 1960s much information about our solar system has come from flybys and landings of spacecraft such as *Ranger, Mariner, Apollo, Pioneer, Viking,* and *Voyager.* This information has been combined with that available from Russian spacecraft and other evidence collected from years of observations by Earthbound astronomers. Coupled with our new understanding of plate tectonics on Earth, new perspectives on the nature and evolution of the solar system have emerged.

What kind of history can we envision for the origin of the elements and early evolution of the solar system on the basis of observable planetary characteristics? The large outer planets, or **Jovian planets,** have a low specific gravity, and are composed largely of hydrogen and its simple compounds, a condition that most likely reflects the primitive composition of the solar cloud and protoplanets. By contrast, the inner, rocky planets, or **terrestrial planets,** such as Earth, are smaller, have high specific gravities (Table 7–1) and relatively little hydrogen. They are composed primarily of elements heavier than hydrogen: oxygen, silicon, aluminum, sodium, calcium, and iron. These elements are rare in the universe as a whole. They probably were produced at the centers of giant stars under extremely high temperatures by the fusion of helium from hydrogen and the addition of neutrons to the nuclei of helium.

We hypothesize that most of the heavier elements formed in giant stars by processes known as neutron capture and decay. Very heavy elements such as uranium may fuse only at very high rates of neutron capture and decay. This may occur when a star implodes as a **nova** or **supernova.** Such activity not only produces the heavier elements, but literally blasts them into space, where they become the "stuff" of cosmic nebulae for the later building of other stars or planets.

In a sense, each new generation of stars and planets builds from the ashes of the last, and the population of elements in any solar system is both a product and a record of its prior history. The abundance and range of heavy elements and isotopes on Earth suggest that matter of our solar system has been recycled through at least one supernova. Our sun is probably a second-generation or third-generation star associated with other stars in the Milky Way galaxy, the origin and evolution of which preceded that of our solar system.

Stellar evolution to the nuclear fusion in our sun produced radiation necessary to heat the inner protoplanets (Mercury, Venus, Earth, and Mars) to such an extent that much of their hydrogen and helium escaped into space, and solid hydrogen compounds such as ammonia and methane were vaporized. The outer protoplanets retained most of their original light gases and solid compounds because they were not heated as much as the inner protoplanets. Satellites separated from these protoplanets in much the same fashion as the protoplanets themselves had separated from the solar disc. Eventually the protoplanets condensed into solid masses, as particles became more concentrated through gravitational attraction.

Protoplanet to Planet

Our present-day interpretive model of Earth's interior structure and composition has been developed from seismological evidence, compositional analy-

Table 7–1
Comparison of Terrestrial and Jovian planets*

	Diameter (km)	Mass (Earth = 1)	Density (Water = 1) (g/cm³)	Gravity (Earth = 1)
Terrestrial				
Mercury	4,835	0.06	5.6	0.38
Venus	12,194	0.82	5.1	0.89
Earth	12,756	1.00	5.5	1.00
Mars	6,760	0.11	3.9	0.38
Jovian				
Jupiter	141,600	318.0	1.2	2.64
Saturn	120,800	95.1	0.6	1.17
Uranus	47,100	14.5	1.6	1.03
Neptune	44,600	17.0	2.2	1.50

*Data from various sources may vary by 10%.

sis of meteorites, studies of the magnetic field, and direct evidence of rocks from Earth and its Moon. What implications does this model have for interpreting thermal history and chemical and physical evolution from protoplanet to differentiated planet?

Nearly all of the elements that occur naturally on Earth were formed prior to the protoplanet stage, probably through a series of complex thermonuclear fusion reactions that represented an evolution from the element hydrogen. A few have formed within the planet as byproducts of radioactive fission or by decay from originally incorporated unstable isotopes. Initial heating of the protoplanet by solar radiation and gravitational contraction, followed by radioactive decay (fission) and to some extent meteoric impact, probably raised the temperature at the center to several thousand degrees Centigrade and caused partial or complete melting.

Presumably, most of the denser elements such as iron and nickel sank into the protoplanet's deep interior and formed a core, probably around 4600 million years ago. Convection and radiation of heat within this early hot interior may have facilitated separation of lighter elements and formation of silicate minerals—essentially a process of fractionization—which then accumulated into a layer called the mesosphere. Persistence of a liquid outer core (Chapter 1) beneath a solid mesosphere is explained by temperatures in that area above the melting points of nickel and iron. However, the melting points of the magnesium- and iron-rich silicate minerals typical of the deep mesosphere are higher than that of the outer core; the mesosphere, therefore, remains in a solid state. Is Earth still getting hotter, or is it becoming cooler? Differentiation of the interior clearly suggests that Earth was once largely molten, but it is not known whether it ever completely melted or if the heating is still increasing, is decreasing, or is remaining steady.

Radiometric dating of meteorites and rocks from the Moon's surface, along with information from lead-isotope ratios and lead-evolution curves (Chapter 6), indicate that Earth evolved from its large, low-density, homogeneous protoplanet stage to a smaller, dense, internally differentiated and heterogeneous planet, with an internal organization of distinct mineral phases, by approximately 4600 million years ago. Developmental events occurring between about 4600 and 3800 million years ago have left no tangible rock record, so much of our interpretation has come from the study of other planets and of meteorites.

As you might expect, ideas about the origin of the lithosphere, atmosphere, and hydrosphere fit into our picture of overall segregation of Earth and

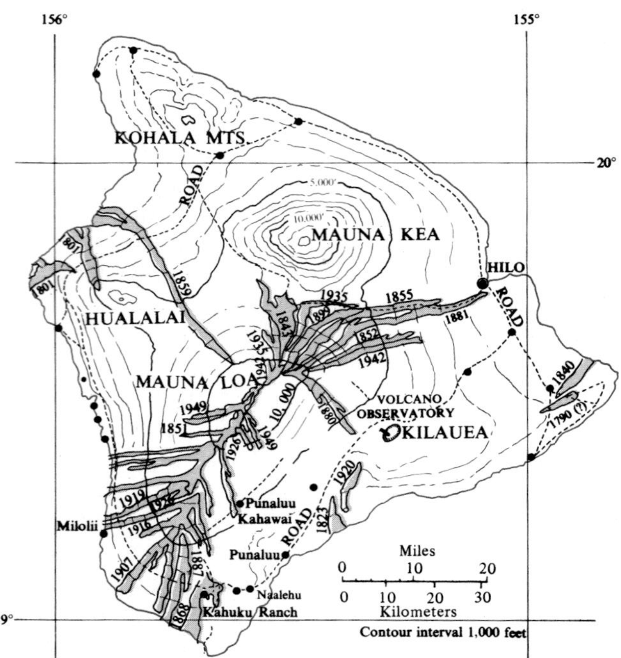

Figure 7–5
Geological map of Hawaii showing the gradual buildup of a basaltic shield volcano. Summits of Mauna Loa and Mauna Kea are over 4000 m and the volcano is forming where ocean water depth is in excess of 3000 m.
(Adapted from G. A. Macdonald and A. T. Abbott, 1970, *Volcanoes in the Sea*, Fig. 45, p. 52: University of Hawaii Press, Honolulu)

are closely related to differentiation of lighter mineral phases from original mesosphere material. The oldest lithosphere very likely was forged through extensive volcanic activity, perhaps similar in style and composition to that occurring on a smaller scale on the island of Hawaii today (Fig. 7–5). Expulsion of associated gases such as carbon dioxide, nitrogen, and steam during eruptive phases can readily account for the formation of an atmosphere and hydrosphere, and consequently these two spheres must also have evolved early, perhaps before 3800 million years ago.

The Lithosphere

Evidence from the Moon and the Planets

Although various lines of evidence point to an age of about 4600 million years for Earth, the oldest remaining rocks are only about 3800 million years old. So the rock record for the first 800 million years of our planet's history appears to have been obliterated, probably by a combination of subduction, metamorphism, weathering, and erosion—processes of the geological and rock cycles on an active planet. It is also possible that for part of this time interval (perhaps for most of it) the lithosphere, in which these oldest rocks are preserved, had not developed to its present thickness and composition and was therefore more readily obliterated by geologic processes. In fact, what little is directly known of the origin and early evolution of Earth's lithosphere is poorly understood, and is the focus of considerable research. In part this research is multifaceted, because it must also consider characteristics and changes in the atmosphere and hydrosphere, both of which would have significantly influenced and been affected by the evolving lithosphere.

What kinds of activity were taking place within the lithosphere and on its surface during the first 800 million years of Earth's history? Although little direct evidence remains on Earth, study of the Moon provides a window through which we are able to glimpse this enigmatic formative period. Exploration of the Moon during the *Apollo* program provided on-site investigations and sample recovery which inaugurated the first studies of the petrologic and geochemical history of a planetary body other than Earth.

This information, together with comprehensive photo coverage of the Moon's surface, has demonstrated that, in contrast to Earth, the Moon's early history is fairly well preserved. Rock debris as old as 4500 million years has been identified from the lunar surface. Cratered highland areas, crater ejecta, and lava flows forming basins (low-lying dark regions) make up a composite of rocks and structures (Fig. 7–6) whose stratigraphy has been interpreted by study of superposition and cross-cutting relationships. We may attribute this preservation of older features to the absence of a significant geologic cycle. In particular, plate tectonics has not been a factor, nor has there been extensive weathering or erosion.

The Moon has a thick, solid crust that formed early in its history from global melting and cooling. The cratered highlands, which dominate the lunar surface, are exposed surface remnants of this early crust. Alteration of the crust occurred primarily by impact of extralunar material, much of which may have been small **planetesimals** remaining from the condensation of the nebula. This cratering was at first extensive but began to decline about 3000 million years ago. Extremely large impacts excavated gigantic depressions and spread ejecta over extensive areas, as evidenced by radially textured deposits; in effect, lunar mountains are basically piles of debris ejected by meteoric impact.

The next stage of lunar history was dominated by emplacement of dark mare plains, which are relatively thick layers of basalt. This major outpouring of lava occurred from 3900 to 3200 million years ago; there probably has been no extensive igneous activity on the surface during the last 3000 million years. The Moon's crust has changed but

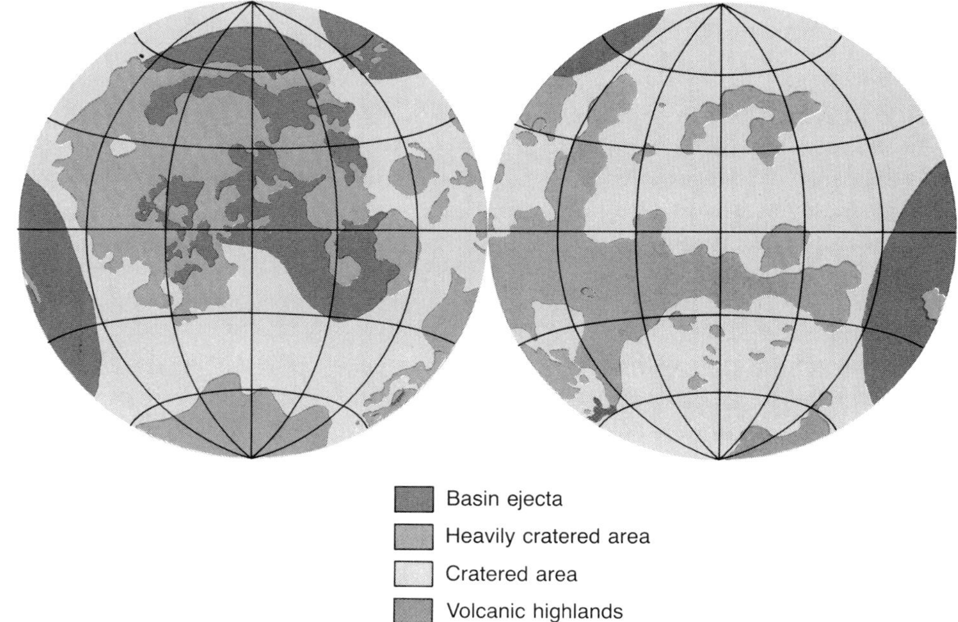

Figure 7–6
Geologic map of our Moon showing volcanic and impact stratigraphy. Compiled from many photographs and very limited sampling by the *Apollo* missions.
(Adapted from D. E. Wilhelms and J. F. McCauley, 1971, U. S. Geological Survey Map I-703, and K. A. Howard, D. E. Wilhelms, and D. H. Scott, 1974, Lunar Basin Formation and Highland Stratigraphy, Fig. 14, *Review of Geophysics and Space Physics*, vol. 12. Copyright by the American Geophysical Union)

Figure 7–7
The Moon's visible surface, illustrating the undestroyed evidence of craters.
(Reproduced by permission of Lick Observatory)

little since then, and evolution of the surface was essentially complete by 2500 million years ago or earlier. In the absence of an atmosphere or hydrosphere to cause weathering, meteoric impact has been the primary process in modifying surface features.

In contrast to the Moon, 98% of Earth's surface is less than 2500 million years old, and 90% is less than 600 million years old. Compared with the Moon, which has essentially been dead for the last 3000 million years, the Earth's lithosphere has been rearranged constantly through plate tectonics activity, and has been effaced by the weathering and erosion processes of a dynamic atmosphere. During the last few thousand million years or so, the geologic cycle has been dramatically more active on Earth than on the Moon.

The key point of this discussion, however, is that our understanding of the early history of the Moon suggests an analogous history for Earth. The pregeologic history (Hadean Eon) of Earth's surface and near surface probably involved basaltic volcanism and meteoric impact, perhaps even as violent as that on the Moon. About 4000 million years ago the surface of Earth probably looked similar to today's lunar surface, which is intensively cratered (Fig. 7–7). Since that time, when infall of meteorites from the solar cloud was much greater than now, comparatively few have hit the Earth. Craters that have survived are called **astroblemes** and are recognized as circular depressions (Fig. 7–8) displaying impact structures and containing materials of meteorite composition in a few places.

Our knowledge of lunar history and processes is only part of the story. We know that meteoric impact has left its mark also on the surfaces of Mercury and Mars. Mars also shows evidence of extensive and varied volcanism, large-scale linear tectonic features, and a complete lexicon of surface features produced by running water (Fig. 7–9). From our accumulating knowledge, though, impact cratering and volcanism are the two processes that have dominated the surface histories of the terrestrial planets in terms of areal coverage, volume, and time duration. Thus it would seem that the early history of the solar system, whose signature has

Figure 7–8
Meteor Crater, Arizona, an astrobleme. The crater is approximately 1.3 km in diameter and 100 m deep and was made by a meteorite.
(Reproduced by permission of Yerkes Observatory)

undergone destruction on dynamic Earth, has been laid before our eyes on the Moon and Mars. The early history of our planet can be interpreted from studies of rocks and events preserved on the other terrestrial planets, because they all share a common early history.

Formation of the Earth's Lithosphere

Our preceding discussion supports a hypothesis that Earth's earliest lithosphere, like that of other inner planets and of the Moon, was thin and composed largely of iron-bearing and magnesium-bearing silicate minerals, giving it a basaltic composition. However, presence of an atmosphere and hydrosphere capable of weathering rocks at the surface began to modify this basaltic layer early in Earth's history. By 3800 million years ago, at the beginning of what is termed Archean time, part of this initial basaltic layer had been altered and probably contained rocks rich in silicon and aluminum; thus it resembled the continental or granitic part of the lithosphere of today (Chapter 1). By what processes did it form?

It is likely that the basaltic crust solidified as Earth cooled from its early molten state. This crustal material would have been exposed to the primitive atmosphere and hydrosphere, and as a result would have been subjected to processes of the rock cycle such as chemical and physical weathering and erosion. Exposed areas of basalt became chemically altered because various silicate minerals making up these rocks break down at different rates. This process produced clastic sediments—perhaps at a relatively low rate geologically, due to low pH values and lack of plant cover—that were enriched in potassium feldspars and quartz relative to basaltic rocks.

These earliest materials were transported and deposited in the primitive seas, and represent the oldest sediments. Burial and lithification, followed by metamorphism and possibly melting of the sediments, resulted in formation of metamorphic and igneous rocks of intermediate rather than basaltic composition. Repetition of these events would eventually form granitic composition, which thereby represented the early continental masses. Although this presents a sketchy outline of the formation of the continental crust of the lithosphere, it fits nicely with our understanding of the rock cycle, hydrologic cycle, and tectonic cycle.

Although much evidence indicates that Earth is about 4600 million years old, the oldest remaining continental crust so far discovered is an area of 3800-million-year-old rocks in southern Greenland (Chapter 8). An important discovery indicating even greater antiquity for crustal rocks is zircons from Australia that have yielded dates of nearly 4200 Ma. The age of these Australian and Greenlandic rocks indicates that formation of continental crust of the lithosphere must have begun before 3800 million years ago, and this indirectly supports our assumption that erosion and sedimentation were operating on Earth's surface at an early date. From these beginnings, the rock record indicates that continental crust has grown thicker and increased in volume throughout Earth's history. Because the specific gravity of granitic rocks is less than that of the basaltic layers from which they were ultimately derived, continental rocks have remained topographically high, in accordance with the principle of isostasy (Fig. 1–12A).

With the development of an internally heterogeneous Earth, and formation of various internal spheres such as the core, mesosphere, asthenosphere, and lithosphere, the basic architecture of our planet was complete by 3800 Ma. Much has

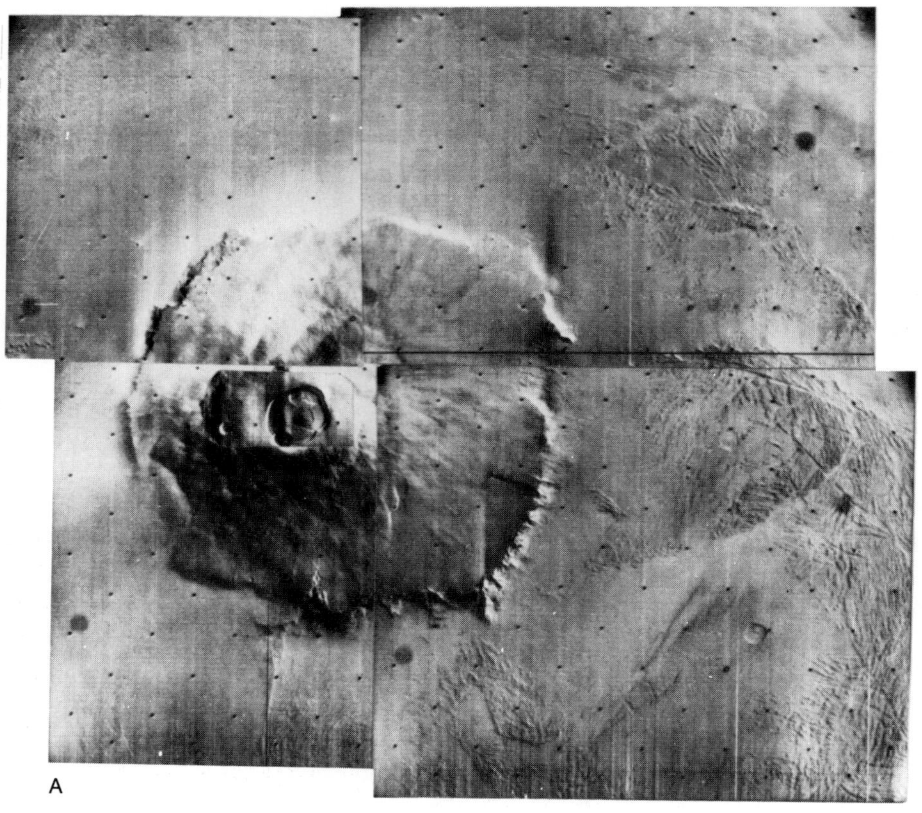
A

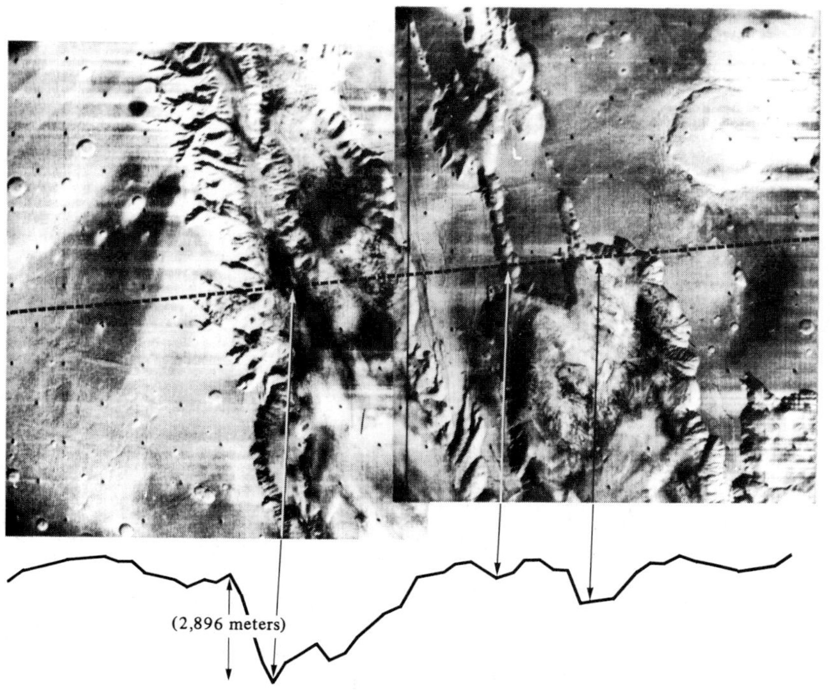

B

C

Figure 7–9
Mars. A. Olympus Mons volcano, 27 km above the plains and 600 km across at the base. How does this compare in size to volcanoes on Earth? B. Evidence of water erosion and mass movements in very large canyons. C. Surface photograph from *Viking 1* showing a dune field.
(Photos courtesy of National Aeronautics and Space Administration)

been modified through geologic time up to the present, but the basic plan has remained the same. Moving our focus of attention to Earth's surface, what can be determined about the origin and early history of the atmosphere and hydrosphere?

The Atmosphere and the Hydrosphere

As primitive Earth heated up and underwent the internal differentiation that produced its core, mesosphere, asthenosphere, and lithosphere, volcanic activity must have been common at the surface, much more so than its local expression at the present time. Along with the pyroclastic debris and lava of these eruptions, it is likely that abundant gases were produced, similar to those associated with modern volcanism. This phenomenon is known as **outgassing** and provides an explanation for the origin of at least part of the atmosphere and hydrosphere (Fig. 7–10). Other evidence suggests that some or perhaps a major portion of the hydrosphere has accreted through time in the form of ice in cosmic dust and meteorites. The gravitational field of the Earth is sufficient to prevent these gases from escaping into space, and a major portion remained to form an atmosphere rich in nitrogen and carbon dioxide and a hydrosphere composed of condensed water vapor. As currently known, no other planet has a dense gaseous atmosphere and a fluid hydrosphere; it is probably no coincidence that life is known only on Earth.

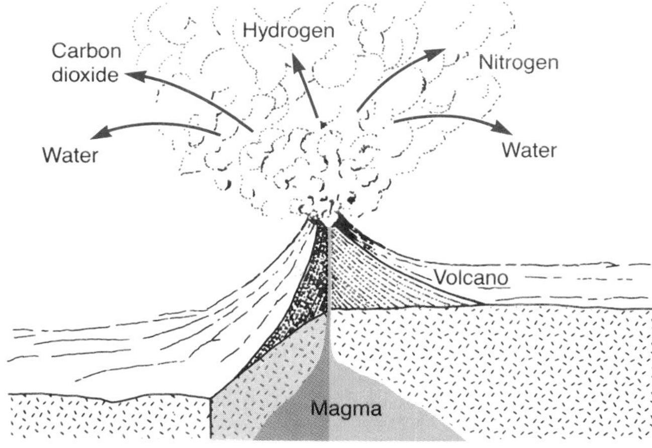

Figure 7–10
Volcanic outgassing of carbon dioxide, hydrogen, nitrogen, and a few other minor gases. Most of the water enters the hydrosphere, nitrogen and carbon dioxide are added to the atmosphere, and hydrogen gas generally escapes into space.

Neither the primitive atmosphere nor the hydrosphere contained oxygen gas, because volcanic activity does not produce it. Therefore, pre-Archean and Archean paleoenvironments were **anaerobic,** or reducing. An absence of oxygen gas also indicates that the atmosphere lacked an **ozone** (O_3) layer. Ozone, formed by bombardment of O_2 molecules by ultraviolet radiation in the atmosphere, serves to screen out much short-wavelength ultraviolet radiation from the surface (Fig. 7–11). Such radiation is lethal to exposed cells: high levels of ultraviolet radiation would have provided a barrier to any developing life near or at the surface. (The ozone layer has been of recent concern and much current study because of mounting evidence that it is being destroyed by human activities in some areas, such as the Antarctic.) As we shall see, the absence of oxygen and ozone and the presence of high levels of ultraviolet radiation at Earth's surface provided important environmental conditions that controlled development and survival of prebiologic molecules, and later, primitive cells.

Characteristics of early Archean sedimentary and metasedimentary rocks preserve some evidence of the conditions in which they were deposited (Chapter 8). For example, although younger sedimentary rocks commonly contain oxidized iron particles and have a characteristic reddish hue, there are few **red beds** of Archean age. This implies that iron particles were not oxidized but rather remained in a reduced state as ferrous iron, even through atmospherically controlled surface processes of weathering, erosion, and deposition. Evidence of locally and periodically abundant oxygen gas in the hydrosphere is provided by layers of chert alternating with layers containing oxidized ferric iron in unusual **banded iron formations** which are known only within age limits of 3400 to 1800 million years ago (Table 8–4).

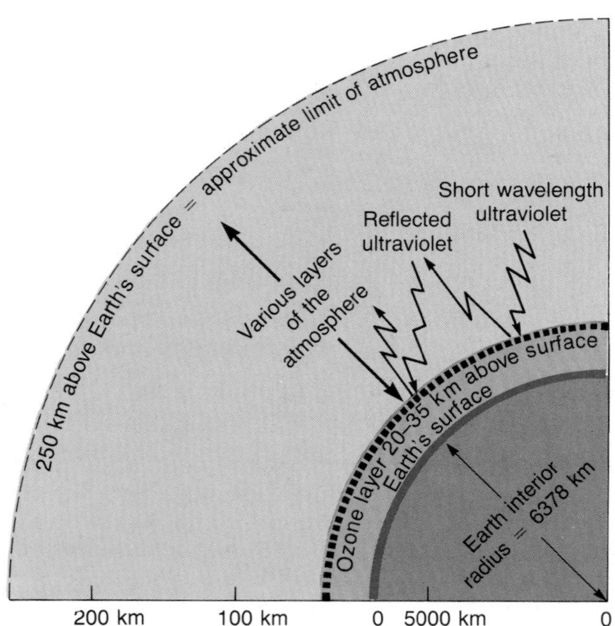

Figure 7–11
Formation of the ozone (O_3) layer (approximately 15 km thick) in the atmosphere serves to screen out a significant amount of solar radiation, especially in the ultraviolet range.

These rocks also provide evidence of the chemical characteristics of the Archean oceans. Abundance of terrigenous rocks and a lack of carbonates can be explained by the existence of an acidic hydrosphere. Carbon dioxide–rich and oxygen-deficient waters favor the formation of bicarbonate ions (HCO_3^{-2}). Such a system would maintain hydrogen-ion concentrations, or **pH,** of less than 7.0, and therefore would be acidic. In such acidic conditions calcium carbonate is soluble and would not be deposited, nor would it be easily available for organisms to use in shell secretions.

Composition and characteristics of the early atmosphere and hydrosphere are in distinct contrast to those existing today. Although we assume that weathering, erosion, and deposition were occurring as they do today, conditions under which they were operating, and the rates and products, were different from those of today's Earth. However, geochemical conditions existing during this early interval favored the formation of a wide spectrum of chemical molecules which eventually produced a living cell, and thus the biosphere. As we shall see, this event had far-reaching consequences, in particular because living organisms alter the chemistry of the hydrosphere and the atmosphere, and thereby affect rates of weathering and types of sediments produced.

The Biosphere

Definition and Characteristics of Life

In the 1950s Stanley Tyler and Elso Barghoorn made a major discovery of microfossils in rocks of Proterozoic age that were previously considered to be unfossiliferous (the Gunflint Formation of the Great Lakes region). Numerous subsequent discoveries of fossil prokaryotes in ancient rocks and concurrent increased precision of radiometric dating techniques indicated that life appeared on Earth during Early Archean time. Further studies have provided a fascinating glimpse of what the earliest life was like, and have considerably altered our perceptions of the biosphere and how it originated.

The boundaries of the biosphere are best defined as corresponding to those areas in which water occurs in a liquid state, as it does in all parts of the hydrologic cycle (Chapter 1). A variety of physical and chemical properties of water are also vital for support of living organisms. One important property of water is that it expands on freezing; thus ice is less dense and floats on water. It may act as an insulator, preventing bodies of water from freezing solid and killing organisms. Because of its bipolar molecular structure, water is also an excellent solvent for a wide variety of chemical reactions; it makes up a major portion of organisms and serves as the transporting and reaction medium for a large variety of materials. Even a casual glance at a chemistry book will provide a list of many important characteristics of this elixir of life.

Other environmental conditions also influence the ability of organisms to exist in the biosphere; some of these include the amount of solar radiation reaching Earth's surface, the temperature of the land surface, atmosphere, and hydrosphere, and the chemical composition of the atmosphere and hydrosphere. Furthermore, as mentioned in Chapter 4, considerable evidence indicates that environmental changes have affected diversity and abundance of organisms, and that variations in Earth's biota throughout geologic time have been controlled by a variety of physical and biological events. We should expect that similar, though perhaps not identical, conditions influenced prebiologic molecules and the development of life.

Living systems are recognized by particular diagnostic characteristics and essentially represent chemical factories that consist primarily of four elements—carbon, hydrogen, nitrogen, and oxygen—that combine to form organic molecules. These elements also combine with lesser amounts of about 20 other elements to provide a large number of complex molecules. We can consider in more detail some other characteristics of life:

1. Organisms consist of one or more **cells** that are capable of reproducing themselves by chemical replication of a wide variety of complex organic molecules.
2. Individual organisms undergo many other chemically related activities such as metabolism, excretion, and growth; important examples of metabolic reactions are **fermentation, photosynthesis,** and **respiration,** which involve carbon dioxide, water, and oxygen along with more complex molecules such as sugars and alcohol.
3. Organisms are able to move or cause motion in water or air; most single-celled and multicelled organisms have appendages such as cilia, tentacles, or other structures capable of such movements.
4. Individuals, whether unicellular or multicellular, have a boundary layer such as a cell membrane, cell wall, or skin that permits selective exchanges of gases and liquids with the environment.
5. All life as we know it has the characteristic ability to adapt to environmental changes, whether by physiological response to small-scale seasonal changes or by genetic change of successive generations through a longer interval of time (Chapter 4).

Living organisms should possess all of these characteristics. Paleontologists recognize that fossils are the remains or traces of once-living organisms, so we may assume that such fossilized organisms also possessed these characteristics when they were living.

The Origin of Life: A Working Model

Excluding various religious explanations of creation, which cannot be subjected to scientific methods, we find that most scientists subscribe to a hypothesis which suggests that life on Earth originated from a series of abiological evolutionary processes during pre-Archean or Early Archean time. As currently envisioned, this evolutionary process consisted of a number of progressively more complex chemical reactions which involved prebiologic molecules within the early hydrosphere. The reactions involved the four main chemical building blocks of carbon, hydrogen, nitrogen, and oxygen, and led to the formation and subsequent recombination of organic compounds into increasingly more complex **organic macromolecules.** These macromolecules responded to environmental changes by undergoing various reactions. Eventually a combination of macromolecules formed that possessed a combination of characteristics which fit our definition of life, and so the simplest living system, the cell, appeared on Earth (Fig. 7–12).

Working models for the origin of life combine a wide range of information obtained from laboratory experiments and from studies of remaining Early Archean rocks. This evidence suggests that living organisms developed (1) by a sequence of succes-

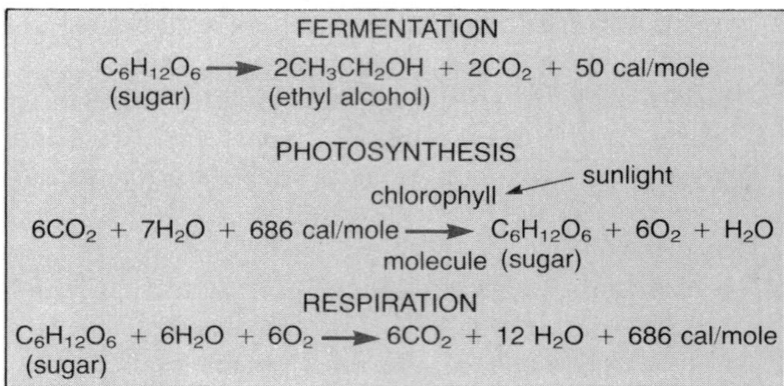

Figure 7–12
Important metabolic reactions in cells. Fermentation is an anaerobic process that produces alcohol and releases about 50 calories of heat energy. In contrast, photosynthesis and respiration are aerobic processes and provide a much larger amount of heat energy.

sively more complex chemical reactions, (2) during an unknown length of geologic time after formation of the lithosphere, atmosphere, and hydrosphere, and (3) within an anaerobic hydrosphere and atmosphere, lacking an ozone layer, that allowed high levels of ultraviolet radiation to reach the surface.

According to this model, life originally formed from chemicals that underwent a succession of many different reactions. These chemical combinations and recombinations may have occurred over a relatively short interval of time. The reactions may have occurred in the primitive hydrosphere, because the various properties of water would have provided appropriate environments for necessary chemical reactions, and would have provided some protection from ultraviolet radiation. It also is possible that this development could have taken place in thermal hot springs, which contain abundant elements.

Within the global primitive hydrosphere, a wide variety of temperatures and chemical and physical energy conditions would have existed. Such different conditions would naturally affect the kinds of chemical reactions and types of molecules produced, much as formation of chemical compounds and their subsequent reactions can be altered by changing the conditions in beakers during chemistry lab experiments. These chemical changes occurring within the primitive hydrosphere represented a form of natural selection, whereby certain organic molecules were favored because of their ability to form and exist in a particular environment. Once formed, these organic molecules, which were adapted to particular conditions within the hydrosphere, could undergo changes in composition in response to changes in environmental conditions. This description suggests that the primitive oceans may have, as the biochemist J. B. S. Haldane described them, "reached the consistency of hot dilute soup."*

As an alternative, these early molecules and reactions may have been bound up within clay minerals, either in the oceans or in hot springs. In this situation the atomic structure of the clay minerals may have acted as a template for the development and restructuring or replication of developing organic molecules. As the organic molecules became more complex the clay mineral templates were eliminated. If this process occurred in hot springs, the newly formed molecules could have gradually migrated to the oceans (Figure 7–13).

Whichever model is considered, for the millions of years of recombinations of molecules, it is not difficult to envision formation of some molecules or combinations of molecules having the characteristics of life that we set forth earlier. By our definition we would have to consider them living organisms. It is important to realize that there was and is no fundamental chemical difference between large nonliving molecules and large living molecules. What was basically different was the *organization and behavior* of the living molecules. Can we document this hypothesis with evidence from the rock record?

The Rock Record

As previously discussed, indirect evidence for a lack of free oxygen in Earth's early atmosphere is preserved in some sedimentary and metasedimentary rocks of Archean age. These rocks contain no oxidized iron minerals such as occur in geologically younger red beds. Also, the rocks are composed predominantly of detrital particles; nonterrigenous rocks such as limestone and dolostone are very rare. This scarcity of nonterrigenous clastic (chemical) rocks is explained by the existence of low pH values in the primitive oceans. Furthermore, many of these old rocks contain unstable minerals, such as uraninite and pyrite, that could not have survived in the presence of oxygen (Chapter 8).

Also within these rocks is preserved carbon that in some instances appears to have been derived from an organic source. At a few localities, micron-sized structures have been found which are interpreted to represent carbonized organic remains of

*1954. *New biology.* Vol. 16. New York: Penguin.

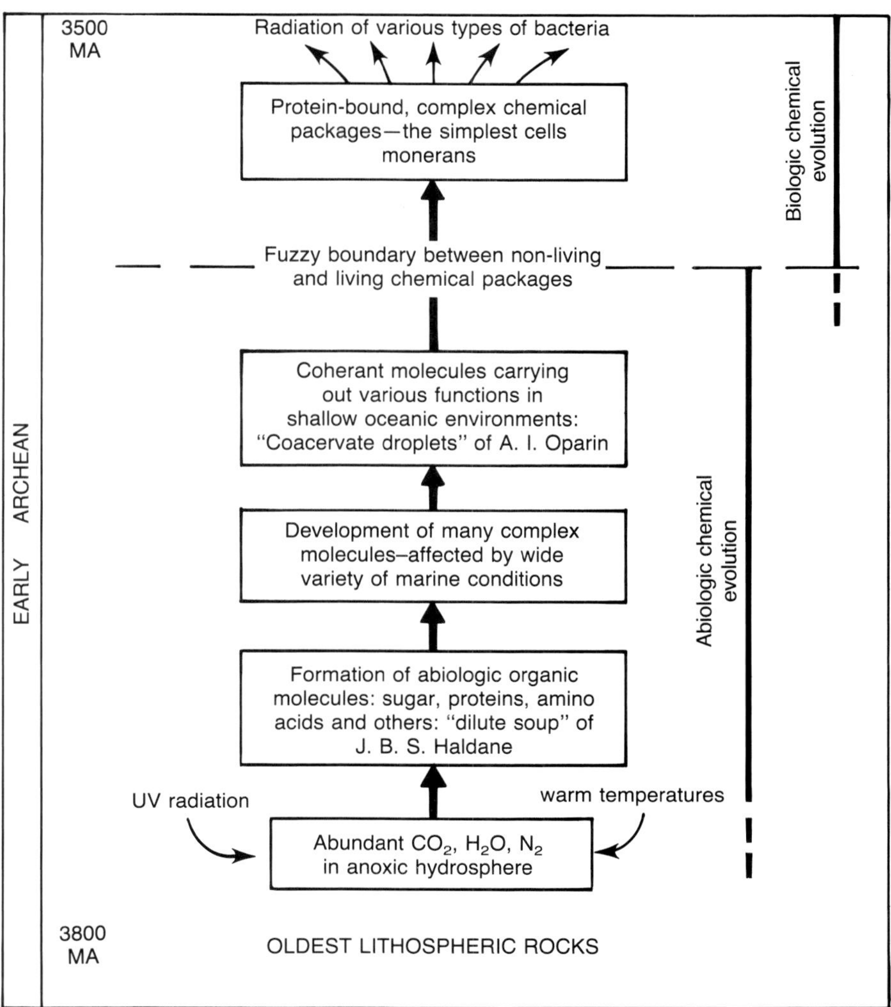

Figure 7–13
Synthesis of hypotheses for the origin of life. Most significantly, these ideas support an origin through gradual chemical evolutionary steps occurring within some part of Earth's hydrosphere over a significant length of Early Archean time. Living systems (cells) represented a change from inorganic chemical evolution to organic chemical evolution.

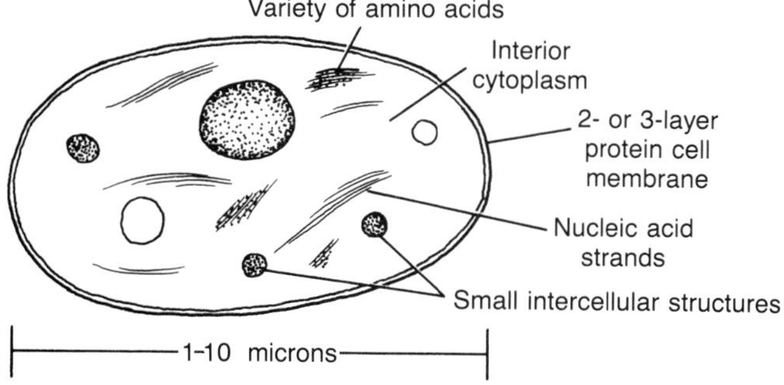

Figure 7–14
The cell is the smallest living system. Procaryotic, or nonnucleated, cells are the simplest type and consist of various organic macromolecules distributed within membrane-bound cytoplasm.

simple cells (Figs. 7–14 and 8–2). These structures have received considerable study, and have been photographed both with electron microscopes and light microscopes. Recognized only since the 1950s, they have been considered to represent bacteria and cyanobacteria (= "blue-green algae"), and consequently are classified in the kingdom Monera.

Organically derived carbon along with these microfossils indicates that life had originated by 3500 million years ago, and perhaps even earlier. As you will see in Chapter 8, younger Archean-age rocks from a number of continents provide evidence of other microscopic and macroscopic monerans, including bacteria and various types of cyanobacteria.

The subsequent geologic history of the biosphere is closely tied to changes in the hydrosphere and atmosphere. In turn, such changes influenced the lithosphere, within which we find the preserved records of events. The history of these changes provides the subjects for the following chapters.

Summary

Study of the origin and early history of Earth and its spheres—lithosphere, atmosphere, hydrosphere, and biosphere—is challenging. Much of the evidence has been obliterated by dynamic processes operating within the geologic cycle. However, evidence of the early history of other, less active, planets has been preserved, and has been studied by a variety of remote-sensing techniques and actual sampling. This information has been applied to understanding Earth's history. The sun and planets appear to have originated at least 4600 million years ago from a condensing gas nebula. Our planet underwent a partial or completely molten state that led to formation of various internal layers: core, mantle, asthenosphere, and lithosphere. Formation of the lithosphere probably began very early, but the oldest remaining rocks are about 3800 million years old.

A process known as outgassing was responsible for our hydrosphere and atmosphere, but as we know from studying modern volcanic eruptions, no oxygen gas was produced. The reducing nature of the atmosphere and hydrosphere is reflected in the general absence of red beds and carbonates of Archean age.

The biosphere, representing life on Earth, originated from chemical reactions involving carbon, hydrogen, nitrogen, and oxygen in the form of complex molecules. These molecules initially existed in a reducing hydrosphere and were influenced by a variety of environmental conditions. By 3500 million years ago, and perhaps considerably earlier, some of these molecules attained characteristics that we use to define living cells. These first organisms were probably much like modern bacteria and cyanobacteria.

Suggestions for Further Reading

Barghoorn, E. S. 1971. The oldest fossils. *Scientific American* 231(5):30–42.

Barghoorn, E. S., and S. A. Tyler. 1965. Microorganisms from the Gunflint Chert. *Science* 147(3658):563–77.

Cloud, P. E. 1970. *Adventures in Earth history.* San Francisco: W. H. Freeman.

Cloud, P. E. 1978. *Cosmos, Earth and man.* New Haven, CT: Yale Univ. Press.

Cloud, P. E. 1987. *Oasis in space: Earth history from the beginning.* New York: W. W. Norton & Co.

Dickerson, R. E. 1978. Chemical evolution and the origin of life. *Scientific American* 239(1):70–109.

Nisbit, E. G. 1986. RNA, hydrothermal systems, zeolites and the origin of life. *Episodes* 9:83–90.

Press, F., and R. Siever, eds. 1975. *Planet Earth.* Readings from *Scientific American.* San Francisco: W. H. Freeman.

Sagan, C. 1973. *The cosmic connection.* New York: Anchor.

Sagan, C. 1980. *Cosmos.* New York: Random House.

Cryptozoic History

8

Eon	Era	Period		Age in Ma*
PHANEROZOIC	CENOZOIC	Quaternary	Quaternary	2
		Tertiary	Neogene	24
			Paleogene	65
	MESOZOIC	Cretaceous		144
		Jurassic		208
		Triassic		245
	PALEOZOIC	Permian		286
		Carboniferous	Pennsylvanian	320
			Mississippian	360
		Devonian		408
		Silurian		438
		Ordovician		505
		Cambrian		570
CRYPTOZOIC (PRECAMBRIAN) — PROTEROZOIC	Late Proterozoic			900
	Middle Proterozoic			1600
	Early Proterozoic			2500
CRYPTOZOIC (PRECAMBRIAN) — ARCHEAN	Late Archean			3000
	Middle Archean			3400
	Early Archean			~3800
HADEAN (Pregeologic history of the Earth)			Origin of Earth	4600

Contents

Key Terms

Cyanobacteria
Prokaryotic
Stromatolite
Eukaryote
Cryptozoic
Phanerozoic
Precambrian
Canadian Shield
Archean
Proterozoic
Geochronometric unit
Orogenic front
Kenoran orogeny
Greenstone belt
Banded iron formation
Red bed
Aulacogen
Diamictite
Methanogen
Autotrophic
Heterotroph

Life Before Trilobites

Until about 40 years ago, one of the great mysteries of geology had been that definitive evidence of life prior to the beginning of the Cambrian Period had not been discovered. Cambrian fauna, dominated by such complex organisms as trilobites (Fig. 8–1), appeared to come into existence abruptly and without known predecessors. How could life have begun with organisms as complex as trilobites? Charles Darwin wrote: "To the question why we do not find rich fossiliferous deposits belonging to . . . periods prior to the Cambrian system, I can give no satisfactory answer. . . . The case at present must remain inexplicable."* During the last several decades, however, an answer has been found; a long pre-Cambrian history of life has been discovered, and it extends back through geologic time almost 3000 million years before the beginning of the Cambrian.

In the early 1950s, the late Stanley Tyler, an economic geologist at the University of Wisconsin, made a startling discovery that was to inaugurate a new dimension in our understanding of early life on this planet. Tyler was involved in a petrographic study of iron-bearing chert deposits in the approximately 2000 million-year-old Gunflint Formation, exposed around the shores of Lake Superior. For decades, this iron-rich formation and the Biwabik Iron Formation, a geologically correlative unit in Minnesota, had provided the ore for the nation's iron and steel industry. Tyler was looking for clues to the precise origin of the minerals.

In several thin sections, Tyler observed some puzzling spherical and elongate microstructures that he believed might be organic in nature. He sent them to Elso Barghoorn, an expert on fossil microorganisms at Harvard University. Barghoorn was convinced that the structures, beautifully preserved in three-dimensional detail in chert, were **cyanobacteria** (formerly referred to as blue-green algae). This discovery from rocks about 2000 million years old represented the first definitive evidence of life before the age of visible animal life (Fig. 8–2). Tyler and Barghoorn published a report on the discovery in 1954. Continuing work on the Gunflint microbiota has identified a diverse paleocommunity of **prokaryotic** microorganisms, including different kinds of bacteria and cyanobacteria.

Prior to Tyler's discovery, the only previously published reports on pre-Cambrian fossils involved peculiar megascopic pillarlike and mound-shaped laminated structures called **stromatolites** (Fig. 8–3A). American paleontologist Charles D. Walcott had hypothesized that stromatolites were fossilized reefs that had been formed by various kinds of algae. However, few people accepted the biologic origin of stromatolites. Barghoorn and Tyler's exami-

*Darwin, Charles. 1859. *On the origin of species by means of natural selection.* London: John Murray. Quotation is from Mentor paperback edition, 1963, p. 309.

CRYPTOZOIC AND PALEOZOIC HISTORY

Formative Stages

Although the Cryptozoic (Precambrian) encompasses the first 85% of Earth history, the record is comparatively obscure. Much of it is missing and most that exists is extremely complex and difficult to decipher. Working out the details of Cryptozoic history presents one of the great challenges in historical geology.

B.

Recent volcanism on the island of Hawaii. This kind of activity was probably commonplace during the early formation of the Earth's lithosphere. Volcanic outgassing is believed to have given rise to the Earth's first hydrosphere and primitive atmosphere.

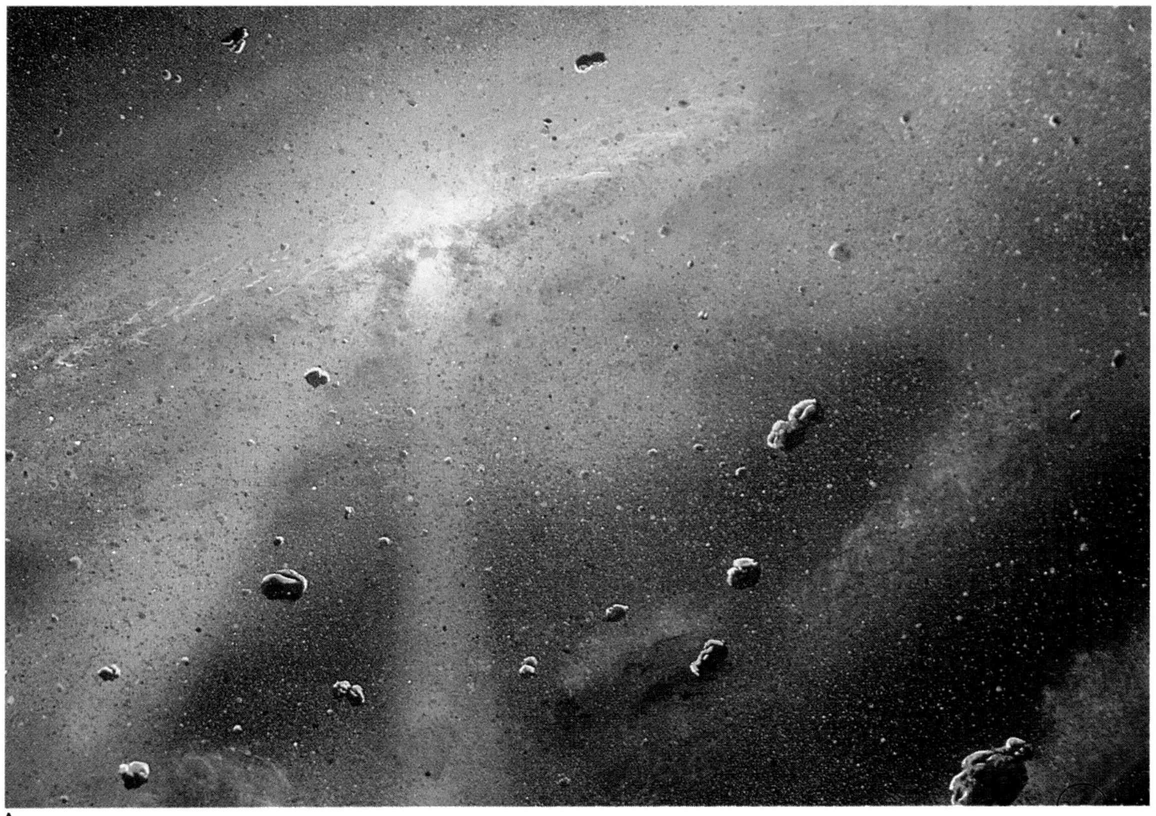

A.

In the beginning . . . . This painting by the astronomer William K. Hartmann depicts the early formation of our solar system by the accretion of chondrites to form planetesimals, which eventually evolved into the planets about 4600 million years ago. Chondrites are chunks of rock, primitive matter of the solar nebula that have broken away from asteroids and occasionally survive passage through the Earth's atmosphere to become meteorites.

Precambrian Rocks

A.

Although the origin of the Earth, interpreted as the beginning of distinct mineral phases, was about 4600 million years ago, the oldest rocks on Earth are less than 4000 million years old and include complex gneisses such as this exposure in Wyoming.

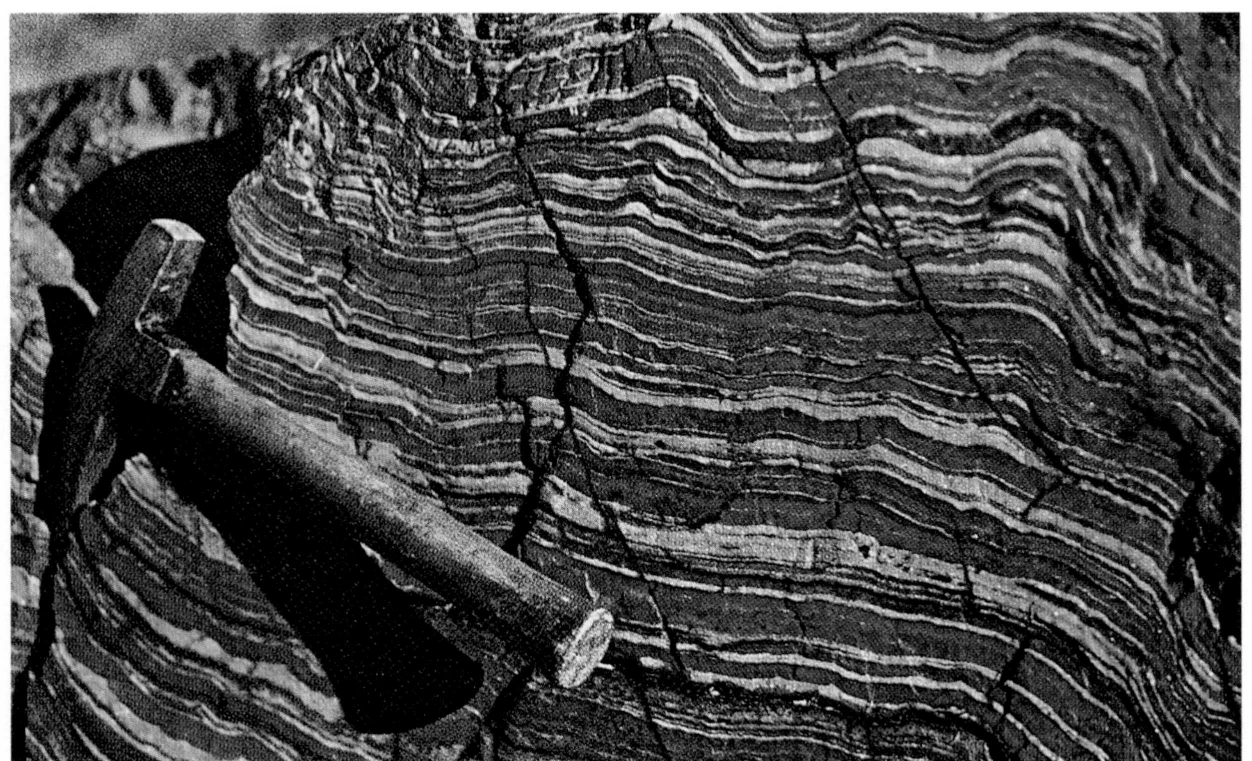

B.

These rocks, called banded iron formations (BIFs) are unique to the Precambrian. The BIFs represent a time and condition when there was episodic abundant production of oxygen by the photosynthetic activities of primitive blue-green algae; however, the oxygen was quickly tied up by free ferrous iron in aqueous environments, producing these alternating siliceous iron-rich (red) and iron-poor (white) layers. These banded iron formations have supplied much of the world's raw iron ore.

These red beds from late Precambrian deposits in the Grand Canyon, Arizona, are detrital sediments oxidized by direct exposure to the atmosphere. Red beds supplanted BIFs about 2000 million years ago, suggesting that by this time, there were consistent levels of free oxygen in Earth's atmosphere of at least 1% present atmospheric level.

A.

These stromatolites from Proterozoic strata in Montana are organic sedimentary structures built by colonial blue-green algae (cyanobacteria). Such colonies literally clogged most shallow marine environments during the Proterozoic. Oxygen produced by widespread photosynthesis may have triggered the formation of BIFs during the Early Proterozoic.

B.

These modern stromatolites from the hypersaline Hamelin Pool Basin in Shark Bay, Western Australia, provide valuable insights to ancient stromatolite growth and development. However, modern stromatolite fields such as this are rare due to competition for space and the herbivorous feeding activities of many post-Precambrian metazoan organisms. Extensive buildups of modern stromatolites are confined to harsh environments that tend to exclude competing metazoans.

C.

Paleozoic Deposits

Paleozoic literally means "ancient animal life." The Paleozoic record is testimony to richly populated shallow seas that periodically invaded the continental interiors. The Paleozoic began with the invasion of warm, shallow seas into the platform regions of several isolated continents and ended with the withdrawal of seas from a supercontinent, coinciding with the dying out of more than 90% of the Earth's species.

A.

Cambrian carbonate rocks, southern Canadian Rockies. Beginning in Cambrian time, continental margin basins and shallow epicontinental seas produced widespread blankets of carbonate deposits.

Lower Paleozoic carbonate rocks exposed in Natural Bridge, Virginia. Thomas Jefferson described this natural wonder as having formed during one sudden supernatural convulsion, a view compatible with the doctrine of strict catastrophism that prevailed during the 18th century.

B.

Monument Valley, southern Utah. Erosion by running water has sculpted these buttes and mesas from flat-lying fluvial red beds and desert dune sands of Permian age. These nonmarine strata are the products of arid environments along the margin of a supercontinent.

C.

Paleozoic Life

A.

Cambrian trilobite, Vermont. Complex animals such as trilobites signify the Cambrian faunal "explosion," inaugurating the Phanerozoic age of animal life. (Scale: trilobite is 12 cm long.)

B.

Delicately preserved crinoid echinoderms in Mississippian limestone, Indiana. Vast crinoid "meadows" covered shallow sea bottoms during the invasion of the last great carbonate epeiric sea. (Scale: base of crinoid calyx is 3.5 cm across.)

C.

Fossil ferns from the deposits of a Late Carboniferous coal swamp, Pennsylvania.

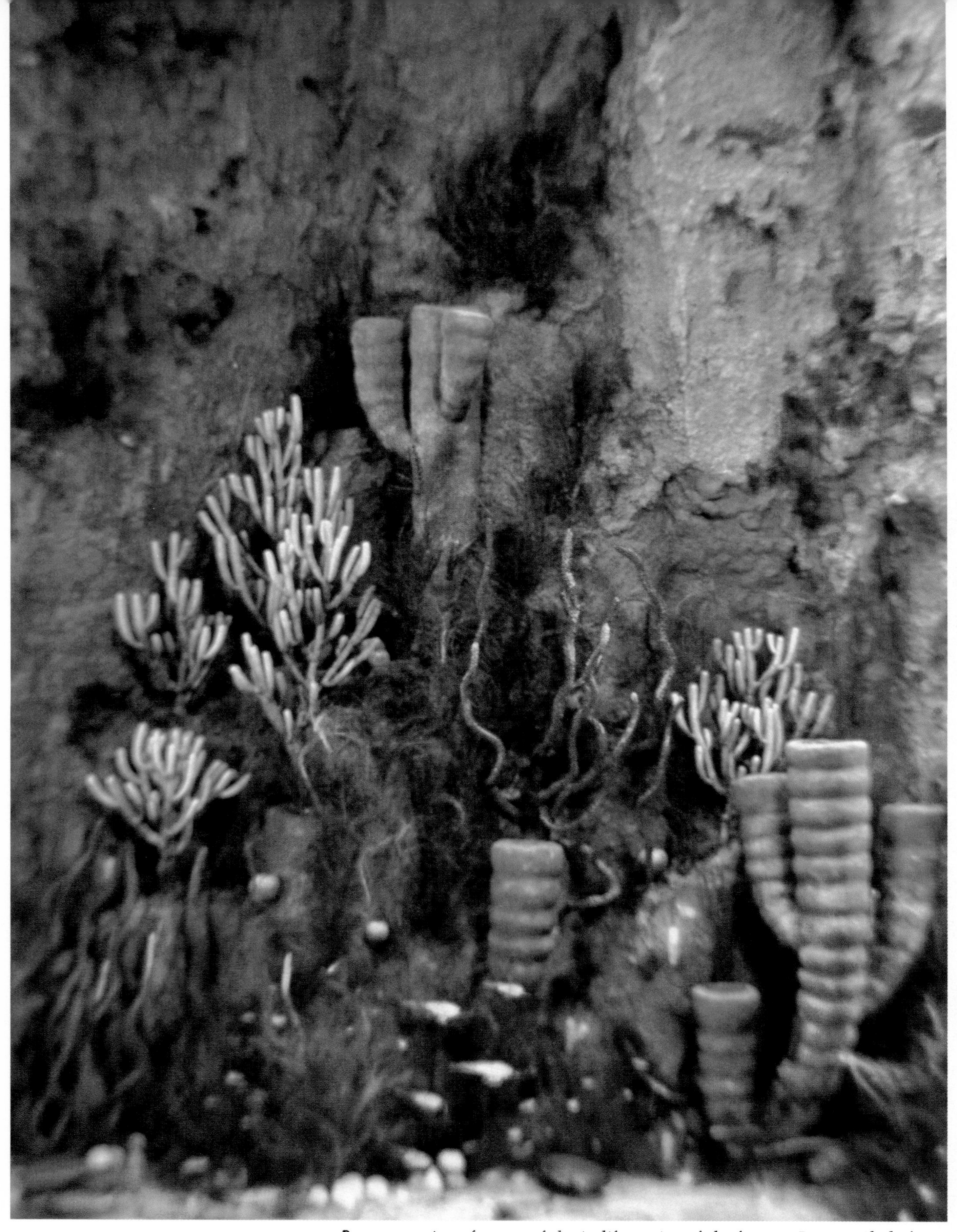

Reconstruction of a part of the in-life setting of the famous Burgess Shale fauna from the Middle Cambrian of Yoho Park, British Columbia. This diorama is on exhibit at the Smithsonian's National Museum of Natural History. It recreates the muddy bottom at the base of the algal reef where delicate soft-bodied species not found elsewhere, as well as sponges, trilobites, and brachiopods, were buried by slumping mud.

Plate II.6

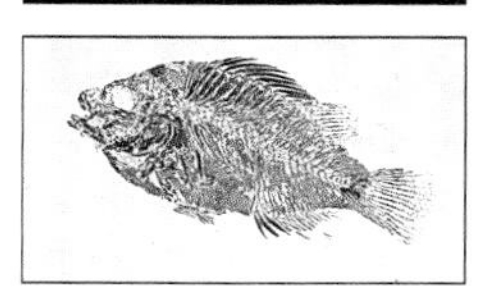

A.

Permian Reef Complex

One of the best-documented ancient reef settings in the geologic record is in the beautifully exposed carbonate rocks of Permian age in the Guadalupe Mountains of New Mexico and West Texas.

A. El Capitan, southern end of the Guadalupe Mountains, in the alpenglow of a West Texas sunset. El Capitan is an exposure of the reef core and fore-reef facies.

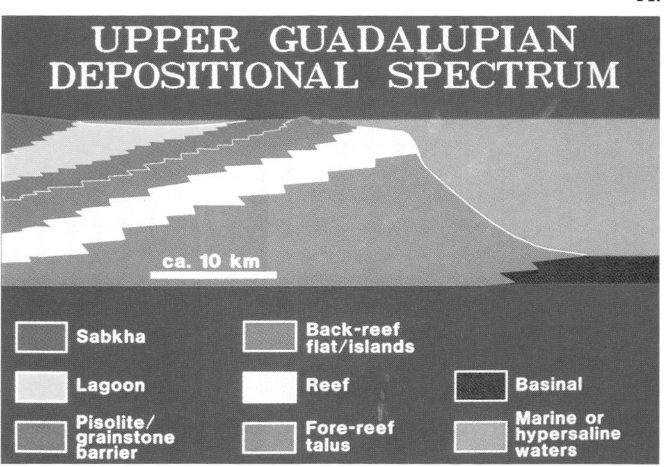

B.

B. Interpretive diagrammatic cross-section of the full spectrum of shelf-to-basin facies of the Capitan Formation and equivalent strata.

C.

C. Polished slab of a laminated, very fine-grained dolostone from the back-reef lagoonal facies. This fabric was most likely produced by intertidal blue-green algal stromatolites. Some of the larger voids are the result of dissolution of evaporite crystals that formed in a hypersaline setting.

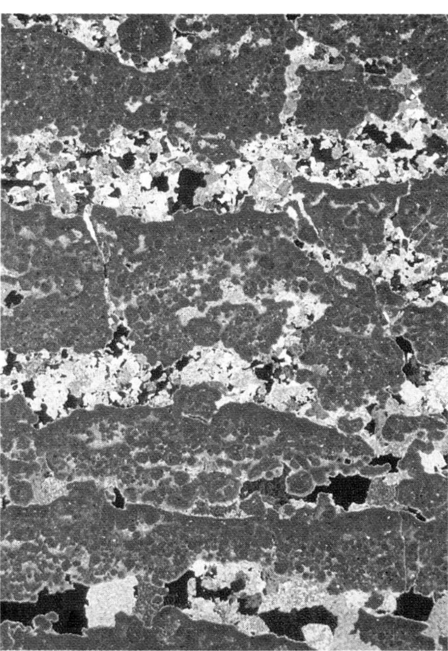

Scale: width is 9 mm D.

Thin-section photomicrograph of hand sample in C. showing anhydrite-filled porosity in stromatolitic dolostone. The anhydrite, an evaporite mineral, attests to hypersaline conditions in this back-reef environment.

Permian Reef Complex

A.

The entrance to Carlsbad Caverns is in the reef facies; the Big Room of the caverns is developed in the fore-reef facies. Carlsbad Caverns formed during the Pleistocene by dissolution along fractures at or near the ground-water table.

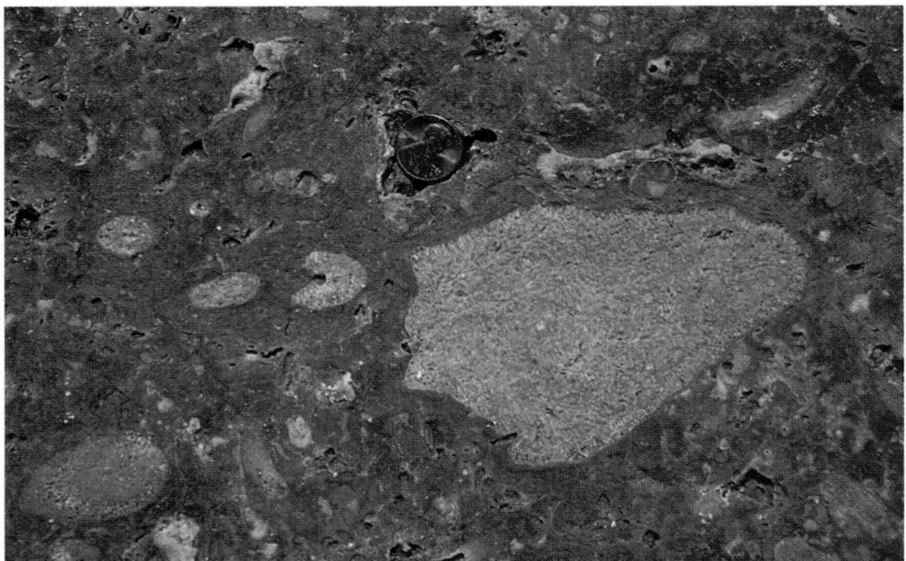

B.

Capitan reef framework shows large calcareous sponges still in oriented living position with long axis perpendicular to the reef trend. Large, irregular light-colored shapes are calcareous sponges.

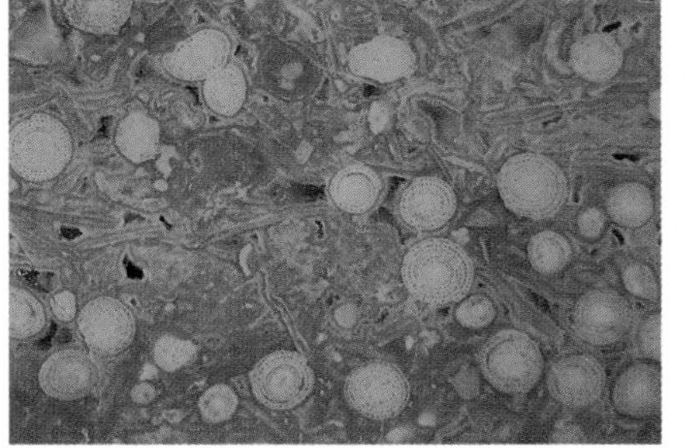

C.

Polished slab of fusulinid limestone from the upper part of the Capitan forereef slope. These fusulinid foraminifera and other grains in the rock were derived from shelf-margin and near back-reef settings and were transported by grainflow and turbidity current processes. (Scale: fusulinids are about 1 mm across.)

D.

Outcrop photograph showing dark, organic-rich, fine-grained, deep-water basinal deposits.

Figure 8–1
Cambrian trilobite. Until recently, the first appearance in the stratigraphic record of complex organisms such as trilobites represented a paradox of major proportion—the sudden appearance of complex organisms with little evidence of prior evolution.
(Photo courtesy of Wards Natural Science Establishment, Rochester, NY; specimen is about 10 cm in length.)

nation of the Gunflint showed that many of their microfossils were from silicified stromatolite structures. This substantiated Walcott's idea, and coupled with discoveries of algal stromatolites in a few modern-day environments (Fig. 8–3B), gave credence to the interpretation that stromatolites are organosedimentary structures, whose laminations are formed by the carbonate sediment trapping-and-binding activities of matlike communities of cyanobacteria.

As an undergraduate geology major at Oberlin College in Ohio, J. William Schopf was enthralled by the mystery of scant evidence of life in the pre-Cambrian record and the sudden appearance of complex, diverse life-forms in the Cambrian. Intrigued by publications on the Gunflint microbiota by Barghoorn and Tyler, he decided to embark on a quest—to learn as much as possible in his lifetime about life before the Cambrian. From Oberlin, Schopf went to Harvard for a program of graduate studies under the supervision of Barghoorn.

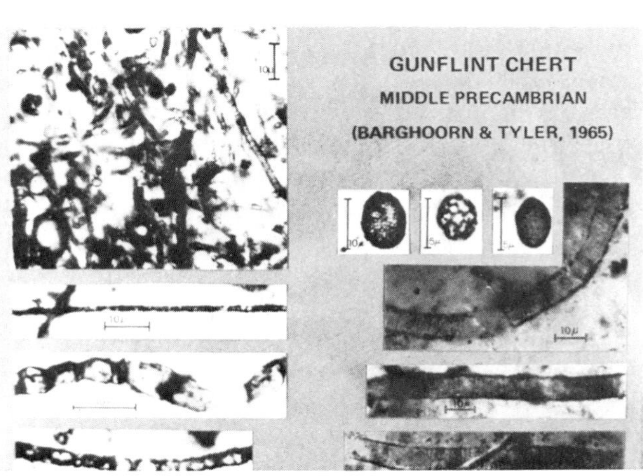

Figure 8–2
Prokaryotic microorganisms from the 2000 million-year-old Gunflint Formation. The discovery of the Gunflint microbiota by Stanley Tyler and its description by Tyler and Elso Barghoorn inaugurated an exciting chapter in the recognition of life before trilobites.
(Photo courtesy of J. William Schopf)

Figure 8–3
Stromatolites. A. Cross-section of 1900 Ma (Early Proterozoic) stromatolites, near east arm of Great Slave Lake, Northwest Territories, Canada. (Pen is 15 cm long.) B. Cross-section of Holocene stromatolite, Hamelin Pool, Shark Bay, Western Australia. Note similar shape to A. and laminated structure. (Stromatolite is 30 cm high.) C. and D. Surface morphology of elongate stromatolites. C. 1900 Ma elongate stromatolites, near east arm of Great Slave Lake, Northwest Territories, Canada. D. Holocene stromatolites, Hamelin Pool, Shark Bay, Western Australia.
(Photos courtesy of Paul F. Hoffman, Geological Survey of Canada.)

In 1965 Barghoorn collected specimens from the Fig Tree Formation in the Barberton Mountains region of South Africa. At that time the Fig Tree rocks were estimated to be slightly in excess of 3000 million years old and were regarded as the oldest known unmetamorphosed sedimentary succession. Schopf joined Barghoorn in a study of the Fig Tree specimens, and from petrographic and electron-microscope examinations, they were able to identify a number of rod-shaped and threadlike filaments, as well as larger spheroidal forms. These finds, identified as certain kinds of bacteria and cyanobacteria, were interpreted as being the inhabitants of the earliest known community of organisms.

Schopf and Barghoorn also studied chert samples from the Bitter Springs Formation in the Northern Territory of Australia. From these rocks, estimated to be about 900 million years old, they found examples of unicellular

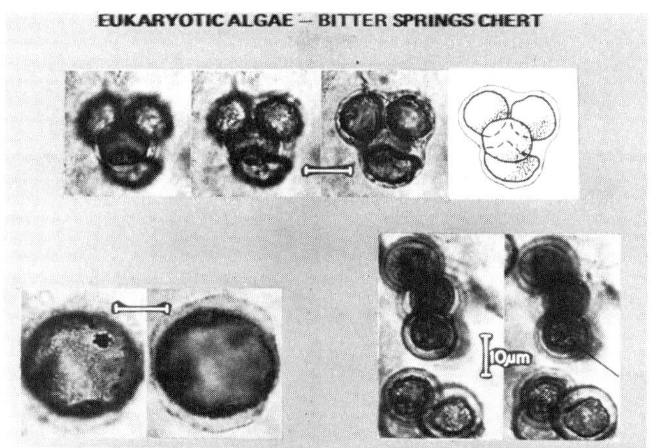

Figure 8–4
Nucleated(?) unicells from the Bitter Springs Formation (approximately 900 million years old), central Australia.
(Photo courtesy J. William Schopf)

eukaryotes: microorganisms with a cell nucleus (Fig. 8–4). This discovery was of great importance for a clearer understanding of pre-Cambrian evolution prior to the dawn of multicellular animal life. Thus, during the 1950s and 1960s, major discoveries not only provided evidence of life before the Cambrian, but also shed light on the crossing of three major evolutionary thresholds:

1. The Fig Tree Formation microfossils were evidence that the transition from chemical evolution to organic evolution had been crossed prior to 3000 million years ago;
2. The Gunflint Formation microbiota was evidence of the crossing of the threshold of diversity at least 2000 million years ago; and
3. The Bitter Springs Formation eukaryotes were evidence that the greatest of all thresholds had been crossed—the evolution of the nucleated cell. Once the nucleated cell evolved, the chromosomes and the DNA and RNA molecules could be confined and organized, paving the way for sexual reproduction, and eventually, the emergence of multicellular life.

After leaving Harvard, Schopf joined the faculty at University of California–Los Angeles, where he has continued to conduct research on pre-Cambrian life and evolution and to make important contributions to our understanding of the age of microscopic life.

Preston Cloud, at the University of California–Santa Barbara, has made many contributions to the study of the early relationships of lithosphere, atmosphere, hydrosphere, and biosphere. Among his many contributions has been a critical examination of the evidence that alleged pre-Cambrian microstructures are in fact organic in nature. This is by no means a simple task. According to Cloud:

> To suggest a biological origin for a given assemblage of nonliving microstructures is permissible only if they are demonstrably carbonaceous, reasonably abundant, show a narrow or approximately polymodal (bell-shaped) size distribution, and have a morphology that is consistent with the proposed origin.*

*1976. Beginnings of biospheric evolution and their biochemical consequences. *Paleobiology* 2:355.

In this chapter we will examine more closely the evidence of life in the pre-Cambrian rock record and the close interconnection of the evolution of biosphere and atmosphere.

Terminology

In 1930, G. H. Chadwick proposed the term **Cryptozoic,** meaning "hidden life," to include all of geologic history prior to the earliest evidence of visible animal life. He likewise introduced the term **Phanerozoic,** meaning "manifest life," to include the geologic record characterized by conspicuous animal life. The term **Precambrian** became popularized as geologists became aware that the stratigraphic systems, recognized by their fossil content (see Chapter 6), subdivided only that part of the geologic column in which remains of organisms were commonly preserved.

Beneath the Cambrian, the lowest of these paleontologically defined systems, they recognized a vast sequence bearing no fossils and not amenable to subdivision into interpretive chronostratigraphic units. It was the seemingly bottomless aspect of this "primitive" rock complex that inspired James Hutton to write "no vestige of a beginning." Thus, the designation Precambrian has long been the popular inclusive term for all of geologic time prior to the beginning of the Cambrian. Because of this, the term Cryptozoic has had only limited use. The name Phanerozoic, embracing the Paleozoic, Mesozoic, and Cenozoic Eras, has enjoyed wide acceptance.

We realize that the deeply entrenched term Precambrian is probably here to stay, but we also know that semantic problems make unambiguous discussion difficult. We would prefer to use terminology that best reflects geologic history as we know it, and thus would favor abandoning the formal term Precambrian and resurrecting the designation Cryptozoic to refer to that phase of geologic history preceding the first appearance of *animal* life on Earth (Phanerozoic). However, we will adhere to convention for the sake of consistency, and for classification purposes, will use the term Precambrian (Table 8–1).

However, where appropriate, we also will employ the informal terms pre-Cambrian or pre-Phanerozoic, for example, when discussing crystalline basement rocks nonconformable beneath Cambrian or younger strata. Whenever possible, we will use more specific time subdivisions of the Precambrian. The first 85% of geologic time deserves a formal name of its own—Cryptozoic, instead of pre-something else, and we will use this term when speaking in a general pre-Phanerozoic historical sense.

Geochronologic Subdivisions

Prior to the widespread use of radiometric dating, the magnitude of the Cryptozoic was not fully appreciated. In the early days of geology, the complex of granites, schists, and gneisses upon which the younger fossiliferous strata rested was regarded as merely a foundation or basement. (Unfortunately, this ambiguous scientific metaphor has been carried to the present day, connoting on one hand a firm foundation, but on the other, an obscure cellar.) These sub-Cambrian rocks showed no clear sequence of events, in marked contrast with the more orderly arrangement of rocks of the Paleozoic, Mesozoic, and Cenozoic. Remember from Chapter 6 that at the turn of this century the oldest accepted estimates of the age of the Earth did not exceed 100 million years. Most of this time was believed to have been required for the Cambrian and younger record, thus allowing relatively little time for the "Precambrian," which was regarded simply as a basement foundation upon which "the wonders of the world were set."

Perhaps the greatest contribution of radiometric dating has been its application to the Cryptozoic (Precambrian) rock record. Many uranium-lead, potassium-argon, and rubidium-strontium dates from all over the world have provided a totally different perspective on the vastness of the Cryptozoic—a time span of some 4000 million years. Because of radiometric dating, there has been a ground swell of renewed interest in Cryptozoic rocks and history. Extreme complexity of the rocks in many places still hampers accurate work. Today, however, we have a considerable body of information on the Cryptozoic.

Because superposition is difficult to work out in many pre-Cambrian terranes, Cryptozoic history has not been subdivided according to a refined scheme such as we have for the Phanerozoic. This

Table 8–1
Classification schemes for Cryptozoic (Precambrian) chronology

	Canada		North America		
Age (Ma)		(Stockwell, 1964)	(U.S. Geological Survey, 1971)		(Harrison and Peterman, 1982)
500	PALEOZOIC	Cambrian	PALEOZOIC Cambrian	PALEOZOIC	Cambrian
		570	570		570
700	PROTEROZOIC	Hadrynian	Precambrian Z	PROTEROZOIC	Late Proterozoic
		880	800		
900					900
1100					
1300		Helikian	Precambrian Y		Middle Proterozoic
1500					
			1600		1600
		1640			
1700					
1900		Aphebian	Precambrian X		Early Proterozoic
2100					
2300					
		2390			
2500	ARCHEAN		2500	ARCHEAN	2500
2700					
2900					Late Archean
					3000
3100		ARCHEAN			
3300			Precambrian W		Middle Archean
					3400
3500					
3700					Early Archean

condition has been imposed by the complexity of the rocks coupled with the fact that Cryptozoic sedimentary rocks do not contain the kind of fossil record that is amenable to subdivision.

As discussed in Chapter 6, the birth and development of the Phanerozoic time scale, based on fossil succession, took place in western Europe. However, the important development of a pre-Phanerozoic chronology occurred primarily in the Great Lakes region of North America in the southern part of the **Canadian Shield.** Early attempts to subdivide the complex history were met with frustration, but with time and effort a number of sequences were described and two very generalized subdivisions emerged: **Archean** and **Proterozoic** (Table 8–1).

The terms Archean and Proterozoic, although representing an early attempt at subdivision of the Cryptozoic record, are still used. Prior to the availability of radiometric dating, there was a tendency to equate Archean with the older-looking pre-Cambrian rocks (plutonic and metamorphic), and Proterozoic with the younger-looking rocks (mostly volcanic and sedimentary). We have already seen (Chapter 6) how this rationale of judging relative age on physical appearance met with failure in early attempts at fashioning a time scale; it is no wonder that this Wernerian approach plagued attempts to organize the more obscure record of the Cryptozoic.

Various regional subdivision schemes have been proposed, but there has been difficulty in correlating Cryptozoic rocks and events from place to place. Until recently there has been little success in putting together a worldwide chronology of the Cryptozoic. In 1972 the U.S. Geological Survey (USGS) adopted an interim scheme for subdividing the Precambrian (Table 8–1) on the basis of significant breaks in Cryptozoic history pinpointed by good control of radiometric dates. The 1974 edition of the USGS's geologic map of the United States uses this scheme, and Precambrian W corresponds closely to Archean. In 1983, the North American Commission on Stratigraphic Nomenclature suggested a classification of **geochronometric units** for divisions of Precambrian time. This scheme employs the terms Archean and Proterozoic as eons, which, in turn, are subdivided into Early, Middle, and Late eras (Table 8–1).

The North American Stratigraphic Code and the International Stratigraphic Guide customarily recognize time-stratigraphic (chronostratigraphic) units and boundaries defined at type sections (stratotypes) as the basis for corresponding geologic time units and boundaries. For the Cryptozoic, however, this procedure has proved impractical, because much of the Cryptozoic record is developed as unfossiliferous nonstratified rocks, which are not amenable to applications of superposition and fossil succession—the two fundamental bases for the Phanerozoic time scale.

As defined in the 1983 North American Stratigraphic Code, geochronometric units are direct divisions of geologic time and do not necessarily have a corresponding rock sequence to which they are referred. Thus, for the Cryptozoic, they are more suitable than standard chronostratigraphic subdivisions. In this scheme, the geochronometric units have been selected on the basis of the temporal positions of the more important geologic events in major regions of the Earth. The boundaries have been selected so as to interrupt as few as possible of the major sequences of sedimentation, igneous intrusion and extrusion, and orogeny. They are defined by chronometric age so as to provide a common basis for region-to-region and continent-to-continent application.

Canadian Shield

Sequence of Events

We shall begin our examination of the Cryptozoic history of North America with the Canadian Shield, a vast lowland rimming Hudson Bay and occupying the eastern two-thirds of Canada, the U.S. margins of Lake Superior, and most of Greenland (Fig. 8–5). Each of the continents of the world has a nucleus or core of predominantly pre-Cambrian basement rocks, either exposed as a shield region or covered with a veneer of younger platform sediments (Fig. 8–6).

The Canadian Shield contains the oldest and most expansive surface exposures of Cryptozoic rock on the North American continent. Granite and granite gneiss are the most abundant rock types, but the shield is a complex patchwork of various kinds of metamorphic rocks, intrusive and extrusive igneous rocks, and sedimentary rocks. As discussed in Chapter 1, the shield represents the exposed part of the nucleus of the continent, and is flanked by younger stratified rocks of Paleozoic and Mesozoic age.

William Logan, who established the Geological Survey of Canada in 1842, was responsible for the pioneering effort in working out the geologic history of the Canadian Shield. It was a herculean task for Logan and his field parties to penetrate the harsh terrain on horseback or foot or by canoe. Ex-

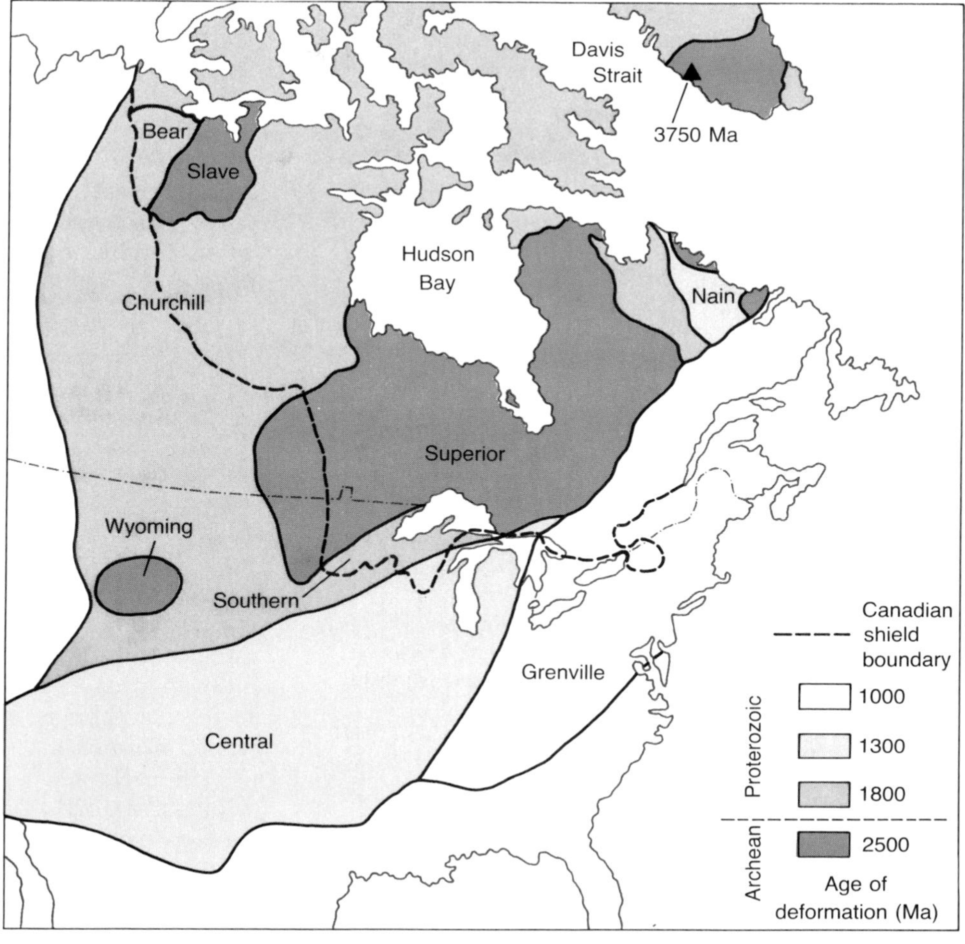

Figure 8–5
Precambrian basement complex of North America showing structural-radiometric age provinces in Canadian Shield and regions outside the Shield that lie beneath younger sedimentary cover.
(From C. W. Stearn, R. C. Carroll, and T. H. Clark, 1976, *Geological Evolution of North America*, 3d edition, Fig. 9–14, p. 164, John Wiley & Sons, New York. Used with permission of the publisher)

cellent field mapping continued to the twentieth century, stimulated in large part by the search for metallic ore deposits (particularly copper, gold, nickel, and platinum), and paved the way for development of a workable pre-Cambrian chronology (Table 8–2). This was a remarkable achievement and speaks highly of the Canadian Survey and its team of hardy, perceptive geologists.

This and subsequent work has shown that in the southern Canadian Shield there are major subdivisions of sedimentary and volcanic rocks, separated by unconformities and intrusive igneous and metamorphic complexes that bear evidence of at least four major orogenies (Table 8–2). This sequence of events is set in a general relative time frame of Archean (early Cryptozoic) and Proterozoic (late Cryptozoic).

Since the early days of geologic investigations of the complicated rocks and structures of the shield, geologists have recognized a major break within the pre-Cambrian complex, marked not only by a widespread unconformity but also by a change in lithology and style of deformation. This boundary, between the Archean and Proterozoic, has a radiometric age of about 2500 million years. It should be emphasized, however, that this date is an approximation, based on a clustering of radiometric dates. The boundary between Archean and Proterozoic actually is a diachronous transition spanning several hundred million years. The Cryptozoic relative chronology of the Canadian Shield was pieced together by use of fundamental principles of historical geology: superposition—layered sequences or "packages" of rock, and cross-cutting relationships—faults, igneous intrusions, and unconformities (Fig. 8–7). Once the sequence of events was worked out, it took the application of radiometric dating to place shield rocks in a regional time frame (Table 8–2).

One of the most significant discoveries from the application of radiometric dating is that the shield can be subdivided into regions or provinces on the basis of isotopic age and rock types. Radiometric dates clustering around 2500, 1800, 1300, and 1000

Ma indicate four major orogenic episodes and major times of regional resetting of radiometric clocks. These orogenies define seven major structural provinces (Fig. 8–5), each of which, in addition to characteristic isotopic age and rock types, has a style of deformation and a structural orientation different from those of adjacent regions. The structural-isotopic age provinces are separated by rather abrupt metamorphic or fault boundaries called **orogenic fronts.**

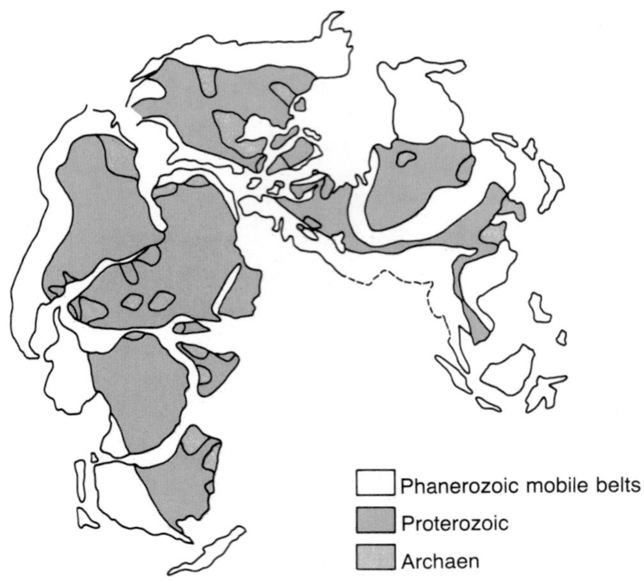

Figure 8–6
Permian continental configuration showing pre-Phanerozoic basement nuclei of continental blocks, including shield areas, flanked by Phanerozoic mobile belts.
(From Brian F. Windley, *The Evolving Continents,* Fig. 1, p. 1. Copyright © 1977, John Wiley & Sons, Ltd. Reprinted by permission of John Wiley & Sons, Ltd.)

Archean Rocks: Greenstone Belts and Granite Gneiss

Rocks of Archean age occur mainly in the Superior and Slave Provinces (Fig. 8–5). As shown in Table 8–2, the orogenic event that brought the Archean to a close is called the **Kenoran orogeny** and occurred approximately 2500 million years ago. Characteristically unique rock suites of Archean terranes are the **greenstone belts,** which occur as giant pods in great elongated downwarps (Fig. 8–8). These belts are thought to be remnants of ancient volcanic-sedimentary basins (Fig. 8–9).

The rock successions in the greenstone belts include ultramafic and mafic volcanic rocks in the lowest parts, overlain by and interstratified with

Table 8–2
Cryptozoic chronostratigraphic classification in relation to orogenies of the Canadian Shield

Eon	Era	Sub-era	Orogeny mean K-Ar mica Age, Ma
PROTEROZOIC	Hadrynian		
	Helikian	Neohelikian	Grenvillian (955)
		Paleohelikian	Elsonian (1370)
	Aphebian		Hudsonian (1735)
ARCHEAN			Kenoran (2480)

From C. H. Stockwell, 1976, Geologic and Economic Minerals of Canada, Table VI–1, p. 51: *Geological Survey of Canada Economic Geology Report,* Vol. 1. Reprinted by permission of Geological Survey of Canada.

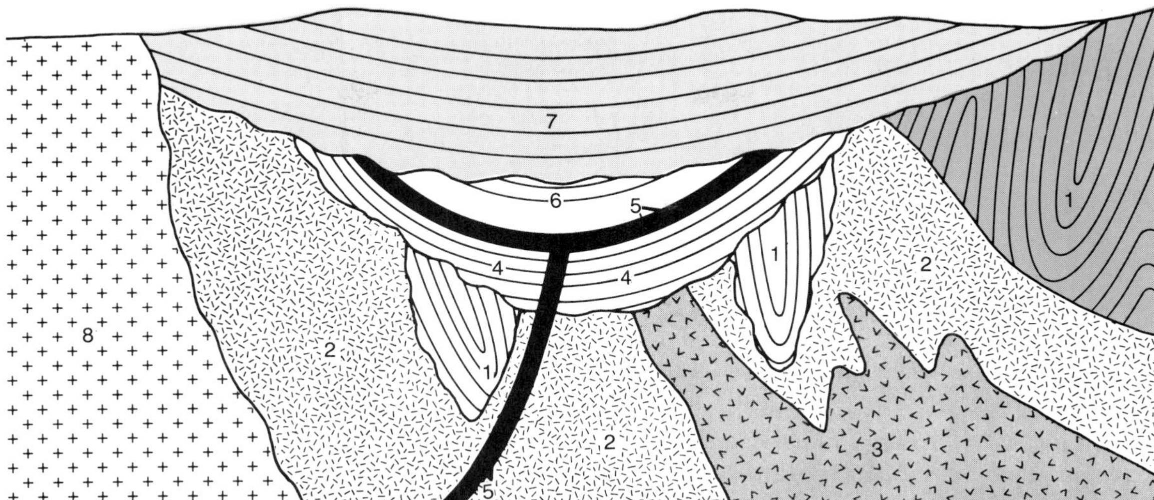

Figure 8–7
Complex superpositional and cross-cutting relationships of rocks in southern Canadian Shield. Numbers indicate oldest (1) to youngest (8).
(Information from C. H. Stockwell, 1976, Geologic and Economic Minerals of Canada: *Geological Survey of Canada, Economic Geology Report No. 1*)

immature graywacke-type sedimentary rocks rich in mafic volcanic rock fragments. These sedimentary rocks in turn are topped by andesitic-to-felsic volcanic rocks and by interstratified pyroclastic rocks and more silicic sedimentary rocks. The name "greenstone" refers to the basaltic rocks in the lower part of the pile; these rocks have been altered by metamorphism to produce green minerals such as epidote, chlorite, and serpentine. Greenstone belts are found in all the Precambrian Shield terranes of the world and are developed in essentially the same fashion.

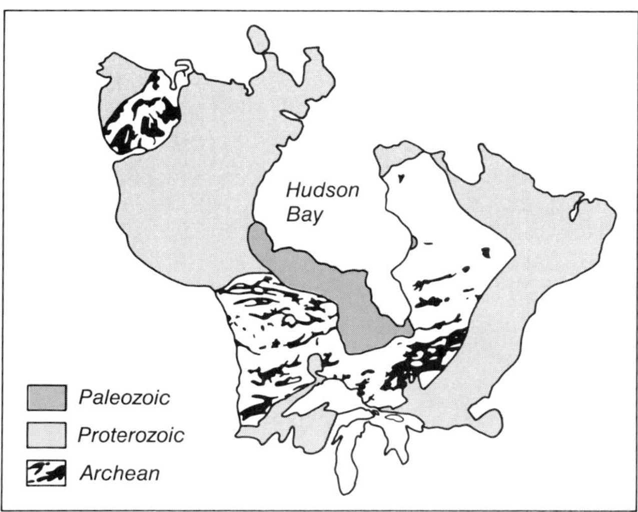

Figure 8–8
Canadian Shield, showing Archean greenstone belts (black).
(From W. R. A. Barager and F. C. McGlynn, 1976, Early Archean Basement in the Canadian Shield: A Review of the Evidence: *Geological Survey of Canada Paper* 76–14. Reprinted by permission of Geological Survey of Canada)

On the Canadian Shield, greenstone belts are concentrated in large tracts several hundred kilometers long and several tens of kilometers across. Between these greenstone-belt tracts lie vast regions of granite and granitoid gneiss and other associated high-grade metamorphic rocks. The relationship of the greenstone belts to the surrounding granitoid terranes is not clearly understood. Some geologists believe that the more ultramafic and mafic lower parts of the greenstone belts are remnants of originally more extensive volcanic-sedimentary successions representing earlier oceanic crust. In this context, these remnants are the deepest downfolds left after massive intrusion of granites (and their close derivatives) and deep erosion. Another school of thought considers the greenstone belts as having been formed along downwarp and fracture zones in an early, thin, brittle granitic crust (Fig. 8–9). In this context, they represent more localized volcanism and orogeny.

Logan originally suggested that the granite and granite gneiss are older than the greenstone belts and are part of an ancient crust; this idea has been revived in recent years. Still another idea proposes that some greenstone belts developed initially as

Figure 8–9
States in evolution of Archean greenstone belts and gneissic terranes.
(From Brian F. Windley, 1973, Crustal Development in the Precambrian, Fig. 3, p. 330: *Philosophical Transactions of the Royal Society of London,* A 273. Reprinted by permission of author)

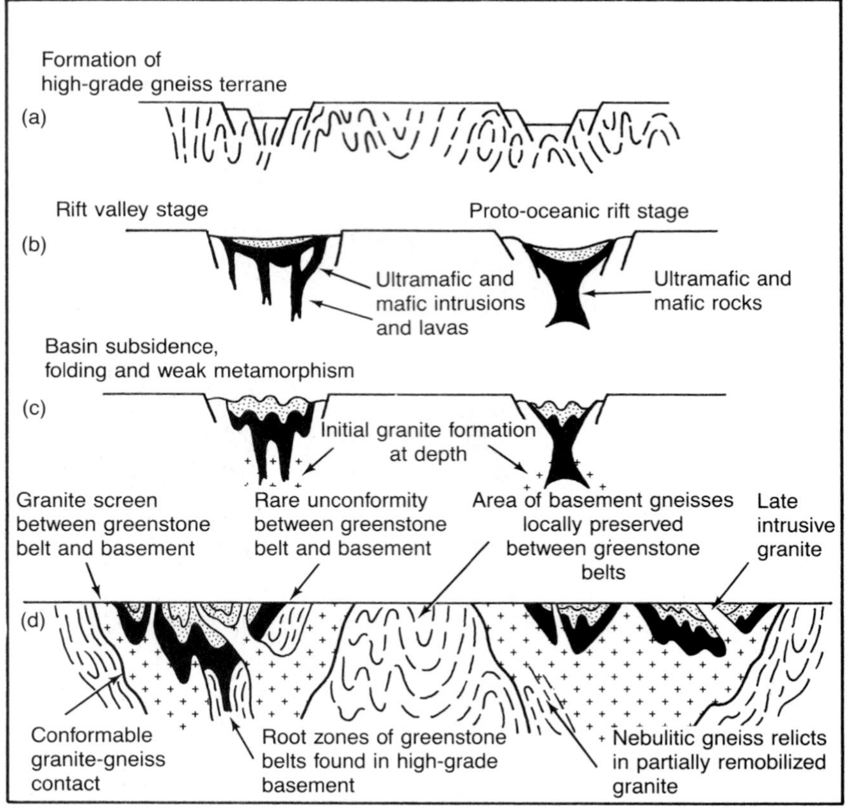

terrestrial equivalents of lunar maria. Certainly the correct model would have important implications for the nature of the Early-to-Middle Archean crust in terms of how much of it was granitic. It is noteworthy that ultramafic volcanic rocks are known only in Archean terranes. Their presence indicates that processes were operating then which no longer occur on such a scale on the Earth.

Chemical analyses of the highly altered volcanic rocks of the greenstone belts indicate rocks ranging from peridotites and basalts, through andesites, to rhyolites and their pyroclastic equivalents. Pillow structures in many of the volcanic rocks show that extrusion was under water. The sedimentary rocks include graywacke sandstones, slates, and conglomerates, as well as peculiar rock sequences called **banded iron formations.** Many of the sandstone beds are graded and have the characteristics of turbidites. Some of the sedimentary rocks in the upper parts of the greenstone belt successions are arkoses and granite pebble conglomerates, indicating derivation from granitic rocks that were present before the belts were formed, or at least before they were completed. The greenstone belt sequences are generally about 10,000 to 30,000 m thick, although seldom are their bases observed. Ages range from less than 3800 Ma to a little less than 3000 Ma.

We know very little about the composition and structure of the Earth's Early Archean crust. The Kenoran orogeny that brought Archean history to a close marks a major change in the development of the Earth's lithosphere. Present estimates put the amount of granitic crust during the Archean at about 10–40% of the present figure. Interestingly, some of the oldest rocks known on the Earth are granitic or are sediments derived from granitic rocks, and some 3700 million-year-old sandstones in Australia contain detrital zircon grains (zircon is a common accessory mineral in granites) radiometrically dated at 4100 to 4300 Ma, implying granitic crust this old. However, most of these Archean granites are sodium-rich, implying influence of mantle geochemistry. It was during the widespread Kenoran event that tremendous volumes of granitic lithosphere formed, transforming what had been comparatively thin slabs of granitic crust into the present thickness of about 40 km. The granites that now surround the greenstone belts comprise some of the thickest and most stable parts of the continental crust.

Unfortunately, it was the emplacement of so much granite that has obscured the original greenstone belt–granitoid crustal relationship, and reset the radiometric clocks. As the Kenoran granites formed, the greenstone belts, being denser pods, progressively sank into synclinal configurations (Fig. 8–9). When the Proterozoic Eon commenced, after a considerable period of erosion, lithospheric conditions were much different than they had been during the Archean.

Proterozoic Rocks: Continental Lithosphere on a Grand Scale

Proterozoic rocks of the shield are quite diverse and have been subdivided into three erathems, separated by two major orogenies: the Hudsonian orogeny (about 1800 million years ago) and the later Grenville orogeny (about 1000 million years ago). These orogenies involved large-scale lithospheric plate collisions, including island arc–to–continent and continent-to-continent interactions. The erathems are called the Aphebian, the Helikian, and the Hadrynian (Table 8–2).

Aphebian rocks include the first widespread quartz-rich sandstones and carbonate rocks, as well as the peculiar but important banded iron formations. Rocks in the Southern Province south and west of Lake Superior contain banded iron formations that have served as North America's main source of iron ore for more than a century. The Gowganda Formation in southern Ontario consists of unsorted and unbedded muddy conglomerates that are believed to represent tillites (Fig. 8–10). Many of the pebbles, cobbles, and boulders in the conglomerates have striated surfaces and in places the conglomerates rest on striated and polished older basement rock. Parts of the Gowganda are developed as isolated outsized cobbles and boulders in a muddy matrix, giving the impression that the large stones were dropped into muddy bottom aquatic environments. These features all point to a major episode of continental glaciation during the Early Proterozoic. Aphebian rocks were folded and intruded by granites during the Hudsonian orogeny (Table 8–2).

Helikian rocks, for the most part, have been severely deformed and metamorphosed by the Grenville orogeny. A mid-Helikian disturbance called the Elsonian orogeny defines a lower Paleohelikian and an upper Neohelikian interval. Thick successions of volcanic rocks, quartzites, marbles, and red beds occur mainly in elongate troughlike areas flanked by granite and gneiss. The Keweenawan Group of the Lake Superior area consists of several thousand meters of basalt flows, arkosic and quartzose sandstones, and shales, and contains metallic copper deposits. Hadrynian rocks are not well represented in the shield proper, but accumulated to great thicknesses in marginal areas of the Appalachian and Cordilleran regions; they will be discussed later.

Figure 8–10
Gowganda tillite; Proterozoic. Note diamictite fabric with exotic clasts in mud matrix. Outcrop has been scoured by Pleistocene glacial activity.
(Photo by J. D. Cooper)

Precambrian Rocks Outside the Shield

Other Provinces

Reference to Figure 8–11 reveals, in addition to the Canadian Shield, scattered smaller exposures of pre-Cambrian rocks in different parts of North America. All of the pre-Cambrian crystalline rocks of these regions are parts of the core or nucleus of the continent generally referred to as the "basement complex" of North America. The Canadian Shield is that part of the basement complex that has been extensively exposed by erosion during the last 1000 million years. The rocks of the shield extend toward the margins of North America beneath the cover of Paleozoic rocks on the platform interior. Radiometric dates from outcrop areas beyond the shield, as well as from the subsurface through drilled core samples, are consistent with the pattern illustrated in Figure 8–5. Structural trends in the basement complex have been mapped by geophysical methods.

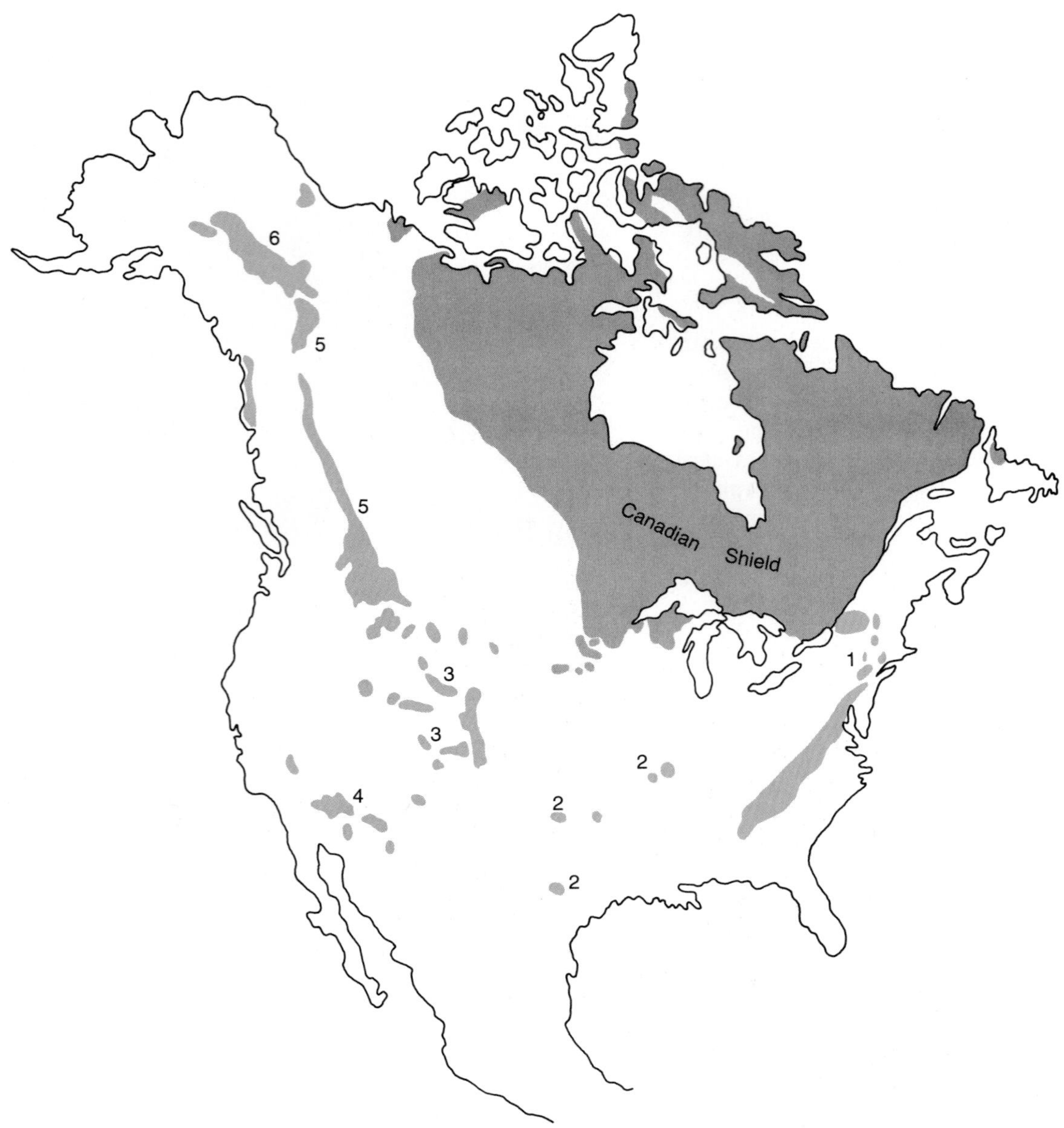

Figure 8–11

North America, showing areas of exposure of Precambrian rocks outside the Canadian Shield. 1. Appalachian region; 2. cores of domes in midcontinent; 3. cores of ranges in Rocky Mountains; 4. southeastern California and Arizona; 5. Canadian Rockies; 6. Alaska.
(From P. B. King, 1979, *Tectonic Map of North America:* U.S. Geological Survey)

Figure 8–5 shows the present state of our knowledge of the isotopic age-structural provinces beneath the continental platform outside the Canadian Shield. Much of the middle part of the United States is underlain by the Central Province, which has a comparatively small outcrop area on the shield itself. The relatively small Wyoming Province is composed of Archean rocks metamorphosed in the Kenoran orogeny. Examples of rocks representative of the various provinces are shown in Figure 8–12. Throughout much of the southern and western mid-continent region (Central Province), shallow *anorogenic* (not related to orogeny) granite and related rocks 1200 to 1500 million years old are present. The tectonic significance of this broad terrane of anorogenic igneous rocks is presently obscure, but some workers have suggested that it may have developed in response to crustal tension, per-

A B C D

Figure 8–12

Precambrian basement rock. A. Gneiss with vertical foliation, Grenville Province, southern Canadian Shield. B. Gneiss in basement rock of Grand Tetons, Wyoming Province. C. Granite and gneiss, Mount Rushmore, Black Hills, Southern Province. D. Gneiss from Blue Ridge Mountains, Virginia; Grenville Province.
(Photos by J. D. Cooper)

haps related to rifting that began along the western margin of the craton at about the same time.

The oldest rocks are in the Lake Superior region in Minnesota (approximately 3700 million years old) and in western Greenland (approximately 3800 million years old). The age of deformation (plutonism, uplift, and metamorphism) shows a crude concentric pattern of progressively younger, more outward bands, suggesting that the North American continent has grown by lateral accretion—the welding of successive orogenic belts. In this regard it should be pointed out that some pre-Cambrian rocks in North America, particularly in the Appalachian Piedmont region and in Alaska, represent *exotic* terranes accreted during later Phanerozoic orogenies, and are not indigenous to the North American continent.

The Precambrian rocks of North America record events that span nearly three quarters of the age of the Earth, from the assembly of the cratonic nuclei in the Middle and Late Archean, through the Proterozoic orogenies that *consolidated* the North American craton, to the Late Proterozoic events that modified it. Paul Hoffman, an expert on Precambrian terranes, summarized this history most succinctly with his catchy title of a symposium keynote address in 1987: "United Plates of America—the Birth of a Craton."

Grand Canyon

The spectacular Grand Canyon and adjacent parts of the Colorado Plateau provide a panoramic view of a significant part of Earth history. This region will serve as a model as we continue our discussion of the geologic history of North America. Well exposed in the narrow, inner gorge of the Grand Canyon (Fig. 8–13) are schists, gneisses, and granites that comprise a complex crystalline assemblage which formed about 1500 to 1300 million years ago during a major orogenic disturbance roughly equivalent to the Elsonian orogeny of the Canadian Shield. Metamorphic rocks such as the Vishnu (Fig. 8–14) and Brahma Schists represent former marine mudstones and sandstones that were subsequently uplifted, deformed, metamorphosed, and intruded by granite during a major orogeny. These rocks later were eroded to a rather subdued landscape. In many respects, these crystalline basement rocks in the Grand Canyon are similar in style to many other pre-Cambrian complexes. They tell a story of sedimentation, volcanism, folding and faulting, metamorphism, igneous intrusion, and erosion—the birth and death of mountain belts.

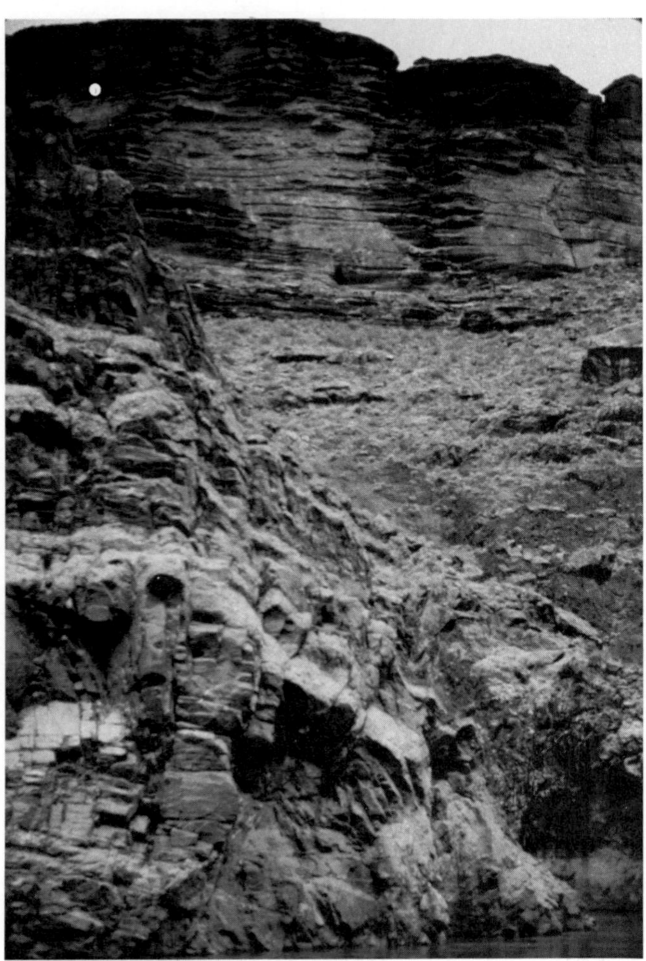

Figure 8–13
Schist with granite intrusions, inner Gorge of Grand Canyon.
(Photo by J. D. Cooper)

All of this happened before a succession of younger pre-Cambrian stratified rocks, the Grand Canyon Supergroup, was deposited. These rocks consist of a thick sequence of quartzites, argillites (compact siltstones and mudstones), **red beds,** limestones, and some lava flows nonconformably overlying the basement complex and underlying a Paleozoic succession in a spectacular angular unconformity (Fig. 8–15). In addition to illustrating classic stratigraphic relationships, the pre-Cambrian rocks of the Grand Canyon also provide an example of how lithology is *not* a good guide to age. The old-looking crystalline basement rocks were originally assigned to the Archean; however, radiometric dating has demonstrated their Middle Proterozoic age.

Sediments of Late Proterozoic Continental Margins

The Grand Canyon Supergroup is only a part of a wedge-shaped belt, 300 km wide and 3500 km long, composed of sandstone, shale, and minor limestone, that was deposited along the western margin of the Middle and Late Proterozoic continent (Fig. 8–16). Rocks of this belt are well exposed in the Death Valley area of California, the Uinta Mountains in Utah, and the northern Rocky Mountains from Waterton-Glacier International Peace Park, Montana, northward into Alberta and British Columbia (Fig. 8–17). At Waterton-Glacier Park they are called the Belt Supergroup.

The Belt stratigraphic succession consists of shale, sandstone, some conglomerate and limestone, and some interstratified basaltic lava flows and sills (Fig. 8–17A). These rocks have a composite thickness of up to 8000 m and comprise an essentially unmetamorphosed section that was deposited in a northwest/southeast-oriented marine-to-nonmarine trough about 1200 to 800 million years ago. Some of the rocks bear the ripple marks and desiccation cracks of shallow-water deposition; others show graded bedding and dark colors (evidence of deeper water deposition) and appear to be turbidites. These rocks of the western Cordillera—as well as generally coeval conglomerates, sandstones, and siltstones comprising the thick (up to 12 km) Ocoee Group of the Great Smoky Moun-

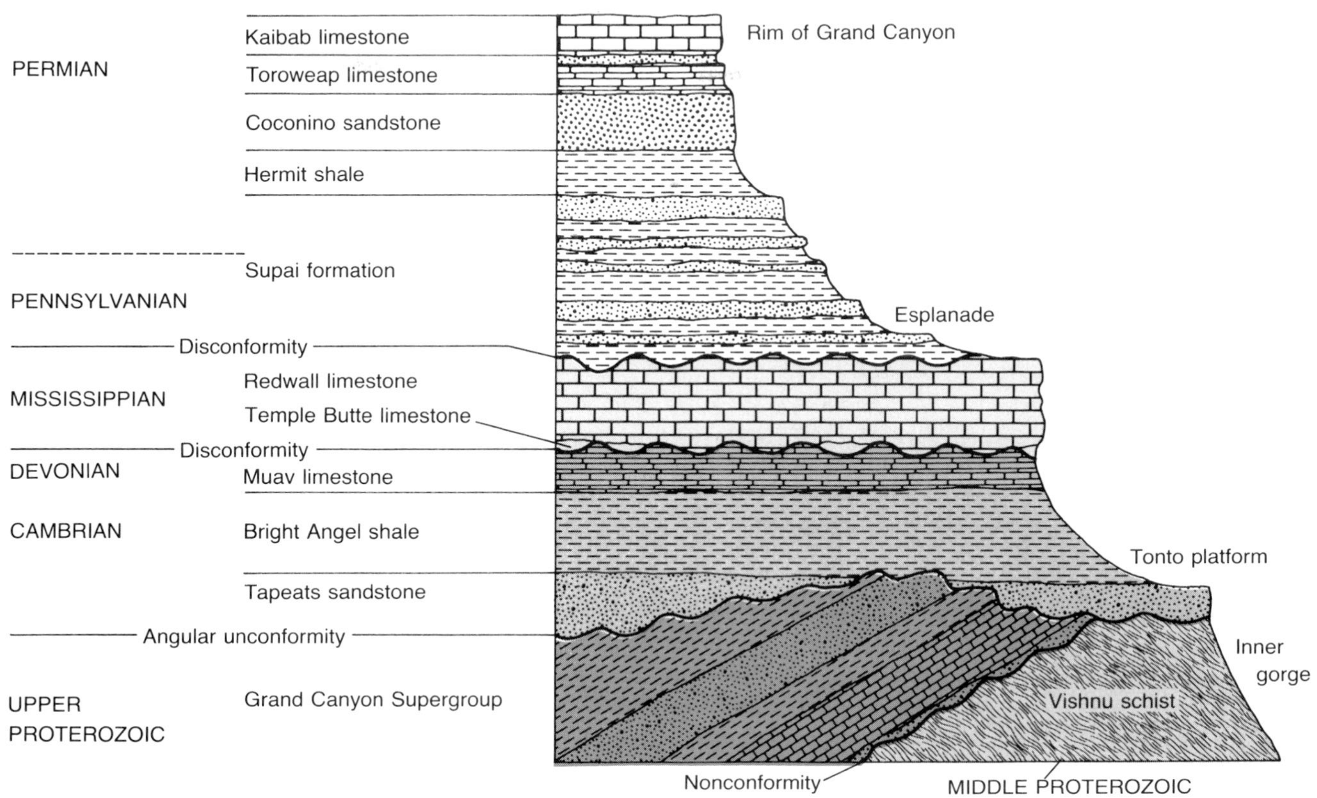

Figure 8–14
Wall of Grand Canyon showing pre-Paleozoic basement rocks (Vishnu Schist); tilted pre-Paleozoic stratified sequence (Grand Canyon Supergroup) nonconformably overlying metamorphic basement; and nearly flat-lying Paleozoic succession unconformably overlying pre-Paleozoic rocks.
(After P. B. King, 1977, *The Evolution of North America,* rev. ed., Fig. 63, p. 105: Princeton University Press. Used with permission of Princeton University Press)

tains in the Appalachian belt—are the early deposits of rifted continental margins as proto–North America was emerging as a separate continental mass (Fig. 8–18).

During the transition from Late Proterozoic to Early Paleozoic, the rifted continental margins evolved into long, linear, subsiding basins called *continental margin basins* (= geosyncline; see Chapter 6). In these there accumulated thick sequences of sediment, which made up a continental shelf–slope-rise wedge. During the initial stages of rifting, three rift arms developed about 120° apart. Two of these evolved into an incipient rift ocean basin to inaugurate the *Wilson Cycle* of ocean-basin opening and closing. The third arm of the rift system, called an **aulacogen,** developed as a linear, fault-bounded basin trending into the interior of the continental block (Fig. 8–18). The aulacogens represent the failed or aborted attempt at complete rifting. These failed arms eventually became filled with sedimentary deposits and were incorporated into the continental structure. The Upper Proterozoic Grand Canyon Supergroup probably represents the sedimentary fill of one of these aulacogens. The continental margin basins became established once large-scale subsidence of thermally cooled lithosphere began, and continued to evolve in a setting marginal to the rift ocean basin.

In a number of localities (Fig. 8–19), peculiar pebbly mudstones called **diamictites** of Late Proterozoic age have been interpreted by many workers as being of glacial origin. The scattered pebbles, embedded in the muddy matrix of some argillite beds, are composed of a great variety of rock types representing a variety of source terranes, and appear to have been dropped onto the site of deposition from above. Similar dropstones occur in the muddy deposits of modern polar seas where floating icebergs have rafted coarse glacial debris away from land areas and delivered it to the ocean floor. Late Proterozoic glaciomarine deposits, as well as tillites, have been recognized on all the continents,

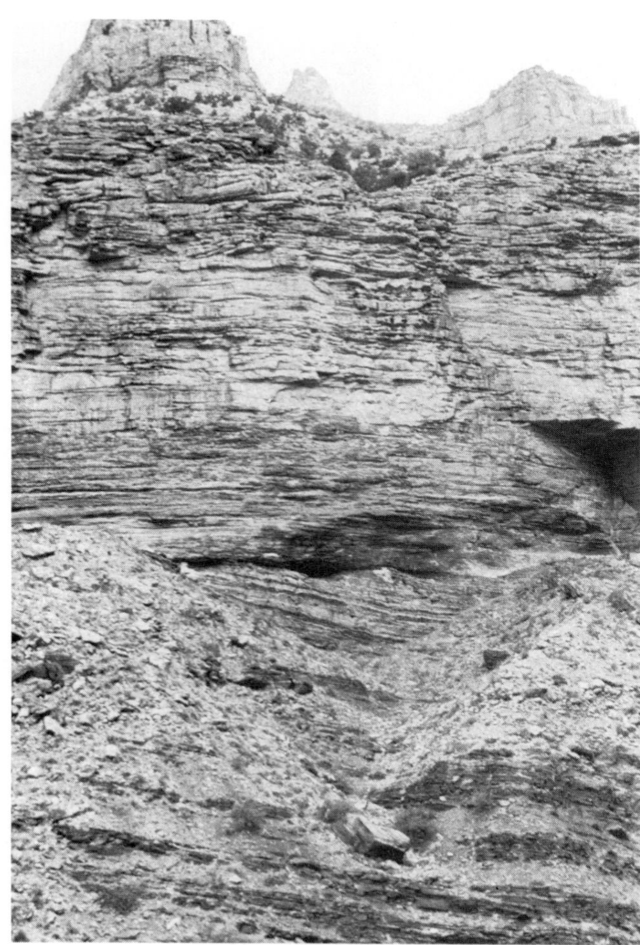

Figure 8–15
Angular unconformity between Cambrian Tapeats Sandstone and strata of Proterozoic Grand Canyon Supergroup, Grand Canyon, Arizona.
(Photo by J. D. Cooper)

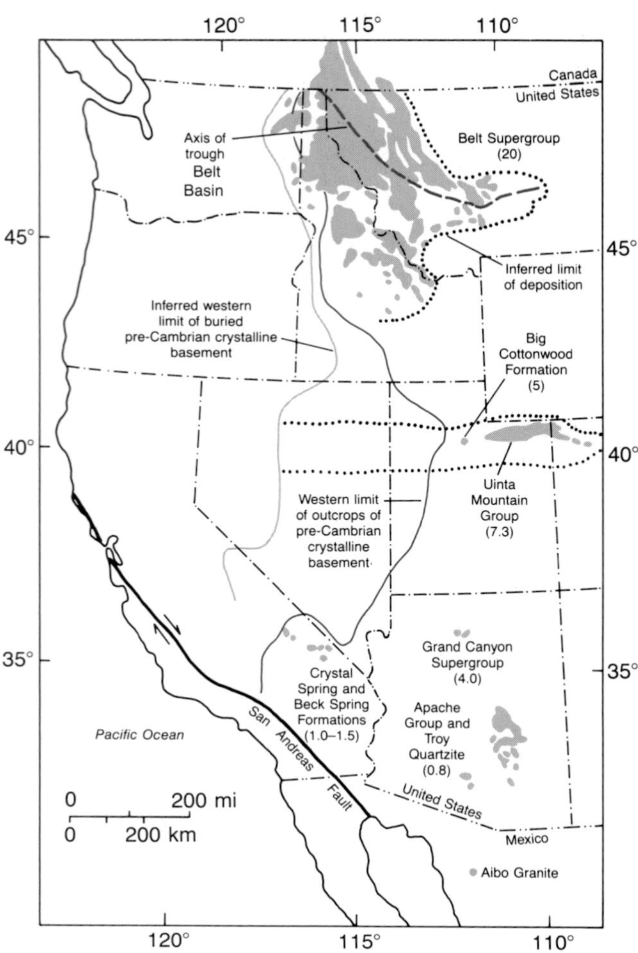

Figure 8–16
Distribution and inferred basins of deposition of Middle and Late Proterozoic (900?–1450? Ma) rocks of the Belt Supergroup and related strata, and known and inferred western limit of Precambrian crystalline basement rocks (1450?–2400 Ma), western United States. Numbers are maximum thicknesses in kilometers.
(From J. H. Stewart, 1982, Regional Relations of Proterozoic Z and Lower Cambrian Rocks in the Western United States and Northern Mexico, Fig. 2, p. 172: Geological Society of America Cordilleran Section Guidebook)

attesting to a time of global refrigeration and large-scale glaciation as a giant supercontinent was beginning to split apart.

Evolution of the Lithosphere

Evidence from the Archean

The progressive increase in granitic lithosphere during the Archean is reflected in the petrologic character of detrital sediments. Most Lower Archean sedimentary sequences typically consist of compositionally and texturally immature rocks rich in plagioclase feldspar, mafic minerals, and mafic rock fragments. Graywackes typically contain abundant basalt fragments. Granites are typically sodium-rich and the rare-earth and large-ion-element content of sedimentary rocks reflect mantle abundances and geochemistries.

In Upper Archean sedimentary rocks, volcanic rock fragments and plagioclase are still abundant, but appreciable amounts of quartz and potassium feldspar are also present. The presence of these last two minerals signals the existence of significant amounts of continental-type granitic rocks, and bears evidence that large tracts of continental lithosphere were being eroded by this time. Poorly sorted and angular detrital grains in Archean sedi-

A

B

Figure 8–17

Proterozoic sedimentary sequences. A. Belt Supergroup, Waterton-Glacier International Peace Park, Montana. B. Uinta Mountain Group, Uinta Mountains, Utah.

(Photos by J. D. Cooper)

LATE-MIDDLE PROTEROZOIC
LATE PROTEROZOIC
EARLY PALEOZOIC

A1. >900? Ma
B2. 900? Ma
B3. 900?–650? Ma
C4. 650?–560? Ma

Incipient rift
Intra-rift deposits
Thermal bulge
Initial rift margin deposits
Spreading center
Rift highlands
Thermal bulge

60N
66N
60N
100E
130E
49N
100W
a
b
c
d
1
2
3
4
5
6
7
8

SIBERIA
NORTH AMERICA
SIBERIA
NORTH AMERICA

A
B
C

Figure 8–18

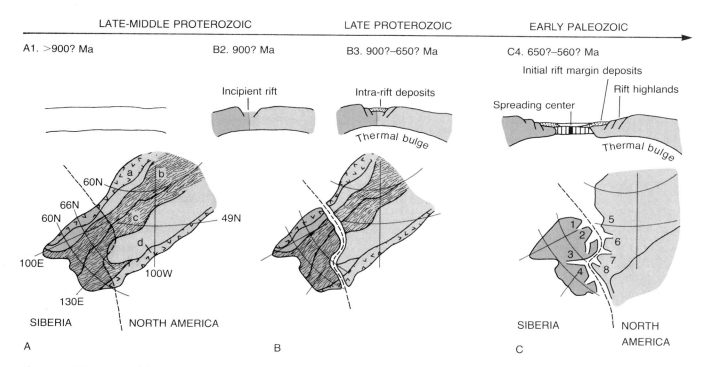

Tectonic model of Late Proterozoic development of continental margin of western United States, invoking a Siberian connection. A. Prerift phase. B. Early rift phase. C. Separation of North American and Siberian continents by rift ocean. Letters in A represent volcanic-plutonic and orogenic belts; numbers in C represent aulacogens along continental margins.

(Cross-sections from J. H. Stewart, 1982, Regional Relations of Proterozoic Z and Lower Cambrian rocks in the Western United States and Northern Mexico, Fig. 11, p. 183: Geological Society of America Cordilleran Section Guidebook, used with permission of the author. Plan views from J. W. Sears and R. A. Price, 1978, The Siberian Connection: A case for Precambrian Separation of the North American and Siberian Cratons, Fig. 2, p. 269: *Geology*, vol. 6, no. 5, reprinted by permission of authors and Geological Society of America)

Figure 8–19
Distribution of Late Proterozoic diamictites plotted on the Late Proterozoic supercontinent reconstruction of Piper (1976). Also shown are boundaries of Proterozoic continental margin basins. (From B. F. Windley, *The Evolving Continents*, Fig. 7–3, p. 121. Copyright © 1977, John Wiley & Sons, Ltd. Reproduced by permission of John Wiley & Sons, Ltd.)

mentary rocks, as well as associated volcaniclastic rocks, suggest rapid erosion and deposition in volcanically active, structurally mobile basins.

These rock suites, generally associated with the greenstone belts described earlier, indicate crustal instability and are similar to present-day island-arc sediments. The comparatively small volumes of quartzite and carbonate rocks suggest that continental shelves were at best poorly developed during most of Archean time. During the Archean the crust was thinner than at present, and microcontinental masses gradually assembled and combined to form larger continents. Large-scale formation of granite during the Kenoran orogeny produced an estimated 60–80% of the present continental lithosphere and the first thick, stable continental platforms.

Evidence from the Proterozoic

The transition from mantle-dominated Archean crust to continental-dominated Proterozoic crust was diachronous and represented a major overturn in the geochemistry of the outer mantle and crust. This transition included major *cratonization* and the large-scale formation of potassium-rich granites. Proterozoic sandstones, in general, consist primarily of quartz-rich graywackes, arkoses, and pure quartz sandstones. The mature quartzose sandstones display abundant ripple marks and cross-stratification; such sedimentary structures, together with the high degree of textural maturity of the sediments, suggest a greater volumetric importance of depositional environments where reworking, sorting, and rounding of grains occurred. The high percentage of quartz is an indication of successive cycles of weathering, erosion, and concentration during which there was progressive enrichment in quartz at the expense of less stable constituents such as feldspar, mafic minerals, and rock fragments.

The Proterozoic sedimentary record thus provides evidence of rapid growth of continental lithosphere, much of it relatively stable and deeply eroded. Associated with the quartz-rich rocks were the first significant amounts of limestone and dolomite and the unique banded iron formations. Abundant carbonate rocks indicate deposition in tectonically stable areas away from the rapid influx of terrigenous clastic detritus. Thus, Proterozoic sediments, in sharp contrast to their Archean forebears, indicate a greater preponderance of more stable environmental conditions, such as we see today on continental shelves. Much Proterozoic sedimentation occurred on broad, relatively flat, slowly subsiding shelves and basins marginal to continental platforms. Early Proterozoic rocks of the Slave Province (Fig. 8–5) represent the oldest well-documented continental margin basin, a long, linear subsiding basin that developed marginal to a continental platform and was the site of accumulation of several thousand meters of sediments. Much of the section is of shallow-marine character.

The continental growth and stability attained by the Early Proterozoic resulted in development of continental margins and interiors that were basically similar to what continents have exhibited during later geologic history to the present. This is in marked contrast to the situation during most of the Archean, when continental masses were small and continental crust was thin. Plate-tectonic activity, as we understand it, probably was not an established phenomenon prior to about 3000 million years ago.

By Early Proterozoic time, however, with increased rigidity of the lithosphere—permanently thick granitic continental lithosphere and formation of relatively stable continental interiors—plate margins became more sharply defined. Continent-to-continent, ocean basin–to–continent, and ocean basin–to–ocean basin interactions and environments began to characterize the global plate-tectonic style that has dominated to the present time. Proterozoic orogenies most certainly are expressions of various plate interactions, including suturing of continental blocks. It was through this tectonic "stitching" together (cratonization) of continental fragments and island arcs, and incorporation of continental margin basin sediment wedges, that the proto–North American continent was forged.

Although the geologic history of many Precambrian terranes is still very sketchy, tremendous advances have been made during the past several decades in providing a clearer understanding of Cryptozoic events and chronology. No longer is the Precambrian as cryptic as its synonym Cryptozoic would imply. The broad outlines of this chronicle have become reasonably clear, but many nagging questions still remain. Several puzzles that are presently occupying the attention of Precambrian researchers are:

How did the Archean continental crust evolve?

Were tectonic processes in the Proterozoic mobile belts different from those along Phanerozoic convergent margins?

What is the significance of the Middle Proterozoic anorogenic igneous terrane?

Evolution of the Biosphere and the Atmosphere

As pointed out in Chapter 7, there are several lines of evidence that strongly suggest the Earth's early atmosphere was devoid of free oxygen. Many laboratory experiments have demonstrated the synthesis of organic compounds under conditions similar to those proposed for the primitive Earth. Such syntheses are inhibited by even very small concentrations of molecular oxygen.

These experiments leave us with the distinct impression that life probably would not have developed at all had the early atmosphere been oxygen-rich. Yet if we look forward from the origin of life to the first appearance of multicellular life, we see organisms with strong oxygen requirements. A paradox? Not at all. The observation simply underscores the close relationship between evolution of the biosphere and of the atmosphere during the Cryptozoic. What were the evolutionary highlights, and their preconditions, from the time when the world was anoxic to the time of oxygen dependency? We will begin our examination of this question by looking at three momentous discoveries made during the 1970s. All shed important light on the earliest life.

Fig Tree Revisited

Until recently, the oldest conclusive evidence of life had come from the Fig Tree Group of South Africa. Recall from the beginning of this chapter that Barghoorn and Schopf in the late 1960s reported cyanobacteria and bacterialike organisms from the Fig Tree. However, with continued work on the material, clouds of doubt arose concerning the true organic nature of the microstructures. Many were of disturbingly large size for prokaryotes and were spheroidal. Spheres—for example, bubbles—can be produced by a host of inorganic processes. Ten years later Barghoorn and associate Andrew Knoll proposed new evidence of life from the Fig Tree, and on the basis of tighter radiometric control, a new age of 3400 Ma. The new evidence from the Fig Tree cherts consisted primarily of nonspheroidal microstructures that were far more convincing than the previous discoveries. Interpretation of these microstructures as being organic rests upon five principal arguments:

1. The new microstructures are within the size range of modern prokaryotes; many of the earlier structures were disturbingly large.
2. The new microstructures form a bell-shaped or polymodal size distribution with a limited range of 1 to 4 microns and have a diagnostic size like that of modern prokaryotes.
3. The new microstructures exhibit a variety of shapes: flattened, wrinkled, and folded, as well as spherical.
4. Some of the microstructures are preserved in what appear to be various stages of cell division.
5. The carbon-12:carbon-13 ratios are too high for inorganic origin, and even suggest carbon fixed by the process of photosynthesis.

These five lines of evidence, considered together, satisfy the requirements set by Preston Cloud to distinguish true fossils from pseudofossils or dubiofossils. So then, if prokaryotes were well established 3400 million years ago, how much further

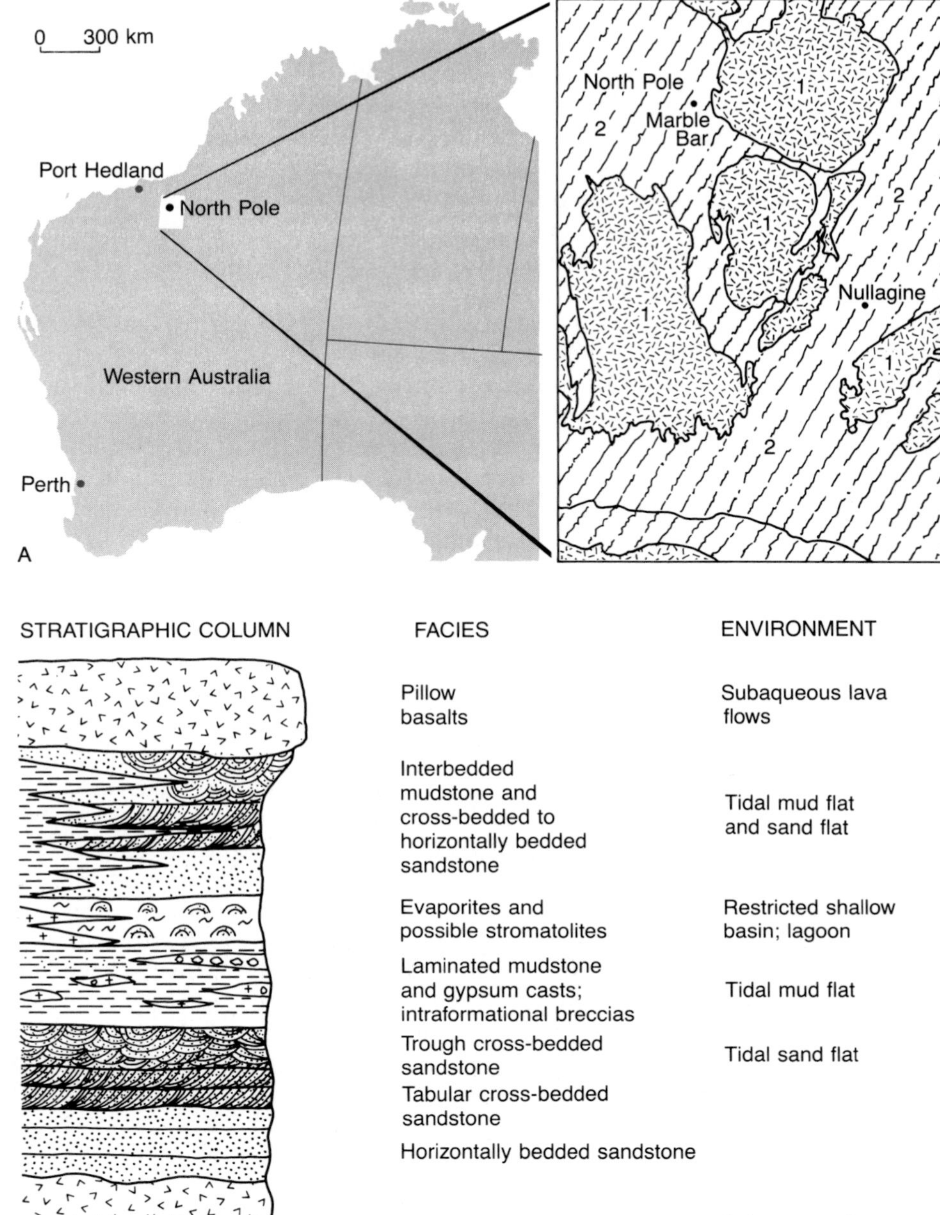

Figure 8–20
A. Western Australia, showing location of North Pole region of the Pilbara block and regional geology of granite basement (1) and greenstone belts (2). B. North Pole sedimentary rocks and volcanics, showing facies and interpreted environments. (Data from D. I. Groves, J. S. R. Dunlop, and Roger Buick, 1981, An Early Habitat of Life: *Scientific American,* vol. 245, no. 4)

back in time shall we seek the origin of life itself? Certainly one constraint on the evidence is posed by the age of the oldest rocks yet discovered on Earth—3800 Ma for the Isua supracrustal terrane of southwest Greenland. The oldest part of this complex is granite gneiss, but from a metamorphosed banded iron formation higher in the succession, Cloud has reported traces of probable organic carbon; no microstructures were found, however. Could it be that life originated prior to 3800 million years ago?

An Unlikely Place Called North Pole

Yet another major discovery at a place called North Pole in Western Australia has produced reasonably convincing microorganisms from a chert-bearing sedimentary sequence perhaps as old as 3500 million years (Fig. 8–20A). This succession, the Warrawoona Group, is part of an Archean greenstone belt assemblage and contains abundant volcanic rocks in the form of pillow basalts and pyroclastics. These interstratified volcanic rocks are amenable to radiometric dating, and abundant isotopic analyses support the approximate age of 3500 million years.

Considering the great antiquity of the North Pole sequence, its degree of preservation is remarkable. As described by geologists D. L. Groves, J. S. R. Dunlop, and Roger Buick at the University of Western Australia, pervasive silicification has preserved primary sedimentary structures such as cross-bedding, ripple marks, intraformational flat-pebble breccias, desiccation features, and structures that look like stromatolites (Fig. 8–20B). Beds of evaporative sulfates in the form of barite are also present. Collectively, the rock types and structures suggest an ancient tidal flat and lagoonal environment, with waters warmed by periodic volcanic emanations, for this paleoenvironment which accommodates perhaps the oldest known biotic community.

Evidence of life in several of the chert beds consists of microstructures in the form of several micron-sized microspheroids and elongate forms resembling filamentous bacteria and cyanobacteria (Fig. 8–21). Stromatolite-looking structures (Fig. 8–22A), some of which are similar in form to modern types growing in a hypersaline lagoon in Shark Bay, Western Australia (Fig. 8–22B, D), also provide evidence of life. Additionally, carbon and sulfur isotope ratios suggest not only the presence of organic carbon, but perhaps also that photosynthesis was going on.

The feature that originally lured researchers to closely investigate these Warrawoona rocks was bedded barite ($BaSO_4$). It was previously thought that such sedimentary sulfate minerals occurred only in much younger rocks, deposited when the atmosphere had attained a significant oxygen concentration. It was also assumed that when the Warrawoona deposits formed, the atmosphere and the oceans were essentially anoxic. The barite appears to have replaced and retained the original crystal form of gypsum ($CaSO_4 \cdot H_2O$), the primary evaporite mineral. Because sulfates are rich in oxygen, the presence of these unusual sulfates at North Pole suggests that local conditions there were more oxidizing than we presume to have been normal for the time. One possibility is that oxygen was being released by oxygen-generating organisms engaged in photosynthesis.

The Methanogens: A Link to the Earliest Forms of Life?

The third major discovery of the 1970s involved biochemical studies of certain modern prokaryotes. Evolutionary paleobiologist Stephen Jay Gould of Harvard University has pointed out that in retracing the course of Cryptozoic evolution it is not necessary to rely solely on the fossil record. An entirely independent signature is preserved in the metabolism and biochemical pathways of living cells. Vestiges of Cryptozoic biochemistries have been retained in certain living organisms. By studying their modern distributions, it is occasionally possible to deduce when certain biochemical capabilities first appeared.

In 1977, a University of Illinois research team announced that a group of bacteria which grow by oxidizing hydrogen and reducing CO_2 to methane (CH_4) are in fact not bacteria at all, but may represent a distinctly different type of prokaryotic life. These microorganisms, called **methanogens,** are an-

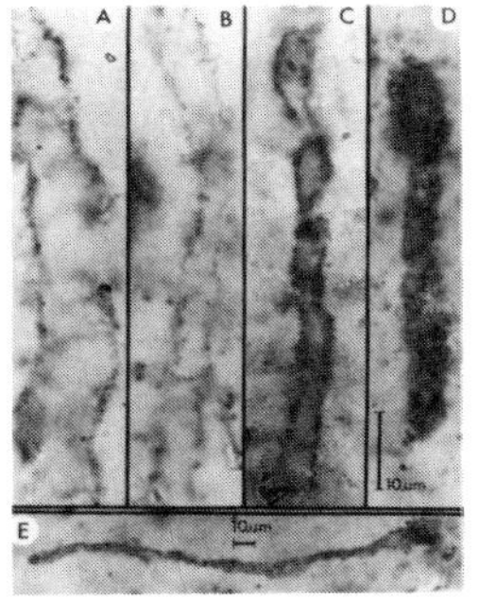

A

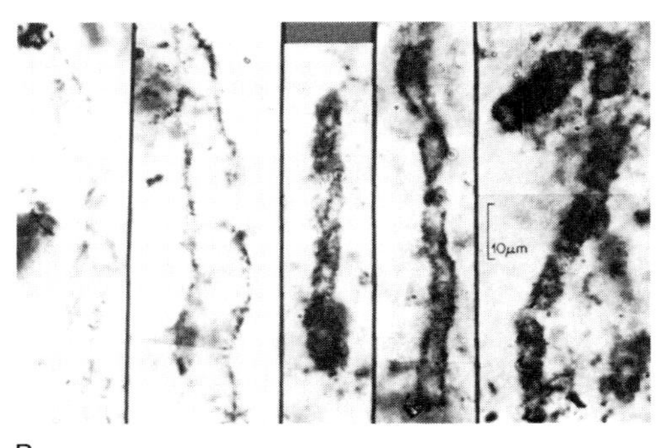

B

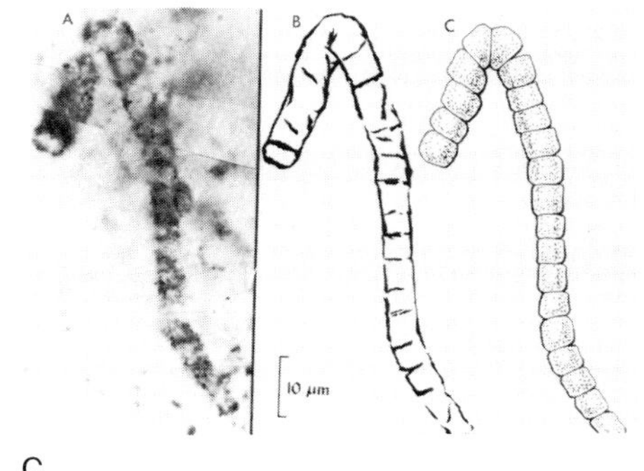

C

Figure 8–21

Microfossils from carbonaceous chert, early Archean Warrawoona Group, North Pole dome region of the Pilbara block, Western Australia. A. Tubular or partially flattened bacterial or cyanobacterial sheaths. B. Elongate, rod-shaped, apparently nonseptate fossil bacteria. C. Unbranched, septate, apparently somewhat tapering filamentous fossil prokaryote shown in petrographic thin section (A) and reconstructions (B, C).
(Photos courtesy of J. William Schopf)

Figure 8–22
Ancient and modern stromatolites. A. Possible stromatolite from 3500 Ma Warrawoona Group, North Pole dome region of Pilbara block, Western Australia. B. Similar-looking, modern-day crinkly laminated stromatolite from Hamelin Pool, Shark Bay, Western Australia. C. Domal morphology and cross-sections of 1900 Ma stromatolites from near east arm of Great Slave Lake, Northwest territories, Canada. (Scale is 40 cm high.) D. Holocene domal stromatolites exposed at low tide, Hamelin Pool, Shark Bay, Western Australia (Scale is 1.5 m).
(Photos A and B by J. D. Cooper; photos C and D courtesy of Paul F. Hoffman, Geological Survey of Canada.)

aerobic; they die in the presence of oxygen. In the modern world, they are confined to unusual oxygen-free environments such as deep hot springs and fetid mud bottoms of stagnant ponds. Methanogens have been known for some time, but the pronouncement that they are different from other prokaryotes came on the heels of the discovery that they have a unique RNA nucleotide sequencing. In fact, the research team that made the discovery believes RNA sequencing to be so significantly different between methanogens and other prokaryotes (bacteria and cyanobacteria) that they are ready to place methanogens in a separate kingdom, distinct from the Monera!

According to Gould, however, the inference of this biochemical difference is that the prokaryotes, including methanogens, bacteria, and cyanobacteria, must have had a common ancestor. Thus, all prokaryotes presumably had the same RNA sequence at one point in their past, and any current measurable differences arose by divergence from this common ancestor. If bona fide monerans (bacteria and possibly even cyanobacteria) had already evolved by the time of deposition of the Fig Tree Group, 3400 million years ago, then the common ancestor of methanogens and monerans must have existed even earlier.

We have good reason to believe that the Earth's original atmosphere was devoid of oxygen and rich in CO_2, the very conditions under which methanogens thrive and under which the Earth's original life might have evolved. Two workers, W. B. N. Berry and P. Wilde at the University of California–Berkeley, have postulated that the world's first biota might have evolved prior to 3900 million years ago—when geothermal energy was more readily available than photic energy—at Archean analogues of modern oceanic hydrothermal vents.

Could methanogens be a remnant of the world's first biota—a biota that evolved to match the

Earth's primordial conditions, but one which now is restricted, because of the rise in oxygen levels, to a few marginal environments? Just as the Moon provides us with information about the pregeologic history of the Earth (prior to 3800 million years ago—see Chapter 7), so might the modern methanogens give us some insight regarding the world's earliest life.

If Gould's interpretation is correct, the Fig Tree organisms, and perhaps also those at North Pole, Australia, were monerans already indulging in photosynthesis. This is direct evidence of life, in the oldest rocks that reasonably could contain it. By reasonably strong inference there is reason to believe that a major radiation of methanogens predated the Fig Tree and Warrawoona monerans. As expressed by Gould, life probably arose on this planet as soon as the lithosphere cooled enough to support it. Given the anoxic atmosphere, the earliest hydrosphere, a lithosphere that could hold bodies of water, and a period of chemical evolution, "the origin of life might have been as inevitable as quartz or feldspar."*

The Oxygen Revolution: Evidence from Sedimentary Rocks

One important line of evidence that our early atmosphere was devoid of oxygen is found in the study of certain sedimentary minerals from Archean greenstone belts. Workers such as Cloud have investigated the possibility that certain very unstable minerals might reflect the concentration of free oxygen at the time they were deposited. One particular mineral of significance is uraninite. In the presence of oxygen, grains of uraninite are readily oxidized and dissolved. Uraninite probably could not have accumulated in Archean deposits if there had been an appreciable concentration of atmospheric oxygen (as much as 1% of present atmospheric level). Significant amounts of unoxidized pyrite also support the notion of anoxic conditions. But what is our evidence in the rock record for the *timing* of the transition from an oxygenless to an oxygen-rich atmosphere?

Perhaps our best evidence comes from iron-rich sedimentary deposits. The banded iron formations (BIFs) contain iron oxides embedded in chert. Banded iron formations occur sporadically throughout the Archean. They are particularly abundant in stratigraphic sequences of Early Proterozoic age between about 2400 and 2000 Ma. The rich prokaryotic microbiota of the Gunflint Formation occurs in a banded iron formation approximately 2000 million years old. Cloud and others believe the banded iron formations represent the deposits of "oxygen sinks": aquatic environments where oxygen released by photosynthesizing cyanobacteria was quickly combined with free ferrous iron. Interestingly, the time interval of the most abundant banded iron formation development coincides with a major development of carbonate rocks and stromatolites in the geologic record.

Stromatolites are known from rocks 3100 and 2800 million years old in South Africa and Rhodesia, and perhaps from rocks as old as 3500 million years old at North Pole, Western Australia (Table 8–3). However, the Early Proterozoic represents a tremendous explosion in stromatolite development, and with it, a major buildup of oxygen produced by the photosynthetic activity of abundant and widespread mats of cyanobacteria. *Thus, the record of major oxygen release is provided by the banded iron formations, and the record of the oxygen-releasing agent is provided by the stromatolites.*

A final note on Proterozoic stromatolites concerns their use in biostratigraphic studies. Some success has been achieved in a few places by use of stromatolites for biostratigraphic subdivision (biozonation) and correlation. Such applications have been limited in scope because of the difficulty in distinguishing between the effects of evolution and the effects of paleoecology on morphology of stromatolites. We know that stromatolite form is a sensitive indicator of environment (Fig. 8–23), but we do not know much about the evolutionary component—the change in morphology through time. Certainly stromatolite biozones are much more difficult to define than those based on metazoan fossils in the Phanerozoic.

Another kind of iron-rich deposit called *red beds* includes detrital sediments whose particles are coated with iron oxides, mostly the mineral hematite (Fe_2O_3). Red beds are common in many sedimentary sequences younger than about 2000 Ma, but rare in older ones. Curiously, banded iron formations are virtually unknown in rocks younger than about 2000 to 1800 Ma. Although there is some stratigraphic overlap between these two different kinds of iron-rich sedimentary rocks (one chemical, the other detrital), red beds essentially supplant BIFs after about 1800 million years ago.

Is this temporal pattern of change in the character of iron-rich sedimentary rocks fortuitous or real? Pervasively iron-stained red sediments are

*Gould, Stephen Jay. 1980. An early start, *in The panda's thumb: More reflections on natural history.* New York: W. W. Norton, p. 218.

Table 8–3
Major evolutionary events during first half of Earth's history

Age in Ma	Eon	Event	Atmosphere	Evidence
2000	PROTEROZOIC	7 Advent of significant O_2 in atmosphere	Oxic atmosphere	7 Earliest major development of red beds
2200	PROTEROZOIC		Oxic atmosphere	
2400	PROTEROZOIC	6 Major development of aerobic photosynthesis; rapid evolution of cyanobacteria	Oxic atmosphere	6 Major development of banded iron formations (B.I.F.) and widespread, diverse stromatolites
2600	ARCHEAN			
2800	ARCHEAN			
3000	ARCHEAN	5 Beginning of aerobic photosynthesis; early evolution of cyanobacteria		5 Oldest definitive stromatolites
3200	ARCHEAN			
3400	ARCHEAN	4 Early diversification of anaerobic bacteria; first primitive anaerobic photosynthesis; simple prokaryotes	Anoxic atmosphere	4 Oldest definitive evidence of life on Earth: moderately diverse prokaryotes in Warrawoona Group, Western Australia; Fig Tree and Onverwacht Groups in South Africa
3600	ARCHEAN		Anoxic atmosphere	
3800			Anoxic atmosphere	
4000				3 Oldest dated rocks on Earth (Isua supracrustal terrane of southwest Greenland, ~3800 Ma); indicates time of metamorphism of sedimentary sequences and plutonic igneous rocks; presence of possible organic carbon and B.I.F.
4200		3 Formation of primitive lithosphere, atmosphere, hydrosphere, biosphere		
4400		2 Major volcanism and meteoric impact		2 Lunar craters and rocks
4600		1 Formation of the Earth		1 Age of meteorites; Pb-evolution curves

Information from P. E. Cloud, Jr., 1974, Evolution of Ecosystems, in *Paleontology and Environment: Readings from American Scientist*; 1976, Beginnings of Biospheric Evolution and Their Biochemical Consequences: *Paleobiology*, vol. 2, p. 351–387; 1983, The Biosphere: *Scientific American*, vol. 249, no. 3, p. 176–189; J. William Schopf, 1978, The Evolution of the Earliest Cells: *Scientific American* Offprint no. 1402, W. H. Freeman, San Francisco; 1983, *Earth's Earliest Biosphere: Its Origin and Evolution*: Princeton University Press, Princeton, NJ.

conventionally attributed to oxidation of iron by free oxygen in the atmosphere, and are most common in nonmarine (subaerially exposed) environments. Could it be that the onset of red beds (and the disappearance of banded iron formations) in the geologic record signals the initial buildup of oxygen in the atmosphere after the oxygen sinks were filled up—perhaps around 2000 million years ago (Table 8–3)?

Photosynthesis

Essentially all of the free oxygen in our atmosphere is, and always has been, the product of organic aerobic photosynthesis. Aerobic photosynthesis is a process whereby the energy of sunlight is employed to make carbohydrates from water and carbon dioxide, and molecular oxygen is released as a byproduct. Aerobic photosynthesis is performed by cyano-

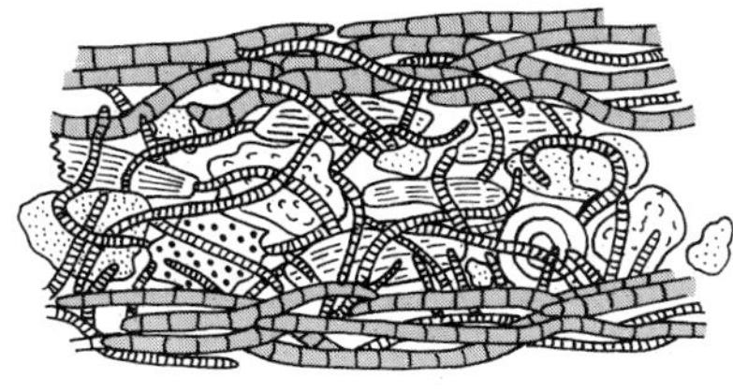

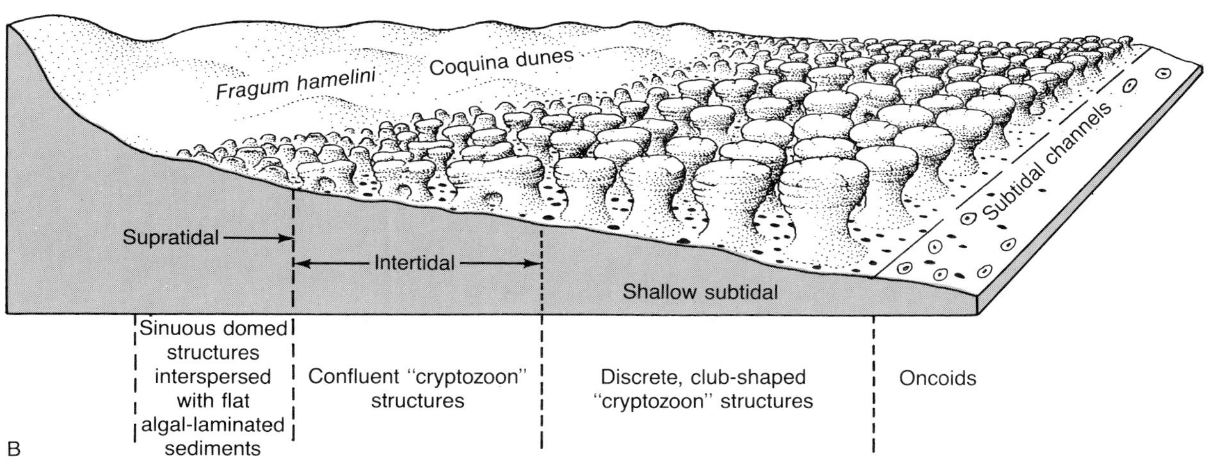

Figure 8–23

A. Day-night accretion cycle in stromatolites. B. Idealized form zonation of stromatolites at Flint Cliff, Hamelin Pool, Shark Bay, Western Australia.
(A, from C. D. Gebelein, 1969, Distribution, Morphology, and Accretion Rate of Recent Subtidal Algal Stromatolites, Bermuda, Fig. 14, p. 60: *Journal of Sedimentary Petrology,* vol. 39, no. 1. Reprinted by permission of Society of Economic Paleontologists and Mineralogists. B, from B. W. Logan, 1961, Cryptozoan and Associated Stromatolites from the Recent, Shark Bay, Western Australia: Fig. 3, p. 528: *Journal of Geology,* vol. 69. Reprinted by permission of University of Chicago Press)

bacteria, algae, and higher plants, all of which are **autotrophic.** Essentially all of the oxygen produced during the early stages of the oxygen revolution was by stromatolitic communities of cyanobacteria. Modern-day bacteria that photosynthesize are of minor importance, but do perhaps provide us with insight regarding the origin of photosynthesis. Bacterial photosynthesis today is entirely *anaero-*

bic. Such photosynthesis does not release oxygen as a byproduct, and cannot proceed in the presence of oxygen. Anaerobic photosynthesizers employ hydrogen sulfide (H_2S) instead of water, and release sulfur instead of oxygen.

Anaerobic bacterial photosynthesis likely evolved to meet the world's first global energy crisis. The first living cells were probably small spheroidal anaerobes that received their energy by fermenting organic molecules formed nonbiologically in an anoxic environment. But as the "organic soup" became depleted by these original anaerobic **heterotrophs,** there arose a need for an alternative energy source. The importance of such ready-made nutrients diminished, however, when the first photosynthetic organisms evolved. Anaerobic photosynthesis probably evolved among primitive bacteria or methanogens early in the Cryptozoic, when the oceans and atmosphere were essentially anoxic, and reduced sulfur from volcanic-vent outgassing persisted due to the high solubility of H_2S.

According to the Berry and Wilde hypothesis, increased competition for available sulfur probably resulted in more dependency on photic energy. These early photic autotrophs might have lived in matlike communities in shallow water, but under conditions of comparatively low light intensity, which was controlled by the cloudy, CO_2-rich, Venus-like atmosphere. Somewhat later, the quantity and range of light reaching the ocean surface improved, and water-splitting accelerated oxidation (water-splitting is the photochemical breaking of the water molecule into hydrogen and free oxygen). Under these conditions, primitive prokaryotes probably gave rise, as a mutant strain, to the first organisms capable of aerobic photosynthesis; these organisms were the ancestors of modern cyanobacteria.

This new brand of photosynthesis was more efficient as a means of energy and nourishment, and it was selected for (i.e., evolutionarily preferred); however, the molecular oxygen released was a toxin that no doubt poisoned many kinds of anaerobic organisms. J. William Schopf suggests one result: that the new aerobic photosynthesizers were able to replace the anaerobic forms in the upper

Table 8–4
Features distinguishing eukaryotes from prokaryotes

Distinguishing characteristics	Unicellular organisms	
	Prokaryotes	Eukaryotes
Cell size	Very small; generally 1–10 microns	Larger; generally 20–100 microns
Cell organization	Poor	Organized
Nucleus	Absent	Present
Organelles	Absent	Mitochondria and chloroplasts
Genetic organization	Loop of DNA in cytoplasm	DNA organized in chromosomes within nucleus
Oxygen requirements	Intolerance to tolerance	Oxygen required
Metabolism	Anaerobic or aerobic	Aerobic
Energy production	Fermentation or respiration	Respiration
Reproduction	Binary fission	Mitosis or meiosis
Organisms represented	Bacteria, methanogens, cyanobacteria	Protists

Data from J. William Schopf, 1978, The Evolution of the Earliest Cells: *Scientific American* offprint no. 1402, W. H. Freeman, San Francisco.

Table 8–5
Eukaryotic microfossils in Proterozoic rocks*

Stratigraphic unit	Location	Bracketed radiometric age (Ma)	Occurrence of eukaryotes
Olkhin Formation	Siberia	725 (680–800)	Branched filaments composed of cells with distinct crosswalls; resembling modern fungi or green algae
Kwagunt Formation	Eastern Grand Canyon, U.S.	800 (650–1150)	Complex, flask-shaped microfossils
Bitter Springs Formation	Central Australia	850 (740–950)	Unicellular algae containing intracellular membranes and organellelike bodies; four sporelike cells in a tetragonal configuration representing mitosis or meiosis
Unnamed shales	Siberia	950 (750–1050)	Spiny cells or algal cysts several hundred microns in diameter
Beck Spring Dolomite	Eastern California	1300 (1200–1400)	Highly branched filaments of large diameter with rare crosswalls similar to those of some green and golden-green algae
Skillogalee Dolomite	South Australia	850 (790–867)	Similar to those of Beck Spring Dolomite; spheroidal microfossils exhibiting two-layered walls and with medial splits on surface, possibly representing encystment stage of eukaryotic algae; tetrahedral group of four small cells resembling spores produced by mitotic cell division of some green algae; well-preserved unicellular fossils containing small membrane-bounded structures
McMinn Formation	Northern Territory Australia	1400 (1280–1450)	
Amelia Dolomite	Northern Territory Australia	1500 (1390–1575)	
Bungle-Bungle Dolomite	Same region and about same age as Amelia Dolomite		

*The task of identifying microscopic, single-celled organisms as eukaryotic is not simple. Also, precise age-dating is limited because ages of the fossiliferous sedimentary deposits are interpolated between the ages of the nearest overlying (youngest bracketing age) and underlying (oldest bracketing age) datable rock units such as lava flows. From the information available, the oldest definitive eukaryotic microfossils are about 1500 million years old. Numerous microfossils from older sediments, such as the well-studied Gunflint Chert (about 2000 million years old), appear to be exclusively prokaryotic.
(Data from J. William Schopf, 1978, The Evolution of the Earliest Cells: *Scientific American* Offprint no. 1402, W. H. Freeman, San Francisco)

portions of the mat communities. The anaerobic forms adapted to the underparts of the mats—a place of less light penetration, but also of little oxygen. Many photosynthetic bacteria occupy such habitats today. As recounted earlier, anaerobic photosynthesis was very likely going on during deposition of the Fig Tree and Warrawoona beds 3400 to 3500 million years ago.

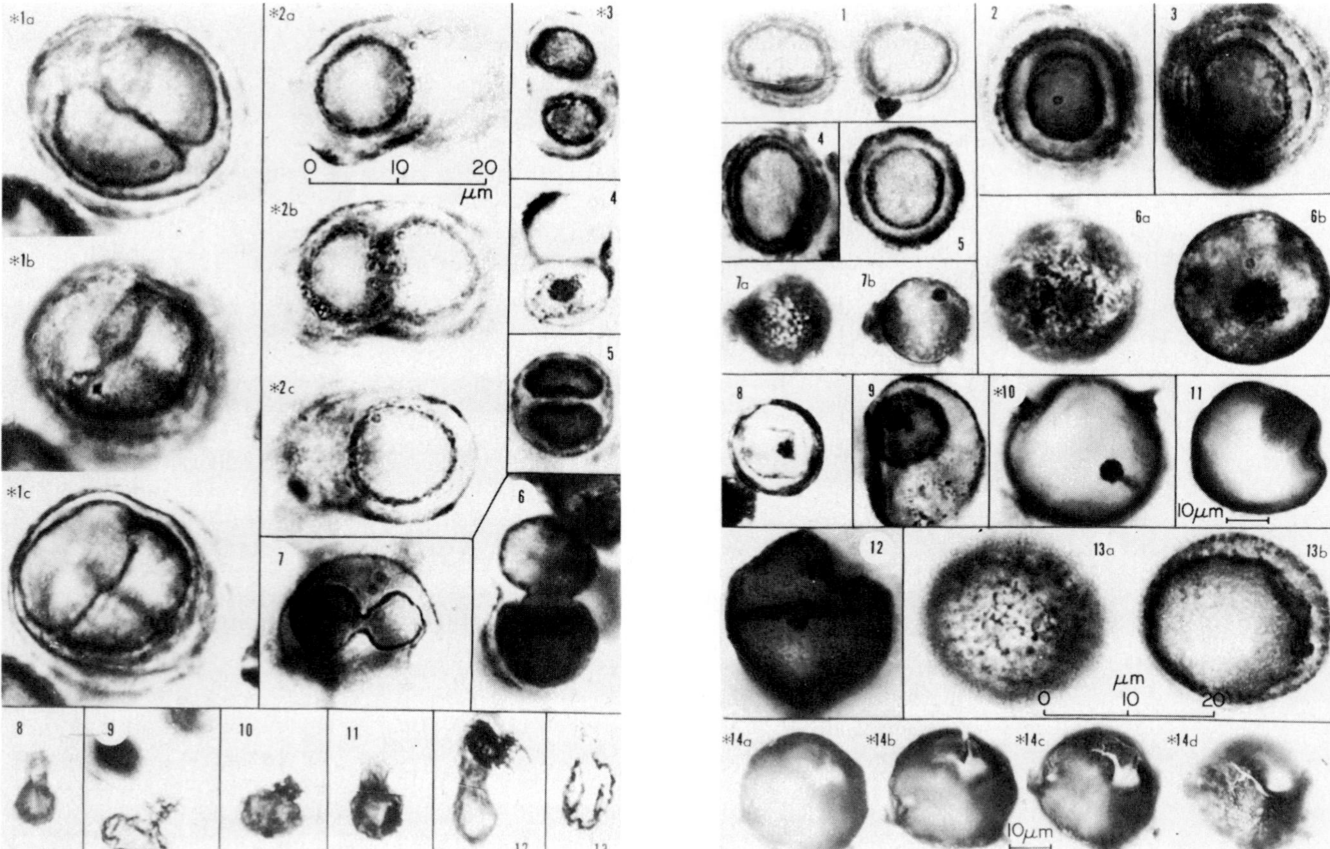

Figure 8–24
Spheroidal eukaryotic algae from bedded, black, stromatolitic chert of the Bitter Springs Formation, Late Proterozoic (about 859 Ma), central Australia.
(Photos courtesy of J. William Schopf)

The cyanobacteria spread rapidly and dominated virtually all accessible habitats by the beginning of the Proterozoic. And with them, the rise of aerobic photosynthesis about 2000 million years ago introduced a change in the global environment that was to profoundly influence all subsequent evolution. Oxygen was here to stay. We customarily think about the effects that the environment exerts on organisms, but during the Cryptozoic organisms had profound effects on the environment.

The Eukaryotes: The Greatest Evolutionary Step

Since the 1960s it has become ever more apparent that the greatest division among living organisms is not between plants and animals, but rather between organisms whose cells have nuclei and those that lack a nucleus. Methanogens, bacteria, and cyanobacteria are the principal types of nonnucleated cells, and belong to the superkingdom Prokaryota. Organisms whose cells have nuclei are called eukaryotes (in Latin, "true kernel"). Table 8–4 shows the important fundamental differences between prokaryotes and eukaryotes.

One particular difference between the two is of great importance in the study of their evolution—namely, the extent to which they tolerate oxygen. As we have already seen, oxygen requirements are quite different among the prokaryotes. Some are totally anaerobic; others can tolerate small amounts of oxygen, and some are fully aerobic. In contrast to this range of adaptations, eukaryotes exhibit a pattern of great consistency; with but a few rare exceptions, eukaryotes have an absolute requirement for oxygen. Comparison of the metabolism and biochemistry of prokaryotes and eukaryotes provides strong evidence that the latter group arose only after a significant quantity of oxygen had accumulated in the atmosphere (Tables 8–3, 8–4). Thus it is appropriate to ask when eukaryotic cells first appeared.

Table 8–5 lists the main stratigraphic occurrences of relatively complex microfossils from Proterozoic strata. Among the oldest definitive eukaryotes are those from the Beck Spring Dolomite of southeastern California—dated at about 1200 to 1300 million years old. These are highly branched filaments of comparatively large diameter and with rare crosswalls; they are similar in some respects to certain green or golden-green eukaryotic algae. Several occurrences of likely eukaryotes have been reported from rocks approximately 1400 million years old in Northern Territory, Australia. Perhaps the most productive stratigraphic unit for early eukaryotes is the approximately 900 million-year-old Bitter Springs Formation in central Australia. Schopf has documented a diverse microbiota of nucleated unicells (Fig. 8–24), some of which may actually show stages of meiotic cell division. If this is the case, simple sexual reproduction had evolved by perhaps 1000 million years ago.

Table 8–6
Major evolutionary events during latest Archean and Proterozoic

Age in Ma	Eon/Period	Event	O_2 level	Atmosphere	Evidence
570	Cambrian	12 Evolution of exoskeletons			12. Calcareous and calcareophosphatic shells
800	Ediacarian	11 Origin and early diversification of multicellular organisms	6–10% PAL O_2	Oxygenated atmosphere	11. Ediacara—soft-bodied metazoan fauna
1000	PROTEROZOIC	10 Diversification of eukaryotes; evolution of sexual reproduction	5% PAL O_2	Oxygenated atmosphere	10. Abundant eukaryotes in Bitter Springs Formation; evidence of meiosis
1200	PROTEROZOIC			Oxygenated atmosphere	9. Increase in diversity of microfossils; increase in size of spheroidal microfossils
1400	PROTEROZOIC	9 Origin of eukaryotes		Oxygenated atmosphere	8. Gunflint and Fortescu diverse microbiotas
1600	PROTEROZOIC	8 Diversification of aerobic prokaryotes			
1800	PROTEROZOIC				
2000	PROTEROZOIC	7 Advent of significant O_2 in atmosphere	1% PAL O_2	Anoxic(?) atmosphere	7. Earliest major development of red beds; youngest detrital uraninites
2200	PROTEROZOIC			Anoxic(?) atmosphere	6. Major development of banded iron formations and widespread, diverse stromatolites; abundant microfossils from stromatolites
2400	PROTEROZOIC	6 Major development of aerobic photosynthesis and respiration; rapid evolution of cyanobacteria		Anoxic(?) atmosphere	
2600	ARCHEAN	5 Early diversification of cyanobacteria; aerobic photosynthesis			5. Definitive stromatolites
2800	ARCHEAN				

Sources as in Table 8–3. PAL = present atmospheric level.

Studies of both the morphology and size (Table 8–5) of unicellular microfossils suggest that in rocks older than 1500 million years eukaryotic cells are rare or absent; in rocks younger than that, such cells become increasingly more abundant. Remember that the moderately diverse Gunflint microbiota, about 2000 million years old, is exclusively prokaryotic; thus it would seem that eukaryotes first evolved sometime between about 2000 and 1500 million years ago; 1500 Ma also is close to the time of abundant occurrence of red beds. Perhaps just prior to 1500 million years ago, an oxygen level was attained in the atmosphere of about one to several percent of the present atmospheric level (PAL), providing an evolutionary opportunity for life to evolve beyond prokaryotes.

The prokaryotes evolved mainly during the time when environmental oxygen concentration in the atmosphere changed from "inconsistently essentially zero" to "consistently slight." However, by the time the eukaryotes appeared, the oxygen levels in the atmosphere were significant and conducive to respiration, which is the central metabolic process of organisms having nucleated cells.

It may seem astonishing that for at least the first 2000 million years in the history of life (more than half!), only the simple prokaryotic level was involved. It is important to remember, however, that major evolutionary breakthroughs, such as the emergence of a new superkingdom (Eukaryota), do not automatically happen with the passage of time. The main prerequisites for evolutionary change are appropriate antecedent biological systems, and evolutionary opportunities. Why the "delay" in the evolution of life beyond simple prokaryotes?

The answer probably lies in the oxygen revolution. The origin of the nucleated cell was the most important, far-reaching step in the history of life. According to Cloud, the evolutionary biogeochemical consequences of this important innovation included, among others: increases in atmospheric O_2 and CO_2, increase in carbonate rocks, formation and stabilization of the *ozone* layer, and the rise of sexual reproduction. The first three underscore the profound influences that life exerted on the total environment. Sexuality coupled with increasing atmospheric oxygen levels (to perhaps 6–10% PAL) may have provided the critical evolutionary triggers that promoted Late Proterozoic eukaryotic diversification and ultimately the evolutionary emergence of multicellular organisms about 700 million years ago (Table 8–6).

Evolution of life during the Cryptozoic occurred under conditions that differed greatly from those prevailing today, but the mechanisms of evolution were the same. Genetic variations made some individual unicells better suited to survive and reproduce in a given environment, and thus able to pass on their heritable traits to succeeding generations. The emergence of new forms of life through this principle of natural selection resulted, in turn, in great changes to the physical and chemical environment, thereby altering the conditions and directions of evolution. *Life as we know it could not have arisen in the presence of oxygen, but it also could not have evolved beyond bacteria without it.*

Summary

Pre-Phanerozoic history is subdivided into Archean and Proterozoic Eons (Table 8–7), whose joint boundary has a radiometric age of about 2500 Ma. The Archean and Proterozoic are further subdivided into Early, Middle, and Late Eras, which are chronometric units not based on stratotypes. Cryptozoic, not Precambrian, is the preferred formal term for pre-Phanerozoic history.

The Canadian Shield contains the oldest and most expansive surface exposure of pre-Cambrian rocks on the North American continent. The shield has been subdivided into seven major isotopic-age/structural provinces, separated from one another by abrupt orogenic fronts that reflect major plate collisions. Archean rocks of the shield are found mainly in the Superior and Slave Provinces and consist of long, narrow greenstone belts within wider tracts of granite, granitoid gneisses, and other metamorphics.

The Kenoran orogeny that brought Archean history to a close was largely responsible for transforming what had been comparatively thin slabs of granitic crust into larger volumes of granite that approached the present average continental thickness of about 40 km. By the beginning of Proterozoic time, general lithospheric conditions were much different than during Ar-

Table 8–7

Summary of major events during the Cryptozoic

Age in Ma	Events	Environment	Atmosphere / other	Eon	Subdivision
600	Origin and early evolution of metazoans	Oxic Environment	6–10% PAL O_2	Proterozoic	Ediacarian
			Glaciation		
800	Diversification of eukaryotes and evolution of sexual reproduction				Late Proterozoic
1000			5% PAL O_2		Middle Proterozoic
1200	Oldest known eukaryotes				
1400					
1600					
1800	Beginning of widespread development of red beds		1% PAL O_2		
2000					Early Proterozoic
2200	Abundant B.I.F.s, stromatolites; diversification of cyanobacteria — Glaciation				
2400					
2600	Kenoran orogeny and formation of large volumes of continental lithosphere	Anoxic Environment		Archean	Late Archean
2800					
3000					
3200	Formation of greenstone belts				Middle Archean
3400	Earliest evidence of life				
3600					Early Archean
3800	Oldest dated rocks on Earth				
4000			Hadean (Pregeologic history of the Earth)		
4200	Origin of lithosphere, atmosphere, hydrosphere, biosphere; widespread volcanism and meteoric bombardment				
4400					
4600	Origin of the Earth				

chean time. Proterozoic sedimentary rocks include quartz-rich deposits, banded iron formations, glacial tillites, true red beds, and carbonates.

Beyond the Canadian Shield, exposures of Precambrian basement rocks are present in the cores of numerous mountain ranges such as the Rockies, in structural domes like the Adirondacks, and in deep canyons like the Grand Canyon. These basement rocks are scattered exposures of the stable nucleus of the continent, consolidated through the process of cratonization during the Proterozoic, and representing extensions of the shield to the margins of the ancient continent beneath the cover of younger, Late Proterozoic and Phanerozoic sediments. Precambrian rocks in the Canadian Shield and elsewhere have yielded important economic mineral deposits; e.g., iron, gold, copper, platinum, and nickel.

The Precambrian sedimentary rock record provides important clues regarding the evolution of the Earth's lithosphere, hydrosphere, atmosphere, and biosphere. Early Archean sedimentary rocks are texturally and mineralogically immature, indicating an unstable, predominantly basaltic crust. Late Archean and Proterozoic sedimentary rocks show progressive enrichment in quartz and potassium feldspar, indicating major increase in granitic, continental crust. Compared with Archean rocks, Proterozoic sedimentary rock suites are more texturally and mineralogically mature, contain more abundant shallow-water sedimentary structures and more carbonates, and indicate widespread deposition in more stable continental shelf settings. Late Proterozoic sedimentary rocks of the Appalachian and Cordilleran belts are the deposits of rifted continental margins, and signify the breakup of a supercontinent.

The Early Archean atmosphere was probably devoid of oxygen but rich in CO_2, as suggested by the presence of unoxidized unstable minerals such as uraninite and pyrite in sediments. The origin of life came about under oxygen-deficient conditions. The oldest known fossils are bacterialike structures preserved in cherts of greenstone belts in South Africa and Western Australia. Free oxygen in the oceans presumably was furnished by water splitting and later by oxygen-releasing photosynthesis. Banded iron formations suggest that oxygen was quickly tied up with iron and silica in aquatic environments that acted as oxygen "sinks." Extensive development of banded iron formations during the Early Proterozoic coincides with significant buildup of carbonate rocks and stromatolites.

True red beds formed extensively sometime after 2000 million years ago, and are signatures of the filling of oxygen sinks and release of free oxygen into the atmosphere in amounts of perhaps 1% present atmospheric level (PAL). The onset of red-bed deposition coincides generally with the cessation of deposition of banded iron formations and represents increased production of oxygen by aerobic photosynthesis.

The origin of the nucleated cell and thus the emergence of the superkingdom Eukaryota was the most important, far-reaching evolutionary step in the history of life. Essentially all known eukaryotes require oxygen for their metabolism. Their first appearance in the geologic record, some time between 2000 and 1500 million years ago, is evidence that significant amounts of free oxygen, conducive to respiration, were present in the environment. Increasing atmospheric oxygen levels, coupled with the rise of sexual reproduction, provided the evolutionary triggers that promoted Late Proterozoic eukaryotic diversification. Change in life and the chemistry of the oceans and atmosphere during the Cryptozoic is largely a story of the oxygen revolution. Life as we know it could not have arisen in the presence of oxygen, but it could not have evolved beyond bacteria without it.

Suggestions for Further Reading

Cloud, P. E. 1983. The biosphere. *Scientific American* 249(3):176–89.

Cloud, P. E. 1988. *Oasis in space: Earth history from the beginning.* New York: W. W. Norton & Co.

Dott, R. H., Jr., and T. L. Batten. 1987. *Evolution of Earth.* 4th ed. New York: McGraw-Hill Book Co.

Gould, Stephen Jay. 1980. An early start. In *The panda's thumb: More reflections on natural history.* New York: W. W. Norton, p. 217–27.

Groves, D. I., J. S. R. Dunlop, and R. Buick. 1981. An early habitat of life. *Scientific American* 245(4):64–74.

Moorbath, S. 1977. The oldest rocks and the growth of the continents. *Scientific American* Offprint No. 357. San Francisco: W. H. Freeman.

Piper, J. D. A. 1976. Paleomagnetic evidence for a Proterozoic supercontinent. *Philosophical Transactions of the Royal Society of London* A280:469–90.

Schopf, J. William. 1978. The evolution of the earliest cells. *Scientific American* Offprint No. 1402. San Francisco: W. H. Freeman.

Schopf, J. William, ed. 1983. *Earth's earliest biosphere: Its origin and evolution.* Princeton, NJ: Princeton Univ. Press.

Walter, M. R. 1977. Interpreting stromatolites. *American Scientist* 65:563–71.

Windley, Brian F. 1984. *The evolving continents.* 2d ed. New York: John Wiley & Sons.

World in Transition: The Precambrian/Cambrian Boundary Interval

Eon	Era	Period		Age in Ma*
PHANEROZOIC	CENOZOIC	Quaternary	Quaternary	2
		Tertiary	Neogene	24
			Paleogene	65
	MESOZOIC	Cretaceous		144
		Jurassic		208
		Triassic		245
	PALEOZOIC	Permian		286
		Carboniferous	Pennsylvanian	320
			Mississippian	360
		Devonian		408
		Silurian		438
		Ordovician		505
		Cambrian		570
CRYPTOZOIC (PRECAMBRIAN) — PROTEROZOIC	Late Proterozoic			900
	Middle Proterozoic			1600
	Early Proterozoic			2500
CRYPTOZOIC (PRECAMBRIAN) — ARCHEAN	Late Archean			3000
	Middle Archean			3400
	Early Archean			~3800
HADEAN (Pregeologic history of the Earth)				
			Origin of Earth	4600

Contents

Key Terms

Ediacarian Period
Vendian System
Laurentia
Tommotian Stage
Adaptive radiation
Boundary stratotype

Miracle of the Ediacara Hills: The Earliest Animals

In 1947 a significant soft-bodied fauna was discovered by paleontologist R. C. Sprigg in the Ediacara Hills of South Australia (Fig. 9–1). Here were found circular impressions resembling jellyfish (Fig. 9–2), preserved in strata of the Pound Quartzite, a stratigraphic unit of presumed Cambrian age. Somewhat later, private collectors found more jellyfishlike imprints and fossils of wormlike forms and traces, as well as some fossils bearing no resemblance to any kind of known organism, fossil or living. These finds stirred considerable interest and prompted the South Australian Museum and the University of Adelaide, under the direction of paleontologist Martin Glaessner, to undertake a joint investigation of the area.

Reexamination of the geology showed that the fossil-bearing strata were nearly 200 meters below the oldest definitive Cambrian shelly fossils in the succession, and were separated from them by several unconformities. Also, preliminary analysis of the soft-bodied fauna indicated that none of these fossils occurred with known Cambrian fossils. These observations conclusively demonstrated a Late Proterozoic age for the Ediacara fauna. Regional correlation with rocks bracketed by radiometric dates indicated that the sediments of the Pound Quartzite were deposited about 670 to 570 million years ago.

From the more than 1500 specimens that have been collected at the type locality, about 30 species in 20 genera have been described. Two-thirds of the specimens have been classified tentatively as coelenterates, about one-

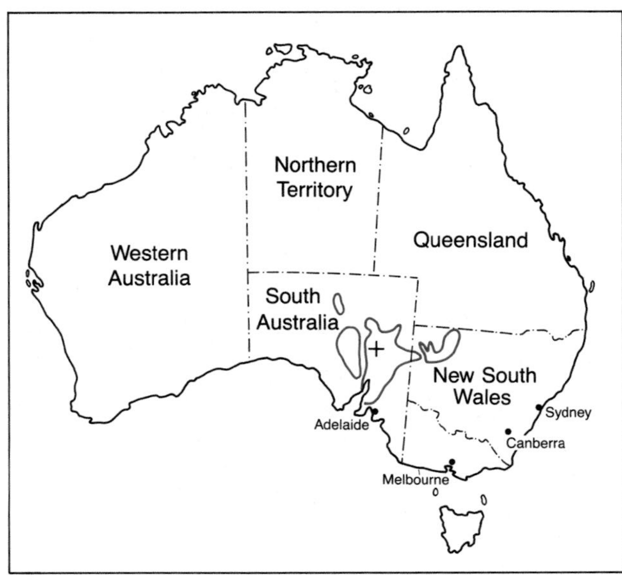

Figure 9–1
Area of exposure of Ediacarian rocks of the Adelaide Basin, Australia, and location of the Ediacara Hills(+), the type locality of the Ediacara fauna.
(From M. F. Glaessner, 1961, Pre-Cambrian Animals, p. 63, *in* L. F. LaPorte, ed., *The Fossil Record and Evolution: Readings from Scientific American*, W. H. Freeman, San Francisco; and M. Wade, 1968, Preservation of Soft-bodied Animals in Precambrian Sandstones at Ediacara, South Australia: *Lethaia*, vol. 1)

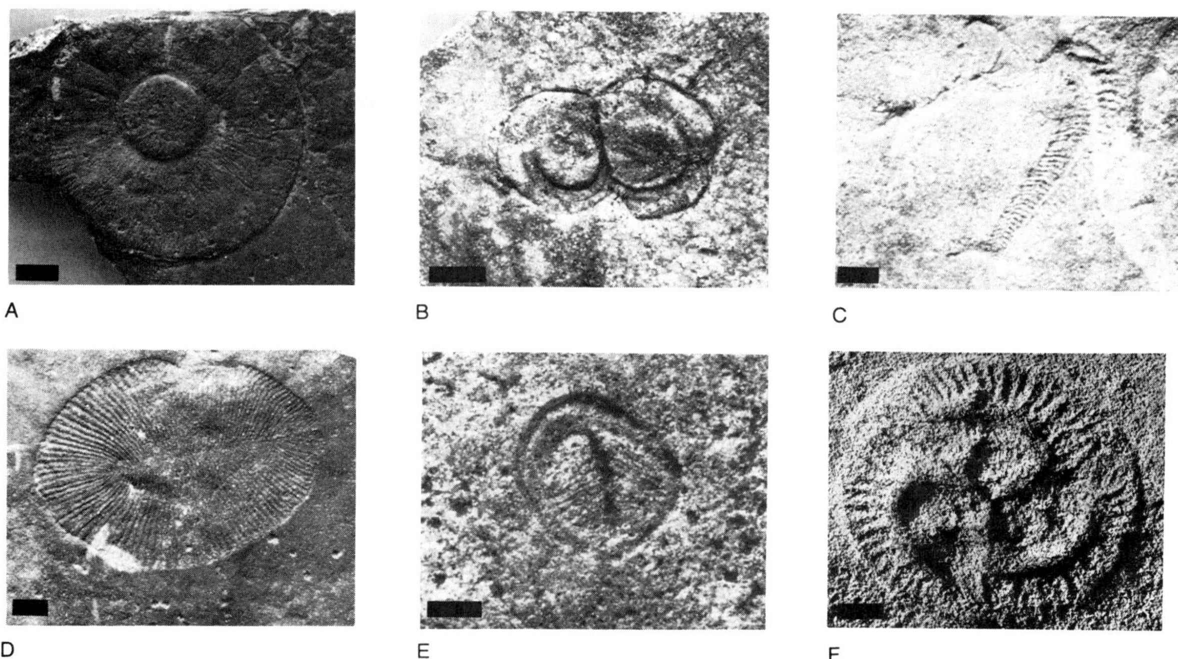

Figure 9–2
Ediacarian fossils from the Pound Quartzite, South Australia. Primitive coelenterates: A. *Charodiscus;* B. *Cyclomedusa.* Primitive annelid flatworms: C. *Spriggina floundersi;* D. *Dickinsonia costata.* Primitive arthropod(?): E. *Parvancorina minchami.* Primitive echinoderm(?): F. *Tribrachidium.* Bars = 1 cm.
(Photos courtesy of M. F. Glaessner)

quarter as annelid worms, and about one-twentieth as arthropods. According to Glaessner, the coelenterates include abundant and moderately diverse medusoid jellyfishlike plans (Fig. 9–2A, B), as well as leaflike or frondlike stalked forms similar to modern-day sea pens. The annelids are represented by small wormlike forms; some had flexible, segmented bodies, paired appendages, and head shields, as displayed by the genus *Spriggina* (Fig. 9–2C), while others, like *Dickinsonia* (Fig. 9–2D), were bilaterally symmetrical, elliptical forms covered with distinctly patterned ridges and grooves.

Primitive arthropodlike animals are represented by *Parvancorina* (Fig. 9–2E), which has a kite-shaped body form with a mid-ridge and hints of legs or gills. The strange-looking disc-shaped *Tribrachidium* (Fig. 9–2F), possibly a primitive echinoderm, has three raised hooked and tentacle-fringed arms radiating at equal angles; nothing like it has ever been described from among the approximately two million species of extinct and living organisms. Trace fossils represented by feeding trails, possibly made by wormlike creatures, are also present.

Most of the specimens are preserved as casts or molds on the bottom surfaces of sandstone beds—a seemingly much more difficult way to preserve soft-bodied structures than by carbonaceous films in shale. Many of the sandstone layers are ripple-marked and cross-bedded, indicating shifting substrate and fluctuating currents—hardly the kind of depositional conditions conducive to preservation of soft-bodied creatures. However, between many of the sandstone layers are seams and stringers of mudstone. As interpreted by Glaessner, the animals themselves probably lived on, or were stranded on, mud flats or mud patches that formed between megaripples and sand ridges during slack-water phases; the soft animal bodies were molded or

Figure 9–3
Interpreted in-life setting of Ediacara fauna. Some creatures shown stranded in small, muddy tidal ponds (a) and on sand flats. Others are shown below the water line. The scene includes jellyfish coelenterates (1); flatworms like *Dickinsonia* (2); segmented worms like *Spriggina floundersi* (3), as well as worm(?) traces (4); the primitive arthropod(?) *Parvancorina* (5); *Tribrachidium,* a possible primitive echinoderm(?) (6); *Rangea* and *Charnia* (sea-penlike coelenterates) (7); hypothetical algae and sponges (8); and a worm in a U-shaped burrow in sandy substrate (9).
(From Martin F. Glaessner, 1961, Pre-Cambrian Animals, p. 72–73; *Scientific American* offprint no. 837. All Rights Reserved. Reprinted by permission of W. H. Freeman and Co., Publishers, San Francisco)

their impressions were cast on the bottom surfaces of layers of shifting sand that washed across the mud as depositional energy increased.

The in-life setting was probably a shallow, nearshore marine environment, perhaps a tidal flat and lagoon (Fig. 9–3). According to Glaessner, some of the animals, such as the frondiform, sea-penlike *Rangea,* lived attached to the sea bottom; some, such as the annelids, crawled along the bottom or burrowed into the substrate; and others, like the medusoid coelenterates, were free-floating or swimming (Fig. 9–3). These strange organisms comprised the world's first known animal community and inaugurated the age of metazoan life.

Ediacarian History

Basis for a New Period

How long before 670 Ma (estimated approximate age of the oldest known metazoan body fossils) did the Metazoa actually originate? The length of prior history of metazoan evolution is unknown. The earliest metazoans must have been the multicellular descendants of protists, but no fossil record of this evolutionary transition has been found. However, if Late Proterozoic metazoans were present prior to about 670 Ma, we should see some evidence of their existence in the form of trace fossils. Interestingly, the oldest definitive animal traces recognized thus far occur in association with documented Ediacara faunas. Some pre-Ediacaran structures described as animal traces have been reported, but their metazoan affinity, not to mention organic, has not been demonstrated. Hence, until proved otherwise, it is logical to assume that metazoans did not make their appearance much before about 700 million years ago.

Ediacaran fossils have been recognized in South-West Africa (Namibia), England, Scandinavia, northern and southwestern Russia, Siberia, China, and

North America. The Namibian fauna was known before the type Ediacara fauna was discovered, but its pre-Cambrian age was not appreciated until later regional correlations were established. The actual number of Ediacara faunal localities is small, but in all these places the stratigraphic position beneath the lowest known Cambrian strata has been demonstrated.

The widespread Ediacara fauna characterizes a distinct interval of *pre-Cambrian* history. Preston Cloud and Martin Glaessner have proposed the **Ediacarian Period** for the geologic time interval beginning with the earliest appearance of soft-bodied metazoans and ending with the earliest appearance of *skeletonized* metazoans. All rocks formed within this period of geologic history constitute the *Ediacarian System.* However, it should be remembered that there is great difficulty in establishing the synchroneity of both the upper and lower boundaries of the Ediacarian. By definition, a chronostratigraphic unit, particularly a formal unit of the time scale, must have isochronous boundaries. Cloud and Glaessner have even proposed that Ediacarian be included in the Paleozoic, and thus the Phanerozoic, to constitute a new pre-Cambrian system (Fig. 9–4).

This idea has merit in terms of the time scale's reflecting more faithfully what we know about the history of life. Recall that Cryptozoic means age of cryptic microscopic life, and Phanerozoic means age of visible animal life (see discussion, Chapter 8). The Ediacara fauna is composed of visible animal fossils and conceptually belongs in the Phanerozoic and Paleozoic. Certainly, the Paleozoic Era has been extended upward on three separate occasions: (1) the original definition by Adam Sedgwick in 1838 included only the Cambrian and Silurian; (2) Devonian, Carboniferous, and Permian were added in 1840 and 1841; and (3) the Ordovician was named in 1879 as the interval of overlap between Sedgwick's Cambrian and Murchison's Silurian (Fig. 9–4). Thus, the concept of the Paleozoic has evolved to accommodate changing knowledge about the record of the rocks and the history of life. Its downward extension to accommodate the more Phanerozoic-like Ediacarian is overdue.

On a worldwide scale, the Ediacarian System, as defined by Cloud and Glaessner, lies between the uppermost Proterozoic tillites (Chapter 8) and the stratigraphically lowest occurrence of shelly fossils that traditionally has marked the base of the Cambrian System in most classification schemes. The geochronologic data derived from the radiometric dates on glauconite from Ediacarian strata and on igneous rocks that bracket the Ediacarian succession in different parts of the world imply a range in time from about 670 Ma at the base to about 570 Ma at the top. The proposed stratotype of the Ediacarian System is about 380 km north of Adelaide, Australia, near the site where the original fauna was discovered.

It should be pointed out, however, that in 1950 the **Vendian System** was proposed for the sequence of formations from the *bottom* of the lowest Upper Proterozoic tillites to the base of the Cambrian in the Russian Platform region, and that this includes strata with an Ediacara fauna. Thus the stratigraphic terminology for the earliest metazoan-bearing stratigraphic interval is in a state of flux. To further complicate the picture, in China the *Sinian System* remains in use for the same general stratigraphic interval. Most workers seem to have adopted the Vendian, although definitions of the interval vary, mainly because of problems in global chronostratigraphic correlations. The 1982 time scale of Harland and others recognizes the Ediacarian as a series (epoch) of the Vendian System (Period) of the Upper Proterozoic Erathem (Era).

In this text we will employ the term Ediacarian, but for the sake of consistency in following the

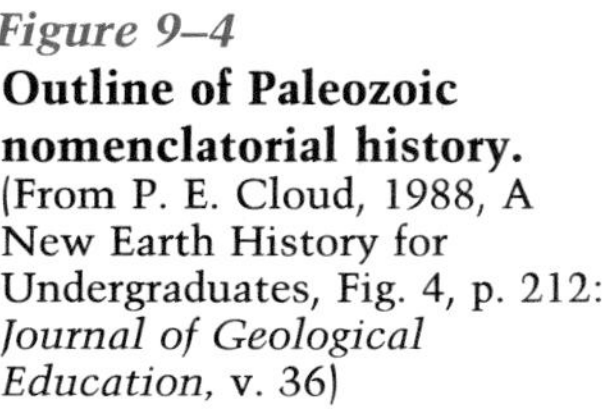

Figure 9–4
Outline of Paleozoic nomenclatorial history.
(From P. E. Cloud, 1988, A New Earth History for Undergraduates, Fig. 4, p. 212: *Journal of Geological Education,* v. 36)

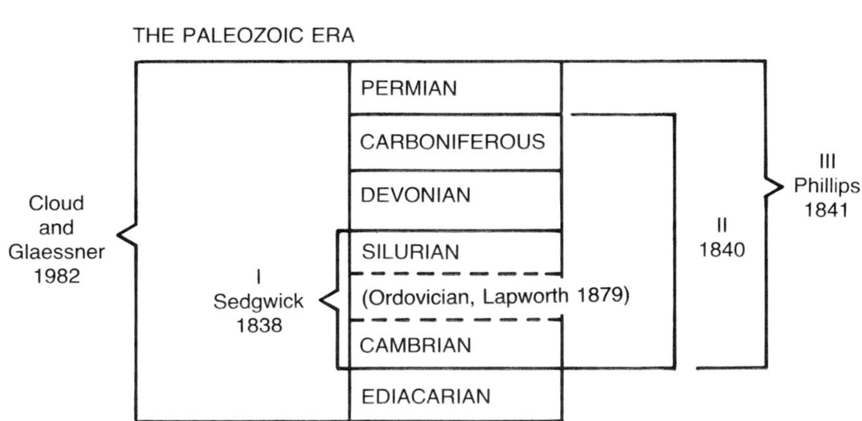

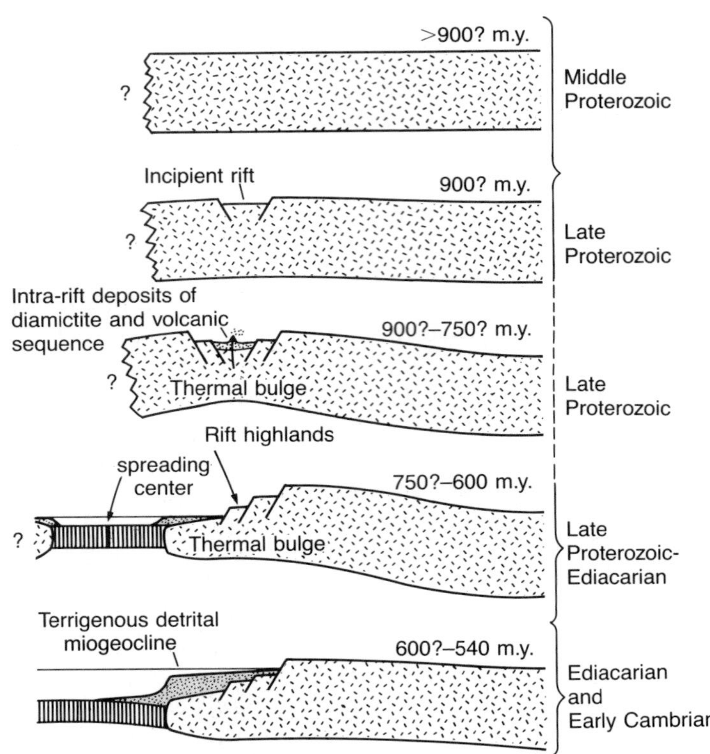

Figure 9–5

Late Proterozoic continental rifting and development of sedimentary deposits of Late Proterozoic, Ediacarian, and Early Cambrian ages along a rifted continental margin—the Cordilleran continental margin basin. (After J. H. Stewart, 1982, Regional Relations of Proterozoic Z and Lower Cambrian Rocks in the Western United States and Northern Mexico, Fig. 11, p. 183: Geological Society of America Cordilleran Section Guidebook)

most up-to-date *published* time scales, we will reluctantly follow convention by keeping it in the Late Proterozoic, even though we believe it conceptually belongs in the Phanerozoic. (Ediacar*ian* will be used for the time interval; Ediacar*a* will be used for the fauna.)

Ediacarian of North America

In North America, Cambrian strata generally rest nonconformably on pre-Cambrian crystalline basement rocks; however, in some places along the margins of the continent, Cambrian rocks appear to be essentially conformable with underlying pre-Cambrian strata. Documented accounts of Ediacarian fossils are rare but do include specimens from stratigraphic successions in Newfoundland and North Carolina. In a number of places, strata of Ediacarian age are presumed to be present on the basis of stratigraphic position and apparent conformity with overlying definitive Cambrian rocks.

Sedimentary rocks in a continental margin basin setting, filling the hiatus of a pre-Cambrian/Cambrian unconformity developed in a more cratonic setting, are believed to be the deposits of rifted continental margins (Fig. 9–5). This rifting of a Late Proterozoic supercontinent resulted in several separate continents, including **Laurentia,** the ancient North American continent. The rifted margins of Laurentia evolved into major subsiding depositional basins. Two major *continental margin basins,* the *Appalachian* and *Cordilleran* (Fig. 9–6), rimmed the tectonically more stable interior platform region or nucleus of the continent, the *craton,* during latest Proterozoic and early Paleozoic time. Subsidence of these long, linear basins was related to lithospheric cooling and sediment loading following thermal stretching during and shortly after initial rifting (Fig. 9–5). Throughout their later history, these continental margin basins were at times active loci for accumulation of thick sedimentary sequences, and at other times sites of active mountain building.

Good exposures of the Upper Proterozoic–Cambrian transition stratigraphic interval occur in the Appalachian Mountain belt (particularly in Newfoundland), the Canadian Cordillera, and the southwestern Great Basin of eastern California and southern Nevada.

Significance of the Ediacara Fauna

Recall from the introduction to Chapter 8 (Life Before Trilobites) that as recently as the middle of this century, the earliest known fossils had all come from rocks of Cambrian age; they included

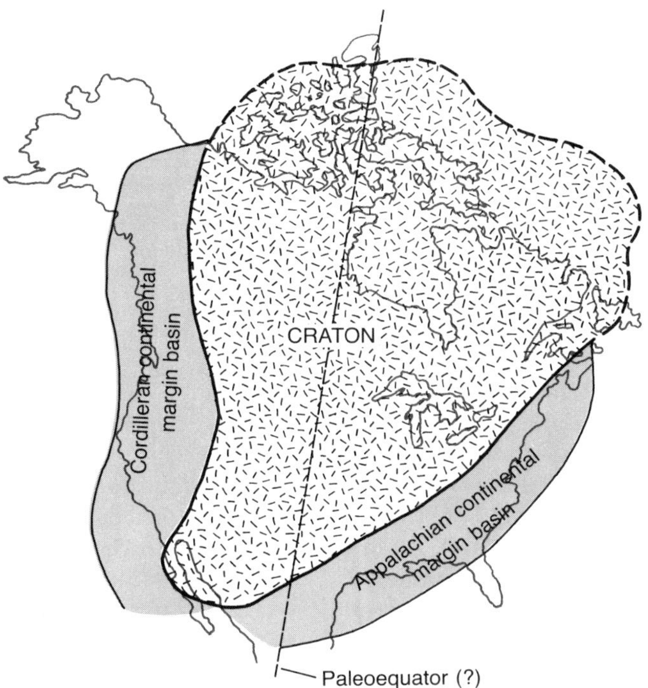

Figure 9–6
Laurentia (proto–North America) during Ediacarian time, showing relationship between exposed craton of Precambrian basement rocks flanked by newly developed continental margin basins (geosynclines).

animal assemblages, dominated by the trilobites, that had body plans similar to those of a number of living animals. The apparently sudden appearance of such animal fossils in the lowest Cambrian strata and the absence of animal fossils in Precambrian rocks made this most important of stratigraphic boundaries comparatively easy to define, but posed a perplexing question: where were the ancestral forms that had given rise to these plentiful, advanced, and diverse early sea animals? This dichotomy made the boundary between the Precambrian and Cambrian the most important of all the dividing lines in the geologic time scale—the boundary separating two great eons of time—the dividing line between the Cryptozoic and Phanerozoic.

Discovery of the Ediacara fauna marked the beginning of laying to rest the speculation about what kind of life existed prior to the Cambrian. The fauna itself marked the beginning of a distinct phase of metazoan life earlier than the Cambrian. Thus its Late Proterozoic (pre-Cambrian) age had important ramifications for what the pre-Cambrian/Cambrian boundary signified in terms of the history of life. In this light, the Ediacara fauna represents Phase I of three evolutionary phases comprising the *transition* from Precambrian to Cambrian (or stated another way, from Cryptozoic to Phanerozoic). Phases II and III of this evolutionary transition include skeletal faunas that predate the first appearance of trilobites.

The Ediacarian partly fills the hiatus that many early stratigraphers long felt existed at the supposed worldwide unconformity between Precambrian and Cambrian. This hiatus, called the *Lipalian interval* by Charles D. Walcott, provided an explanation for the abundant shelly animal megafossils in Cambrian rocks immediately above Precambrian igneous and metamorphic rocks (Fig. 9–7). The explanation for this seemingly abrupt and mysterious appearance of advanced animals was that the *first* metazoans originated and underwent a long period of evolution in ocean basin areas where sediments accumulated but did not become accessible for examination. Much later, according to this idea, as

Figure 9–7
Nonconformity (contact has been enhanced) between Upper Cambrian sandstone (2) and Precambrian crystalline rocks (1). Colorado River, near Glenwood Springs, Colorado.
(Photo by J. D. Cooper)

seas encroached onto the continental platform interiors during the Cambrian, populations of organisms migrated into environments that produced sedimentary rocks that are accessible (Fig. 9–8). This is an understandable conclusion reached by Walcott, when one considers his devotion to Darwin's gradualistic ideas on evolution. Although representing the triumph of hope over experience, the Lipalian interval, as viewed by Walcott, accommodated that supposed long period of metazoan evolution required by the gradualistic model to lead up to the basal Cambrian fauna of diverse animals.

During the twentieth century, and particularly during the past several decades, increased knowledge of pre-Cambrian rocks and the magnitude of time involved has stimulated a search for the biological conditions that existed prior to the explosive appearance of complex shell-bearing organisms. According to Cloud and Glaessner, this search has revealed the existence of some well-preserved sedimentary successions that extend beneath the base of the Cambrian without apparent major interruption (Fig. 9–8). Evidence of marine origin in these sub-Cambrian deposits fueled the expectation that if there were antecedents to the Cambrian biota, they would be found in these rocks. The Ediacara fauna represents the realization of that expectation and gives us a critical look at the earliest known metazoan life forms.

Events of the Ediacarian World

As suggested by its first appearance worldwide above glaciogenic sediments, the Ediacara fauna must have evolved not long after the last major episode of Late Proterozoic continental glaciation. Various levels of tillites and glaciomarine deposits, dated between 600 and 670 Ma, seem to provide a lower limit to the fauna. Sea-level low-stands during glacial maxima would have exposed new tracts of continental margin areas to weathering and ero-

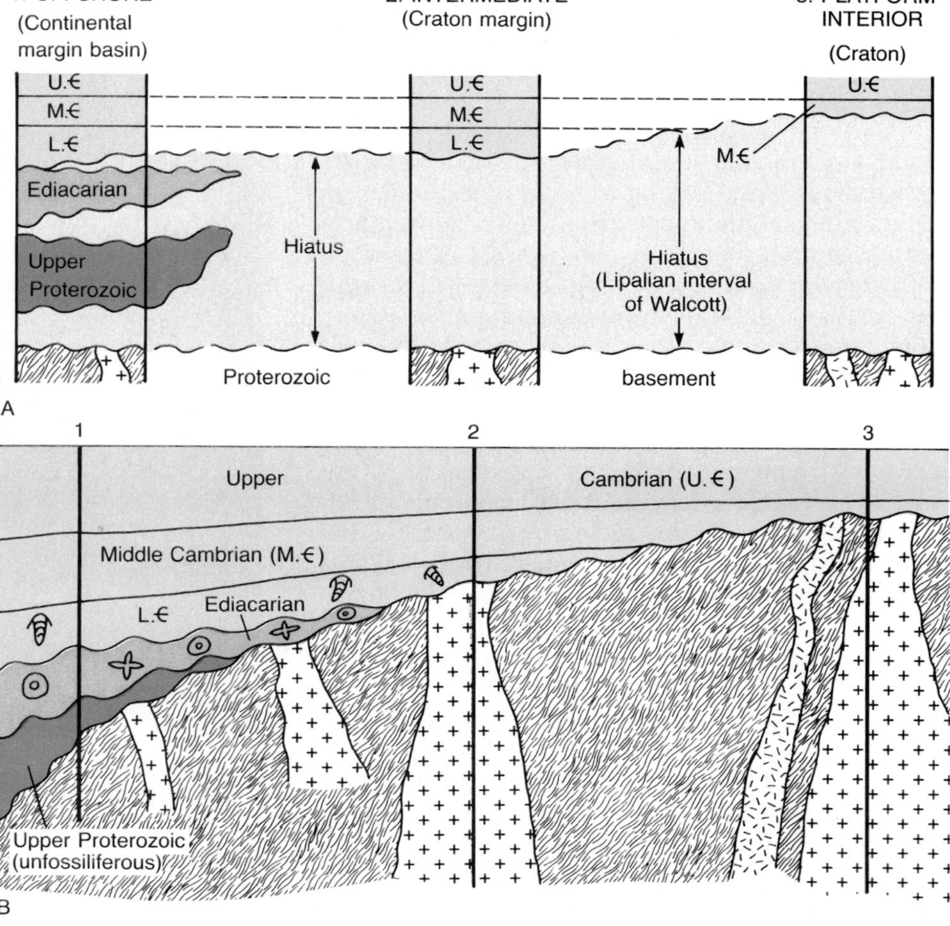

Figure 9–8
Precambrian-Cambrian boundary in cratonic, craton margin, and continental-margin basin regions. A. Stratigraphic relationships superimposed on chronostratigraphic diagram showing hiatus of Precambrian-Cambrian unconformity (the Lipalian interval of Walcott). B. Natural stratigraphic relationships showing progressive overlap of older stratigraphic packages by younger ones, as marine conditions gradually invaded the continental margin and continental interior from Late Proterozoic on into Cambrian time.

sion, resulting in peneplanation. Postglacial sea-level rise presumably would have drowned these flat shelf areas, thus providing extensive habitats for the newly evolved inhabitants of the shallow sea floor.

Geologic and paleomagnetic evidence suggests that during the Late Proterozoic, much of the Earth's land mass was concentrated in a single supercontinent (Fig. 9–9). Continental rifting occurred during the transition from Precambrian to Cambrian, and this breakup produced additional shoreline and shallow marine habitats. This, coupled with the close proximity of the newly separated continental margins, made it possible for the Ediacara fauna to migrate rapidly and widely from one continental shelf to another. The equatorial position of these continental masses (Fig. 9–9), as suggested by paleomagnetic evidence, was conducive to warm, equable climatic conditions along much of the shoreline. General similarities of Ediacara faunal associations worldwide probably reflect the absence of major ecological barriers on continental shelves.

This largely equatorial position, with its lack of temperature extremes, likely had a pronounced effect on food resource level and stability. A lowered temperature gradient between the poles and Equator would have sustained a smaller seasonal overturn of ocean waters. This condition would have resulted in fewer deep ocean nutrients reaching shallow marine waters, thus causing food supplies to stabilize at relatively low levels.

The flattened, flimsy, almost filmlike body plans of most Ediacarian animals (e.g., the pancake-looking *Dickinsonia* in Fig. 9–2D had a maximum thickness of about 6 mm, but a diameter up to a meter or more!) may represent an adaptation to this limited food supply. A body plan with a high ratio of surface area to volume would have facilitated efficient uptake of nutrients from seawater, or perhaps efficient absorption of light by symbiotic algae that may have released nutrients to the host metazoans and removed waste products.

The flattened, air mattress-like body plans of Ediacarian animals might also reflect the comparatively low oxygen level at the time (between 5% and 10% present atmospheric level, or PAL). Barely necessary oxygen levels of about 5% PAL would have limited respiration in early metazoans to be accomplished by simple oxygen diffusion through the exposed body surface, a process favored by naked organisms having high surface-to-volume ratios. Thus, at first glance, the Ediacara fauna appears to have been well adapted to the marine

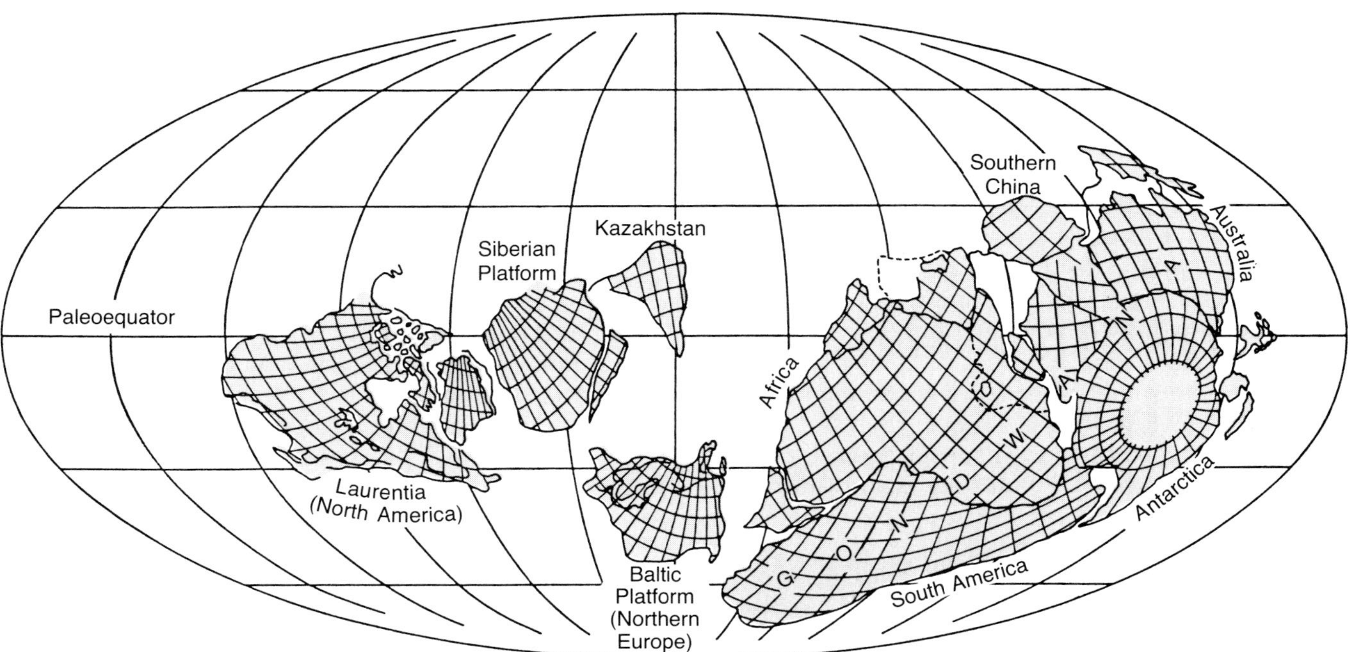

Figure 9–9

Geography of the Ediacarian world.

(From C. R. Scotese, 1986, *Phanerozoic Reconstructions: A New Look at the Assembly of Asia.* University of Texas Institute for Geophysics Technical Report No. 66, Paleoceanographic Mapping Project Progress Report No. 19–1286. Used with permission of the author)

conditions that prevailed during the latest Proterozoic—shallow marine environments characterized by low nutrient and oxygen levels.

Yet another perspective on the flattened body plan shared by most Ediacarian animals is that it is only rarely utilized by modern organisms—and not by any living creature believed to be linked (in an evolutionary sense) to an Ediacarian animal. Adolf Seilacher of West Germany, one of the world's leading authorities on trace fossils and animal-sediment relationships, has argued that interpretation of Ediacarian fossils in terms of modern soft-bodied animals must be reconsidered. He feels that all Ediacarian animals have been forced, often with considerable difficulty, into modern taxonomic groups. Seilacher questions the jellyfish nature of the medusoidlike fossils, preferring instead to relate them to a heterogeneous group of trace fossils and discoid benthic organisms. He attributes impressions of supposed sea pens and annelid worms to unknown benthic organisms having a quasi-autotrophic mode of nutrition.

Seilacher believes the Ediacara fauna represents a distinct low-diversity episode in the evolution of multicellular organisms, and not the beginning of metazoan radiation. The implication here is that the world's first metazoan fauna represents a "first try," a "failed experiment"—that it was replaced after a mass extinction, not simply improved upon and expanded. This is a contentious interpretation at odds with the picture of Ediacarian jellyfish, corals, and worms—a picture suggesting continuity of evolutionary relationships across the Precambrian/Cambrian boundary.

Does the Ediacara fauna represent a unique and extinct "experiment"—composed of small groups that never achieved much diversity, and which bear, at best, only distant relationships with any modern animal? Perhaps we should expect that the early history of any new grade of organic complexity should meet with some failure, but does this mean that the metazoa had to be "reinvented" in the Cambrian? Regardless of the answer, these soft-bodied, flimsy creatures formed the earliest known communities of animals, and they occupy a unique position in the evolutionary history of the Metazoa.

The Cambrian Radiation Event

Earliest Shelly Faunas

Proterozoic–to–Lower Cambrian sedimentary successions in continental margin basins have been studied intensively in recent years, in the quest for data on which a clearer definition of the base of the Cambrian might be developed. These rocks are confined to ancient continental margin basins that developed along the newly rifted continental margins. Work on them has shown clearly that the Ediacara fauna of soft-bodied animals disappeared or became very scarce in the preserved record after Ediacarian time. The Ediacara forms were succeeded by a fauna of small shelly fossils representing organisms *not* descended from members of the Ediacarian assemblage.

As stated earlier, the Ediacarian time interval (period or epoch, depending on which classification one accepts) represents Phase I in the transition from Cryptozoic (age of microscopic life) to Phanerozoic (age of visible animal life). Phase II in this transition (Fig. 9–10), as defined by paleobiologist M. A. S. McMenamin, began about 570 Ma (±30 million years) with the disappearance of the Ediacara soft-bodied fauna and the appearance of the first assemblages of shelly faunas of low diversity, in which about 5 species of shelled animal are found together. These are small, chitinous, calcareous, and phosphatic metazoan fossils of mostly problematic affinity, and are best known from sections in the Siberian Platform region.

An example of one of these early shelly forms is the small (a few mm in length), phosphatic, tusk-shaped fossil called *Prothertzina* (Fig. 9–11A), which is believed to be a grasping spine similar to that of modern arrow worms. If this association is correct, it is the first fossil that can be identified with any confidence as having been linked to a *predatory* animal.

Another common taxon from this phase is *Anabarites* (Fig. 9–11B), a small tube-shaped fossil, with three distinct interior ridges, composed of calcium carbonate. It is a stratigraphically long-ranging but geographically widespread fossil that has been found in Australia, China, India, Iran, Kazakhstan, Mongolia, Siberia, and western and eastern North America.

It should be emphasized here that Phase II does not record the very first shelly fossils, but rather the *first low-diversity assemblages.* Significantly, a few small tube-shaped shelled fossils, including *Cloudina* and *Sinotubulites* (Fig. 9–11C, D), both composed of calcium carbonate, represent the oldest shelly fossils, and occur in association with Ediacarian soft-bodied fossils. Thus it would appear that skeletonization began with a trickle rather than a flood of forms. Although an important evolutionary phenomenon, skeletonization occurred in a number of evolving groups, and developed sequentially, not absolutely abruptly, even though it appears to have been explosive on a scale of several

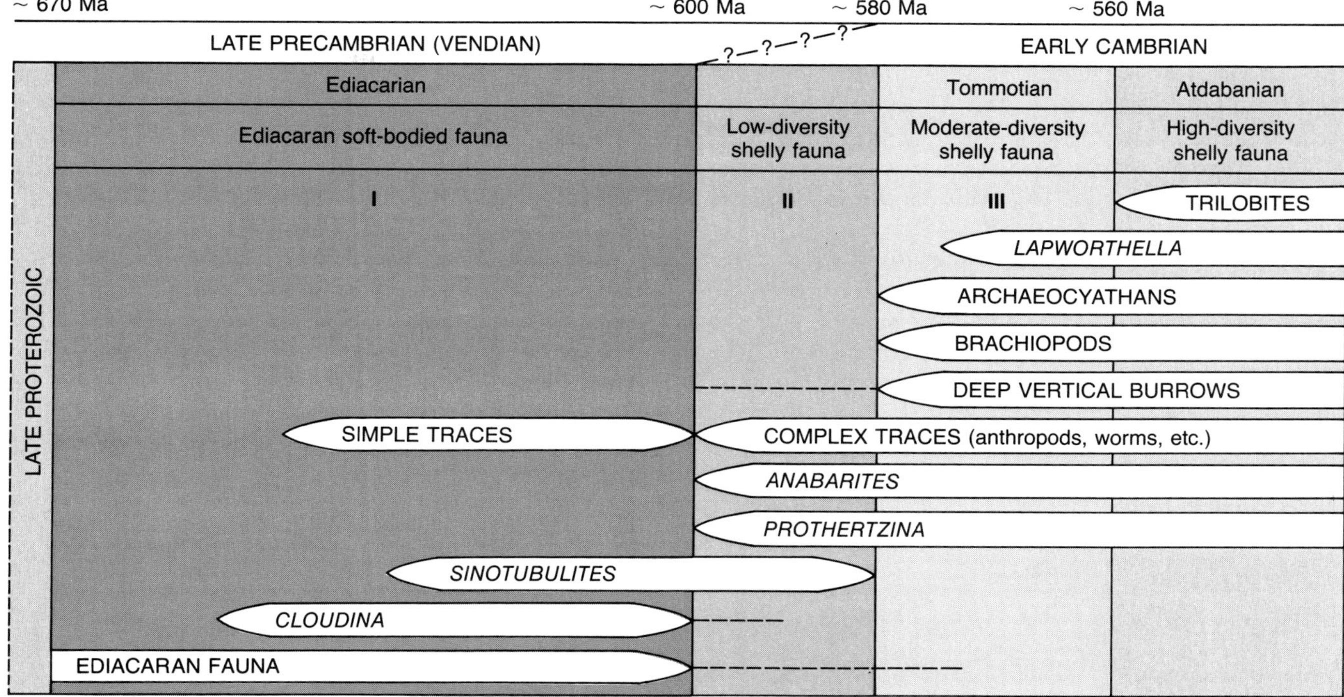

Figure 9–10

Late Proterozoic–Early Cambrian time scale illustrating the three evolutionary phases in the transition from Precambrian to Cambrian.

(From M. A. S. McMenamin, 1987, The Emergence of Animals, *Scientific American,* vol. 257, no. 4, p. 96–97. Copyright © 1987 by Scientific American, Inc. All rights reserved.)

tens of million years. As paleontologist Steven Stanley suggests, it was simply a part, albeit an important one, of the overall early metazoan diversification.

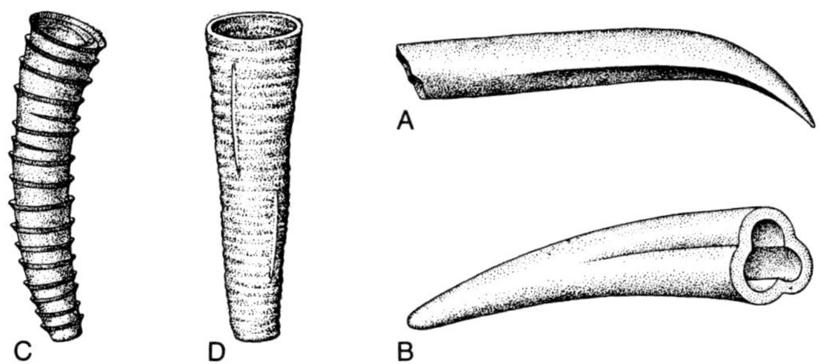

Figure 9–11

Early skeletonized fossils from Phases I and II of the Precambrian-Cambrian transition. A. *Prothertzina,* the probable calcium phosphate grasping spine of an early predator. B. *Anabarites,* a common associate of *Prothertzina* in Phase II assemblages. C. *Cloudina* and D. *Sinotubulites,* tube-shaped fossils of calcium carbonate composition representing the earliest known skeletonized organisms.

(From M. A. S. McMenamin, 1987, The Emergence of Animals. *Scientific American,* vol. 257, no. 4, p. 96–97. Copyright © 1987 by Scientific American, Inc. All rights reserved.)

Along with the first shelly assemblages characterizing Phase II in the transition, there is a tremendous increase in the number and diversity of trace fossils in seafloor sediments. In contrast to Ediacarian trace fossils, which are mostly simple, two-dimensional shallow feeding burrows and poorly oriented search trails on bedding surfaces, the traces in Phase II sediments are more complex three-dimensional forms and include diverse, deep, vertical burrows, intricate galleries and networks, and a variety of trackways. One might argue that the apparent increase in diversity of life from Phase I (Ediacarian) to Phase II is an artifact of preservation bias, whereby hard shells are more apt to leave a record than soft-bodied animals. However, the increase in abundance and diversity of trace fossils in Phase II sediments provides a good index that the increase in diversity of metazoans is real because trace fossils have a more constant preservability.

Phase III in the transition from Precambrian to Cambrian (Fig. 9–10), as defined by McMenamin, and which lasted for about 10 to 20 million years, is characterized by shelly faunas of moderate diversity in which more than 5, but generally fewer than 15, species of shelled animals are found together. This fauna of small shelly fossils underlies the lowermost trilobite-bearing beds in many areas of the world. The stratigraphic interval comprising Phase III is generally referred to as the **Tommotian Stage,** best known from a richly fossiliferous sequence of carbonate strata exposed in the Aldan River area in southwestern Siberia.

The Tommotian Stage also marks the first appearance of the archaeocyathids, a group of unusual, vase-shaped, double-walled, calcium carbonate-shelled creatures that are presently classified within a separate phylum (Archaeocyatha), but which also show many characteristics of certain sponges. Other described taxa from Tommotian sections include hyolithids (extinct mollusclike creatures), monoplacophorans (primitive molluscan class), possible gastropods, inarticulate brachiopods, sponges, probable pogonophorans, protoconodonts, and a variety of problematica that cannot be assigned with certainty to any known phylum (Fig. 9–12).

Tommotian faunas have been found in a number of areas, including Kazakhstan, Russia, Poland, Scandinavia, England, Newfoundland, Nova Scotia, New England, northwestern Canada, California, Mexico, Mongolia, China, and Australia, although precise correlation with the type Siberian Tommotian is commonly questionable. During the time interval in which overlying strata were deposited that are clearly of traditional Cambrian age (the Atdabanian Stage), the geographic range of archaeocyathids expanded greatly, and trilobites, those hallmarks of Cambrian faunas, appeared for the first time and diversified rapidly (Fig. 9–10). Both Phase

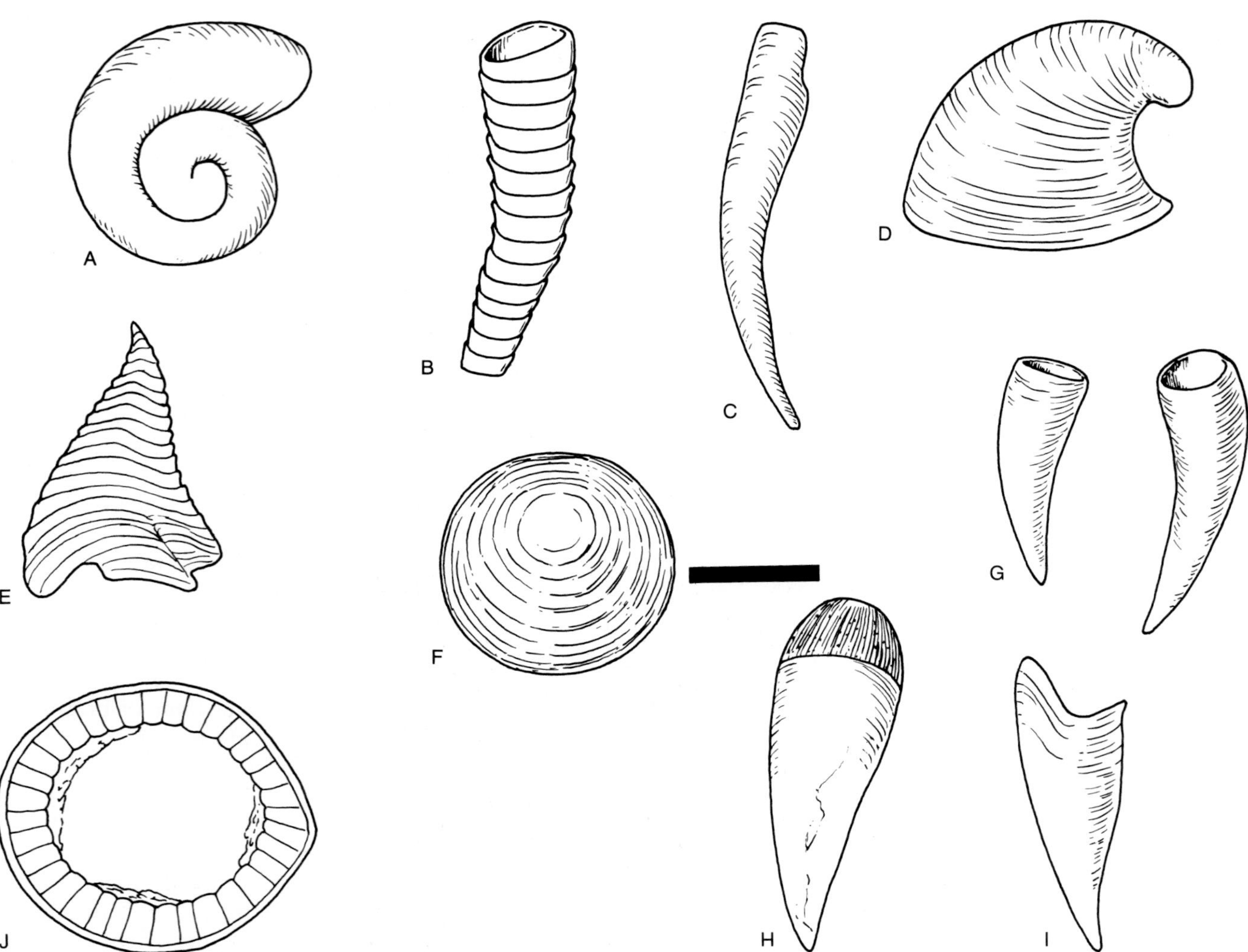

Figure 9–12

Enigmatic earliest shelly fossils from Tommotian strata, U.S.S.R. A–I. Mollusclike calcareous cone and coiled shells. J. Transverse section of archaeocyathid showing double-walled structure. Bar is 1 cm.

(From M. E. Raaben, 1981, The Tommotian Stage and the Lower Cambrian Boundary (trans. from Russian): U.S. Department of the Interior and National Science Foundation, Washington)

II and Phase III shelly faunas also partly fill the gap between the Precambrian and Cambrian, thus further reducing the apparent abruptness of appearance of the first trilobites.

Adaptive Radiation

Thus we see that major skeletonized faunas made their appearance over an interval of perhaps 20 to 30 million years. When viewed in light of the stratigraphic occurrences, this constitutes a major **adaptive radiation**—not as sudden and mysterious as once believed, but nonetheless truly dramatic. The most dramatic aspect of this faunal radiation is the number of high-level taxa, namely phyla and classes, representing radically different kinds of organisms, that made their appearance in such a short time interval (Fig. 9–13).

This appearance of natural new phyla and classes occurred at a scale and rate that has not been matched since. One logical explanation for this "explosion" is that the world was essentially an ecological vacuum for metazoans. This certainly would have been the case if the Ediacara fauna suffered a mass extinction, as some believe. A tremendous number of unoccupied ecological niches were waiting to be filled. New animals burst onto the scene without competition and became the "founders" of separate evolutionary lineages. The environmental opportunities were there; the time was ripe for a major adaptive radiation.

This rapid diversification of animals, although in some ways unique, is consistent with current punctuational models of macroevolution (Chapter 4). Initially, many of these higher-level taxa were themselves of relatively low diversity, consisting of only a few (perhaps in some cases only one or two) natural families, genera and species. (Remember, any single species must belong to a single genus, family, order, class, and phylum.) Later in the Early Cambrian, as we shall see in the next chapter, successful groups flourished to give us the diverse familiar phyla and classes of the Phanerozoic (Fig. 9–13). The unsuccessful groups became extinct, mostly before the end of the Cambrian.

Several factors probably combined to create the niche and habitat availability. One of the important contributors may have been extensive grazing and cropping of cyanobacterial colonies and mats by early evolving herbivorous invertebrates, thus opening up new ecospace. This competitive exclu-

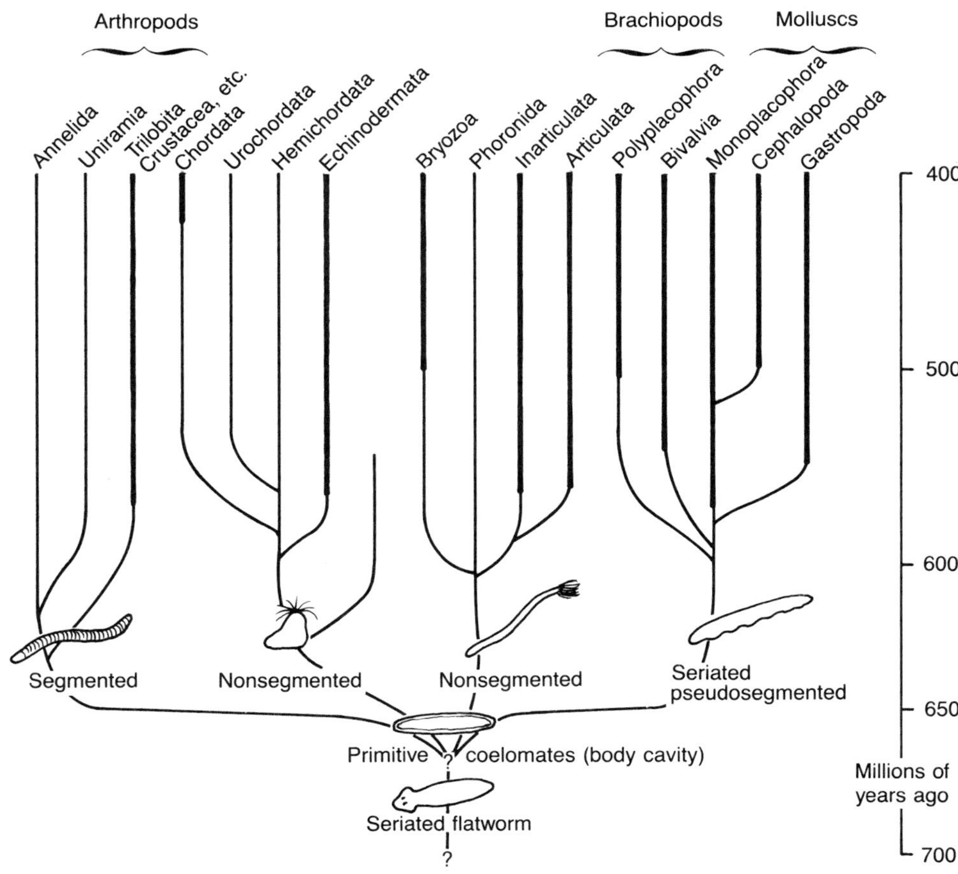

Figure 9–13
Evolution of the metazoan phyla. Heavier lines indicate that the lineage of the phylum had acquired a mineralized skeleton.
(After J. W. Valentine and Kathryn Campbell, 1975, Genetic Regulation and the Fossil Record, Fig. 3, p. 478: *American Scientist,* vol. 63. Reprinted by permission of *American Scientist*)

sion of cyanobacteria, which may have literally saturated many Late Proterozoic shallow marine environments, appears to be borne out by a marked decline in stromatolites in carbonate strata of the transition interval. The herbivory itself attests to changing feeding strategies whereby heterotrophy (the consumption of other organisms) became more important.

Another aspect of the early diversification of skeletal metazoans was the initiation of complex communities of animals linked by food chains. One important link in some food chains was predation. The impact of predators on early metazoan communities may have been great and may well have exerted selective pressure favoring skeletonization as a strategy for protection. Evidence of early predation includes:

Actual fossils of predators such as *Prothertzina* (Fig. 9–11) and *Anomalocaris* (Fig. 9–14A),

Specimens of damaged (and healed) fossils (prey) such as examples of wounded trilobites (Fig. 9–14B), and

Antipredatory adaptations such as the mail-like coat-of-armor shells that probably protected the upper surface of slow-crawling animals like *Lapworthella* (Fig. 9–14C).

Many of the small tubular and conical Tommotian shelly fossils may actually have been *sclerites,* disarticulated single elements or parts of such mail-like coats of armor.

Geochemical Signatures

It is logical to assume that skeletonization became selected for, as free oxygen levels continued to increase (perhaps to 10% PAL or more) and more advanced organic respiratory and circulatory systems evolved. Exoskeletons of calcareous, phosphatic, and chitinous composition seemingly would have provided an adaptive advantage for bottom living, leverage, articulation, protection, security, and accommodation for size increase. This would suggest that the rapid, yet sequential early evolution of exoskeletons was related to *intrinsic,* biologically or ecologically controlled factors. Certainly there is compelling evidence for this interpretation, but could the onset of skeletonization also be related to *extrinsic* factors such as physicochemical changes in the oceans?

In this regard, consider the abundant occurrence of calcium phosphate in the boundary interval in some sections. Deposits of phosphorite, the amount of secreted calcium phosphate skeletal material, and the amount of phosphatic replacement (phosphatization) of calcium carbonate shells are significant. What caused the release of substantial quantities of phosphorus into shallow marine waters? Figure 9–15 shows two chemical trends near the boundary; they are related to the ratio of sulfur isotopes ^{32}S and ^{34}S (expressed as ^{34}S) and carbon iso-

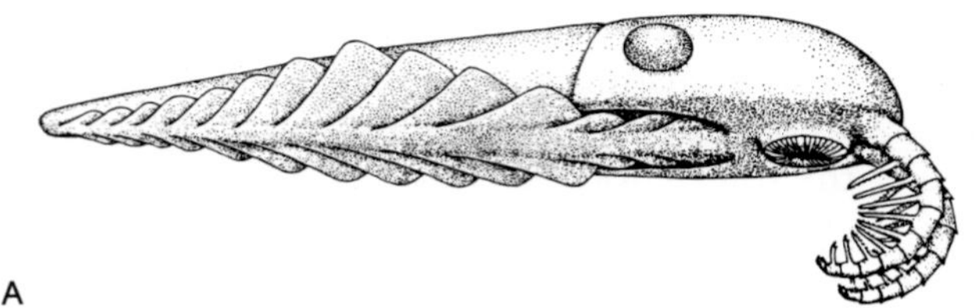

A

B

C

Figure 9–14
Three expressions of predation in the Early and Middle Cambrian. A. The predator. *Anomalocaris,* known as "the terror of the trilobites," was a predaceous arthropod that occasionally grew to 45 cm length, considerably larger than most Cambrian animals. Note the gripping appendages to carry food to its mouth. B. The victim. *Ogygopsis klotzi,* a Middle Cambrian trilobite from the Stephen Formation, British Columbia. Note the bite mark on the pygidium (lower right tail) of the specimen, probably inflicted by *Anomalocaris.* C. The protected. *Lapworthella,* an animal armored with sclerites. This coat-of-mail was probably an adaptation for protection against predaceous animals like *Anomalocaris.*
(A, C, from M. A. S. McMenamin, 1987, The Emergence of Animals, p. 96–97 and 101: *Scientific American,* vol. 257, no. 4. Copyright © 1987, *Scientific American,* Inc. All rights reserved. B, photo courtesy of Derek E. G. Briggs, Department of Geology, University of Bristol, England)

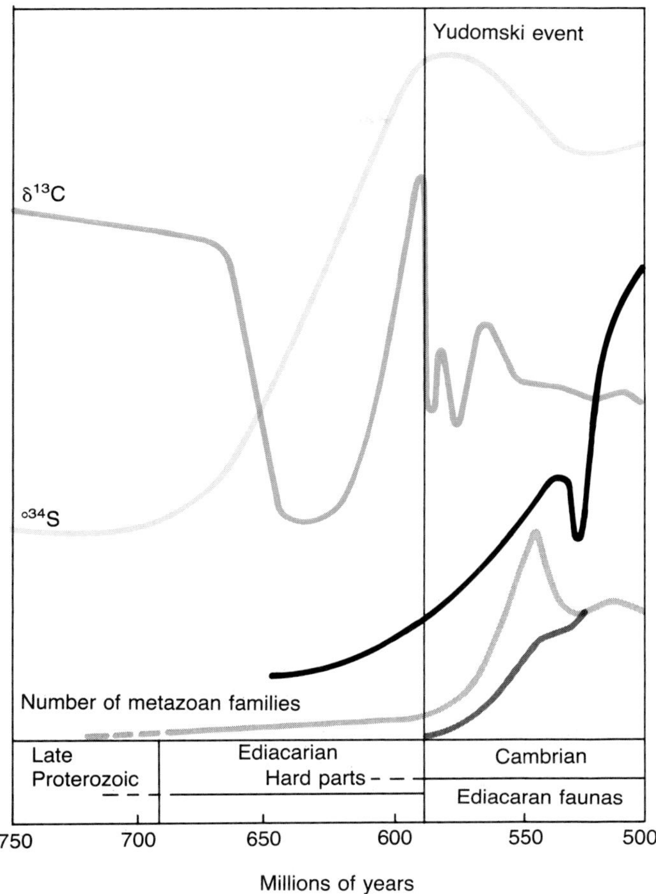

Figure 9–15
Combination of geochemical, geological, and paleobiological data that contribute to understanding the events that occurred during the Precambrian-Cambrian transition interval. The sharp peak in the number of metazoan families (light gray curve) is largely a reflection of the Archaeocyatha. The sea-level curve, based on interpretation of depositional facies patterns and disconformities, reflects the Early Cambrian transgression, followed by a regression at the end of the Early Cambrian. Changes in geochemistry of the oceans are expressed by sulfur and carbon isotopes.
(From Simon Conway Morris, 1987, The Search for the Precambrian-Cambrian Boundary: *American Scientist,* vol. 75, fig. 9, p. 175. Reproduced with permission of *American Scientist*)

topes ^{12}C and ^{13}C (expressed as ^{13}C), and may have some bearing on this question.

The largest of three major ^{34}S excursions with extreme positive values is called the *Yudomski Event* and reflects sulfide accumulation. Sulfide-rich brines may have been stored in restricted incipient rift ocean basins between continental fragments in the early stages of supercontinent breakup during the latest Proterozoic. Progressive continental separation during the transition time interval and widening of rift ocean basins may have promoted more overturn of oceanic waters, resulting in large-scale upwelling of isotopically heavy waters. The massive upwelling of the Yudomski Event probably introduced substantial quantities of nutrients and phosphorus that were formerly trapped in the brines. Rapid shifts in the ^{13}C values near the boundary (Fig. 9–15) may reflect changes in oceanic productivity related to the Yudomski Event.

Yet another change in ocean chemistry that might be linked to biological development involves variations in CO_2 content in the oceans and atmosphere. A possible scenario envisions increased rates of plate subduction related to accelerated seafloor spreading, which produced metamorphic reactions that released elevated amounts of CO_2. The result was a rise in CO_2 levels, which caused the shift in carbonate precipitation across the boundary interval and influenced the development of calcitic skeletons. Thus we see another manifestation of the transition from Precambrian to Cambrian: chemical changes, perhaps induced by plate-tectonic activity, that not only left geochemical signatures in the rock record, but also may have been important influences upon the biological changes that we observe.

In summary, the metazoan adaptive radiation probably was related to a combination of factors, including rising atmospheric oxygen levels, continued continental fragmentation and flooding of continental shelves by transgressing seas, and ecological interactions within the biosphere. More oxygen allowed for more complex anatomical grades. Land-sea changes created a greater diversity of shallow marine habitats and niches, which were rapidly filled by opportunistic, unique kinds of metazoans. Continental separation also produced more genetic isolation and may also have triggered changes in ocean chemistry, both of which influenced biological development. Relative sea-level rise and marine transgression drowned low-relief continental margins, producing new tracts of shallow-water habitats. The evolutionary emergence of herbivores, which resulted in extensive cropping of cyanobacteria mats and eukaryotic algae, opened up new niches for a variety of other organisms.

In Search of the Golden Spike: The Precambrian/Cambrian Boundary

Evolution of a Concept

In recent years, perceptions of the Precambrian/Cambrian boundary have changed significantly. According to British paleontologist Simon Conway

Morris, the documentation of a long Precambrian microfossil record (Chapter 8), the discovery of the latest Precambrian (Vendian, Ediacarian) animal fossils (the Ediacara fauna), and the development of a Precambrian chronometric scale have enabled us to view boundary events in the context of 3000 million years of prior biological evolution. Furthermore, improved documentation of early shelly faunas has provided a clearer picture of the sequential appearance of skeletonized organisms.

Decades ago the definable stratigraphic boundary between the Precambrian and Cambrian was relatively easy to find because the areas then under study were mostly in cratonic regions where Cambrian sedimentary rocks unconformably overlie Precambrian rocks. As the twentieth-century database expanded to areas originally occupied by ancient continental margin basins, where sedimentation was more continuous from Proterozoic to Cambrian, the task of precisely locating the boundary in conformable sequences has become increasingly complicated.

In a nutshell, the boundary problem has been reversed. Originally the stratigraphic boundary was relatively easy to pick, but the evolutionary implications were an enigma. Now that we know much more (but certainly not all) about the evolutionary events (Phases I–III of the transition interval), the precise placement of the stratigraphic boundary has become increasingly difficult.

So where exactly should the boundary be placed, and why is this so important? This is the most cardinal boundary in the time scale. It is important to determine where this boundary lies in any given sequence if paleontologists are to correlate the information gathered at one site with that from another. This is the rationale expressed by the International Union of Geological Sciences–International Geological Correlation Project Working Group on the Precambrian/Cambrian Boundary, whose prime

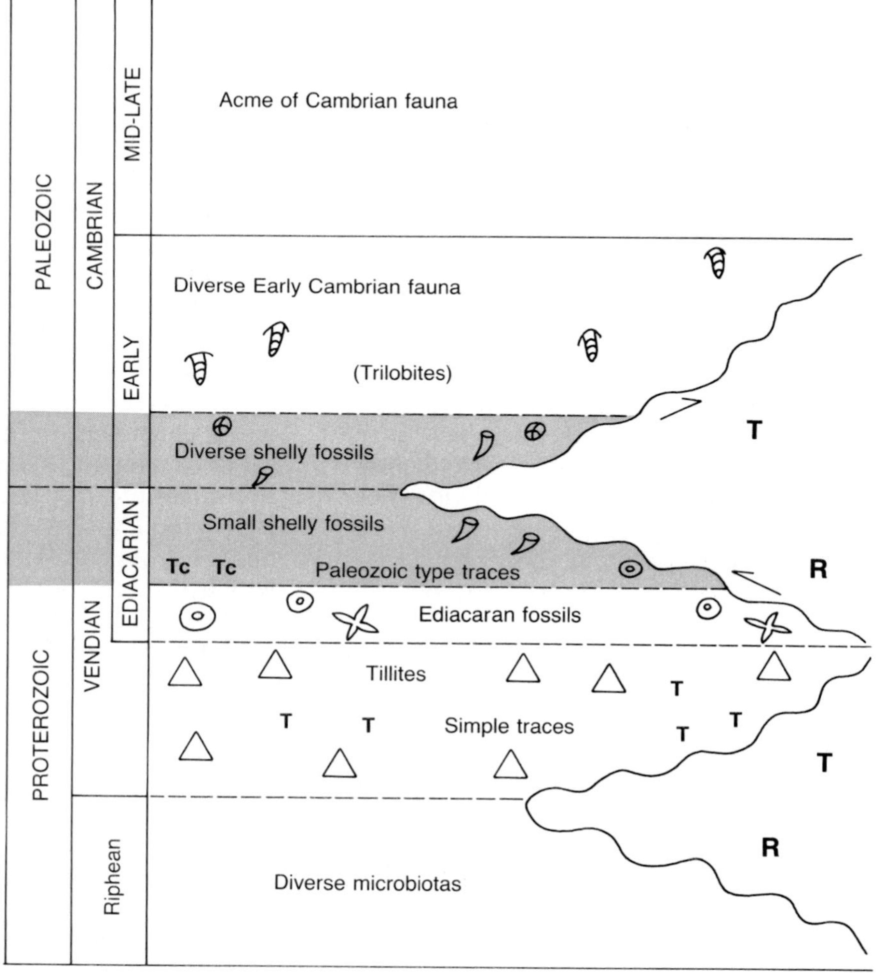

Figure 9–16
Stratigraphic framework for the appearance of complex animals in the latest Precambrian (Vendian and Ediacarian) and Cambrian. (From J. John Sepkoski, Jr. and Andrew H. Knoll, 1983, Precambrian-Cambrian Boundary: The Spike is Driven and the Monolith Crumbles: *Paleobiology*, vol. 9, no. 3, Fig. 1, p. 201. Reproduced with permission of editors of *Paleobiology*).

task is to designate a precise location and horizon for the boundary. Focus of the Working Group has been on the stratigraphic interval comprising Phases II and III of the transition interval (Fig. 9–10). In this regard, few dispute the Ediacarian fossils as being unquestionably pre-Cambrian, or trilobites as being unquestionably Cambrian. At the very center of attention is the interval comprising the Tommotian Stage (Phase III), a thin slice of the time scale comprising perhaps 20 million years or more (Fig. 9–16).

Shelly Fossils

Most workers agree that the boundary should be placed as close as practicable to the earliest known appearance of diverse shelly fossils having a good potential for correlation. This is nice in theory, but here lies the rub in terms of practicality. Keep in mind that this boundary selection will be only as meaningful as its ability to be correlated on an intercontinental scale. Over the past few decades, an international consensus has emerged concerning the recognition and definition of formal chronostratigraphic units by means of **boundary stratotypes.** This procedure rests on detailed documentation of candidate stratigraphic sections that straddle the interval in which the boundary is likely to be located. Ultimately this selection process leads to a specific geographic locality and stratigraphic horizon (nicknamed "the golden spike"), which represents, by definition, the boundary.

The establishment of the Precambrian/Cambrian Boundary Working Group has stimulated much research on the problem, and by the decade of the 1980s the number of candidate sections had been distilled to a short list of three: (1) a section along the Aldan River in eastern Siberia, (2) a section in a phosphate quarry near Meishucun (Yunnan Province) in southern China, and (3) a section on the Burin Peninsula in southeastern Newfoundland (Fig. 9–17).

Each section has its supporters and detractors, and at various times each has enjoyed favor over the others. Several problems prolong the decision of selecting one: deciding which criteria to use, the transitional nature of the boundary interval, the influence of facies controls on the distribution of fossils, taxonomic uncertainties, and correlation resolution. Certainly, where best to place the Precambrian/Cambrian boundary depends on understanding the events during the span of time encompassing the transition interval.

The problem in using the evolution of hard parts to define the boundary is that the onset of biomi-

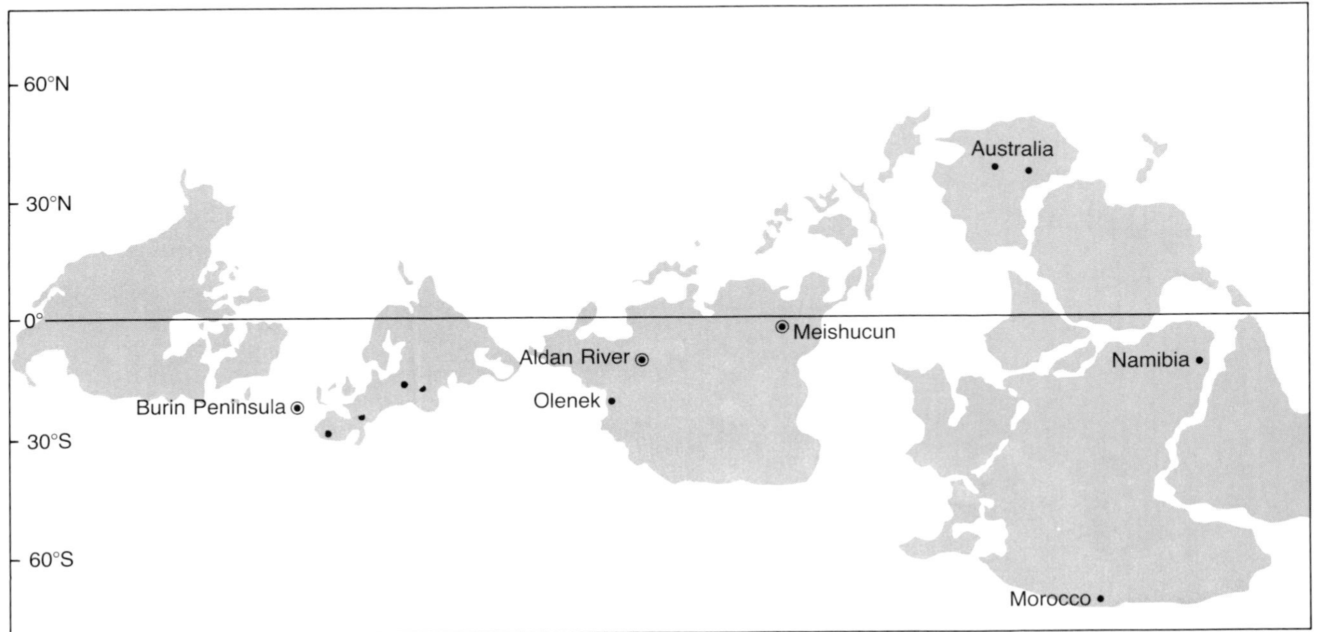

Figure 9–17
World geography reconstruction for the Precambrian-Cambrian boundary interval showing location of potential boundary stratotype sections.
(From Simon Conway Morris, 1987, The Search for the Precambrian-Cambrian Boundary: *American Scientist*, vol. 75, Fig. 5, p. 161. Reproduced with permission of *American Scientist*)

neralization appears to have occupied millions of years, with different groups acquiring skeletons at various times in the latest Proterozoic to earliest Cambrian. How good a biostratigraphic potential many Tommotian fossils have is still problematic. This is exacerbated by the fact that some Tommotian fossils have long stratigraphic ranges, extending downward into sub-Tommotian strata as well as into higher parts of the Cambrian. Furthermore, taxonomy of many of the small shelly fossils has become a quagmire. Also, marked provincialism of the earliest skeletal fossils and their virtual restriction to carbonate facies have hampered global correlation in the boundary interval. If there is to be a "golden spike" definition of this most cardinal of all stratigraphic boundaries, then, like the other boundaries of the time scale, it must depend primarily on biostratigraphic decisions that revolve around accurate fossil identifications and the laborious assembling of taxonomic range charts.

How meaningful is a "golden spike" unless it can be correlated globally? It was not until post-Tommotian (Atdabanian) time that archaeocyathids and early trilobites became widespread. Some experts have argued that this is the only point in the stratigraphic record where intercontinental correlation is sufficiently precise to permit definition of the boundary based on body fossils. However, this argument has met with heavy resistance because such a definition would consign to the Precambrian substantial thicknesses of strata that teem with shelly fossils. Many boundary stratigraphers find this unsettling—historically the concept of the base of the Cambrian has been the first major appearance of hard parts.

This brings to mind the argument about who "discovered" America—Leif Ericson or Christopher Columbus? Ericson landed first, but the voyages of Columbus opened the sea lanes and paved the way to establishing trade routes and European settlement of the Americas. Which was the more meaningful? Perhaps too much attention has been paid to megascopic shelly fossils. Some workers have been impressed with the possibilities of *acritarchs* (organic-walled microfossils), which may turn out to have good potential biostratigraphic utility in the boundary interval.

Trace Fossils

A vocal group of boundary-interval researchers believes that trace fossils may hold the key to driving the "golden spike." The pattern of diversification of trace fossils broadly mirrors the adaptive radiations of the skeletal metazoans across the Precambrian/Cambrian boundary (Fig. 9–18), although trace-fossil diversification begins stratigraphically below the radiation of shelly fossils. This pattern of trace-fossil diversification strongly suggests that the Early Cambrian fossil record reflects the initial adaptive radiation of marine animals in general and not simply the advent of skeletonization. Thus, the scant and equivocal traces in sediments older than 700 to 800 Ma, together with the pattern of diversification in the Ediacarian and Cambrian, strongly suggests

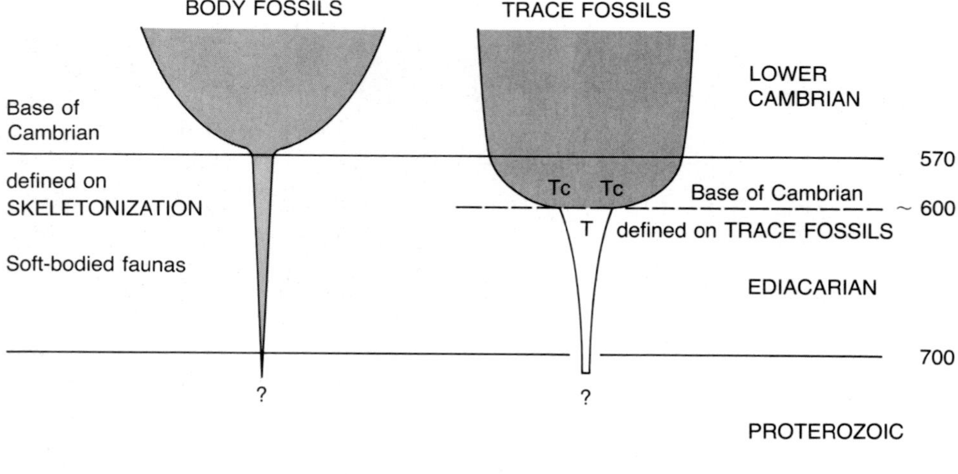

Figure 9–18
Diversity trends in trace fossils and body fossils from Late Proterozoic to Early Cambrian. Note the appearance of Paleozoic-type trace fossils prior to the "explosive" development of skeletonized faunas about 570 million years ago.

an evolutionary trend rather than a chance occurrence or facies controls.

Tremendous advances have been made during the past few decades in the study of trace fossils (ichnology). Classification schemes relating to behavioral patterns such as feeding, dwelling, locomotion, grazing, resting, and escape (Chapter 3) have made trace-fossil associations important paleoenvironmental indicators. However, because of facies controls on the benthic trace-makers and the long stratigraphic ranges of many *ichnogenera* (form types with taxonomic generic names), trace fossils have enjoyed little success as biostratigraphic tools. This is understandable for the remainder of the Phanerozoic, where an abundant body-fossil record provides detailed comparison of boundary faunas. However, in terms of initial patterns in the very early history of metazoans, the potential contribution that trace fossils could make in solving the boundary problem should not be overlooked.

Until recently, most workers were of the opinion that, by themselves, trace fossils are unlikely to provide the biostratigraphic resolution necessary for precise definition of the boundary. However, trace fossils are especially common in terrigenous clastic facies where shelly fossils typically are rare and poorly preserved. Correlation in terrigenous clastic facies is critical because such deposits comprise nearly 75% of exposed rocks in the boundary interval. Furthermore, many boundary-interval trace fossils are cosmopolitan, and several globally correlatable trace fossil biozones that occur below the lowest trilobites have been documented. Thus, the flowering of trace fossils may provide more than just a first approximation of the boundary.

Interestingly, in the proposed boundary stratotype section in Newfoundland, the boundary is placed at the abrupt appearance of complex Phanerozoic-type trace fossils, which approximately corresponds with the first appearance of simple small shelly fossils. This choice seems to have excellent prospects for global correlation, and at this writing is favored by a majority of the Boundary Working Group Committee.

Is There A Finite Boundary?

The Precambrian/Cambrian boundary problem was originally a one-dimensional problem in evolutionary paleontology: where were the ancestors of the trilobites? Now the boundary problem is a series of smaller problems relating to studies in sedimentology, taxonomy, trace fossils, small shelly fossils, and precise correlation. Seemingly, in a nonstratigraphic sense, the Precambrian/Cambrian boundary has become a metaphor for the concept of a transition interval—an evolutionary transition that reflects a world in transition. Even so, stratigraphic systems such as the Cambrian are supposed to have isochronous boundaries, at least within the limits of stratigraphic resolution.

These are the constraints that workers have imposed upon the natural stratigraphic record. We must organize it so that it suits our use and purpose. But can the transitional nature of the change from the Precambrian world to the Cambrian world be reduced to a finite isochronous horizon? (Remember that it was just a "changing world," before we tried to neatly subdivide it.) How synchronous would this horizon be when defined on the *first-occurrence* biostratigraphic data that most workers favor?

Uniquely, the base of the Cambrian System, unlike the bases of the other Phanerozoic systems, is defined on first occurrences rather than comparison of "before and after" stratigraphic data. Should we return to the first appearance of trilobites globally to define a correlatable base of the Cambrian, and thus leave a thick sequence containing shelly fossils as Precambrian? Should trace fossils be used in the selection process for this most cardinal of all stratigraphic boundaries, when they do not figure in the definition of any subsequent time-scale boundary? Suppose it could be demonstrated that a particular geochemical signature represented an abrupt, even catastrophic chemical event? Such a record might provide a widespread and even global method of synchronous correlation, possibly at a resolution superior to any available biostratigraphic scheme. Would it not be nice if the "golden spikes" were driven for us? Nature, of course, does not work that way. Time-scale boundaries are human-made—human attempts at organizing and subdividing the natural stratigraphic record. Occasionally there are parts of the record that defy the drawing of boundaries.

The Precambrian/Cambrian boundary is a problem in chronostratigraphy, but what about the absolute age of the boundary? The most widely accepted date is 570 Ma, but dates range from 615 to 530 Ma. The latter date has support from radiometric ages and stratigraphic relationships in Newfoundland. Alas, challenging problems continue to be researched and remain to be solved regarding the base of the Cambrian—the beginning of Paleozoic, of Phanerozoic time—the most hallowed boundary of our time scale, and various stratigraphic philosophies govern the process.

Summary

The Ediacarian and earliest Cambrian together represent the transition from Late Proterozoic to Paleozoic (Precambrian to Cambrian). This transition, which can be divided into three informal evolutionary phases based on the fossil record, is confined to continental margins; in cratonic regions, a profound unconformity separates Cambrian and Precambrian rocks. Phase I of the transition is the Ediacarian Period, which was formally proposed in 1982 as the time interval (approximately 670 to 570 Ma) beginning with the earliest appearance of soft-bodied metazoans and ending with the earliest appearance of skeletonized metazoans.

The Ediacarian is based on the distinct soft-bodied Ediacara fauna originally described from the Ediacara Hills in South Australia. Rocks of the Ediacarian System are confined to continental margin basin stratigraphic sequences on several continents, and lie between the uppermost Proterozoic tillites and the stratigraphically lowest occurrence of moderately diverse shelly fossils. Although presently included in the Late Proterozoic in the most widely published time scales, the Ediacarian conceptually and rightfully belongs in the Phanerozoic as a pre-Cambrian system because of its significance in the history of visible animal life.

In North America, documented accounts of Ediacarian fossils are rare, but strata of Ediacarian age are presumed to be present on the basis of stratigraphic position and apparent conformity with overlying definitive Cambrian rocks. These strata lie above glaciogenic sediments and are early deposits of both the Appalachian and Cordilleran continental margin basins, which developed along the newly rifted margins of Laurentia.

The world's first metazoan fauna of soft-bodied creatures evolved at a time postdating Late Proterozoic glaciation and during the breakup of a supercontinent. Postglacial drowning of rifted continental margins provided stable but low-resource-level environments that accommodated these earliest animal communities. General similarity of Ediacara faunal associations worldwide attests to widespread ecological conditions and lack of barriers. Evidence suggests that the Ediacara fauna represents an initial evolutionary "experiment," with collapse of community structure and mass extinction terminating the fauna before the onset of widespread biomineralization.

The appearance of exoskeletons represents an important evolutionary milestone and a major aspect of the early metazoan diversification. Skeletonization, which had many adaptive advantages for bottom living, probably became selected for as oxygen levels continued to increase, perhaps to about 10% PAL, and more advanced respiratory and circulatory systems evolved. Skeletonized faunas appear sequentially, over an interval of about 20 million years, which presents problems in selecting an ideally synchronous Precambrian/Cambrian boundary.

The oldest assemblages of skeletal fossils include small tube and cone-shaped calcium carbonate and phosphatic and chitinous shells of uncertain biologic affinity. This low-diversity skeletal fauna constitutes Phase II of the Precambrian/Cambrian transition. Phase III of the transition, comprising the traditional Tommotian Stage, is characterized by abundant and diverse small shelly fossils as well as sponges, archeocyathids, primitive molluscs, coelenterates, echinoderms, and brachiopods, and predates the first appearance of trilobites.

These early skeletal faunas and associated trace fossils are significantly more diverse than the Ediacara fauna, and do not appear to have evolved from Ediacara-type animals. These faunas evolved during world conditions of:

Continued continental breakup and separation (promoting genetic isolation),

Marine transgression (producing greater expanses of shallow marine habitats),

Rising oxygen levels (allowing for more advanced anatomical systems),

Predation (inducing secretion of protective exoskeletons),

Cropping of cyanobacterial colonies (opening up additional new ecospace), and

Changing chemistry of the oceans (enhancing biomineralization).

Favorable environmental conditions and vacant ecological niches combined to produce a major adaptive radiation of opportunistic, enterprising early skeletal metazoans.

The discovery of pretrilobite skeletal faunas in a number of places around the world not only underscored the problem of finding a synchronous base for the Cambrian System, but added a new perspective on the transition from rocks without metazoan fossils to rocks containing the oldest trilobites, which historically was the main criterion for drawing the base of the Cambrian in continuous Proterozoic/Cambrian sequences.

Three candidate Precambrian/Cambrian boundary stratotype sections have become the focal points of research on the boundary problem. An international working group has galvanized this research by emphasizing clearer understanding of events during the time span of the boundary interval. This has been played up as the most cardinal boundary in the time scale. Defining the "golden spike" (metaphor for the Precambrian/Cambrian single-horizon boundary) will depend on biostratigraphic data, but the most meaningful approach is an integrated one whereby studies in sedimentology, paleoecology, biostratigraphy, and geochemistry are being carried out in conjunction with taxonomic studies to assess the relative importance of evolution, ecology, preservation, and ocean chemistry in controlling the stratigraphic distribution of the fossils.

Search for the "golden spike" has produced an abundance of data on the boundary interval, but also frustrations in selecting a boundary stratotype. Various stratigraphic criteria have been used to define the boundary, including occurrence patterns in shelly megafossils, microfossils, and even trace fossils. But taxonomic uncertainties, facies controls, provincialism, and long biostratigraphic ranges have hampered resolution. The transitional nature of the boundary interval may not be amenable to single-horizon boundary definition. A world in transition has left a transitional record.

Suggestions for Further Reading

Cloud, P. E., Jr. 1987. *Oasis in space: Earth history from the beginning.* New York: W. W. Norton and Co.

Cloud, P. E., Jr. 1988. A new Earth history for undergraduates. *Journal of Geological Education* 36:208–14.

Cloud, P. E., Jr., and M. F. Glaessner. 1982. The Ediacarian Period and System: Metazoa inherit the Earth. *Science* 217(4562):783–92.

Conway Morris, Simon. 1987. The search for the Precambrian-Cambrian boundary. *American Scientist* 75: 157–67.

Cowie, J. W., and M. D. Brasier, eds. 1989. *The Precambrian-Cambrian boundary.* New York: Oxford Univ. Press.

Glaessner, M. F. 1961. Precambrian animals. *Scientific American* Offprint No. 903. San Francisco: W. H. Freeman.

Glaessner, M. F. 1984. *The dawn of animal life: A biohistorical study.* New York: Cambridge Univ. Press.

Gould, Stephen Jay. 1983. The Ediacarian experiment. *Natural History Magazine* 92(11):18–23.

McMenamin, M. A. S. 1987. The emergence of animals. *Scientific American* 257(4):94–102.

Early Paleozoic History

10

Eon		Era	Period		Age in Ma*
PHANEROZOIC		CENOZOIC	Quaternary	Quaternary	2
			Tertiary	Neogene	24
				Paleogene	65
		MESOZOIC	Cretaceous		144
			Jurassic		208
			Triassic		245
		PALEOZOIC	Permian		286
			Carboniferous	Pennsylvanian	320
				Mississippian	360
			Devonian		408
			Silurian		438
			Ordovician		505
			Cambrian		570
CRYPTOZOIC (PRECAMBRIAN)	PROTEROZOIC	Late Proterozoic			900
		Middle Proterozoic			1600
		Early Proterozoic			2500
	ARCHEAN	Late Archean			3000
		Middle Archean			3400
		Early Archean			~3800
HADEAN (Pregeologic history of the Earth)					
			Origin of Earth		4600

Contents

Key Terms

Craton
Epeiric sea
Transcontinental arch
Grand cycle
Cratonic sequence
Taconic orogeny
Ophiolite
Clastic wedge
Flysch
Molasse
Iapetus Ocean
Laurentia
Baltica
Gondwana

The Wonders of the Burgess Shale

During a field excursion to the majestic Canadian Rockies in 1909, Charles D. Walcott, the great American geologist and student of the Cambrian, made a fantastic discovery high on the west face of Mt. Wapta near Field, British Columbia. As one apocryphal but colorful version of the story goes, his packhorse stumbled over a fallen chunk of shale, and when the specimen split apart, Walcott's trained eyes caught the gleam of reflection from some glossy markings on the bedding plane surface. A closer examination revealed *carbonaceous* imprints and films of soft-bodied creatures preserved in amazing detail (Fig. 10–1). Further search and the eventual opening of a quarry produced thousands of specimens that represent an unusual association of species, most of which are unique to this locality.

These remarkable fossils occur in the Burgess Shale member of the Stephen Formation of Middle Cambrian age. The biota includes more than 150 species representing at least eight known phyla of animals, and perhaps as many more unknown phyla. Most of the fossils represent taxa that became extinct by the end of the Cambrian. Approximately 40% of the presently recognized fauna consists of arthropods, but sponges, coelenterates, echinoderms, molluscs, annelid worms, and even a primitive chordate number among the finds, as well as animals that cannot be assigned to any living taxonomic group. Not only is the fauna unique; it is amazingly well preserved, and many of the arthropod specimens show preservation of appendages, bristles, and even internal organs.

Despite the early major research effort by Walcott and some of his associates, significant gaps remained in knowledge of the Burgess Shale paleoenvironment, conditions of preservation, faunal composition, and phylogenetic relationships. Walcott himself shoehorned all of the animals into familiar groups, and some of the more troublesome ones he lumped into a catchall taxonomic "wastebasket" of wormlike creatures called Vermes. In the late 1960s, under the direction of the Canadian Geological Survey, renewed interest in the Burgess Shale fauna, stimulated in large part by investigations of the depositional paleoenvironments of Cambrian strata in this region, resulted in temporary reopening of Walcott's quarries and a new period of collecting. Both the new material and major portions of Walcott's original collections have been studied by systematic paleontologists at Cambridge University in England. This work, combined with analysis of the depositional and postdepositional settings of the Burgess Shale by Canadian Survey geologists, has narrowed the areas of uncertainty about this remarkable fauna.

As described by British paleontologists H. B. Whittington and Simon Conway Morris, the Burgess Shale soft-bodied fauna represents a rare mode of preservation. This fauna reflects a combination of circumstances in a paleoenvironment that had optimum accumulation rates of organic-rich mud, and

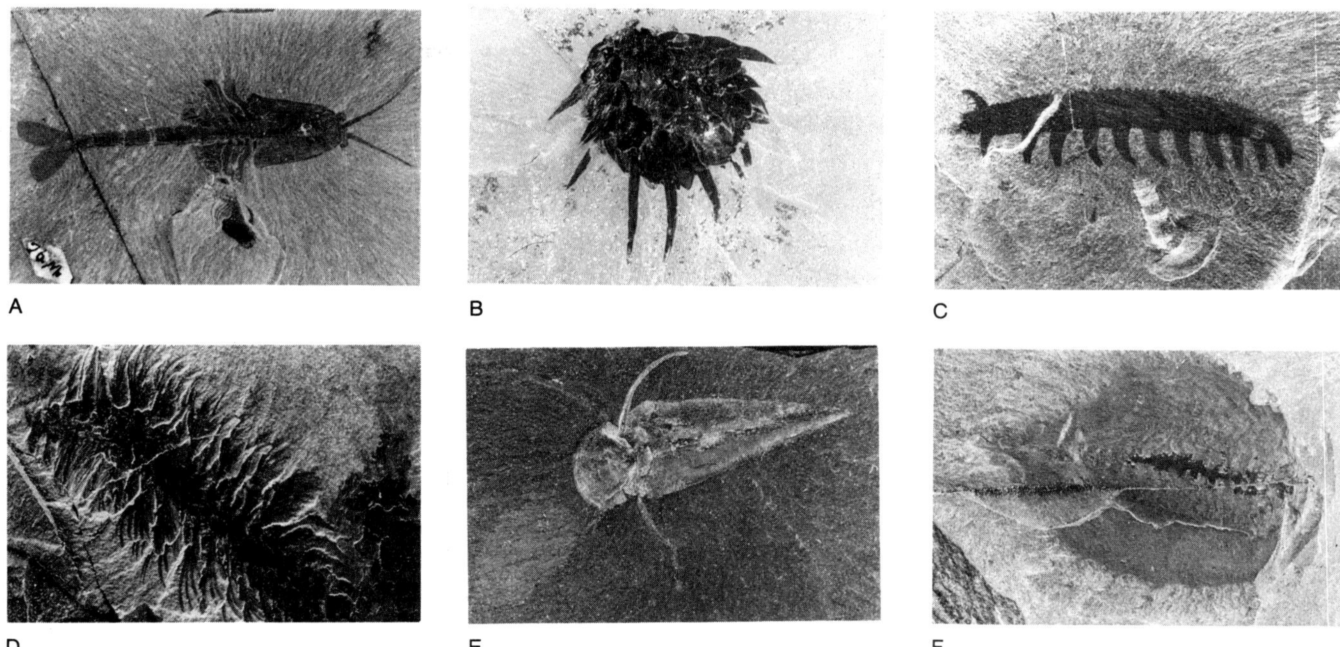

Figure 10–1

Burgess Shale fossils. A. *Waptia fieldensis,* an arthropod. B. *Wiwaxia corrugata,* affinity uncertain. C. *Aysheaia pedunculata,* an arthropod. D. *Canadia irregularia,* a polychaete worm. E. *Hyolithes carinatus,* a mollusc(?). F. *Naraoia spinifer,* an arthropod.
(Photos courtesy of National Museum of Natural History. Smithsonian Institution Photo Nos. 114259/52.FS, 65056/29.FS, 83942/18.FS, 17.FS, 137509/37.FS, 83946/20.FS)

a lack of bottom-scavenging organisms to devour the carcasses that had settled there. More recent investigation of the unique deposit paints a paleoenvironmental picture of a moderately deep marine bottom situated at the toe of an embayed carbonate algal reef (Fig. 10–2). The bottom waters in this setting probably were restricted in circulation and poisoned by the buildup of hydrogen sulfide. Talus mounds of mud accumulated against the base of the reef and had surfaces presumably elevated above the noxious bottom waters. These perched surfaces provided habitats for a complex community of invertebrates, predominantly soft bodied, but also some shell-bearing.

However, the tranquility of this community structure periodically was interrupted by slumping of these mud piles, with the catastrophic result that the bottom dwellers were swept into the stagnant and poisonous bottom waters where they were annihilated and rapidly buried. Lack of aerobic bacteria allowed the organisms to be faithfully preserved in the sediment. Later, slow compaction of the muds to shale and the eventual uplift of a mountain range made the deposit available for discovery.

The Burgess Shale fauna is one of the most important paleontological discoveries ever made. This example of rare preservation provides a hint of the nature, complexity, and full array of Cambrian life. As Stephen Jay Gould has pointed out, the fossils from this one small quarry in western Canada exceed, in *anatomical diversity,* all modern organisms of the oceans. For example, to appreciate this Burgess Shale diversity, consider the phylum Arthropoda. Burgess Shale arthropods, composed of vastly fewer *species,* contain about 20 more basic anatomical designs than what we observe today

Figure 10–2

Reconstruction of the Burgess Shale fauna. The fauna is depicted here as inhabiting a muddy bottom at the base of an algal reef that stood more than 100 m high and whose top was near sea level. The scene depicts a pre-slide environment showing the scars of previous slumps as well as incipient failures, both signatures of the impending catastrophe that will transport part of the fauna to the less hospitable post-slide environment of deposition. No attempt has been made to show the animals in numbers proportional to their fossil abundance. The taxa are identified by number, starting at the bottom left; only about a fifth of the species fossilized in the shale are shown.

Most of the immobile animals of the seafloor are sponges: *Pirania* (12), seen with brachiopods (11) attached to its spicules; *Eiffelia* (22); the gregarious *Choia* (25); a gracile species of *Vauxia* (5), with a more robust species at the top right (5a), and *Chancelloria* (27).

Three other immobile animals are *Mackenzia* (21), a coelenterate; *Echmatocrinus* (16), a primitive crinoid, seen attached to an empty worm tube, and *Dinomischus* (17), one of the Burgess Shale species that represent hitherto unknown invertebrate phyla.

The burrow-dwelling animals are *Peronochaeta* (1), a polychaete worm that fed on food particles in the silt; *Burgessochaeta* (2), a second polychaete that captured food with its long tentacles; *Ancalogon* (4), a priapulid worm possibly ancestral to some modern parasites; *Ottoia* (7), another priapulid worm; *Selkirkia* (8), a third priapulid, seen here in a burrow front end down; and *Louisella* (9), a fourth priapulid that inhabited a double-ended burrow and undulated its body to drive oxygenated water over its gills.

***Peytoia* (10) is a free-swimming coelenterate shaped like a pineapple ring. The seafloor dwelling molluscs, in addition to *Hyolithes* (6), are *Scenella* (23), its soft parts hidden under "Chinese hat" shells, and *Wiwaxia* (24), with its covering scales and defensive spines, seen here plowing a trail through the silt.**

Among the many arthropod genera of the seafloor are *Yohoia* (3), with its distinctive grasping appendages; *Naraoia* (13), an atypical trilobite that retained some larval characteristics; *Burgessia* (14), with its long tail spine; *Marrella* (15), which may have swum just above the seafloor; *Canadaspis* (20), an early crustacean, and *Aysheaia* (26), a stubby-legged animal suggestive of the living land dweller *Peripatus*.

Other representatives of new phyla seen in addition to *Dinomischus* (17) are *Hallucigenia* (18), one preparing to feed on a dead worm and another approaching it, and *Opabinia* (19), seen here grasping a small worm with its single bifurcated appendage.

Finally, seen swimming alone at the top left is *Pikaia* (28), the sole representative of the chordate phylum in this Middle Cambrian fauna. *Pikaia* probably used its zigzag array of muscles to propel itself above the seafloor. The phylum of chordates includes the subphylum of vertebrates, which evolved later.

(From Simon Conway Morris and H. B. Whittington, The Animals of the Burgess Shale, *Scientific American*, July 1979, p. 72.

within known groups of arthropods! Some 15 to 20 Burgess shale fossils cannot be placed in any modern phylum, and represent unique forms of life, "failed experiments," if you will, in metazoan design.

In Gould's view, Walcott's failure to appreciate the large-scale taxonomic diversity and unique body plans represented in the Burgess Shale fauna was conditioned by his strict adherence to Darwin's view that the Cambrian fauna demanded a long gradual Precambrian evolution. (Recall the discussion of the Lipalian interval in Chapter 9.) Darwin's so-called artifact theory (that the Cambrian fauna was a preservational artifact of the long Lipalian interval of prior evolution, which was not preserved) provided the cornerstone for Walcott's approach to interpreting Cambrian life.

So, instead of drastically increasing the known Cambrian diversity, Walcott interpreted the Burgess Shale fauna in light of 30 previous years of trying to substantiate the artifact theory. Thus we can understand (and excuse) Walcott, who was virtually forced into this ultraconservative account of the Burgess Shale animals. According to Gould, "A profusion of new Burgess phyla would have undermined this approach. Walcott wanted to prove the artifact theory, if for no other reason than as an ultimate tribute to Darwin from a Cambrian paleontologist."*

Even though he misinterpreted its evolutionary significance, it is only fitting that Walcott discovered the Burgess Shale fauna, because his name ranks high in the annals of North American geology, particularly in studies of the Cambrian Period and its life. Walcott was the world's leading expert on Cambrian rocks and fossils and a powerful scientific administrator. He was chief of the U.S. Geological Survey, Secretary of the Smithsonian Institution, and influential in establishing the Carnegie Institute of Washington. His accomplishments are particularly remarkable in light of his having little in the way of formal education. Adam Sedgwick named the Cambrian, but it was Charles Doolittle Walcott who really "put the Cambrian on the map" through his many published reports on faunas and correlation.

*Gould, S. J. 1986. A short way to big ends. *Natural History* 95(1):18–30.

Cambrian History

Sedimentation Patterns

The newly formed Cordilleran and Appalachian continental margin basins received predominantly terrigenous clastic sediments derived from exposed Precambrian crystalline rocks in the interior part of the **craton** (Fig. 10–3). As seas slowly spread out from the basin margins, the craton, which had been subject to a prolonged interval of weathering and erosion, was gradually inundated by shallow marine waters. This major transgression and flooding of the continental interior platform by shallow seas, called **epeiric seas,** was nearly complete by Late Cambrian time except for a few emergent island areas that are collectively referred to as the **transcontinental arch** (Fig. 10–4).

Sedimentary rock types from North American miogeoclines are essentially identical in composition and texture to those deposited in the shallow epeiric seas of the cratonic interior. The main differences in these two suites of strata is the stratigraphic thickness, which is greater in the miogeoclinal sections because of more continuous subsidence. Here subsidence accommodated more sediment, and sedimentation kept pace with subsidence, thus producing a preponderance of shallow marine environments. In accordance with present-day basin subsidence models, this miogeoclinal subsidence during the Cambrian was related to a combination of thermal cooling of the lithosphere and sediment loading. James Hall recognized the basic tenets of this idea when he formulated the "geosyncline" concept in the mid-nineteenth century (Chapter 6).

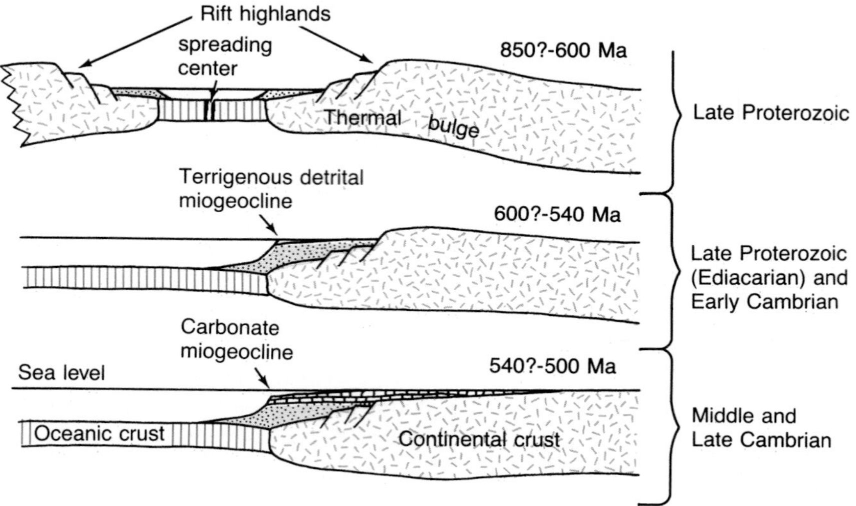

Figure 10–3

Evolution of Cordilleran margin of North America from a Late Proterozoic–Early Cambrian terrigenous clastic miogeocline to a mid-Late Cambrian carbonate miogeocline as terrigenous source lands were denuded and progressively drowned by shallow seas advancing from the miogeocline into the craton.
(After J. H. Stewart, 1982, Regional Relations of Proterozoic Z and Lower Cambrian Rocks in the Western United States and Northern Mexico, Fig. 11, p. 183: Geological Society of America Cordilleran Section Guidebook)

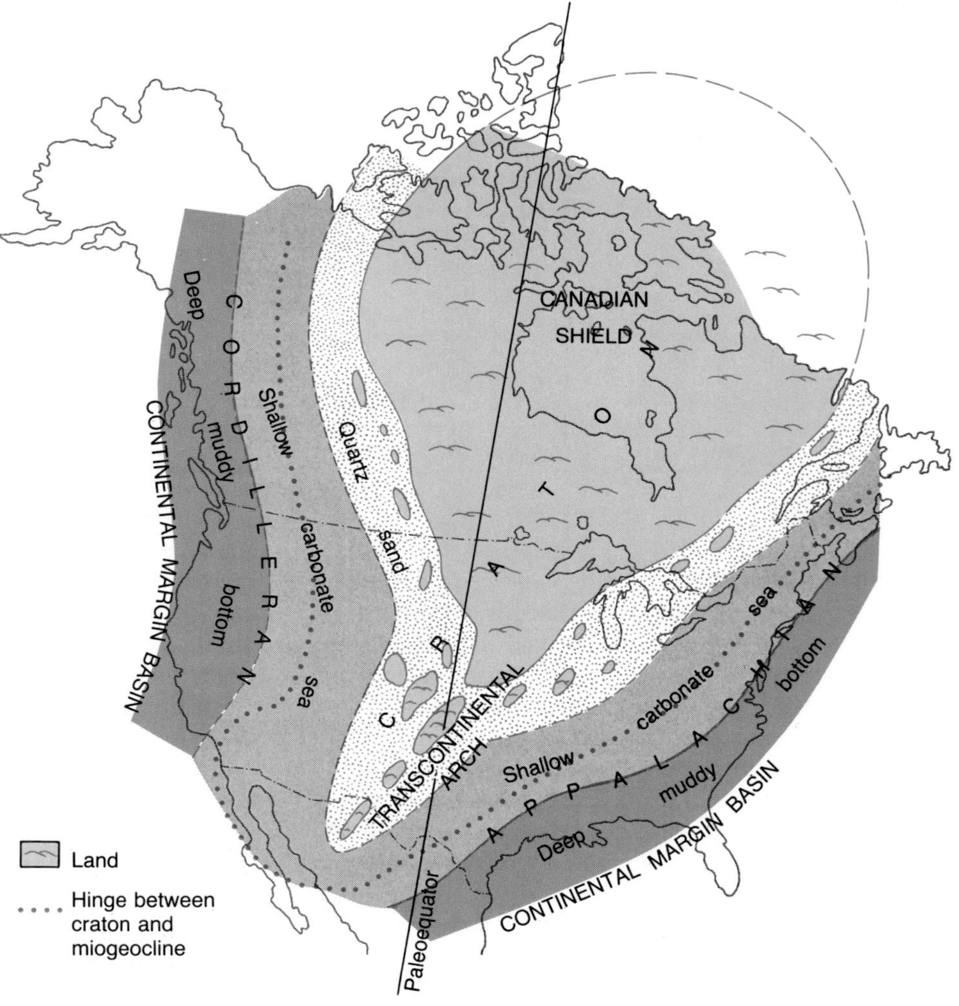

Figure 10–4

Paleogeography of Late Cambrian superimposed on outline map of present-day North America.
(Data from C. Lochman-Balk, 1971, Cambrian System, Fig. 14, p. 74, *in Geologic Atlas of the Rocky Mountain Region:* Rocky Mountain Association of Geologists, Denver)

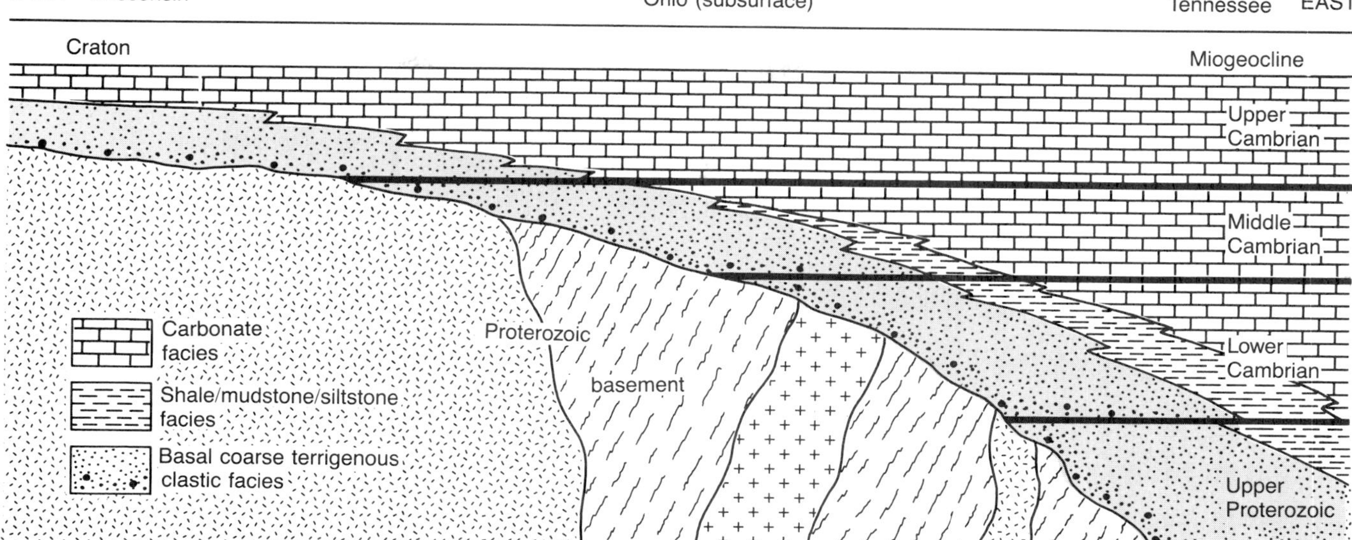

Figure 10–5

Stratigraphic cross-section showing three main Cambrian depositional facies from Appalachian continental margin basin to cratonic interior. Time-transgressive nature and progressive development of carbonate facies are shown during the time when terrigenous source areas were gradually drowned by advancing Late Cambrian seas. High vertical exaggeration and not to scale.

Figure 10–5 shows that transgressing seas spread nearly pure quartz sand, derived from the craton, as a widespread blanket that ranges in age from Early Cambrian in the continental margin basins to Late Cambrian in the cratonic interior. A more seaward belt of finer, muddy detrital sediments, developed as shale and siltstone, accumulated in subtidal environments below *wave-base.* During the Late Cambrian, after most of the pre-Cambrian basement-rock source areas had been drowned by shallow seas in one of the highest sea-level stands of the entire Phanerozoic, carbonate sedimentation predominated in the miogeoclinal and cratonic regions (Figs. 10–3 and 10–5).

Transgression resulted in progressive overlap of successive Lower, Middle, and Upper Cambrian deposits, with extensive carbonate facies topping off the sequence (Fig. 10–5). In the miogeoclinal belt, carbonate sedimentation was established earlier because the carbonate-rich seas were further removed from the emergent parts of the craton, and calcium carbonate could be deposited without being overwhelmed and smothered by terrigenous clastic detritus (Figs. 10–3 and 10–5).

Miogeoclinal and cratonal sedimentary rocks show abundant evidence of shallow-water deposition. Ripplemarks and cross-stratification are common sedimentary structures (Fig. 10–6A). Limestones contain such shallow-water features as stromatolites and *oncoids,* oolitic beds and lenses, bioclastic layers, and intraformational limestone-pebble conglomerates (Fig. 10–6B, C). Abundant and laterally extensive intraformational conglomerates are a hallmark of Cambrian carbonate sequences. They attest to the reworking of desiccation clasts on tidal flats, as well as to frequent storms that shredded cohesive, thin, carbonate-mud sea-bottom layers into tabular clasts and quickly redeposited them, commonly in edgewise orientations (Fig. 10–6C).

Limestone and dolomite beds commonly display various kinds of desiccation features, indicating periodic emergence of the depositional surface. Shallow-water trace fossils are present as a variety of locomotion, resting, and feeding burrows (Fig. 10–6D). The shallow epeiric seas that invaded the craton most likely ranged in depth from shoal waters to several tens of meters, and large areas of tidal flats were commonplace.

An illustration of the rock record and depositional patterns produced as the result of gradual encroachment of Cambrian seas is shown in Figure 10–7. Upper Proterozoic and Lower Cambrian rocks of the Cordilleran miogeocline progressively thin and pinch out toward the craton, and are overlapped by Middle and Upper Cambrian deposits. Note also the drastic change in thickness between the miogeoclinal, platform edge, and cratonic sedi-

Figure 10–6
Shallow-water features from Cambrian sedimentary rocks. A. Tidal herringbone (bidirectional) cross-bedding. B. Oncoids (shallow, subtidal rolled stromatolites). C. Edgewise intraformational limestone-pebble conglomerate. D. Trace fossils (feeding burrows).
(Photos by J. D. Cooper)

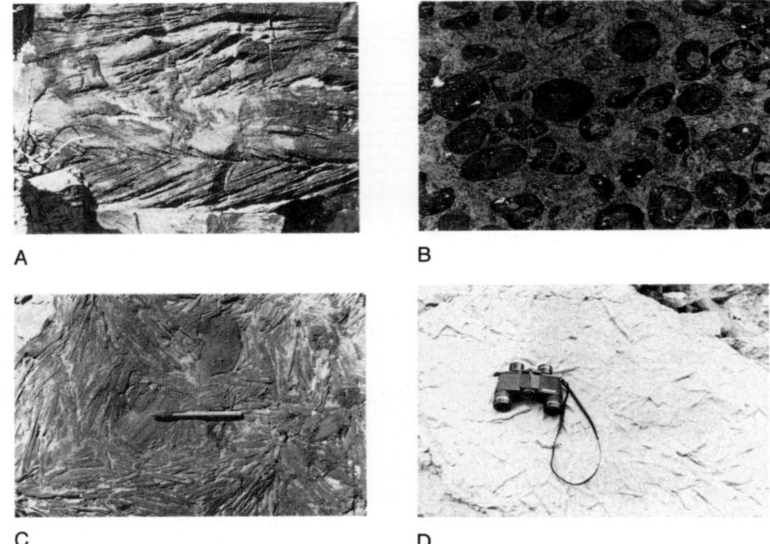

mentary successions. By the time we reach the Grand Canyon, relatively flat-lying sandstone of late Early Cambrian to Middle Cambrian age nonconformably overlies Proterozoic basement in some places, and in others overlies Upper Proterozoic sedimentary rocks of the Grand Canyon Supergroup.

In north-central Nevada, parts of California, and the Pacific Northwest, there are some very different-looking Cambrian rocks that include graded sandstone and impure limestone beds, argillite, chert, and greenstone, as well as deposits bearing slump features and transported blocks. These rocks are believed to represent deeper marine-slope and

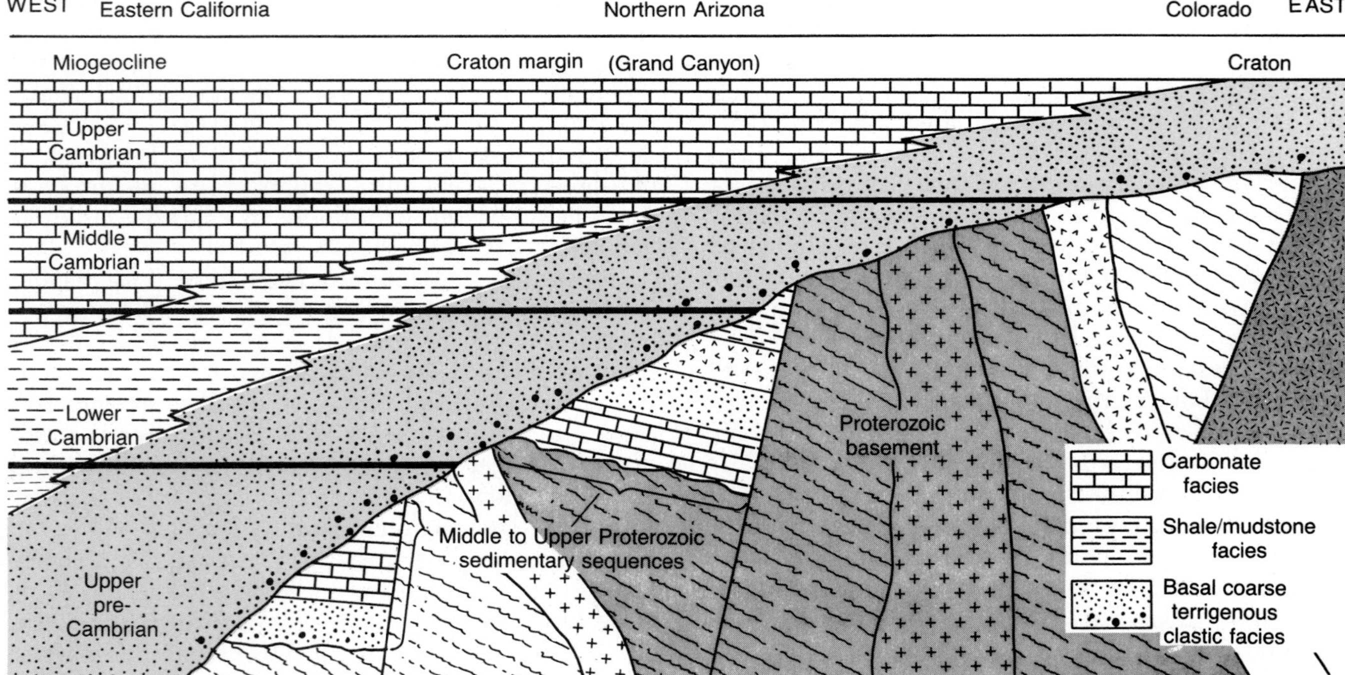

Figure 10–7
Stratigraphic cross-section from Cordilleran continental margin basin to cratonic interior, highlighting time-transgressive nature of depositional facies, the product of gradually advancing marine encroachment into the craton during the Cambrian. High vertical exaggeration and not to scale.

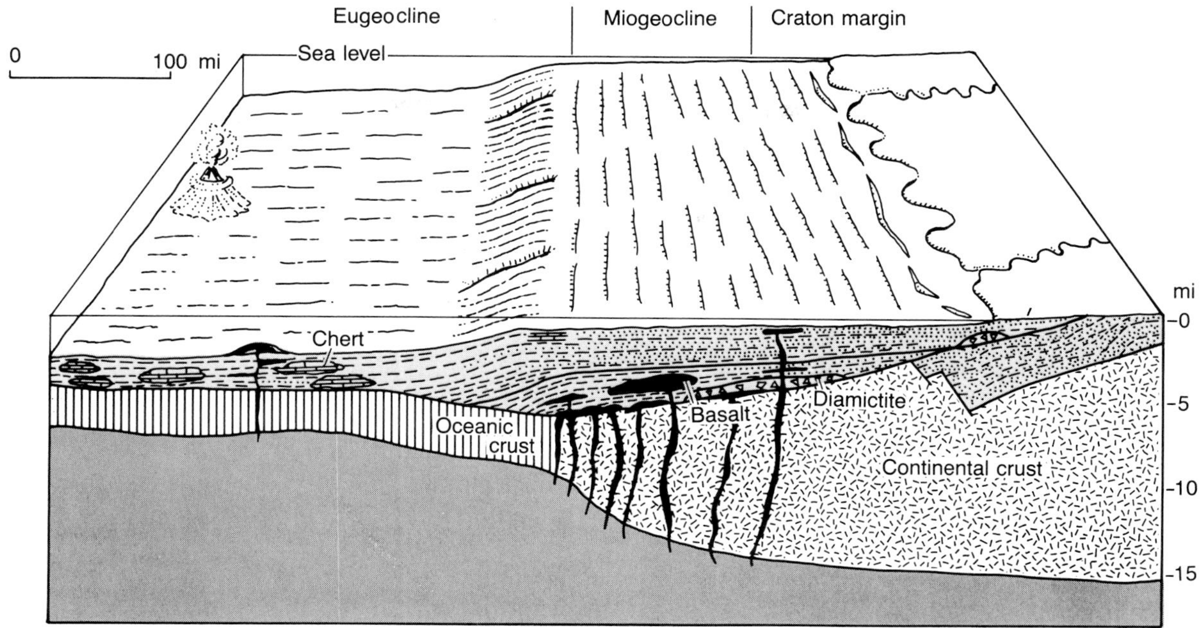

Figure 10–8

Depositional settings of the Cordilleran margin for Upper Proterozoic and Lower Cambrian rocks in the northern Great Basin, Nevada and Utah.

(From J. H. Stewart, 1972, Initial Deposits in the Cordilleran Geosyncline: Evidence of a Late Precambrian (<850 m.y.) Continental Separation, Fig. 3, p. 1350: *Geological Society of America Bulletin,* vol. 83, no. 5. Reprinted by permission of Geological Society of America and author)

basin deposits, and are related to an outer, deeper water belt, the *eugeocline* (Fig. 10–8).

A Facies Model: Cambrian of the Grand Canyon

The Cambrian rocks of the Grand Canyon provide an instructive model for appreciating sedimentation patterns in the advancing sea and for illustrating Walther's Law of the correlation of facies (Chapter 2). The section of rock includes three major lithofacies, which correspond generally to the formally named Tapeats Sandstone, Bright Angel Shale, and Muav Limestone (Fig. 10–9). The Tapeats Sandstone represents the basal braided-fluvial deposits and transgressive shoreface deposits of beach, bar, and sandflat environments—sediments that accumulated as marine waters slowly inundated the western margin of the craton during the late Early and Middle Cambrian. As transgression continued during the Middle Cambrian, terrigenous mud and silt of the Bright Angel Shale and carbonate sediments of the Muav Limestone were deposited over the Tapeats in a classic transgressive onlap succession.

The vertical sequence of sandstone-shale-limestone exposed in any one section comprises the well-known **grand cycle,** which records the cratonward migration of progressively more seaward depositional environments through time. Figure 10–9 depicts how the three major lithofacies are intertongued; they represent the products of depositional environments that coexisted at any one time. The dynamics of cyclic sedimentation have been responsible for the intertonguing stratigraphic patterns that emerge in such a reconstruction. The formally named formations—superposed layer-cake units of convenience in geologic mapping and regional correlation—are but local expressions of these intertonguing facies.

Figure 10–10 shows slightly older, similar facies further basinward on the craton margin. Although different formation names are employed in this section, the large-scale grand cycle facies are contiguous with the same succession in the Grand Canyon.

Cambrian Life

The Cambrian is the lowermost subdivision of the geologic time scale having a well-preserved, abundant fossil record that can be recognized and correlated worldwide. Remember, it is the Cambrian and younger record—containing skeletonized faunas—

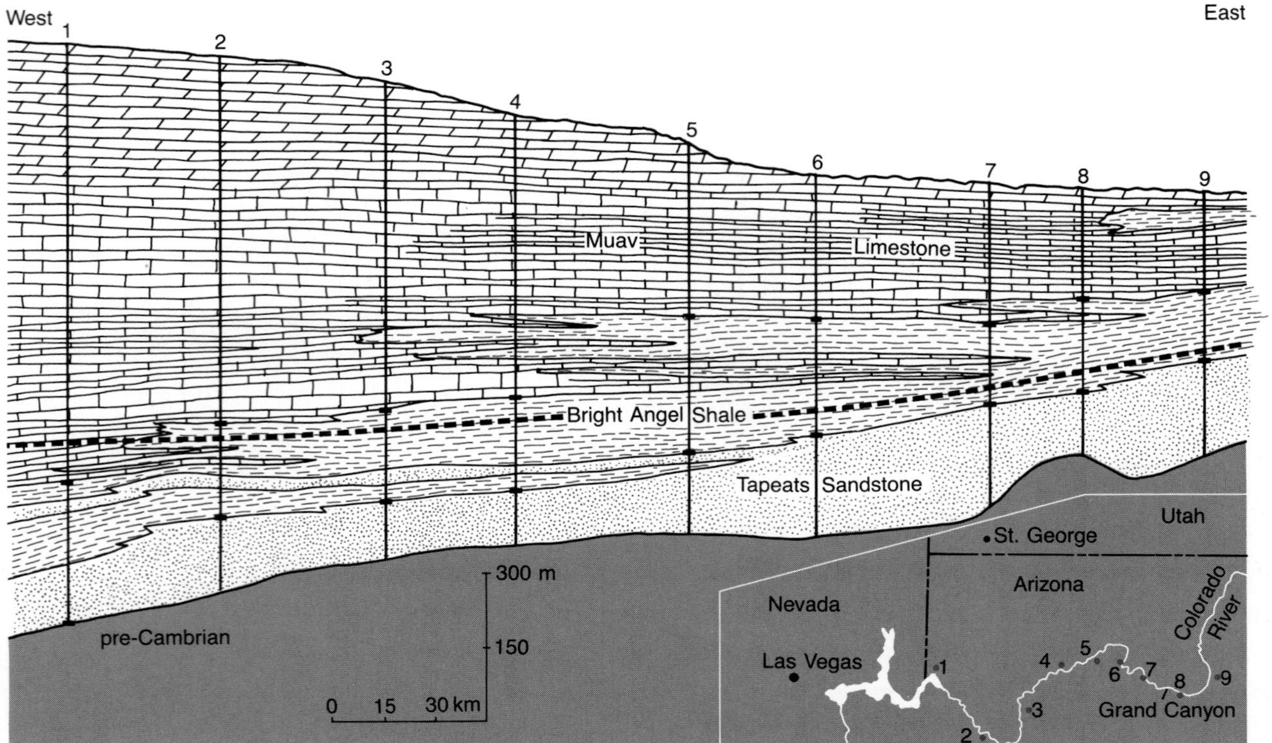

Figure 10–9

Stratigraphic cross section from Lake Mead to the eastern part of the Grand Canyon showing the classic Grand Canyon onlap cycle of Cambrian facies (map inset shows section locations). Note the mappable boundaries in each section (horizontal bar) between the three formations and their relationships to the complex onlap-offlap facies boundaries. Dashed line is time line based on faunal horizon. High vertical exaggeration.

(From E. H. McKee, 1945, Cambrian History of the Grand Canyon Region, Part I. Stratigraphy and Ecology of the Grand Canyon Cambrian, Fig. 1, p. 14: *Carnegie Institution of Washington, Publication* 563. Reprinted by permission of Carnegie Institution of Washington)

whose chronostratigraphic subdivision is deeply rooted in the principle of fossil succession, and subdivision boundaries are defined by time-significant evolutionary changes. Although the base of the Cambrian is conceptually defined on the first appearance of moderately diverse skeletal faunas, this criterion does not necessarily represent a synchronous event (as we have discussed in Chapter 9—In Search of the Golden Spike). This boundary is not as precise as those at the bases of succeeding stratigraphic systems. The base of each succeeding system, although recognized on first occurrences of particular faunas, also is determined on the comparison of fossil faunas with those of the preceding system. The base of the Cambrian does not enjoy that luxury.

By the end of the Cambrian, all living (extant) phyla that are now well skeletonized had appeared, except perhaps the Bryozoa. These phyla came into existence during the Ediacarian and Cambrian, and (except for the sponges, which are believed to have descended independently from a protistan ancestor) probably represent evolution from four or five major "superphylum"-level ancestral worm groups (Fig. 9–13, Chapter 9). The fossil record sheds little light on the details of the origin of the metazoan phyla.

The post-Tommotian Cambrian fossil record is dominated by the trilobites (Figs. 10–11 and 10–12), which are an extinct class of the phylum Arthropoda and provide most of the data for the biostratigraphic zonation and correlation of Cambrian strata. Trilobites secreted carapaces of calcium phosphate and were present in amazing diversity early in the period. They include about 75% of known Cambrian life forms that secreted exoskeletons. In their initial adaptive radiation, the trilobites explored a variety of niches in the marine environment. Morphologic diversity is expressed by differences in size (most were only a few centimeters long, but some attained lengths of 20 cm), shape, and ornamentation, and by eyes: some tri-

Figure 10–10
Cambrian section, Marble Mountains, eastern California. This sequence, more outboard (Craton margin) than the Cambrian of the Grand Canyon, shows similar succession of major facies (sandstone-shale-carbonate), but is Early-to-Middle Cambrian in age. 1 = Proterozoic gneissic basement; 2 = fluvial and shallow-marine sandstone equivalent to the Tapeats Sandstone of the Grand Canyon; 3 = shale-siltstone-limestone equivalent to the Bright Angel Shale; 4 = limestone and dolomite equivalent to Muav Limestone.
(Photo by J. D. Cooper)

lobites had very advanced compound eyes, while some were completely blind. Trilobites shed their exoskeletons much like their living cousins, shrimp and crayfish, and thus an individual had the potential for leaving not one but several fossils through a succession of molt stages.

The phylum Brachiopoda makes up 15–20% of the Cambrian skeletonized fossil record. Most

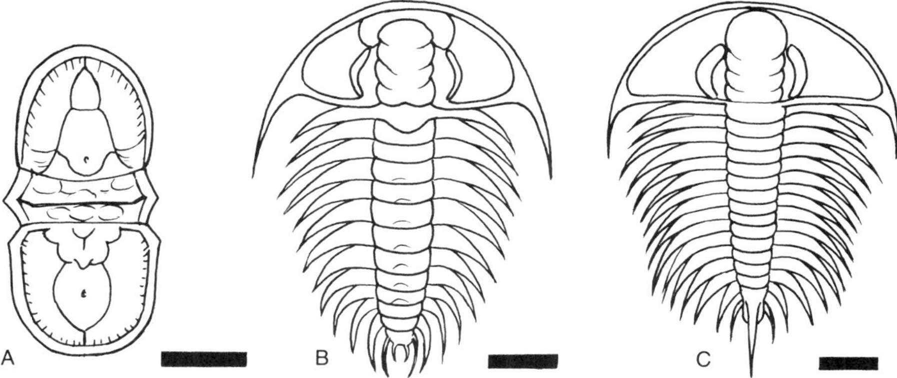

Figure 10–11
Representative Cambrian trilobites. A. Agnostid trilobite. Bar = 0.25 cm. B, C. Nonagnostid trilobites. Bars = 1 cm.
(From A. R. Palmer, 1974, In Search of the Cambrian World, Fig. 1, p. 217: *American Scientist*, vol. 62. Reprinted by permission of *American Scientist*)

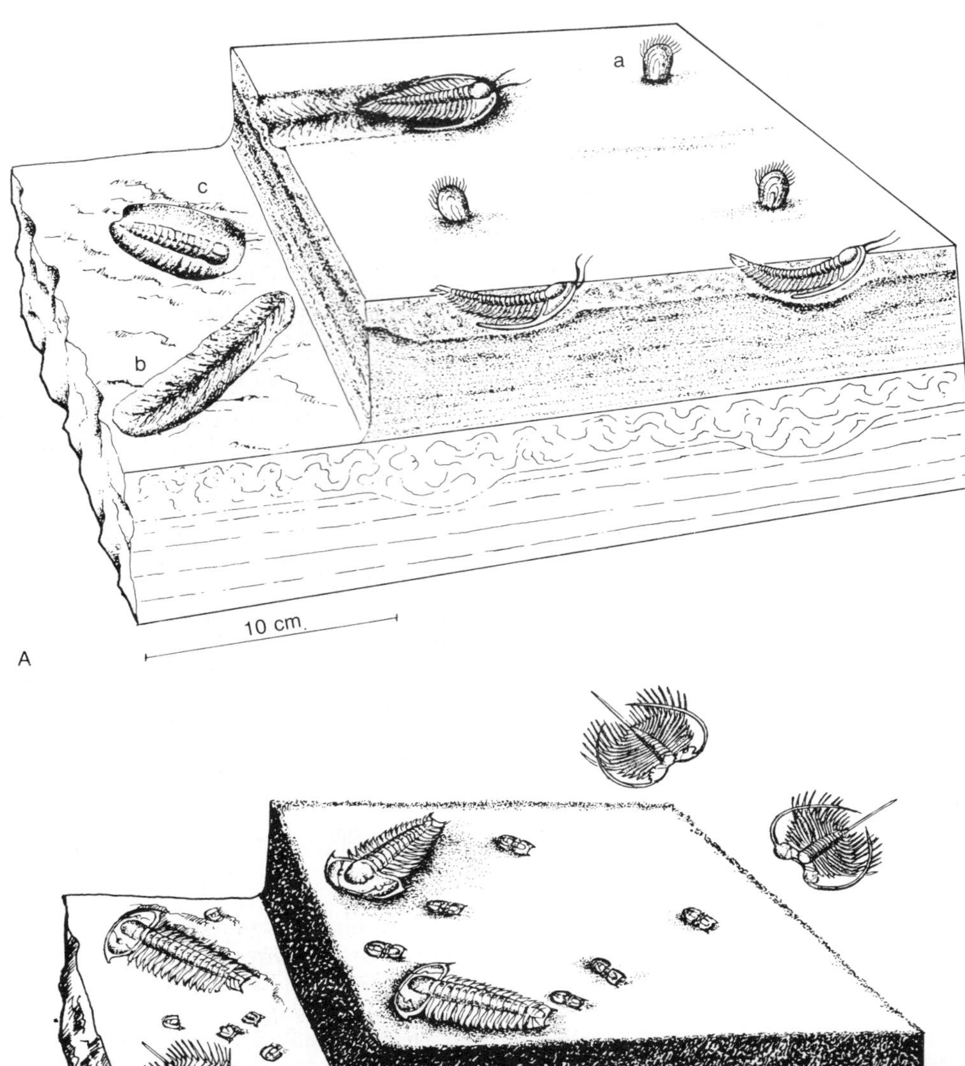

Figure 10–12
In-life Cambrian faunal associations. A. *Cruziana-Lingulella* community: a, *Lingulella*, an inarticulate brachiopod; b, *Cruziana*, a trilobite crawling trace; c, *Rusophycus*, a trilobite resting trace. B. Community of trilobites belonging to the family Olenellidae.
(From W. S. McKerrow, 1978, *Ecology of Fossils*, Figs. 1, 4, p. 53, 61: MIT Press. All rights reserved. Reproduced with permission of MIT Press)

Cambrian brachiopods (Fig. 10–13A, B, C) had phosphatic shells and belong to the class Inarticulata; the great evolutionary expansion of forms bearing calcium carbonate shells and belonging to the class Articulata was yet to come in the explosive Ordovician faunal radiation.

An enigmatic Cambrian group consisted of spongelike creatures having a double-walled calcium carbonate shell (Fig. 10–13J, K), the Archaeocyatha, which are classified as a separate, extinct phylum. The cup-shaped archaeocyathids were abundant and widespread during the Early Cambrian and formed meadowlike patches on shallow limy sea bottoms. By the Middle Cambrian they had dwindled in numbers to a few enclaves in what is now Australia. They became extinct during the Middle Cambrian, the victims of environmental foreclosure.

In addition to the Archaeocyatha, a number of other Cambrian animal groups were short lived: several minor arthropod and echinoderm classes (Fig. 10–13G, H, I) and primitive molluscan classes

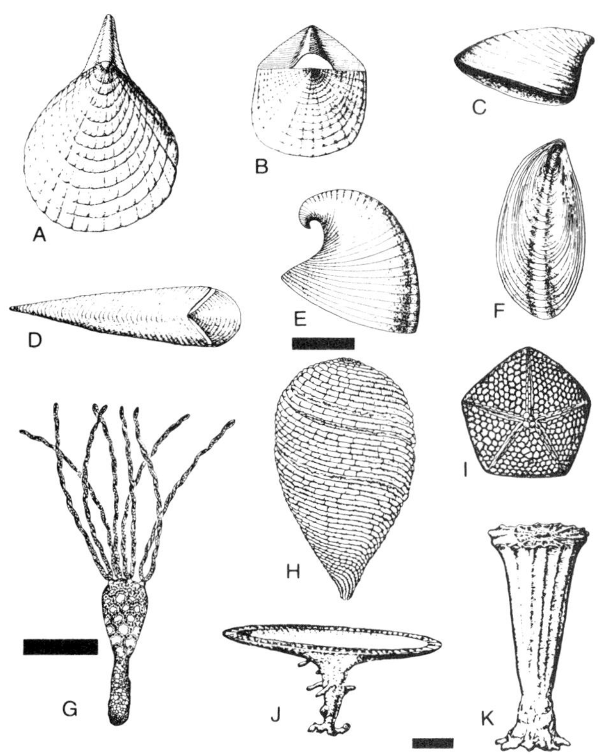

Figure 10–13
Representative nontrilobite Cambrian fossils. A–C. Brachiopods. D. Hyolithid (Primitive mollusc or separate phylum?). E, F. Molluscs. G–I. Echinoderms. J, K. Archaeocyathids. Bars = 1 cm.
(From A. R. Palmer, 1974, In Search of the Cambrian World, Fig. 1, p. 217: *American Scientist*, vol. 62. Reproduced by permission of *American Scientist*)

(Fig. 10–13E, F), as well as at least a half-dozen primitive and poorly known phyla, became extinct before the period ended. Extinction of phyla and class-level taxa during the Cambrian occurred at a scale never to be repeated.

Stromatolites, so prevalent during the Late Proterozoic, also became significantly reduced in Cambrian carbonate rocks, most likely a reflection of large-scale cropping of cyanobacterial colonies by grazing, herbivorous metazoans. Cambrian stromatolites (as well as later ones) developed mainly in hypersaline and other harsh environments where grazing herbivorous predators were not common.

Interesting in this regard, however, is the abundance, particularly in *Upper* Cambrian carbonates, of organosedimentary structures called *thrombolites.* These are like stromatolites in terms of gross morphology, but differ in that they are nonlaminated, possessing instead a clotted fabric (thus the prefix thrombo = blood clot). Thrombolites were formed by skeletal-secreting cyanobacteria and eukaryotic algae, and developed as reeflike banks and mounds. These colonies may represent a short-lived evolutionary strategy against metazoan browsing and cropping activities, and a reef-type existence after the demise of the reef-building archaeocyathids and prior to the onset of large-scale metazoan reef development.

To what degree does the Burgess Shale reflect the norm of Cambrian paleocommunity structure and composition? Although the composition of the fauna is unique in terms of the preserved fossil record (our only look at the representatives of perhaps as many as a dozen otherwise unknown phyla), the faunal assemblage probably was not particularly unique in the Cambrian. The uniqueness is more a reflection of the remarkable preservation than of the composition of the fauna. According to Simon Conway Morris, if the extraordinary conditions of fossilization had not occurred, so that only animals with shells survived to be fossilized, the resulting assemblage would consist of components of most Cambrian fossil faunas: trilobites, brachiopods, sponges, a few echinoderms, and hyolithids (primitive molluscs?). In this light, perhaps the Burgess Shale fauna can be rightly considered an approximate guide to the original diversity of at least some Cambrian invertebrate communities that lived in moderately deep, muddy bottom environments.

In many respects, the Cambrian was a harsh time that brought many different selective pressures to bear on animal groups. Only the hardier, ecologically flexible, and well-established taxa survived.

Uniqueness of the Cambrian Fauna

The explosive emergence and diversification of new higher taxa, the dominance of trilobites, and the extinction of several primitive phyla and classes of low diversity give the Cambrian a unique character. After the Cambrian, no new phyla appeared, and none became extinct (to our knowledge). It is important to remember that the basic evolutionary designs that were successful during the remainder of the Phanerozoic were *established* during the Cambrian, and the poorly suited, unsuccessful designs were *eliminated* during the Cambrian. Later Phanerozoic evolution was simply a modification of what had previously been established during the Cambrian.

After an initial evolutionary burst early in the period, diversification slowed markedly through the remainder of the Cambrian. Diversification increased exponentially during the Ordovician (Fig.

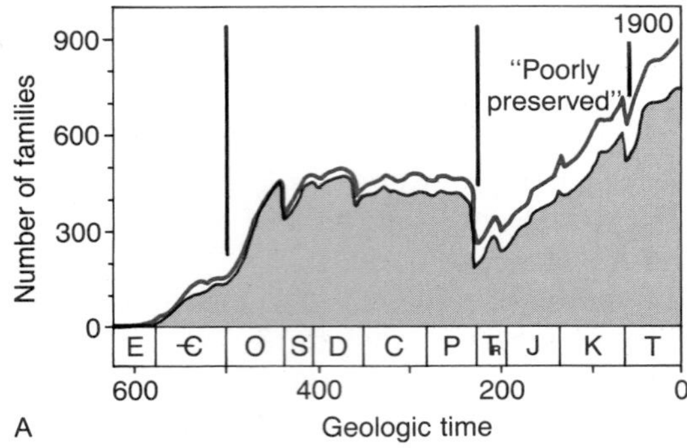

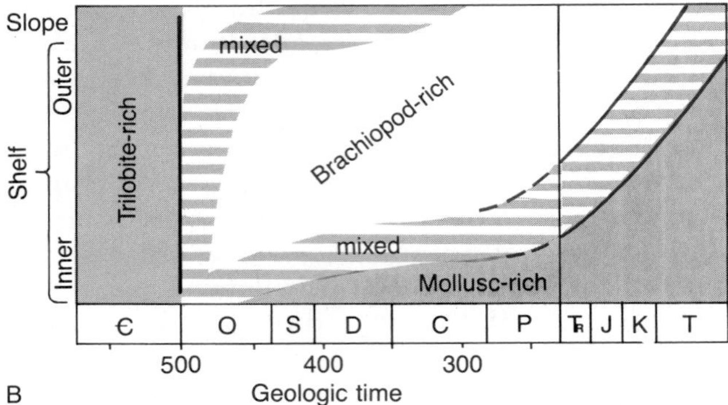

Figure 10–14

Faunal changes through time. A. Phanerozoic history of diversity of marine animal families. The total standing number of families described from the marine fossil record is indicated by the upper curve of the graph. The lower curve, bounding the medium brown field, represents the family diversity of "shelly" taxa that constitute the bulk of the fossil record. The unshaded field between the two curves indicates the diversity of nonskeletal taxa. Note the abrupt increase in diversity in the Early Ordovician after a pronounced leveling off during the Middle and Late Cambrian. B. Changes in general environmental distribution of marine invertebrate communities. The Cambrian trilobite-rich shelf communities were largely replaced during the Ordovician by the brachiopod-rich communities of the late Paleozoic.

(From J. J. Sepkoski, Jr., 1981, The Uniqueness of the Cambrian Fauna, Figs. 1 and 3, p. 203, 206, *in* Short Papers for the Second International Symposium on the Cambrian System: *U. S. Geological Survey Open File Report* 81–743. Reprinted by permission of author)

10–14A) as the more typical *Paleozoic fauna* came into prominence (Fig. 10–14B), but the basic evolutionary stocks had been successfully established in the Cambrian. As Stephen Jay Gould writes, "The message of the Burgess Shale is that the history of metazoan life is a tale of winnowing and culling and stabilization of a few surviving anatomies, not a story of steady expansion and progress."*

*1988. A web of tales. *Natural History* 97(10):16–23.

Some workers share the opinion that the Ediacarian and Cambrian together comprise a sufficiently unique and long interval of geologic time to be considered as a separate *era.* This interval of at least 175 millon years duration (about as long as the Mesozoic and considerably longer than the Cenozoic) has a truly unique fauna in terms of diversity, taxonomic composition, ecological organization, and evolutionary grade when compared to the Cryptozoic and post-Cambrian Phanerozoic—a truly distinctive chapter in the history of metazoan life and exemplary of what an era represents. Certainly the Ediacara fauna, displaying the world's first multicellular grade of anatomical organization, is very different from the algae and prokaryote-dominated Proterozoic biota.

On the other hand, according to paleontologist J. J. Sepkoski, Jr., the differences between the faunas of the Cambrian and of the later Paleozoic are rivaled only by the differences observed between the faunas of the Paleozoic and of the combined Mesozoic and Cenozoic eras. This uniqueness of the Cambrian fauna (and of the Ediacara fauna as well) arises from its special position in the history of life; it represents the completion of the transition from a pre-Phanerozoic autotroph-dominated world ocean to a Phanerozoic heterotroph-dominated world ocean.

Ordovician History

Continued Flooding of the Continent

Sedimentation patterns continued generally uninterrupted from Late Cambrian into Early Ordovician. A large volume of limestone and dolomite is exposed today in parts of the Appalachian, cratonal, and Cordilleran regions, attesting to vigorous and continuous depositional activity in calcium carbonate-rich, shallow-marine waters during the Late Cambrian and Ordovician. A major regression of epeiric seas from the craton occurred near the end of the Early Ordovician. As a result, Lower Ordovician and Upper Cambrian sedimentary rocks were exposed to erosion. Very pure quartz sand, typified by the St. Peter Sandstone (Chapter 2) of the eastern craton, was then reworked and redeposited during a major marine transgression that inaugurated the Middle Ordovician, with the consequent covering of the erosion surface (Fig. 10–15). The epeiric sea continued to advance and flood almost the entire craton by Late Ordovician. Shelly limestones were deposited over most of the continental platform in water depths to a few tens of meters or less, cover-

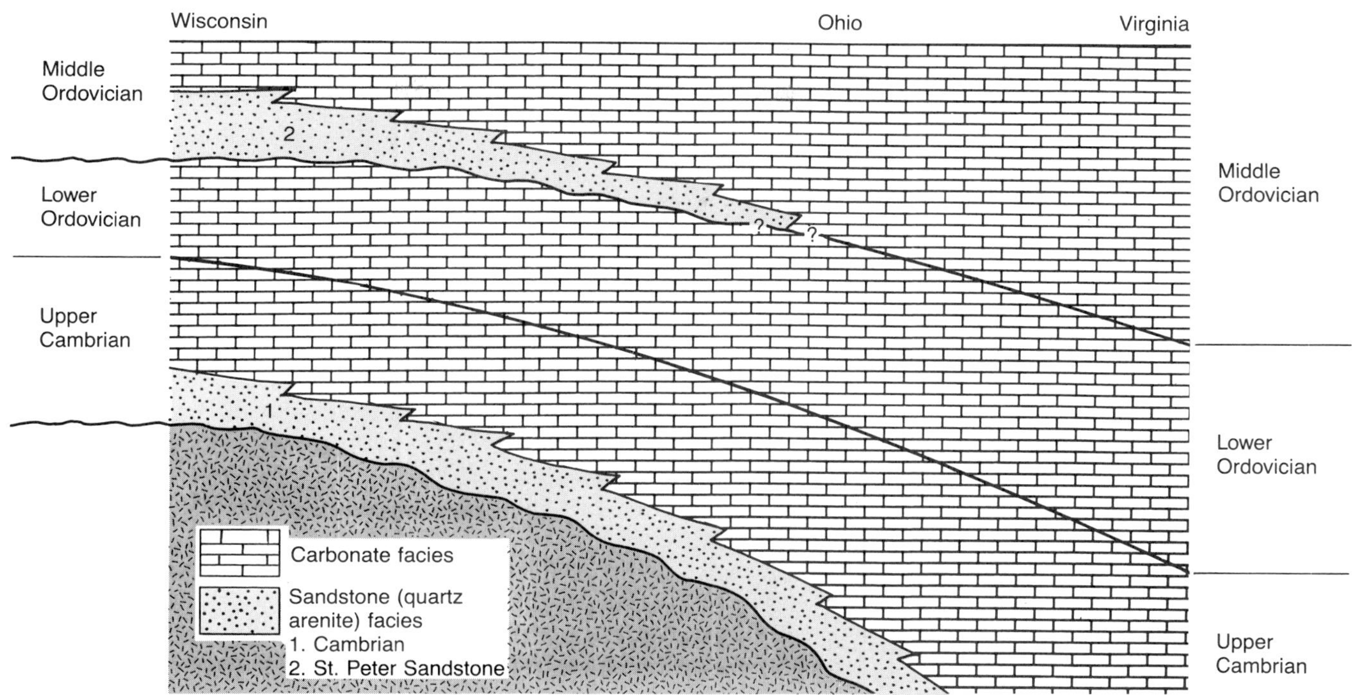

Figure 10–15
Lower and Middle Ordovician facies relationships from the Appalachian continental-margin basin to the central craton. High vertical exaggeration and not to scale.

ing more of the erosion surface and producing a major cratonwide unconformity.

These shallow, warm, calcium carbonate–rich epicontinental or epeiric seas, so characteristic of Paleozoic time, have no modern-day counterparts on the same scale. Extensive *carbonate* sedimentation does not occur today on continental shelves. At present, the North American continent is relatively emergent, with a large percentage of its surface elevated more than 100 m above sea level. Erosion of positive areas produces great volumes of terrigenous clastic detritus that is responsible for smothering carbonate production in potential carbonate environments of continental shelf areas.

One important place where present-day carbonate sedimentation is the rule is the Great Bahama Bank. This is a region of high calcium carbonate productivity, and one that is geographically removed from the influx of terrigenous detritus. The Bahamas are part of a major carbonate platform that has been a locus for limestone production since the Late Mesozoic. This region provides an instructive actualistic model for studying carbonate sedimentation. Figure 10–16, a Holocene facies map of an area adjacent to Andros Island, is probably a reasonably accurate present-day *small-scale* analogue for much of the North American craton during the Late Cambrian and much of the Ordovician—a large-scale shallow-marine platform containing a mosaic of carbonate environments that produced complex intertonguing facies.

The large-scale cyclic pattern of transgression and regression, which we have already considered for the Early-Middle Ordovician transition, was repeated several more times during the Paleozoic (Fig. 10–17). American geologist L. L. Sloss has applied the term **cratonic sequence** to the large-scale (greater than supergroup) rock-stratigraphic packages that represent major transgressive-regressive (onlap-offlap) cycles, bounded by unconformities of cratonwide extent.

The large-scale (cratonwide) unconformity-bounded sequences also have been recognized in continental areas outside North America. Some geologists believe these major onlap-offlap cycles reflect the dynamic responses to fluctuations in holding capacity of the Paleozoic ocean basins, as influenced by lithospheric plate motions. The crux of this idea is that, during times of accelerated seafloor spreading, bulging, spreading ridges caused a decrease in ocean-basin holding capacity, with the result that continental margins were drowned by land-transgressing displaced waters. Figure 10–18 shows how these sequences relate to global cycles of relative changes of sea level during the Paleozoic.

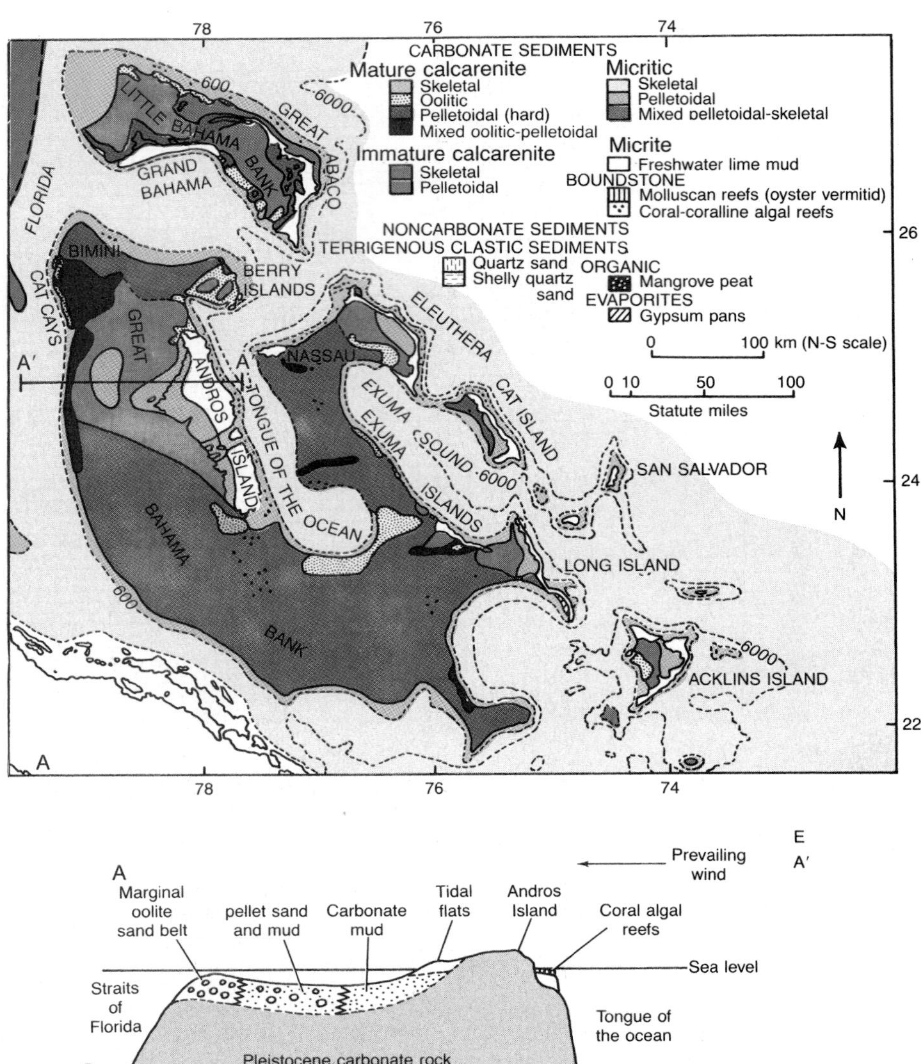

Figure 10–16
Present-day carbonate sediments in the Bahamas. A. Areal distribution of carbonate sediments. B. Schematic cross-section of western part of the Bahama platform showing distribution of modern carbonate facies.
(A after R. B. Halley, P. M. Harris, and Albert C. Hine, 1983, Bank Margin Environment, in Carbonate Depositional Environments, Fig. 2, p. 245: *American Association of Petroleum Geologists Memoir* 33. Reproduced by permission of American Association of Petroleum Geologists; B from R. E. Garrison, 1975, Carbonate Sedimentation on Shelves and Platforms, Fig. 4–4, p. 4–4, *in Current Concepts of Depositional Systems with Applications for Petroleum Geology:* Short course volume. Reproduced by permission of San Joaquin Geological Society)

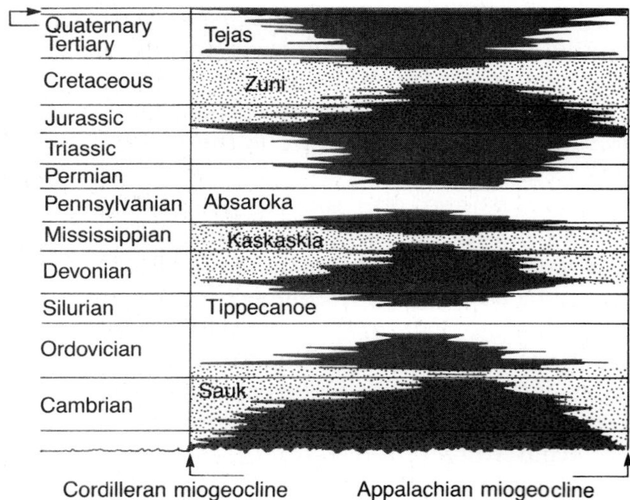

Figure 10–17
Time-stratigraphic relationships of the major onlap-offlap sequences of the North American craton. Black represents hiatuses (erosion + nondeposition time magnitude of sequence-bounding unconformities). White and stippled patterns represent deposition of tangible rock record of the sequences.
(After L. L. Sloss, 1963, Sequences in the Cratonic Interior of North America, Fig. 6, p. 110; *Geologic Society of America Bulletin,* vol. 74. Reprinted by permission of author and Geological Society of America)

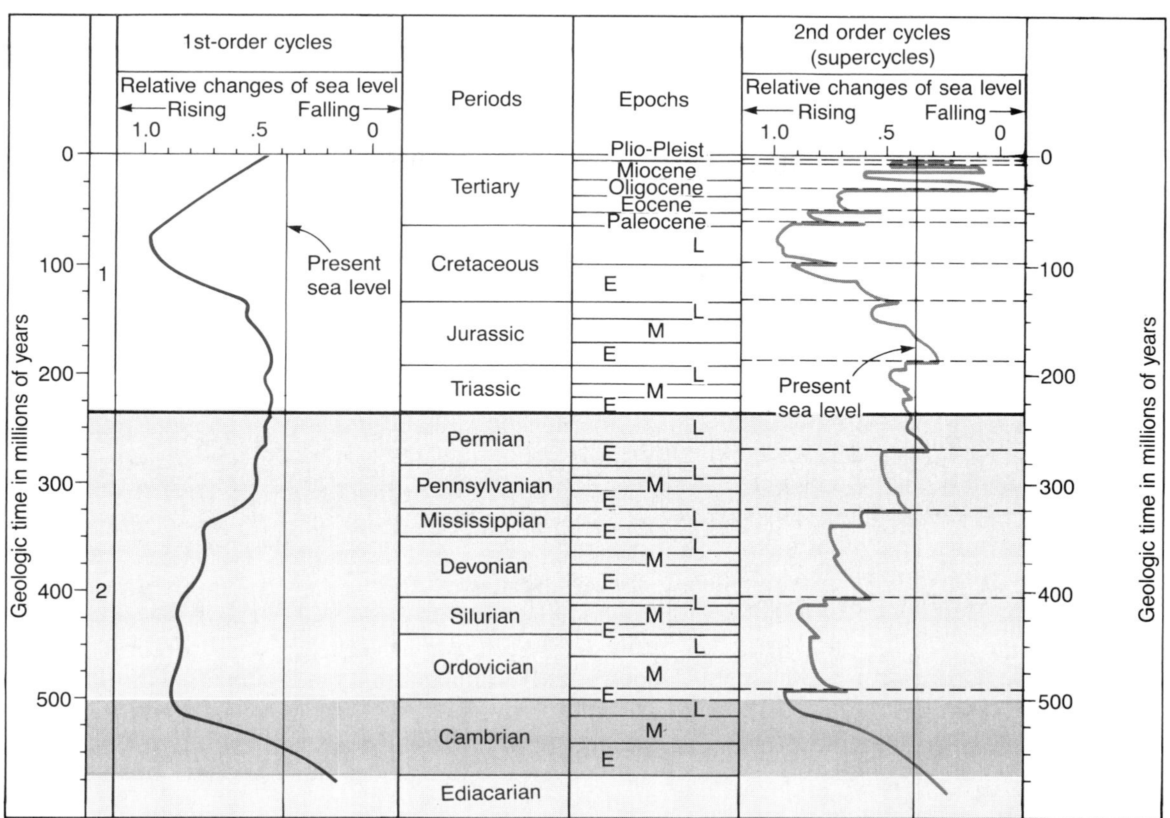

Figure 10–18
First- and second-order global cycles of relative change of sea level during Phanerozoic.
(From R. R. Vail, R. M. Mitchum, and S. Thompson III, 1977, Seismic Stratigraphy and Global Changes of Sea Level, Fig. 1, p. 84, *in* Global Cycles of Relative Changes of Sea Level: *American Association of Petroleum Geologists Memoir* 26. Reproduced by permission of American Association of Petroleum Geologists)

The Calcium Carbonate Shell: A Success Story

Ordovician faunas differ considerably from Cambrian faunas, an expression of the great evolutionary development of the calcium carbonate shell, as tremendous increases in diversity of shell-secreting organisms accompanied the reinvasion of epeiric seas into the cratonic interior during early Middle Ordovician. Selection pressure may have been exerted on marine invertebrates to evolve rigid, external, calcium carbonate shells as adaptations for anchoring on shallow-sea bottoms, for muscle and organ support, for possible protection from cosmic radiation in shallow water, and for protection against early predators. Also, stabilization of O_2 in seawater and attainment of supersaturation with $CaCO_3$ were likely geochemical factors that enhanced carbonate productivity.

Whatever the reasons, many diverse groups of organisms found it to their evolutionary advantage to be encased in a hard shell. Abundant Middle and Upper Ordovician shelly limestones attest to a sea teeming with life. Richly fossiliferous limestones in the Cincinnati, Ohio, area sparked the childhood curiosity of several prominent North American paleontologists.

Of particular importance in this expansion of the calcium carbonate shell was the phylum Brachiopoda. The articulate brachiopods (Figs. 10–19 and 10–20A, B), rare in Cambrian seas, experienced a fantastic diversification in the Ordovician. They are comparatively rare in modern seas, but contributed to large volumes of shelly limestone during the Paleozoic. Middle and Late Ordovician seas were abundantly populated with diverse brachiopods, bryozoans, ostracodes, conodonts, graptolites, nautiloid cephalopods, gastropods, echinoderms, corals,

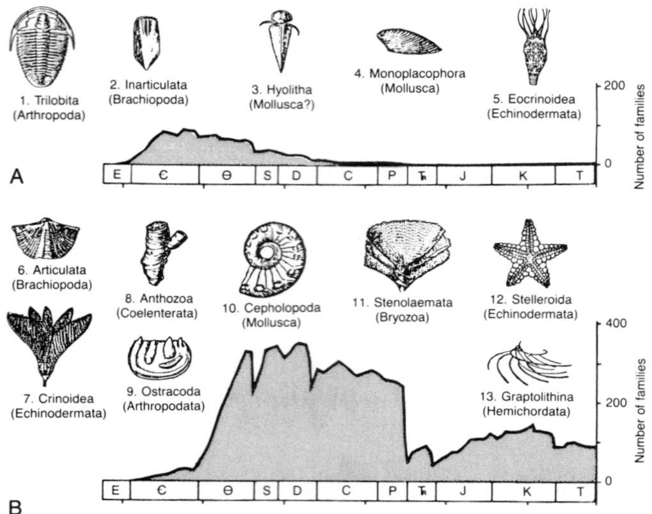

Figure 10–19

Phanerozoic history of taxonomic diversity of marine animal families comprising the two principal evolutionary faunas of the Paleozoic. A. The Cambrian fauna, characterized by the classes Trilobita, Inarticulata, Hyolitha, Monoplacophora, Eocrinoidea (phyla shown in parentheses). B. The Paleozoic fauna, characterized by the classes Articulata, Anthozoa, Cephalopoda, Stenolaemata, Stelleroida, Crinoidea, Ostracoda, Graptolithina (phyla shown in parentheses). (From J. J. Sepkoski, Jr., 1984, A Kinetic Model of Phanerozoic Taxonomic Diversity. III. Post-Paleozoic Families and Mass Extinctions, Fig. 2: p. 250. *Paleobiology,* vol. 10, no. 2. Reproduced by permission)

and bivalve molluscs (Figs. 10–19 and 10–20A, B)—faunal groups that were of minor significance during the Cambrian.

The dominant Cambrian groups, on the other hand, contributed very little to the great Ordovician faunal radiations (Fig. 10–19). Trilobites, although nearly as abundant and diverse as during the Cambrian, were greatly outnumbered by other Ordovician invertebrate groups, in particular the articulate brachiopods, and, along with inarticulate brachiopods, enjoyed greatest diversity in outer-shelf and slope environments. According to paleontologist J. J. Sepkoski, Jr., the Ordovician pattern of expansion of new major taxa and contraction of typical Cambrian taxa involved the largest turnover in composition of marine faunas in the Phanerozoic history of the oceans.

As mentioned previously, the Cambrian Period appears to have been a time of initial adaptive radiation and evolutionary trial and error among major phyla of invertebrate organisms. Nature's search for workable combinations among the new metazoan life forms produced some success stories, but resulted in numerous extinctions. In contrast, the Ordovician, when viewed in the history of life, was a time of *secondary adaptive radiation* and accelerated diversification, as successful evolutionary lines became established and stabilized. This increase in diversity and evolutionary success may, in part, have been an expression of stabilization of oxygen levels and environments in the marine realm.

By late in the period, all of the *invertebrate phyla* and most of the *classes* that we are familiar with today were firmly established. Since that time, the changes in invertebrate life have been mostly smaller-scale evolutionary radiations and extinctions within these classes at lower taxonomic levels. This contrast further accentuates the difference between the Cambrian fauna and the more typical Paleozoic fauna (Fig. 10–14).

Of great importance in dating and correlating Ordovician strata are the *graptolites* (Fig. 10–19), colonial organisms that evolved rapidly during the Ordovician and Silurian and became extinct during the Carboniferous. Graptolites are preserved most abundantly and characteristically as carbonaceous films on the surface of dark shale layers that were deposited in eugeoclinal areas. This association of graptolites with a particular lithology has inspired the expression "graptolite facies."

True *vertebrate* organisms, represented by primitive jawless fish of the class Agnatha, first appear in the geologic record in rocks of Late Cambrian age in North America. Abundant fragments of bone and external plates of an agnathan group called *ostracoderms* occur in Middle Ordovician sandstone in Colorado, and represent the oldest known diverse vertebrate fauna in North America. Were agnathans the first vertebrates, and if so, what were their evolutionary roots? The fossil record sheds little light on this important evolutionary step, although arguments for an echinoderm ancestry have been favored. The presence of several primitive chordates in the Middle Cambrian Burgess Shale strongly suggests that the vertebrates had their origin during the Cambrian as part of the metazoan explosion.

Conodonts—those enigmatic, microscopic "tooth-like" structures (see Chapter 3) composed of calcium phosphate—are abundant in Ordovician rocks. Although we are not certain of the biologic affinity of conodonts, the suggestion has been made that they are structural parts of a primitive eel-like chordate; if this is true, yet another line of evidence suggests that the chordate record extends back at least as far as the Middle Cambrian. Current ideas have also favored a caetognath-like (arrow worm) or lophophorate invertebrate affinity. But regardless of what they were biologically, conodonts are useful

Figure 10–20

Ordovician faunal communities. A. Shallow-marine Ordovician bottom community: a, articulate brachiopods; b, crinoid echinoderms; c, gastropod mollusc. B. Diverse brachiopod community: articulate brachiopods (a–d); trilobites (e–g); monoplacophoran mollusc (h); nautiloid cephalopod mollusc (i); *Tentaculites,* an enigmatic mollusc (j). C. Graptolite assemblage. Planktonic graptolite colonies sank through the water column to come to rest on deep-sea muddy bottoms.

(From W. S. McKerrow, 1978, *The Ecology of Fossils,* Figs. 9, 11, 12, p. 77, 81, 83: MIT Press.

for biostratigraphic correlation. Because they commonly survive recrystallization and dolomitization of limestones (unlike calcareous body fossils), they are particularly good biostratigraphic tools in carbonate sequences. Much of the Ordovician-through-Devonian chronostratigraphic subdivision of the Cordilleran and cratonal stratigraphic successions is being reexamined by use of conodonts.

Mass extinctions of marine invertebrates at the family level occurred near the end of the Ordovician (Fig. 10–14). Raup and Sepkoski have computed an extinction rate of 19.3 families per million years for the Late Ordovician. This figure represents a diversity drop of 12% and a rate significantly greater than the "normal" background rate of about 8.0 families per million years. Possible causes may have included increased predation and competition, and cooling of marine waters due to glaciation.

Tectonic Unrest in the Appalachians

During the last half of the Ordovician and extending into the Early Silurian, a mountainous land mass emerged in the northern part of the Appalachian continental margin basin (Fig. 10–21). The growth of this structurally complex mountain range was a result of the first in a series of major regional Paleozoic orogenic disturbances that affected the Appalachian belt, and which deformed rocks deposited in the Appalachian continental margin basin. This Ordovician event, called the **Taconic orogeny,** is named after the Taconic Moun-

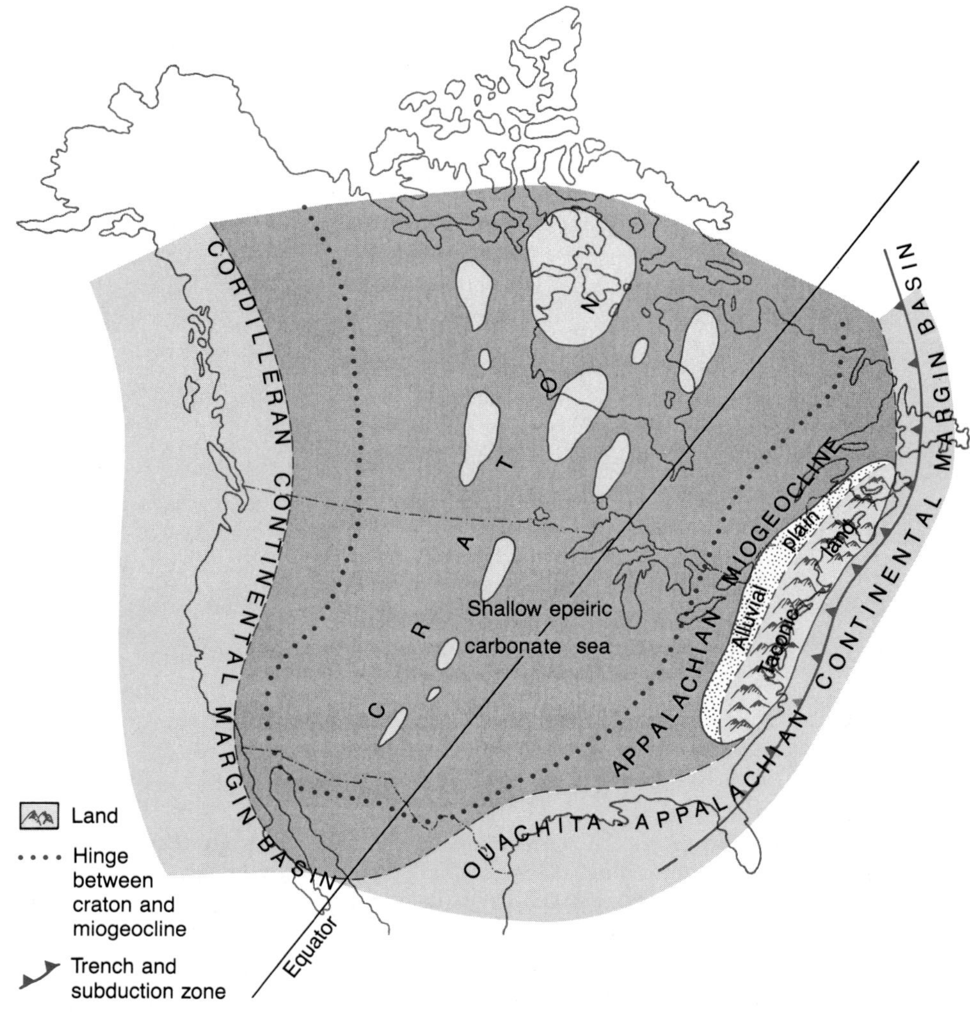

Figure 10–21
Paleogeography of Late Ordovician superimposed on outline map of present-day North America.

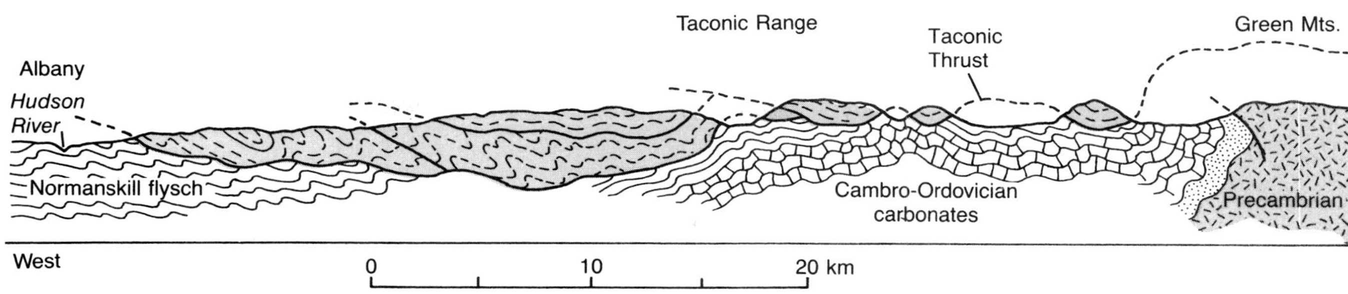

Figure 10–22
Taconic eugeoclinal slices overlying miogeoclinal rocks of about the same age.
(From Philip B. King, *The Evolution of North America.* Copyright © 1959, rev. ed. 1977 by Princeton University Press, Fig. 36, p. 60, reprinted by permission of Princeton University Press)

tains in eastern New York, Vermont, and central Massachusetts. The mountains that were produced during a complex series of Taconic disturbances have long since eroded, but their existence, location, and growth can be deduced from the geologic evidence both within and peripheral to the disturbed belt.

The Taconic orogeny was a significant event in Paleozoic history. It provides a model for understanding mountain-building and the unraveling of geologic history through interpretation of the rock record. One critical aspect of the orogeny involved the tectonic emplacement (Fig. 10–22) of a large mass of previously formed Cambrian and Ordovician eugeoclinal rocks on top of a miogeoclinal section of about the same age. The eugeoclinal rocks are characterized by rhythmically interbedded graded sandstones and shales and associated volcanics; the miogeoclinal rocks are mostly shallow-marine, shelf carbonates with shelly fossils. The stratigraphic and structural relationships have been worked out through painstaking field investigations, aided significantly by graptolite biostratigraphic studies. Here we see the advantage of paleontology: it provides a critical tool that is not available for working out details of pre-Paleozoic orogenies.

Additional structural, stratigraphic, petrologic, and sedimentologic evidence for orogeny has provided much information on timing and magnitude as well as origins of this early Paleozoic disturbance. For example, in a number of places within the Taconic belt, steeply tilted Lower Ordovician and older rocks are overlain by less-deformed Silurian and younger rocks, presenting a pronounced angular unconformity. Yet another line of evidence includes volcanic activity, which was more prevalent in the orogenic belt in New England during the Ordovician Period than during the Cambrian. Rocks produced by this volcanism include eugeoclinal seafloor lava flows, as well as successive levels of widespread volcanic ash beds that punctuate Ordovician successions of the miogeoclinal belt.

Igneous activity also included emplacement of *plutonic* bodies from Georgia to Newfoundland, but particularly in New England, with radiometric dates clustering around 480 to 440 Ma. These plutonites, in part, may represent "plumbing" for some of the volcanics. Mafic and ultramafic rocks occur from Pennsylvania through New England to Newfoundland, and in part represent pieces of oceanic lithosphere (**ophiolites**) that became incorporated into continental structure during the orogeny. Pervasive regional metamorphism, much of which coincided with the Taconic orogeny, has overprinted New England eugeoclinal rocks, and represents yet another manifestation of orogenic-belt activity.

A final body of evidence for the Taconic orogeny is the great volume of sediment that was shed from the western front of the Taconic Mountains, from North Carolina to southern maritime Canada. A voluminous **clastic wedge** of gravel, sand, and mud spread westward from the belt of deformed eugeoclinal rocks and was thickest and coarsest along the eastern margin of the miogeoclinal belt (Fig. 10–23). Red shales and sandstones of the Queenston Formation in New York and southern Ontario, Canada, have given rise to the name "Queenston clastic wedge." Significant amounts of terrigenous clastic material were derived from the east for the first time in the history of the Appalachian continental margin basin; this pattern was to be repeated throughout the remainder of the Paleozoic.

For more than 100 years, geologists have wrestled with various aspects of the Taconic orogeny, in particular with the Taconic eugeoclinal terrane (the *Taconic allochthon*) and the mechanism of its emplacement. What was responsible for the tremen-

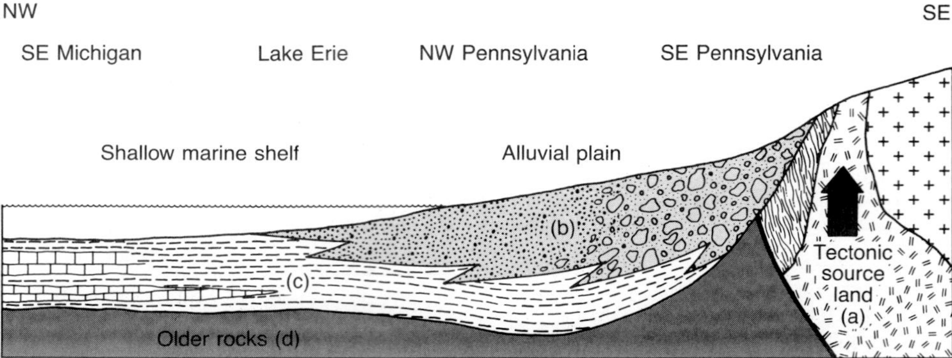

Figure 10–23

Relationship among (a) tectonic source land of Taconic orogen; (b) postorogenic clastic wedge deposits of coarse terrigenous sediments of alluvial fan, stream, and marine shoreface environments; (c) synorogenic and postorogenic shallow marine shelf shale and foreland basin turbidite (flysch) facies; and (d) preorogenic older rocks.

(Modified from G. Marshall Kay, 1948, North American Geosynclines: *Geological Society of America Memoir 48*)

dous crustal shortening and the westward displacement, for tens of kilometers, of one colossal rock suite over another?

Plate tectonics has provided a new model within which to view the various lines of geological evidence. With respect to present-day orientation, the Taconic orogeny is interpreted to have been caused by eastward subduction of oceanic lithosphere beneath a volcanic island arc (Fig. 10–24). Subduction can occur only along the advancing side of a plate; therefore the subduction zone consumed the ocean between the arc and the ancient North American continent until they collided (Fig. 10–24). Evidently the continental crust tried to go down the subduction zone, and part of the oceanic crust was pushed up (*obducted*) onto the continental crust along with continental-rise eugeoclinal deposits which are now the slate and graywacke masses of the Taconic allochthon.

This arc-continent collision was the Taconic orogeny, beginning in early Middle Ordovician and spreading westward through most of the remainder of Ordovician time. Plate convergence caused westward overthrusting, surficial volcanism (perhaps in part related to island-arc activity), and deep-seated igneous intrusion. Also, terrigenous detritus expelled from the uplifted eugeoclinal continental slope–and–rise sediments was redeposited as turbidites in a foreland basin that had developed to the west (Fig. 10–25). These **flysch** deposits were subsequently deformed as tectonism spread westward. Sediments eroding from the resulting tectonic highlands spread westward as a great clastic wedge (**molasse**), producing the nonmarine–to–shallow-marine deposits of the Queenston assemblage (Figs. 10–23 and 10–25).

The northern part of the Appalachian continental margin basin, from its beginning as a rifted continental margin shelf–slope–rise prism in the latest Proterozoic-Cambrian, to its crustal mobility in the Ordovician, evolved from depositional phase to orogenic phase. What had been a passive, trailing-edge setting bordering the **Iapetus Ocean*** during the Cambrian and Early Ordovician became an active, convergent plate margin during the latter part of the Ordovician, as a subduction zone developed and underthrusting of oceanic lithosphere produced compression which caused deformation of the continental margin basin rocks.

The major features of the history of this orogeny can be read from the character of the Ordovician sedimentary sequence: preorogenic stable platform carbonates at the base; succeeded by synorogenic rhythmically bedded turbidites of *flysch* character; topped by postorogenic nonmarine–to–shallow-marine conglomerates, sandstones, and shales (the Queenston clastic wedge) of *molasse* character (Fig. 10–25). Stratigraphic sequences provide a sensitive index to tectonic framework and history.

*The proto-Atlantic. In Greek mythology, Iapetus was the father of Atlas, for whom the Atlantic was named.

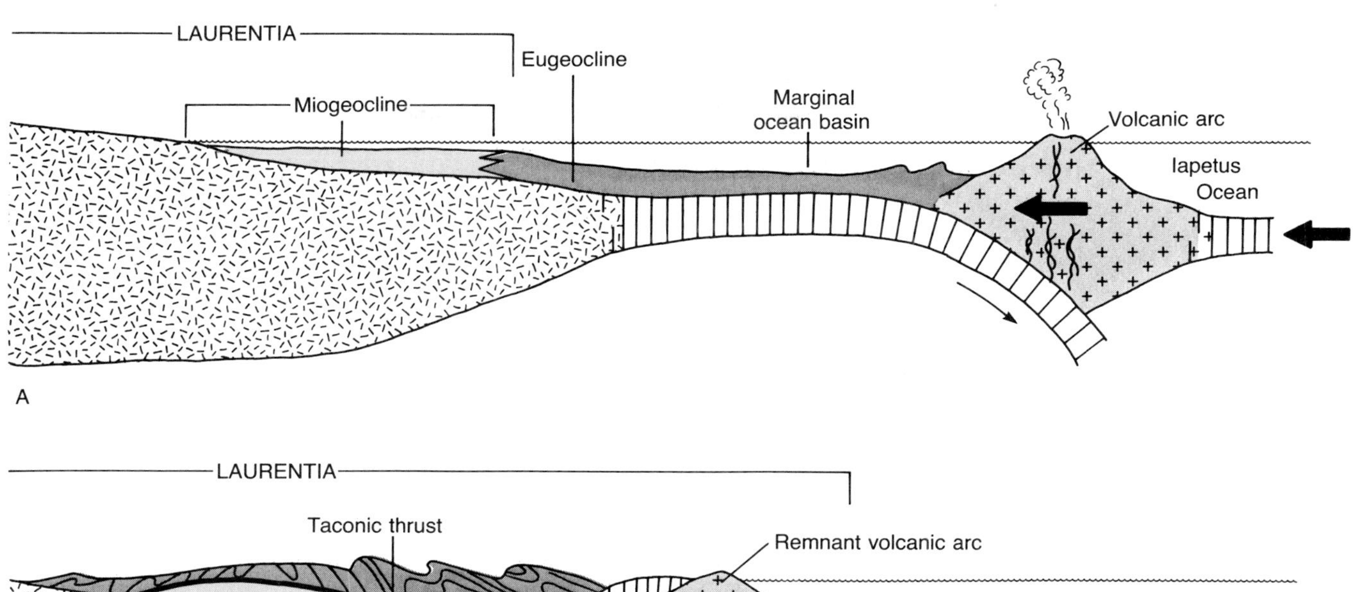

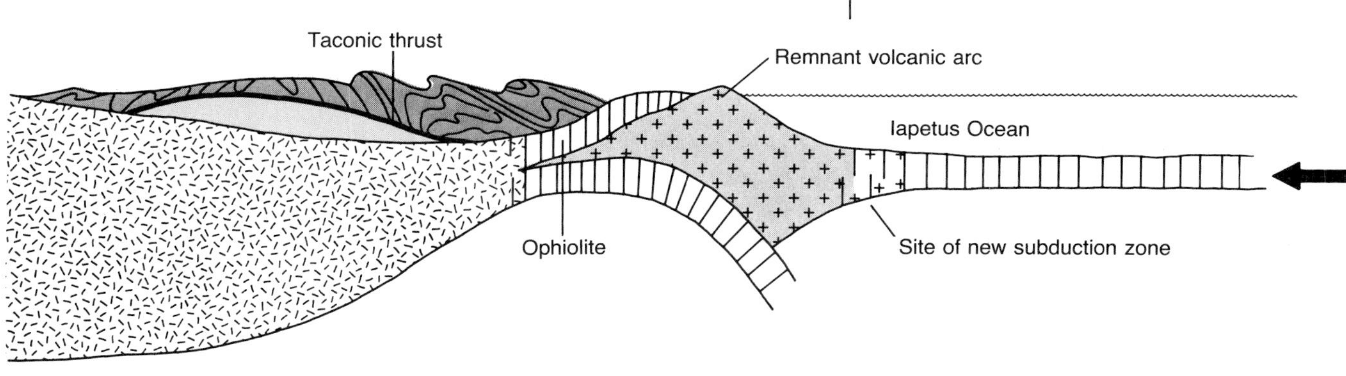

Figure 10–24

Late Ordovician Taconic orogeny. A. Pre-Taconic development of miogeoclinal (shelf) and eugeoclinal (slope, rise) deposits in continental margin basin bordered by volcanic island-arc system. B. Increase in convergence rates produced collision of the volcanic arc with the edge of the continent, causing telescoping of this portion of the continental margin basin, which resulted in thrusting (the Taconic thrust) of eugeoclinal rocks (the Taconic allochthon) over miogeoclinal rocks.

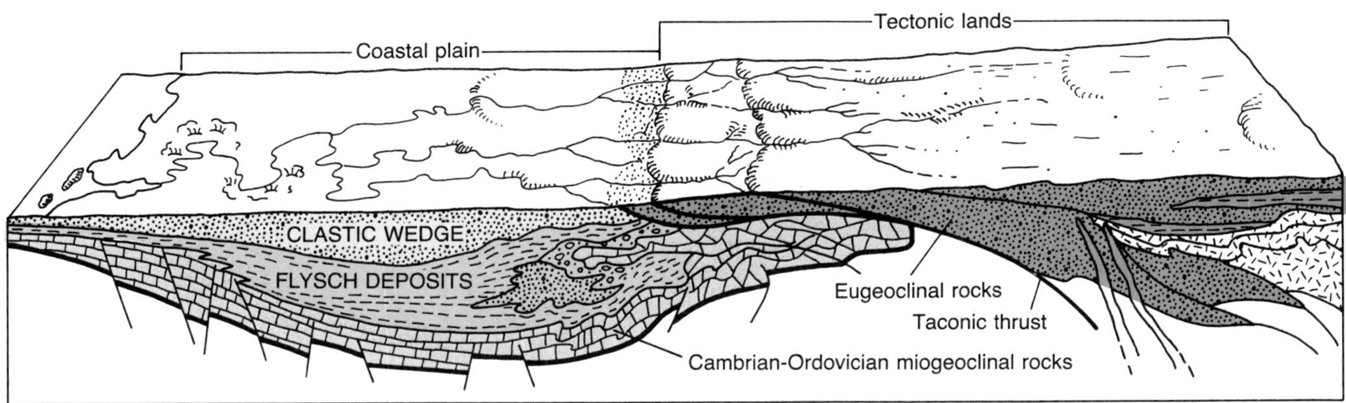

Figure 10–25

Block diagram depicting paleogeography of northern Appalachian region shortly after Taconic orogeny. Taconic tectonic lands were worn down by erosion, and the resulting detritus was carried by westward-flowing streams to be deposited as a coastal-plain clastic wedge.

(Modified from J. F. Bird and J. M. Dewey, 1970, Lithosphere Plate–Continental Margin Tectonics and the Evolution of the Appalachian Orogen, Fig. 7, p. 1043: *Geological Society of America Bulletin,* vol. 81, no. 4. Used with permission of Geological Society of America and the authors)

Silurian History

Salt Deposits, Reefs, and Cratonic Basins

The Taconic Mountains continued to be worn down during the Silurian Period, and the post-Taconic clastic wedge containing abundant *red beds* built out from east to west. Hematite-rich sandstones and mudstones of this sequence serve as the source of iron for the Birmingham, Alabama, steel mills. By the end of the Silurian, the tectonic highlands had been reduced to low relief, and carbonate sedimentation succeeded deposition of terrigenous clastics in the Appalachian miogeoclinal area.

Except for the waning stages of Taconic disturbance in the Appalachian continental margin basin, Silurian history in North America was comparatively quiet tectonically. Major parts of the continental interior were covered by shallow epeiric seas that produced widespread limestone and dolostone deposits. A well-known section exposed along the walls of the gorge below Niagara Falls contains a basal unit of beach sandstone overlain by shallow-marine shale and dolostone (Fig. 10–26). Silurian shallow-marine faunas include abundant articulate brachiopods, bryozoans, cephalopods, crinoids, and corals (Fig. 10–27A); planktonic graptolites populated the near-surface waters of continental margin

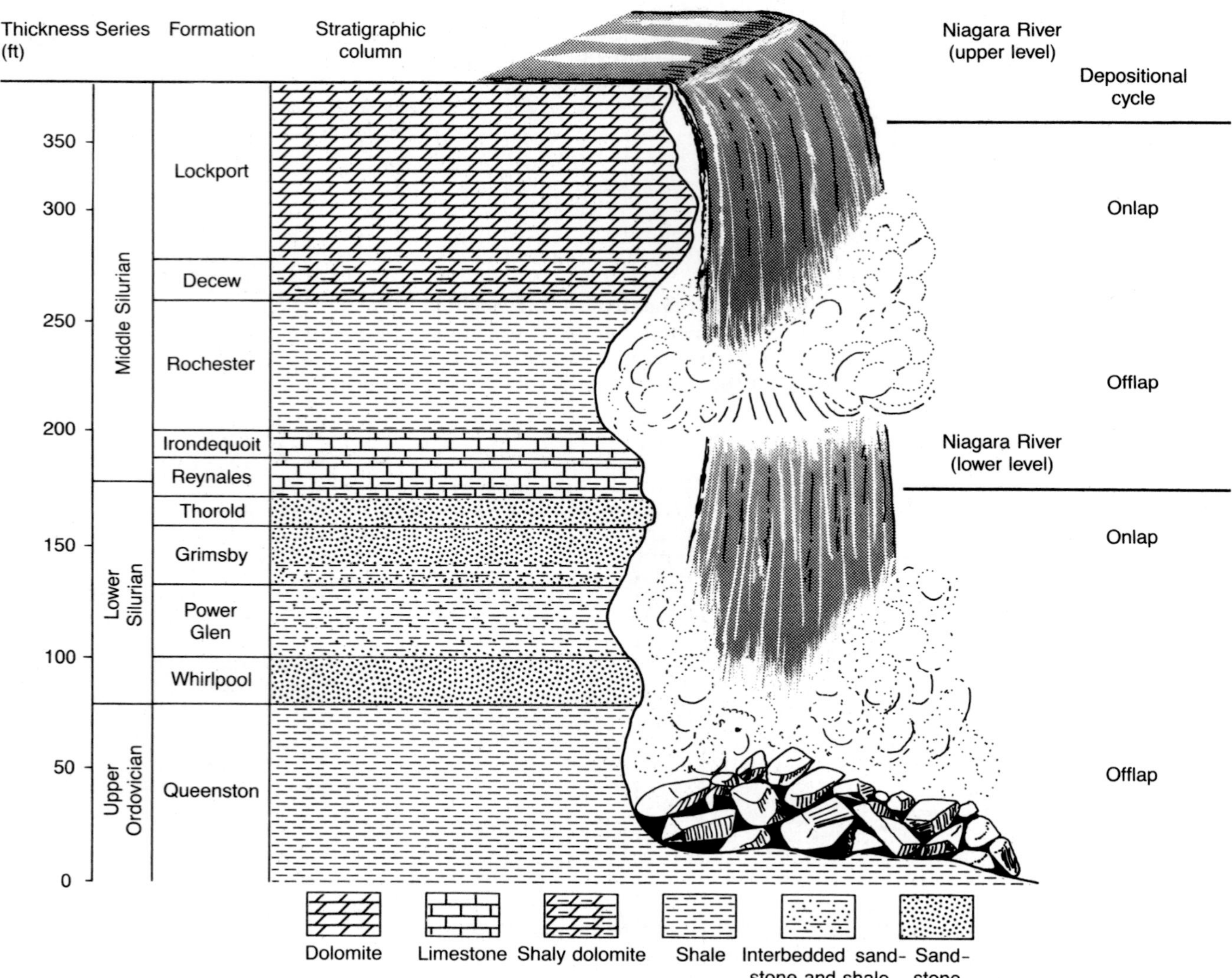

Figure 10–26
Stratigraphic column, Niagara Gorge, United States–Canadian border.

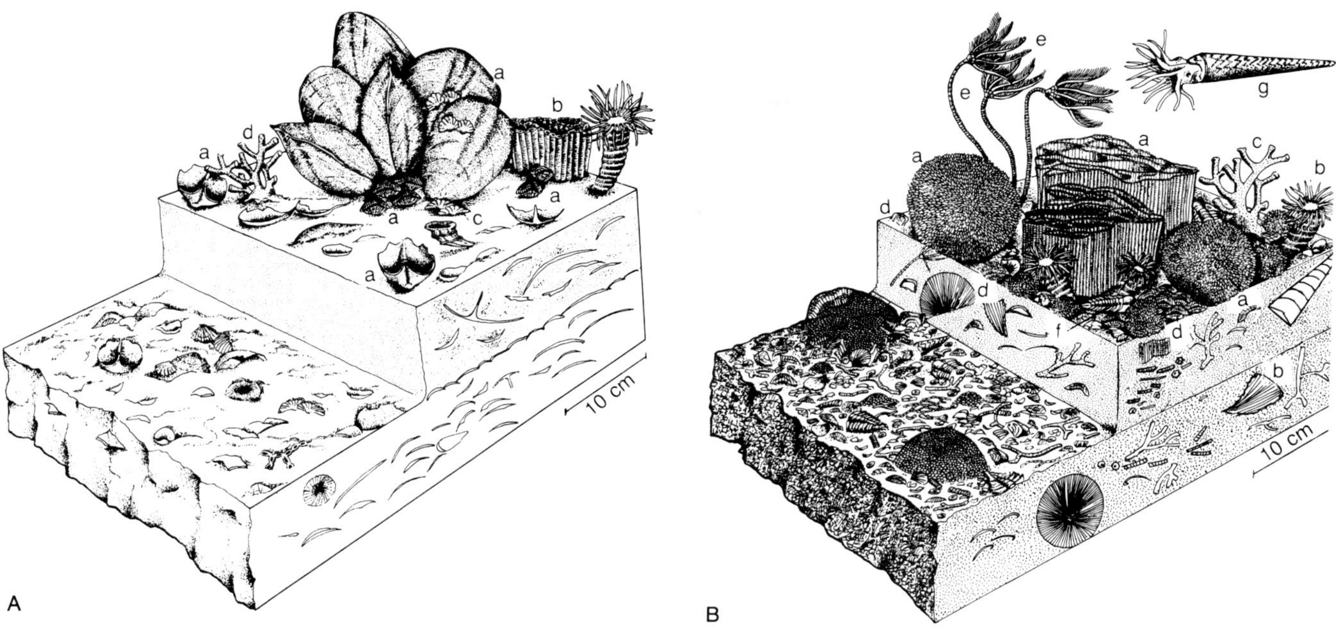

Figure 10–27

A. Silurian shallow-marine bottom community: a, Articulate brachiopods; b, tabulate coral; c, rugose coral; d, bryozoan. B. Silurian reef assemblage: a, tabulate corals; b, rugose coral; c, bryozoan; d, articulate brachiopods; e, crinoid echinoderm; f, trilobite; g, nautiloid cephalopod mollusc.

(From W. S. McKerrow, 1978, *The Ecology of Fossils;* Figs. 22, 24, p. 109, 111: MIT Press.)

basin seas. Unusual arthropods, the eurypterids (Fig. 10–28) and ostracodes, also are locally abundant in some Silurian deposits.

Thick deposits of salt and gypsum accumulated in restricted basins that developed within the eastern part of the craton in a large area encompassing most of Michigan and parts of Ohio, Pennsylvania, New York, and southern Ontario (Fig. 10–29). Evaporite basins, such as the Michigan Basin, were cut off from the open seas by a complex of organic reefs that were built by corals, stromatoporoid sponges, and calcareous algae. The reefs were rigid, wave-resistant, moundlike frameworks of calcium carbonate skeletons that created barriers to circulation. The physical setting that promoted reef growth involved the development of several basins and adjacent arches within what previously had been a stable craton. This warping of the craton was a byproduct of the Taconic orogeny. Abnormally thick cratonic Silurian sections in the Michigan Basin (Fig. 10–29) and Williston Basin (in North Dakota) attest to subsidence and sediment accumulation in these areas.

Reef communities flourished, and the wave-resistant, moundlike structures that formed profoundly affected the development of adjacent sedimentary facies. The reefs are important paleoecologic and stratigraphic features. During the Silurian, tabulate and rugose corals, stromatoporoid sponges, and bryozoans contributed to the reef ecosystem (Fig. 10–27B). This important marine ecosystem represents a major evolutionary advance at the community level and was tied strongly to physical changes in the architecture of the craton.

Paleogeography of the Early Paleozoic World

Paleogeographic Reconstructions

As discussed in Chapter 2, paleogeography is a prime goal of historical geology. To know what the world looked like at various times in the past involves reconstruction of ancient geographies, including land-sea relationships, character of land and marine areas, location of mountain belts, and inferences about paleoclimatic patterns and oceanic circulation.

Figure 10–28
Diorama of Silurian brackish-marine bottom scene near Buffalo, New York. Shown are algae (a), eurypterids (e), worms (w), and shrimp (s).
(Photo courtesy National Museum of Natural History, Smithsonian Institution Photo No. 659A)

Reconstructing global paleogeography involves:

1. Positioning the paleocontinents with respect to latitude and longitude,
2. Determining the geographic features and paleoclimates,
3. Interpreting the paleoenvironmental conditions on each paleocontinent, and
4. Depicting the above features within the limits of stratigraphic dating.

The databases for these determinations include paleomagnetic information; rocks and structures indicative of tectonic belts; and climatically, environmentally, and temporally sensitive rock types and fossils. As indicated by paleogeographer R. Van der Voo, *meaningful paleogeographic reconstructions must show strong agreement among all three: paleomagnetism, paleobiogeography, and paleoclimatology.* Each is discussed below.

Paleomagnetism. Reliable paleomagnetic results depend on a number of factors. First and foremost is the assumption (hopefully correct) that a similar geomagnetic field—a geocentric, coaxial, dipolar one—existed in the geologic past, which exists at present and during the more recent past. This is of utmost importance, in order that paleomagnetic inclinations with respect to the paleohorizontal yield direct information about geographic paleolatitude. Critical also is the quality of the paleomagnetic analysis itself, whereby the true remanent magnetization must be isolated from unwanted later magnetic overprints. Also of critical importance is the accurate determination of the age of the rock being studied, and the age of the magnetization in that rock. There is always a danger of the magnetization's being significantly younger than the rocks in which it has been preserved.

Fortunately, current techniques allow for repeated testing by carefully designed experiments, to

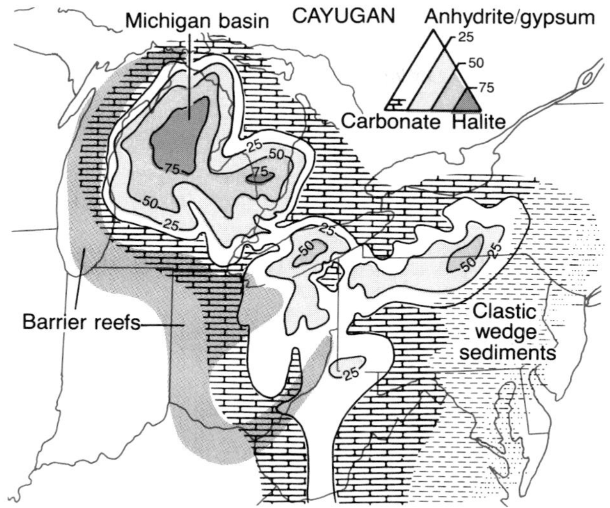

Figure 10–29
Upper Silurian facies map of northeastern United States showing distribution of three principal chemical sediment types: carbonate rock (limestone and dolomite), anhydrite/gypsum, and halite, the products of an evaporite setting.
(After H. L. Alling and L. I. Briggs, 1961, Stratigraphy of Upper Silurian (Cayugan) Evaporites; Fig. 8, p. 541: *American Association of Petroleum Geologists Bulletin,* vol. 45. Reproduced by permission of American Association of Petroleum Geologists)

enable accepting or rejecting each hypothesis that a given magnetization was acquired during a given time interval. The idea here is to identify and screen out (demagnetization) any younger remagnetization that was produced at low temperatures.

One additional unfortunate limitation on paleomagnetic data is that the axially symmetrical nature of the dipole field model which is used to determine paleolatitude will not permit determination of the longitude.

Paleobiogeography. A useful test of predicted paleolatitudes or relative longitudinal proximity may be provided by *faunal provinces.* Although different faunal provinces in time intervals of noncosmopolitan faunas may still span large geographical distances, their boundaries usually must be interpreted in terms of geographic barriers or other reproduction-isolation mechanisms. At the same time, a faunal province found to occur in tectonic elements which are now far apart implies that reproductive communication was possible. Biogeographic relationships, therefore, provide excellent control on relative positioning of individual tectonic elements, and can indicate changes in relative paleolongitudes. However, they are by themselves less able to position the continents in a latitude framework.

Paleoclimatology. Paleoclimatology involves study of the motion of all three complex systems: hydrosphere, atmosphere, and lithosphere. Assertions about paleoclimatic conditions require a rather complete paleogeographic knowledge about the distribution of land, shallow seas, and oceans. Climatically sensitive sedimentary facies generally provide reasonably good estimates: correlations of coal swamps, thick terrigenous clastic sequences, and glacial tillites with wet belts are usually reliable; similarly dry climates are indicated by evaporites. The main problem is developing a model that translates dry or wet conditions (combined with warm or cold temperature indicators) into latitudinal position. Warm-water carbonate rocks, particularly reef facies, help constrain the possibilities to within about 30° latitude, but this depends somewhat on the zonal arrangement and size of continental blocks, and their drift history (rapid or slow, latitudinal or longitudinal drift path).

Despite the problems and constraints, it has been through the integration of paleomagnetic, paleobiogeographic, and paleoclimatic interpretations that the almost kaleidoscopically changing configuration of early Paleozoic (and later) continents has been determined. The most accurate pictures are a function of the quality of the data and the density of data control points.

Cambrian Paleogeography

The reconstruction of Late Cambrian paleogeography of the North American continent (ancient Laurentia, Fig. 10–4) is made possible by careful geologic mapping and analysis of the rock and fossil record, and interpretation of depositional paleoenvironments and of unconformities. But what about the larger, global context of which Laurentia was only a part? What did the Cambrian *world* look like?

Figure 10–30 suggests that it was a world strange and different from the present-day configuration of continents and ocean basins. According to a synthesis of recent paleogeographic studies, six major continental blocks existed during the Cambrian (Fig. 10–30). Much of what is now North America and Greenland, together with parts of the British Isles, comprised the ancient continent of **Laurentia.** Figure 10–30 shows Laurentia lying astride the Equator and in an orientation roughly 90° clockwise from the present-day orientation of North America. This determination is made possible by paleomagnetic evidence derived from Upper Cam-

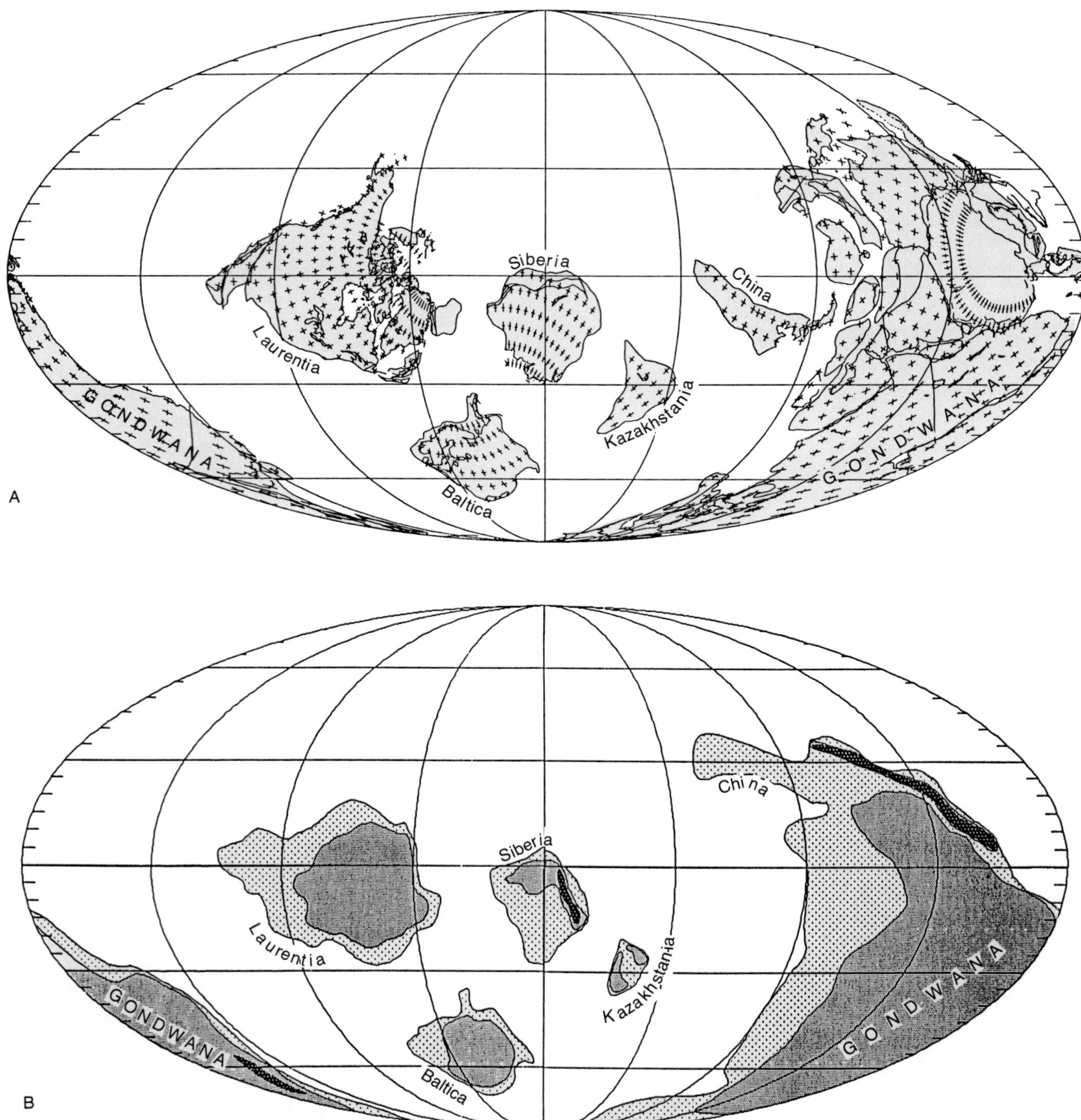

Figure 10–30

World paleogeography reconstructions for the Cambrian. A. Early Cambrian. B. Late Cambrian. Note the equatorial position of Laurentia.
(From C. R. Scotese, 1986, *Phanerozoic Reconstructions: A New Look at the Assembly of Asia.* University of Texas Institute for Geophysics Technical Report No. 66. Paleoceanographic Mapping Project Progress Report No. 19–1286. Used with permission of the author)

brian rocks on the present-day continent—rocks determined to be indigenous to the continent. Nearly horizontal inclinations of magnetized particles tell the ancient latitude, and orientation of the particles permits positioning of Laurentia with respect to the magnetic poles.

Paleomagnetic evidence suggests that all the paleocontinents except **Baltica** and China straddled the Equator during the Late Cambrian and occupied much of the space available in the equatorial belt. Their relative order of longitudinal sequence has been determined by the distribution of faunal provinces. Although Laurentia cannot be related to an absolute longitude (relative to the prime meridian), the space constraints imposed by paleobiogeography and paleomagnetism fix longitudinal position within rather narrow limits.

An example of Cambrian paleobiogeographic data involves trilobite provinces. Cambrian trilobites in eastern North America belong to two distinct faunal provinces, the American and European (Fig. 10–31). Both provinces contain a diverse assemblage of trilobite genera, but share few genera in common. These two distinctive faunal complexions suggest that some kind of barrier was present to prevent mixing. There is compelling information—both geologic and paleontologic—which strongly suggests that Laurentia and Baltica were separated during Cambrian time by the *Iapetus* Ocean.

Through the synthesis of many diverse kinds of data derived from different subfields of geology and geophysics there has emerged a picture of a Late Cambrian world in which the continents were dispersed around the globe in tropical latitudes, ocean basins were extensively interconnected, all the continents except **Gondwana** were awash with shallow seas, and the polar regions lay in open ocean (Fig. 10–30). These paleogeographic features made Late Cambrian time climatologically unique. If the general structure of atmospheric circulation has not changed radically, prevailing winds and ocean currents would have been almost wholly parallel to latitude, especially above 50° to 60° north and south.

Recent heat-budget calculations suggest that the peculiar distribution of land and sea in the Late Cambrian meant that the amount of absorbed solar radiation was probably lower than for any other time during the Phanerozoic, and that the Cambrian was a relatively cool period. This is in marked contrast to the modern world:

> Today's continents are grouped in three extensive north-south-oriented masses which partly isolate three equatorially centered oceans;

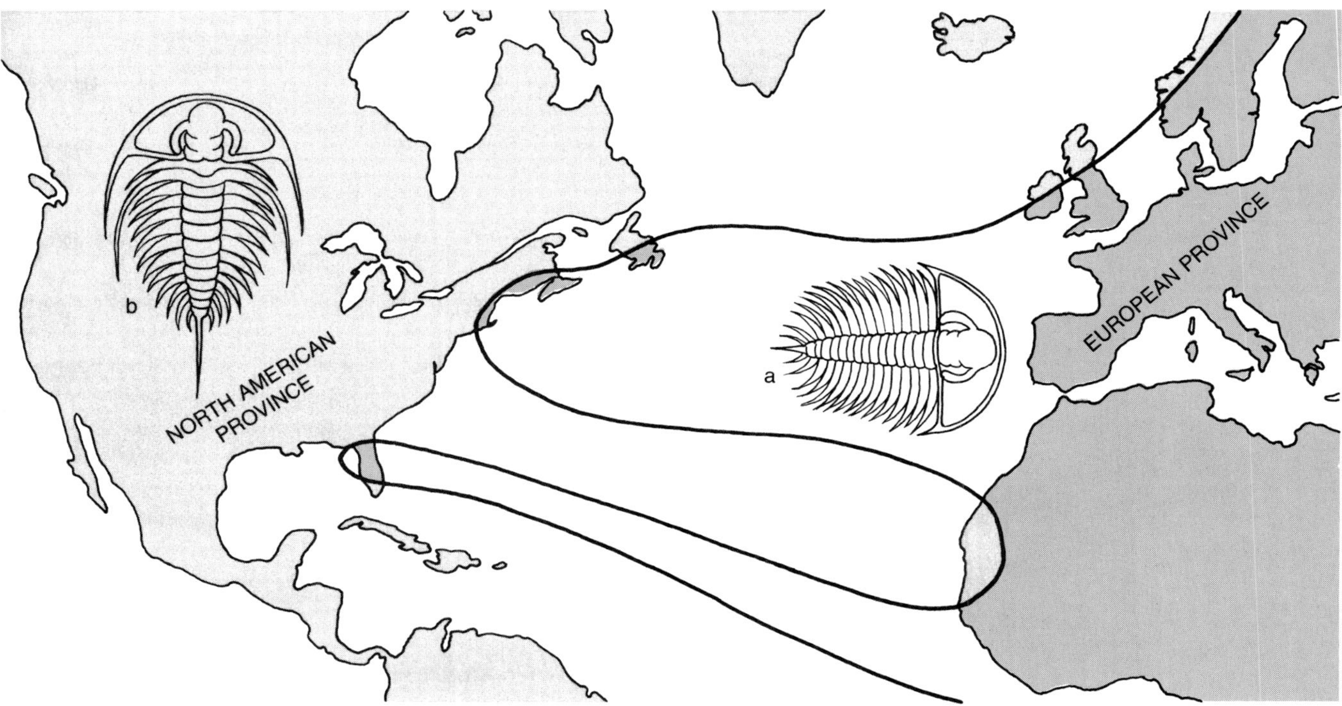

Figure 10–31
Trilobite provinces. The solid line represents the boundary between two distinctly different Cambrian faunal realms (represented by the trilobite genera *Paedeumius,* in North America, and *Holmia,* in Europe). An oceanic barrier originally separated the two biogeographic provinces which are connected today in Scandinavia, the British Isles, parts of eastern North America, and northwestern Africa. The odd pattern of contact between the two provinces is the result of post-Cambrian continental collisions and later separations.

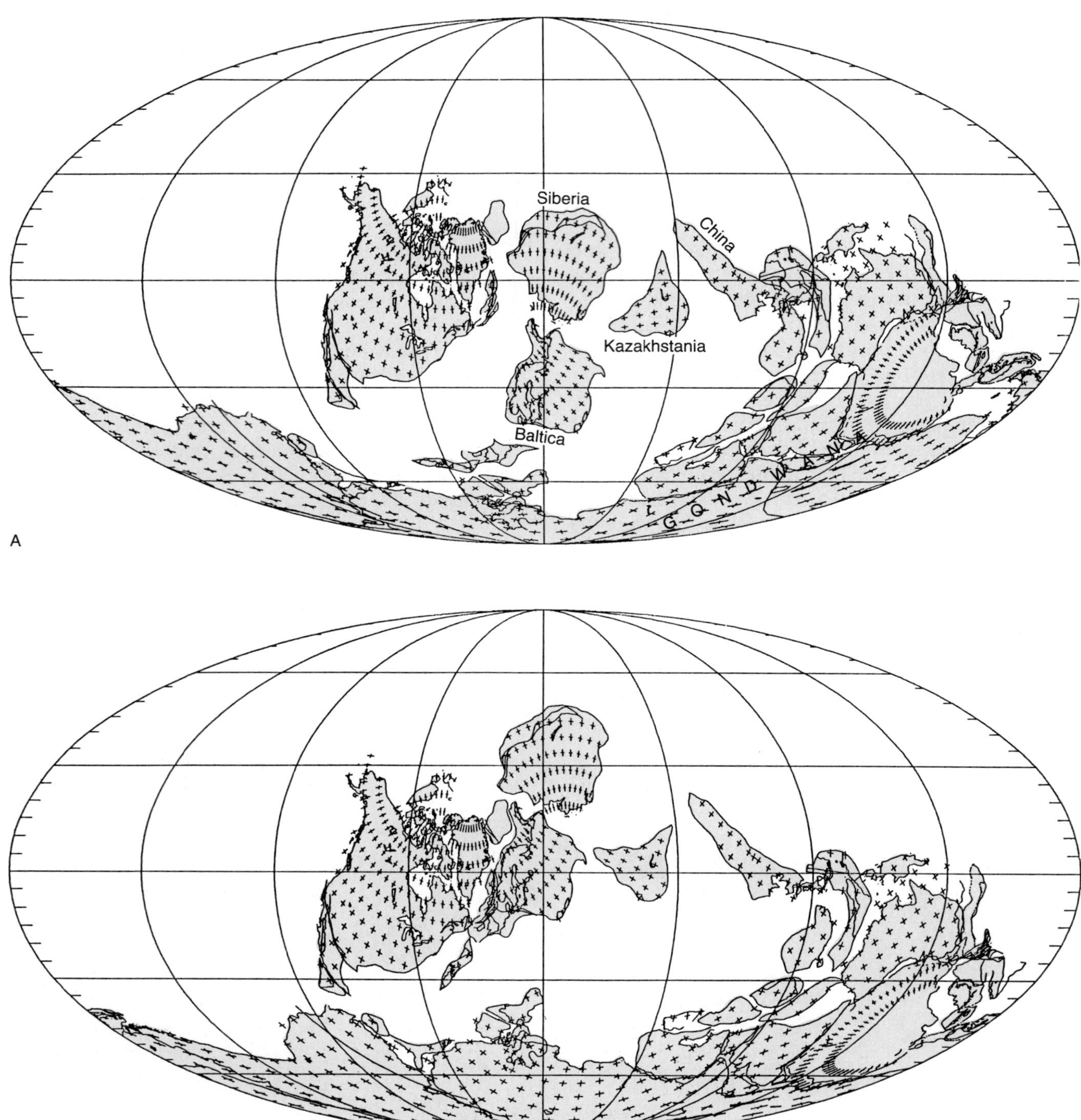

Figure 10–32
Early Paleozoic world paleogeography reconstructions. A. Middle Ordovician. B. Middle Silurian. Note the counterclockwise rotation of Laurentia since the Cambrian (Fig. 10–30) and the convergence between Laurentia and Baltica from Ordovician to Silurian.
(From C. R. Scotese, 1986, *Phanerozoic Reconstructions: A New Look at the Assembly of Asia.* University of Texas Institute for Geophysics Technical Report No. 66. Paleoceanographic Mapping Project Progress Report No. 19–1286. Reproduced with permission of the author)

- Today's continents are largely emergent, with major mountain belts representing zones of earlier plate collisions;
- Today's polar regions are either covered or surrounded by land masses; and
- Today's climates are strongly zoned.

Ordovician and Silurian Paleogeography

According to recently acquired paleomagnetic data, a major rotation occurred during the Ordovician. Laurentia (which included the present-day North American craton, Greenland, Scotland, and northern Ireland) rotated, while remaining on the Equa-

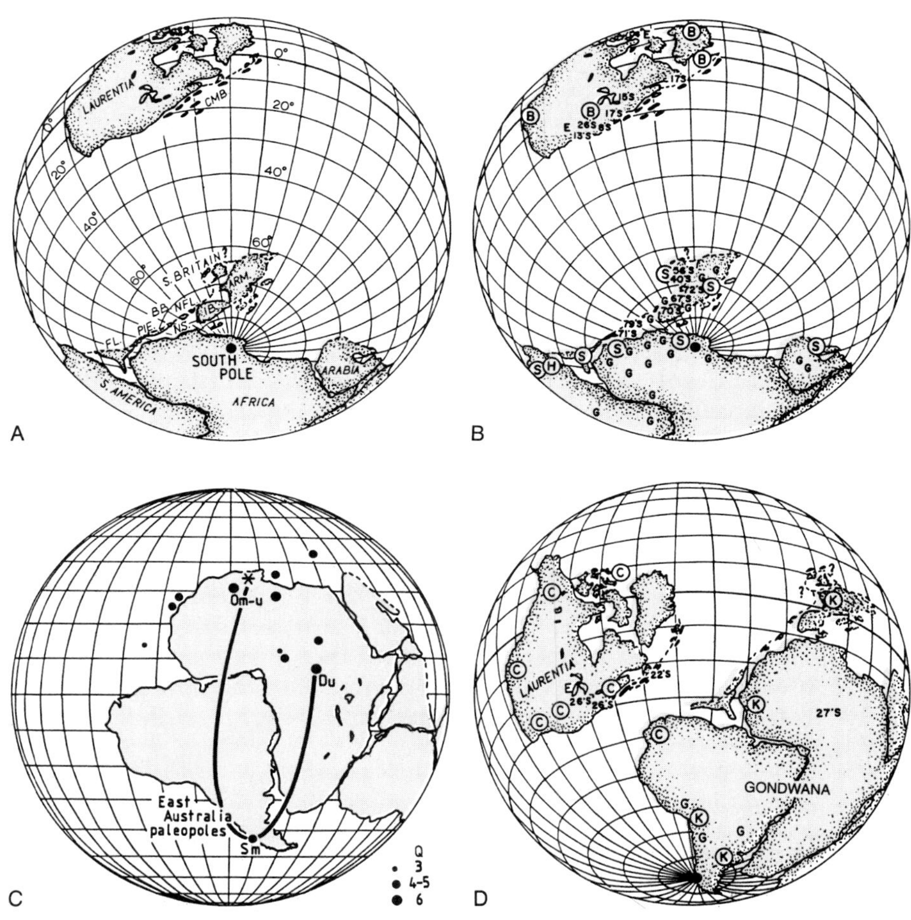

Figure 10–33

A. Middle-to-Late Ordovician paleogeographic reconstruction, showing names of the separate tectonic elements. CMB = Central Mobile Belt of the northern Appalachians, ARM = central Europe, and IB = Iberian Peninsula, together constituting Armorica; NFL = eastern Newfoundland; NS = Novia Scotia; BB = Boston Basin; PIE = Avalonian part of the Piedmont province; FL = northern Florida. B. Same map, but with paleomagnetic paleolatitudes (numbers), biogeographical indicators (circled letters), and paleoclimatological indicators (letters). B = Bathyurid fauna, S = *Selenopeltis* fauna, and H = Hungaiid-Calymenid trilobite fauna. G = glacial relicts; E = evaporite occurrences. C. Ordovician-through-Devonian apparent polar-wander path for Gondwana. Om-u = Middle-to-Late Ordovician; Sm = Middle Silurian; Du = Late Devonian. D. Middle Silurian paleogeography reconstruction. Numbers represent paleomagnetic paleolatitudes; G = glacial relicts; E = evaporite occurrences; C = cosmopolitan brachiopod fauna; K = more endemic *Clarkeia* brachiopod fauna.
(From Rob Van der Voo, 1988, Paleozoic Paleogeography of North America, Gondwana, and Intervening Displaced Terranes: Comparisons of Paleomagnetism with Paleoclimatology and Biogeographical Patterns, Figs. 2, 3, 6, p. 315, 316, 318: *Geological Society of America Bulletin*, Vol. 100, No. 3. Reproduced with permission of Geological Society of America and the author)

tor, in a counterclockwise sense by about 45° (Fig. 10–32A).

Paleoclimatological indicators for the Middle Ordovician of North America consist of evaporites symmetrically distributed at about 15° latitude north and south of the Equator, thus confirming the equatorial paleomagnetic latitudes. Early-to-Late Ordovician phosphorites in Nevada have been interpreted to mark the west-facing margin of Laurentia. Ordovician trilobite faunas that occur in present-day North America, Scotland, northern Siberia, and northern China are not found in the Baltic shield area, southern England and Wales, southern Europe (Armorica), South China, or Gondwana; this suggests that no connection existed between Laurentia and Gondwana or these other areas.

Gondwana moved southward from its Late Cambrian equatorial position (compare Figs. 10–30 and 10–32A), and its North African portion was the first land area to drift into polar latitudes. This region straddled the South Pole during the Late Ordovician, as evidenced by *tillites* of this age in what is now the Sahara Desert! These tillites represent the oldest Paleozoic record of glaciation, and in accordance with our present-day climatic models, suggest that a polar region became landlocked for the first time during the Paleozoic. This resulted in a zonation of climates and refrigeration at the South Pole. The geographic poles of the earlier Ordovician and Cambrian presumably were located in open ocean areas; the shift from equable Cambrian and Early Ordovician climates, to more zoned later Ordovician climates, was a consequence of the more widespread dispersal of continents.

An alternative paleogeographic reconstruction by R. Van der Voo focuses upon Early Paleozoic Laurentia, Gondwana, and intervening small terranes. The latter include the *Avalonian* and *Armorican* loosely comprised mosaic of islands, several exotic terranes in the present central and southern Appalachian Piedmont, and northern Florida. Paleomagnetic, geologic, and biogeographic data on these islands in the Ordovician Iapetus Ocean suggest a significant distance from the equatorial North American craton and a fringing proximity to the northwest African margin of Gondwana (Fig. 10–33A,B).

Evaporites and reefs in the Michigan Basin agree with the paleomagnetic results, thus confirming a paleolatitude of about 25° south for this region during the Silurian (Fig. 10–33B). A recent reconstruction by Van der Voo is based on an apparently well-confirmed paleomagnetic polar-wander path that describes a track between northwest Africa and the area west of Chile for the Silurian movement of Gondwana (Fig. 10-33C). Paleoclimatologically, this new Silurian pole agrees with the presence and absence of mid-Paleozoic glacial relics that describe a path of glacial centers moving across Gondwana. Van der Voo's reconstruction shows that during the Silurian, island terranes in the Iapetus Ocean were swept up by the northerly migration of Gondwana and bulldozed along toward a collision course with Laurentia (Fig. 10–33D).

Summary

During the Cambrian Period, metazoan diversification continued as continental margins and interiors were flooded by marine transgression. The transgressive Cambrian epeiric seas spread a blanket of quartz-rich sand ranging in age from Early Cambrian (in the miogeoclinal belt) to Late Cambrian (in the cratonic interior). By Late Cambrian, most of the cratonic interior of Laurentia was flooded by shallow epeiric seas, and widespread carbonate deposition was the rule.

North American cratonal and miogeoclinal strata contain abundant features of shallow-water deposition, and areally extensive tidal flats were common. Turbidites, black shales, chert, and slump deposits characterize Cambrian eugeoclinal slope and deep basin deposits.

Cambrian world paleogeography was such that six identified major continents were positioned at low latitudes. Much of what is now North America and Greenland, together with parts of the British Isles, made up the ancient continent of Laurentia, which lay astride the Equator in a position roughly 90° clockwise from the present-day orientation of North America.

Post-Tommotian Cambrian skeletal faunas are dominated by trilobites, which make up about 75% of the taxa and provide most of the biostratigraphic biozonation. Of the remainder, inarticulate brachiopods (15–20%), archeocyathids (about 10%, but extinct after the Middle Cambrian), primitive molluscs, and echinoderms are the most abundant taxa. Trace fossils are abundant and diverse, and show a distinct parallelism with the pattern of increased body-fossil diversity from the Ediacarian well into the Cambrian.

One of the most unique fossil assemblages in the geologic archives is the Middle Cambrian Burgess Shale fauna, which includes more than 150 species representing at least eight known and perhaps even more previously unknown phyla. Most of the fossils are unique to the single locality, and represent taxa that became extinct by the end of the Cambrian. The Cambrian, containing the world's first skeletal faunas, was not only a time of rapid diversification and appearance of high-level taxa, but was also a time of extinction of numerous short-lived, low-diversity higher taxa. The Cambrian fauna is unique when compared to post-Cambrian Phanerozoic faunas, reflecting harsh, unstable conditions and changing Cambrian paleoenvironments.

Carbonate deposition in the miogeoclines and craton continued generally uninterrupted from the Late Cambrian into the Early Ordovician, but near the end of the Early Ordovician major regression of epeiric seas produced a craton-wide erosion surface. By the Late Ordovician, nearly the entire craton was inundated once again by shallow epeiric seas that contained a complex mosaic of carbonate environments.

This renewed Ordovician transgression was accompanied by an evolutionary explosion of the calcium carbonate shell, reflecting major adaptive radiation of such shell-bearing taxa as articulate brachiopods and bryozoans. Other important faunal groups that participated in the Ordovician radiation, but were of only minor importance in the Cambrian, included molluscs, echinoderms, and corals, and noncalcareous-secreting taxa such as graptolites and conodonts. This represented a tremendous turnover of marine taxa from Cambrian times, and the stabilization of marine communities and higher-level taxa. After the "Cambrian experiment," no known phyla and very few classes of marine animals became extinct. Primitive jawless fish, the ostracoderms, were present in moderate diversity, and represent an early radiation of vertebrates after their origin in the Cambrian.

From the mid-Ordovician to Early Silurian, the Taconic Orogeny deformed the northern part of the Appalachian continental margin basin. The Taconic, the first of several phases in the deformation of the Appalachian belt, resulted from the subduction of oceanic lithosphere beneath an island-arc terrane and eventual collision of the arc with the continent, telescoping the continental margin and thrusting Cambro-Ordovician eugeoclinal deposits over coeval miogeoclinal carbonates. Erosion of the Taconic land mass produced a voluminous, westward-prograding clastic wedge. During the Silurian, Taconic highlands continued to be worn down, an alluvial plain blanketed a strip of eastern Laurentia, and carbonate epeiric seas covered much of the cratonic interior. Evaporite deposits accumulated in several intracratonic basins which were rimmed with organic reefs.

During the Ordovician and Silurian, Laurentia remained in an equatorial position, while rotating counterclockwise. The northwest-African part of Gondwana was in high southerly latitudes during the Late Ordovician, as evidenced by glacial tillites in the Sahara region. During the Silurian, this region drifted to lower southern latitudes and was fringed by a number of island terranes.

Suggestions for Further Reading

Bambach, R. K., C. R. Scotese, and A. M. Ziegler. 1980. Before Pangea: The geographies of the Paleozoic world. *American Scientist* 68(1):26–38.

Briggs, D. E. G., and H. B. Whittington. 1985. Terror of the trilobites. *Natural History* 94(12):34–40.

Conway Morris, Simon, and H. B. Whittington. 1979. The animals of the Burgess Shale. *Scientific American* 241(1):122–35.

Gould, Stephen Jay. 1985. Treasures in a taxonomic wastebasket. *Natural History* 94(12):22–34.

Gould, Stephen Jay. 1986. Play it again life. *Natural History* 95(2):18–26.

Hallam, A. 1972. Continental drift and the fossil record. *Scientific American* Offprint No. 903. San Francisco: W. H. Freeman.

McAlester, A. L. 1977. *The history of life.* 2d ed. Foundations of Earth Science Series. Englewood Cliffs, NJ: Prentice-Hall.

Palmer, A. R. 1974. Search for the Cambrian world. *American Scientist* 62:216–25.

Raup, D. M., and J. J. Sepkoski, Jr. 1982. Mass extinctions in the marine fossil record. *Science* 215:1500–04.

Valentine, J. W. 1978. Evolution of multicellular plants and animals. *Scientific American* Offprint No. 1403. San Francisco: W. H. Freeman.

Valentine, J. W., and E. M. Moores. 1974. Plate tectonics and the history of life in the oceans. *Scientific American* Offprint No. 912. San Francisco: W. H. Freeman.

Whittington, H. B. 1985. *The Burgess Shale.* New Haven, CT: Yale Univ. Press.

Late Paleozoic History

11

Eon		Era	Period		Age in Ma*
PHANEROZOIC		CENOZOIC	Quaternary	Quaternary	2
			Tertiary	Neogene	24
				Paleogene	65
		MESOZOIC	Cretaceous		144
			Jurassic		208
			Triassic		245
		PALEOZOIC	Permian		286
			Carboniferous	Pennsylvanian	320
				Mississippian	360
			Devonian		408
			Silurian		438
			Ordovician		505
			Cambrian		570
CRYPTOZOIC (PRECAMBRIAN)	PROTEROZOIC	Late Proterozoic			900
		Middle Proterozoic			1600
		Early Proterozoic			2500
	ARCHEAN	Late Archean			3000
		Middle Archean			3400
		Early Archean			~3800
HADEAN (Pregeologic history of the Earth)				Origin of Earth	4600

Contents

Key Terms

Acadian orogeny
Pangaea
Antler orogeny
Ouachita
Alleghany orogeny
Cyclothem
Panthalassa
Tethys Sea
Laurasia

*The Snout**

It began as such things always begin—in the ooze of unnoticed swamps, in the darkness of eclipsed moons. It began as a strangled gasping for air.

The pond was a place of reek and corruption, of fetid smells and of oxygen-starved fish breathing through laboring gills. At times the slowly contracting circle of the water left little windrows of minnows who skittered desperately to escape the sun, but who died, nevertheless, in the fat, warm mud. It was a place of low life. In it the human brain began.

There were strange snouts in those waters, strange barbels nuzzling the bottom ooze, and there was time—three hundred million years of it—but mostly, I think, it was the ooze. By day, the temperature in the world outside the pond rose to a frightful intensity; at night the sun went down in smoking red. Dust storms marched in incessant progression across a wilderness whose plants were the plants of long ago. Leafless and weird and stiff they lingered by the water, while over vast areas of grassless uplands the winds blew until red stones took on the polish of reflecting mirrors. There was nothing to hold the land in place. Winds howled, dust clouds rolled, and brief erratic torrents choked with silt ran down to the sea. It was a time of dizzying contrasts, a time of change.

On the oily surface of the pond, from time to time a snout thrust upward, took in air with a queer grunting inspiration, and swirled back to the bottom. The pond was doomed, the water was foul, and the oxygen almost gone, but the creature would not die. It could breathe air direct through a little accessory lung, and it could walk. In all that weird and lifeless landscape, it was the only thing that could. It walked rarely and under protest, but that was not surprising. The creature was a fish.

In the passage of the days the pond became a puddle, but the Snout survived. There was dew one dark night and a coolness in the empty stream bed. When the sun rose the next morning the pond was an empty place of cracked mud, but the Snout did not lie there. He had gone. Down stream there were other ponds. He breathed air for a few hours and hobbled slowly along on the stumps of heavy fins.

It was an uncanny business if there had been anyone there to see. It was a journey best not observed in daylight, it was something that needed swamps and shadows and the touch of the night dew. It was a monstrous penetration of a forbidden element, and the Snout kept his face from the

*Loren Eiseley. 1957. *The Immense Journey.* Random House, Inc. Reprinted by permission of Random House Publishers, New York.

light. It was just as well, though the face should not be mocked. In three hundred million years it would be our own.

There was something fermenting in the brain of the Snout. He was no longer entirely a fish. The ooze had marked him. It takes a swamp-and-tide-flat zoologist to tell you about life; it is in this domain that the living suffer great extremes, it is there that the water-failures, driven to desperation, make starts in a new element. It is here that strange compromises are made and new senses are born. The Snout was no exception. Though he breathed and walked primarily in order to stay in the water, he was coming ashore.

He was not really a successful fish except that he was managing to stay alive in a noisome, uncomfortable, oxygen-starved environment. In fact the time was coming when the last of his kind, harried by more ferocious and speedier fishes, would slip off the edge of the continental shelf, to seek safety in the sunless abysses of the deep sea. But the Snout was a freshwater Crossopterygian, to give him his true name, and cumbersome and plodding though he was, something had happened back of his eyes. The ooze had gotten in its work.

Devonian History

Depositional Patterns

From their adaptive success in the Silurian, reef-building organisms continued to flourish well into Devonian time. Devonian reef complexes buried in the subsurface of western Canada are important petroleum reservoirs. The reef cores represent carbonate facies that commonly had favorable *porosity* and *permeability*, and were situated updip from more basinal deposits that were rich in organic matter. This raw organic matter subsequently became converted to hydrocarbons with time and depth of burial, and eventually migrated updip to become entrapped in the reef facies. The Golden Spike reef complex in Alberta is a representative example (Fig. 11–1). Carbonate rocks comprise only about 20% of the stratigraphic column worldwide, but roughly half of the Earth's petroleum reservoirs are in these carbonates, mostly in dolostone. A good proportion of these are associated with reef facies.

The widespread, carbonate-rich epeiric seas that characterized the Silurian receded, and much of the continental interior underwent erosion during the Early and Middle Devonian. Early Devonian was a time of continued warping of the craton as basins and arches continued to grow and to influence sedimentation patterns. The Michigan Basin and the Williston Basin of North Dakota and southern Canada continued to subside and receive deposits of dolomite, anhydrite, and some gypsum and salt. In these areas, downwarping attendant with deposition preserved sedimentary sequences so that Upper Silurian and Lower Devonian rocks are conformable. Through much of the rest of the cratonic region, Lower and Middle Devonian rocks are absent. The Middle Devonian transgressive sea deposited fossiliferous sandstones, shales, and limestones. This transgression inaugurated another major onlap-offlap stratigraphic *sequence* cycle (Fig. 10–17, Chapter 10) in the cratonic interior.

Much of the Cambrian-Devonian carbonate section in North America consists of dolostone, composed of the mineral dolomite, $CaMg(CO_3)_2$, which formed mainly by secondary replacement of original limestone. Dolomitization of much of the lower Paleozoic carbonate section in the Great Basin Province of the Cordillera is believed to have resulted from shallow subsurface mixing of marine and fresh water, the latter having filtered into the subsurface from exposed tracts of tidal flats as well as from emergent surfaces that acted as freshwater

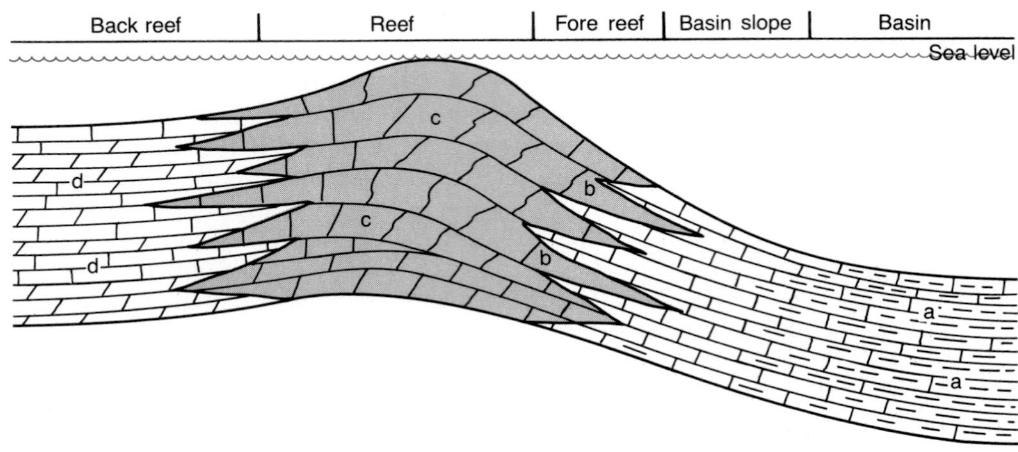

Figure 11–1

Schematic cross section across reef tract showing back-reef lagoonal facies (d), reef core (c), reef flank (b), and basinal facies (a). Hydrocarbons (oil and gas) are generated from raw organic matter that accumulates under low-oxygen bottom conditions in (a). Maturation of organic material to petroleum involves burial under sediment load and subsequent heating, with expulsion of hydrocarbons into basin-slope and reef-flank carrier beds (b). Hydrocarbons become trapped mainly in highly porous and permeable carbonates of the reef core, which is situated along edge of platform in attractive position to receive migrating fluids. Favorable reservoir porosity and permeability characteristics of reef core are related to initial organic framework fabric of reef as well as postdepositional solution and dolomitization.

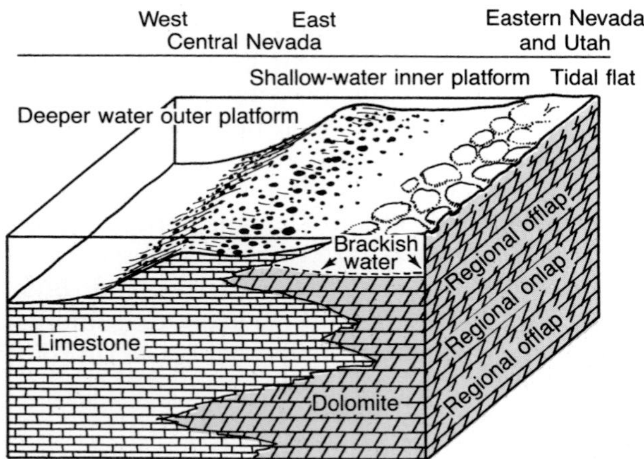

Figure 11–2

Generalized paleogeography of early Paleozoic Cordilleran miogeocline and its influence on regional dolomitization of subtidal limestone deposits. Open tracts of supratidal environments and areas exposed during regressive phases acted as areas of freshwater recharge. Subsurface mixing of fresh and marine waters provided optimum Mg/Ca ratios and slow crystallization rates, promoting extensive dolomitization. Lateral migration of recharge areas with regional onlap and offlap resulted in migration of limestone-dolomite boundary with time. Limestones in west-central Nevada escaped pervasive dolomitization because of distance from areas of freshwater recharge. Horizontal dimension represents tens to hundreds of kilometers; vertical dimension represents tens to hundreds of meters.

(From J. B. Dunham and E. R. Olsen, 1978, Diagenetic Dolomite Formation Related to Paleozoic Paleogeography of the Cordilleran Miogeocline in Nevada; Fig. 1, p. 557: *Geology*, vol. 6. Reproduced by permission of the authors and Geological Society of America)

recharge areas (Fig. 11–2). Significant amounts of dolomite may also have formed as early postdepositional replacement of limestone in supratidal environments where magnesium-rich brines were concentrated.

Devonian limestones have offered some of the finest fossil collecting in North America. It was primarily a comparison of fossiliferous Devonian strata in New York and Iowa that led James Hall to his ideas on "geosynclines" (Chapter 6). Abundant articulate brachiopods, corals, bryozoans, sponges, crinoids, and trilobites comprise an invertebrate fauna that reached its greatest diversity in Middle Devonian seas (Fig. 11–3). Ammonoid cephalopods underwent a major adaptive radiation, and the earliest forms, those with *goniatite sutures,* are important taxa for biostratigraphic subdivision and correlation of Devonian and Carboniferous rocks. Devonian carbonate rocks also are commonly rich in conodonts, which have been important to biostratigraphic studies. Near the end of the Devonian, mass extinction decimated the ranks of marine invertebrates (Fig. 10–14A, Chapter 10), marking another faunal crisis in the history of Phanerozoic life.

A Calendar in the Coral

Annual and daily growth increments—analogous to growth rings of trees—of some Middle Paleozoic rugose corals can be compared with those of modern scleractinian corals. The number of daily layers between annual layers generally ranges from 410 to 420 in Devonian species, a significant difference from the 360 to 370 in modern specimens. This comparison suggests that there were more days in a Devonian year than in our present year. The inference here is that, if the path of the Earth's orbit around the sun has not changed significantly, then the speed of the Earth's rotation about its own axis has. If such is the case, the cause was probably the braking action of the gravitational attraction of the Moon on the Earth's rotation. If we have correctly

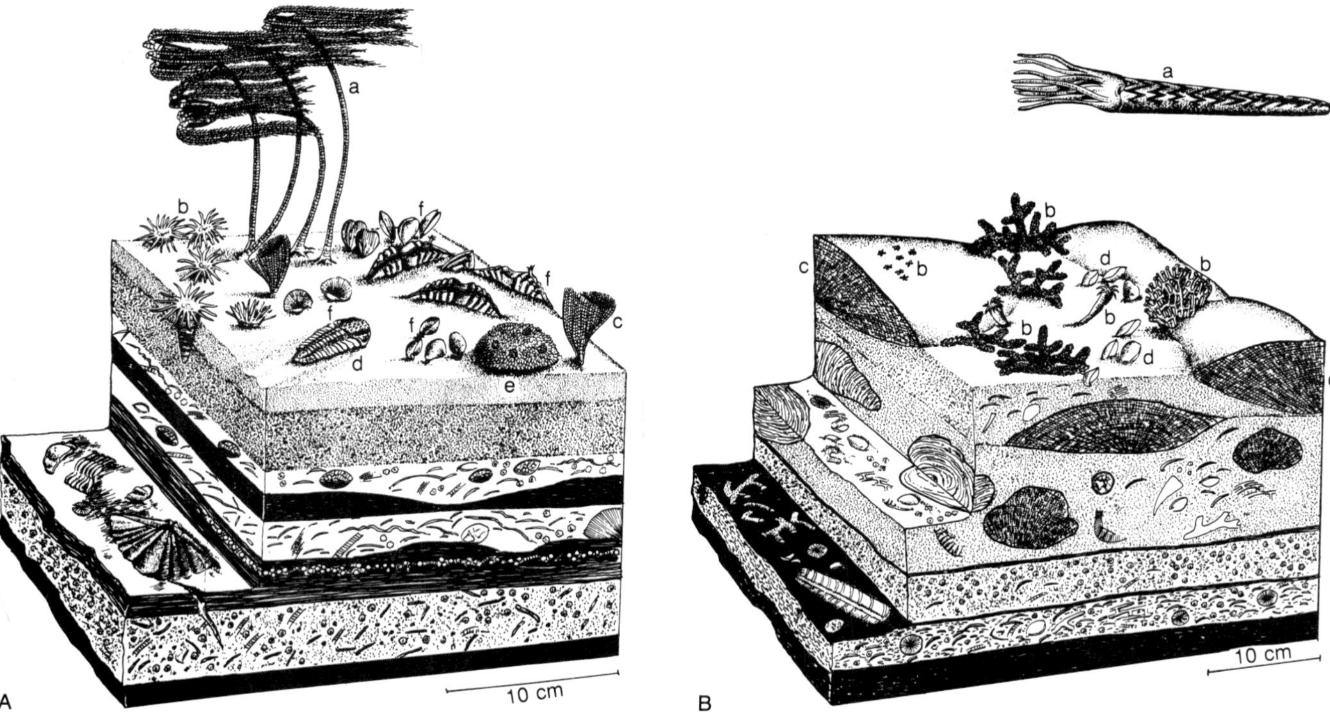

Figure 11–3
A. In-life Middle Devonian muddy-shelf marine-bottom community: a, crinoid echinoderms; b, rugose coral; c, bryozoan; d, trilobite; e, tabulate coral; f, articulate brachiopods. B. In-life Middle Devonian off-reef community: a, nautiloid cephalopod mollusc; b, tabulate corals; c, stromatoporoid sponge; d, articulate brachiopods.
(From W. S. McKerrow, 1978, *The Ecology of Fossils;* Figs. 34, 35, p. 136, 137: MIT Press, all rights reserved. Reproduced with permission of MIT Press)

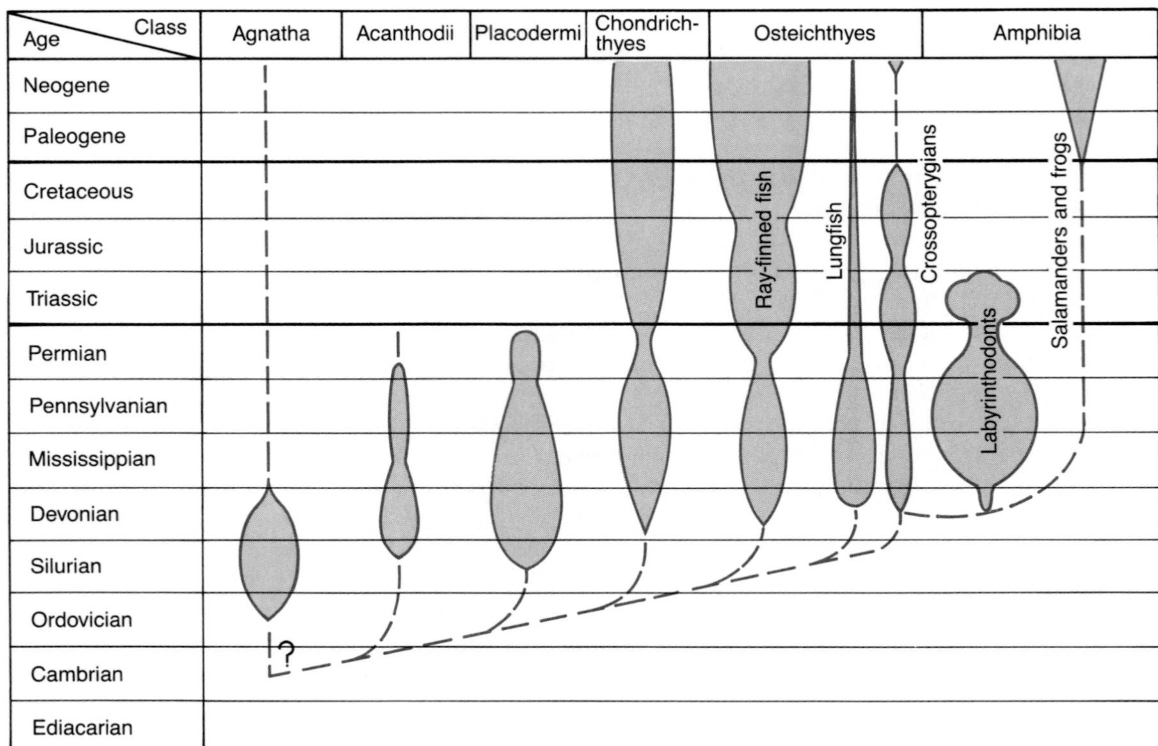

Figure 11–4
Large-scale evolutionary history of fishes and amphibians. Dashed lines show the most probable evolutionary relations. The width of the patterned areas indicates the approximate diversity and abundance of each group.

extrapolated from the Devonian coral data, then the slowdown in the Earth's rotation has been about one second every 50,000 years since the origin of the Earth-Moon system. This figure has been confirmed by independent astrophysical studies.

The Age of Fish and the Vertebrate Transition to Land

Vertebrate life also diversified during the Devonian. Five classes of fish had evolved by early in the period. Because of the rapid evolutionary adaptive radiation the Devonian has commonly been referred to as "the age of fish." The five fish classes include:

1. The jawless Agnatha, represented today by the parasitic lampreys and hagfish.
2. The Acanthodii, jawed armored fish—extinct.
3. The Placodermi, jawed armored fish—extinct.
4. The Chondrichthyes, including true sharks, skates, and rays.
5. The Osteichthyes, which are the bony fishes.

Because of their great efficiency in the aquatic environment, the last two groups rapidly replaced the other classes during the Late Devonian, and have been dominant ever since (Fig. 11–4).

Geologic evidence suggests that fish initially evolved in marine environments. However, as part of the Devonian radiation, several groups invaded freshwater habitats.

One of the milestones in the evolutionary history of the vertebrates was the development of the jaw. The jaw of primitive placoderms is believed to have evolved from the anterior gill arches of agnathan ancestors. By early in the Devonian, fish had evolved jaws lined with cutting teeth and they represented a new level of predation.

The bony fishes are divided into two main groups, one of which, the ray-finned fish, includes the forms with which we are most familiar today. The other group of bony fishes, the so-called *lobe-finned fish,* were the ancestors of nonfish vertebrate classes. A group of Devonian lobe-finned fish called the *crossopterygians* possessed paired fins that consisted of bones around a strong central axis and attached to the body by a shoulder girdle, structurally

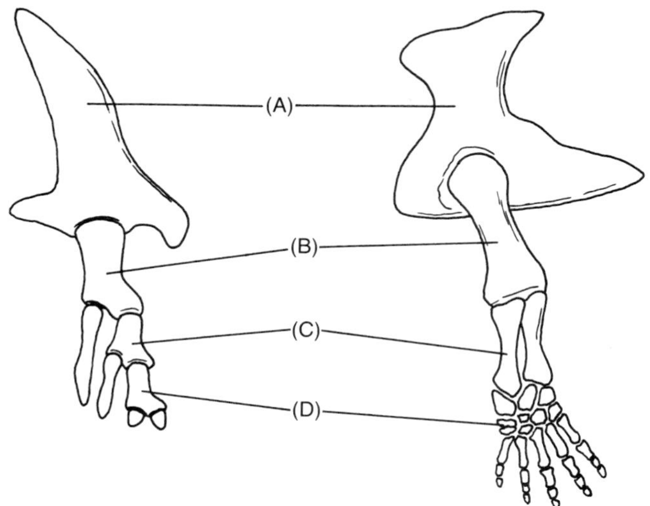

Figure 11–5

Comparison of pelvic region and the hind limb in Devonian crossopterygian fish *Eusthenopteron* (left) and Permian labyrinthodont amphibian *Trematops* (right): (A) pelvis, (B) femur, (C) tibia-fibula, (D) pes.

(From E. H. Colbert, *Evolution of the Vertebrates—A History of the Backboned Animals Through Time,* 3d ed.; Fig. 26, p. 71. Copyright © 1980 by John Wiley & Sons, Inc. Reprinted by permission of John Wiley & Sons, Inc.)

different from those of ray-finned fishes (Fig. 11–5). This bone arrangement allowed the lobe fins more freedom of movement at the point of attachment to the body, and their muscles extended into the fin to permit greater control of fin movement. In addition to the specialized fin, crossopterygians had lungs for breathing air, presumably an adaptation for existence in oxygen-depleted terrestrial ponds.

Lobe fins, ideally suited to develop into flexible supportive limbs, combined with lungs for breathing air, proved to be a beautiful *preadaptation* for making vertebrate life on land a possibility. Before the end of the Devonian, primitive amphibians evolved from a group of crossopterygians called the *rhipidistians,* exemplified by our friend, the Snout, eloquently described by anthropologist Loren Eiseley in the introduction to this chapter.

Having adapted to freshwater environments that occasionally dried up or became depleted of oxygen, the rhipidistians were constantly vulnerable. Their lobed fin and lung evolved to cope with such harsh conditions. These structures were adaptations for survival, not for the luxury of walking on land. However, the lobed fin possessed the basic tetrapod (four-legged) limb plan (Fig. 11–5), and this paved the way for the evolutionary transformation of a water-dwelling creature to a land creature, and for the emergence of a new class of vertebrates, the Amphibia.

Living crossopterygians are represented by the *coelacanths,* an evolutionary branch that diverged during the Devonian (Fig. 11–6). Coelacanth fossils have been reported from rocks as young as Cretaceous, but the creatures were long thought to be extinct. However, in 1939, off the coast of South Africa, a fisherman landed a live coelacanth in his nets; several dozen have been reported since. These "living fossils" have helped clarify the structures of the Paleozoic lobe-finned fish.

The amphibians were not the first inhabitants of the terrestrial environment, however. Land plants, which probably evolved from green algae (see Chapter 16 for a thorough discussion of plant evolution), first appear in the Upper Silurian rock record, and are represented by forms no longer than matchsticks. During the Devonian, several divisions of *seedless vascular plants* evolved rapidly; by late in the period, diverse forests, including large trees, covered extensive lowland areas. Many elements of this diverse flora provided food for the amphibian invaders. Among the animals, the first amphibians were preceded in their invasion of the land by early insects, spiders, and some gastropods.

Terrestrial Vertebrates: The Earliest Amphibians

The oldest known amphibians come from Old Red Sandstone deposits in eastern Greenland, and are well represented by the genus *Ichthyostega.* Similar in form to their crossopterygian ancestor, the ichthyostegids had streamlined bodies, long tails, and fins, all well suited for efficient swimming. However, in addition, they had four legs and strong hip girdles, shoulders, and rib cages, all structural adaptations for walking on land. These adaptations must have taken place slowly and involved changes in a variety of physiological and structural characters. Problems of breathing, hearing, and feeding, in addition to locomotion, had to be overcome. Such changes occurred through a succession of populations before the amphibian condition became a reality.

The transition is well documented in the fossil record. During the Carboniferous, the amphibians that followed the ichthyostegids were the *labyrinthodonts,* so named for the intricately grooved, labyrinthine structure of their teeth. A group of labyrinthodonts called *rhachitomes* (Fig. 11–6) were squat, bulky creatures with stout limbs and looked somewhat like stubby alligators. They were the dominant land vertebrates on the scene when

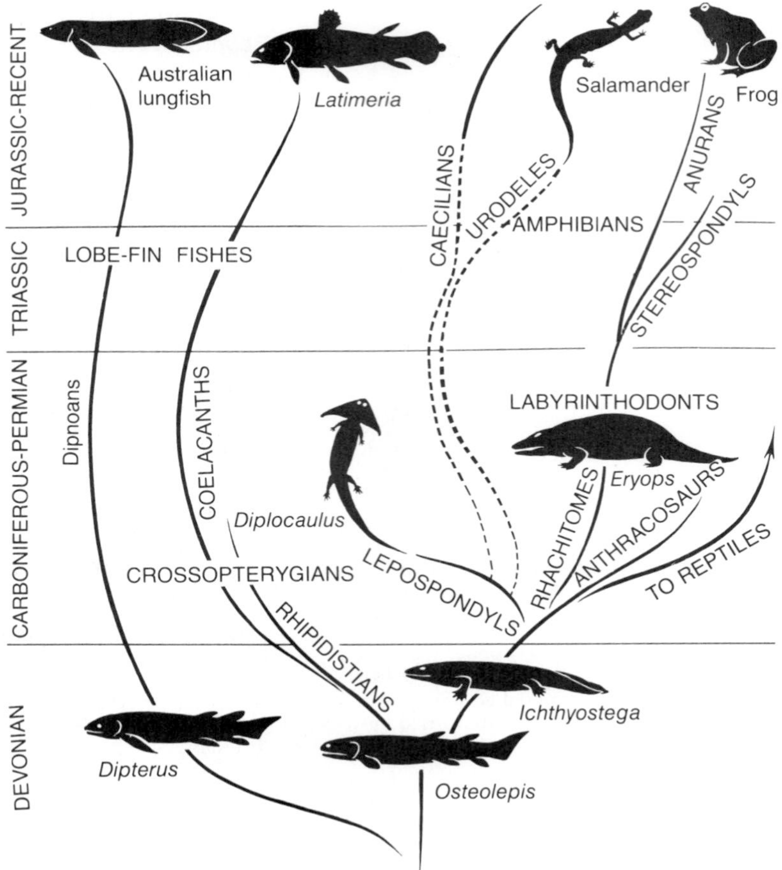

Figure 11–6
Evolution of the lobe-finned fishes and amphibians.
(From E. H. Colbert, 1980, *Evolution of the Vertebrates—A History of the Backboned Animals Through Time*, 3d ed.; Fig. 29, p. 87. Copyright © 1980 by John Wiley & Sons, Inc., New York. Reprinted by permission of John Wiley & Sons, Inc., and Lois M. Darling)

the first reptiles evolved from them in the Carboniferous.

Today's amphibians, including toads, frogs, newts, and salamanders, play a subordinate role among land vertebrates. Like their ancestors, they are still linked to the aquatic environment. They were able to surmount the crucial obstacles of air-breathing and locomoting on land, but one final requirement for a pure land life has eluded them: amphibians must return to the water to reproduce, because their delicate, naked eggs, like those of fish, would quickly desiccate if deposited in a subaerial environment.

More Tectonic Unrest

Middle Paleozoic orogenic disturbances resulted in yet another phase of mountain building in eastern Laurentia (northeastern North America and Greenland) and northwestern Baltica (Western Europe). This major tectonic event, the **Acadian orogeny,** was superimposed across the deeply eroded roots of the Taconic orogenic belt. From South Carolina to Newfoundland, the Appalachian eugeocline, which had been compressed during the Taconic disturbance, was deformed again. The resulting Acadian tectonic land covered an even larger area and shed a tremendous volume of terrigenous clastic debris (Fig. 11–7). Evidence of this major orogenic event is read from the rock record in the same fashion as described for the Taconic orogeny.

This disturbance involved events typical of orogenic belts: folding, faulting, metamorphism, and igneous intrusion. Profound angular unconformities separating Lower Devonian and older rocks from Upper and post-Devonian rocks tell part of the story. Granite intrusives and regional metamorphism also were more widespread than during the Taconic orogeny. Isotopic dates from throughout the crystalline Appalachians indicate extensive plutonism and crustal disturbance during the Devonian.

One result of the Taconic arc–continent collision was to force a new westward-dipping subduction zone to form east (outboard) of the accreted volcanic arc terrane. This new subduction zone would have "swallowed" Iapetus oceanic crust between eastern Laurentia and other continental terranes (Fig. 11–8). Recent paleomagnetic and

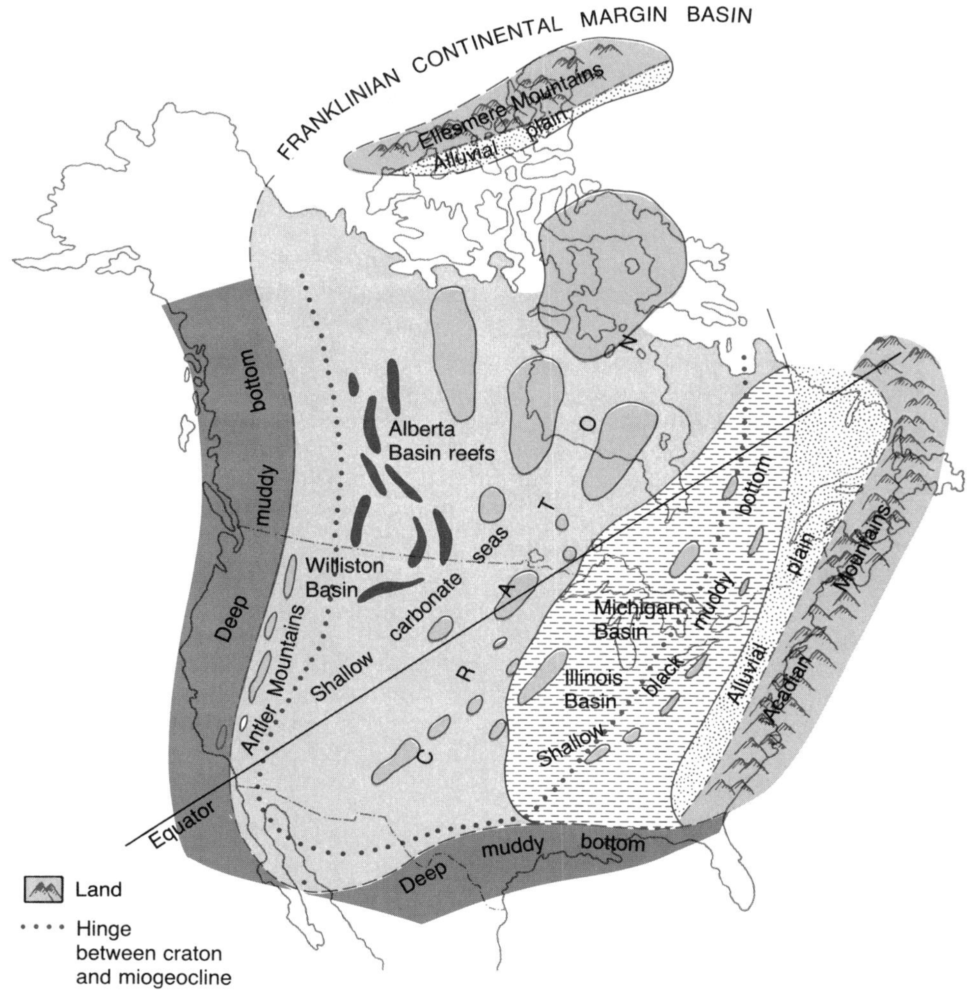

Figure 11–7
Paleogeography of Late Devonian superimposed on outline map of present-day North America.

geologic data suggest that lithospheric plate interactions involving Laurentia and Gondwana, and possibly Baltica, deformed the Appalachian continental margin basin. By Middle Devonian, suturing of the northeastern part of Laurentia and the northwestern part of Gondwana was nearly complete, and the Iapetus Ocean Basin closed, thus completing a Wilson cycle.

This collision sandwiched several displaced island terranes (Fig. 10–33, Chapter 10), including *Armorica,* between the Laurentian and Gondwanan continental blocks. According to paleogeographer R. Van der Voo, Armorica consisted of central Europe, the Iberian Peninsula, and southern Ireland, southern England, and Wales. Another complex of basement terranes caught in this squeeze was the *Avalon* terrane, parts of which is now recognized in the Appalachian Piedmont Province, New England, and Newfoundland.

The convergent plate margins that existed in a *continent–to–ocean basin* relationship in the Late Ordovician changed to a *continent-to-continent* relationship in the Devonian (Fig. 11–8). The present-day Appalachian Piedmont Province contains a complex assemblage of plutonic and metamorphic rocks which are generally Devonian and older. The main part of this province is made up of (1) terranes representing Paleozoic Appalachian eugeoclinal rocks that were subjected to repeated deformation and intrusion, (2) remnants of volcanic island arcs, and (3) perhaps one or more microcontinents accreted onto the continental margin during the Acadian orogeny (Fig. 11–8).

The Caledonian orogenic belt of the British Isles and Scandinavia represents a now-disjunct segment of the Acadian orogenic belt. The Acadian and Caledonian belts match up well when North America and Europe are restored to their interpreted Devonian positions. The contact between Cambrian trilobite provinces (Fig. 10–31 in Chapter 10), seen on both sides of the Atlantic, was formed during the Middle Paleozoic suturing of the continental mar-

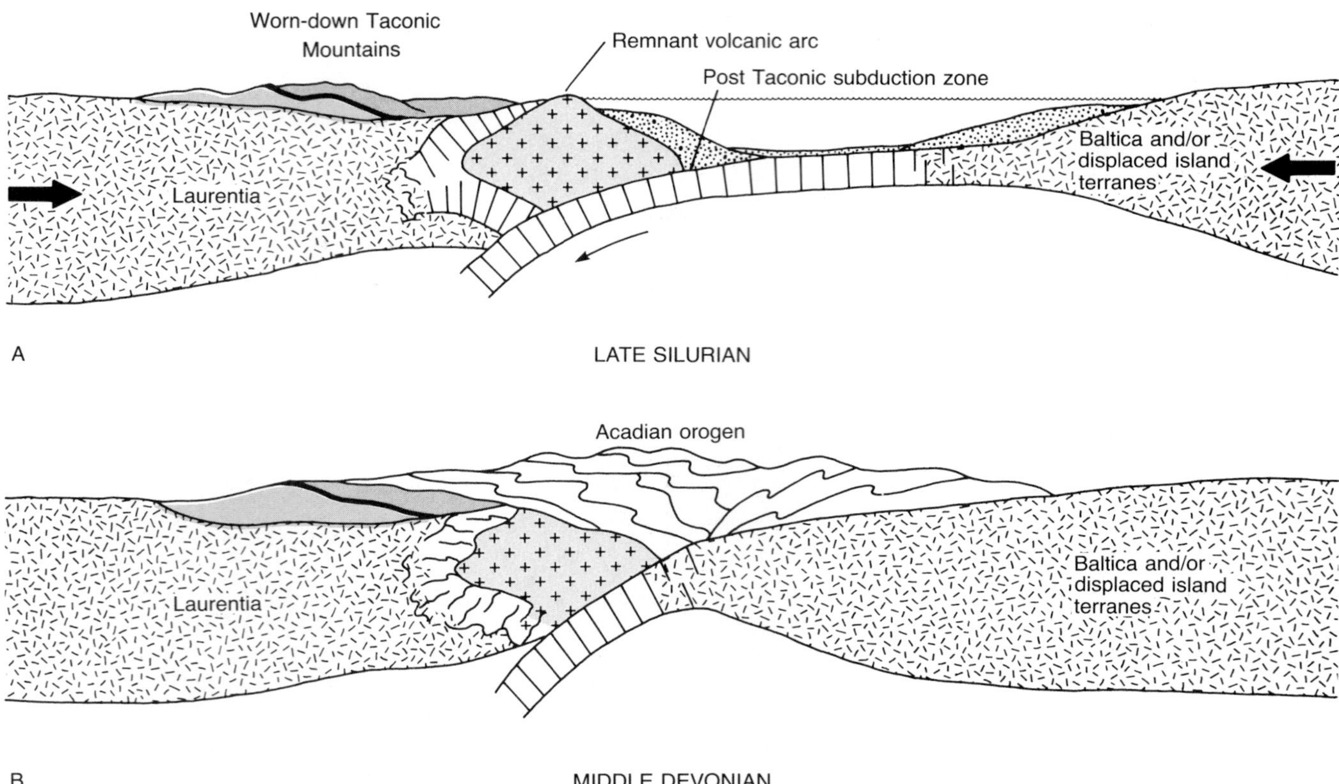

Figure 11–8
Acadian orogeny. A. Post-Taconic subduction and constriction of Iapetus Ocean. B. Continued subduction and eventual collision of Baltica and/or displaced island terranes with the eastern margin of Laurentia during Middle Devonian time to produce the Acadian orogen.

gins of northeastern Laurentia and northwestern Baltica and Armorica.

The Acadian orogeny also produced its own clastic wedges (Fig. 11–9). In fact, the volume of detritus shed westward from growing Acadian highlands was roughly twice that of the clastic wedge complex produced from the Taconic mountains. The Late Devonian–to–Early Mississippian clastic wedge is named for the Catskill Mountains in upstate New York, where we find exposed numerous examples of these postorogenic continental deposits and shallow, nearshore-marine deposits.

The Catskill clastic wedge provides a most instructive model within which to appreciate the fundamental distinctions between lithostratigraphic and chronostratigraphic units, and to understand how formally named mappable rock units are related to major lithofacies. From east to west, major facies grade laterally from coarse sandstones and conglomerates, containing abundant red beds of terrestrial origin, to shallow-marine sandstones and siltstones, and finally to marine shales and limestones (Fig. 11–10). The Catskill clastic wedge has received considerable attention through the years, and some 75 years after the concept was formulated in Europe, was the subject of one of the first serious studies in this country incorporating the notion of sedimentary facies.

The famous Old Red Sandstone of the British Isles is a Devonian clastic wedge that was shed eastward from the Caledonian highlands. Like its North American Catskill counterpart, the Old Red contains fossil land plants, freshwater fish, and early amphibian remains, and it interfingers eastward with marine shelly limestones. The apparent mirror imagery of the Old Red and Catskill clastic wedges (Fig. 11–9) is no accident; it resulted from the bilateral symmetry of the Acadian-Caledonian orogenic belt, suggesting that the northern part of the Appalachian continental margin basin was bordered by at least two cratons, the North American (Laurentian) and the European (Baltican and Armor-

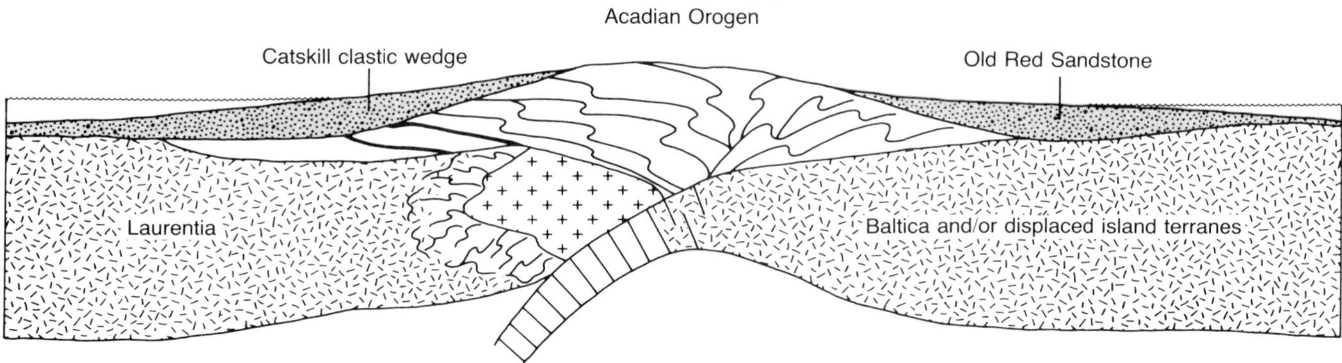

Figure 11–9
Relationship between Acadian orogen (the Acadian-Caledonian mobile belt) and mirror-image Late Devonian postorogenic clastic wedges: the Catskill and Old Red.

ican). This bilaterally symmetrical orogenic belt is further suggested by such geologic features as (1) opposite direction of overthrusting and (2) zones of intense metamorphism bounded on either side by less-deformed rocks.

It is interesting to note that the zone of suturing does not coincide with the seam of desuturing and fragmentation that formed in the Mesozoic when the supercontinent **Pangaea** broke up. Pieces of Baltica, Gondwana, and other displaced terranes remained as part of the North American continental block. This is why the contact between Cambrian trilobite provinces, formed during the Acadian orogeny, now is found on both sides of the Atlantic (Fig. 10–31 in Chapter 10).

There is an unmistakable correspondence among the increase in land area as a result of orogeny, the explosive evolution of Devonian land plants, and the origin of the first terrestrial vertebrates (the amphibians). Mountain building, together with the resulting voluminous incursion of clastic-wedge sediments to form alluvial plains and deltas, resulted in emergent expanses of continental areas, particularly lowlands. This physical setting provided a host of new, previously unexplored ecological niches.

Rapid niche-filling and niche-partitioning promoted major adaptive radiation among the new invaders. Enterprising floras and faunas were quick to seize such evolutionary opportunities. Widespread lowland vegetation also had a profound effect on weathering, erosion, and deposition, particularly in fluvial environments. Pre-Devonian landscapes, naked of vegetation, were probably drained by *braided streams,* characterized by shallow, broad channels with voluminous sediment discharge. Vegetation

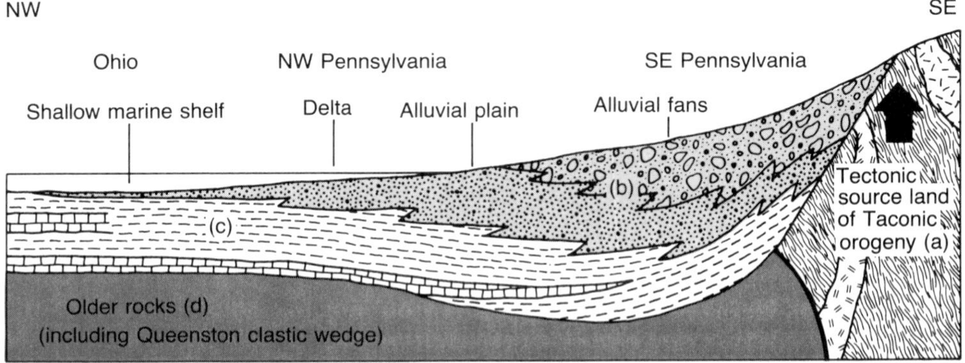

Figure 11–10
Catskill clastic wedge. Note relationship to Acadian orogen, interfingering facies relationships showing onlap-offlap cycles, overall progradational character of the facies, and progressive fining of sediments with distance from Acadian highland source terrane. A postorogenic molasse deposit.

stabilized loose sediment and promoted meandering streams with deeper, more confined channels and smaller sediment discharge.

The Cordillera

During the Cambrian Period, North America was similar to present-day Africa in that both eastern and western margins originated from Late Proterozoic rifting and were either static or trailing edges. The developing continental margin basins were similar to the present-day Atlantic margin of North America. We have already discussed how this comparatively passive setting was interrupted in the Appalachian belt as eugeoclinal rocks were deformed repeatedly from Ordovician through Devonian time.

The Cordilleran continental margin basin was relatively quiet until the Late Devonian (Fig. 11–11), when subduction of oceanic lithosphere along the western continental margin resulted in pre-Carboniferous eugeoclinal deposits being thrust eastward over miogeoclinal carbonate rocks, in a manner somewhat reminiscent of the Taconic orogeny. This event, called the **Antler orogeny,** occurred along a belt known as the Roberts Mountains thrust, and is best displayed from central Nevada to Idaho (Fig. 11–12). Here the thrust relationships can be seen, and a pronounced angular unconformity separates the structurally deformed rocks from overlying, less-disturbed Carboniferous strata. The overthrusting presumably resulted from the constriction of a small marginal ocean basin as a volcanic island–arc complex converged on the continental block. The Antler event was on a smaller scale than the Taconic and Acadian disturbances, and deposits shed from Antler highlands accumulated mainly in marine environments, with little or no development of red-bed alluvial plains.

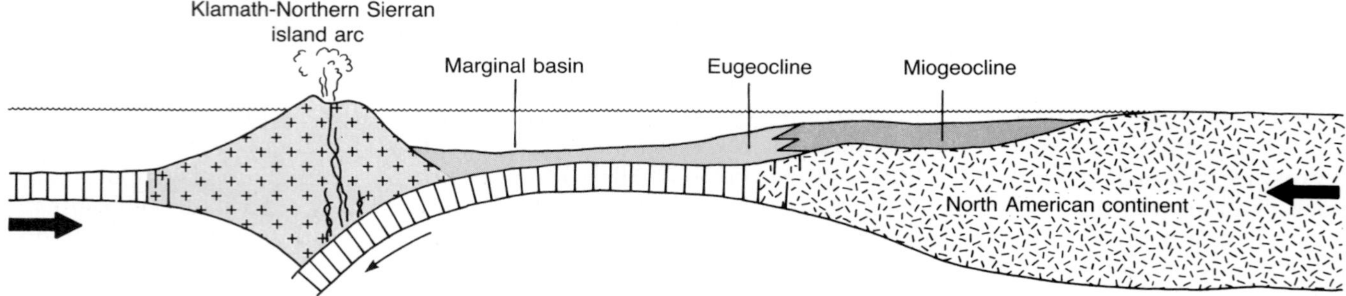

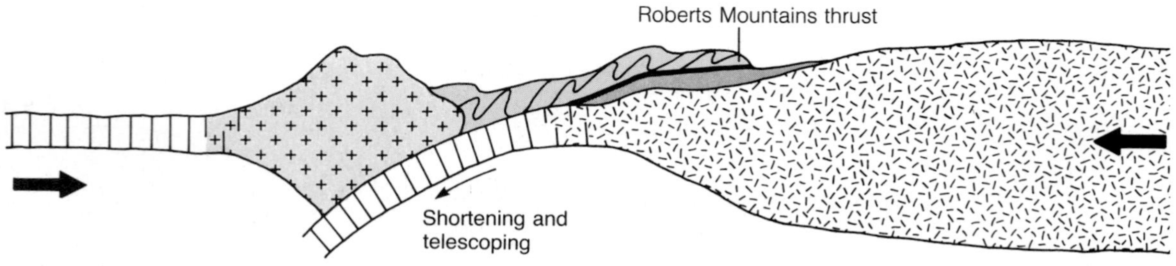

Figure 11–11

Antler Orogeny. A. Relationship between early Paleozoic volcanic island-arc system and the western margin of the North American continent (Laurentia), based on the model of a west-dipping subduction zone. B. Late Devonian increase in convergence rates between western margin of Laurentia and volcanic arc, resulting in shortening of marginal basin and thrusting of eugeoclinal rocks eastward over miogeoclinal rocks.

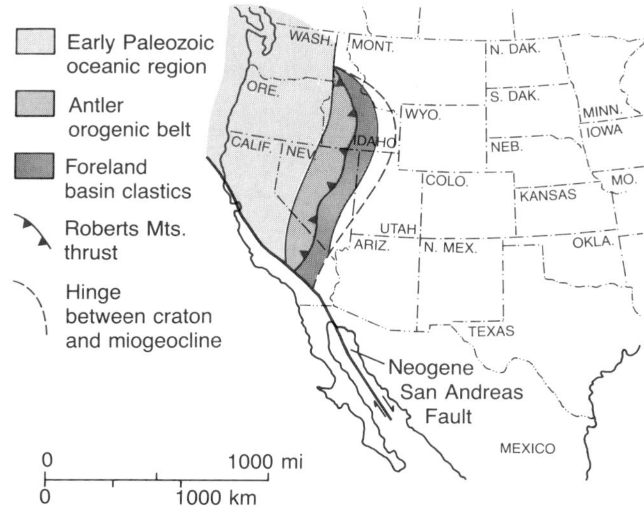

Figure 11–12
Western United States showing principal tectonic features of the Devonian-Mississippian Antler orogeny.

Carboniferous History: The Mississippian and Pennsylvanian

Mississippian Deposits

The Mississippian System is named for exposures in the Mississippi Valley, particularly in Iowa and Missouri, where limestones rich in oolites and crinoids are characteristic (Figs. 11–13 and 11–14). Some refer to the Mississippian as the "age of crinoids" because of the widespread abundance of columnals and stem fragments. We should remember that, unlike the other stratigraphic system names, Mississippian and Pennsylvanian are provincial names, enjoying usage only in North America. The Mississippian represents the lower part of the worldwide Carboniferous System, and the Pennsylvanian the upper part; the stratotype for the Carboniferous is in England.

The Mississippian includes some unusual sedimentary deposits. Throughout much of the eastern craton, west of the Acadian Mountains, accumulation of black, organic-rich mud—the Chattanooga Shale and related deposits—occurred under somewhat restricted anaerobic conditions in a thermally stratified inland equatorial sea during the Late Devonian and Early Mississippian. These conditions were probably related to interactions between climatic and tectonic factors. Specifically, during times of tectonic activity, the rising Acadian mountains created a barrier to moisture-laden easterly trade winds, reducing clastic input and favoring deposition of organic-rich muds. These black shales interfinger eastward with coarser clastics of the Catskill clastic wedge, which prograded cratonward during times of tectonic quiescence.

Another carryover from the Late Devonian was extensive formation of chert. Some of the chert occurs as nodules in limestones and probably represents localized pockets of secondary replacement of host carbonate mudstone. Other chert occurrences

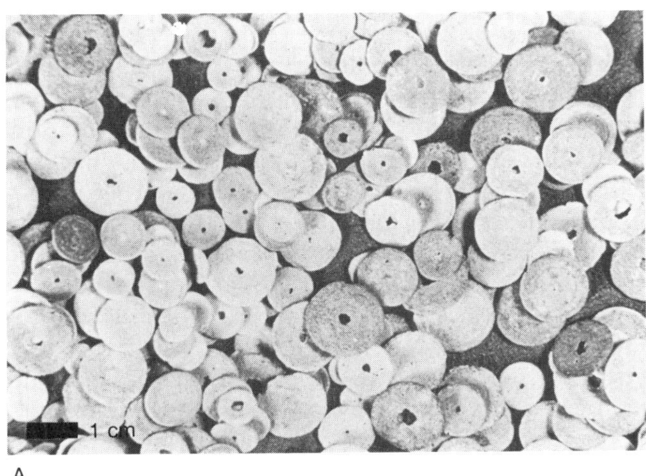

A

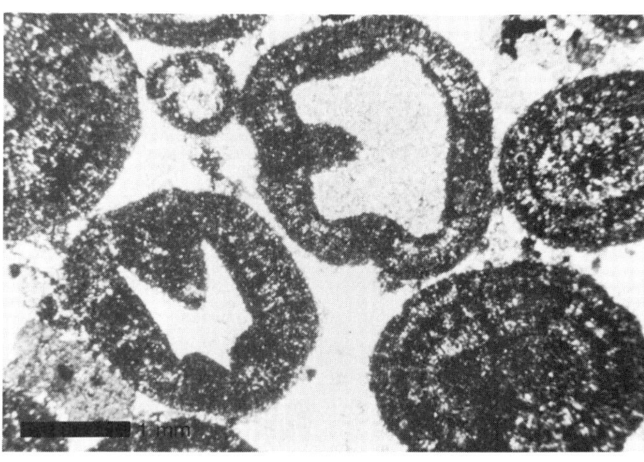

B

Figure 11–13
A. Crinoid stem fragments in Mississippian limestone. B. Thin-section photomicrograph of oolitic limestone. Most of the nuclei of ooids are crinoid columnals.
(A, photo courtesy of Ward's Natural Science Establishment; B, photo courtesy of American Association of Petroleum Geologists)

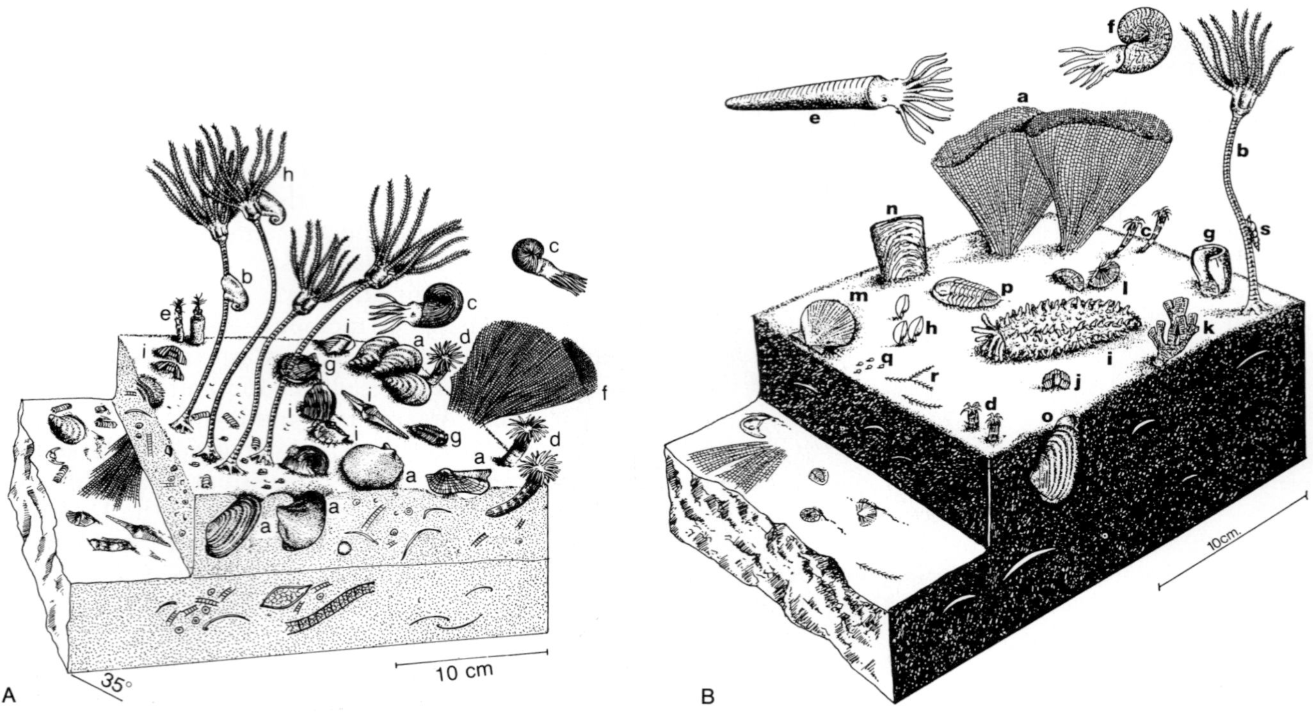

Figure 11–14

A. In-life restoration of Mississippian shallow-marine bottom community: a, bivalve molluscs; b, gastropod mollusc; c, ammonoid cephalopod molluscs; d, rugose corals; e, serpulid annelid worm; f, bryozoan; g, trilobite; h, crinoid echinoderm; i, articulate brachiopods. B. In-life restoration of Mississippian muddy-bottom invertebrate community: a, k, r, bryozoans; b, crinoid; c, d, rugose corals; e, nautiloid cephalopod; f, ammonoid cephalopod; g, h, j, l, articulate brachiopods; i, echinozoan; m, n, o, bivalve molluscs; p, trilobite; q, ostracodes; s, gastropod mollusc.

(From W. S. McKerrow, 1978, *The Ecology of Fossils;* Fig. 46, 51, p. 163, 173: MIT Press, all rights reserved. Reproduced with permission of MIT Press)

include thin-bedded to thick-bedded units, presumably of primary origin. The source of silica was probably mostly biogenic, having been derived from the siliceous skeletal material of sponges and radiolarians.

The Mississippian Period witnessed the last widespread Paleozoic carbonate-rich epeiric sea in the cratonic interior of North America (Fig. 11–15). The evidence is plentiful. In the Midwest, creamy-white oolitic and foraminiferal limestone near Salem, Indiana, has been quarried extensively for choice building stone. In western North America, thick ridge-and-cliff-forming limestone units attest to the richly populated carbonate seas; examples are the Redwall Limestone in the Grand Canyon and correlative formations in the northern Rockies, the southern Great Basin, and the Canadian Rockies. These limestones contain rugose corals, brachiopods, crinoids, bryozoans, ammonoids, and sponges.

Thick deposits of Upper Mississippian terrigenous clastic sediments, mainly of flysch style, accumulated in the **Ouachita** continental margin basin (Fig. 11–15) and are visible in the Ouachita Mountains of Arkansas and Oklahoma. Voluminous incursions of terrigenous clastics also accumulated in a foreland basin and shelf area east of the Antler orogenic belt (Fig. 11–16). These deposits include shales to the east and thick flysch accumulations to the west. Late Mississippian deposition throughout the Appalachian miogeocline changed from predominantly carbonates to terrigenous muds and sands, a harbinger of extensive uplift and mountain building that was to climax deformation of the Appalachian continental margin basin throughout the remainder of the Paleozoic. Swampy lowlands on alluvial plains and deltas were sites of accumulation of plant remains that became Mississippian coal beds, presaging the great coal swamps of the Pennsylvanian.

Figure 11–15
Paleogeography of mid-Mississippian, superimposed on outline map of present-day North America.

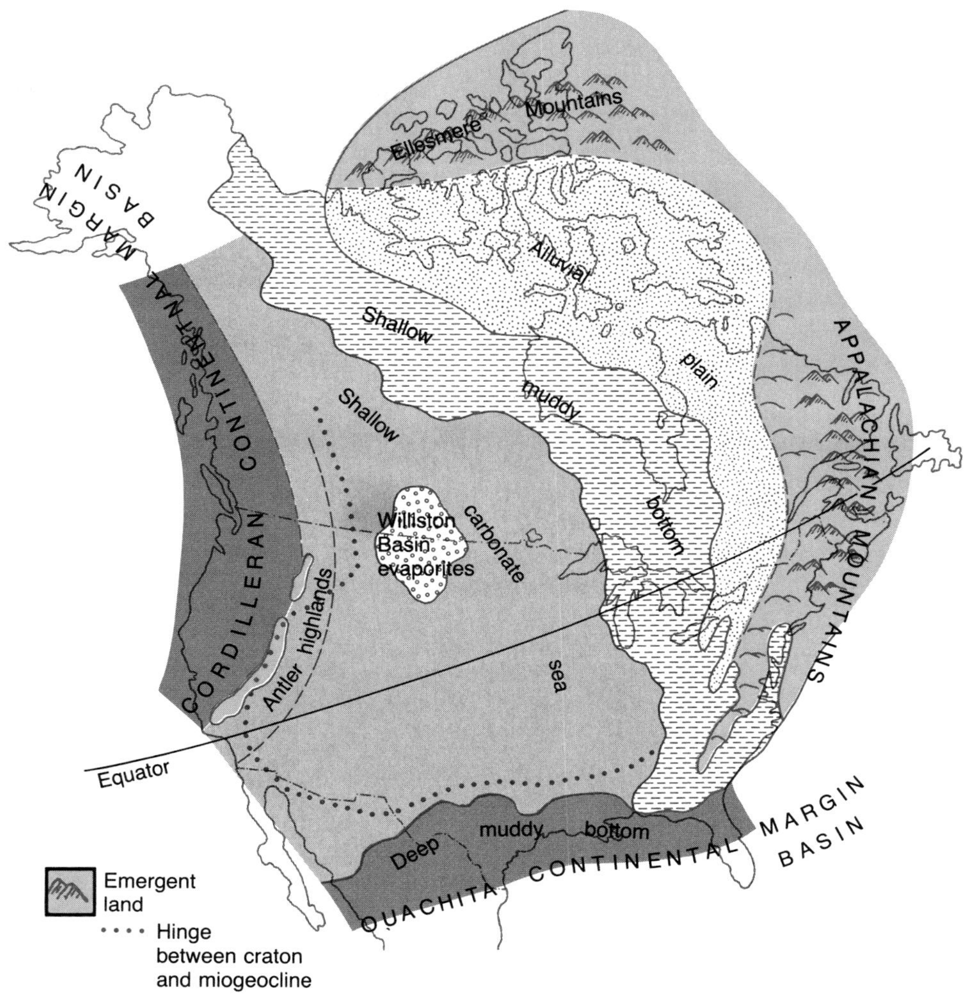

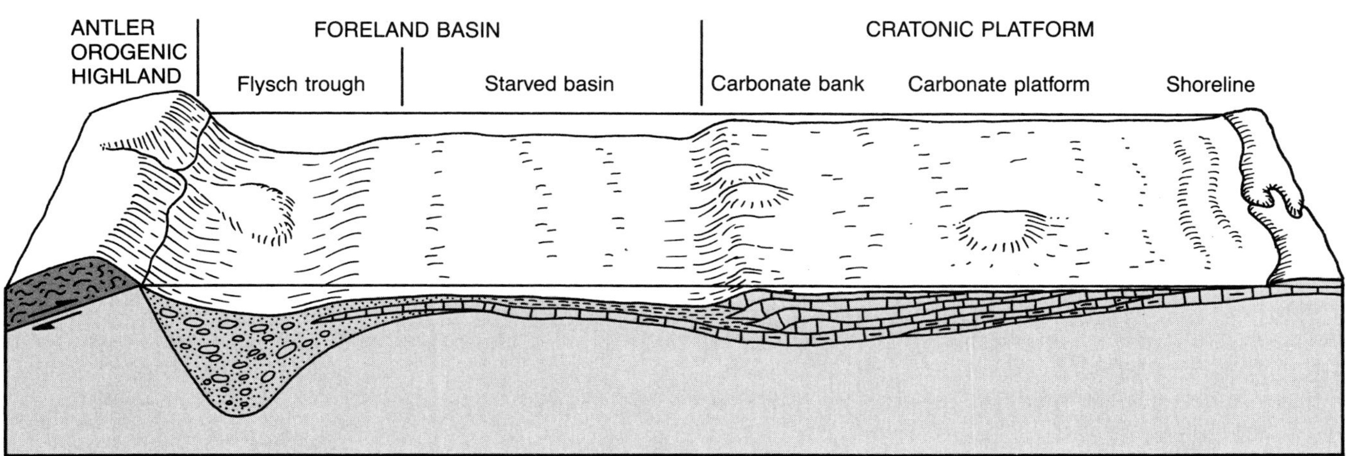

Figure 11–16
Depositional setting of Cordilleran foreland basin and cratonic platform during Early Mississippian.
(From F. G. Poole and C. A. Sandberg, 1977, Mississippian Paleogeography and Tectonics of the Western United States; Fig. 3, p. 74: Pacific Section SEPM Paleozoic Paleogeography Symposium Volume. Reproduced by permission of Pacific Section, Society of Economic Paleontologists and Mineralogists)

Late Paleozoic Orogenic Disturbance

In eastern North America, the **Alleghany orogeny** climaxed the final phase of a succession of orogenic events that had been occurring in the Appalachian mobile belt since the Ordovician. We have already examined how post–Lower Ordovician miogeoclinal rocks were developed as alternating carbonate and terrigenous clastic packages, signifying times of relative quiescence or mobility in the eugeoclinal belt. During the Pennsylvanian and Permian, the miogeoclinal rocks themselves, particularly in the region from New York southward to Alabama, were folded and thrust-faulted. The folds in general are asymmetrical and in places even overturned toward the craton (Fig. 11–17). Rocks of the Appalachian Plateau provinces (Fig. 11–17) were warped into a huge synclinorium.

Deposits of the Appalachian Plateau Province accumulated in a foreland basin setting whose subsidence was triggered by flexural loading of stacked thrust sheets of the Appalachian orogen. The thrust faults are eastward-dipping and occur mainly in Virginia and Tennessee (Fig. 11–17). This Appalachian fold-and-thrust belt is the present-day geologic and physiographic Valley and Ridge Province. The youngest rocks affected are Early Pennsylvanian in Tennessee, Late Pennsylvanian in western Pennsylvania, and Early Permian in the Appalachian Plateau provinces.

What was responsible for this Late Paleozoic wave of deformation? The intensity of both folding and thrusting diminishes toward the craton; the Appalachian Plateau Province includes relatively undisturbed upper Paleozoic strata that thicken to the east. The cratonic basement acted as a buttress against which the miogeoclinal rocks were pushed from the southeast. If we are consistent in looking to major lithospheric plate interactions for an answer, then perhaps it is reasonable to invoke a model of continental collision whereby Gondwana impinged against the southern margin of Laurentia, thus completing the closing up of the intervening ocean basin. This plate interaction was part of the late Paleozoic global suturing of continental masses into a supercontinent assembly called Pangaea. Just as the Taconic and Acadian orogenic structures have their counterparts in the Caledonian mobile belt of western Europe, so does the Alleghanian structural belt of eastern North America match the Late Pennsylvanian Hercynian orogenic trend of western Europe, northwestern Africa, and southern Asia.

In recent years, some startling relationships have been revealed by seismic-reflection profiling data from the Consortium for Continental Profiling Project (COCORP), and by detailed geologic studies across the southern Appalachian belt in the Carolinas and Georgia. The Precambrian and lower Paleozoic crystalline rocks that make up the Blue Ridge and Piedmont Provinces appear to overlie an eastward-thickening wedge of younger sedimentary rocks at depth. The implication is that a colossal slab of crystalline rocks has been thrust westward for several hundred kilometers. This great subsurface thrust fault that transported the present Blue Ridge and western Piedmont Provinces northwestward was probably the "piston" or "plunger" that folded and faulted the strata in the Valley and Ridge, and to a lesser extent, the Appalachian Plateau provinces.

One preliminary model interprets the thrust sheet as having been emplaced initially during the Taconic orogeny, when part of the floor of a marginal basin, together with part of the crust of a volcanic island arc, were thrust onto the continental margin of Laurentia (Fig. 11–18). Later, during the Acadian orogeny, various displaced island terranes which were pushed along by an advancing Gondwana land mass (and perhaps Baltica), collided with, became accreted to, and moved with the thrust sheet. Finally, during the Alleghany orogeny, the African part of Gondwana collided again with Laurentia, moved the thrust sheet even farther westward, and folded and faulted the miogeoclinal strata into their present configuration in the Valley and Ridge Province (Fig. 11–18).

The Appalachian orogenic belt plunges beneath younger deposits of the continental shelf on its southeastern side, and under the deposits of the Gulf coastal plain in Georgia and Alabama. It would appear at first glance that the southern terminus of the outcrop of the Appalachian belt is the last we see of it, but is it?

A separately named structural trend, the *Ouachita*, begins near the southwestern terminus of the Appalachian belt and extends for at least 1800 km across the southern United States, and probably into Mexico (Fig. 11–19). Unlike the almost continuously exposed Appalachian belt, the Ouachita belt is exposed for only 450 km of this distance—in the Ouachita Mountains of Arkansas and Oklahoma and in the Marathon region in West Texas. The remainder is covered by Mesozoic and Cenozoic deposits of the Gulf Coastal Plain (Fig. 11–19). However, from deep drilling, much is known about the covered part. Could it be that the Paleozoic orogenic belts which border the eastern and southern margins of North America are part of a *continuous* continental margin basin and mobile-belt trend?

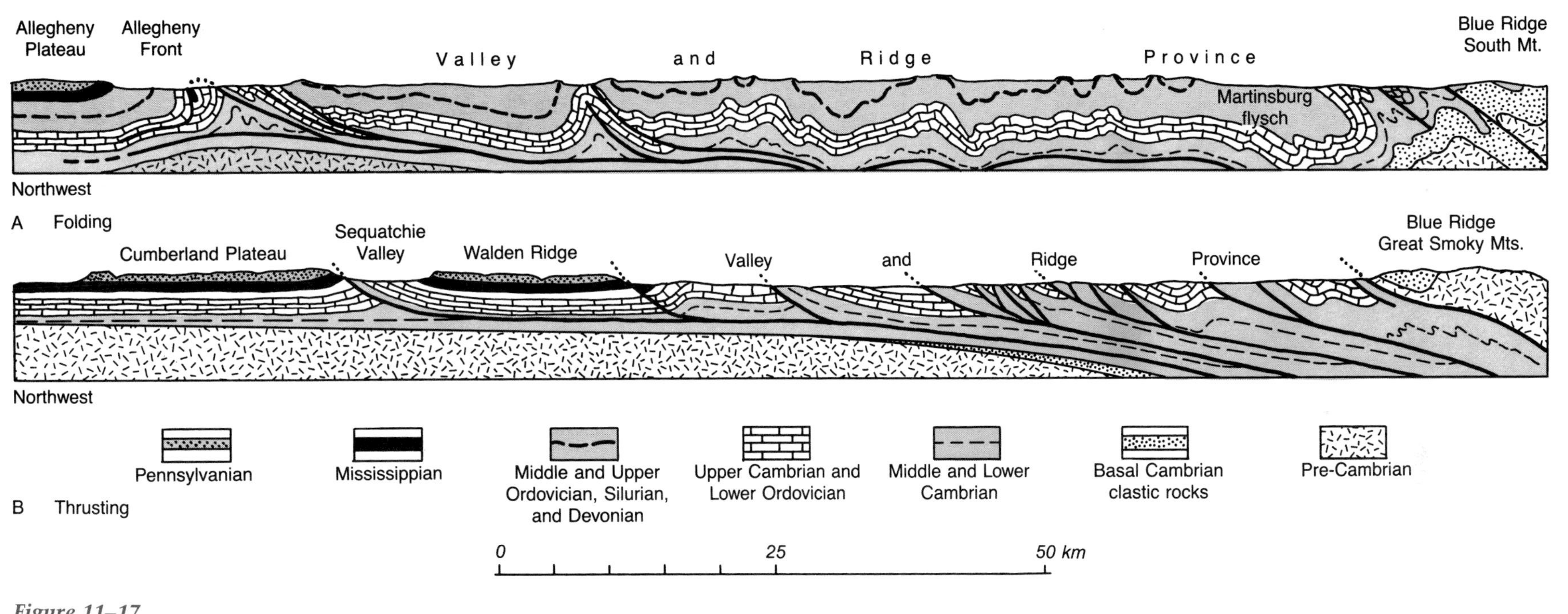

Figure 11–17

Structural style across Appalachian belt. A. Central Appalachians of Pennsylvania, where folding is dominant style. B. Southern Appalachians of Tennessee, characterized by thrust faults.

(From Philip B. King, *The Evolution of North America.* Copyright © 1959, rev. ed. © 1977 by Princeton University Press. Fig. 29, p. 48, reprinted by permission of Princeton University Press)

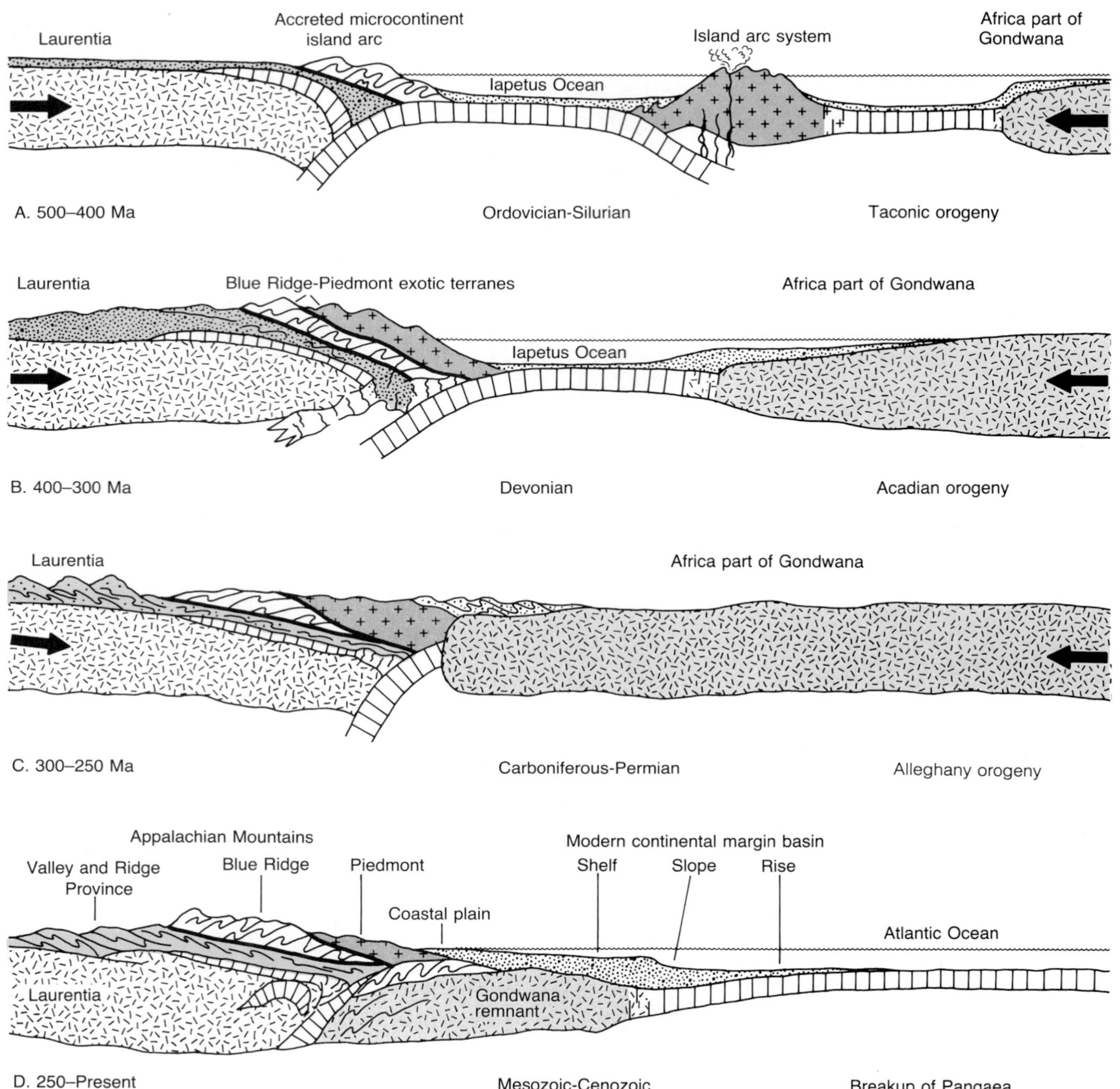

Figure 11–18

Evolution of the southern part of the Appalachian orogen as a result of collisions among ancient North America (Laurentia), an island arc system, and the African part of Gondwana. A series of plate collisions resulted in the overthrusting of parts of the continental margin of North America, culminating in the folding and thrusting of miogeoclinal rocks that now comprise the Valley and Ridge Province. Post-Paleozoic breakup of a supercontinent left a remnant of Gondwana as part of the North American continent. This tectonic model is based on a combination of geologic data and COCORP reflection seismic profiling.

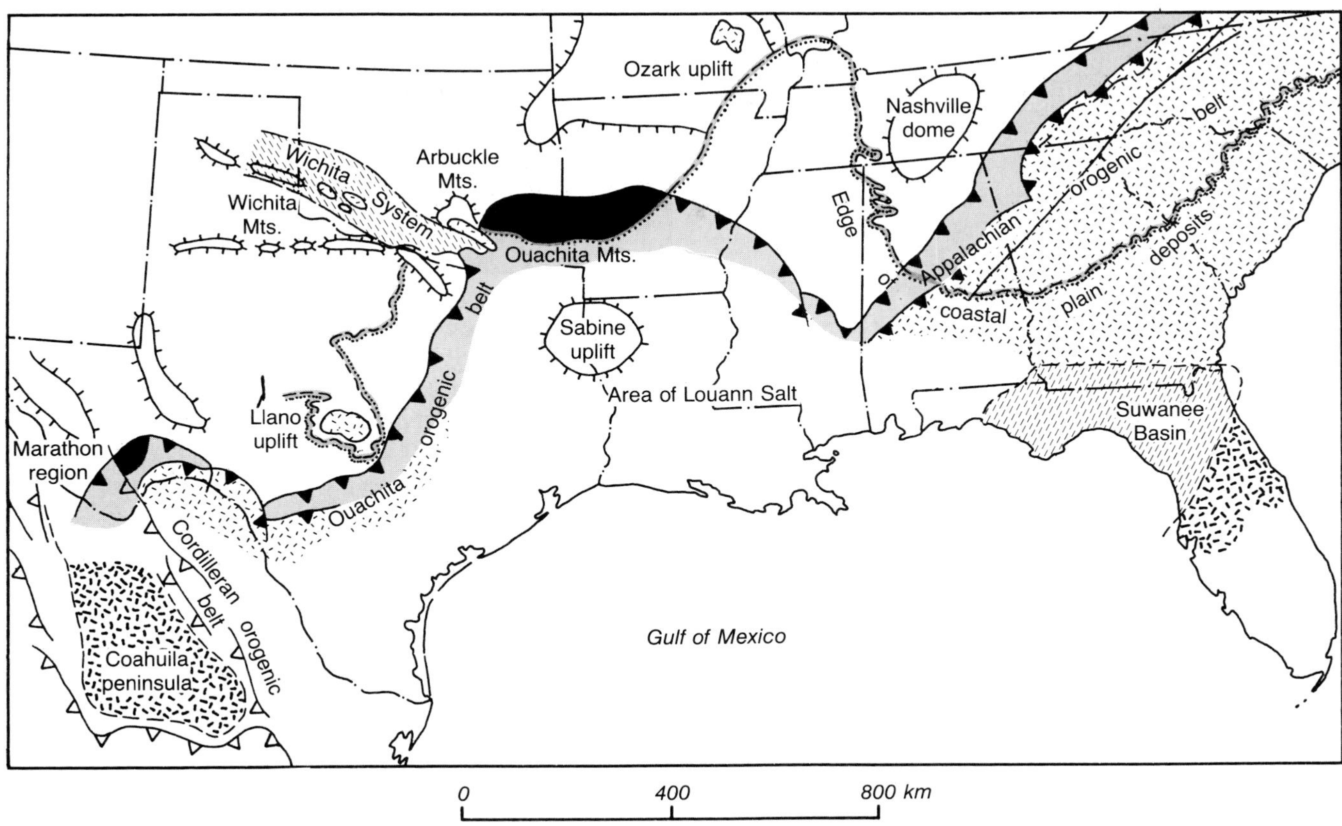

Figure 11–19

South-central United States showing regional relations of Ouachita orogenic belt in surface exposures (black) of Marathon region, West Texas, and Ouachita Mountains, Oklahoma and Arkansas, and in subsurface beneath younger sediments of Gulf Coastal Plain Province.
(From Philip B. King, *The Evolution of North America:* Copyright © 1959, rev. ed. © 1977 by Princeton University Press. Fig. 44, p. 71, reprinted by permission of Princeton University Press and author)

The exposed rocks and geologic structures of the Ouachita and Marathon regions suggest a history that began with deposition of a modest thickness of pre-Carboniferous sandstone, shale, and finally chert. This entire pre-Carboniferous section is noticeably thinner than the contemporaneous shelf and platform carbonate sections cratonward!

P. B. King, a geologist with the U.S. Geological Survey and longtime student of the Ouachita trend, attributed this odd relationship to slow accumulation of sediments in a subsiding trough. In both the Marathon and Ouachita Mountains segments there is a dramatic change from chert to Mississippian and Pennsylvanian flysch deposits (Figs. 11–20, 11–21). The thick Carboniferous flysch is composed of sand and mud and occasional boulders derived mainly from tectonic source areas to the south and southeast. The tectonic source areas resulted from subduction of oceanic lithosphere beneath the northern margin of an approaching continental block and deformation of earlier deposits (Fig. 11–22). During the Late Pennsylvanian, the deformation spread northward and westward and folded and faulted the flysch deposits of the Ouachita trough. This deformation culminated during Late Pennsylvanian and Early Permian time by the overthrusting of deformed continental margin basin rocks many kilometers toward the continent.

During the Pennsylvanian Period, a west-to-northwest-trending belt of the craton of Colorado and Utah was moderately shortened to form broad basins and basement uplifts (Fig. 11–23), bounded by high-angle reverse faults. This disturbance in the ancestral Rocky Mountains elevated large masses of Precambrian crystalline basement, which served as source areas for thick deposits of nonmarine con-

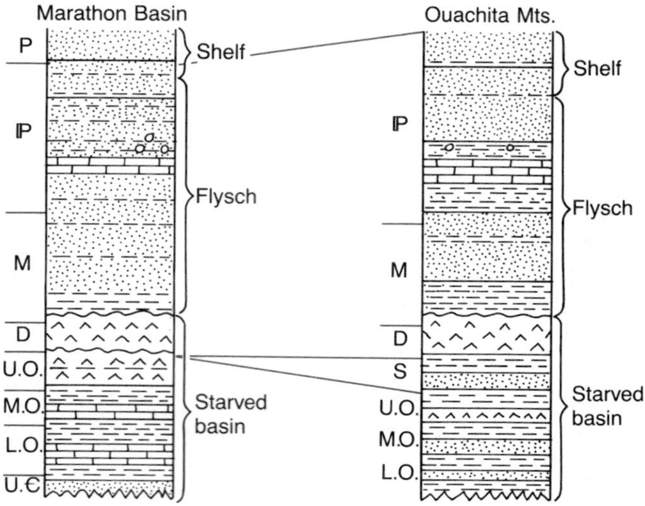

Figure 11–20
Paleozoic stratigraphic sections for Marathon Basin and Ouachita Mountains, showing similarity in succession of facies. Depositional history shows change from deep starved basin sediments in early Paleozoic to thick turbidite flysch sedimentation in late Paleozoic.

glomerate, arkosic sandstone, and red shale that graded out into marine strata (Fig. 11–24). Several marine basins within the ancestral Rockies, such as the Paradox Basin, received thick deposits of Pennsylvanian clastics, carbonates, and evaporites (Figs. 11–23 and 11–24). The crustal shortening likely was a byproduct of the collision between the African and South American parts of Gondwana, and the southern edge of North America (Laurentia).

Coal-Bearing Cycles

By the close of the Paleozoic, eastern North America had become sutured to western Europe and northwestern Africa. The plate collisions that brought about the assembly of continents to form Pangaea had definite mountain-building effects, which in turn exerted much influence on the patterns of sedimentation. The Pennsylvanian records a marked change in the dynamics of sedimentation in the eastern part of the North American craton. Enormous volumes of sand and mud, derived from emerging highlands in the Appalachian-Ouachita mobile belt, were spread westward and northward (Fig. 11–25). Nonmarine, deltaic, and marginal marine deposits of brackish-water bays and lagoons became progressively more widespread as the continent was tilted upward along its collision edges.

However, the retreat of epeiric seas was not a simple one; numerous oscillations of sea level and changes in position of shoreline occurred, and these produced rhythmically repetitious sedimentary successions called **cyclothems.** Larger-scale cycles containing bundles of cyclothems represent tectonic-climatic cycles—related to episodic uplift in the Appalachian-Ouachita belt and to Gondwana glaciation—and changes in sediment budget. The individual cyclothems are more closely related to

A

B

Figure 11–21
A. Rhythmically bedded turbidite flysch, Haymond Formation, Marathon Basin, Texas. B. Ouachita Mountains flysch, southern Oklahoma, used in wall of building in Talihina, Oklahoma, and artistically masoned to display soles of Pennsylvanian sandstone beds exposing flute and groove casts.
(Photos by J. D. Cooper)

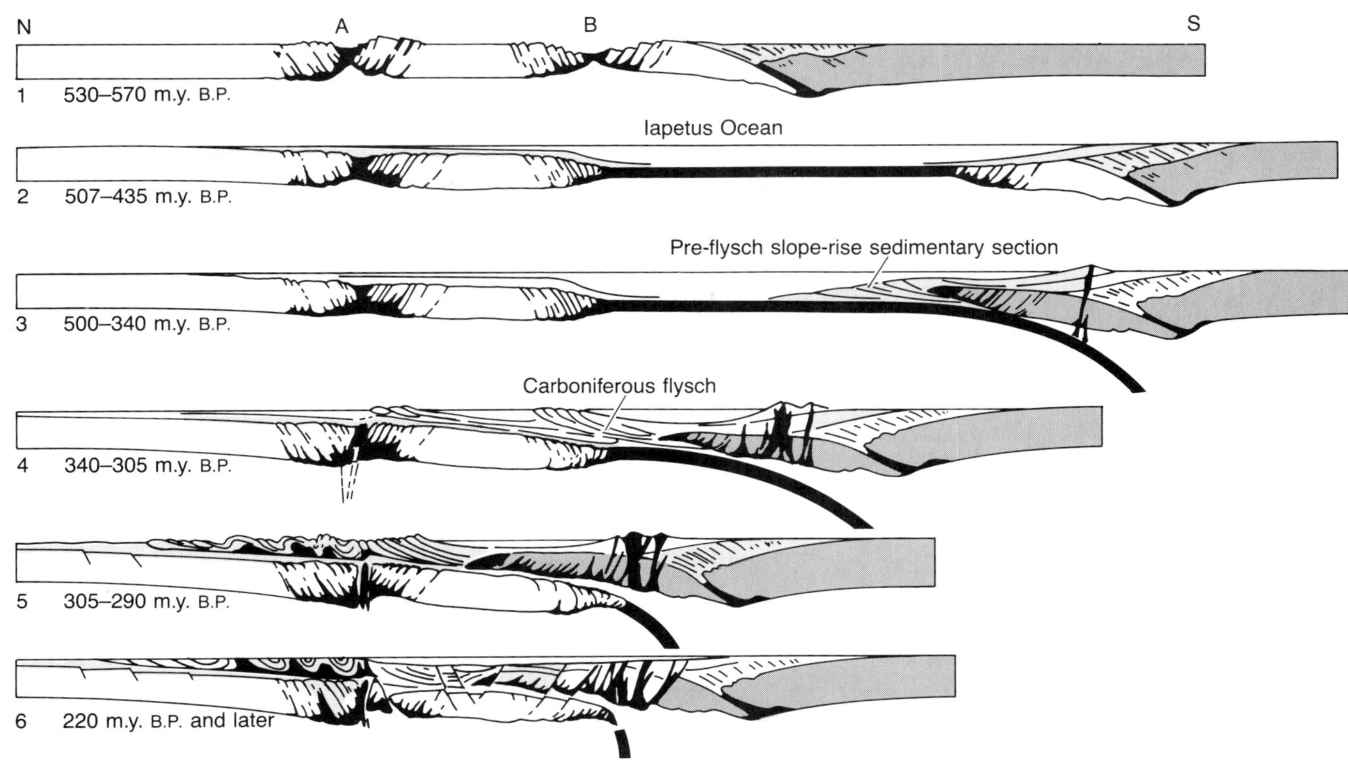

Figure 11–22
Plate-tectonic model of the Ouachita orogenic belt. Oceanic crust shown in black. 1. Middle to Late Cambrian; rifting to form Anadarko aulacogen (A) and Mississippi aulacogen (B). 2. Ordovician; open spreading across the Mississippi aulacogen to form a southern extension of Iapetus Ocean, with subsidence and deposition along continental margins. 3. Ordovician to Mississippian; continued open spreading of rift ocean, with southward subduction along northern margin of South America. 4. Mississippian to Pennsylvanian; incipient continental collision. The orogenic front along the southern continental margin overrides continental remnants of the northern margin, supplying increasing volumes of clastics to form thick flysch deposits. 5. Pennsylvanian; continued continental collision. Dislocated masses of flysch and preflysch are thrust cratonward. 6. Permian; rifting, normal faulting, and fault-block tilting incipient to seafloor spreading in the Gulf of Mexico Basin.
(After G. Briggs, and D. Roeder, 1975, Sedimentation and Plate Tectonics, Ouachita Mountains and Arkoma Basin, Fig. 6, *in A Guidebook to the Sedimentology of Paleozoic Flysch and Associated Deposits, Ouachita Mountains and Arkoma Basin, Oklahoma:* Dallas Geological Society. Reprinted by permission of Dallas Geological Society)

the delicate interplay between nonmarine deltaic and shallow-marine interdeltaic and shelf environments. Switching of deltaic distributaries resulted in numerous small-scale onlap-offlap cycles.

The cyclothem model (Fig. 11–26), produced by the migration of closely related environments and expressed by a characteristic superposition of facies, is a good illustration of *Walther's Law.* These Pennsylvanian cyclic successions of the Appalachian Plateau Province and craton display rapid vertical and lateral facies changes involving sediments that were deposited at or near sea level in alternating nearshore marine and terrestrial coastal environments. They also characteristically contain coal beds.

The coal beds of the Pennsylvanian cyclothems are the compacted accumulations of stems and leafy vegetable matter in coastal swamps, delta plains, and lagoons—settings similar to the present-day Dismal Swamps of Virginia and North Carolina and the bayou country of the Mississippi delta in southern Louisiana. These coal deposits have given rise to the abundant coal fields of Pennsylvania, West Virginia, Kentucky, and Illinois, as well as other parts of the Appalachian plateaus and mid-continent. Land plants were abundant and varied

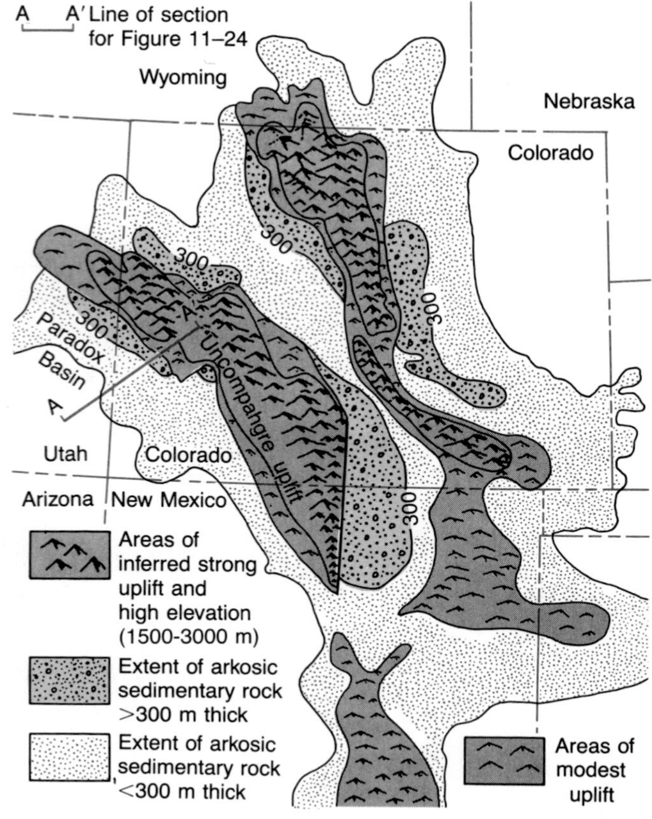

Figure 11–23

Restoration of ancestral Rockies during Pennsylvanian, and distribution and thickness of associated arkosic sedimentary rocks.

(Redrawn from W. W. Mallory, 1972, Pennsylvanian Arkoses and the Ancestral Rocky Mountains, Fig. 1, p. 132, *in Geologic Atlas of the Rocky Mountain Region:* Rocky Mountain Association of Geologists. Used by permission of Association)

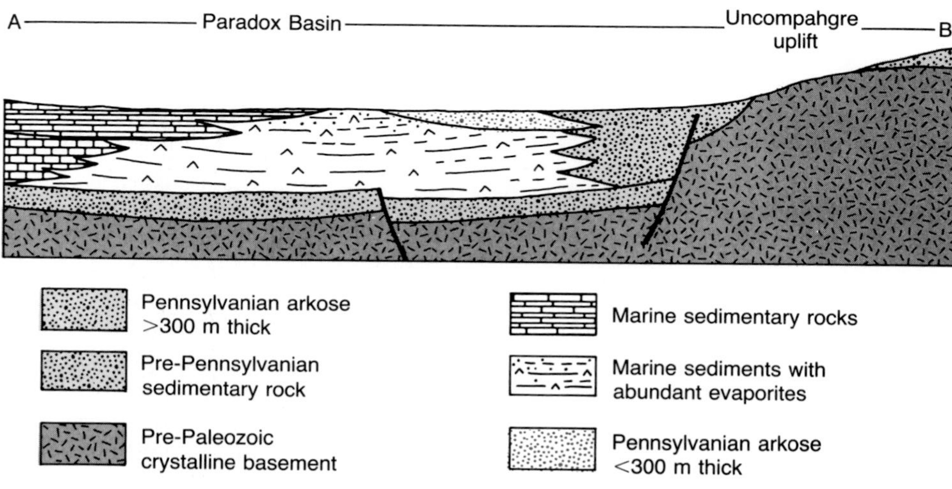

Figure 11–24

Example of ancestral Rocky Mountains uplift (Uncompahgre uplift) of pre-Paleozoic crystalline basement blocks, and development of adjacent basin (Paradox Basin) and depositional facies in western Colorado and eastern Utah.

(Redrawn from R. J. Hite and F. W. Carter, 1972, Pennsylvanian Rocks and Salt Anticlines, Paradox Basin, Utah and Colorado, Fig. 48, p. 138, *in Geologic Atlas of the Rocky Mountain Region*: Rocky Mountain Association of Geologists. Used by permission of Association)

Figure 11–25
Paleogeography of mid-Pennsylvanian superimposed on outline map of present-day North America.

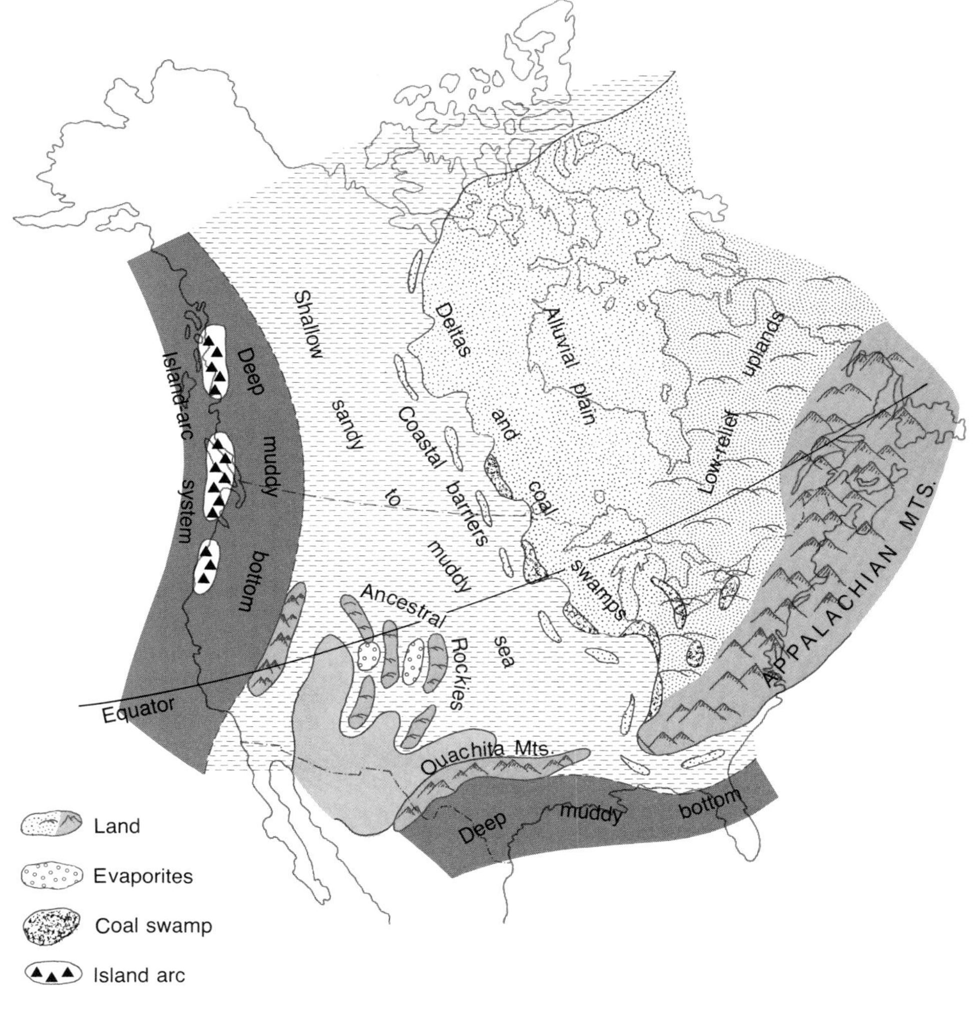

Figure 11–26
Cyclothem deposition. A. Vertical succession of facies (not to scale) of cyclothem showing characteristic cyclic repetition. B. Delta–to–shallow-marine environments that result in cyclothem deposition. The numbers relate the type of environment to the type of sediments deposited in A. Facies in A represent the migration of environment of B through time at one place, in accordance with Walther's Law.

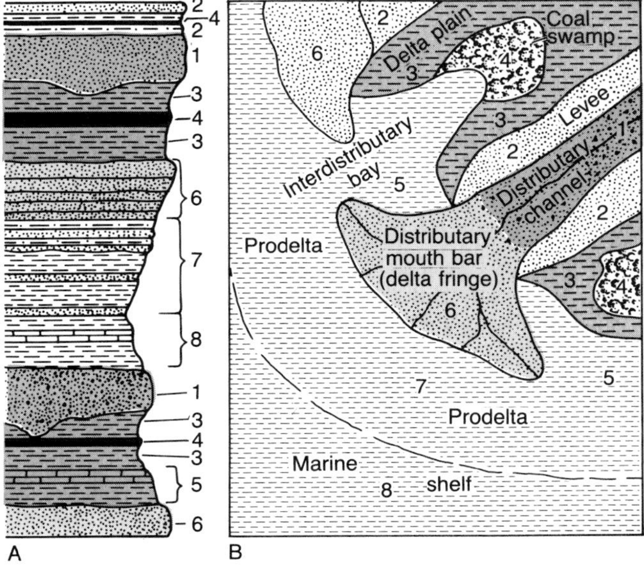

Figure 11–27
Restoration of Pennsylvanian coal-forest scene in Illinois showing scale trees, club mosses, and ferns.
(Photo courtesy of Field Museum of Natural History, Chicago. Photo No. 75400)

during the Pennsylvanian, and coal-forming swamps included lush stands of scale trees, scouring rushes, and ferns (Fig. 11–27) (see Chapter 16). Insects were uncommonly large and abundant in the coal swamps; winged forms similar to dragonflies, as well as giant cockroaches, were numbered among a diverse fauna. Deltaic-plain deposits at Mazon Creek, Illinois, contain small concretions that entomb exquisite fossils of a variety of plant compressions (Fig. 11–28), as well as spiders, centipedes, and insects.

Terrestrial Vertebrates: Emergence of the Reptiles

The oldest reptiles discovered thus far were found in sedimentary rocks of Early Pennsylvanian age near the Bay of Fundy in Nova Scotia. Today the Bay of Fundy is rimmed by cliffs that are battered daily by 15-meter tides, but 280 million years ago, the district lay near the Equator and was a tropical lowland covered by dense swamps. Hollow trunks of scale trees and giant club mosses, relics of the lush flora that grew in the swamps, are fossilized in the sediments exposed in the cliffs; entombed

Figure 11–28
Fossil plants in concretions from Pennsylvanian deposits, Mazon Creek locality, Will County, Illinois. A. *Neuropteris.* B. *Annularia.*
(Photo courtesy of Field Museum of Natural History, Chicago. Photos No. 81443-A 81011)

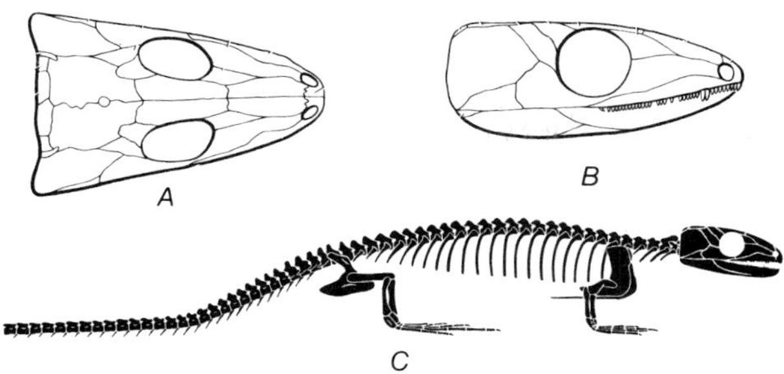

Figure 11–29
The oldest known reptile, *Hylonomus*, a small, slender, and agile cotylosaur. A. Dorsal view of skull. B. Lateral view of skull. C. Skeleton.
(From E. H. Colbert, *Evolution of the Vertebrates—A History of the Backboned Animals Through Time*; 3d ed., Fig. 42, p. 113. Copyright © 1980 by John Wiley & Sons, Inc., New York. Reproduced by permission of John Wiley & Sons, Inc.)

within the hollows of some of the trunks are the skeletons of a small, primitive reptile called *Hylonomus* (Fig. 11–29). These earliest-known reptiles were small animals that lived in a terrestrial realm dominated by amphibians. However, amphibians were limited in their colonization of the land because of their dependence on water in which to lay their delicate eggs.

Reptiles solved this problem with an egg that could resist drying out. Thus began one of the greatest adaptive success stories in the history of life. The problem of reproduction on land was surmounted by the evolution of a shelled egg within which the embryo could float in a liquid-filled sac, the *amnion* (Fig. 11–30). The protective layers provided strength and resistance to desiccation. The amnion provided the liquid environment and acted as a shock absorber. Reptilian offspring were able to emerge from the eggs as miniature adults; amphibians had to progress through a larval stage.

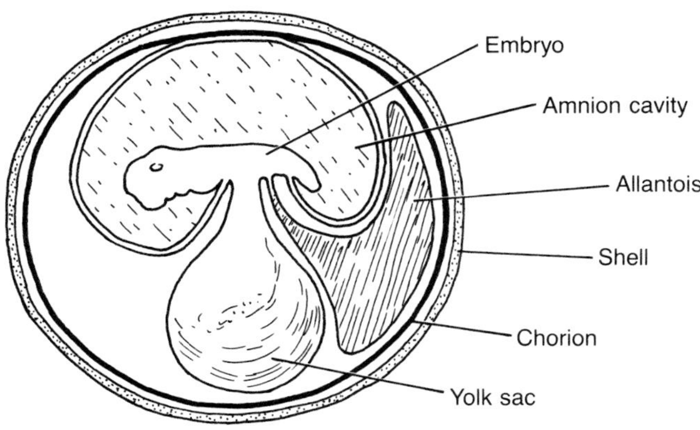

Figure 11–30
Amniotic egg.

Key differences between the reptiles and amphibians are mostly physiological, and are not well preserved in the fossil record. This is especially true for the evolutionary transition from amphibian ancestor to reptile descendant. However, fossil evidence showing subtle differences in skull structure, limb-bone construction, jaw and dental patterns, position of the ear, shape of ribs, and vertebral construction suggests that by Early Pennsylvanian the first reptiles had evolved from closely similar labyrinthodont amphibian ancestors. It is only in later reptiles that the more easily detected skeletal differences between reptiles and amphibians developed. These differences allowed the reptiles to move about on land more efficiently than could amphibians.

Hylonomus and its close relatives from the Bay of Fundy tree stumps belong to the group involved in the initial reptile radiation, the order Cotylosauria (Fig. 11–29). The early cotylosaurs were small forms that most likely fed on insects and grubs. The evolutionary innovations that accompanied the initial radiation of the cotylosaurs were so successful that by early in the Permian several other major reptile groups had evolved from this stock.

Permian History: The Paleozoic Drama Ends

An Arid Continent

During the Permian Period, the final chapter of Paleozoic history, major regression of seas and gradual emergence of the continent continued. Lower Permian rocks in the Alleghany Plateau and in the New Brunswick Basin in maritime Canada are only gently folded, suggesting that the compressional forces which folded and faulted the rocks of the Appalachian miogeocline had diminished by Early Permian time. No Middle or Upper Permian rocks have been recognized east of the Mississippi River, but the Lower Permian strata show essentially a continuation of Pennsylvanian depositional patterns. These rocks consist of cyclically bedded sandstones, siltstones, shales, and some coal, and are the products of coastal stream, lake, and swamp continental environments. In the Ouachita and Marathon regions, later Permian deposits, such as fossiliferous limestone in the Glass Mountains of West Texas, unconformably overlap the older

Permo-Carboniferous deformed rocks and provide an upper time limit to major deformation.

The Permian inaugurates a long interval of extensive *red bed* deposition in the western part of the craton (Fig. 11–31). The occurrence of red beds signifies depositional environments periodically exposed to the atmosphere—environments such as coastal tidal flats, river floodplains, alluvial fans, and lakes. During the Permian, interior North America was the scene of widespread distribution of such environments, fed by northward- and westward-draining streams that carried iron-rich sediment loads from marginal highlands. The various hues of the red beds—red, maroon, orange, vermilion, purple, and lavender—have been brought about by oxidation through direct exposure to the atmosphere.

Red beds can form under both humid and dry conditions; however, during the Permian, widespread conditions of aridity are suggested by evaporite deposits of anhydrite and gypsum. Extensively cross-bedded sandstone units with well-rounded, sorted, and frosted quartz grains suggest ancient sand-dune deposits, and evoke a picture of coastal deserts. Perhaps the aridity was the result of continentality that came about through the continental collisions and suturing of fragments into the super landmass Pangaea. The mountain belts that developed along the sutures no doubt acted as barriers to moisture, thus creating rain shadows that contributed to this change in world climatic patterns.

Last Vestiges of Paleozoic Seas

In North America open-marine deposition during the Permian was confined principally to the western part of the United States and Canada (Fig. 11–31). The Middle Permian Kaibab Limestone forms

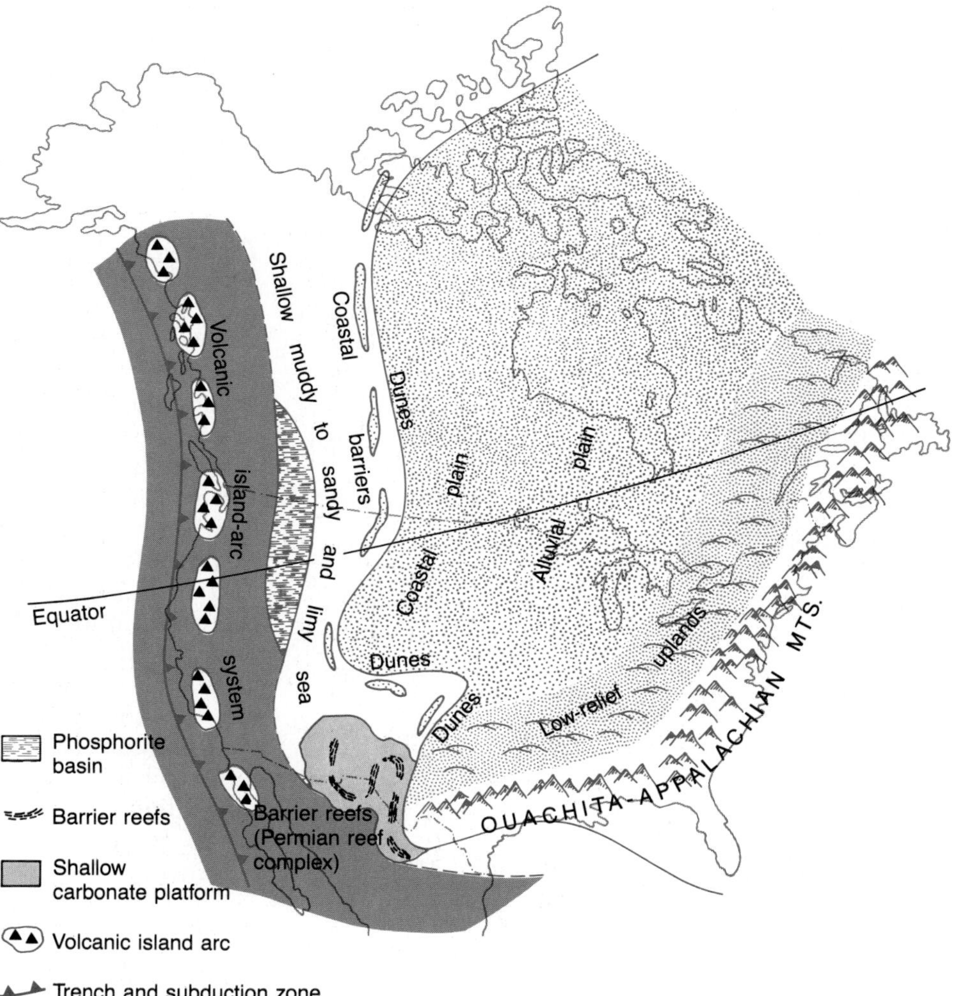

Figure 11–31
Paleogeography of Late Permian superimposed on outline map of present-day North America.

the spectacular rimrock of the Grand Canyon and is widely exposed over the surrounding plateau and as far west as southern Nevada. The Kaibab is the deposit of a marine invasion from the Cordilleran miogeocline onto the cratonic shelf. Sandwiched between the Kaibab and the Mississippian Redwall Limestone, in the walls of the Grand Canyon, are Pennsylvanian and Permian red beds that signify deposition on coastal mudflats and river floodplains. A prominent cross-bedded quartz sandstone, the Coconino, represents ancient sand dunes of a Permian desert.

Northward from the Kaibab sea, a moderately deep and restricted basin (Fig. 11–31) was the site of accumulation of the phosphate-rich sediments of the Phosphoria Formation. This unit has been extensively mined for fertilizer in the northern Rocky Mountain states of Wyoming, Idaho, and Montana. A tremendous thickness of limestone and sandstone accumulated in the Oquirrh Basin in northwestern Utah and southern Idaho. Thick eugeoclinal deposits in northern California, Oregon, British Columbia, and Alaska are composed largely of volcanic material. Permian volcanism in the eugeocline was an expression of oceanic plate subduction in the western borderland (Fig. 11–31).

To the south, in the Midland and Delaware basins (together called the Permian Basin) of West Texas and southeastern New Mexico, thick deposits of the famous Permian reef and associated lithofacies were formed (Fig. 11–31). A splendid platform–to–deep basin succession (see discussion, Chapter 2) is exposed in the east-facing escarpment of the Guadalupe Mountains. Platform-edge carbonate rocks buried in the subsurface have produced abundant hydrocarbons. The stratigraphic succession in this region serves as the North American standard Permian reference section.

Life of the Permian

Invertebrate life in the seas during Permian time was highlighted by the great abundance of fusulinid Foraminifera (Fig. 11–32). After their first appearance in the Late Mississippian, fusulinids flourished during the Pennsylvanian and Permian, and they provide excellent index taxa for the upper Paleozoic. Their biostratigraphic usefulness has contributed importantly to time-stratigraphic subdivision and understanding of the depositional history of the petroleum-rich, reef-rimmed Permian Basin.

Paleobiogeographic differences in Permian fusulinid faunas within the Cordilleran orogen suggest post-Permian convergence of what were presumably separate Asiatic and American faunal provinces—a consequence of lithospheric plate interactions (see later discussions on accreted terranes, Chapter 12). Spinose productid brachiopods, such as the beautiful silicified specimens from the Glass Mountains of West Texas, are characteristic of the Permian; calcareous algae, sponges, molluscs, echinoderms, and corals were also abundant (Fig. 11–33). Although the diversity of marine invertebrate life had experienced a marked decline since reaching a zenith in the mid-Devonian, there were several rich faunal provinces during the Permian, particularly at low, tropical latitudes.

The dominant tetrapods during the Early Permian were the pelycosaurs. They evolved into a diverse assemblage of plant-eating and predatory forms, and many were up to 3 m long. The genera *Edaphosaurus* and *Dimetrodon*, from the Permian red beds of north-central Texas, exemplify the main characteristics of the pelycosaur line (Fig. 11–34). It is interesting that the teeth of the powerful carnivore *Dimetrodon* show a fairly marked degree of adaptation for different functions, foreshadowing the mammalian condition of well-differentiated incisors, molars, and canines that was yet to come. The real hallmark of the pelycosaurs, however, was the erect "sail" along the back of the animal, formed by vertebral spines covered with skin (Fig. 11–35). This elaborate structural feature probably functioned as a heat receptor and radiator that evolved as a special adaptation to meet requirements determined by selection pressures of the environment.

By Late Permian, the pelycosaurs had been replaced largely by their more successful descendants, the therapsids, better known as the mammal-like reptiles (Fig. 11–34). The therapsids evolved from the carnivorous pelycosaur line, but following the pattern repeated over and over by groups of tetrapods, they rapidly diversified into separate carnivore and herbivore lines. This pattern has proved to be an evolutionary success because a few carnivores can keep the herbivore population in check. The therapsids made up at least 90% of the known reptile genera during the Late Permian, and occupied diverse ecological niches.

End-of-Paleozoic Faunal Crisis

In spite of this seemingly rich array of life, the Permian was a time of calamity and crisis for many groups of organisms, both invertebrate and vertebrate, both marine and terrestrial. Before the period ended, roughly 50% of the invertebrate families,

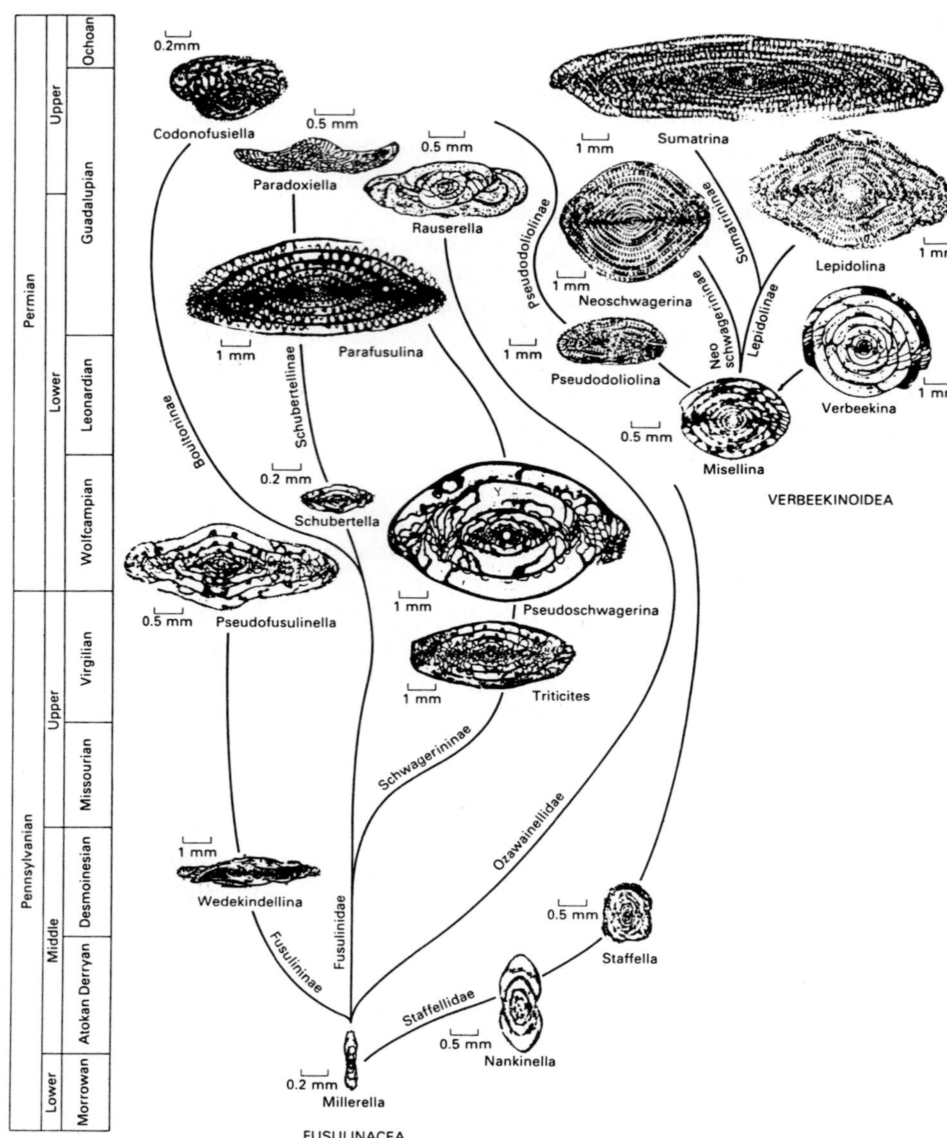

Figure 11–32

Fusulinid phylogeny. Simplified phylogeny of two superfamilies illustrated with a few representative genera, all shown in axial section. Smaller forms shown at greater magnification.

(From R. S. Boardman, A. H. Cheetham, and A. J. Rowell, eds., 1987, *Fossil Invertebrates,* Fig. 8.33, p. 82: Blackwell Scientific Publications)

75% of amphibian families, and 80% of reptilian families became extinct (Figs. 11–36 and 11–37). This makes the end-of-the-Permian mass-extinction event the most devastating crisis in the history of metazoan life. Raup and Sepkoski have calculated a Late Permian extinction rate of about 14.0 families per million years, significantly greater than the "normal," or background, rate of about 8.0 families per million years. Plants (Chapter 16) did not suffer quite the calamity at the end of the Paleozoic as did the animals, although Permian plant forms did decline in comparison to the lush, diverse Pennsylvanian coal-forest flora.

Trilobites, which had been on the wane since the end of Devonian, did not survive the end of the Paleozoic. Nor did fusulinid Foraminifera (Superfamily), rugose and tabulate corals (Orders), many kinds of brachiopods (several Orders), two orders of bry-

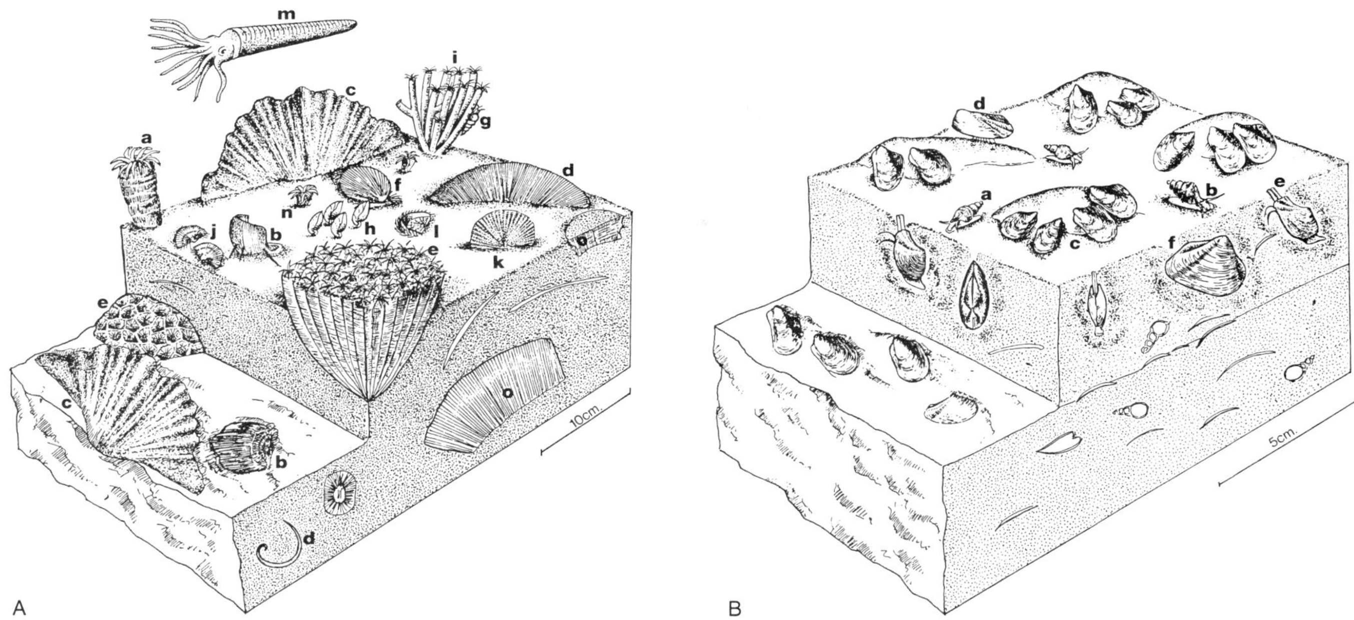

Figure 11–33

Late Paleozoic in-life restorations. A. Pennsylvanian brachiopod calcarenite community. a, e, i, n, rugose corals; b, c, d, h, j, k, l, articulate brachiopods; f, bivalve mollusc; g, gastropod mollusc; m, nautiloid cephalopod mollusc; o, sponge(?). B. Permian hypersaline sea community. a, b, gastropod molluscs; c–f, bivalve molluscs.

(From W. S. McKerrow, 1978, The Ecology of Fossils, Figs. 50, 60, p. 170, 192: MIT Press, all rights reserved. Reproduced with permission of MIT Press)

Figure 11–34

Evolution of the pelycosaur and therapsid reptiles.

(From E. H. Colbert, *Evolution of the Vertebrates—A History of the Backboned Animals Through Time;* 3d ed., Fig. 48, p. 127. Copyright © 1980 by John Wiley & Sons, Inc., New York. Reproduced by permission of John Wiley & Sons, Inc., and Lois M. Darling)

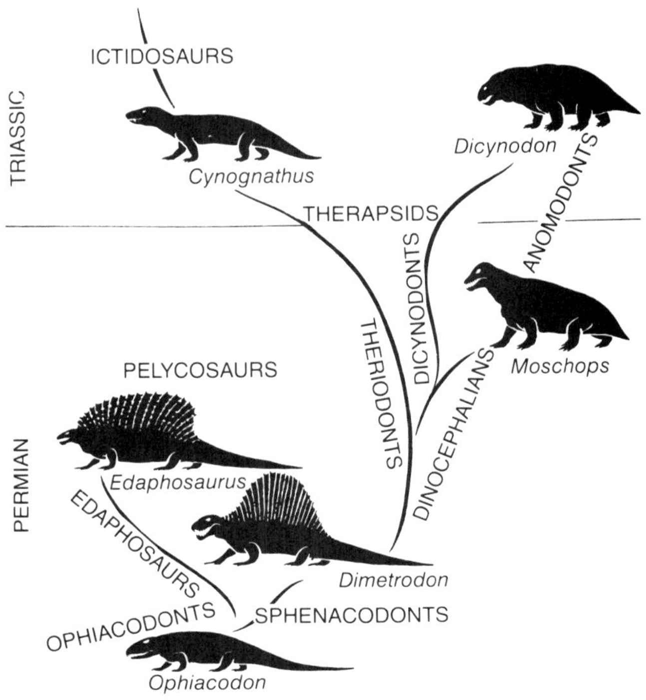

Figure 11–35
Skeleton of pelycosaur *Edaphosaurus* from Permian red beds, north-central Texas.
(Photo courtesy of National Museum of Natural History. Smithsonian Institution Photo No. 36248-A)

ozoans, cephalopod molluscs, and several groups of attached echinoderms (including the Subphylum Blastozoa), all of which became extinct (Fig. 11–36). All of these taxa had been highly successful, and some even dominant, during the Paleozoic.

Although the most reliable data set on mass extinctions is at the taxonomic level of family, experts have estimated that over 90% of marine invertebrate species died out by the end of the Permian. This suggests that a number of families were represented by only a few species (perhaps in some cases one or two) at the Paleozoic's end (the so-called "Cheshire cat" effect). Even though this was a tremendously devastating faunal crisis, most of the extinctions occurred at lower taxonomic levels (family, genus, species); relatively few suprafamily taxa became extinct in the Late Permian. This presents an interesting contrast with Cambrian extinctions, which included a number of low-diversity phyla and classes (Chapter 10).

Physical and biological causes for mass extinctions were discussed in Chapter 4. Regarding the end-of-Paleozoic extinctions, the unifying concept of plate tectonics may well hold the key. We have already mentioned the possible causal relationship between plate tectonics and the onset of climatic aridity as the Paleozoic drew to a close. This may have been responsible for some of the terrestrial floral and faunal extinctions. However, what about the large number of marine invertebrates? Continental convergence toward the end of the Paleozoic and the formation of Pangaea caused a draining away of epeiric seas and the consequent loss of marine habitats and ecospace. Previously separated—even isolated—faunas were brought into closer proximity and had to compete for the same dwindling resources. Highly specialized organisms like the ornately spinose productid brachiopods, with a limited range of environmental tolerance (*stenotopic*), were unable to cope with the pressures of the changing world. Stenotopic taxonomic groups became perched in positions of vulnerability. As long as environmental conditions remained within their narrow range of adaptations, they could carry on, but when environments changed, their community structures collapsed, and large-scale extinctions resulted.

From Late Devonian to the end of Permian there is a marked gradual decrease in total diversity among marine invertebrates, presumably a biologi-

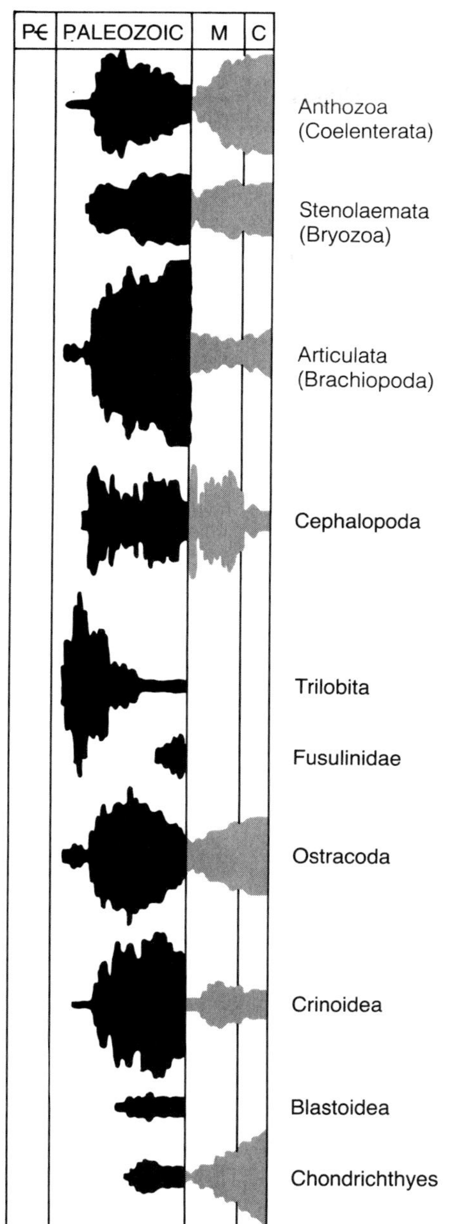

Figure 11–36

Diversity patterns of 10 higher-level (suprafamilial) taxa that were severely affected by the end-of-Paleozoic faunal crisis. Note the abrupt drop in diversity of all taxa, and complete extinction of some.

(From J. John Sepkoski, Jr., 1982, A Compendium of Fossil Marine Families: *Milwaukee Public Museum Contributions in Biology and Geology,* No. 51)

cal consequence of continental convergence, the closing of seaways, and total reduction of provinciality. The Paleozoic faunal patterns suggest general correlations, first between comparatively higher diversity and continental separation, and

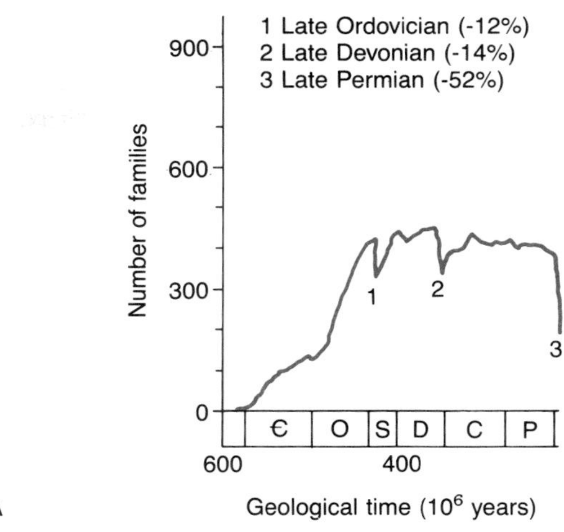

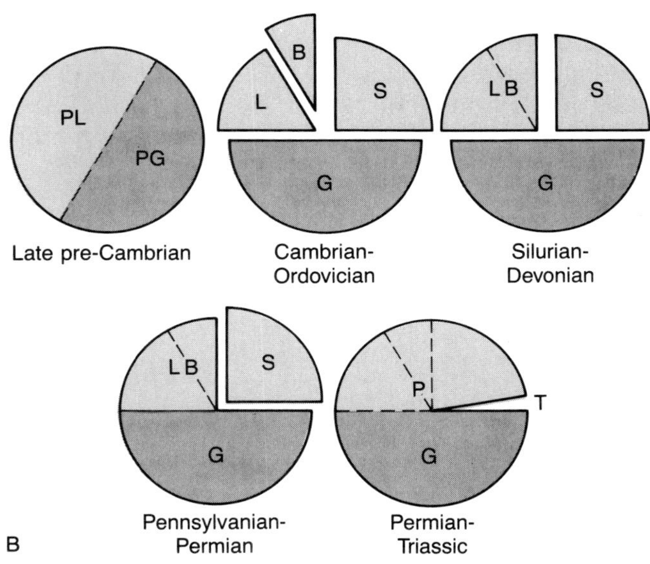

Figure 11–37

A. Standing diversity through Paleozoic for families of marine invertebrates and vertebrates, highlighting abrupt drop in diversity (mass-extinction event) at the end of the Permian. Late Ordovician mass-extinction event may have been influenced by rapid cooling of marine waters brought on by glaciation. B. Schematic continental configuration during Paleozoic showing relationship between diversity and degree of continental separation. (B, Baltica; G, Gondwana; L, Laurentia; LB, Laurentia and Baltica; P, Pangaea; PG, proto-Gondwana; PL, proto-Laurasia; S, Siberia; T, Tethys.)

(A from D. M. Raup and J. J. Sepkoski, Jr., 1982, Mass Extinctions in the Marine Fossil Record; Fig. 2, p. 1502: *Science,* vol. 215. Copyright 1982 by the American Association for the Advancement of Science. B from J. W. Valentine and E. M. Moores, 1972, Global Tectonics and the Fossil Record; Fig. 2, p. 170: *Journal of Geology,* vol. 80, no. 2. Reproduced by permission of University of Chicago Press)

second between lowered diversity (involving extinctions) and times of continental assembly (Fig. 11–37). Perhaps changes of large magnitude in the relative configuration of the continents may have had far-reaching effects on environments, and in turn, environmental changes exerted fatal stress on numerous groups of organisms. For example, continental clustering, resulting in a more arid climate, was the underlying cause of the formation of extensive marginal–marine evaporite deposits. The tying up of salts in these environments may have caused the oceans to become less saline, a condition that would have affected populations of organisms having narrow salinity-tolerance ranges.

Although it represents the greatest calamity in the Phanerozoic history of life, the end-of-the-Permian faunal crisis does not stand alone. Figure 11–37 shows two additional Paleozoic faunal crises—one at the end of the Ordovician and the other during the Late Devonian. And as we shall see in the Mesozoic and Cenozoic (Chapters 12, 13, 14), mass extinction was not limited to the Paleozoic. What are some of the common denominators related to environmental deterioration and collapse that might shed light on the causes of mass extinctions? One interesting commonality among the Ordovician, Devonian, and Permian crises relates to continental glaciation in Gondwana. Major continental glaciation may have caused widespread lowering of oceanic temperatures. Major collapse of tropical reef communities, in particular, during these times lends credence to the notion of drastic changes in water temperature.

Paleogeography of the Late Paleozoic World

Devonian Paleogeography

Paleomagnetically, Devonian and Silurian paleolatitudes for Laurentia are very similar, placing the Early-to-Late Devonian Equator through southern Greenland, Hudson Bay, and British Columbia or Montana (Fig. 11–38A, B). Paleoclimatologically,

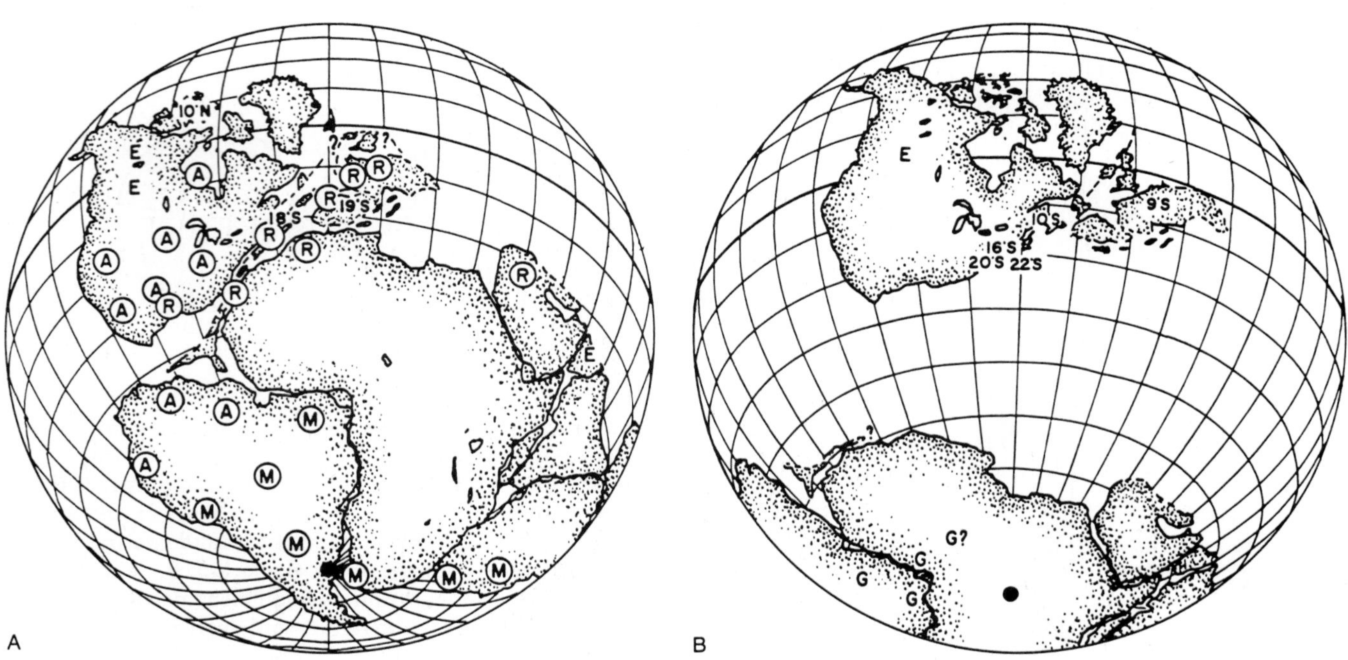

Figure 11–38

A. Early Devonian paleogeographic reconstruction. A, R, M are faunal realms; E = evaporites; numbers represent paleolatitudes. B. Late Devonian paleogeographic reconstruction. E = evaporites; G = glacial deposits; numbers represent paleolatitudes.

(From Rob Van der Voo, 1988, Paleozoic Paleogeography of North America, Gondwana, and Intervening Displaced Terranes: Comparisons of Paleomagnetism with Paleoclimatology and Biogeographical Patterns, Figs. 4, 5: *Geological Society of America Bulletin*, Vol. 100, No. 3. Reproduced with permission of Geological Society of America and the author)

Lower-to-Upper Devonian evaporites in the Yukon, Hudson Bay, and Williston Basin regions are located between 15°N and 15°S, which is in agreement with the paleomagnetic results. Paleobiogeographically, Lower Devonian faunal realms (Fig. 11–38A) show marked provinciality and endemic patterns consistent with regressive sea levels and an Acadian-Caledonian barrier land mass. The Late Devonian, by contrast, was characterized by a highly cosmopolitan marine brachiopod, coral, and conodont fauna, with no particular biogeographic realms to be distinguished (Fig. 11–38B).

The biggest problem in Devonian paleogeographic reconstructions is how to interpret the movement history of Gondwana. According to R. Van der Voo, new paleomagnetic data from western Australia yield a pole in central Africa. This requires the apparent polar wander path for Gondwana to loop from a mid-plate Ordovician location in northern Africa, through the mid-Silurian pole in western Chile, back to the Equator in Africa in the Late Devonian (Fig. 10–33B, Chapter 10). Van der Voo feels that the path of glacial centers migrating across Gondwana is in agreement with this paleomagnetic polar wander path. After a mid-Silurian–to–mid-Devonian interval with a warmer climate in Gondwana, strong evidence for Late Devonian glaciations can be found in northern Brazil. This indicates to Van der Voo that the north African part of Gondwana moved rapidly southward from Early to Late Devonian, from subtropical latitudes near Laurentia to intermediate latitudes.

This indeed represents a dramatic change in world geography after Early Devonian convergence and collision between Gondwana and Laurentia, a collision that sandwiched several intervening displaced terranes (viz., Armorica and Avalonia) between the two continental masses and formed the Acadian-Caledonian orogen (Fig. 11–38A). Basins in eastern Greenland, Norway, Great Britain, and the northern Appalachians were sites of extensive red bed deposition (Old Red Sandstone; Catskill clastic wedge) during the Middle and Late Devonian, a signature of major continent-continent collisions.

However, the problem is: to what extent was Gondwana involved? How far, and along what path, did the Gondwana supercontinent move during the Silurian and Devonian? The movement history depicted in Figure 11–38 has some support, but the density of control is weak, and the movement history suggested seems bizarre. According to this interpretation, during the Late Devonian, following the collision that produced the Acadian-Caledonian orogen, Gondwana promptly became separated from Laurentia and the Armorica, Avalon, and Baltica terranes by a medium-width ocean. (The Armorica, Avalon, and Baltica terranes became part of an enlarged Laurentia—Fig. 11–38B.)

Figure 11–39 shows an alternative reconstruction that does not require the unusually rapid movement history and directional changes. Here, after the mid-Devonian collision of Laurentia with the northern fringe of Gondwana, the two continents moved northward together across the Equator.

Carboniferous and Permian Paleogeography

The pageant of changes for Carboniferous reconstructions (Fig. 11–40A) shows that Gondwana, according to the scenario depicted in Fig. 11–38, moved northward once again from its Late Devonian position, and gradually converged on Laurentia, closing the ocean basin between them. Thus, if this more radical scenario is true, North America maintained a generally stable latitudinal position during the Paleozoic, but Gondwana was much more footloose, making a rapid northward voyage during the Silurian to visit Laurentia in the Early Devonian, returning to southern latitudes during the later Devonian, only to venture forth once again in the Early Carboniferous to suture with Laurentia once more in the Late Carboniferous.

In light of what we know about plate motions, this requires the almost dizzying speed of 25 to 30 cm/year (more than 50° in 40 million years), which is considerably faster than lithospheric plates are moving now (or in the recent geologic past). However, we should not be lulled into taking a too-uniformitarian approach to this problem. Further well-dated paleomagnetic and paleobiogeographic data will be required to resolve this dilemma. On the other hand, if we accept the more easily accommodated scenario depicted in Figure 11–39, Gondwana and Laurentia moved in consort during the Carboniferous, with perhaps a tightening up along the suture zone to produce the Alleghany and Ouachita orogens.

One of the main problems with making Paleozoic global paleogeographic reconstructions is that we have no preserved oceanic crust and magnetic anomaly patterns. This is in marked contrast to the last half of Mesozoic and the Cenozoic (Chapters 12, 13, 14), where the "tape recording" of present ocean-floor anomalies aids importantly in tracking the separation and movement paths of the continents during the past 180 million years.

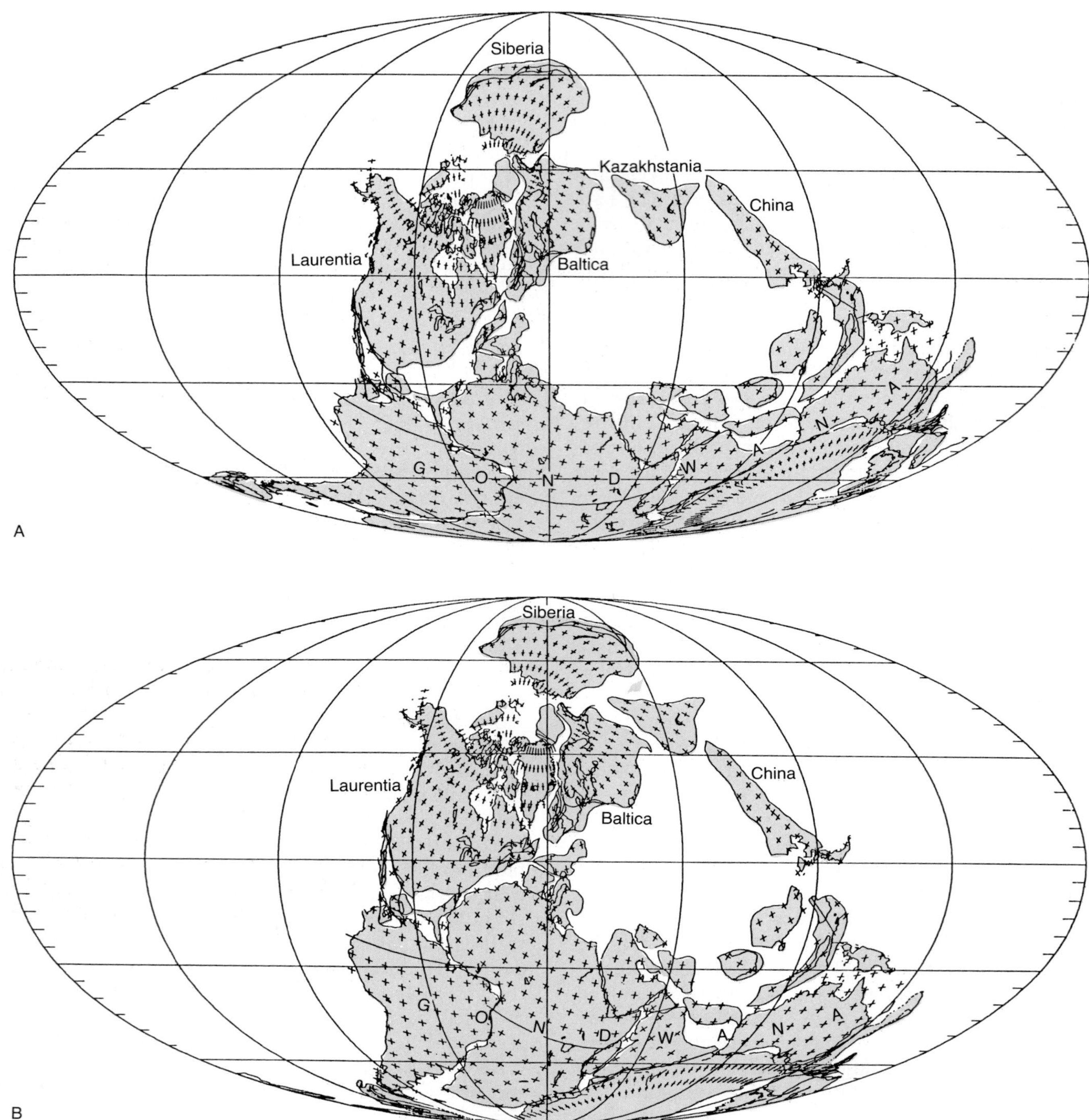

Figure 11–39
World geography reconstructions. A. Early Devonian. B. Late Devonian. Note the difference between this interpretation and that depicted in Figure 11–38, particularly for the movement history of Gondwana.
(From C. R. Scotese, 1986, *Phanerozoic Reconstructions: A New Look at the Assembly of Asia.* University of Texas Institute for Geophysics Technical Report No. 66. Paleoceanographic Mapping Project Progress Report No. 19–1286)

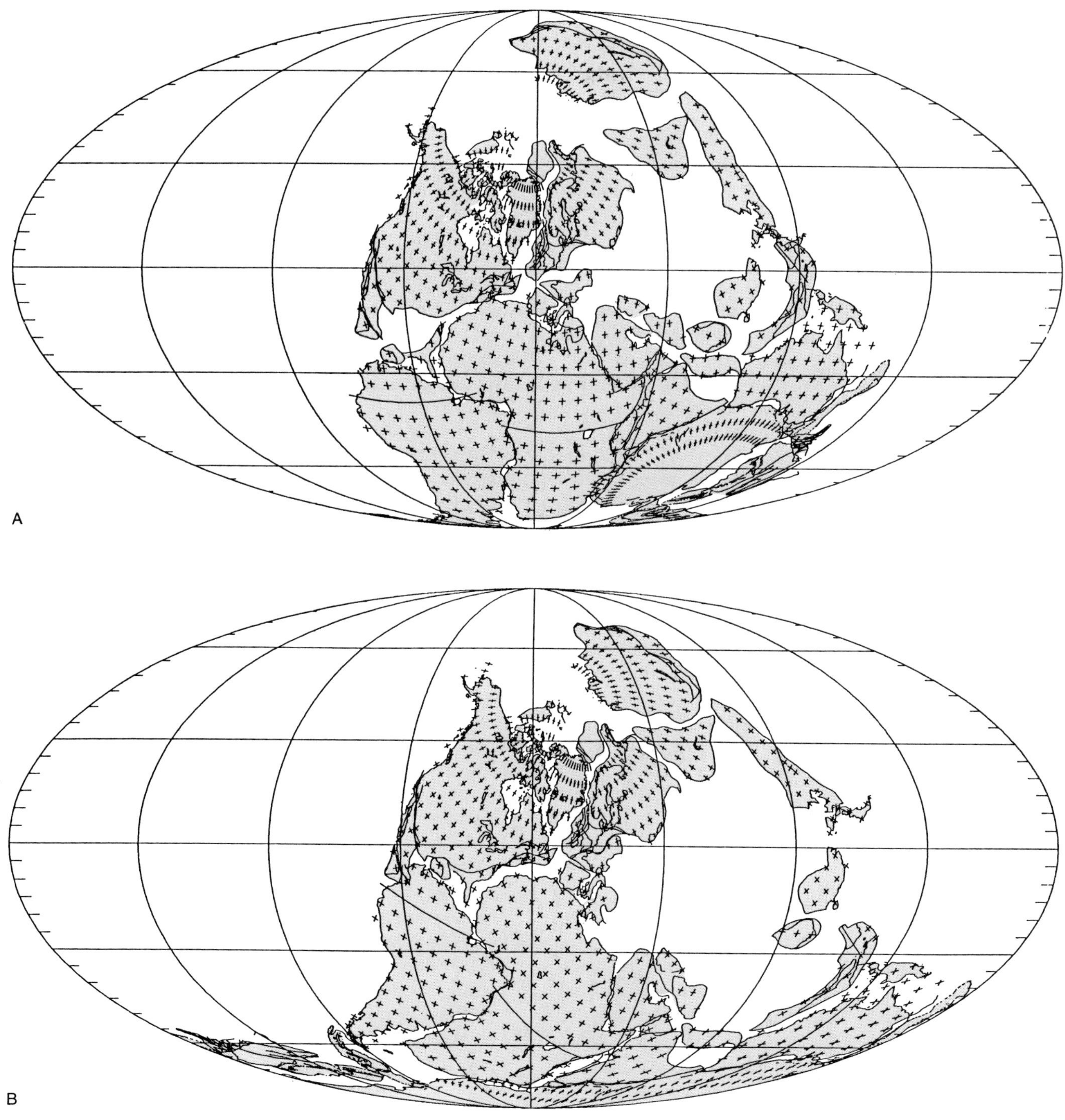

Figure 11–40

World paleogeography reconstructions. A. Mississippian. B. Pennsylvanian. Note the accretion of what is now Florida to Laurentia during the Pennsylvanian.
(From C. R. Scotese, 1986, *Phanerozoic Reconstructions: A New Look at the Assembly of Asia.* University of Texas Institute for Geophysics Technical Report No 66. Paleoceanographic Mapping Project Progress Report No. 19–1286)

The Hercynian and Alleghany orogenies produced mountain belts in what are now eastern North America, North Africa, and central Europe. During collision between Gondwana and Laurentia, the Armorica and Baltica parts of enlarged Laurentia were displaced northward along a series of megashears that developed on the original suture zone. These large-scale strike-slip faults presently can be mapped from coastal New England across Newfoundland and through Scotland. The Great Glen fault of Scotland and the Cabot fault of Newfoundland match up when western Europe is restored to its interpreted post-Devonian/pre–late Carboniferous position with respect to northeastern North America.

The Late Carboniferous orogenic belt straddled the Equator, as suggested by the distribution of climatically sensitive Upper Carboniferous deposits. As with the preceding Caledonian-Acadian disturbances, great volumes of terrigenous clastic sediments were shed from the mountainous highlands. This time the deltaic plains and coastal-lagoon and marsh paleoenvironments of the clastic-wedge successions were the sites of extensive coal swamps, where vegetation accumulated under conditions of heavy rainfall. These environments gave rise to the great coal deposits of the eastern United States, western Europe, and Donetz Basin of the USSR. The plant fossils in the coal-bearing cyclothems of these regions do not show strong seasonal growth rings; this implies that the vegetation grew in a wet but constantly warm tropical belt. Coal deposits developed also in Siberia and China, but here the plant fossils have growth rings, indicating seasonal climates; this in turn implies that these continental blocks occupied a north temperate belt during the Late Carboniferous (Fig. 11–40B).

Tillites in southern Gondwana attest to major continental glaciation during the Permo-Carboniferous time interval, supporting the reconstruction of the south polar position of this region at that time. Plant fossils with seasonal growth rings also are found in the south temperate latitudes of Gondwana, marginal to the ancient ice sheets. Recall that it was this evidence of late Paleozoic glaciation in modern-day South America, South Africa, India, and Australia that inspired Edward Suess, in the late nineteenth century, to support the notion that these continents were once part of a larger assembly (Chapter 1). Eustatic sea-level changes, brought about by the waxing and waning of these Gondwana ice sheets, are recorded in the Carboniferous and Permian cyclothems on the continents.

Paleomagnetic information suggests a Late Permian geographic configuration that is supported by distribution of evaporites and other climatically sensitive deposits (Fig. 11–41A). The formation of Pangaea resulted in an enormous ocean, **Panthalassa,** which spanned the globe from pole to pole and encompassed nearly 300° of longitude! Such a configuration would have exerted a major control on oceanic circulation, which, in turn, would have profoundly influenced Permian climates. These climates were characterized by aridity. In accordance with present-day climatic models, the equatorial currents, driven by the trade winds, would have flowed uninterrupted around five-sixths of the circumference of the Earth, impinging against the east-facing coast of Pangaea, making it extremely warm. The warm waters of the **Tethys Sea,** the indented eastern margin of Pangaea, probably were circulated by gulf streams that extended warm conditions into higher latitudes.

The paleobiogeography of some Permian cotylosaurs and pelycosaurs has contributed importantly to the interpretation of continental positions. The Permian cotylosaur *Mesosaurus* has been found in Brazil and South Africa. The plant-eating pelycosaur *Edaphosaurus* and an associated fauna of other reptiles, crossopterygian fish, and labyrinthodont amphibians have been found in Permian deposits of both northern Texas and Czechoslovakia. These now disjunct occurrences, which reinforce the paleomagnetic data and other lines of geological evidence, support the reconstruction of continents for Permian time (Fig. 11–41B).

The mountain belts between Gondwana and **Laurasia** formed barriers that created giant rain shadows, even in tropical latitudes. These desert conditions are recorded by extensive dune deposits and evaporites. Major withdrawals of shallow seas (brought about by plate collisions), together with changes of volume of seafloor spreading ridges, left large areas of exposed land, which contributed to the climatic extremes of severe aridity. Abundant evaporites accumulated along the margins of these retreating seas, and red beds blanketed wide areas of the exposed supercontinent. We have already seen how this inhospitable world presented a real survival test for a major part of the biosphere. Only the hardy, adaptable groups of organisms survived.

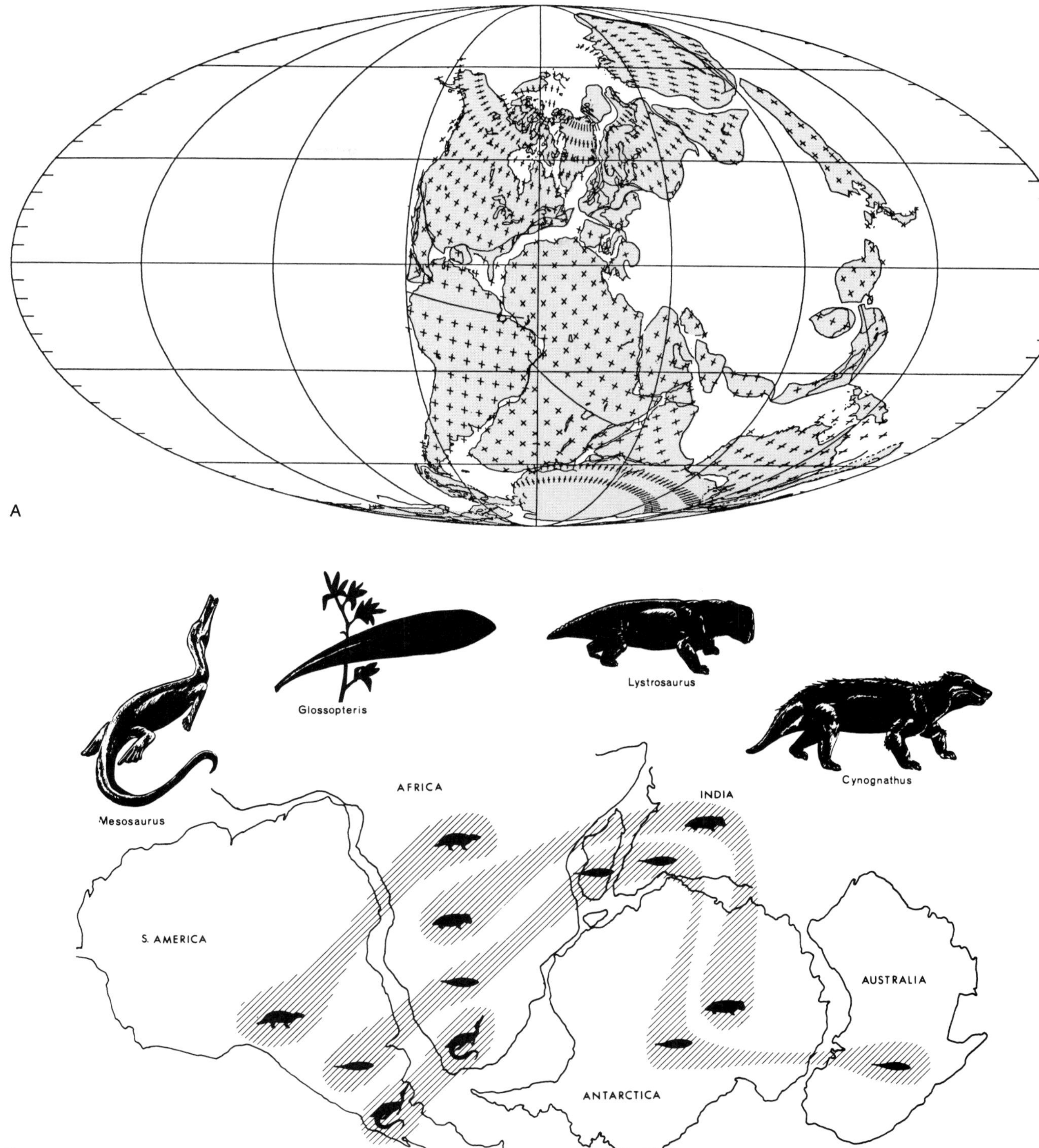

Figure 11–41

A. World paleogeography reconstruction for the Late Permian—the formation of Pangea. B. Gondwanaland reassembled, and some of the paleontological links that bind it together. *Mesosaurus,* a Permian reptile, occurs in southern Brazil and South Africa; *Glossopteris,* a Permian plant, occurs across all of the Gondwana components; *Lystrosaurus,* a Lower Triassic therapsid reptile, occurs in South Africa, peninsular India, southeast Asia, and Antarctica; *Cynognathus,* a Lower Triassic reptile, occurs in Argentina and South Africa. Late Paleozoic continental glacial deposits are also present on the five continents shown.

(A from C. R. Scotese, 1986, *Phanerozoic Reconstructions: A New Look at the Assembly of Asia.* University of Texas Institute for Geophysics Technical Report No. 66. Paleoceanographic Mapping Project Progress Report No. 19–1286. B. from E. H. Colbert, 1973, *Wandering Lands and Animals;* Figs. 30, 31, p. 68, 72: E. P. Dutton, New York. Reproduced by permission of author)

Summary

Withdrawal of epeiric seas during the Early and Middle Devonian resulted in extensive erosion on the craton, with consequent removal of much of the Silurian section. Renewed invasion of cratonic seas in the Middle Devonian produced fossiliferous carbonate deposits. Coral and stromatoporoid reefs continued to flourish around the margins of intracratonic basins. The Paleozoic record of North America consists of four large-scale onlap-offlap cycles, called sequences, that are bounded by unconformities of cratonwide extent. The sequences are the first-order rock-response products of interactions among global tectonics, climate, and eustatic sea-level changes.

Vertebrate organisms diversified greatly during the Devonian, and by early in the period five fish classes were well represented. A group of freshwater bony fish—the lobe-finned crossopterygians—gave rise to the class Amphibia late in the period, thus beginning the vertebrate transition to land. Primitive vascular plants, which had appeared during the Silurian, also experienced dramatic diversification, and by the Late Devonian much of the land surface was cloaked with vegetation. The Devonian was a time of maximum Paleozoic diversity. Marine invertebrates, however, experienced a wave of mass extinctions late in the period; from the Late Devonian onward there was a gradual decline in diversity, culminating in the end-of-Paleozoic faunal crisis.

In the Appalachian region, mid-Devonian mountain building—the Acadian phase of the Appalachian orogeny—resulted from final closing of the northern part of the Iapetus Ocean as Baltica, Gondwana, and a number of island terranes collided with Laurentia. The Catskill sediments of northeastern North America and the Old Red Sandstone of Greenland and western Europe are parts of clastic-wedge facies associations that developed symmetrically on opposite sides of the suture orogen.

A major question regarding Late Devonian world paleogeography revolves around the position of Gondwana with respect to Laurentia. Did it separate from Laurentia and migrate back to high southern latitudes, or did it remain in close proximity before colliding with Laurentia once again in the Late Carboniferous?

In the Late Devonian and Early Mississippian, subduction along the Cordilleran margin of the continent caused telescoping of a marginal basin and produced the Antler orogeny. The Devonian-Mississippian transition also was a time of abundant chert formation and deposition of black, organic-rich shales. Clean oolitic and crinoidal deposits characterize the central craton and much of the Cordilleran belt, and attest to widespread invasion of the last great carbonate-producing epeiric sea during the Mississippian. Deposits of flysch accumulated in the Ouachita basin, signaling the beginnings of orogeny, and coal beds presaged the great coal swamps of the Pennsylvanian.

The Pennsylvanian was a time of tectonic activity in the ancestral Rocky Mountains and the Appalachian-Ouachita belt, and of cyclic sedimentation in tectonic foreland basins and the craton. Thick piles of Upper Mississippian and Pennsylvanian flysch in the Ouachita trough were derived from erosion of tectonic sourcelands raised along the northern margin of Gondwana as a result of plate collisions. Compressional folding and thrust-faulting in the Appalachian miogeoclinal belt resulted from collision between southeastern Laurentia and Gondwana and the closing of the intervening ocean. The Alleghany orogeny represents the climax of a long Appalachian orogeny involving interactions among a number of oceanic and continental plates and the final forging of the Appalachian orogen. Folding and thrusting of Carboniferous flysch and older deposits in the Ouachita belt during the Late Pennsylvanian to Permian signify the completion of suturing of Gondwana and Laurentia.

Coal-bearing cyclothems of the midcontinent and Appalachian foreland basins reflect global effects of cyclicity in Gondwana glaciation, regional cyclicity in tectonic activity, and local-to-regional cyclicity of sediment input. Coal-forming swamps represent deltaic-plain and coastal-lagoon environments that developed along the margins of prograding clastic wedges. The swamps contained lush stands of scale trees, club mosses, rushes, and ferns, which provided the raw organic matter for the coal. The oldest known reptiles have been found in Lower Pennsylvanian cyclothem deposits and signify a new adaptive breakthrough in the vertebrate conquest of land.

The Permian was a time of final suturing of continental masses to form the supercontinent Pangaea. Elevated mountain chains and withdrawal of epeiric seas brought about widespread aridity on Pangaea; this favored extensive deposition of red beds and evaporites on alluvial plains and coastal tidal flats. In present-day North America, post–Lower Permian deposits are confined to two areas—the western craton, where continental and coastal marine red beds, dune sands, and shallow-marine mudstones and carbonates formed, and to the Cordilleran belt, where shallow-to-deep marine deposits accumulated. The Permian Basin of West Texas and southeastern New Mexico was rimmed by a major barrier reef; extensive marine phosphorite deposits formed in the northern Rockies; and thick volcaniclastic eugeoclinal deposits formed in the western Cordillera.

The Permian was a period of crisis in the history of life. Near the end of the period, roughly 50% of marine invertebrate families and more than 75% of terrestrial vertebrate families became extinct in the most devastating wave of mass extinctions of the Phanerozoic. A number of higher taxa became extinct, including fusulinid Foraminifera, the echinoderm subphylum Blastozoa, several subclasses of crinoids, the last of the trilobites, several orders of bryozoans and articulate brachiopods, rugose and tabulate corals, and the reptilian order Pelycosauria.

Drastically increased continentality, increased aridity, withdrawal of epeiric seas with consequent loss of ecospace, salinity changes, and increased competition combined to place exorbitant demands on many highly specialized, vulnerable taxonomic groups. Most, if not all of the environmental changes that contributed to the end-of-Paleozoic faunal crises were byproducts of global tectonics—the suturing of continents and closing of ocean basins.

Suggestions for Further Reading

Bambach, R. K., C. R. Scotese, and A. M. Ziegler. 1980. Before Pangaea: The geographies of the Paleozoic world. *American Scientist* 68(1):26–38.

Dietz, R. S. 1972. Geosynclines, mountains, and continent-building. *Scientific American* Offprint No. 899. San Francisco: W. H. Freeman.

King, P. B. 1977. The Evolution of North America. Rev. ed. Princeton, NJ: Princeton Univ. Press.

Laporte, Leo. 1979. Ancient environments. 2d ed. Foundations of Earth Science Series. Englewood Cliffs, NJ: Prentice-Hall.

McAlester, A. L. 1977. The history of life. 2d ed. Foundations of Earth Science Series. Englewood Cliffs, NJ: Prentice-Hall.

Newell, N. D. 1963. Crises in the history of life. *Scientific American* Offprint No. 901. San Francisco: W. H. Freeman.

Newell, N. D. 1972. The evolution of reefs. *Scientific*

American Offprint No. 901. San Francisco: W. H. Freeman.

Oliver, Jack. 1980. Exploring the basement of the North American continent. *American Scientist* 68(6):676–83.

Raup, D. M., and J. J. Sepkoski, Jr. 1982. Mass extinctions in the marine fossil record. *Science* 215:1501–04.

Runcorn, R. K. 1966. Corals as paleontologic clocks. *Scientific American* Offprint No. 871. San Francisco: W. H. Freeman.

Valentine, J. W. 1978. Evolution of multicellular plants and animals. *Scientific American* Offprint No. 1403. San Francisco: W. H. Freeman.

Valentine, J. W., and E. M. Moores. 1974. Plate tectonics and the history of life in the oceans. *Scientific American* Offprint No. 912. San Francisco: W. H. Freeman.

Van der Voo, Rob. 1988. Paleozoic paleogeography of North America, Gondwana, and intervening displaced terranes: Comparisons of paleomagnetism with paleoclimatology and biogeographical patterns. *Geological Society of America Bulletin* Vol. 100 p. 311–24.

Early Mesozoic History

12

Eon		Era	Period		Age in Ma*
PHANEROZOIC		CENOZOIC	Quaternary	Quaternary	2
			Tertiary	Neogene	24
				Paleogene	65
		MESOZOIC	Cretaceous		144
			Jurassic		208
			Triassic		245
		PALEOZOIC	Permian		286
			Carboniferous	Pennsylvanian	320
				Mississippian	360
			Devonian		408
			Silurian		438
			Ordovician		505
			Cambrian		570
CRYPTOZOIC (PRECAMBRIAN)	PROTEROZOIC	Late Proterozoic			900
		Middle Proterozoic			1600
		Early Proterozoic			2500
	ARCHEAN	Late Archean			3000
		Middle Archean			3400
		Early Archean			~3800
HADEAN (Pregeologic history of the Earth)				Origin of Earth	4600

Contents

Key Terms

Blueschist
Seamount
Sonoma orogeny
Tethys
Nevadan orogeny
Farallon plate
Accretionary wedge
Mélange
Cordilleran orogeny
Tectonostratigraphic terrane

The Bone Hunters

Mesozoic, translated literally, means "middle life," an apt description for the intermediate stage of evolution of life present in that era, as compared to the more primitive life of the Paleozoic and the more modern life of the Cenozoic. The Mesozoic is also the "age of reptiles"—not the kinds of reptiles we see today, but forms that included the largest beasts ever to walk the Earth. The Mesozoic was a fantastic time of dinosaurs, giant sea "monsters," and pterodactyls—creatures that would sooner suggest creation by the minds of science-fiction writers than by nature (Fig. 12–1). Nonetheless, the bizarre reptiles of the Mesozoic were real. Their bones and skeletons adorn the halls of the great natural-history museums in this country and abroad, captivating the imaginations of millions.

Who were the people responsible for collecting these tremendous specimens, and where were the fossils found? These questions take us back to the golden age of vertebrate paleontology and to those heroes of the American West—the bone hunters.

During the pre–Civil War period of the nineteenth century, there was no organized program for collecting fossils in North America. But after the Civil War, when the great expanses of the West were being opened, the really serious business of collecting fossils on a grand scale mushroomed. The U.S. government, in an effort to assess the natural resources of this new land, instituted a series of territorial surveys. Because much of the emphasis of these surveys was on geology, many fossils were discovered, and word soon spread of the fantastic fossil fields of the West. Thus began a new and highly exciting period in American paleontology, centered around two intriguing individuals.

Othniel Charles Marsh (1831–1899), nephew of the wealthy banker and philanthropist George Peabody, acquired an early interest in paleontology; he was inspired by the richly fossiliferous rocks exposed by the diggings of the Erie Canal near his home in Lockport, New York. Having broken away from what he considered the drudgery of farm life, Marsh, with financial assistance from rich Uncle George, got a first-rate education at Phillips Academy and later at Yale, where he studied geology under J. D. Dana of geosynclinal fame. While at Yale, Marsh began amassing a collection of fossils that would later become one of the finest of its kind in the world.

During the summer of 1861, he explored the newly discovered gold fields of Nova Scotia, and the writing style of his published report clearly demonstrated his penchant for capitalizing on the dramatic. His report aroused attention even in Europe. In 1863, George Peabody gave Yale a museum of natural history, the famous Peabody Museum, with the proviso that his nephew be given a professorship. Marsh gratefully accepted the unpaid professorship because such a post left him without teaching obligations, and gave him free rein to conduct research. Allowances and a bequest from his

Figure 12–1
Mounted skeleton and restoration of Jurassic sauropod dinosaur *Apatasaurus (Brontosaurus).*

uncle gave him enough money to live comfortably and to amass his rich collection of fossils.

Edward Drinker Cope (1840–1897), nine years younger than Marsh, was a child prodigy. At the age of 6 he began recording his own journal, and by 10 was making scientific observations and sketches. His formal education at Quaker schools ended at 16 when his wealthy father decided that the frail, undersized youngster should prepare for the life of a practical farmer. Like Marsh, however, Cope had other ideas; he was impatient with the slow process of crop cultivation and longed for the excitement of science. In the winter of 1860, Cope enrolled in a series of lectures given by the eminent Joseph Leidy at the University of Pennsylvania. The following year Cope became a member of the Philadelphia Academy of Sciences, and four years later accepted an unpaid curatorial post at the Academy. From 1864 to 1868 he was Professor of Natural History at Haverford College.

Cope supported himself and his family with the rent from a farm his father had given him a few years earlier, and he plunged headlong into his exciting career of science. Although he had been publishing for several years on modern vertebrates, he published his first scientific paper on fossil vertebrates in 1870. He roamed the East in search of fossils and made at least one collecting trip with a friend from Yale University—O. C. Marsh. In 1871, Cope made his first trip to the western fossil fields.

When the railroad opened up the West and made its fossils accessible, Cope and Marsh, who began their careers as friends, were employed by competing scientific surveys. Cope was collecting fossils with the Hayden Survey, led by Ferdinand Hayden, while Marsh was affiliated with the King Survey, led by Clarence King.

The competitive spirit of both men exploded into full-fledged rivalry, and by 1873 they were using that ultimate battleground—the scientific literature—for airing their differences. Both men became obsessed with being the first to discover and publish. From 1870 to 1875 staggering amounts of material were obtained by the collecting parties, under the direction of the rivals. However, much of the systematic work on the specimens was hastily done, and the rapid-fire publications that followed were occasionally laced with inaccuracies.

After 1874, Marsh spent little time in the field, being content to delegate responsibility to trusted subordinates. He devoted most of his time to research and lab work, and he revolutionized existing procedures for fossil collection and preparation. Cope, on the other hand, realized the importance of seeing the vertebrate fossil in its relation to the outcrop; he continued to make forays, often alone, into the fossil fields of the west. The bone-hunting teams of Cope and Marsh raked across the Dakota Badlands, the Smoky Hill River country of Kansas, the Morrison beds of Como Bluff, Wyoming, and Canon City, Colorado, and numerous other virgin fossil localities of the Great Plains and Rocky Mountain basins.

The number of species of Mesozoic reptiles and Tertiary mammals described by Cope and Marsh is stunning. Perhaps the rivalry between the two men stimulated both to herculean efforts much greater than they would have made if all had been pleasant and serene.

In their last years, the feud abated somewhat, as both men fell into poor health and financial straits. Marsh had to give up his home and request a salary for his professorship at Yale. When he died in 1899, he left to Yale and to the U.S. National Museum in Washington, DC, perhaps the greatest collection of vertebrate fossils ever assembled. He described more than 450 new species, and his restorations of dinosaurs will always be a monument to his genius. Marsh was a sure and methodical thinker, of lesser intellect than Cope, but nonetheless a scholar of ability; he possessed a rare genius for organization, for recognizing the key elements of situations, and for delegating responsibility and capitalizing on the hard work of others.

Cope died at his home in Philadelphia, which, along with the Marsh laboratories at Yale, served as one of the important world centers for research in vertebrate paleontology during the last half of the nineteenth century. His deathbed was a cot that lay amid a veritable plethora of fossil bones. Cope is remembered as a quick, witty, incisive individual who had boundless energy and enthusiasm. He was a man of extraordinary brilliance and ability, perhaps one of the greatest true scholars this country has ever produced.

To Cope and Marsh we owe much about the knowledge of life of the past, in particular of the great reptiles (Fig. 12–1) of the Mesozoic and the mammals of the Early Cenozoic. The new techniques of collecting, preparing, and studying fossils established by these men formed the basis for modern vertebrate paleontology in this country, and for the entire world. They also transformed vertebrate paleontology from a passive, chance-collection activity into a vigorous, dynamic science. Discovery of the great dinosaur fossil-hunting grounds in the west, and collection of great numbers of skeletons, completely revolutionized both the concept and construction of natural-history museums.

Triassic History

More Red Beds

The Triassic, the initial period of the Mesozoic, was named for a three-part stratigraphic subdivision in Germany. This sequence of red sandstone and shales, separated by fossiliferous limestones, does not closely resemble the Triassic succession in other parts of the world, but the presence of red beds is characteristic of many sections and attests to much continental deposition. In North America, Mesozoic history began rather undramatically with a continuation of Permian depositional patterns,

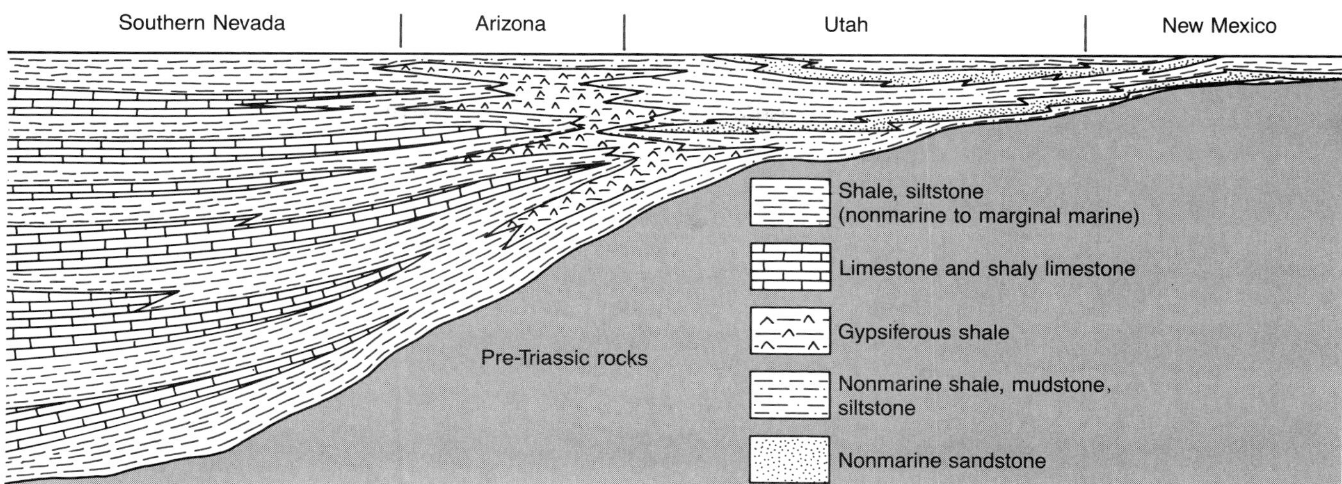

Figure 12–2
Restored east-west cross section of Moenkopi Formation, showing nonmarine-to-marine transition from western craton to continental margin basin.
(Data from M. F. MacLachlan, 1972, *Geologic Atlas of Rocky Mountain Region:* Rocky Mountain Association of Geologists)

characterized by continental red beds in the western interior part of the craton. Variegated Triassic sediments, in particular the red beds, underlie some of the most spectacular and colorful scenery in the American west.

One of the most varied and interesting rock units in western America is the Moenkopi Formation, a succession of red and chocolate mudstones of Early Triassic age, laid down in a variety of coastal-nonmarine and shallow-marine environments. Mudcracked and ripple-marked siltstone beds are common, and local beds of gypsum and casts of halite crystals indicate a relatively arid climate, a carryover from the dry Permian Period.

Several tongues of limestone that thicken westward punctuate the Moenkopi mudstone succession (Fig. 12–2) and attest to periodic marine encroachments across coastal mudflats and floodplains. Marine fossils in these carbonate tongues provide good biostratigraphic tie-ins for the sparse amphibian and reptile fossils in the continental facies.

Unconformably overlying the Moenkopi is a widespread unit, consisting predominantly of mudstone and siltstone in a dazzling array of colors ranging from red, pink, and purple to chocolate, blue, ash gray, and even white. This variegated unit, the Chinle Formation of Late Triassic age, is widely exposed over the Colorado Plateau, and is famous for its petrified wood. The abundant and beautifully preserved conifer logs in Petrified Forest National Park, Arizona (discussed in Chapter 16) are products of silicification of the wood, commonly in exquisite detail, by red, yellow, orange, and purple agate. Much of the silica was probably from volcanic ash beds within the fluvial and delta-plain Chinle sediments. The logs were not preserved as a fossilized forest, but were transported during flood stages, eventually being deposited in sand bars and on floodplains, and later petrified by silica that precipitated from ground water.

Fossil cycads and ferns also have been recovered from the Chinle, and together with the abundant conifer logs, they provide a fair representation of what Triassic land floras were like. The Chinle is not known for its fossil vertebrates, but in a few places it has produced remains of labyrinthodont amphibians, peculiar crocodilelike phytosaurs, and some small bipedal dinosaurs (Fig. 12–9).

Tectonic Unrest in the Western Cordillera

The miogeoclinal and eugeoclinal belts that had characterized the Cordilleran continental margin basin during much of the Paleozoic underwent major changes during the late Paleozoic and Triassic. Intense volcanism within an island-arc system that extended from California to Alaska, and orogeny throughout much of the western Cordillera, affected the continental margin basin. The Permo-Triassic volcanic belt was probably similar to the present-day Japanese archipelago and was related to a major zone of subduction. This volcanic island-arc system (Fig. 12–4) was separated from the main-

A

B

Figure 12–3

Chinle Formation at Petrified Forest National Park, Arizona. A. Exposure showing lens-shaped fluvial channel deposits (c) with petrified log (l) protruding from outcrop face. B. Petrified log–strewn landscape.
(Photos by J. D. Cooper)

Figure 12–4

Paleogeography of Early Triassic superimposed on outline map of present-day North America.

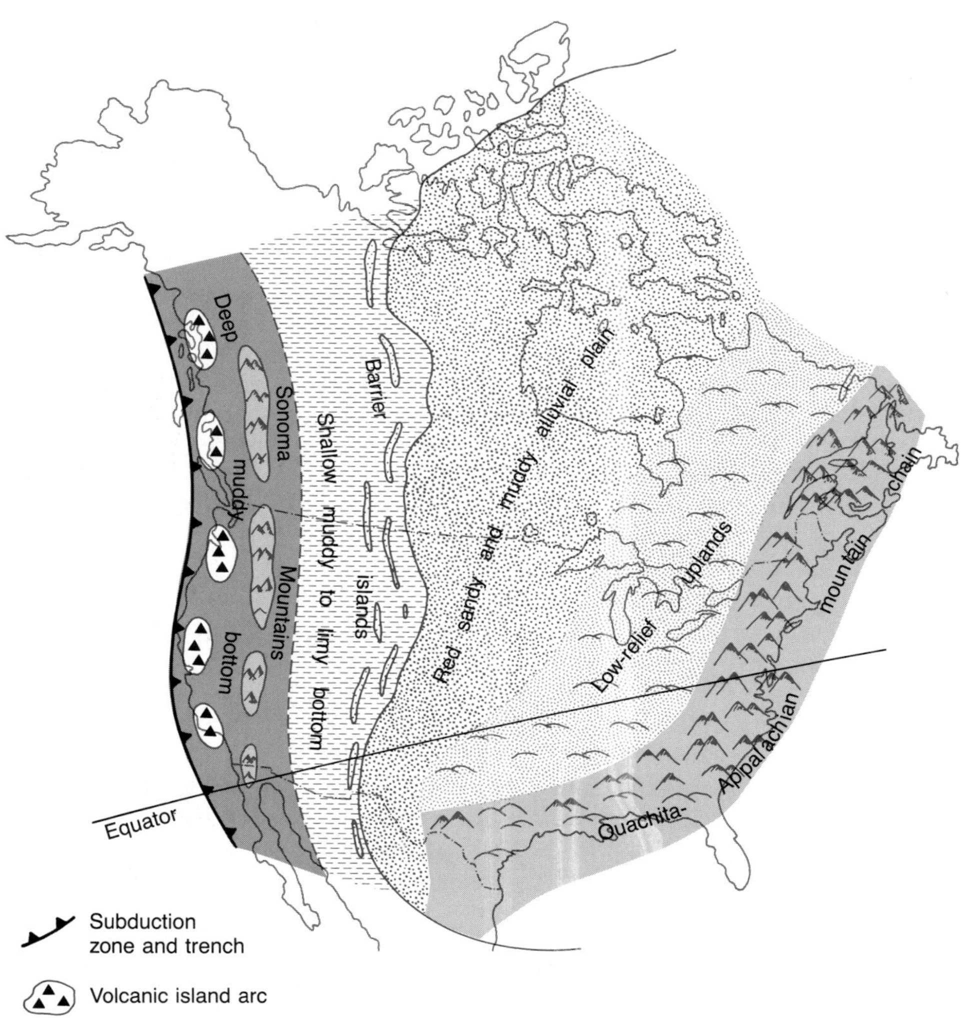

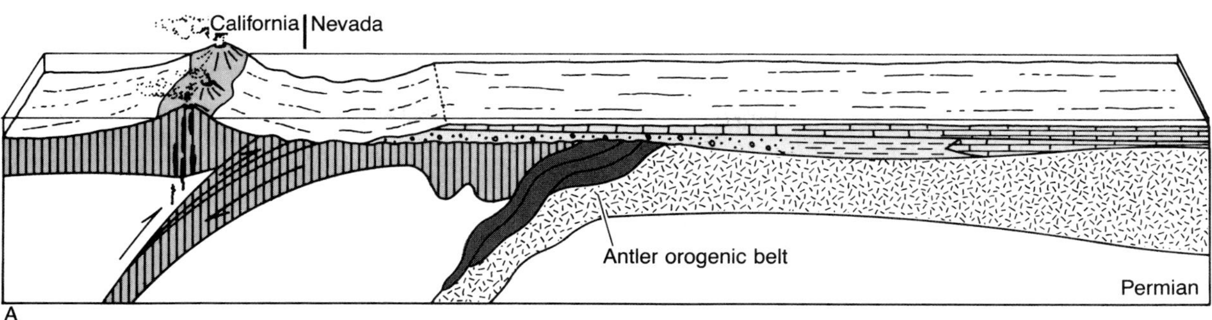

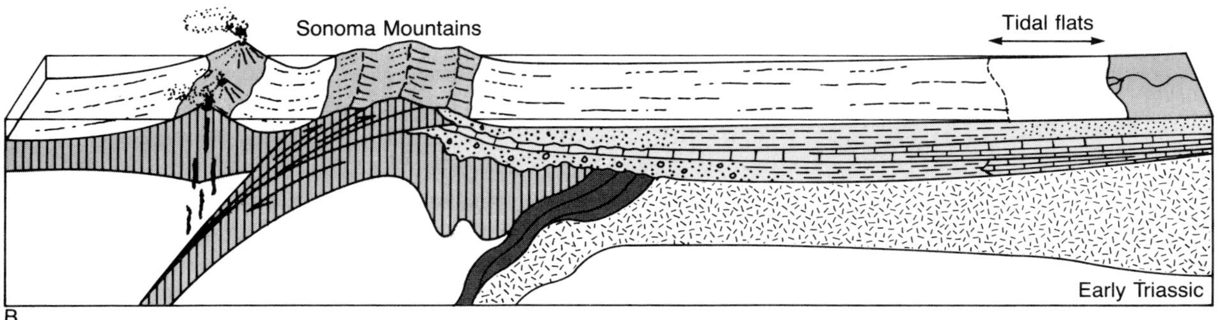

Figure 12–5
Inferred paleogeography and tectonic activity culminating in Permian-to-Triassic Sonoma orogeny in western North America.

land by a small ocean basin similar to the modern Sea of Japan.

The tectonic belt is well expressed in the Pacific Northwest, particularly in British Columbia and in the Klamath Mountains. Here, major orogenesis is attested by deformed Permian rocks intruded by acidic and mafic plutons, together with remnants of ophiolites, volcanic-arc andesites, and **blueschist.** Throughout much of the western Cordillera, angular unconformities separate Permian and older rocks from Upper Triassic strata. The Upper Triassic sediments are varied and complex. Some show the influence of the last vestiges of volcanism; some are thick sequences of shales, graywacke turbidite sandstones, and conglomerates; and some are developed as local carbonate banks and reefs that grew around foundering volcanic islands and topped **seamounts,** in a fashion similar to some modern-day small Pacific Islands.

The Permo-Triassic orogenic event involved *westward* subduction of oceanic lithosphere, the closing of the late Paleozoic back-arc basin, and the convergence of the volcanic arc complex against the western edge of the continental plate (Fig. 12–5). In Nevada, upper Paleozoic rocks of the marginal back-arc basin were overthrust eastward in a style reminiscent of the Late Devonian–Early Mississippian Antler Orogeny (Fig. 11–11 in Chapter 11). Overthrusting occurred along the major westward-dipping Golconda thrust, which overrode the Roberts Mountains thrust. This episode of deformation in Nevada is commonly referred to as the **Sonoma orogeny.**

The eastward-migrating oceanic island arc, which collided with the continent to produce the deformation, became attached and is now exposed in northwest Nevada and the eastern Klamath Mountains of California. During the later Triassic and Early Jurassic, there were again island arcs offshore. Subduction beneath the continent during Late Triassic time produced voluminous silicic volcanic ash that was dispersed to the southwest, and furnished the silica that petrified the logs in the Chinle Formation. These plate interactions were most likely related to the Early Mesozoic breakup of Pangaea (Fig. 12–6), and more specifically to the formation of the embryonic Atlantic rift-ocean and the beginning of major westward movement of the North American continent as it began to drift away from the new oceanic (Atlantic) spreading center.

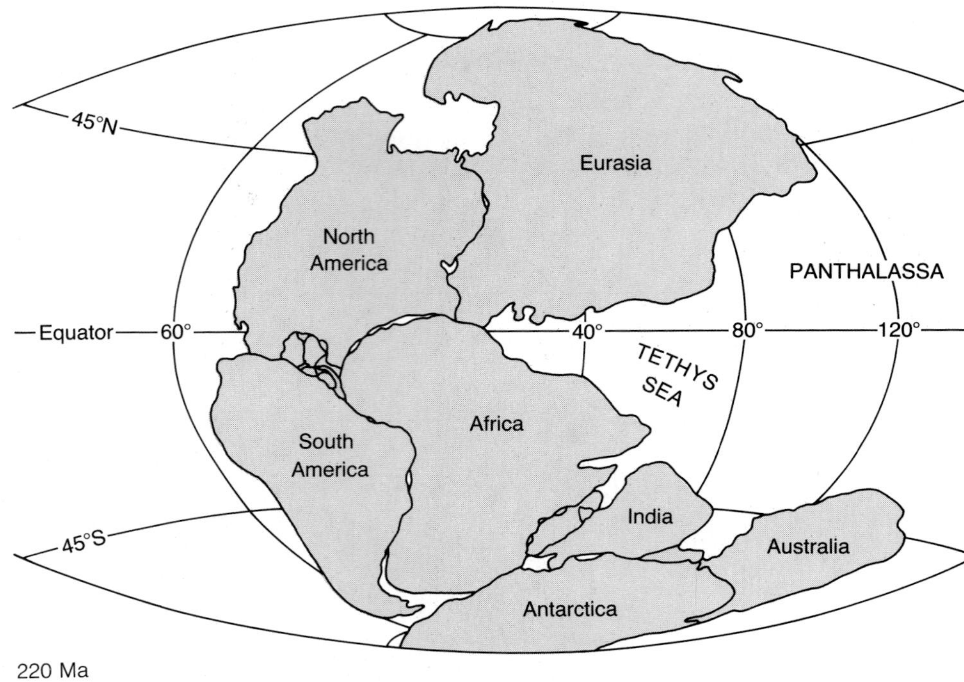

Figure 12–6
Pangaea supercontinent reconstruction for Late Triassic.
(From Critter Creations, San Diego, CA; and A. G. Smith and J. C. Briden, 1977, Mesozoic and Cenozoic paleocontinental maps, no. 7, p. 18; Cambridge University Press. Used with permission)

Triassic Events in the Appalachians

The Triassic record in North America is not confined exclusively to the Cordillera. During the Late Triassic and Early Jurassic (Fig. 12–7), a discontinuous chain of variously sized downfaulted basins formed in the crystalline part of the Appalachian region, from maritime Canada to the Carolinas (Fig. 12–8A). These structural troughs were sites of accumulation of thick sedimentary sequences collectively called the Newark Supergroup, named for exposures near Newark, New Jersey. The Newark rocks consist of conglomerate and sandstone of arkose composition, and shale and mudstone; they are commonly developed as red beds. Flaggy brown sandstones from the Newark assemblage have furnished the building blocks of the well-known brownstone houses of the eastern United States. The sediments were derived from highlands of crystalline rock that formed during the middle Paleozoic Acadian orogeny, and later uplifted during the Late Triassic along high-angle normal faults.

The rocks are coarsest adjacent to the upfaulted basin margins, where sands and gravels were deposited in alluvial fans. Farther out in the continental basins, finer sand and mud were deposited in stream channels, floodplains, and lakes. Associated with the sedimentary rocks are basaltic lava flows, diabase dikes, and sills such as the Palisades along the Hudson River (Fig. 12–8B).

The Late Triassic block-faulting and near-surface mafic igneous activity have important implications for the Early Mesozoic tectonic history of eastern North America. The high-angle normal faults indicate tensional stress, producing extension of continental lithosphere—a structural style superimposed on the older Appalachian compressional mountain structures. This Late Triassic disturbance, also evidenced in northwestern Africa and western Europe, was a prelude to later rifting of North American, European, and African continental fragments from the Pangaea assembly.

Terrestrial Life and the Beginning of a Dinosaur Dynasty

No evidence of marine life has been found in the Newark beds, but fossils of land plants and freshwater fish are locally abundant, particularly in gray, organic-rich beds. The plant remains are mainly foliage (as opposed to the petrified logs in the Chinle Formation), and are most common in Virginia and the Carolinas, where gray mudstones are more abundant. The plant fossils represent a swamp flora of ferns and scouring rushes (see Chapter 16).

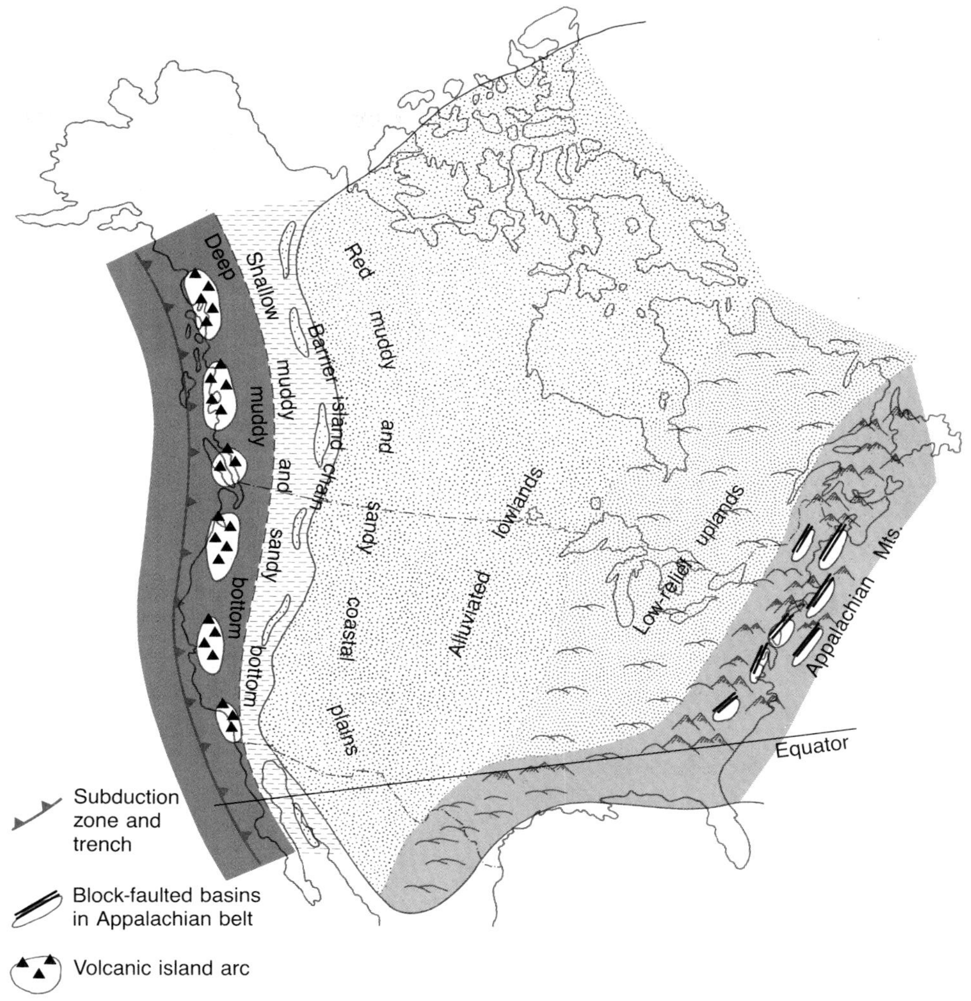

Figure 12–7
Paleogeography of Late Triassic superimposed on outline map of present-day North America.

Leaves and needles from cycads and conifers were washed into the swamps from forests on the slopes and uplands. A few coal beds suggest that more humid climatic conditions existed here than in the northern basins.

The Newark strata have yielded more dinosaur footprints than any other place in the world. In fact, the first evidences of dinosaurs discovered in North America were odd-looking three-toed footprints in sandstone in the Connecticut Valley. These footprints are the theme of Dinosaur State Park, Rocky Hill, Connecticut, where some sandstone slabs contain prints in patterns that suggest gregarious reptiles traveling in herds. Curiously, despite the hundreds of footprints, very few early dinosaur bones have been found in the Upper Triassic of the East.

Half a continent away from the Newark Basins, brilliantly colored Chinle beds at a locality named Ghost Ranch, New Mexico, yielded the bones of a small light-boned dinosaur that Edward Cope named *Coelophysis.* Many years later, Edwin H. Colbert of the American Museum of Natural History headed an expedition that produced numerous bones and several complete skeletons of *Coelophysis,* thus increasing significantly the knowledge of one of the earliest dinosaurs. *Coelophysis* ran on almost birdlike hind limbs and hunted prey with clawed forelimbs. Unlike the giants of the Jurassic and Cretaceous, most Triassic dinosaurs were similar to their thecodont ancestors, being nimble, light-boned, rather small carnivores (Figs. 12–9 and 12–10). They represent the beginning of a fantastic dynasty that lasted for more than 100 million years.

However, as one dynasty was beginning, there were major extinctions among other terrestrial vertebrates as the Triassic drew to a close. Principal victims among the reptiles were the thecodonts

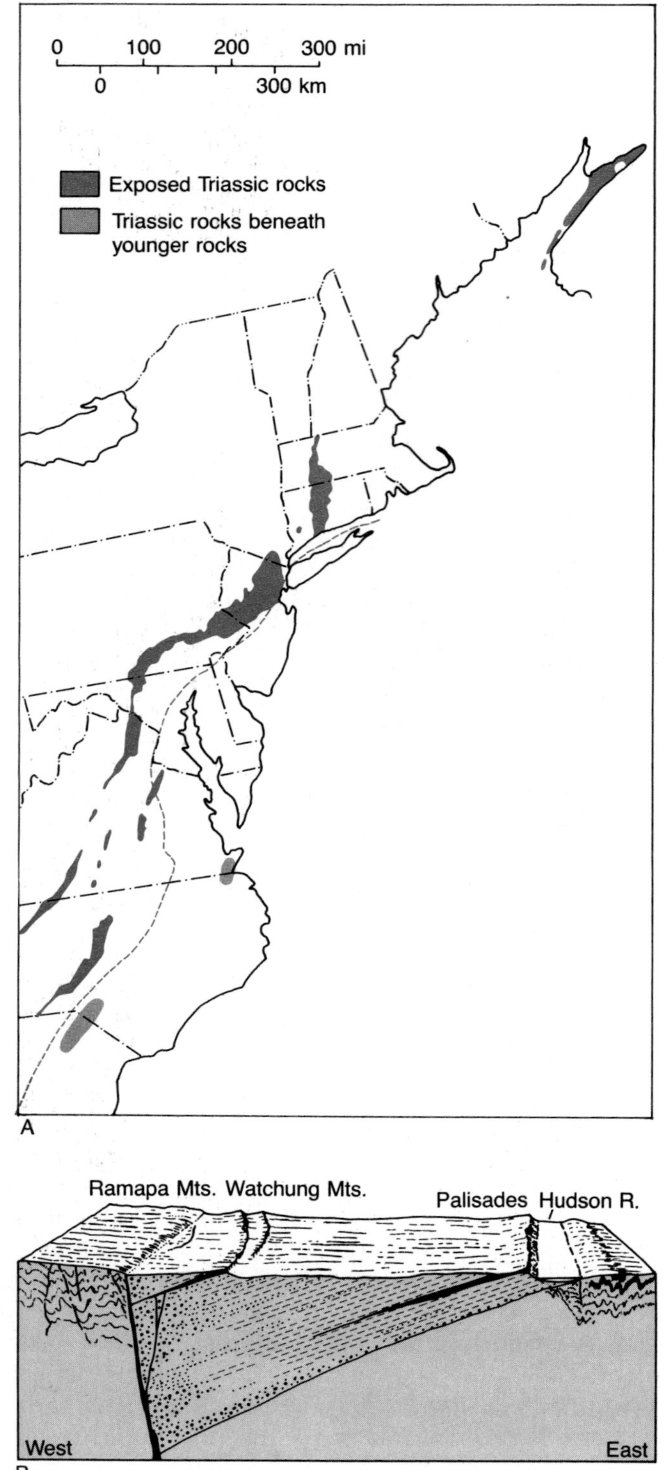

Figure 12–8
A. Northestern United States and maritime Canada, showing distribution of Triassic basins. B. Present-day Triassic basin, showing nonmarine sedimentary facies (brown) and diabase sills (black).
(From Morris S. Peterson, J. Keith Rigby, and Lehi F. Hintze, *Historical Geology of North America,* 2d ed., Figs. 10.4, 10.5, p. 143, 144. © 1973, 1980 Wm. C. Brown Publishers, Dubuque, IA. All Rights Reserved. Reprinted by permission.)

(Fig. 12–11), the cotylosaurs, and the mammal-like therapsids (Fig. 12–11), the reptile group that gave rise to the earliest true mammals in the Late Triassic (see Chapter 17). Labyrinthodont amphibians also died out.

Marine Life

The original Triassic type section in Germany, with its preponderance of red beds and sparse fossil record, was an unfortunate choice because of its in-

Figure 12–9
Restoration of scene in eastern United States during the Late Triassic Period (200 million years ago). Dominant plants are conifers and cycadeoids. Animals, left to right: small, slim dinosaurs, *Coelophysis;* larger dinosaurs (two) in background, *Trilophosaurus;* crocodilelike forms to right, phytosaurs.
(Photo courtesy of National Museum of Natural History. Smithsonian Institution Photo No. 2526C)

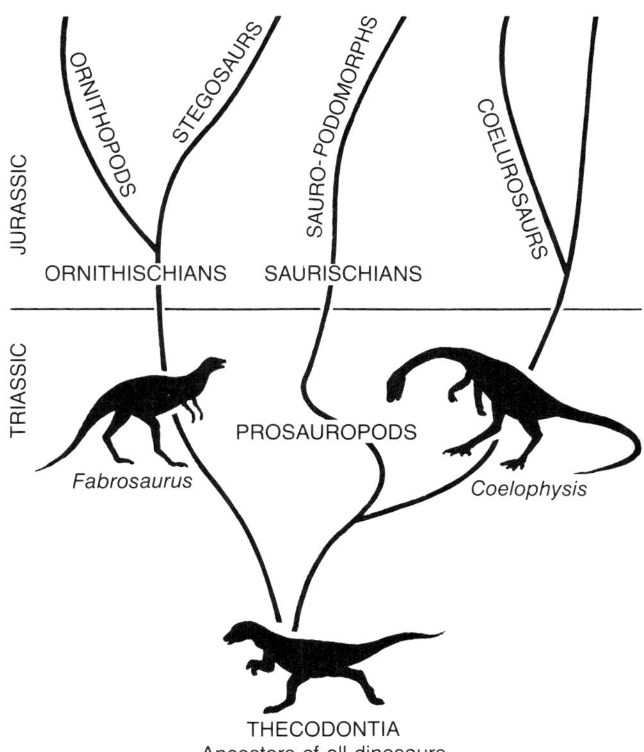

Figure 12–10
Early evolution of the dinosaurs.
(From E. H. Colbert, 1980, *Evolution of the Vertebrates—A History of the Backboned Animals Through Time;* 3d ed., Fig. 61, p. 160. Copyright © 1980 by John Wiley & Sons, Inc., New York. Reprinted by permission of John Wiley & Sons, Inc.)

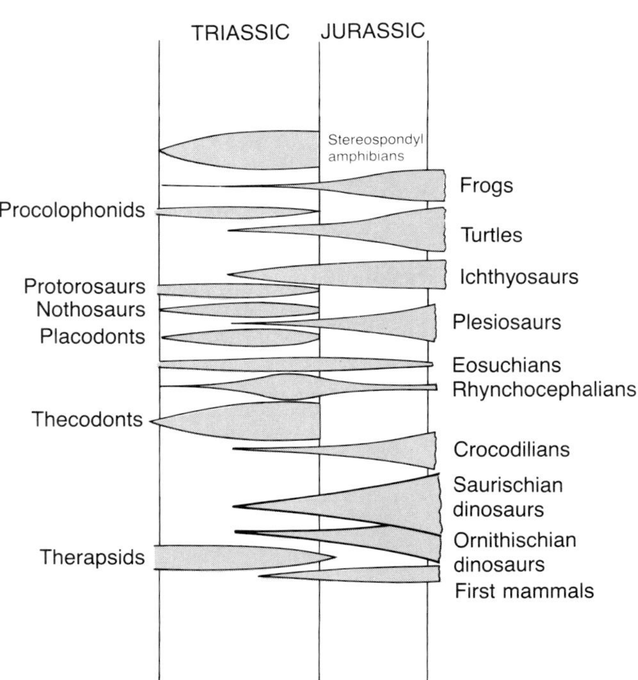

Figure 12–11
Range and relative abundance of tetrapods (four-legged terrestrial vertebrates) within and beyond the Triassic.
(From E. H. Colbert, *Evolution of the Vertebrates—A History of the Backboned Animals Through Time;* 3d ed., Fig. 64, p. 162. Copyright © 1980 by John Wiley & Sons, Inc., New York. Reprinted by permission of John Wiley & Sons, Inc.)

adequacy in providing a good reference standard. Subsequently, a sequence of predominantly fossiliferous marine carbonate rocks in the Alps was designated as the standard for Triassic reference and correlation. This situation is not unique, and it underscores the difficulties posed by a number of the original type sections for geologic systems. It also underscores the importance of using fossiliferous sections of marine strata, which give the concept of "system" its integrity. Several of the original type sections turned out to be poor choices because of their lack of fossils, and later, after the importance of paleontologic control was realized, and it was appreciated that systems are interpretive units based on aggregates of fossils, additional sections were selected as standards of reference and correlation.

By far the best Triassic fossiliferous sequences in North America are in the western Cordilleran belt, particularly in the foothills of northern British Columbia and the Sverdrup Basin of the Arctic islands. Middle and Upper Triassic sequences in these and other areas contain ammonoid biozones that provide excellent correlation and a composite standard reference section for the marine Triassic of North America. The Triassic marine record consists of isolated remnants. Most of the rocks were uplifted and eroded or buried during later Mesozoic and Cenozoic events. Fortunately, abundant ammonoid faunas have allowed good correlation among these separated sequences, as well as general correlation with the Alpine section of the European Triassic.

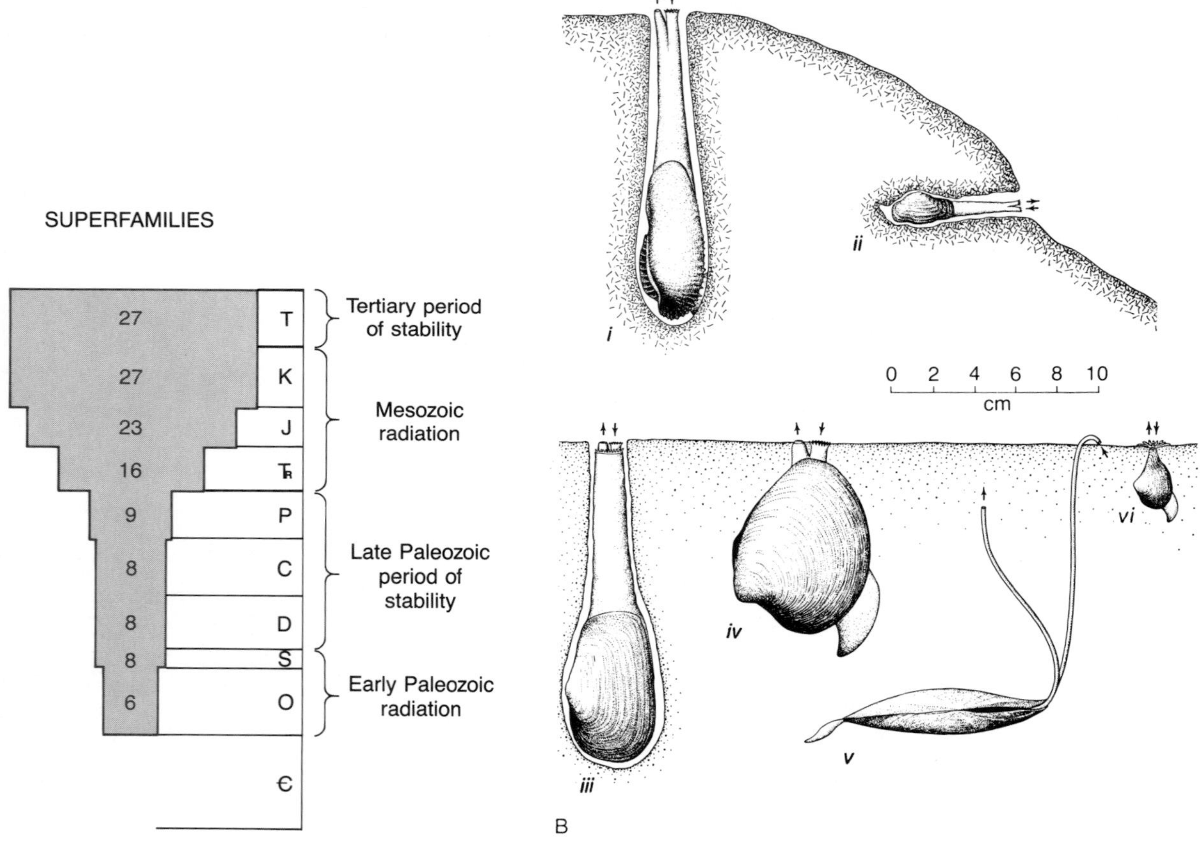

Figure 12–12
A. Diversity of marine bivalve molluscs through the Phanerozoic, measured in number of superfamilies existing per geologic period. Most of the Mesozoic radiation involved new groups of infaunal siphon-feeding forms. B. Representative kinds of infaunal siphon-feeding bivalve molluscs: *i, ii*—borers inhabiting rock; *iii–vi*, burrowers in soft sediment. Arrows indicate direction of water currents.
(From S. M. Stanley, 1968, Post-Paleozoic Adaptive Radiation of Infaunal Bivalve Molluscs—A Consequence of Siphon Formation; Text-Figs. 1 and 6, p. 215 and 219: *Journal of Paleontology*, vol. 42, no. 1. Reproduced by permission of Society of Economic Paleontologists and Mineralogists)

The main difference between Triassic and Permian rocks is expressed in the fossil assemblages. The major faunal extinctions that marked the close of the Paleozoic were followed by repopulation of Triassic seas by very different faunas. This change is indelibly impressed in the stratigraphic record, and of course, inspired the drawing of a boundary that separates the Paleozoic and Mesozoic Eras of Earth history. The rich populations of ammonoid cephalopods were characteristic of Triassic seas worldwide and contributed importantly to the composition of marine early Mesozoic invertebrate faunas. However, the ammonoids, whose swimming mode of life made them so well adapted and successful during the Triassic, almost died out near the end of that period. The entire subclass Ammonoidea apparently survived as one lone family that gave rise to the great adaptive radiation of ammonites in the Jurassic.

The Triassic also marks the beginning of a major adaptive radiation of bivalve molluscs (Fig. 12–12A). New groups evolved and achieved marked ecological success in the aftermath of the late Paleozoic extinctions. Part of this success stemmed from ecological replacement of extinct epifaunal brachiopods. However, most of the diversification can be linked to evolution of the siphon, an anatomical feature that developed from fusion of folds in the fleshy mantle (Fig. 12–12B). This evolutionary breakthrough allowed for both filter-feeding from the water column and an infaunal existence.

Modern types of reef-building corals belonging to the order Scleractinia replaced the tabulate and rugose orders of the Paleozoic. Extensive fossil reefs in the alpine region of southern Europe and in North Africa represent the tropical conditions of the **Tethys** Seaway (Fig. 12–6). Mobile echinoderms such as sea urchins and starfish became more abundant, and largely replaced the predominantly attached forms of the Paleozoic—the crinoids, blastoids, and cystoids. There were major extinctions in the marine realm during the Late Triassic, most noteworthy being the ceratite ammonoids and the conodonts.

Jurassic History

Sand, Sand Everywhere

In western North America, Jurassic strata, like the underlying Triassic, form parts of many familiar landmarks. Magnificent arches, alcoves, spires, and pinnacles have been sculptured in cross-bedded sandstone and red beds, and are featured in national parks and monuments throughout the Rocky Mountain region. Among the best known of these rocks is the Navajo Sandstone, a vast blanketlike deposit that is widely exposed over the western part of the craton. The quartz-rich sand was derived from the continental interior and the Canadian Shield by recycling of grains from older quartzose sandstones.

The chief distinguishing feature of the Navajo, beautifully exposed in the walls of Zion Canyon, Utah (Fig. 12–13), is the large-scale cross-stratification; some individual cross-bed sets are more than 25 m thick. This prominent feature, together with the generally excellent sorting and rounding of the quartz grains, has made the Navajo a classic example of a dune deposit, and has evoked the picture of a large Early Jurassic coastal desert (Fig. 12–14). The Navajo is the uppermost unit of a succession of formations collectively referred to as the Glen Canyon Group, named for magnificent exposures in Glen Canyon, Utah, now partially submerged beneath the waters of Lake Powell.

Jurassic Marine Sediments

Except for some continental deposits in Michigan and the upper part of the Newark Supergroup, Jurassic sedimentary rocks are not exposed in eastern North America. However, their presence beneath the cover of younger rocks in the Atlantic and Gulf Coast area has been demonstrated by deep drilling. In the Atlantic shelf margin, Upper Jurassic terrigenous clastics interfinger seaward with carbonates. This relationship has its actualistic analogue in the facies patterns in the Gulf of Elat (Aqaba), an early-stage rift-zone setting that is the northern continuation of the Red Sea rift.

These Jurassic sediments in the subsurface of the Atlantic margin represent the initial continental margin deposits after the Early-to-mid-Jurassic continental breakup and the newly formed Atlantic Ocean invaded the rifted eastern margin of the continent. These postrift sediments rest upon an extensive erosion surface, the *postrift unconformity*, and clearly postdate the syn-rift deposits of the Late Triassic to Early Jurassic Newark Supergroup. As the eroded basement subsided from thermal cooling of the lithosphere, shallow marine sediments progressively onlapped the postrift erosion surface. Seismic profiles have revealed thick wedges of seaward-dipping strata lying astride the boundary between oceanic and transitional crust. These have been interpreted to be thick wedges of interlayered

A

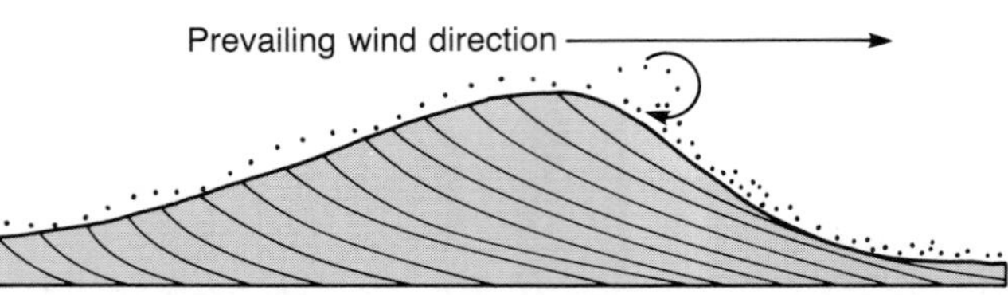

B1. Development of dune by movement of sand up windward side and down slip face or leeward side

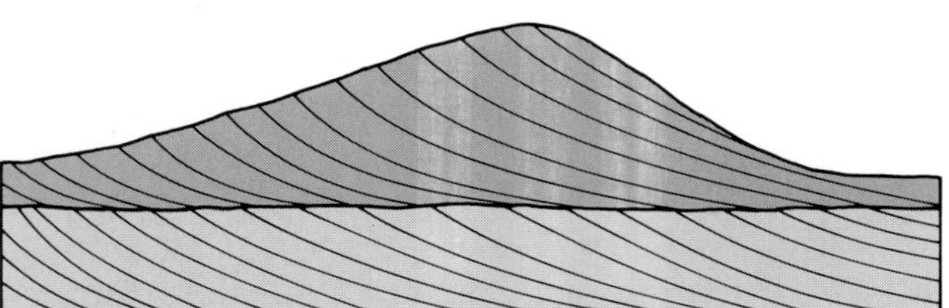

B2. Erosion of first dune level and development of second dune

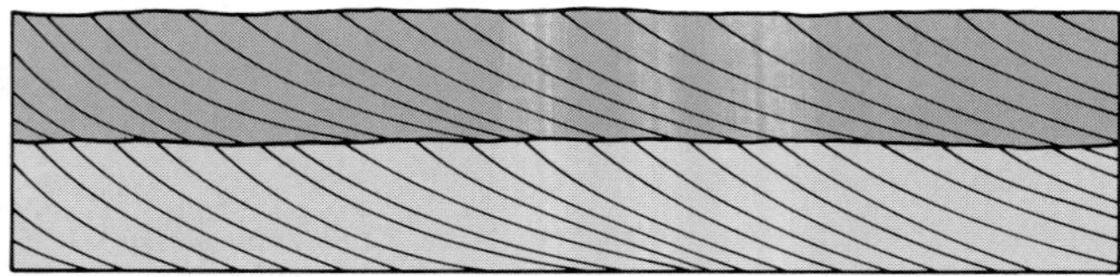

B3. Multiple dune sets separated by erosional truncation surfaces

Figure 12–13
A. Large-scale, high-angle cross-stratification in beds of eolian (dune) origin, Navajo Sandstone, Zion National Park, Utah. B. Development of succession of truncation surfaces in eolian sandstones.
(A, photo by J. D. Cooper)

sedimentary rocks and basalts which formed at the time of initial rifting and continental breakup.

In the U.S. Gulf Coast, Jurassic rocks occupy a crescent-shaped subsurface belt extending from Alabama to northeastern Mexico, and comprise a seaward-thickening wedge that grades from a shoreward facies of red beds to shallow-marine carbonates. The Smackover Limestone in the Louisiana subsurface has yielded significant amounts of petroleum. Evaporites are locally common in the section; a thick evaporite unit, the Louann Salt, was deposited in the poorly circulated shallow waters of the embryonic Gulf of Mexico Basin during the early stages of separation of southeastern North America from northwestern Africa and northern South America (Fig. 12–15). The Jurassic rocks of the Atlantic and Gulf Coast regions are overlapped by Cretaceous deposits, but their presence in the subsurface indicates the earliest marine deposition on the trailing margin of the North American continent as Pangaea began to split apart.

Beginning in the Early Jurassic, marine encroachments advanced widely into the western craton on at least three different occasions and deposited a complex association of sandstones, shales, and limestones. The sedimentary succession is comparatively thin, generally not exceeding several hundred meters, and indicates tectonic stability of the craton. The Jurassic interior seaway (Fig. 12–16), commonly referred to as the Sundance Sea, extended from the Arctic almost to the newly formed Gulf of Mexico. This cratonic shelf sea spread eastward from a miogeoclinal trough that is well represented by thick sections of fossiliferous marine shale in western Canada. Life flourished in the Sundance seaway, and abundant fossils are found in its deposits, characterized especially by belemnite and ammonite cephalopods.

Along the very western margin of the continent from California to Alaska, thick sequences accumulated which were typical of a eugeoclinal setting. Graywackes, dark shales, bedded cherts, and

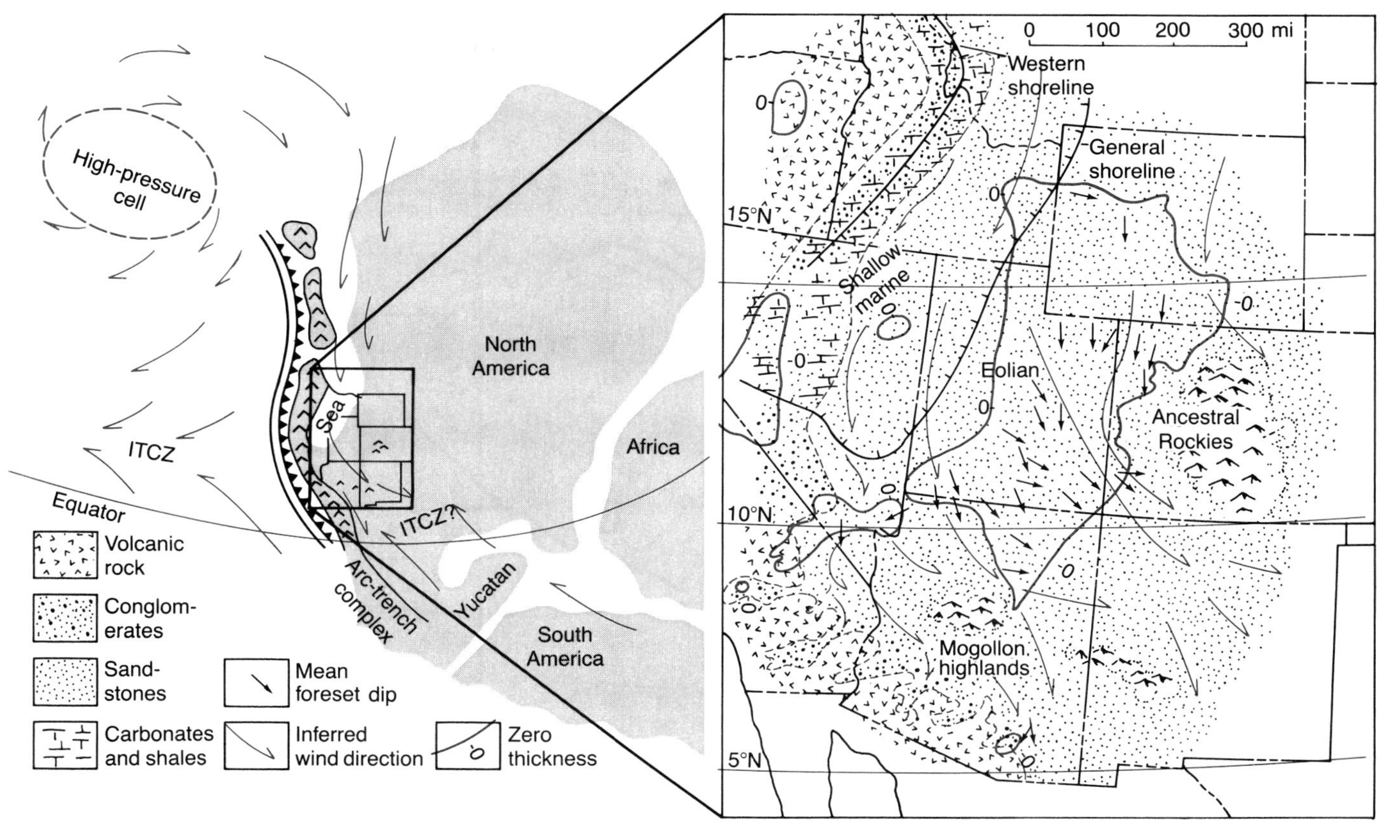

Figure 12–14

Early Jurassic paleogeography. A. Western interior of United States. ITCZ is intertropical convergence zone. B. Detail for southwestern United States.

(From G. Kocurek, and R. H. Dott, Jr., 1983, Jurassic Paleogeography and Paleoclimate of the Central and Southern Rocky Mountain Region, Fig. 3, p. 106, *in Mesozoic Paleogeography of the West-Central United States,* M. W. Reynolds and E. D. Dolly, eds.: Rocky Mountain Section SEPM. Reproduced by permission of Rocky Mountain Section, Society of Economic Paleontologists and Mineralogists)

conglomerates, together with volcaniclastic sediments and submarine basalt flows, make up a great thickness of deposits. However, as in the Triassic eugeoclinal section, later Mesozoic and Cenozoic orogenies have overprinted much of the western Cordillera and have disrupted the original continuity in rock assemblages.

Sedimentation and Plate Convergence

The Klamath Mountains and western Sierra Nevada of northern California display remnant composite Jurassic island arcs. These arcs are expressed mainly as low-grade metamorphic assemblages of basaltic and andesitic volcanics and volcaniclastic sediments intruded by plutons. These arcs, which formed offshore in the manner of the modern Philippine Islands, and which formed after the Sonoma orogeny, were partly assembled by arc-arc collisions. The aggregate collided with the western margin of the North American continent in Late Jurassic time (Fig. 12–17). This event is commonly referred to as the **Nevadan orogeny** and heralded the beginning of a long phase of eastward subduction of the **Farallon Plate** beneath the western edge of the continent.

Westward-moving North America was enlarged by this Late Jurassic collision of composite island arcs. Convergence continued between continental and oceanic plates, and a new subduction system broke through along the western margin of the enlarged continent (Fig. 12–17). It is believed that many subduction systems beneath continents have been initiated similarly by reversals of subduction

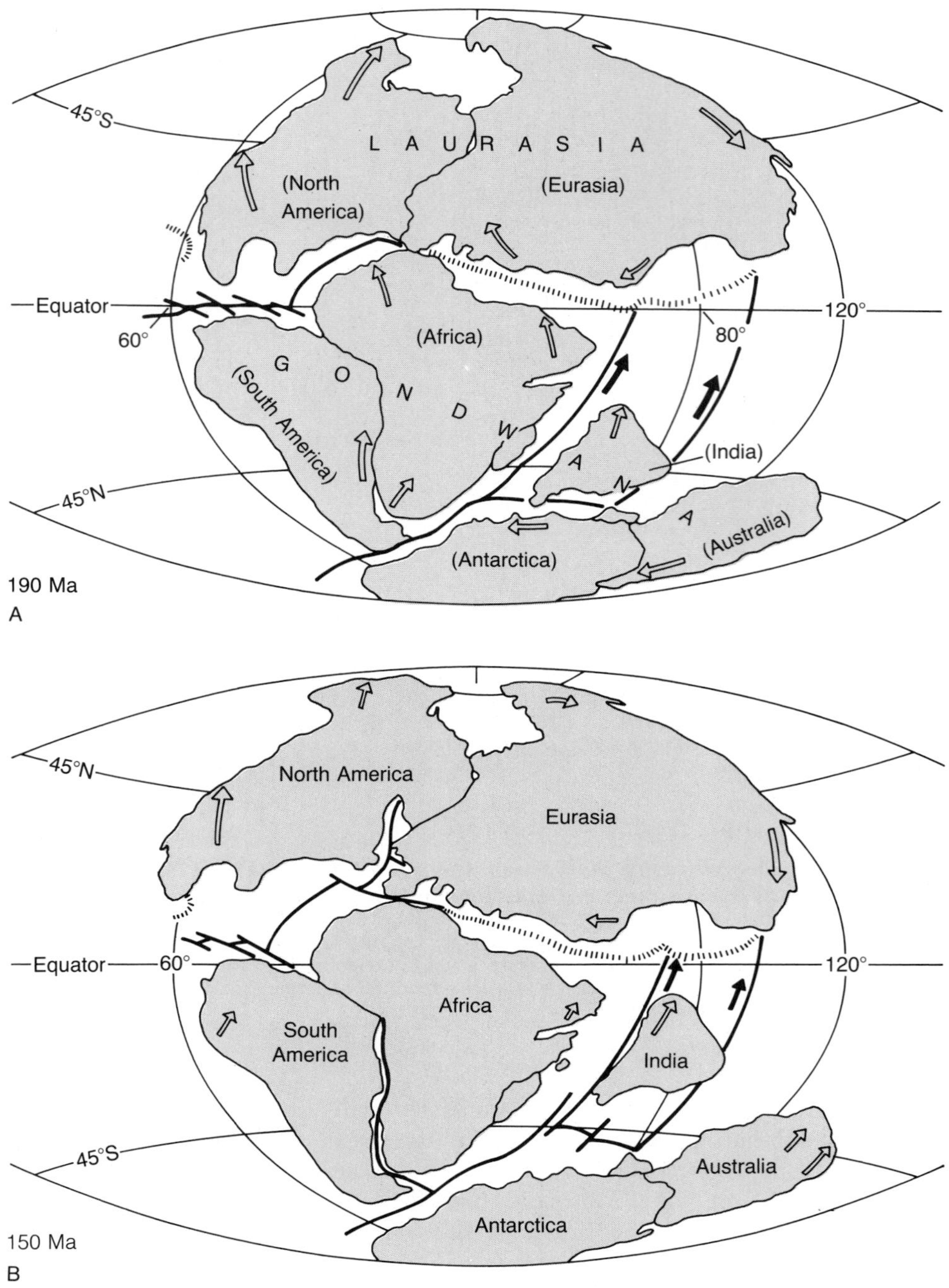

Figure 12–15
World paleogeography reconstructions. A. Early Jurassic. B. Late Jurassic.
(From Critter Creations, San Diego, CA; and A. G. Smith and J. C. Briden, 1977, Mesozoic and Cenozoic paleocontinental maps, no. 9, p. 19: Cambridge University Press, New York. Used with permission)

following collision. With the Nevadan orogeny, the western margin of North America became part of a plate-tectonics regime similar to that of the western margin of present-day South America, where the Andes mountain range has formed. Throughout the remainder of the Mesozoic, a deep trench and associated magmatic arc, related to subduction of Farallon Plate oceanic lithosphere, characterized the western edge of the continent, giving it the character of an *Andean-type* margin.

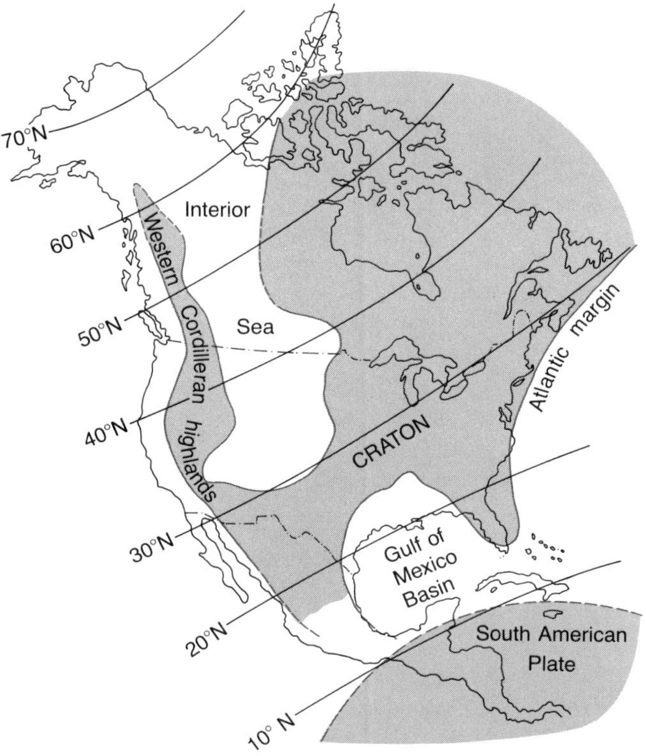

Figure 12–16
Paleogeography of North America showing paleolatitudes and distribution of Late Jurassic land and sea.
(After R. Brenner, 1983, Late Jurassic Tectonic Setting and Paleogeography of Western Interior, North America, Fig. 1, p. 120, *in Mesozoic Paleogeography of the West-Central United States,* M. W. Reynolds and E. D. Dolly, eds.: Rocky Mountain Section SEPM. Reproduced by permission of Rocky Mountain Section, Society of Economic Paleontologists and Mineralogists)

As the westward-moving North American continent continued to override the Pacific oceanic lithosphere during the Late Jurassic, an unusual rock assemblage, the Franciscan Formation of the California Coast Ranges, began to accumulate in a submarine trench and its associated **accretionary wedge** (Fig. 12–18). The Franciscan is a complex unit of unknown thickness (in places at least 7000 m) that ranges in age from Late Jurassic to Late Cretaceous. It consists predominantly of graywacke, but also includes siltstones, conglomerates, black shales, chert, pillow basalts, and greenstones. Some sections contain rhythmically bedded flysch and peculiar pebbly mudstones and boulder beds.

Franciscan lithologies indicate a mixing of rocks that originally formed in abyssal-plain, continental-slope, and continental-shelf environments, and were brought together in the submarine trench. Chaotic mixtures of various-sized blocks of Franciscan materials contained within a pervasively sheared matrix are called **mélange.** These mélanges comprise major parts of the subduction accretionary wedges, and some contain exotic remnants of carbonate atolls bearing western Pacific, near-equatorial Carboniferous and Permian faunas. Parts of the Franciscan terrane have been metamorphosed to the blueschist facies, and ophiolite complexes also are present. The mélange and blueschist indicate subduction along the western edge of the continent, and the ophiolites indicate accretion of unsubducted oceanic crust. Fossils are rare in the Franciscan, but radiolarians in the thin chert beds indicate a Late Jurassic age for the lower part of the assemblage.

To the east of the Franciscan complex, a thick succession of sandstone and mudstone comprising the Great Valley Group (Fig. 12–18) was deposited on the continental slope and shelf in a *fore-arc* basin setting, from Late Jurassic through the Cretaceous. No volcanics are associated with the Great Valley Group. In comparison to the Franciscan, the stratigraphy is more regularly organized, and benthic fossils are moderately abundant. Much of the Jurassic part of the Great Valley Group was deposited as mudstone facies in deep basin environments.

This Pacific-margin setting generally was separated from the interior seaway by land masses that were uplifted by lithospheric deformation. The deformation heralded the beginning of a wave of orogenic disturbance that would continue through the Mesozoic into the Cenozoic. This major phase of deformation is called the **Cordilleran orogeny,** and, like the Appalachian orogeny of the Paleozoic, it was a protracted event, consisting of separate pulses that manifested themselves in particular regions. The history of the Cordilleran orogeny is related primarily to the underthrusting of Pacific Ocean lithosphere beneath the western margin of the North American Plate along an eastward-dipping subduction zone. Recall that subduction also was largely responsible for late Paleozoic orogeny in the western Cordillera. However, the rate of plate convergence, intensity of deformation, orientation of structures, and plate-boundary architecture were quite different during the Cordilleran orogeny.

The initial phase of the Cordilleran orogeny, the Nevadan orogeny, was related to an increase in the relative rate of convergence of Pacific oceanic lithosphere and the North American continent, produced mainly by the westward movement of the

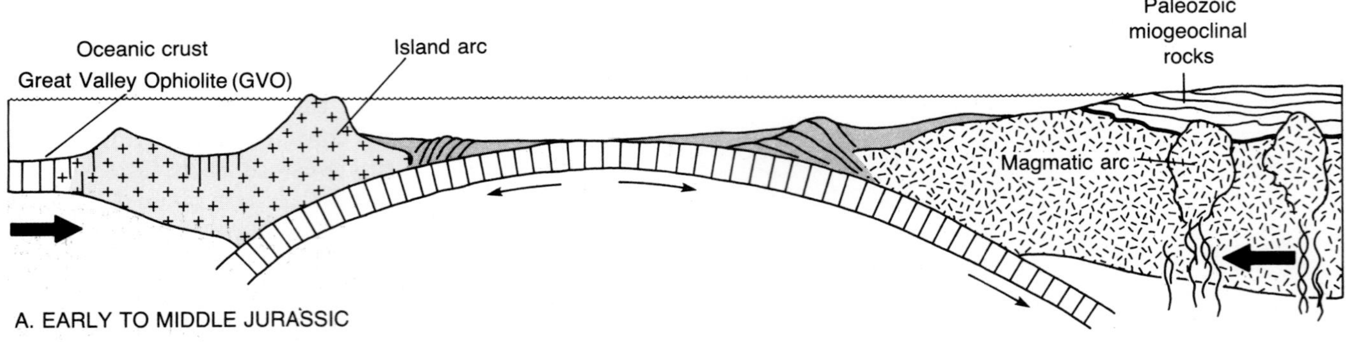

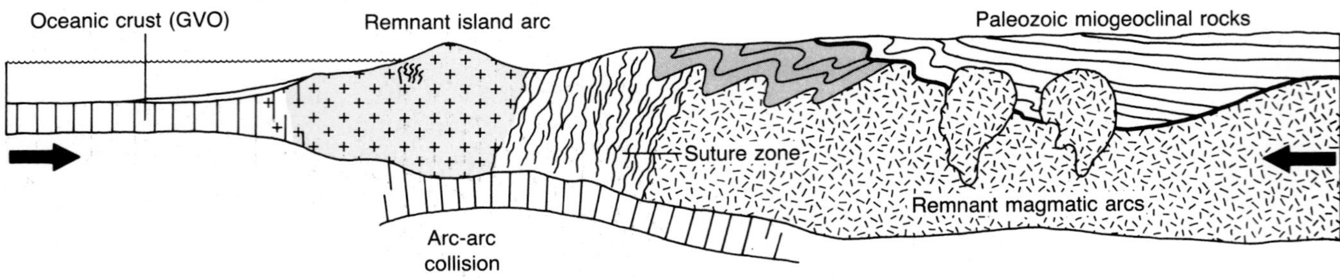

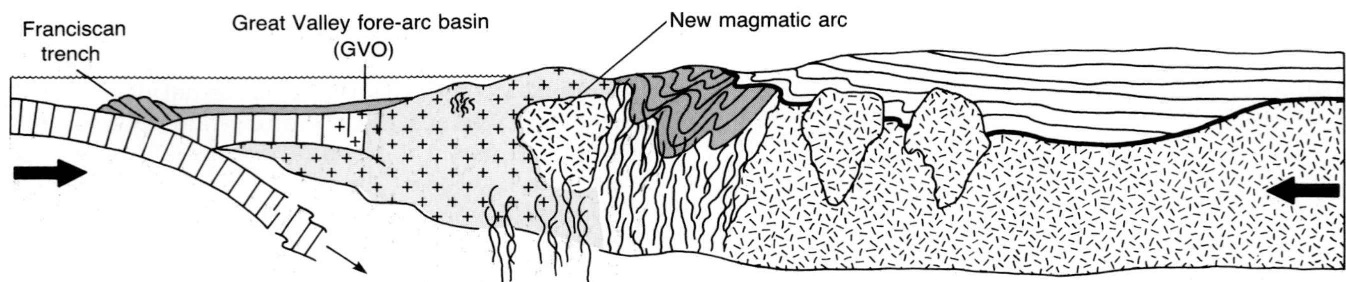

Figure 12–17

Development of Andean-type continental margin, western North America. A. Early Jurassic bipolar subduction and closing of back-arc basin. B. Arc-arc collision (Nevadan orogeny) and beginning of development of Andean-type margin in Late Jurassic. C. New east-dipping subduction zone and development of trench, fore arc basin, and new magmatic arc in Late Jurassic.

latter as the mid-Atlantic Ridge spreading center developed. This increase in plate convergence was responsible for a change from a Japanese-type margin to an Andean-type margin for western North America (Fig. 12–19). The Japanese-margin analogue, which was expressed as a volcanic island-arc system and interarc basin, characterized the western edge of North America from mid-Paleozoic through Early Mesozoic. The Andean-margin setting, manifested by a continental-margin magmatic-arc and fore-arc basin, characterized the western edge of North America from the mid-Mesozoic through Early Cenozoic (Fig. 12–19).

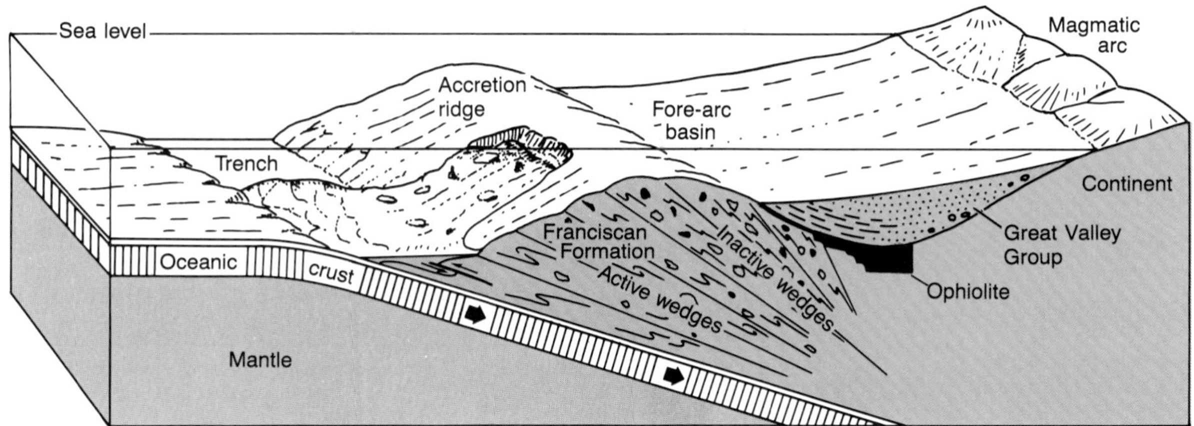

Figure 12–18
Inferred depositional setting of Franciscan Formation in active trench along Cordilleran margin. Olistostromes—deposits of submarine slumps—incorporate variously sized fragments called olistoliths (various kinds of sedimentary rocks, blueschists, and oceanic basalt), derived from previously formed rock. These fragments are reinvolved in subduction and reincorporated into successively younger mélange accretionary wedges during continued underthrusting. Mélanges differ from olistostromes in that they involve chaotic fragments in a pervasively sheared matrix—fragments that are stirred, mixed, and sheared in the subduction zone. Sediments, mostly turbidites, of the Great Valley Group were deposited in a fore-arc basin, behind the accretion ridge.
(After B. M. Page, 1977. Effects of Late Jurassic–Early Tertiary Subduction in California, Fig. 5–9, p. 66, *in Late Mesozoic and Cenozoic Sedimentation and Tectonics in California:* San Joaquin Geological Society Short Course. Reproduced by permission of San Joaquin Geological Society)

The Morrison Formation: Graveyard of the Dinosaurs

The Nevadan orogeny was characterized by intrusive igneous activity and associated volcanism; it produced tectonic highlands that contributed great volumes of sediment to the east. Following a pattern we have already seen in the Paleozoic record of the eastern part of the continent, orogeny in the western Cordillera during the Late Jurassic is shown by the sedimentary record of the western interior part of the continent. Colorful gray, green, red, and maroon sediments of the Morrison Formation were deposited over an immense region (Fig. 12–20). A great regression of the Sundance Sea occurred northeastward into Canada as the Morrison clastic wedge built eastward.

Most of the Morrison consists of mudstone and siltstone, with local beds and lenses of sandstone and conglomerate, punctuated by a few volcanic ash horizons, all deposited on an expansive floodplain that was built up by streams that carried detritus eastward from rising mountains. The presence of calcareous nodules (called *caliche*) throughout much of the Morrison attests to seasonal conditions of dryness. Stream-channel facies within the Morrison, as well as similar sediments in the Triassic Chinle Formation, have been the sites of significant uranium mineralization in the Colorado Plateau Province.

The Morrison Formation has achieved its fame from the great wealth of dinosaur remains. Dinosaurs in great numbers walked the surfaces of Morrison floodplains, seeking vegetation. After death, their bones were entombed and preserved in stream-channel sand bars. Museums of the world feature Morrison dinosaur fossils (Fig. 12–21) and Dinosaur National Monument near Vernal, Utah, has a splendid display of a diverse assemblage of bones chiseled into relief on the surface of a thick sandstone bed.

Another famous Morrison locality is the Bone Cabin quarry in southern Wyoming. Here, near the turn of the century, a collecting party from the American Museum of Natural History happened across an isolated sheepherder's cabin only a few miles from the famous Como Bluff site where Marsh's diggers had discovered great quantities of dinosaur bones a quarter-century before. But this was no ordinary cabin. It was constructed entirely of agatized dinosaur bones from a nearby site that eventually yielded freight-car loads of dinosaur fossils!

Terrestrial Life

The dinosaurs diversified rapidly during the Jurassic into an amazing array of forms (Fig. 12–22). Perhaps the most popularized of the Jurassic dinosaurs

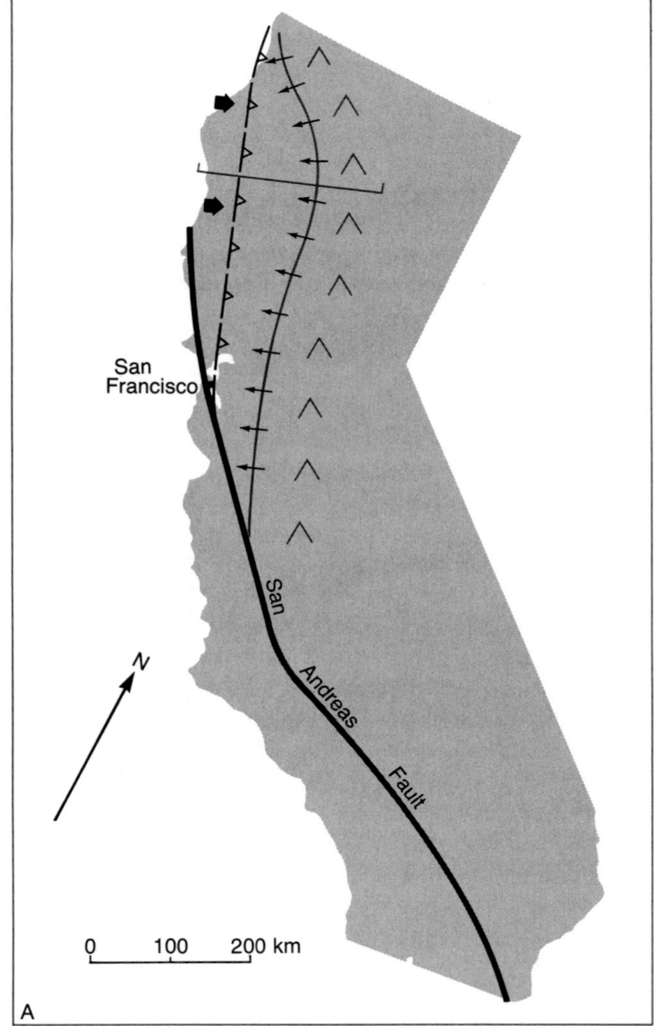

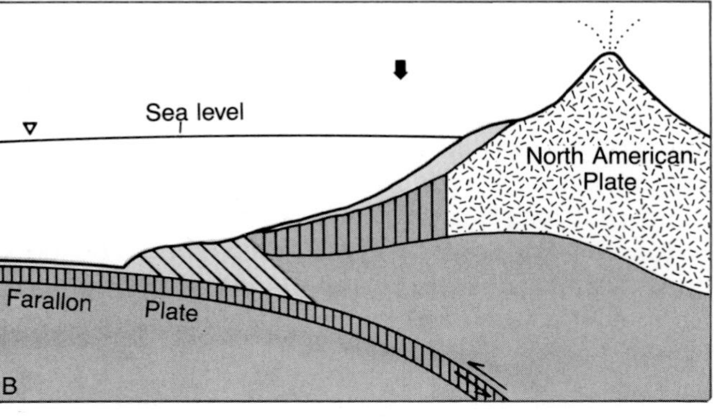

Figure 12–19

Late Jurassic, northern California. A. Map. The two heavy arrows at upper left show eastward subduction of Farallon Plate. Small arrows indicate westward sediment dispersal. Brown line shows location of paleoshoreline. Sawtooth pattern indicates position of trench and eastward dip of subduction zone. San Andreas fault zone (Neogene) truncates Late Mesozoic paleotectonic trends. Mountain symbols show location of magmatic front, as expressed by the westward limit of plutonism. B. Cross-section X–X′.

(After R. V. Ingersoll, 1978, Paleogeography and Paleotectonics of Late Mesozoic Forearc Basin of Northern and Central California; Figs. 3 and 4, p. 475: *In Mesozoic Paleogeography of the Western United States:* Pacific Section SEPM Paleogeography Symposium, vol. 2. Reproduced by permission of Pacific Section, Society of Economic Paleontologists and Mineralogists)

Figure 12–20

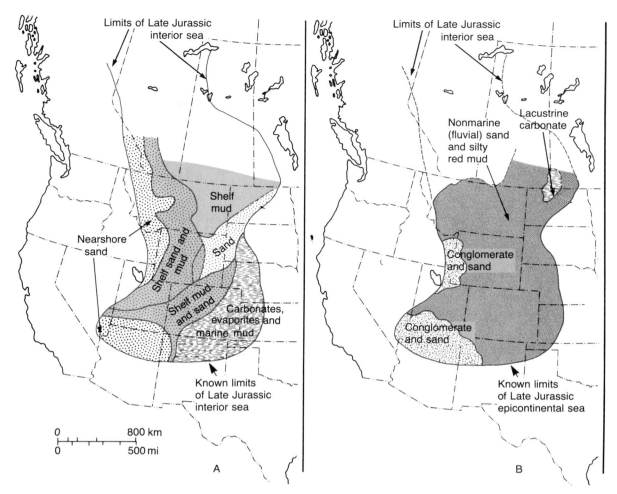

Major lithofacies and environments during late part of Late Jurassic in western interior of North America. A. Approximately 150 Ma. B. Approximately 155 Ma.
(From R. L. Brenner, 1983, Late Jurassic Tectonic Setting and Paleogeography of Western Interior, North America, Fig. 9, p. 129, *in Mesozoic Paleogeography of West-Central United States,* M. W. Reynolds and E. D. Dolly, eds.: Rocky Mountain Section SEPM. Reproduced by permission of Rocky Mountain Section, Society of Economic Paleontologists and Mineralogists)

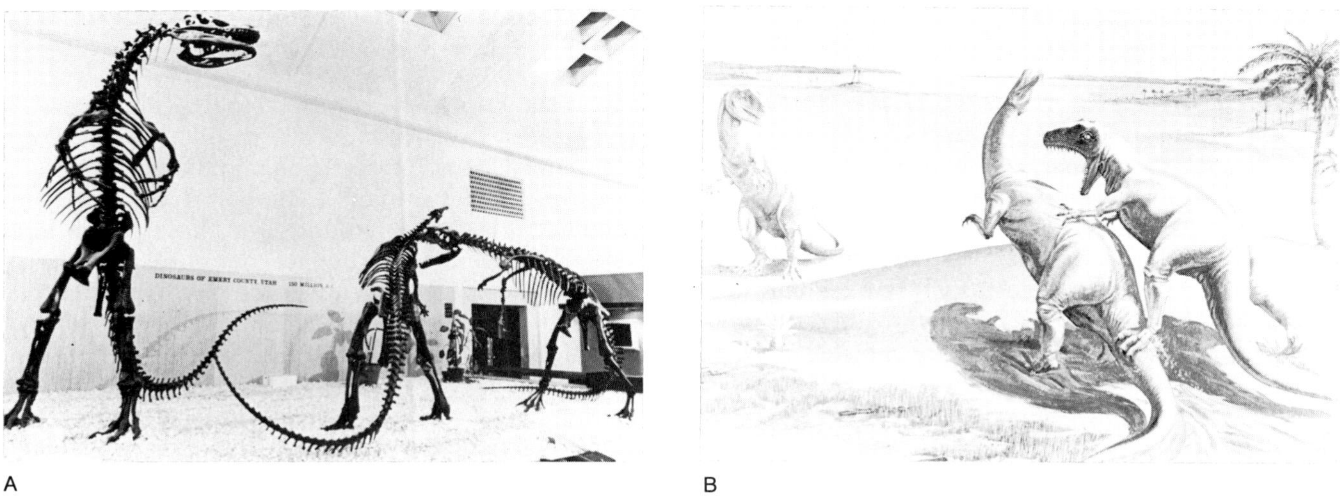

Figure 12–21

Morrison Formation fauna. A. *Allosaurus* (left), a theropod, and *Camptosaurus* (right), a sauropod. B. Restored scene from Morrison alluvial plain; combatants are *Camptosaurus* and *Allosaurus*.
(A, B courtesy of Utah Museum of Natural History)

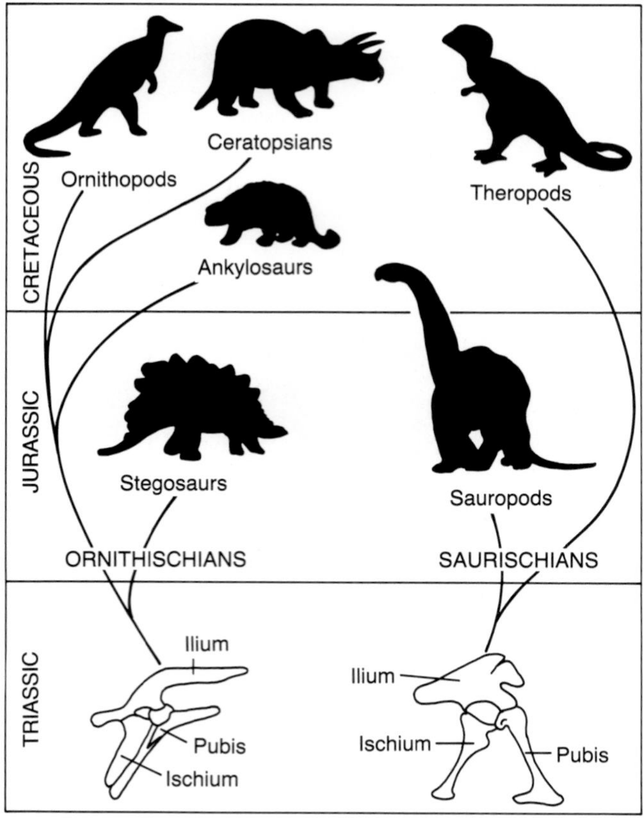

Figure 12–22
General Jurassic and Cretaceous history of the six suborders of dinosaurs, and pelvis structure in the two orders: Saurischia and Ornithischia. The Saurischia are characterized by a pelvis with a forwardly developed pubis. In the Ornithischian pelvis, the pubis is parallel to the ischium.
(From E. H. Colbert, 1969, Evolution of the Vertebrates—A History of the Backboned Animals Through Time, 2d ed. Figs. 68, 70, p. 197, 200: Copyright © 1980 by John Wiley and Sons, Inc. Reprinted by permission of John Wiley and Sons, Inc., and Lois M. Darling)

are the great herbivorous sauropods *Apatosaurus* (formerly *Brontosaurus*), *Brachiosaurus,* and *Diplodocus,* and the voracious flesh-eating theropod *Allosaurus* (Fig. 12–21). *Apatosaurus* possessed an unusually large pelvic outlet, which has led some dinosaur experts to suggest that female "brontosaurs" may have given birth to live young. If this is true, it was very unreptilelike, for reptiles are egg-layers. Also, there is evidence (such as fossilized gizzard stones) that many sauropods did most of their chewing and macerating of vegetation in a gizzard, much like certain birds. Jurassic sauropods also may have traveled in herds, as evidenced by trackways and localized bone accumulations. The foregoing better describes the traits of warm-blooded tetrapods than of cold-blooded reptiles, and figures into an ongoing controversy over just how reptilelike the dinosaurs really were (see discussion, Chapter 13).

Translated literally, dinosaur means "terrible lizard." The image of dinosaurs as superior lizards persisted well into the 1960s, and dinosaurs were reconstructed and illustrated in lizardlike poses, with elbows bent and tails dragging the ground. Not only were they not lizards, but most were not terrible, and some were probably quite peaceable giants, being more gentle grazers and browsers. To dispel another myth, all dinosaurs were not large. Many were of only modest size, and some were no bigger than a chicken; even a few chipmunk-sized adults have been found. Sir Richard Owen (1804–1892), who established the science of vertebrate paleontology in England, was the first to recognize that these extinct reptiles needed a name, and it was he who coined the word "Dinosauria," later anglicized to dinosaur. Dinosauria is not a formal taxonomic name in modern classification of vertebrates. Dinosaurs include two extinct orders of the reptilian subclass Diapsida: Saurischia and Ornithischia (Fig. 12–22).

In the process of filling the available ecological niches, some reptiles took to the air, as exemplified by the gliding and flying pterosaurs. Jurassic mammals include four principal orders, known best from small bits of skeleton, jaws, and teeth obtained mostly from the Morrison Formation. These creatures left a very meager Jurassic fossil record, but enough has been learned to determine that they underwent an initial radiation of small, primitive forms after their origin in the Late Triassic (see discussion, Chapter 17). Jurassic land floras were dominated by seed-bearing plants, including cycads, gingkos, and conifers (see Chapter 16).

All the known specimens (about a half dozen) of the earliest bird, *Archaeopteryx* (Fig. 12–23A), are from the Upper Jurassic Solenhofen Limestone in Bavaria, West Germany. The soft lime mud that provided the burial grounds for these fossils preserved feathers in exquisite detail. However, as some vertebrate paleontologists have pointed out, without the feathers *Archaeopteryx* looks very reptilian. It has been suggested that *Archaeopteryx* was actually a theropod dinosaur whose feathers were more an adaptation for thermal insulation than for powered flight (Fig. 12–23B). Perhaps *Archaeopteryx* represents an evolutionary transition from theropod saurischian to bird (Fig. 12–24).

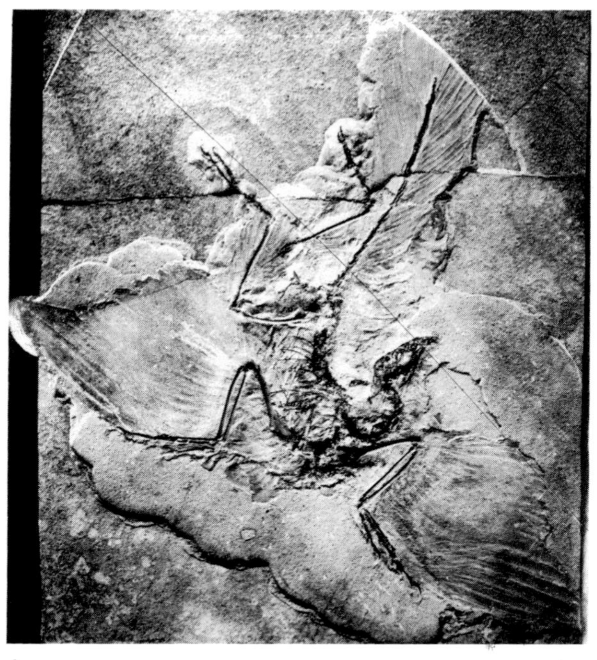

A

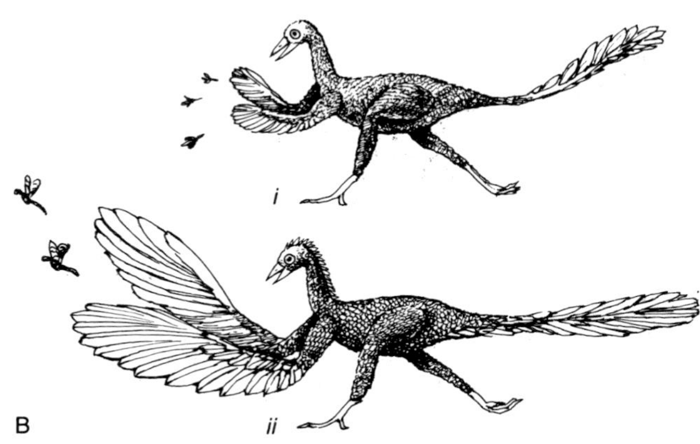

Figure 12–23
A. *Archaeopteryx* preserved in Jurassic Solenhofen Limestone. Note impressions of feathers. Skeleton is like that of a small, running insectivorous dinosaur. B. Origin of powered flight from the ground up (cursorial theory), as envisioned by Yale University paleontologist John Ostrom. Proto-Archaeopteryx (*i*) illustrates an early stage in the enlargement of feathers on the hands and arms as an aid in catching insects (insect-net theory). The enlarged tail feathers are hypothesized as aerodynamic stabilizers, enhancing agility and quick maneuvering during chase after prey. *Archaeopteryx* (*ii*) presumably was at or just past the threshold of powered flight, but is shown here in a similar predaceous pose. Ostrom's version of the cursorial theory has the "insect nets" providing the lift for flight. Three scientists at the University of Northern Arizona have conducted experiments that suggest jumping may have supplied the necessary lift.
(A, Photo courtesy of National Museum of Natural History, Smithsonian Institution Photo No. 15771. B, from John H. Ostrom, 1979, Bird Flight, How Did It Begin? Fig. 10, p. 55; *American Scientist*, vol. 67. Reproduced by permission of *American Scientist)*

Marine Life

The Jurassic is the least-widespread system in North America. Although some sections are abundantly fossiliferous (see Fig. 12–25 for representative communities), strata on this continent are not nearly as rich in fossils, nor are species as well represented as in Europe. Jurassic strata in Great Britain provided the substance for William Smith's monumental principle of fossil succession. The impact of this principle on the science of stratigraphy can hardly be exaggerated. Somewhat later, from studies of Jurassic strata, refinement of Smith's ideas led to the concepts of stage and zone (Chapter 6). Also, the observation that rock types change laterally within certain Jurassic ammonite zones led to the formulation of the facies concept. Because Jurassic strata and their contained fossils fostered these fundamental stratigraphic principles, the Jurassic System commonly is referred to as the "cornerstone of stratigraphy."

The organisms largely responsible for the recognition of stratigraphic units based on their fossil content were the ammonoid cephalopod molluscs (ammonites) (Fig. 12–25). These swimming cephalopods were the most abundant invertebrates in Jurassic seas, and they displayed a remarkable degree of diversity in shell form and in intricacy of shell sutures. Jurassic ammonite successions also illustrate several detailed evolutionary lineages, and the

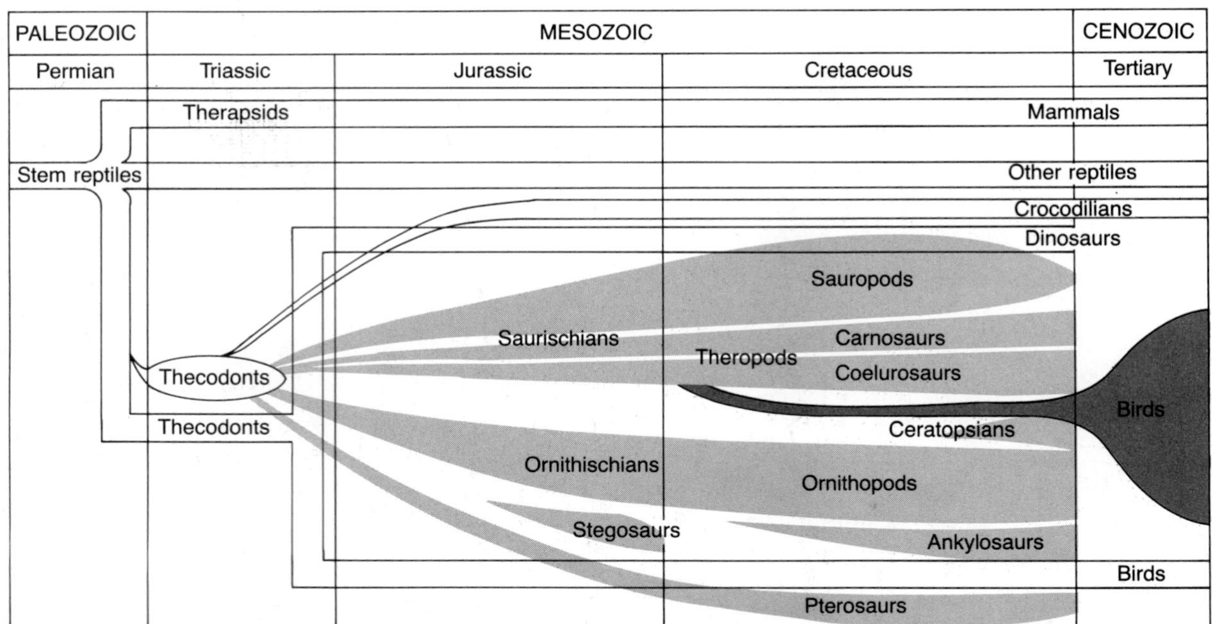

Figure 12–24

Evolution of birds from theropod dinosaurs. New idea on bird evolution in relation to other dinosaur groups shown in shading, superimposed on earlier idea of reptilian evolution viewing birds as direct descendants of thecodonts.

(After John H. Ostrom, 1978, New Ideas about Dinosaurs; p. 166; *National Geographic*, vol. 154, no. 2. Used by permission of National Geographic Society)

rapid vertical stratigraphic change in ammonite-species composition has allowed a refined biozonation scheme which has resolved the Jurassic system into increments with an average duration of approximately one million years.

The belemnites (Fig. 12–25B) were squidlike cephalopods whose bullet-shaped internal shells are common Jurassic fossils. Paleotemperature determinations on the calcite shells of belemnites point to seawater temperatures at midlatitudes that were about 15°C warmer during the Jurassic than at present. The quantitative paleotemperature data are derived from oxygen-18:oxygen-16 ratios, which vary according to the temperature of the seawater in which the organisms lived. The amount of oxygen-18 in shells decreases as temperature increases.

Jurassic invertebrate faunas, exclusive of the ammonites, definitely had a strong semblance of modernization. Bivalve and gastropod molluscs continued to thrive and diversify, as did the sea urchins and corals. Also numbered among the marine fauna were abundant vertebrates. Several groups of reptiles which had invaded the sea during the Triassic were well represented by the ichthyosaurs (Fig. 12–26), plesiosaurs, and marine turtles, all of which shared the seas with a great variety of bony fishes.

Microplates and the Accretion of Western North America

In Suspect Terrane

Although subduction was the major underlying cause of Early Mesozoic orogeny in the Cordilleran region, it does not represent the complete story of mountain building. A growing number of plate tectonicists contend that dozens of crustal blocks in the North American western Cordillera, lying side-by-side, are not genetically related. Also, they contend that much more lithosphere was added to western North America during the Mesozoic than reasonably can be accounted for by volcanism along island arcs, accretion of sediments from the seafloor, or magmatic-arc activity.

Several lines of geologic evidence brought into focus during the late 1970s and early 1980s suggest that much of North America, from Alaska to Baja California (in particular the Alaskan and Canadian Cordillera), consists of accreted lithospheric blocks of various sizes—*microplates* as described in Chapter 1—called **tectonostratigraphic terranes** (Fig. 12–27).

These terranes are of varying composition and have features that sharply contrast with those of

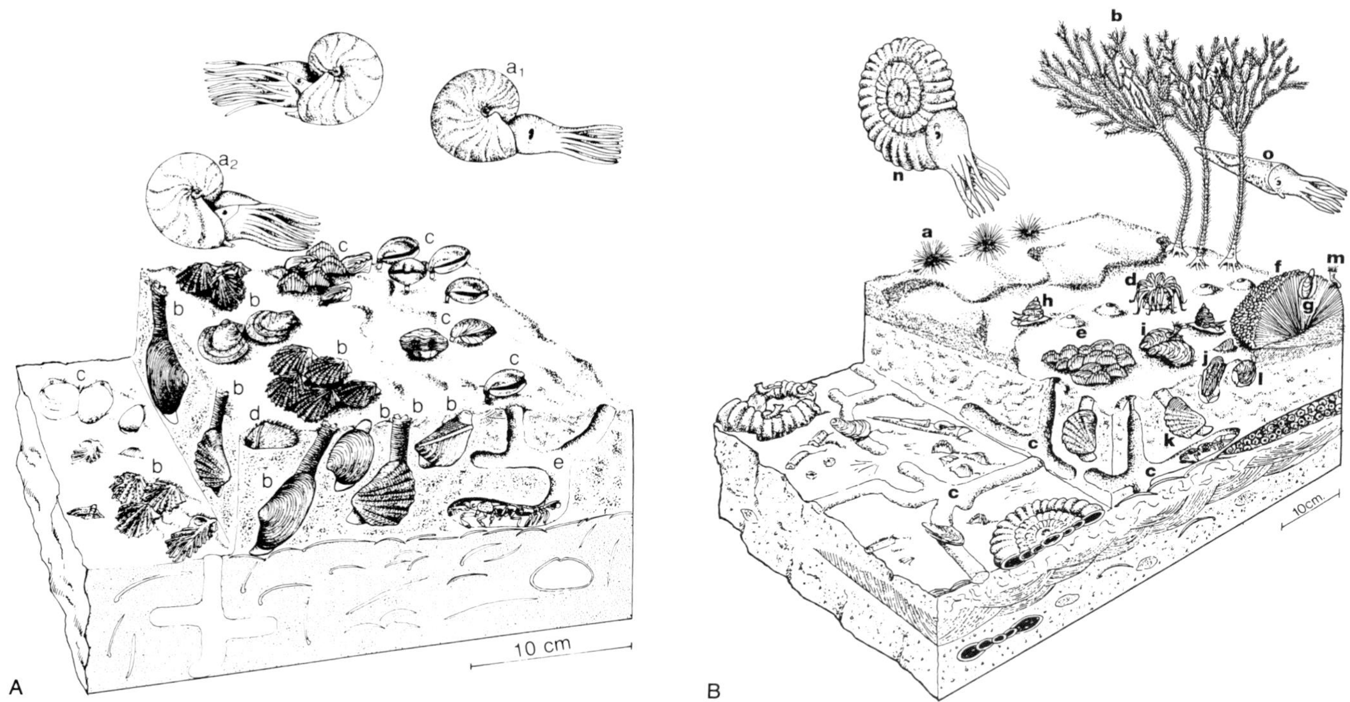

Figure 12–25

A. Jurassic calcareous sand-bottom community; a_1, ammonoid cephalopod mollusc; a_2, Nautiloid cephalopod mollusc; b, bivalve molluscs; c, articulate brachiopods; d, echinoid echinoderm; e, trace fossil (burrow) containing crustacean. B. In-life restoration of Jurassic calcarenite invertebrate community: a, echinozoan; b, crinoid; c, crustacean feeding/dwelling traces; d, f, scleractinian coral; e, articulate brachiopod; g, i, j, k, l, bivalve molluscs; h, gastropod mollusc; m, polychaete worm; n, ammonoid cephalopod; o, belemnoid cephalopod.

(From W. S. McKerrow, 1978, *The Ecology of Fossils;* Fig. 78, p. 245; Fig. 70, p. 225; MIT Press, all rights reserved. Used by permission of MIT Press)

Figure 12–26

Fossilized skeleton of ichthyosaur, Jurassic of western Europe.

(Photo courtesy of National Museum of Natural History. Smithsonian Institution Photo No. 1142)

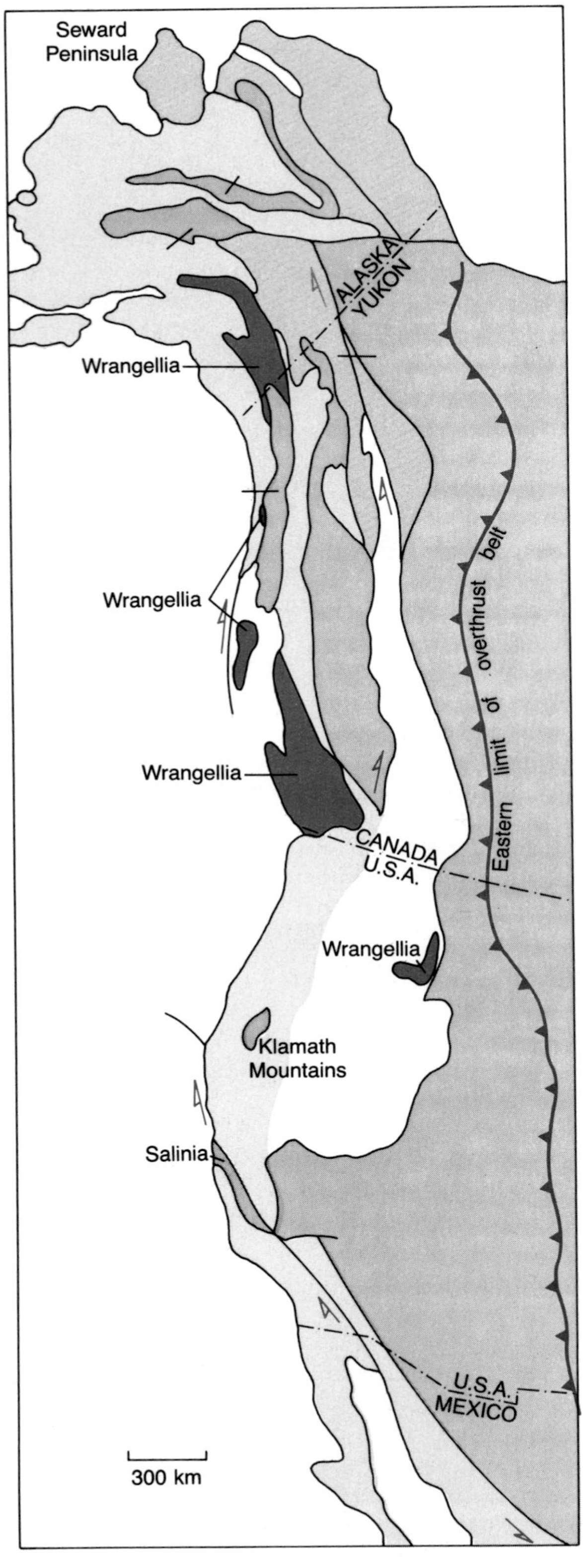

Figure 12–27
Western North America showing the vast region composed of suspect and exotic accreted terranes (brown). One such terrane, named Wrangellia (dark brown), has been dismembered and strung out by post-docking transcurrent faulting. Cratonic North America is shown in light gray. Also shown is the eastern limit of the Mesozoic–Early Cenozoic Cordilleran orogeny. (After Zvi Ben-Avraham, 1981, The Movement of Continents; Fig. 9, p. 298: *American Scientist*, vol. 69, no. 3. Reproduced by permission of *American Scientist)*

nearby crustal blocks. Each terrane is bounded by major faults and records a geologic history so different from that of neighboring terranes that it is unlikely that they formed originally in close proximity. Some of the terranes clearly have a foreign origin, in that they are of unknown paleogeography with respect to the ancient Cordilleran continental margin and western craton. Such terranes are referred to as *exotic terranes;* others of probable foreign origin, but not conclusively proved to be exotic, are called *suspect terranes,* emphasizing paleogeographic uncertainty. Some workers are convinced that some of the more exotic accreted lithospheric blocks were prefabricated elsewhere and carried thousands of kilometers east and north on spreading oceanic lithosphere from their sites of origin in various parts of the Pacific basin.

Most of the exotic terranes that have been identified are of ocean origin and consist of oceanic lithosphere that once included volcanic islands, plateaus, seamount chains, ridges, or island arcs. A few blocks represent fragments of continents. The accreted terranes are viewed as having been rafted along on moving and subducting lithosphere into collision with the margin of the North American continent. As the oceanic plate plunged beneath the continent along the subduction zone, the island arc, volcanic plateau, or microcontinent riding on the oceanic plate resisted subduction and was scraped off and accreted to the edge of the continent, after which the subduction zone migrated (stepped) westward. In such a context, much of western North America (for an average distance inland of about 500 km) is viewed as a collage of accreted terranes—a western North America that has been shaped to its present configuration over the past 200 million years by the impact of oceanic plates (Fig. 12–27).

A prime example is Alaska. Extensive work in the 1970s by the U.S. Geological Survey, performed to assess the mineral resources of this vast piece of the continent, produced the startling observation that adjacent crustal blocks were amazingly different. This investigation demonstrated that the straightforward application of plate-tectonic theory (viz., model of subduction of oceanic lithosphere along a continental margin) failed to account for the geology of Alaska. Almost the entire state proved to be a patchwork of separate crustal fragments—the flotsam and jetsam of ancient Pacific Basin lithosphere—a collage of terranes repositioned during the past 160 million years by the wanderings and collisions of crustal plates.

The original suspicions about some of the western Cordillera terranes came about through observations of discontinuities in stratigraphy, paleontology, structure, and paleoclimatology. Later, the explanation that these geologic anomalies were the results of enormous displacements and dislocations of large crustal blocks was advanced mainly on the basis of dramatic differences in *paleomagnetism* when compared to the stable craton of North America. Terrane analysis is one aspect of paleogeographic reconstructions. In order to determine the geologic history of any terrane, paleomagnetic information must agree with the paleobiogeographic and paleoclimatologic data, as discussed in Chapter 10.

In this regard, the characteristics of a microplate (terrane) that define its uniqueness or individuality are rock types and ages, internal structural style and tectonic boundaries, fossil faunas and floras and their biogeographic implications, climatically sensitive facies and fossils, and paleomagnetic signatures. Many sedimentary sequences of terranes that formed originally in oceanic areas have been dated by microfossils, especially radiolarians retrieved from acid-treated cherts, and conodonts from acid-treated limestones.

Microplates are the subject of continuing and ever-increasing analysis and interpretation. At present, many workers share the opinion that docking of microplates coincides with, and was instrumental in, producing deformation associated with the Sonoma and Nevadan orogenies of the Early Mesozoic, as well as later orogenies during the Cretaceous and Paleogene. A number of these terranes have been greatly modified by postdocking tectonic activity. In this regard, the well-studied *Wrangellia Terrane* (Fig. 12–27) has been sliced up and strung out over a considerable distance by later transcurrent faulting since its presumed Early Mesozoic collision and incorporation into western North America.

The time of docking of terranes, either at the ancient continental margin or against each other, can be dated within reasonable limits by certain common denominators (Fig. 12–28):

- The age of similar cover rocks, called "overlap assemblages,"
- The depositional age of detritus shed from one terrane upon another, or from the continent onto a terrane (sedimentologic linkage), or
- Similar postdocking intrusive events.

In the last regard, an interesting recent study claims that the Wrangellia and Alexander terranes (Fig. 12–27), where they are juxtaposed in the Wrangell Mountains in Alaska, are "stitched" together by a pluton of Pennsylvanian age, implying docking of both terranes no later than late Paleozoic!

Think of the Mesozoic margin of western North America as a colossal harbor, receiving variously sized merchant ships (microplates), each carrying an exotic cargo (rocks, fossils, and paleomagnetic signatures), and each docking in the harbor, to eventually clog it and create a junkyard (collage of microplates).

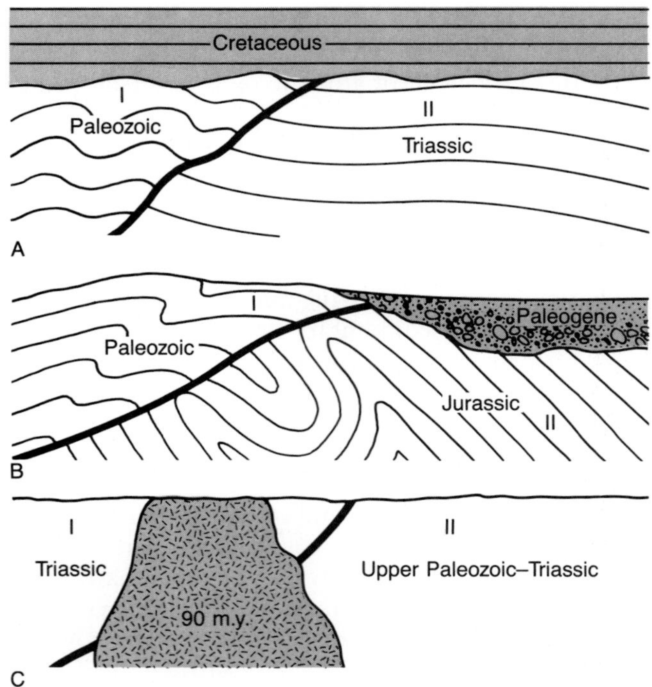

Figure 12–28
Pinning the time of docking of accreted terranes. A. Age of cover rocks. B. Age of detritus shed from one upon the other. C. Welding by intrusion. Docking cannot be earlier than youngest exotic rocks involved or later than pinning rocks. Bold lines represent fault boundaries, between tectonostratigraphic terranes.

A New Model and New Questions

The concepts of *exotic tectonostratigraphic terranes* and *collage tectonics* add a complicated wild card to our understanding of the geologic history of western North America. However, they also offer an explanation of why active continental margins grow much faster than passive trailing margins: accreted terranes of oceanic origin indeed are new additions to the continent, rather than the recycling of older continental material. The adherents of the microplate model believe that western North America has grown by more than 25% through piecemeal accretion since the Early Triassic.

A number of terranes in the older Appalachian orogen also are highly suspect. Some workers think the western margin of the ancient Iapetus Ocean (Chapter 10) is poorly defined, and that a significant number of suspect terranes such as Armorica and Avalonia are present along the eastern flank of the orogen. Nearly all of these terranes are defined by their distinctive early Paleozoic rocks, fossils, and paleomagnetic signatures. These suspect terranes are not easily incorporated in a simple model of a single symmetrical Iapetus Ocean. It is highly likely that some terranes, now east of the ancient miogeocline, were not previously connected to or evolved near the ancient continent of Laurentia.

The microplate concept provides a fresh approach to gaining a better understanding of the true history and anatomy of both the Appalachian and Cordilleran orogens, as well as those on other continents. Problems of relating episodic and more local orogenic events to continuous orogenic processes are more easily accommodated. Orogeny occurred in a particular region whenever an appropriate seafloor feature, such as an island arc, or seamount, or submarine plateau, impinged on that region. Finally, such a model is more compatible with the actualistic perspective of modern oceans, which are cluttered with submerged plateaus, sea mount chains and islands of various sizes (e.g., the tangled complexities of the Melanesian region in the western Pacific).

The more simplified, large-scale plate interactions, described in this and previous chapters, remain basically unchanged in the microplate model. However, many of the stratigraphic, structural, paleontologic, and paleomagnetic details may have radically different implications. Although they represent the secondary effects of global plate motion, microplate accretions may have been the primary factor in the forging of continental geology. The essence of the concept of collage tectonics is the individuality of the separate terranes; each exotic terrane records a geologic history significantly different from that of neighboring terranes.

In its early, simplest versions, plate-tectonics theory suffered from the deficiency of failing to account in detail for most of the geology of the continents. Consequently, during the decade of the 1970s, considerable effort went into developing and refining the theory to better explain the observations of continental geology. The microplate concept has played a major role in this refinement. The decade of the 1980s is witnessing a new revolution in our understanding of continental lithosphere evolution.

Summary

Triassic depositional patterns in the western craton of North America were similar to those of the preceding Permian Period and included extensive continental red beds and evaporites. Marine deposition was confined to the western part of the continental margin.

Major orogeny occurred during the Permo-Triassic in the western Cordillera. This event, the Sonoma orogeny, involved subduction of oceanic lithosphere. Convergence of a volcanic island-arc system on the western margin of the continent caused telescoping of a marginal ocean basin and major overthrusting of continental-margin basin sediments along the continental margin.

Although most of the Triassic record of North America is in the western craton and Cordilleran belt, a significant Upper Triassic and Lower Jurassic section—the Newark Supergroup and related rocks—occurs in surface and subsurface block-fault basins within the crystalline part of the Appalachians. Basalt sills, together with the crustal extension that produced the basin-opening faults, provide a signature of Early Mesozoic rifting, which heralded the breakup of Pangaea.

Land life during the Triassic was highlighted by dramatic adaptive radiations of gymnosperm plants and reptiles, but some major extinctions of tetrapods also occurred. Dinosaurs and the first mammals made their appearance late in the period.

Triassic seas swarmed with ammonoids, bivalve molluscs diversified rapidly, and scleractinian corals built extensive reefs. The richest marine province was the tropical, equatorial Tethys seaway, which indented the eastern margin of Pangaea.

During the Early Jurassic, the western craton of North America continued to receive nonmarine deposits. The thickly cross-stratified Navajo Sandstone of the Colorado Plateau Province represents a vast sandy desert like the Sahara. Later in the Jurassic an interior seaway, the Sundance, stretched from the Arctic almost to the newly formed Gulf of Mexico Basin. Jurassic marine sediments are present in the subsurface of the Atlantic and Gulf Coast regions, and represent the earliest marine deposition along the rifted continental margin as Pangaea began to split apart. A thick evaporite unit, the Louann Salt, was deposited in the embryonic Gulf of Mexico Basin. In the western part of the Cordillera, deep marine sediments were deposited from California northward to Alaska. The enigmatic, chaotic Franciscan Formation of the California coast ranges began to accumulate as an accretionary wedge in a deep-sea trench.

Magmatic-arc igneous activity along the Andean-type continental margin and back-arc thrusting began after the early, Nevadan phase of the protracted Cordilleran orogeny. This orogeny was the response to subduction of the Farallon oceanic plate beneath the western margin of the North American continent. Growing tectonic highlands provided source areas for the fore-arc basin Great Valley Group of California, and for the massive incursion of sediments that formed the Morrison alluvial plain of the western craton. The Morrison Formation is famous for its wealth of dinosaur fossils. Natural-history museums of the world feature reconstructions of the giant Jurassic sauropod genera *Apatosaurus, Brachiosaurus,* and *Diplodocus,* and the voracious meat-eater *Allosaurus. Archaeopteryx,* the first "bird," represented by about a half-dozen specimens from the Solenhofen Limestone in Bavaria, may actually be the remains of a small feathered theropod dinosaur which was not capable of powered flight.

Unlike North American counterparts, Jurassic marine strata in Europe are widely exposed and very fossiliferous. They served as the cornerstone for development of such important stratigraphic concepts as fossil succession, stage, zone, and facies. Abundant, rapidly evolving ammonite cephalopod faunas, squidlike belemnites, and bivalve and gastropod molluscs indicate a major diversification of molluscs. Fossils of marine reptiles, including ichthyosaurs, plesiosaurs, and turtles, bear evidence that some reptiles had invaded the sea.

Several orogenies shaped the western part of North America during the early Mesozoic. These orogenies involved subduction of oceanic lithosphere and various continent–island arc interactions. After the Nevadan orogeny, the western margin of North America developed as an Andean-type margin.

During these various plate interactions, the westward-drifting continental block acted like a bulldozer, and scraped off parts of the ocean floor at different places and different times along much of the Cordilleran margin. Island arcs, seamounts, submarine plateaus, split-off continental fragments, and a few slivers of oceanic lithosphere itself became accreted to the edge of the continent as exotic terranes. Some traveled thousands of kilometers before their final docking. Anomalous stratigraphy, paleontology, and paleomagnetic signatures have allowed their recognition and have provided information on origins, migration routes, and times of docking. The recognition of over 50 separate, highly diverse exotic terranes in the Cordillera, as well as others in other orogens of the world, has carried plate tectonics beyond definition of large-scale megaplate interactions to consideration of microplates and collage tectonics.

Suggestions for Further Reading

Bakker, R. T. 1975. Dinosaur renaissance. *Scientific American* Offprint No. 916. San Francisco: W. H. Freeman.

Bakker, R. T. 1986. The dinosaur heresies. New York: William Morrow & Co.

Ben-Avriham, Zvi. 1981. The movement of continents. *American Scientist* 69(3):291–300.

Dietz, R. S., and J. C. Holden. 1970. The breakup of Pangaea. *Scientific American* Offprint No. 892. San Francisco: W. H. Freeman.

Howell, D. 1985. Terranes. *Scientific American* 253(5):116–26.

Jones, D. L., Allan Cox, Peter Coney, and Myrl Beck. 1982. The growth of western North America. *Scientific American* 247(5):70–128.

King, P. B. 1977. *The evolution of North America.* Rev. ed. Princeton, NJ: Princeton Univ. Press.

Lanham, Url. 1973. *The bone hunters.* New York: Columbia Univ. Press.

McPhee, John. 1980. *Basin and range.* New York: Farrar, Straus & Giroux.

McPhee, John. 1982. *In suspect terrain.* New York: Farrar, Straus & Giroux.

Ostrom, J. H. 1978. A new look at dinosaurs. *National Geographic* 154(2):152–85.

Ostrom, J. H. 1979. Bird flight. How did it begin? *American Scientist* 67:46–56.

Late Mesozoic History

13

Eon		Era	Period		Age in Ma*
PHANEROZOIC		CENOZOIC	Quaternary	Quaternary	2
			Tertiary	Neogene	24
				Paleogene	65
		MESOZOIC	Cretaceous		144
			Jurassic		208
			Triassic		245
		PALEOZOIC	Permian		286
			Carboniferous	Pennsylvanian	320
				Mississippian	360
			Devonian		408
			Silurian		438
			Ordovician		505
			Cambrian		570
CRYPTOZOIC (PRECAMBRIAN)	PROTEROZOIC	Late Proterozoic			900
		Middle Proterozoic			1600
		Early Proterozoic			2500
	ARCHEAN	Late Archean			3000
		Middle Archean			3400
		Early Archean			~3800
HADEAN (Pregeologic history of the Earth)					
				Origin of Earth	4600

Contents

Key Terms

Chalk
Granitization
Foreland fold-thrust belt
Sevier orogeny
Bentonite
Endothermy
Ectothermy

Nemesis, Asteroids, Iridium, and the Death of Dinosaurs

Extraterrestrial Cause for the Cretaceous-Tertiary Extinction—this was the imposing title of the lead article in the June 6, 1980, issue of *Science,* the principal publication of the American Association for the Advancement of Science. This article turned the scientific community on its ear by proposing that a large body (bolide) impact with the Earth was the cause of the "sudden" demise of dinosaurs and other animals at the end of the Cretaceous.

The authors were Luis Alvarez (a Nobel laureate) and his son Walter, working in conjunction with two University of California–Berkeley colleagues, Frank Asaro and Helen Michel. They found an anomalously high concentration of the rare platinum-group element *iridium* in a clay layer marking the Cretaceous-Tertiary (K/T) boundary in the proposed boundary stratotype section near Gubbio, Italy (see Chapter 6). Because the anomaly was identified precisely at the K/T boundary, and because iridium is normally almost absent from the Earth's crust, but relatively much more abundant in some types of meteorites, an extraterrestrial interpretation for the mass extinctions marking the end of the Cretaceous (the so-called terminal Cretaceous event) seemed reasonable.

The basic thesis presented by the Alvarez group was that a large asteroid (perhaps 10 km in diameter) hit the Earth 65 million years ago, and the force of the impact sent into the atmosphere a tremendous volume of pulverized rock, dust, and fragments of the asteroid itself (with its iridium). According to the scenario, the atmosphere became so clogged with the dust that sunlight was blocked and photosynthesis by phytoplankton and green plants was inhibited or arrested completely. This, in turn, broke down food chains and triggered a domino effect that led to the extinction of the most vulnerable animal groups—the most famous being the dinosaurs. The logic presented here was that the iridium anomaly in the K/T boundary clay layer is a geochemical signature of a bolide impact and subsequent fallout, and because the boundary marks a major mass faunal crisis, the impact must have been the major cause of the extinctions—the coincidence was too strong to dismiss as happenstance.

Interestingly, the Alvarez group did not start out by formulating a hypothesis about the cause of extinction, and then going to Gubbio to test the hypothesis. It seems that Walter Alvarez was working on a geologic project in northern Italy, and needing reliable information on depositional rates, he turned to the thick, continuous section at Gubbio for data. The Gubbio section, consisting mostly of pelagic limestone of late Mesozoic and early Cenozoic age, has a tightly defined, fossil-based chronology which has been carefully analyzed. Fossils, remember, are invaluable for assembling a sequence of events, but are not data of sufficient resolution to provide quantifiable information on elapsed time. What Walter Alvarez needed was a tracer in the sedimentary rocks that could tell him about depositional rate.

Luis Alvarez entered the picture by suggesting a unique approach to the problem, which involved calculations of relative amounts of meteoritic dust in the sedimentary rocks. The idea here was that, if the rate of meteoritic dust fall were known (and it was assumed to be fairly constant), normal sedimentation rate (expressed as mm per 1000 years) could be calculated from the percentage of meteoritic dust occurring in a total sediment sample. The problem, however, was to distinguish the particles of meteoritic origin from normal terrestrially derived clay particles.

Luis Alvarez recognized the importance of isolating some easily measurable property of the meteoritic material that could substitute for the actual amount of micrometeoritic particles. It was at this point that they decided to analyze chemically for the concentration of the trace element iridium, largely because of its near-absence in rocks of the Earth's crust, and its known presence in meteorites.

So, with the aid of analytical facilities at Berkeley, and the expertise of chemists Asaro and Michel, a succession of Gubbio limestones and claystones, spanning the paleontologically defined K/T boundary, was analyzed for iridium. Remember that the results, hopefully, were to give Walter Alvarez the indicator of sedimentation rates that he needed for his study. The surprise was that the analysis indicated far more iridium than was expected, or than was found in rocks above or below the boundary clay (Fig. 13–1). These results provided not the answers Walter was looking for, but instead the kickoff for an exciting new look at the Cretaceous-Tertiary boundary—a boundary that marks one of the great mass-extinction events of the Phanerozoic record, and a boundary separating two eras of geologic time. Needless to say, he placed his original project on the back burner for a time.

Such is often the course of scientific research—investigations in one area may lead to a breakthrough in another area. Once the geologic community was introduced to the data and conclusions, the search was on to find other iridium anomalies. Since 1980, iridium anomalies have been described from dozens of K/T boundary sections all over the world, both on the continents and in the ocean basins. The K/T boundary iridium spike (Fig. 13–1) and its proposed significance have been greeted with loud and mixed reactions by the scientific community.

Prior to the Alvarez-group paper, most paleontologists had settled into a posture of resigned complacency about the subject of mass extinctions. Most agreed that it was a fascinating subject, but of such a complex, interactive nature that it could not be resolved by simple solutions. Many had taken the general approach that large-scale plate motions, resulting in repatterning of environments, had been the ultimate cause. Changing land-sea relationships, dwindling resources and increased competition, breakdown of genetic isolating mechanisms, and changing climates had coalesced to bring about the downfall of taxonomic groups—a sort of environmental foreclosure.

A number of more specific theories had been advanced, but none of the more popular earthbound ideas were totally satisfactory explanations. Even extraterrestrial impact had been proposed previously by several prominent workers, but with little or no supporting evidence.

The Alvarez group's pronouncement had the effect of polarizing paleontologists into two camps. On one side were those who jumped on the bandwagon, and saw this as the ticket they were looking for to explain not only the Cretaceous terminal event, but perhaps others as well (such as the Late Ordovician, Late Devonian, end of Permian, Late Triassic). On the other side were the skeptical and cautious, at times vehement in their opposition, who still clung to the notion that the K/T extinction patterns for individual taxa were sequential, not abrupt, and that the Cretaceous ended with a

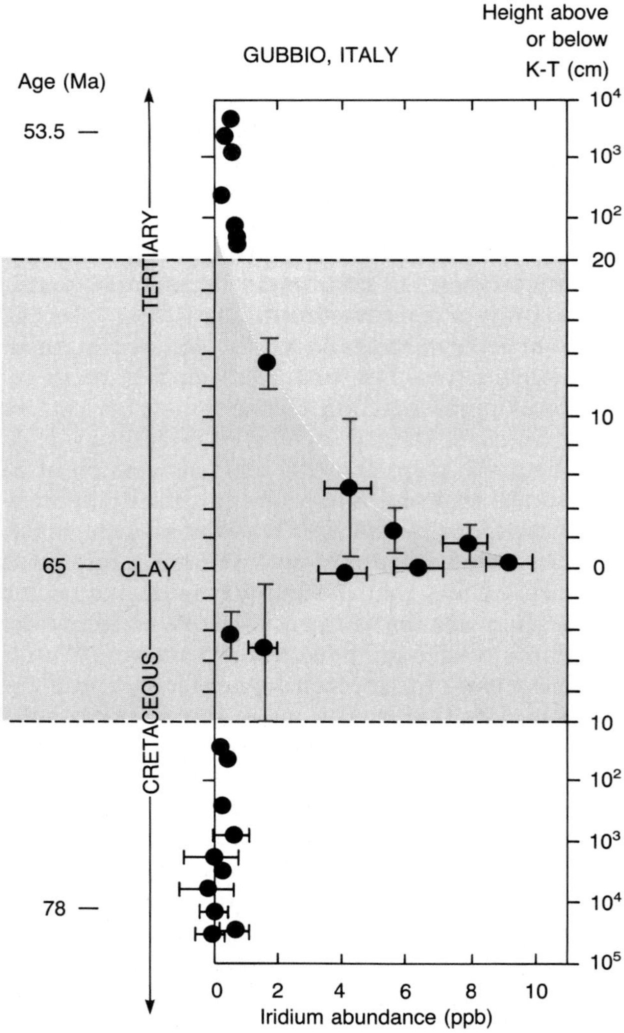

Figure 13–1

Iridium curve showing the K-T boundary anomaly at the stratigraphic section near Gubbio, Italy. Iridium abundance is shown in parts per billion (ppb). One part per billion is about one ten-millionth of 1%. The vertical scales show age in Ma and centimeter thickness below and above the K-T boundary clay layer. The spike in the curve shows the iridium anomaly. The horizontal error bars indicate the uncertainty in chemical analysis, and the vertical error bars show the thickness of rock over which each sample was collected.

(From L. W. Alvarez, 1983, Proceedings of the National Academy of Sciences, *USA*, vol. 80, Fig. 4, p. 627–42)

whimper, not a bang. Many were willing to accept the evidence for an impact (and a growing body of evidence indicates that indeed there was one), but would not concede it to have been a major factor in the extinctions.

In 1980, two paleontologists at the University of Chicago, John Sepkoski and David Raup, proposed that major extinction events since the end of the Paleozoic (i.e., those significantly above "normal" background rates of extinction) have occurred at regular intervals of about 26 million years. This was based on rigid mathematical treatment of a great abundance of paleontological data. With no known earthbound phenomena to trigger such a periodicity, this suggested to the authors that extraterrestrial influence was likely. This lent further credence to the impact theory for the terminal Cretaceous event.

A subsequent study on *astroblemes* (fossil impacts), involving much less hard data, proposed a similar periodicity for impact during the Phanerozoic. The periodicity idea had the effect of sweeping several prominent astrophysicists into the maelstrom of excitement, and from a number of ideas concerning extraterrestrial perturbations there emerged the theory of *Nemesis*, the "Death Star." Nemesis is the name given to a hypothesized small companion star to our sun. As the story goes, Nemesis is said to be moving away from the Earth, and is presently about 2 light years away, but in another few million years its orbit will bring it back toward the Earth. The return trip supposedly will take another dozen or so million years, and before the orbit is complete, Nemesis will have passed through the Oort Cloud, an envelope of billions of comets that revolve closely around the Sun.

Supposedly, this disturbance of the Oort Cloud will cause a number of its comets to radically change their orbits, sending some toward the Earth, with one or more actually colliding with our planet. Of course, Nemesis's orbit is considered to have a fixed period of 26 million years. Hence, what we have with the Nemesis idea is a big "clock" in the sky that controls biological destinies on Earth. In this light, dinosaurs were not the victims of bad genes, but rather of bad luck.

The Nemesis story has appeared in popular newsmagazines, newspapers, and television specials, and has even been likened to a nuclear-winter scenario. Despite all the hype, a few facts remain inescapable according to Raup. First, no one has ever seen Nemesis or the Oort Cloud. The demise of dinosaurs by comet (or asteroid) impact is highly debatable, and the 26 million-year periodicity in mass extinctions may or may not be real. Yet, there is some evidence for all parts of the story. It is a novel hypothesis of cosmic proportions (as well as cosmic connections), and it is in the process of being tested—the scientific method at work.

If the hypothesis turns out to be true, the repercussions for how we view Earth history and mass extinctions would be great. The range of disciplines covered by the research is vast, including evolutionary biology, paleontology, biostratigraphy, sedimentology, geochemistry, mathematical modeling, atmospheric science, and astrophysics—a true cross-fertilization of scientific endeavors.

As David Raup stated in his book, *The Nemesis Affair*, "the Nemesis theory may turn out to be a major step forward in our understanding of the natural world or an embarrassing period of near insanity in scholarship."* But science always has, and will continue to have, its so-called lunatic fringe—that cadre of imaginative workers who are not afraid to break from conventional wisdom and boldly pursue a radical new idea. Remember that the early devotees of continental drift were branded as mavericks, and their hypothesis was officially quashed, but they were later vindicated. Similarly, the Nemesis affair might be guilty until proven innocent. As with continental drift, where we wonder why it took so long to recognize the "obvious" phenomenon of seafloor spreading, we may one day wonder how we ever thought the Earth could have been unaffected by all that real estate whirling above our heads. Consider the known ancient astroblemes, and the asteroid that missed us by 450,000 miles in March, 1989!

---

*Raup, David. 1987. *The Nemesis Affair.* New York: W. W. Norton & Co.

Cretaceous History

An Abundant Record

The Cretaceous System is well represented in North America. Anyone who has cast even a cursory glance at the Geologic Map of the United States cannot help but be impressed by the amount of area colored green, representing Cretaceous sedimentary rocks. Significant areas of plutonic rocks are also present. Cretaceous sediments were deposited over a wide region by marginal and interior seas that spread beyond the limits of Jurassic deposition. With the gradual encroachment of Cretaceous seas onto the continent, the Pacific Coast and Atlantic and Gulf Coasts were submerged, and thick stratigraphic sections accumulated. When considering Cretaceous depositional patterns, one must keep in mind the plate tectonics of the period. The Pacific margin was the leading edge, and the Atlantic and Gulf of Mexico margins represented the passive trailing edge of the North American continent. We shall discuss the effects of plate tectonics on sedimentary patterns by first examining the trailing margin.

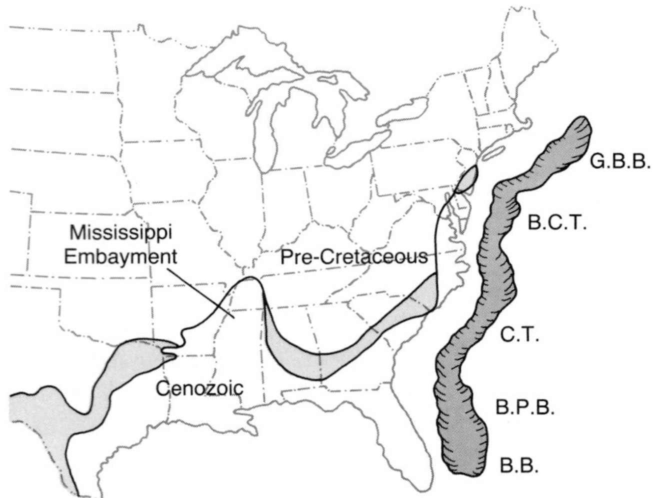

Figure 13–2
Outcrop pattern of Cretaceous sedimentary rocks, eastern and southern United States, and major basins in the continental shelf region.

Sedimentation on a Trailing Margin

The earliest onlapping sediments of the modern Atlantic margin were mid-Jurassic–to–earliest-Cretaceous limestone, dolomite, and anhydrite. These carbonates and evaporites were deposited in warm, shallow seas developed on the postrift erosion surface, and all along the margin there developed a pronounced carbonate paleoshelf edge. The carbonate deposits formed a stable structure along this edge from Georges Bank to the Bahamas (Fig. 13–2). This carbonate bank was eroded periodically so that steep escarpments are now buried beneath the continental slope (they have been detected by seismic profiling). Apparently, the northward drift of the North American continental plate carried the U.S. Atlantic margin progressively north of 30°N latitude (the general present-day northern limit of extensive carbonate deposition) from earliest Cretaceous time. Thus, carbonate deposition terminated progressively from north to south, but still exists on the Bahaman Platform.

As seafloor spreading continued and North America moved steadily away from the hot spreading center, thermal cooling of the lithosphere caused subsidence along the continental margin. By latest-Jurassic–to–earliest-Cretaceous time, the sediment loading on the cooling lithosphere caused flexural downbending of the adjacent crust to form the coastal plain landward of this hinge zone. Continued cooling, subsidence, and flexure increased the width and thickness of the coastal plain wedge. Along the trend of the hinge, the flexing of the lithosphere varied, and several prominent basins and platforms developed within the Atlantic continental margin. These included, from north to south, the Georges Bank Basin, Long Island Platform, Baltimore Canyon Trough, Carolina Platform, Blake Plateau Basin, Florida Platform, and Bahaman Basin (Fig. 13–2). This architecture of salients and reentrants along the Atlantic margin was inherited from structures in the Paleozoic orogen.

On the Atlantic coastal plain, Cretaceous sediments are exposed in a narrowing band from Georgia to Long Island (Fig. 13–2), and have been traced in the subsurface as far north as Newfoundland. The outcrop belt represents the exposed, gently upturned edges of a wedge-shaped succession that thickens seaward and comprises a sizeable bulk of the present Atlantic continental shelf. The sediments include sandstones, with local development of *glauconitic* sand (greensand), siltstones, and mudstones, and minor amounts of conglomerate. Units of marl (clayey limestone) are present, but few bona fide limestones occur in the succession.

The terrigenous clastic material was derived from erosion of the Appalachian Mountains. The morphology of the Atlantic coastline during the Cretaceous was probably somewhat similar to that of the present and included beach, bay, lagoon, barrier-island, delta, and marine-shelf environments.

In the Gulf Coast Province, Cretaceous sediments are exposed in a large crescent-shaped belt from the southern margin of the Atlantic coastal plain in Georgia to the Mexican-Guatemalan border. The outcrop belt is interrupted around the Mississippi Embayment (Fig. 13–2), where a prominent reentrant of coastal Cenozoic deposits overlaps the Cretaceous. The Mississippi Embayment is probably the expression of an *aulacogen,* developed during an earlier rifting phase but still expressing a structural template on the Gulf margin. As in the Atlantic coastal region, Gulf Coast Cretaceous sediments form a seaward-thickening wedge, but unlike the Atlantic section much of the Gulf section is developed as carbonates. In the eastern Gulf Coast areas of Alabama and Mississippi only Upper Cretaceous rocks crop out at the surface, but to the west an expansive terrane of Lower Cretaceous rocks is exposed in the Edwards Plateau of central Texas and the Sierra Madre Oriental of northeastern Mexico.

From Alabama to southeastern Mexico, Early Cretaceous carbonate deposition was influenced by a major barrier-reef complex called the Edwards Reef (Fig. 13–3). The reef trend had a particularly strong influence on carbonate-platform deposition in the Texas region. The barrier-reef trend itself lies in the subsurface of the Coastal Plain Province, but the varied flat-lying deposits of the back-reef area are widely exposed throughout the dissected Edwards Plateau. Here the carbonate rocks are every bit as complex in facies patterns as Paleozoic carbonates of the great platform-interior seas. Most of the rocks were deposited in shallow water in a mosaic of carbonate tidal flats, oolite and skeletal banks and bars, lagoons, bays, and small patch reefs (Fig. 13–4).

One formation, the Glen Rose Limestone, contains some individual beds that can be traced for hundreds of kilometers, suggesting deposition on broad tidal flats. Other shallow-water features include ripple marks that commonly show interference patterns, cross-bedding, flat-pebble intraformational conglomerates, mud cracks, evaporites, and even dinosaur footprints, some of which contain raindrop impressions. During Glen Rose deposition the 600 km trip from Dallas to Del Rio, Texas, could have been made in a rowboat and a good pair of wading boots.

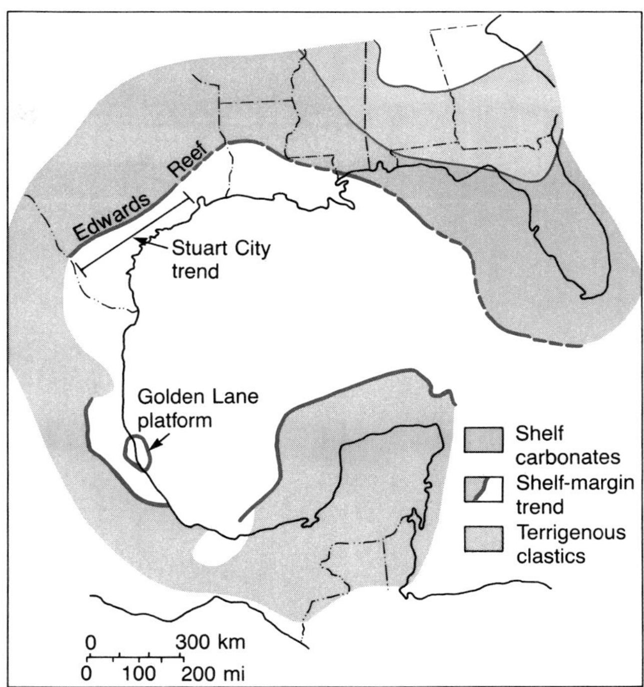

Figure 13–3

Distribution of Lower Cretaceous shelf-margin facies around Gulf of Mexico Basin. Reef trend shown as dark band.

(After A. A. Meyerhoff, 1967, Future Hydrocarbon Provinces of Gulf of Mexico–Caribbean Region, Fig. 8; p. 231; *Gulf Coast Association of Geological Societies Transactions,* vol. 17; and D. G. Bebout and C. H. Moore, Jr., eds. Carbonate Depositional Environments, Fig. 1, p. 441; *American Association of Petroleum Geologists Memoir,* 33. Used by permission of Gulf Coast Association of Geological Societies and American Association of Petroleum Geologists)

In contrast to the Lower Cretaceous, the Upper Cretaceous in the western part of the Gulf Coast region contains large amounts of terrigenous clastic material, probably derived from Late Cretaceous uplift in the Rocky Mountain region. The Upper Cretaceous of the eastern Gulf Coast contains more carbonates, indicating that the region was largely isolated from major sources of terrigenous influx. Today major carbonate deposition is confined principally to the Florida Bay area of the west Florida shelf and to the Yucatán shelf, reflecting again favorable latitudes and lack of proximity to terrigenous influence. Both the eastern and western Gulf Coast Upper Cretaceous sections contain prominent units of fine-grained limestone called **chalk**. It was the chalk deposits on both sides of the English Channel that served as the original type section for the Cretaceous System ("creta" is the Latin word for chalk).

Cretaceous rocks in the Gulf Coast Province have yielded abundant hydrocarbons. The produc-

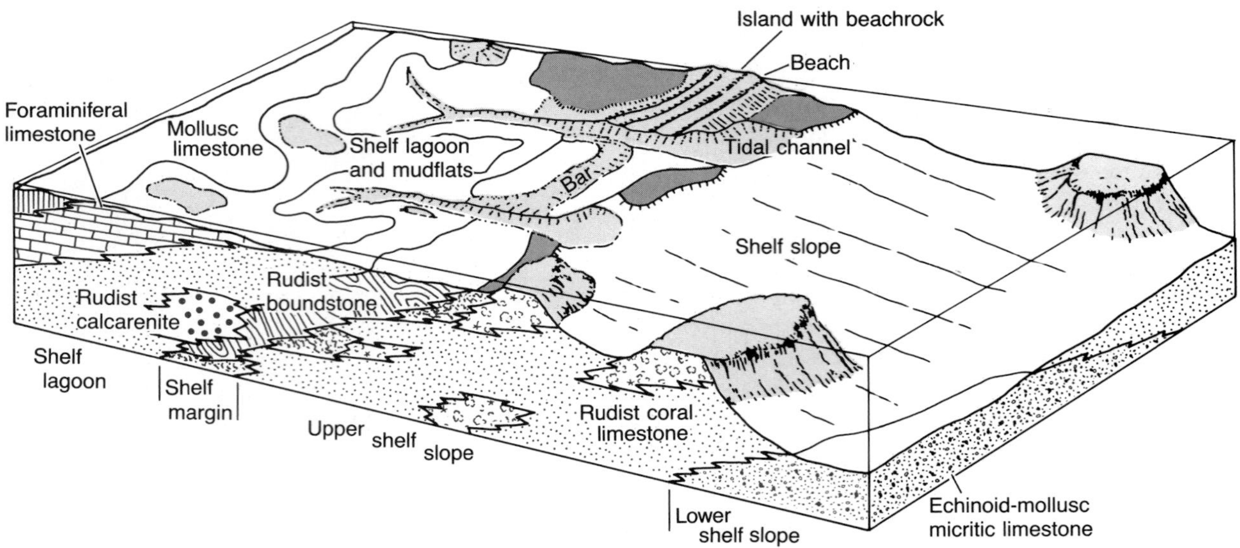

Figure 13–4

Facies and interpreted depositional environments across the Lower Cretaceous reef trend, South Texas.

(After D. G. Bebout, and R. G. Loucks, 1974, Stuart City Trend, Lower Cretaceous, South Texas—A Carbonate Shelf Margin Model for Hydrocarbon Exploration, Fig. 3, p. 443, *in* Carbonate Depositional Environments: *American Association of Petroleum Geologists Memoir,* 33. Used by permission of American Association of Petroleum Geologists)

tive oil fields of eastern and northeastern Mexico have tapped carbonate reservoir rocks of the Edwards Reef, Golden Lane, and other reef trends and associated platform facies. The truncation of a prominent unit, the Woodbine Sandstone, beneath an unconformity has given rise to the East Texas field (Fig. 13–5), a multibillion-barrel producer that has been one of the largest oil fields on the North

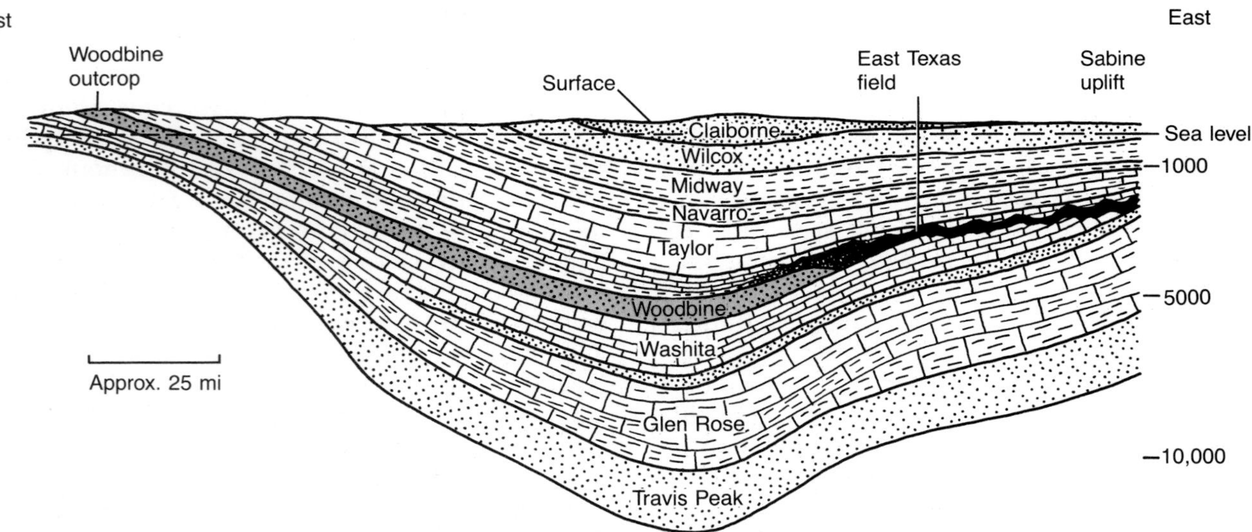

Figure 13–5

East Texas petroleum accumulation. Wedging of eroded Woodbine Sandstone between limestone units, forming traps for East Texas field on western flank of Sabine uplift.

(After M. T. Halbouty and J. J. Halbouty, 1982, Relationships Between East Texas Field and Sabine Uplift in Texas; Fig. 2, p. 1045: *American Association of Petroleum Geologists Bulletin,* vol. 66, no. 8. Used by permission of American Association of Petroleum Geologists)

Figure 13–6

Western North America showing trend of Cretaceous batholiths. A. Coast Ranges batholith. B. Idaho and Boulder batholiths. C. Sierra Nevada batholith. D. Peninsular California batholith.

(Data from P. B. King, comp., 1969, *Tectonic Map of North America:* U.S. Geological Survey)

American continent. Here, the Woodbine, sealed beneath the unconformity, is a shallow-marine shoreline facies in which are trapped hydrocarbons that migrated from more seaward and basinal organic-rich mudstones.

The Continent's Leading Edge

Let us now examine some Cretaceous events in the western Cordillera along the dynamic, leading edge of the continent. The beginnings of the Cordilleran orogeny in Late Jurassic continued into Cretaceous time as immense volumes of granite were formed from Alaska to Baja California (Fig. 13–6). These granitic plutons include the Peninsular California, Sierra Nevada, Idaho, Boulder, and Coast Range batholiths. This chain of batholiths is interpreted as representing a late Mesozoic magmatic arc related to subduction of Pacific oceanic lithosphere along the western margin of the North American continental plate (Fig. 13–7).

Gold nuggets that lured prospectors to California in the Gold Rush of 1849 came from gold-bearing quartz veins in the plutonic rocks, the Mother Lode. Metallic ores of the Coeur d'Alene district in Idaho as well as Butte, Montana and British Columbia were deposited by hydrothermal solutions which accompanied the magmatic activity and formation of the batholithic rocks. The formation of granite, originally thought to be a product of slow cooling of parent magma at depth, also has been ascribed to an essentially metamorphic process, **granitization,** whereby preexisting rocks have been transformed into granite through replacement. The granites of orogenic belts may be related to subcrustal melting and replacement involving a heat source generated from subduction below the edge of the continental lithosphere.

The Andes belt of South America contains abundant granite and andesite, as part of the magmatic arc related to the subduction of Pacific lithosphere beneath the western edge of the continent (Fig. 13–8). As mentioned previously, the western margin of North America was probably an Andean-type margin during most of late Mesozoic time. Parts of the batholith complexes are as old as mid-Jurassic, but most of the dates indicate an Early-to-Middle Cretaceous age.

Deposition of the chaotic Franciscan Formation in the trench and accretionary wedge, and Great Valley turbidite-fan assemblage in the fore-arc basin of the active plate margin continued generally uninterrupted through the Cretaceous (Fig. 13–9). The western part of the thick Great Valley Group

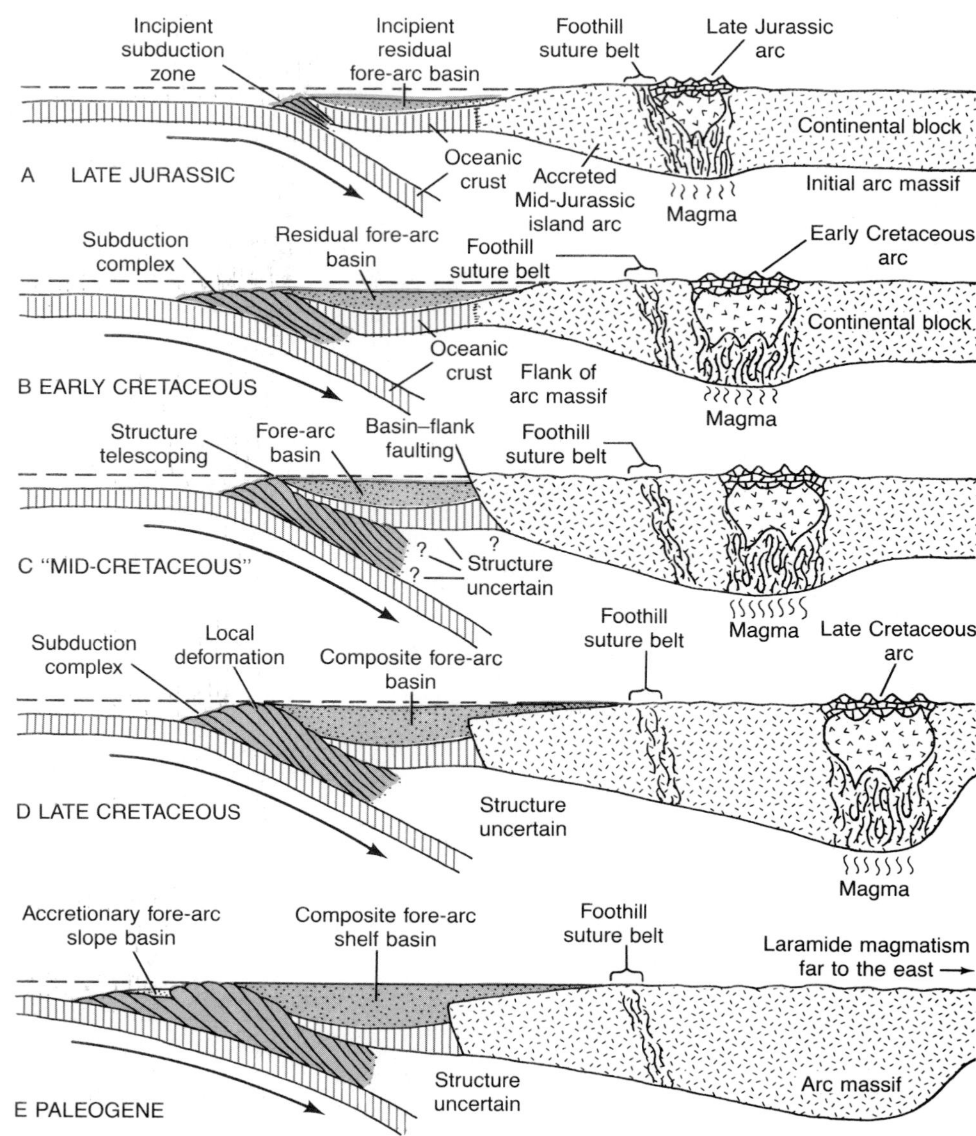

Figure 13–7
Late Mesozoic–Paleogene plate-tectonic model for western margin of North America at latitude of northern California. Note subduction zone and associated trench (site of deposition of Franciscan Formation), formation of accretionary ridge and fore-arc basin (Great Valley Group) in arc-trench gap, and magmatic arc (which coincides with batholithic trend of Fig. 13–6). Foothill suture belt is zone of collision between mid-Jurassic island-arc system and continental-margin magmatic arc to initiate Nevadan phase of Cordilleran orogeny and the change from a Japanese to an Andean (South American) type of margin. (From W. R. Dickinson and D. R. Seely, 1979, Structure and Stratigraphy of Fore-Arc Basins, Fig. 11, p. 25: *American Association of Petroleum Geologists Bulletin*, vol. 63. Used by permission of American Association of Petroleum Geologists)

was probably deposited on oceanic basement, which represents a strip of marginal basin oceanic lithosphere that formed behind the eastward-migrating composite Jurassic arc (Fig. 12–17 in Chapter 12). This was left attached to the upper plate alongside California during the subduction reversal, and thus became the leading edge of the overriding continental plate of Cretaceous time (Figs. 13–7 and 13–9).

This oceanic lithosphere, in addition to forming the basement beneath the western Great Valley of California, is also exposed as a thick *ophiolite* sheet in the coast ranges. The preservation of the thin ophiolitic leading edge of Cretaceous California demonstrates that the continent was not crumpled against the oncoming Pacific oceanic lithosphere (Farallon Plate). The original physical relationship between the Great Valley and Franciscan rock assemblages has been masked by Cenozoic faulting.

The late Mesozoic rocks of central California consist of three side-by-side assemblages which evolved during the same time span:

- the Franciscan—a poorly organized trench and accretionary wedge assemblage;
- the Great Valley—a more rhythmically bedded fore-arc basin accumulation; and
- the Sierra Nevada batholith—a magmatic arc complex.

The Franciscan Formation, which is exposed onshore mostly as deep-water deposits of Cretaceous age, continued from its Late Jurassic beginnings to

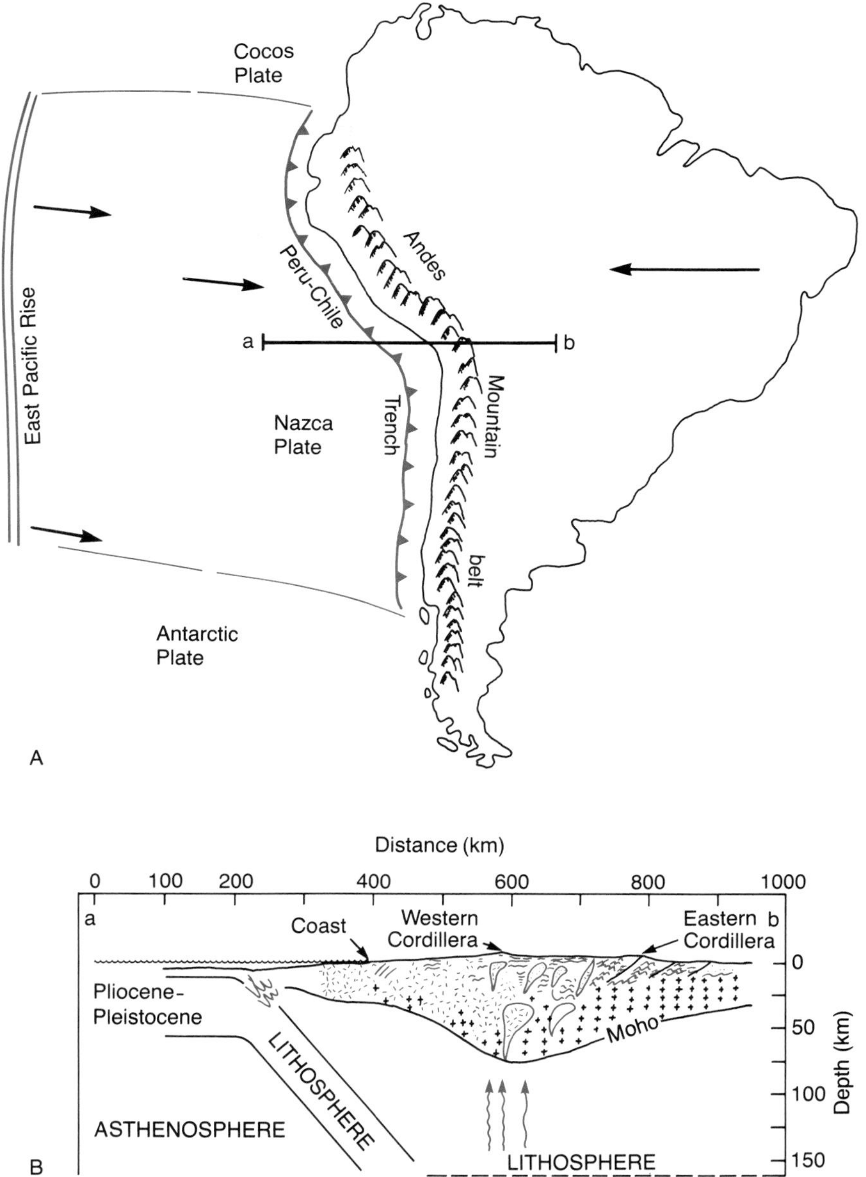

Figure 13–8
Western margin of South America. A. Andes trend, Peru-Chile trench, and East Pacific rise spreading center—a modern plate-tectonic analogue for the Late Mesozoic–Early Cenozoic western margin of North America. B. Cross section showing similarity to western margin of North America during Late Cretaceous Sevier orogeny. (A, courtesy Critter Creations; B, after D. E. James, 1971, Plate Tectonic Model for the Evolution of the Andes, Fig. 10, p. 3341; *Geological Society of America Bulletin*, vol. 82. Reproduced by permission of author)

form as a complex assemblage of deep-water terrigenous clastic sediments and mélange that lies structurally beneath the ophiolite in the Coast Ranges. The mélange, characterized by a pervasively sheared matrix, accumulated as an accretionary wedge and contains pieces of ophiolite, abyssal pelagic sediments, and high-pressure blueschist metamorphic rocks, as well as enclosed pieces of seamounts and atolls conveyed from more distant southern latitudes. The Great Valley Group contains abyssal-plain deposits overlain by deep-sea turbidite fan-and-slope deposits.

The distance of the Cretaceous batholiths inland from correlative accretionary-wedge complexes indicates a moderate angle of inclination of the subducting oceanic lithosphere. At any one time, the Cretaceous magmatic-arc activity was confined to a narrow belt, with successive belts becoming younger eastward. In southern California, these belts of Jurassic and Cretaceous igneous, metamorphic, and sedimentary rocks cut across the trend of the major Paleozoic paleotectonic features and facies belts (Fig. 13–10). This relationship probably resulted from the different angle of convergence of the North American and Pacific Plates once the mid-Atlantic rift opened and the North American continent began its westward movement in mid-Mesozoic time.

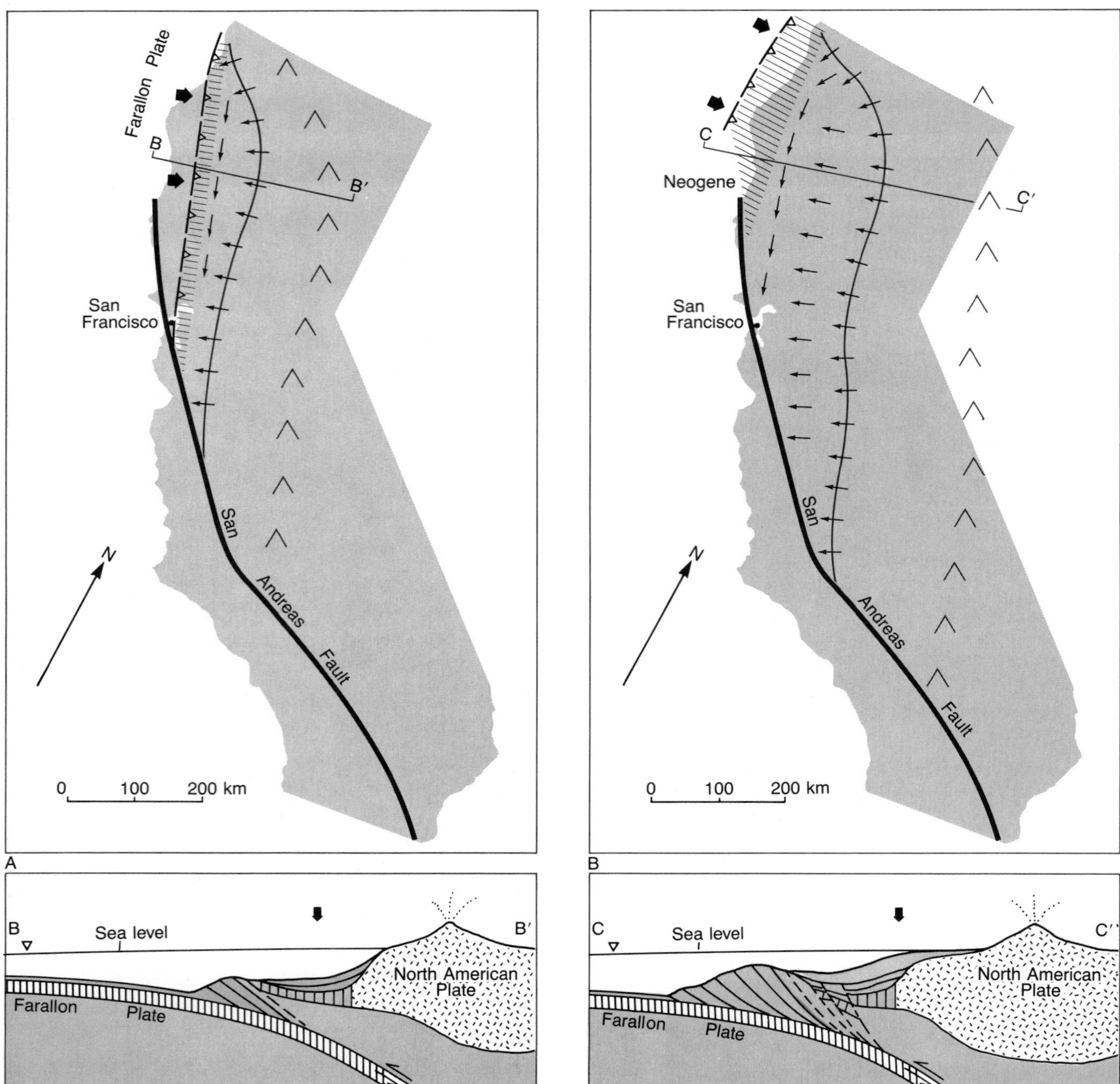

Figure 13–9

Cretaceous, northern California. A. Early Cretaceous. B. Late Cretaceous. Symbols the same as for Figure 12–19. By Cretaceous time the subduction complex (Franciscan Formation) had enlarged and the fore-arc basin had subsided sufficiently so that arc-derived detritus was trapped behind a bathymetric barrier. Most sediments (Great Valley Group) accumulated in deep-marine basin-plain environments within the arc-trench gap during Early Cretaceous, but by Late Cretaceous, sedimentary progradation of turbidite-fan, slope, and shelf deposits was beginning to fill the fore-arc basin.

(After R. V. Ingersoll, 1978, Paleogeography and Paleotectonics of the Late Mesozoic Forearc Basin of Northern and Central California; Fig. 5–8, p. 476–477, *in Mesozoic Paleogeography of the Western United States:* Pacific Section SEPM Paleogeography Symposium, vol, 2. Reproduced by permission of Pacific Section, Society of Economic Paleontologists and Mineralogists)

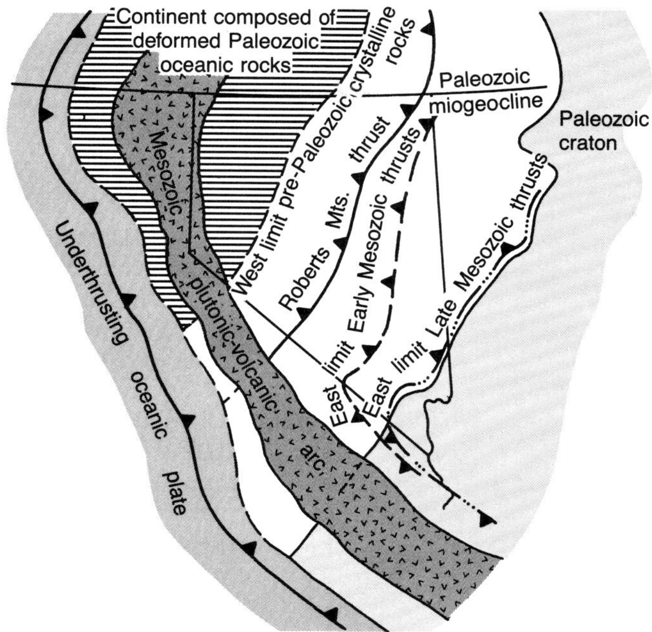

Figure 13–10
Late Mesozoic, showing truncation of Paleozoic miogeoclinal and deformational trends by a Mesozoic plutonic-volcanic arc of Andean type. An inferred southward convergence of Early and Late Mesozoic thrust zones is also shown, as is the change in trend of such faults and their departure from the miogeoclinal terrane in southeastern California.
(From B. C. Burchfiel and G. A. Davis, 1972, Structural Framework and Evolution of the Southern Part of the Cordilleran Orogen, Western United States; Fig. 7, p. 111; *American Journal of Science,* vol. 272)

As with the preceding Triassic and Jurassic Periods, reconstructions of Cretaceous paleogeography of the Pacific Coast are sketchy because of overprinting by Cenozoic tectonics. The evidence, however, points to continued subduction, with development of shallow-water coastal deposits along a narrow shelf, and rapid subsidence and thick sediment accumulations in deeper water offshore. Turbidite-fan complexes are well represented in northern California and Oregon, and abundant coal-bearing deltaic deposits are found in the north slope of Alaska.

Sevier Foreland Fold Thrust Belt

From southern Nevada to southern Canada, a **foreland fold-thrust belt,** comprising a tectonic wedge consisting of the Cordilleran miogeoclinal uppermost Proterozoic and Paleozoic strata, formed during the great Cretaceous batholith time of growth (Fig. 13–11A). Compressional imbricate overthrust and fold structures, varying widely with the competence of stratigraphic units, formed within the thickening and eastward-spreading tectonic wedge. The cratonic basement beneath the eastern part of the sliding wedge subsided by flexural loading and sloped upward toward the east (Fig. 13–11B).

According to regional-tectonics expert Warren Hamilton, because crustal shortening–compressive structures are continuous from batholiths to thrust front, arc-magmatic crustal thickening can be invoked as the prime mechanism for this eastward overthrusting. In this perspective, thrusting was a response to gravitational spreading due to crustal thickening further west. By analogy with active thrust belts in the central Andes and New Guinea, the surface of the magmatic arc may have been at an altitude of 4 km or so.

Thus the style of deformation during the Cretaceous in much of the Cordilleran belt was characterized largely by back-arc thrusting, which displaced gigantic slabs of Paleozoic miogeoclinal rocks and shoved them eastward, along low-angle westward-dipping thrust planes in almost ramplike fashion, over younger Paleozoic and Mesozoic rocks (Fig. 13–12). Imbricate thrust slices stacked like huge shingles can be traced the length of the Mesozoic Cordillera. This crustal shortening, related to the **Sevier** phase of the Cordilleran orogeny, was as much as 50 to 100 km in places, and was a principal manifestation of the subduction-generated compression that affected the Cordilleran margin from Late Jurassic to early Cenozoic time. In recent years, the Cordilleran overthrust belt has been the focus of active exploration for hydrocarbons, with targets being attractive reservoir facies and structures beneath the soles of thrust faults.

Cretaceous Interior Seaway

In the western part of the craton, flooding of marine waters from both the Arctic and Gulf of Mexico formed a broad interior seaway (Fig. 13–13) by mid-Cretaceous time—somewhat reminiscent of the Sundance Sea of the Jurassic. This mid-Cretaceous transgression, also documented on the other continents, probably resulted from accelerated seafloor spreading as Pangaea underwent major fragmentation (Fig. 13–14); marine waters, displaced by inflated spreading centers, flooded the margins and interiors of drifting continents.

The mid-Cretaceous flooding represents the last major marine transgression into the heartland of the continent and the highest sea-level stand (Fig.

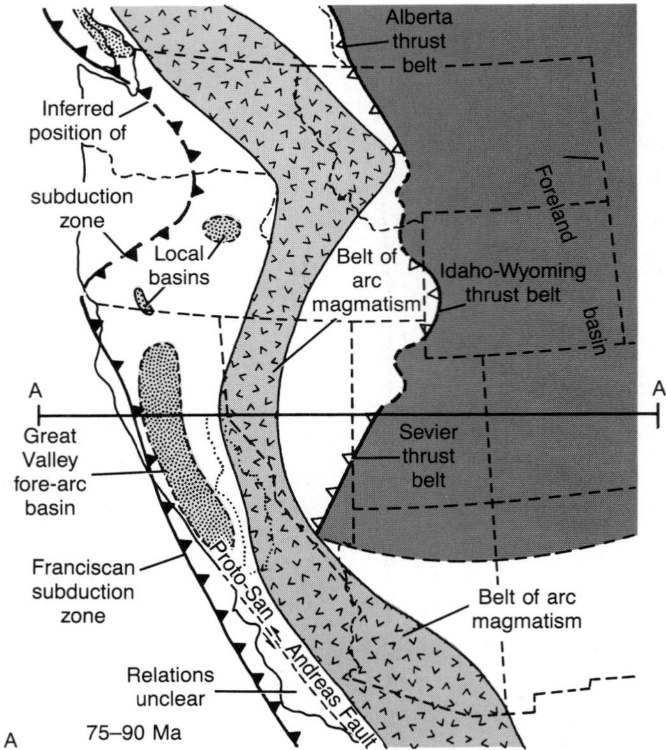

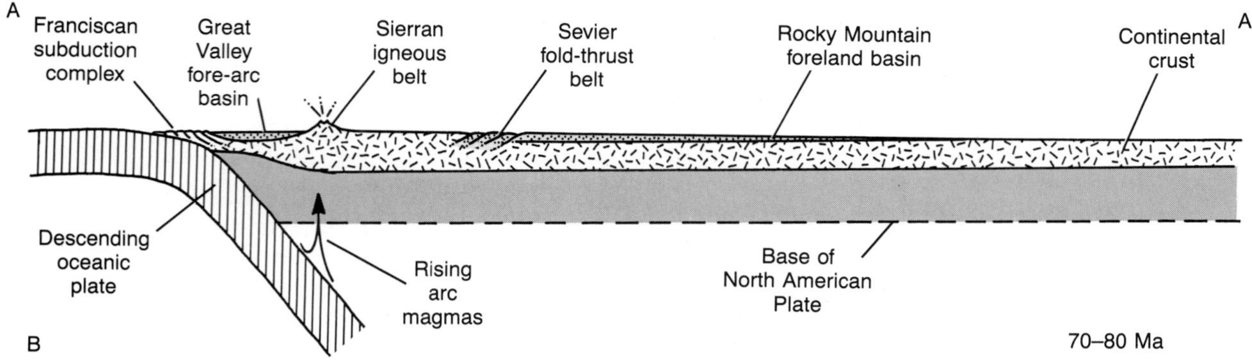

Figure 13–11

A. Paleotectonic and paleogeographic sketch map of Cordilleran region. Late Cretaceous, 75–90 Ma. B. Inferred configuration of subducted slab and associated tectonic elements during early Late Cretaceous Sevier orogeny phase of evolution of the Cordillera. Note Cretaceous interior seaway occupying a foreland basin cratonward of Sevier orogenic belt, itself a zone of back-arc thrusting related to subduction along continental margin.

(From W. R. Dickinson, 1979, Cenozoic Plate Tectonic Setting of the Cordilleran Region in the United States, Figs. 2a and 10, p. 4 and 11, *in Cenozoic Paleogeography of the Western United States:* SEPM Pacific Section, Pacific Coast Paleogeography Symposium 3. Used by permission of Pacific Section, Society of Economic Paleontologists and Mineralogists)

13–15) of the entire Phanerozoic, slightly exceeding that estimated for the Late Cambrian (Fig. 13–14). At its maximum extent, during the early Late Cretaceous, the seaway was more than 1500 km wide, stretching from Utah to Iowa. The eastern margin of the seaway sloped gently and subsided slowly. Comparatively little sediment was introduced from the emergent parts of the craton to the east, resulting in thickness of generally less than 100 m for the Cretaceous deposits in the eastern part of the inte-

Figure 13–12

East face of Spring Mountains (looking northwest), west of Las Vegas, Nevada, showing Keystone thrust, one of the major faults in the Sevier overthrust belt. Dark-colored rocks of upper plate are lower Paleozoic miogeoclinal and craton-margin carbonates; light-colored rocks of lower plate belong to eolian Lower Jurassic Aztec Sandstone (equivalent to Navajo).
(Photo courtesy of John S. Shelton)

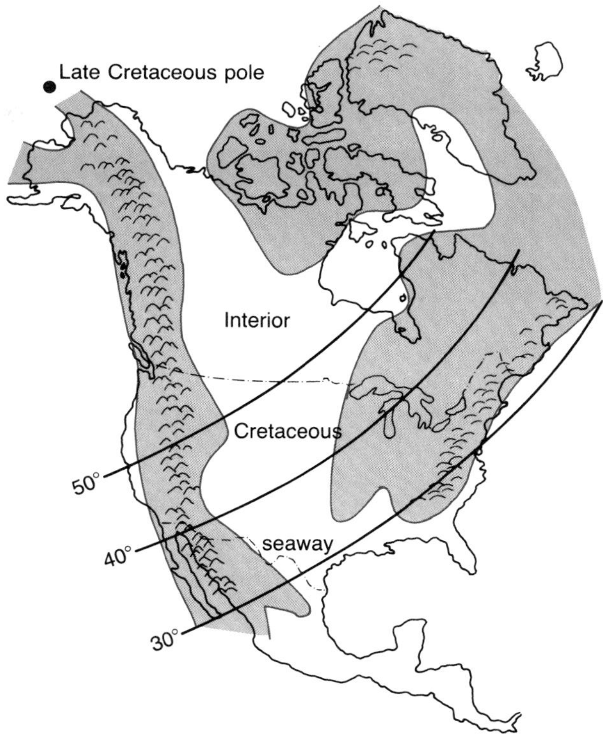

Figure 13–13

Generalized Late Cretaceous paleogeography of North America, showing extent of interior Cretaceous seaway.

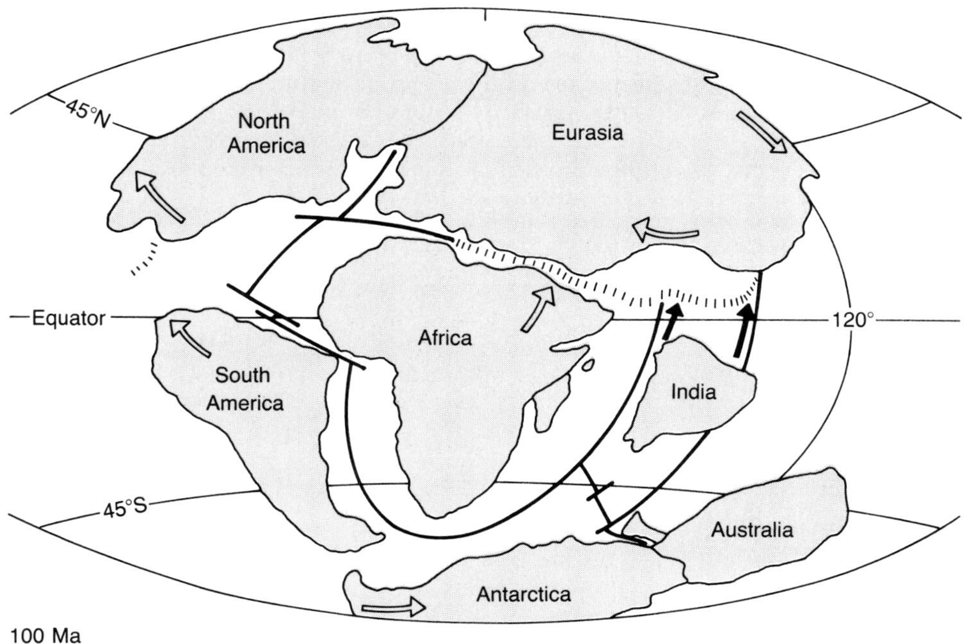

Figure 13–14

World paleogeography reconstruction for Early Cretaceous.
(From Critter Creations, San Diego, CA; and A. G. Smith, and J. C. Briden, 1977, Mesozoic and Cenozoic paleocontinental maps, no. 10, p. 21: Cambridge University Press, New York. Used with permission)

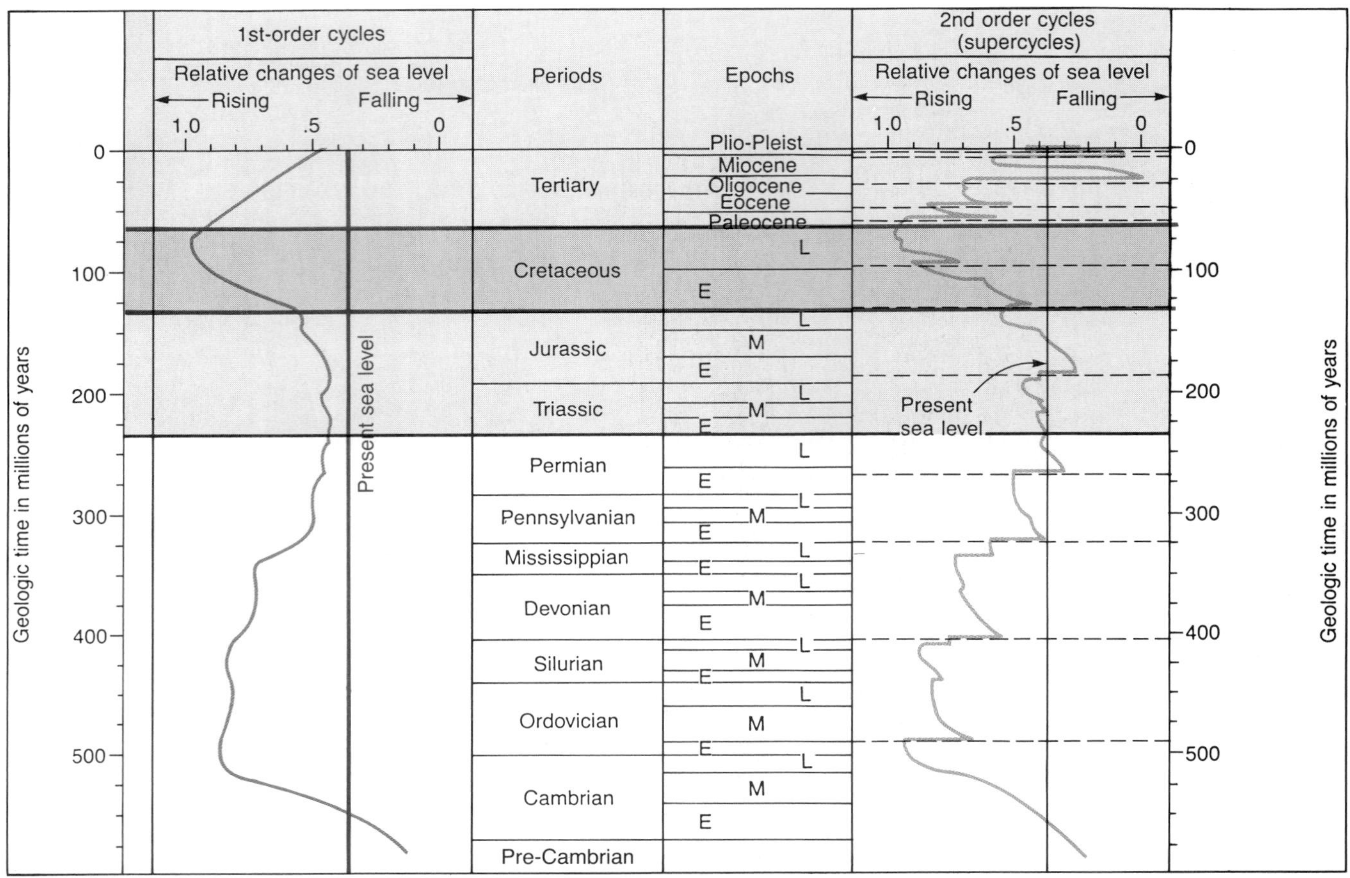

Figure 13–15
First- and second-order global cycles of relative sea-level change during Phanerozoic, highlighting early Late Cretaceous transgressive maximum. In recent years, detailed knowledge of ancient Phanerozoic sea-level changes has been enhanced by seismic stratigraphic techniques developed primarily within the petroleum industry. In such a context, subsurface discontinuities have been revealed that identify transgressive and regressive events. Cycles identified in the subsurface of continental margins commonly can be correlated with outcrop sections on land.
(After P. R. Vail, R. M. Mitchum, and S. Thompson II, 1977. Seismic Stratigraphy and Global Changes of Sea Level; Figs. 1, 2, p. 84, 85; *American Association of Petroleum Geologists Memoir,* 26. Reproduced by permission of American Association of Petroleum Geologists)

rior seaway. The Dakota Sandstone, a famous aquifer in the western interior of the United States, is a nearshore deposit of the initial transgression of the sea.

The depositional and stratigraphic patterns of this interior seaway bear evidence of the continuously growing Cordilleran mountain belt to the west Fig. 13–16). Abundant thin volcanic ash beds called **bentonites** are present in many Cretaceous sections in Montana, Wyoming, and Colorado and attest to continued volcanism in the western and central Cordilleran belt. The bulk of the sediment was supplied from Cordilleran highlands raised during the Sevier orogeny, along the western margin of the seaway. Here pronounced subsidence and sediment influx resulted in sequences more than 6000 m thick in places. The facies relationships show a progressive change from coarse sandstone and conglomerates adjacent to the source areas on the west, to finer sandstones, siltstones, and shales with a few tongues of limestone to the east.

Figure 13–16 depicts the dynamic transgressive-regressive patterns as recorded in onlap-offlap stratigraphic cycles, and the progressive offlap pattern of the sedimentary succession. These facies reflect alluvial-fan, coastal-plain, fluvial, beach, lagoon, barrier bar, delta, and marine-shelf paleoenvironments (Fig. 13–17). The stratigraphic patterns faithfully record the migration of these various environments over one another through time in response

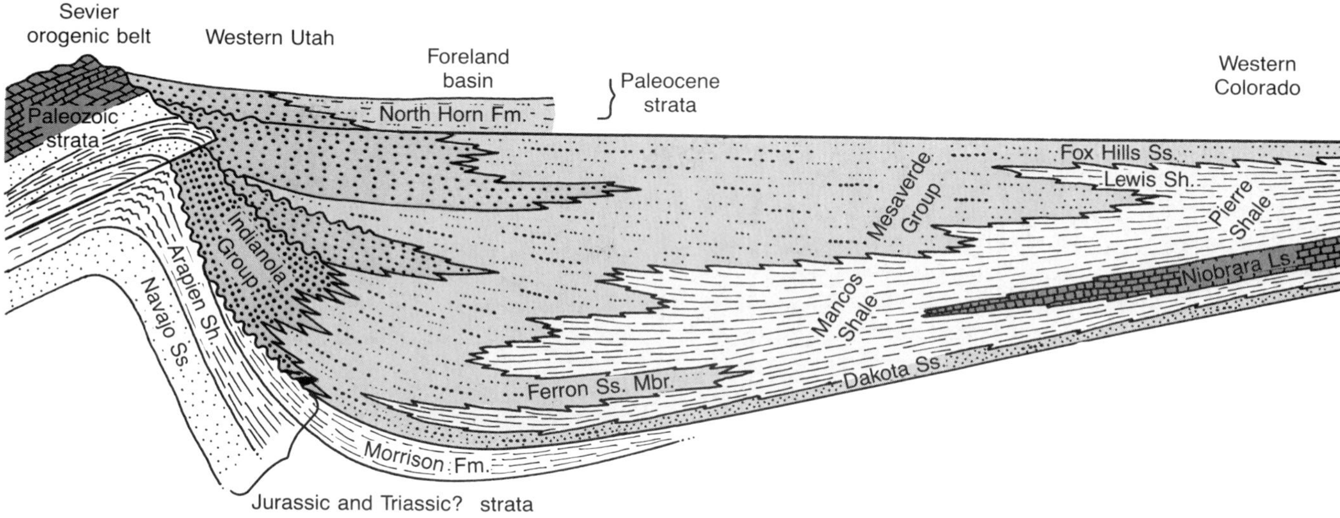

Figure 13–16

Restored west-east cross section of Cretaceous facies of western interior seaway and relationship to Sevier orogenic belt.

(From R. L. Armstrong, 1968, Sevier Orogenic Belt in Nevada and Utah; Fig. 5, p. 446: *Geological Society of America Bulletin,* vol. 79. Reproduced by permission of Geological Society of America and author)

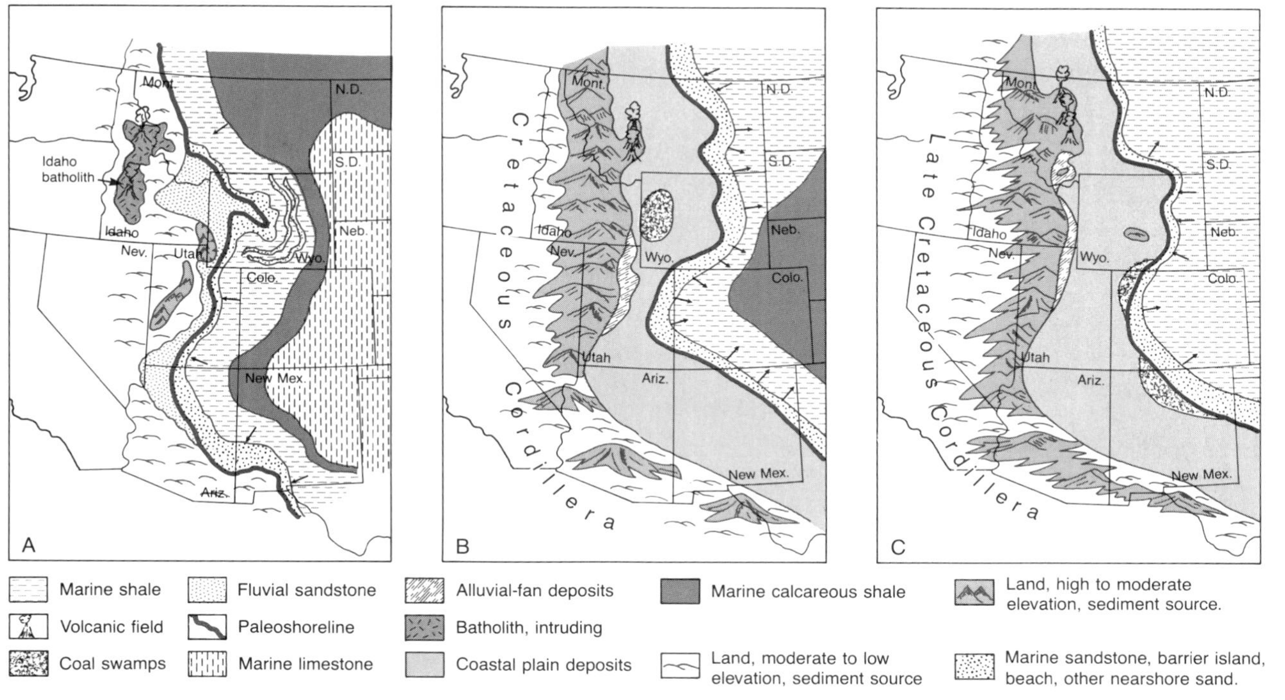

Figure 13–17

Paleogeography of western interior of United States. A. Early Late Cretaceous. B. middle Late Cretaceous (Campanian). C. Late Late Cretaceous (Maestrichtian).

(After D. P. McGookey, coord., 1972, Cretaceous System, Figs. 27, 40, 49, p. 209, 218, 224, *in Geologic Atlas of the Rocky Mountain Region:* Rocky Mountain Association of Geologists, Denver. Reproduced by permission of Rocky Mountain Association of Geologists)

to the relationship among tectonic activity (Sevier orogeny) in the source area, subsidence, and the varying amounts of detritus delivered to the depositional systems. In this context, the Cretaceous interior seaway is viewed as occupying a subsiding foreland basin whose subsidence was related to flexural loading of stacked imbricate thrust sheets. In this tectonic setting, the Cretaceous interior seaway was not an epeiric sea in the sense of the classic Paleozoic craton interior-platform shallow seas.

The thick sequence of Cretaceous terrigenous clastics that prograded from west to east comprises a great clastic wedge (Figs. 13–16 and 13–17). The relationship of this clastic wedge to the Cordilleran orogeny is reminiscent of the Ordovician Queenston, Devonian Catskill, and Carboniferous clastic wedges and their relationships to the Taconic, Acadian, and Alleghany phases, respectively, of the Appalachian orogeny. With regard to the last comparison, Cretaceous outcrops in the Four Corners region (junction of Arizona–Colorado–New Mexico–Utah) are progradational offlap sequences that record numerous fluctuations of strandlines and cyclic deposition. Examples of such outcrops are in Mesa Verde National Park, Colorado; in the San Juan Basin of northwestern New Mexico; and in the Book Cliffs in north-central Utah (Fig. 13–18). Much of the coal in the Rocky Mountains and Colorado Plateau is from these Cretaceous cyclic deposits that record deltaic, coastal-barrier, and lagoonal environments. Cretaceous sandstones in the subsurface of Wyoming, Colorado, and Montana also have produced significant hydrocarbons.

Black, organic-rich muds were the chief deposits of the more offshore shelf and slope parts of the Cretaceous interior seaway; they also occur in Cretaceous continental-margin deposits and in deep ocean cores. Black shales are particularly widespread in Europe and have become a facies trademark of the Cretaceous. Organic-rich black muds are the products of unusual environmental conditions, including a source of abundant organic carbon and preservation of the carbon from oxidation. It seems that major phases of black-mud deposition have corresponded with times of unusually deep transgressions. In its central portions, the Cretaceous interior seaway was oftentimes a deep marine basin. During the last half of the Cretaceous, warm, ice-free poles, and high sea-level stands (Fig. 13–15) favored black, organic-rich mud accumulation by promoting stagnant, anaerobic, bottom-water conditions. Climatic cycles might have caused repetitive intervals of unusually high organic production, and less vigorous deep oceanic circulation could explain the preservation through anoxia.

A

B

C

Figure 13–18
Cretaceous marine shelf and shoreface deposits. A. Book Cliffs, eastern Utah. B. Mesa Verde National Park, Colorado. C. Mesa de los Cartujanos, Sabinas Coal Basin, northeast Mexico.
(Photos by J. D. Cooper)

Such organic-rich black shales have provided the source beds for hydrocarbons that subsequently migrated into sandy reservoir facies in various parts of the Cordillera and other regions.

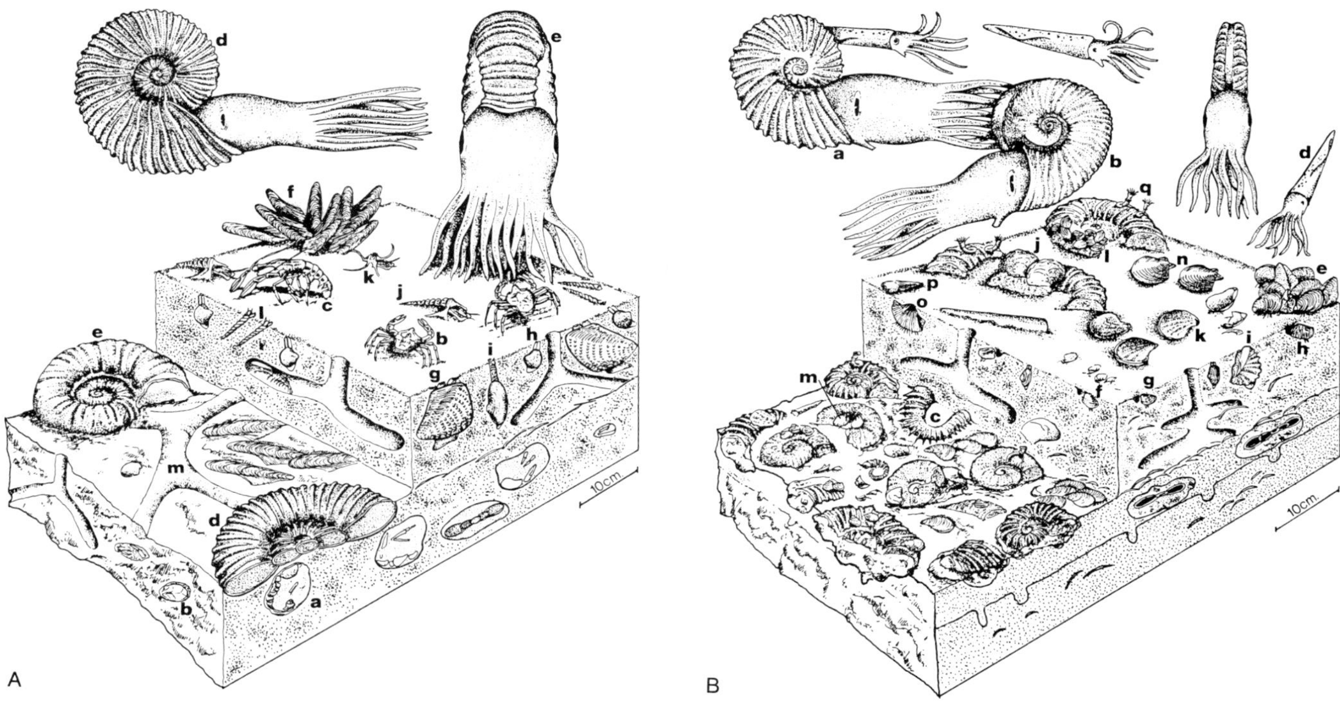

Figure 13–19

Cretaceous in-life community restorations. A. Early Cretaceous sandy-bottom invertebrate community: a–c, decapod crustaceans; d, e, ammonoid cephalopod molluscs; f–i, bivalve molluscs; j–l, gastropod molluscs; m, crustacean feeding trace. B. Early Cretaceous phosphate nodule-bed invertebrate community: a–c, ammonoid cephalopod molluscs; d, belemnoid cephalopod molluscs; e–o, bivalve molluscs; p, *Ichthyosaurus* tooth; q, annelid worms.

(From W. S. McKerrow, 1978, *The Ecology of Fossils,* Figs. 94, 96, p. 292, 296: MIT Press, all rights reserved. Reproduced with permission of MIT Press)

As the Cretaceous drew to a close, heightened tectonic activity and massive incursions of terrigenous clastics from the west, together with a slowing of global seafloor spreading, forced the withdrawal of this last great interior sea from the continent. The marine waters retreated to the north and south, and marginal marine and continental deposition took place. Widespread coastal-plain deposits formed as the seaway retreated. These deposits are locally coal-bearing, and include diverse fossil plants—and the last of the dinosaurs.

Marine Invertebrates

The nearshore and offshore marine-shelf environments of the interior sea and coastal regions teemed with life (Figs. 13–19A, B). Exceptionally fossiliferous deposits in the Gulf Coast and in the Great Plains areas of Alberta, eastern Montana, the Dakotas, Nebraska, and Kansas attest to seas populated with diverse cephalopod, bivalve, and gastropod molluscs (Figs. 13–19A, B). Many of the ammonite cephalopods from the Pierre Shale in the western interior are beautifully preserved and still retain the pearly luster of their aragonitic shells.

Rapidly evolving Cretaceous ammonite faunas have permitted refined biostratigraphic zonations that have greatly facilitated both intracontinental and intercontinental correlation. Cretaceous ammonites show an amazing diversity (Fig. 13–20) related to many different adaptations and life habits in the marine realm. Unfortunately, the lack of modern-day close relatives of this fascinating group of marine invertebrates has severely limited our understanding of their paleoecology.

Cretaceous rocks also contain the first evidence of planktonic foraminifera, as well as the microscopic plates of calcareous floating marine algae, the coccolithophorids. The fine-grained calcareous skeletal material of these organisms contributed to the deposits of chalk on marine shelves. Diatoms also became abundant for the first time during the Cretaceous, and their photosynthesis, coupled with that of the coccolithophorids, may have resulted in significant increases of atmospheric oxygen.

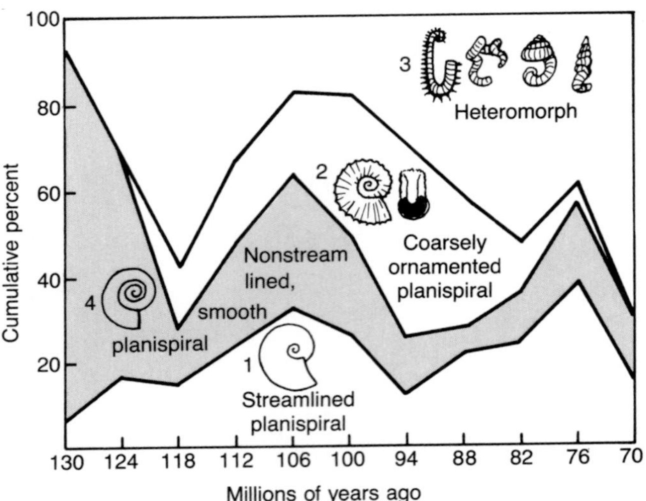

Figure 13–20

Three evolutionary trends in Cretaceous ammonite shell types—1, streamlined; 2, ornamented; 3, heteromorphic. All developed at the expense of 4 (non-streamlined, smooth planispiral forms that characterized most Jurassic ammonoids). Paleontologist Peter Ward interprets this trend as an expression of adaptation to the selective pressures exerted by progressively more sophisticated marine predators, such as teleost fish and marine reptiles, that evolved during the Jurassic and Cretaceous. The smooth exterior and laterally compressed cross section in 1 reduced drag, and tight coiling increased hydrodynamic stability, both factors contributing to agility and speed in swimming, an advantage in outmaneuvering and escaping predators. Broad cross section and comparatively loose coiling in 2 made shell less well adapted for swimming, but coarse ornamentation may have evolved to discourage shell-crunching predators. As shown by the graph, however, this trend was the least successful. Most of the heteromorphs (3) were probably well-poised and balanced floaters.

(Adapted from Peter Ward, 1983. The Extinction of the Ammonites, p. 139; *Scientific American*, vol. 249, no. 4, copyright 1983 by Scientific American. All rights reserved. Used with permission)

Peculiar oysters assigned to the genera *Exogyra* (Fig. 13–21A) and *Gryphaea* are locally abundant in Cretaceous invertebrate faunas. Another interesting group of Cretaceous bivalve molluscs were asymmetrical, sessile clams called rudists (Fig. 13–21D). Most bivalve molluscs, modern and ancient, have shell forms that are sensitive indicators of their life habits. The rudists were no exception; the shape, size, and robustness of rudist shells are good paleoecologic indicators of shallow-water depth and high energy. Because of their superficial resemblance to certain rugose corals, rudists provide a good example of convergent evolution. Rudists, along with scleractinian corals, coralline algae, and bryozoans, were important contributors to Cretaceous reefs and were the most important frame builders for the Edwards Reef and smaller patch reefs of back-reef platform areas.

Cretaceous reefs of the Gulf Coast region are yet another example of the reef ecosystem. The geologic history of reef communities is testimony to the resiliency of a most important association of organisms. Prior to the Cretaceous, the reef ecosystem had suffered two major calamities: the first near the end of the Devonian, and the second at the end of the Permian, as part of the end-of-Paleozoic faunal crisis. After each collapse, reef communities resurged with renewed vigor as new populations and taxa of reef-builders and reef-dwellers filled niches in the ecosystem. Rudists possessed a shell form well adapted for existence in high-energy reefs. One species found in Cretaceous reef limestones in Jamaica has a shell more than 1 m long and more than 10 cm thick.

The presence of rudists in Cretaceous deposits of the West Indies and Gulf Coast regions reflects the spread of Tethyan-realm faunas and tropical paleoecologic conditions. When Pangaea formed during the late Paleozoic, a large oceanic indentation developed on its eastern side in tropical latitudes. This body, the Tethys Sea, was a most hospitable marine realm during the Permian, and spawned some of the richest reef faunas that have ever existed. The Tethyan realm extended westward during the Mesozoic as Africa separated from Europe and North America (Fig. 13–22).

The Tethys Sea, generally synonymous with the tropical marine belt during the Mesozoic, provided a region of stable conditions for invertebrate life. Extensive Triassic reefs in the Alps were nurtured in the resource-rich western end of Tethys. The break up of Pangaea, the opening of the Atlantic, the establishment of a major zone of east-to-west tropical currents, and the flooding of parts of the continents in the mid-Cretaceous paved the way for expansion of the stable Tethyan-type conditions to other regions in the tropical belt. The rudists exemplify the spread of Tethys paleobiogeography from the Mediterranean into the Caribbean and Gulf Coast regions during the late Mesozoic as continental breakups reached the point where the tropical marine belt nearly circumscribed the globe (Fig. 13–22).

Cretaceous Vertebrates

Marine vertebrates found the Cretaceous seas much to their liking. Ray-finned bony fishes diversified dramatically during the period, and the western interior seaway in particular included among its in-

Figure 13–21

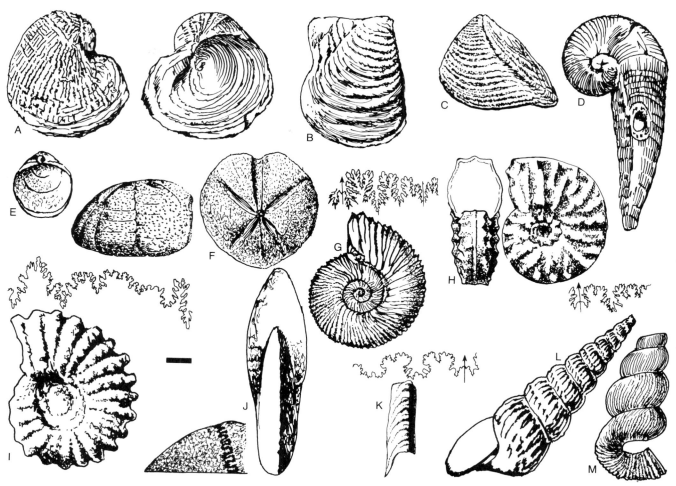

Representative Cretaceous invertebrate fossils. A–D. Bivalve molluscs (D, rudist clam); E. Articulate brachiopod. F. Echinoid echinoderm. G–M. Ammonite cephalopod molluscs with suture patterns highlighted. (K–M are heteromorph forms.) Bar is 1 cm.

(From *Treatise on Invertebrate Paleontology,* Geological Society of America and University of Kansas Press)

Figure 13–22

Mid-Cretaceous world geography showing extent of tropical Tethyan conditions.

(From E. G. Kauffman and C. C. Johnson, 1988, The Morphological and Ecological Evolution of Middle and Upper Cretaceous Reef-Building Rudistids, Fig. 1, p. 195: *Palaios,* vol. 3, no. 2)

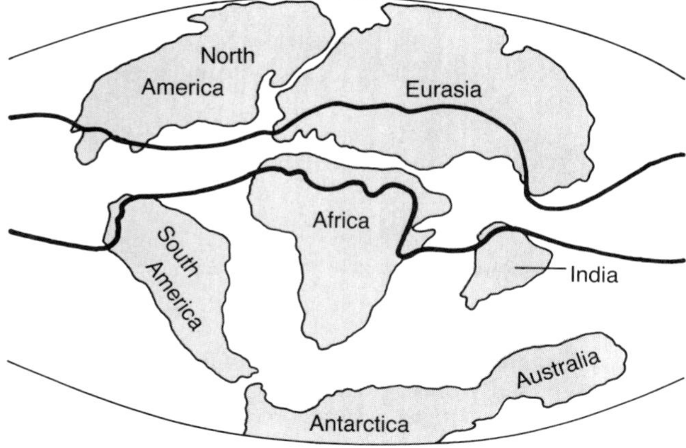

Figure 13–23
Giant marine turtle from deposits of Cretaceous interior seaway.
(Photo courtesy of Peabody Museum of Natural History)

habitants a horde of aquatic reptiles. Fossils of large sea turtles (Fig. 13–23), marine lizards called mosasaurs (Fig. 13–24), and the ichthyosaurs and plesiosaurs grace many museum halls. In the fossils, paddle-shaped limbs and streamlined bodies are the most characteristic structural adaptations that accommodated reptilian life in the sea (Fig. 13–25).

After the delicate preservation of *Archaeopteryx* in the Late Jurassic Solenhofen Limestone, there is a 50-million-year gap in the fossil record of bird evolution. Cretaceous bird fossils, although rare, include specimens representing several of the modern orders: ducks, grebes, and pelicans. Perhaps best known is the large, flightless bird *Hesperornis,* well adapted to life in the sea, where it could swim and dive. Pterosaurs (Fig. 13–26) were also present, and were probably outcompeted by birds before the end of the Cretaceous. Recent research has demonstrated that pterosaurs were probably more efficient fliers than once thought, and were capable of fully powered flapping flight as opposed to simple gliding. A Late Cretaceous pterosaur from western Texas had a wing span of over 10 m.

Cretaceous mammals, although somewhat more advanced than their Jurassic predecessors, were nonetheless small, primitive forms that played a distinctly subordinate role to the dinosaurs. Skeletal material beyond the customary jaws and teeth has been collected at Bug Creek and Hell Creek, Montana. Marsupials (some probably ancestral to the common opossum) and early placental mammals number among the more than 25,000 specimens that have been recovered from these significant localities. It is interesting to consider that mammals evolved at the same time as dinosaurs and lived, for a span of time nearly triple that of their later success, as small creatures in the nooks and crannies of a world dominated by dinosaurs.

Cretaceous dinosaurs reached a range of adaptive types not previously attained. Like other groups of tetrapods, the dinosaurs evolved many specialized herbivores and relatively few carnivores. The meat-eating theropods, although in the minority, served an important role in maintaining a balanced eco-

Figure 13–24
Fossilized skeleton of *Tylosaurus,* a mosasaur from the Cretaceous interior seaway. Skeleton is nearly 3 m in length.
(Photo courtesy of National Museum of Natural History. Smithsonian Institution Photo No. 1145)

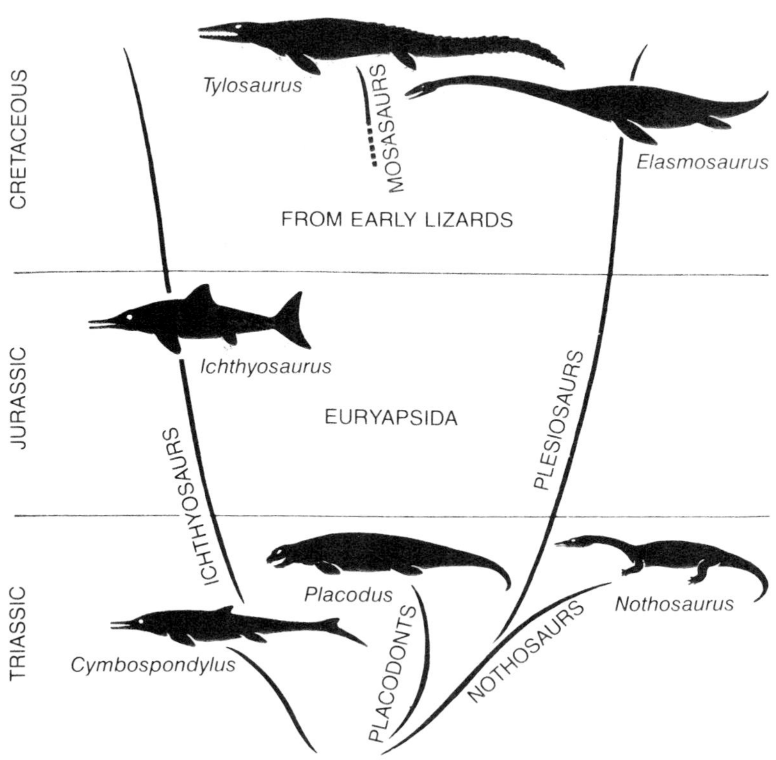

Figure 13–25
Evolutionary relationship of Mesozoic marine reptiles.
(From E. H. Colbert, *Evolution of the Vertebrates—A History of the Backboned Animals Through Time;* 3d ed., Fig. 68, p. 175. Copyright © 1980 by John Wiley & Sons, Inc., New York. Reproduced by permission of John Wiley & Sons, Inc., and Lois M. Darling)

system by functioning as a form of population control. The most popularized of the Cretaceous theropods is *Tyrannosaurus rex,* a voracious flesh eater who reached lengths of more than 12 m, stood about 6 m high, and weighed 5 to 10 metric tons (Fig. 13–27). Although varied in size, the theropods typically possessed large, strong hind limbs with large hooked claws protruding from the three toes. Their forelegs were much smaller, but also bore sharp claws, and the oversized powerful jaws were lined with doubly serrated stabbing teeth.

The herbivorous ornithischians diversified into a fantastic array of adaptive types and had a range of dental patterns well adapted for browsing, cutting, cropping, and chewing. The stegosaurs (Fig. 12–22, Chapter 12) possessed a double row of about 20 alternating, erect, immovable plates along their arched backs. These dorsal plates, laced with blood

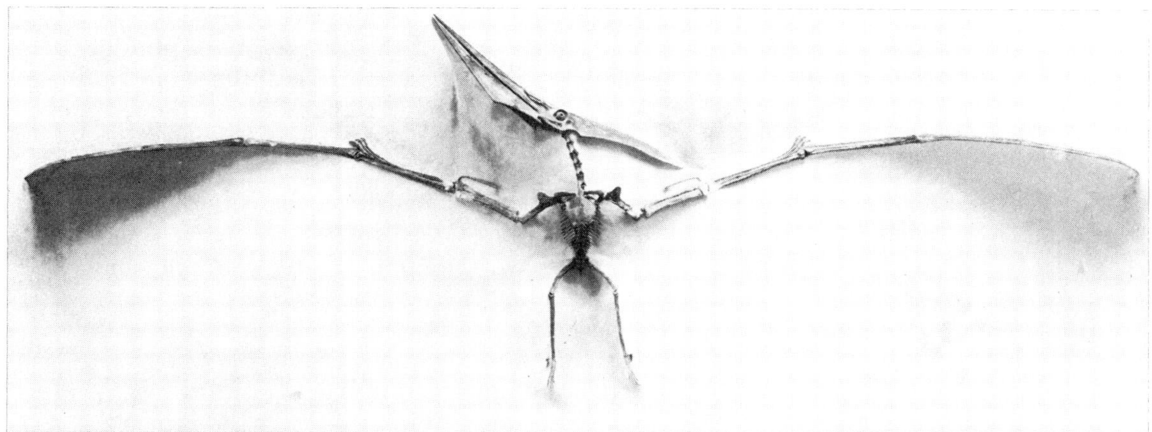

Figure 13–26
Fossilized skeleton of *Pteranodon,* a pterosaur from the Cretaceous of the western interior of the United States. Specimen is about 5 m from wingtip to wingtip.
(Photo courtesy of National Museum of Natural History. Smithsonian Institution Photo No. 28138)

Figure 13–27
Restoration of scene in northern Rockies and Great Plains region during the Late Cretaceous (80 Ma). Plants include angiosperms, some of which resemble living types. Dinosaurs, left to right: duck-billed ornithopod *Edmontosaurus*, aquatic plant eater; *Triceratops*, horned plant eater; and two voracious theropod predators—*Gorgosaurus* (left) and *Tyrannosaurus* (right)—confronting each other.
(Photo courtesy of National Museum of Natural History. Smithsonian Institution Photo No. 81-16573)

vessels, probably functioned mainly for thermoregulation. They also may have afforded some protection, as did two tail spikes. Stegosaurs had an enlarged opening at the spinal base that may have housed nerves from the legs and body mass where they entered the spinal cord, or they may have been air space to aid in cooling during periods of heightened activity.

During the Cretaceous, the stegosaurs were succeeded by a group of bulky, squat ornithischians, the ankylosaurs (Fig. 13–28), which had tough bony plates that covered their 6-m-long bodies and short, sharp, sturdy spikes along their flanks. Their tails terminated in a bludgeonlike knot of bone. With their compact construction and surface armor, the ankylosaurs show definite evolutionary advances toward protection against predators.

A third ornithischian suborder was the Ornithopoda (Fig. 13–28), a bipedal group that diversified dramatically during the Cretaceous. Commonly called duckbilled dinosaurs because of their flattened jaw, the ornithopods had cheek teeth well adapted for grinding vegetation. Some dental patterns were particularly well-suited for grinding and macerating coarse, abrasive plants such as the newly evolved angiosperms. The first dinosaur remains ever reported (teeth and a few bone fragments) were found in 1822 and belonged to what later would become known as the ornithopod genus *Iguanodon*. These unusual fossils were presented to the great French anatomist, Baron George Cuvier, who suggested they belonged to a large extinct reptile about the size of a rhino.

Near the end of the Cretaceous, a group of ornithopods called hadrosaurs became large and abundant, and many evolved bony crests, domes, and tubular outgrowths of the nasal passages on the top of the skull (Fig. 13–29). The first recorded dinosaur skeleton discovered in North America was a hadrosaur from Cretaceous beds near Haddonfield, New Jersey. Different crest forms may have been adapted for a variety of functions, but were not, as commonly hypothesized, snorkels for underwater activity. Some domal outgrowths may have cushioned the impact from butting during courtship ritual. The more-tubular outgrowths may have been structural adaptations for improved sense of smell and perhaps for making hooting and honking sounds as a means of verbal communication. Remarkable preservation of nests and egg clutches in

MESOZOIC HISTORY

Dinosaur footprint on mudstone bed of Newark Supergroup, Dinosaur State Park, Connecticut. This is one of dozens of footprints in trackway patterns left by early dinosaurs in their trek across a late Triassic mud flat.

A.

Mesozoic history began with a supercontinent largely intact and ended with supercontinent breakup and another mass extinction event, highlighted by the demise of dinosaurs and ammonoid cephalopods. One characteristic of the early Mesozoic is the pervasive occurrence of red beds. This widespread production of red beds is a holdover from late Permian time when there was large-scale oxidation of nonmarine sediments on a supercontinent.

Red beds in late Paleozoic-Triassic section exposed in canyon of the Colorado River, Deadhorse Point State Park, near Moab, Utah.

B.

A.

B.

C.

In Patterns of Red

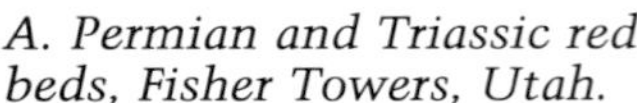

A. Permian and Triassic red beds, Fisher Towers, Utah.

B. Petrified conifer logs weathered out from Upper Triassic Chinle Formation, Petrified Forest National Park, Arizona.

C. Colorful succession of Triassic strata, Capitol Reef National Park, Utah.

A.

B.

A. Triassic sequence, Vermillion Cliffs, Arizona.

B. Lower Jurassic red beds of fluvial channel and overbank origin near St. George, Utah.

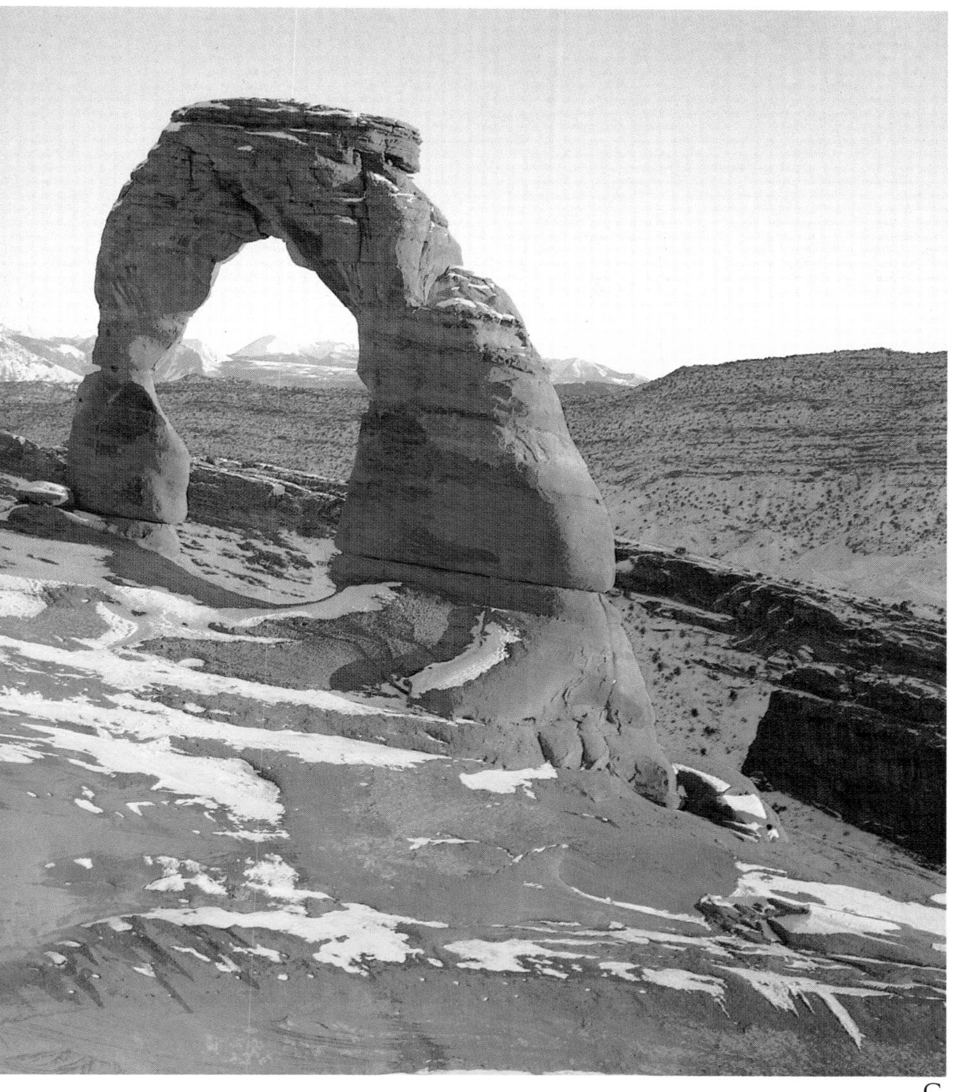

C.

Exquisite erosional sculpturing of Jurassic sandstone, Arches National Park, Utah. Scenery such as this, featuring curious and beautiful landforms developed on Triassic and Jurassic red beds and eolian sandstones, has inspired the creation of several western national parks.

Sand, Sand, Everywhere

During the Early Jurassic, much of western North America was the site of a gigantic dune field, similar to the modern Sahara. This produced extensive sheets of windblown sand, now expressed as fossilized dunes in stratigraphic units such as the Navajo Sandstone.

A.

A. Outcrop exposure of cross-bedded eolian sandstone of the Lower Jurassic Navajo Sandstone, Zion Canyon National Park, Utah.

B. Modern dune analogue serves as an actualistic model for the environment of the Navajo Sandstone.

C. Thin-section photomicrograph showing details of the well-rounded, well-sorted pure quartz sand grains of the Navajo Sandstone.

B.

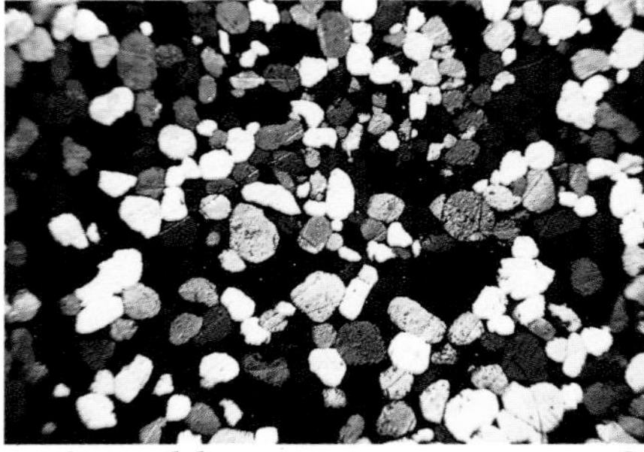

Scale: width is 2.5 mm

C.

Cretaceous Deposits

A.

White cliff exposures of chalk, Dover Coast, England. Chalk is a fine-grained limestone composed of microscopic shells of planktonic calcareous microorganisms. Cretaceous, from creta, the Celtic word for chalk, was a time of extensive development of these pelagic chalk deposits.

B.

Upper Cretaceous delta plain deposits, northwestern Colorado. The dark layer is a coal seam representing accumulation of delta plain vegetation. Mining of Cretaceous coal in the Rocky Mountain west has produced an important source of energy, but has also raised environmental concerns regarding degradation of scenic lands and air pollution.

Mesozoic Life

A

Jurassic ammonoid cephalopods, Germany. Mesozoic seas swarmed with schools of swimming ammonoid cephalopods, but they were victims of a major mass extinction event that defines the end of an era. (Scale: specimen in upper left is 4 cm across.)

B

Cretaceous oysters of modern type—a survivor of the mass extinction. The genus Crassostrea *has continued a successful lineage to the present day; however, several other kinds of Mesozoic oysters did not survive the end-of-Cretaceous calamity.*

C

Cretaceous sea urchin. Mesozoic echinoderms were dominated by bottom-crawling echinoids in contrast to the attached crinoids that flourished during the Paleozoic. (Scale: specimen is 10 cm across.)

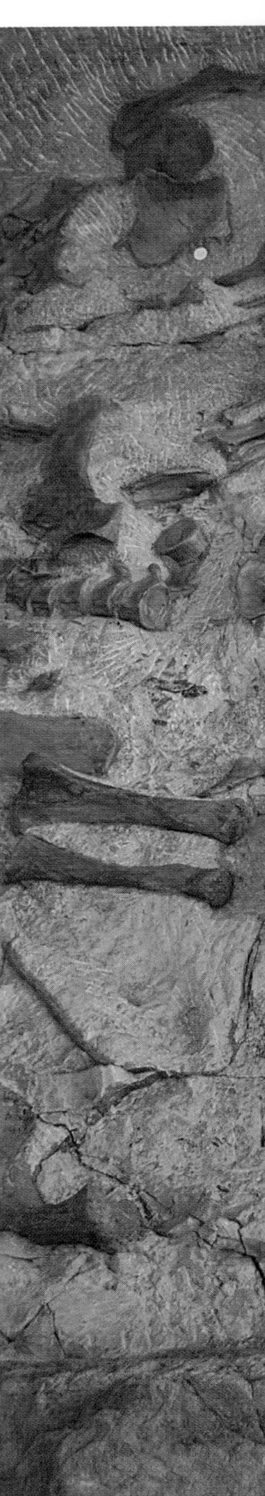

Graveyard of the Dinosaurs

This bedding surface in the Upper Jurassic Morrison Formation, exposed in the working quarry at Dinosaur National Monument, Utah, contains a plethora of bones from several kinds of dinosaurs that dwelled on a Late Jurassic flood plain. So successful and dominant among land vertebrates for more than 130 million years, the dinosaurs were victims of the mass extinction event that brought the Mesozoic, the age of reptiles, to a dramatic close.

THE END OF AN ERA

Does a thin clay layer hold the key to the mystery of the "great dying" at the end of the Mesozoic?

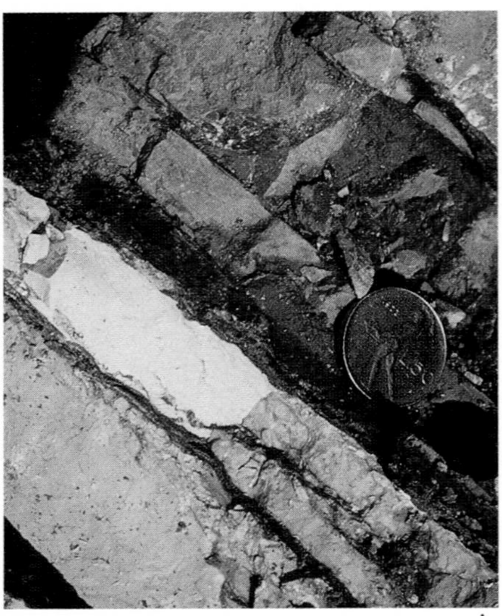

A.

The K-T boundary clay layer (highlighted by white strip just below 2 cm diameter 50 Lira coin) at the Cretaceous-Tertiary boundary stratotype section near Gubbio, Italy. Anomalously high occurrences of the rare platinum group element iridium, as well as concentration of tiny altered basaltic spherules (interpreted as impact droplets) in this thin layer suggest fallout from the impact of a large comet or asteroid 65 million years ago. The boundary clay layer is sandwiched between the uppermost Cretaceous pelagic limestone, typically white in this region, and the lowermost red limestone of the Tertiary.

B.

C.

D.

B., C., D. Could such an impact 65 million years ago have triggered a chain reaction through the biosphere that resulted in the mass extinction of such disparate groups of organisms as terrestrial dinosaurs, planktonic foraminifers, and swimming marine ammonoid cephalopods? Did the dinosaurs succumb to bad genes or bad luck?

Figure 13–28
Cretaceous ornithopods, right and left; ankylosaur at lower center.
(C. R. Knight mural, courtesy Field Museum of Natural History)

Upper Cretaceous alluvial-plain sediments in Montana suggest that hadrosaurs nested in large, densely packed colonies, guarded their eggs, and guarded and fed their young in the nest. This is behavior more characteristic of warm-blooded animals than of cold-blooded reptiles.

Figure 13–29
Examples of crest forms in some Cretaceous hadrosaurs.
(C. R. Knight mural, courtesy Field Museum of Natural History, Chicago)

The fourth group of ornithischians included the quadrupedal, horned forms of the suborder Ceratopsia. The earliest form, *Protoceratops,* was small and lacked horns, but had the characteristic beaklike jaw front. Fossilized *Protoceratops* eggs were found in Lower Cretaceous rocks in Mongolia during the highly publicized Central Asiatic Expedition of the American Museum of Natural History in the 1920s. *Triceratops* had a pair of horns that projected from the skull over the eyes, and a median horn just above the nostrils (Fig. 13–27). The head was large and had a shieldlike posterior extension for protection and for attachment of jaw and neck muscles. In the very Late Cretaceous, vast herds of *Triceratops* had spread to all continents, and the uppermost stratigraphic occurrence of *Triceratops* fossils helps define the Cretaceous-Paleogene boundary in continental deposits of the western interior.

The Hot-Blooded Dinosaur Controversy

Historically, dinosaurs have been regarded as the epitome of extinction. They have been viewed as evolutionary failures and oversized, inefficient hulks that plodded through life toward ultimate extinction. The 1970s witnessed a rebirth of dinosaur research highlighted by pronouncements that dinosaurs, like their vertebrate cousins the mammals and birds, were warm blooded. This idea has become a subject of controversy between more traditional vertebrate paleontologists and a small but vocal group of nontraditionalists.

Cast into the role of unreptilelike reptiles, dinosaurs have become the subject of renewed research aimed particularly at obtaining a better understanding of their bioenergetics and behavior. This research has shed new light on the dinosaurs' role in past tetrapod ecosystems. This new perspective regards them as anatomically efficient and behaviorally complex—an amazing group of animals with a wide range of adaptations, and much more than just an evolutionary novelty. Regardless of the final outcome of the hot-blooded dinosaur controversy, this research has dispelled many myths concerning these fascinating beasts.

Paleontologist Robert Bakker is one of the leaders in the renaissance of dinosaur research. Bakker asserts that most, and perhaps all, dinosaurs were not true reptiles, but were **endothermic** (warm-blooded) animals, more like mammals and birds in their physiology. The radical idea of warm-blooded dinosaurs was sparked during the 1960s by John Ostrom's discovery in Montana of a small bipedal dinosaur, named *Deinonychus,* that he described as fleet-footed, highly predaceous, extremely agile, and very active—anything but reptilian in its behavior, responses, and way of life. The suggestion was that this dinosaur, and perhaps others, might have had a metabolic rate similar to that of birds or mammals—a radical idea that conflicted with conventional wisdom. Bakker, a student of Ostrom's at Yale, felt this made perfect sense, and he has devoted a career to trying to prove it.

Bakker's hot-blooded dinosaur argument has advanced along several fronts. He cites predator-prey ratios as being one of the most reliable lines of evidence to support the notion that dinosaurs were warm blooded. The idea here is that a given population of prey animals can support far fewer warm-blooded predators than cold-blooded ones, because of the much larger energy requirements of the more active warm-blooded predators. Bakker compared the numbers of flesh-eating dinosaurs versus herbivores from several assumed predator-prey paleoecologic assemblages representing different stratigraphic levels and geographic localities. He found the ratio of predators to prey, expressed as biomass percent, to be very low—generally less than 20%—which is comparable to the ratio of modern lions to zebras. Predator-to-prey ratios among ectotherms are higher, generally greater than 50%. This line of evidence alone supports the idea that only the predators were warm-blooded, but even then only if the critical assumption is correct that the specimens collected from each locality accurately portray the abundance of the kinds of dinosaurs that coexisted, and more importantly, truly represent in-place assemblages.

Bakker has suggested that the erect limbs of dinosaurs were associated with high body temperatures and activity levels, as they are in modern mammals. Their great size actually may have been a help rather than a hindrance in keeping active. Since large animals have much less surface area in relation to body mass than smaller animals, there is relatively less surface exposed for heat gain or loss. This could have been the key to sauropod success, and perhaps to dinosaur success in general—the maintenance of a rather constant body temperature. Bakker further cites *bone histology,* in particular, as strong evidence of endothermy in dinosaurs. He noted that the density of capillaries and Haversian canals (loci for complex calcium-phosphate exchanges) in dinosaur bone cross-sections shows striking similarity to the patterns in birds and mammals.

Paleontologist John Horner, from his laborious and meticulous field work in Upper Cretaceous beds in the Willow Creek anticline of the Montana badlands, has collected a number of dinosaur growth series, with individuals within a species ranging from fossilized embryos, to babies, to juveniles, to full-grown adults. Horner pursued the idea of collecting growth series to get data on growth rate; fast-growing bone, characteristic of mammals, has a high density of vascular canals. **Ectotherms,** like reptiles, grow slowly, and their bone structure has a low density of canals and has growth-arrest lines.

Horner's work has demonstrated the combination of very fast growth rate (up to 3 m in one year!) and bone structure that is more characteristic of an endotherm (Fig. 13–30). Horner's sharp eye for fossils has also uncovered a number of fossilized nesting sites, including eggs (some with embryos), hatchlings, and various stages of young, together with fossilized regurgitated food. These remarkable fossilized nesting sites bear evidence of care for the young, yet another endothermic trait.

Bakker has also calculated the "cruising" speeds of a number of fossil dinosaurs. Based on the way their limbs were constructed and the style of preserved footprint trackways, he maintains they were adapted for moving continuously, not lying about like lizards. He believes some dinosaurs were fast cruisers, and that even some of the gargantuan sauropods were capable of cruising at speeds over 3 miles per hour. Such a pace, Bakker maintains, would have been necessary if they migrated, as for example, looking for fresh new vegetation, much

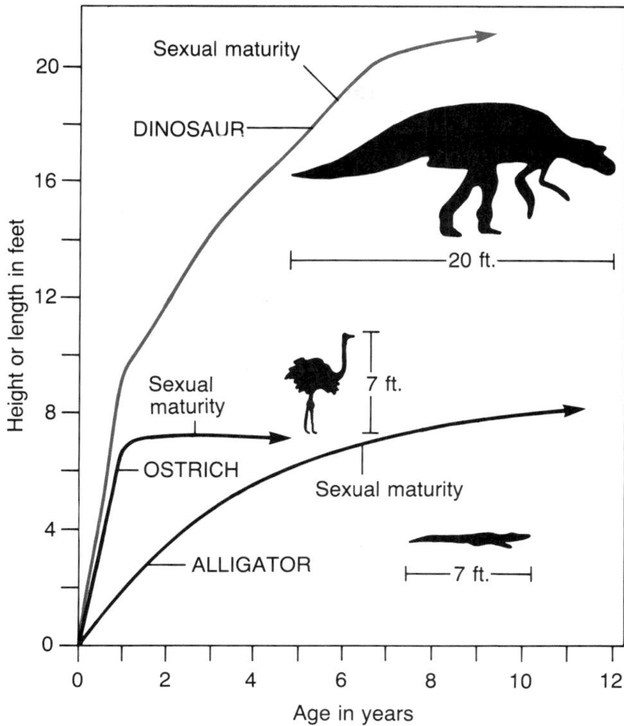

Figure 13–30

In the rapid growth of their early years, dinosaurs are closer to the warm-blooded ostrich than to the cold-blooded alligator.

(From Virginia Morrel, 1987, Announcing the Birth of a Heresy, p. 41: *Discover*, vol. 8, no. 3. Reproduced with permission of *Discover*)

like herds of elephants in present-day East Africa. Cold-blooded animals like reptiles do not migrate; they do not have the sustained capacity for exercise because they do not have the high metabolism required for such activity. There is abundant evidence that many hadrosaurs were gregarious and traveled in herds, perhaps for social contact and protection.

Some researchers have drawn on the herding behavior of East African elephants, and closer to home, musk oxen and caribou, to explain the vast dinosaur bone beds at Dinosaur Provincial Park in Alberta, Canada, only 200 km north across the border from Horner's Montana sites. Along Alberta's Red Deer River, for a distance of 250 km, complete skeletons of various ceratopsians and hadrosaurs lie together in groups of 10 or more.

An interesting comparison between the coeval Alberta and Montana beds is that the former have yielded no fossil nesting sites. Sedimentologic studies suggest that the Montana area was in a somewhat more upland setting, closer to highlands, where the dinosaurs preferred to nest. The Alberta area was in a more coastal, low relief, vegetation-rich setting, subject to wetting and drying—a good place to feed, but not to nest.

Perhaps the most difficult problem facing the endothermy hypothesis concerns the gargantuan size of many dinosaurs, particularly the ponderous sauropods. If the large sauropods were endothermic, they would have required an enormous daily food consumption. True endotherms, which regulate their body heat internally, require much more fuel to generate that internal heat than ectotherms, which depend on external heat sources to warm up to optimal temperatures. The real stumbling block then becomes one of size: if an adult African elephant, weighing 7 or 8 metric tons, consumes 125 to 250 kilograms of fodder every 24 hours, should we believe that *Brachiosaurus* ate the same amount as a dozen elephants?

In recent years, the hot-blooded dinosaur has become a popular subject of research and discussion at scientific meetings. A number of critics of endothermy are willing to accept the possibility that many dinosaurs, although not truly endothermic like mammals and birds, were nonetheless capable of achieving a nearly stable body temperature through various styles of thermoregulation, such as basking. The elephantine bodies of such sauropods as *Apatosaurus* and *Brachiosaurus* might have acted as huge heat reservoirs; once heated up they would have cooled off slowly in an equable subtropical climate, and thus maintained operating temperature without a critical need for internal heat regulation. This kind of semiconstant body temperature maintenance is called *homeothermy*, and may have allowed some of the larger dinosaurs to have frequent, short-term, high-exercise metabolism, permitting bursts of high activity.

Undeniable, though, is the erect posture of dinosaurs, whereby walking and running were accomplished with the legs held in near-vertical position. This erect posture is found today in mammals and birds, all of which are endothermic and capable of prolonged activity. By contrast, most living ectothermic land vertebrates have a more sprawling posture, and their walking and running gaits take the form of a more cumbersome sideways, waddling motion.

Perhaps the real answer to the endothermy-versus-ectothermy riddle is couched in compromise: some dinosaurs probably were ectotherms like modern reptiles; many may well have been homeothermic, capable of sustaining frequent bursts of energy and activity; and perhaps the most active, smaller bipedal hunting carnivores were true endotherms. Also undeniable is that in their 140 million years on Earth, the dinosaurs not only thrived, but occupied a wide variety of ecological niches. They also achieved an amazing diversity, which has only recently come to light; at least 40% of all known species have been described since the early 1960s.

Another Faunal Crisis and the End of an Era

The Cretaceous Period was a rich time in the history of life, and the fossil record presents a dazzling array of forms. The end of the period, however, was a time of crisis as numerous groups of organisms became extinct. Cretaceous marine invertebrate faunas had a distinctly modern look, despite abundant forms such as the ammonites that did not survive the end of the period. Separation of continents and the onset of latitudinally zoned climates promoted increased provincialism and faunal diversity (Fig. 13–31). During the Triassic and Jurassic, marine faunal provinces were few, and the number of cosmopolitan species was great. By the Late Cretaceous, however, faunas were less cosmopolitan as geographic isolation resulted in a greater number of indigenous species. The same pattern holds true in general for terrestrial faunas; Cretaceous dinosaurs reached a range of adaptive types not previously attained, and mammals diversified and evolved into forms more advanced than their Jurassic predecessors.

On land the close of the Cretaceous is marked by the extinction of the dinosaurs. But as one dynasty ended, another began. During the Cretaceous the flowering plants—the angiosperms—underwent explosive evolution (see Chapter 16). Colored petals and pollen represent major breakthroughs in plant reproduction. By the Late Cretaceous, angiosperms dominated land floras. Not only was the emergence of angiosperms a milestone in plant evolution; their presence has had a tremendous effect on the evolution of birds and mammals.

By the end of the period, many taxa that had played important roles in Cretaceous biotas died out. Ammonites, rudist clams, *Exogyra* and *Gryphaea* oysters, inoceramid clams, dinosaurs, pterosaurs, plesiosaurs, ichthyosaurs, and mosasaurs all disappeared. Primary producers—the coccolithophorids—and primary consumers—the planktonic foraminifera—suffered heavy losses. All of these previously successful terrestrial and marine organisms, and forms as different as ammonites and dinosaurs, became extinct. Why?

The end-of-Mesozoic faunal crisis is more difficult to explain when invoking earthbound causes than the mass extinctions near the close of the Paleozoic. We called upon plate tectonics and the formation of a supercontinent as the ultimate cause of late Paleozoic mass extinctions, and perhaps global tectonics is partly the explanation for the end-of-Mesozoic extinctions (see Chapter 4). Certainly major retreats of the sea occurred, perhaps reducing shallow-marine ecospace, but the separation of continents (Fig. 13–31) was one that would seemingly favor increased provincialism, and thus a net increase in diversity.

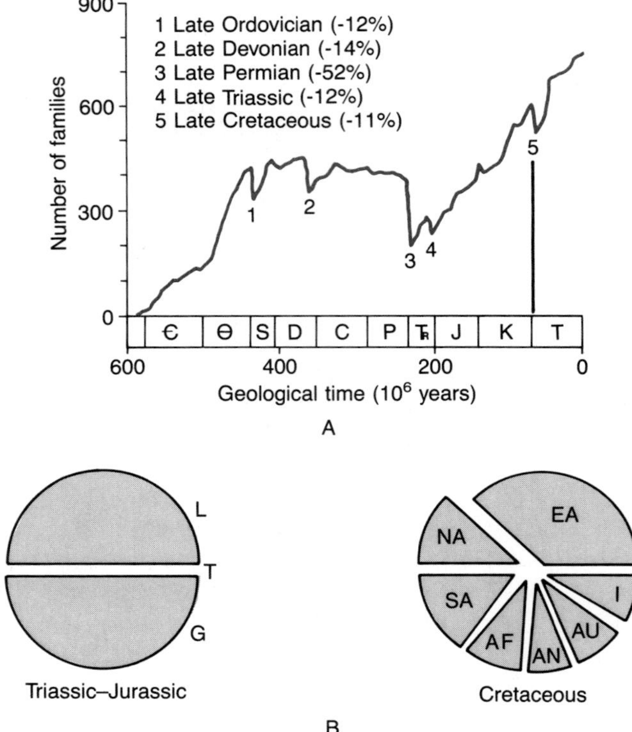

Figure 13–31

A. Standing diversity through Phanerozoic for families of marine invertebrates and vertebrates, showing abrupt drop in diversity at end of Cretaceous (5), a reflection of mass-extinction event. B. Configuration of continental masses. (AF, Africa; AN, Antarctica; AU, Australia; EA, Eurasia; G, Gondwana; I, India; L, Laurasia; NA, North America; SA, South America; T. Tethys.) Note that the relationship to diversity patterns is different than for late Paleozoic (Fig. 11–37), suggesting that factors other than plate tectonics are required to explain the terminal Cretaceous extinction event.

(A from D. H. Raup and J. J. Sepkoski, Jr., 1982, Mass Extinctions in the Fossil Record, Fig. 2, p. 1502: *Science*, vol. 215. B after J. W. Valentine and E. M. Moores, 1972, Global Tectonics and the Fossil Record, Fig. 2, p. 170: *Journal of Geology*, vol. 80. Reproduced by permission of American Association for the Advancement of Science and the University of Chicago Press)

The close of the Cretaceous was a time of major environmental disruption. The continued fragmentation and separation of continents and the north-south distribution of continents (Fig. 13–32) may have brought about the beginning of modern latitudinally zoned climates, and the onset of a cooling trend. Possibly, cooler mean annual temperature led to the downfall of some organisms. As discussed in Chapter 4, breakdowns in primary links in the food chain may explain many late Mesozoic extinctions.

There is abundant evidence in ocean-floor Deep Sea Drilling Project cores, as well as in outcrop samples, for massive reduction in the numbers of coccolithophorids and planktonic foraminifera near the end of the Cretaceous. The loss of primary producers such as coccolithophorids might have disrupted the foodchain of marine organisms, both invertebrate and vertebrate. In addition, the significant loss of these photosynthesizing marine plankton, together with reduction of productivity in the oceans, might have caused excessive buildups of atmospheric carbon dioxide, triggering a greenhouse effect that resulted in a temporary warming trend. The suggestion has been made that such a sudden rise of the global temperature might have had a devastating effect on the reproductive capabilities of large land dwellers such as dinosaurs.

Yet another direct casualty of massive extinctions among the marine plankton might have been the ammonites. Paleontologist Peter Ward has suggested that ammonite larval stages may have been planktonic, thus rendering the ammonites vulnerable to environmental changes that wiped out other planktonic organisms. Ward further suggests that nautiloid cephalopods, who survived the end-of-Cretaceous extinction event, may have had benthic larval stages that gave them higher survival value.

The decade of the 1980s has witnessed renewed interest in the terminal Cretaceous event, sparked by the discovery of a widespread *iridium* anomaly at the K/T boundary, as recounted in the introduction to this chapter. The resulting controversy over whether or not there was an extraterrestrial impact, and, if there was, whether or not it had a major influence on the mass extinctions, has stimulated a great amount of research in a number of disciplines. Results from dozens of independent studies presently favor an impact or a series (swarm) of impacts about 65 million years ago. In addition to several studies on iridium, discovery of anomalous concentrations of other rare elements, shocked metamorphosed quartz, and soot residues in the K/T boundary layer have solidified the impact theory.

Also, an unusual K/T boundary sandstone bed, with chaotic internal fabric, in the Brazos River

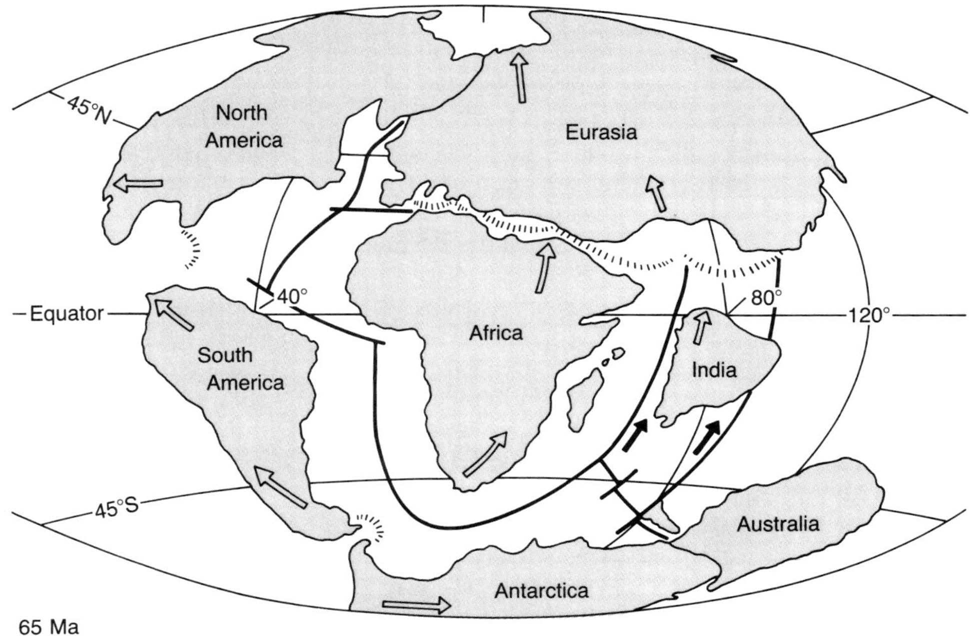

Figure 13–32
End of Cretaceous world geography.
(From Critter Creations, San Diego, CA; and A. G. Smith and J. C. Briden, 1977, Mesozoic and Cenozoic paleocontinental maps, no. 12, p. 23: Cambridge University Press, New York. Used with permission)

Valley of Texas, has recently been interpreted as the catastrophic depositional product of a 50 m or higher tsunami caused by a bolide/water impact within 5,000 km of the site. According to the scenario envisioned by paleontologists who embrace the impact theory as the primary cause of the K/T faunal crisis, the impact of a meteor or comet might have resulted in mass mortality in any of several ways:

1. By producing dust that may have cooled the climate as well as retarding photosynthesis of plants, with a domino effect all the way up the food chain;
2. By producing cyanide poisoning in the oceans and killing off marine plankton; or
3. By flash-heating of the atmosphere during entry of the extraterrestrial body, resulting in catastrophic extinctions.

A catastrophe to many geologists still means something unfamiliar. However, bolide impact is a real phenomenon. Its results are perhaps catastrophic on a geologic time scale, but then again actualism (substantive uniformitarianism) accommodates these natural catastrophes. This "catastrophic" theory has met with considerable resistance from those who invoke a combination of more gradual causes, such as:

1. Terminal Cretaceous worldwide regression of epicontinental seas;
2. Decrease in habitat space and breakdown of genetic isolating mechanisms;
3. Lowering of speciation rates;
4. Upward shift toward the ocean's surface of the level at which carbonate dissolves (the CCD);
5. Competitive replacement of dinosaurs by mammals; and
6. Increase in seasonality at higher latitudes.

The end of the Cretaceous also was a time of intense volcanic activity. Interestingly, volcanic dust from the 1883 explosion of Krakatoa in the East Indies contained anomalously high concentrations of iridium and other platinum-group metals. Some researchers maintain that the K/T boundary iridium anomaly can be explained by extensive volcanism alone, and that heightened volcanic activity, in terms of effects on atmospheric chemistry and density, might well have created the unstable environment that resulted in large-scale extinction.

One particular line of study represents a sort of reconciliation between bolide impact and volcanic influence, and involves and describes an end-of-Cretaceous bolide impact on the west side of the Indian subcontinent, near present-day Bombay. Here, a 600-km-diameter crater has been described that is filled with the thick basalt lavas that comprise the *Deccan Plateau.* This crater is judged to be large enough to have caused pressure-relief melting in the asthenosphere. Basalt then flooded the crater to form an immense lava lake, the terrestrial equivalent of a lunar mare. The close age relationship between the basalts and the K/T boundary, and the discovery of shocked metamorphosed quartz beneath the lavas, has some researchers more than eager to claim this as evidence of *the* impact that caused the terminal Cretaceous extinction event. This idea would see the impact as initiating the road to mass extinction, as well as triggering massive outpourings of lava, which produced harmful changes in the atmosphere that finished off the extinction process—a one-two punch that might explain some of the gradual extinction trends in certain taxonomic groups.

The subject of mass extinctions, as brought out in Chapter 4, is a fascinating topic for research, as well as for speculation. Probably nearly as many hypotheses have been advanced to explain mass mortality as there are major taxonomic groups that have become extinct. Certainly, any meaningful theory or combination of theories must agree with the fossil record as currently understood. Extinctions resulting from catastrophic impact should be expected to show tight synchroneity. Those resulting from more gradually changing earthbound phenomena would, perhaps, be less synchronous.

With regard to the dinosaurs, there appears to have been a gradual dwindling of species in the Late Cretaceous. Reduction from about 35 species 75 million years ago, to about 24 species 70 million years ago, to about six species at the end of the Cretaceous, suggests that dinosaurs were already on the wane when the asteroid hit. There are also reports of a few species of dinosaurs above the K/T boundary in China and a few other places. Bakker sees this pattern as not the work of a Death Star, but rather a pattern coincidental with the end-of-Cretaceous elimination of terrestrial geographic diversity that had promoted earlier speciation. He believes the few remaining dinosaur species at the end of the Cretaceous, already weakened by "topographic boredom" wherein normal rates of extinction were outpacing rates of speciation, may have succumbed to parasites and diseases.

Evolutionist Stephen Jay Gould, on the other hand, accepts the bolide-impact theory to explain the terminal Cretaceous event. He offers this interesting perspective:

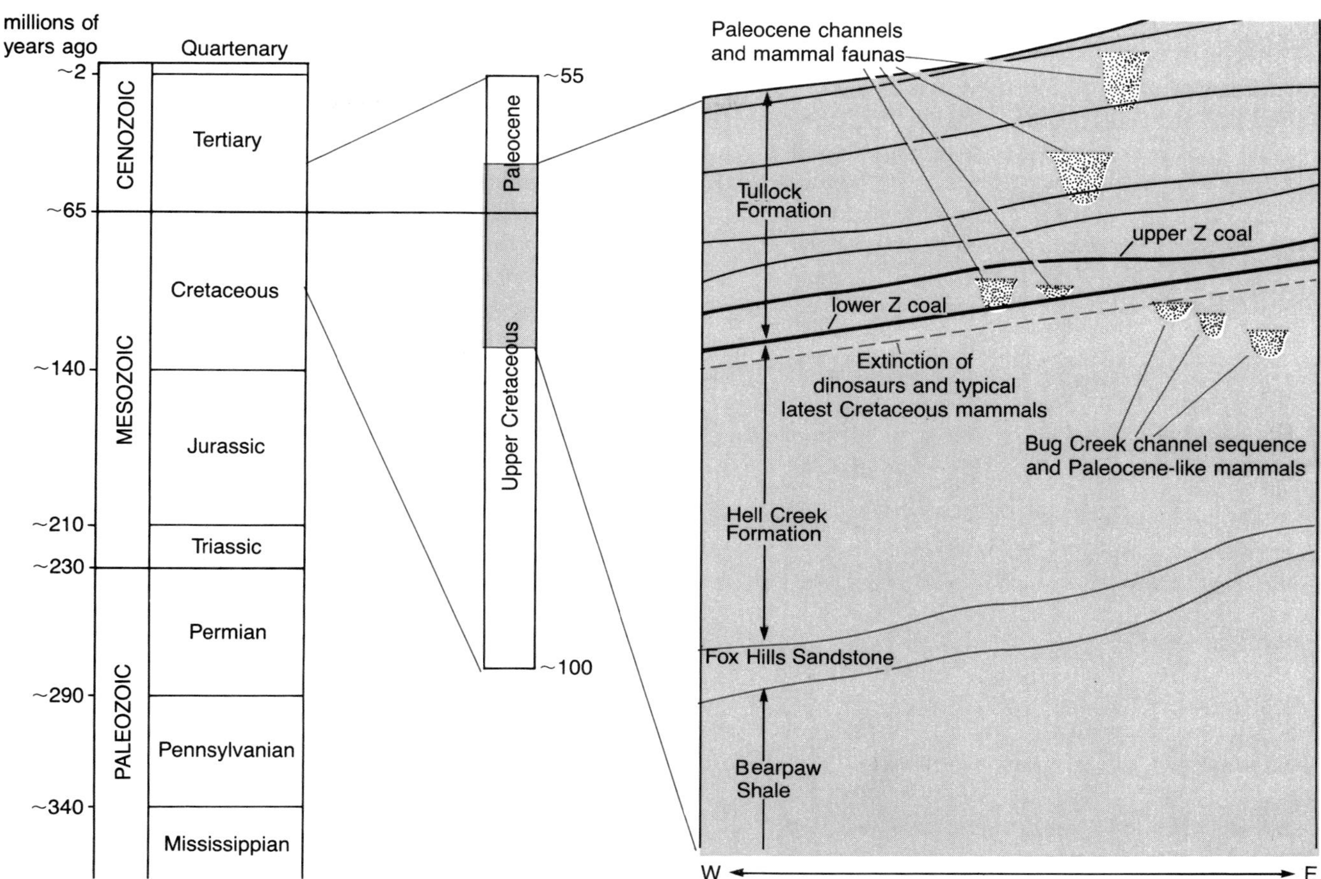

Figure 13–33

Time-stratigraphic diagram of sedimentary sequence in northeastern Montana showing some discrepancies in Cretaceous-Tertiary boundary definition and regional correlation. The boundary between the Hell Creek and Tullock Formations is the base of the lower Z coal. The Cretaceous-Tertiary boundary, as defined by the disappearance of dinosaurs, is, on the average, about 3 m below this level. The major floral changes occur well above this boundary, in places as high as the upper Z coal bed.

(From J. D. Archibald and W. A. Clemens, 1982, Late Cretaceous Extinctions, Fig. 4, p. 381: *American Scientist,* vol. 70, no. 4. Reproduced by permission of *American Scientist)*

Extinction is no sign of ineptitude but the inexorable result of life on an uncertain planet. Life is a series of complex and unpredictable events, not a straight and narrow path to progress. Wind back the tape of life to the midst of dinosaur hegemony and let it play again, but without asteroid or cometary impact. This time perhaps, as our own day is reached, no tyrannosaur graces a T-shirt. Rather great-grandson of tyrannosaur gazes down at his feet and wonders how those odd little furry things continue to eke out such a marginal life in his glorious world. We didn't have to evolve at all.*

One of the problems that continues to hamper solution of the causes and effects of mass mortality at the end of the Cretaceous involves the definition of the Cretaceous-Tertiary boundary, and the imprecision of correlation (Fig. 13–33). In some areas, particularly marine sections on the continents, mega-invertebrates have been used to define the boundary. Within the terrestrial realm, changes in fossil floras and dinosaur extinction define the boundary. In the ocean basins, microfossils such as foraminifera and calcareous nannoplankton provide the data. Most commonly, these biotic changes are not concordant. For example, in a continuous stratigraphic section of marine pelagic sediments that spans the Cretaceous-Paleogene boundary near Zu-

*Gould, S. J. 1987. The lesson of the dinosaurs: Evolution didn't inevitably lead to us. *Discover* vol. 8, no. 3, p. 51.

maya, Spain, coccolithophorids and planktonic foraminifera show abrupt extinctions coincident with the iridium-rich boundary clay layer (Fig. 13–34).

Peter Ward, on the other hand, has documented a more gradual decline of ammonites in the same section, with the youngest specimens occurring some 12 m below the boundary clay, implying that the last species may have died out some 100,000 years before the event that produced the iridium fallout. The application of radiometric dating and magnetostratigraphy should allow for more refined correlations to be made among disparate faunas, geographic areas, and paleoenvironments. Also, the fossil record is being examined more closely in areas where Cretaceous-Tertiary boundary stratotypes have been defined. This more detailed resolution will, no doubt, give us more information on the magnitude, selectivity, and ultimately the causes of the extinctions, and on the time interval over which they occurred.

Whatever the causes, be they catastrophic-extraterrestrial or gradual-terrestrial, or a combination, the affected groups of organisms were not able to adapt to the environmental changes; they succumbed to the stresses of a changing world. The mystery of the great dying-out that marks the close of the Mesozoic Era still awaits an answer. The Cretaceous Period lasted some 70 million years, beginning with the continents still largely clustered, but ending with most of the continental land masses fragmented. The age of reptiles was over, and mammals would inherit the Earth.

A

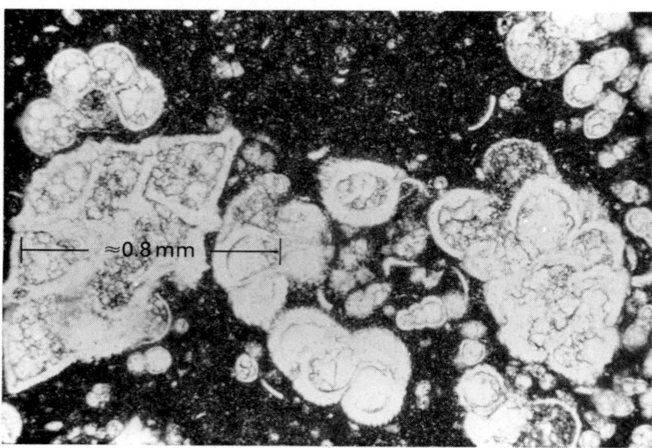

B

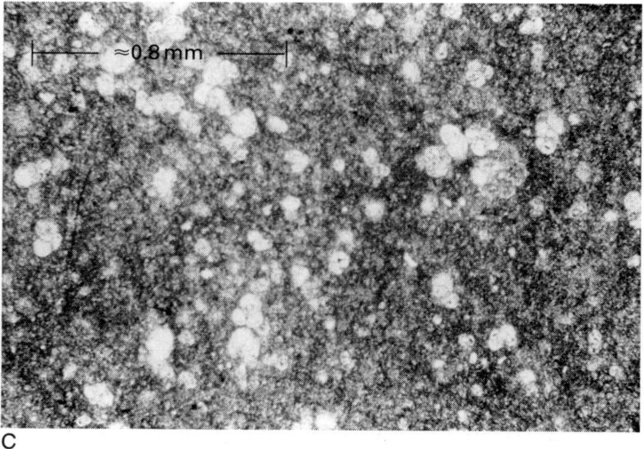

C

Figure 13–34

The Cretaceous/Tertiary boundary. A. K-T boundary interval and boundary clay layer near Zumaya, Spain. The iridium anomalies in this thin clay layer, together with basaltic spherule concentrations and shocked metamorphosed quartz grains, are interpreted to be the signatures of a major bolide impact. B. Photomicrograph showing the assemblage of Foraminifera in the uppermost Cretaceous limestone at the Gubbio, Italy section. Note the size and the many different forms of these planktonic foraminifers. Compare this with the assemblage in photomicrograph C, which represents the lowermost limestone layer of the Tertiary. This assemblage includes only simple and tiny forms. The implication of this abrupt change on either side of the boundary clay layer is that the diversified assemblage of complex Cretaceous forms was abruptly wiped out by the K-T extraterrestrial impact, represented world-wide by the thin iridium-rich clay layer. Only tiny, simple forms survived the catastrophe in the pelagic realm, and they constitute the root evolutionary stock for a new adaptive radiation in the early Tertiary.

(A, photo courtesy of J. F. Mount; photos B and C courtesy of Alessandro Montanari)

Summary

Cretaceous sediments were deposited over a wide region by marginal and interior seas that spread beyond the limits of Jurassic deposition. Sedimentation on the trailing margin of the continent produced thick stratigraphic sections in the Atlantic and Gulf Coast areas. Terrigenous clastic sediments typify the Atlantic Coast region. In the Gulf Coast, abundant carbonate sediments were deposited, and during the Early Cretaceous, a major barrier-reef system rimmed much of the western Gulf.

Continued subduction of the Farallon Plate beneath the western margin of the North American continent was responsible for extensive magmatic-arc activity manifested by emplacement of granitic batholiths from Alaska to Baja California during the Late Jurassic to mid-Cretaceous. Deposition of the Franciscan Formation in the trench and of the Great Valley Group in the fore-arc basin in California continued through the Cretaceous. To the east, extensive back-arc thrusting produced the Sevier foreland-fold thrust belt. Erosion of the Sevier tectonic highlands produced a tremendous volume of sediment that accumulated as a great clastic wedge and prograded eastward along the edge of an interior seaway that stretched from the Arctic to the Gulf of Mexico. The interior seaway, at times some 1500 km wide, was the result of mid-Cretaceous major marine transgression into the subsiding depression of a foreland basin. This Cretaceous transgression resulted in the highest sea-level stand of the entire Phanerozoic.

The Cretaceous was a time of exceptionally rich faunal and floral diversity. Among the marine invertebrates, ammonite cephalopods, bivalve and gastropod molluscs, and sea urchins flourished. The peculiar sessile rudist bivalves were reef-builders that lived in the tropical waters of the expanding Tethyan realm. Diatoms, planktonic foraminifers, and planktonic calcareous algae—the coccolithophorids—made a dramatic appearance; the last two groups contributed to great volumes of Cretaceous chalk. A variety of marine vertebrates—bony fish as well as large sea turtles, mosasaurs, ichthyosaurs, and plesiosaurs—rounded out the gallery of marine life.

On land, flowering plants—the angiosperms—first appeared in the Early Cretaceous, and by late in the period had ecologically displaced most of the gymnosperms, particularly in lowland areas. Mammals continued to increase in diversity, but remained small, mainly nocturnal, forms that played a secondary role in land ecosystems. By late in the period, early marsupials and placentals had evolved. Birds (represented mainly by seagoing varieties) and pterosaurs graced the skies. It was truly a bountiful time in the history of life. Increased diversity levels reflected continued rifting and rafting of continental fragments as Pangaea broke up. What had been very cosmopolitan faunas during the Jurassic became progressively more provincial with continental breakup and separation.

The dinosaur dynasty reached its zenith during the Cretaceous, with six suborders and an impressive array of adaptive types, including many specialized herbivores and relatively few carnivores. Renewed interest in research on dinosaurs during the decade of the 1970s has shed light on the bioenergetics and social patterns of these amazing animals, as well as on their role in tetrapod ecosystems. This new look at dinosaurs has dispelled many of the traditional myths about their being evolutionary failures, and has portrayed them as some of the most successful organisms that ever lived. This renewed research has also precipitated a controversy over whether the dinosaurs were cold blooded, warm blooded, or both.

Despite the richness and diversity of Cretaceous life, the end of the period was a time of mass extinction as many marine plankton, some marine invertebrates, most marine reptiles, and the dinosaurs died out. This wave of mass extinction is difficult to explain in light of the plate-tectonics situation of separated continents and increased provinciality. Lowered sea-level stands accompanying end-of-Cretaceous regressions probably caused stress for many marine organisms. However, the story of this mass extinction defies simple, singular explanation. One popular recent extinction theory, based in part on the anomalously high iridium content in the Cretaceous-Tertiary boundary clay in oceanic and some land sections, invokes the impact of a large asteroid or comet. Such an event might have triggered a domino effect by upsetting the marine food chain, changing $O_2:CO_2$ ratios in the atmosphere, and causing a short-term global greenhouse-type warming trend that might have had disastrous consequences for large terrestrial vertebrates like the dinosaurs.

Suggestions for Further Reading

Alvarez, L. W., W. Alvarez, F. Asaro, and H. V. Michel. 1980. Extraterrestrial cause for the Cretaceous-Tertiary extinction. *Science* 208(4448):1095–1108.

Archibald, J. D., and W. A. Clemens. 1982. Late Cretaceous extinctions. *American Scientist* 70(4):377–86.

Bakker, R. T. 1975. Dinosaur renaissance. *Scientific American* Offprint No. 916. San Francisco: W. H. Freeman.

Bakker, R. T. 1986. *The dinosaur heresies.* New York: William Morrow & Co.

Ben-Avriham, Zvi. 1981. The movement of continents. *American Scientist* 69(3):291–300.

Dietz, R. S., and J. C. Holden. 1970. The breakup of Pangaea. *Scientific American* Offprint No. 892. San Francisco: W. H. Freeman.

Ganapathy, R. 1980. A major meteorite impact on the Earth 65 million years ago: Evidence from the Cretaceous-Tertiary boundary clay. *Science* 209:921–23.

Gore, Rick. 1989. Extinctions: What caused the Earth's great dyings. *National Geographic* 175(6):662–700.

Gould, Stephen Jay. 1987. The lesson of the dinosaurs: Evolution didn't inevitably lead to us. *Discover* 8(3):51.

Horner, John R., and James Gorman. 1988. Digging dinosaurs. Workman Publ. Co.

Jones, D. L., Allan Cox, Peter Coney, and Myrl Beck. 1982. The growth of western North America. *Scientific American* 247(5):70–128.

King, P. B. 1977. *The evolution of North America.* rev. ed. Princeton, NJ: Princeton Univ. Press.

Lanham, Url. 1973. *The bone hunters.* New York: Columbia Univ. Press.

Morrell, Virginia. 1987. Announcing the birth of a heresy. *Discover* 8(3):26-50.

Newell, N. D. 1963. Crises in the history of life. *Scientific American* Offprint No. 867. San Francisco: W. H. Freeman.

Ostrom, J. H. 1978. A new look at dinosaurs. *National Geographic* 154(2):152–85.

Padian, K. 1988. The flight of pterosaurs. *Natural History* 97(10):58-69.

Raup, D. M. 1986. *The nemesis affair.* New York: W. W. Norton & Co.

Silver, L. T., and P. Schulz, eds. 1982. *Geological interpretations of impacts of large asteroids and comets on the Earth.* Geological Society of America Special Paper 190.

Stanley, S. M. 1984. Mass extinctions in the oceans. *Scientific American* 250(6):64–84.

Ward, Peter. 1983. The extinction of the ammonites. *Scientific American* 249(4):136–47.

14 Cenozoic History

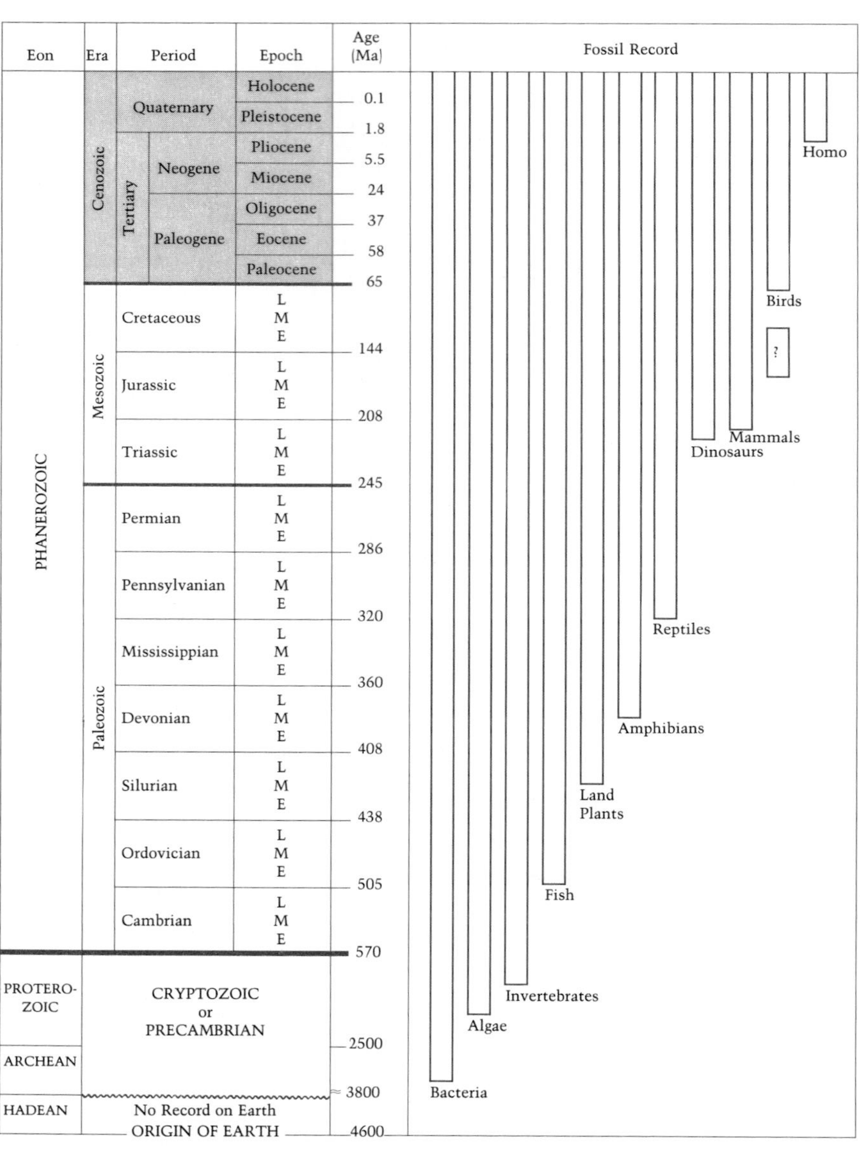

Eon
Era
Period
Epoch
Age (Ma)
Fossil Record
Holocene
Quaternary
Pleistocene
0.1
1.8
Pliocene
5.5
Cenozoic
Neogene
Miocene
24
Tertiary
Oligocene
37
Paleogene
Eocene
58
Paleocene
65
Cretaceous
L
M
E
144
Mesozoic
Jurassic
L
M
E
208
Triassic
L
M
E
245
PHANEROZOIC
Permian
L
M
E
286
Pennsylvanian
L
M
E
320
Mississippian
L
M
E
360
Paleozoic
Devonian
L
M
E
408
Silurian
L
M
E
438
Ordovician
L
M
E
505
Cambrian
L
M
E
570
PROTERO-ZOIC
CRYPTOZOIC
or
PRECAMBRIAN
2500
ARCHEAN
3800
HADEAN
No Record on Earth
ORIGIN OF EARTH
4600
Homo
Birds
?
Mammals
Dinosaurs
Reptiles
Amphibians
Land Plants
Fish
Invertebrates
Algae
Bacteria

Contents

Key Terms

Base level
Laramide orogeny
Kerogen
Epeirogeny
Salt dome
Diapir
East Pacific Rise
Diatomite
Graben
Horst

Conquering the Colorado

The magnificent mountains, plateaus, and deep canyons of the Cordilleran region were formed mainly in Cenozoic time, during the last 65 million years. Every bit as colorful as the geology and scenery of this vast and grandiose region is the story of geological exploration of western North America during the last half of the nineteenth century. It is a story of adventure, hardship, and privation, but mostly of discovery.

After the Civil War, the United States government authorized a geological exploration along the 40th parallel, and geological and geographical surveys of the western territories. These expeditions were ambitious, and even though rivalry developed among several of the surveys, their undaunted probing into the strange and often forbidding new land of the West resulted in a rapid succession of important geologic discoveries. Of particular significance was the discovery of countless fossil localities which yielded the remains of previously undescribed species of reptiles, mammals, and plants (Chapter 12). Discovery of valuable mineral resources not only stimulated a period of mining activity, but also led to revolutionary theories on the formation of metallic ores. The continuity of rock exposures presented a panorama of stratigraphy and structure not previously seen in other regions of North America, and new concepts were developed of how landscapes evolve.

Perhaps the most significant byproduct of early geologic exploration of the West was the recognition that portions of this magnificent land should be preserved. The accomplishments of the Hayden survey (1870–1878), directed by Ferdinand Hayden and including landscape artist Thomas Moran and pioneer photographer W. H. Jackson, were in large measure responsible for creation of America's first national park, Yellowstone, in 1872.

One of the most remarkable figures to emerge from the period of western geologic discovery was Major John Wesley Powell (Fig. 14–1). Powell led two expeditions down the Colorado River and its canyons, and was influential in the shaping of the geological sciences in America. Powell was born in western New York in 1834, but later moved with his family to Ohio, where he had the good fortune to be influenced in his early education by several naturalists. He quickly developed a strong interest in science, and when the Powell family moved to Illinois, young John nurtured this interest by attending Illinois College and Wheaton College.

His early twenties were spent teaching school, exploring rivers by boat, and collecting specimens. When the Civil War broke out, he enlisted in the Union Army, serving as a military engineer and artillery officer; he lost his right forearm in the Battle of Shiloh. After the war, Major Powell became Professor of Geology at Illinois Wesleyan University, and curator of the Illinois State Natural History Society. He also offered courses at Illinois Nor-

Figure 14–1
John Wesley Powell converses with unidentified Paiute Indian during northern Arizona Survey more than 100 years ago. (Photo from National Anthropological Archives. Smithsonian Institution Photo No. 1591)

mal University and earned a reputation as a first-rate teacher who combined learning from books with experience in the field and lab.

In 1867, while on a field trip with students to Colorado, he climbed Pikes Peak; the next summer he was one of a party of seven to first climb Longs Peak. It was during these trips to Colorado that Powell became infused with an intense desire to explore the Colorado River by boat. On May 24, 1869, he began his first trip down the Colorado, leading an expedition of ten men, departing from Green River, Wyoming, in four boats. Money for this expedition came both from Powell's own pockets and from various sources whom he had convinced of the trip's value. The Illinois Natural History Society sponsored the expedition. Transportation of men, boats, and supplies to Green River was provided by the Burlington and Union Pacific Railroads, and the Smithsonian Institution loaned surveying instruments. The U.S. War Department furnished the rations.

Powell's expedition reached the mouth of the Virgin River in southern Nevada (Fig. 14–2A) on August 30, some three months after leaving Green River. Although the expedition of 1869 was a hasty reconnaissance, it nevertheless was billed as a plunge into the great unknown, and it created much attention and public interest. Major Powell was a hero, and he encountered no difficulty in obtaining from Congress an appropriation for further exploration of the Colorado River country. The entire year of 1870 was spent in detailed preparation.

The Colorado River expedition of 1871 was intended to gather more scientific data than the first expedition, and more elaborate preparations were made toward this end. An important addition was a photographer, E. D. Beamon of New York City, and his assistant, J. K. Hillers. Photography was no easy task in 1871, especially on a river expedition. Imagine lugging heavy, cumbersome equipment in and out of a boat, and up and down canyon

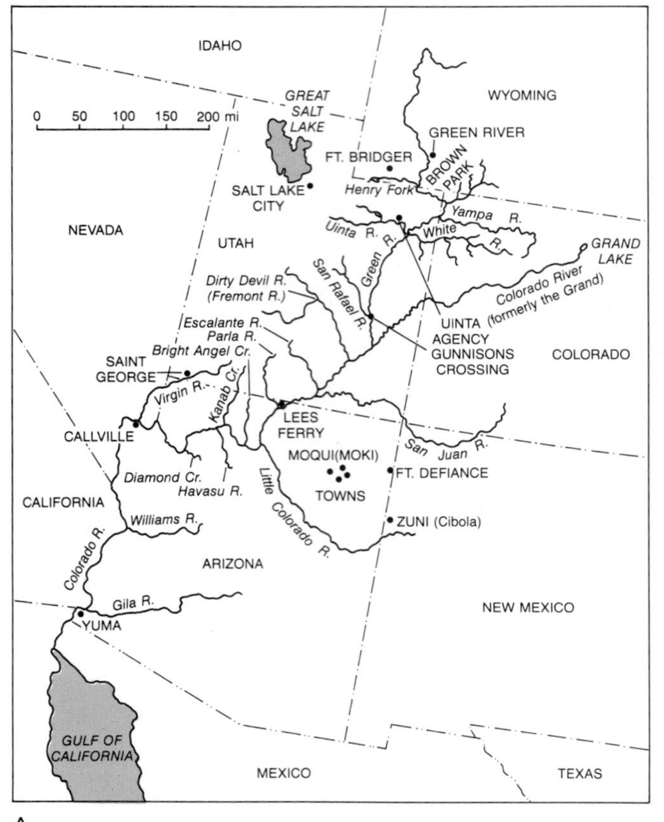

A

B

Figure 14–2
A. Colorado River region and route of John Wesley Powell's first expedition (indicated by dots). B. The Grand Canyon country.
(A, from William Culp Darrah, *Powell of the Colorado.* Copyright 1951, © renewed 1979 by Princeton University Press. Map, p. 121, reprinted by permission of Princeton University Press. B, from J. W. Powell, *The Exploration of the Colorado River and Its Canyons,* p. 16: Dover Publications, New York. The Dover edition, first published in 1961, is an unabridged and unaltered republication of the work first published in 1895 by Flood and Vincent under the title, *Canyons of the Colorado.* Used by permission of Dover Publications, Inc.)

walls, and using glass photographic plates. Beamon and Hillers had stamina equal to the task, and they took over 350 plates, many of them truly excellent. In addition to the photographers, the exploration party included a surveyor and three topographers.

On May 22, 1871, almost two years to the day after the first expedition was launched, the party of twelve men in three boats left from the same point—Green River, Wyoming—with Major Powell the only member of the 1869 crew to repeat the trip. This second effort spent considerably more time charting the detailed courses of the Colorado and its tributaries, and in making topographic surveys and geologic maps of the canyons and plateaus. The actual boating part of the expedition ended on September 7, 1872, when the party reached Kanab Creek in Arizona (Fig. 14–2A), but mapping continued through 1873.

Powell's effort had become recognized and was sponsored as a full-fledged survey, one of four operating in the West. In 1879, after much cajoling and coercion of government officials for support, these surveys became merged into one—the U.S. Geological Survey. Its first director was Clarence King, and Powell served as its very capable second director for 14 years. (In 1968, to commemorate Powell's second expedition, the U.S. Geological Survey launched its own expedition to retrace Powell's journey as accurately as possible, and succeeded in retaking most of his historic photographs from the same vantage points.)

The Powell Survey filled in the last large blank on the geographic map of North America. This was a gigantic region that extended from the Uinta Mountains on the north to the Virgin River on the south, and from the Green River westward to the high plateaus (Fig. 14–2A). From Powell's work in the canyons and plateaus of the Colorado River country there grew a new understanding of the processes of erosion and the evolutionary development of land forms. Powell introduced the concept of **base level** and the classification of drainage as antecedent, consequent, and superposed. Geomorphology became a recognized discipline, and the interplay among stratigraphy, structure, erosional processes, and land morphology was seen in a dramatic new perspective.

Powell's goal was to understand the land of the West and the native Americans who inhabited it. Known as "Kapurats," meaning "one-arm-off," Powell befriended and gained the trust of Indians in the plateau country (Fig. 14–1). He learned their customs and language, and became one of this country's most vigorous proponents of their protection. His zeal both for science and humanity led to establishment of both the U.S. Geological Survey and the Bureau of Ethnology in the Smithsonian Institution, and he was one of this country's loudest spokesmen for the wise use of the public domain and natural resources.

John Wesley Powell's gifts to science and to his country are perhaps rivaled only by the beauty of the Grand Canyon itself. The last few sentences in his book, *The Exploration of the Colorado River and its Canyons,** provide some insight into the man and his keen vision:

> You cannot see the Grand Canyon in one view, as if it were a changeless spectacle from which a curtain might be lifted, but to see it you have to toil from month to month through its labyrinths. It is a region more difficult to traverse than the Alps or the Himalayas, but if strength and courage are sufficient for the task, by a year's toil a concept of sublimity can be obtained never again to be equaled on the hither side of Paradise.

*Dover ed., 1961. First published in 1895 by Flood and Vincent under the title, *Canyons of the Colorado.*

The Western Interior

The Rocky Mountains

We shall begin our examination of the Cenozoic of North America in the Rocky Mountain region of the western interior. The Cordilleran orogeny continued from the Cretaceous into the early Cenozoic. The Late Cretaceous–to–early Cenozoic phase is commonly referred to as the **Laramide orogeny;** its effects were most evident in the eastern part of the Cordilleran belt in what now are referred to as the northern, central, and southern Rocky Mountain Provinces.

Remember that the Cordilleran orogeny, which began during the Jurassic in the western part of the Cordilleran belt, progressed eastward during the late Mesozoic and early Cenozoic like a rippling wave, finally culminating in the Eocene (Table 14–1). The Laramide phase tilted, folded, and faulted the Cretaceous beds that had been deposited in the interior seaway, among other rocks. These Cretaceous strata, in turn, had been formed from erosional debris shed from tectonic highlands farther west, during earlier phases (e.g., the Sevier) of the Cordilleran orogeny.

In the northern Rocky Mountains—from Wyoming to the Northwest Territories in Canada and

Table 14–1
Timing of phases of Cordilleran orogeny during Mesozoic and Cenozoic

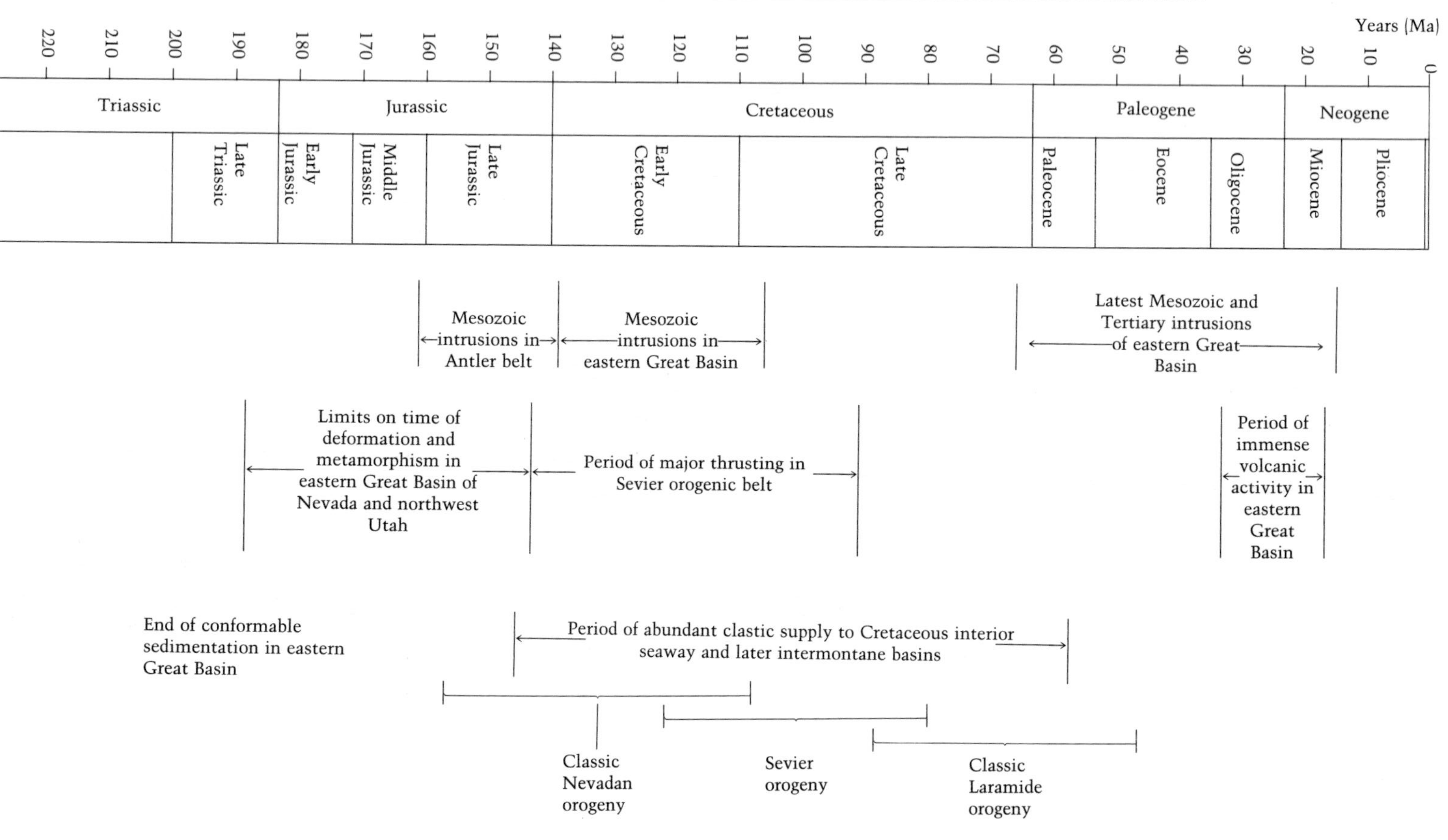

Source: After R. L. Armstrong, 1968, Sevier Orogenic Belt in Nevada and Utah, Fig. 7, p. 452: *Geological Society of America Bulletin,* vol. 79, no. 4.

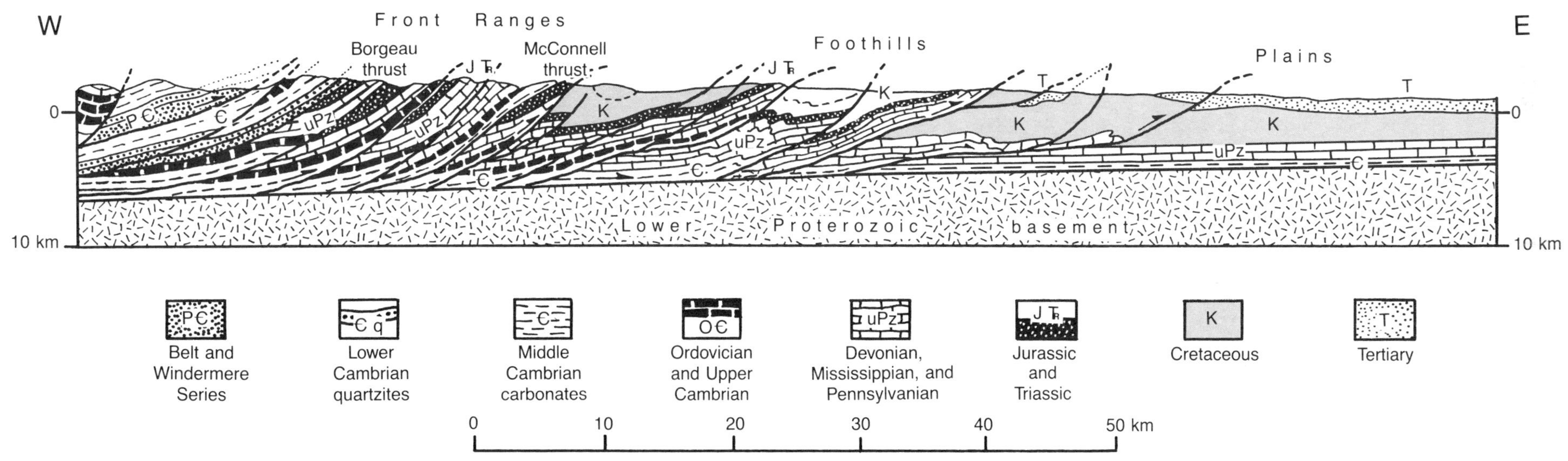

Figure 14–3
Laramide deformational style of imbricate thrusts in Alberta, Canada.
(From Philip B. King, *The Evolution of North America,* Fig. 86 (A1): Copyright © 1959, rev. ed. © 1977 by Princeton University Press, Princeton, NJ. Reprinted by permission of Princeton University Press)

northward into Alaska—thrust-faulting and folding, which began in Cretaceous time, continued to deform Proterozoic, Paleozoic, and Mesozoic strata of the Cordilleran miogeocline, as well as Mesozoic rocks of the Rocky Mountain interior seaway. This orogenic phase, somewhat reminiscent of the late Paleozoic disturbance in the southern Appalachians, exhibited a characteristic compressional shortening tectonic style involving asymmetrical folding and eastward thrusting. In some parts of the overthrust belt, the thrust plates are imbricated; some of the thrusts have displacements measured in tens of kilometers (Figs. 14–3 and 14–4).

In northeastern Mexico, the Sierra Madre Oriental, a southern extension of the Rocky Mountain system, is a chain of mountains that records the Laramide deformation of Jurassic and Cretaceous marine carbonate rocks. It is primarily a fold province, characterized by tight, strongly compressed doubly plunging anticlines and synclines with a frontal (eastern) belt of broader, open folds. The individual mountain ranges are typically anticlinal in structure; in the cores of some of the anticlines, Jurassic evaporites have been deeply eroded to form picturesque hidden valleys.

In the central Rocky Mountains of Colorado, Wyoming, and New Mexico, large areas of the craton were uplifted during the Laramide event. Such was the situation in the Colorado Front Range (Figs. 14–5 and 14–6) where broad-backed, asymmetrical uplifts, many with pre-Cambrian crystalline basement exposed in the cores, illustrate the principal tectonic style. Most of the majestic Colorado peaks, such as Pikes Peak, Mount Elbert, and Longs Peak, have been sculptured from pre-Cambrian crystalline basement. These unusually high uplifts, formed by vertical fault movements of pre-Cambrian basement blocks, represent in part the

A

B

Figure 14–4
A. Chief Mountain, Montana, a klippe (erosional remnant of thrust sheet) of Lewis overthrust, composed of pre-Paleozoic strata of Belt Supergroup, tectonically underlain by Upper Cretaceous shale. B. Sun River Canyon, Montana, showing Mississippian Madison Limestone (cliff exposure) in upper plate of major overthrust and Cretaceous strata (in canyon) in lower plate.
(Photos by J. D. Cooper)

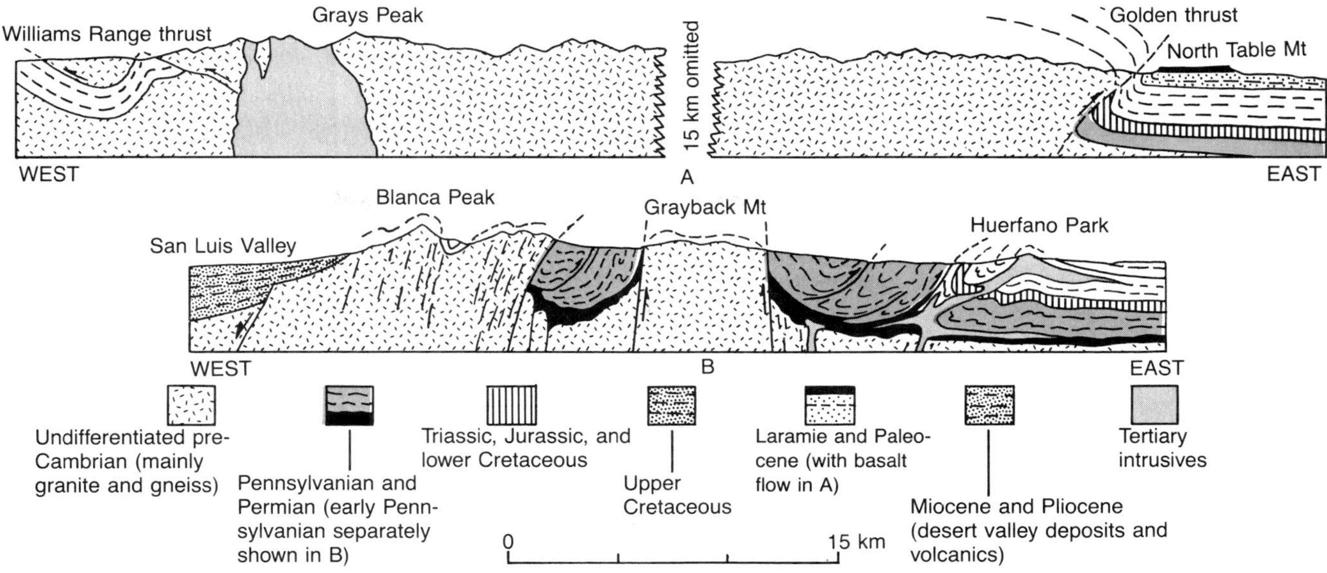

Figure 14–5

Vertical uplift of pre-Paleozoic basement style of Laramide deformation in southern Rocky Mountains. A. Colorado Front Range. B. Sangre de Crusto Mountains, Colorado.

(Redrawn from P. B. King, 1977, *The Evolution of North America:* Princeton University Press. Reproduced by permission of Princeton University Press and the author)

Figure 14–6

Looking south over Boulder, Colorado, at Rocky Mountain front. Pre-Paleozoic basement (dark, vegetated) to right (west). Pennsylvanian arkoses form steeply dipping "flat-irons" in right center along foot of escarpment. Permo-Triassic lies in central valley. Jurassic Morrison Formation capped by Cretaceous Dakota Sandstone forms ridge to left (east).

(Photo coutesy of John S. Shelton)

reactivation of ancestral Rocky Mountain fault blocks originally uplifted during the Pennsylvanian Period (Chapter 11).

This uplift of cratonic basement blocks is a characteristic feature of the Laramide structural belt, and illustrates that some mountain-building events have included regions not within continental-margin basin settings. As such, this is truly a tectonic enigma, and represents one of the oddest occurrences in the tectonic history of the world. In his colorful book about the geology of Wyoming, *Rising from the Plains,* author John McPhee metaphorically describes this "popping" up of mountains from beneath the cratonic sedimentary cover as like "a family of hogs waking up beneath a huge blanket of mud."* What caused mountain-building to advance so far into the continental interior?

The plate-tectonics model that so far seems to best explain the Laramide phase of the Cordilleran orogeny involves a change in plate-convergence rates and angles that began at the boundary between North American continental lithosphere and

*McPhee, John. 1986. *Rising from the Plains.* New York: Farrar, Straus & Giroux.

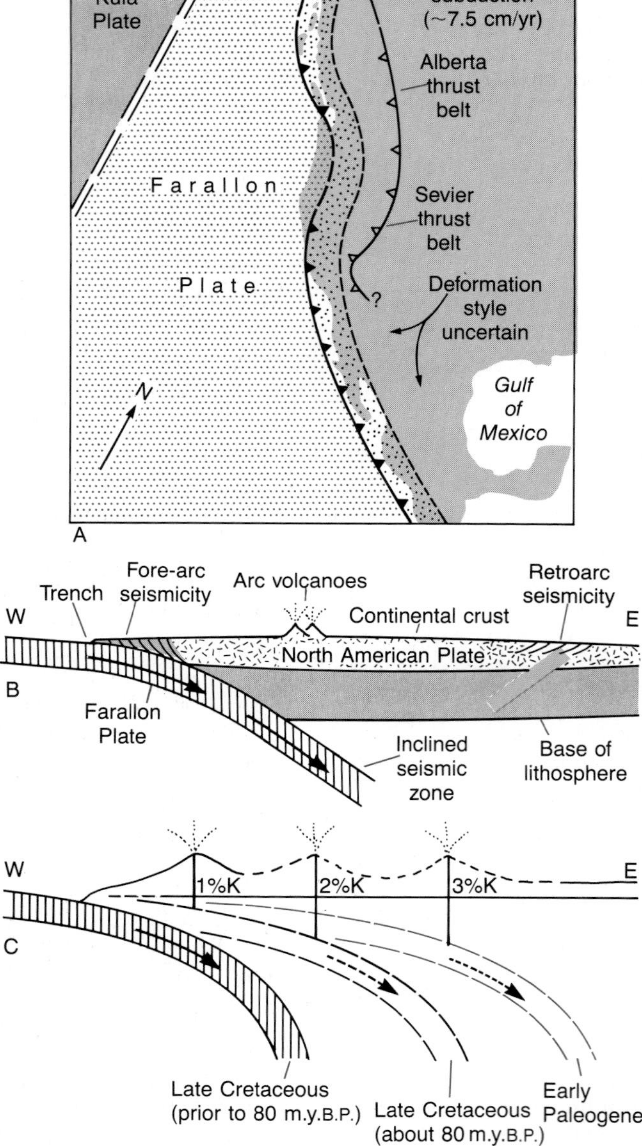

Figure 14–7

A. Plate configurations and plate motions, western North America and eastern Pacific Basin, approximately 80 Ma. B. Style of subduction (steep mode) and related arc magmatism and back-arc (Sevier) thrusting, approximately 80 Ma. C. Percentage of potassium (K) varies with distance from trench; volcanic activity farthest from trench has highest percentage of potassium. This relationship provides a guide to depth at which melting occurred and thus to determining the dip angle of the subduction zone, which decreased during latest Cretaceous.

(A from W. R. Dickinson, 1979, Cenozoic Plate Tectonic Setting of the Cordilleran Region in the United States, Fig. 1A, p. 2, *in* Cenozoic Paleogeography of the Western United States: SEPM Pacific Section Paleogeography Symposium, vol. 3. Reproduced by permission of Pacific Section, Society of Economic Paleontologists and Mineralogists. B. from W. R. Dickinson and W. S. Snyder, 1978, Plate Tectonics of the Laramide Orogeny, Fig. 2, p. 359, *in* Laramide Folding Associated with Basement Block Faulting in the Western United States: *Geological Society of America Memoir* 151. Reproduced by permission of authors. C, data from S. B. Keith, 1978, Paleosubduction Geometries Inferred from Cretaceous and Tertiary Magmatic Patterns in Western North America: *Geology,* vol. 6, p. 516–521)

Pacific oceanic lithosphere (the Farallon Plate) about 80 million years ago (Fig. 14–7A). These motions of the lithospheric plates, whose interactions controlled late Mesozoic and Cenozoic Cordilleran tectonics, have been determined by use of evidence from offshore data, particularly seafloor magnetic-anomaly patterns.

In a scenario described by William R. Dickinson and Warren Hamilton, prior to 80 million years ago, Pacific oceanic lithosphere belonging to the Farallon Plate was subducted beneath the North American continental plate, approximately at right angles to the Cordilleran margin and at a rate of somewhat less than 10 cm/year. The motion of the North American Plate was northwestward at a rate in excess of 5 cm/year. This Late Cretaceous convergence rate is believed to be similar to standard values for modern arc-trench systems. The angle of dip of the subducted slab (Fig. 14–7B) is believed to have been about 50°, a rather normal value for modern arc-trench systems. This angle of Late Cretaceous subduction is inferred from the potassium gradient in granitic rocks of the Cretaceous batholiths (Fig. 14–7C). The leading edge of the westward-drifting North American Plate was continually pressed against the zone of flexure in the Farallon Plate. This produced contraction inland behind the magmatic arc, resulting in thrusting in the Sevier belt (Chapter 13).

Associated with this Late Cretaceous subduction mode was a belt of *arc magmatism* that was positioned some 150 to 200 km distant from a trench that apparently extended continuously from Mexico to Alaska. The Cretaceous batholith trend, subparallel to the present-day coastline from Mexico to Alaska, represents the eroded roots of the once-continuous magmatic arc that was positioned cratonward of, and parallel to, the subduction zone along the continental margin.

Magnetic-anomaly patterns in the Pacific suggest that from about 80 million years ago (Late Cretaceous) to 40 million years ago (Late Eocene), unusually high convergence rates prevailed at the Farallon–North American trench. Subduction of the Farallon Plate (Fig. 14–8A) was abnormally rapid, perhaps about 15 cm/year, and was oblique to the Cordilleran margin. The motion of the continental block had changed to generally due west at about 5 cm/year.

On the basis of interpretations of the distribution of arc magmatism and the potassium gradient in arc-volcanic rocks (Fig. 14–7C), it is inferred that the increase in plate-convergence rate was accompanied by a progressive decrease in the angle of dip of the subducted slab (Fig. 14–8A). As the angle of

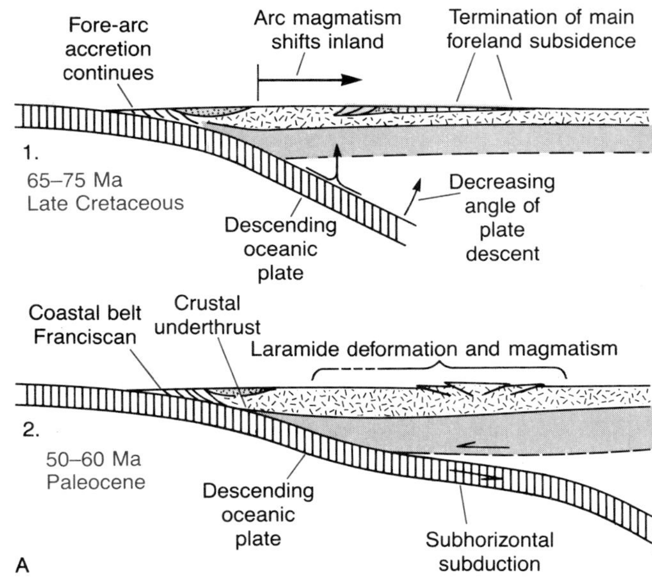

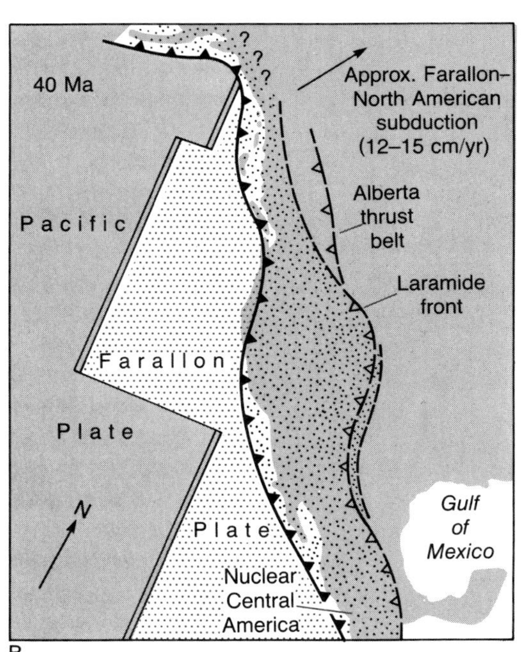

Figure 14–8

A. Plate interactions along Cordilleran margin of North America. 1. Late Cretaceous. Note the decreasing angle of oceanic plate descent, and attendant eastward shift of arc magmatism. 2. Paleocene. Note subhorizontal subduction and Laramide deformation and magmatism. B. Inferred plate configuration and plate motions, western North America and east Pacific Basin, Paleogene, approximately 40 Ma.

(From W. R. Dickinson, 1979, Cenozoic Plate Tectonic Setting of the Cordilleran Region in the United States, Figs. 1B, 2B, 2C, *in* Cenozoic Paleogeography of the Western United States: Pacific Section SEPM Paleogeography Symposium, vol. 3. Reproduced by permission of Pacific Section, Society of Economic Paleontologists and Mineralogists) subduction decreased to perhaps only 10° in the early Paleogene, arc magmatism crept inland and became greatly diminished in magnitude, a behavior that probably can be attributed to a change in the locus of melting beneath the arc. The place at which the descending slab penetrated the asthenosphere shifted progressively farther eastward with respect to the westward movement of the overriding continent (Fig. 14–8A). As the thin zone of arc magmatism migrated inland, back-arc tectonism also shifted eastward (Fig. 14–8B) and changed in structural style from "thin-skinned" thrusting in the old miogeoclinal belt to the characteristic cratonic basement-cored uplifts in the central Rockies.

In essence, the flattening of the subduction angle resulted in the increased coupling between the subducting plate and the base of the overriding continental plate. The effects of this coupling were thickening of the crust and mountain-building that spread as far east as Wyoming and the Black Hills of South Dakota, and Colorado, New Mexico, and West Texas.

According to Warren Hamilton, the continental lithosphere was in essence "eroded" from below against hot, young, oceanic lithosphere that could not sink fast enough (due to the shallowing of subduction) to "get out of the way" of the rapidly and steadily advancing continent. The product of this interaction was the Laramide crustal shortening of the Rocky Mountain region, manifested by large asymmetrical anticlines cored by Precambrian basement rocks, bounded on one or both sides by reverse faults or steep monoclines against deep basins that subsided and received sediments concurrent with rise of uplifts (Fig. 14–9). Individual uplifts were inaugurated at various times from Late Cretaceous to mid-Eocene, but there was continuity in timing of shortening throughout the region as a whole. *In this context, Laramide deformation is viewed as a response to the effects of rapid plate convergence and plate descent at an abnormally shallow angle.*

The arrival and collision of exotic terranes, as a mechanism that contributed to the Laramide deformation, should not be ruled out. As suggested by plate tectonocists, Laramide folding and faulting might be an expression of the final phases of exotic-terrane collision with North America, representing the "tightening up" of a "soft," fragmental continental crust composed of terranes accreted during the earlier Mesozoic (Chapter 12). Interaction of the terranes with the adjoining ancient crust would presumably cause rotations, uplifts, and overthrusts in a broad band encompassing both the North American craton and the terranes themselves. The

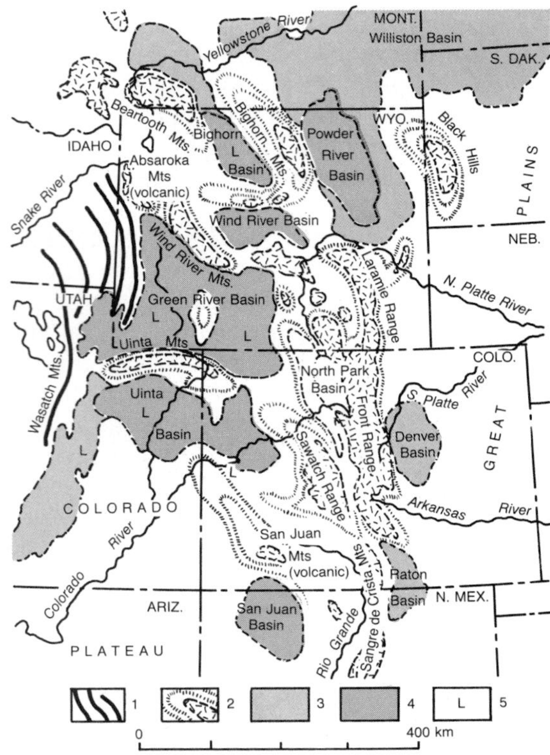

Figure 14–9

Central and southern Rocky Mountains showing uplifts and basins of Paleogene 1. Folds and fault blocks in sediments. 2. Laramide uplifts east of miogeoclinal area with outcrops of pre-Paleozoic basement rocks in their higher parts. 3. Basins that received Paleocene sediments. 4. Basins in which Eocene sediments were deposited over Paleocene sediments. 5. Areas of lake deposits, mainly of Eocene age.

(From Philip B. King, 1977, *The Evolution of North America*, Fig. 74, p. 116. Copyright © 1959, rev. ed. © 1977 by Princeton University Press. Reproduced by permission of Princeton University Press)

driving force of such a process would have been the continuing subduction of oceanic plates under North America.*

As mentioned in the previous chapter, the Mesozoic and early Cenozoic Cordillera of western North America has often been referred to as an "Andean-type" margin. Eastward subduction (much of it "flat-slab" style) during the late Mesozoic and early Cenozoic beneath the continental margin of western North America, and eastward subduction during the Neogene beneath the continental margin of South America, have produced remarkably similar structures and suites of tectonic provinces. Thus

*1982. The Growth of Western North America. *Scientific American* 247(5):84.

the Cordilleras of North and South America represent, respectively, deeply eroded and active examples of the same kind of orogenic system.

Rocky Mountain Basins

Uplift of the Rocky Mountains during the very Late Cretaceous and early Cenozoic brought to a close the final vestiges of marine conditions in the western interior of North America. Downwarping between the Rocky Mountain uplifts resulted in *intermontane basins* that became the dumping grounds for thick accumulations of Paleogene nonmarine sediments in alluvial-fan, stream, and lake environments (Fig. 14–9). Intermontane-basin sediment fills have produced important economic mineral deposits, including petroleum, coal, and uranium.

Of particular interest regarding hydrocarbons are the Green River and Uinta Basins in adjacent parts of Wyoming, Colorado, and Utah (Fig. 14–9). These basins provide instructive examples of nonmarine depositional models: during the Eocene they were occupied by a system of shallow lakes in which accumulated the delicately laminated shale, chemically complex carbonate mudstones, and dolostones of the Green River Formation. This formation (Fig. 14–10) is famous for its fish fossils and the oil shales that have figured prominently in recent discussions of America's petroleum reserves. The oil shales actually contain a hydrocarbon substance called **kerogen,** which is an early-stage oil. Kerogen is a product of bacterial transformation of organic matter derived from plant and animal life in the lakes. Abundant organic matter accumulated because of anaerobic conditions that existed at and below the sediment-water interface in the lake-bottom environments (Fig. 14–11).

These Green River kerogen-rich rocks are petroleum source beds. Geological history has not favored maturation of the oil and has not permitted expulsion of hydrocarbons into more porous and permeable carrier and reservoir layers. Usable petroleum is obtained only after an elaborate and expensive heating process, which reduces the viscosity of the kerogen. At present, these rocks, even though estimated to contain several hundred billion barrels of oil, do not constitute a viable source of petroleum to meet the nation's fossil-fuel requirements.

By Oligocene time, the intermontane basins were filled with sediments, and the last pulses of Rocky Mountain Laramide deformation had ceased. In places, flat-lying Upper Eocene deposits unconformably overlie tilted and folded older Eocene and Paleocene strata. At a few localities, Paleozoic and Mesozoic rocks have been thrust over lower Eocene conglomerates. By the end of the Oligocene, the Rocky Mountains had been nearly buried in their

A

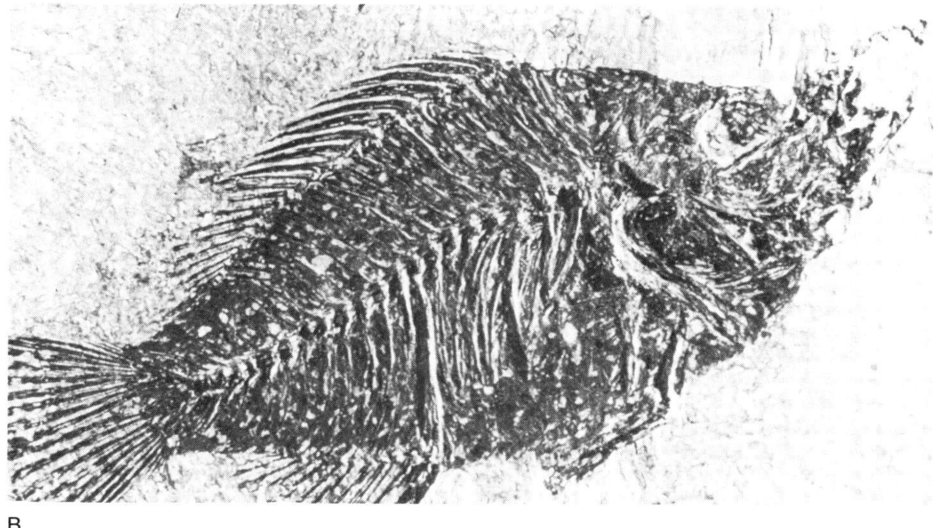

B

Figure 14–10
Eocene Green River Formation. A. Outcrop near Rifle, Colorado. Dark layers are kerogen-rich mudstone. B. Fossil freshwater fish from outcrop in southwestern Wyoming. Fish is 10.5 cm.
(A, photo by J. D. Cooper; B, photo courtesy of Wards Natural Science Establishment)

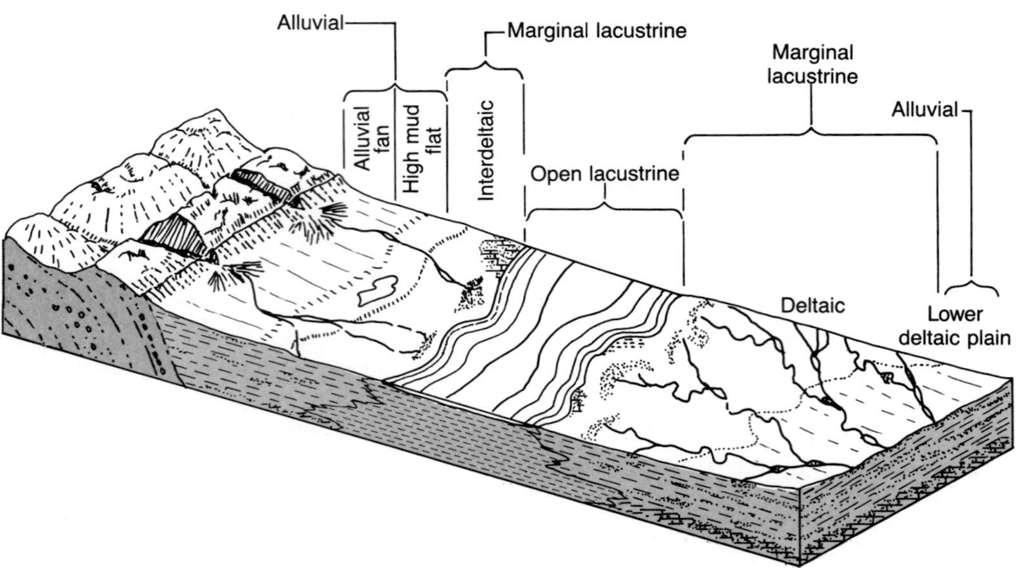

Figure 14–11
Distribution and interpretation of depositional environments of open-lacustrine, marginal-lacustrine, and alluvial facies of western Lake Uinta, Uinta Basin, Utah. Width of Lake Uinta in diagram is approximately 40 km; vertical exaggeration 15–20×.
(After R. T. Ryder, T. D. Fouch, and J. H. Elison, 1976, Early Tertiary Sedimentation in the Western Uinta Basin, Utah, Fig. 6, p. 502; *Geological Society of America Bulletin*, vol. 87, no. 4. Used by permission of author)

own debris, and their summits were worn down to peneplain surfaces. Some of these Rocky Mountain intermontane basin fills are over 10,000 feet thick. A spectacular example is comparatively tiny Jackson Hole Basin, in the shadow of the Teton Range, where almost 20,000 feet of nonmarine Miocene sediments accumulated—a testimony to truly dramatic subsidence and filling.

Voluminous amounts of erosional debris had accumulated along the front of the Rocky mountains in a great eastward-sloping apron (Fig. 14–12). Oligocene sediments of the White River Group, exposed in the spectacular badlands of South Dakota and in erosional escarpments of northwestern Nebraska, have yielded abundant fossils of a diverse assemblage of mammals. These include, among others, the giant titanotheres and sheeplike oreodonts (Fig. 14–13) (see Chapter 17). During the late nineteenth century, persistent and seasoned teams of bone hunters combed these beds in search of mammal-bone treasures.

Stratigraphic sections in the intermontane basins also yielded tons of mammal fossils, making the Rocky Mountain region one of the most productive areas in the world for specimens and data on Paleogene mammals. These fossils have provided important information on mammalian evolutionary patterns, community structure, taxonomic composition, and biostratigraphy. The Rocky Mountain Paleogene section has provided a standard for comparison with other nonmarine Paleogene sections on the continent.

Igneous Activity in the Cordillera

All through the Rocky Mountain region, from Mexico to Alaska, intrusive masses were emplaced during the Late Cretaceous and early Cenozoic. Much of this intrusion of granite and related rocks was accompanied by copper, lead, zinc, iron, gold, and silver mineralization that later led to extensive mining activity and spawned many of the colorful mining camps and towns of the American West. Examples are the vast copper deposits of Bingham, Utah, Morenci, Arizona, and Santa Rita, New Mexico; the silver of the Comstock lode and Tonopah, Nevada; the gold of Cripple Creek, Colorado, the Black Hills of South Dakota, and Goldfield, Nevada; and other famous localities. These deposits are the results of disseminated and widespread arc magmatism that also produced the Henry Mountains laccolith in Utah and the picturesque Devils Tower in Wyoming.

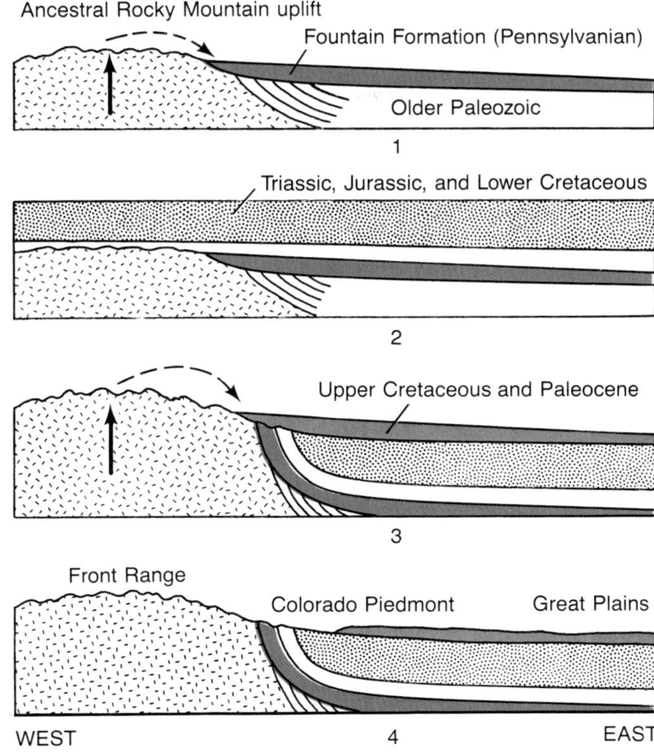

Figure 14–12

Structural evolution of the Front Range of Colorado. 1. Late Paleozoic; ancestral Rocky Mountain uplift (see Chapter 11). 2. Late Mesozoic, when range was tectonically quiet and buried. 3. Early Paleogene, immediately following Laramide Orogeny; formation of clastic apron of Great Plains. 4. Present relations following Cenozoic regional uplift and dissection.

(From Philip B. King, *The Evolution of North America*, Fig. 66, p. 108. Copyright © 1959, rev. ed. © 1977 by Princeton University Press. Reprinted by permission of Princeton University Press)

In addition to the intrusive activity, widespread eruptive centers formed in the Absaroka Range of Montana and Wyoming during Eocene and Oligocene time, and covered with lavas and volcanic breccias a vast area that includes the present Yellowstone Plateau. Amethyst Cliff in the eastern part of Yellowstone Park exposes a stratigraphic section of sedimentary beds interlayered with volcanic ash deposits and flows in which are preserved some 27 levels of fossilized tree stumps, trunks, and leaf impressions (Chapter 3). Volcanic activity in the Yellowstone area continued into the Miocene. The geysers, boiling mud pots, and hot springs are graphic testimony that volcanic heat, the so-called *Yellowstone hotspot*, still lingers below the surface.

Canyon Cutting

Early Neogene history of the Rocky Mountain region involved a broad, gentle regional arching called **epeirogeny.** This upwarping inaugurated a new erosion cycle by elevating the previous erosion surface and causing the streams to be rejuvenated. Previously buried mountain ranges were exhumed and carved anew by streams seeking base level. Large volumes of erosional debris were carried beyond the ranges to form the Miocene and Pliocene beds of the high plains. Remnants of several Paleogene intermontane basin fills—for example, North and South Park Basins, Colorado—were elevated to high levels on the flanks and within several of the ranges.

Spectacular canyons, such as Royal Gorge of the Arkansas River, Black Canyon of the Gunnison River, and Wind River Canyon and Bighorn Canyon of the Bighorn River were cut during the epeirogeny by streams whose courses were *superposed* across the structural grain of Rocky Mountain ranges. This superposition of major streams is particularly well illustrated in the Wyoming Rockies (Fig. 14–14). These rivers flowed across completely buried structural mountains during the Miocene and were let down across them at anomalously odd angles during uplift and stripping of the Paleogene and Miocene cover. The Gangplank (Fig. 14–14), on the east flank of the Laramie Range, is a finger of ground nearly 100 km long that somehow escaped removal; it extends from deroofed Precambrian granite high in the range eastward to Miocene sediments in Nebraska. It is the only place between Mexico and Canada where the surface that once covered the mountains still reaches to a summit.

The exhumed Rocky Mountains that we see today were formed structurally during the Late Cretaceous–Eocene Laramide orogeny, but the topography reflects a history of upwarping followed by erosion, with major streams incising deep canyons. The finishing touches of the final scene have been magnificently etched by glacial ice during the Pleistocene (Chapter 15).

The Colorado Plateau Province includes adjacent parts of Utah, Arizona, New Mexico, and Colorado (Fig. 14–26). Flat-lying–to–moderately tilted Paleozoic and Mesozoic rocks indicate that the region was not severely affected by the deformation that accompanied the Cordilleran orogeny. Although comparatively minor deformation affected the Colorado Plateau, the major Laramide structures lie in a belt trending northward and widening through New Mexico into Colorado, where they splay out in successive arcs to the west across Utah and

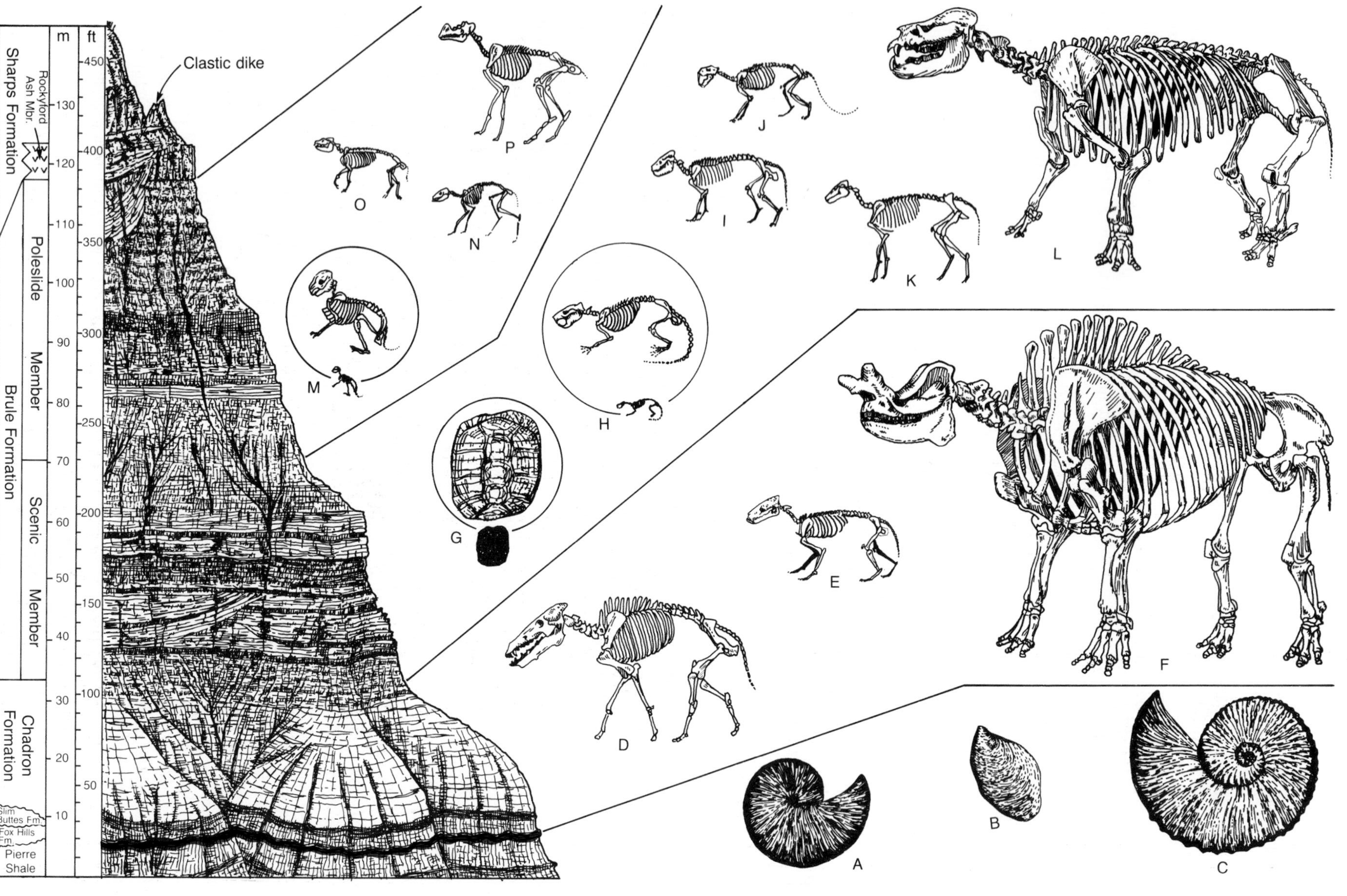

Figure 14–13

Upper Cretaceous, upper Eocene, and Oligocene formations and fossils of Badlands National Park, South Dakota. A, C. Upper Cretaceous ammonites. B. Bivalve mollusc. D–F. Early Oligocene mammals (D, entelodon; E, oreodont; F, titanothere). G–L. Early late Oligocene tortoise and mammals (G, land tortoise; H, squirrel-like rodent; I, horse, *Merycoidodon*; J, saber-toothed cat; K, *Messohippus*, three-toed horse; L, amphibious rhinoceros). M–P. Mid-late Oligocene mammals (M, archaic rabbit; N, chevrotainlike ruminant; O, oreodont; P, deerlike ruminant).

(From G. J. Retallack, 1983, A Paleopedological Approach to the Interpretation of Terrestrial Sedimentary Rocks: The Mid-Tertiary Fossils Soils of Badlands National Park, South Dakota, Fig. 4, p. 826: *Geological Society of America Bulletin,* vol. 94. Reproduced by permission of author)

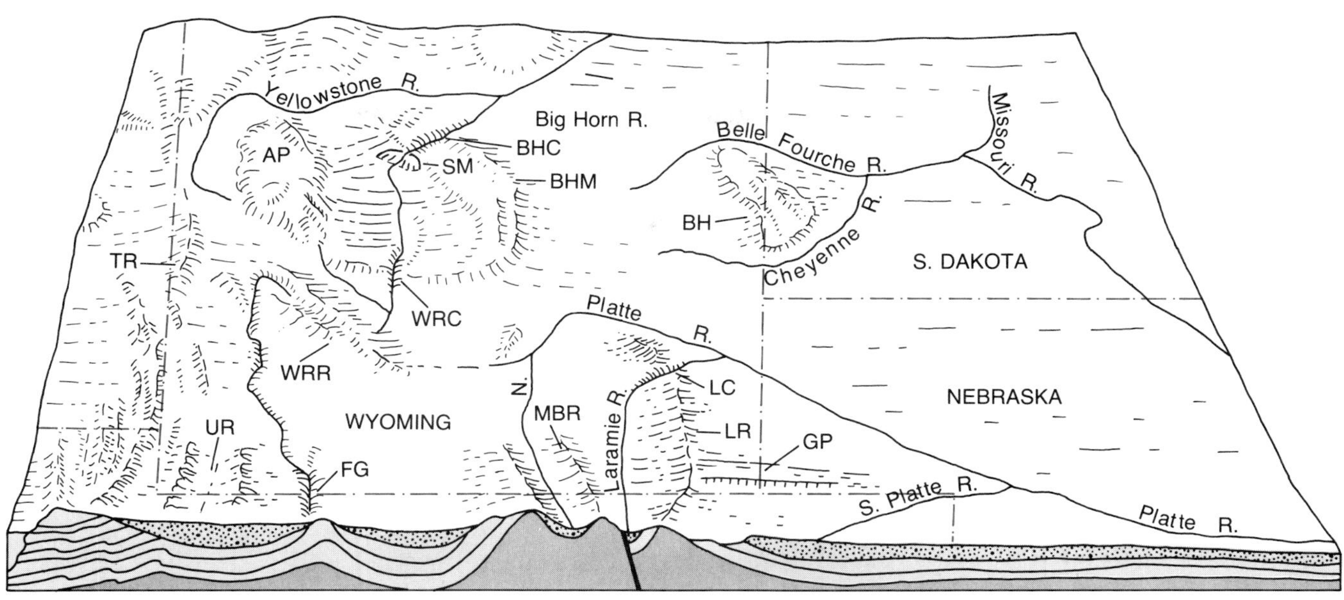

A

B

Figure 14–14

Canyon-cutting in the Rocky Mountain region. A. Rocky Mountain structural ranges cut by superposed streams. B. Sheep Mountain anticline, Wyoming, crossed by Bighorn River.

(A from C. A. Dunbar and K. Waage, *Historical Geology*, Fig. 17–12, p. 415. Copyright © 1969 by John Wiley & Sons, Inc., New York. Used with permission of John Wiley & Sons, Inc. B, photo courtesy of John S. Shelton. Used with permission)

northwest across Wyoming and into Montana (Fig. 14–15). According to Warren Hamilton, the shortening across the Rocky Mountains represents a rotation of the Colorado Plateau block relative to the continental interior. The geometry of the compressive structures indicates that this rotation was about 4° clockwise and is inferred to record a slowing to the southwest, by drag against subducting lithosphere, relative to the faster-advancing interior of the continental plate.

There has been no satisfactory single explanation for the uplift of the Plateau block itself, although underplating of continental crust above a deep crustal "hotspot" and resulting isostatic adjustments should not be ruled out. The region is characterized by plateaus and erosional escarpments that rise steplike to the north of its most famous feature, the Grand Canyon. Mesas and deeply incised canyons expose rocks ranging in age from Proterozoic to Cenozoic. Mesozoic formations, such as the sequence exposed in the area of Glen Canyon, Utah, once covered the region like a blanket, but have been eroded during the Cenozoic. The erosion was accomplished by streams rejuvenated during the late Cenozoic epeirogeny, which affected a major part of the Cordilleran region. Exploration of the plateaus and canyons by venturesome scientific surveys after the Civil War (see beginning of the chapter) contributed new concepts of erosion in arid regions, and inaugurated a fascinating chapter in the history of geologic investigations in western North America.

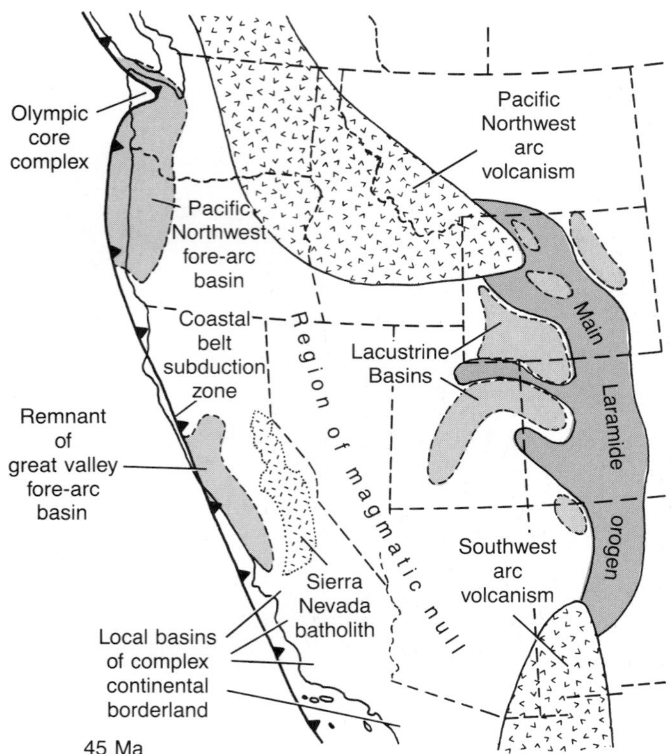

Figure 14–15

Main tectonic features associated with Eocene subduction along Andean-type western continental margin of North America.

(From W. R. Dickinson, 1979, Cenozoic Plate Tectonic Setting of the Cordilleran Region in the United States, Figs. 8, 10, p. 10, 11, *in* Cenozoic Paleogeography of the Western United States: Pacific Section SEPM Paleogeography Symposium, vol. 3. Reproduced by permission of Pacific Section, Society of Economic Paleontologists and Mineralogists)

The Continent's Trailing Edge

The Atlantic Margin

After the end of the compressional deformation of the Appalachian orogeny, and following extensional block-faulting during the Late Triassic (Chapter 12), the Appalachian Mountains were eroded to an almost flat surface by Cretaceous time. The modern topography of the Piedmont, Blue Ridge, Valley and Ridge, and Appalachian Plateau Provinces (Fig. 14–16) has evolved through several cycles of late Mesozoic and Cenozoic erosion. Early Cenozoic epeirogenic uplift of the Appalachian region caused major streams to become incised; resultant downcutting and erosion etched out the weaker rocks and created local relief on the more resistant rocks. This differential erosion is particularly well illustrated in the Valley and Ridge Province, where streams seeking new base level carved extensive lowlands in the weak formations of the folded belt.

Elevated remnants of old erosion surfaces suggest that several such cycles of upwarping, erosion, and peneplanation occurred in the Appalachians during the Cenozoic. Today we see only the roots of Appalachian folds (Fig. 14–16), structures inherited from the late Paleozoic deformation of the Appalachian miogeoclinal sedimentary succession. The topographic mountains are products of a complex cyclic Cenozoic erosional history. What caused the epeirogenic upwarping in the Appalachian region? The complete answer is not known, but as in the Rocky Mountain area, upwarping probably was related to isostatic adjustments of continental lithosphere.

The Appalachian belt has been comparatively stable tectonically since the beginning of the Jurassic, although occasional earthquakes, such as the 1872 tremor in Charleston, South Carolina, testify to renewed activity on some faults. A seaward-thickening wedge of terrigenous sediments comprises the Cenozoic section of the Atlantic Coastal Plain and continental shelf (Fig. 14–17). The great

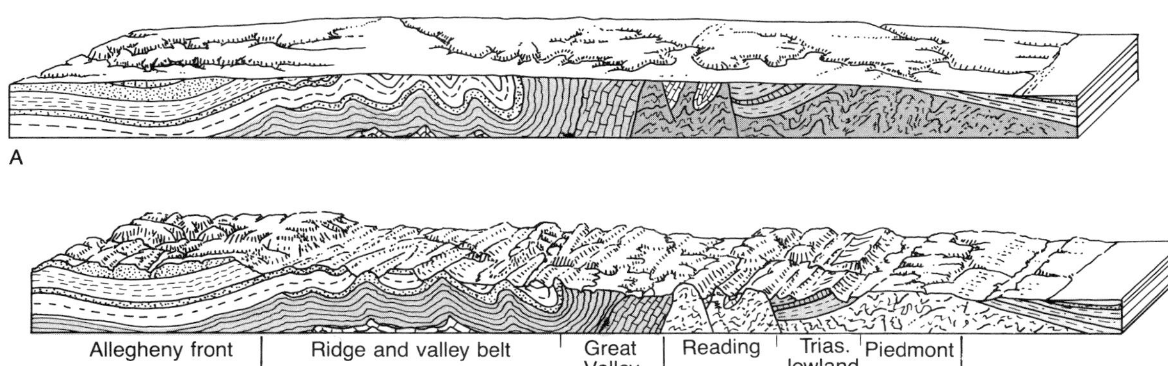

Figure 14–16

Cenozoic landscape evolution of Appalachian region in Pennsylvania. A. Cenozoic, Neogene dissection of earlier erosion surface. B. Continued sculpturing of landscape to form present-day Appalachian Plateau, Valley and Ridge (valleys eroded in shales; ridges developed on more resistant limestones and quartzites), crystalline Appalachians and Piedmont, and Coast Plain physiographic provinces. Note superposition of streams, entrenched meander patterns, and relationship between topography and rock type.

(From Douglas Johnson, 1931, *Stream Sculpture on the Atlantic Slope,* Figs. 1–9, p. 15, 17, 19: Columbia University Press, New York. Reproduced by permission of Columbia University Press)

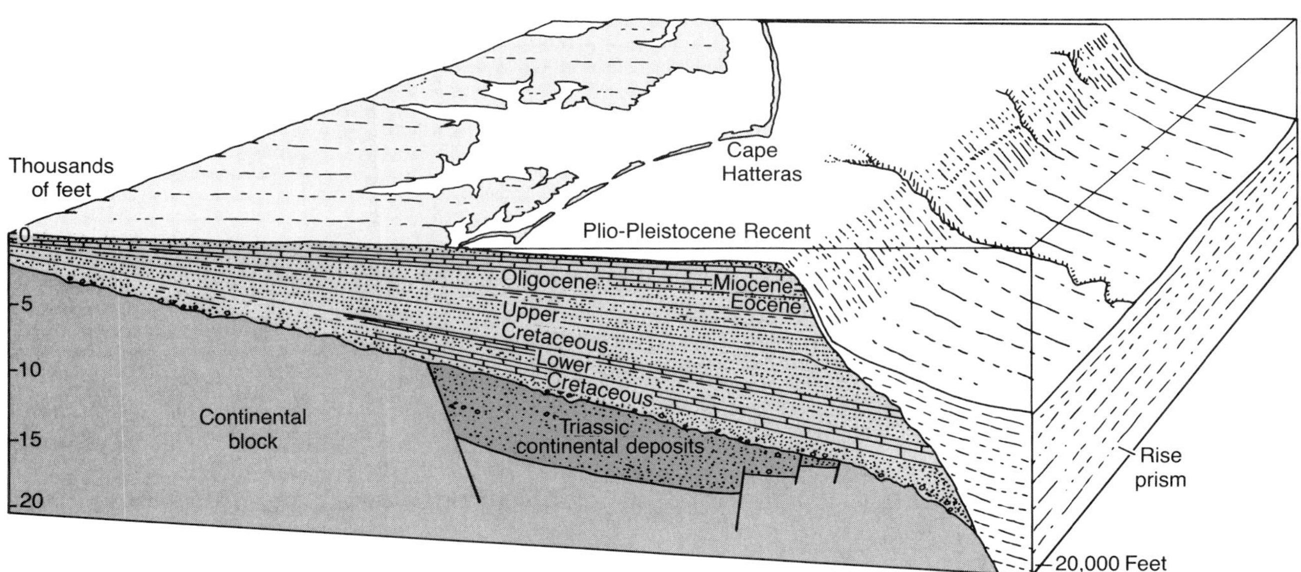

Figure 14–17

Modern continental-shelf sedimentary-terrace prism (miogeocline, medium brown) along eastern U.S. coast in vicinity of Cape Hatteras, North Carolina. Cretaceous and younger strata dip seaward and thicken at continental slope. The sedimentary prism was desposited on an Early Cretaceous peneplain, and basement rocks (gray) include pre-Paleozoic and early Paleozoic igneous and metamorphic complexes of the crystalline Appalachians. Late Triassic–Early Jurassic (Newark) rift basins and sedimentary fill (dark brown) developed during initial rifting of North America from North Africa about 180 Ma.

(From R. S. Dietz and J. C. Holden, 1974, Collapsing Continental Rises: Actualistic Concept of Geosynclines—A Review, Fig. 5, p. 20: *Society of Economic Paleontologists and Mineralogists Special Publication* 19. Reproduced by permission of the Society of Economic Paleontologists and Mineralogists)

bulk of this material was derived from erosion of the Appalachians. Remember that beginning in the Jurassic and continuing through the Cretaceous, the North American continent moved away from Europe and Africa. We already have reviewed Mesozoic sedimentation along this drifting margin. Cenozoic deposits along the eastern seaboard (Fig. 14–17) and in the Gulf Coast region represent the addition, during the last 65 million years, of sediments on the tectonically passive trailing margins of the continent.

The Gulf Coast

In the Gulf Coast, outcrop sections of fluvial and nearshore-marine sedimentary sequences change facies seaward in the subsurface to more offshore, finer-grained marine-shelf deposits. Important oil and gas accumulations occur in sandstone facies that lie updip from deeper marine organic-rich mudstones. The sandstones represent barrier-bar, delta-fringe, beach, and stream-channel environments. The porosity and permeability of these sandstone facies provide a hydrocarbon reservoir potential that is in sharp contrast to that of the downdip source-bed mudstone facies of relatively low permeability.

A most interesting petroleum-entrapment situation is related to peculiar structures called **salt domes,** which are more abundant in the Texas and Louisiana Gulf Coast than any other place in the world. The domes are vertical, fingerlike projections of intrusions called **diapirs** that have penetrated the continental-shelf sedimentary wedge (Fig. 14–18). Some have moved close to the surface, such as the famous Spindletop Dome in Texas. The salt in the structures has come from the Louann Salt, a thick Jurassic evaporite unit that was deposited during the early stages of formation of the Gulf of Mexico Basin (Chapter 12). Hydrostatic loading caused by subsequent deep burial of the Louann Salt beneath the thick Cretaceous and Cenozoic section has resulted in plastic behavior, upward flow, and diapiric intrusion of the less dense salt. The original loci for flowage were probably irregularities on the upper surface of the salt; such irregularities would have been accentuated by compac-

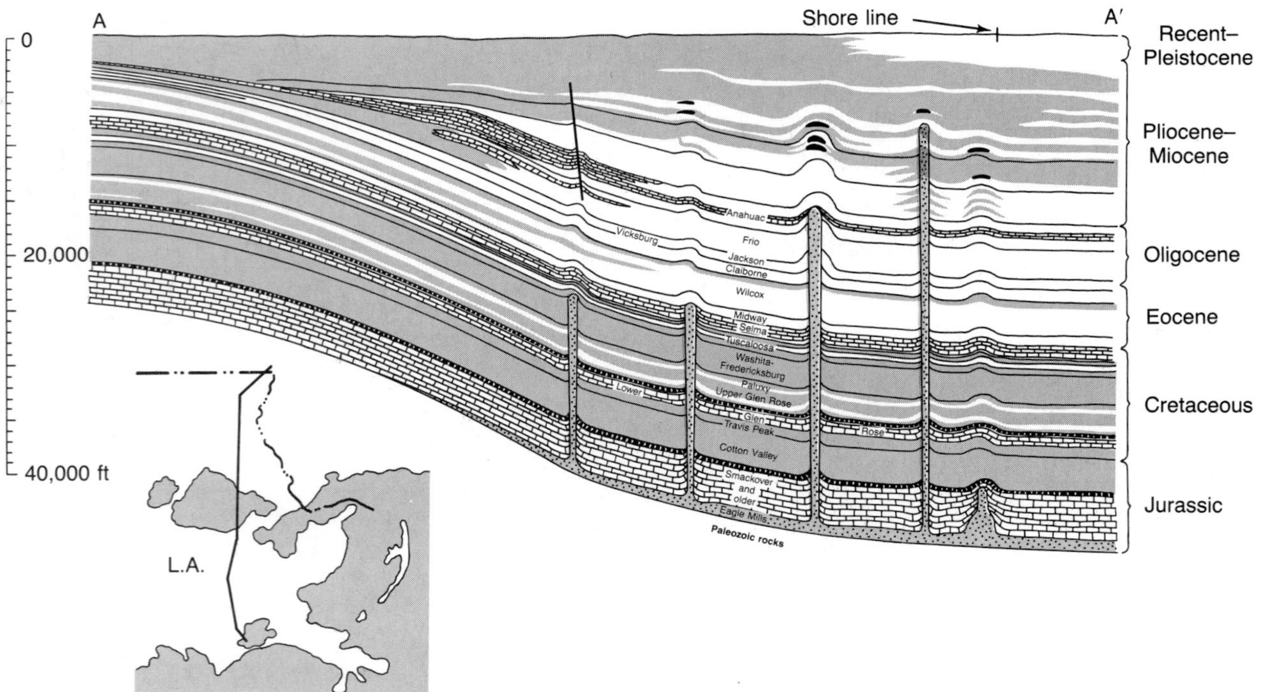

Figure 14–18

Cross section through Louisiana showing Gulf Coast sedimentary section and salt domes. Note petroleum accumulations (dark bands) in traps created by doming of sediments.

(From J. B. Carsey, 1950, Geology of Gulf Coast Area and Continental Shelf, Fig. 2, p. 362: *American Association of Petroleum Geologists Bulletin,* vol. 34. Reproduced by permission of American Association of Petroleum Geologists)

tion during sediment loading. In addition to having influenced the entrapment of recoverable hydrocarbons (Fig. 14–18), the domes themselves are sources of commercial salt and sulfur.

With regard to hydrocarbons, it is noteworthy that the Gulf Coast, both onshore and offshore, has yielded large amounts of oil and gas from the Mesozoic and Cenozoic continental-shelf and coastal-plain succession, whereas the Atlantic coastal-wedge sequence has contributed little. Much of this discrepancy may be a result of the comparatively small concentration of exploration effort along the Atlantic seaboard. However, a significant oil and gas venture could be in the offing for the Atlantic margin: recent geophysical profiles across the Atlantic shelf have identified attractive subsurface structures that might be favorable hydrocarbon traps. Our nation's critical energy needs may push us beyond the present environmental constraints to test for the presence of oil and gas in the Atlantic offshore. Gas-producing but immature hydrocarbons have been discovered in the Baltimore Canyon region of the Atlantic margin.

An Actualistic Basin Model

The present-day Atlantic margin provides an instructive actualistic model wherein the Atlantic and Gulf Coast regions are viewed as continental margin basins. In this model, the continental-shelf and coastal-plain sedimentary wedge represents the miogeocline, and the continental slope and continental-rise prism of sediments at the toe of the continental slope, developed on the transition from continental to oceanic lithosphere, represents the eugeocline (Fig. 14–17). The Atlantic margin-type continental margin basin is considered the model for those ancient analogues that developed marginal to a rift ocean on the trailing edge of a drifting continent. The Atlantic miogeoclinal continental-terrace prism was deposited on peneplaned continental crust that was formed by continental accretion—during the Acadian orogeny—of an earlier eugeoclinal rock assemblage and exotic terranes.

The actualistic model envisions the possibility of the present eugeoclinal sedimentary prism collapsing in the future and becoming welded to the continent by plate tectonics in the same fashion. In this light, one can envision a simplified scenario for the opening, closing, and reopening of the Atlantic Ocean, incorporating the notion of Atlantic margin-type basins and the formation of marginal orogenic belts (orogens), an illustration of the *Wilson cycle.* This geotectonic cycle also explains how the North American continent has grown by lateral accretion of orogens, a phenomenon that James Dwight Dana had described during the 1870s as part of his geosynclinal cycle.

The Continent's Leading Edge

Plate Collisions

In marked contrast to the broad continental shelf along the trailing-edge Atlantic and Gulf Coast margins, the shelf along the western margin of the continent is much narrower. This is because it is the tectonically more dynamic, leading edge of the westward-drifting continent, and has been engaged in collision with the eastern, leading edge of Pacific Ocean basin lithosphere since Mesozoic time. Today, deep-marine environments are present a short distance offshore, a setting that has been prevalent throughout the Cenozoic. This is evidenced by thick sections of deep-marine sedimentary rocks in the coastal ranges and basins of Washington, Oregon, and California. These deep-water sequences, commonly developed as turbidite-fan complexes, represent a continuation of Cretaceous depositional patterns. Many of these sections change facies rather rapidly in a landward direction to shallow-marine and even continental deposits.

As discussed in Chapters 12 and 13, from the early Mesozoic to late Paleogene, the western edge of North America was developed as an Andean-type margin with a margin-edge subduction zone and associated magmatic arc. Subduction activity along this margin was responsible for the deformation associated with the Cordilleran orogeny.

Perhaps no segment of the entire circum-Pacific rim has undergone a more complex tectonic evolution during the Cenozoic than the Cordilleran region of the western United States, and perhaps no other region has been the subject of more intense scrutiny and tectonic analysis than the Cordilleran belt. In 1970, Tanya Atwater, then a graduate student in geophysics at Scripps Institute of Oceanography, proposed a model to explain the implications of plate tectonics for the Cenozoic evolution of western North America. Her detailed analysis of seafloor magnetic-anomaly patterns revealed that at least three oceanic plates—including the now almost completely subducted *Kula Plate,* the *Farallon Plate,* and the *Pacific Plate*—interacted with the western margin of North America during the last 80 million years (Figs. 14–7, 14–8, and 14–19). Extrapolating back in time by unspreading and un-

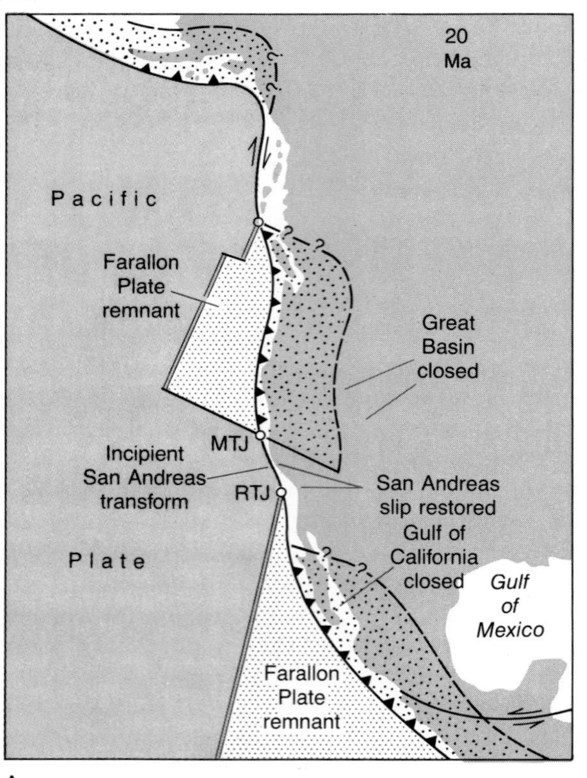

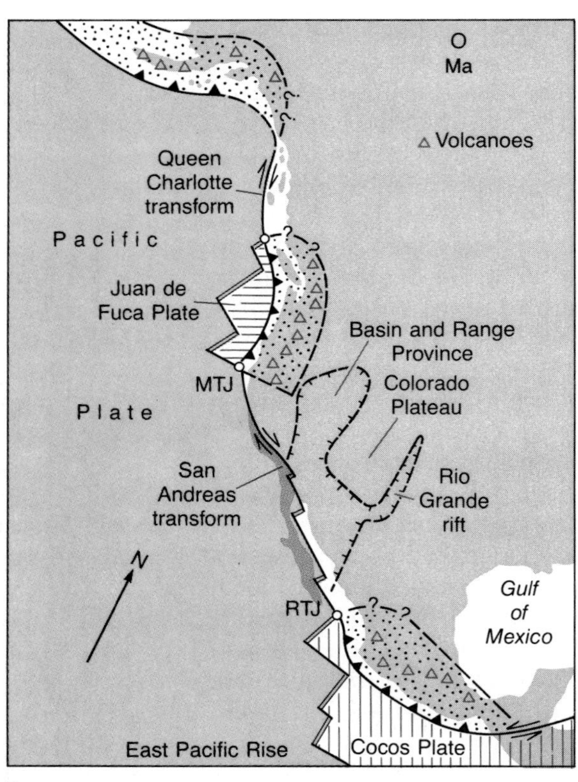

Figure 14–19
Evolution of the San Andreas transform system. A. 20 Ma. B. Present. MTJ = Mendocino triple junction; RTJ = Rivera triple junction.
(From W. R. Dickinson, 1979, Pacific Section SEPM Paleogeography Symposium Vol. 3—Cenozoic Paleogeography of the Western United States, Fig. 1, p. 2. Reproduced by permission of Pacific Section, Society of Economic Paleontologists and Mineralogists)

subducting various segments of plates, Atwater and others during the 1970s reconstructed the changing, almost kaleidoscopic pageant of plate configurations that have most influenced western North America during the Late Cretaceous and Cenozoic.

From Late Cretaceous through the Paleogene, the Farallon Plate was subducted continuously beneath the entire Cordilleran margin (Fig. 14–8); its remnants continue to be subducted beneath the western edge of North America off northern California, Oregon, and Washington (Juan de Fuca Plate) and off southern Mexico (Cocos Plate). Convergence was faster than spreading, and in the Late Oligocene (about 30 million years ago), the junction between the **East Pacific Rise** and the great Mendocino transform fault intersected the trench off northern Mexico (Fig. 14–19), thus inaugurating a major change in plate geometry. As spreading continued north and south of the intersection, the Pacific Plate west of the rise was enlarged toward the continent, whereas eastern oceanic plate segments were progressively subducted (Fig. 14–19).

In essence, initial contact began at a corner of the Pacific Plate, but with continued subduction north and south of the initial contact, the actual zone of contact lengthened. Along this zone, subduction no longer occurred, being replaced by lateral *shear,* resulting in the San Andreas transform boundary (Fig. 14–19). The Pacific Plate has continued to move northward relative to the United States. The result of the plate interactions has been the formation of a right-lateral strike-slip boundary (the San Andreas fault system), between the Pacific and North American plates, which has enlarged with time by the northward and southward migration of triple junctions.

The Pacific margin of the United States and Mexico today lies along the join between the North American lithospheric plate and the Pacific, Juan de Fuca, and Cocos Plates (Fig. 14–19). The diverse geology and topography along a broad belt well over 100 km inland from the coast is the result of the tectonic interaction between these plates, overprinted upon the products of previous plate interactions. Along this continental margin, three major styles of plate interaction occur: *transform, divergent,* and *convergent.* These are exemplified, respectively, by the San Andreas fault, the Gulf of California and Salton Trough, and the Juan de Fuca and Cocos Plates.

The San Andreas Fault

The 1906 San Francisco earthquake first drew attention to the San Andreas fault, the principal rupture in a family of right-lateral strike-slip faults (the San Andreas system) that is traceable through California for about 1000 km—from near the head of the Gulf of California to Cape Mendocino (Fig. 14–19). Throughout its length the San Andreas fault appears as a gash across the landscape, in many places displaying alarming amounts of offset (Fig. 14–20) on young features such as drainage courses and even cultural features such as fence lines.

Right-lateral slip of as much as 6 m accompanied the 1906 earthquake, and a total cumulative right-lateral displacement of more than 300 km has been suggested for the San Andreas since the beginning of the Miocene. Abundant press coverage has made San Andreas a household name and synonymous with earthquakes, but only during the last decade has it been appreciated that the San Andreas system of faults has played a most significant role in the Neogene structural evolution of not only the *California mobile borderland belt,* but much of the western Cordillera as well.

The San Andreas fault is now known to be one of the principal battle scars of the complex interaction between the leading edge of North America

A

B

C

Figure 14–20
San Andreas fault zone. A, B. Trace of San Andreas Fault, Carizzo Plain area, California. C. Trace of San Andreas Fault, Tembler Range, north of Carizzo Plain, southern California.
(Photos courtesy of John S. Shelton)

and the eastern margin of Pacific Ocean basin lithosphere. Once established, the San Andreas lengthened through time by northward migration of the *Mendocino triple junction* among the Juan de Fuca, Pacific, and North American Plates, and the southward migration of the *Rivera triple junction* among the Cocos, Pacific, and North American Plates (Fig. 14–19). Farther inland, arc magmatism has died out during the last 20 million years along a gradually lengthening segment of the continental margin. This extinguishing of arc magmatism resulted from the change of plate interaction along the edge of the continental block from subduction to right-lateral shear. In this context, the strike-slip San Andreas fault represents an unusual transform-fault boundary between the North American and Pacific Plates (Fig. 14–21).

The several hundred kilometers of cumulative right-lateral movement on the San Andreas fault system has been revealed through detailed geologic mapping and matching of identifiable geologic terranes on both sides of the fault. This matching has involved, among other comparisons, the restoration of sedimentary deposits containing distinctive rock types with the parent source rocks, as well as locating separated sedimentary facies on opposite sides of the fault.

Cenozoic Marine Basins

In addition to the effect on landscape and the offset of rock terranes and other geologic features, the San Andreas fault, as mentioned earlier, has played a key role in the structural evolution of California during the Neogene. Combined movements on the master San Andreas fault and related faults of the system have been responsible for the formation of sedimentary basins. Movements along the San Andreas system also have caused uplift of the California coast ranges.

This complex interaction between the Pacific and North American Plates has fragmented much of western California into a mosaic of horizontally and vertically moving crustal blocks. It was within this setting that a number of coastal sedimentary basins formed. Examples are the Ventura and Los Angeles Basins, as well as those in the offshore southern California borderland (Fig. 14–22). These were tectonically active marine basins which formed as downdropped sags and pull-apart troughs. These basins became filled with sediments because of their position close to high-standing sediment source areas in the mountain ranges along the continental margin. Throughout most of their Neogene history they were dynamic, fault-bounded, rapidly subsiding basins that received tremendous thicknesses of sediment, including some of the thickest Miocene and Pliocene sections in the world. These basins have received considerable attention through the years because of their tremendous yield of oil and gas. Much of the sedimentary section was developed as turbidites deposited in deep-water submarine-fan systems.

Just prior to the voluminous deposition of terrigenous clastics, one very unusual sedimentary unit, the Monterey Formation, was deposited in marginal basins of the California borderland during the mid-

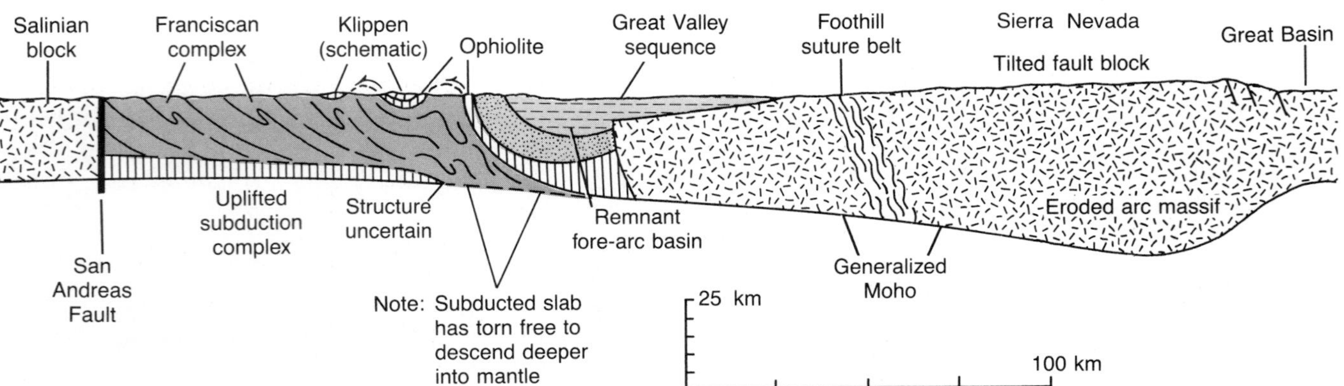

Figure 14–21
California-type margin that has evolved during the Neogene, highlighted by San Andreas fault zone (transform system). Salinian block has been offset from Sierra Nevada block by San Andreas fault system.
(From W. R. Dickinson, and D. R. Seely, 1979, Fig. 11, p. 25: Structure and Stratigraphy of Forearc Basins: *American Association of Petroleum Geologists Bulletin*, vol. 63. Reproduced by permission of American Association of Petroleum Geologists)

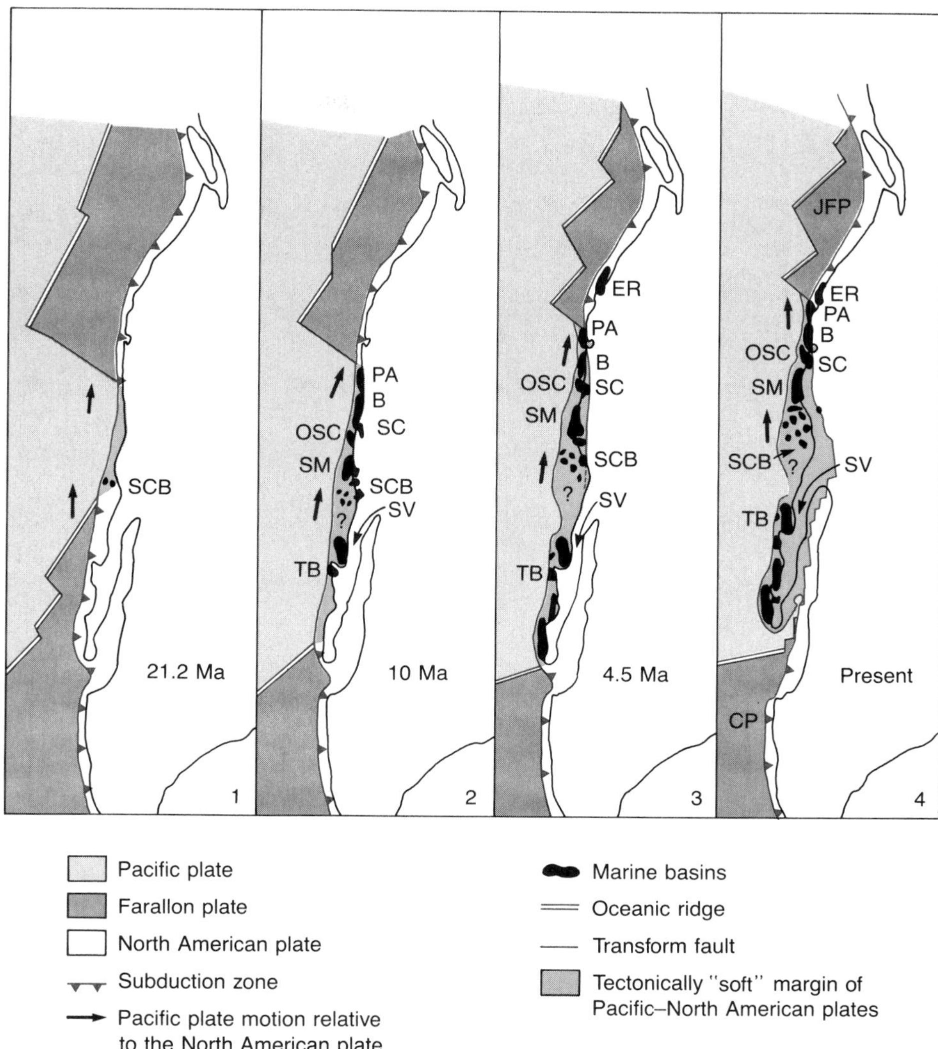

Figure 14–22
Interaction of Pacific, Farallon, and North American Plates for Cenozoic time intervals, showing time of initial development, locations, and general shape of Neogene basins that formed in tectonically "soft" or pliant zones between Pacific and North American Plates. B. = Bodega Basin; ER = Eel River Basin; OSC = Outer Santa Cruz Basin; PA = Point Arena Basin; SC = Santa Cruz Basin; SCB = Southern California Basin (includes Los Angeles and Ventura Basins); SM = Santa Maria Basin; SV = Sebastián Vizcaíno Basin; TB = Tortugas Basin; JFP = Juan de Fuca Plate; CP = Cocos Plate.
(After M. C. Blake, Jr., and others, 1978, Neogene Basin Formation and Hydrocarbon Accumulation in Relation to Plate Tectonic Evolution of the San Andreas Fault System, California, Fig. 2, p. 396–397: American Association of Petroleum Geologists Bulletin, vol. 62, no. 3. Reproduced by permission of American Association of Petroleum Geologists)

dle-to-late Miocene. One of the principal rock types of this finely textured unit is **diatomite,** a soft, white, siliceous rock composed largely of microscopic diatom skeletons. Tremendous diatom blooms were responsible for staggering numbers of diatom skeletons that accumulated during the Miocene. For example, a 1-square-mile, 1-foot-thick bed of pure diatomite would contain 10^{19} diatoms—only a small fraction of total Monterey diatomite! This widespread rapid deposition of diatom *oozes* records astronomically high plankton productivity, spawned by late Miocene climatic deterioration and intensified oceanic upwelling. Thus, the Monterey Formation represents the deep basinal phase of a major Neogene cycle of basin formation and filling associated with *wrench-fault* tectonism and terrigenous sediment-starved conditions along the California margin.

During Monterey deposition, climatic, oceanographic, and tectonic events combined to produce a unique set of circumstances. These included variable but generally high plankton production in surface waters; subsurface waters conducive to the preservation of organic-rich pelagic sediments; and a series of rapidly subsiding, restricted basins essential for accommodating these deposits. A unique association of facies formed as basin, slope, and shelf deposits within or near the fluctuating boundaries of a well-developed oxygen-minimum zone (Fig. 14–23). This depositional setting was similar to the present Gulf of California, western margin of South America, and southern California borderland. These organic-rich deposits are the primary source beds for the rich hydrocarbon accumulations in California's coastal Tertiary basins (Fig. 14–22).

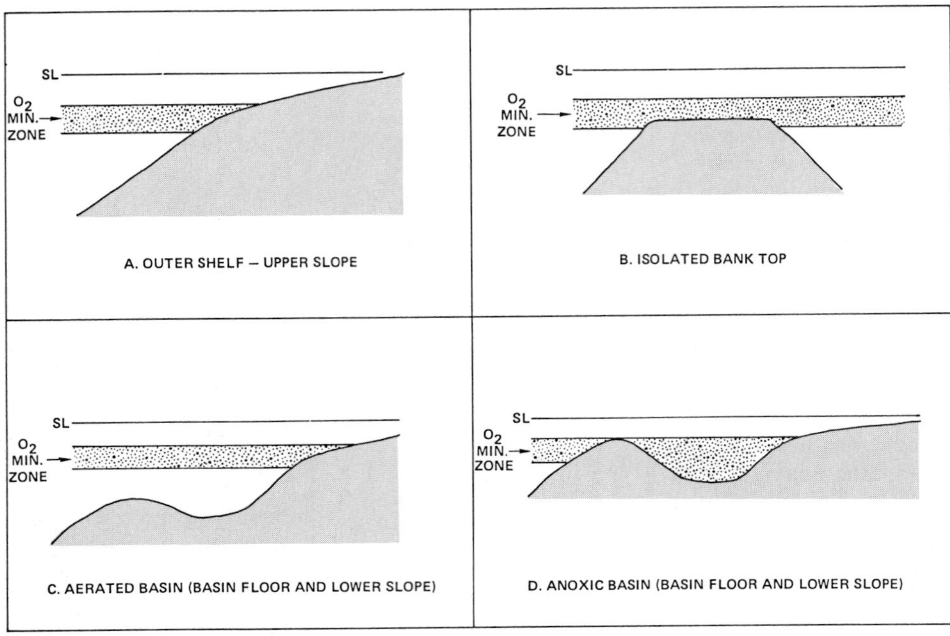

Figure 14–23
Simplified sketches of depositional environments represented by the Monterey Formation.
(From K. A. Pisciotto and R. E. Garrison, 1981, Lithofacies and Depositional Environments of the Monterey Formation, California, Fig. 19, p. 115: Pacific Section, Society of Economic Paleontologists and Mineralogists Symposium Volume. Reproduced by permission of the Pacific Section, Society of Economic Paleontologists and Mineralogists)

Anatomy of a Hydrocarbon Basin

The Los Angeles Basin is a deep pull-apart basin with complex substructure. In its deepest sediment-filled part, the top of the Miocene lies at a depth of 6 km. The basin is now filled to form a broad plain upon which the Los Angeles megalopolis sprawls. The predominantly marine sedimentary fill is Neogene and Quaternary in age, and deposition began when the basin initially opened in the early-to-middle Miocene. This thick sedimentary fill was subsequently compressed and deformed during the Pleistocene.

The Los Angeles Basin is one of the most prolific oil basins in the world, for its size (10^6 barrels of recoverable crude oil per cubic mile of sediment). Its ultimate production of crude oil will approach 10 billion barrels, and it provides an instructive illustration of the optimum incubator and habitat for oil. Organic matter, preserved in muddy sediments that were slowly deposited between times of turbidity currents, accumulated under oxygen-deficient conditions on the deep basin floor. The organic matter was subsequently transformed into hydrocarbons through deep burial, heating, and slow bacterial decay. Late in the Cenozoic the hydrocarbons were expelled from their source beds by overburden pressure. They migrated into the adjacent, more porous and permeable turbidite sands, and then moved upward along the flanks of the basin to become trapped in basin-margin anticlines, against faults, and in sand pinchouts (Fig. 14–24).

The timing of formation of basin-margin faults and anticlines was particularly critical for the entrapment of so much petroleum in the subsurface. In fact, many of the anticlines in southern California are so geologically young that they still have surface topographic expression. This correspondence between topography and structure was realized quickly by oil finders during the first half of this century, and all of these structures have been drilled extensively. The search for oil today involves looking for deeper, subtler traps onshore and similar geological situations offshore. Imagine the contrast between the present-day land of freeways, movie studios, and Disneyland, and the subsiding Miocene deep-marine basin with its turbidite fans and surrounding uplifted highlands!

Gulf of California

An interesting manifestation of Neogene plate-tectonics activity along the western edge of the continent is the Gulf of California rift (Fig. 14–25). This rift has been formed by plate *divergence* along transform faults and small spreading-ridge segments beneath the modern-day Gulf of California. The divergence is expressed by detachment of the Baja California peninsula, which consists of thick continental rocks, from the mainland Mexico con-

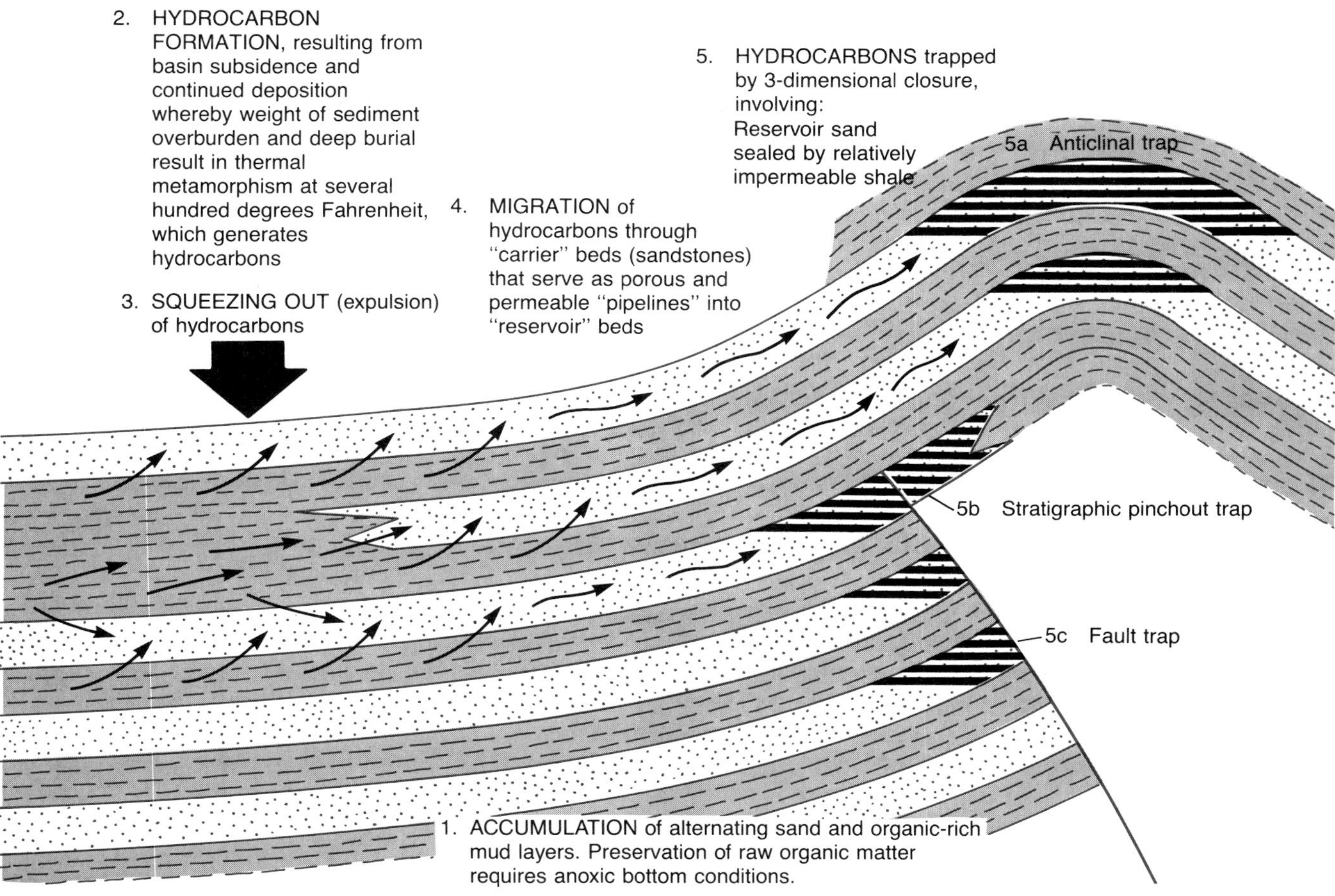

2. HYDROCARBON FORMATION, resulting from basin subsidence and continued deposition whereby weight of sediment overburden and deep burial result in thermal metamorphism at several hundred degrees Fahrenheit, which generates hydrocarbons
3. SQUEEZING OUT (expulsion) of hydrocarbons
4. MIGRATION of hydrocarbons through "carrier" beds (sandstones) that serve as porous and permeable "pipelines" into "reservoir" beds
5. HYDROCARBONS trapped by 3-dimensional closure, involving:
Reservoir sand sealed by relatively impermeable shale
5a Anticlinal trap
5b Stratigraphic pinchout trap
5c Fault trap
1. ACCUMULATION of alternating sand and organic-rich mud layers. Preservation of raw organic matter requires anoxic bottom conditions.

Figure 14–24
Optimum habitat of petroleum and the evolution of a petroleum basin from accumulation of organic matter, to formation of hydrocarbons, to expulsion from source beds and migration up flanks of basin, to entrapment in basin-margin structures and stratigraphic pinchouts.

tinental lithospheric block portion of the North American Plate.

During the last 5 million years, the Baja California peninsula has rifted and rafted away from the Mexican continental block in a clockwise rotation, moving obliquely northwestward parallel to a series of transform faults in the floor of the Gulf between active seafloor-spreading centers (Fig. 14–25). This extension of the lithosphere occurred as a component of the relative shear between the Pacific and North American Plates. Baja California, along with the entire coastal sliver of California west of the San Andreas fault, is now attached to the Pacific Plate, and is moving relatively northwestward along the San Andreas shear system at the rate of about 6 cm/year.

The Gulf of California is not an arm of the Pacific Ocean that has invaded the continent. It is an incipient small ocean basin, floored with oceanic basalt lithosphere that has been generated and spread from the fragmented East Pacific Rise. The Gulf of California narrows within the United States to form the Salton Trough, a complex **graben** now occupied by the Salton Sea. The Salton Trough formed in the Early Pliocene, accompanied by regional crustal arching that is interpreted to be the result of thermal expansion of the lithosphere above the northern continuation of the East Pacific Rise. High thermal gradients, which have provided the opportunity for geothermal power plants, and the presence of Holocene volcanic activity indicate active spreading centers at depth. The Salton trough contains a 6-km thick sedimentary fill of Pliocene and Pleistocene alluvial-fan, fluvial, and playa lake deposits; these are folded and faulted, attesting to ongoing deformation in the region. Most

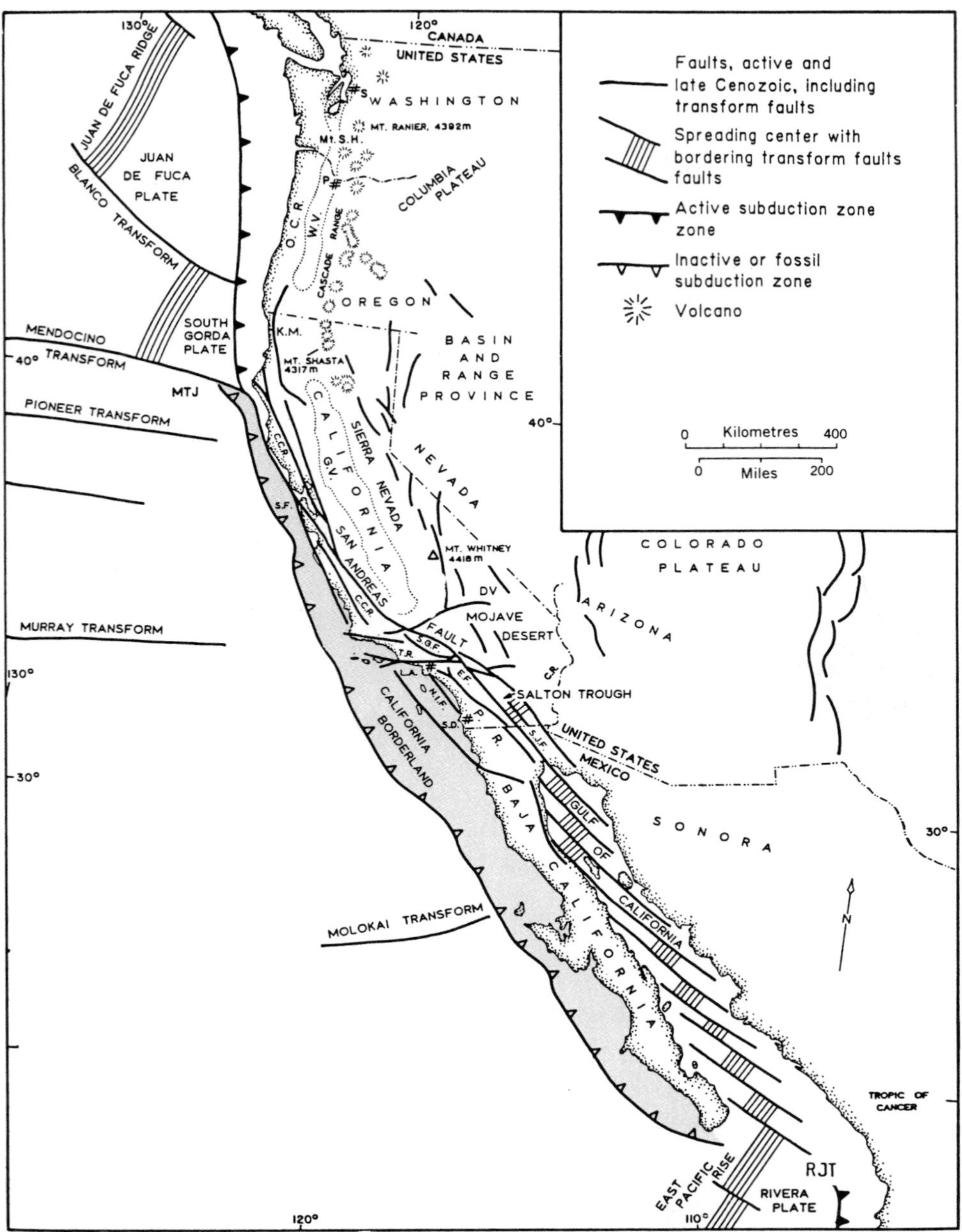

Figure 14–25
Tectonic sketch map of the westernmost U.S. and adjoining Mexico and Canada. CCR = California coast ranges; CR = Colorado River; DV = Death Valley; GV = Great Valley; KM = Klamath Mountain; LA = Los Angeles; MTJ = Mendocino Triple Junction; MT. SH = Mount St. Helens; P = Portland; PR = Peninsular Ranges; S = Seattle; SD = San Diego; SF = San Francisco; TR = Transverse Ranges; WV = Willamette Valley–Seattle Lowland.
(From J. C. Crowell, 1987, The Tectonically Active Margin of the Western U.S.A.: *Episodes—International Geoscience Newsmagazine,* vol. 10, no. 4, Fig. 1, p. 279)

of the sediment was delivered by the Colorado River, and much was derived from the carving of the Grand Canyon.

Basin and Range Province

From the Nevada-Oregon border, southward through Nevada and eastern California to the central highlands of Mexico, east-west extensional tectonics during the Neogene resulted in pronounced north-south block faulting, producing the characteristic features of the *Basin and Range Province* (Figs. 14–26 and 14–27). This is a vast region of uplifted fault-block mountain ranges, including **horsts** and tilted blocks and adjacent graben and asymmetrical half-graben downdropped basins. The unmistakable basin-and-range topography is an expression of the north-south-oriented basin-and-range structures—an unusual physiography that has inspired the analogy of a "horde of giant caterpillars crawling north out of Mexico."

This begs the question, "how did this vast region come under the influence of extensional tectonics, when for most of its late Paleozoic and Mesozoic-to-Paleogene history, it was a region subjected to

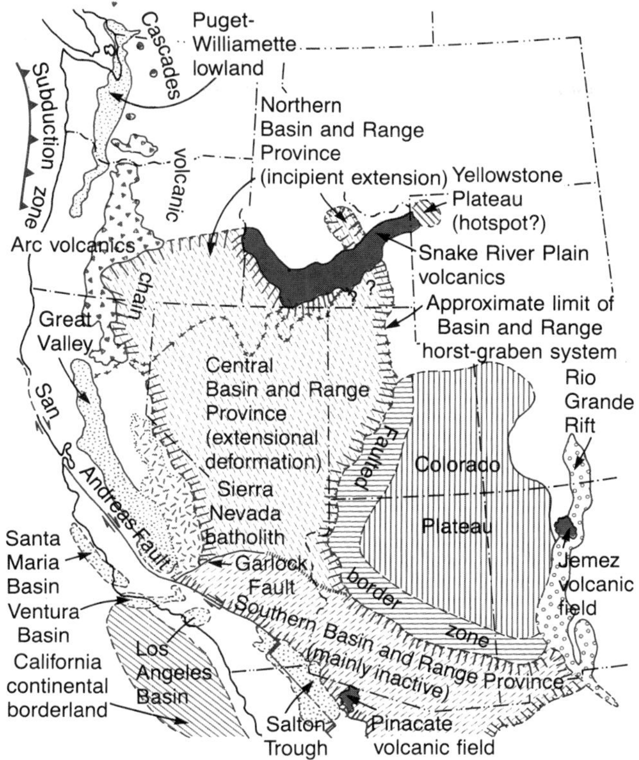

Figure 14–26
Tectonics and paleogeography of the Cordilleran region of the United States at present, highlighting Basin and Range Province.
(From W. R. Dickinson, 1979, Cenozoic Plate Tectonic Setting of the Cordilleran Region in the United States, Fig. 4, p. 8 *in* Cenozoic Paleogeography of the Western United States: Pacific Section SEPM, Paleogeography Syposium, vol. 3. Reproduced by permission of Pacific Section, Society of Economic Paleontologists and Mineralogists)

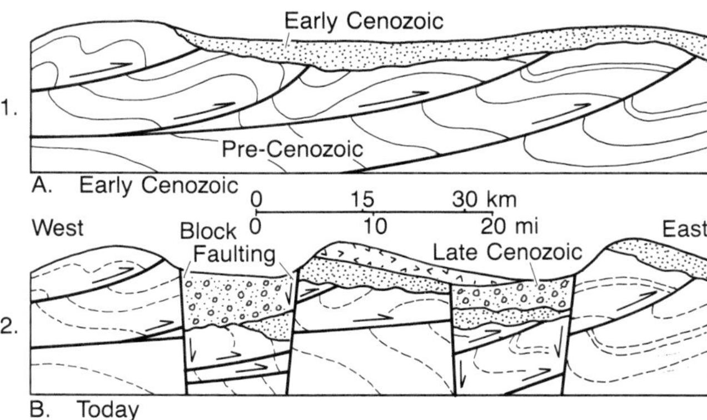

Figure 14–27
History of the Basin and Range region. 1. Thrust faulting and folding of Paleozoic and early Mesozoic miogeoclinal rocks, late Mesozoic–to–early Cenozoic Cordilleran orogeny. 2. Block faulting superimposed on older structural grain, formation of fault-block basins and ranges, and filling of basins with erosional debris. Older rocks and structures are still preserved with ranges.
(From D. H. Dott, Jr., and R. L. Batten, *Evolution of the Earth*, Copyright © 1981 McGraw-Hill Book Co., New York. Fig. 17.15, p. 465. Reproduced by permission of McGraw-Hill Book Co.)

strong compressional stresses?" Remember that from about 80 Ma to about 40 Ma, subduction along the Cordilleran margin was unusually rapid and the subduction angle was abnormally shallow. About 40 Ma, however, subduction rates slowed abruptly, and compressional shortening stresses in the lithosphere decreased. This was followed by a phase of widespread volcanism which lasted until about 20 Ma. The thermally weakened continental lithosphere became stretched and extended, perhaps because of this decreased rate of subduction. During the late Paleogene and early Neogene, the region of the Basin and Range Province was involved in the same broad epeirogenic upwarping that rejuvenated the Rocky Mountains. It was then an expansive, rugged highland, standing at generally higher elevations than other parts of the Cordillera. It had exterior drainage, and consequently contains virtually no Paleogene deposits.

Beginning in Late Oligocene, about 30 Ma, subsidence between major low-angle normal faults occurred, resulting in broad basins whose orientations were somewhat oblique to present-day structures. This early extension phase was then followed about 20 Ma by a second phase of major extensional deformation, the so-called basin-and-range event. It became pronounced during the Late Miocene, about 10 to 5 Ma, and has continued to the present, giving rise to the characteristic north-south-oriented horsts and grabens, bounded by high-angle normal faults, and the characteristic basin-and-range physiography.

Cumulative lithospheric extension (lengthening) has been on the order of 100 km or more, and perhaps as much as 250 km near the latitude of Las Vegas, Nevada. As the crustal blocks were uplifted, they were eroded, and terrigenous sediments were deposited in adjacent intermontane basins. Associated volcanism produced rhyolitic-to-basaltic flows and pyroclastic deposits, and was an integral part of early basin-and-range tectonism; however, the later Neogene phase of extension was not accompanied by major volcanism.

The basin-and-range block faulting, involving high-angle normal faults, was superimposed on earlier vintages of compressional deformation that had folded and thrust-faulted Paleozoic and Mesozoic rocks during several phases of the Cordilleran orogeny. This overprinting of one structural style on another (Fig. 14–27) represents the latest chapter in a deformational history that goes back some 300 million years in this part of the Cordilleran belt. More than that, it is a signature of a profound structural change that has affected western North America during the last 30 million years. This change has involved vertical and large-scale shearing fault motions which have resulted in extreme fragmentation of the lithosphere, in contrast to the predominantly compressional tectonic style that characterized the Late Jurassic–to–late Paleogene Cordilleran orogeny.

Interestingly, basin-and-range extensional tectonics coincides with the origin of the San Andreas fault system and its early evolution, and with crustal fragmentation within a right-lateral megashear regime in California (Fig. 14–28). Could the two be related? Basin-and-range tectonism, long an enigma, presents an alluring subject for application of plate-tectonics models, but unanimity has not been reached on a single interpretation. One view sees the second phase of extension as having been induced by an unstable plate configuration, with gaps forming between plates, as subduction gave way to transform motion.

An interesting idea proposed by Dickinson relates extension to the absence of a subducted oceanic plate beneath the North American Plate adjacent to the gradually lengthening transform (Fig. 14–28). Shearing stresses, originating at the transform plate boundary but propagated inland, may have given rise to a component of extension perpendicular to the plate boundary. Several major right-lateral strike-slip faults in the region of the Nevada-California border may represent a transition from predominantly shear to east-west extension.

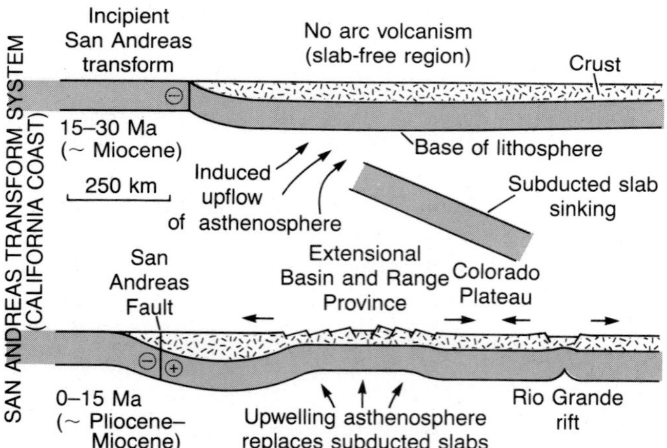

Figure 14–28

Inferred configurations of subducted slabs and associated tectonic elements during Neogene evolution of the Cordillera. Upper portion is 15–30 Ma; lower portion is 0–15 Ma.

(From W. R. Dickinson, 1979, Cenozoic Plate Tectonic Setting of the Cordilleran Region in the United States, Figs. 3E, 3F, p. 6, *in* Cenozoic Paleogeography of the Western United States: Pacific Section SEPM Paleogeography Symposium, vol 3. Reproduced by permission of Pacific Section, Society of Economic Paleotologists and Mineralogists)

Regardless of the exact mechanism, the extensional stresses appear to be associated with the transform boundary. When viewed in historical context, the initial phase of extension accompanied by major volcanism, prior to the basin-and-range event, was probably a response to the abrupt slowing of subduction, but when the lithosphere was still relatively "hot." The more pronounced east-west extension that began about 20 Ma, and which produced the rifting of crustal blocks that formed the typical basin-and-range style, was probably a response to the shear stresses along the developing transform when the continental lithosphere had cooled and was more brittle. The actual rifting, however, as a tectonic response to the extensional stress field, may have developed only because the continental lithosphere had been weakened by previous (prior to 30 Ma) thermal activity and mountain-building related to subduction.

The eastern-most margin of the Basin and Range Province occupies a narrow 1000 km long zone between the Colorado Plateau province and the Great Plains (Figs. 14–26 and 14–28). This is the Rio Grande Rift, a major zone of narrow horsts and grabens, volcanism, and nonmarine basin sedimentary fill that has been active for the past 10 million years. As a classic example of a continental rift, the Rio Grande Rift provides important insights into the upper mantle and lithosphere processes of intracontinental rifting—the kind that may eventually lead to the formation of a rift ocean basin.

The western margin of the Basin and Range Province is the abrupt eastern escarpment of the Sierra Nevada range in California. The Sierra Nevada block was uplifted in a series of pulses and attained most of its elevation during the Neogene. It has created an orographic barrier, blocking moisture-laden air from the Pacific, and producing a so-called rain shadow east of the range front. The Basin and Range Province embraces the Great American Desert and includes some of the most spectacular scenery to be enjoyed on the North American continent.

The Volcanic Provinces

Extensive volcanic activity occurred from Alaska to Mexico during the Neogene. Giant calderas and associated widespread ash-flow sheets are impressive volcanic features in the western United States. Many of these were produced by eruptions so voluminous as to stagger the imagination. Immense volumes of basalt poured from fissures in the Columbia River region of Washington, Oregon, and Idaho (Figs. 14–26 and 14–29A), and great masses of more rhyolitic lavas spread all through the Sierra Madre Occidental of western Mexico. The Columbia Plateau Province covers an area greater than 150,000 square km and contains more than 60,000 cubic km of basalt, making this one of the most impressive products of lava flooding in the world. Topographic valleys were filled in and older geology covered up as the plateau was constructed. Most of the basalt flooding occurred during the Miocene and Pliocene. The Snake River Downwarp of Idaho (Figs. 14–26 and 14–29B) was a volcanically active region whose trend tracks the Neogene movement of the northwestern United States across a fixed magmatic hotspot, now positioned beneath the Yellowstone area.

To the west of this basaltic plateau, a great chain of late Cenozoic andesite volcanoes comprises the majestic Cascade Mountains Province, extending from British Columbia southward to northern California (Figs. 14–26 and 14–29B). Cascade volcanoes such as Mount St. Helens, Mount Rainier, Mount Baker, Mount Hood, Mount Shasta, and Mount Lassen are expressions of a young magmatic arc that was superimposed on older geologic terranes and was related to a subduction margin, where the Juan de Fuca Plate is moving relatively eastward and downward beneath the continental rocks of western North America. This comprises the Cascadian *convergent* belt. The tectonic and topographic features on the continent to the east of the subsea subduction zone are related to this tectonic style. As the Mendocino triple junction moved northward during late Cenozoic time (Fig. 14–29), in conjunction with the lengthening of the San Andreas transform, the belt of plate convergence moved with it. Thus, the track of old volcanic centers, cut off in their activity by these movements, is recognized to the south in California.

As mentioned earlier, part of the western margin of North America has changed since the late Oligocene, from an Andean-type margin to what is generally referred to as a California-type margin, characterized by the right-lateral San Andreas fault system (Fig. 14–21). Remember that once the triple junctions between Farallon Plate segments and the Pacific and North American Plates had been established, their migration produced right-lateral transform motion, which replaced subduction. However, north of Cape Mendocino, which marks the terminus of the San Andreas fault, subduction of the Juan de Fuca segment of the Farallon Plate has continued through the Neogene (Fig. 14–29); the Cascade volcanic arc is part of an arc-trench system that lies north of the San Andreas fault. The volcanic chain of southern Mexico and Central America is part of an arc system lying south of the San Andreas fault zone.

Although the Cascade Province of andesite volcanism can be explained by subduction, a suitable explanation for the eruption of immense Neogene basalt fields in the back-arc region in the Pacific Northwest has been slow in developing. In some ways, these Columbia Plateau lavas remain as puzzling as they were before the advent of plate-tectonic models. However, some recent ideas on basalt plateaus may be on the right track. In this context, the Columbia Plateau, like the Deccan Plateau in India (Chapter 13), might represent yet another terrestrial equivalent of a lunar mare—the basalt flooding of an *impact crater.* The southern Oregon part of the Columbia Plateau appears to be closely related tectonically to the continental rifting in the northern Basin and Range Province and the Yellowstone hotspot track along the Snake River Plain (Fig. 14–29B).

One currently popular idea is that impact cratering apparently starts hotspots by initiating pressure-relief melting in the asthenosphere. Impacts may even initiate oceanic-spreading ridges and continental rifts by causing a crack in stressed lithosphere, which then lengthens in a direction perpendicular to that of maximum tensional stress. If this is so, random encounters with vagrant asteroids or comets play an important role in plate-tectonic events. As with the theory that bolide impacts have caused at least one mass-extinction event, this influence on plate tectonics suggests another possible example of how the Earth may not control its own agenda.

Most of the Cascade volcanic activity occurred during the Pliocene and Pleistocene, although some has continued to the present, such as the 1914–1917 eruptions of Mount Lassen and the 1980 eruptions of Mount St. Helens. Such recent activity suggests that major volcanic peaks are sleeping giants, and that Pacific Northwest volcanoes are dormant, not extinct.

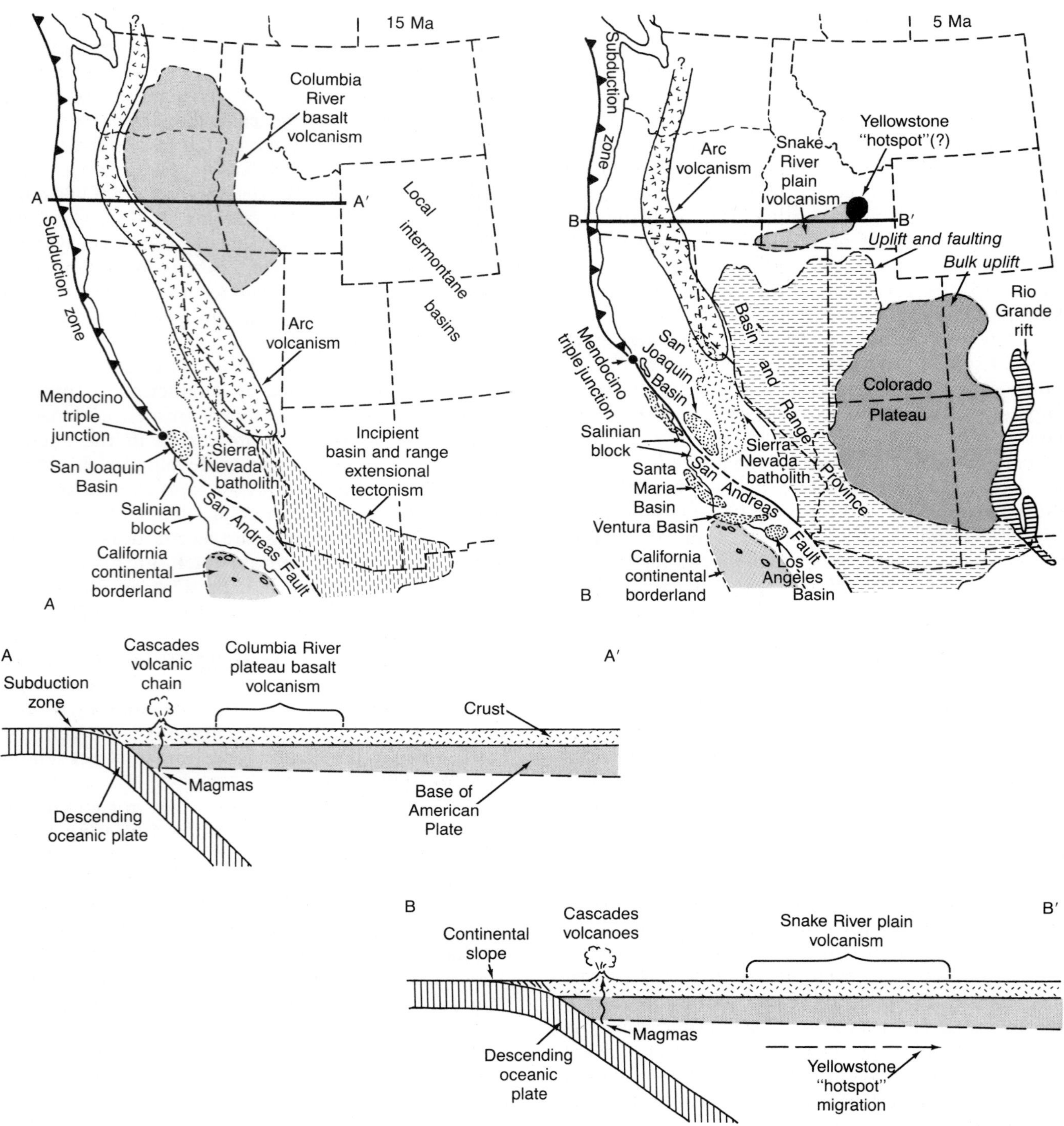

Figure 14–29

Paleotectonics and paleogeography of the Cordilleran region, highlighting volcanic activity. A. Miocene (15 Ma), showing formation of Columbia River basalts. B. Near the beginning of the Pliocene (5 Ma), showing Cascade magmatic arc and Snake River Plain. Schematic cross sections for A and B show inferred relationship between subducted slab and volcanism in western Cordillera.

(From W. R. Dickinson, 1979, Cenozoic Plate Tectonic Setting of the Cordilleran Region in the United States, Figs. 3E, F, 5–7, p. 6, 9, *in* Cenozoic Paleogeography of the Western United States: Pacific Section SEPM, Paleogeography Symposium, vol. 3. Reproduced by permission of Pacific Section, Society of Economic Paleontologists and Mineralogists)

Global Tectonics

Pacific Region and Ancient Tethys

A major tectonic revolution, involving large-scale shearing motions and block-faulting, has dominated the tectonic style of western North America and the northern Pacific Ocean Basin during the last 30 million years. The impetus for tectonic behavior has been interaction between the North American and Pacific Plates.

However, this tectonic disturbance of the eastern Pacific Basin and western North America is only a part of late Cenozoic changes that were of global importance. Throughout the entire Pacific rim, plate interactions have fostered heightened tectonic activity. Earthquakes and volcanic activity in Japan, Alaska, California, Central America, and South America are testimony to the continuation of this unrest. Within the Pacific Plate, the Hawaiian Island chain continues to grow as it migrates across a fixed mantle-plume hotspot (now positioned beneath the southeastern margin of the island of Hawaii). The pronounced bend in the Emperor Chain of seamounts, at about Midway Island, may reflect changing plate motions in the Pacific Plate, beginning about 30 million years ago (Fig. 14–30).

Outside the Pacific region, one of the most active mobile belts during the last half of the Cenozoic has been the Tethyan region between old Gondwana and Laurasia, where continued plate interactions resulted in formation of the Alps and Himalayas in the late Cenozoic. The great Alpine-Himalayan system of southern Europe and Asia displays plastically deformed Mesozoic and Cenozoic rocks in structures that we do not see in older mountain belts such as the Appalachians, because of dramatic differences in erosional history. The Himalayan Mountain system was formed during the collision between India and southern Asia.

The subcontinent of India is an excellent example of an accreted terrane of continental origin. The block that is now India was rafted along on spreading and subducting oceanic lithosphere into collision with the Eurasian continent. The converging lithosphere blocks telescoped some 800 km or more along thrust faults, forming the Himalayas and a lithosphere twice the thickness of normal continental crust. In the 40 million years since the initial collision, the Indian subcontinent has continued to move northward, tightening up the suture zone and shoving Asian crustal rocks to the north and east. The continuing convergence has caused major disruptions far into China, and has resulted in many devastating earthquakes.

The Alps resulted from collisions between northern Africa and southern Europe, and even today, Mediterranean islands such as Cyprus, which is experiencing uplift, attest to the squeezing between two major lithospheric plates. Indeed, structural disturbances of great magnitude occurred with amazing frequency during late Cenozoic (Fig. 14–31).

In the words of John McPhee, in his book *Basin and Range,* if the essence of plate tectonics could be captured in one sentence, it would be "There is marine limestone on top of Mount Everest."

Messinian Salinity Crisis: When the Mediterranean Dried Up

One of the truly remarkable geologic discoveries of the past several decades involves the late Neogene history of the Mediterranean Basin. Some 5.5 to 5.3 million years ago, during the so-called Messinian part of the late Miocene epoch, the Mediterranean was a region of basinwide evaporite deposition. Here an evaporite unit up to 2 km thick accumulated during a 200,000-year interval. Desiccation and restriction were brought on by the collision of Africa with Eurasia (Fig. 14–31), during which time a number of Mediterranean subbasins formed along the collision zone.

In the 1970s the Mediterranean was the site of intense geologic investigation and controversy. At a majority of Deep Sea Drilling Project (DSDP) Leg-13 drill sites—13 out of 22—researchers recovered gypsum and anhydrite, and/or halite, of Messinian age from sediments now covered by 2000 m of ocean water. A team of scientists led by K. J. Hsu postulated that the evaporites of the deeper parts of the Mediterranean subbasins had been laid down in relatively shallow–to–ephemeral water, and further that the Mediterranean was a deep, desiccated basin whose floor was some 2,000 m below sea level. Yet, it was covered by shallow-water desert lakes and playas!

This radical idea and nonuniformitarian conclusion stirred the fires of controversy among many land-based geologists who viewed the Messinian evaporite in light of a classic deep marine-basin model. However, in the consensus report that followed a later DSDP drill program (Leg 42A), an almost unanimous interpretation emerged: the Messinian evaporites of the Mediterranean were deposited in shallow water, interspersed with an

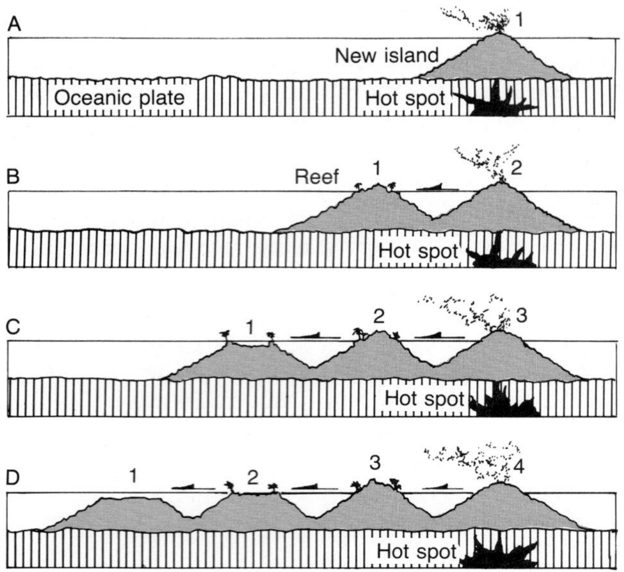

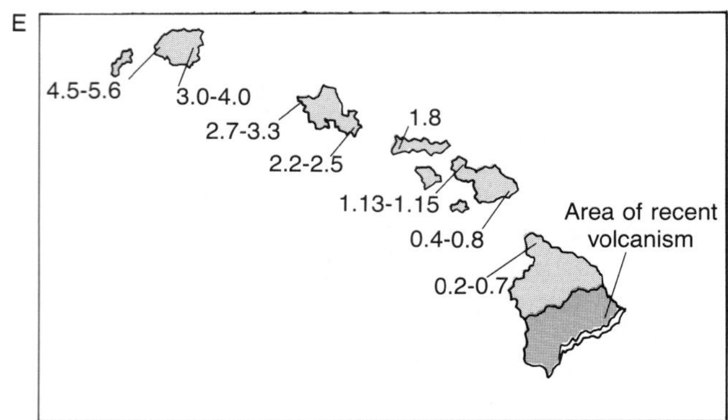

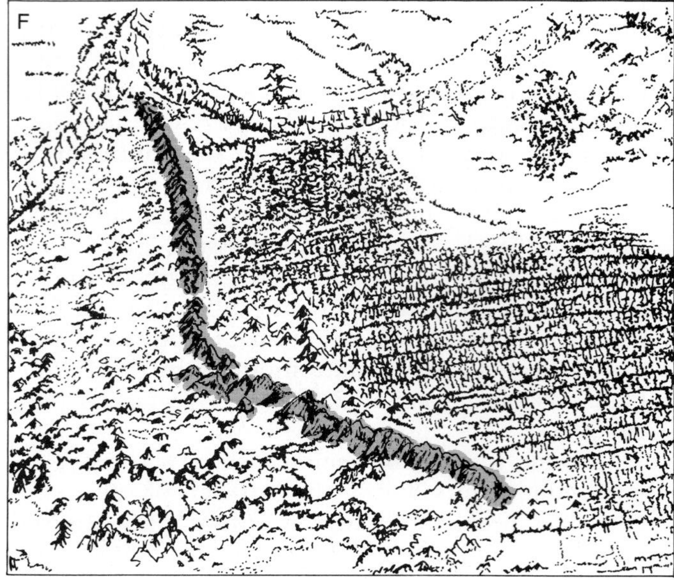

Figure 14–30
Intraplate volcanic activity in the Pacific Ocean illustrating the origin of linear chains of volcanic islands and seamounts. A. Volcanic island is formed by extrusions from a fixed (stationary) mantle-plume hotspot. B. As the plate moves, the volcanic island passes over the hotspot and becomes dormant. The surface of the island may be eroded to sea level, and reefs may grow to eventually form an atoll with further sinking. A new island is formed over the hotspot. C. Continued movement produces a chain of islands that become progressively older away from the hotspot, as in D. E. The Hawaiian Island chain has developed during the past 5 to 6 million years in a similar fashion (numbers are ages of volcanic basalts, in Ma). F. The Hawaiian chain is part of a more extensive chain called the Hawaiian-Midway chain, which, in turn, is connected to the Emperor Seamount Chain. An abrupt change in the direction of Pacific Plate movement is indicated by the change in orientation of the entire chain. The Emperor Seamount Chain began to form more than 60 million years ago when the plate was moving northward. About 30 million years ago, the plate began to move northwesterly, and the Midway-Hawaiian chain formed. This shift in plate motion corresponds in timing to the inception of the transform boundary between the Pacific and North American Plates.
(From W. K. Hamblin, 1989, *The Earth's Dynamic Systems,* 5th ed., Fig. 19.19, p. 414: Copyright 1989 by Macmillan Publishing Company. Reprinted with permission of Macmillan Publishing Company)

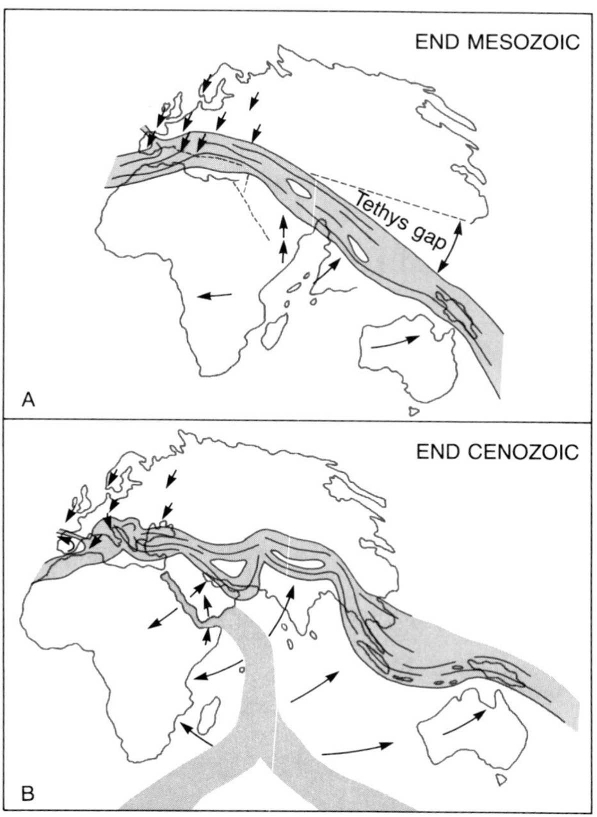

Figure 14–31
Plate interactions and deformation in Tethyan region. Light-gray bands represent orogenic belts; brown represents seafloor spreading centers. Short arrows show continental displacements; long arrows represent magnetization directions.
(From R. H. Dott, Jr., and R. L. Batten, *Evolution of the Earth*, Fig. 17.31, p. 479). Copyright © 1981 by McGraw-Hill Book Co., New York. Reproduced by permission of McGraw-Hill Book Co.)

occasional deeper-water deposit. If this idea is correct, and it has yet to be disproved, the depositional setting of the Messinian evaporites is unusual, and perhaps unique—no known modern counterparts can be invoked.

According to the Hsu team scenario, prior to the Messinian, the western end of the Mediterranean was supplied with seawater by a current flowing continually from the Atlantic, and the eastern end was supplied by water flowing in from the Tethys. The collision of Africa with Eurasia restricted the inflow, and then some 5.5 million years ago a tectonic dam cut off the surface inflow of seawater. Within 1,000 to 10,000 years, the Mediterranean dried out, creating a series of ephemeral and perennial lacustrine basins on what was previously the deep seafloor of the Mediterranean. These lakes were scattered across the old abyssal plain of the former seafloor at a level 2 km or more below the level of the Atlantic. Needless to say, the final refilling of the Mediterranean Sea some 5.3 million years ago must have been a spectacular event, with Atlantic waters reentering the deep hole in a series of colossal waterfalls.

Hsu and others contend that the opposing model of deep-water salt deposition is inapplicable, because it is proven wrong by many facts, such as the faunal evidence (e.g., indigenous faunas of freshwater benthic ostracodes that could not have lived in a salt-depositing sea). According to them, the deep-desiccation model explains many natural wonders of the Mediterranean world, such as post-Miocene plant and animal dispersal patterns. Geophysicists find the model attractive because it helps explain the existence of a seismically defined "grand canyon" beneath the city of Cairo, presumably cut by the Nile River into the deposits of its former delta when base-level was drastically lowered.

The deep-desiccation model has been challenged a number of times, but has withstood these challenges when details of the evidence were examined. Some of the challenges have been made because the deep-desiccation model "doesn't seem right," reflecting personal predelictions rather than science. If the model is correct, it not only represents a remarkable bit of geologic history, but a triumph of the spirit as well. It shows that scientists are not afraid to support a radical idea if it is well documented, and to believe in the unexpected, the unconventional, and the nonuniformitarian history of the Earth.

Life of the Cenozoic

The Age of Mammals

Mammals inherited the Earth from the reptiles, and diversified rapidly in an initial adaptive radiation that filled many niches left vacant by the extinction of Mesozoic reptiles. As will be elaborated more fully in Chapter 17, two mammal groups—marsupials and placentals—that had emerged during the Cretaceous had a major influence on early Cenozoic mammal evolution. The real mammal success story involved the placentals; probably because of their better-organized brain, they generally won in competition with other kinds of mammals. An early placental group, the shrewlike insectivores, was the stem stock from which the other placental orders evolved during the Paleocene and Eocene. By the Eocene, early ancestors of most modern mammal orders were present, including such familiar groups as rodents, carnivores, odd-toed and even-toed hoofed mammals, elephants, whales, as well as primates, the order to which apes and man (see Chapter 17) belong.

In a pattern reminiscent of many other groups, placental mammals underwent an initial phase of "trial-and-error" and "experimental" evolution during which time a number of archaic groups became extinct. A mass-extinction event occurred near the end of the Eocene. Real stabilization of mammalian evolution took place during the Neogene. The tremendous diversification of flowering plants—the angiosperms—had a profound effect on the evolution of animal groups, such as insects, birds, and particularly mammals. This is quite evident in the Miocene, when prairie grasses evolved and influenced a change in many groups of mammalian herbivores, from browsers to grazers. This change is well illustrated by the pattern of horse evolution, in which changes in dental patterns and limb and toe structure (Chapter 17) can be viewed.

During the dawn of mammal evolution, the supercontinent Pangaea had begun to split apart. Through the Cenozoic, the pieces moved and slipped farther apart, drifting passively on their moving plates. Terrestrial life forms had been comparatively uniform across the supercontinent, but during the Cenozoic each drifting land mass developed its own environmental conditions. Such was the situation in North America: the birth of the Rockies and the formation of the Great Plains opened up new niches for enterprising mammals. In Australia, the critical timing of its isolation as an island spared the indigenous marsupial fauna from early Cenozoic competition with placentals. Plate movement, and the resulting continental separations, were responsible for more endemism and comparatively greater diversification among the total world mammal fauna than we see in Mesozoic land reptiles, which have a decidedly more cosmopolitan complexion.

The Marine Realm

Cenozoic fragmentation and isolation of continents created the best of all possible worlds for marine invertebrates. After the end-of-Mesozoic extinctions wiped out the ammonites and several other major groups, the composition of invertebrate faunas gradually took on a modern look, as familiar groups evolved successfully—bivalve and gastropod molluscs, bryozoans, echinoderms, worms, arthropods, and corals (Fig. 14–32). Marine invertebrates probably have a greater total diversity today than during any time in geologic history. This modern diversity is the result of isolation and north-south configuration of land masses and continental shelves. This situation, which has evolved steadily through the Cenozoic, has influenced climatic patterns and important changes in oceanic circulation.

More than 30 modern marine-shelf benthic-invertebrate provinces have been defined. These provinces are separated longitudinally by continental masses and ocean basins, which provide major barriers to migration and mixing. The provinces are partitioned latitudinally (principally by temperature barriers) and their boundaries coincide with those of major climate belts (e.g., Fig. 3–40, Chapter 3). These temperature boundaries also have created migratory barriers, thus facilitating geographic speciation and formation of endemic faunas. In contrast, for example, during the Jurassic there were fewer than a half-dozen separate provinces, and faunas were much more cosmopolitan, resulting in lowered total diversity.

Foraminifera (Fig. 14–32, I–L), diatoms, radiolarians, dinoflagellates, coccolithophorids, and other single-celled groups have flourished through the Cenozoic. Foraminifera are widespread in Cenozoic sediments and have been studied extensively because of their use in biostratigraphic correlation in subsurface sections and in reconstructing paleoenvironments and *paleobathymetric* patterns. Certain planktonic forms have allowed precise correlations of deep-basin sections with shallow-marine sections. Spores and pollen also have served as useful microfossils in stratigraphic studies. Because of their subsurface stratigraphic value, all of these microfossil groups have proved useful in the search for petroleum. Many local and regional Cenozoic chronostratigraphic subdivision schemes have been erected on the basis of terrestrial mammal faunas, marine mega-invertebrates, and marine and nonmarine microfossils (including foraminifera, radiolarians, and diatoms, as well as spores and pollen).

In addition to the biostratigraphic data, and tied in with it, is an ever-growing network of radiometric dates derived from interbedded volcanic ash units and continental and marine volcanic flows and shallow intrusives. Paleomagnetic events recorded as geomagnetic reversals also have furnished a powerful tool for chronostratigraphic correlations and subdivisions in some sections of Cenozoic sediments and volcanic rocks, especially when tied to biostratigraphic and radiometric dates.

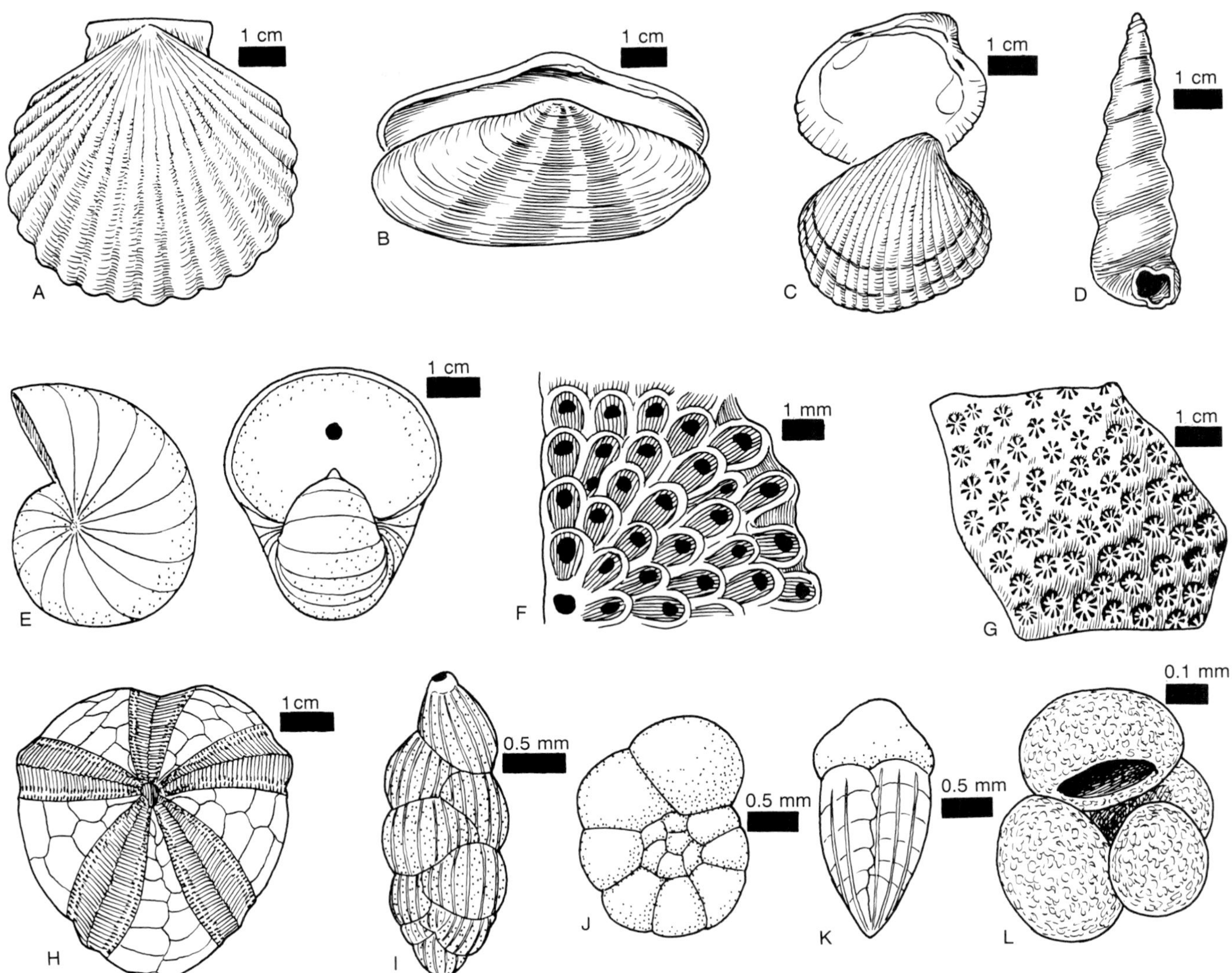

Figure 14–32
Representative Cenozoic marine inverterbrate fossils. A–C. Bivalve molluscs. D. Gastropod mollusc. E. Nautiloid cephalopod. F. Bryozoan, G. Scleractinian coral. H. Echinoid echinoderm. I–K. Benthic foraminifer. L. Planktonic foraminifer.
(A–C, E–H from *Treatise on Invertebrate Paleontology,* University of Kansas and Geological Society of America; D from M. S. Petersen and J. K. Rigby, 1982, *Interpreting Earth History,* Pl. 8, p. 115; Wm. C. Brown Publishing Co.; I–K from R. M. Kleinpell, 1938, Miocene Stratigraphy of California, Pls. XX, XIV, Figs. 17, 12a, 3a; *American Association of Petroleum Geologists;* L from R. Z. Poore and others, 1981, Microfossil Biostratigraphy and Biochronology of the Relizian and Luisian Stages of California, Pl. 1, *in* The Monterey Formation and Related Siliceous Rocks of California: Pacific Section, Society of Economic Paleontologists and Mineralogists)

"Twenty Seconds 'Til Midnight": The Quaternary

If all of geologic history were scaled down to a 24-hour day (another way of metaphorically depicting deep time), the latest 2 million-year interval of the Cenozoic—the Pleistocene and Holocene Epochs, comprising the Quaternary Period—would consume only the last 20 seconds! The Pleistocene is characterized by great continental glaciers that covered much of the northern hemisphere, moving southward from the Arctic region on at least four separate occasions. The diverse effects of Pleistocene glaciation and its possible causes are treated

A B C D

Figure 14–33
Glacially influenced landscapes. A. Grand Tetons, Wyoming, showing glaciated U-shaped valley. B. Grand Tetons and terraces along the Snake River, Wyoming. Terraces formed of sediment deposited during sea-level highstands, elevated by downcutting during sea-level lowstand. C. Peyto Lake and lacustrine delta of outwash plain, Columbia ice fields area, Canadian Rockies, Alberta. D. Cross-section view of a gravel bar that formed as a tombolo in pluvial Lake Manly, which occupied Death Valley during the late Pleistocene. Death Valley National Monument, California.
(Photos A–C by J. D. Cooper. D from John S. Shelton, used with permission)

in Chapter 15; we mention it here only to put this fascinating epoch in its historical context. The onset of frigid climates during the Cenozoic is indicated by cooler marine temperatures and lowered sea levels during the Oligocene. Pleistocene glaciation may well have been strongly influenced by late Cenozoic plate motions that resulted in the North Pole being surrounded by continents.

During the Pleistocene, alpine glaciation occurred in the higher-altitude regions of the Rockies, Cascades, and Sierra Nevada. The powerful erosive force of glacial ice and the influence of glacial activity upon landscapes is graphically exhibited in such places as Yosemite Valley, California; Waterton-Glacier International Peace Park, Montana/Canada; Jasper Ice Fields, Alberta; Rocky Mountain National Park, Colorado; and the Grand Tetons of Wyoming (Fig. 14–33), among others—testimony to ice having sculptured the final scene. Today some alpine glaciers remain, but they are small in comparison to their Pleistocene counterparts, and their numbers have been greatly reduced.

Pleistocene glacial and interglacial phases had tremendous impact on marine sedimentation. Great volumes of sediment were carried by major streams to the shelves of the continent's trailing edge and to the turbidite fans of its leading edge. Much of the construction of the gigantic Mississippi River delta occurred during the Pleistocene, and submarine fans filled the trench between the Juan de Fuca Rise and the Cascade magmatic arc (Fig. 14–29). Also, rainsoaked areas of the continent south of the ice front were the sites of major landslides and debris flows. Many effects of continental glaciation can be seen in southern Canada, the Great Lakes region, and New England. For instance,

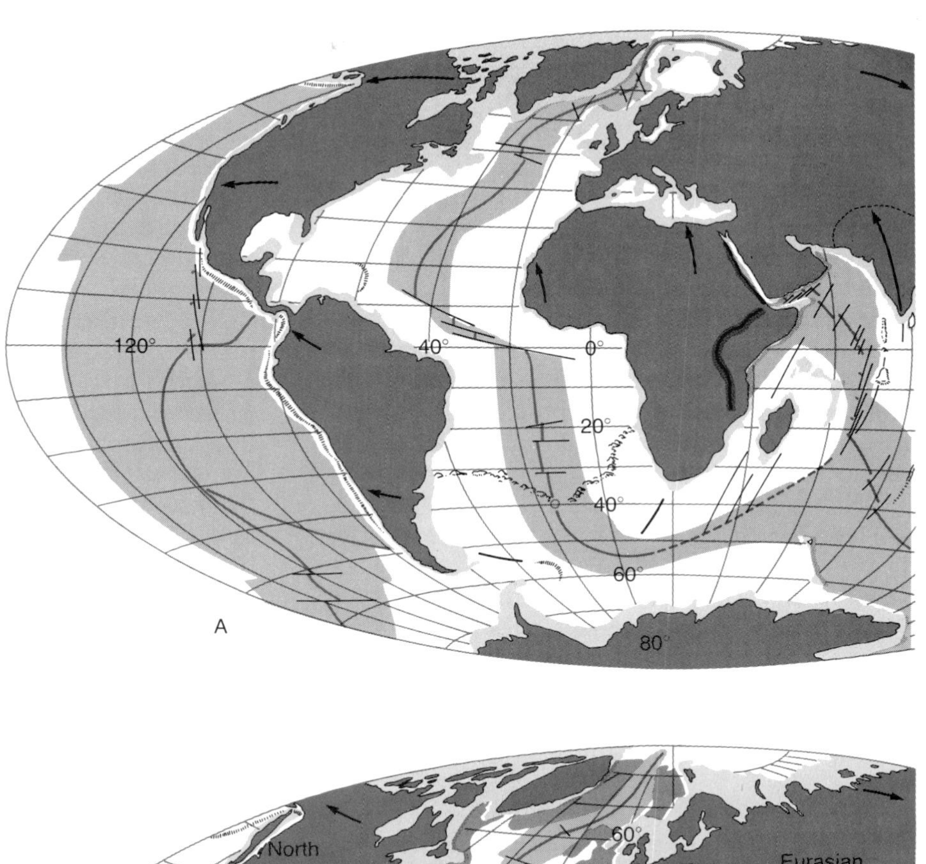

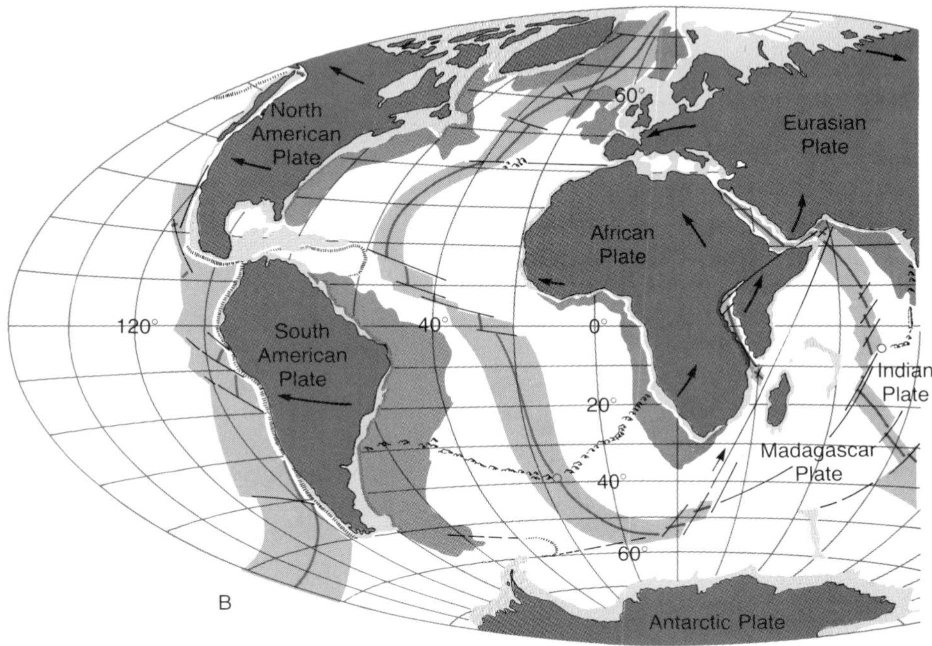

Figure 14–34

Present and future plate configurations. A. Modern world B. World 50 million years from now; present-day continental positions shown in brown. Note the change in position of the sliver of North American continent west of the San Andreas fault.
(From R. S. Dietz and J. C. Holden, 1970, The Breakup of Pangaea, p. 38, 39; *Scientific American*, October. Copyright 1970 by Scientific American, Inc. All rights reserved)

Long Island, New York, is the remnant of a terminal moraine whose deposits rest upon Precambrian schist.

The Pleistocene was also a time of major tectonic uplift and deformation in California, a consequence of continued interactions between the Pacific and North American Plates along the San Andreas fault system. Vertical uplift, overthrusting, and overturning of Pleistocene sedimentary beds were commonplace. Many of the anticlines and faults that trap hydrocarbons in California's Neogene coastal basins developed during the Pleistocene wave of deformation; elevated marine terraces veneered with Pleistocene sediments bear evidence of major coastal uplift. Volcanic activity in the magmatic-arc belts north and south of the San Andreas fault is evidence of continued subduction along much of the continental margin during the Pleistocene. Crater Lake, Oregon, occupies the collapsed caldera of an andesite volcano that blew its top during the Pleistocene.

The Holocene Epoch is generally considered to be the last 10,000 years: the time since retreat of the last great continental ice sheet, and the beginning of postglacial sea-level rise. Could the Holocene be just another interglacial phase, with more ice advances in the offing? Or will all the polar ice melt, thus raising sea level worldwide another 100 m, with severe consequences for coastal cities? This provocative subject will be treated in Chapter 15.

During the Pliocene, human beings evolved in Africa (Chapter 17) and by the late Pleistocene had entered the scene on the North American continent, probably by way of the Bering land bridge between Asia and North America. Humans quickly made their presence felt, and through hunting activities may have been instrumental in the extinction of a number of large mammals about 30,000 to 10,000 years ago. At first, human activities were geographically confined and compatible with the physical environment, as exemplified by the Mesa Verde cliff dwellings that blend into the sandstone ledges. Later, however, since the era of European discovery and colonization, the industrial revolution, and the automated age, human beings have spread across the land from shore to shore, at times obtrusively.

Despite the presence and influence of *Homo sapiens,* the natural geologic forces of the Earth will continue unabated, uncaring for those who choose to live near the San Andreas fault or in the shadow of a Guatemalan volcano. As historian and philosopher Will Durant said, "Human civilization exists by geologic consent—subject to change without notice." Time and process will march on, and 50 million years from now plate tectonics will have molded and shaped an Earth that may look something like that portrayed in Figure 14–34. In the context of exotic terranes, the narrow slice of continent west of the San Andreas fault—coastal California and Baja California—will have accreted along the continental margin of Alaska, adding yet another foreign piece of real estate to this collage.

Summary

The Laramide phase of the Cordilleran orogeny continued from the Cretaceous into the early Paleogene, and affected the eastern part of the Cordilleran belt. Uplift of pre-Paleozoic basement in the southern and central Rockies and folding and thrusting of Proterozoic, Paleozoic, and Mesozoic rocks in a belt extending from Alaska to Mexico were related to continued subduction along the continental margin. Laramide deformation began about 80 million years ago with the onset of oblique and unusually rapid subduction of the Farallon oceanic plate, accompanied by shallowing of the subduction zone. As the angle of subduction gradually decreased, arc magmatism and back-arc tectonism migrated eastward.

Laramide uplift of the Rocky Mountains during the Late Cretaceous and early Paleogene caused the last vestiges of interior seas to recede from the North American continent. The Cretaceous interior seaway was replaced by Rocky Mountain ranges and intermontane basins. Paleogene deposits of the Rocky Mountain basins and the Great Plains are the sites of some of the richest fossil mammalian faunas in the world.

The Late Cretaceous to early Paleogene was also a time of intense volcanic activity and intrusion of small plutons—a manifestation of broadly disseminated magmatic-arc activity associated with the Laramide phase of the Cordilleran orogeny. Much of the intrusive activity was accompanied by formation of economic metal deposits. Epeirogenic upwarping in late Paleogene and early Neogene inaugurated a new erosion cycle. Previously peneplaned and buried mountain ranges were exhumed, and some were cut across by superposed streams, which carved spectacular deep canyons. The Colorado Plateau, largely spared by Cordilleran orogeny deformation, was intricately dissected into a landscape of plateaus, benches, mesas, buttes, arches, and deep canyons by streams rejuvenated during Neogene epeirogeny.

In the Appalachian region, several cycles of Cenozoic epeirogenic uplift likewise rejuvenated streams that carved valleys in weak strata and sculptured ridges in more resistant rocks. The present-day Appalachian Mountains expose the deeply eroded roots of an earlier, more majestic range. Mesozoic and Cenozoic erosion cycles in the Appalachians produced great volumes of sediment that were carried to the Atlantic coastal plain and continental shelf—the passive, trailing margin of the continent.

The Atlantic and Gulf Coast margins of North America are actualistic continental margin basins. The coastal plains and continental shelves represent the miogeocline, and the continental slope and rise represent the eugeocline. The Atlantic–Gulf Coast model provides insight into those ancient continental margin basins that developed marginal to a rift ocean on the trailing edge of a drifting continent.

In contrast to the passive trailing Atlantic and Gulf Coast margins, the Pacific margin of North America has involved interaction of continental and oceanic plates on a grand scale. One of the most dramatic manifestations of this plate interaction is the San Andreas fault system, which is the boundary between the North American and Pacific Plates. According to the Atwater model, about 30 million years ago the San Andreas fault was initiated by collision and overrunning of a segment of the East Pacific Rise spreading ridge by the edge of the North American continent. The San Andreas lengthened during the Neogene by northward and southward migration of the Mendocino and Rivera triple junctions, respectively.

The San Andreas fault system, a giant megashear and transform-plate boundary, has played a key role in the tectonic evolution of California. The right-lateral shearing motion between the North American and Pacific Plates has been responsible for uplifting the coastal ranges and fragmenting the continental crust into a great number of differentially moving blocks. The splintered margin of the North American Plate in California provided a setting for development of dynamic, fault-bounded basins that received thick accumulations of sediments. Several of these, such as the Los Angeles Basin, became sites for major hydrocarbon accumulations. Other manifestations of Neogene plate-tectonics activity in the western Cordillera include opening of the Gulf of California rift and pronounced block-faulting to form the Basin and Range Province. Extensive Neogene magmatic-arc volcanism in the Cascades of the northwest, and Mexico and Central America to the south, is related to underflow of oceanic lithosphere north and south of the San Andreas transform.

Throughout the entire Pacific rim, plate interactions have generated earthquakes and volcanic activity in Japan, Alaska, California, Mexico, Central America, and South America. Formation of the Alpine–Himalayan Mountain belt during the Cenozoic is evidence that dramatic plate motions were occurring over much of the globe during Cenozoic history. This activity set the stage for the complete drying out of the Mediterranean Basin about 5 million years ago.

Cenozoic life is highlighted by the rise to dominance of the most advanced class of organisms—the mammals. Continental separations, promoting genetic isolation and provincialism, were responsible for increased diversification of the total world mammalian fauna. Rapid diversification of angiosperm plants paralleled the radiation of insects and birds. Cenozoic fragmentation and isolation of continents, together with ecologic partitioning of north-south-oriented continental shelves, promoted provincialism and diversity levels of marine invertebrates to a degree previously unattained in the Phanerozoic.

Pleistocene history was characterized by northern-hemisphere glaciation and higher-altitude alpine glaciation, the culmination of a global refrigeration trend that began in the Oligocene. Pleistocene glacial and interglacial stages had a profound influence on marine sedimentation, owing to abundant precipitation, increased runoff, and delivery of detritus to the continental shelves and ocean basins. Neotectonic activity in the Pacific-coast region produced dramatic uplift and deformation over a short period of time. The late Pleistocene witnessed the arrival of humans in North America—the main migratory route from Asia being the Bering land bridge. Their hunting activities may have contributed to extinction of many large land mammals between 10,000 and 30,000 years ago.

The Holocene Epoch, comprising the last 10,000 years since the retreat of the last glacial ice sheets, may be just another interglacial stage. Either the return of glacial conditions to grip the northern hemisphere, or the melting of present polar ice caps, causing a dramatic rise in sea level, will have dire environmental consequences. Fifty million years from now, southern California may be an accreted terrane of southern Alaska.

Suggestions for Further Reading

Baldridge, K. C., and K. H. Olsen. 1989. The Rio Grande Rift. *American Scientist* 77(3):240–48.

Burke, K. C., and J. Tuzo Wilson. 1976. Hot spots on the Earth's surface. *Scientific American* Offprint No. 920. San Francisco: W. H. Freeman.

Dalrymple, G. B., E. A. Silver, and E. D. Jackson. 1973. Origin of the Hawaiian Islands. *American Scientist* 61:294–308; also *in* B. J. Skinner, ed. 1980. *Earth's history, structure, and materials.* Readings from *American Scientist.* Los Altos, CA: William Kaufmann.

Dietz, R.S. 1972. Geosynclines, mountains, and continent-building. *Scientific American* Offprint No. 899. San Francisco: W. H. Freeman.

Heezen, B. C., and I. D. MacGregor. 1973. The evolution of the Pacific. *Scientific American* Offprint No. 911. San Francisco: W. H. Freeman.

Hsu, K. J. 1972. When the Mediterranean dried up. *Scientific American* Offprint No. 904. San Francisco: W. H. Freeman.

James, D. E. 1973. The evolution of the Andes. *Scientific American* Offprint No. 910. San Francisco: W. H. Freeman.

Jones, D. L., Allan Cox, Peter Coney, and Myrl Beck. 1982. The growth of western North America. *Scientific American* 247(5):70–128.

Jordan, T. H., and J. B. Minster. 1988. Measuring crustal deformation in the American West. *Scientific American* 259(2):48–60.

Kurten, Bjorn. 1969. Continental drift and evolution. *Scientific American* Offprint No. 877. San Francisco: W. H. Freeman.

McPhee, John. 1980. *Basin and Range.* New York: Farrar, Straus & Giroux.

McPhee, John. 1986. *Rising from the Plains.* New York: Farrar, Straus & Giroux.

Molnar, Peter, and Paul Tapponier. 1977. The Collision between India and Eurasia. *Scientific American* Offprint No. 923. San Francisco: W. H. Freeman.

Powell, J. W. 1961. *The exploration of the Colorado River and its canyons.* Dover Publications, Inc., New York. Unabridged and unaltered republication of the work first published in 1895 by Flood and Vincent under the title, *Canyons of the Colorado.*

Rosenfeld, C. L. 1980. Observations on the Mount St. Helens eruption. *American Scientist* 68:494–509; also *in* B. J. Skinner, ed. 1980. *Earth's history, structure, and materials.* Readings from *American Scientist.* Los Altos, CA: William Kaufmann.

Stephens, H. G., and E. M. Shoemaker. 1987. *In the footsteps of John Wesley Powell: An album of comparative photographs of the Green and Colorado Rivers, 1871–1872 and 1968.* Denver: Johnson Books.

Valentine, J. W., and E. M. Moores. 1974. Plate tectonics and the history of life in the oceans. *Scientific American* Offprint No. 912. San Francisco: W. H. Freeman.

The Big Freeze: Glaciers and Glaciation

15

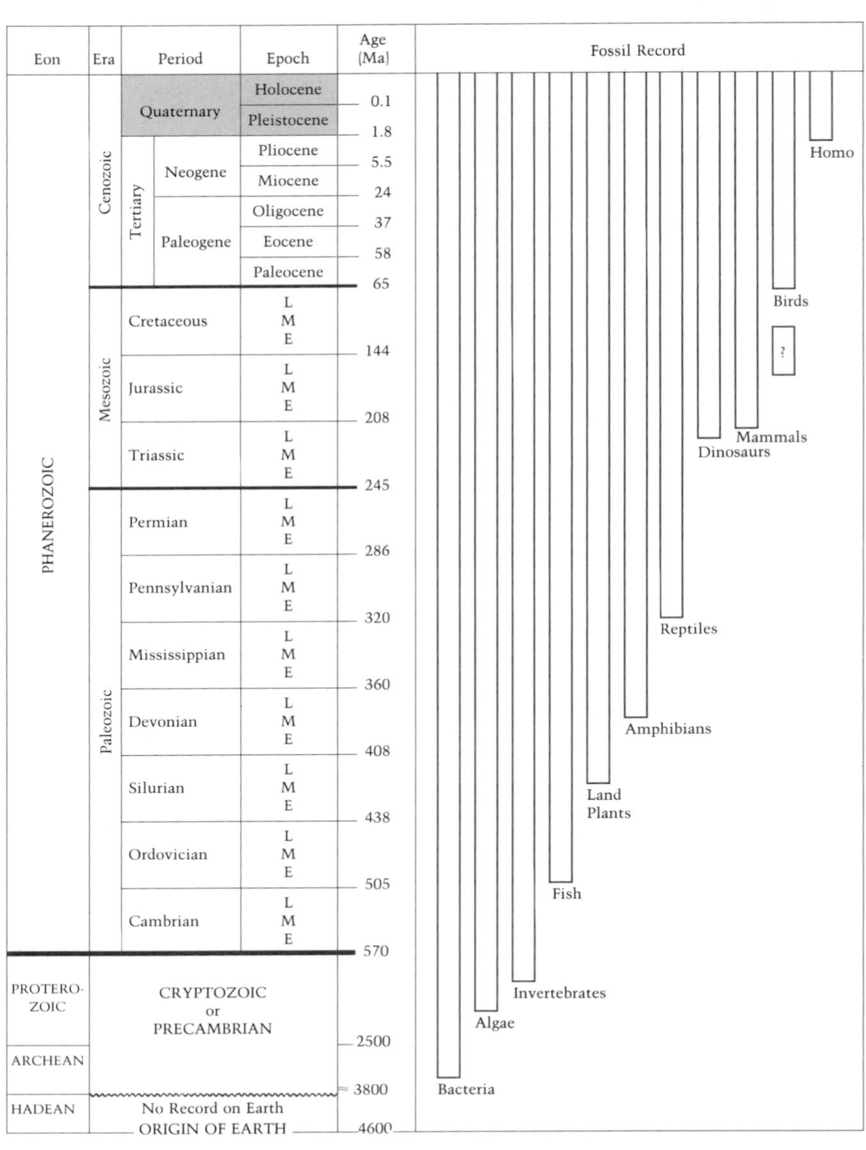

Contents

Key Terms

Erratic boulder
Moraine
Till
Interglacial
Polarity event
Boundary stratotype
Lake varve
Isostatic rebound
Pluvial lake
Submarine canyon
Land bridge
Heat budget
Greenhouse effect

Birth of a "Preposterous Hypothesis"

Among the writings of most of the world's religions are descriptions of a widespread catastrophic event involving floodwaters. In western religions, this event is called the Noachian deluge, or great flood; it is described in the Old Testament of the *Bible*. What appeared to be obvious evidence for such a flood were boulders resting in flat-lying areas, far-removed from their place of origin; these are now called **erratic boulders,** and some are very large. Erratics were known to have been transported many miles from their areas of origin and deposited in a haphazard fashion.

Well into the 1800s distribution of these boulders in northern and central Europe was attributed to action of very strong currents of water and mud, or to boulder-laden icebergs drifting on the floodwaters. As could be expected, these ideas fit very well with the hypothesis of neptunism advocated by Abraham Werner and his students in the late 1700s (Chapter 6). However, there are major problems with this explanation.

Recalling our previous discussions of the concept of actualism, and considering our current knowledge of the science of meteorology, it seems highly unlikely that a flood of worldwide scale would occur. Floods are produced by runoff from excessive rainfall. Because rainfall is part of the hydrologic cycle and occurs when the atmosphere is saturated with water vapor, there would be no mechanism to produce water vapor if rain were falling worldwide. Thus, there does not seem to be a scientific mechanism to produce enough rainfall for such a global flood. Furthermore, where would the waters recede to after such a hypothetical flood?

At the beginning of the 1800s, many major geological concepts were undergoing birth and early development, and controversy was the rule. In Europe, much controversy raged over an explanation for the origin of rocks, and to many geologists the idea of a worldwide flood still held considerable attraction. To those scientists who observed the evidence—huge erratics; polished, often-grooved surfaces of exposed bedrock in some areas; and large mound-shaped hills and ridges of poorly sorted sediments—the idea of a great flood seemed to provide a reasonable explanation.

An alternative scientific explanation, both for the distribution of erratics and for the occurrence of flooding, had been proposed as early as 1787. However, it took 50 years before scientists seriously considered this new concept, and perhaps another 25 years for it to achieve general acceptance. This concept has become known as the "glacial theory."

John Playfair, most noted for his explanations of the Huttonian theory, suggested in 1802 that glaciers, rather than floodwaters, could have been the cause of these geomorphologic features:

> For the moving of large masses of rock, the most powerful engines without doubt which nature employs are the glaciers. . . . In this manner, before the valleys were

> cut out in the form they now are, and when the mountains were still more elevated, huge fragments of rock may have been carried to a great distance. . .*

However, Playfair's idea was virtually ignored for 30 years. This example brings to mind other ideas that were proposed, and either rejected or forgotten. Two examples are Gregor Mendel and his experiments in the mid-1800s leading to the concept of genetics (Chapter 4), and Alfred Wegener in the early 1900s and his concept of continental drift that led to the doctrine of plate tectonics (Chapter 1).

As the science of geology progressed into the middle 1800s, explanations for natural events relying on worldwide flooding or other catastrophic events gradually lost credibility and were replaced by other explanations. Beginning in the 1820s, Jean de Charpentier and Ignace Venetz revived interest in the concept of glaciation. Venetz, a Swiss engineer, proposed that the peculiar features on the Swiss plains were produced by an ancient extension of alpine glaciers. This hypothesis seemed outrageous to most scientists. However, Louis Agassiz, a Swiss biologist, went to investigate the evidence. By 1837, he had become convinced by the evidence described by Venetz and by his own observations in the field, and decided to present a paper to the annual congress of Swiss scientists.

In this paper he suggested a number of rather startling ideas: First, he said that movement of glacial ice, not floodwaters, was responsible for all purported diluvial phenomena. Second, he proposed that glaciation was not a local phenomenon but was part of a major change in climate that had affected all of Europe. Third, and most startling, he stated his belief that in the recent past, vast ice sheets had covered much of Europe and that only isolated mountain peaks rose above the ice in northern Europe.

Agassiz, already a well-respected scientist in Europe by the late 1830s as a result of extensive studies of fossil fish, had a monumental task to convince the scientific community of the existence of former glaciers. The hardest part for Agassiz was to convince Europe's foremost geologists. William Buckland and Charles Lyell, for example, had by 1840 become staunch supporters. However, as John Imbrie and Katherine Palmer Imbrie noted in their book, *Ice Ages,* it took another 20 years before most British geologists accepted the glacial theory.

By the 1840s, Agassiz had become the leading proponent for the existence of widespread ancient glaciers. He traced the evidence of glaciation throughout Europe. In 1847 he accepted a teaching position in the United States at Harvard University, where he devoted many years to the study of similar glacial evidence in North America. He essentially started the branch of geology called *glaciology.* Agassiz travelled extensively, presented many lectures, and did much to convince skeptics in North America, as well as Europe, of the former existence of widespread glaciers on both continents. Along with these interests, he maintained his interest in fossil fish and founded the now-famous Museum of Comparative Zoology at Harvard.

From this discussion it is evident that Agassiz was a fine example of a naturalist. His formal training was in zoology, but he became renowned in other fields of natural science as well. In earlier chapters we have noted other well-rounded naturalists, such as E. D. Cope, J. W. Powell, Georges Cuvier, and James Hutton.

In the 140 years since the pioneering work of Agassiz, geologists have amassed vast information about glaciers and glaciation. There is consider-

---

*From Mather, K. F., and S. L. Mason. 1939. *A source book in geology.* Cambridge, MA: Harvard Univ. Press, p. 137.

able evidence indicating that glaciers have advanced and retreated over much of the northern hemisphere a number of times during the Pleistocene Epoch. Thus, the Pleistocene has become popularly known as the "ice age." In this chapter, we will consider the nature of historic and prehistoric evidence for glaciation, discuss its effects on the Earth, and delve into hypotheses proposed to explain the phenomenon.

Distribution of Glaciers

Active glaciers in North America occur in Alaska and Canada and to a lesser extent in the Sierra Nevada, Cascade Range, and Rocky Mountains of the United States (Fig. 15–1). However, a variety of preserved physical evidence attests to the existence of much more widespread ancient glaciers. These features can be readily observed on visits to the Sierra Nevada and the Rocky Mountains. Somewhat less obvious but more widespread evidence can be observed in the midwestern and northeastern United States and Canada. Numerous and widespread erosional and depositional features provide proof for the previous presence of vast ice sheets in these regions in the not-too-distant past. Similar features are known from northern Europe and from central and northern Asia.

This evidence indicates that perhaps as much as two-thirds of the land area in the northern hemisphere was covered by thick sheets of ice (Fig. 15–2). In some areas, such as northern Canada, the thickness of these glaciers may have exceeded 3 km! The landscape in many areas of the northern hemisphere has been dramatically altered by glacial erosion or deposition. Today only remnants of these ice sheets exist, in Greenland and around the North Pole.

The Pleistocene Ice Ages

Development of a Glacial Chronology

By the early 1870s, about 30 years after Louis Agassiz first proposed his hypothesis for glaciation, the concept had been accepted as theory by most geologists. Major research then focused upon constructing a history of the ice ages. Within 10 years, mechanisms of ice formation and movement were recognized and the geographic distribution of ancient glaciers was known. By mapping the distribution of **moraines,** erratic boulders, and other features, it was recognized that glaciers had in the past covered about 27 million km^2, or approximately

A

B

Figure 15–1
A. Relatively small valley glaciers at Mt. Rainier, Washington. B. Example of large valley glacier, part of a large ice field; the Columbia Glacier.
(Photos from R. Miller)

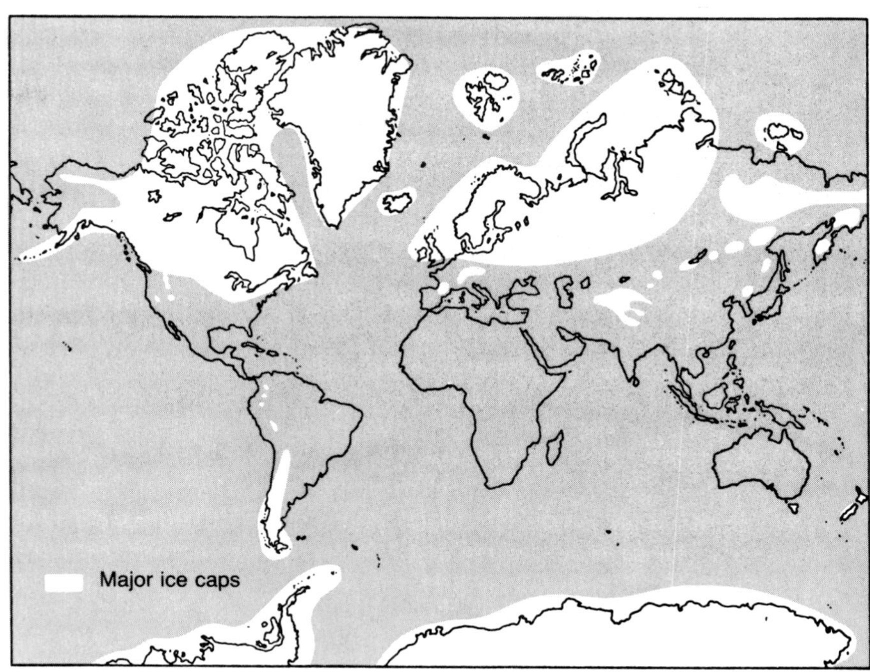

Figure 15–2
Extent of maximum glaciation during Pleistocene time. In North America, glacial ice sheets extended southward into the Midwest and covered most of what is now the eastern seaboard megalopolis (see Fig. 15–4). (From L. W. Mintz, *Historical Geology: The Science of a Changing Earth*, Fig. 20.39, p. 535. © 1977 by Merrill Publishing Co.)

three times the area covered by ice today. Most of this area was in the northern hemisphere.

A major discovery made during these initial studies was the cyclicity of ice advances and retreats. Subsequent careful mapping of the distribution of terminal moraines and correlation of **till** deposits indicated that at least four, and perhaps more, stages of ice advance had occurred during the Pleistocene Epoch. Each of these advances was followed by retreat of the ice: an **interglacial** stage (Fig. 15–3). Fortunately for geologists, each successive major advance of ice did not completely cover and remove evidence of the preceding stages!

More recent studies have provided considerable refinement of the early evidence. In particular, a variety of radiometric dating techniques (such as carbon-14, potassium-40:argon-40, uranium-234, thorium-230, and fission track—see Chapters 5 and 6) have provided a chronology for Pleistocene glacial and interglacial stages, and information for determining the age of the Pliocene-Pleistocene boundary. These dating techniques also indicate that each glacial advance had a different duration, and that advances and retreats occurred as irregular pulses over tens of thousands of years. The glacial features that are observed most readily today were produced by the most recent ice sheet, the Wisconsinan glaciation. Maximum glacial advance occurred during the Wisconsinan glacial age, and as Figure 15–4 indicates, ice extended as far south as 40° north latitude in parts of the Great Plains.

Recognition of multiple glacial and interglacial events of the Pleistocene and development of radiometric chronology have provided valuable information for geologists. However, determination of the Pliocene-Pleistocene boundary has presented a

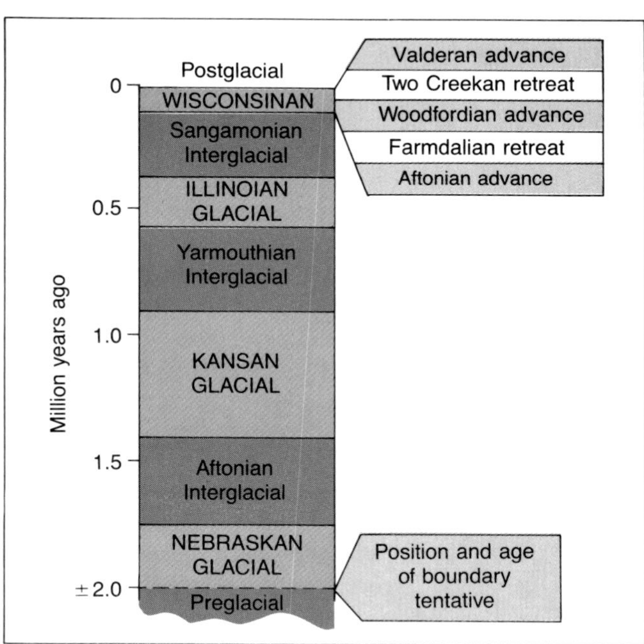

Figure 15–3
Glacial chronology for North America during the Pleistocene and Holocene Epochs.

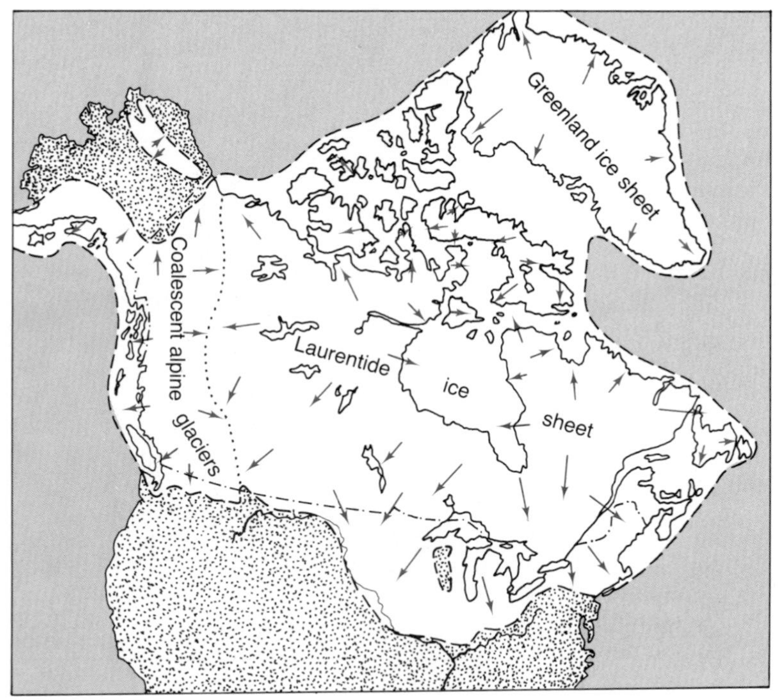

Figure 15–4
Maximum extent of ice sheets in North America during Wisconsinan glacial advance. Glaciers also occurred in mountainous regions of the western United States such as the Rockies and Sierra Nevada. Arrows show presumed direction of movement.
(From R. J. Foster, *General Geology*, Fig. 10.24, p. 204. © 1978, Merrill Publishing Co.)

number of difficulties. These problems illustrate a number of complications involved in trying to fit natural events into a preconceived set of ideas such as the geologic time scale.

How should the Plio-Pleistocene boundary be defined? Possible methods are:

1. Determine radiometric dates of volcanic rocks.
2. Establish the onset of the oldest glacial advance.
3. Note changes in land-mammal taxa.
4. Recognize changes in planktonic Foraminifera and isotopic content of deep-sea sediments.
5. Use changes in human lineages.
6. Choose a particular magnetic field reversal.
7. Combine two or more of these techniques.

In actuality, all of these have been used, but difficulty arose when we recognized that few, if any, of these events occurred simultaneously (Fig. 15–5). A significant attempt to correlate the boundary by comparing all of these features was published by the American Association of Petroleum Geologists in 1978 (*The Geologic Time Scale*). There is by no means universal agreement, but many geologists use a figure of between 1.8 and 2.0 million years before present (Ma) for the boundary. This number corresponds to the Olduvai magnetic normal **polarity event** within the Matuyama Polarity Epoch, and

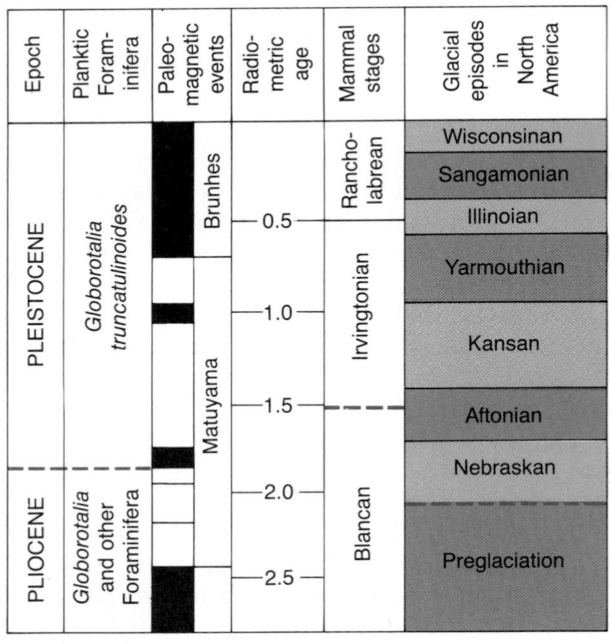

Figure 15–5
Position of the Pliocene-Pleistocene series boundary (heavy dashed line). Note the lack of synchroneity. Position of this boundary must be determined by agreement on what events are most significant and widespread.

to a widespread microfossil boundary. The Plio-Pleistocene **boundary stratotype** is in Italy.

A Record of Changing Climates

One significant aspect of the Pleistocene ice age was climatic change on a global scale: glacial stages and interglacials were associated with worldwide decrease or increase in average temperature. These large-scale climatic changes affected temperature, humidity, rainfall, and wind patterns in regions far removed from the direct influence of glacial ice. These climatic variations caused expansion of cool temperatures to lower latitudes, formation of large lakes in currently dry desert areas of the southwestern United States, and increased rates of erosion with development of large river systems. We have no evidence to suggest that these variations have ceased; thus we may expect long-term changes to continue. Change is recognized by study of **lake varves,** tree-growth rings, the coiling direction of Foraminifera, and changes in isotopic ratios in sediments.

Along with indicating climatic conditions, varved lake sediments provide a method for determining geologic time. Paired layers of lake sediments (Fig. 15–6) record seasonal fluctuations of freezing and thawing of the upper layers of the water. Each couplet represents sediments that accumulate during the year. The layer that forms during the winter when the lake surface is frozen is thinner, darker in color, has a higher organic content, and is finer grained than the layer that forms during the summer. The existence of varved lake sediments is, therefore, an indicator of rigorous climate with freezing winter temperatures; today, lakes at high latitudes or at high elevations form yearly varves. The distribution of these sediments can therefore provide an indication of past climate conditions. The number of paired varves in a lake also records the duration of the freezing climate for the lake. For example, many lakes in the northern United States contain varves representing about 8700 years of deposition; these provide an indication of when the ice retreated from this region.

Seasonal or longer-term fluctuations of climate are recorded by plants in the form of growth rings (see Chapter 16, Figs. 16–4 and 16–27). Most plants forming these yearly rings exist in temperate-to-arctic climates; they are rarely found in the tropics. Therefore, the geographic distribution of fossil plants having such growth rings can be used to map the extent and location of cool or cold climatic zones. In addition, a vertical succession of fossilized plant remains preserved in rocks at one location, where some layers contain plants with rings and some contain plants without rings, could indicate periodic fluctuation in climate. Spacing and thickness of the rings indicate dry or wet climatic cycles, and these can be related to regional climatic changes (Chapter 16).

Figure 15–6
Varved lake sediments deposited on glacial till and exposed in this core sample. Dark layers represent winter deposits, and light layers represent summer deposits. Many years are represented by this sample from the Eocene of Colorado. Width of sample is 5 cm.
(From R. J. Foster, *General Geology,* Fig. 10.27, p. 205. © 1978, Merrill Publishing Co.)

Change in climate is also recorded by changes in water temperature of the world's oceans. During glacial advances, ocean-surface temperatures decrease; this change significantly affects many marine organisms. As a consequence, some species of planktonic Foraminifera undergo changes that are quite spectacular, considering their microscopic size. In water temperatures above 10°C, one species, *Globorotalia truncatulinoides,* forms its shell in a right-hand coil; in water below 8–10°C, this same species coils in a left-hand direction (Fig. 15–7)! Since first noted by D. B. Ericson and other scientists in 1954, this geologic thermometer has been used to chronicle temperature changes in the oceans during the Pleistocene Epoch.

Other species of foraminifers and other plankton may have disappeared because they could not tolerate the temperature changes. These changes in plankton in the water column are recorded by the sediments; the record of changes in taxa in the sedimentary record is used to recognize temperature changes that correspond with glacial and interglacial stages.

Another possibility for a geologic thermometer was suggested by Harold C. Urey in the late 1940s, and work by Cesare Emiliani, Samuel Epstein, and others in the 1950s quantified his concept. This bit of detective work involved the discovery that ratios of two isotopes of oxygen—oxygen-18 and oxygen-16—change as ocean temperatures change. The amount of oxygen-16 decreases as the temperature of seawater decreases. Because Foraminifera and many other organisms construct their calcite tests from elements in the surrounding seawater, long-term fluctuations in ocean temperatures associated with glacial or interglacial episodes would affect the oxygen-isotope ratios in tests of successive populations of planktonic Foraminifera. Accumulation of these Foraminifera in the sediments would provide a picture of changing climates (Fig. 15–8).

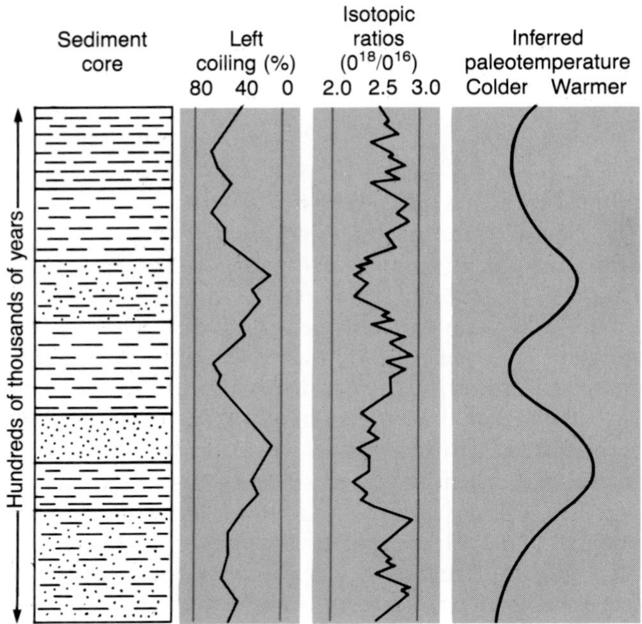

Figure 15–8
Simplified paleotemperature curve for ocean water, based on oxygen-18/oxygen-16 ratios and coiling of planktonic Foraminifera. Colder water is indicated by higher O^{18}/O^{16} ratios and greater numbers of left-coiled forams preserved in sediments.

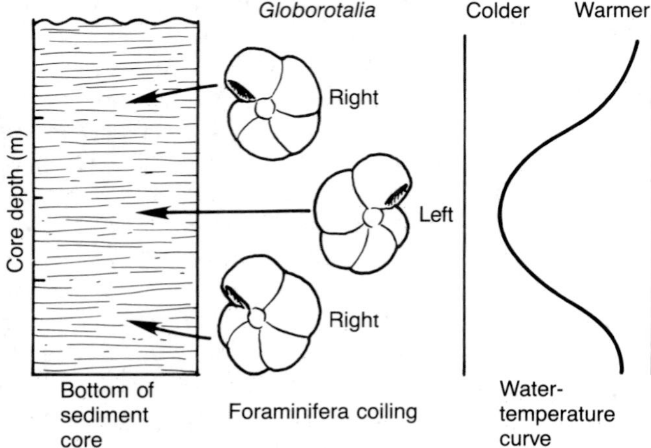

Figure 15–7
Coiling direction of the planktonic formaminifer *Globorotalia truncatulinoides* is controlled by water temperature. Preservation of their tests in ocean sediments provides a clue to recognizing temperature changes.

The heavier isotope, oxygen-18, becomes more concentrated in seawater during times of high evaporation and high snowfall accumulation on the ice caps. The decreasing percentage of oxygen-16 and consequent gain of oxygen-18 in marine waters during times of glaciation is reflected in the geochemistry of shells in Foraminifera that accumulate in sediments. Because of their high oxygen-18:oxygen-16 ratios, shells of deep-water benthic Foraminifera, living where water temperatures seldom rose more than a few degrees above freezing, also serve as sensitive indicators of glacial advances and retreats.

Much of this evidence became available through the Deep Sea Drilling Project, which was begun in 1968 with funds from the National Science Foundation. As mentioned in Chapter 1, the DSDP has also furnished considerable evidence that has proven invaluable in constructing many hypotheses of seafloor-spreading rates and directions.

Cenozoic—the age of mammals—the modern world unfolds. During the Cenozoic Era, the last 65 million years of Earth history, the continents drifted into their present positions, and life on Earth rebounded with amazing diversity after the terminal Cretaceous extinction event. During the past 3 million years climatic deterioration has been expressed by several phases of continental and alpine glaciation. During this same period our own species evolved rapidly.

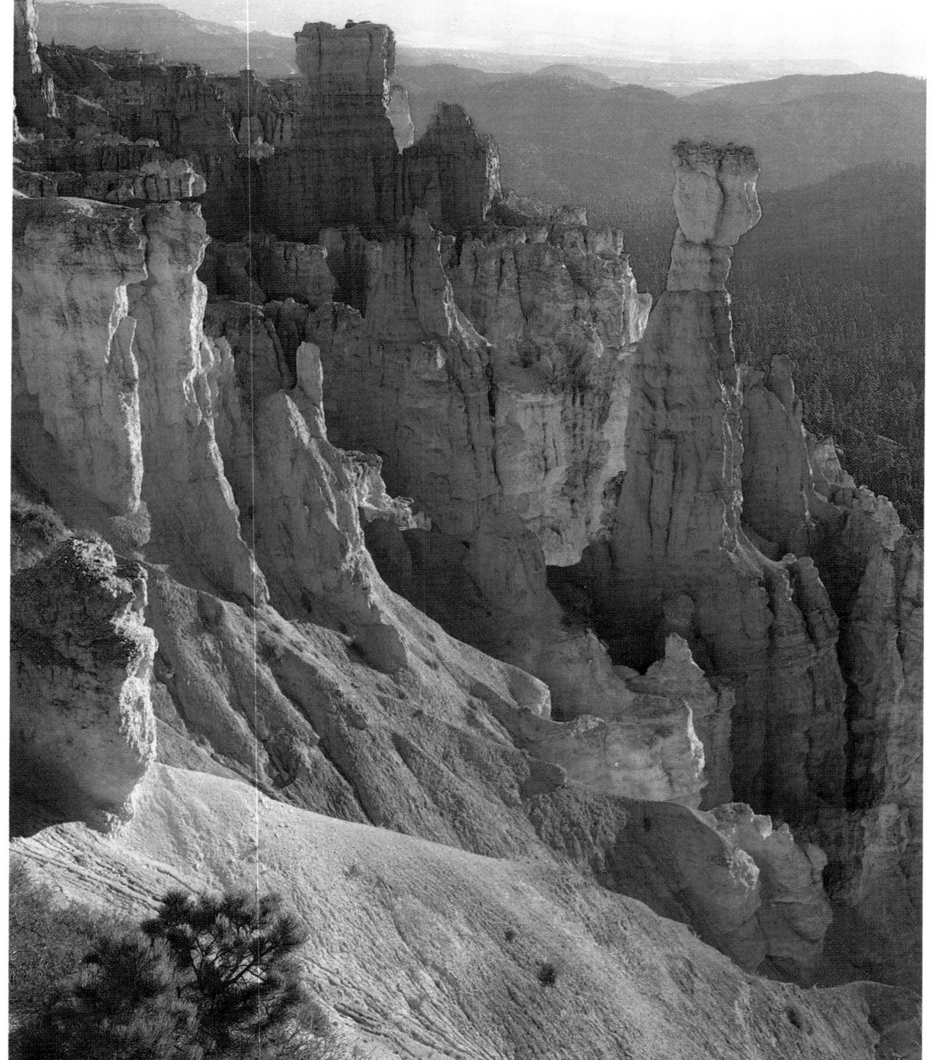

A

B

Canyon-Cutting

A. Colorful Eocene lake beds make up the scenic escarpment at Bryce Canyon National Park, Utah. During the early Cenozoic, many of the intermontane basins in the Rocky Mountain region were occupied by extensive lake systems.

B. Deeply entrenched meanders on the San Juan River near Mexican Hat, Utah, have inspired the name "Goosenecks" and bear evidence of rapid downcutting by streams rejuvenated by regional uplift.

Block Faulting on a Grand Scale

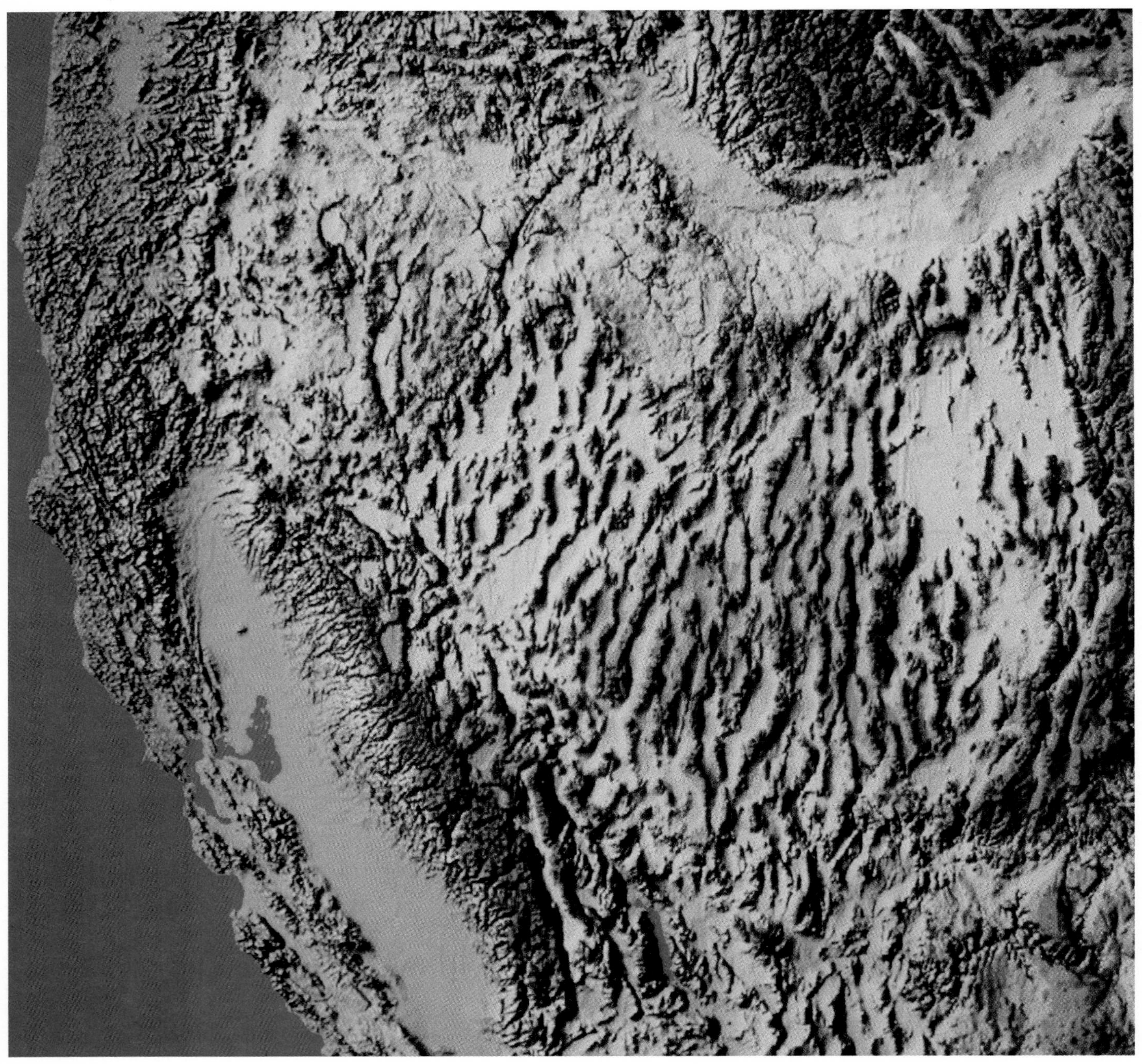

Computer-enhanced image of the Basin and Range Province of the western United States, a vast region of east-west crustal extension that produced north-south oriented block-faulted mountains and intervening basins.

Computer-enhanced image (scale is approximately 1:450,000), from Landsat's thematic mapper, of a region in the southern part of the Basin and Range Province along the Nevada-California border. The large purple area in the center is the Spring Mountains, Nevada. The light-dark boundary along the curved eastern end of the Spring Mountains is the Keystone Thrust. The cluster of red squares in the lower left part of the image is Pahrump, Nevada. Note also the clear expression of stratigraphy in the western part of the image and the extensive alluvial fans. In this southern Great Basin part of the Basin and Range Province, the basins and ranges are oriented more NW-SE because of Cenozoic movements along major right-lateral shear zones. Remote-sensing techniques such as this can greatly facilitate geologic mapping and the detection of subtle tectonic features.

Volcanic Activity in the Western Interior

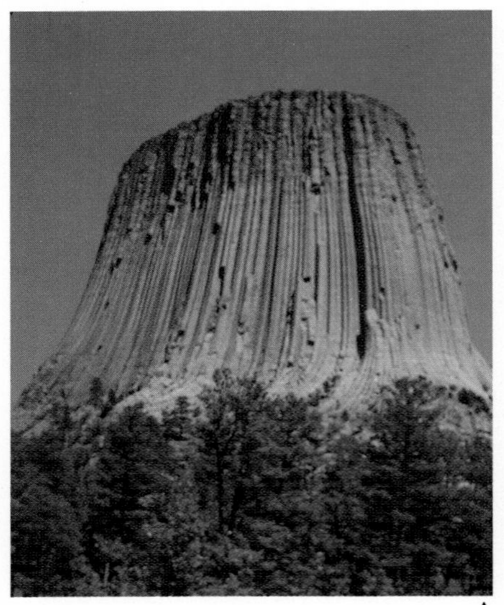

A

Devil's Tower, Wyoming, a Tertiary volcanic plug (diatreme). Note the pattern of columnar joints formed by cooling stresses. Erosion has exhumed the solidified volcanic neck.

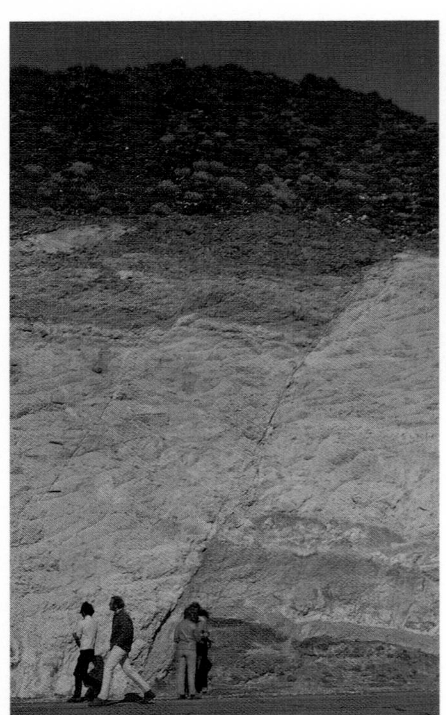

B

Roadcut exposure of faulted Tertiary tuffs in eastern California. Cenozoic volcanism was commonplace throughout much of the Cordilleran region.

C

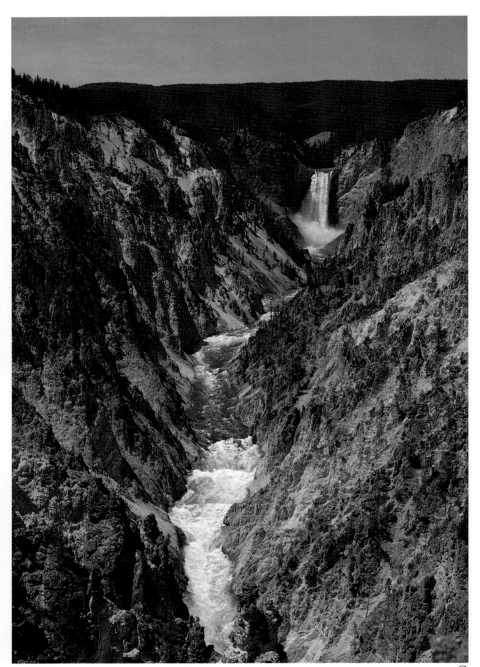

Scenic canyon of the Yellowstone River, Wyoming, cut into thick Tertiary volcanic deposits of the Yellowstone Plateau.

Volcanic Activity Along the Continent's Leading Edge

A

Crater Lake, Oregon. Part of the chain of composite volcanoes comprising the Cascade Range, the mountain that contains Crater Lake "blew its top" during the Pleistocene. Crater Lake occupies the collapsed caldera of a once more lofty Mt. Mazama.

B

Volcan Fuego, Guatemala, part of a magmatic arc trend related to subduction of the Cocos plate.

C

The eruption of Mt. St. Helens, Washington. This violent eruption in 1980 served to underscore the volatile nature of parts of the Cascade magmatic arc province. This volcanism is related to continuing subduction of the Juan de Fuca plate.

The Continent's Western Margin

A

Landsat infrared photograph showing the San Andreas fault north of metropolitan Los Angeles. The San Andreas fault zone is the active boundary between the North American and Pacific plates. Rapidly subsiding Cenozoic basins such as the Los Angeles Basin developed along this splintered plate margin and were filled with thick sequences of Neogene sediments, many of which are of deep marine origin.

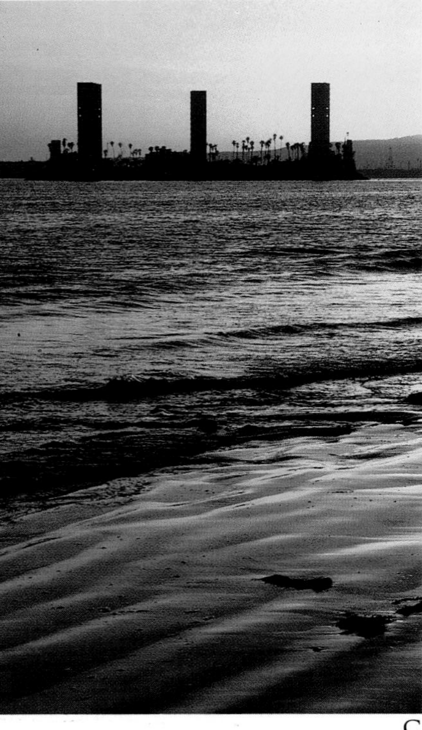

C

As the sun sinks slowly in the west, the silhouettes of offshore camouflaged oil drilling rigs off Long Beach, California, are sharpened against the skyline. These wells produce from the offshore extension of the Wilmington oil field, a multi-billion barrel producer that ranks as one of the five most prolific oil fields in North America. Much of the oil in the Los Angeles basin has been produced from turbidite deposits.

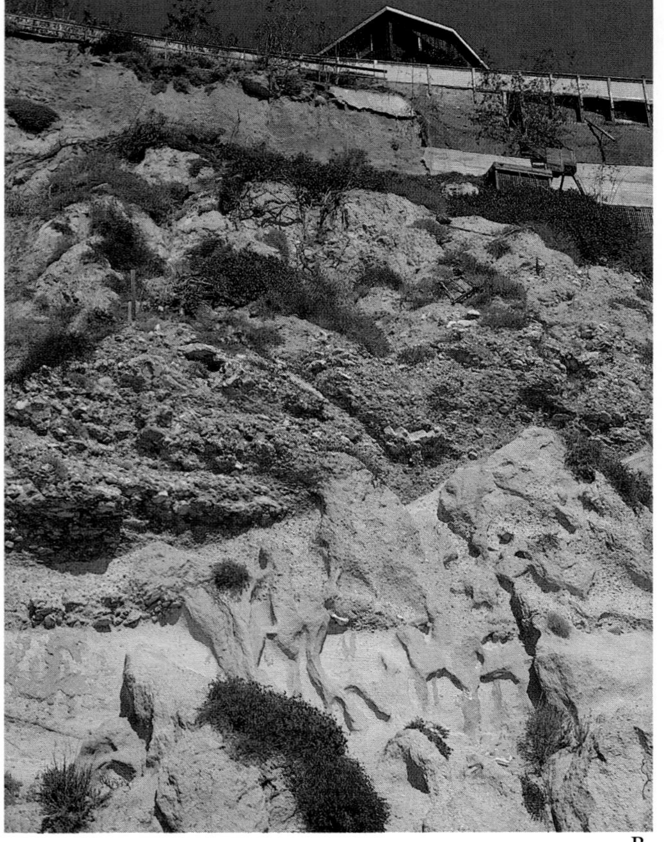

B

Deep-sea turbidite fan channel deposits of Neogene age at Dana Point, California. The gravel-filled channel and surrounding sandy deposits show large-scale similarities with fluvial or alluvial fan deposits; however, closely associated mudstone facies containing deep-water foraminifera place these coarse deposits in a deep marine setting.

A

The "incomparable valley," as naturalist John Muir called it, Yosemite Valley is one of the most dramatic expressions of Pleistocene alpine glaciation.

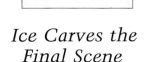

Ice Carves the Final Scene

B

The Greenland ice cap. This is what much of the northern hemisphere may have looked like during Pleistocene times of glacial advance when thick continental ice sheets covered the landscape.

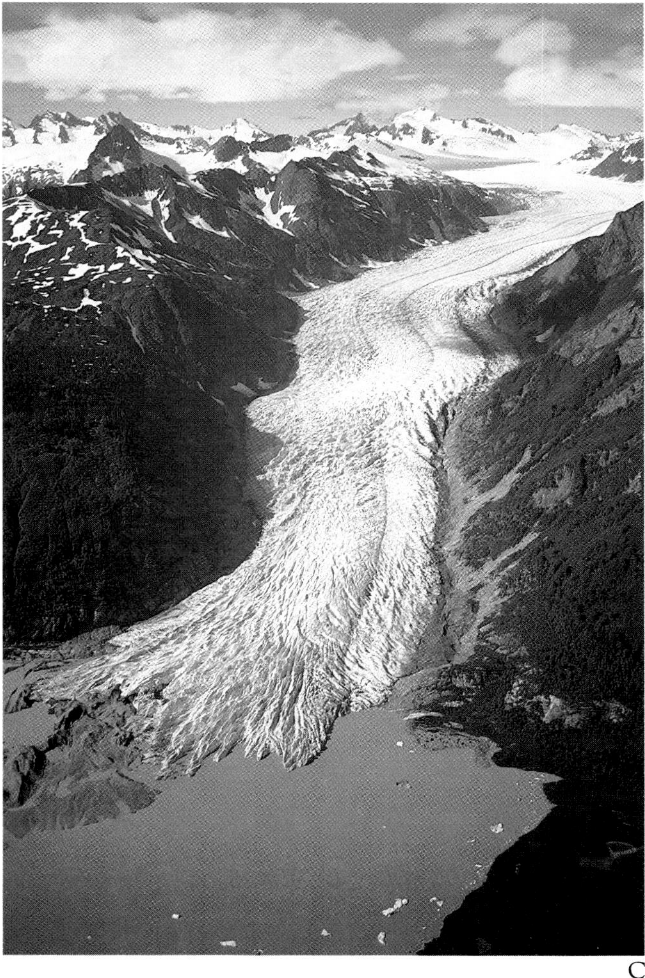

C

Davidson Glacier, Glacier Bay, Alaska, a modern-day tidewater glacier. Glaciers that advance to the edge of the sea commonly deposit coarse sediments offshore onto muddy bottoms.

Cenozoic Life

Scale: width is 15 cm A

Fossil fish from Eocene lake bed deposits, southwestern Wyoming.

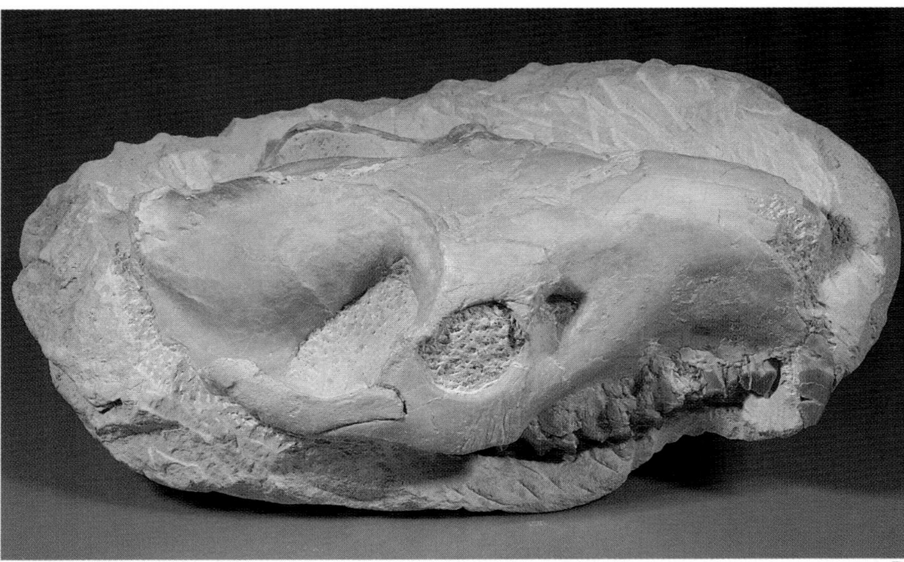

Scale: width is 30 cm B

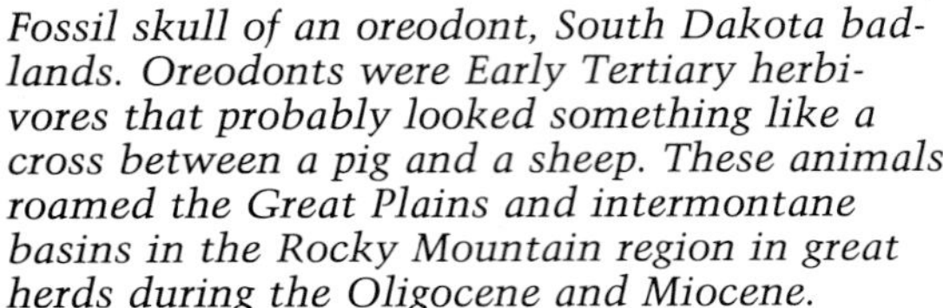

Fossil skull of an oreodont, South Dakota badlands. Oreodonts were Early Tertiary herbivores that probably looked something like a cross between a pig and a sheep. These animals roamed the Great Plains and intermontane basins in the Rocky Mountain region in great herds during the Oligocene and Miocene.

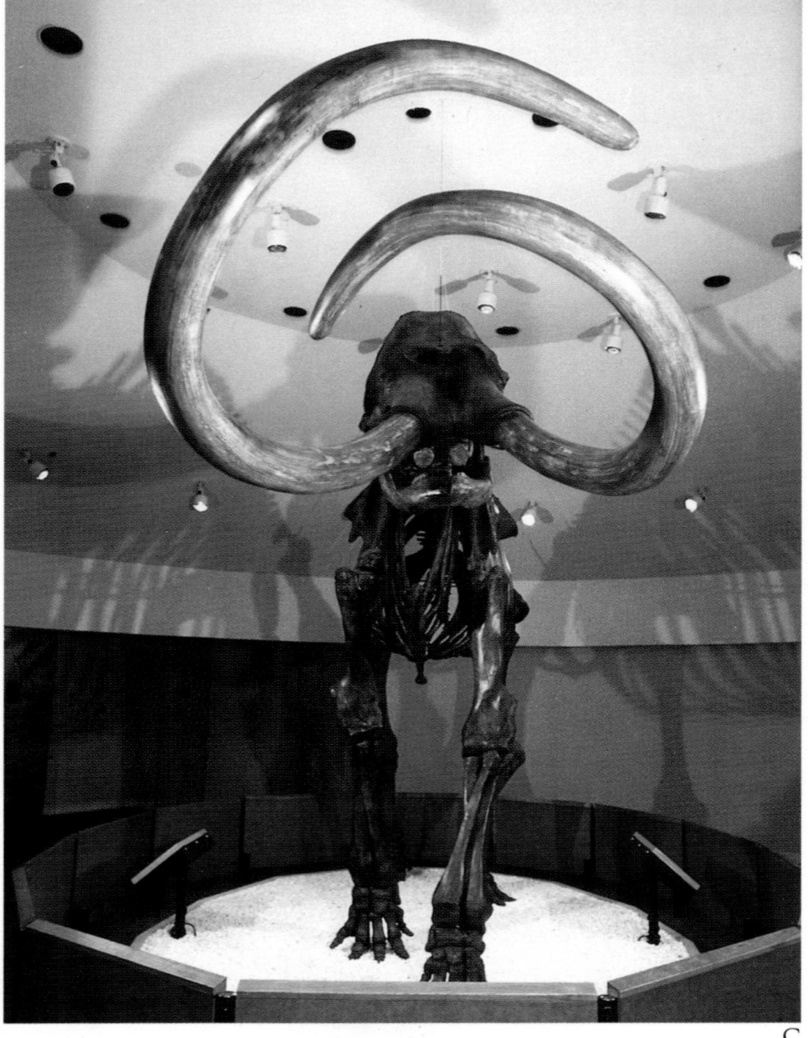

C

Reconstruction of Pleistocene Imperial mammoth from the LaBrea Tar Pits, southern California. Large Pleistocene terrestrial vertebrates became extinct 30,000 to 10,000 years ago, possibly from hunting by humans.

Some Unusual Effects of Glaciation

As depicted in physical geology textbooks, the erosive power of large masses of ice produces distinctive geomorphologic features. Some features, including U-shaped valleys like Yosemite Valley in the Sierra Nevada and peaks such as the Matterhorn in the Alps, are very beautiful. Other features, such as the fjords in northern Europe, glacial deposits in the Midwest, and the very large Great Lakes, represent excavation and deposition on a grand scale. Such features are widespread and often have important implications for interpreting geologic history.

Of particular significance are the formation of large lakes and the deposition of lake sediments such as varves; accumulation of large volumes of clastic particles which may form major deltas; and development of submarine canyons and deep-sea fan deposits. The indirect effects of climatic change associated with glaciation are often no less significant, and include distributional and evolutionary changes in plants and animals. Migration of hominids and other mammals in Pleistocene and Holocene time was and is strongly influenced by temperature and the position of sea level. We will consider some of these conditions and events.

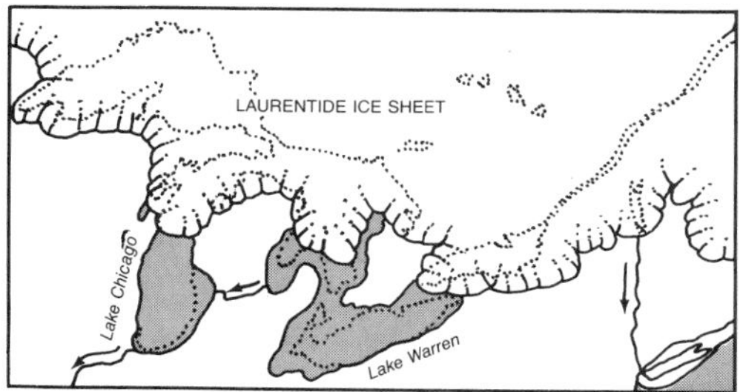

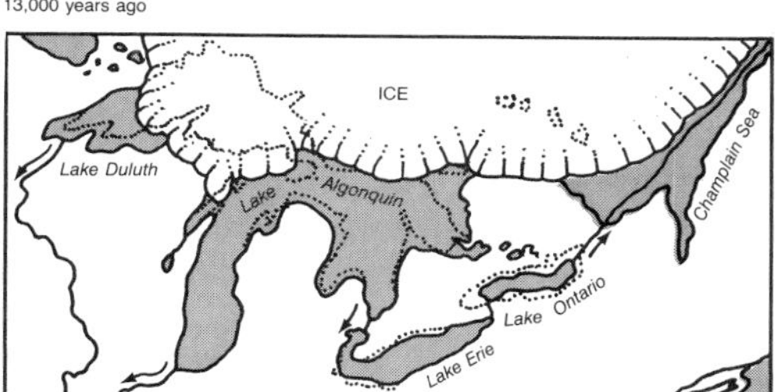

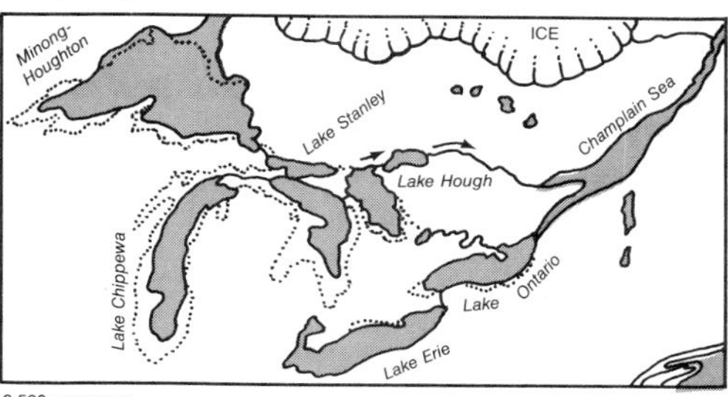

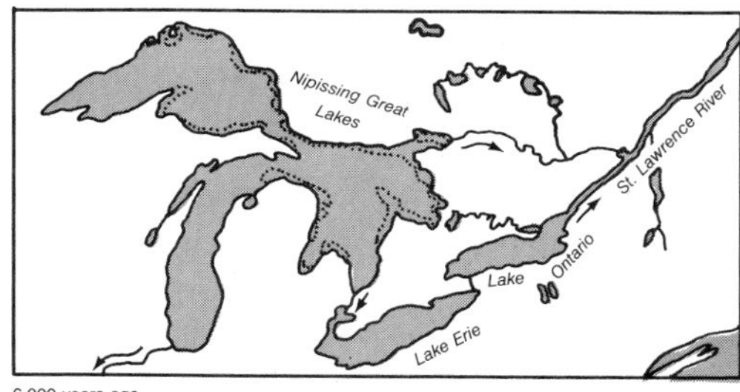

Figure 15–9
Sequence illustrating formation of the Great Lakes, from erosion by glacial ice to subsequent filling by meltwater during melting of the Wisconsinan ice sheets.
(From V. K. Prest, 1970, Quaternary Geology of Canada, Fig. 7–6, p. 90, 91, *in* Geology and Economic Minerals of Canada: *Department of Energy, Mines and Resources Economic Geology Report,* 1, 5th ed.)

The Great Lakes and Pluvial Lakes

Figure 15–4 is a reconstruction of the ice sheets that covered North America during Pleistocene time; in some areas the ice attained a thickness of over 3 km. Other glaciers, such as valley and piedmont glaciers, were a result of climatic change coupled with the uplift of mountain ranges that resulted from extensive tectonic activity that began in the Miocene (Chapter 14). The Rocky Mountains and Sierra Nevada were extensively glaciated. Numerous large inland lakes formed from glacial runoff in the Midwest, and these drained southward into the Gulf of Mexico by way of a vast drainage system, represented today by smaller rivers such as the Mississippi.

The Great Lakes, along with many other northern lakes, were formed by ice erosion during the latest Wisconsinan glacial episode and were filled with meltwater as the ice retreated some 8000 to 12,000 years ago. Figure 15–9 is a time-lapse sequence of the Great Lakes, beginning 13,000 years ago; first Lake Warren, followed by the giant Lake Algonquin, occupied the sites of modern Lake Michigan and Lake Huron and covered areas now occupied by Chicago and Detroit. By 11,500 years ago the ice had retreated enough to expose eastern outlets to the Atlantic, and drainage reduced the size and levels of these ancestral lakes so that they look nearly modern. As one might expect, this change in drainage had considerable effect on the previously developed massive southward-flowing drainage systems, and resulted in a decrease of flow and sediment volume in those rivers flowing into the Gulf of Mexico.

Following retreat of the ice sheets, an immense weight of up to 23 metric tons per square meter was rapidly removed from the underlying rocks of Proterozoic and Paleozoic ages. These rocks, which had been depressed by the weight of overlying ice, began to undergo **isostatic rebound,** which continues to the present day. In the future this continued rebound may tilt the Great Lakes southward, much like a large shallow plate of water, resulting in major changes in volume of discharge.

Although the climate of the southwestern United States is hot and dry and the region generally lacks major rivers and lakes, conditions were different during the Pleistocene glaciations. For example, during the Wisconsinan glacial age, changing climate produced glaciers in many of the mountains. Meltwater as runoff and increased precipitation combined to produce a large number of inland lakes, some of which reached enormous sizes. These inland lakes, known as **pluvial lakes** (Fig. 15–10), partially or completely filled many of the intermontane basins of the Basin and Range Province. If you are familiar with the extreme conditions of aridity found today in Death Valley, California, it is difficult to visualize in that location a lake 150 km long and almost 200 m deep! This pluvial lake, named Lake Manley after one of the pioneers who crossed the valley, has completely vanished, but old shoreline terraces and lake deposits testify to its previous existence (Fig. 14–33D, Ch. 14).

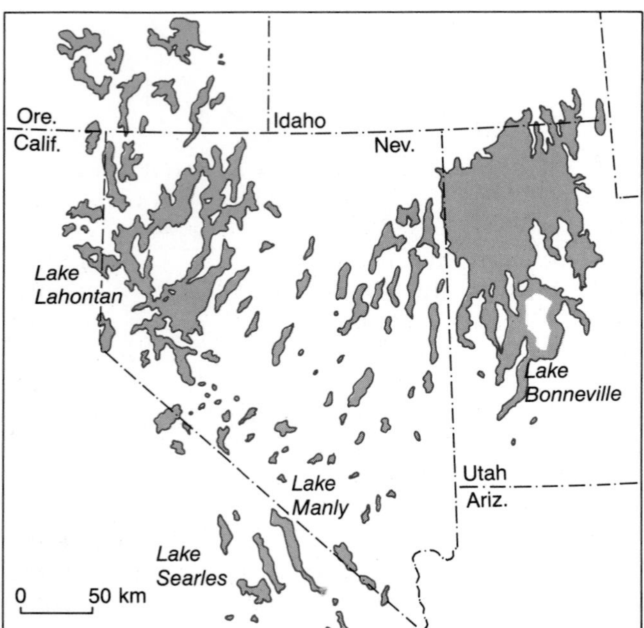

Figure 15–10
Pluvial lakes in the southwestern United States during the latest Pleistocene (Wisconsinan) ice age. Great Salt Lake is a remnant of Lake Bonneville, and Death Valley contains evidence of ancient Lake Manley.
(From H. E. Wright, Jr., and D. G. Frey, eds., Quaternary Geology of the United States, Fig. 1, p. 266. Copyright 1965 by Princeton University Press, Princeton, NJ. Reproduced by permission of Princeton University Press)

Another pluvial lake was ancient Lake Bonneville; a remnant of this giant lake exists today in Utah as the Great Salt Lake. Unusually wet winters since 1980 have fed considerable water into Great Salt Lake, causing a rapid rise in water level and threatening to inundate large portions of the cities on its borders. Other notable examples of pluvial lakes include giant Lake Winnipeg in Canada and Lake Lahontan in California and Nevada. Both are represented today only by remnant lakes.

Deltas, Submarine Canyons, and Fans

During Pleistocene time an enormous amount of sediment was transported by large rivers that flowed from the eastern Rocky Mountains, the Great Lakes region, and the western Appalachians, and emptied into the Gulf of Mexico. For example, at the mouth of the Mississippi River, the Pleistocene delta that prograded into the Gulf contains sediments exceeding 6000 m in thickness. These sediments reflect a very rapid rate of sedimentation not representative of average sedimentation rates through geologic time. During the Pleistocene, however, some of the most rapid rates of sedimentation in history may have been recorded by this and other deltaic systems in various parts of the world.

During times of active glacial advance, vast amounts of water were locked up in ice, and sea levels were lowered worldwide by as much as 100 m. Thus, as the last ice age ended approximately 8000 to 10,000 years ago, melting of these ice sheets raised sea level nearly 100 m. Many old shoreline features are now submerged, including ancient beaches, wave-cut terraces, and stream valleys. In addition, some prehistoric human settlements and campsites have been submerged.

Other evidence of glacial activity during lowered sea-level conditions is provided by the existence of **submarine canyons** (Fig. 15–11). These canyons, which are especially distinctive along the west coast of the United States, may have originally begun as stream-cut channels eroded into parts of continental shelves that were emergent during intervals of lowered sea level. Some of these canyons were lengthened seaward, probably as a result of erosion by submarine turbidity flows. With the rise of sea level in the last 8000 to 10,000 years, these canyons have been submerged; however, they have

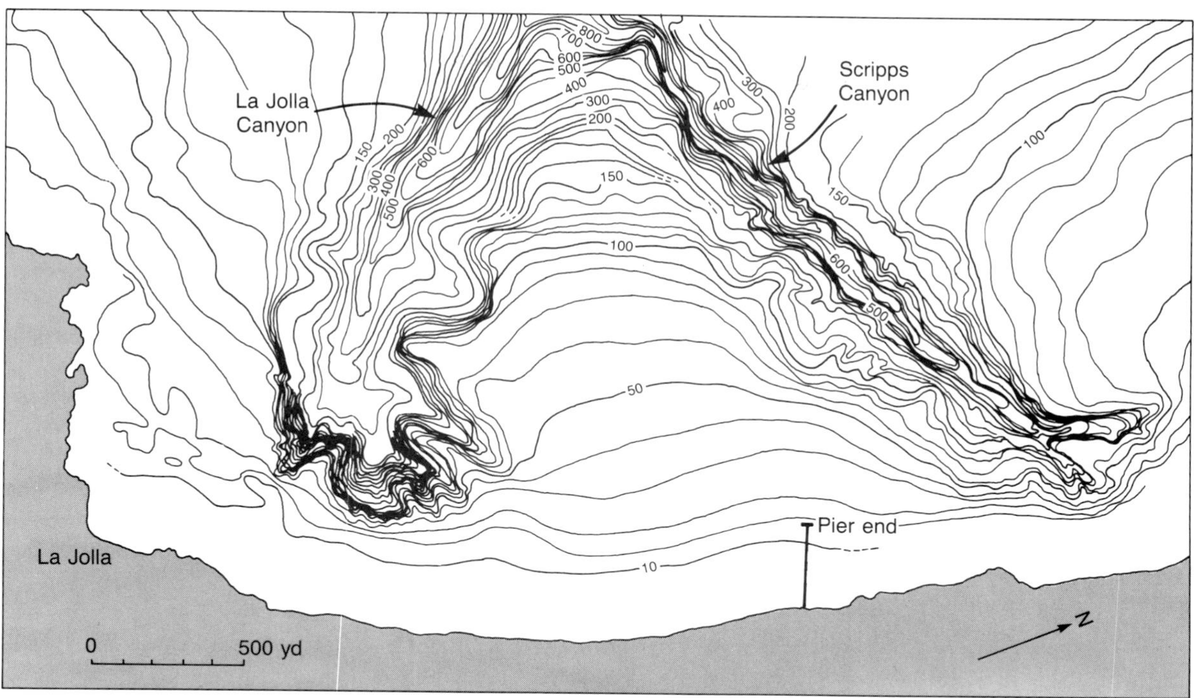

Figure 15–11
Modern submarine canyons, such as Scripps Canyon extending offshore from La Jolla, California, probably began as river-eroded channels during lowered sea level and currently serve as funnels for large amounts of sediment transported offshore into deeper marine environments. Such sediments may accumulate as deep-sea fan deposits.
(Adapted from F. P. Shepard, 1971, *The Earth Beneath the Sea*, Fig. 55, p. 117: Atheneum Press, reprinted by permission of Johns Hopkins University Press, Baltimore)

been maintained—and even enlarged—by various processes of submarine erosion.

Another manifestation of accelerated erosion and deposition during the Pleistocene is abnormally thick submarine turbidite deposits, which accumulated at the mouths of submarine canyons or at the toes of basin slopes. Coalescing fans along the toe of the Atlantic continental slope have contributed heavily to the sediments forming the continental rise.

Plant Extinctions and Animal Migrations

As we have described, climatic changes associated with glaciation had significant effects on physical characteristics globally, and on the basis of our discussions of evolution (Chapter 4), we would expect to see changes in plant and animal taxa in the Pleistocene record. In fact, cumulative changes in climate resulted in extinction of a variety of taxonomic groups, redistribution and migration of many taxa, and appearance of new species. This highly complex interaction of organisms and environment bears a closer look. You might also consider the following discussion in relation to the evolutionary history of humans (Chapter 17).

Evidence of the influence of changes in climate is afforded by the modern distribution of plants. From your own experience you can recall the most obvious examples: abundance of cacti in arid climates; abundant grasslands of the prairies, which are now mostly converted to farmland; tundra in the Arctic; and rain forests in the tropics. Each of these plant associations is the result of a set of climatic conditions, and to a lesser degree, of soil characteristics. Changes in climate from cooler glacial to warmer interglacial, and corresponding changes in rainfall, have influenced the distribution of many of these plant taxa. Cold-temperature floras spread during glacial phases, whereas tropical and arid floras become more widespread during the interglacial phases.

Redistribution of plants also affects the distribution of animals. Two examples that illustrate migration patterns of animals involve the history of the Bering Strait (Fig. 15–12) and the Isthmus of Panama. The Bering Strait in the North Pacific is

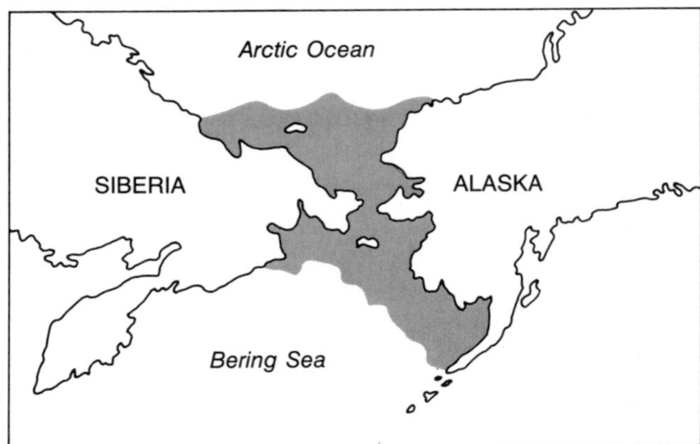

Figure 15–12
The Bering Straits provided a wide migratory pathway for terrestrial vertebrates during lowered sea level, but is completely covered during integlacial episodes such as are occurring today. Area in brown indicates approximate extent of land during lowered sea-level stages.
(Adapted from C. I. Matsch, 1976, *North America and the Great Ice Age,* Fig. 3, p. 101: McGraw-Hill Book Co., New York. Reproduced by permission of McGraw-Hill Book Company)

today a region of shallow water between Asia and North America and is a barrier to migration by land. However, paleontologic evidence indicates that the two land areas were connected during early Cenozoic time, thereby affording terrestrial animals a migratory pathway. In the late Miocene the straits were submerged, thus curtailing terrestrial migrations. During low-water stages of Pleistocene glacial advances, however, the area was episodically exposed and again served as a migratory corridor. Humans migrated across from Asia to North America during an episode of lowered sea level.

The Isthmus of Panama is a thin strip of land that was uplifted tectonically in late Cenozoic time. Its width is greatly affected by sea level. The isthmus has provided a convenient pathway for animal and plant migrations between North and South America, and many mammal species migrated southward and northward between the two continents. Emergence of the isthmus was enhanced by the lowering of sea level at times during the Pleistocene, thus providing a **land bridge.** Some South American taxa used the bridge to extend their range northward, including ground sloths, armadillos, and opossums. The same bridge also enabled many species to invade South America; although some South American taxa were little affected by this invasion, a major extinction did occur in South American mammals.

On a larger scale, the Pliocene fossil record indicates relatively few extinctions in mammalian taxa. By the beginning of the Pleistocene, however, major changes can be observed. Many taxa were severely reduced or became extinct, and new mammals evolved and became adapted to the recurring severe ice-age climates. Examples are the mammoths and mastodons, the Irish elk, and a variety of other giant species. Warmer climates also supported such well-known forms as the saber-toothed cats and giant ground sloths. Large numbers of these and many other taxa are preserved in the La Brea Tar Pits in southern California. The Pleistocene-Holocene boundary is marked by the extinction of many large mammals. Perhaps these extinctions were a product of climatic changes, but another influence of major significance may have been the spread of humans.

Middle and late Cenozoic climatic changes may have exerted significant selective pressure on the evolutionary history of primates. As we have previously noted, extensive grasslands had developed by Miocene time, probably in response to cooling and increasing aridity that had begun in the late Eocene. Coincidentally, the fossil record of the late Miocene provides examples of ground-dwelling higher primates, including ancestors of apes and humans. In Pliocene and Pleistocene time most hominid evolution occurred in Africa, today a region of relatively warm climate, but during the Pleistocene, long-term fluctuations in rainfall would have corresponded to glacial and interglacial stages. This variable harshness of Pleistocene climate may have made early humans more resourceful and adaptive.

Appearance and early migration patterns of *Homo* were controlled by climatic conditions in much the same fashion as that of other terrestrial animals. For example, it is probable that humans migrated northward from Africa into Europe and eastward into Asia during a middle Pleistocene interglacial age. Evidence for existence of *Homo* in Europe and Asia is provided by preserved fossils and artifacts. Particularly well documented are the fossils of "Peking man" (*Homo erectus pekinensis*). These fossils, along with evidence of fire and remains of plants and other animals, provide evidence that caves near the modern city of Beijing (Peking), China, were inhabited from about 460,000 to 230,000 years ago during an interglacial age. It is probable that descendants of this species in the form of *Homo sapiens* reached North America by crossing the Bering land bridge much later during lowered sea levels of the Wisconsinan glacial age (Chapter 17).

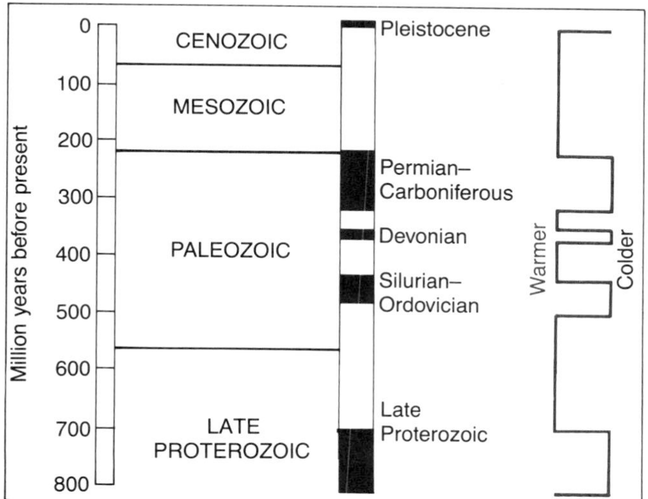

Figure 15–13
Paleotemperature curve for the past 800 million years indicates a number of major glacial episodes (dark color), including that of the Pleistocene Epoch.

Evidence of Pre-Pleistocene Glaciation

Evidence obtained from a variety of disciplines during the last 100 years has allowed a broad understanding of the global effects associated with glacial and interglacial intervals. A variety of climatic indicators and distinctive geomorphologic and sedimentologic features is known to be associated with glaciation and can be used to recognize the extent of ancient ice advances. Geologists have applied this information to the rock record and have recognized several Phanerozoic and pre-Phanerozoic glacial intervals prior to the Pleistocene ice age.

The evidence from many widely scattered localities on several continents indicates that glacial intervals occurred in the middle and late Proterozoic, early and late Paleozoic, and of course the Pleistocene (Fig. 15–13). These climatic interpretations are based on lithologic features such as glacial pavement and tillites, on preserved fossil plants that indicate cold climates, and on paleomagnetic data that indicate paleolatitudes of continents. A combination of this evidence, plus that of other climatic indicators such as red beds, evaporites, and isotopic ratios, has been used to construct paleoclimatic conditions and paleotemperature curves for late Proterozoic and Phanerozoic time. As you might expect, the accuracy of these curves diminishes with increasing antiquity of the record.

Recently reported evidence indicates that cooler climates and polar ice caps may have occurred more commonly in the past than previously thought. Such conditions, however, may not have been rigorous enough to produce major glacial episodes. For example, sedimentary rocks occurring between radiometrically dated lava flows on Iceland have yielded pollen from conifers, angiosperms, and other cold-temperature-adapted vascular plants, suggesting a rapid drop in temperature between 9 and 10 million years ago. This palynological evidence indicates that cooling, and possibly glaciation, occurred in parts of the northern hemisphere as early as the late Miocene, considerably predating the traditional concept of Pleistocene ice ages.

Cooler climate conditions and the associated glacial interval of the late Paleozoic illustrate how evidence obtained from different disciplines can provide support for a hypothesis. In our discussion of late Paleozoic time, a reconstruction of Pangaea was described (Chapter 11). Paleomagnetic evidence from volcanic rocks of this age indicates that much of the Pangaea supercontinent was located in high latitudes of the southern hemisphere, with the land masses generally clustered around the geographic South Pole. Sedimentary rocks of late Paleozoic and early Mesozoic age in what are now South America, Africa, Australia, and India contain glacial pavement and tillite. Associated plant fossils of the *Glossopteris* flora show by their leaf shapes and the presence of growth rings on stems that they were adapted to cool or cold climates.

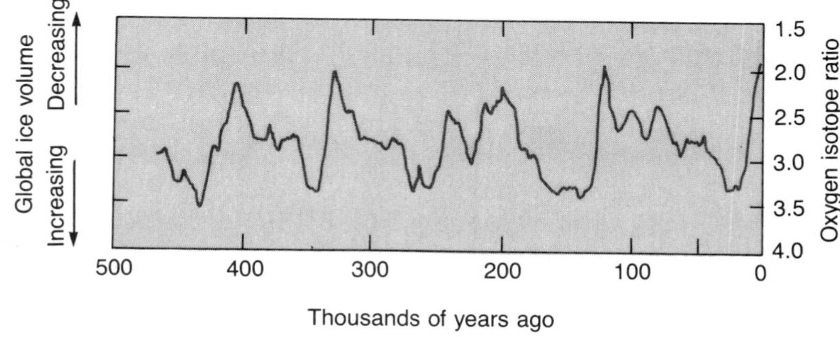

Figure 15–14
One example of a relatively detailed paleotemperature curve for the last 500,000 years; based on oxygen isotope ratios of Indian Ocean sediments.
(Adapted from *Ice Ages: Solving the Mystery*, Fig. 40, p. 169, by J. Imbrie and K. P. Imbrie, 1979, Enslow Publishers, Hillside, NJ)

Compared with the unavoidably imprecise graphs for older events, a relatively precise graph of temperature changes has been developed for the Pleistocene ice ages (Fig. 15–14). It provides a well-documented record of temperature fluctuations, especially for the last 500,000 years. It is evident that larger-scale temperature changes are punctuated by small-scale pulses, thus providing a rather jagged curve. An interesting aspect of the graph is the cyclicity of climatic fluctuations. If this information is used to predict future climate, the present warm interglacial interval will cool as we begin to enter a new ice age.

Glaciation: Search for a Cause

The Earth's Orbit and Heat Budget

We have noted that climatic and geomorphic changes are associated with past episodes of glaciation and that these episodes are cyclic. Furthermore, although the Earth has experienced major glacial events at least five times in the last 800 million years, much of this geologic time was characterized by mild climate. Knowledge of this climatic history and glaciation provokes some questions. How can we explain advances and retreats of the ice? What conditions are responsible for initiating glaciation? Are these factors the same for each glaciation, or could different sets of conditions occurring at different times have produced the same effect?

There are a few assumptions we can use to establish the groundwork for developing more complex ideas. One main assumption is that there has been only one source of external heat reaching the Earth's surface for the last 4600 million years. This source is the sun. On the surface and within the interior of this star, nuclear reactions fuse hydrogen to helium to produce heat in the form of solar radiation. Incoming solar radiation provides a **heat budget** for the Earth. We have evidence that indicates the sun's output has remained relatively constant through the Phanerozoic. Small variations in solar radiation do occur and are associated with increased sunspot activity, but sunspots are of short duration and are not a significant factor in climatic controls over the tens or hundreds of thousands of years associated with major advances and retreats of the ice caps. However, it is possible that sunspot activity could act as a trigger mechanism in conjunction with other phenomena.

A second assumption is that the Earth's orbit around the sun has remained a relatively constant elliptical pathway over geologic time. Our distance from the sun fluctuates yearly from about 146 million km to 151 million km; we assume that these distances have remained nearly constant since Early Archean time. Fluctuations in the rotational axis of the Earth itself appear to be cyclic and may have an important bearing on global temperatures.

Search for an explanation of the ice ages has provided varied hypotheses. The search is still incomplete, but we can distill a number of ideas and discuss some of them. Of the many proposed explanations, the following are the most common: (1) increase in tectonic activity and volcanic activity, (2) changes in atmospheric composition, (3) variations in ocean-water circulation, and (4) astronomical fluctuations. We will examine these ideas below. (These explanations and others are discussed in detail in *Glacial and Quaternary Geology,* by Richard F. Flint—see Suggestions for Further Reading at the end of this chapter.)

Changes in the Atmosphere

At intervals during the Earth's geologic history, widespread tectonic activity has produced extensive mountain systems; this activity is most evident in (but is not restricted to) the late Paleozoic, the late Mesozoic, and the Cenozoic. Early in the history of glacial studies, an association was recognized between extensive mountain building and Pleistocene glaciation. Alteration of wind patterns resulting from the high elevation of many young mountain ranges, such as the Alps and Rockies, provides conditions favorable for the formation of valley glaciers, and such glaciers may be extensively developed. These mountain systems, however, cannot provide the large-scale and cyclic climatic changes necessary to explain the waxing and waning of the Pleistocene ice sheets, so there does not appear to be a causal association between mountains and major glaciation.

The spectacular eruption of the volcanic island of Krakatoa in 1883 was heard 5000 km away in Australia, caused a large tsunami, and created a vast amount of dust that remained in the upper part of the atmosphere for many years. This atmospheric dust resulted in a measurable cooling of the Earth's surface and led to the suggestion that episodes of glaciation could be initiated by large-scale eruption of one or more volcanoes, with the consequent production of large quantities of dust. This idea held that such dust would decrease the amount of solar radiation reaching the Earth's surface, thereby producing a cooler climate and initiating the onset of widespread glaciation. As the dust gradually settled, the climate would warm and the glaciers would recede.

However, a comparison of episodes of volcanic activity, including major caldera eruptions, fails to provide a close correlation between volcanism and widespread glaciation. However, a major volcanic eruption might trigger a glacial episode in conjunction with other causes. Just such an idea was discussed in a recent article in the journal *Science* by J. R. Bray,* who showed that major volcanic eruptions closely preceded the Pleistocene glacial ages and may have triggered them.

A related idea suggests that variation in carbon dioxide concentration in the atmosphere affects surface temperatures. Although there is some disagreement as to the actual climatic response, most scientists consider that an increase in CO_2 would cause temperatures to rise. This phenomenon, known as the **greenhouse effect,** has been discussed at length in many recent newspaper and magazine articles. Much concern has been expressed about the significant increase in atmospheric carbon dioxide produced by burning of vast quantities of wood, coal, and petroleum materials in the last 250 years. There is as yet no evidence that episodic fluctuations of CO_2 have occurred in the past, or that this could trigger glaciation or melting of ice caps. However, we do not know the overall changes to the Earth's climate that could occur because of the induced greenhouse effect.

Variations in Ocean Water and Circulation

In 1956 Maurice Ewing and William Donn of Lamont-Doherty Geological Observatory proposed an interesting hypothesis involving alternating episodes of freezing and thawing of water in the Arctic Ocean, to account for cyclic glaciation. In their model, an ice-free Arctic Ocean would provide a source area for evaporation of large amounts of water vapor that could then precipitate as snow and ice on polar land areas. The buildup of ice would cause a drop in sea level and shut off circulation between the Arctic and the North Atlantic Oceans. This shallowing and decrease in circulation of the Arctic Ocean would allow it to freeze, thus eliminating the source of moisture for glaciers. As the glaciers melted, sea level would rise and the Arctic Ocean would thaw. This process would theoretically be cyclic. However, the hypothesis suffers from the fact that studies of Arctic bottom sediments provide no evidence that the Arctic Ocean has been ice-free at any time during the last few million years.

Astronomical Fluctuations

Our last hypothesis suggests that climatic fluctuations could be caused by variations in the Earth's orbit. An early version of this idea was proposed in 1842 by the mathematician J. A. Adhemar, but his ideas, along with subsequent revisions by James Croll, were rejected by most geologists. Beginning in the early 1900s, the Serbian astronomer Milutin Milankovitch provided mathematical evidence of irregularities in the Earth's orbit. From years of study, beginning in the early 1900s, he recognized a cyclicity to these irregularities and in the early 1940s proposed his hypothesis of orbital variations. Subsequent work by many scientists has substantiated and refined this evidence and provided a correlation between orbital variations and climatic conditions; these correlations are recognized in cores from the Deep Sea Drilling Project (DSDP).

Milankovitch proposed that recognized irregularities in the Earth's orbit are cyclic, and involve:

1. Ellipticity of the Earth's orbit, with a 92,000-to-123,000-year bimodal cyclical variation;
2. Inclination or obliquity of the Earth's axis, with a 41,000-year cycle (Fig. 15–15); and
3. Precession of equinoxes, with a 21,000-year cycle (Fig. 15–15).

Variations of these orbital conditions affect the amount of solar radiation received at the Earth's surface, and thus influence the global heat budget. Each factor by itself is not very significant, but at approximately 40,000-year intervals the three conditions reinforce each other and would be especially pronounced at higher latitudes.

The Milankovitch hypothesis has recently been strongly supported by geologists John Imbrie and James D. Hays. Along with a team of scientists from around the world, they have provided paleontologic and isotopic evidence from many DSDP sediment cores that indicate close correlations of paleoclimatic changes with the astronomical cycles

*Pleistocene volcanism and glacial initiation. *Science* 197:251–53.

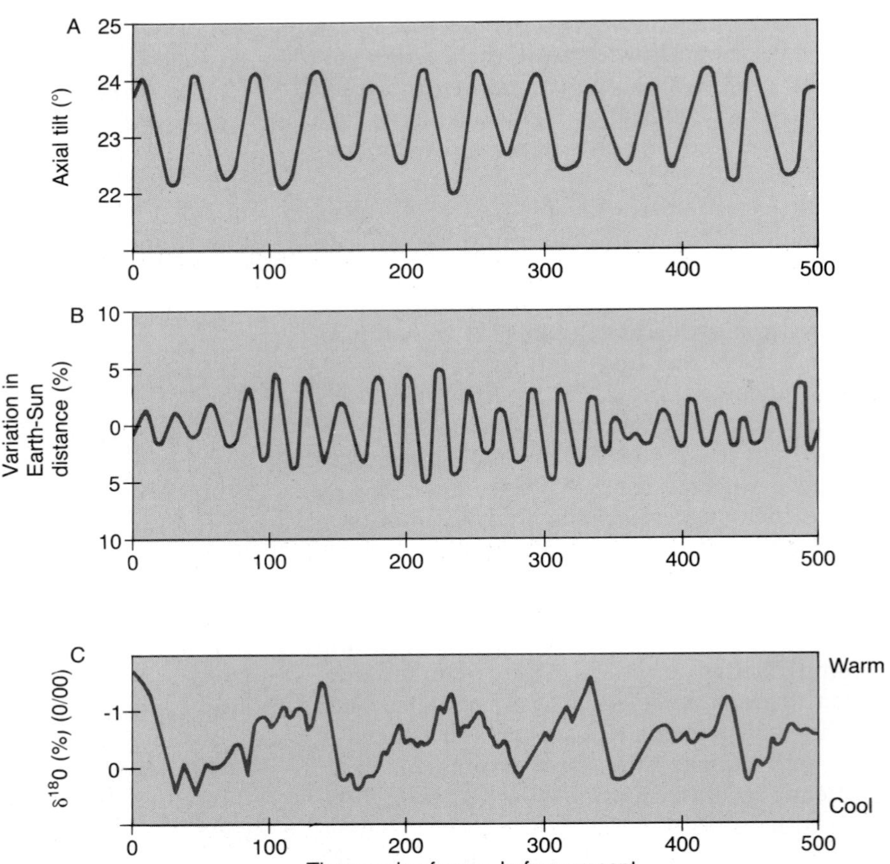

Figure 15–15
Curves comparing (A) changes in inclination (41,000-year cycle) with (B) astronomical variations of precession of equinoxes (21,000-year cycle) and (C) variations of oxygen-18 content of deep-sea sediments.
(A, B, from W. Broecker and J. van Donk, p. 188, *Reviews of Geophysics*, vol. 8, 1970. Copyright by the American Geophysical Union. C from C. Emiliani, 1978, The Causes of the Ice Ages, p. 351, 353: *Earth and Planetary Science Letters*, Elsevier Science Publishers, Inc.)

of Milankovitch. Further evidence indicates that these cycles can be recognized in oceanic sediments nearly 10 million years old. Apparently, however, paleotemperature curves indicate that the effects of the 100,000-year cycle were stronger over the last 2 million years than between 2 and 8 million years ago. It would appear that the influence of Milankovitch cycles is enhanced at certain times by one or more other events; a recent idea is that size of the ice sheets themselves may influence the Earth's heat budget.

Although each of the hypotheses discussed has provided a possible explanation for Pleistocene glaciation, all have at least one drawback, or fail to explain some aspect of glaciation. A strong possibility exists that a more complete and satisfactory answer lies in a combination of hypotheses. For example, combining plate motions and position of the continents with the patterns of the Milankovitch cycles might offer a solution. Possibly some new concept, by itself or in conjunction with previously proposed ideas, might provide the answers.

* * * * *

Summary

Extensive work by Louis Agassiz beginning in the 1830s established a foundation for modern concepts of glaciation. Glacial pavement, erratic boulders, moraines, and other features were recognized in many areas of Europe, Asia, and North America and indicated the existence of extensive ice sheets in these regions. Mapping of glacial features such as till deposits indicated the cyclic nature of glacial and interglacial stages, and demonstrated that at least five major advances of ice sheets occurred during the last 2 million years. Maximum advance occurred during the Wisconsinan glacial age, as ice covered much of North America as far south as 40° north latitude.

Along with waxing and waning of ice, other global changes occurred as a result of climatic variations. Formation of large pluvial lakes, major alteration of drainage systems, fluctuations in sea level, and other features have been documented by a variety of techniques. Of particular usefulness are studies of varved lake sediments, plant growth rings, variations in coiling directions of some species of planktonic Foraminifera, and isotopic ratios in deep-sea sediments. All of these track changes in climate; they are especially significant if they can be used in combination.

Late Cenozoic climatic changes have affected evolutionary history and distribution of many plant and animal taxa. Adaptations to arid or cold conditions have been followed by large-scale extinctions. Sea-level changes have opened or closed migratory pathways and subsequently contributed to invasions and extinctions of taxa on various continents. It is likely that fluctuations during the Pleistocene influenced evolutionary history and distribution of hominids, including those of our own genus *Homo.*

Search for a causal explanation for cyclic glaciation has resulted in a number of diverse hypotheses. At present, the most promising idea invokes the Milankovitch cyclic irregularities in the Earth's orbit. These fluctuations combine at intervals and may influence the global heat budget enough to slightly cool or heat the atmosphere, thereby initiating either a glacial or interglacial stage. One appealing aspect of this hypothesis is its potential for explaining other episodes of glaciation noted in the geologic record of the last 800 million years. Further understanding of the Milankovitch cycles and collection of considerable data from modern weather studies may allow us to provide accurate short-term and long-term climate predictions.

Suggestions for Further Reading

Agassiz, L. 1967. *Studies on glaciers.* Ed. and trans. by A. V. Carozzi. New York: Hafner.

Beaty, C. B. 1978. The causes of glaciation. *American Scientist* 66(4):452–59.

Eddy, J. A. 1977. The case of missing sunspots. *Scientific American* 236:80–92.

Flint, R. F. 1971. *Glacial and Quaternary geology.* New York: John Wiley & Sons.

Imbrie, J., and K. P. Imbrie. 1976. *Ice ages.* Short Hills, NJ: Enslow Publishers.

Lurie, E. 1960. *Louis Agassiz: A life in science.* Chicago: Univ. of Chicago Press.

Matsch, C. L. 1976. *North America and the great ice age.* New York: McGraw-Hill Book Co.

Matthews, S. W. 1976. What's happening to our climate. *National Geographic* 150(5):576–615.

Rukang, W., and L. Shenglong. 1983. Peking man. *Scientific American* 248(6):86–94.

16

Matchsticks to Magnolias: The Evolutionary History of Plants

Eon		Era	Period		Age in Ma*
PHANEROZOIC		CENOZOIC	Quaternary	Quaternary	2
			Tertiary	Neogene	24
				Paleogene	65
		MESOZOIC	Cretaceous		144
			Jurassic		208
			Triassic		245
		PALEOZOIC	Permian		286
			Carboniferous	Pennsylvanian	320
				Mississippian	360
			Devonian		408
			Silurian		438
			Ordovician		505
			Cambrian		570
CRYPTOZOIC (PRECAMBRIAN)	PROTEROZOIC	Late Proterozoic			900
		Middle Proterozoic			1600
		Early Proterozoic			2500
	ARCHEAN	Late Archean			3000
		Middle Archean			3400
		Early Archean			~3800
HADEAN (Pregeologic history of the Earth)					
			Origin of Earth		4600

Contents

Key Terms

Vascular plant
Tracheophyte
Xylem
Phloem
Chloroplast
Stoma
Pith
Epidermal layer
Cambium
Cortex
Thallophyta
Embryophyta
Spore
Terminal sporangia
Sporophyte
Gametophyte
Gymnosperm
Growth ring
Angiosperm
Dicotyledon
Monocotyledon
Pollen
Palynology
Dendrochronology

The Remains of an Ancient Petrified Forest

Historical evidence indicates that fossilized plants have been known for over 3000 years, and that many remains served as curios in the cabinets of collectors. However, these interesting objects, along with the remains of invertebrates and vertebrates, were considered mostly "sports of nature" as late as the eighteenth century—recall the story of Johann Beringer described in Chapter 3. Scientific study of plant fossils began in the early 1800s, and in 1818 the Reverend Henry Steinhauer published the first descriptions of fossil plants in which binomial nomenclature was used to name the specimens. Recall from our discussion of taxonomy that binomial nomenclature was used for animals by Linnaeus in the 1750s, almost 60 years earlier. Evidently the taxonomic study of plant fossils lagged behind the study of other branches of paleontology.

Beginning in the 1820s, the study of paleobotany advanced rapidly. Outstanding for his early contributions was Adolphe Brongniart, who combined understanding of botanical classification with a thorough knowledge of the distribution of living plant taxa. Although recognizing the great differences between living and fossil floras of Europe, he was a catastrophist and applied Cuvier's hypothesis of sudden extinctions to explain the abrupt changes in flora seen in the fossil record. To his credit, Brongniart also recognized that knowledge of the environmental conditions affecting living plants could be used to interpret paleoenvironmental conditions, and that these conditions determined the distribution of fossil taxa, and that plants could be reliable indicators of ancient climatic conditions. As paleobotanist Erling Dorf of Princeton University has pointed out, Brongniart can be rightfully considered the "Father of Paleobotany" for these early insights into the study of plant fossils (Fig. 16–1).

Many early reports of plant fossils involved specimens recovered from strata associated with coal deposits of Carboniferous age. This is not surprising, for coal had been a familiar source of energy for over 200 years, supplying fuel for the industrial revolution. Interest in coal deposits and their formation fostered many studies of the associated plant fossils. In North America, the most important deposits containing coal-bearing strata are (1) Pennsylvanian rocks extending in a band parallel to the Appalachian Mountains, and (2) Cretaceous rocks in the Rocky Mountain and Colorado Plateau areas.

Less important from an economic standpoint, but of major scientific interest and aesthetic beauty, are plant fossils found in the Chinle Formation in Arizona's Petrified Forest National Park. The Chinle, of Late Triassic age, is exposed widely in the Colorado Plateau. These distinctive rocks consist of variable and often beautifully colored shales, sandstones, and siltstones. You can observe this formation in the Petrified Forest and Painted Desert in Arizona, the Capitol Reef National Park in Utah, and in many other locations.

Figure 16–1
Photograph of Adolphe Brongniart, considered the father of paleobotany. From the frontispiece of his book (1881, G. Masson, Paris). (From H. N. Andrews, 1980, *The Fossil Hunters*, p. 65. Copyright © 1980, Cornell University Press; used by permission)

The Chinle has been studied by many geologists since the 1850s, but was first formally named by H. E. Gregory in 1917. Over the years, many changes to the formal status of these rocks were proposed by geologists working in the region, which provides an excellent illustration of stratigraphic methodology and principles. (A discussion of these changes and of other studies involving the Chinle is provided in *Investigations in the Triassic Chinle Formation,* published by the Museum of Northern Arizona.)

Scientific interest in the Chinle resulted in part from its excellent and widespread exposures. However, more important was evidence indicating that these rocks were deposited in a variety of paleoenvironments—ponds, lowland swamps, and floodplains—and that ancient paleoclimates were warm and humid and gradually changed through time, eventually becoming more arid. These conditions combined to produce the abundant red beds of the formation, and helped to preserve more than 20 species of molluscs and arthropods; 16 genera of fish, amphibians, and reptiles; and most impressively, over 50 species of plants. As discussed in Chapter 12, the Chinle can be correlated with other Triassic rocks in the United States, allowing accurate reconstruction of the paleogeography of that time.

Most plant fossils preserved in the Chinle occur as impressions of leaves, stems, and reproductive parts. The most spectacular remains are the petrified stems, some of which are quite large. Indians had discovered the remains of these fossils, as evidenced from arrowheads and axes fashioned from the silicified logs, but the first written report of these spectacular remains was that of Army Lieutenant James H. Simpson in 1850. Numerous subsequent studies indicated that the most commonly preserved logs are conifers, and that they consist of agate, jasper, and chalcedony, which are microcrystalline varieties of quartz. Replacement of the buried logs occurred

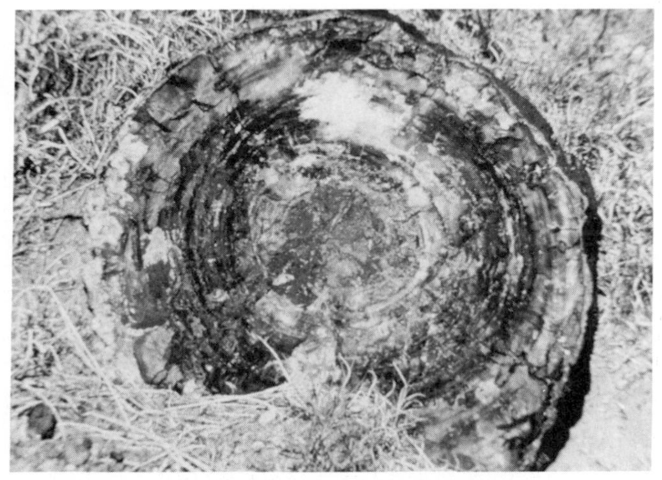
A

B

Figure 16–2
Petrified wood. A. Completely silicified log from the Chinle Formation at Petrified Forest National Park, Arizona. This is an end view of a stem, and shows the basic structure of the old woody tissue. B. Thin section of a similar log, showing well-preserved internal cellular structure. No original woody tissue is present; all features are silicified, representing complete replacement.
(Photos by R. H. Miller)

very slowly, by action of groundwater containing siliceous solutions and minute amounts of impurities; these became incorporated into the mineral crystal structure, and impart the beautiful colors. Replacement was so precise that thin sections of some of the logs show very well-preserved internal cellular structure of the original wood (Fig. 16–2).

By the 1890s many exposures of petrified wood were known from areas in northern Arizona, and vast amounts were collected by scientists and the public for study and as curios. A mill for crushing the silicified wood for use as an abrasive was built, but apparently never went into operation. Concern that the fossils would soon disappear prompted the Arizona Territorial Legislature (Arizona was not yet a state) to petition Congress to preserve the area. Lester F. Ward of the U.S. Geological Survey examined the region and wrote a report in 1900 proposing that the area be preserved as a national park. In December 1906, President Theodore Roosevelt declared the region a national monument; in 1962 more area was added and President John Kennedy declared the entire location a national park.

The World of Plants

Characteristics of Plants

Land surfaces of the Earth are covered by a myriad of immobile and generally green organisms known as plants. At least some plant species are found growing in all but the most extreme environments. Examples of harsh conditions that inhibit or prevent plant growth are the salt pan in Death Valley, the shifting sand dunes in parts of the Sahara and other deserts, and the ice cap of the Antarctic; but in most other places there exists a profusion of green plants. Plants play a critical role in the biosphere, hydrosphere, and atmosphere, and have a lesser (but still important) role in the lithosphere.

Plants are the basic source of food for most terrestrial animals; they produce a significant proportion of atmospheric oxygen as a byproduct of photosynthesis; and their woody tissues provide humankind with a source of heat energy in many parts of the world. Remains of ancient plants that have been altered to various kinds of coal also provide an important energy source—a fossil fuel. In fact, as supplies of oil and gas become depleted, coal may again become a major source of energy, as it was in the 1800s and early 1900s.

Distribution of plants on the Earth's land areas is controlled by conditions such as type of soil and overall climate. For example, compare the various types of plant species that exist in arid regions, such as deserts, with those that exist in tropical rain forests, in redwood forests, or on the Arctic tundra (Fig. 16–3). Differences in overall morphology—height, shape, leaf size, type of bark, and other features—of plants living in different environments have been produced by natural selection operating on successive generations. Important controlling factors are differences in climatic conditions that exist in different regions.

Information obtained from observations and studies of the characteristics and distribution of modern land plants provides important guidance for interpretation of ancient plant fossils; it also illustrates actualism. For example, the fossil record provides evidence that changes in plants may have influenced evolutionary adaptive radiations and extinction of animals (Chapter 4). Also, interpretation of the distribution of ancient climatic zones, based on plant-fossil distribution, provides useful information to support the concept of plate tectonics (Chapter 1).

A definition provides the appropriate entry into our subject. In Chapter 3, plants are listed as multicellular organisms that manufacture food from inorganic materials. However, a more generalized definition of "plant" is "an organism generally capable of manufacturing food from inorganic substances by photosynthesis." This definition allows us to include as plants organisms currently classified in the kingdoms Monera and Protista as well as in the kingdom Plantae. However, monerans lack a cell nucleus and are single-celled organisms considerably distinct from protistans or true plants. For our purpose, we will modify the definition and restrict the term "plant" to "single-celled or multicellular organisms that contain a cell nucleus, and which are capable of photosynthesis." Thus, we are primarily interested in the origin and history of the kingdom Plantae, and especially **vascular plants,** which are those having internal water and nutrient transport systems.

A

B

C

Figure 16–3

Various types of vegetation which reflect prevailing climatic conditions. A. Various cactus species, characteristic of arid climates of high desert areas of the southwestern United States. B. Lush vegetation characteristic of tropical humid climates, such as in Puerto Rico. C. Various evergreen conifers, characteristic of cool-temperature climates.

(A, C, photos courtesy of R. Miller; B, photo courtesy of Fred Sundberg)

Our goals in this chapter are fourfold:

1. To describe the basic classification of divisions within the plant kingdom,
2. To discuss the origin and subsequent evolutionary history of plants, focusing upon highlights of various groups,
3. To provide an introduction to the study of microscopic plants, and
4. To consider the geologically useful applications of fossil plants.

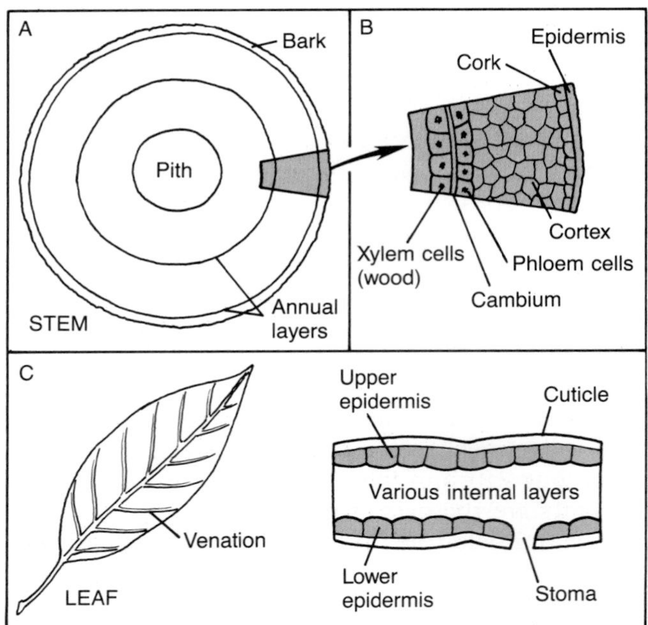

Figure 16–4
External and internal vascular plant structures. A. Stem cross section of two-year-old plant. B. Enlarged portion of stem showing various layers. C. Leaf and enlarged cross section; internal layers include vascular system and cells where photosynthesis occurs.

Morphology of Plants

Vascular plants occur in a wide variety of shapes and forms and can be recognized by a number of common morphologic features. Except for some of the algal groups and the most primitive multicellular taxa, all higher plants contain a vascular system and are known as **tracheophytes.** Most also have some form of root system, leaves, a cuticle epidermis, and woody tissues. Later in this chapter we will trace the evolution and development of these morphologic structures, and describe how they relate to the successful colonization of land. Interestingly, there are living representatives of some of the most primitive vascular plant groups; some of these ancient survivors lack one or more of the characteristic structures. "Living fossils" such as these plants provide important clues that help paleobotanists unravel the details of plant evolution.

The vascular system of plants consists of internal tubelike structures made of cells called **xylem** and **phloem** that transport water and nutrients to various parts of the plant (Fig. 16–4). Xylem cells develop in the stem and represent woody tissue, which is the most preservable part of the plant. The outer layers, especially epidermis and cork, provide protection from harmful parasites and excessive ultraviolet radiation. In some trees, such as redwoods, a thick, well-developed epidermis also provides protection against fire and insect predators.

Root systems are basically a subsurface continuation of the stem. Most roots grow in soil, anchor the plant, and absorb water and nutrients from the soil. Leaves are the site of food production; photosynthesis occurs there in **chloroplasts.** Small pores known as **stoma,** which allow for exchange of carbon dioxide, oxygen, and water vapor with the atmosphere, are found on the lower sides of leaves.

The internal structure of a plant stem is shown in Figure 16–4. The major parts are the central **pith,** woody tissue, and outer **epidermal layers** known as bark. Woody tissue consists primarily of xylem cells: these cells also transport water from roots to other parts of the plant. The epidermis consists of a number of layers. The innermost of these consists of **cambium** cells and is the locus for plant growth. The next layer consists of living phloem cells, which transport nutrients. External to the phloem are the **cortex,** cork, and epidermal layers. Phloem, cortex, cork, and epidermis comprise what is commonly called the bark. Differences in thickness and structure of these layers are useful criteria for classification of various plant taxa.

Classification of Plants

With this brief introduction to plant morphology we can now consider classification of plants—not a simple task, because of many conflicting concepts among botanists and paleobotanists. We will use a modified system combining some of the ideas of botanist Harold C. Bold and paleobotanists Henry N. Andrews and Thomas N. Taylor. In our classification, the plant kingdom is divided into two subkingdoms: Thallophyta and Embryophyta.

Thallophyta consist of unicellular or multicellular aquatic forms that lack true root systems, woody stems, or leaves; these are commonly

Table 16–1
Classification of subkingdom Thallophyta

Division	Common Name	Geologic Range
Chlorophycophyta	Green algae	Proterozoic–Holocene
Rhodophycophyta	Red algae	Proterozoic–Holocene
Phaeophycophyta	Brown algae (seaweeds)	Proterozoic–Holocene
Chrysophycophyta	Diatoms	Jurassic(?)–Holocene
Euglenophycophyta	Euglenids	Cretaceous–Holocene
Charophycophyta	Charophytes	Silurian–Holocene

known as *algae.* Thallophytes are divided into green, red, and brown algae; diatoms; euglenids; and charophytes (Table 16–1). These plants are classified on the basis of differences in the type of chlorophyll molecule and of other pigments found within cells, and on differences in other internal cellular structures. It should be noted, however, that in many classifications (see Chapter 3), thallophyte divisions are considered to be within the kingdom Protista, because most of them are represented by unicellular organisms.

Thallophytes have played an important role in Phanerozoic history and are of major importance in the fossil record. For example, diatoms (chrysophytes) (Fig. 16–5A) have played an important role as primary producers in the ocean since Cretaceous time. During Cenozoic time they were important rock formers. Diatomite is a marine sedimentary rock consisting almost entirely of diatom remains, which are often associated with other algal groups and occasionally with fish beds that represent unusual paleoenvironmental conditions leading to local mass-mortality events (Fig. 16–5B). Diatomites are economically valuable as material for filters.

Red algae (rhodophytes) and some green algae (chlorophytes) secrete calcareous walls and thus have been important contributors to wave-resistant organic structures such as reefs (Fig. 16–6) throughout Phanerozoic time. The mechanical breakdown of the calcareous wall structures of these algae provides considerable fine-grained calcareous material for the formation of limy sediments. Such organically produced sediments may become lithified into fine-grained limestone, known as lime mudstone, which is found abundantly in all systems of the Phanerozoic (Figure 16–7). Today lime muds are accumulating in areas such as southwestern Florida and the Bahamas.

Brown algae (phaeophytes), commonly known as kelp or seaweeds, attach to the bottom with structures called *holdfasts.* Some may grow to over 30 m in height and form forests in shallow shelf seas, which provide important habitats for many other

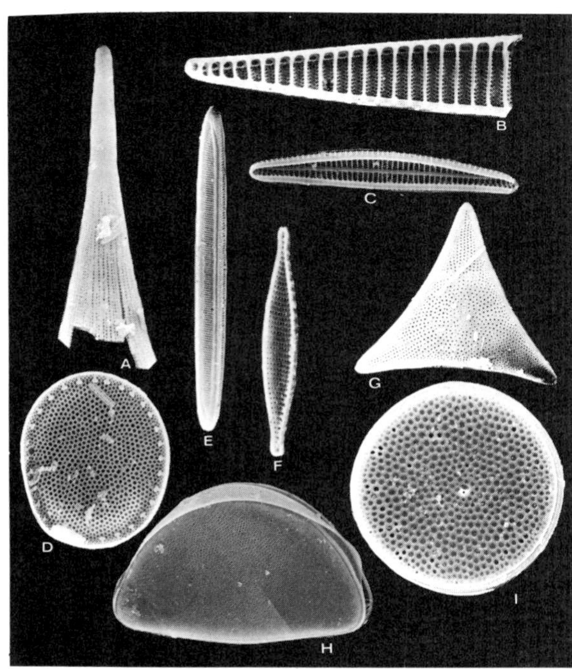

A

B

Figure 16–5
A. Various kinds of marine diatoms (A–I) illustrated by scanning electron microscope photomicrograph (×500). B. Photograph of marine diatomite and fish fossil from the Monterey Formation, Miocene, California. (scale in cm)
(A, from B. U. Haq and A. Boersma, *Introduction to Marine Micropaleontology,* Fig. 3, p. 247. Copyright 1978 by Elsevier Science Publishing Co., Inc., New York. Reprinted by permission of the publisher. B, photograph by J. D. Cooper)

Figure 16–6
A. Calcareous reef-forming red algae. B. Calcareous green algae. Both Holocene specimens from tropical regions.
(Photos by R. Miller)

Figure 16–7
Example of lime mudstone; very fine-grained, lithographic, lime mudstone, Jurassic Solnhofen Limestone, Bavaria.
(Photo courtesy of Critter Creations, Inc.)

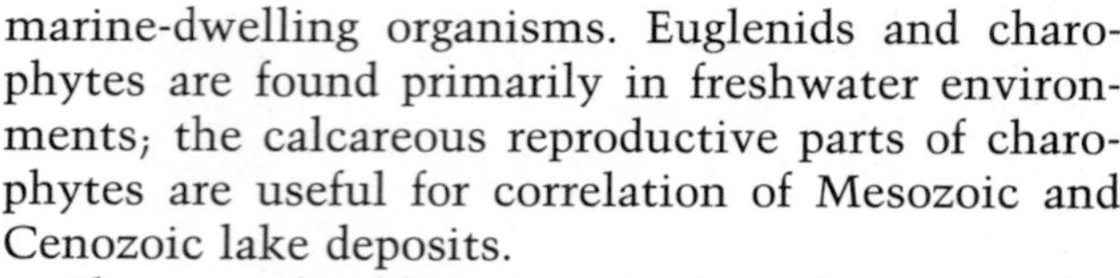

marine-dwelling organisms. Euglenids and charophytes are found primarily in freshwater environments; the calcareous reproductive parts of charophytes are useful for correlation of Mesozoic and Cenozoic lake deposits.

The second subkingdom, **Embryophyta,** includes *all terrestrial plants.* Except for the less complex molds, liverworts, and mosses, all embryophytes have a vascular system. They are generally termed *tracheophytes* and can be assigned to eleven divisions. Table 16–2 provides a reference for our subsequent discussion of the evolutionary history of these land plants.

Fossil Record of the Plant Kingdom

Preservation

Paleobotanical concepts of evolutionary history and classification of land plants are dependent upon knowledge of living plants and interpretation of specimens recovered from the fossil record. Thus, it is important to have a thorough understanding of the methods and types of plant preservation. Before proceeding with our historical journey we will take a brief look at factors in plant preservation.

Table 16–2
Classification of subkingdom Embryophyta—Generally regarded as the "true" plants

Division	Common Name	Geologic Range	Extant Species
Seedless plants			
Rhyniophyta	—	Silurian–Devonian	0
Zosterophyllophyta	—	Silurian–Devonian	0
Microphyllophyta	Club mosses	Devonian–Holocene	1100
Anthrophyta	Horsetails	Devonian–Holocene	20
Pteridophyta	Ferns	Devonian–Holocene	10,000
Seed-bearing plants			
Pteridospermophyta	Seed ferns	Devonian–Jurassic	0
Coniferophyta	Conifers	(?)Mississippian–Holocene	550
Cycadophyta	Sago palm	(?)Mississippian–Holocene	100
Ginkgophyta	Maidenhair tree	(?)Pennsylvanian–Holocene	1
Gnetophyta	—	(?)Permian–Holocene	70
Flowering plants			
Anthophyta	Flowering plants	(?)Jurassic–Holocene	300,000

Because vascular plants live mainly in terrestrial environments, many of which are located away from areas of sediment deposition, the plants are not preserved in the fossil record as commonly as are many invertebrate phyla. A further problem is the tendency for various parts of the plant to become separated at death. Thus, seeds, leaves, roots, and stems of a single plant species may not be found together in the fossil record. There have been cases in paleobotanical taxonomy where separate specimens of fossilized roots, leaves, and stems were described, with each part assigned a different taxonomic name—but at a later date, the separate parts were found together and determined to belong to the same plant. The life of a taxonomist is sometimes difficult!

Plants are preserved as microfossils, and macroscopically as carbon films (carbonization), impressions, and mineralized replacements. Carbonization is a common type of plant preservation. When volatile organic compounds of the plant—consisting of nitrogen, hydrogen, and oxygen—are driven off by heat and pressure after burial, only carbon remains as a residue. Thus, a thin film of carbonized stems or leaves is preserved on bedding surfaces of rocks (Fig. 16–8). The slow process of carbonization can also transform plant remains into coal (Fig. 16–9), therefore providing us with one of our most important fossil fuels:

Increasing heat and pressure →

Plant remains → Peat → Lignite → Bituminous coal (soft coal) → Anthracite coal (hard coal)

Figure 16–8
Carbonized remains of plant stem, illustrating leaf scars. Compare with drawing of Fig. 16–14. Carboniferous age, location unknown.
(Photo by R. Miller)

Figure 16–9
Bituminous coal (left) and anthracite coal (right).
(Photo by R. Miller)

A second type of plant preservation is leaf or flower impressions, which usually form in fine-grained sedimentary rocks such as siltstone or shale, or in volcanic ash beds deposited in lake or swamp environments. The leaves are compressed by the weight of overlying sediments, and the structures are impressed into the still-soft sediments. When lithification occurs such impressions are preserved. These impressions may preserve very fine details of the leaf structures, but the fossil itself is essentially two-dimensional—lacking any depth. Normally none of the original organic material is left, but clearly this type of preservation can grade nicely into carbonization.

Woody tissue of stems may become buried and completely mineralized by groundwater. The end result of this process is *petrified wood,* commonly consisting of microcrystalline quartz. If replacement occurs very slowly, essentially cell by cell, the original cellular structure and other features of the wood may be preserved almost perfectly, and can be studied in thin section (Fig. 16–2B). The beautiful colors of some petrified wood, such as the conifer trunks and logs in the Petrified Forest National Park of Arizona, resulted from very small amounts of such elements as iron or copper in the groundwater. These elements were incorporated into the silica that replaced the wood. Petrified wood is an example of a fossil that is both beautiful and very useful to paleobotanists, because the plant structures provide taxonomic information and indicate the paleoclimatic conditions in which the organisms lived.

Microscopic-sized **spores** and pollen are also preserved in fine-grained sedimentary rocks (Fig. 16–

26). These tiny particles commonly were windborne or transported by rivers out to sea—sometimes over hundreds of kilometers—where they were buried in marine sediments. Because the original organic outer layer of these reproductive parts is durable, these microfossils may be recovered as part of the undissolved residue which remains if one treats the rocks with acid. Spores and pollen also may be studied in thin section. Identification of species and inference of ancient climatic conditions can be made by studying the abundance and diversity of these microfossils. As we shall see, fossil spores and pollen may provide clues to unraveling the early evolutionary history of tracheophytes.

Origins and Evolutionary Highlights

The fossil record of vascular plants records a number of important events (Fig. 16–10). The history of these plants extends back only about 450 million years (Late Ordovician), under one-tenth of the total time of Earth history (4600 million years) and about 200 million years less than the first known metazoan (animal) fossils. The fossil record presently provides well-documented evidence of terrestrial plant fossils existing in latest Silurian time. This interpretation is based on evidence of body fossils containing preserved vascular systems of xylem and phloem cells, and on reports of characteristic spores.

The actual origin of vascular plants occurred earlier in time, as suggested by some questionable Cambrian vascular plant fossils and more plausible reports of Late Ordovician–to–Early Silurian spores reported by Jane Gray and Arthur Boucot of Oregon State University. The Cambrian fossils do not appear to have vascular systems, and have not been accepted by most paleobotanists as truly vascular in nature. Very recent reports describing the size and structural complexity of some Ordovician spores indicate that they very probably were formed by vascular plants.

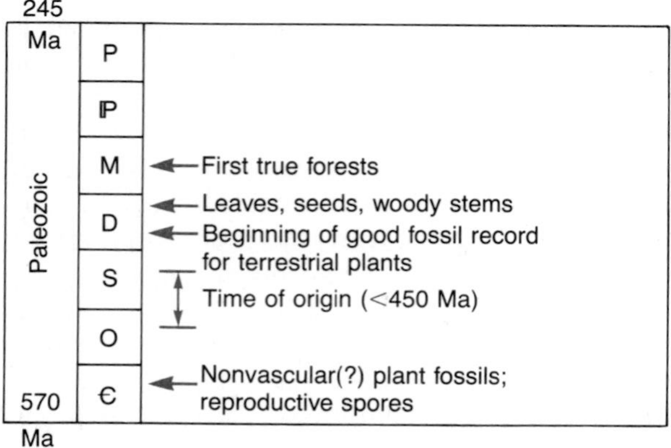

Figure 16–10
Major events in the early history of land plants. Appearance of flowering plants in the early Mesozoic is not shown.

Although the fossil record indicates that vascular plants existed as early as Ordovician or possibly Cambrian time, only limited evidence points to their ancestors. So far this evidence indicates that the most likely available ancestors were the algal groups. For a number of reasons, most paleobotanists believe that green algae were ancestral to vascular plants:

First, the fossil record of this division extends back into the Ediacarian, and possibly even earlier. Thus, these algae had a long evolutionary history prior to the first appearance of a vascular plant, and were therefore an available ancestral group.

Second, green algae live in freshwater environments as well as in the oceans, permitting a much easier transition to terrestrial existence than would be possible for a similar group or groups that existed only in the marine realm.

Third, the type of chlorophyll molecule and other biochemical characteristics of green algae are relatively close to those of vascular plants.

Fourth, the life cycle and reproductive features of green algae are similar to those of the more primitive vascular plants.

On the basis of these similar characteristics and of available fossil evidence of early vascular plants, a simplified chart of plant evolution can be constructed (Fig. 16–11). Evidently one or more taxa of green algae made the transition to land by the Late Ordovician and had evolved into primitive vascular plants. One of these early plant groups was the Rhyniophyta. This division is considered to be ancestral to most of the other vascular plant divisions. The other major group of early plants is represented today only by the club mosses.

Once they established a grip on land, primitive vascular plants began to fill available terrestrial niches at an ever-increasing pace. Between Late Silurian and Mississippian time, a span of approximately 75 million years, vascular plants developed many of their characteristic features: woody tissues, complex root structures, leaves, and seeds. This record of the first evolutionary radiation of land plants into previously unfilled terrestrial niches serves as a good example of adaptive radia-

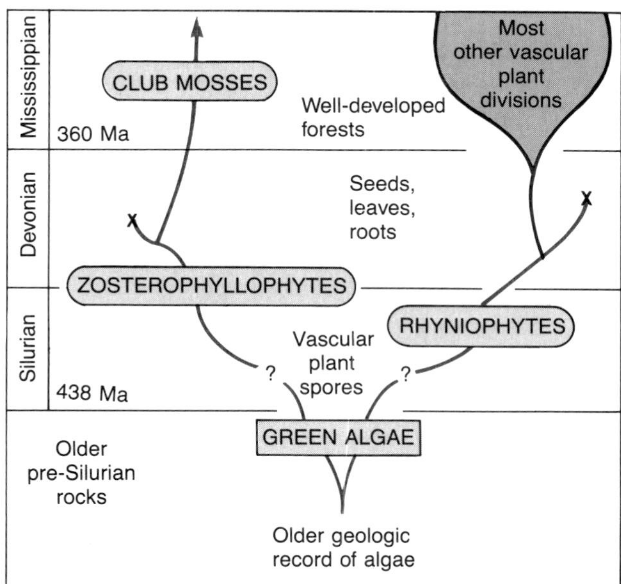

Figure 16–11
Origin and early evolutionary history of vascular land plants; includes some of the important morphologic features shown in Fig. 16–10. Appearance of seeds was an important prerequisite to late Paleozoic adaptive radiation.

tion (Chapter 4). It is interesting, but not surprising, to find that the history of terrestrial vertebrates indicates a similar evolutionary pattern. Colonization proceeded slowly at first, as amphibians made the transition from water to land. Through Devonian and Carboniferous time many morphologic and physiologic features evolved, allowing these vertebrates to cope with the requirements for living and reproducing on land.

Although they may have evolved earlier, simple root systems are first found in Lower Devonian rocks and become more complex in Middle Devonian rocks; leaves are known from Middle Devonian and seeds from Upper Devonian rocks. By the end of the Devonian Period plants had undergone an extensive evolutionary radiation onto land. Many diverse groups had appeared, and the first true forests developed.

Evidence for the existence of forests is provided by well-preserved floras in terrestrial deposits of the Catskill clastic wedge near Gilboa, New York (Chapter 11). Similar floras found in what are now Belgium, Scotland, the Russian platform, and other areas, suggest that similar paleoclimatic conditions existed throughout these regions, perhaps because of their close proximity in Devonian time. Much of our knowledge of Devonian plants has come from the painstaking work of Professor Suzanne Leclercq of the University of Liège, Belgium, whose career as a paleobotanist has spanned 50 years.

The evolutionary radiation of post-Devonian plants was brought about by an advance in reproductive capabilities in the form of seeds, which are durable structures resistant to desiccation. Seeds helped plants to colonize drier highland environments as well as lowland swamps, and fostered the development of widespread forests. The Carboniferous Period was the heyday for development of these forests. Evidence of the extensive distribution of forests is provided by major accumulations of coal in what are now the central and eastern United States and western Europe. During late Paleozoic time these areas were parts of ancient Laurasia. In some areas these coal-bearing rocks (the coal measures) are parts of unusual sedimentary packages known as cyclothems (Chapter 11).

Another major event in plant evolution occurred in Mesozoic time, possibly during the Jurassic Period, but more likely in the Early Cretaceous. This was the appearance of the first flowering plants, which subsequently became the dominant vascular plant group. They have provided the base of the food chain for most terrestrial communities in late Mesozoic and Cenozoic time. Flowering plants underwent an adaptive radiation, becoming very diverse and abundant by the Late Cretaceous. Later, during the middle Cenozoic, many of these older taxa were replaced by new taxa such as grasses, shrubs, vegetables, and hardwood trees, many of which are common today. These changes in plants may have initiated the changes in mammals recorded in Cenozoic sedimentary rocks (Chapters 14 and 17).

Evolutionary History of Major Plant Taxa

Seedless Vascular Plants

At this point we can trace a more detailed history of the plant divisions listed in Table 16–2. Five divisions produce spores as part of their reproductive cycle, and these can be conveniently termed *seedless vascular plants.* The oldest are rhyniophytes and zosterophyllophytes.

Rhyniophyte remains were first discovered about 60 years ago in the Middle Devonian Old Red Sandstone in Scotland (see Chapter 11). Because of excellent preservation of these fossils within silicified layers of the Rhynie Chert, internal structures such as xylem and phloem cells were recognized, and thus the evolutionary significance of these plants

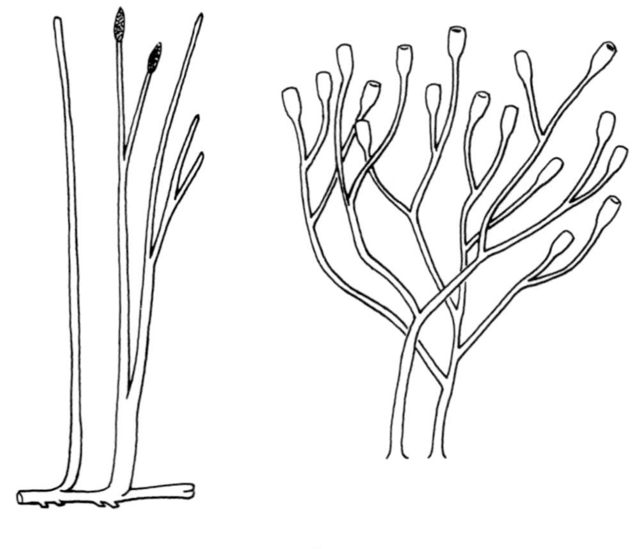

Figure 16–12
Devonian vascular land plants. A. *Rhynia,* simple reconstruction. B. *Cooksonia,* simple reconstruction. Note lack of root structures, simple thin stems, and terminal sporangia. Width of stems 1.5 to 2.0 mm.
(A, from H. N. Andrews, Jr., 1966. *Studies in Paleobotany.* Copyright © 1966 by John Wiley & Sons, Inc., New York. Reprinted by permission of John Wiley & Sons, Inc. B from D. Edwards, 1970, Fertile Rhyniophitina from Britain, Fig. 4b, p. 459: *Palaeontology,* vol. 13, pt. 3)

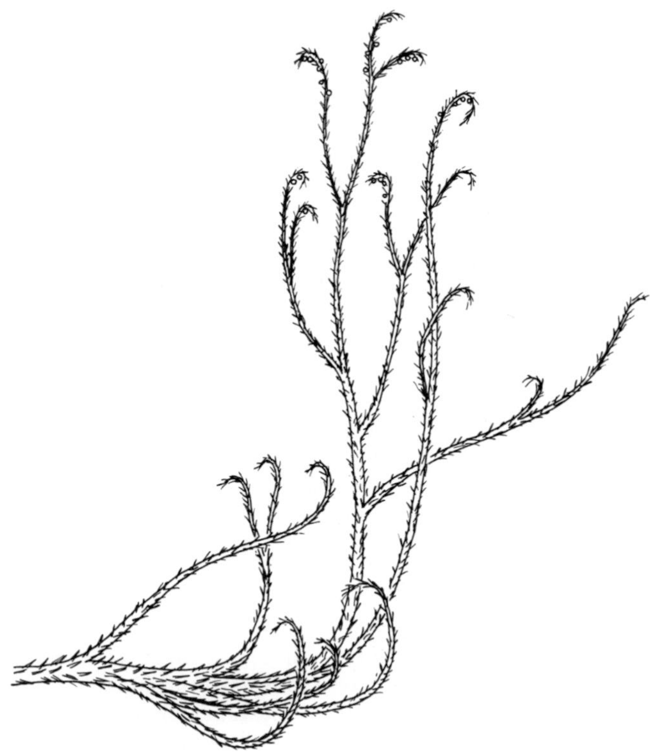

Figure 16–13
Reconstruction of a zosterophyllophyte, *Sawdonia,* approximately 30 cm tall.
(After H. N. Andrews, 1974, Paleobotany 1947–1972, p. 186: *Annals of Missouri Botanical Gardens,* vol. 61)

was apparent. Fossilized specimens indicate that rhyniophytes lacked well-developed root structures and had no leaves. Reproductive organs were located at the tips of the stems and are called **terminal sporangia;** these sporangia were the sites of spore production. No seeds have been found associated with the plants. Modern reconstructions indicate that none of these plants were more than half a meter tall, and they lacked woody tissue (Fig. 16–12).

The second group, zosterophyllophytes (Fig. 16–13), is represented by fossils found in Lower and Middle Devonian rocks. These plants also lacked true roots or leaves, but had branching stems with the sporangia located along the axes of the stems rather than at the tips. This division is considered to be ancestral to the club mosses, which are known as Microphyllophyta or Lycopsida in some classifications. Club mosses have poorly developed roots and distinct stems and leaves. During the Carboniferous Period some genera attained heights of up to 40 m, with trunk diameters of 1 to 2 m (Fig. 16–14).

It is interesting to speculate on the appearance of the Earth's land surfaces in Late Silurian and Early Devonian time (Fig. 16–15). The only existing vascular plants apparently were rhyniophytes and zosterophyllophytes, and none of these were much over one-half meter in height. This early vegetation certainly provides a sharp contrast to today's. If we go back further in time, previous to the Late Silurian, there is no record of land plants at all, although nonvascular plants such as bryophytes and mosses probably existed. It is difficult to visualize our world without abundant plants, and certainly this lack of plant cover would have affected chemical weathering and rates of erosion as well as development of fluvial systems on land surfaces.

The lack of vascular plants as producer organisms at the base of terrestrial food chains (Chapters 3 and 4) would have placed severe constraints on the existence of other land-dwelling organisms. Arthropod remains are known from terrestrial deposits of Silurian age, but are very rare. Land-dwelling vertebrates do not appear in the record until the Devonian Period—after vascular land plants had become relatively well established.

Although most of the other plant divisions appeared during the Devonian Period, comparison of anatomical features among these groups suggests to

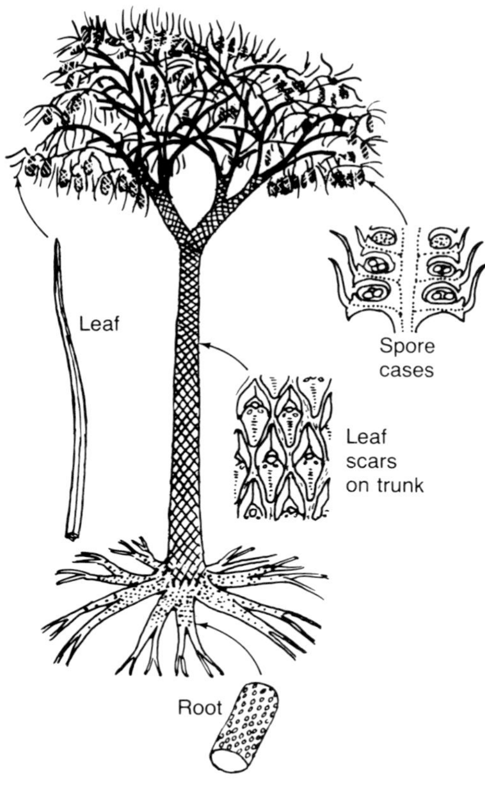

Figure 16–14
Reconstruction of the microphyllophyte (club moss) known as *Lepidodendron*, a common "scale tree" of Carboniferous age. Compare to Fig. 16–8.
(From L. W. Mintz, *Historical Geology: The History of a Changing Earth*, Fig. 7.122, p. 183. © 1977 by Merrill Publishing Co.)

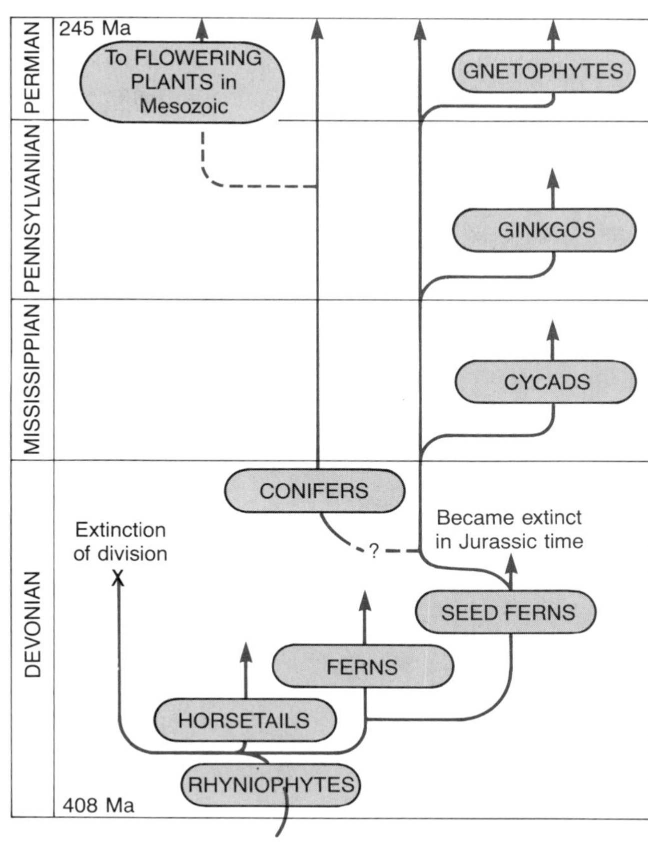

Figure 16–16
Evolutionary history of many vascular plant divisions; much of this information is speculative. Note that the flowering plants first appear in Triassic(?) or Jurassic rocks. Arrows indicate continuing geologic history.

most paleobotanists that the rhyniophytes were ancestral (Figure 16–16). The evolutionary relationships among these plant groups are discussed later in this chapter.

The arthrophytes, more commonly known as horsetails or scouring rushes (Fig. 16–17), also first appeared in Devonian rocks. Fossil and living specimens have stems with horizontal joints and may

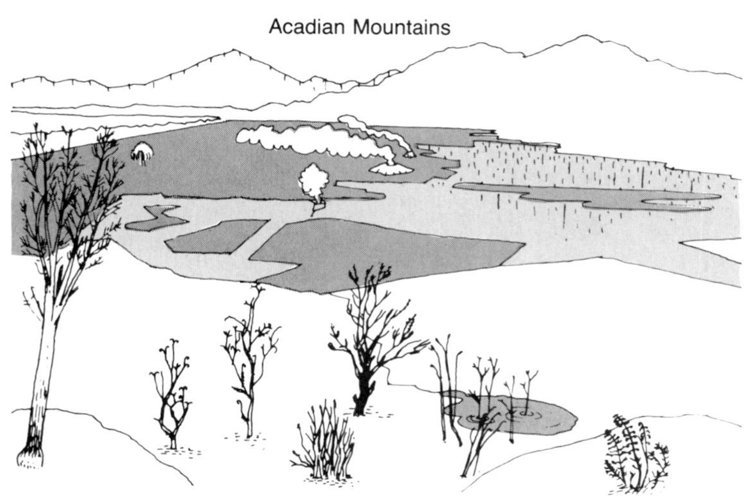

Figure 16–15
Reconstruction of a Devonian landscape showing rhyniophytes dwelling in shallow-water swampy areas.
(From L. W. Mintz, *Historical Geology: The History of a Changing Earth*, Fig. 17.60, p. 428. © 1977 by Merrill Publishing Co.)

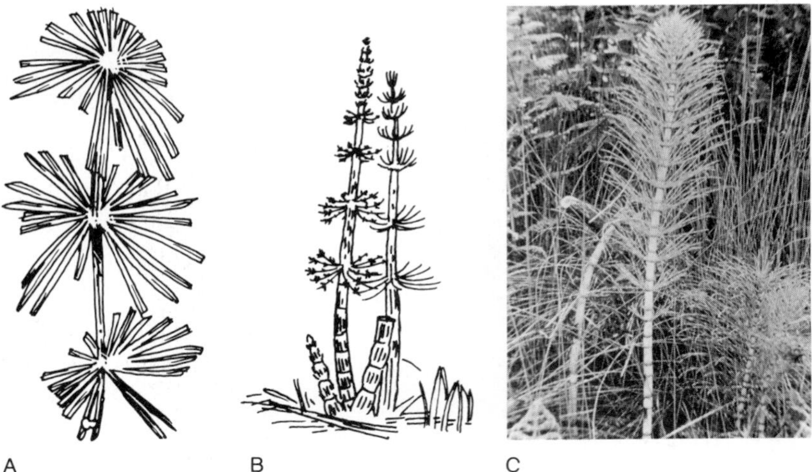

Figure 16–17
Arthrophytes. A. Leaf impressions of *Annularia;* Carboniferous. B. Reconstruction of *Calamites,* showing horizontal joints and round scars where smaller branches attached; Carboniferous. C. Modern *Equisetum* showing horizontal joints and sporangia.
(A, B from L. W. Mintz, *Historical Geology: The History of a Changing Earth,* Figs. 7.123, 7.125, p. 184. © 1977 by Merrill Publishing Co. C, photo courtesy of Critter Creations, Inc.)

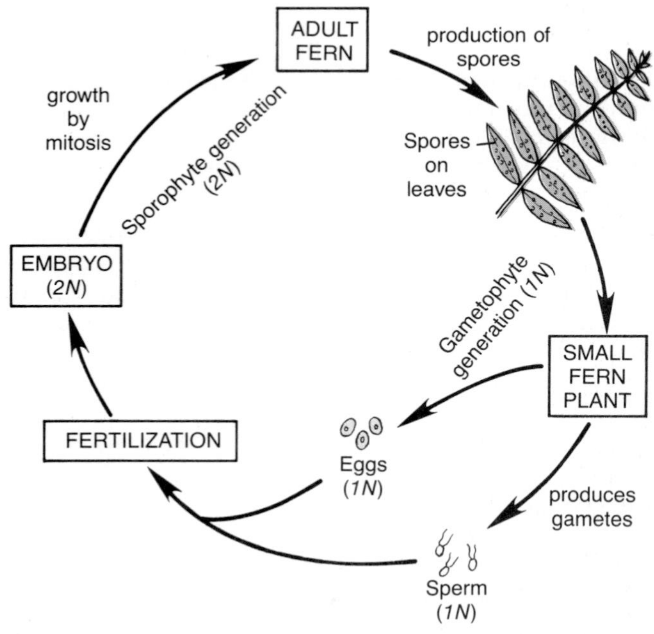

Figure 16–18
Life cycle of Pteridophyta. Ferns and other seedless vascular plants have an adult stage (sporophyte) that is diploid (2*N*) and produces spores. These grow and become a small gametophyte generation that undergoes meiosis and produces eggs and sperm (each haploid = 1*N*). These may unite (fertilization) to produce a zygote (diploid) which grows into a sporophyte adult stage.

have leaves in whorls at nodes. These plants lack well-developed root systems and produce spores which develop in sporangia located on upright stems. Some Paleozoic arthrophyte species were large trees and were common in Carboniferous forests, and their remains provided a significant contribution to coal deposits. Today only a single genus—*Equisetum*—survives; it grows in moist environments.

Pteridophytes, the last division of seedless vascular plants, commonly known as ferns, are the most common of the five divisions today. Ferns have true root systems and well-developed distinctive leaves. In their reproductive cycle ferns go through a **sporophyte** and **gametophyte** generation (Fig. 16–18). Sporophyte adults produce haploid spores and are the dominant form in the life cycle of ferns and other seedless vascular plants. To most of us, ferns are recognizable by their relatively distinct leaf shape and by the development of spores on the underside of the leaves. Ferns flourished in the widespread, warm, moist, swampy environments of the late Paleozoic, but today they are more restricted. Some living species of tree ferns in Australia, New Zealand, and tropical areas may grow to a few tens of meters in height (Fig. 16–19A).

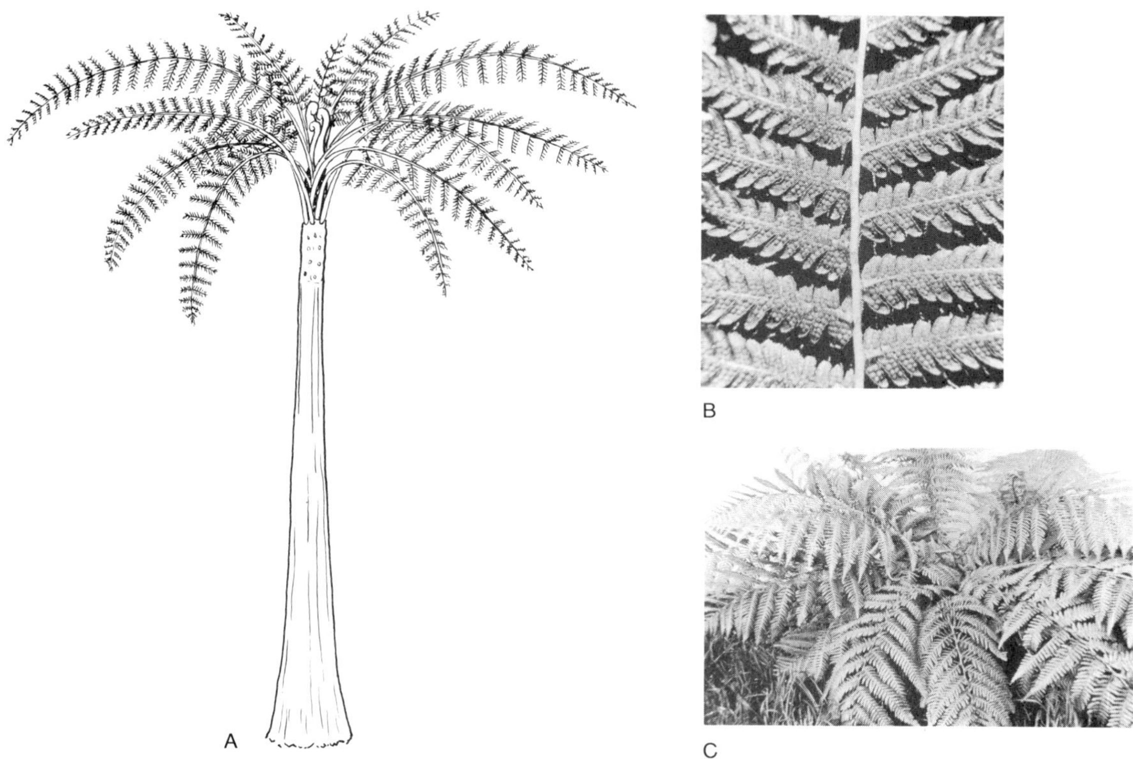

Figure 16–19

Ferns. A. Reconstruction of a tree fern *Psaronius*, about 8 m tall; Carboniferous. B. Fossilized fern leaves. C. Modern New Zealand tree fern, which may grow to heights of 10 to 15 m.

(A, Morphology and Anatomy of American Species of *Psaronius*, Fig. 1–108: from J. Morgan, 1959, Illinois Biology Monthly 27, University of Illinois Press, Champaign, IL. B, C, photos courtesy of Critter Creations, Inc.)

Seed-bearing Vascular Plants

Except for the division Anthophyta—the flowering plants—the remaining plant divisions can be described loosely as **gymnosperms,** or more commonly, as naked-seed plants. These divisions include seed ferns, conifers, cycads, ginkgos, and gnetophytes.

Seed ferns (Pteridospermophyta) were the dominant taxonomic group during the Carboniferous. Because of their fernlike vegetation, it was originally assumed that these plants were the remains of true ferns, but discovery of seed-bearing structures on some fronds revealed their gymnosperm affinity. This division represents the most primitive seed-bearing vascular plants. They were abundant and diverse in the Paleozoic, but became extinct in the Jurassic. Many of the well-preserved impressions found in ironstone concretions of the famous Pennsylvanian Mazon Creek flora in Illinois represent leaves of seed ferns (Fig. 16–20).

Fossil remains of seed ferns have been found in Permian and Triassic rocks of Australia, South Africa, South America, Antarctica, and India. These plants, dominated by the genus *Glossopteris* (Fig. 16–18C), had lanceolate leaves, were deciduous, and had **growth rings.** Such characteristics are common in plants that grow in temperate (or perhaps cooler) climates having distinct seasonal climatic changes. Lithologic evidence, such as the presence of tillites, suggests that these land areas—the southern megacontinent of Gondwana—were glaciated during the late Paleozoic (Chapter 11). The *Glossopteris* flora seems to support this hypothesis.

Coniferophyta, or conifers—the evergreens—are the most abundant gymnosperms today, and are represented by about 550 species. They have well-developed root systems, woody stems, leaves, and in some cases, seed-bearing cones. Modern conifers are most abundant in relatively harsh climates, particularly very cold or dry regions or areas having poor soils. In contrast, however, the fossil record

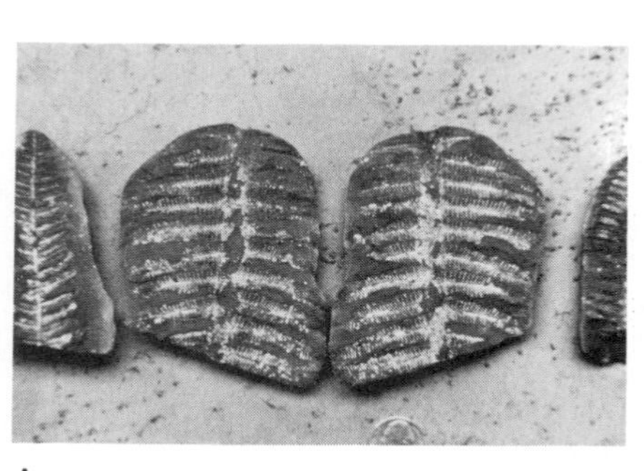
A

B

C

Figure 16–20
Seed ferns. A. Fossil leaves in ironstone concretions from Mazon Creek (Francis Creek Shale), Illinois, of Carboniferous age. B. Leaf with seed (arrow). C. *Glossopteris* leaves of Permian age from the southern hemisphere.
(A, C, photos courtesy of Critter Creations, Inc.; B from L. W. Mintz, *Historical Geology: The History of a Changing Earth,* Fig. 7.128, p. 185. © 1977 by Merrill Publishing Co.)

A

B

C

D

E

F

G

Figure 16–21
Conifers. A, B. *Sequoia* (redwood tree) trunks in growth position and showing foliage and seed cone; Oligocene, Florissant Fossil Beds National Monument, Colorado. C. Living specimens of the coast redwood near Eureka, California. D, E. *Pinus*, living specimen and needle-shaped leaves. F. *Araucarioxylon* log; Triassic, Chinle Formation, Petrified Forest National Park, Arizona. G. *Araucaria* (star pine), living specimen, about 2 m tall.
(A, D, E–G, photos courtesy of Critter Creations, Inc.; B, photo courtesy U.S. National Park Service, C, photo courtesy Fred Sundberg)

suggests that they lived in regions having milder climates. This in turn suggests that conifers may have been displaced from many habitats by the flowering plants. Included in this group are evergreen trees such as pine, fir, juniper, and spruce (Fig. 16–21). Some unusual species are conifers, such as the bristlecone pine, California coastal redwood, and giant sequoia.

Cycads (Cycadophyta) are short plants having a stem topped by a crown of leaves. They resemble pineapples with leaves when small, and palm trees when larger (Fig. 16–22). In fact, their common name is sago palm, although true palms are flowering plants. Cycads were one of the dominant divisions during the Mesozoic and are thus associated with the giant ruling reptiles discussed in Chapters 12 and 13. Today about 100 species survive, mostly in tropical environments.

The ginkgos (Ginkgophyta) are represented by only one living species, *Ginkgo biloba,* commonly known as the maidenhair tree (Fig. 16–23). This species had nearly become extinct, but living specimens were discovered in China and have been spread around the world by humans. The species truly deserves the term "living fossil," and along with the cycads, is one of the most primitive gymnosperms.

The Gnetophyta consist of three poorly known genera (Fig. 16–24). They tend to live in environments not conducive to preservation. For example, the genus *Ephedra* exists in arid-to-semiarid climates; thus the fossil record for the group is poorly known. However, pollen grains recovered from marine and lacustrine sediments and from sedimentary rocks indicate a geologic range extending back at least to the Permian Period. Most living and extinct species are relatively small.

Flowering Plants

The final division we will consider is the Anthophyta, more commonly known as the **angiosperms,** or flowering plants. These organisms are the most advanced tracheophytes, and are characterized by flowers and seed-bearing fruits. Today they make up about 95% of living terrestrial plant species. Their brightly colored and often scented flowers attract birds and insects (and even humans!) who transport pollen, and in so doing may fertilize the seeds. The seeds are covered or enclosed and some develop a fruit covering; animals and birds eat the fruit covering and excrete the undigested seeds, providing a transport mechanism for the plant. Angiosperm pollen and seeds also can be transported by wind and water; the phenomenon of wind transport is well known to hay-fever sufferers at certain times of the year! These reproductive methods have played an important role in allowing the rapid evolutionary radiation of the angiosperms.

The two main groups of angiosperms—**dicotyledons** (dicots) and **monocotyledons** (monocots)—are

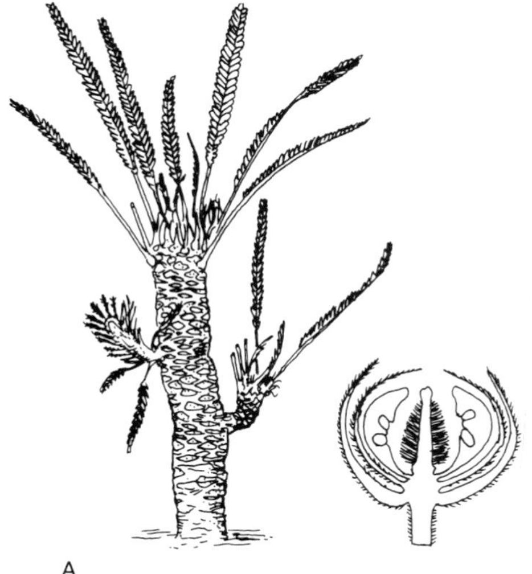

Figure 16–22
Cycads. A *Cycadeoidea,* a reconstruction of Mesozoic cycadlike plant. B. Living cycad, *Cycas,* about 1 m tall.
(A from L. W. Mintz, *Historical Geology: The History of a Changing Earth,* Fig. 7.129B, p. 186. © 1977 by Merrill Publishing Co. B, photo courtesy of Critter Creations, Inc.)

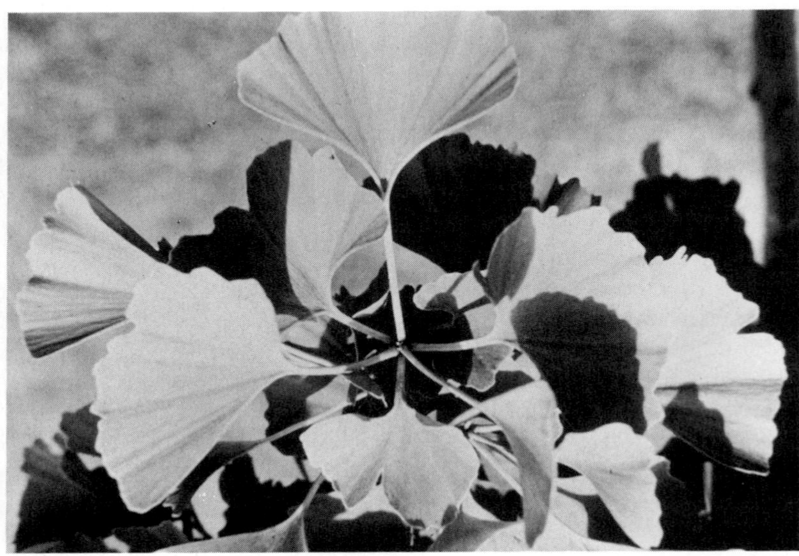

A B

Figure 16–23
***Ginkgo.* A. Living tree. These trees may attain heights of over 40 m and develop a very large canopy of branches; they can be quite spectacular. B. Distinctive lobate leaf.**
(Photos courtesy of Critter Creations, Inc.)

easily distinguished on the basis of differences in leaf venation (Fig. 16–25). Dicots are considered to be the older group. The exact time of origin of angiosperms is not yet known, but discoveries from the fossil record suggest that they had evolved from earlier seed-bearing plants by the Early Cretaceous. During Cretaceous time they underwent an evolutionary radiation, and by the end of the Cretaceous

Figure 16–24
Living gnetophyte, *Ephedra,* from California high desert.
(Photo courtesy of Critter Creations, Inc.)

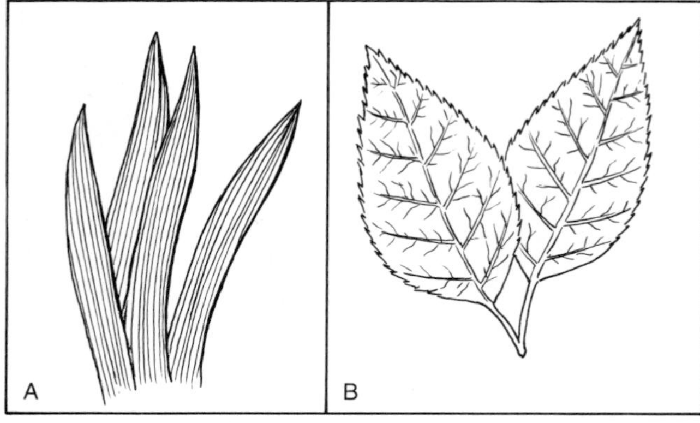

Figure 16–25
A. Parallel venation of monocot leaf. B. Radiating venation of dicot leaf.

had become the most abundant and diverse land-dwelling plants. In the middle Cenozoic, many taxa became extinct, and earlier taxa were replaced by groups which are more similar to those with which we are familiar. This replacement was followed by an evolutionary radiation of these new taxa.

Evolutionary changes in angiosperms during Cenozoic time were associated with, and probably were influenced by, changing climatic conditions such as global cooling and increasing aridity. These changes, which began in the Oligocene Epoch, resulted in a gradual decrease in abundance of forests containing woody angiosperms (dicots) and an ecological replacement by grasses and shrubs, most of which are monocots. By Miocene and Pliocene time extensive grasslands had developed in areas that are now the prairies of the Great Plains. These climatic changes and resultant redistribution of plant taxa greatly affected the mammals. The fossil record indicates that major changes in this class of vertebrates occurred during Miocene time, including extinction of many early Cenozoic browsing forms and the appearance of more agile grazing taxa (Chapter 17).

Special Applications of Paleobotany: Spores, Pollen, and Tree Rings

Palynology

A somewhat different approach to the study of plants is the investigation of their microscopic reproductive parts, including spores and **pollen.** This subdiscipline of botany, called **palynology,** is a relatively new area of study. The term palynology was proposed as recently as 1944, although a few pioneers were publishing reports on plant microfossils in the late 1800s and early 1900s. Impetus for palynological studies was provided by the petroleum industry; plant microfossils are obtained with relative ease from surface outcrops or drill-hole samples, and like Foraminifera and other protist or animal microfossil groups, are used to correlate sedimentary rocks. Spores and pollen also provide information on the distribution and diversity of plant species even where larger fossilized remains such as stems and leaves are not preserved. This information can, in turn, be used to interpret ancient climatic conditions.

Pollen and spore fossils are most commonly obtained as insoluble residues from rocks that have been dissolved in various acids. Most are recovered from fine-grained marine sedimentary rocks such as shale, siltstone, or lime mudstone. Such remains of terrestrial plants are common in marine sedimentary rocks because they are durable and can be easily transported to the oceans by wind and water, and their durable nature allows them to be readily preserved. Commonly, detailed interpretations of the taxonomic composition and diversity of ancient plant communities are made on the basis of studies of the distribution and characteristics of preserved pollen and spores.

Spores are reproductive structures of algae, mosses, club mosses, horsetails, psilophytes, and ferns; the extinct rhyniophytes and zosterophyllophytes also produced spores. Some plant taxa are *heterosporous* and produce two different sizes of spores. The smaller-sized microspore is male and the larger megaspore is female. In other plants, the spores are equal in size and are considered *homosporous;* these spores may be bisexual or may germinate into male or female plants and produce gametes. Microspores in heterosporous plants evolved into the pollen grains of seed-bearing plants. Pollen is the male gamete in seed-bearing plants and in flowering plants (Fig. 16–26).

The oldest known complex spores are from Ordovician rocks. These spores predate any verified body fossils of vascular plants. Remember that the first commonly accepted tracheophyte stems are found in Upper Silurian strata; thus these Ordovician spores provide possible evidence of plant history earlier than the Late Silurian. On a cautionary note, however, some groups of algae and the fungi also produce complex spores, so possibly the Ordovician spores do not represent vascular plant remains. The final word on the antiquity of the first higher plants awaits further discoveries.

Dendrochronology

As noted earlier in this chapter, the distribution of living plants provides valuable evidence useful for interpretation of fossil plants and the events and conditions preceding their preservation in the fossil record. One aspect of this study is the relatively new technique—known as **dendrochronology**—that involves interpretation of tree rings.

Formation of new plant cells during growth is controlled similarly by climatic conditions: larger, thin-walled cells are added during optimum conditions, which occur in spring and early summer; smaller, thicker-walled cells are added near the end of the growing season in late summer and fall. Within plant stems, a sharp boundary is apparent between the zone of small cells and the new larger

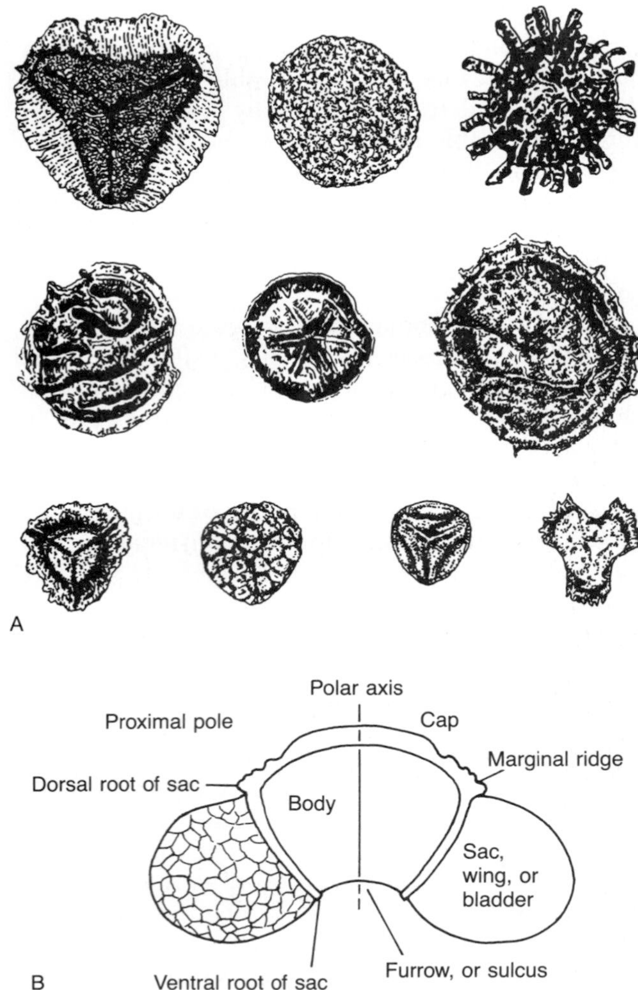

Figure 16–26
Palynological samples. A. Paleozoic spores. B. Pollen grain illustrating morphological features useful for identification.
(A, from H. N. Andrews, Jr., *Studies in Paleobotany,* Fig. 17–4, p. 451. Copyright © 1966 by John Wiley & Sons, Inc., New York. Reprinted by permission of John Wiley & Sons, Inc. B, from B. U. Haq and A. Boersma, *Introduction to Marine Micropaleontology,* Fig. 3, p. 329. Copyright 1978 by Elsevier Science Publishing Co., Inc., New York. Reprinted by permission of the publisher)

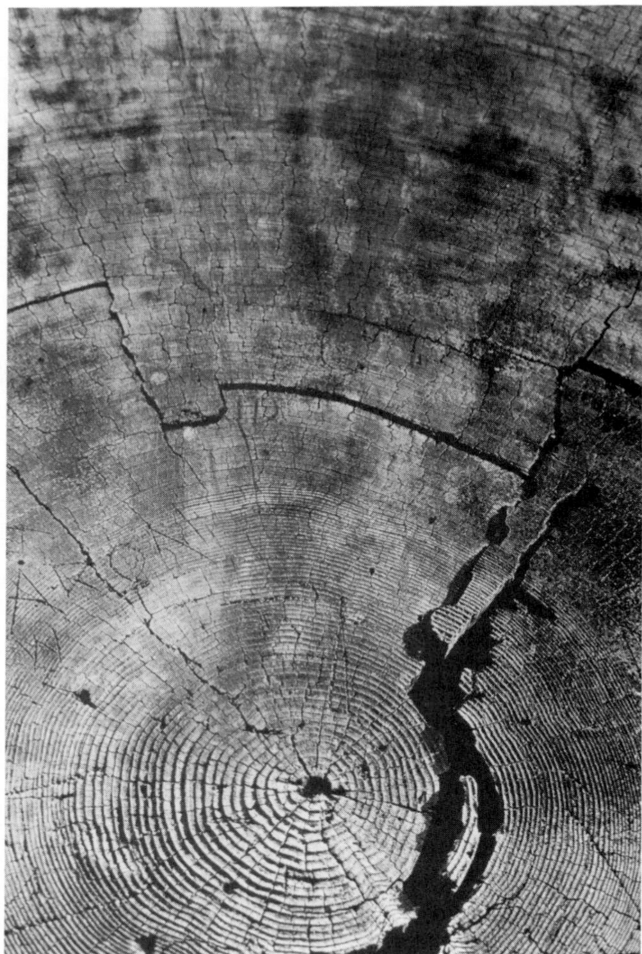

Figure 16–27
Redwood stem illustrating growth rings.
(Photo by R. Miller)

cells added each subsequent year. Over successive years these alternate zones of cells form rings, which are known as growth rings (Fig. 16–27). These rings are most characteristic of plants that grow in arid, temperate, or cold climates, especially where there are distinct seasonal changes. Thus, yearly rates of growth and the climatic conditions are recorded by these annual rings. Because many seed-bearing plants grow in harsher climates, they commonly exhibit well-developed growth rings.

Some giant sequoias of the Sierra Nevada, for example, have more than 4000 rings. Even more impressive are some specimens of the bristlecone pine, which grows in the high peaks of the western United States. Some of these trees have over 4500 rings. Not only do tree rings provide evidence of age; they also record climatic variations during the life of the tree. For example, excessively wet or dry years, or even fires, are recorded by tree rings. These events often occur on a regional scale, such as the droughts of the 1930s in the Midwest and the drought of 1976–1977 that affected many western states. Such conditions and events are recorded by tree rings, which then become a useful correlation tool. This use of tree rings has provided evidence of prehistoric climatic events back through the Holocene and later part of the Pleistocene.

Dendrochronology can be coupled with radiocarbon dating to provide very detailed age determinations and correlations for several tens of thousands of years back in time. This area of study promises to provide important evidence in correlation of Pleistocene and Holocene events, and is useful in interpreting climatic changes associated with glaciation and in providing age-datum lines for correlating human fossil remains.

Summary

In this description of the major taxonomic groups of plants we have noted the successive appearance of features that have allowed vascular plants to become progressively better adapted to a terrestrial mode of life. Of paramount importance was the first colonization of land by the seedless vascular plants in Silurian and Devonian time. The evolution of seeds allowed expansion into many new niches in late Paleozoic and Mesozoic time. A significantly more successful reproductive feature was the evolution of protected seeds and flowers in the Mesozoic, and subsequent radiation of flowering plants in the Cretaceous Period and then in the Cenozoic. These progressive reproductive and other morphologic features provide the basis for classification of plant taxa. Parallel types of change can be seen in the development of land-dwelling vertebrates; it is evident that the evolutionary histories of terrestrial plants and vertebrates are closely related.

Our very broad definition of "plant" is a nucleated, single-celled or multicellular organism that uses photosynthesis to obtain food. Thallophyte divisions are commonly considered to be protists and are important primary producers. Such groups as diatoms, red algae, and calcareous green algae have left a relatively good fossil record, and their remains contribute to the rock record.

Embryophytes are known as vascular plants or tracheophytes; most have roots, stems, leaves, and seeds. However, early Paleozoic vascular plant fossils and a few living taxa lack one or more of these structures. Body fossils of seedless vascular plants are known from Upper Silurian rocks, and spores tentatively interpreted to be of tracheophyte origin are known from Upper Ordovician rocks. Major evolutionary advances occurred in the Devonian Period, with the appearance of well-developed roots, leaves, and seeds. True forests containing both seedless and seed-bearing taxa became widespread in the Carboniferous, and may have provided a major impetus for the development and spread of amphibians and reptiles.

The appearance of flowering plants and their rapid diversification are highlights of plant evolution in the late Mesozoic. Subsequent ecologic replacement during the Cenozoic, with gradual reduction in hardwood forests and the spread of grasslands, affected the distribution of other organisms, in particular the mammals.

The distribution of land plants is controlled by climate and this fact has been applied to the fossil record to decipher paleoclimatic conditions. Characteristics of plant fossils—e.g., presence or absence of growth rings, shape and kind of leaves—have provided important clues for recognition of ancient tropical and cold climates. The overall distribution of plant fossils during short intervals of geologic time is used to define ancient climatic zones. Interpretation of the displacement of paleoclimate zones on the continents has played an important role in our understanding of plate tectonics and the changes in positions of continents through time.

Suggestions for Further Reading

Andrews, H. N. 1961. *Studies in paleobotany.* New York: John Wiley & Sons.

Andrews, H. N. 1980. *The fossil hunters.* Ithaca, NY: Cornell Univ. Press.

Banks, H. P. 1968. The early history of land plants. *In* H. T. Drake, ed. *Evolution and environment.* New Haven, CT: Yale Univ. Press.

Bold, H. C. 1977. *The plant kingdom.* Englewood Cliffs, NJ: Prentice-Hall.

Breed, C. S., and W. J. Breed, eds. 1972. Investigations in the Triassic Chinle Formation. *Museum of Northern Arizona Bulletin* 47.

Dorf, E. 1964. The petrified forests of Yellowstone Park. *Scientific American* 210(4):106–15.

Taylor, T. N. 1981. *Paleobotany.* New York: McGraw-Hill Book Co.

Tidwell, W. D. 1975. *Common fossil plants of western North America.* Provo, UT: Brigham Young Univ. Press.

The Meek Inherit the Earth: Evolutionary History of the Mammals

17

Eon		Era	Period		Age in Ma*
PHANEROZOIC		CENOZOIC	Quaternary	Quaternary	2
			Tertiary	Neogene	24
				Paleogene	65
		MESOZOIC	Cretaceous		144
			Jurassic		208
			Triassic		245
		PALEOZOIC	Permian		286
			Carboniferous	Pennsylvanian	320
				Mississippian	360
			Devonian		408
			Silurian		438
			Ordovician		505
			Cambrian		570
CRYPTOZOIC (PRECAMBRIAN)	PROTEROZOIC	Late Proterozoic			900
		Middle Proterozoic			1600
		Early Proterozoic			2500
	ARCHEAN	Late Archean			3000
		Middle Archean			3400
		Early Archean			~3800
HADEAN (Pregeologic history of the Earth)					
			Origin of Earth		4600

Contents

Key Terms

Occipital condyle
Endothermy
Monophyletic
Polyphyletic
Arboreal
Nocturnal
Molar
Omnivorous
Marsupial
Placental
Asylum area
Insectivore
Grazing
Browser
Land bridge
Ungulate
Artiodactyl
Perissodactyl
Binocular vision
Prehensile tail
Prosimii
Anthropoidea
Stereoscopic vision
Bipedal gait
Opposable thumb

Mammals and Evolutionary Theory

The study of mammalian evolution is but one discipline within vertebrate paleontology. This discipline's history is sprinkled with spectacular fossil discoveries which, coupled with more mundane ones, have helped piece together interpretations of the origin and development of this class of chordates. As in other branches of paleontology, there is laborious field work which is occasionally spiced with the discovery of new or exciting fossil evidence. Highly independent and colorful individuals have been attracted to the field, as exemplified by E. D. Cope and O. C. Marsh (Chapter 12). Not surprisingly, the stories of some of these collectors and scientists provide a fascinating glimpse into the history of science.

We all know Thomas Jefferson as a statesman and U.S. President, but few know of his scientific interest in paleontology. During the late 1700s he collected fossil bones from Virginia, and in 1797 published an article describing some of these as fossil mammals. Because of his interest in natural science, he helped push a bill through Congress in 1803 supporting the now-famous Lewis and Clark expedition for exploration of the United States west of the Mississippi River. Published accounts of this and other expeditions during the first half of the nineteenth century described the wonders of the West, and prompted further expeditions and settlement following the Civil War.

These expeditions are an adventuresome chapter in the history of the "wild West," and they foreshadow the massive exploitation of western resources that was to follow in the last half of the century. Stories and specimens collected on these expeditions fostered increasing interest in western rocks and fossils, and the more serious collectors soon followed. In previous chapters we briefly told of the more colorful fossil collectors and scientists of the middle-to-late 1800s, such as Joseph Leidy, Edward Cope, and O. C. Marsh.

In their footsteps followed other paleontologists who concentrated their work in the western interior, particularly in the badlands areas on the eastern slopes of the Rocky Mountains. Cenozoic terrestrial deposits in these areas yielded some of the world's most abundant and well-preserved remains of early and middle Cenozoic mammals. Major collections of these fossils were established at Yale University, the American Museum of Natural History, and other institutions. A number of vertebrate paleontologists spent major parts of their careers studying these remains.

Among the second-generation American vertebrate paleontologists were scientists such as Samuel Wendell Williston (1852–1918), Henry Fairfield Osborn (1857–1935), and William Berryman Scott (1858–1947). These men began their scientific studies amidst the turmoil of the Cope-Marsh feud, and they tended to support Cope. The careers of all three extended well into the twentieth century, especially those of Osborn and Scott. From 1900 to the mid-1930s they dominated vertebrate paleontology; Osborn in particular was a prolific writer and published over 400 papers during his career.

Figure 17–1
Expedition to the Gobi Desert in the 1920s; led by Roy Chapman Andrews of the American Museum of Natural History.
(Photo courtesy of the American Museum of Natural History. Smithsonian Institute Photo No. 251648)

In 1891 Osborn became curator of a newly created Department of Mammals at the American Museum of Natural History. Later, as a trustee, he helped organize many of the great collecting expeditions sponsored by the museum. One famous expedition of the 1920s, to the Gobi Desert in Mongolia (Fig. 17–1), was led by Roy Chapman Andrews. These expeditions made spectacular discoveries of reptiles and mammals, including the first dinosaur eggs and the first remains of Cretaceous mammals. The treks were not for the soft: automobiles were primitive, and roads and maps were virtually nonexistent. Despite these conditions, vast collections were brought back to the museum, and numerous specimens were pieced together. Many of the skeletons of large extinct mammals and dinosaurs found in museums throughout the world are replicas of specimens that were painstakingly reconstructed by these scientists.

An interesting aspect of Osborn's career was his collection of recent and fossil horse remains, and compilation of the available literature on the evolution of the horse family (Equidae). This turned into a monumental task involving many collectors and staff at the museum. Although numerous publications resulted from this work, Osborn never completed his major monograph on horses. The task was accomplished in 1951, sixteen years after his death, when the important book *Horses* was published by paleontologist George Gaylord Simpson. In a tribute to Osborn's original work, Simpson acknowledged that his publication was "on a scale incomparably more modest than was anticipated by Osborn and his staff."

Simpson was among the most outstanding and best-known vertebrate paleontologists of this century, publishing numerous scientific and semipopular books on evolution. He is especially known for his studies of Cenozoic mammals, particularly the evolutionary history of horses. Simpson used extensive and detailed evidence from horse lineages to support his ideas on evolution. His concepts combine Darwin's ideas with modern insights in paleontology and genetics. The distribution of fossil horses in the rock record showcases a complex series of morphological changes that represent genetic response to environmental change through nearly 55 million years, and this serves as an instructive introduction to the study of mammals.

Side-by-side with these remarkable discoveries and successful careers is a darker facet of science: occasional fabrication of data, or outright hoaxes. Most scientific hoaxes are rapidly recognized and exposed, but a few have gone uncovered for years. An example from paleoanthropology is the famous "Piltdown Man" hoax.

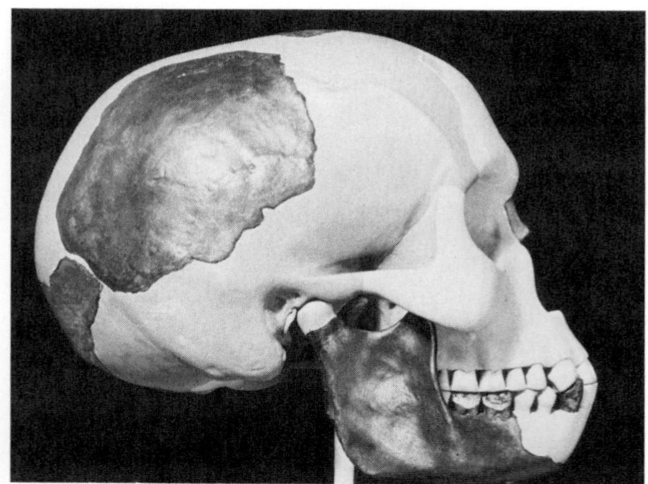

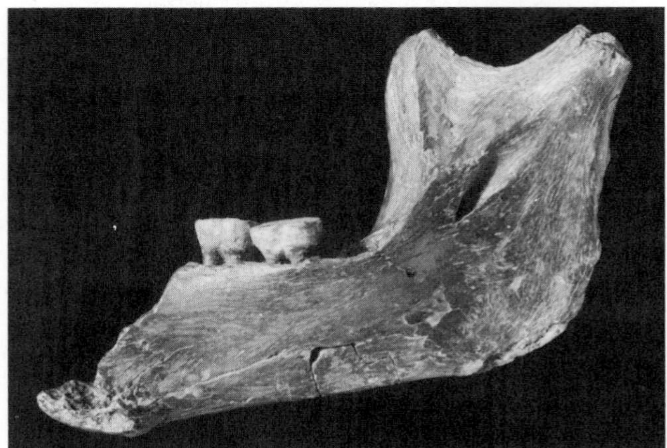

Figure 17–2
Skull and lower jaw with two crooked molar teeth of *"Eoanthropus dawsoni."* This skull is evidently that of a modern human *(Homo sapiens)* and the jaw is that of a modern orangutan—the famous "Piltdown man" hoax.
(Photos courtesy of British Museum of Natural History)

Toward the end of 1912, a human-fossil discovery was reported in the prestigious British journal *Nature.* A skull and lower jaw with two teeth were found by a fossil collector named Charles Dawson in river gravels at Piltdown Common, near Sussex, England. So began the saga of Piltdown Man. This famous fossil was given the name *Eoanthropus dawsoni.* It had a skull very human in appearance, but the lower jaw was apelike and contained two relatively small, evenly worn molars.

For about 40 years after discovery of the bones—into the 1950s—anthropologists struggled to place Piltdown Man into the framework of human evolution, with little success. Then, in 1953, comprehensive restudy, including carbon-14 dating of the fossils, revealed peculiarities. Anthropologist Kenneth Oakley saw that the remains were a hoax. In fact, the bones had been artificially colored and the teeth had been filed smooth and crookedly set into the jaw (Fig. 17–2). The skull was from a recent (modern) human being, and the jaw was that of a modern orangutan!

The author of this elaborate and successful hoax has never been identified. Several eminent British geologists have been suggested as perpetrators—including A. W. Sollas, Professor of Geology at Oxford University in the early 1900s—but none ever confessed, and all now deceased are unable to do so. A new twist to this mystery was the recent addition of still another suspect. The authors of an article in the September issue of *Science 83* presented circumstantial evidence linking Sir Arthur Conan Doyle, creator of Sherlock Holmes, to the hoax. As a physician and writer of clever mysteries, Doyle had the knowledge, ability, and perhaps the motivation to fake the specimens. However, as with other suspects proposed through the years, he went to his grave without comment, and so the plot only thickened. The elaborate Piltdown Man hoax had a long run; it brings to mind the hoax perpetrated on Johann Beringer in the late 1700s (Chapter 3).

Inauspicious Beginnings

Introduction

During the last 65 million years of the Earth's history—the Cenozoic Era—mammals have evolved into a wide variety of species that have filled many terrestrial and marine niches. Consequently, mammals have become the most abundant and diverse class of terrestrial vertebrates during the Cenozoic, and not surprisingly this era is known as the "age of mammals." However, the evolutionary history of this class of vertebrates is much longer, extending back to Late Triassic time, about 215 million years ago. The origin and early evolutionary history of mammals in the Mesozoic and their subsequent expansion in the Cenozoic provides a fascinating chapter in the history of life.

The study of reptile history (Chapters 12 and 13) indicates that they were the dominant consumers in terrestrial and marine communities for most of the 160 million years of Mesozoic time. Extinction of a majority of reptile taxa in the Cretaceous provided opportunities for mammals, who underwent an evolutionary radiation, expanding from a few orders in the Mesozoic to nearly 30 orders by mid-Cenozoic time. Mammalian diversity can be illustrated by noting some of the orders that have appeared.

The enormously abundant rodents (Order Rodentia) exceed all other orders combined in diversity of species and are very widespread on land areas. Marine mammals such as the whales (Order Cetacea) represent a return to the sea, as did the marine reptiles earlier. One group, the bats (Order Chiroptera), developed flight, but have not become abundant, probably because of competition with birds. Lemurs, tarsiers, monkeys, apes, and humans (Order Primates), although not very diverse, represent an unusual order, and to us a very important one.

The history of mammals provides good examples of many evolutionary patterns. In particular, we recognize an important adaptive radiation in the Paleogene, replacement of archaic taxa by more modern forms in Miocene time, and the overall mechanisms of evolution illustrated by the 55-million-year history of horses. The geographic distribution of mammals in the Cretaceous and during the Cenozoic also illustrates the effects plate tectonics may have on evolutionary history of major taxa. In this chapter we will discuss (1) the Mesozoic origin and early evolutionary history of mammals, (2) the significance of the fossil record of horses, and (3) the adaptive radiations of new orders in the Cenozoic.

Mammalian Characteristics and Classification

Mammals can readily be distinguished from reptiles by a variety of physiological and anatomical features. When comparing fossils of primitive mammals with reptiles, many of these differences are not easily recognized; this indicates the close evolutionary history of the two groups in early Mesozoic time. We recognize mammals on the basis of:

- A bony palate between the nose and mouth;
- A single lower jaw bone;
- The presence of complex dentition, including a variety of teeth such as incisors, canines, premolars, and molars;
- Three very small inner ear bones known as the hammer, anvil, and stirrup; and
- The double **occipital condyle** at the back of the skull, which allows free movement of the head.

These features (in particular the single bone of the more durable lower jaw, and the varied teeth) are most useful to paleontologists because they are more easily preserved than subtle physiological characteristics such as suckling and endothermy.

Mammals have a high metabolic rate that produces internal body heat, a condition known as **endothermy.** They also have a four-chambered heart, mammary glands, and external insulation such as hair or fur. However, as discussed in Chapters 12

Table 17–1
Mammal orders of the Mesozoic

Taxon	Geologic Range
Subclass Uncertain	
Docodonta	Triassic–Jurassic
Triconodonta	Jurassic
Subclass Allotheria	
Multituberculata	Jurassic–Eocene
Subclass Theria	
Symmetrodonta	Jurassic–Cretaceous
Pantotheria	Jurassic–Cretaceous
Marsupialia	Cretaceous–Holocene
*Condylartha	Cretaceous–Eocene
*Creodonta	Cretaceous–Pliocene
*Insectivora	Cretaceous–Holocene

*Placental mammals. Note that the marsupials and the placentals first appear in rocks of Late Cretaceous age.

and 13, the presence of some of these features may not be unique to mammals. Some evidence from fossil reptiles suggests that archosaurs may also have been endothermic; evidence has been reported of preserved archosaur epidermis having external insulation in the form of hair and feathers.

Some of the morphologic features used to recognize mammals also can be used to classify them. Some orders, as listed by vertebrate paleontologist Alfred S. Romer, occur only in Mesozoic rocks (Table 17–1). Other orders known from Mesozoic rocks are more common in Cenozoic rocks, and are also included in Table 17–2. Fossils representing the Mesozoic orders are rare and their remains consist mainly of teeth and a few jaw and skull fragments. Most were relatively small and none of the species discovered so far was larger than a modern house cat. A great many more Cenozoic orders are

Table 17–2
Mammal orders of the Cenozoic

Taxon	Common Examples	Geologic Range
Subclass Allotheria		
Multituberculata		Jurassic–Eocene
Subclass Theria		
Marsupialia		Cretaceous–Holocene
*Condylartha		Cretaceous–Eocene
*Creodonta		Cretaceous–Pliocene
*Insectivora	Shrews	Cretaceous–Holocene
*Taeniodontia		Paleocene–Eocene
*Tillodontia		Paleocene–Eocene
*Astrapotheria		Paleocene–Miocene
*Amblypoda		Paleocene–Oligocene
*Edentata	Sloths, armadillos	Paleocene–Holocene
*Lagomorpha	Rabbits	Paleocene?–Holocene
*Rodentia	Rodents	Paleocene–Holocene
*Primates	Primates	Paleocene–Holocene
*Carnivora	Dogs, cats	Paleocene–Holocene
*Litopterna		Paleocene–Pleistocene
*Notoungulata		Paleocene–Pleistocene
*Chiroptera	Bats	Eocene–Holocene
*Cetacea	Whales	Eocene–Holocene
*Artiodactyla	Deer, cattle	Eocene–Holocene
*Perissodactyla	Horses	Eocene–Holocene
*Proboscidea	Elephants	Eocene–Holocene
*Sirenia	Sea cows	Eocene–Holocene
*Tubulidentata		Eocene–Holocene
*Hyracoidea	Hyrax	Oligocene–Holocene
*Pholidota		Oligocene–Holocene
*Embrithopoda		Oligocene
*Demostyla		Miocene–Pliocene
Subclass Prototheria		
Monotremata		Pleistocene–Holocene

*Placental mammals. Note that most first appear in rocks of Paleocene-Eocene age.

known, and many attained very large body sizes, such as whales and ungulates. As a result, a much better fossil record exists for Cenozoic mammals. Many mammalian evolutionary lineages have been studied, including the classic example of horse evolution, and all provide support for evolutionary theory.

Origin of Mammals

By use of teeth, skulls, and bones—the parts most likely to be preserved in the fossil record—it is possible to provide an estimate of when mammals first evolved. By careful study of the record, paleontologists have reconstructed events leading up to the first mammals, and have traced their subsequent history through the Mesozoic and Cenozoic Eras. This early history is intricately interwoven with the history of reptiles, with major changes in land plants, and with the relative movements of the lithospheric plates through the 200 million years since the Triassic.

Evolutionary relationships between mammals and reptiles are illustrated in Figure 17–3. As described in Chapter 11, reptiles first appeared in the Early Pennsylvanian and were descended from labyrinthodont amphibians. One subclass, the Synapsida, became the most diversified and abundant reptile group of the late Paleozoic. Therapsids, an order of synapsids, are very abundant in Permian rocks and continue into the Triassic record. These fossils reveal a number of mammalian anatomical characteristics such as a second bony palate and a single lower jawbone. Also, preservation of epidermis of some therapsids suggests that in life the animals may have had fur and whiskers, which are insulators and indicate the possibility that this group was endothermic.

Therapsids dominated terrestrial environments until the close of the Permian Period, when approximately 85% of them became extinct. Remains of these creatures have been recovered from rocks on the southern-hemisphere continents of ancient Gondwana, but some are also known from red beds in Texas and New Mexico. The red beds were deposited in lacustrine and floodplain environments under arid climatic conditions perhaps similar to those existing in the American Southwest today.

During the Triassic, remnants of mammal-like therapsids that survived the Permian extinctions underwent significant evolutionary changes and a variety of new lineages appear in the rock record (Fig. 17–3). Near the end of Triassic time at least one of these new lineages, and possibly more, crossed a physiological threshold and made the evolutionary transition from mammal-like reptile to true mammal. Other therapsid lineages did not make the transition, and by Early Jurassic time all the therapsids were extinct. As Figure 17–4 sug-

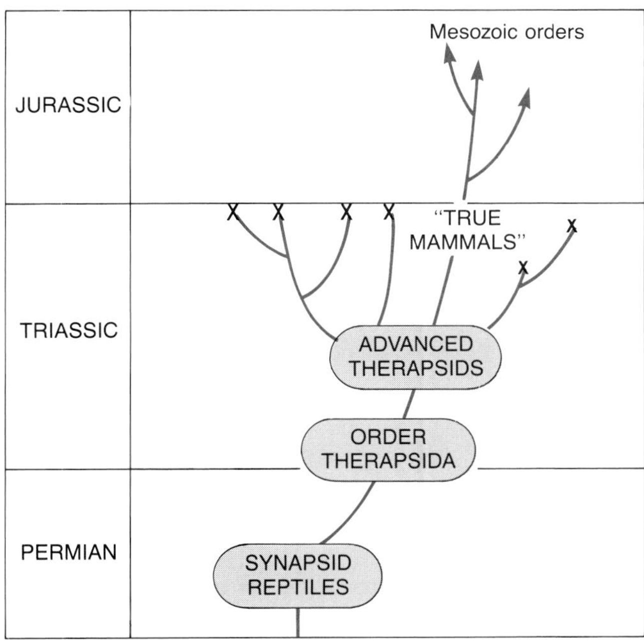

Figure 17–3
Late Paleozoic–to–early Mesozoic mammal-like reptiles leading to the first true mammals, which appear in rocks of Late Triassic age.

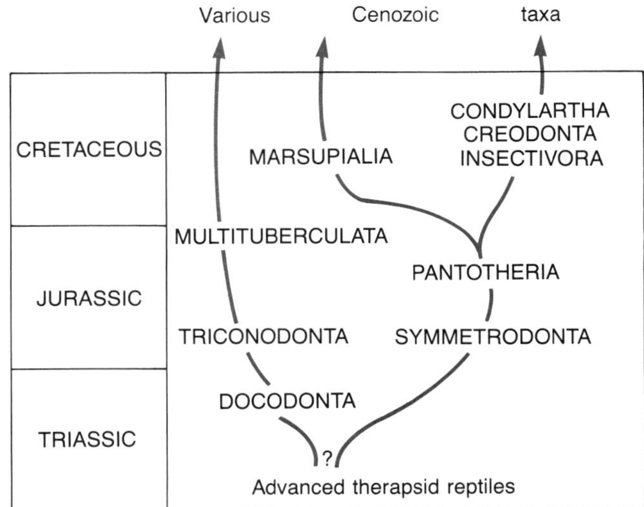

Figure 17–4
Interpretation of evolutionary history of Mesozoic mammals based primarily on remains of teeth and lower jaws (see Fig. 17–5)

gests, only one therapsid lineage evolved into true mammals, but herein lies controversy. If all mammals descended from one lineage of therapsid reptiles, they would be considered to have a **monophyletic** origin. If the mammals evolved from two or more lineages of therapsids, they would have a **polyphyletic** origin.

To distinguish between monophyletic or polyphyletic origin for mammals, considerable fossil evidence must be available; abundant jaws, skeletal material, and especially teeth are the main prerequisites. Such material is abundant for mammal-like reptiles, but is lacking for the early mammals, and at present there is no conclusive evidence for either monophyly or polyphyly. Compounding the complexity of the reptile-mammal evolutionary transition is evidence that specific mammalian characteristics appeared at different times in different evolving lineages. However, the morphological features of teeth and other skeletal evidence suggest to some vertebrate paleontologists that mammals evolved from a single lineage of small-sized, carnivorous therapsids. The genus *Cynognathus,* although belonging to the cynodont lineage of therapsids, is commonly cited as having features transitional between reptile and mammal (Fig. 17–5).

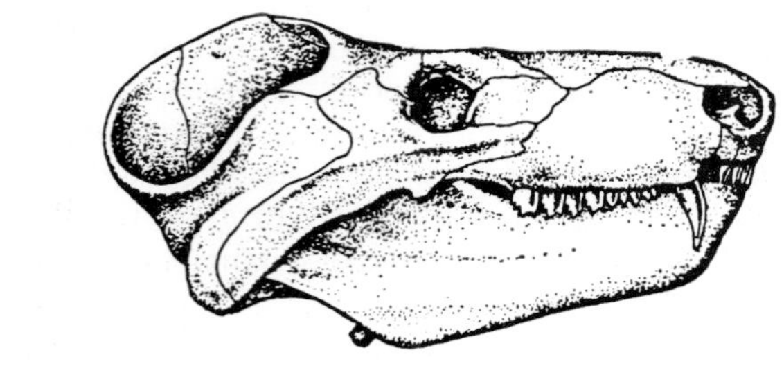

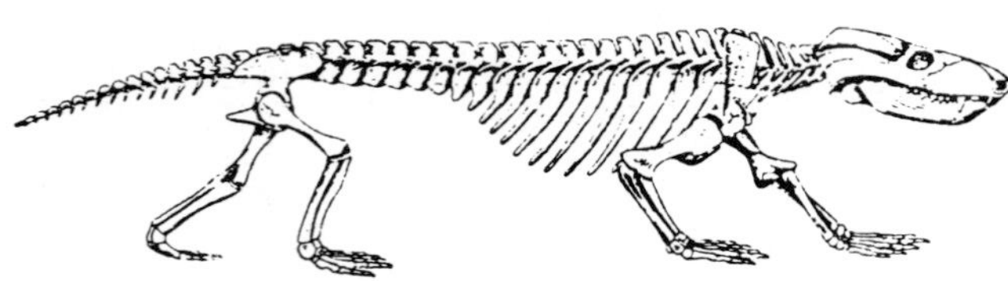

Figure 17–5
Examples of cynodonts, a group of mammal-like reptiles of Triassic age. A. Skull of *Cynognathus,* a therapsid reptile, illustrating skull, lower jaw bone, and complex dentition, all of which represent mammal-like characteristics. Specimen approximately 46 cm long. B. lateral view of reconstructed skeleton of *Thrinaxodon,* a therapsid reptile. Specimen approximately 0.5 m long.
(Modified from A. S. Romer, *Vertebrate Paleontology,* 3d ed., Figs. 276 and 277, p. 179. University of Chicago Press. © 1966 by the University of Chicago. All rights reserved)

As discussed in Chapter 11, it is difficult to distinguish between amphibians and the earliest reptiles in fossils of Early Pennsylvanian age. This same difficulty plagues interpretation of the transitional fossils that led from therapsid to mammal in Late Triassic time. Furthermore, study of such transitional fossils indicates that the first mammals were probably distinct from therapsids primarily in physiological features which are not usually preserved; not until somewhat later in mammalian history do distinctive skeletal differences appear. These difficulties, while presenting challenging problems for paleontologists, are excellent examples of the process of evolution, because they document the transitional nature of evolutionary changes.

Mammals survived the wave of extinction at the end of Triassic time, as a result of a number of characteristics that had survival value. Endothermy allowed them to retain a small body size and still produce enough body heat to remain active, even in cold climates. The distinctive differentiation of mammalian teeth permitted a diet that could include a wide variety of foods. Further evidence suggests that many early mammals were **arboreal** and

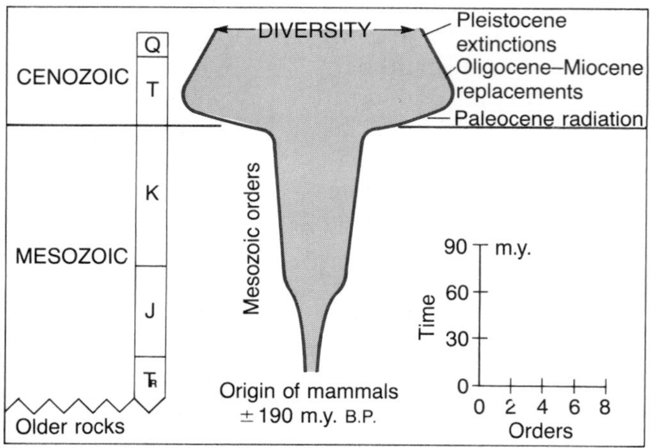

Figure 17–6
Evolutionary history of the class Mammalia. The chart illustrates diversity at the order level. A major adaptive radiation occurred early in the Cenozoic. Evolutionary replacement of Cretaceous and many early Cenozoic orders occurred during latest Eocene to Miocene time. Climatic changes and emergence of humans may have contributed to Pleistocene extinctions of many mammal lineages.

probably were **nocturnal**; thus they inhabited niches unoccupied by other vertebrates.

The large-scale evolutionary history of mammals for the last 190 million years can be divided into three main phases (Fig. 17–6). An early phase included the time of origin and early history during Mesozoic time. This interval represents about two-thirds of the entire history of mammals; at that time they were uncommon, small, and subordinate to the dinosaurs, and presumably evolutionary opportunities favoring major diversification did not exist.

A change in fortunes occurred with the extinction of dinosaurs at the end of Cretaceous time. This paved the way for a second phase, represented by a rapid evolutionary radiation in the early Cenozoic, followed by an interval of extinction in mid-Cenozoic time. The third phase was another adaptive radiation in the middle Cenozoic, during which time most of the modern taxa appeared. We will consider these phases next.

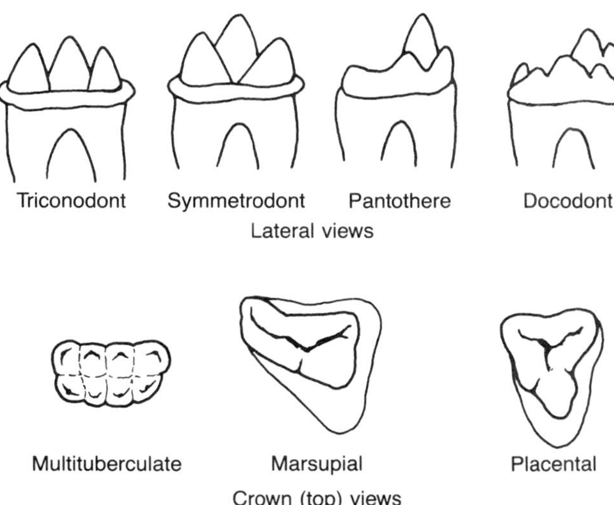

Figure 17–7
Sketches of molar (cheek) teeth of Mesozoic mammals. Note the distinct cusp pattern used to distinguish among the various orders.
(Modified from A. S. Romer, *Vertebrate Paleontology*, 3d ed., Fig. 307, p. 199; University of Chicago Press. © 1966 by the University of Chicago. All rights reserved)

Mesozoic Mammals

Despite extensive searches of the rock record for over 100 years, Mesozoic rocks have yielded fossils representing only nine orders of mammals. These orders are distinguished from one another on the basis of shape of the **molars,** or cheek teeth, primarily because these teeth are by far the most commonly preserved hard parts and because they show recognizable morphologic differences. Until the recent discovery of skull and bone fragments of Cretaceous pantotheres at Bug Creek, Montana, few skeletal parts of Mesozoic age had been found.

Early mammals were small, on average about the size of modern rats, with a few perhaps reaching the size of small house cats. Their bones were small, fragile, and easily broken—and easy to overlook in the rock record, especially if they occur with huge reptile bones. It is interesting to compare the tools and techniques used to discover and collect huge dinosaur bones (many meters long) and tiny mammal teeth (3 mm to 10 mm in diameter) from the same collecting sites. Certainly the collecting of each type of fossil presents its problems!

Construction of evolutionary history (Fig. 17–4) is based upon teeth and jaws, most of which have been found in North America, Europe, and eastern and central Asia. The various orders of Mesozoic mammals are differentiated on the basis of crown position, crown complexity, and outline of molar teeth (Fig. 17–7). The shape of these teeth supports suggestions that primitive mammals had an **omnivorous** diet, probably of the insectivorous type; their teeth are adapted for grinding various types of food such as insects, seeds, and eggs.

Of greatest interest to us are the pantotheres (Figure 17–8), because this order is considered to be ancestral to the more advanced **marsupials** and **placentals.** The other orders of Mesozoic mammals represent evolutionary dead ends, although one, the multituberculates, was very successful in terms of longevity. Multituberculates survived well into the Cenozoic; however, they did not lead to more advanced groups. In contrast to other early mammalian orders, multituberculates had molars with longitudinal rows of cusps adapted for grinding, and thus were probably herbivorous (Figs. 17–7 and 17–8).

Before considering the history of Cenozoic mammals, let us review some events that occurred during the Cretaceous period. As discussed in Chapter 13, the breakup of Pangaea began in the Triassic and had progressed considerably by Late Cretaceous time. This fragmentation affected the number of terrestrial habitats and altered climatic patterns. These changes are recognized also in the fossil record of vascular plants—seed-bearing gymnosperms were replaced by the flowering plants. Finally, and

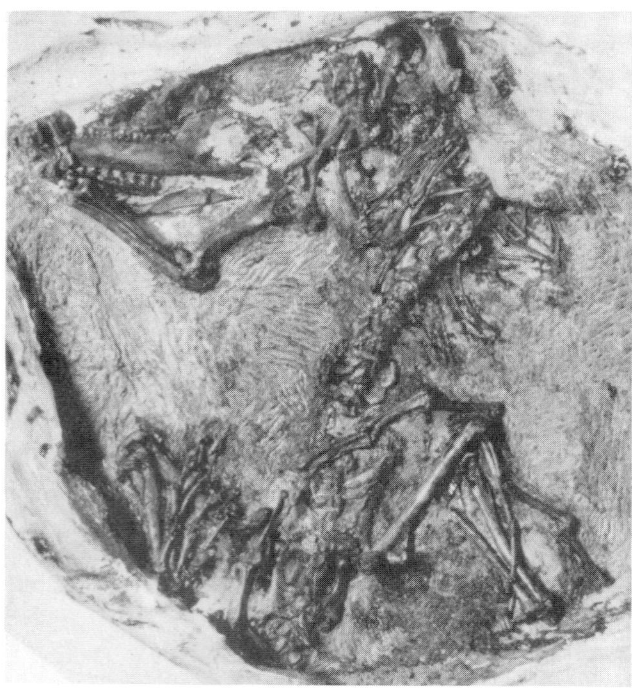

Figure 17–8
Photograph of the fossilized skeleton of an undescribed Mesozoic pantothere from the Late Jurassic of Portugal (×2).
(From R. L. Carroll, *Vertebrate Paleontology and Evolution,* Fig. 19–5, p. 428. © 1988 W. H. Freeman & Co.)

perhaps most importantly, the end of the Cretaceous was the time of dinosaur extinctions. These events all influenced mammalian evolution in the Cretaceous, and helped set the stage for the subsequent explosive radiation of mammals in the Cenozoic.

Mammals Take Center Stage

Refugees from the Mesozoic

Mammal fossils from earliest Cenozoic—the Paleocene Epoch—are much more abundant than in Mesozoic rocks, and show a dramatic increase in diversity. Comparison of Tables 17–1 and 17–2 indicates that only five orders survived the Cretaceous extinctions, but more significantly, eleven new orders of placental mammals appeared. Of the holdovers, multituberculates represent what A. S. Romer described as a highly specialized but very successful order. As mentioned, they hold the longevity record for mammalian orders, having survived from Cretaceous to Eocene time, a span of nearly 100 million years! As noted previously, these mammals were herbivorous, and may have filled niches later occupied by the rodents. In the early Cenozoic some species attained large size (Fig. 17–8), a characteristic common to the evolutionary history of many herbivorous vertebrate lineages. Extinction of the multituberculates in the Eocene may have been due to competition with more advanced placentals.

Another order first appearing in Cretaceous time, marsupials, have a pouch for nursing newborn, a distinctive pelvic structure, an inturned lower jawbone, and three premolar and four molar teeth (Fig. 17–9). The geologic history of this order illustrates unusual evolutionary patterns. During the Cretaceous, the marsupials had a nearly worldwide distribution, but they were apparently "outcompeted" in the early Cenozoic by rapidly diversifying placental orders; today they are uncommon in most parts of the world. In Australia and South America, however, Cenozoic marsupials were not affected by the placentals, and remained diversified; during the Cenozoic these regions became **asylum areas** for the order, although South American marsupials were affected by placentals once the Panamanium land bridge formed in the Pliocene.

This pattern of marsupial survival is closely related to plate tectonics. By Cretaceous time the breakup of Pangaea had progressed to the point that Australia and South America had become isolated from other land masses before placental mammals could become established. Thus marsupials, free from competition with placentals, evolved into a wide variety of species. Many of these, such as the marsupial dog, wolf, and various rodentlike animals, are similar to their placental counterparts, and fill equivalent niches in terrestrial communities. Today most South American marsupials are extinct because of competition with the placentals that migrated southward across the Panamanian land bridge that formed in the late Neogene, about 3 million years ago (Chapter 15). One exception to these extinctions is the opossum, a marsupial that has managed to survive in South America and even migrate to and spread in North America. Survival of this creature is undoubtedly related to its adaptability; opossums can eat almost anything, are a prolific producer of young, and are able to survive in a wide variety of climatic conditions. Other organisms with these characteristics have also survived over long intervals of geologic time; examples of other adaptive generalists are turtles, cock-

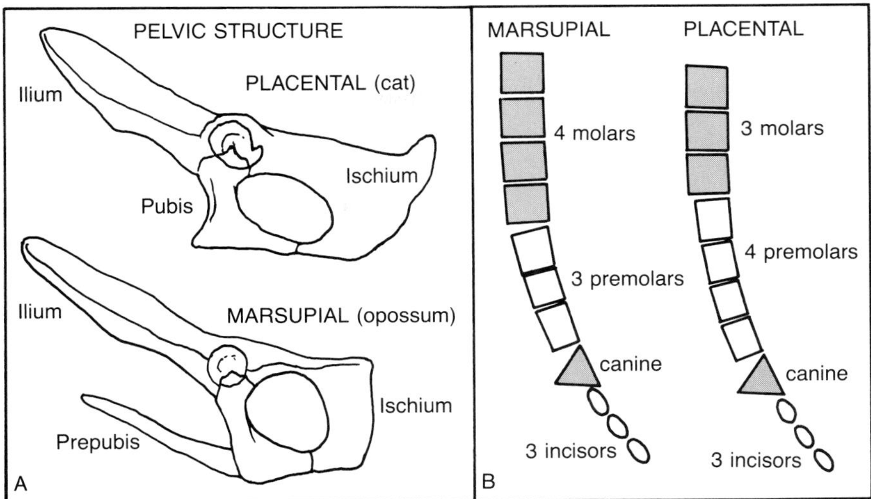

Figure 17–9

Marsupial and placental anatomy. A. Pelvic bones illustrating forward projection in marsupials. B. Lower right tooth row indicating the differences in number of molar and premolar teeth in marsupials and placentals.

(A, modified from A. S. Romer, 1962, *The Vertebrate Body,* Fig. 142, p. 190. W. B. Saunders Company, Philadelphia, PA. B, modified from A. S. Romer, *Vertebrate Paleontology,* 3d ed., Fig. 312, p. 202: University of Chicago Press.)

roaches, and some genera of inarticulate brachiopods.

Early Cenozoic Placental Radiations

The second phase of mammal evolutionary history began in early Cenozoic time with the appearance and rapid proliferation of placental mammals. Placentals are by far the most abundant and diversified group of Cenozoic mammals. They are characterized by having a placenta for prenatal development, distinctive pelvic bones, a relatively enlarged brain, and four premolar and three molar teeth on each side of the jaw (Fig. 17–9). Three primitive orders first appear in uppermost Cretaceous rocks, and one, the **Insectivores** (shrews, moles, hedgehogs), is probably the ancestral stock that gave rise to many other orders. Rapid evolutionary radiation of placentals occurred during the Paleocene and Eocene Epochs, when 18 new orders appeared (Fig. 17–10).

A brief scan of the placental orders shown in Figure 17–10 indicates that these mammals rapidly diversified into habitats left vacant by the demise of the major reptile groups, and exploited new habitats as well. For instance, placentals of the Order Carnivora include terrestrial types such as dogs, cats, bears, raccoons, and hyenas, and marine forms such as seals (Fig. 17–11). Carnivores underwent adaptive radiation in the Oligocene following the decline of a more primitive order, the creodonts, which had occupied carnivore niches in Paleocene and Eocene communities. The rodents, generally known as gnawing mammals, are the most abundant order and include diverse groups such as rats, mice, squirrels, porcupines, and beavers. Rodents underwent an expansion in the early Cenozoic and have continued to diversify to the present time.

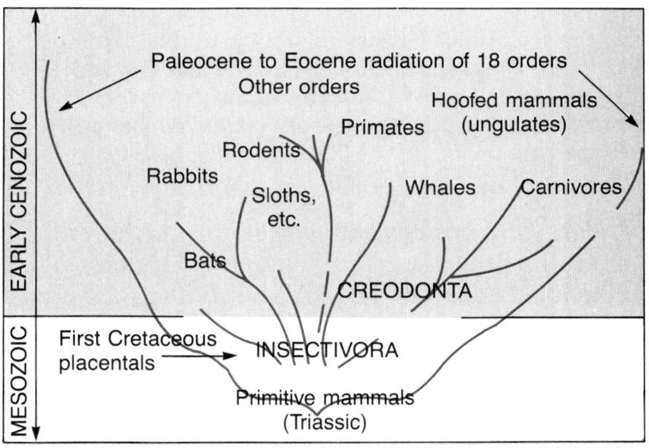

Figure 17–10

An early order of placentals, the insectivores, appears to have given rise to many Paleocene and Eocene orders.

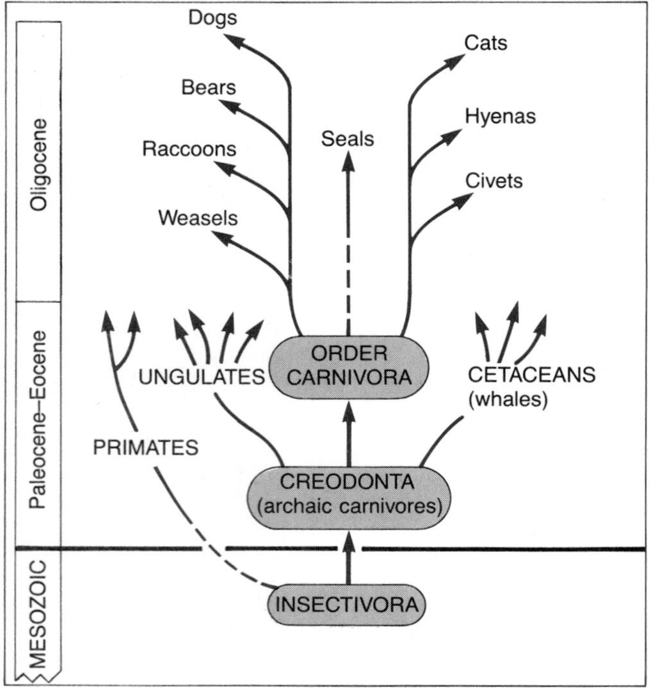

Figure 17–11
Evolutionary history of some placental orders. Carnivores replaced the older creodonts in Oligocene time. The pattern illustrated by these placental carnivores followed a pattern similar to that exhibited by carnivorous reptiles in the Jurassic and Cretaceous Periods. Seals represent aquatic forms (suborder Pinnipedia); the other groups are terrestrial (suborder Fissipedia).

Hoofed mammals, known as ungulates, are the most important large herbivorous placentals. They are characterized by hoofed feet and by well-developed molar teeth which are very efficient for grinding vegetation. Many of these herbivorous mammals attained large sizes during the Cenozoic; many such as the titanotheres and other extinct primitive ungulates were at least 3 to 4 m in length and weighed several metric tons.

Other orders of placentals first appeared during the early Cenozoic, and some of these are of general interest. The cetaceans include most of the marine mammals, such as whales and porpoises. First appearing in the Eocene as relatively small organisms, they rapidly increased in size. Today some, such as the blue whale, may exceed 30 m in length and are the largest animals known. Although whales have diverse feeding patterns today, early Cenozoic species were carnivores, and probably inherited their dentition pattern from their creodont ancestors.

Also of interest are the primates. Although not abundant in the fossil record, this order includes humans among its ranks. The order evolved from a primitive insectivore ancestor during the Paleocene and subsequently diversified into a number of lineages. Tracing of this evolutionary history is difficult because of a notoriously poor fossil record. As we shall see, a number of different hypotheses are currently under consideration.

Middle and Late Cenozoic Placental Evolution

The end of the Eocene Epoch is marked by the extinction of many orders and families of mammals that had appeared in the Cretaceous and Early Paleocene. Fossils found in central Oregon, the Rocky Mountain basins, and the Great Plains indicate that, during Oligocene and especially Miocene time, many new mammal taxa appeared in the fossil record. These new taxa were much more similar to living mammals than were the earlier forms. One notable aspect of this middle and late Cenozoic radiation was the development of increasingly distinctive mammal faunas on different continents. We already mentioned the marsupials in Australia and South America. By Miocene time, significant differences can also be seen between the placentals of North America and Eurasia. Some examples of these differences are:

1. By late Miocene, primates had disappeared from North America, but were evolving new lineages in Europe and Africa.
2. Ungulates such as the horse family were evolving rapidly in North America, but were absent in Europe.
3. Divergence of ungulate lineages occurred on these separated land masses.

As you may suspect, this increasing diversity and divergence was stimulated by opening of the Atlantic Ocean. Increased continental fragmentation produced geographic isolation and thus fostered increasing genetic divergence.

The evolutionary changes in mammals may be linked to changes in climate, vegetation, and plate tectonics. During Miocene time widespread angiosperm grasslands developed, and new taxa of **grazing** mammals evolved, especially in North America and parts of Africa, to replace the more primitive early Cenozoic **browsers.** By Pleistocene time a combination of events produced widespread climatic cooling, which culminated in glaciation in the northern hemisphere and affected many mammal taxa. Fluctuations in sea level associated with the waxing and waning of large ice sheets exposed and submerged **land bridges** across the Bering Straits in the Arctic and the Isthmus of Panama between North and South America. When emergent, these land bridges allowed increased migration of placentals between Asia and North America and between North and South America; when submerged, these areas acted as barriers to migration of terrestrial mammals.

The myriad mammalian changes that began in the latest Pliocene and accelerated in the Pleistocene Epoch have continued into the Holocene. Significant aspects of these changes have been the appearance of humans and the rapid extinction of larger mammals such as the giant ground sloths, cave bears, mammoths, mastodons, and saber-toothed cats, to name a few. That this trend is continuing is obvious from the rapidly increasing number of species on endangered species lists.

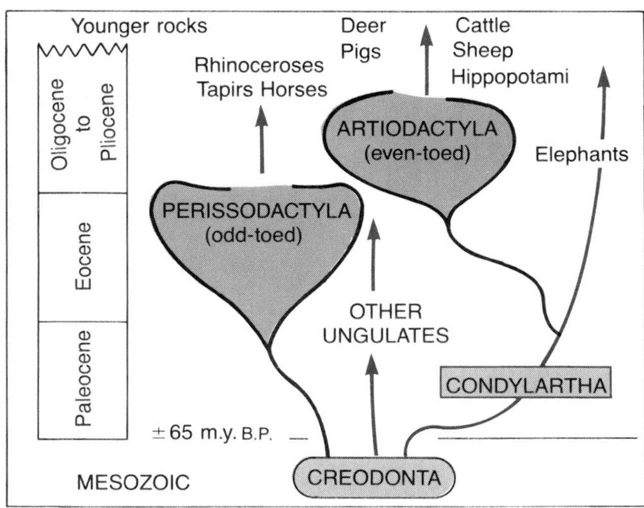

Figure 17–12
Ungulate evolutionary history through the Cenozoic. Maximum diversity of the odd-toed and even-toed orders occurred at different times during the Cenozoic.

A Model of Mammalian Diversity

Even-Toed and Odd-Toed Ungulates

Fossils of a variety of herbivorous placentals, loosely grouped as **ungulates,** provide an example of mammalian evolutionary patterns during the Cenozoic. Ungulates are a diverse group of mammals that possess in common a wide variety of morphological features. In general they are represented by medium-to-large-sized, herbivorous, hoofed mammals with well-developed, complex grinding teeth. They probably evolved from creodonts (Fig. 17–12), a group of Late Cretaceous–to–early Cenozoic carnivorous mammals of relatively small size.

The first ungulates, known as condylarths, show modification of their molar teeth into grinding types, but still retain skeletal features of their carnivorous creodont ancestors. Other ungulates appear in the record by middle Cenozoic time and represent most major lineages of modern ungulates. Two orders that we will consider in greater detail are even-toed ungulates, called **artiodactyls,** and odd-toed ungulates, or **perissodactyls.** Other ungulates are elephants and the South American notungulates, most of which are extinct.

Artiodactyls are the most diversified order of ungulates existing today. They include most familiar groups of herbivorous mammals: deer, cattle, pigs, and sheep, among many others. The fossil record indicates that primitive artiodactyls had evolved from condylarths by Eocene time and subsequently underwent rapid diversification, reaching maximum diversity in the late Cenozoic. During the Oligocene and Miocene the most abundant artiodactyls belonged to a group known as oreodonts (Fig. 17–13). Numerous skull and other skeletal remains of these sheeplike animals have been recovered from terrestrial deposits of the White River Group in the badlands of South Dakota.

Diagnostic anatomical features include the existence of either two or four toes on each foot, distinctive articulation of the ankle bones, and teeth somewhat like those of their early Cenozoic carnivorous ancestors. Except for the hippopotamus and large hogs, most are well adapted for running and live in semiarid grassland environments such as plains and prairies. The evolutionary history of the group indicates a progressive increase in overall size and reduction in toes on each foot from four to two (Fig. 17–13C).

Perissodactyls also first appear in the lower Eocene fossil record. This group subsequently underwent rapid diversification into five main branches, including three that exist today: tapirs, rhinoceroses, and horses (Fig. 17–14). Odd-toed ungulates underwent evolutionary trends paralleling those of the even-toed ungulates:

1. Gradual increase in size,
2. Adaptation for running, with a consequent decrease in toes on each hoof from five to three and in some groups to only one, and
3. Development of complex molar teeth for grinding vegetation.

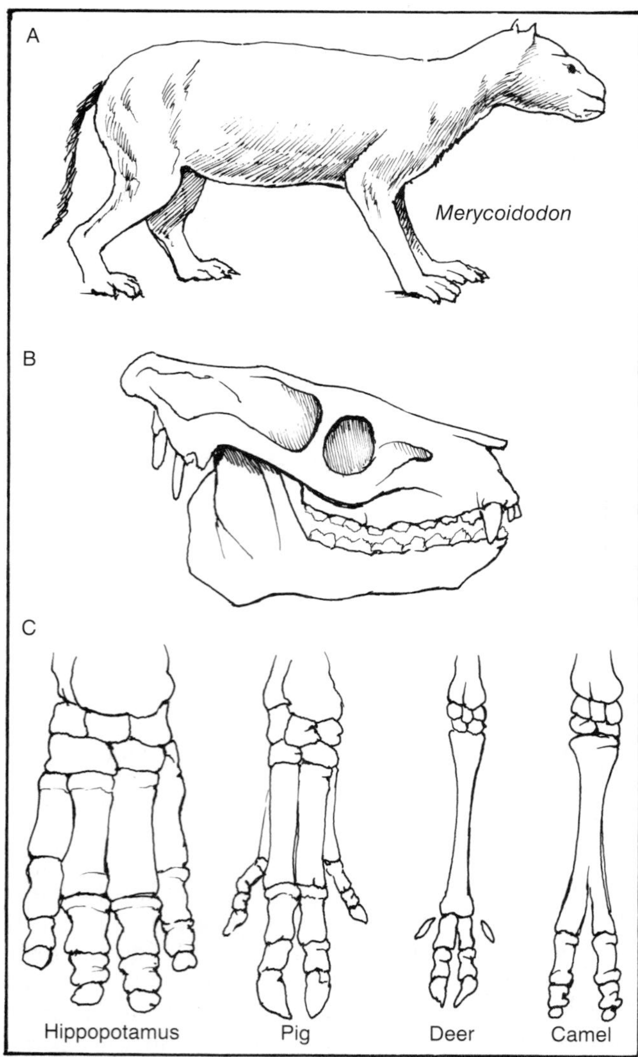

Figure 17–13
Even-toed ungulates. A. Reconstruction of Oligocene sheep-sized oreodont. B. Skull of Oligocene genus *Oreodon*. Note well-developed high-crowned teeth and placental mammal dentition (skull 12.5 cm long). C. Comparison of forelimb foot bones in modern artiodactyls.
(A, redrawn from E. H. Colbert, *Evolution of the Vertebrates*, 3d ed., Fig. 147, p. 408. Copyright © 1980 by John Wiley & Sons, Inc., New York. Reproduced by permission of John Wiley & Sons, Inc., and Lois M. Darling. B, modified from A. S. Romer, *Vertebrate Paleontology*, 3d ed., Fig. 408, p. 280: University of Chicago Press. © 1966 by The University of Chicago. All rights reserved. C, modified from A. B. Howell, *Speed in Animals*, Fig. 20, p. 159: University of Chicago Press. © 1944 by The University of Chicago. All rights reserved)

In contrast to artiodactyls, perissodactyls attained their maximum diversity in the early Cenozoic. Of interest, because they grew to sizes approaching that of the dinosaurs, were titanotheres and chalicotheres (Fig. 17–15). Both of these groups

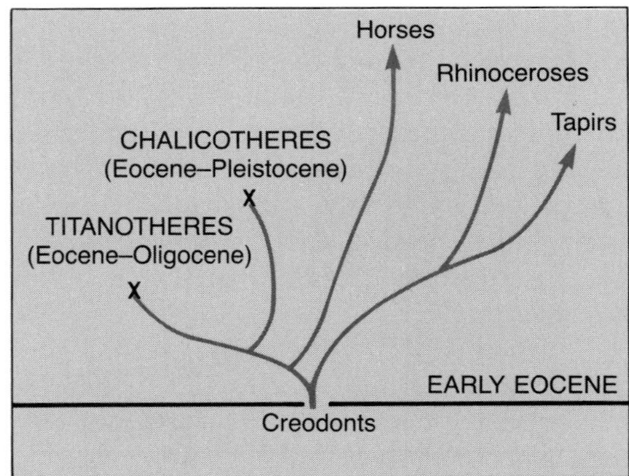

Figure 17–14
Cenozoic lineages of odd-toed ungulates. Early Cenozoic titanotheres and chalicotheres reached large sizes, but are extinct. The other lineages are represented by a few living taxa.

were abundant in the early Cenozoic but became extinct by the early Neogene.

Evolutionary History of Horses

Another group of perissodactyls, the horses, have received intensive study by such vertebrate paleontologists as H. F. Osborn and G. G. Simpson. These men studied the fossil record of horses for many years and gradually recognized many major evolutionary trends and characteristics within this lineage (see introduction to this chapter). Their published papers are classic studies and illustrate many patterns and processes of evolution we have discussed in previous chapters.

The horse family first appears in the fossil record in rocks of early Eocene age which are about 50 to 55 million years old. Except for the modern horse of the genus *Equus*, all other taxonomic groups within the family are extinct. As indicated in Figure 17–16, horse evolution has proceeded in a steplike manner with many side branches and lineages (only a few of these branches are indicated). A major pattern is the repeated trend for evolutionary radiation into many lineages, indicating the complexity of horse phylogeny.

It is fortunate that the fossil record of this group is good and that Osborn, Simpson, and other collectors have been so meticulous. By piecing together the fossil record, most of the stages of various lineages can be reconstructed. It is evident that modern *Equus* represents just one branch within a lineage, rather than the result of any directed

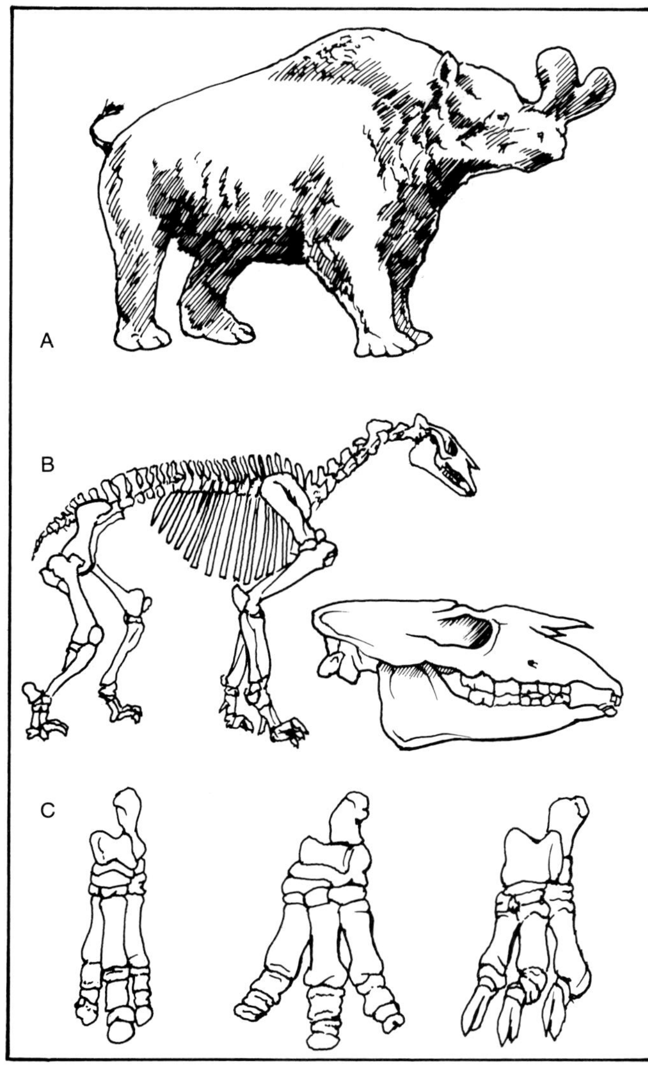

Figure 17–15
Odd-toed ungulates. A. Reconstruction of an Oligocene titanothere of the genus *Brontotherium,* which was 3 to 4 m long. B. Skeleton (3 m long) and skull of a Miocene chalicothere of the genus *Moropus.* C. Rear-limb foot bones of various odd-toed ungulates.
(A, C, redrawn from E. H. Colbert, *Evolution of the Vertebrates,* 3d ed., Figs. 133, 136, p. 377, 385. Copyright © 1980 by John Wiley & Sons, Inc., New York. Reproduced by permission of John Wiley & Sons, Inc., and Lois M. Darling. B, modified from A. S. Romer, *Vertebrate Paleontology,* 3d ed., Figs. 387, 395, p. 267, 270: University of Chicago Press. © 1966 by The University of Chicago. All rights reserved)

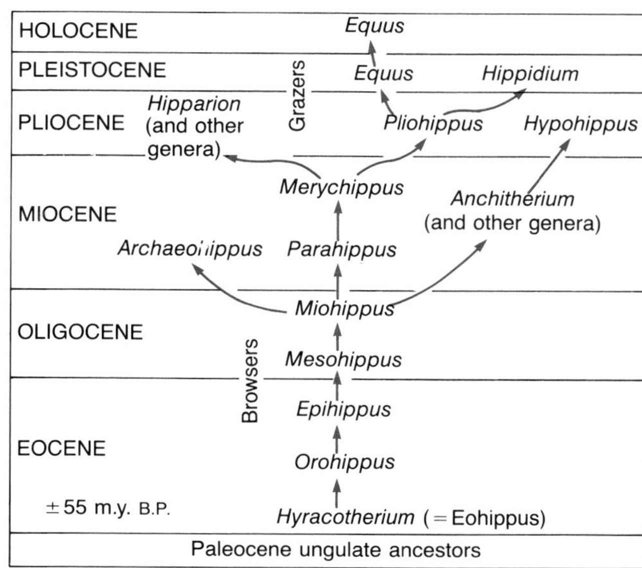

Figure 17–16
Cenozoic horse evolution, based mainly on fossils from North America. Evolutionary radiations occurred in Oligocene, Miocene, and Pliocene times. Major trends were an increase in body size, reduction in number of toes, and change from browsing to grazing habit.
(Modified from G. G. Simpson, *Horses,* © 1951 by Oxford University Press, New York)

evolutionary trend. It will be interesting to see whether the history of horses remains an example of *phyletic gradualism,* as interpreted by Simpson, or is found to support the idea of *punctuated equilibrium* of Niles Eldridge and others (Chapter 4).

Many morphological traits within the horse family underwent changes that can be traced through the fossil record. The most useful of these features are:

1. Increase in length of the legs;
2. Progressive reduction in number of toes from four to one on each foot (Fig. 17–17);
3. Increase in tooth size and complexity;
4. Increase in skull size and cranial capacity, indicating an increase in brain size; and
5. Overall increase in body size.

Such evolutionary changes can be explained as representing genetic changes which occurred rapidly in populations as a response to changing environmental conditions; this would support the punctuated-equilibrium model. This would mean that small local populations were subjected to selective pressures at various times through the Cenozoic. For example, reduction in number of toes, increases in overall body size, and development of complex molar teeth did not occur simultaneously. Some of these changes provided opportunities for expansion and diversification, especially evident in the later Cenozoic.

The earliest members of the horse lineage, found in lower Eocene rocks, were relatively unspecialized odd-toed ungulates now known as *Hyracother-*

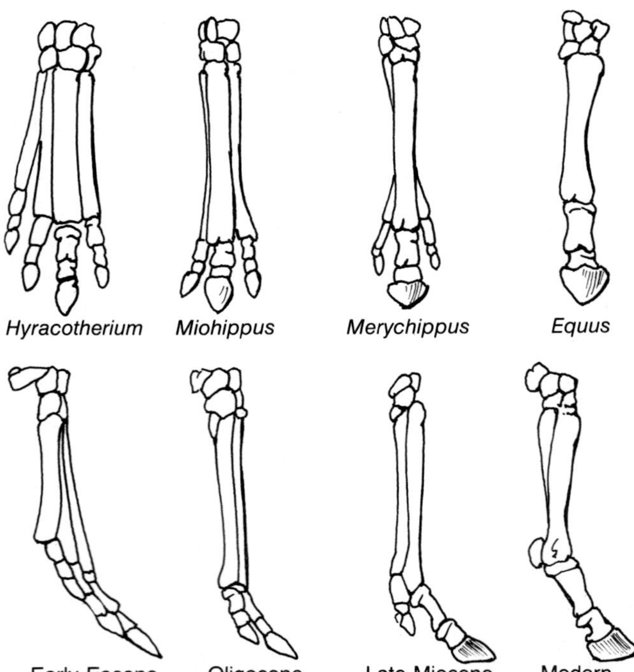

Figure 17–17
Reduction in number of toes in horses illustrates one of a number of evolutionary patterns evident from the Cenozoic fossil record of the group.
(Redrawn from A. S. Romer, *Vertebrate Paleontology*, 3d ed., Fig. 383, p. 263: University of Chicago Press. © 1966 by The University of Chicago. All rights reserved)

ium (*Eohippus* in earlier texts). These were small-dog-sized animals with three functional hoofed toes on each foot and unspecialized teeth adapted to browsing on shrubs and bushes. During Eocene and Oligocene time there was a slight increase in body size and development of more complex molar teeth. At least four different genera have been named.

Beginning in Miocene time, horses got larger, lost some of their toes, developed larger teeth, and evidently were becoming adapted to more open grasslands. At least 11 genera of horses representing four separate lineages are known from Miocene and Pliocene deposits. By this time, horses had become more modern in appearance and were larger, with well-developed grinding molar teeth and large skulls with a larger brain. Each foot had only one toe and the animals were clearly adapted for life in open grassland environments such as the Great Plains of the United States. Fossils representing the lineage leading to the modern genus *Equus* first appear in Pliocene rocks.

Changes in tooth size and shape are characteristic of horse evolution, and because teeth are durable they provide an important source of paleontologic evidence. Horses have developed larger molars, increased the complexity of the crown pattern on the grinding surface of the molar teeth, and formed a thicker enamel coating on the tooth. These changes are related to the change from the browsing habit of Eocene, Oligocene, and early Miocene species to the grazing habit of later Miocene, Pliocene, Pleistocene, and modern species. They probably represent adaptations for better grinding of tough angiosperm grasses.

Another major adaptive feature was the increase in size and complexity of the brain. This is particularly evident in Pliocene and modern forms, and parallels the increase of body size. Both of these changes are related to the gradual adaptation for living in open grasslands, where speed and agility, coupled with increased body size and mental alertness, would provide protection from predators.

Eocene and Oligocene horse fossils are known in Europe and North America. Horse evolution from Miocene to Pleistocene occurred almost entirely in North America. Well-known collecting areas are located in the Great Plains, Oregon, and Florida. Famous Pleistocene localities such as the Rancho La Brea Tar Pits in California and other localities in Texas, Idaho, and Kansas have yielded many excellent specimens. Thus, evolutionary history of horses is well documented by fossil evidence from extensive Cenozoic continental deposits (Chapter 14). During the Pleistocene, horses migrated to Eurasia over the Bering land bridge, but may have become extinct in North America. They were reintroduced in the 1600s during colonization by Spain, France, Portugal, and England.

Evolutionary History of Primates

Although the fossil record of primates extends back to the Paleocene Epoch, it is important to realize in the following discussion that the fossil record of this order is poor when compared with that of marine invertebrates or many other mammalian orders. The environments in which primates dwell explain this scanty evidence. Highlands, forests, and plains areas are regions in which most primates have lived throughout the Cenozoic, but they are not good sites for preservation of fossils. Through considerable effort, however, enough evidence has been collected to provide a reasonably clear picture of primate evolution (Fig. 17–18). However, there remain many muddy areas within this picture. Much of the evidence consists of fragmentary bones and skulls and well-preserved teeth. These remains

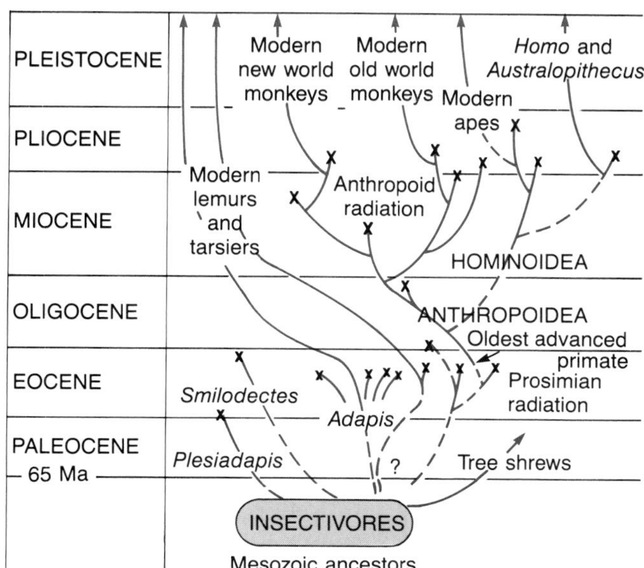

Figure 17–18
Evolutionary history of primates. Taxa noted in text are named. Dashed lines represent uncertain evolutionary relationships or lack of fossil evidence. "X" indicates extinct lineage.

are found in lake deposits, volcanic ash beds, fluvial sands and gravels, and cave deposits.

Older, more primitive primates commonly have five-digit hands and feet, **binocular vision,** and distinctive teeth characteristic of an omnivorous diet, and in some taxa a **prehensile tail** (or grasping tail); these are all characteristic of tree-dwelling (arboreal) organisms. Some more recent (or advanced) primates have a pelvic structure and bones to support semierect-to-erect posture, allowing bipedal locomotion, and a relatively large skull and brain capacity compared to total body weight. Organisms containing some or all of these features include fossil and living lemurs, tarsiers, monkeys, apes, and humans. Lemurs and tarsiers are considered primitive primates and are included in the suborder **Prosimii;** more advanced primates such as monkeys, apes, and humans are classified in the suborder **Anthropoidea.**

Extant prosimians retain characteristics of the early primates in that they are arboreal, are generally omnivorous, have five-digit hands and feet, and have nonstereoscopic vision. Today prosimians have a somewhat restricted distribution and are found only in tropical regions of Asia, Africa, Madagascar, and India. However, the fossil record indicates that these organisms and their ancestors had a much wider distribution earlier in the Cenozoic, and were abundant and diversified on most continents during the Paleocene and Eocene Epochs. The decrease of once-diverse prosimians probably corresponds with gradual continental fragmentation, northward drift of some land masses out of mild tropical climatic zones, and appearance and diversification of higher primate groups. In this example we again see the effects of plate tectonics on distribution of organisms; similar patterns occurring in invertebrates, plants, reptiles, and other groups of mammals have been described in previous chapters.

Advanced primates include Ceboidea (new world monkeys) and Cercopithecoidea (old world monkeys), and Hominoidea, which includes apes and humans. These more advanced groups have relatively larger brains and **stereoscopic vision** because both eyes are positioned at the front of the skull; some are ground-dwelling rather than arboreal species. Distribution of modern monkeys and apes—known from South and Central America, Africa, India, and Asia—is much more widespread than that of prosimians. The fossil record indicates that monkeys existed during Oligocene time. By that time, however, they possessed distinct anatomical features, suggesting that they may have originated as early as the Eocene.

Apes are most abundant today in Africa and southeast Asia and include four groups commonly termed gibbons, chimpanzees, orangutans, and gorillas. Anatomically and physiologically, apes rather than monkeys more closely resemble humans.

Humans are represented today by only one species, *Homo sapiens,* and are adapted to a ground-dwelling habitat despite an occasional aching back and fallen arches. Humans are characterized by erect, or upright, posture, a **bipedal gait,** an enlarged brain, distinctive canine teeth, well-developed **opposable thumbs,** the unique ability to speak and use abstractions, and of course, our distinctive social structures. Our species is distributed worldwide and has a population of about 4 billion; thus *Homo sapiens* is the most abundant and widespread primate species.

Much controversy surrounds our understanding of primate evolution over the past 10 million years. Evidence to support a number of different interpretations has been provided by widely diverse data, including fossils, radiometric dating, and molecular studies of blood proteins and nuclear and non-nuclear DNA. These new techniques have revised earlier interpretations of a mid-Cenozoic divergence and established that hominids branched off from the ape line only around 5 million years ago.

A spectacular discovery of footprints in the Laetoli Ash Beds of Northern Tanzania indicated that some of the oldest hominids were bipedal and walked upright. Found in 1976 by Mary Leakey and a group from the University of California at Berkeley, these footprints closely resemble those of modern humans, but were made by people of smaller stature—no more than four feet nine inches tall (Fig. 17–19). Actual remains of such humans were found at about the same time, in 1974, about 1,200 miles north in the Afar Triangle of Ethiopia. The first specimen, known as "Lucy," was followed by many others, all of which are known to be about 3.5 million years old (Fig. 17–19). One further fossil, found in 1985 near Lake Turkana in northern Kenya, is a 2.5 million-year-old skull which contains primitive features (ape-like jaw and small braincase) and more highly evolved features (bony crest at the top of the skull).

This evidence, when combined with previously known material and molecular studies of modern humans, suggests that hominids probably evolved around five million years ago in Africa; that a number of species (possibly five) and genera (probably two—*Australopithecus* and *Homo*) have appeared; and that at least some of these coexisted during the past three million years (Fig. 17–20). The genealogical tree of modern humans, as reconstructed from the evolution of mitochondrial DNA, shows the common ancestral stock as having lived no more than 250,000 years ago.

Homo sapiens, named by Linnaeus in 1758, is considered to have appeared about 300,000 years ago, and fossils are known from all parts of the world. The oldest subspecies, here termed *H. sapiens neanderthalensis* (Fig. 17–21), is very well known and is named for the Neander Valley location in Germany where the fossils were first discovered in 1856. Neanderthals were originally considered a separate species, *H. neanderthalensis.* The change in classification indicates a change in our concepts of these fossils and provides an interesting story.

The first reconstruction of a Neanderthal was based on specimens from France and pictured a short, squat, and quite brutelike individual. Restudy of the fossils, however, indicated that this

A

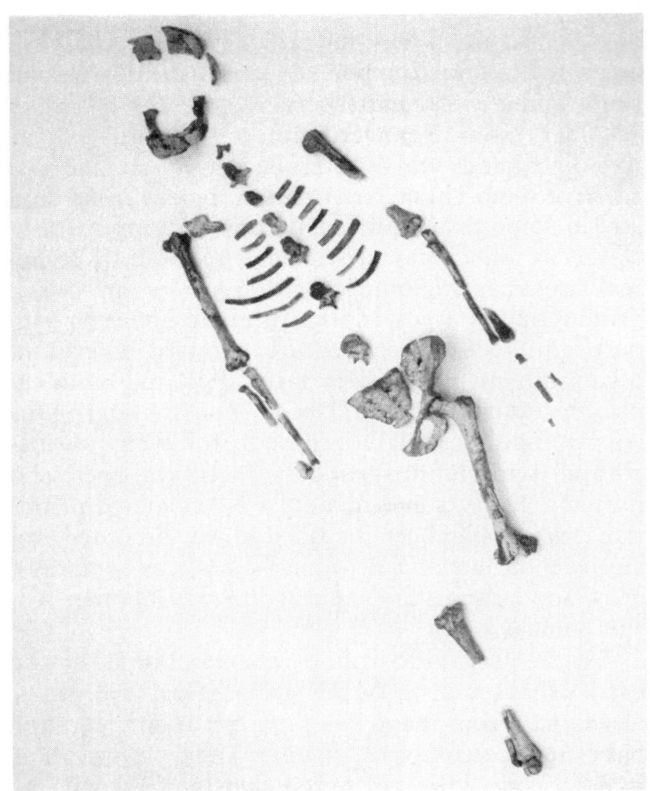

B

Figure 17–19
A. Photograph of a portion of over 70 human footprints preserved in 3.6–3.8 million-year-old volcanic ash at Laetoli, Northern Tanzania. B. Reconstructed skeleton of "Lucy" from 3.0–3.5 million-year-old deposits in the Afar Triangle, Ethiopia.
(A, *National Geographic.* B. Smithsonian Institution, *Mosaic.* Reproduced with permission)

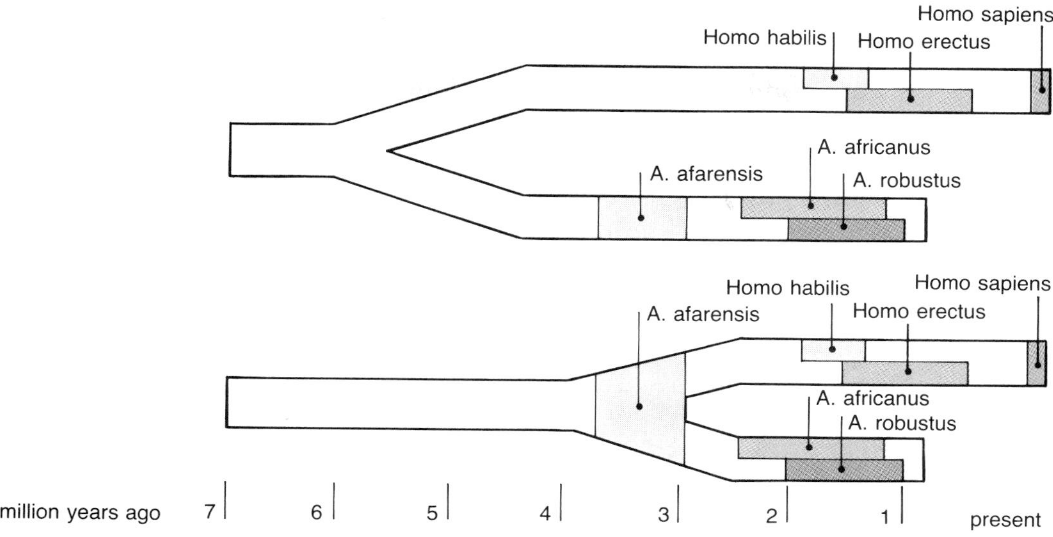

Figure 17–20

Simplified diagram of various species of hominid genera *Australopithecus* and *Homo* known from the past four million years of the fossil record. Note that some taxa appear to have lived simultaneously, and possibly could have had contact.
(Modified from *Mosaic,* Smithsonian Institution, vol. 19, p. 32, © 1988)

original specimen was, in fact, afflicted with severe and perhaps crippling bone disease! Further discoveries from various parts of the world have altered our concepts of Neanderthals. This subspecies had an erect posture, had a brain size averaging approximately 1500 cubic centimeters, formed and used well-shaped stone tools, and apparently had developed social structures. In Europe the group is considered to have become extinct approximately 35,000 years ago. The one missing ingredient for continued success may have been failure to develop a spoken language. This may have set the Neanderthals apart from the Cro-Magnons, who did develop speech. However, according to anthropologist C. Loring Brace, distinctive features of the cranium link modern western Europeans to Neanderthals.

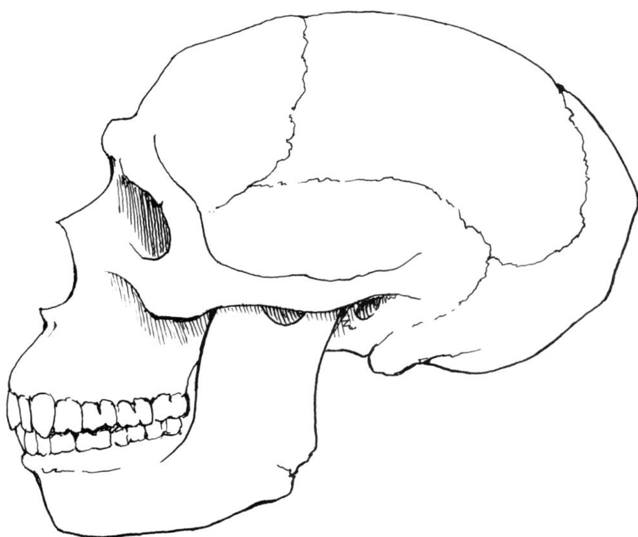

Figure 17–21

***Homo sapiens.* Cast of neanderthal-type specimen found by three priests from La Chapelle-aux-Saints in southwestern France in 1908. A nearly complete skeleton was also found with tools in a shallow grave. Age of specimen 40,000 to 75,000 years; cranial capacity 1620 cm^3.**
(Drawing courtesy of Harry Nelson)

The first modern humans, *Homo sapiens sapiens,* appeared between 35,000 and 50,000 years ago during the last ice age (Chapter 15). Anatomically, they were somewhat more robust than living humans. Within the last 5,000 years humans have evolved complex social structures, have developed writing, and have invented many complex tools and machines.

The most recent evolutionary history of *H. sapiens* seems to have been cultural rather than physical. In the last few hundred years we have been influenced by development of many sources of energy, by the industrial revolution and automation, and by an unprecedented population explosion. Our civilizations have developed, or perhaps evolved, at an exceedingly rapid rate; in fact, it has been suggested that we have advanced too far too fast, and are on a collision course with extinction because of the global political and environmental problems we have created.

The preceding is not intended as a detailed treatment of human evolution (a subject more appropriate for anthropology); however, it is important that we view our species in total context against the backdrop of 4600 million years of Earth history. Our species is not apart, but rather intricately tied to the biosphere. Although we are "johnny-come-latelys" on the evolutionary scale, we do have a biological heritage that can be traced backward through the record of the rocks. What are some of the lessons that we can learn from the past? Will we be witness to or be a part of the next great crisis in the history of life? Will our activities hasten such a crisis? We are the custodians of a fragile planet. As the only thinking, speaking, truly inventive, and manipulative species, it is our obligation to discharge our stewardship responsibilities.

The future evolution of our species no doubt will continue to be largely cultural. As the noted geneticist G. L. Stebbins has suggested, humans are in an evolutionary position *culturally* that is analogous to that of invertebrates during the earliest Phanerozoic, when a wide range of habitats were available. Perhaps we are on the threshold of a major cultural adaptive radiation or explosive evolution that will carry our species beyond present national and global crises to unimagined limits. What scenario would you envision for our future?

Summary

Mammals play a major role in terrestrial communities today and have done so throughout the 65-million-year history of the Cenozoic Era. However, the fossil record indicates that mammals originated in Late Triassic time, about 215 million years ago. Their ancestors were therapsids, or mammal-like reptiles, whose geologic history began in late Paleozoic time and ended with extinction at the end of Triassic time.

Mesozoic mammals are known mainly from teeth, jaws, and a few skulls and bones. From this evidence nine orders have been recognized, none of whose members were larger than a modern house cat. Characteristically they had a single lower jawbone with a variety of teeth, a bony palate, a double occipital condyle, and, presumably, physiological characteristics such as endothermy.

Pantotheres, with a geologic range of Jurassic to Cretaceous, appear to have been ancestral to the various Cenozoic orders. In the early Cenozoic, placental mammals underwent rapid diversification and by the end of Eocene time had become dominant consumers in terrestrial communities. Mammalian fossils in Oligocene and Miocene deposits indicate that earlier forms had become extinct and that new families, more similar to those living today, had appeared. One obvious change was the appearance of grazing herbivores, representing orders such as even-toed and odd-toed ungulates. Even-toed ungulates of deer, cattle, and sheep lineages became very widespread.

One lineage of odd-toed ungulates, the horses, has received intensive study, aided by large fossil collections that represent the 55-million-year history of the group. Studies of horse phylogenetic trends have provided evidence of major evolutionary patterns. Changes in various anatomical features—increasing body size, reduction in number of toes, and increase in size and complexity of molar teeth—illustrate various episodes of adaptive radiations and change in feeding habits from browser to grazer. These patterns indicate that horses became progressively more adapted to grassland environments through the Cenozoic.

Another Cenozoic mammal order, the primates, includes our own species, *Homo sapiens.* Not surprisingly, the evolutionary history of this order is of considerable interest. Primitive primates are known from Paleocene rocks; as for most primate taxa, fossil evidence is scarce and often fragmentary. Fossils of more advanced primates are known from upper Eocene rocks but are more numerous in Oligocene strata. Approximately two million years ago the first representatives of our genus, *Homo,* appeared in Africa and approximately 300,000 years ago *H. sapiens* appeared. Within the past 30,000 years most changes in our species have been cultural rather than physical.

Suggestions for Further Reading

Colbert, E. H. 1980. *Evolution of the vertebrates.* 3d ed. New York: John Wiley & Sons.

Fisher, A. 1988. The more things change . . . *Mosaic* 19(1):23–33.

Hopson, J.A. 1967. Mammal-like reptiles and the origin of mammals. *Discovery* 2(2):25–33.

Isaac, G., and R. E. F. Leakey, eds. 1979. *Human ancestors.* San Francisco: W. H. Freeman.

Leakey, M. D. 1979. Footprints in the ashes of time. *National Geographic* 155(4):446–58.

Leakey, R. E. 1976. Hominids in Africa. *American Scientist* 64:174–78.

Millar, R. 1972. *The Piltdown men.* New York: St. Martin's Press.

Romer, A. S. 1966. *Vertebrate paleontology.* 3d ed. Chicago: Univ. of Chicago Press.

Simpson, G. G. 1951. *Horses.* New York: Oxford Univ. Press.

Tattersall, I., and N. Eldridge. 1977. Fact, theory and fantasy in human paleontology. *American Scientist* 65:204–11.

Glossary

Acadian orogeny Mountain-building event (*see* orogeny) affecting the Appalachian belt from South Carolina to Newfoundland during mid-Paleozoic time; associated with closing of the proto-Atlantic basin (Iapetus); European counterpart is the Caledonian orogeny.

Accretionary wedge A wedge of sediment that is piled up along the continent side of a deep-sea trench in the upper part of a subduction zone where sediments accumulate faster than they can be subducted. The more active wedges are immediately adjacent to the subduction zone of underthrusting and consist mainly of mélange. Successive wedges accrete to form an outer arc ridge.

Actualism Modified view of the concept of uniformitarianism; recognizes that Earth processes of past and present are similar, but that rates, intensities, and relative importance of these processes have varied through time. *See* uniformitarianism.

Adaptive radiation Proliferation of new species (or higher taxa such as genera, families, etc.) from one or a few ancestral stocks; adaptive radiation is a major evolutionary pattern and has produced much of the present diversity of life forms.

Alleghany orogeny Late Paleozoic mountain-building event (*see* orogeny) that completed the deformation of the Appalachian continental margin basin; manifested mainly by folding and thrust-faulting of rock of the Appalachian miogeocline, including the present-day Valley and Ridge Province and Allegheny Plateau. European and North African counterpart is the Hercynian orogeny.

Allopatric speciation Model of formation of new species (speciation) where a reproductively isolated portion of a population changes rapidly through a succession of generations and becomes a genetically distinct new species; once formed these new species undergo little further genetic or morphologic change through time.

Anaerobic Capable of living in an environment characterized by a lack of free (uncombined) oxygen (anoxic environment).

Andesite The fine-crystalline igneous rock of intermediate composition that makes up volcanic island arc chains and magmatic arcs.

Angiosperm Flowering plant, the most advanced type of terrestrial plant; characterized by flowers and seed-bearing fruits; seed is protected. *See* gymnosperm.

Angular unconformity Stratigraphic surface (erosional surface) between underlying deformed strata that dip at a different angle than the younger overlying strata. *See* unconformity.

Animal Multicellular organism (metazoan) that obtains nutrients by consumption of other organisms.

Anthropoidea Suborder of advanced primates, including monkeys, apes, and humans. *See* Prosimii.

Antler orogeny Mid-Paleozoic mountain-building event (*see* orogeny) in the Cordilleran continental margin basin; best displayed in northern Nevada and Idaho (Roberts Mountains thrust).

Aphebian Era Earliest era of the Proterozoic Eon; 2500–1600 million years ago. *See* Helikian and Hadrynian Eras.

Aragonite A calcium carbonate mineral that crystallizes in the orthorhombic system. It is less stable than calcite, the more common calcium carbonate mineral. It occurs as a major constituent of shallow marine lime mud (micrite) and is an important constituent of the shells of many invertebrate organisms.

Arboreal Tree-dwelling.

Archaeocyathid Extinct animal form of uncertain biological affinity, but generally classified as a separate phylum; probably intermediate between Porifera and Coelenterata; confined to the Cambrian Period.

Archean Earliest major subdivision (eon) of Cryptozoic time for which there is a rock record on Earth; beginning with the oldest rocks of the Earth's crust about 3800 million years ago and closing with the Kenoran orogeny 2500 million years ago. The pregeologic eon, for which there is no known rock record on Earth, is the Hadean. *See also* Proterozoic.

Arthropod Organism belonging to the most abundant and diverse group of animals; characterized by segmented body and jointed limbs; includes extant crabs, shrimps, spiders, insects, and extinct trilobites, among many others.

Artiodactyl Any of an order of even-toed (two or four toes on each foot) ungulates (hoofed mammals), including deer, cattle, pigs, and sheep. *See* perissodactyl.

Asthenosphere Weak "plastic" zone of the Earth's interior structure characterized by relatively low seismic wave velocities; lies below the Earth's lithosphere.

Astrobleme Crater on the surface of the Earth that was formed by impact of meteoric or cometary debris.

Asylum area Geographic area in which a population of organisms becomes isolated and is not affected by evolutionary trends that occur elsewhere; *example:* Australia and its distinctive marsupial mammals.

Atmosphere Gaseous layer surrounding the Earth and held to the Earth by gravity; composition 78% nitrogen, 21% oxygen, plus traces of argon, carbon dioxide, water vapor, and other gases.

Atomic number Number of protons in an atomic nucleus; this number characterizes each specific chemical element and determines the position of an element on the periodic chart (*see* Appendix A).

Aulacogen Transverse, long-lived, deeply subsiding, linear trough, at times fault bounded, that extends at a high angle from a miogeocline into the adjoining craton. The aulacogen basin fill is generally contemporaneous with and lithologically similar to the sedimentary wedge of the related miogeocline, but in addition contains periodically erupted basalt.

It is hypothesized that deep mantle convection plumes produce three-armed rift systems in continents. Two of the arms unite and spread to produce a rift ocean basin, initiating a Wilson Cycle (*see*); the third arm, the aulacogen, remains as an abandoned rift extending into the continental interior from a reentrant on the new continental margin.

Australopithecine One of a group of Pliocene-Pleistocene fossil hominids (humans) found in eastern and southern Africa.

Autotroph Producer organism. *See* producer.

Back reef Lagoonal area between reef and mainland; typically characterized by quiet water and deposition of limy muds.

Baltica One of six major continental blocks believed to have been in existence by Cambrian time; essentially equivalent to what is now western Europe.

Banded iron formation (BIF) Iron precipitate deposits formed by the combination of ferrous iron in the sea with oxygen generated by early photosynthesizers; interbedded with chert; unique to strata of Cryptozoic age.

Base level Lowest elevation to which a portion of the Earth's surface may be eroded; usually sea level.

Basin Depressed area into which the surrounding slopes drain.

Benioff zone A plane beneath the trenches of the circum-Pacific belt, dipping toward the continents at an angle of about 45°, along which earthquake foci cluster. The zone is defined along the upper boundary of a subducting plate as it sinks into the asthenosphere.

Benthos Bottom-dwellers; organisms that live *on* (epifauna) or *within* (infauna) a seafloor or lake bed.

Bentonite Clay formed by the alteration in place of volcanic ash beds; correlatable bentonite beds provide good chronostratigraphic markers because they are formed by individual eruptive events.

Binocular vision Vision employing both eyes at once. An animal having side-mounted eyes, like a rabbit or deer, sees a wide field of view, useful in detecting predators. An animal having front-mounted eyes, like a wolf or a human, sees two overlapping fields of view; this allows three-dimensional viewing with depth-of-field, or stereoscopic vision.

Biofacies Sedimentary facies defined on the basis of fossil content rather than lithology.

Biogeographic province Geographic area that supports similar flora and fauna; such an area is typically defined by environmental factors such as climate, temperature, topography, water depth, and salinity.

Biosphere All living organisms of the Earth; the array of life forms.

Biostratigraphic unit Rock unit whose boundaries are defined on fossil content (one or more species or other taxonomic rank); fundamental biostratigraphic unit is the biozone.

Biozone Interval of strata that is characterized by one or more fossil taxa; fundamental biostratigraphic unit.

Bipedal gait Characteristic of walking with two feet.

Bivalve Mollusc characterized by two shells typically of equal size and shape (some sedentary forms are asymmetrical); each valve is nonbilaterally symmetrical; includes clams, scallops, and oysters.

Blocking temperature The temperature below which a particular mineral becomes a closed chemical system for a particular radioactive decay series.

Blueschist Metamorphic rock characterized by the presence of the mineral glaucophane (blue amphibole); forms in a high-pressure, low-temperature metamorphic environment.

Boundary stratotype Stratigraphic sequence that is a type section for a chronostratigraphic (time-stratigraphic) boundary; *example,* the Plio-Pleistocene boundary stratotype is in Italy. *See* stratotype, type section.

Brachiopod Marine animal that secretes two shells (valves) typically unequal in size and/or shape; each shell bilaterally symmetrical; popularly called "lampshell."

Brain capacity Amount of space (usually measured in cubic centimeters) within the skull that is occupied by the brain; has been used as a measure of development in primate evolution.

Browser Land-dwelling animal that feeds on shoots, twigs, and leaves of trees and shrubs.

Bryozoa Small colonial animals that secrete calcareous structures of various size and shape; popularly called "moss animal."

Caledonian orogeny *See* Acadian orogeny.

Cambium Innermost portion of three epidermal layers (bark) of a plant stem; location for growth of the plant. *See* cortex, epidermal layer.

Canadian Shield Vast lowland rimming the Hudson Bay region and making up the eastern two-thirds of Canada, the U.S. margins of Lake Superior, and most of Greenland; the most extensive area of exposed Precambrian rock on the North American continent. *See* shield.

CCD (carbonate compensation depth) In the ocean, that level below which the rate of solution of calcium carbonate exceeds the rate of its deposition. In the Pacific Ocean this depth is at about 4000–5000 m; in the Atlantic, it is somewhat shallower.

Carbonaceous film Mode of fossil preservation by which a carbon residue forms the shape of the former living organism; most often found on bedding surfaces of dark shales.

Carbonization The accumulation of residual carbon by the changes in organic matter and decomposition products; or the accumulation of carbon by the slow, underwater decay of organic matter; or the conversion into carbon of a carbonaceous substance such as coal by driving off the other components.

Cast Filling of a void left by the removal (dissolution) of a shell or other form of organic material. *See* mold.

Catastrophism Concept that geologic changes were the result of sudden, violent, worldwide supernatural catastrophic events.

Cell Mass of protoplasm enclosed within a membrane (often a cell wall) and usually including one or more nuclei (monerans lack a nucleus); basic unit of living organism.

Cephalopod Mollusc characterized by a well-developed head with eyes, tentacles, and the ability to jet-propel through the water; univalve shell takes various forms; includes extant squid, octopus, chambered nautilus, and extinct ammonoids.

Chalk A finely textured, generally white, pure marine limestone composed predominantly of calcareous shells and fragments of planktonic microorganisms such as foraminifera and coccolithophorids.

Chloroplast Site of the photosynthesis reactions of plants; located in the cells of most algae (not in cyanobacteria) and in the cells of the leaves of higher plants.

Chromosome One of the bodies in the cell nucleus containing genes in a linear order.

Chronostratigraphic unit (time-stratigraphic unit) Succession of strata formed during a specific interval of geologic time and defined by isochronous boundaries; includes the fundamental units of the chronostratigraphic scale such as eonothem, erathem, system, series, stage, chronozone.

Chronozone A biozone that is interpreted to have isochronous boundaries; the smallest-scale chronostratigraphic unit.

Class Major subdivision in the classification of life forms; category just below phylum level.

Clastic wedge Thick sequence of clastic sediments derived from and often deposited adjacent to a tectonic land mass.

Coacervate droplet Very small organic globule that possibly existed as an intermediate form before appearance of living cells.

Collage Assemblage of fragments of materials; collage *tectonics* refers to an accretion of fragments called microplates; much of western North America is viewed as a collage of accreted terranes.

Community Association of organisms living in close proximity with one another; part of an ecosystem.

Conodont Tiny tooth-shaped form of unknown, but possibly eel-like vertebrate zoological affinity; important Paleozoic fossil.

Consumer Organism that is not able to directly produce its own food by photosynthesis, but consumes other organisms; animals and some protistans.

Continental margin basin (geosyncline) A long, linear basin situated marginal to the craton of a continent. This large-sized basin gradually subsides through an appreciable span of time and receives a thick accumulation of sediments. The classic continental margin basins have formed along the passive, trailing edges of continents where continental shelf and continental slope/rise prisms of sediment have accumulated. Most of the ancient continental margin basins have evolved from a trailing-margin depositional phase to a collision-margin deformation (mobile belt) phase, and have become orogens (mountain belts) as part of a geotectonic cycle. *See* eugeocline, miogeocline.

Convergent plate boundary Boundary characterized by lithospheric plates moving *toward* one another; includes ocean-ocean convergence along island arcs, oceanic lithosphere underthrusting continental lithosphere, and continental collisions. *See* subduction zone.

Coral Marine coelenterate that occurs as both a solitary individual and in colonies; secretes a calcareous external skeleton; reef builder.

Cordilleran orogeny Mountain-building event (*see* orogeny) in western North America extending from Jurassic time into the Early Cenozoic Era; began in the western part of the Cordilleran belt and progressed eastward through time. *See* Laramide, Nevadan, and Sevier orogenies.

Correlation (1) Matching of rock units on the basis of lateral continuity of lithology (*lithostratigraphic* correlation), typically on a local or regional basis; (2) matching of rock units on the basis of fossils (*biostratigraphic* correlation) on local, regional, and worldwide levels; (3) matching of rock units on the basis of similar age (*chronostratigraphic* correlation) on local, regional, and worldwide levels; or (4) matching of rock units on the basis of paleomagnetic signatures (*magnetostratigraphic* correlation) on local or regional levels. Correlation of rock units on a physical basis most often does *not* mean correlation in a time sense.

Cortex Outermost portion of three epidermal layers (bark) of a plant stem. *See* cambium, epidermal layer.

Cosmopolitan Having a wide, unrestricted geographic distribution. Opposite, *see* endemic.

Craton Relatively tectonically stable interior region of a continent; usually of large size and including both shield and adjacent platform; *example,* the North American craton includes the Canadian Shield and the adjacent interior lowland.

Cratonic sequence Large-scale, lithostratigraphic sequence that represents major onlap-offlap cycles; bounded by unconformities of cratonwide extent.

Crinoid Marine echinoderm characterized by a cup-shaped body and a series of branching arms; popularly called "sea lily."

Cross-cutting Principle of relative dating: rock units (such as igneous intrusions) and geologic features (such as faults) that cut across preexisting rocks and structures are younger than the rocks/features they cut.

Cryptozoic (Precambrian) Largest span of geologic time; the age of microscopic life; defined to include all of geologic history prior to the advent of major animal diversification; 4600 to approximately 600 Million years ago. *See* Precambrian.

Cyanobacteria (blue-green "algae") Blue-green bacteria.

Cyclothem One of a series of rhythmically repetitious sedimentary sequences that include fluvial, brackish-water, and marine sediments; characteristically contains coal beds.

Deduction Reasoning from a known principle to an unknown, from the general to the specific, or from a premise to a logical conclusion.

Dendrochronology Interpretation of tree rings, especially in applications of tree-ring dating; when coupled with radiocarbon dating, dendrochronology provides very detailed age determination and correlation for the last several tens of thousands of years.

Desiccation crack Crack formed in fine-grained sediment, such as clay, due to shrinkage of the sediment as it dries.

Diagenesis All chemical, physical, and biologic changes experienced by a sedimentary deposit after its initial deposition, and during and after its lithification, exclusive of surface alteration (weathering) and metamorphism. Diagenetic changes most commonly involve such processes as cementation, recrystallization, replacement, dissolution, and compaction.

Diamictite General term referring to any poorly sorted, terrigenous conglomerate or breccia with a muddy matrix; term does not imply a specific depositional environment.

Diapir Intrusion of less dense rock material in a viscous solid state through overlying rocks (core of such an intrusion often is salt). *See* salt dome.

Diastem Depositional break within conformable strata; break generally expressed as a bedding plane and represents a very short hiatus (days, weeks, centuries) in a sequence of rocks expressing essentially continuous sedimentation; not characterized by significant faunal or floral changes. *See* unconformity.

Diatom Single-celled plant that secretes a siliceous frustule (shell) of diverse and often ornate form; microscopic in size; important base of some food chains.

Diatomite Siliceous sedimentary rock composed mainly of diatom frustules (skeletons).

Dicotyledon Plant belonging to one of two main groups of angiosperms (flowering plants); dicots are the more primitive group and evolved earlier (Triassic Period). *See* monocotyledon.

Disconformity Unconformable surface between essentially parallel strata; erosional surface is evident and represents a significant gap in the stratigraphic record; typically characterized by a change in fauna and/or flora. *See* unconformity, diastem, hiatus.

Divergence of species Separation of species into two or more distinct new species.

Divergent plate boundary Boundary characterized by lithospheric plates moving *away* from one another; *example,* an ocean-floor spreading center such as the Mid-Atlantic Ridge.

DNA molecule (deoxyribonucleic acid) Complex organic molecule (protein) that contains the genetic material of an organism; these molecules form genes located along strands (chromosomes) that control critical chemical reactions within cells that are significant in controlling physical characteristics.

East Pacific Rise Portion of the global oceanic ridge system that extends north-south on the eastern side of the Pacific Ocean floor.

Echinoderm One of a diversified group of marine animals that is typically characterized by five-rayed symmetry; *examples,* starfish, sea urchins, crinoids.

Echinoid Mobile echinoderm characterized by globular body without arms or stem; *examples,* sea urchins and sand dollars.

Ecosystem Complex interrelationships within a group of organisms and between the group and the environment; interaction of both the living and the nonliving components; *examples,* pond ecosystem, forest ecosystem.

Ectotherm Cold-blooded animal; organism lacking the ability to produce internal body heat, so body temperature fluctuates readily; *example,* reptiles.

Ediacarian Period Formally named by Cloud and Glaessner (1982) as the time interval—from approximately 700(?) Ma to 570(?) Ma—during which lived the Ediacara soft-bodied fauna (the world's earliest-known animal community). Most classifications regard the Ediacarian time interval as the last major division of the Proterozoic. Cloud and Glaessner include it as the initial period of the Paleozoic.

Elsonian orogeny Mountain-building event (*see* orogeny) that occurred approximately 1300 million years ago in the Canadian Shield (during the Helikian Era).

Embryophyta Subkingdom of plants that includes the terrestrial plants; with the exceptions of mosses and liverworts, embryophytes are vascular plants (tracheophytes).

Endemic Restricted to a specific region (biogeographic province); *example,* specialized finches of the Galapagos Islands. Opposite, *see* cosmopolitan.

Endotherm Warm-blooded animal; organism has the ability to produce internal body heat and thus it maintains a near-constant body temperature; *examples,* mammals and birds. *See* homiothermy.

Eon Largest abstract unit of geochronologic (time) scale (e.g., *see* Proterozoic and Phanerozoic Eons); subdivided into eras. *See* eonothem.

Eonothem Highest ranking chronostratigraphic subdivision; used for a sequence of rocks formed during a specific eon of geologic time; designation above erathem in rank; *example,* Phanerozoic Eonothem.

Epeiric sea Widespread shallow sea that inundates portions of the interior of a continent; brought about by sea-level changes affecting entire continents or major portions thereof.

Epeirogeny Broad, relatively gentle crustal arching-type uplift over a wide geographic region (as opposed to the more intense deformation of an orogeny).

Epidermal layer One of the three outer layers of the structure of a plant stem; bark. *See* cambium, cortex.

Epifauna Benthic (bottom-dwelling) organisms that live on a seafloor or lake bed.

Epoch Abstract unit of geologic time; formally named geochronologic unit; subdivision of a period and subdivided into ages; *examples,* Late Cambrian Epoch, Early Ordovician Epoch; time equivalent of series. *See* series.

Era Abstract unit of geologic time; formally named geochronologic unit; subdivision of an eon and subdivided into periods; *examples:* Cenozoic Era, Mesozoic Era. *See* erathem.

Erathem Chronostratigraphic term for those rocks formed during a specific era of geologic time; designation above system in rank; *examples,* Cenozoic Erathem, Mesozoic Erathem. *See* era.

Erect posture Standing/walking/running in an upright position.

Erratic boulder Boulder foreign to the area in which it is found; usually deposited by a glacier.

Eugeocline Outer belt (seaward side) of a continental margin basin (geosyncline); characterized by deepwater clastic sediments with associated volcanics. *See* continental margin basin; miogeocline.

Eukaryote Life form with a cell (or cells) that contains an organized nucleus; includes protistans, fungi, plants, and animals. *See* prokaryote.

Eurytopic Able to survive and reproduce under a wide range of environmental conditions; wide tolerance of conditions. Opposite, *see* stenotopic.

Evolutionary theory Concept of organic evolution (development of life forms through time); supported by considerable biological and paleontological evidence. *See* organic evolution.

Exotic terrane Terrane in which the rocks are foreign to the general area; believed to have originated at some other location and transported to its present position by lithospheric plate movement. *See* suspect terrane.

Extinction "Dying out" of a taxon.

Facies The aspect, appearance, and characteristics of a rock unit, usually reflecting the conditions of its origin; a sedimentary facies is the distinctive product of a depositional environment.

Facies tract Spectrum of laterally adjacent facies that are different but genetically related; *example:* adjacent subenvironments of stream channel, natural levee, and backswamp of a fluvial complex.

Family Subdivision in the classification of life forms; below the level of order and above the level of genus.

Farallon Plate Portion of Pacific Ocean lithosphere subducted beneath the western margin of the North American Plate during the Cordilleran orogeny.

Fermentation Decomposition of complex organic molecules caused by the activity of yeast (fungi) and some bacteria in an oxygen-poor environment.

Flysch European term referring to marine rocks characterized by thinly bedded shales (term flysch derived from their fissile nature) alternating with coarser graywacke-type sandstones; graded bedding common; often associated with rapid erosion of an adjacent rising land mass in the early stages of an orogenic event; commonly deposited as turbidites in foreland basins that develop during the early stages of orogeny; companion term to molasse (*see*) and a fundamental part of the geotectonic cycle.

Food chain Relatively simple feeding sequence within a community of organisms; *example,* plankton eaten by small fish which are eaten by big fish. *See* food web.

Food web Complex interweaving of feeding patterns formed by the interlinking of individual food chains; *example:* connections between food chains in a pond and those in an adjacent meadow. *See* food chain.

Foraminifera Abundant and diverse group of single-celled, microscopic marine organisms (protistans) that secrete calcareous tests; include both benthic and planktonic forms.

Foreland fold-thrust belt A major zone of folding and thrust-faulting directed inboard toward the foreland or more stable margin of the continental interior; it lies between the main zone of plate collision and the more stable cratonic interior of a continent, commonly inboard (cratonward) of a magmatic arc complex.

Fore reef Seaward margin of a reef structure; typically composed of a slope of debris eroded from the face of the reef (reef talus).

Formation Mappable rock unit with distinctive physical properties by which it may be identified; the fundamental lithostratigraphic unit.
Fossil Remains of an ancient life form or traces of an organism preserved in rocks of the Earth's crust (does not include remains less than about 10,000 years old).
Fossil fuel Energy-producing fuel derived from organic sedimentary deposits; *examples,* coal, petroleum, natural gas.
Fossil succession Changes in fossil content within a vertical succession (chronological sequence) of rocks due to evolutionary change through time.

Gametophyte Stage in the reproductive cycle of vascular plants during which the sex cells (gametes) are produced.
Gastropod Mollusc characterized by coiled univalved shells, each shell being a single chamber; snails.
Gene A unit of heredity that is transmitted in the chromosome and which by interaction with internal and external environment, controls the development of a trait; capable of self-replication. The sequence of nucleotides in a DNA molecule that dictates the nucleotide sequence of an RNA molecule.
Gene pool Collective genetic material of a population of one species of organism.
Genera *See* genus.
Genotype Genetic makeup of an individual organism.
Genus Subdivision in the classification of life forms; below the level of family and above the level of species. *Plural,* genera.
Geochronologic unit (time unit) Abstract unit of geologic time; formally named unit of the geochronologic scale; time equivalent of chronostratigraphic unit; *examples:* eon, era, period, epoch, age, phase.
Geochronology "Science of Earth time"; relates geologic events to time, especially by use of absolute time (radiometric time ascribing a specific number of years before present to an event).
Geochronometric unit Direct division of geologic time defined by chronometric age (radiometric dating); a time unit that does not have a corresponding rock sequence or stratotype to which it is referred; *examples:* subdivisions of Precambrian such as Late Archean, Middle Proterozoic.
Geologic cycle Schematic portrayal of the interrelated way the Earth works; includes the physical, chemical, and biological processes; hydrologic cycle, rock cycle, and tectonic cycle are all incorporated into the larger picture of the geologic cycle. *See* hydrologic, rock, and tectonic cycles.
Geotectonic cycle Relates to the life of a continental margin basin (geosyncline), from depositional phase in a passive plate margin setting to deformational phase in a collision plate margin setting (i.e., from depositional basin to orogen) to post-orogenic clastic wedge. Originally defined by Stille (1940).
Gondwana One of six major continental blocks believed to have been in existence by Cambrian time; formed a southern-hemisphere block which included South America, Africa, India, Australia, and Antarctica.
Graben Elongate depressed (downdropped) fault block; commonly forms the basins of basin-and-range topography. *See* horst.
Graded bedding Stratification characterized by an upward change in texture from coarse-grained sediment (base of stratum) to finer-grained sediment (top of stratum); especially characteristic of deposition from a turbidity current. *See* turbidite.
Grand cycle A stratigraphic cycle expressed by a thick terrigenous facies overlain by a carbonate facies, reflecting the retrogradation of an offshore marine carbonate environment (and facies) over a more nearshore terrigenous environment (and facies); a transgressive terrigenous-carbonate couplet.
Granitization Transformation of preexisting rocks into granite through recrystallization and/or replacement; essentially metamorphic formation of granite.
Graptolite One of a class of extinct, colonial, floating organisms of problematic zoological affinity, but usually classified as nonvertebrate chordates (hemichordates); important guide fossil in Paleozoic time (Ordovician through Devonian Periods).
Grazing Feeding on herbage: grasses on land, and algae in oceans.
Greenhouse effect Concept that introduction of greater amounts of carbon dioxide into the atmosphere (such as from burning of fossil fuels) will cause a rise in atmospheric temperature; the mechanism works thus: short-wavelength solar energy passes through Earth's atmosphere (like greenhouse glass) and is converted to longer-wavelength heat energy upon striking the Earth's surface; this longer-wavelength heat energy is absorbed by carbon dioxide, so the greater the amount of CO_2 in the atmosphere, the greater is the heat retained.
Greenstone belt Belt of ancient volcanic-sedimentary rock successions found in all Archean shield terranes of the world; name derived from the presence of green alteration minerals in the lower part of the rock succession.
Grenville orogeny Mountain-building event (*see* orogeny) that occurred approximately 1000 million years ago in the Canadian Shield (Proterozoic Eon).
Group Lithostratigraphic unit next in rank above formation; includes two or more related formations.
Growth ring Tree rings indicating yearly growth; especially distinct in plants that grow in climates characterized by seasonal changes; also found in secreted calcareous skeletons of some invertebrates.
Gymnosperm "Naked seed" plant; the seed is not enclosed as in fruit-bearing plants; *examples:* cycad, conifer, ginkgo. *See* angiosperm.

Habitat Environment to which an organism is best adapted; the place where the requirements to support an organism are available.
Hadrynian Era Most recent era of time in the Proterozoic Eon; 900–700 million years ago. *See* Aphebian and Helikian Eras.
Half-life The time necessary for a radioactive substance to lose half of its radioactivity (provided there are a large number of atoms involved). Each radioactive nuclide has a characteristic half-life; *examples:* uranium-238 half-life = 4510 million years, uranium-234 half-life = 247 thousand years, radon-222 gas half-life = 3.8 days, lead-214 half-life = 26.8 minutes.
Heat budget Analysis of the distribution of solar radiation within the geosystem; based on amount of incoming solar radiation, amount of that radiation absorbed by clouds, and amount of that radiation reflected back into space by particulate matter in the atmosphere, among other factors.
Helikian Era Middle era of time in the Proterozoic Eon; 1600–900 million years ago. *See* Aphebian and Hadrynian Eras.
Hercynian orogeny *See* Alleghany orogeny.
Heredity Genetic material that is distinctive for each species and is passed on to successive generations through the reproduction cycle. This genetic material plays a major role in the physical characteristics of individuals and species.
Heterotroph Consumer organism. *See* consumer.
Hiatus Time interval not represented by rocks of a stratigraphic sequence; span of time when nondeposition, erosion, or both occurred. *See* unconformity.

Homiothermy Maintenance of relatively constant body temperature; warm-bloodedness. *See* endotherm.

Horst Elongate uplifted fault block; commonly forms the relatively higher ranges of basin-and-range topography. *See* graben.

Hudsonian orogeny Mountain-building (*see* orogeny) that occurred approximately 1800 million years ago in the Canadian Shield (Proterozoic Eon).

Hydrologic cycle Basic circulation of the hydrosphere (water) of the Earth: ocean-to-atmosphere by evaporation; to land in the form of precipitation; and back to ocean by runoff and other systems. Includes many important subsystems such as river systems, groundwater systems, and glacial systems. Component of the general geologic cycle. *See* geologic cycle.

Hydrosphere All forms of water associated with the Earth: oceans, rivers, lakes, groundwater, glacial ice, and water vapor in the atmosphere.

Iapetus Ocean Early Paleozoic proto-Atlantic Ocean in existence by the beginning of the Cambrian Period; closed during Paleozoic time because of convergence of plates bearing Laurentia (northeastern North America and Greenland), Baltica (western Europe), and Gondwana.

Induction Drawing a conclusion on the basis of specific facts; reasoning from the specific (a body of facts) to a general conclusion. Opposite, *see* deduction.

Infauna Benthic (bottom-dwelling) organisms that live within the sediments of the seafloor or lake bed; *example,* burrowing clams.

Insectivore Primitive mammal order exemplified by moles and hedgehogs and characterized by small size, nocturnal habits, and dependency on insects for food.

Interglacial Span of time between two glacial advances.

Invertebrate Animal lacking a spinal column (backbone) or notochord (skeletal rod).

Isostasy Concept of a theoretical balance between large portions of the Earth's lithosphere, such as continental areas "floating" on more dense substratum. *See* isostatic rebound.

Isostatic rebound Uplift of a portion of the Earth's crust following the removal of a great weight such as glacial ice. *See* isostasy.

Isotope Form of a chemical element resulting from change of the number of neutrons in the atomic nucleus.

Jovian planet Any of the four large outer planets of the solar system (located relatively farther from the sun): Jupiter, Saturn, Uranus, Neptune; gaseous planets composed predominantly of hydrogen. *See* terrestrial planet.

Kenoran orogeny Mountain-building event (*see* orogeny) that occurred approximately 2500 million years ago; closing event of Archean time; produced major additions to continental lithosphere.

Kerogen Hydrocarbon substance (bitumen) dispersed in some sedimentary rocks (such as the so-called oil shales) that yields petroleum when heated.

Kingdom Major subdivision in the classification of life forms; most inclusive ("largest") of the various subdivisions.

Lake varve *See* varve.

Land bridge Segment of land that connects two larger land areas; *example:* the Isthmus of Panama is a modern land bridge connecting the continents of North America and South America.

Laramide orogeny Youngest phase (Late Cretaceous through Early Cenozoic) of the more inclusive Cordilleran orogeny (*see* orogeny); most evident in the Rocky Mountain provinces. *See* Cordilleran orogeny.

Lateral continuity Principle that sedimentary strata, when originally deposited, are three-dimensional and extend laterally in all directions until they thin to a zero-thickness edge or terminate abruptly against the margin of the depositional basin.

Laurasia The protocontinent of the Northern Hemisphere (corresponding to Gondwana in the Southern Hemisphere) from which the present continents of the Northern Hemisphere have been derived by separation and continental displacement. The protocontinent Laurasia included most of North America, Greenland, and Eurasia, excluding India.

Laurentia One of six major continental blocks recognizable by Cambrian time; included present-day North America and Greenland.

Law of inclusions A principle of relative dating: fragments of rocks that are included within other rocks are older than the rocks that contain them.

Lineage Succession of evolution-related species through geologic time; ancestry.

Lithofacies Sedimentary facies defined on the basis of rock type (lithology).

Lithosphere Earth's outer rigid rind; it is fragmented and consists of a mosaic of plates that move over the underlying asthenosphere.

Lithostratigraphic unit Rock unit defined on the basis of physical aspects (lithology) and not on fossil content; therefore it may not be the same age everywhere; fundamental lithostratigraphic unit is the formation.

Ma Abbreviation for "millions of years ago" or "millions of years before present."

Magmatic arc Volcanic mountain chain along a continental margin; major zone of igneous intrusive and extrusive activity associated with a convergent plate boundary; *examples:* Andes Mountains of South America, Cascade Mountains of northwestern United States.

Magnetic anomaly Any measurement of the intensity or the polarity of the Earth's magnetic field that is a departure from the normal or expected measurement; *examples:* in terms of polarity, a positive magnetic anomaly measured in rocks indicates an ancient magnetic field parallel to the present field; a negative magnetic anomaly indicates that the former field was oriented opposite to the Earth's present magnetic field (in terms of north and south magnetic poles).

Magnetostratigraphic unit An interval or body of rock characterized by remnant magnetic properties. The boundaries of such a unit are determined by change in paleomagnetic signature. The fundamental unit is the magnetic polarity zone.

Marsupial Mammal that is characterized by the presence of an abdominal pouch to carry the young; *examples:* kangaroo, opossum.

Meiosis Cell reproduction accomplished by replication of DNA strands (chromosomes) and two successive cell divisions; each resulting cell contains only half the genetic information of the parent. *See* mitosis.

Mélange Deposit composed of a tectonic mixture of rock materials; fragments of various composition, texture, and age consolidated in a sheared matrix indicative of intense deformation; commonly developed in accretionary wedges related to subduction zones.

Member Lithostratigraphic unit that is a subdivision of a formation.

Mesosphere Solid middle zone of the Earth's interior structure; located between the plastic asthenosphere and the core of the Earth.

Methanogen Distinctive form of prokaryotic microorganism that grows by oxidizing hydrogen and reducing carbon dioxide to form methane; thrives in anoxic (oxygen-deficient) environments.

Microplate Relatively small-sized lithospheric plate. *See* collage.

Milankovitch hypothesis Hypothesis that climatic fluctuations causing glacial cyclicity are due to variations of the Earth's axis and orbit.

Miogeocline Inner belt (closer to the continent) of a continental margin basin (geosyncline) characterized by thick sequences of shallow-water sediments (similar in type to those deposited on the craton margin, but much thicker) and lack of major volcanic materials. *See* continental margin basin; eugeocline.

Mitosis Cell reproduction accomplished by replication of DNA and division into two smaller cells that are essentially identical to the parent cell. *See* meiosis.

Moho Abbreviated form of Mohorovičić discontinuity, which is the boundary surface or sharp seismic discontinuity that separates the Earth's crust from the subjacent mantle; it marks the level in the Earth at which P-wave velocities change abruptly from 6.7–7.2 km/sec in the lower crust to 7.6–8.6 km/sec at the top of the upper mantle part of the lithosphere; depth ranges from about 5–10 km below the ocean floor to about 35 km below the continents, although it may reach 60 km beneath some mountain ranges. This seismic discontinuity probably represents a change from basalt (above) to peridotite (below).

Molar One of the cheek teeth in mammals, located behind the incisors and the canine teeth; characterized by a wide-crowned surface suitable for grinding food.

Molasse European term for a postorogenic clastic wedge; represents the terrigenous clastic debris shed from the erosional wearing down of an orogen (mountain belt). Molasse facies include deposits in a spectrum of environments (facies tract) ranging from alluvial fan, to fluvial, to paralic. Molasse is a companion term to flysch (*see*), and both are parts of the geotectonic cycle.

Mold Impression left in sediment after shells or other organic materials are dissolved or otherwise removed; both internal and external molds are formed, depending upon whether the form of the inside or outside of the shell is preserved. *See* cast.

Mollusc One of an abundant and diverse group of animals popularly called "shellfish"; soft bodied and often with a hard shell, unsegmented, with a head and a muscular foot; mostly aquatic; *examples:* bivalves (such as clams), gastropods (snails), and cephalopods (such as squids).

Moneran Single-celled organism lacking a discrete nucleus.

Monocotyledon Plant belonging to one of two main groups of angiosperms (flowering plants); monocots are the more advanced group. *See* dicotyledon.

Monophyletic Originating from a single ancestral lineage. *See* polyphyletic.

Moraine Unsorted sedimentary debris transported by a glacier, and when the ice melts, deposited in hummocky mounds as terminal moraine, recessional moraine, lateral moraine, or medial moraine, or deposited in an irregular sheet as ground moraine.

Mutation Sudden changes in the chemical structure of genetic material of organisms that can be passed on to subsequent generations.

Natural selection Evolutionary mechanism whereby environmental conditions affect survival rates of variants within a population of organisms; organisms best-adapted to the environment will survive and produce viable offspring.

Nekton Organisms that have the ability to swim and to control their movements in water.

Neptunism Late eighteenth/early nineteenth-century doctrine that *all* rocks were formed by precipitation from an original, primeval ocean; championed by Abraham Werner (1750–1817).

Nevadan orogeny Initial phase (Late Jurassic through mid-Cretaceous) of the more inclusive Cordilleran orogeny (mountain-building event in western North America); characterized by intensive igneous activity including the formation of the major batholith complexes of the western margin of North America. *See* Cordilleran orogeny.

Niche Specific role or function that an organism has in a living community; *example:* in a shallow-marine environment worms fill the niche of deposit-feeders, and some bivalves (clams) fill the niche of filter-feeders.

Nocturnal Active at night.

Nonconformity Unconformable surface that separates older crystalline rock (igneous or metamorphic) from younger, overlying sedimentary strata. *See* unconformity.

Nova/supernova Star that collapses inward (implodes) and produces a sudden increase in brilliancy; such an event produces heavy elements and blasts them into space where they become "seed" matter for the development of new stars and planets.

Nuclide Atom defined by the number of protons and neutrons in its nucleus.

Occipital condyle Bony knob (double structure in mammals) at the base of the skull; it articulates with the first vertebra.

Offlap Vertical succession of sedimentary facies reflecting the regressive movement of the sea *off* the land; typically characterized by a fine-to-coarse-grained top-to-bottom sedimentary sequence (limestone-shale-sandstone). Opposite, *see* onlap.

Omnivorous Adapted to feeding on both animals and plants.

Onlap Vertical succession of sedimentary facies reflecting the transgressive movement of the sea *upon* the land; typically characterized by a coarse-to-fine-grained bottom-to-top sedimentary sequence (sandstone-shale-limestone). Opposite, *see* offlap.

Ontogeny Process of growth (from young to old) in an *individual* organism. *See* phylogeny.

Ophiolite suite Association of ultramafic rocks (peridotite), mafic rocks (gabbro and basalt—often pillow basalts), radiolarian cherts, and rocks rich in serpentine, chlorite, and other metamorphic minerals that are all representative of oceanic lithosphere; an exposed ophiolite suite indicates uplifted deep-sea floor, and incorporation into continental structure.

Opposable thumb Primate thumb that can be moved into a position opposite the fingers, thereby increasing dexterity.

Order Subdivision in the classification of life forms; category just below the level of class and above the level of family.

Organic evolution Process of unidirectional genetic change of life forms; controlled by genetics and natural selection. *See* evolutionary theory.

Organic macromolecule Large molecule of organic compound formed during a series of chemical reactions that in Early Archean time may have led to evolution of the living cell (may be similar to coacervate droplets).

Original horizontality Principle that sediments are originally deposited in an essentially horizontal position (parallel to the Earth's surface) because they accumulate on an essentially flat depositional surface; tilted strata, therefore, imply post-depositional deformation.

Orogen A linear or arcuate region that has been subjected to folding and other deformation during an orogenic cycle. Orogens were mobile belts during their formative stages, and most of them later became mountain belts by postorogenic processes. *See* orogenic belt.

Orogenic belt Region of lithospheric mobility and unrest (relative to stable blocks of the crust) that has been deformed into mountain chains; typically long and linear regions (former continental margin basins) characterized by folded and faulted rocks.

Orogenic front Boundary (contact) between orogen (deformation belt) and less disturbed rocks.

Orogeny Process of forming mountains; may involve folding, faulting, and igneous activity; often related to lithospheric plate convergence.

Ouachita The Ouachita segment of the Appalachian-Ouachita continental margin basin and mountain system. The Ouachita Mountains of Arkansas and Oklahoma contain Paleozoic strata deposited in the Ouachita continental margin basin and deformed by orogeny near the end of the Paleozoic.

Outgasing Process of expelling gases from the Earth's interior by volcanic activity.

Ozone O_3 chemical form of oxygen caused by bombardment of the normal atmospheric O_2 molecules with ultraviolet radiation in the upper atmosphere.

Paleoecology Branch of paleontology that is concerned with the relationships of ancient organisms to their environments and to one another.

Paleogeographic map Graphic representation of ancient environments, such as shorelines, basins, river systems, and mountain belts; small-scale maps may depict ancient continental-oceanic arrangements.

Paleontology Branch of geology that is the study of prehistoric life preserved as the fossil record.

Palynology Field of study within paleobotany that investigates spores and pollen (reproductive parts of plants).

Pangaea "All lands"; single supercontinent resulting from the Late Paleozoic global suturing of continental masses.

Panthalassa All-inclusive ocean that surrounded Pangaea; spanned the globe from pole to pole and encompassed nearly 300° of longitude.

Paraconformity Unconformable surface between essentially parallel strata; "hardly distinguishable from a simple bedding plane" and characterized by a change in fauna or flora. *See* unconformity.

Paralic Depositional realm that embraces the transitional belt between continental and marine; includes coastal environments such as deltas, beaches, bays, estuaries, coastal barriers, lagoons.

Period Abstract unit of geologic time; fundamental unit of the geochronologic scale; subdivision of an era and subdivided into epochs; *examples,* Cambrian Period, Ordovician Period; time equivalent of system. *See* system.

Perissodactyl Any of an order of odd-toed (one, three, or five toes on each foot) ungulates (hoofed mammals), including horses and tapirs. *See* artiodactyl.

Permineralization Preservation of fossils by deposition of mineral material in the pore spaces of organic hard parts, indurating the original organic material.

pH Measure of the acidity or basicity of a solution on a scale from 0 to 14: pH 0 = maximum acidity (concentration of H^+ ions); pH 7 = neutral; pH 14 = maximum basicity or alkalinity (OH^- in solution). (The numbers 0–14 are logarithms of the reciprocal of the hydrogen-ion concentration.)

Phanerozoic Most recent eon; defined to include all of geologic history characterized by conspicuous animal life (from the present to approximately 600 million years ago); includes the Paleozoic, Mesozoic, and Cenozoic Eras.

Phenotype Physical characteristics of an organism as determined by its genotype (genetic makeup) and environmental conditions.

Phloem Type of cell in the vascular system of plants; transports liquids and nutrients to various parts of the plant. *See* vascular plant.

Photosynthesis Chemical synthesis of organic compounds from water and carbon dioxide, using chlorophyll molecules and energy from sunlight; a function of monerans, protistans, and green plants.

Phyla *See* phylum.

Phyletic gradualism Model of formation of new species (speciation) whereby one species gradually evolves into another species through a span of time.

Phylogeny Process of change in taxa (species, genus, family, etc.) through geologic time; history of development of a collective *group. See* ontogeny.

Phylum Major subdivision in the classification of life forms; broad and inclusive category just below kingdom level and above class level. *Plural,* phyla.

Pith Central portion of the internal structure of a plant stem; soft, spongy tissue.

Placental Type of mammal characterized by the presence of a placenta, the organ that unites a fetus to the maternal uterus.

Planetesimal Small, solid, and cold body in space; planets may have formed by accretion of a cloud of planetesimals (the dust-cloud or planetesimal hypothesis).

Plankton Organisms that float freely in water; *example:* diatoms.

Plant Generally multicelled organism (although some classifications include chlorophyll-bearing protists) that possesses the ability to manufacture food from inorganic materials by photosynthesis.

Plate tectonics Concept in which the Earth's outer "rind," the lithosphere, consists of a mosaic of rigid pieces (plates) that move and interact. *See* tectonic cycle.

Pluvial lake Lake formed during a time of exceptionally heavy rainfall; used specifically for a lake formed during Pleistocene glacial advances.

Polarity event Change of polarity of the Earth's magnetic field that is of relatively short duration; occurs during a polarity epoch; *example,* a small span of time when normal polarity occurs within an epoch of reverse polarity.

Pollen Microspores produced in seed-bearing vascular plants; usually appears as fine dust.

Polyphyletic Originating from two or more lineages of ancestors. *See* monophyletic.

Precambrian Often-used term referring to all of geologic time prior to the beginning of the Cambrian Period (conventionally placed at 570–600 million years ago). *See* Cryptozoic.

Prehensile tail Tail that has the ability to wrap around an object, such as in grasping a branch; characteristic of South American monkeys.

Producer Organism that is able to produce its own food and energy by the process of photosynthesis; monerans, some protistans, and plants. *See* autotroph.

Progradation The building outward (or forward) toward the sea of a shoreline or coastline (e.g., a beach, delta, or fan). Through time this is expressed as the migration of more landward environments and facies over more seaward environments and facies, producing an offlap cycle. *Opposite* of retrogradation (*see*).

Prokaryote Single-celled, nonnucleated life form; *examples,* bacteria, cyanobacteria, and methanogens. *See* eukaryote.

Prosimii "Primitive" primates, including lemurs and tarsiers.

Proterozoic An eon, the younger subdivision of Cryptozoic (Precambrian) time; from about 2500 Ma to about 600 Ma. *See* Archean.

Protistan Single-celled organism having a nucleated cell.

Protoplanet "First planet"; orbiting mass of dust and gas clouds that gradually condensed into a solid planetary body; precursor of a present planet.

Punctuated equilibrium Model of formation of new species (speciation) whereby an evolving lineage has relatively rapid and substantial morphological change within "geologically short moments"; these "moments" of rapid change punctuate (separate) longer intervals of time when the characteristics of the lineage were relatively constant (had equilibrium).

Radioactive decay Spontaneous emission of atomic particles from the atom nucleus causing disintegration of the atom; *examples:* decay of uranium-238 to lead-206, decay of potassium-40 to argon-40.

Radioactive emission Emission of particles or energy from the atomic nucleus to produce radioactive decay; the three types are (1) alpha particle (two protons and two neutrons), (2) beta particle (electron expelled when a neutron is split into a proton and an electron), and (3) gamma radiation.

Radiogenic Produced by radioactive decay; *example:* radiogenic lead.

Radiolarian Microscopic, single-celled organism (protistan) that secretes a complex, often ornate siliceous shell.

Radiometric Pertaining to the measurement of radiation; applicable to determination of age of a rock by measurement of radioactive decay of some isotopes (radiometric dating).

Recrystallization Fossil preservation by conversion of unstable forms of shell material (such as aragonite) to more stable forms (such as calcite); microstructure of the original shell is destroyed in the process; not restricted to fossil preservation, but also applicable to recrystallization of inorganic minerals.

Red bed Detrital sedimentary rock (most commonly sandstone and shale), the particles of which are coated with iron oxides, usually the mineral hematite; most often formed in nonmarine environments due to thorough oxidation of the iron by free (uncombined) oxygen in the atmosphere.

Reef Wave-resistant structure built up from the seafloor by accumulation of skeletal material from marine organisms such as calcareous algae, corals, and bryozoans; important organic feature in the sedimentary rock record; complex ecologic community of reef-building organisms.

Regression Fall of sea level relative to the shore, with resulting movement of the sea *off* the land. Opposite, *see* transgression.

Replacement Fossil preservation by removal of original material in solution and concurrent deposition of new compounds in its place (such as in petrified wood); not restricted to fossils, but also applicable to replacement of inorganic minerals, such as calcite replacement by dolomite.

Reproductive isolation Situation in which individuals of one species are biologically unable to reproduce with individuals of any other species because of genetic differences, although these species may coexist in the same geographic area.

Respiration Chemical processes associated with breathing; removal of oxygen from the atmosphere and emission of carbon dioxide.

Retrogradation The backward (landward) movement or retreat of a shoreline or coastline. Through time this results in the migration of more seaward environments and facies over more landward environments and facies, producing an onlap cycle. *Opposite* of progradation (*see*).

Ripple mark Wavelike (undulating) form on the surface of sediment; caused by water or air currents flowing over the surface or by back-and-forth motion of waves or currents.

Rock cycle Schematic portrayal of interrelationships among the three rock classes; illustrates the basic concept that new rocks are formed from older rocks; component of the general geologic cycle. *See* geologic cycle.

Salt dome Vertical, fingerlike projection of salt that has intruded into overlying rocks from a lower salt stratum. *See* diapir.

Seamount Isolated mountain rising from the ocean floor; typically a volcanic cone.

Sedimentary basin A low area on the surface of the Earth's lithosphere, of tectonic origin, in which sediments have accumulated. These negative areas subside by one or more of the following mechanisms: thermal cooling of lithosphere, faulting, sediment loading, tectonic loading, or downwarping. *Examples,* Appalachian continental margin basin, Michigan Basin, Los Angeles Basin.

Sedimentary cycle Vertical succession of sedimentary rocks formed during a transgression-regression cycle. *See* onlap, offlap.

Sedimentary facies Lateral variation in sedimentary rock units partly or wholly equivalent in age; deposits produced by different but laterally adjacent environments of deposition. Facies in a vertical sequence; *see* Walther's Law.

Septa *See* septum.

Septum Partition, such as a radiating plate of the skeletal structure of coral or the wall between the chambers of cephalopod shells. *Plural,* septa.

Series Chronostratigraphic term for those rocks formed during a specific epoch of geologic time; below system in rank; *examples,* Lower Cambrian Series, Pliocene Series. *See* epoch.

Sevier orogeny Middle phase (Cretaceous) of the more inclusive Cordilleran orogeny; characterized by back-arc folding and thrusting. *See* Cordilleran orogeny; orogeny.

Shield Precambrian nucleus of a continent typically containing the roots of ancient orogenic belts; relatively stable for a long span of time and topographically a low-lying region. *See* Canadian Shield.

Sonoma orogeny Permo-Triassic mountain-building event (*see* orogeny) expressed by structures in the western Cordillera.

Speciation Evolutionary processes of species formation; *examples: see* allopatric speciation, phyletic gradualism, punctuated equilibrium.

Species Subdivision in the classification of life forms; least inclusive ("smallest") of the various subdivisions.

Sponge Invertebrate animal with two-layer body and a cellular level of organization with no organs; spicules are the predominant skeletal part of the sponge found in the fossil record.

Spore Asexual reproductive body produced by spore-bearing vascular plants; has the capability to develop into a new individual.

Sporophyte Stage during which spores are produced in the reproductive cycle of spore-bearing vascular plants.
Stage Chronostratigraphic term for those rocks formed during a specific age of geologic time; below series in rank; *examples:* Trempealeauan Stage, Franconian Stage (both divisions of the Upper Cambrian Series).
Stenotopic Able to survive and reproduce only in a narrow range of environmental conditions; narrow tolerance of conditions. Opposite, *see* eurytopic.
Stereoscopic vision Perception of an object in three-dimensional form because of having two eyes with overlapping fields of view; an important characteristic of humans and other predators.
Stoma Pore in the epidermis of plant leaves; allows gaseous exchange (oxygen, carbon dioxide, water vapor) between the plant and the atmosphere. *Plural,* stomata.
Stratigraphy Science of layered (stratified) rocks, including spatial and time relationships of different strata, interpretation of dynamic depositional patterns, and organization of rock sequences.
Stratotype Type section for any formal stratigraphic unit; ideally a stratigraphic sequence of essentially continuous sedimentation (not interrupted by unconformities).
Stromatolite Sedimentary structure formed by the sediment trapping and binding of cyanobacteria; characterized by laminated, mound-shaped form.
Stromatoporoid Extinct reef-building animal of uncertain biological affinity, but generally classified as a form of sponge in phylum Porifera; fossils typically calcareous laminated masses.
Subduction zone Zone of descent of one plate margin (leading edge) beneath the edge of the adjacent plate at a convergent boundary; expressed topographically by an oceanic trench; *example:* subduction of the Nazca Plate under the western margin of the South American Plate along the Peru-Chile Trench. *See* convergent plate boundary.
Submarine canyon Seafloor canyon that typically crosses the continental shelf and extends down the continental slope; acts as an avenue of transport for sedimentary debris to the deep-sea floor.
Supergroup Lithostratigraphic unit that is an assemblage of related groups, or of formations and groups; associated groups often have significant similar lithologic features.
Supernova *See* nova.
Superposition Principle that in a sequence of essentially undisturbed layers of sedimentary rocks, the oldest layer is at the bottom and the youngest layer is at the top.
Suspect terrane Terrane in which the rocks are suspected to be foreign to the general region; the terrane is suspected to have originated at some other location and moved into its present position as a result of lithospheric plate movement. *See* exotic terrane.
Suture Line or groove; line of junction of a septum in a cephalopod shell to the inside of the outer shell, a significant feature in classifying cephalopods; in a tectonic sense, the line of union at a convergent plate boundary; *example,* suturing of the continents together by convergence to form Pangaea.
System Chronostratigraphic term for those rocks formed during a specific period of geologic time; below erathem in rank; *examples,* Cambrian System, Triassic System. *See* period.

Taconic orogeny Late Ordovician mountain-building event (*see* orogeny) affecting the northern Appalachian belt (Taconic Mountains of eastern New York, Vermont, and central Massachusetts); associated with partial closing of the proto-Atlantic basin (Iapetus) due to plate convergence.
Taxa *See* taxon.
Taxon *Any* level of classification of organisms; *examples:* species, genus, family. *Plural,* taxa.
Taxonomy Classification of organisms.
Tectonic cycle Model that explains the major structures of the Earth (such as ocean basins, folded mountain belts, volcanic mountain chains) as a result of the interaction of the Earth's lithospheric plates as they move about on a weak asthenosphere ("plastic" layer); individual plates move away from one another, toward one another, or slide past each other; component of the general geologic cycle. *See* geologic cycle.
Tectonostratigraphic terrane A crustal block, not necessarily of uniform composition, bounded by faults. It is a geologic entity having a history distinct from the histories of adjacent crustal blocks. Such tectonically bounded blocks are generally considered to be accreted (not indigenous) to the continental structure of which they are now a part.
Terminal sporangium Reproductive spore-producing organ of seedless vascular plants; located at tip of stem or branch. *Plural,* sporangia.
Terrane Geographic area in which a specific rock type or assemblage of rocks is prevalent; *examples:* shield terrane, coastal-plain terrane.
Terrestrial planet Any of the inner planets of the solar system (located close to the sun); Mercury, Venus, Earth, Mars; rocky and Earthlike in composition. *See* Jovian planet.
Tethys Sea East-west seaway between Gondwana (continents of the southern hemisphere) and Eurasia; existed from Paleozoic to Early Cenozoic.
Thallophyta Subkingdom of plants including unicelled or multicelled aquatic forms that lack true root systems, woody stems, or leaves; *examples,* diatoms, brown algae (kelp).
Till Ice-deposited debris, typically unsorted and unstratified.
Tommotian Stage Time-stratigraphic unit especially significant because it contains the earliest known shell-bearing fossils—primitive molluscs, brachiopods, archaeocyathids, and others; lowest Cambrian, but predates first appearance of trilobites.
Trace fossil Preservation of an indication of an organism's presence and activity, such as feeding or locomotion tracks and trails, and dwellings on or in sediment; structural parts of the organism's body are not present; *examples:* animal tracks, burrows.
Tracheophyte Plant having a vascular system of xylem and phloem.
Transcontinental arch Series of emergent areas trending in a northeast-southwest direction across the central part of the North American craton (Lake Superior to Arizona) during Early Paleozoic time; these individual land areas collectively reflect the existence of a structural high.
Transform fault Strike-slip fault associated with lateral motion between lithospheric plates; *examples:* San Andreas fault zone in California, seafloor fracture zones between offset segments of the oceanic ridge system.
Transgression Rise of sea level relative to the shore with resulting encroachment of the sea *onto* the land. Opposite, *see* regression.
Trilobite One of an extinct class of arthropods with a significant Paleozoic fossil record; characterized by trilobed body.
Triple junction Point that marks the complex intersection of three lithospheric plates; *example:* junction of Pacific Plate, North American Plate, and Cocos Plate.
Turbidite Sedimentary deposit produced by a turbidity current (generally developed as graded sandstone and mudstone); common in deep-sea fan environment. *See* turbidity current, graded bedding.

Turbidity current Dense, sediment-laden water current that moves rapidly downslope; common in submarine-canyon and basin-slope environments. *See* turbidite.

Type section Particular stratigraphic section that was used to *originally* define a formal stratigraphic unit and that serves as a standard. *See* stratotype.

Unconformity Buried surface of erosion or nonaccumulation of sediments; produces a gap in the sedimentary record. *See* angular unconformity, diastem, disconformity, nonconformity.

Ungulate Any of the hoofed mammals; *examples:* horse, elephant. *See* artiodactyl, perissodactyl.

Uniformitarianism Doctrine that ancient Earth processes may be understood by studying present-day processes, that the same physical principles have existed throughout geologic time; concept ascribed to James Hutton (1726–1797); strict interpretation of the concept implies uniformity in rates, intensities, and importance of the various processes. *See* actualism.

Varve (lake varve) Paired layers of lake sediments that record an annual deposit; composed of a light-colored, typically thicker summer lamina and a dark-colored, typically thinner, finer-grained winter lamina.

Vascular plant Plant that contains internal tubelike structures called xylem and phloem, which form a vascular (liquid-conducting) system. *See* xylem, phloem, tracheophyte.

Vendian System Uppermost system of the Upper Proterozoic Erathem; based on a stratotype in the Siberian Platform; the **International Stratigraphic Guide** recognizes the Vendian System (Period) to include the Ediacarian Series (Epoch).

Vertebrate Animal that possesses a spinal column (backbone).

Volcanic island arc Oceanic, volcanic mountain chain that parallels a seafloor trench—both features are associated with plate convergence; results from igneous activity produced by subduction of a lithospheric slab into the asthenosphere; *examples:* Japanese islands parallel to the Japanese Trench; Aleutian Islands parallel to the Aleutian Trench.

Walther's Law Within a sedimentary cycle, the same succession of facies occurs laterally and vertically; the facies are products of environments that occur laterally adjacent to one another and succeed or precede one another in a sedimentary cycle.

Wave base The depth below the surface of a body of water at which wave action no longer stirs the bottom sediments. Under fair weather conditions, it is at significantly more shallow depths (10 m or so) than during storm conditions (commonly 50 m or more).

Wilson cycle Sequence of plate-tectonic events producing (a) the opening of an ocean basin by continental rifting, and (b) the closing of an ocean basin by continental collision; *example:* formation of the proto-Atlantic Ocean (Iapetus) and subsequent Paleozoic closing of the ocean to form the supercontinent Pangaea.

Xylem Type of cell in the vascular system of plants; transports water to various parts of the plant. *See* vascular plant, phloem.

Zone *See* biozone.

Appendix A: The Periodic Table

Key:

Atomic weight → 1.00797
Atomic number → 1 H ← Symbol
Hydrogen ← Name
Electron configuration → $1s^{1}$

When atomic weight is given in parentheses, best known isotope is indicated.

1.00797 1 **H** Hydrogen $1s^{1}$								
6.94 3 **Li** Lithium $1s^{2}2s^{1}$	9.012 4 **Be** Beryllium $1s^{2}2s^{2}$							
22.99 11 **Na** Sodium $[Ne]3s^{1}$	24.31 12 **Mg** Magnesium $[Ne]3s^{2}$							
39.10 19 **K** Potassium $[Ar]4s^{1}$	40.08 20 **Ca** Calcium $[Ar]4s^{2}$	44.96 21 **Sc** Scandium $[Ar]3d^{1}4s^{2}$	47.90 22 **Ti** Titanium $[Ar]3d^{2}4s^{2}$	50.94 23 **V** Vanadium $[Ar]3d^{3}4s^{2}$	52.00 24 **Cr** Chromium $[Ar]3d^{5}4s^{1}$	54.94 25 **Mn** Manganese $[Ar]3d^{5}4s^{2}$	55.85 26 **Fe** Iron $[Ar]3d^{6}4s^{2}$	58.93 27 **Co** Cobalt $[Ar]3d^{7}4s^{2}$
85.47 37 **Rb** Rubidium $[Kr]5s^{1}$	87.62 38 **Sr** Strontium $[Kr]5s^{2}$	88.91 39 **Y** Yttrium $[Kr]4d^{1}5s^{2}$	91.22 40 **Zr** Zirconium $[Kr]4d^{2}5s^{2}$	92.91 41 **Nb** Niobium $[Kr]4d^{4}5s^{1}$	95.94 42 **Mo** Molybdenum $[Kr]4d^{5}5s^{1}$	(98)[b] 43 **Tc** Technetium $[Kr]4d^{5}5s^{2}$	101.1 44 **Ru** Ruthenium $[Kr]4d^{7}5s^{1}$	102.9 45 **Rh** Rhodium $[Kr]4d^{8}5s^{1}$
132.9 55 **Cs** Cesium $[Xe]6s^{1}$	137.3 56 **Ba** Barium $[Xe]6s^{2}$	Lanthanides 57–71	178.5 72 **Hf** Hafnium $[Xe]4f^{14}5d^{2}6s^{2}$	180.9 73 **Ta** Tantalum $[Xe]4f^{14}5d^{3}6s^{2}$	183.8 74 **W** Tungsten $[Xe]4f^{14}5d^{4}6s^{2}$	186.2 75 **Re** Rhenium $[Xe]4f^{14}5d^{5}6s^{2}$	190.2 76 **Os** Osmium $[Xe]4f^{14}5d^{6}6s^{2}$	192.2 77 **Ir** Iridium $[Xe]4f^{14}5d^{7}6s^{2}$
87 **Fr** Francium $[Rn]7s^{1}$	88 **Ra** Radium $[Rn]7s^{2}$	Actinides 89–103						

Lanthanides →	138.9 57 **La** Lanthanum $[Xe]5d^{1}6s^{2}$	140.1 58 **Ce** Cerium $[Xe]4f^{1}5d^{1}6s^{2}$	140.9 59 **Pr** Praseodymium $[Xe]4f^{3}6s^{2}$	144.2 60 **Nd** Neodymium $[Xe]4f^{4}6s^{2}$	(145) 61 **Pm** Promethium $[Xe]4f^{5}6s^{2}$	150.4 62 **Sm** Samarium $[Xe]4f^{6}6s^{2}$	151.9 63 **Eu** Europium $[Xe]4f^{2}6s^{2}$
Actinides →	227.0 89 **Ac** Actinium $[Rn]6d^{1}7s^{2}$	232.0 90 **Th** Thorium $[Rn]6d^{2}7s^{2}$	231.0 91 **Pa** Protactinium $[Rn]5f^{2}6d^{1}7s^{2}$	238.0 92 **U** Uranium $[Rn]5f^{3}6d^{1}7s^{2}$	237.0 93 **Np** Neptunium $[Rn]5f^{4}6d^{1}7s^{2}$	(244) 94 **Pu** Plutonium $[Rn]5f^{6}7s^{2}$	(243) 95 **Am** Americium $[Rn]5f^{7}7s^{2}$

								1.00797 1 H Hydrogen $1s^1$	4.0026 2 He Helium $1s^2$
			10.81 5 B Boron $1s^2 2s^2 p^1$	12.01 6 C Carbon $1s^2 2s^2 p^2$	14.00 7 N Nitrogen $1s^2 2s^2 p^3$	15.999 8 O Oxygen $1s^2 2s^2 p^4$	18.998 9 F Fluorine $1s^2 2s^2 p^5$	20.179 10 Ne Neon $1s^2 2s^2 p^6$
			26.98 13 Al Aluminum $[Ne]3s^2 p^1$	28.08 14 Si Silicon $[Ne]3s^2 p^2$	30.97 15 P Phosphorus $[Ne]3s^2 p^3$	32.06 16 S Sulfur $[Ne]3s^2 p^4$	35.45 17 Cl Chlorine $[Ne]3s^2 p^5$	39.95 18 Ar Argon $[Ne]3s^2 p^6$
58.70 28 Ni Nickel $[Ar]3d^8 4s^2$	63.54 29 Cu Copper $[Ar]3d^{10} 4s^1$	65.38 30 Zn Zinc $[Ar]3d^{10} 4s^2$	69.72 31 Ga Gallium $[Ar]3d^{10} 4s^2 p^1$	72.59 32 Ge Germanium $[Ar]3d^{10} 4s^2 p^2$	74.92 33 As Arsenic $[Ar]3d^{10} 4s^2 p^3$	78.96 34 Se Selenium $[Ar]3d^{10} 4s^2 p^4$	79.91 35 Br Bromine $[Ar]3d^{10} 4s^2 p^5$	83.80 36 Kr Krypton $[Ar]3d^{10} 4s^2 p^6$
106.4 46 Pd Palladium $[Kr]4d^{10}$	107.9 47 Ag Silver $[Kr]4d^{10} 5s^1$	112.4 48 Cd Cadmium $[Kr]4d^{10} 5s^2$	114.8 49 In Indium $[Kr]4d^{10} 5s^2 p^1$	118.7 50 Sn Tin $[Kr]4d^{10} 5s^2 p^2$	121.7 51 Sb Antimony $[Kr]4d^{10} 5s^2 p^3$	127.6 52 Te Tellurium $[Kr]4d^{10} 5s^2 p^4$	126.9 53 I Iodine $[Kr]4d^{10} 5s^2 p^5$	131.3 54 Xe Xenon $[Kr]4d^{10} 5s^2 p^6$
195.1 78 Pt Platinum $[Xe]4f^{14} 5d^9 6s^1$	197.0 79 Au Gold $[Xe]4f^{14} 5d^{10} 6s^1$	200.6 80 Hg Mercury $[Xe]4f^{14} 5d^{10} 6s^2$	204.4 81 Tl Thallium $[Xe]4f^{14} 5d^{10} 6s^2 p^1$	207.2 82 Pb Lead $[Xe]4f^{14} 5d^{10} 6s^2 p^2$	209.0 83 Bi Bismuth $[Xe]4f^{14} 5d^{10} 6s^2 p^3$	(209) 84 Po Polonium $[Xe]4f^{14} 5d^{10} 6s^2 p^4$	(210) 85 At Astatine $[Xe]4f^{14} 5d^{10} 6s^2 p^5$	(222) 86 Rn Radon $[Xe]4f^{14} 5d^{10} 6s^2 p^6$

157.3 64 Gd Gadolinium $[Xe]4f^7 5d^1 6s^2$	158.9 65 Tb Terbium $[Xe]4f^9 6s^2$	162.5 66 Dy Dysprosium $[Xe]4f^{10} 6s^2$	164.9 67 Ho Holmium $[Xe]4f^{11} 6s^2$	167.3 68 Er Erbium $[Xe]4f^{12} 6s^2$	168.9 69 Tm Thulium $[Xe]4f^{13} 6s^2$	173.0 70 Yb Ytterbium $[Xe]4f^{14} 6s^2$	175.0 71 Lu Lutetium $[Xe]4f^{14} 5d^1 6s^2$
(247) 96 Cm Curium $[Rn]5f^7 6d^1 7s^2$	(247) 97 Bk Berkelium $[Rn]5f^9 7s^2$	(251) 98 Cf Californium $[Rn]5f^{10} 7s^2$	(252) 99 Es Einsteinium $[Rn]5f^{11} 7s^2$	(257) 100 Fm Fermium $[Rn]5f^{12} 7s^2$	(258) 101 Md Mendelevium $[Rn]5f^{13} 7s^2$	(259) 102 No Nobelium $[Rn]5f^{14} 7s^2$	(260) 103 Lw Lawrencium $[Rn]5f^{14} 6d^1 7s^2$

Appendix B: A Synoptic Classification of Organisms

All classifications are human-made schemes. Classifying anything—minerals, rocks, fossils, stars, or cars—into related groups is an endeavor to make order out of diversity—to put items into a series of cubbyholes that our minds can grasp. Classification is a tool of study. Being human constructs, classifications do not meet with universal acceptance; thus synoptic classifications of organisms in different texts will vary. A key point in the classification of organisms is the thread of genetic relationships between groups; evolutionary concepts must be taken into account when assigning organisms to their groups. This is not just a descriptive classification, therefore, but phylogenetic as well; evolutionary relationships are honored as much as possible. As indicated in Chapter 3 (see discussion of conodonts), some fossil organisms are of unknown biologic affinity and are difficult to fit into the present classification scheme.

The synoptic classification that follows is not meant to include all known life forms, but rather includes the major organic groups and the important fossil forms discussed in this text.

Kingdom MONERA (unicellular: nonnucleated cell structure)

- **Division*Schizomycophyta**—bacteria; Cryptozoic—Holocene
- **Division Cyanophyta**—cyanobacteria (blue-green bacteria), stromatolites; Cryptozoic–Holocene

Kingdom PROTISTA (unicellular: nucleated cell structure)

- **Phylum Protozoa**
  - **Class Sarcodina**
    - **Order Foraminifera—**most commonly with calcareous tests; Cambrian–Holocene; planktonic forms; Cretaceous–Holocene
      - **Family Fusulinidae**—fusulinids; Mississippian—Permian
    - **Order Radiolaria**—radiolarians; siliceous, perforate shell; Cambrian–Holocene

**Division* is a botanical classification term, generally equivalent to *phylum* of zoological classification.

Kingdom PLANTAE (unicellular and multicellular [metaphyte]: nucleated cell structure; photosynthetic; see Chapter 16 for more detailed discussion)

Subkingdom Thallophyta—primarily aquatic forms lacking true root systems; some unicellular algal groups that are commonly classified under Protista.

- **Division Chlorophycophyta**—green algae; Cryptozoic–Holocene
- **Division Rhodophycophyta**—red algae; Crytozoic–Holocene
- **Division Phaeophycophyta—**brown algae (seaweeds); Cryptozoic–Holocene
- **Division Chrysophycophyta**—diatoms; Jurassic?–Holocene
- **Division Euglenophycophyta**—euglenids; Cretaceous–Holocene
- **Division Charophycophyta**—charophytes; Silurian–Holocene

Subkingdom Embryophyta—terrestrial plants

- **Division Rhyniophyta**—Silurian–Devonian
- **Division Zosterophyllophyta**—Silurian–Devonian
- **Division Psilophyta**—Devonian–Holocene
- **Division Microphyllophyta**—club mosses; Devonian–Holocene
- **Division Arthrophyta**—horsetails and sphenopsids; Devonian–Holocene
- **Division Pteridophyta**—ferns; Devonian–Holocene
- **Division Pteridospermophyta**—seed ferns; Devonian–Jurassic
- **Division Coniferophyta**—conifers; Devonian?–Holocene
- **Division Cycadophyta**—cycads; Mississippian?–Holocene
- **Division Ginkgophyta**—maidenhair tree; Pennsylvanian?–Holocene
- **Division Gnetophyta**—Permian?–Holocene
- **Division Anthophyta**—flowering plants; Triassic?–Holocene

Kingdom ANIMALIA (multicellular [metazoan]; nucleated cell structure; nonphotosynthetic)

- **Phylum Porifers**—sponges, stromatoporoids; Cambrian–Holocene
- **Phylum Archaeocyatha**—soft-tissue structure unknown; conical, double-walled calcareous shell; extinct; Early and Middle Cambrian
  - **Phylum Coelenterata;** Ediacarian? Cambrian–Holocene
  - **Class Anthozoa**—corals and sea anemones
    - **Order Tabulata**—extinct forms without (or with poorly developed) septa; horizontal tabulae supported the animal; important contributors to Paleozoic reefs; Ordovician–Permian

Order Rugosa—extinct forms with septal development; includes horn corals; major Paleozoic reef builders; Ordovician–Triassic

Order Scleractinia—coral reef builders of Mesozoic and Cenozoic times; predominantly colonial types; Triassic–Holocene

Phylum Bryozoa—colonial encrusting or branching forms; Ordovician–Holocene

Phylum Brachiopoda—marine forms with two-valved shell; Cambrian–Holocene

Class Inarticulata—two valves lacking tooth and socket hinge structure; chitino-phosphatic shell composition; Cambrian–Holocene

Class Articulata—two valves, with well-developed hinge structure; typically calcareous shell; fossils more abundant; Cambrian–Holocene

Phylum Mollusca—diverse group of both fossil and modern forms; Cambrian–Holocene

Class Bivalvia—two hinged, commonly mirror-image calcareous shells; muscular, creeping foot; clams, oysters, scallops; Cambrian–Holocene

Class Gastropoda—most with single, coiled calcareous shell; muscular, creeping foot; distinct head; snails; Cambrian–Holocene

Class Cephalopoda—shelled or shell-less forms; calcarceous shelled forms commonly with chambers and sutures; jet-propulsion system of locomotion; extinct ammonoids comprise one of the most important guide-fossil groups; Late Cambrian–Holocene

Subclass Nautiloidea—simple sutures; Cambrian–Holocene

Subclass Ammonoidea—fluted sutures; Devonian–Cretaceous; suture types: goniatite, Devonian–Permian; ceratite, Mississippian–Triasic; ammonite, Permian–Cretaceous

Subclass Coleoidea; Mississippian–Holocene

Order Belemnoidea—belemnites; Mississippian–Eocene

Class Scaphopoda—curved, tusk-shaped calcareous shells open at both ends; common as Cenozoic fossils; Ordovician–Holocene

Class Polyplacophora—segmented shell of the chiton; Cambrian–Holocene

Class Monoplacophora—conical calcareous shell typically with several pairs of muscle scars on its inner surface; biologically an important form suggesting common ancestry of molluscs, annelids, and arthropods; Cambrian–Holocene

Phylum Annelida—segmented worms (earthworm an example); trace fossils as burrows and trails; Ediacarian? Cambrian–Holocene

Phylum Arthropoda—segmented bodies and jointed appendages; diverse forms; most abundant phylum—80% of all known animals; Ediacarian? Cambrian–Holocene

Class Trilobita—extinct trilobites; Cambrian–Permian

Class Crustacea—ostracodes, barnacles, lobsters, and crabs; Cambrian–Holocene

Class Insecta—insects; relatively rare as fossils, although the most abundant of living invertebrate classes; Silurian–Holocene

Class Arachnoidea

Order: Eurypterida—eurypterids; Ordovician–Permian

Phylum Echinodermata—internal calcareous skeleton; commonly five-rayed symmetry; Ediacarian? Cambrian–Holocene

Subphylum Crinozoa—mainly sessile (attached to the seafloor) echinoderms

Class Crinoidea—crinoids; Ordovician–Holocene

Subphylum Echinozoa—predominantly vagrant (not attached) echinoderms; Ordovician–Holocene

Class Echinoidea—sea urchins; Ordovician–Holocene

Class Asteroidea—starfish; Ordovician–Holocene

Phylum Hemichordata—some affinity to chordates; small dorsal stiffening rod

Class Graptolithea—extinct graptolites; Cambrian–Mississippian

Phylum Chordata—most often with a segmented vertebral column as in subphylum Vertebrata; diverse; Ordovician–Holocene

Subphylum Vertebrata

Class Agnatha—jawless fish; Ordovician–Holocene

Class Placodermii—primitive armored fish; Ordovician–Mississippian

Class Chondrichthyes—cartilaginous fish (sharks); Silurian–Holocene

Class Acanthodii—may be ancestral to bony fish; spiny sharks; Silurian–Permian

Class Osteichthyes—bony fish; Silurian–Holocene

Class Amphibia—amphibians; water-dependent stages in life cycle; Devonian–Holocene

Class Reptilia—reptiles; Pennsylvanian–Holocene (see Chapters 12 and 13 for more detailed discussion)

Subclass Anapsida—includes turtles; extinct cotylosaurs; Pennsylvanian–Holocene

Subclass Synapsida—includes extinct pelycosaurs and therapsids; Pennsylvanian–Triassic

Subclass Euryapsida—extinct marine forms including icthyosaurs and plesiosaurs; Triassic–Cretaceous)

Subclass Diapsida—most diverse subclass; includes lizards, snakes, crocodiles; extinct thecodonts, dinosaurs, pterosaurs; Triassic–Holocene

Class Mammalia—mammals; Triassic–Holocene (see Chapter 17 for more detailed discussion)

Subclass Prototheria—monotremes; Pleistocene?–Holocene

Subclass uncertain—includes docodonts and triconodonts; Triassic–Jurassic

Subclass Allotheria—includes multituberculates; Jurassic–Eocene

Subclass Theria—includes symmetrodonts, marsupials, insectivores, pantotheres, and all Cenozoic placental mammals; Jurassic–Holocene

Class Aves—birds; Jurassic? Cretaceous–Holocene

Unknown affinity: "toothlike" conodonts—utilitarian order Conodontophorida phylum and class unknown; Cambrian–Triassic

Index

Note: Boldface numbers indicate pages with only figures of the entry.